KU-556-390

136° 138°

40°

AOMORI
Aomori
L. Towada

Akita Morioka

AKITA   IWATE

YAMAGATA

MIYAGI

PAN SEA

Yamagata

Sendai

38°

Sado Is.

Niigata

Fukushima

NIIGATA   FUKUSHIMA

ISHIKAWA Toyama

TOCHIGI

GUMMA Utsunomiya

Kanazawa

TOYAMA Nagano Maebashi

Mito

IBARAKI

36°

Fukui

NAGANO SAITAMA

L. Kasumigaura

FUKUI HONSHU

Urawa

GIFU

Kofu TOKYO Tokyo

YAMANASHI

Yokohama Chiba

Nagoya

Gifu

KANAGAWA CHIBA

L. Biwa

SHIGA Otsu

AICHI

Shizuoka

Nara

Tsu

SHIZUOKA

NARA MIE

Oshima Is.

34°

YAMA

PACIFIC OCEAN

136°

128° 130°

32°

OKINAWA

JAPAN

1:8,000,000

0 50 100 150 200 250

:15,000,000

KILOMETERS

200km

138° 140° 142°

May 1991

Contributed to the
King Alfred's College
Library by
Winchester Shoei College

JAPAN

KING ALFRED'S COLLEGE
WINCHESTER
Library: 01962 827306

To be returned on or before the day
marked below, subject to recall

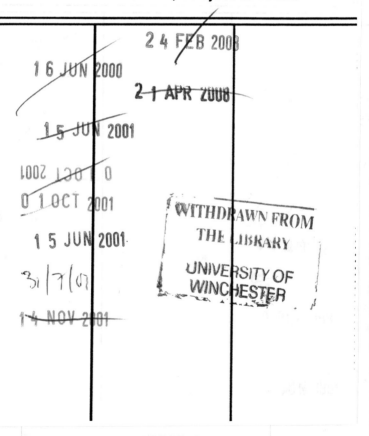

24 FEB 2008

1 6 JUN 2000

2 1 APR 2008

1 5 JUN 2001

0 1 OCT 2001

0 1 OCT 2001

WITHDRAWN FROM
THE LIBRARY

UNIVERSITY OF
WINCHESTER

1 5 JUN 2001

31/7/01

1 4 NOV 2001

KA 0123505 2

Published by
BUREAU, INC.

©1991 by Japan Travel Bureau, Inc.
ALL RIGHTS RESERVED
ISBN 4-533 01681-2
First edition 1914

Donated to the Library

King Alfred's College

by Winchester Shoei College

May 1991

KING ALFRED'S COLLEGE
WINCHESTER

915.2
JAP   0123805

Foreword

I take considerable pleasure in introducing this revised edition of THE NEW OFFICIAL GUIDE JAPAN, published after two years of exceptional, tireless efforts by Japan Travel Bureau, Inc. This window on Japan has gained an unparalleled reputation in the travel world spanning its more than seventy years as being one of the most reliable guidebooks on Japan ever prepared under one cover. I am further delighted to mention that cooperation in its compilation was rendered to JTB by the Japan National Tourist Organization.

The present volume contains a diverse range of the most up-to-date and authentic information on Japan considered to be useful and interesting to the visitor to our land. It deals extensively with almost every aspect of Japan from one end of the country to the other covering her natural environment, culture, government, economy and the daily life of her people as well as her cities and towns, resorts, means of transport, accommodations and other related facilities.

I am thus especially confident that this new volume will ably succeed the previous edition as one of the foremost guidebooks on Japan.

I additionally wish to express my sincere hope that this guidebook will serve not only as the most reliable companion available to the traveler to our shores, but that it will also afford delightful armchair reading for all those with a keen interest or even a sense of curiosity about our country, and thereby contribute to a better understanding in the international community of Japan and her people.

S. Sumita

Shunichi Sumita
President
Japan National Tourist Organization

February 1991

Preface

We, the Japan Travel Bureau, with the cooperation of the Japan National Tourist Organization, decided to compile a new, comprehensive guidebook more than two years ago to replace the current edition of The New Official Guide: Japan issued in 1975. The New Official Guide: Japan has been regarded as the most authoritative and reliable guidebook about Japan over the past half century. We earnestly desired to bring the most up-to-date as well as the most accurate cyclopedic travel guide to our country, one that would be different–not only in appearance but also in the arrangement of the contents–from its predecessor.

The new volume consists of two parts. The first one provides general information about Japan aimed at helping people know this country better and gain a general insight into the life and cultural background of the Japanese people. The latter volume offers practical information to foreign travelers on all the principal sights and places of interest throughout Japan. The new volume will also serve as a complete "thesaurus" on things Japanese.

We are deeply indebted to all those institutions and individuals who rendered valuable assistance to us in the way of information and material. Our special thanks are due to the authorities who contributed information, in parts or in whole, on various subjects for this book.

Contributors
  Chuzenji Tokiji
    Architect
  Furuta Shokin
    Theologist
  Kawatake Toshio
    Dramaturgist   Professor, Waseda University
  Kishimoto Shigenobu
    Economist   Professor, Yokohama National University
  Miyazawa Juichi
    Music Critic
  Okada Jo
    Art Critic
  Yoshida Seiichi
    Literary Critic
  Yui Masami
    Historian   Professor, Waseda University

Lastly, we would like to acknowledge our indebtedness to Mr. Andrew M. Adams without whose diligence in looking over this manuscript this book would not have been possible.

February 1991

Contents

General Information

5

Contents

Travel Information

Contents

Contents

Contents

11

Contents

Contents

NOTES

1. In this guidebook, Japan is described in eight sections from North to South, in addition to general introductory information. Honshu, the largest of the four islands forming Japan, is treated in five sections (Northeastern, East Central, Central, West Central and Western Honshu), while Hokkaido,Shikoku plus the Inland Sea, and Kyushu plus Okinawa make three independent sections.
2. Listing of tourist information services, airlines, package tours, hotels, youth hostels, foreign diplomatic delegations, Japanese embassies, consulates-general and consulates abroad, and sister cities are placed in the supplement.
3. Names of Japanese people are given in Japanese manner, with surname before the given name.
4. For weights and measures, the metric system is used.
5. The population of each city is as of march 1989.
6. All data, unless otherwise stated, are based on those of June 1990.
7. All maps are inserted at the end of this guidebook.
8. The code number enclosed and put after a place of interest, such as Nagoya ⟨57⟩, indicates the map page to be referred to.
9. The mark ☎ followed by numbers put after city names, such as Kyoto ☎075, indicates local area codes.
10. The following abbreviations are used in this guidebook:

A.D. = Anno Domini
alt. = altitude
B.C. = before Christ
C = Centigrade
cc = cubic centimeter(s)
cm = centimeter(s)
d. = died
gr. = gram(s)
hr(s). =hour(s)
kg. = kilogram(s)
kl. = kiloliter(s)

km = kilometer(s)
kw. = kilowatt(s)
lit. = liter(s)
lit. = literally
m = meter(s)
min. = minute(s)
mm = millimeter(s)
Mt(s). = Mount(s)
pop. = population
t. = ton(s)

GENERAL INFORMATION

I. Introductory Remarks

The Japanese archipelago consists of four main islands—Hokkaido, Honshu, Shikoku and Kyushu—and about 4,000 smaller islands, including Okinawa. Japan's total land mass makes up only 0. 3% of the landportion of the earth's surface. However, the Japanese population accounts for 3% of the earth's population.

The archipelago stretches over 2,798 km from north to south, with the upper limit situated at lat. 45°33' N. and the southern extreme at lat. 20°25' N. The majority of the land lies in the Temperate and Subtropic Zones. Despite the limited amount of available land and the many typhoons and earthquakes that strike Japan, it is unique in Asia as the only major, fully industrialized economic power.

As of April 1989, the total area of land actually under Japanese jurisdiction was 377,719 sq.km. The population was 122,335,313 with 60,200,209 men and 62,135,104 women—an increase of 520,000 during the previous year. In population terms, Japan is the seventh-largest nation in the world. After excluding areas unsuitable for living, the Japanese population density is the highest in the world. Approximately 70% of the nation is covered by mountainous areas, with the majority of the residential and industrial regions concentrated from the middle to the southern part of the main island of Honshu. The total land area is slightly less than that of the American state of California or the European nation of Sweden.

Japan meets 70% of its need for foodstuffs domestically, but because of the steady reduction in the number of people engaged in agricultural activities and the competition from lower-priced imports, this is one area that is currently presenting many problems for the nation. Due to the mountainous nature of Japan, the amount of land available for agriculture and industry is quite limited. The coast is covered with numerous harbors and bays, and stretches over a total of 26,505 km. The abundance of mountains and the twisting shoreline provide a natural setting that is unique to Japan.

The central section of the main island of Honshu is traversed by the Fuji Volcanic Chain and Fossa Magna fault from the Japan Sea in the west to the Pacific Ocean in the east. These divide the island into a northeastern half and a southwestern half. There is another mountain range that cuts across from the north to the west. Thus, it can be said that the island is composed of four geographical sections. The Japan Sea side of the northeastern half, the Pacific Ocean side of the northeastern half, the Japan Sea side of the southwestern half and the Inland Sea(Seto-Naikai) side of the southwestern half. Each region has its own particular climate, customs, and manners.

In terms of geographic regions, Honshu consists of five districts: Tohoku District

This district is located in the northern part of Honshu and contains the six prefectures of Akita, Aomori, Fukushima, Iwate, Miyagi and Yamagata.

Kanto District

This district is located south of the Tohoku District and contains the Tokyo metropolitan area and the six prefectures of Chiba, Gumma, Ibaraki, Kanagawa, Saitama and Tochigi.

Chubu District

This district is located in the central part of Honshu and contains the nine prefectures of Aichi, Fukui, Gifu, Ishikawa, Nagano, Niigata, Shizuoka, Toyama and Yamanashi.

Kinki District

This district is located in the southwestern part of Honshu and contains the seven prefectures of Hyogo, Kyoto, Mie, Nara, Osaka, Shiga and Wakayama.

Chugoku District

This district is located in the westernmost part of Honshu and contains the five prefectures of Hiroshima, Okayama, Shimane, Tottori and Yamaguchi.

In addition to these five districts, there are several other popular ways of dividing Honshu. The regions thus categorized are also called districts. Some of the more familiar ones are the Hokuriku District (Fukui, Ishikawa and Toyama prefectures), the Sanriku District (Aomori, Iwate and Miyagi prefectures), the Shin-etsu District (Nagano and Niigata prefectures), the San-in District (Shimane and Tottori prefectures and the northern half of Yamaguchi Prefecture) and the San-yo District (Hiroshima and Okayama prefectures and the southern half of Yamaguchi Prefecture).

In feudal times, the four main islands were divided into various administrative provinces. At present, the country is made up of 47 regional divisions consisting of one *to* (Tokyo Metropolis), one *do* (Hokkaido), two *fu* (Kyoto and Osaka) and 43 *ken* (prefectures) — 31 in Honshu, four in Shikoku, and eight in Kyushu and Okinawa. This system corresponds somewhat to the British system of counties. The capital, Tokyo, is situated in the middle part of Honshu on the Pacific Coast. The port city of Yokohama lies approximately 30 km south of Tokyo, and has continued to serve as a major port since the early days of sea travel. The old capital of Kyoto is in the west-central part of Honshu. Osaka—one of the main manufacturing and commercial centers of Japan—is located 43 km southwest of Kyoto. Kobe, located near Osaka, is situated on the eastern end of the lovely Seto-Naikai (Inland Sea) and still serves the western part of Japan as a major port. At the western end of the Inland Sea is Shimonoseki, which is connected on the other side to Moji in Kyushu by road and rail through underwater tunnels and across bridges. Nagasaki, the oldest open port in Japan, is situated on a peninsula in western Kyushu.

Despite the problems posed by Japan's many mountains, the nation's network of railways is the most modern and technically advanced in the world. Thanks to the "Seikan Tunnel"—an ocean-floor tunnel that connects Honshu and Hokkaido and the Seto-Ohashi Bridge going from Honshu to Shikoku, the rail system now extends to all four main islands. The vast majority of the railways are operated by Japan Railways (JR). In addition, there are other rail lines, bus networks and airports in the major regional cities that provide fast, convenient land and air service throughout the country. Recent years have seen a dramatic increase in the popularity of boats. Fully-equipped cruise ships and ferries ply the waters from major cities throughout Japan.

Transportation to Japan

Japan is located along the main air routes to the Orient. Many flights heading east, west and south make stopovers along the way.

In addition to flights out of Tokyo, there are international departures from Osaka, Nagoya, Fukuoka and Okinawa as well as some flights leaving from Kagoshima, Kumamoto, Nagasaki, Komatsu (Kanazawa), Niigata, Sendai and Sapporo. Tokyo is served by two airports. Tokyo International Airport at Haneda mainly serves domestic flights and New Tokyo International Airport in Narita serves international flights. In Osaka, New Kansai International Airport is scheduled to open in 1994.

Entry, Landing and Registration
Passport and Visa

Passport: Any foreign visitor desiring to enter Japan must have a valid, unexpired passport bearing a visa for residence in a given status under the Immigration Control Order.

Visa: In principle, it is necessary to receive a visa before entering Japan. However, agreements have been concluded between Japan and many other countries permitting their citizens to enter Japan without applying for a visa in advance. This is particularly true for travelers who come to Japan for tourism.

Issuing of Visas: Visas are issued at Japanese Consular Offices abroad, and in areas that do not have a Consular Office, they are issued by the Ambassador or an Attache at a Japanese Embassy. A visa must be received prior to arrival in Japan.

Applying for Visas: Visas issued in cases that are determined solely by Consular Offices abroad can be obtained within two or three days. Visas that must be referred to the Ministry of Foreign Affairs for approval (those who enter Japan for employment, studies or to accompany someone) require between two and three months.

Those Who Do Not Require a Visa: As of April 1, 1989, Japan had completed agreements with the following 51 countries excluding their citizens from the necessity of applying for a visa before coming to

Japan. Citizens of these countries who plan to stay in Japan no longer than the period agreed to in these agreements do not require a visa. However, a visa is required by anyone who desires to obtain employment or engage in any paid activity or stay past the specified period.

Citizens of the following countries are exempted from the requirement of obtaining a visa:

For a stay not exceeding six consecutive months:

Australia, Federal Republic of Germany, Ireland, Liechtenstein, Mexico, Switzerland and the United Kingdom.

For a stay not exceeding three consecutive months:

Argentina, Bahamas, Bangladesh, Barbados, Belgium, Canada, Chile, Colombia, Costa Rica, Cyprus, Denmark, Dominica, El Salvador, Finland, France, Greece, Guatemala, Honduras, Iceland, Iran, Israel, Italy, Lesotho, Luxembourg, Malta, Malaysia, Mauritius, New Zealand, Netherlands, Norway, Pakistan, Peru, Portugal, San Marino, Singapore, Spain, Surinam, Sweden, Tunisia, Turkey, Uruguay, USA and Yugoslavia. (Temporarily suspended for Bangladesh and Pakistan)

For stays of up to 14 days:

Brunei

Visa Types: Some visas are valid for a single entrance to Japan and others are valid for multiple entries. Multiple entry visas are issued to citizens of countries that have reciprocal agreements providing for them.

Validity of Visas: In principle, visas are valid for three months from the date of issue. However, in cases where there are reciprocal agreements, visas are issued for extended periods.

Entry and Exit Formalities

Entry Formalities: At the port of entry into Japan, visitors are requested to fill in an Application for Landing/Exit Record and produce the following items for examination by the immigration inspector:

1) In the case of a transit traveler: A ticket or a written guarantee made by the carrier concerned for onward transportation and valid travel documents (passport, etc.) permitting entry into countries other than Japan.

2) In the case of a tourist: A ticket or a written guarantee made by the carrier concerned for onward or return transportation, travel documents valid for the duration of the authorized stay and for onward or return travel from Japan and a reasonable sum of money to cover the expenses of his/her stay in Japan.

Exit Formalities: When a foreign visitor leaves Japan, he/she must have his/her passport stamped for certification of departure by the immigration inspector at the port of departure from Japan, whether or not he/she intends to seek permission to re-enter the country. If a foreigner wishes to leave Japan temporarily and return with the same status of residence, he/she may obtain a re-entry permit on application to an Immigration Inspector at one of the immigration offices.

Quarantine

There are no requirements for foreign travelers from any country regarding certificates of vaccination. However, there are some cases in which a traveler will be required to see a quarantine doctor. Those who have experienced diarrhea or other symptoms of illness during a voyage should register an address or telephone number in Japan where they can be contacted if the need arises.

Customs

Upon arrival, foreign visitors must make an oral declaration of accompanied baggage or fill out a Declaration of Accompanied / Unaccompanied Goods. Forms are available on board aircraft and ships.

a) Those whose accompanied baggage exceeds the duty-free limits.... one form

b) Those who have unaccompanied goods (articles sent on a different ship or plane or mailed from abroad)....two forms

Those who have unaccompanied goods must fill out both parts of the Declaration of Accompanied / Unaccompanied Goods and receive an approval stamp which will allow for their unaccompanied articles to pass through customs upon arrival. The stamped section should be kept in order to claim the goods. Declaration of goods, both accompanied and unaccompanied, must be made upon arrival; otherwise, the declaration will not be accepted by customs after entry. When passengers take delivery of their unaccompanied goods, they must present the stamped portion of their declaration to customs. If they fail to do so, they will not be able to get their unaccompanied goods exempted from duties and taxes.

There is no limit on the amount of cash that a traveler is allowed to bring into Japan. Travelers may take up to ¥5 million out of Japan. There is no limit on the amount of foreign currency or travelers cheques that a foreigner can take out of Japan.

When bringing in or carrying out from Japan a large amount of goods, if the total value exceeds ¥300,000, such goods will be treated as general freight and the necessary forms must be filled out.

Tax-Free Articles: No duties or taxes are levied on the personal effects of travelers, whether accompanied or unaccompanied goods, as long as they do not exceed the following limits.

Alcoholic beverages: 3 bottles, each containing approximately
                              760 cc.

Tobacco: 400 cigarettes
               100 cigars
               500 grams of pipe tobacco
               500 grams of powdered tobacco

500 grams of chewing tobacco

The total weight of cigars, cigarettes and tobacco may not exceed 500 grams.

Perfume: 2 ounces

Others: Up to ¥200,000

The total overseas value of all articles other than the above items must be under ¥200,000. Items whose overseas market value does not exceed ¥10,000 are free of taxes and duties and are not included in the ¥200,000 total. There is no duty-free allowance for articles or sets of articles with a market value of over ¥200,000.

Minors (under 20 years old) may bring in such personal effects as are deemed reasonable by Customs Officers. However, minors may not bring in alcoholic beverages or tobacco.

Clothing, cosmetic articles, personal effects and portable articles used for professional purposes during travel such as typewriters, 8mm cameras, VTRs, projectors and tape recorders are free of duties and taxes. Household personal effects, automobiles, boats etc., which have been used for over a year and are brought into Japan for personal use, are free of duties or taxes.

The following items are not allowed to be brought into Japan:

1) Opium and other narcotic drugs and utensils involved in their use.

2) Counterfeit, altered or imitation currencies in coins, bank notes or other securities.

3) Any books, pictures, carvings and other items deemed harmful to public order and morals.

4) Articles that infringe upon patent rights, utility model rights, design rights or copyrights.

5) Pistols, revolvers and all types of ammunition.

6) All products specified in the Washington Convention (Convention on International Trade in Endangered Species of Wild Fauna and Flora)

For the following items, permission for entry must be secured prior to the customs examination:

1) Plants not contrary to the Plant Protection Law.

All plants brought into Japan must be inspected by a Quarantine Officer. This includes orchid seedlings, shrubs, pineapples, oranges and other fruit, tulip bulbs, seeds of vegetables and flowers, medicinal ginseng and straw products. All plants and products thereof must be inspected by a Quarantine officer and be approved before being brought into Japan. When importing plants, a certificate of inspection should be received from the plant-quarantine organization of the country of origin.

2) Animals not contrary to the Domestic Animal Infectious Disease Prevention Law.

When animals, meat products, horns, etc., are brought into Japan, they must be inspected by a quarantine officer at the time of their import, as specified in the Animal Infectious Diseases Control Law.

Dogs are inspected by a Quarantine officer under the Rabies Prevention Law.

3) Gunpowder and other explosives.

4) Firearms, swords and other weapons.

Tax-Free Purchases of Souvenir Articles: Purchases of tax-free articles at designated stores can be made by having a form titled "Record of Purchase of Consumption Tax-Exempt for Export" duly filled in and attached to the visitor's passport. The form can be obtained at duty-free stores.

At these stores, a "Tax Free" sign is put up at the entrance and the price tag has a note explaining that the article is tax-free. Tax-free articles will be checked by a Customs Officer at the port of departure.

Duty-Free Entry of Automobiles for Re-Export: An automobile may be imported free of customs duties, either by bringing it into Japan at the time of entry (except for those who are moving their residence to Japan) or by sending it to Japan separately by presenting a "Temporary Importation Paper" ("Carnet de Passages en Douane"), based on the Customs Convention on Temporary Importation of Private Road Vehicles, to the Customs Officer, provided that the vehicle is to be re-exported.

Driver's License: Japan is a member country of the 1949 Convention on Road Traffic. This means that anyone possessing a valid International Driver's License may drive a car in Japan without applying for a Japanese License. However, in addition to the International Driver's License, citizens of the member countries to the agreement which was reached in 1968 in Vienna are required to apply for a Japanese Driver's License. In all cases, Japanese traffic laws apply.

Currency

Foreign visitors to Japan may bring in and take out with them any currency, personal ornaments and other valuables as long as they are confirmed by a Customs Officer.

The Japanese unit of currency is the yen, indicated by the symbol ¥. There are ¥ 1, 5, 10, 50, 100 and 500 coins. Bank notes are available in denominations of ¥ 1,000, 5,000 and 10,000 . There are many coin-operated vending machines, which are used to purchase short-distance rail tickets and subway tickets as well as a variety of products used in daily life, including cigarettes, soft drinks, and even beer and other alcoholic beverages. It costs ¥10 to make a three-minute local call on public telephones.

Credit cards can be used at most hotels, department stores, duty-free shops, restaurants as well as at most stores. Among the major credit cards generally accepted are Diner's Club, American Express, VISA and Master Card. Since there are relatively few establishments that accept travelers cheques, it is best to convert them into yen at banks or other officially recognized exchanges. Foreign currency can be exchanged for yen at foreign exchange banks. Japan participates in the floating exchange rate system. As of December 1990, the US $1.00 was equivalent to approximately ¥130.

Currencies that are convertible into yen are the U.S. dollar, Canadian dollar, British pound sterling, German mark, Swiss franc, French franc, Dutch gilder, Belgian franc, Danish krone, Norwegian krone, Swedish krone, Australian dollar, New Zealand dollar, Italian lira, Austrian schilling, Hong Kong dollar, Singapore dollar and Portuguese escudo. However, not all currencies can be converted into Japanese yen at every foreign exchange bank. Travelers cheques can be cashed into yen from the following currencies: the U. S. dollar, Canadian dollar, British pound sterling, German mark, Swiss franc, French franc, Dutch gilder, Belgian franc, Danish krone, Norwegian krone, Swedish krone, Australian dollar, New Zealand dollar, Italian lira, Austrian schilling, Chinese yuan, Hong Kong dollar, Singapore dollar, Spanish peseta, Portuguese escudo, etc.

Weights and Measures

The metric system has been in use since 1893 and was adopted in 1924 as the official system of weights and measures.

Concise Conversion Table of Weights and Measures

Metric Unit	U.K. and U.S. Equivalents ※
Length:	
1 centimeter (cm)	0.39370 inches
1 meter (m)	3.28084 feet or 1.09361 yards
1 kilometer (km)	0.62137 miles
Area:	
1 square centimeter (sq. cm)	0.1550 square inches
1 square meter (sq. m)	10.7639 square feet
1 square kilometer (sq. km)	0.3861 square miles or 247.105 acres
Weight:	
1 gram (g)	15.4324 grains
1 kilogram (kg)	35.2740 ounces or 2.20464 pounds
1 ton (t)	0.9842 tons (U.K.) or 1.1029 tons (U.S.)
Volume:	
1 cubic centimeter (cc)	0.06102 cubic inches
1 cubic meter (cu. m)	35.3147 cubic feet or 1.30795 cubic yards
1 liter (l.)	0.21998 gallons (U.K.) or 0.26418 gallons (U.S.)

※ U.K. = British Imperial System　U.S. = U.S. Customary System

Sanitation and Medical Services

Japan maintains high standards in the sanitation and medical fields. Matters related to public hygiene are supervised by the government. High standards are established for all fruit, vegetables, milk, fish, fowl and processed foods offered for sale. Most towns and cities have complete waterworks and sewage networks that assure an abundant supply of fresh water and efficient disposal of waste water.

There is no need for a traveler in Japan to be concerned about infectious diseases or fevers. Japanese medical practitioners make full use of the most advanced techniques available in Europe and the United States, and many doctors understand either English or German.

Japanese pharmaceutical products are of the highest quality. Medicines are dispensed at hospitals and clinics, where medical treatment is provided, and at drug stores, where prescriptions can be filled.

There are many hospitals with emergency medical treatment facilities that provide a complete range of services at all times.

Emergency and Security

Dial 110 for police and 119 to report a fire or to call an ambulance. If you require first-aid treatment, contact your hotel or ask someone for assistance.

Japan is proud of its low crime rate. Police boxes are located at major street intersections in most neighborhoods. Patrol cars are always cruising and dispatched on call throughout the city.

Seasonal Attractions

Japan offers a variety of unique attractions to the tourist. All of the months and seasons are blessed with their own special features. January brings three days of lively New Year's celebrations. This is the most important holiday of the year on the Japanese calendar. In February, the blooming of the plum trees begins the succession of flowers that continues all year round. Excursions to famous locations offering picturesque floral scenery mark the beginning of the outdoor recreation season. In summer, the beaches, mountains and hot-springs resorts are at their best. In autumn, people head for the country to see the blazing colors of the changing leaves as well as the chrysanthemums. The crisp autumn air is perfect for outdoor athletic activities. Spring and autumn are the most popular seasons for travel in Japan. However, there are many fine winter and summer resorts, making Japan an ideal vacation spot all year.

Japan is often called the land of flowers and has probably supplied more flowering shrubs and trees to the gardens of the world than any other country. In spring, the most important of all flowers—the *sakura* (cherry blossoms)—spread their pink canopy across the land.

There are more than 50 varieties of *sakura* trees. The date when the cherry blossoms open differs depending on the type and location, but the cherry trees generally begin to bloom in March in the south and continue into May in the north. As the temperature rises, the blossoms open further and further north. If one starts in the south and travels north, it is possible to view them many times over.

Other Japanese flowers noted for their beauty in the spring and summer are *ume* (plum), *nanohana* (rape flower), *tsubaki* (camellia), *momo* (peach blossom), *yamabuki* (Japanese globeflower), *fuji* (wisteria), *tsutsuji* (azalea), *botan* (tree peony), *shakuyaku* (peony), *hanashobu* (Japanese iris), *hasu* (lotus) and *asagao* (morning glory).

The Japanese summers are hot, with average temperatures in July of 26.8°C in Osaka, 25.2°C in Tokyo and 20.2°C in Sapporo. Summer is a time for outdoor sports. With its long coastline, Japan offers many opportunities to go swimming, windsurfing, sailing and scuba diving. Japanese youth have shown an increasing interest in marine sports in recent years. Yachts and boats are also popular, especially in the Sagami Bay area south of Tokyo and around the many islands that dot the Inland Sea. Angling may be enjoyed all year round at the numerous fishing grounds along the coast as well as at the rivers and lakes, but summer and autumn are the best seasons for sports fishing.

Completely surrounded by water, Japan is blessed with many beautiful scenic sea areas. The best place to appreciate the beauty of the ocean is at the southern tip of the archipelago on the islands of Amami and Okinawa, where the beauty of the coral reefs attracts divers from around the world.

In order to escape the summer heat, many Japanese go to the mountains. Some of the most popular areas are the Chubu Sangaku (Japan Alps) National Park in Nagano, Toyama, Gifu and Niigata prefectures, Nikko, Hakone, the Fuji-Five-Lake district and Izu Peninsula. There are many vacation resorts in the mountains and along the lake shores.

Mountain climbing and camping are also popular summer pastimes. Many areas have been set aside and equipped with facilities to accommodate climbers and campers. Japan's most famous mountain is undoubtedly Mt. Fuji (alt. 3,776 m). Although it is the highest mountain in Japan, it is rather easy to climb, and in summer, long columns of hikers can be seen wending their way up and down its trails.

With many lofty peaks of over 2,500 meters, the Japan Alps sprawl across the central part of Honshu. The best time to climb these mountains is from mid-July to mid-August.

Japan's mountains are mainly of volcanic origin and have a cone-shaped or truncated form that adds to the natural beauty of the landscape. Typified by Mt. Fuji, they often have many lakes and plateaus in their foothills as well as on their summits. They are mainly composed of granite and quartz, and the surrounding foothills have many swift-flowing streams that attract boaters looking for an exciting descent. The mountains are covered with a thick growth of broad-leaved trees that presents a scene of sylvan beauty.

The most beautiful sight in summer is undoubtedly the lush greenery that spreads across the countryside. The green leaves of cherries, maples, *haze* (Japanese wax tree), oaks, chestnuts, birches and elms make a subtle but lovely contrast against the deeper hues of the evergreen pines that are found everywhere. At the height of summer, Japan is covered by a thick carpet of greenery, which, in autumn, is transformed into a richly colored tableau as the leaves change colors. The most beautiful autumnal sight is the changing colors of the leaves of some 20 varieties of maple trees. In addition to maple viewing, visitors to Japan will find the climate at its best in the autumn.

In autumn, Japan is famous for its *kiku* (chrysanthemums) which have been cultivated for over 1,500 years and used as the Imperial Crest. Skillful Japanese horticulturists have developed a large number of varieties with a subtle diversity of form and color. Chrysanthemum shows are held annually throughout the country. Since chrysanthemums can be raised in many inspirational shapes, florists delight in creating *kiku-ningyo* (chrysanthemum dolls). Backed by a tableau of chrysanthemum blossoms on a wire frame, these figures are arranged to depict scenes of important traditional and historical events. Only a true craftsman of this art can bring the figures to life and create a perfect harmony of colors and shapes.

Among the many autumnal plants, *nanakusa* (seven flowering herbs) are the most popular. These consist of *hagi* (bush clover), *kikyo* (balloon flower), *susuki* (pampas grass), *ominaeshi* (patrina scabiosaefolia), *nadeshiko* (pink), *kuzu* (arrowroot) and *fujibakama* (fragrant thoroughwort). Although these plants grow naturally in the wild, they are cultivated in gardens as well.

Except for the northern regions, winter in Japan is usually quite mild with clear skies. Winter sports are very popular. The winter visitor will find a wide range of ski slopes and skiing conditions. The season begins in mid-December and continues through April. Japanese ski lodges are fully equipped with facilities that match top winter resorts anywhere in the world. Only an hour's ride on the Shinkansen ("bullet train") from Ueno (Tokyo), these resorts offer a convenient getaway from the metropolis. In addition to skiing, many of the lodges provide hot-springs bathing.

National Holidays and Events

According to the White Paper on labor, 58.3% of all companies had adopted five-day work week at the end of 1989. Government and public offices are open from Monday to Saturday with two Saturdays off each month. In February 1989, banks, many of the post offices and financial institutions adopted a complete five-day work week. There is a debate currently under way concerning the possibility of closing schools on Saturdays as well.

National Holidays

Japan observes the following 13 national holidays (If a holiday falls on a Sunday, the following day is treated as a holiday.) If a day falls between two holidays then it too is treated as a national holiday. May 4 is an (and the only) example of this.

January 1: *Ganjitsu*, or New Year's Day. Comparable to Christmas in Western countries, this is the most important of all holidays in Japan. It is a time when people celebrate the beginning of the new year and recall the events of the old.

January 15: *Seijin-no-Hi*, or Coming of Age Day. In Japan, children are considered adults on their 20th birthday. This day is set aside for those who have turned 20 during the previous year. They are encouraged to become mature adults.

February 11: *Kenkoku Kinen-no-Hi*, or National Foundation Day. On this day, people recall the legends of the founding of Japan and rejoice in their national legacy. Legend holds that over 2,600 years ago on this day, Jimmu, the first Emperor of Japan, ascended the throne.

March 21 (or 20): *Shumbun-no-Hi*, or Vernal Equinox Day. This day is devoted to promoting the love of nature and all its creatures.

April 29: *Midori-no-Hi*, or Greenery Day. This day was the birthday of the late Emperor Showa. Upon his death in January 1989, it was renamed Greenery Day and designated as a national holiday.

May 3: *Kempo Kinen-Bi*, or Constitution Memorial Day. This anniversary marks the adoption of the Constitution of Japan. It is celebrated in order to increase the people's awareness of the Constitutuion.

May 5: *Kodomo-no-Hi*, or Children's Day . Since ancient times, May 5 has been celebrated as the Boy's Festival. However, after World War II, it was designated as a holiday to pray for the happiness and prosperity of all children.

September 15: *Keiro-no-Hi*, or Respect-for-the-Aged Day. On this day, people wish the elderly of the nation a long life and thank them for their contribution to society for so many years.

September 23 (or 24): *Shubun-no-Hi*, or Autumnal Equinox Day. On this day, people worship their family ancestors.

October 10: *Taiiku-no-Hi*, or Sports Day, is celebrated to promote the mental and physical health of the people through the enjoyment of sports.

November 3: *Bunka-no-Hi*, or Culture Day. This day is set aside to foster the love of peace and freedom as well as the advancement of culture. Cultural awards are given by the government to those who have made significant contributions to the nation's culture.

November 23: *Kinro Kansha-no-Hi*, or Labor Thanksgiving Day. On this day, the nation honors the working people, promotes respect for labor and rejoices over a bountiful production.

December 23: *Tenno Tanjo-Bi*, or the Emperor's Birthday. On this day, the Emperor and his family appear on the balcony of the Imperial Palace and greet the crowds of well-wishers, who are allowed to enter the Palace.

How the Japanese Spend Their Holidays

In some rural districts, annual functions are observed according to the lunar calendar. As a result, the New Year's holidays generally come during the first half of February.

New Year's Festival (January 1-3): The biggest holiday of the year. Though greatly simplified in many respects nowadays, the traditional way of celebrating the New Year's Festival in ordinary homes is as follows: Special preparations are made to celebrate the occasion in the most jovial manner, with nearly all business suspended during this period. The front of the house is decorated on both sides of the entrance with a combination of pine boughs, plum-tree sprigs and bamboo stalks called *kado-matsu* — all from trees that are regarded as symbols of longevity, constancy, prosperity and purity. The *kado-matsu* decoration is thus set up in the hope that the new year will bring vigor, long life and strength to the members of the family.

Across the top of the gate or at the entrance to the house is hung the *shime-nawa*, a rope of twisted straw decorated at brief intervals with strips of white paper. According to Shinto beliefs, this purifies the house and keeps out all evil spirits.

Placed among the decorations at the entrance are fern leaves, an orange and a lobster. The fern, with its multiplicity of fronds, represents a prayer that the family's good fortune will continue to grow throughout the year. The Japanese word for a bitter orange is *daidai*, a homophone that also means "from generation to generation." This double meaning is the reason it is included among the offerings. The curved back of the lobster is supposed to suggest old age and the special wish that one may enjoy long life—until his back is bent like a lobsters.

Special food is eaten during the New Year's holidays, the first meal on New Year's Day being a great event. For this meal, fresh water is brought at daybreak—if possible, from a well. This is called *waka-mizu* (young water) and is believed to have the power of preserving health throughout the year. A special dish called *o-zoni* (literally "boiled assortment")—a broth that contains *mochi* (rice-cakes or rice-paste) and vegetables— is served. *O-zoni* is a "must" during the New Year's holidays.

Many other delicacies are served, including *kazunoko* (lit. numerous children—herring roe); *mame* (black beans), because it is pronounced the same way as another Japanese word meaning "robust;" *kachiguri* (hulled, dried chestnuts), which indicates success since the word *kachi* means "victory;" dried *kombu*, a seaweed signifying happiness, and lotus root—the lotus being a sacred plant, which, though growing in muddy waters, has a straight stem and a pure white flower.

The yellow petals of a variety of chrysanthemum (eaten in salads) are frequently used to enrich the color scheme of the table. The preparation of this meal—and, in fact, all Japanese meals—is arranged with an eye for color.

Besides the food mentioned above, a ceremonial drink—*toso*—is served at this time in the belief that it has the power to prevent sickness. *Toso* is *mirin* (a sweet sake) flavored with cassia bark and other spicy ingredients. *Mochi*, a kind of solidified rice-paste made into flat, round or square cakes of many sizes, is baked and eaten throughout the holidays.

These traditional New Year's dishes differ somewhat from one region to another in terms of ingredients and preparation. In these days of fast food and frozen dishes, the people take great joy and pride in preparing their particular family dishes for the New Year's holidays.

Early in the morning of New Year's Day, many people pay their first visit of the year—called *hatsumode* or *hatsumairi* (first prayer visit)—to their guardian shrines or celebrated Buddhist sanctuaries in their district. At midnight, just as the temple bells ring out the old year, the shrine and temple precincts are crowded with bustling, cheerful people, who are worshipping, exchanging greetings with friends and buying *engi-mono* (a good luck talisman) at the booths in the precincts. In the Kanto District, including the Tokyo Metropolis, people excitedly flock to Meiji Shrine, Asakusa Kannon Temple, Kawasaki Daishi Temple, Naritasan Shinshoji Temple and Kamakura's Tsurugaoka Hachimangu Shrine to celebrate. Women and children clad in beautiful *kimono* highlight the New Year's celebration.

To express their joy for the new year, people exchange *nengajo* (New Year's greeting cards) and give *otoshidama* (New Year's monetary gifts) to children, a custom similar to the Western one of exchanging Christmas cards and gifts.

During the first few days of the year, it is customary for people to visit the homes of their good friends, family and relatives where everyone rejoices and greets the new year.

Quite commonly, it is customary for company workers living in big cities to return to their hometowns with their families during the New Year's holidays. However, during recent years, many young families have also chosen to spend the holiday together at a ski lodge or hot-springs resort or even at city hotels in order to avoid the preparations and complications involved with the traditional New Year's holidays. However, the traditional New Year's customs remain strongly entrenched, particularly if one goes out into the countryside, where they still prevail.

Of the many indoor games played at New Year's, the most popular is the *utagaruta* game. *Utagaruta* (lit. poem-cards), or *hyakunin-isshu*, is a collection of 100 *tanka* (31-syllable poems) written by 100 celebrated poets. The collection is said to have been compiled by Fujiwara-no-Sadaie (often called Fujiwara-no-Teika, refer to p.157). In the *utagaruta* game, two decks of cards are used. On each of the cards of one deck is written one of the poems from the *hyakunin-isshu*, and on the cards of the other deck appear the last two lines of the corresponding poem. The cards in this latter deck are spread out on the *tatami*-mat-covered floor, and as "reader" recites the poems aloud, the players try to be the first one to pick up the matching card. The one collecting the most cards is declared the winner. Although such traditional games have become quite rare in many families, they are still enthusiastically followed by private groups and associations.

Outdoor games played at this time include kiteflying, which is done by boys, and *hanetsuki* (battledore and shuttlecock), which is played by girls.

Passing through the streets on the fourth day of the New Year's holidays are wagons and trucks piled high with merchandise and decorated like parade floats with flags and streamers. These are the vehicles of the wholesale dealers making the first deliveries of the year. These deliveries are called *hatsuni* (first merchandise) and are undertaken in the hope that good luck will come during the year. In recent years, however, this custom has become rare.

On the fourth day, all normal functions of the country are resumed, and government as well as private company offices reopen. Usually on the sixth day, the *dezome-shiki* (fire-brigade parades) are held in many parts of the country. In Tokyo, the parade is held along Chuo-dori Avenue in Harumi. *Dezome-shiki* is particularly interesting since it has been one of the special attractions of the capital since the Edo period. The festival's acrobatic performances on ladder tops were first introduced in the old days to show the agility of Edo firemen when confronted with danger. Even today, they are always eagerly applauded by the many spectators.

On the seventh day, as a rule, all New Year's decorations — both inside and outside the house—are taken down, and the main New Year's celebration comes to an end. The seventh day is also known as *Nanakusa-no-Hi* (the Day of Seven Herbs) because of the special dish served on that day—a rice gruel seasoned with *nanakusa*, or seven herbs.

Seijin-no-Hi (Coming of Age Day): On this day, local governments stage ceremonies to congratulate young people who have reached their 20th birthday during the previous year. Young women appear in lovely *kimono* to celebrate their good fortune in having come of age.

Setsubun ("Changing of the Seasons"): Taking place in the first part of February, this is a popular festival marking the end of winter and the birth of spring (*risshun*), according to the lunar calendar. *Setsu-bun* is observed throughout the country with *mame-maki*, or bean-throwing, and loud cries of *"Fuku-wa-uchi, oni-wa-soto!"* (In with good luck, out with the demon!) to ensure their good luck for the year. At big temples, such rites are open to the public. To draw the public to such festivities, famous personalities in the entertainment world or stars in the sports world are selected as the *toshi-otoko* or *toshi-onna* (a man or woman born under the zodiac sign for that year) to throw the roasted beans, thereby expelling the demons and ensuring good luck for all present.

Momo-no-Sekku ("Peach Blossom Fete"): Popularly known as *Hina Matsuri* (Doll Festival or Girls' Festival), it is held every year on the third day of the third month. When the lunar calendar was in general use, the third month witnessed the blossoming of peach flowers; hence, the name. The dolls displayed on this occasion, however, are not those which children play with every day. They are ceremonial dolls, many of which are handed down from generation to generation as family heirlooms. In some homes, they are actually the principal heritage. They are displayed in the best room of the house for several days centering around March 3, after which they are carefully boxed and stored away until the following year. Parents who do not possess such heirlooms buy a new set of dolls when a baby girl is born. Relatives and friends also present such dolls as gifts. A formal set usually consists of 15 dolls, customarily dressed in ancient costumes. The display is not complete unless it includes, besides the traditional dolls, miniature household articles and appliances, which are often exquisite works of art. These include a chest of drawers, *hibachi* (brazier), a dining-table set, a cosmetic stand, musical instruments, a palanquin in which the dolls are supposed to be carried and other tiny articles. The most highly valued dolls are the *dairi-bina*, which represent the Emperor and Empress dressed in resplendent ancient court costumes of silk. They are attended by their ministers and other dignitaries as well as by court ladies and musicians. All are displayed on a *hina-dan* (doll-stand), a tier of usually five or seven shelves covered with bright red cloth. The *dairi-bina* always occupy the top shelf, the Emperor on the left and the Empress on the right (facing the stand). Behind them are miniature folding screens, which form a background for decorated toy candleholders and vases containing peach blossom sprigs. Court ladies, and toy banquet trays and dishes usually occupy the second shelf, while musicians, ministers and court officials together with delicacies of many kinds in elaborately decorated miniature boxes are placed on the lower shelves.

Peach blossoms, symbolizing marital bliss, are indispensable parts of the display. The peach blossoms also signify the feminine traits of gentility, repose and tranquillity. The main offerings are small cakes, *hishi-mochi* (diamond-shaped rice cakes), *shiro-zake* (mixture of ground rice with sweet *sake*), *sekihan* (rice boiled with red beans) and colored wheat gluten.

Buddha's Birthday: The birthday of Gautama Buddha, the founder of Buddhism, is celebrated throughout Japan on April 8. Every important temple observes the ceremony of *kambutsu-e*, or "Baptizing Ceremony of Buddha." This consists mainly of pouring "sweet tea" in tiny ladles over a small statue of the infant Buddha as an expression of devotion. The statue is placed in a miniature, temporary temple decorated with flowers called *hana-mido* (flowery temple). Little children dressed in festival robes walk in a procession through the temple yard. Of the temples in Tokyo where Buddha's birthday is celebrated, the more popular ones are the Sensoji (Kannon) Temple in Asakusa and the Gokokuji Temple in Otsuka.

Boys' Festival (or Shobu Fete): This has been celebrated every year for centuries on the fifth day of the fifth month. Actually, May 5 is as much a day of festivity for small boys as March 3 is for girls. It is called *Shobu-no-Sekku* because of the display of leaves of the *shobu* (iris), the long, narrow leaf of which is shaped somewhat like a sword blade. The festival is also called *Tango-no-Sekku*.

Iris leaves are used in the display because they and another word implying "respect for bravery" are both pronounced *shobu* even though they are written with different characters. The leaves are steeped in the *shobu-yu*, or *shobu* hot bath, on May 5, imparting their peculiar fragrance to the water. There is a traditional belief that the *shobu-yu* possesses a miraculous preventive power effective against all kinds of diseases.

For the festival, finely chopped iris leaves are mixed with *sake* to produce a drink, which was a favorite among the *samurai* warriors of the past because of its good taste. The *chimaki* and *kashiwa-mochi* (rice dumplings: the former is wrapped in iris or bamboo leaves and the latter in oak leaves) are special dainties prepared for the occasion. Iris leaves are also placed along the eaves of the house on this day to ward off evil spirits.

Although there is no one set form for this festival, it is traditionally carried out in the following way: A stand similar to that used in the Dolls' Festival is erected in the parlor. On it are displayed dolls representing famous feudal generals and legendary or fairy-tale heroes as well as a paraphernalia of miniature swords, armor, helmets, banners and saddles. The walls are also decorated with images of heroic warriors. Among the dolls usually displayed are Kato Kiyomasa; Minamoto-no-Yoshitsune; Kintoki, a figure of Herculean stature; Momotaro, the Japanese equivalent of Jack the Giant-Killer, and the legendary Chinese deity, Shoki.

On one side of the stand is a long, lacquered bow with a quiver of arrows; on the other, a valuable sword with a richly decorated hilt and scabbard. Near it, a lacquered rack is often placed holding exquisite miniatures of spears and other weapons as well as silk banners bearing the family crest.

On a tall bamboo or wooden pole erected in the yard or sometimes attached to the roof, *koinobori* (carp-shaped cloth streamers) are hoisted so that they flap in the breeze and seem to swim in the air like real fish. Originally, a carp was hoisted for each son—a very large *koinobori* (10 m or more in length) for the eldest and ranging down to a small one if there was a baby boy in the family.

Several legends account for the choice of the carp, the most popular of which is based on the fact that this fish, like the salmon, has the energy and power to fight its way up swift- running streams, cascades and falls. Because of its strength and determination to overcome all obstacles, it is held up as a good example to growing boys symbolizing ambition, energy, strength and perseverance. The festival theme is the encouragement of manliness, the overcoming of life difficulties and the eventual achievement of success.

Tanabata Matsuri (Star Festival): On July 7, the festival—perhaps the most romantic of all of Japan's annual events—owes its inception to a popular belief originating in China. The story goes that two stars in love, *Kengyu* (Altair, or the Cowherd Star) and *Shokujo* (Vega, or the Weaver Star), which are divided on opposite sides of the Milky Way, hold a joyous union on that single night of each year. The popular custom of praying to the Cowherd for a good harvest and to the Weaver for skill in weaving has been observed in Japan for centuries in connection with the Star Festival.

Young people celebrate this festival by writing down their wishes on small strips of paper and hanging them on bamboo branches set up in the garden. This custom has become widespread even in school, where young pupils hope to acquire skill in handwriting by praying to the stars for success in their studies. In Sendai in Miyagi Prefecture, Hiratsuka in Kanagawa Prefecture and Sayama in Saitama Prefecture as well as in other localities, the Star Festival is observed with great gaiety.

Bon Festival: This festival has been observed yearly in Japan on July 13-15 by Buddhist families ever since the introduction of that faith to Japan some 1,400 years ago. Likened to the Christian All Souls' Day, it is sometimes called the "Festival of Souls" as well as the "Feast of the Dead" or the "Festival of Lanterns." In many country districts, it is celebrated according to the lunar calendar and held in the middle of August. Most businesses and stores close, as people living in the metropolitan areas return to their hometowns to be with their families.

The purpose of the festival is to perpetuate the memory of one's ancestors, to stimulate ancestor worship and filial piety, and to remind people of the deeds of their forefathers. While it is a solemn occasion, the *Bon* Festival is also a time of joy because honored relatives have returned from the spirit world for a brief visit. In Japan, it is believed that the dead are never very far away and that their souls long to return to their living relatives for the *Bon* Festival.

While the detailed manner in which *Bon* is celebrated varies some-what in different parts of the country, its essential features are the same.

In preparation for *Bon*, the Buddhist faithful, in addition to clean-ing their house and beautifying the family grave in honor of the dead, purchase offerings for the various rituals at the *kusa-ichi* (grass market)—the Bon street fairs held throughout the country.

In the best room in front of the *butsudan* (family altar), a small mat is spread. On it are placed the *ihai* (monumental tablet) and other ancestral tablets together with various articles purchased in prepara-tion for the festival. Around these, a tiny leaf fence is set up. A meal for the dead is then served in minute portions. Besides the favorite dishes of the departed spirit, such dishes as potatoes and sesame cooked together and a dish of sesame, eggplants and squash are offered.

On the 13th, the graveyards are the scene of pious devotion to family ancestors and the burning of much incense. As darkness sets in, more and more families arrive at the graves, inviting the spirits to visit their old homes and offering to escort them there. Paper lan-terns are set throughout the cemeteries, and a night visit to one of them, as the lanterns flicker in the darkness and the incense rises in clouds, presents an interesting spectacle. In rural areas, lanterns are carried to escort the spirits home. The guides are careful to point out the bad places in the road and generally show the greatest concern over their spirit-guests. The head of the family kindles a welcome fire in front of the house to which the spirit is being guided. At the entrance, dried hempseed placed in a dish is set ablaze. This is called the *mukae-bi* (welcome fire). In the house, members of the family talk to the spirits as if they were actually present in the flesh. At night all during the festival, lanterns shed a subdued light throughout the house. On the 15th, the last day of the *Bon* Festival, *okuri-dango* (farewell rice dumplings) are offered to the spirit-guests to cheer their departure to the *Meido*—that mysterious celestial world of the dead. On the 16th, *okuri-bi* (farewell fire) is lit in front of the house to serve as a beacon to show the departing spirits the way back to their abode.

The *Bon Odori* (*Bon* Dance) is held on evenings around the 15th. These dances nowadays are part of festivals held in commercial areas in cities and towns. However, in order to see a true *Bon Odori*, one must go out to the countryside. Among the most famous dances are the ones held at the Gujo Hachiman in Gifu Prefecture, Yatsuo in Toyama Prefecture, Yamagata in Yamagata Prefecture, Tokushima in Shikoku and Shiraishi Island in the Inland Sea.

Shichigosan: This is held on November 15. The word *shichi-go-san* literally means "seven-five-three." On this day, parents with girls of seven, boys of five, and either boys or girls of three years of age take their children to their guardian shrines or to large shrines in the neighborhood. Here, they express their thanks to the deity for allowing their children to reach their respective ages safely and to invoke future blessings. They purchase red-and-white talisman candies called *chitose-ame* (*chitose* meaning 1,000 years; hence, longevity) and distribute them to neighbors and friends. The most popular shrines in Tokyo for this festival are the Meiji Shrine, the San-no-Hie Shrine, the Kanda Myojin Shrine, the Fukagawa Hachiman Shrine and the Hikawa Shrine. They are all crowded on this day with children dressed up in their Sunday best.

Local Festivals

There are few days in the year when there is not a festival being celebrated somewhere in Japan. Most of the festivals are of a religious nature and generally include a street procession of the adherents of the shrine or temple, honoring the tutelary deity. They carry the *mikoshi* (portable shrine) of the deity or draw *dashi* (floats) on which musicians and sometimes dancers perform.

Some of the more spectacular of the important annual festivals and functions are as follows:

January 1: New Year's Day is the "festival of festivals" for the Japanese and is celebrated throughout the country. People dressed in traditional *kimono* pay homage at nearby shrines, offering visitors a good "shutter chance," but it is primarily an occasion for family reunions just like Christmas in Western countries.

January 7: *Usokae*, a Bullfinch Exchange Festival of Dazaifu Temmangu Shrine in Dazaifu, Fukuoka Prefecture.

January 9-11: *Toka Ebisu* is a festival for praying for prosperity in business. It takes place in three parts— *Yoi Ebisu* on the 9th, *Hon Ebisu* on the 10th and *Nokorifuku* on the 11th—and is attended by about a million people. (Imamiya Ebisu Shrine in Osaka)

January 15: Grass Fire Ceremony on Wakakusayama (Wakakusa Hill)in Nara.

January 17: *Bonten* Festival of Miyoshi Shrine in Akita.

Early February: Snow Festival in Sapporo, Hokkaido. Huge, elaborate snow and ice sculptures are erected on the O-dori-Koen Promenade.

February 3 or 4: *Setsubun*, or Bean-Throwing Festival, is observed at main temples across the country.

February 3 or 4: Lantern Festival of Kasuga Taisha Shrine in Nara is known for its fantastic scene created by 3,000 lighted lanterns.

February 15-16: *Kamakura* in Yokote, Akita Prefecture, has a unique snow-country event. Igloo-like snow houses enshrining the God of Water are erected and children enjoy indoor parties in them.

February 17: In the *Bonten* festival, special shrine decorations called *bonten*, each carried by 20 to 30 young men, are taken to a shrine for consecration. (Asahiokayama Shrine in Yokote, Akita Prefecture)

Third Saturday in February: *Hadaka Matsuri* (Festival of the Naked) of Saidaiji Temple in Okayama. A multitude of half-naked, stout-bodied youths perform ablution in the water of the Yoshii River. Afterwards, pushing and jostling and filing into the temple grounds uttering peculiar yells, they scramble for a pair of sacred wands called *shingi* thrown at them in the darkness by the priest.

March 1–14: *Omizutori*, or Water-Drawing Festival, of Todaiji Temple in Nara is solemnly observed at 2 a.m. on the 13th day to the accompaniment of ancient Japanese music. For many Japanese, the *Omizutori* ritual signals the advent of a long-awaited spring.

March 3: *Hinamatsuri* or Doll Festival, is celebrated throughout the country.

March 13: *Kasuga* Festival of Kasuga Taisha Shrine in Nara features the staging of a 1,100-year-old classic dance.

April 14–15: *Takayama Matsuri* Festival of Hie Shrine in Takayama, Gifu Prefecture, is known for its gala procession of gorgeously decorated floats.

May 3–4: *Hakata Dontaku* Festival in Fukuoka features a parade of citizens in fancy attire, escorting masqueraders of legendary gods on horseback.

May 11–October 15: Cormorant Fishing on the Nagara River, Gifu. This ancient method of catching a trout-like fish called *ayu* with trained cormorants takes place nightly under the light of blazing torches.

Saturday and Sunday in mid-May: *Kanda Matsuri* of Kanda Myojin Shrine is one of the three biggest festivals of Edo (the old name of Tokyo). Seventy *mikoshi* take part, the biggest being the *Sengan* (lit. 3,750 kg)—the *Mikoshi* of Kanda Ichiba. The *dashi* (festival floats) parade is also attractive with its traditional music and graceful dancing. The other two major Edo festivals are *Sanja Matsuri* and *Sanno Matsuri*.

Third Saturday and Sunday in May: *Sanja Matsuri* Festival of Asakusa Shrine in Tokyo. Citizens carrying a colorful, portable shrine on their shoulders parade through the streets.

May 15: *Aoi Matsuri*, or Hollyhock Festival, of Shimogamo and Kamigamo shrines in Kyoto features a magnificent pageant, reproducing the colorful Imperial Procession that paid homage to the shrines in ancient times.

May 17–18: Grand Festival of Toshogu Shrine in Nikko. Its highlight is a spectacular procession of over 1,000 armor-clad men escorting three sacred, portable shrines through the streets.

Third Sunday in May: *Mifune Matsuri* Festival on the Oi River in Kyoto reproduces an ancient, graceful boat festival.

June 14: Rice-Planting Festival of Sumiyoshi Shrine in Osaka. Young girls in traditional farmers' costumes ceremoniously transplant rice seedlings in the shrine's paddies as a prayer for a good harvest.

June 15: *Chagu-Chagu Umakko*, or Horse Festival, in Morioka, Iwate Prefecture. A number of colorfully decorated horses parade through the streets on their way to Komagata Shrine.

June 10-16: *Sanno Matsuri* Festival of Hie Shrine in Tokyo features a procession of portable shrines through the busy streets around the Akasaka district.

July 7: *Tanabata*, or Star Festival, is celebrated nationwide.

July 15: *Hakata Yamagasa* Festival in Fukuoka reaches its climax on the 15th with a fleet of giant floats topped with elaborate decorations parading through the streets.

July 13-16 (August in other areas): *Bon* Festival. Religious rites in memory of the dead who, according to Buddhist belief, revisit this world during this period are observed throughout the country. A *Bon* dance party is held nightly in practically every community, and visitors are encouraged to join this easy-to-learn folk dance.

Mid-July: *Kangensai* Music Festival of Itsukushima Shrine in Miyajima, Hiroshima Prefecture. Classical court music and dances are performed on the brightly decorated boats.

July 16-17: *Gion Matsuri*, the biggest festival in Kyoto, dates back to the ninth century, when people tried to seek the protection of the gods against a pestilence that was ravaging the city. Gorgeous floats parade through the main streets on the 17th.

July 23-25: *Soma Nomaoi*, or Horse-Chasing Festival, in Haramachi and its vicinities, Fukushima Prefecture. This is a dynamic, horse-riding contest in which a thousand mounted men dressed in ancient *samurai* armor vying for three sacred flags. This is the climax of the festival and takes place on the 24th.

July 24-25: *Tenjin Matsuri* Festival of Temmangu Shrine in Osaka. A fleet of boats bearing portable shrines sail down the Dojima River.

August 1-7: *Nebuta Matsuri* Festival in Aomori from the 2nd to the 7th and *Neputa Matsuri* Festival in Hirosaki from the 1st to the 7th are spectacle summer festivals televised nationwide. Enormous, illuminated papier mâché dummies are paraded through the streets on floats in the evening.

August 5-7: *Kanto Matsuri* Festival in Akita features a parade of men vying in skill at balancing *kanto*, or long bamboo poles hung with many lighted lanterns, on their shoulders, forehead, chin or hips.

August 6-8: *Tanabata* or Star Festival in Sendai is the largest and brightest of its kind. The main streets are decorated with numerous colored paper streamers and banners.

August 6-8: *Hanagasa* Festival in Yamagata features a dance parade through the streets by more than 10,000 townspeople wearing *hanagasa*—a low, round straw hat adorned with brightly colored artificial flowers.

August 12-15: *Awa Odori* Folk Dance Festival in Tokushima. The entire city resounds with singing and dancing, and visitors are encouraged to join this joyful, dancing parade.

August 16: *Daimonji* Bonfire on Mt. Nyoigatake in Kyoto. A spectacular bonfire in the shape of the Chinese ideograph meaning "big" can be viewed from downtown Kyoto.

September 16: *Yabusame*, or Horseback Archery, of Tsurugaoka Hachimangu Shrine in Kamakura.

October 7–9: *Kunchi* Festival of Suwa Shrine in Nagasaki features a dragon dance of Chinese origin and floats with umbrella-shaped decorations.

October 9–10: *Takayama Matsuri* Festival of Hachimangu Shrine in Takayama, Gifu Prefecture is noted for its gala procession of ornate floats.

October 14–15: *Kenka Matsuri* Festival of Matsubara Shrine in Himeji, Hyogo Prefecture reaches its climax on the 15th, when portable shrines are shouldered by half-naked youths, who jostle each other and vie in displaying their skill at balancing the shrines.

October 17: Autumn Festival of Toshogu Shrine in Nikko features a colorful procession of armor-clad parishioners escorting a sacred portable shrine.

October 22: *Jidai Matsuri*, or Festival of the Eras, of Heian Shrine in Kyoto is one of the three grandest festivals of Kyoto. Its highlight is a procession of citizens in colorful costumes representing various eras of Kyoto's 1,200-year-old-history.

October 22: Fire Festival of Yuki Shrine in Kurama, Kyoto. Long rows of torches imbedded along the approach to the shrine are set on fire, as children with burning torches march to the shrine.

November 3: *Daimyo Gyoretsu* in Hakone is a faithful reproduction of a feudal lord's procession that was once a familiar scene along the old Tokaido Road.

November 2–4: *Okunchi Matsuri* Festival of Karatsu Shrine in Karatsu, Nagasaki Prefecture is well known for its parade of huge, colorful floats.

Mid-November: *Tori-no-Ichi*, or Rake Fair, of Otori Shrine in Tokyo. Dozens of makeshift stalls selling *kumade*, or ornate bamboo rakes, are set up in the shrine's precincts.

November 15: *Shichi-go-san* is the shrine visiting day for children aged 3, 5 and 7 in appreciation of their good health given to them by the guardian gods. (refer to p.36)

December 2–3: *Chichibu Yomatsuri* of Chichibu Shrine in Saitama Prefecture is noted for the gorgeously decorated festival floats pulled through the streets. When night falls, countless paper lanterns are lit on the floats, creating a beautiful sight.

December 17: *On-Matsuri* Festival of Kasuga Taisha Shrine in Nara features a procession of people masquerading as courtiers, retainers and *sumo* wrestlers of ancient times.

Mid-December: *Hagoita-Ichi*, or Battledore Fair, of Asakusa Kannon Temple in Tokyo is the year-end mart where ornate battledores and various New Year's decorations are sold.

December 31: *Namahage* in Oga Peninsula, Akita Prefecture, is a unique annual event in which groups of grotesquely masked men disguised as devils make door-to-door calls at homes with children, enquiring: "Are there any good-for-nothing kids around here?"

December 31: *Okera Mairi* Ceremony of Yasaka Shrine in Kyoto. A sacred fire is kindled in the shrine's precincts. It is believed that the fire will bring happiness to those cooking their first meal with the embers of the fire, and visitors are encouraged to take some of the embers of the sacred fire back to their homes.

* Note: Some festival dates change from year to year.

Postal, Telegraph and Telephone Services

The Japanese postal system provides complete service for both domestic and foreign mail. Post office operations come under the control of the Ministry for Posts and Telecommunications, while telegraph and telephone communication services are handled by the privatized Nippon Telegraph and Telephone Corporation(NTT). Overseas telecommunication services are provided by Kokusai Denshin Denwa Co., Ltd. (KDD), International Digital Communications, Inc. (IDC) and International Telecom Japan, Inc. (ITJ). Communications between principal domestic cities are handled competitively by three other corporations in addition to NTT: Daini Denden Co., Ltd., Nihon Telecom and Nihon Kosoku Tsushin Co., Ltd.

Postal Service

Postal supplies and stamps are sold at all post offices. Post offices are open from 9:00 a.m. to 5:00 p.m., Mondays through Fridays, while major post offices are open on Saturdays from 9:00 a.m. to 12:30 p.m. One can also buy stamps and obtain postal information from clerks at the front desk of hotels. Letters should be deposited in mail boxes, which can be found along the street. The simplest way to post mail or packages is to ask for assistance from one's hotel front desk. Postal rates for letters addressed within Japan are ¥62 for up to 25 grams and ¥72 for up to 50 grams in the case of standard-sized envelopes (between 9 × 14 cm and 12 × 23.5 cm). The rate for nonstandard-sized mail is ¥120 for up to 50 grams and ¥175 for up to 100 grams. Domestic postcards require ¥41.

Foreign Money Orders

The issuance of ordinary money orders to foreign countries is handled by post offices, while telegraphic money orders are issued by post offices designated as exchange offices for foreign postal money orders. All post offices can be used for the disbursement of money orders sent from overseas to Japan. Charges for issuing foreign money orders (as of April 1989):

1) Ordinary Money Orders: Up to ¥10,000—¥800, up to ¥50,000—¥1,000, up to ¥100,000—¥1,200 and up to ¥200,000—¥1,500. ¥500 for each additional ¥100,000.

2) Telegraphic Money Orders: These require the same charges as for ordinary money orders plus the actual charges for the telegram.

Foreign Parcel Post

Foreign parcels can be sent and received between Japan and most foreign nations under the Agreement Concerning Postal Parcels of the Universal Postal Union as well as under bilateral parcel post agreements.

While the maximum weight for a single parcel is 10 kg for all destinations, the type of contents of a parcel acceptable and the maximum measurements of a single parcel differ depending on its destination. Although there are some restrictions, a service called SAL (Surface Air Lifted, operated by the Ministry of Posts and Telecommunications) provides cheaper air mail service than normal air mail rates but not as cheap as sea mail rates.

Many international private delivery services such as DHL and Federal Express provide fast and efficient service between Japan and many other nations. This service is especially useful for business firms.

Telegraph Service

Telegrams in Japanese *kana* characters can be sent from NTT branch offices and main post offices. International telegrams sent in the Roman alphabet are handled by KDD. The following offices are open 24 hours a day and handle not only telegrams, but also facsimiles, photo-telegrams, ISD (International Subscriber Dialing) and telex services.

Tokyo Telegraph Office   (03) 3211-5588
Nagoya Telegraph Office (052) 971-4222
Osaka Telegraph Office (06) 228-2151
The following services are available:
1) ordinary telegrams, 2) letter telegrams (night letters) and 3) urgent, reply pre-paid, inquiry and radio marine telegrams.

Public Facsimile Service

Three types of services are available: direct transmission and reception, bureau to bureau service and household-to-bureau service. The rates vary depending on destination, size and method.

Telephone Service

There are four different types of public telephones, each of which can be differentiated by its color.

A buzzer will sound when one has used his last coin or card unit. Put in more coins or another card to continue talking. Change is not given for ¥100 coins, but unused ¥10 coins are returned when the phone is hung up. Intra-city calls are charged at the low rate of ¥10 for three minutes. Magnetic, prepaid card can be purchased at NTT sales offices, train station kiosks and other stores.

Type of Phone	Coins used
Red or Pink Phones (In and in front of stores)	¥10 only
Blue Phones (Street booths)	¥10 only
Yellow Phones (Street booths and in public places)	¥10 & ¥100
Green Phones (Street booths and in public places)	Magnetic, prepaid card & ¥10, ¥100 or only magnetic, prepaid card

Long-Distance Calls: When placing a long-distance call, it is first necessary to dial the area code. Area codes for principal Japanese cities are indicated in the subsection on each city in the Travel Information Section.

International Calls: As stated in the above, KDD, IDC and ITJ all offer international calling services. As their rates vary, it is advisable to compare them when placing international calls. A service charge may be added to the charge for telephone calls placed from hotel rooms. International calls can be classified as direct-dial calls and operator-assisted calls.

International calls can be placed directly in the same way as domestic calls. First dial 001 (0061 for IDC, 0041 for ITJ), then the country code, area code and telephone number. The rate is charged in 6-second units and decreases after the first minute. An economy rate with a 20% discount is in effect between 7:00 p.m. and 11:00 p.m. from Monday to Friday, and from 8:00 a.m. to 11:00 p.m. on Saturdays, Sundays and holidays. A late-night discount of 40% is available between 11:00 p.m. and 5:00 a.m.

The following is an explanation of how to place an international call, using KDD's system as an example:

Example of a Directly Dialed International call:
001-1-212-976-1212
  001: KDD's access number
    1: country code
  212: area code
  976-1212: telephone number
Telephone calls can be placed directly to most advanced countries from certain types of public telephones.

Operator-Assisted International Calls: Dial 0051 and a KDD operator will connect one to the number desired. The following options are available:

1. Person-to-person call: Give the name and telephone number of the person to whom one wishes to speak. No charge is made until the connection is made.

2. Station Call: Just give the telephone number to the place that one wants to call. The charge is less than that for a person-to-person call.

3. Collect Call: Tell the operator that a "collect call" is desired and the connection will be made when the person called agrees to accept the charges.

4. Credit-Card Call: Tell the operator to place a "credit card call."

One can also use ISD (International Subscriber Dialing) to place international calls. If one wants to use this method to place a collect call or credit-card call, dial the appropriate number from the following list and an operator from that country will answer:

Area	Number
Continental USA	0039-111
Canada	0039-161
Hawaii	0039-181
U.K.	0039-441
France	0039-331
Italy	0039-391
Netherlands	0039-311
Korea	0039-821
Hong Kong	0039-852
Taiwan	0039-886
Thailand	0039-661
Singapore	0039-651
Australia	0039-611
New Zealand	0039-641

Luggage Delivery Services

Luggage delivery services are available at all the major airports. At New Tokyo International Airport in Narita, for instance, QL Liner, ABC Co., Ltd. and other firms have counters in the arrival lobby from which they deliver luggage directly to hotels or to any designated address. Luggage is delivered the following day. From Narita to hotels in downtown Tokyo,an example of the rate is ¥1,550 for each piece of luggage up to 30 kg and an additional ¥100 for pieces that weigh more than 30 kg, with a maximum limit of 40 kg (as of July 1990). This Service is also available from hotels to the airport.

II. Tourist Facilities and Available Services

Reception of Foreign Visitors

Efforts are being made in Japan to improve and expand tourist facilities for visitors from abroad so that they can travel in Japan in comfort and safety.

Entry and exit formalities have been simplified to a considerable extent. For the benefit of tourists planning to stay in Japan for a brief period, a special system permitting them to enter Japan without visas has been adopted.

In Tokyo, Kyoto and at the New Tokyo International Airport in Narita, Tourist Information Centers (TIC), operated by the Japan National Tourist Organization (JNTO), have been set up to provide all necessary travel information on tours in Japan in English and other foreign languages. In addition, all the principal cities and tourist areas are equipped with information centers named "i" system (refer to p.63). They usually have English-speaking staff. A visit to any one of them will provide the tourist with a sufficient amount of information on travel in Japan. Tourist information is also available by telephone. (refer to p.63 and 64)

All travel agents are required to register with the government in order to ensure the reliability of their service. The agencies can make travel arrangements for foreign visitors and offer various package tours.

Since there are very few foreigners who can speak Japanese, there is a great need for translators and interpreters. The government has established standards for guide-interpreters. Those who have passed the national examination are qualified as licensed guide-interpreters in English, French, German, Italian, Spanish, Russian, Chinese, Portuguese and Korean. In addition, volunteer "Good-will Guides" are organized throughout the country. (refer to p.63)

As for accommodations, there are a large number of Western-style hotels located throughout the country, including government-registered hotels that meet international standards. Foreign visitors staying at such hotels will find all the conveniences that they expect from quality establishments without encountering any problems with differences in culture and manners.

In addition, there are numerous *ryokan*, or traditional Japanese inns. The *ryokan*, which meet standards of modern requirements, are also registered with the government. They are ideal for the foreign visitor who wants to get a feel for the traditional Japanese life-style.

At major cities throughout the nation, travelers can find reasonably priced hotels often used by economy-minded business people known as "business hotels" and low-priced *minshuku* (Japanese family-style inns). In resort areas, one may find lodge-style pensions as well as government-run "People's Lodges" and "National Vacation Villages." These are open for use by foreign guests as well. Furthermore, there are many publicly and privately run youth hostels throughout the nation. These are widely used by young travelers.

Japanese cooking is one of the most pleasing. In addition to the wide range of locally raised produce, foodstuffs are imported from all over the globe. Japanese agricultural cultivation methods are highly advanced and ensure that many farm products are available all year round. In addition to such traditional Japanese favorites as *sukiyaki*, *tempura*, *sashimi*, *sushi* and *kaiseki ryori*, there are many foreign restaurants specializing in French, Italian, German, Russian and Spanish cuisine as well as spicy Indian and Mexican food, and Chinese and Korean delicacies, etc. Japan is proud of the high quality of its fresh water, and there is never any need to worry about drinking tap water or the availability of commercial mineral water.

It may be said that Japan is a fantasyland for the traveler who is interested in shopping. It is perhaps best known for the superior quality of such electronic goods as cameras, video-tape recorders, CD players, color TV sets, portable stereo radios and personal computers. However, Japanese pearls, ceramics and such traditional craftwork as dolls, silk goods and cotton wear can also be found. Since electrical voltage and cycles change from one country to another, many products are expressly manufactured for export to meet foreign specifications. Foreign visitors can take advantage of discounts at duty-free shops, where they will find a friendly staff capable of speaking their language and helping them to fill out the necessary forms. They can also find many discount shops that carry high-tech electronic goods as well as deluxe products that are sure to leave visitors with a long-lasting memory of their stay in Japan.

Consumption Tax: (as of April 1990)
Charge (per person/per day)
Restaurants

Under ¥5,000	3%
Over ¥5,000	6%

Hotels

Under ¥10,000	3%
Over ¥10,000	6%

Air and rail fares are priced with the tax included.

The nationwide transportation network is fully equipped. Advances in the development of air service have brought practically every part of the country to within a few hours of the major urban centers. The railway network extends to every corner of the country, and travel by means of comfortable, deluxe buses has also become very popular. As a result of the increase in the number of people traveling by car in recent years, the need for car-ferry service has grown. Long-distance ferries cross from Tokyo to Hokkaido, Shikoku and Kyushu, and from the Osaka/Kobe area to Shikoku and Kyushu.

By making systematic use of the above-mentioned tourist facilities, it is possible for foreign visitors to enjoy in comfort and safety the natural beauty of Japan and to come into personal contact with the nation's age-old history and culture.

Accomodation Facilities

Western-Style Hotels

Japan's dramatic economic growth has given the Japanese people more and more time to spend on leisure activities. People are moving around a great deal, and the need for good accommodations has greatly increased. As a result, almost every town and city offers a range of accommodations that includes fully equipped, first-class luxury hotels such as Tokyo's Hotel Okura, Imperial Hotel and Hotel New Otani as well as business hotels with limited services but reasonably priced accommodations to say nothing of the resort areas that cater to tourist.

Travelers who prefer a wide choice of restaurants and shops, a spacious lobby and such luxuries as secretarial and laundry services will be at ease at any of Japan's top luxury hotels. Those seeking simpler accommodations will find satisfaction at the business hotels, which are generally priced at a half or one-third the cost of the luxury hotels.

As of March 1990, there were 400 member hotels in the Japan Hotel Association: 42 in Tokyo, 25 in Osaka, 21 in Kyoto, 11 in Nagoya and 8 in Yokohama. The Japan Business Hotel Association counts 431 members.

All these hotels are equipped with modern conveniences, including central heating and air-conditioning. Many have special facilities that include restaurants serving Western food and such traditional Japanese dishes as *sukiyaki*, *tempura* and *sushi*. Many hotels also have beautiful Japanese landscape gardens, although business hotels generally have only limited facilities.

The following is a list of average prices charged at member hotels of the Japan Hotel Association:

Rooms	For One Person	For Two Persons
single	¥8,000–10,000	
twin		¥13,000–28,000
suite		¥35,000–600,000
Meals		
breakfast	¥1,300–1,800	
lunch	¥2,500–5,000	
dinner	¥5,000 –	

Business hotels are very convenient for travelers who desire an economical trip with simple, low-priced accommodations. These hotels usually do not provide porter or room services. Drink and cigarette vending machines are conveniently located in the hallways. As they cater mainly to business travelers, most rooms are singles. Many of these hotels have a restaurant. Since they are conveniently located in urban centers and close to stations, these reasonably priced hotels are also commonly used by tourists.

Prices are approximately as follows:

Rooms	For One Person	For Two Persons
single with bath	¥3,500–7,000	
twin with bath		¥5,000–10,000

A service charge of 10–15% is levied on hotel accommodations and hotel restaurants and bars. Except for baggage porters, tipping is not customary in Japan.

Japanese-Style Inns, or Hotels (Ryokan)

Ryokan, traditional Japanese-style inns, or hotels, have been improved to such an extent that they now play an important role in providing accommodations for both foreign and Japanese guests.

Recent years have seen a particular increase in the number of foreign guests who want to expand their knowledge and experience of Japan by staying in a traditional Japanese room and eating Japanese food. Sleeping on a *tatami* mat, and bathing in a large bath and in outdoor hot springs have come to be appreciated as a unique experience not to be missed by the traveler in Japan. Foreign visitors should make a point of staying at least one night in one of the traditional *ryokan* in Kyoto, Nara or Hakone. Although several *ryokan* have made great efforts to employ an English-speaking staff to assist in accommodating foreigners, the language barrier still exists for non-Japanese-speaking foreigners at most *ryokan*.

As of March 1990, there were about 2,200 members of the Japan Ryokan Association (JRA). Of these, about 1,500 were registered with the Ministry of Transport to ensure that they offer suitable facilities for all visiting guests.

The accommodations, facilities and service at *ryokan* differ widely from those provided by Western-style hotels, but foreign guests will enjoy the relaxing, home-like atmosphere and receive personalized service that will please even the most seasoned traveler.

Ryokan are usually two or three-story wooden structures with the outward appearance of ordinary Japanese houses. However, solid ferro-concrete buildings eight or nine stories high are becoming quite popular in thriving tourist centers. Many of these now call themselves "hotels" rather than *ryokan*. Still, whatever the outward appearance or name, the interior is invariably built in the traditional Japanese style. Furthermore, most *ryokan* are equipped with a wide range of modern facilities.

A guest at a *ryokan* is usually led into a sitting room with an adjoining anteroom and a veranda. Each section is partitioned off from the others by sliding, paper-paneled doors. As the rooms can be locked from both inside and out, complete privacy is ensured throughout. The floor is matted with snug-fitting *tatami*, each section of which measures 180 cm by 90 cm (6'×3') and is 6 cm thick. The *tatami* is topped by a smoothly woven rush cover, soft and pleasant to the touch. Customarily, the size of the room is determined by the number of *tatami* mats used.

The furnishings are simple but graceful. In the middle of the room is a low, lacquered table with cushions arranged around it. In one corner is a slightly elevated alcove with a flower arrangement, while on the alcove wall hangs a scroll with a painting or poem written in artistic calligraphic style. The veranda/sun-room is provided with a table and chairs so that guests may sit and take in the surrounding scenery. The Japanese sitting room can quickly be converted to a dining room or bedroom. Everything is kept clean and tidy, with clothing and baggage stored away in the built-in closets.

Japanese-style inns, or "hotels," customarily charge a daily rate for lodging, which includes dinner and breakfast. Lunch is not included, but may be ordered separately. Local specialties or seasonal delicacies may also be ordered for an additional charge. Alcoholic drinks and soft drinks are usually not included with the meal and must be ordered separately. Usually these are contained in a refrigerator installed in the room and anything consumed will be added to your bill. At check-out time, guests will be billed for anything that they consume. Prices of food and beverages are provided on a list, often placed on a table nearby. Although it is possible to stay at a *ryokan* without taking any meals, the experience of enjoying a wide range of traditional Japanese delicacies is without doubt one of the main reasons for staying at a *ryokan*. Furthermore, for guests who do not take breakfast or dinner, the charge is only reduced by about 5% and 15%, respectively.

Ryokan rooms are generally designed to accommodate 4–5 guests, with the actual charge depending on how many people stay in a room. Unlike hotels, room rates at *ryokan* vary greatly, especially on Saturdays, on the day before a holiday and during peak seasons. By avoiding weekends and times when many people are traveling, one can experience the same service and quality for a considerably reduced rate.

Average room rates (when shared by two persons) per night, including two meals, at a *ryokan* are as follows:

Deluxe	¥18,000–30,000
Superior	¥12,000–18,000
Standard	¥ 8,000–12,000

A 10–15% service charge is added to these rates. Therefore, if no special services are requested, there is no need for any tipping.

One of the major charms of *ryokan* at hot-springs resorts is their *rotemburo* (outdoor hot-springs baths). There is nothing better to relieve stress and fatigue than gazing at a beautiful natural setting while relaxing in a hot, soothing bath. Visitors can bathe in the privacy of their own room since many *ryokan* provide rooms with a private bath, but they are welcome to try the public bath, generally used by all guests in common. *Ryokan* base their image on and take great pride in their hot springs and baths. Travelers often select a *ryokan* based on its hot-springs and bathing facilities. Japanese guests usually take their bath before supper, which is usually served at 6:00 p.m. It should be remembered that since all guests bathe together, it is not proper to wash oneself inside a Japanese bath. The body is washed and rinsed outside the bath with the use of a basin and a small stool provided for that purpose. Both hot and cold-water faucets are provided, and it is here that one washes and shaves. Afterwards, one enters the bath to relax and enjoy the soothing warm water, rinsing off at the faucet after leaving the bath if one feels the need. While the guests are in the bath, dinner preparations take place in their room. The relaxed mood of that moment immediately after the bath is just right for enjoying a delicious meal. It is important to arrive at a *ryokan* early enough so that one can relax and bathe in time to enjoy dinner.

At purely traditional *ryokan* with a wooden construction, guests are requested to take off their shoes at the entrance. Slippers are provided for walking along the hallway, but they should be removed before entering a room with a *tatami* floor. At *ryokan* that have adopted a more modern outward appearance, guests are usually allowed to walk to their rooms without taking off their shoes. Despite the outward modern appearance, however, rooms in such *ryokan* are always designed in the traditional style. Most rooms in such *ryokan* have a television, refrigerator and safe for keeping valuables. Like Western-style hotels, most leading *ryokan* are equipped with central heating and air-conditioning.

A light Japanese *kimono* called *yukata* (often used as a sleeping garment) is supplied to guests. It comes in handy, not only when walking around the *ryokan* and going to the bath, but also when relaxing in the sitting room, as sitting on *tatami* in Western-style clothes can be rather uncomfortable. When the weather is cold, *dotera* or *tanzen* (padded *kimono*) are supplied to guests.

Beds are made up directly on the *tatami* floor in the evening by the room attendant. A thick, sponge-rubber mattress is first laid out with one or two layers of soft, fluffy quilts set on top. The sheets are then spread over this, and down- or cotton-filled quilts—the number and thickness depending on the season—serve as blankets.

The dishes served at *ryokan* are almost all Japanese style. If orders are placed in advance, guests will be served a Western-style breakfast of coffee, toast and eggs. Although not everyone may enjoy Japanese cooking, one can rest assured that all the ingredients are fresh and that the chef has considerable training in the art of food preparation. The meals served at *ryokan* are of such a variety and quality that many of the dishes cannot be found in the average household any-more. If only for the sake of experiencing something entirely differ-ent from Western-style cooking, every visitor to Japan should at least once try a true, Japanese-style *ryokan* dinner. Meals at *ryokan* are usually served to guests in their own rooms. Due to the shortage of labor in recent years, however, there is a tendency for meals at many *ryokan* to be served in large dining areas.

Economy Inns

In order to meet the needs of foreign visitors who would like to experience the traditional Japanese *ryokan* at a more affordable price, a group of *ryokan* owners have joined together to form the Japanese Inn Group. This group has members not only in the com-mon travel spots of Tokyo, Kyoto and Nara, but in Shikoku, Kyushu and Hokkaido as well. All offer similar services at reduced prices. As of March 1990, there were a total of 75 member locations. Reservations can be made by letter or over the phone. Standard rates for one night without meals are as follows:

Room rate	¥3,500-9,000
Breakfast	¥ 300-1,000

Youth Hostels

Youth hostels are simple, neat and inexpensive accommodation facilities. They are operated to promote wholesome travel by the youth, to encourage the cultivation of a sound mind and body, and to strengthen international friendship through travel between the youth of Japan and foreign countries.

As of October 1990, there were about 440 youth hostels throughout Japan. Of these, 75 were built with government subsidies and are managed by local authorities. The others are managed or contracted by Japan Youth Hostels, Inc. (JYH).

Youth hostels are equipped with separate bedrooms for men and women, dining rooms, showers and heating systems. Common kitchens equipped with utensils are also available. Most foreign visitors staying at youth hostels are young and these facilities offer wholesome, safe accommodations for the youthful traveler.

As of October 1990, average rates at youth hostels in Japan were as follows:

Bed	¥2,500 (includes sheets and heating charge)
Breakfast	¥ 350-450
Dinner	¥ 650-850
Meeting Hall	¥50 per person

Note: Further information is available at Japan Youth Hostels Inc., located on the 3rd fl., Hoken Kaikan Bldg., 2 Sadoharacho 1-chome,

Ichigaya, Shinjuku-ku Tokyo: ☎ (03)3269-5831/3. Refer to "the supplement."

Minshuku

Minshuku are family-style inns that are operated within private homes. These inns are usually found in coastal and mountainous areas where travelers seek simple accommodations in a natural environment. They are also often used for training sessions by various groups and are especially popular among young travelers and families. There are 304 Japan National Tourist Organization (JNTO)-listed *minshuku* located throughout Japan. Rates for one night with two meals for adults start at ¥6,000.

Pensions

Pensions are the newest addition to Western-style accommodations in Japan. They are family-style inns with a relaxed atmosphere and delicious home-style cooking. Located at such resorts as ski grounds mountain and lake areas, they are very popular especially among young people. With average rates of ¥7,000 - 8,000 for a night and two meals, pensions offer substantial savings when compared to city hotels and deluxe *ryokan*. There are 325 JNTO-listed pensions located throughout Japan.

Public Accommodations

Many public recreational accommodations have been set up in areas of beautiful natural scenery and places that offer the chance to build a wholesome mind and body through athletic activities. Prices at these accommodations are kept low to allow anyone to take advantage of them.

Kokumin Shukusha (People's Lodges)

This is the most popular type of the public accommodation for sightseeing and can be found all over the country. In addition to public facilities (292 as of March 1990), there are other privately run facilities that are designated and regulated by the National Parks Association of Japan (148 as of March 1990).

Average rates for one night with two meals are as follows:

Adults	¥5,300
Children	¥4,800

Kokumin Kyuka-mura (National Vacation Villages)

National Vacation Villages are health resorts established in national parks and quasi-national parks that are blessed with beautiful natural surroundings. As of March 1990, a total of 32 villages were used by 1,160,000 people annually. In addition to the basic accommodations, these areas offer recreation facilities such as ski grounds, swimming pools, tennis courts and camping grounds. Their popularity among foreign visitors is steadily increasing.

Average room rates are:

    Adults ¥7,000-9,000
    Breakfast (Japanese and Western-style)   ¥700
    Dinner (Japanese-style)   ¥2,300
  Meals at these villages include local specialties, seafood, steak and a variety of Japanese food.

  In addition to the above facilities, there are many travel and resort facilities that are run with funds from the national pension and national health insurance. Most of these are open to use by foreign visitors as well.

Domestic Traffic Facilities

Air Service

  Regularly scheduled domestic flights are maintained on the major routes connecting Sapporo, Tokyo, Osaka, Fukuoka and Naha as well as on routes linking other principal cities. In addition to the main routes operated by Japan Air Lines (JAL), All Nippon Airways (ANA) and Japan Air System (JAS) also offer service on these lines. Local routes are mainly served by ANA and JAS.

  Japan has 79 airports and seven companies offer a total of 163 service routes. Under the present network, it is generally possible to travel to any city from Tokyo within 2 hrs. 30 min. In Tokyo Haneda Airport is for domestic destinations, while Narita Airport (New Tokyo International Airport) is for international flights.

  The largest number of flights is offered between Tokyo and Sapporo—30 round-trip flights daily. There are 23 round-trip flights between Tokyo and Fukuoka daily. Since the distance from Tokyo to Osaka can be covered by the JR Shinkansen rail service in only 2 hrs. 52 min., there are many more rail passengers on that route than air travelers. Among the local routes that have many flights are those between Osaka and cities in Shikoku and Kyushu. There are 21 daily round-trip flights between Osaka and Kochi, six between Osaka and Kagoshima, and ten between Osaka and Tokushima, while the routes between Tokyo and Kyushu/Shikoku/Hokkaido are sufficient to provide ample service. Many travelers fly up to Hokkaido to take advantage of the excellent skiing conditions there. Others escape the cold of winter with a quick flight down to the sunny, sandy shores of Okinawa.

  In Okinawa Prefecture at the southern end of Japan, South West Air Lines (SWAL) operates an inter-island service. In an area like Okinawa, which consists of a string of islands, air service is regarded as one of the principal means of transportation. With Naha as the center, the air service covers such islands as Miyako, Ishigaki, Kume, Aguni, Shimoji, Kita-Daito, Minami-Daito and Yonaguni. Hokkaido Prefecture lies at the northern end of Japan and is serviced by regularly scheduled flights on Air Nippon (ANK), even to the distant Rishiri, Rebun and Okushiri islands. Sapporo, Nagoya, Osaka and Fukuoka are connected with international routes via the New Tokyo International Airport at Narita. There are still relatively few scheduled flights, but the convenience of these direct flights from regional cities has proved very popular. Regular helicopter service is available between Narita and Haneda Airport or to Yokohama, taking about 30 min.

Notes on Air Fare

∗ 1. Round-trip fares are double one-way fares. For travel that is completed within 7 days, there is a discount of 10% on round-trip tickets. (10 days for Okinawa and SWAL routes)

∗ 2. A 35% reduction is available for youths, a 20% reduction for senior-citizen couples, a 20% reduction for women's groups more than two persons and a 10% reduction for air-excursion tickets. (Certain limitations apply to these reductions).

∗ 3. Certain JAL and ANA flights have deluxe seats called "super seats," which can be obtained for an additional fee.

Railway Service

Japan Railways (JR)

The first rail service in Japan opened between Shimbashi (in Tokyo) and Yokohama in 1872. Under governmental direction, the Japanese rail system soon expanded significantly to keep abreast of the country's rapid modernization. The Japanese National Railways (JNR) continued its development until all areas of the country were connected in an extensive network. In April 1987, JNR was privat-ized as one aspect of governmental reform. Six independent new rail companies serving travelers in Hokkaido, east Japan, central Japan, west Japan, Shikoku and Kyushu are recognized under the name "Japan Railways (JR)." The privatization of JNR led to the closing of unprofitable routes and the introduction of bus service in these areas as well as the establishment of new railway lines to serve these areas. At present, Japan Railways operates three types of services in a mutually interlinked network: Shinkansen lines, main lines and regional lines. The entire rail system is organized and operated in a single, extensive network called the JR Group, allowing uninhibited travel on JR lines throughout the nation.

Japan offers probably the most efficient and convenient rail service in the world. The JR Group maintains the world's most tightly scheduled train service. JR trains are safe, speedy and punctual. Exploring Japan by rail is also a rewarding experience: the scenery viewed through train windows changes practically every minute, thanks to the country's diversified topography. JR operates more than 25,000 trains daily including Shinkansen super-expresses on its nationwide system that extends over 20,000 km. In urban areas, rail companies besides JR also have an extensive rail network linking cities and towns. Within big cities like Tokyo, Osaka, Kobe, Kyoto, Nagoya, Yokohama, Sapporo, Fukuoka and Sendai, subways are available for convenient intra-city transportation.

Trains: JR passenger trains are classified according to their speed and accommodations. The Shinkansen and limited-express trains are the fastest and offer the best accommodations. Ordinary expresses are somewhat slower and have fewer passenger facilities. Rapid trains are operated over short distances of around 100 km. Local trains cater mainly to commuters and students.

Some long-distance limited-express sleeper trains are equipped with dining cars, which offer reasonably priced Western and Japanese meals as well as beer, spirits and soft drinks. For those wishing to eat at their seats or desiring to purchase souvenirs, attendants with vending carts pass through the cars selling boxed lunches, coffee, spirits and local specialties. Train conductors can be identified by their uniforms, and are ready to give information and assistance on train changes and other passenger requests. On Shinkansen trains, announcements are made in English. However, for the non-Japanese-speaking foreigner, there are still some difficulties to be overcome when taking a rail journey in Japan.

Shinkansen: Literally "The New Trunk Line," the Shinkansen is the nationwide, high-speed train service run on standard gauge (1,435 mm or 4 ft. 8.5 in.) double tracks. In constructing this railway, the most advanced technology and engineering skills from every industrial field were employed, making it one of the fastest, most reliable and most traveled rail transport systems in the world.

Shinkansen service is now available along the following routes:

1. Tokaido / San-yo Shinkansen (Tokyo – Hakata ⟨Fukuoka⟩)
This route was first developed in 1964 to service the area between Tokyo and Shin-Osaka. Service is provided by both "Hikari" trains and "Kodama" trains.

Tokyo – Shin-Osaka (552.6 km)	Hikari	2 hrs. 52 min.
Tokyo – Okayama (732.9 km)	Hikari	3 hrs. 50 min.
Tokyo – Hiroshima (894.8 km)	Hikari	4 hrs. 36 min.
Tokyo – Hakata (Fukuoka) (1,176.5 km)	Hikari	5 hrs. 57 min.

2. Tohoku Shinkansen (Ueno, Tokyo – Morioka)
The "Yamabiko" and "Aoba" trains run on this route.

Ueno – Fukushima (272.8 km)	Yamabiko	1 hr. 35 min.
Ueno – Sendai (351.8 km)	Yamabiko	2 hrs.
Ueno – Morioka (535.3 km)	Yamabiko	3 hrs. 19 min.

3. Joetsu Shinkansen (Ueno, Tokyo – Niigata)
The "Asahi" and "Toki" trains run on this route.

Ueno – Takasaki (105.0 km)	Asahi	47 min.
Ueno – Nagaoka (270.6 km)	Asahi	1 hr.34 min.
Ueno – Niigata (333.9 km)	Asahi	2 hrs.

＊ Work is under way to extend the Shinkansen from Ueno Station to Tokyo Station (as of January 1990). Due to be completed in June 1991 this will allow for direct connections between the Tokaido Shinkansen and the Tohoku and Joetsu Shinkansen lines.

Some Shinkansen trains stop only at major stations, while others make local stops as well. As a result, the traveling time required varies between different trains on the same line. All trains consist of ordinary-class cars and first-class cars called Green Cars, both with smoking and non-smoking sections. Ordinary cars have both reserved and non-reserved seats, while Green Cars have only reserved seats. In addition to these, there are private rooms (except on the Joetsu Line), buffet cars and telephone booths. On the Tokaido, San-yo and Tohoku lines, cars that have private rooms are designed in a two-floor structure. Telephones on board Shinkansen trains are exactly the same as all public telephones and offer high-performance service.

One of the main reason for the popularity of rail transport in Japan is the extremely high percentage of departures and arrivals that are made exactly on schedule. As the number of travelers on any given route tends to be quite high, it is best to reserve a seat to ensure a comfortable journey.

The following is a list of ways to make one's rail journey in Japan more pleasant and interesting:

Japan Rail Pass: This pass allows for passage on all trains in the JR Group, including the Shinkansen, limited express, ordinary express, local trains, buses and a ferry. It is the most economical, flexible and easy way to travel in Japan.

There are two types of rail passes: Green (First Class) and Ordinary (Tourist Class).

Japan Rail Pass	Green		Ordinary	
	Adults	Children	Adults	Children
7 days	¥37,000	¥18,500	¥27,800	¥13,900
14 days	¥60,000	¥30,000	¥44,200	¥22,100
21 days	¥78,000	¥39,000	¥56,600	¥28,300

* Children between the ages of 6-11 are eligible for the children's fare.

Passes are only sold outside of Japan. Take your passport to any office of JAL (JAL passengers only), JTB or other JR-designated agent, where you can purchase an exchange order for a pass. Upon arrival in Japan, go to the *ryoko* center or travel service center in Narita Airport or any of the designated JR travel service centers in Tokyo, Ueno, Ikebukuro, Shinjuku, Shibuya, Sapporo, Sendai, Misawa, Yamagata, Fukushima, Niigata, Tsukuba, Yokohama, Nagoya, Kyoto, Osaka, Shin-Osaka, Hiroshima, Shimonoseki, Kokura, Hakata, Kumamoto or Nishi-Kagoshima stations, where the pass is activated and its period of validity determined. Show your pass at any *Midori-no-Madoguchi* (Green Window) at major JR stations or at JR travel service centers and a seat can be reserved without charge. During your trip, remember to stop in at a JR station when making further reservations.

Train Fares: In addition to the basic passenger fare, there are separate charges for reserved seats, sleepers and green cars (first class) as well as supplementary charges for Shinkansen, limited-express and ordinary-express trains. Children 12 years or older are charged the full fare and children 6-11 years old are eligible for half-price children's fare, while the fare for young children and infants under the age of six is determined by the number of children traveling. Once a ticket is purchased, it may be canceled but a charge is levied, depending on the conditions of the cancellation. Short-distance tickets are issued for a limited period of validity. It is always wise to check with a station clerk when buying a ticket.

For a round trip, when the one-way distance on JR trains exceeds 600 km, the return portion of this round-trip fare will be discounted by 20%.

Buying Tickets: When purchasing tickets for short distances that do not require reserved seats, go to the automatic ticket machines located near the entrance of train stations. Above the machines will be found maps indicating the fare. If you cannot find your destination on the map, it is best to purchase the cheapest ticket and show it at the fare adjustment office of the station where you get off so you can pay the remaining fare. Some machines accept coins as well as ¥1,000 bills. If you plan on traveling frequently on the JR trains, it is convenient to purchase a pre-paid "Orange Card." These magnetized cards come in fixed units and can be used in machines instead of cash.

For medium and long-distance trips, go to the Green Window at a JR station or major travel agents office where you buy reserved-seat tickets. Since reservations can be made from one month prior to the date of travel, it is best to go as early as possible to ensure that you get a seat on the train that fits your schedule.

Other (Non-JR) Railways

In addition to JR, there are many railway companies with a long history of excellent service to local areas. In large cities, these railways provide a level of service equal to or greater than that provided by the JR Group. This is quite unique among the world's railway networks. There are presently 132 railway companies other than JR, 14 of which are large-scale corporations and the other 118 are medium- to small-scale firms. There are also 11 municipal rail systems and the Teito Rapid Transit Authority.

The following is a list of the major railway companies (not including JR):

Tokyo

Tobu Railway, Seibu Railway, Keisei Electric Railway, Keio-Teito Electric Railway, Odakyu Electric Railway, Tokyu, and Keihin Electric Express Railway

Nagoya

Nagoya Railroad

Kyoto, Osaka and Kobe

Kinki Nippon Railway, Nankai Electric Railway, Keihan Electric Railway, Hankyu, and Hanshin Electric Railway

Kyushu

Nishi-Nippon Railroad

Compared to Europe and America, the role played in Japan by railway networks in metropolitan transport systems is much more important than that of automobiles.

Subways: The importance of underground subway systems has grown, as ground transportation systems have become more and more congested in large metropolitan areas where they are serving greater and greater areas to accommodate the many people commuting between the suburbs and the downtown metropolitan areas. At present, the following cities have subway systems: Tokyo, Osaka, Nagoya, Yokohama, Kobe, Kyoto, Sapporo, Fukuoka and Sendai.

New Transportation Systems: With the aid of computers and advanced technologies, new transportation systems are being developed with features that save energy and manpower. Reductions in exhaust fumes, noise and other forms of pollution have also been achieved as transport capacity and speeds have been improved. Examples of these are the fully-automated, computer-controlled Kobe City Port Liner, the Newtram of Osaka City and the Yokohama Seaside Line. Progress is continuing on the linear motor car for the high-speed, post-Shinkansen-generation system. This project has attracted great interest and expectations.

Road Traffic

The Japanese road network is composed of nationally administered expressways and roads that traverse the nation as well as prefectural, city, town and village roads. At the beginning of 1990, there was a total of 4,560 km of expressways, the longest of which runs from Aomori at the northern tip of the island of Honshu directly down to Hitoyoshi City in Kumamoto Prefecture on the island of Kyushu with the distance of 1999 km. The majority of Japanese expressways are toll roads.

Car Rentals: Toyota, Nissan, Nippon Rent-A-Car and other major and minor firms have offices throughout the country where most types of Japanese-made automobiles can be rented. Most rental cars have automatic transmissions. If a reservation is made for a rental car by combining it with JR (with the condition of taking JR trains more than 200 km) or airline tickets at travel agents or JR travel service centers at major JR stations, one can obtain discounts both on the rental fee and JR or airline tickets.

Road Signs: Japanese roads signs follow internationally accepted standards and can easily be understood by anyone, but it is advisable to review them briefly before driving in Japan.

A Note on Driving in Japan: In Japan, automobiles are driven on the left side of the road and the steering wheel is located on the right side of the car. Signposts showing the name of the street are quite rare, and except for those in large cities, there are few destination signs in English, so it is very important to obtain a good map and have a sharp navigator. Traffic on some city streets is in only one direction and many streets are narrow, with no distinction between the road and the pedestrian walkway. The maximum and minimum speeds on expressways are 100 km and 50 km, respectively. Stay in the left lane except for passing, in which case one should use the middle or right lane.

Long-Distance Buses: Long-distance buses cover many routes such as the one between Tokyo and Fukuoka (1,161 km). Super double-decker buses are used on many routes along with deluxe buses for night-time travel, a service that has gained much popularity in recent years. Travel by bus is a safe and inexpensive means of transportation.

Dining

Western-style restaurants can be found in all the cities of Japan, and even in remote areas simple foreign dishes may be obtained in many Japanese restaurants. Restaurants in the large cities offer almost every style of European and Chinese cooking at reasonable prices in addition to the finest Japanese dishes. Many famous French and Italian restaurants operate branches in Tokyo and Osaka. Ethnic food, whether it be Korean, Thai, Indian or any other, can be found throughout the country. Prices vary greatly, depending on the kind of food and the quality level of the restaurant.

Member restaurants of the Japan Restaurant Association are always equipped with clean, excellent facilities. They can easily be identified by the emblem posted at the entrance reading "International Tourist Restaurant," which indicates that they have been designated as a "Registered International Tourist Restaurant" that meets the standards of the Department of Tourism, Ministry of Transport.

When the charge per person does not exceed ¥5,000, only a 3% consumption tax is levied. If it goes over ¥5,000, the tax is raised to 6%. Furthermore, most high-class restaurants charge an additional 10% service charge.

A high-class *ryoriya* (Japanese-style restaurant) can accommodate hundreds of guests in tastefully decorated rooms usually looking out on exquisitely designed gardens. Typical Japanese dishes, the arrangement of which varies according to the occasion—ceremonial or ordinary—are as follows: *sashimi* (thinly sliced raw fish), *yakimono* (broiled fish and fowl), *nimono* (boiled fish and fowl with vegetables), *shirumono* (soup), *mushimono* (steamed fish, fowl and eggs), *sunomono* (vinegared fish or shellfish with vegetables) and *konomono* or *tsukemono* (pickled vegetables).

It is said that Japanese food is eaten with the eyes and not with the mouth. The dishes in which the food is served are of many sizes, shapes and designs to suitably match their contents. The dishes are meant to combine subtlety with the food to stimulate the appetite of the viewer.

One way to differentiate restaurants in Japan is that, in general, restaurants with wax samples which are uncannily similar to real food are reasonably priced. The prices are usually given with the samples, and even if you cannot speak Japanese, you need only point to the dish that you desire and you can get what you want. You will surely be amazed at how similar the actual dish is to the sample in the window. This system of window samples is found throughout Japan.

Large cities have many family restaurant chains that offer good food at reasonable prices. For ¥800–1,500, you can be sure to get a satisfying meal. There are many fast-food chains in Japan as well. In addition to such internationally known chains as McDonalds, Denny's, Wendy's, Kentucky Fried Chicken, Mr. Donut and Dunkin Donuts, there are many Japanese chains such as Lotteria and Sky-lark. In railway stations, you can find small booths selling *ramen* (Chinese noodles) and other noodle dishes for ¥250–400. You can also purchase a *bento* (lunch-box meal) on the platform and enjoy it during a long-distance ride.

Night Life

Japanese cities are second to none in the world when it comes to night life. The number and variety of night clubs, discos, bars, restaurants and other night spots are enough to keep even the most energetic traveler entertained. Some of these are quite expensive and cater only to businessmen with inflated expense accounts, while others are patronized by average company workers looking for a few drinks and some laughs after a hard day at the office. Some large clubs feature top musicians and singers who perform to their guests' delight. Such places usually run between ¥15,000–25,000 per person. There are many discotheques that are popular among young people. Admission is usually from ¥3,000–5,000. Western-style bars serve Western drinks in a light and friendly atmosphere. Recent years have seen the appearance of many small, casual pubs that serve light meals and drinks. Cafe bars serve a wide range of alcoholic and non-alcoholic beverages and foods. In addition, there are, of course, the traditional "*akachochin*" (red lantern bars) and *yakitori* (skewered barbecued chicken) bars.

Beer is the most popular drink in Japan and can be ordered at almost any restaurant or bar. It comes in large, medium and small bottles with prices in the range of ¥400-900, depending on the type of establishment.

Sake, a fermented liquor made from rice is the national drink. It is usually served hot in a small carafe (180ml: ¥300-500), from which it is poured into a tiny cup used for drinking. It has a smooth and mellow taste and goes well with Japanese dishes. It has an alcoholic content of 15-16%.

Shochu is a distilled spirit made from sweet potatoes, corn, barley, etc. Like vodka, it is used as a base liquor for cocktails. *Shochu* is very popular among workers and young people.

In addition to beer, *sake* and *shochu*, you can find just about any kind of alcoholic drink in Japan that is available elsewhere. Whiskey, brandy, wine and other alcoholic beverages are not only imported in great variety and quantity, but are produced by Japanese manufacturers locally as well.

Shopping

Japan is a paradise for the shopper who values variety. Whether it be traditional handicrafts or high-tech electronic goods, one can find whatever he wants at reasonable prices. Silks, pearls, pottery, bamboo ware, dolls, damascene, cloisonne, lacquerware, wood-block prints and other fine-quality articles can be found at specialty shops and department stores, most of which are open for business on Sundays and national holidays as well as on weekdays.

Department stores are well stocked with modern Japanese consumer goods. In addition, these stores are usually designed with a view to keeping their interiors visually pleasing. A wide selection of electronic and audio goods are available at any of the many discount stores. These shops offer not only reduced prices, but also articles with variable voltage switches that allow them to be used outside of Japan without any additional converter. Electronic rice cookers are particularly popular among Asian visitors. Television sets, VTRs and CD players are highly popular with most tourists.

Foreign visitors can take advantage of duty-free shopping. By presenting one's passport at duty-free shops, a Record of Purchase of Consumption Tax-Exempt for Export will be attached to it, allowing one to pass Customs freely with his purchase. Articles purchased in this way must be shown at Customs when leaving Japan.

Department stores can usually be found in the main downtown areas of cities. Although they do not always offer the lowest prices, they provide a wide range of fine merchandise, allowing one to shop in confidence with the knowledge that all the goods are guaranteed to be of the finest quality.

Most stores usually open at 10:00 a.m. and close at 8:00 p.m. In general, department stores close at 7:00 p.m. They close one day during the week (not on Saturday or Sunday). Most specialty shops and department stores have some clerks who can speak English or some other languages.

Large hotels have shopping arcades with stores that can deliver or send goods anywhere in the world. If one is looking for traditional Japanese souvenir goods, the Oriental Bazaar at Harajuku or Asakusa in Tokyo is recommended, since they offer a wide range of fans, paper lanterns for room decorations, *kimono*-clad dolls, paper dolls, silk and cotton *kimono*, *happi* coats and paper craft goods. Even if no purchases are made, seeing the bazaar is an experience all its own.

Tourists looking for personal and light goods during their trip will easily find them in any of the underground shopping arcades, many of which have opened at large train stations and other areas through which a large number of people pass.

In large cities such as Tokyo or Osaka, stores in wholesale business districts sell a variety of standard items to individuals, ranging from saucepans to stereo equipment, at wholesale prices. It is a good idea to visit these areas.

For camera and audio gear:
.....Shinjuku; Ikebukuro (Tokyo)
For electrical and computer equipment:
.....Akihabara (Tokyo); Nippombashi (Osaka)
For food and general merchandise:
.....Tsukiji; Okachimachi (Tokyo)
For clothing:
.....Yokoyamacho (Tokyo); Dobuike (Osaka)
For cooking implements:
.....Kappabashi (Tokyo)

Travel Information

Tourist Information Centers (TIC)

Tourist Information Centers are operated by the Japan National Tourist Organization (JNTO) to provide information and asistance to foreign travelers in Japan. They can be found in Tokyo, Kyoto and Narita (at the New Tokyo International Airport). Information is available not only on travel but also on Japanese culture, industry, customs and other subjects which might interest the visitor. Additional services include arranging home visits (but not at the Kyoto Office), the Tele Tourist and Japan Travel Phone services and acting as a liaison with the "i" system information center (see below).

JNTO is a semi-governmental organization founded in 1959 as a part of the Ministry of Transport to promote travel in Japan. In addition to the three offices in Japan, there are sixteen offices in twelve countries (as of April, 1990) handling inquiries and providing information.

"i" System Information Centers

The "i" system is a network of local public entities organized under JNTO to provide information to foreign travelers. As of April, 1990 there are 70 offices providing information in foreign languages (mainly English). Refer to the supplement.

Guide Service

Guide-interpreters may be hired through hotels as well as travel agents. In accordance with the Guide-Interpreter Business Law, any person who intends to engage in the guide business must pass a national examination conducted by JNTO and supervised by the Ministry of Transport and obtain a license from the prefectural governor. Licensed guides are available for interpretation in English, French, Spanish, German, Chinese, Italian, Portuguese, Russian and Korean. As of April 1990, there were about 3,500 licensed guides, of whom about 1,000 were members of the Japan Guide Association.

Charges for guide-interpreter services depend on the level of expertise required and the length of the assignment. Average rates are in the range of ¥17,000–30,000 per day. In addition, transportation costs, meal and accommodation costs for the duration of the assignment are borne by the person engaging a guide-interpreter.

Good-will Guides

In addition to professional interpreting services, the Japan National Tourist Organization (JNTO) organizes volunteer guides (Good-will guides) who are capable of performing simple interpretation and tourist guidance. As of April 1990, more than 34,000 Good-will guides were registered. In principle, this service is provided at no charge and is especially useful for providing assistance to foreigners at train stations, in shops, on the street everywhere else. Good-will guides attend events for foreigners sponsored by local autonomous bodies in order to assist them, provide tourist information and act as a sort of "private diplomat" in the interest of furthering international relations, exchanging cultures and sharing experiences. They also offer tourist information at such places as the Asakusa Tourist Center, the JR Kyoto Station, Osaka Station and tourist information offices in Nara. They can be identified by the badge on their breast.

Japan Travel-Phone

This free telephone service is provided to help foreigners traveling in Japan who encounter problems due to the communication barrier and need precise information concerning their trip. Just dial the toll free number from anywhere in Japan between 9:00 a.m. – 5:00 p.m. This service is offered by JNTO.

For information on eastern Japan 0120-222800

For information on western Japan 0120-444800

When calling from Tokyo or Kyoto, the call is treated as a paid local city call. In Tokyo, dial (03)3502-1461. In Kyoto dial, (075)371 -5649.

Teletourist Service

Tape-recorded telephone information on travel topics, entertainment and major calendar events in and around Tokyo and Kyoto is also available around the clock. This "Teletourist Service" is provided in English (03-3503-2911) and French (03-3503-2926) in Tokyo and in English in Kyoto (075-361-2911). This service is offered by the JNTO's TIC centers in Tokyo and Kyoto, respectively.

In addition to these, East Japan Railways offers telephone information services on railways called "JR East-Infoline" (03-3423-0111).

Travel Hints

Package Tours

In major tourist areas such as Tokyo, Kyoto, Nikko and Hakone, sightseeing buses with English-speaking guides are available (refer to "the supplement"). All major cities have sightseeing buses so one can easily see the sights, even if English speaking guides are not provided.

Home Visit System

It is great fun to meet the local people and learn about their life-style when you go abroad. The Home Visit System, which operates entirely on the basis of goodwill, is offered in the 19 cities listed below. Through this system, you can visit a home, talk with family members for a few hours and get a glimpse of Japanese domestic life. Longer stays, however, cannot be arranged through this program.

Written applications should be submitted at least one day in advance to one of the tourist associations listed below or others.
Sapporo

Sapporo Tourist Association: ☎ (011)211-3341
Tokyo

JNTO Tokyo Tourist Information Center (TIC): ☎ (03)3502-1461
Narita

Narita City Tourist Information Office: ☎ (0476)24-3198

JNTO Narita Tourist Information Center (TIC), located at New Tokyo International Airport: ☎ (0476)32-8711

Narita Tourist Pavilion Tourist Information Center, Narita
Tourist Pavilion: ☎ (0476)24-3232
Yokohama
Yokohama International Tourist Association: ☎ (045)641-5824
Nagoya
Nagoya International Center: ☎ (052)581-5678
Otsu
Otsu International Goodwill Association, International Affairs
Division, Otsu City Office: ☎ (0775)23-0404
Kyoto
Kyoto City International Foundation: ☎ (075)752-3511
Osaka
Osaka Tourist Information Center: ☎ (06)305-3311
Osaka Tourist Information Office: ☎ (06)345-2189
Shirahama
Shirahama Tourist Information Center: ☎ (0739)42-2900
Kobe
Kobe International Tourist Association: ☎ (078)303-1010
Okayama
Okayama International Plaza: ☎ (0862)22-0457
Kurashiki
Kurashiki Association for International Friendship:
☎ (0864)22-5141
Mihara
Mihara Kokusai Shinzen Shinko Kyokai: ☎ (0848)63-1000
Hiroshima
Hiroshima International Relations Organization:
☎ (082)247-8007
Fukuoka
Fukuoka International Association (Rainbow Plaza):
☎ (092)733-2220
Nagasaki
Tourist Section, Nagasaki Prefectural Government:
☎ (0958)24-1111   Ext. 2644/5
Kumamoto
Sightseeing Section, Kumamoto City Office: ☎ (096)328-2394
Miyazaki
Miyazaki Bridge of Fellowship: ☎ (0985)56-2822
Kagoshima
Tourist Section, Kagoshima City Office: ☎ (0992)24-1111
City Tourist Information Service Center: ☎ (0992)53-2500

These are operated under the auspices of 19 councils in each of the above cities in cooperation with municipal and prefectural governments. In 1989, a total of 958 families took part in the network and 920 visits were arranged for 1,914 foreign visitors.

Home Stay

In recent years in Japan there has been a great increase in recognition of the importance of home stay experiences in the promotion of exchanges of international culture and the expansion of good will between the peoples of the world. There are many organizations involved in activities related to home stays, with regional public organizations playing central roles. However, few of these organizations are designed to help members of the general public who are interested in participating in home stay programs.

The following organization is available to help anyone who is interested in participating in a home stay experience.

The Japanese Association of the Experiment in International Living (EIL):6th floor Tachibana Bldg., 4-5 Kojimachi, Chiyoda-ku, Tokyo 102 ☎(03)3261-3451

Applications should be made at least eight weeks in advance. Application forms are available at the above EIL office. Contact the EIL office directly for details concerning application procedures, conditions and related matters. EIL is the international education and cultural exchange organization in the world, and has evolved into a worldwide federation representing member organizations in over 25 nations.

Industrial Tourism

Japan's scenic beauty, its cultural properties and historical relics are indeed well known throughout the world and are perhaps the main attraction for foreign visitors. However, it cannot be denied that many foreigners traveling to Japan are interested in seeing for themselves what has led to the recent dramatic Japanese economic success. JNTO has compiled a mini-guide entitled "Industrial Japan." It introduces various firms and factories that welcome foreign visitors.

From such light industries as cameras, television sets, watches, precision machines and electronics to heavy industries such as machinery, chemicals and steel, the modernity of Japanese manufacturing systems, their technological capabilities and the large scale of industrial plants hold great interest for many foreign visitors. Although many plants offer guided tours, the areas that are of most interest are usually kept off-limits to visitors in order to preserve their industrial secrets.

The institutions listed below provide industrial tours. For more information and reservations, contact them directly or go to the closest JNTO Tourist Information Center (TIC), where detailed information on submitting applications and arranging transportation can be obtained.

Automobile Manufacturing:
Toyota Motor Corporation

A 2 and 1/2 hr. tour of the plant in Toyota City, Aichi Prefecture
Nissan Motor Co., Ltd.
  A 2 hr. tour of the Zama Plant in Zama City and the Murayama
  Plant in Musashi-Murayama City

Computer and Home Electronics:
NEC Showroom C & C Plaza (Uchisaiwai-cho, Tokyo)

Electric appliances and electronics:
Toshiba Science Institute
  A 1 hr. tour in Kawasaki City, Kanagawa Prefecture

Industrial Robot and Factory Automation:
Tokyo National FA (Robot) Center
  30–60 min. tour in Shimbashi, Tokyo

Brewery, Distillery and Winery:
Suntory Co., Ltd.
Suntory Tamagawa Plant (Kawasaki City, Kanagawa Prefecture)
Suntory Yamazaki Distillery (Yamazaki, Osaka)
Suntory Yamanashi Winery (Futabacho , Yamanashi Prefecture)
Suntory Musashino Brewery (Musashino City, Tokyo)

Newspapers:
Asahi Shimbun Publishing Ltd.
  1 hr. tour in Tsukiji, Tokyo

Others:
Tsukiji Fish Market (Tokyo Central Wholesale Market)
  1–2 hrs.   (Tsukiji, Tokyo)
Tokyo Stock Exchange
  30–60 min.   (Kabutocho, Tokyo)
NHK Broadcasting Center
  1 hr.   (Shibuya, Tokyo)
Noritake Co., Ltd. (chinaware)
  1 hr.   (Nagoya)
Tsukamoto Seito Pottery Workshop
  30 min.   (Mashiko Town, Tochigi Prefecture)
Yuzen Cultural Hall
  9:00 a.m. – 5:00 p.m.   (Kyoto)
Nishijin Textile Museum
  9:00 a.m. – 5:00 p.m.   (Kyoto)
Kyoto Handicraft Center
  9:00 a.m. – 6:00 p.m.   (Kyoto)
Inaba Cloisonne
  9:00 a.m. – 5:30 p.m.   (Kyoto)
Kyoto Municipal Museum of Traditional Industry
  9:00 a.m. – 5:00 p.m.   (Kyoto)
In Tokyo, JTB organizes the Sunrise Tour for industrial tourism.
  Sights: Tokyo Stock Exchange, Isuzu Motors Ltd., Japan
          Airlines maintenance facilities
  Total time: 9 hrs. (only on Tuesdays and Thursdays)
  Cost: ¥9,980 (children: ¥8,960) (As of April 1990)

"Explore Japanese Culture" System

Recent data on tourism indicates that over 40% of the foreign visitors to Japan are interested in learning about Japanese people, the Japanese way of life and traditional Japanese culture. Many aspects of Japanese culture are already well known abroad. Some of the more popular examples include the tea ceremony, flower arranging, *judo*, *kendo* and *karate*. However, there are many other, less well-known aspects of Japanese culture that are certain to be of interest to the visitor willing to seek them out. By visiting places and seeing with one's own eyes and actually participating in some of these cultural activities, the visitor is sure to learn more about Japan and deepen the cultural aspects of his or her voyage in this country.

In order to assit visitors in learning about Japanese culture, JNTO has established the "Explore Japanese Culture System." This system is operated with voluntary participation of over 300 private homes and cultural and sports facilities in 54 cities. Some of the more than 100 aspects of Japanese culture featured in this program are the tea ceremony, flower arranging, monochrome painting, calligraphy, Japanese musical instruments (*samisen*, *koto*) and *kimono* dressing. The system is outlined in the "Explore Japanese Culture" pamphlet published by JNTO. This pamphlet can be obtained at overseas offices of JNTO, Tourist Information Centers (TIC) in Japan and local government-operated tourist information offices affiliated with the "i" system (refer to p.63) organized by JNTO. Applications to participate in the "Explore Japanese Culture" System are available at any TIC or "i" office in cities where affiliated events are held.

New Sites of Discovery

Major sightseeing areas such as Kyoto, Nara, Nikko, Fuji and Hakone are, of course, well known to tourists interested in Japan. These places are certainly rich in Japanese character and not to be missed, but they are not all there is to sightseeing in Japan. There are many other places throughout the country that allow one to come into contact with the long history, natural beauty and unique traditional culture of Japan. By visiting these places, the tourist can discover a new side of Japan and thus obtain a deeper understanding of the country.

To this end, 36 areas have been designated as New Sites of Discovery by the Japanese government. When going to any of these areas, consult one of JNTO's Tourist Information Centers (TIC) or "i" system information centers, and refer to the Travel Information pages (62-64) in this book.

List of the "New Sites of Discovery"

Prefectures	Areas Major Tourist Spots
Hokkaido	① Sapporo—Lake Shikotsu Area Sapporo, Chitose ② Hakodate—Onuma Area Hakodate, Nanae, Mori
Iwate	③ Morioka—Hachimantai Area Morioka, Shizukuishi, Nishine, Ashiro, etc.
Miyagi	④ Sendai—Matsushima Area Sendai, Shiogama, Matsushima, etc.
Yamagata	⑤ Zao—Yamadera—Dewasanzan Area Zao, Dewasanzan
Fukushima	⑥ Aizu-Wakamatsu—Bandai Area Aizu-Wakamatsu, Bandai, Inawashiro, etc.
Niigata	⑦ Niigata—Sado—Yahiko Area Niigata, Sanjo, Shibata, Tsubame, Ryotsu, Toyosaka, Yahiko, Yoshida, Ogi, etc.
Nagano	⑧ Matsumoto—Japan Alps Area Matsumoto, Omachi, Hotaka, etc.
Ibaragi	⑨ Tsuchiura—Tsukuba Area Tsuchiura, Yatabe, Tsukuba, Kukizaki, etc.
Tochigi	⑩ Nikko—Utsunomiya Area Utsunomiya, Nikko, Imaichi, Kuroiso, Mashiko, Nasu, Shiobara, etc.
Chiba	⑪ Narita Area Narita, Sakura, Sakae, Shibayama
Kanagawa	⑫ Kanagawa Area Yokohama, Kamakura, Fujisawa, Odawara, Hakone
Yamanashi	⑬ Mt. Fuji—Five Lakes Area Fuji-Yoshida, Oshino, Lake Yamanaka, Lake Kawagchi, Ashiwada, Narusawa, etc.
Toyama	⑭ Toyama—Tateyama—Kurobe Area Toyama, Oyama, Tateyama, Kamiichi, Unazuki
Ishikawa	⑮ Kanazawa—Minami-Kaga Area Kanazawa, Komatsu, Kaga, etc.
Gifu	⑯ Hida—Takayama Area Takayama, Furukawa, Gero, etc.
Shizuoka	⑰ Izu Higashi-Kaigan Area Atami, Ito, Shimoda, Higashi-Izu, Kawazu
Aichi	⑱ Nagoya—Inuyama Area Nagoya, Inuyama
Shiga	⑲ Biwako-Otsu—Hikone Area Otsu, Hikone
Hyogo	⑳ Kobe—Himeji—Takarazuka Area Kobe, Himeji, Takarazuka
Nara	㉑ Nara-Hokuwa—Ikoma—Ikaruga Area Nara, Tenri, Yamato-Koriyama, Ikoma, Ikaruga, etc.
Wakayama	㉒ Kinokuni-Kuroshio Area Tanabe, Oto, Shirahama, Kushimoto, etc.
Okayama	㉓ Okayama—Kurashiki Area Okayama, Kurashiki

Shimane	㉔ Matsue—Izumo Area Matsue, Izumo
Hiroshima	㉕ Hiroshima Area Hiroshima, Kure, Miyajima, Etc. ㉖ Setouchi Chuo Area Fukuyama, Mihara
Kagawa	㉗ Kagawa-Setouchi Area Takamatsu, Marugame, Sakaide, Zentsuji, Kan-onji, Shido, Kotohira, Takuma, Nio, etc.
Ehime	㉘ Matsuyama—Imabari Area Matsuyama, Imabari, Hojo, etc.
Fukuoka	㉙ Fukuoka-Chikushi Area Fukuoka, Chikushino, Kasuga, Onojo, Dazaifu, Nakagawa
Saga	㉚ Saga Ceramic Vallay Area Imari, Takeo, Arita, Ureshino, Nishi-Arita, Yamauchi
Nagasaki	㉛ Nagasaki—Unzen Area Nagasaki, Obama
Kumamoto	㉜ Aso—Kumamoto—Amakusa Area Kumamoto, Aso, Oguni, etc.
Oita	㉝ Beppu—Yamanami Area Beppu, Yufuin, Kokonoe
Miyazaki	㉞ Miyazaki Area Miyazaki, Saito, Nichinan, Kushima, Kobayashi, Ebino
Kagoshima	㉟ Kagoshima Area Kagoshima, Ibusuki, Sakurajima, etc.
Okinawa	㊱ Southern Okinawa Area Okinawa

III. Natural Features

Geographical Features

Japan is formed by an arc of islands lying east of the Asian continent. It stretches for 2,798 km from northeast to southwest. Included as part of the Circum-Pacific Zone, the area in which Japan lies contains orogenic, volcanic and earthquake belts spreading across its land as well as its coastal waters. The activities of these belts have combined to create the scenic beauty of the country and its many hot springs.

Mountains (*yama, san* or *zan, take* or *dake* and *mine* in Japanese)

Four-fifths of the area of Japan consists of mountains, with a chain of mountains running through each of the four main islands.

The mountains of Hida, Kiso and Akaishi in central Honshu are characterized by sheer cliffs and peaks reaching a height from 2,500 m to over 3,000 m. These mountains are respectively called the Northern, Central and Southern Japan Alps. The Hidaka Mountain Chain in Hokkaido, the Echigo and Kanto mountain chains in Honshu and the Shikoku Mountain Chain in Shikoku are also steep-sided, with many high peaks rising from 1,500 m to 2,500 m. These steep mountain chains contrast strikingly with the Kitakami, Abukuma and Chugoku mountain chains, which are marked by gentle slopes and crests forming comparatively broad plateaus.

Volcanic Mountains (*kazan*)

As a result of frequent eruptions and internal explosions, the volcanic mountains of Japan have assumed a great variety of shapes, adding to the natural beauty of the country. The cone-shaped Mt. Fuji in central Honshu is Japan's highest mountain with a height of 3,776 m above sea level. Mountains located in various districts resembling Mt. Fuji in shape are often named after the areas (generally, the ancient provincial names) in which they are located with the addition of the word "Fuji." For instance, Mt. Yotei in Hokkaido is also called Ezo-Fuji, while Mt. Iwaki in Aomori Prefecture is popularly known as Tsugaru-Fuji. Others are Nambu-Fuji (Mt. Iwate in Iwate Prefecture), Hoki-Fuji (Mt. Daisen in Tottori Prefecture) and Satsuma-Fuji (Mt. Kaimon in Kagoshima Prefecture).

There are volcanic mountains of many other shapes as well. To cite a few examples—Mt. Yarigatake on the boundary between Nagano and Gifu prefectures has a spear-like peak and Mt. Myogi in Gumma Prefecture has a saw-toothed summit. Still more fantastic in shape are Mt. Bandai in Fukushima Prefecture and the mountains of Ontake and Norikura, both on the borders of Nagano and Gifu prefectures.

Following are the different volcanic systems:

The Chishima Chain: This mountain range stretches from central Hokkaido to the Kurile Islands in the northeast. In Hokkaido are Mt. O-Akan, Mt. Me-Akan (active), Mt. Daisetsu and Mt. Tokachi (active).

The Nasu Chain: This starts at Rishiri Island near the northern tip of Hokkaido, crosses the southern land area of Hokkaido, leaps over to central Honshu and ends at Mt. Asama on the borders of Nagano and Gumma prefectures. The chain takes in Mt. Tarumae, Mt. Yotei and Mt. Komagatake in Hokkaido; Mt. Hakkoda (Aomori Prefecture), Mt. Iwate (Iwate Prefecture), Mt. Zao (the boundary between Yamagata and Miyagi prefectures), Mt. Bandai (Fukushima Prefecture) and Mt. Nasu (Tochigi Prefecture) in Honshu. The chain also extends to Mts. Akagi, Haruna and Myogi in Gumma Prefecture.

The Chokai Chain: These mountains start at Mt. Iwaki (Aomori Prefecture) and end at Mt. Asama, with Mts. Chokai, Gassan, etc. in between.

The Fuji Chain: Cutting diagonally across mid-Honshu, the Fuji Chain runs from Mt. Yakeyama (Niigata Prefecture) all the way to the Mariana Islands. Running through Mt. Yatsugatake, it includes Mt. Myoko (Niigata Prefecture), Mt. Fuji, the Hakone mountains, and the mountains on the Izu Peninsula and the Seven Isles of Izu. Mt. Mihara (active) on Oshima Island is also included.

The Norikura Chain: This short chain covers the Hida mountains and includes Mt. Tateyama (Toyama Prefecture) and Mts. Yakedake (active), Norikura and Ontake on the borders of Nagano and Gifu prefectures.

The Hakusan Chain: This chain extends from Mt. Hakusan on the borders of Ishikawa and Gifu prefectures to Mt. Unzen in Nagasaki Prefecture. The most famous mountain in this chain is Daisen in Tottori Prefecture.

The Kirishima Chain: This chain starts at Mt. Aso in Kumamoto Prefecture in Kyushu and includes Mt. Kirishima on the borders of Kagoshima and Miyazaki prefectures plus the well-known Sakurajima overlooking the Bay of Kagoshima. This contains most of the mountains in Kirishima National Park.

Rivers (*kawa* or *gawa* in Japanese)

The rivers of Japan are short and rapid for the most part. The longest is the Shinano River, which flows 367 km and empties into the Japan Sea at Niigata City. Next comes the Teshio River of Hokkaido followed by the Tone River, which empties into the Pacific at Choshi, Chiba Prefecture. Draining an area of 16,840 sq.km, the Tone River basin is the largest in Japan, with the Ishikari and Shinano river basins next in size.

Since they are short and rapid, the rivers of Japan are of little use as a means of traffic. The upper sections, as a rule, are blocked by rocks. The shallower rivers are suitable only for small boats if they keep to mid-stream. Small steamboats are in use only on the lower courses of some of the larger rivers such as the Yodo in Osaka, the Sumida in Tokyo, the Shinano and the Tone, mentioned above. Numerous dams have been constructed on the upper reaches of these swift-flowing rivers, which are used mostly for hydraulic power stations and land irrigation.

Floods are likely to occur when there is an extra concentration of rain during the rainy season in June and July as well as during the heavy rains that accompany the typhoons in August and September.

In many cases where a river has its source in a mountain lake, the water flows down in cascades. In some cases, the river is marked by many rapids such as the Kiso near Nagoya, the Hozu in Kyoto, the Fuji and Tenryu in Shizuoka Prefecture and the Kumagawa in Kumamoto Prefecture. The descent of these rapids by boat affords an exciting and interesting trip.

The streams that flow in torrents through thickly wooded gorges are unique compared to those of Europe and America with a beauty all their own. Both Kurobe and Tenryukyo in central Honshu offer especially inspiring scenic views as does the Sounkyo Gorge in the upper reaches of the Ishikari River in Daisetsuzan National Park in Hokkaido.

Plains (*heiya*), basins (*bonchi*) and tablelands (*daichi*)

Only one-fifth of the entire land area of the country is flat, areas characterized by plains, basins and tablelands.

Plains are found along the lower courses of the larger rivers. They are fertile, arable land devoted mainly to the production of rice. Chief among the well-known plains are the Kanto Plain, where the Tone River flows; the Niigata Plain, watered by the Shinano and Agano rivers; the Nobi Plain around Gifu and Nagoya on the lower reaches of the Kiso River; the Ishikari Plain in Hokkaido, watered by the Ishikari River, and the Sendai Plain in the Tohoku District, where the Kitakami River flows.

Among the more important basins in Japan are the Yamagata Basin in the Tohoku District, which includes Yamagata City; the Kofu Basin in central Honshu with Kofu City, and the Kyoto Basin, centered around Kyoto.

The extensive tablelands found in Hokkaido and Kyushu as well as in the central and western parts of Honshu are utilized primarily as farms and pastures.

Lakes (*ko, numa* and sometimes *ike* in Japanese)

Of Japan's many lakes, the largest is Lake Biwa (694.5 sq.km) near Kyoto, while the deepest is Lake Tazawa (425 m) in northern Honshu. Among the scenic lakes located in high altitudes are Lakes Akan,

Mashu (one of the clearest lakes in the world with a water transparency of 25 m) and Shikotsu in Hokkaido; Lakes Towada and Inawashiro in the Tohoku District; Lake Chuzenji in Nikko; Lake Ashi in Hakone, and the Fuji Five Lakes on the northern skirts of Mt. Fuji. All are in Japan's national parks. Lakes Akan, Mashu, Shikotsu, Towada and Ashi were formed by waters collected in volcanic craters or calderas, while Lake Inawashiro, Lake Chuzenji and the Fuji Five Lakes were created by the natural damming of rivers by lava.

Then there are the man-made lakes, where water is used for power generation or irrigation. In central Honshu, there is the Sakuma Dam, which blocks the upper waters of the Tenryu River, which, in turn, has its source in Lake Suwa. The Tama River is dammed on its upper reaches, forming Lake Okutama, while the Sagami River creates Lake Sagami.

Seacoasts (*kaigan* in Japanese)

Surrounded by seas, Japan has an unusually long coastline in comparison with its area. Compared to the approximate 377,000 sq. km of land area, the seacoast has a total length of about 26,500 km.

Offshore islands, large and small, are common along the coast. Formed of rocks peculiar to their districts, some islands are covered with luxuriant greenery, while others are sparsely dotted with trees or shrubs. The shoreline usually consists of beaches of white sand or precipitous cliffs. In some places, the shoreline is fronted by fantastic rock formations marked by caves, caverns, natural bridges and gates.

The best known is the Seto-Naikai (Inland Sea) with nearly 1,000 picturesque islands. Along the Japan Sea coast are the Oga Peninsula in Akita Prefecture, the Noto Peninsula in Ishikawa Prefecture and Sotomo Beach in Fukui Prefecture. The Oki Islands of Daisen-Oki National Park and the Kujukushima Islands of Saikai National Park are also well known. The Pacific coast includes the Sanriku seascapes of Iwate Prefecture, the Kumano coastline of the Kii Peninsula in Mie and Wakayama prefectures and Capes Muroto and Ashizuri in Kochi Prefecture. Geologically, the coasts of Sanriku in northern Honshu as well as Kumano and Shima peninsulas in Wakayama and Mie prefectures, respectively, are quite jagged. The jagged bays with their various inlets offer great scenic beauty, enhancing the splendor of the national parks in which they are located.

In contrast to the above, there are long expanses of white, sandy beaches bordered by groves of green pines. Such scenes can be found at Uchiura Bay in Hokkaido, Kujukurihama in Chiba Prefecture, Miho-no-Matsubara in Shizuoka Prefecture, Katsurahama in Kochi Prefecture, Niji-no-Matsubara at Karatsu in Saga Prefecture, and Kagoshima Bay and Fukiagehama in Kagoshima Prefecture.

Plants and Animals

Japan has an abundant rainfall and many thick forests. Taken on a global scale, forest areas occupy a total of one-third of the total land mass. In contrast, 70% of the Japanese land mass is covered by forest. Since the nation stretches from north to south, the northern parts are covered by coniferous trees, the middle areas by deciduous, broad-leaved trees and the southern areas by broad-leaved oaks, evergreen oaks, camellias and evergreens. Japan is unique in the world in that its forests are not influenced by dry, subtropic weather and stretch uninterruptedly from north to south, displaying a tremendous variety of fauna and flora. In southern Kyushu, southern Shikoku and particularly in Okinawa, one can find subtropic plants such as fountain palms and Japanese fern palms. Pine trees and Japanese cedar grow profusely throughout the country, even in the warm southern sections.

The flora of Japan is marked by a tremendous variety of species. Different seasons offer different colors. The autumn change of foliage is particularly impressive. Many people take advantage of this time to escape to the countryside to enjoy the seasonal atmosphere and scenic views. This type of excursion, called *Momijigari,* is very popular among Japanese.

The Sekiryo (meaning "backbone") mountains run through the central part of the Japanese Archipelago, separating the Japan Sea coast from the Pacific Ocean coast. As a result, the flora on either side of the mountain range differ considerably. Japanese flora are classified into the Northern Species—one of the world's six categories of flora. This category includes species prevalent in the non-tropical areas of the Euroasian Continent and the North America Continent. The approximately 30,000 species that are grouped in this category under the term "forest flora" reveal many similarities. In spite of the relatively small Japanese land mass, there is great confusion among the distribution patterns of Japanese flora because of the topographical, environmental and geo-historical influences. The Japanese flora can further be subdivided into seven districts: Hokkaido District, Hokuriku District, Kanto District, Chubu-Sangaku (Japan Alps) District, Western-Japan District, Ryukyu District and the Ogasawara District.

The woodlands are inhabited by a wide variety of animals. Depending on the regional characteristics, each area has its own particular species, including many herbivores and carnivores— animals ranging in sizes from very small species to large bears, antelope and other mammals.

Japanese fauna are classified into the former Northern Sector, one of the six categories into which the world's fauna are classified. This category includes species prevalent in the Euroasian Continent, Central and North America and North Africa. Although many aspects of the fauna of Southeast Asia (known as the Oriental Sector) can be found in Japanese fauna, Japan is not included in that sector. The Watase Line separates these two sectors from all areas south of Amami-Oshima Island falling into the Oriental Sector. Although this division can be made for land animals, it is not entirely applicable to birds and fresh-water fish.

The brown bear makes its home in Hokkaido, while monkeys can be found in the forests and mountains of all other areas. Deer and wild boar are commonly found in broad-leaved forest zones. Although the *kiji* (native pheasant) and the *yamadori* (copper pheasant) both have colorful plumage and are peculiar to Japan, neither is found in Hokkaido.

The *kamoshika* (antelope) and the *raicho* (snow grouse) are found in the highlands, but since their number has dwindled, they are now under special government protection.

Climatic Conditions

Honshu, Shikoku and Kyushu lie within the Temperate Zone, with the annual average temperature ranging from 22.4°C at Naha in Okinawa to 5.6°C at Kushiro in Hokkaido. The four seasons in Japan are clear cut and each possesses its own distinctive scenery.

Owing to its location on the Pacific Ocean, Japan has a relatively higher humidity and heavier rainfall in summer than Europe does. Conversely, it has a lower humidity in winter. The amount of rainfall is greater, as a rule, in the southwestern part of the country than in the northeastern, and in the summer time there is more rainfall on the Pacific seaboard than on the Japan Sea side of the country. The *tsuyu* or *baiu* (rainy season), which is welcomed by farmers as the proper time for rice planting, sets in about the middle of June and lasts until the middle of July, although it is interspersed by fair days.

Northern Japan is covered with snow for two or three months every winter, while snowfall is much heavier on the Japan Sea coast than on the Pacific coast side. In the southern sectors, however, snowstorms are rare, and when snow does fall, it seldom remains on the ground for more than a day or two. No snowfall is ever seen in the Okinawa Islands.

Average temperatures and rainfall in major cities in Japan are given in P.77

National Parks and Quasi-National Parks

Japan lacks the grand-scale scenery found in America and Europe, but it has a unique beauty all its own that makes it one of the most picturesque countries in the world. Seasonal changes, the time of day and even weather conditions enhance the natural beauty of the country. The infinite variety found in the coastline, islands, mountains, valleys, lakes, rivers, rocks, forests and plains is a characteristic feature of Japanese scenery. Temples, shrines, feudal castles—

Average Temperatures in Japan   (In Centigrade)

Location	Winter (Jan.)	Spring (Apr.)	Summer (Jul.)	Autumn (Oct.)	Annual Average
Asahikawa	-8.5	4.7	20.3	8.5	6.3
Sapporo	-4.9	6.2	20.2	10.6	8.0
Aomori	-1.8	7.5	20.9	11.9	9.6
Akita	-0.5	8.8	22.6	13.1	11.0
Sendai	0.9	10.0	22.2	14.3	11.9
Niigata	2.0	10.7	24.2	15.5	13.01
Kanazawa	2.9	11.9	25.0	16.1	14.0
Utsunomiya	1.4	11.6	23.6	15.1	12.9
Nagano	-1.2	10.2	23.6	13.3	11.4
Tokyo	4.7	13.9	25.2	17.3	15.3
Shizuoka	6.0	14.4	25.2	18.2	16.0
Nagoya	3.6	13.5	25.6	16.9	14.9
Kyoto	3.9	13.7	26.3	17.0	15.2
Osaka	5.6	14.5	27.0	18.3	16.2
Kobe	4.8	13.9	25.9	17.8	15.6
Hiroshima	4.3	13.3	25.6	17.0	15.0
Matsuyama	5.3	13.9	26.2	17.7	15.6
Kochi	5.6	15.4	26.2	18.4	16.3
Fukuoka	5.7	14.2	26.7	17.8	16.0
Nagasaki	6.4	15.0	26.5	18.9	16.6
Kumamoto	4.9	15.1	26.8	17.9	16.1
Oita	5.5	13.8	26.0	17.6	15.6
Kagoshima	7.0	16.1	27.2	19.6	17.3
Naha	16.0	21.0	28.1	24.3	22.4

Average Rainfall and Humidity in Japan

Location	Spring	Summer	Autumn	Winter	Annual Total
Sapporo	64 (80)	90 (74)	104 (75)	118 (68)	1,141 (74)
Aomori	80 (83)	106 (76)	86 (81)	194 (70)	1,424 (78)
Sendai	85 (86)	170 (77)	132 (71)	42 (67)	1,245 (75)
Tokyo	122 (79)	140 (74)	203 (57)	49 (66)	1,503 (69)
Kyoto	145 (76)	239 (74)	122 (72)	56 (67)	1,638 (73)
Hiroshima	156 (82)	276 (75)	111 (71)	51 (71)	1,644 (75)
Fukuoka	134 (80)	252 (76)	100 (69)	77 (74)	1,705 (75)
Naha	142 (82)	174 (74)	149 (70)	122 (79)	2,118 (78)

(Rainfall given in milliliters)
(Figures in parenthesis indicate humidity percentage)

both restored and left in ruins—farmhouses and other typical Japanese structures blend harmoniously with the natural scenery.
The natural parks in Japan are regional parks whose natural scenery is unspoiled. They are classified into national parks, quasi-national parks and prefectural natural parks. There are 28 areas of outstand-

ing natural beauty typical of Japanese scenery that have been designated as national parks. They occupy a total area of 20,500 sq. km, or approximately 5.43% of the entire area of Japan.

The Shiretoko, Akan, Daisetsuzan, Shikotsu-Toya and Rishiri-Rebun-Sarobetsu national parks, all in Hokkaido, are generally comprised of volcanoes, mountain lakes, swamps and virgin forests as well as numerous hot springs. The Daisetsuzan, with an area of 2,320 sq.km, is the largest of the 28 national parks.

The Towada-Hachimantai National Park is well known for its lake and volcanic scenery. The Bandai-Asahi National Park consists of four sections—the district centering around Lake Inawashiro, the Bandai-Azuma mountains, Mt. Iide and the Asahi-Gassan mountains.

Nikko National Park's special attraction is the harmonious blending of nature and art in which Lake Chuzenji, Kegon Waterfalls and the Toshogu Shrine form a single, harmonious whole.

The Jo-Shin-Etsu-Kogen (Plateau or Highland) National Park covers two volcanic districts rising to an altitude of about 2,000 m. The two active volcanoes of Asama and Shirane are located here as well as Mt. Tanigawa with its unique alpine contours. Sugadaira Kogen (Plateau or Highland) and Shiga Kogen (also called Shiga Heights) are both popular hiking and skiing resorts.

The Chichibu-Tama National Park embraces mountains, valleys and forests northwest of Tokyo. It consists of the Chichibu mountain district (alt. 1,500–2,400 m), Tama mountain district (alt. 600–1,500 m) and Shosenkyo Gorge.

The Ogasawara National Park, formed by the group of Ogasawara Islands and located some 1,100 km south of Tokyo, is one of the nation's southernmost parks. Situated between tropical and subtropical zones, this national park is famed for its picturesque islands and coastal scenery as well as numerous virgin forests of subtropical trees.

The Fuji-Hakone-Izu National Park boasts magnificent Mt. Fuji, the five lakes that lie at its base, Hakone hot-springs resorts, a part of the Izu Peninsula and the Seven Isles of Izu.

The Chubu-Sangaku (Mountains) National Park is also called the Japan Alps National Park and comprises more than 100 peaks. Several mountains more than 3,000 m high, sharply slashed cliffs and snowy valleys present a truly spectacular sight.

The Minami Alps (Southern Japan Alps) National Park, together with the Japan Alps National Park, is one of the most representative mountain parks in Japan.

Mt. Hakusan (alt. 2,702 m), which together with Mt. Fuji and Mt. Tateyama (alt. 3,015 m) has formed the "Three Mountains" for religious climbers since olden times, is the focal point of the Hakusan National Park. Special attractions of the park include Japanese beeches covering the mountainside, pines creeping up to the northern slope and a large variety of alpine plants growing near the mountaintop.

Capes jutting out into the ocean, calm inlets, marine terraces worn away by erosion—these are some of the aspects that make the Ise-Shima National Park famous.

A fantastic seacoast, deep gorges and towering peaks combine to create the Yoshino-Kumano National Park.

The San-in-Kaigan (Coast) National Park extends for 77 km on the Japan Sea coast of Honshu between the Oku-Tango Peninsula with its famous Amanohashidate and the Tottori Sand Dunes near Tottori City. The seacoast with its grotesque rock formations and the Sand Dunes are interesting features of this national park. The Daisen-Oki National Park features the graceful figure of Mt. Daisen (alt. 1,729m) and the seascape of the Oki Islands with their rugged mountains.

The Seto-Naikai (Inland Sea) National Park, which covers the Inland Sea together with sections of its coast, stretches from Mt. Rokko at Kobe in the east to Mt. Takasaki near Beppu in the west. The sea is studded with numerous islands of all sizes, the most famous of which is the picturesque Miyajima Island where the Itsuku-shima Shrine is located.

The Ashizuri-Uwakai National Park is located at the southernmost tip of Shikoku Island. Cape Ashizuri, a major tourist attraction, offers a magnificent view of many high, steep granite cliffs directly facing the Pacific Ocean.

Mt. Aso in Kumamoto Prefecture and Mt. Kuju in Oita Prefecture are the centers of attraction in Aso National Park. The seacoast around Sasebo and the outlying islands to the west plus the coastline of the Goto Islands are the highlights of the Saikai National Park, while the two districts of Mt. Unzen and the Amakusa Islands make up the Unzen-Amakusa National Park. For its part, the Kirishima-Yaku National Park is characterized by volcanic scenery and a natural forest not to mention its many hot springs. It also includes areas on Kagoshima Bay and Yakushima Island off the southern extremity of Kyushu.

The Iriomote National Park, Japan's southernmost national park, is located some 1,200 km south of Kagoshima in the East China Sea. The main feature of the park is Iriomote Island with its virgin forests of subtropical trees. This park also represents one of the most beautiful "marine park districts" in Japan.

The National Parks are designated as such and administered by the Environment Agency on the basis of recommendations by the National Park Council. Although the quasi-national parks are also designated by this agency on the basis of recommendations by the council, they are administered by the local prefectural authorities. Almost equal to the national parks in scenic beauty, the 55 quasi-national parks occupy a total area of 13,346 sq. km, or 3.54% of the entire area of Japan.

Since Japan has many rocky shores, the sea in the high latitudes is characterized by stone corals and a great variety of fish. "Marine Parks" are set up in some parts of national or quasi-national parks in order to conserve the beautiful seascapes and marine life. As of March 1989, there were 123 marine parks in 57 areas of Japan.

National Parks (From North to South)

Name	Location (Prefecture)
1. Rishiri-Rebun-Sarobetsu	Hokkaido
2. Shiretoko	Hokkaido
3. Akan	Hokkaido
4. Kushiro-Shitsugen (Marshland)	Hokkaido
5. Daisetsuzan	Hokkaido
6. Shikotsu-Toya	Hokkaido
7. Towada-Hachimantai	Aomori, Akita, Iwate
8. Rikuchu Kaigan(Coast)	Iwate, Miyagi
9. Bandai-Asahi	Yamagata, Niigata, Fukushima
10. Nikko	Fukushima, Tochigi, Gumma, Niigata
11. Jo-Shin-Etsu-Kogen (Plateau or Highland)	Gumma, Niigata, Nagano
12. Chichibu-Tama	Saitama, Tokyo, Yamanashi, Nagano
13. Ogasawara	Tokyo
14. Fuji-Hakone-Izu	Kanagawa, Yamanashi, Tokyo, Shizuoka
15. Chubu Sangaku (Japan Alps)	Niigata, Toyama, Nagano, Gifu
16. Hakusan	Toyama, Ishikawa, Fukui, Gifu
17. Minami Alps (Southern Japan Alps)	Nagano, Yamanashi, Shizuoka
18. Ise-Shima	Mie
19. Yoshino-Kumano	Mie, Nara, Wakayama
20. San-in Kaigan (Coast)	Kyoto, Hyogo, Tottori
21. Seto-Naikai (Island Sea)	Wakayama, Hyogo, Okayama, Hiroshima, Yamaguchi, Toku-shima Kagawa
22. Daisen-Oki	Tottori, Okayama, Shimane
23. Ashizuri-Uwakai	Kochi, Ehime
24. Saikai	Nagasaki
25. Unzen-Amakusa	Nagasaki, Kumamoto, Kago-shima
26. Aso-Kuju	Kumamoto, Oita
27. Kirishima-Yaku	Miyazaki, Kagoshima
28. Iriomote	Okinawa

Quasi-National Parks (From North to South)

1.	Abashiri	Hokkaido
2.	Shokambetsu-Teuri-Yagishiri	Hokkaido
3.	Niseko-Shakotan-Otaru Kaigan (Coast)	Hokkaido
4.	Hidaka Sammyaku-Erimo (Mountains)	Hokkaido
5.	Onuma	Hokkaido
6.	Shimokita Hanto (Peninsula)	Aomori
7.	Tsugaru	Aomori
8.	Hayachine	Iwate
9.	Kurikoma	Iwate, Miyagi, Akita, Yamagata
10.	Minami (Southern) Sanriku-Kinkazan	Miyagi
11.	Zao	Yamagata, Miyagi
12.	Oga	Akita
13.	Chokai	Akita, Yamagata
14.	Echigosanzan-Tadami	Niigata, Fukushima
15.	Suigo (Water-District)-Tsukuba	Ibaraki, Chiba
16.	Myogi-Arafune-Saku Kogen (Plateau or Highland)	Gumma, Nagano
17.	Minami (Southern)-Boso	Chiba
18.	Meiji-no-Mori (Meiji Woods)-Takao	Tokyo
19.	Tanzawa-Oyama	Kanagawa
20.	Sado-Yahiko-Yoneyama	Niigata
21.	Noto Hanto (Peninsula)	Toyama, Ishikawa
22.	Echizen-Kaga Kaigan (Coast)	Fukui, Ishikawa
23.	Wakasa Wan (Bay)	Fukui, Kyoto
24.	Yatsugatake-Chushin Kogen (Plateau or Highland)	Yamanashi, Nagano
25.	Tenryu-Oku-Mikawa	Nagano, Shizuoka, Aichi
26.	Ibi-Sekigahara-Yoro	Gifu
27.	Hida-Kiso Gawa (River)	Aichi, Gifu
28.	Aichi Kogen (Plateau or Highland)	Aichi
29.	Mikawa Wan (Bay)	Aichi
30.	Suzuka	Shiga, Mie
31.	Murou-Akame-Aoyama	Mie, Nara
32.	Biwako (Lake Biwa)	Shiga, Kyoto
33.	Meiji-no-Mori-Mino-o (Meiji Woods)	Osaka
34.	Kongo-Ikoma	Nara, Osaka
35.	Hyonosen-Ushiroyama-	Hyogo, Tottori, Okayama

	Nagisen	
36.	Yamato-Aogaki	Nara
37.	Koya-Ryujin	Nara, Wakayama
38.	Hiba-Dogo-Taishaku	Hiroshima, Tottori, Shimane
39.	Nishi (Western) Chugoku Sanchi (Plateau or Highland)	Shimane, Hiroshima, Yamaguchi
40.	Kita (Northern) Nagato Kaigan (Coast)	Yamaguchi
41.	Akiyoshidai	Yamaguchi
42.	Tsurugisan (Mt. Tsurugi)	Tokushima, Kochi
43.	Muroto-Anan Kaigan (Coast)	Tokushima, Kochi
44.	Ishizuchi	Ehime, Kochi
45.	Kita (Northern) Kyushu	Fukuoka
46.	Genkai	Fukuoka, Saga, Nagasaki
47.	Yaba-Hita-Hikosan	Fukuoka, Kumamoto, Oita
48.	Iki-Tsushima	Nagasaki
49.	Kyushu Chuo-Sanchi (Central Mountains)	Kumamoto, Miyazaki
50.	Nippo Kaigan (Coast)	Oita, Miyazaki
51.	Sobo-Katamuki	Oita, Miyazaki
52.	Nichinan Kaigan (Coast)	Miyazaki, Kagoshima
53.	Amami-Gunto (Islands)	Kagoshima
54.	Okinawa Kaigan (Coast)	Okinawa
55.	Okinawa Senseki (Old Battlefields)	Okinawa

Hot Springs

The custom of bathing in hot springs in Japan dates back over 2,000 years. The climate of Japan is characterized by high levels of humidity, leading people to develop the habit of bathing at regular intervals, especially in hot springs.

There is no country in the world that boasts more natural hot springs than Japan, which has over 19,500 different springs. Areas in which there is a great deal of volcanic activity offer the best and most famous hot springs. Since long ago, hot springs have been said to be of great medicinal value and people have sought out the different health benefits offered by hot springs in different areas throughout the nation. Hotels, *ryokan* and other tourist accommodations have developed around most hot springs. Traveling to such resort areas is a favorite form of recreation among the people. In particular, agricultural and fishing villages depend on hot springs as a source of economic and spiritual vitality. Although many large resort areas have developed around famous hot springs, there are still numerous springs along sea coasts and in the mountains that remain undeveloped in their natural state.

Health Benefits: Each hot spring has been analyzed to determine the contents of the water and its beneficial effects. These are listed on signs posted nearby. Most Japanese hot springs can be classified into the following types:
1) Mild Hot Springs
2) "Heart Baths," so-called plain, carbonic acid hot springs
3) Bicarbonate Acid Earth Hot Springs that are good for diabetes
4) "Beauty Baths," so-called alkaline hot springs
* Warming Hot Springs that refresh and warm the body
5) "Hot Baths," so-called common salt hot springs
6) "Apoplexy Baths," so-called sulfur hot springs (bitter-tasting water)
* Divided into the three categories of saltpeter hot springs, gypsum hot springs and bitter hot springs
7) Iron Hot Springs said to be good for anemia
* Divided into the two categories of carbonic-acid hot springs and green vitriol hot springs
8) "Eye Baths," so-called alum hot springs
9) Sulfur Hot Springs said to smell like rotten eggs
10) Acidic Hot Springs good for the skin
11) "Radium Hot Springs," so-called radioactive hot springs
* The water from these hot springs is used not only for soaking, but it can have medicinal effects when it is drunk. A list of contraindications against soaking and drinking is posted at the entrance. It is important to inform oneself about their efficacy before using these baths.
Alternate uses of hot springs
1) Mineral Sand Baths are known for their beautifying benefits.
2) Palatable hot-spring water is good for the digestive system.
3) Breathing the air at hot springs is good for the respiratory tract.
  There are certain types of hot springs in Japan that are indeed quite unique.
1) Steam Hot Springs that use the surrounding steam and currents
2) Sand Baths in which people lie down and are buried in ocean sand
3) Sleeping Baths in which people remain for an extended period of time
4) Cascading Baths that give the same effect as a body massage
5) Timed Baths which can give a strong stimulation
  Refer to the nearest JNTO Tourist Information Center (TIC) for more detailed information on hot springs and their benefits.

IV. History

Founding of the Country and First Foreign Contacts (‒ 600 A.D.)

It is generally believed that the Japanese Archipelago was first inhabited by man in the later Stone Age, known as the Neolithic Age. Some archaeological findings indicate that man lived in this part of the world in the early part of the Stone Age. The clay vessels used in the Neolithic Age are of two types — the *Jomon* type and the *Yayoi* type. *Jomon*-type clay vessels, so called from the *jomon* (wavy, mat-markings) encircling them, have been found in many parts of the country. It appears that this type of earthenware was used for several thousand years.

About a century before the time of Christ, a new phase of primitive culture made its appearance in northern Kyushu and the area now known as Nara Prefecture, gradually spreading to other regions. The clay vessels used by the people under the influence of this phase of culture were of the *Yayoi* type, so named because specimens were first unearthed at a place called "Yayoi" in the present city of Tokyo.

About this time, bronze and iron were introduced from the Asian continent. The bronze culture was apparently short-lived, with the Stone and Bronze Ages gradually merging into the Iron Age. Chief among the representative bronze articles uncovered at excavation sites are swords and spears found mostly in western Japan and bells found in central Japan. It is not difficult to imagine, then, that the tribes who used these implements must have been the ancestors of the present Japanese race. But expert opinion is divided as to the origin or origins of the Japanese race. In all probability, several races from northeastern as well as southern Asia gradually merged into a single race to form the ancestral source of the Japanese.

Ancient Japanese lived in small communities, each made up of several *uji*, or family groups. These family groups were gradually unified until they were able to form a state around the beginning of the fourth century. The nucleus of this state was the Yamato Court in the present Nara Prefecture. The first leader of this Court was named Hatsukunishirasu Sumeramikoto, whom the Japanese later referred to as Jimmu Tenno, or Emperor Jimmu.

Ancient Japan had contacts with only two continental countries — Korea and China. About the time Japan achieved unification, Korea was divided into four kingdoms struggling for supremacy—Kokuli (Kokuri in Japanese) in the north, Silla (Shiragi in Japanese) in the southeast, Paikche (Kudara in Japanese) in the southwest and Mimana sandwiched between Silla and Paikche. Japan had some political influence in south Korea, and at one time even fought Silla and Kokuli in an alliance with Paikche and Mimana. In 660, Silla unified Korea, and, having joined with Tang-Dynasty China, over-threw Paikche, which had been friendly with Japan. Japan fought the Chinese on the side of Paikche, but was crushed in 663, leading to the end of its influence in Korea.

As might be expected, continental culture reached Japan's shores, first through Korea and then directly from China. Both Confucianism and Buddhism, destined to exert a tremendous influence upon the Japanese people in subsequent years, were introduced from Paikche. Together with this inflow of culture from the continent, there was a great movement of people from Korea and China coming to live in this island country. They taught the local people the practical arts of sericulture, weaving, metalcasting and brewing as well as the cultural arts of writing and literature.

Period of Political Reforms, Growth of Buddhism and Nara Period (600–784)

The social structure of ancient Japan was based on a system of family groups, or *uji*, as they were called. With the natural increase in population from generation to generation, the *uji* system gradually disintegrated so that the social structure underwent a series of radical changes. Such social upheavals inevitably resulted in corresponding changes in the political organization of the country. It was just at such a juncture that Shotoku-Taishi, or Prince Shotoku (574–622) entered the stage of national history as regent to Empress-Regnant Suiko (reigned 592–628) to administer the affairs of state. Not only did he Japanize Buddhism, but he also attempted important political reforms. The political thought of Prince Shotoku focused on the state as the nucleus of all activity. He insisted on profound reverence for the gods. In his Constitution of Seventeen Articles, he instructed the nation to be obedient and prudent when commanded by the Emperor. Furthermore, he not only framed and perfected various administrative systems, but also greatly improved and encouraged culture and education.

Under his leadership, Japanese civilization made excellent progress. Without deviating from his fundamental position of profound reverence for the gods, the Prince gave wholehearted protection to Buddhism. He built such colossal Buddhist temples as the Shitennoji —generally called Tennoji—in the province of Settsu (Osaka) and the Horyuji in the province of Yamato (near Nara). He also ordered the carving of Buddhist images and delivered lectures himself on Buddhist sutras.

Twenty some years after the death of Prince Shotoku, Prince Naka-no-Oe (626–671) arrived on the scene. He achieved a political reformation on a grand scale with the assistance of Fujiwara-no-

Kamatari. This prince began his work by overthrowing the Soga family, which was then wielding unwarranted authority. Thus, he firmly secured the centralization of political power in the court. As a result, the land and people of the empire were placed under the direct control of the Imperial Court as public land and subjects. Every person, male or female, over six years of age was granted a uniform plot of land fixed by law that he or she was expected to cultivate until death, when it was returned to the state. In 645, a series of political reforms known as The Great Reform of Taika were launched.

Meanwhile, Prince Naka-no-Oe ascended the throne. Posthumously called Emperor Tenchi, he never slackened in his efforts to bring his reforms to a successful consummation. Thus began the great work of compiling a code of laws and regulations. This code, first laid down during the reign of Emperor Tenchi, was called *Omi-ryo*. It was revised in the reign of Emperor Temmu and renamed *Asuka-no-Kiyomihara-ryo*. During the reign of Emperor Mommu (reigned 697–707), it became a completed code, which is now popularly known as *Taiho Ritsuryo*. But a short time later—during the reign of Empress-Regnant Gensho (reigned 715–724), it was revised again and finally completed under the name of *Yoro Ritsuryo*.

Although it had been the custom in earlier times for Emperors to change the nation's capital at the time of their accession, Empress-Regnant Gemmei (reigned 707–715) established a permanent court and government seat in the province of Yamato in 710 and called it Heijokyo, which later became known as Nara. Because the succeeding seven emperors lived in Nara over a period of 74 years, this age is commonly called the Nara period.

The Nara period was characterized by the great popularity and prosperity of Buddhism. It was also during this time that the famous image of the Great Buddha, or *Daibutsu*, of Nara—which is still standing—was cast. The bronze casting was authorized by Emperor Shomu (reigned 724–749), the most devout Buddhist among the Emperors of this period. In those days, there was active contact with China, which was then governed by the Tang Dynasty; official missions were frequently sent there and Buddhist priests crossed and recrossed the waters between the two countries. This contact with China greatly strengthened the national self-consciousness of the Japanese people.

Thus were published the "Kojiki" (Record of Ancient Matters) and the "Fudoki" (Typographical and Cultural Accounts of the Provinces) under Empress-Regnant Gemmei as well as the "Nihonshoki", or "Nihongi" (Chronicles of Japan) under Empress-Regnant Gensho. The "Kojiki" and "Nihonshoki" are the two most valuable sources of information to the student of the ancient history, religion and culture of Japan.

The outstanding literary work of this period is the "Man-yo-shu", literally "A Collection of Ten Thousand Leaves"—an anthology containing more than 4,500 poems of various lengths. The general tone of the poems is simple, unaffected and full of vigor. Their style and phraseology are free and grand in their expression of natural, unfeigned emotions and sentiments as well as sincere and reverent thoughts (refer to p.153).

Along with the growing popularity and prosperity of Buddhism, art and industry also made great progress. Many splendid specimens have been preserved of the temple architecture, Buddhist sculpture, metal casting, painting, embroidery, lacquer work and other arts that flourished in these days. In the art history of Japan, this period is called the Tempyo Age. In the precincts of the Todaiji Temple at Nara is a repository known as the Shoso-in, which houses more than 9,000 articles of impressive beauty and craftsmanship. These treasures, most of which were used by Emperor Shomu, include several articles brought from Greece, the East Roman Empire (Byzantine Empire), Persia, India, China (of the Tang Dynasty) and Paikche (Korea). Redolent of exoticism, these age-old art specimens, mostly in a fine state of preservation, speak eloquently of the international character of Nara culture.

Heian Period (794-1185)

Emperor Kammu (reigned 781-806) moved the capital in 784 from Nara to Nagaokakyo in Yamashiro Province (now, part of Kyoto Prefecture). Ten years later, he built a new city at a spot remarkable for its natural beauty, naming it Heiankyo. This was the origin of the present Kyoto. This era, which lasted about four centuries, is therefore called the Heian period.

The early part of the Heian period was characterized by the great influence and prosperity of the Imperial House. At home, the nation rejoiced over the conquest and pacification of the Ezo people, who had until then dominated northern Japan. Abroad, trade was carried on with Pohai (a kingdom occupying part of an extensive region in what is now the southern part of the northeastern area of China), whose missions frequently visited Kyoto. Political reforms were carried out, while Buddhism produced such celebrated priests as Saicho (posthumously called Dengyo-Daishi) and Kukai (posthumously, Kobo-Daishi).

In the Heian period, the idea gradually gained strength that Shinto gods and Buddhas were essentially identical, with the result that the Japanese national tendency toward reverence of the gods became more completely harmonized with Buddhism than ever before, thus contributing still further to its popularization. As in the Nara period, the study of Buddhism was eagerly pursued, and many famous scholars versed in the Chinese classics flourished. Learning was promoted not only by the *daigaku* (central university) and *kokugaku* (provincial colleges), both state institutions, but also by a number of private schools established for the sons and daughters of aristocratic families.

This era of glory for the Imperial House was followed by the ascendancy of the Fujiwaras. Under Emperor Montoku (reigned 850 - 858), Fujiwara-no-Yoshifusa, a descendant of Fujiwara-no-Kamatari, became *dajo-daijin*, or prime minister, and rose to the exalted position of regent to the throne under the next Emperor, Seiwa (reigned 858-876). In the reign of Emperor Uda (reigned 887-897), Yoshifusa's adopted son, Mototsune, became *kampaku*, an official corresponding to supreme adviser to the Emperor. As a result of these important appointments, the Fujiwaras gradually grew very powerful.

Meanwhile, the Imperial House itself produced many wise Emperors and Empresses. The wisdom and foresight of Emperor Kammu, founder of Heiankyo, or Kyoto, were more than amply demonstrated by his memorable achievements. Emperor Saga (reigned 809-823) was not only an able writer in prose and verse, but also a skillful calligrapher. His consort, generally known as Empress Danrin, was a devout Buddhist, whose life was marked by deeds of mercy and charity. No less devoted to Buddhism was the consort of Emperor Junna (reigned 823-833), who also dedicated much of her time and energy to philanthropic work.

The reign of Emperor Daigo (reigned 897-930) produced a great many scholars versed either in Japanese or Chinese literature. As a result, an exceptional number of literary masterpieces were produced. This notable age is generally known as the Engi Era of Enlightenment. The reign of Emperor Murakami (reigned 946-967), who also exerted himself to ensure good government, is known as the Tenryaku era. Native Japanese literature began to flourish in the Engi-Tenryaku years, and among the elite there developed a taste for things Japanese. By command of Emperor Daigo, Ki-no-Tsurayuki (868-945) and other poets selected a considerable number of old and new Japanese poems, then compiled them in an anthology called "Kokin Wakashu" (A Collection of Japanese Poems, Ancient and Modern, refer to p.154). It is valued as the most important anthology of Japanese verse published after the "Man-yo-shu".

About the time of Emperor Ichijo (reigned 986-1011), a brilliant group of talented beauties, including a number of lady literati, gathered at the Imperial Court. They included such famed writers as Sei-Shonagon, who wrote a collection of essays called "Makura-no-Soshi" (Pillow Book, refer to p.156), and Murasaki-Shikibu, who produced the novel "Genji Monogatari" (Tale of Genji, refer to p.156). Art and industry also became highly refined while remaining typically Japanese. As many Buddhist temples were built, architecture, sculpture and painting made considerable progress.

The most famous of these edifices is the *Ho-odo*, or Phoenix Hall, attached to the Byodo-in Temple built in 1053 at Uji (near Kyoto) by

Fujiwara-no-Yorimichi. The image of Buddha Amitabha enshrined in the structure is attributed to the celebrated artist Jocho, while the mural paintings that adorn the interior of the hall are said to have been done by Takuma Tamenari. Both the image of Buddha and the wall paintings are works of art resplendent with aristocratic delicacy and refinement.

Aristocratic life in those days was a merry and many-splendored affair. The nobles led a life of luxury and ease, going on morning drives in stately carriages to view lovely flowers or admiring the evening moon from beautifully decorated boats on a lake, river or sea. They dwelled in palatial residences and enjoyed all the privileges and pleasures that noble birth and wealth could command.

In striking contrast to the gaiety of metropolitan life was the corruption that was slowly eating into provincial government. Emperor Gosanjo (reigned 1068–1072) was convinced that all these political malpractices and social evils were, in the final analysis, due to the usurpation of political and administrative authority by the Fujiwara regents and supreme advisers to the throne. Accordingly, he tried to reduce their power and influence by gathering all the reins of government into his own hands to rule the country personally.

His successor, Emperor Shirakawa (reigned 1072–1086), followed his example, endeavoring to weaken the system of regency and advisership. By maintaining a powerful voice in the affairs of state after his retirement from the throne, he gave rise to what came to be known as *insei*, or government by retired emperors. But *insei* had various undesirable features of its own, finally resulting in the civil wars of the Hogen and Heiji eras (1156–1160). It was during these domestic disturbances that Taira-no-Kiyomori, a scion of the military caste, distinguished himself by deeds of valor, thus winning for himself repeated promotions at the court and in the government. Eventually, he attained the position of *dajo-daijin*, or prime minister. All members of the Taira family were given prominent official posts, to the exclusion of the other aristocratic families in a period of unchallenged ascendancy for the Tairas that lasted about 20 years. Their life of pride and luxury was such that it gradually aroused the envy and hatred of the rest of the nation, high and low. At last, the Tairas (or Heike, as they are often called) were overthrown by Minamoto-no-Yoritomo in 1185.

Kamakura Period (1192–1333)

Minamoto-no-Yoritomo took up his position at Kamakura, laying the foundations for a military government that lasted nearly 680 years until 1867. Yoritomo and his counselors obtained permission from the Emperor in 1185 to establish the posts of *shugo* (guards) and *jito* (heads of districts, or squires) throughout the country. As might be expected, the posts were given to his retainers. The *shugo* were entrusted mainly with military affairs and police duties, while the *jito* were in charge of the landed estates as well as the collection of land-taxes, paid in rice.

From that time onward, actual political power was in the hands of Yoritomo. In 1192, Yoritomo was appointed *Sei-i-Taishogun* (or *shogun* for short; lit. Generalissimo for the Subjugation of the Eastern Barbarians). It was then that he founded the *bakufu* (lit. camp office), or shogunate government, at Kamakura. Yoritomo was succeeded as *shogun* by his sons, Yoriie and Sanetomo, but Yoriie was killed in 1204 and Sanetomo was also assassinated in 1219 by his nephew Kugyo. Thus, the Minamotos were brought to an abrupt end after only 27 years of ruling prosperity, during which the three of them succeeded one another as supreme military commander of the country.

After the downfall of the Minamoto (or Genji, as they are often called), Kamakura officials invited Fujiwara-no-Yoritsune from Kyoto to fill the post of *shogun*, but actual government control was now in the hands of Hojo Yoshitoki .

The military families constituted a newly risen class, or social stratum. The culture of the Kamakura period, therefore, was simple, straightforward and vigorous. During the Kamakura period, for the first time in Buddhist history, Japanese-born sects of Buddhism sprang into being such as the Jodoshu (Jodo sect), the Jodo-Shinshu and the Hokkeshu. In the field of literature, composing poetry in the native tongue was as popular as ever. Emperor Gotoba (1180–1239), Fujiwara-no-Shunzei, Fujiwara-no-Teika, the priest Saigyo, and Minamoto-no-Sanetomo (third Shogun at Kamakura) were among the more celebrated poets of the time.

There also arose a new and masculine form of literature—the war narrative, which dealt with the changing fortunes of military leaders engaged in civil strife. These included "Hogen Monogatari", "Heiji Monogatari", "Gempei Josuiki" ("Seisuiki") and "Heike Monogatari" —all historical narratives respectively describing the civil wars of the Hogen and Heiji eras, the rivalry and struggles between the Minamotos (Genji) and Tairas (Heike) and the rise, prosperity and fall of the Taira family.

Fine and useful arts, emancipated from their traditional patterns, achieved free and vigorous development. The most notable progress was seen in sculpture, in which such great artists as Unkei, Tankei and Kaikei gave the world masterpieces replete with manly strength and vigor. In painting, *emakimono* (scrolls illustrating stories) were popular. *Emakimono* show very ingenious methods of expression. For instance, the passage of time was aptly conveyed by painting different scenes and episodes in proper sequence on a long scroll. Only a section may be unrolled at one time and duly appreciated before proceeding to the next section.

In the art of making weapons and armor, phenomenal progress was achieved by those who made helmets and armor with the production of elaborate suits of armor. It was in the Kamakura period that such celebrated swordsmiths as Masamune appeared. It was also during this period that the virile national spirit of the Japanese people was fostered and strengthened through *bushido*, or the way of the warrior.

And it was just when the military families had developed their martial virtues to a high degree of efficiency that the Yuan Dynasty of China sent expeditions to Japan. The Yuan Dynasty was founded by Kublai Khan (1216-1294), grandson of the great Genghis Khan, who had previously conquered most of the known world in Asia and Europe. Wishing to extend his suzerainty over the Japanese islands, he sent an official message to Japan during the reign of Emperor Kameyama (reigned 1259-1274).

Hojo Tokimune, regent of the Kamakura Shogunate, resolutely refused to consider or even to reply to the message, and all subsequent Mongol missions were turned away by his order. In 1274, therefore, during the reign of Emperor Gouda (reigned 1274-1287), the Yuan government sent an expeditionary force, including Korean contingents, to the port of Hakata in Kyushu. The Mongol invaders were defeated, however. After failing in his first invasion attempt, Kublai Khan sent a second force of 100,000 strong in 1281.

The battle with this Mongolian force ended in an overwhelming victory for the Japanese defenders due to the timely arrival of a violent typhoon, which the Japanese in those days believed to be a *kamikaze* (divine wind), as well as to the stubborn resistance of the warriors. The Japanese soldiers who had fought and survived demanded rewards from the government, but the *bakufu* was in such desperate financial straits that it could not possibly satisfy their demands. As a result, it gradually lost the confidence of the *bushi* (warriors), and local governments lost considerable power.

Seeing this, Emperor Godaigo (1288-1339) plotted to overthrow the *bakufu* together with the nobles, who had been nourishing an ambition to regain the political power they had lost to the military class. The *bakufu* got wind of what was brewing and exiled the Emperor to the island of Oki in the Japan Sea in 1332. After escaping from the island in the following year, the Emperor with the assistance of such able generals as Nawa Nagatoshi (?-1336), Kusunoki Masashige (1294-1336), Nitta Yoshisada (1301-1338) and Ashikaga Takauji (1305-1358) eventually succeeded in causing the downfall of the *bakufu*. The cherished ideal of the nobility was thus realized, if only temporarily, as the reins of government passed into the hands of the Emperor once again. This is called the Kemmu Restoration.

Muromachi and Azuchi-Momoyama Periods (1336-1598)

The nobles, monks and court ladies were rewarded more generously than the generals who had rendered meritorious service in helping Emperor Godaigo restore the Imperial regime. The warriors were upset over this unfair treatment. Moreover, local warriors were compelled to bear the cost of the palace construction and other expenses, intensifying their anger. All this gave impetus to a craving for the return of military government.

Ashikaga Takauji was not slow to capitalize on this discontent. Gathering the disgruntled warriors under his banner, he rose in revolt against Emperor Godaigo. The Imperial army met with defeat and the Emperor fled Kyoto, taking refuge in the Yoshino mountains (in the present Nara Prefecture, refer to p.737). When Takauji entered the capital, he established a *bakufu* there in 1336 and enthroned a new Emperor.

The nation now had two Emperors—one in Kyoto and the other at Yoshino. The Kyoto Court was known as the Northern Court and the other as the Southern Court. This double Court was destined to continue to exist in rivalry for 57 years, a period popularly known as the Nambokucho (South-North Dynasty) period. In 1392, the Yoshino Court merged with the Kyoto Court, but the real power still rested with the *bakufu* set up by Takauji at Muromachi in Kyoto. The period resulting from the establishment of the *Kyoto bakufu* (1336) until the year 1573, when the Ashikaga Shogunate was overthrown, is called the Muromachi period.

Ashikaga Yoshimitsu (1358-1408), who succeeded in controlling a large number of military leaders and their subordinates, dominated the nation. Living a luxurious life, he constructed a villa at Kitayama in Kyoto, where he built a gilded, three-story structure called Kinkakuji Temple, or Gold Pavilion, encircled by a picturesque garden (refer to p.690). After Yoshimitsu's death, the real center of power shifted from the *shogun* to his nominal subordinates, among whom an unceasing struggle for supremacy ensued. Things went from bad to worse until the time of Shogun Ashikaga Yoshimasa (1436-1490). He was so addicted to a life of luxury and so indifferent to the affairs of state that it became necessary to resolve financial difficulties by increasing taxes.

The inevitable consequence was that the country was soon seething with discontent and threats of war. Finally, in 1467, the two powerful retainers of the *bakufu*, Hosokawa Katsumoto and Yamana Sozen, carried their rivalry to such extremes that it resulted in an open clash of arms. This was the signal for the beginning of prolonged and nationwide internecine strife. For more than 100 years scores of military leaders took up strategic positions in their respective districts, striving with one another for supremacy. Thus, they earned for their time the truly fitting opprobrium of *Sengoku-jidai*—the Age of Civil Wars.

Though he was a political failure, Yoshimasa had his strong points: he was well versed in literature and art criticism. On his retirement as *shogun*, he had a villa built at Higashiyama in Kyoto, with the Ginkakuji Temple, or Silver Pavilion, as the central structure, where he indulged in epicurean pursuits. (Refer to p.676). Because of the many masterpieces in fine arts that were created in those days, art history has given this period a name of its own—the Higashiyama Age.

Among the great painters of the Higashiyama Age were Mincho, skilled in painting Buddhist images; Sesshu, a landscape artist, Kano Motonobu, an eclectic, adopting whatever he thought good either in Japanese or Chinese art, and Tosa Mitsunobu, who breathed new vigor into what is known as *yamato-e* (lit. Japanese pictures, refer to p.183). The art of metal engraving was best represented by Goto Yujo, while the art of making lacquerware attained a higher degree of refinement and delicacy than any other art form.

As for the manners and customs of the time, it should be noted that they were greatly influenced by Zen Buddhism, then in great vogue. In fact, it was so popular that in matters of taste such traits as frankness and disinterestedness were valued by both high and low. The tea ceremony and the art of flower arrangement were especially fashionable. Originating about this time were the three arts of jointly writing link verse, or *renga* (refer to p.159); of *noh* recitation, properly called *yokyoku* or *utai* (refer to p.158 and 166), and of the *noh* farce known as *kyogen*(refer to p.158).

Gaining ascendancy in Owari Province toward the end of the Muromachi period, Oda Nobunaga (1534-1582) brought the neighboring provinces under his control. In 1568 he entered Kyoto intending to restore the shogunate, but the Ashikaga Shogun had already become more nominal than real. As a result, Nobunaga ousted the *shogun* from the capital and devoted himself to the task of unifying the country by force of arms. On the verge of achieving his goal after some ten years of strenuous efforts, he was assassinated by one of his generals—Akechi Mitsuhide—in 1582. But another of Nobunaga's illustrious generals took up the task where the master had left off and succeeded in making himself master of the entire country. This man was Toyotomi Hideyoshi (1536-1598). He did not stop there, however. He sent his forces to Korea in 1592 to fight against the Chinese forces. During the Korean struggle, however he died in 1598, and the Japanese forces were withdrawn from the peninsula.

The age in which Nobunaga and Hideyoshi flourished is known as the Azuchi-Momoyama period (1573-1598), so called from the respective names of the castles of these two generals. This age is characterized, among other things, by the great progress made in the realm of art.

In architecture, the art of castle construction made remarkable progress. Chief among these citadels were Azuchi Castle, Osaka Castle and Fushimi Castle (in Momoyama). The first was built by order of Nobunaga and the latter two by Hideyoshi. Each had a donjon, or keep, of from five to seven stories. The thick stone walls of Osaka Castle give one an idea of the Herculean task involved in erecting these castles. The architecture of dwelling houses is well typified by the residences of various generals such as the magnificent Jurakudai mansion erected for Hideyoshi. The interior of this mansion was elaborately decorated with paintings done in bold strokes and rich colors. Quite a number of these paintings, executed by such masters as Kano Eitoku (1543-1590), Kano Sanraku (1559-1635) and Kaiho Yusho (1533-1615), have survived the ravages of time.

The *chanoyu*, or tea ceremony (refer to p.209), which had already become an institution in the previous Muromachi period, was practiced with religious zeal during this period. Both Nobunaga and Hideyoshi developed a passion for the tea ceremony. The noted tea master Sen-no-Rikyu, who flourished during this period, raised the tea ceremony to the dignity of a national art.

The temperament of the Japanese people in the Azuchi-Momoyama period was such that they loved grandeur and splendor, as is evident from the practical as well as the fine arts, which were full of manly vigor and rich in delicate designs and colors. The general taste also tended towards magnificence and breadth of vision. Dancing, singing and music were in great vogue. It was during this period that *joruri* (a kind of ballad drama, refer to p.161), *ayatsuri* (puppet show, refer to p.169) and *kabuki* drama (refer to p.161) had their beginnings.

Edo (Tokugawa) Period (1603-1867)

Next to Hideyoshi himself, Tokugawa Ieyasu (1542-1616) was the most influential man in the country. After Hideyoshi died, Ishida Mitsunari plotted to oust Ieyasu, and in 1600 he took up arms against him. In the famous battle of Sekigahara (Gifu Prefecture), Ieyasu defeated him. Three years later in 1603, the victor Ieyasu was appointed *Sei-i-Taishogun* (or *shogun* for short; generalissimo) and established his *bakufu* in Edo (now, Tokyo). In two more battles, one in 1614 and the other in 1615, he annihilated the Toyotomi Clan and its adherents, who made their last stand at Osaka Castle.

Efforts were then directed toward the readjustment and consolidation of the various administrative systems and institutions, with the result that the *bakufu* was placed on firmly secure foundations. The social structure of the Edo period consisted of strata divided into *kuge* (court nobles), *buke* (warriors or *samurai*), farmers and *chonin* (townspeople). The nobles occupied the most exalted social rank, but had little political power or economic influence. The warriors, on the contrary, wielded the real power. With the *bakufu* (shogunate) as their central authority, about 270 *daimyo* (feudal lords) divided the country among themselves into domains or fiefs, which they governed with the assistance of their retainers and subordinates. Subject to the rule of this military class, the townspeople engaged in trade and industry and the farmers in agriculture. Thus, the feudal system of Japan was established.

It was during the previous age—the war-torn Muromachi period — that the number of ships sailing to the Far East from Europe began to increase. Among the visitors to Japanese waters were a group of Portuguese sailors who drifted to the island of Tanegashima to the south of Kyushu in 1543 when Emperor Gonara was on the throne. They were the first foreigners to introduce firearms into Japan.

It was only natural in a strife-ridden age like the Muromachi period that firearms were quickly and eagerly adopted in every province, thus affecting tactics, fortification and other military strategy. Some time later came the Spaniards, who, like the Portuguese, engaged in commercial relations with the Japanese. Because these European traders came to Japan by way of the south seas, they were called *namban-jin* (southern barbarians).

Shortly after the first arrival of the Portuguese, Francisco de Xavier came to this country in 1549 and preached the tenets of the Jesuits. The Japanese called the new teaching *Kirishitanshu* (Christianity) or *Tenshukyo* (Religion of the Heavenly Father). From that time on, Christianity gradually spread until the advent of Oda Nobunaga, who further encouraged it by granting official sanction for its propagation. Three *daimyo* of Kyushu—Otomo, Omura and Arima—went so far as to send messengers to Rome, where they were received in audience by the Pope.

Christianity, however, was officially banned by Hideyoshi, who feared that it would constitute a disturbing factor to public peace and order.

In 1600, when Tokugawa Ieyasu was rapidly gaining supremacy, a merchant vessel of the Dutch East India Company drifted into Japanese waters. Ieyasu summoned crewmembers Jan Joosten, a Hollander, and William Adams (refer to p.441), an Englishman, and asked them questions concerning the state of affairs abroad. In 1609, permission was granted the Hollanders to engage in trade, and similar permission was given the English in 1613. Hirado and Nagasaki in Hizen Province (now, Nagasaki Prefecture) were opened as ports to foreign traders of these two nations.

The overseas adventures of the Japanese people since the Muromachi period were characterized by extraordinary vigor. In Hideyoshi's time, many a merchant vessel left Japan for trade with distant lands. At the beginning of the Edo period, the spirit of adventure abroad became so intense that great numbers of Japanese ships, with *shuinjo* (lit. vermilion-stamped permits) issued by the *bakufu*, sailed between Japan and Macao, Luzon, Siam and other countries south of Japan. Ieyasu even sent commercial representatives across the Pacific to Nueva Hispania, as Mexico was then called, to open trade relations with that distant country.

With regard to Christianity, Ieyasu adopted and pursued the policy of prohibition initiated by Hideyoshi, but it was not rigidly enforced throughout the country. Date Masamune (1565-1636), lord of Mutsu Providence (now, Fukushima, Miyagi, Iwate and Aomori prefectures) in northern Japan, for example, sent his retainer, Hasekura Tsunenaga (1571-1622), to Rome with the avowed object of acquiring the esoteric details of the Catholic faith (refer to p.341). Foreign relations were so active that it was not possible to entirely prevent European missionaries from smuggling themselves into this country to preach the Gospel. Iemitsu, the third of the Tokugawa Shogun, accordingly, tightened control over Christianity by prohibiting the importation of Christian literature, the emigration of Japanese to any foreign country and the return of any Japanese who had left the country.

In protest against these measures, the Jesuits of Amakusa and Shimabara in Kyushu rose in revolt in the winter of 1637, but the rebellion was suppressed the following spring (refer to p.860). The *bakufu* enforced an even stricter ban on Christianity, and in 1639 it closed the country to the Portuguese. As both the English and the Spaniards had stopped coming to Japan some time before, only the Dutch continued to trade, using Nagasaki as their port of entry. From that time on, the Dutch, Chinese and Koreans were the only foreigners admitted to Japan. With its foreign contacts thus sadly declining, the nation found itself in a state of virtually complete seclusion.

Many institutions of Western civilization had been introduced into Japan while the country was still open to the people of various European countries. As Christianity spread across various districts of the country, schools were founded and books published under its influence. Astronomy, geography, medicine, literature, architecture and painting made significant progress, fields of knowledge that soon greatly flourished. Many European goods were also imported.

Shogun Iemitsu was succeeded by Ietsuna, and the latter by Tsunayoshi. The period of Tsunayoshi's tenure of office is known as the Genroku era (1688-1704). While this era saw a general relaxation of political morals, phenomenal advances and achievements were made in the sciences, literature and the arts. Among the eminent scholars of this period were such men as Yamazaki Ansai (1618-1682), Yamaga Soko (1622-1685), Ito Jinsai (1627-1705) and Ogyu Sorai (1666-1728). A plebeian literature also developed, producing such masters as novelist Ihara Saikaku (1642-1693, refer to p.160), the *haiku* poet Matsuo Basho (1644-1694, refer to p.160) and the playwright Chikamatsu Monzaemon (1653-1724, refer to p.161). Among the artists of the time were the *ukiyo-e* painter Hishikawa Moronobu (1618-1694), the lacquerware artist Ogata Korin (1658-1716, refer to p.185), and Hanabusa Itcho (1652-1724), who excelled in portraits and paintings of flowers and birds. All these artists produced works full of sensuous charm or breadth of vision.

Wallowing in the blessings of peace, the people tended more towards extravagance. They frequented *joruri* recitations and play-houses, dressed in expensive and gorgeous *kimono*, etc. In fact, all their personal belongings were excessively elaborate in keeping with the times. The modes and fashions current in those days are known by the general term—Genroku style.

Ienobu succeeded Tsunayoshi as *shogun*, and was, in turn, succeeded by Ietsugu. While Ienobu and Ietsugu were in office, Arai Haku-seki (1657-1725) was appointed a *bakufu* official and carried out reforms to correct the malpractices inherited from the previous era. Hakuseki's reforms were based on civilian principles, whereas Yo-shimune—the next *shogun*—made steadfastness and sturdiness his guiding principles in carrying out political reforms of his own. About that time, the nation also made notable progress in all fields of economic activity.

Yoshimune as *shogun* was succeeded by his son Ieshige, who in turn gave the office to his son Ieharu. Ieharu's period of office was clouded by Tanuma Okitsugu (1719-1788), who usurped much of the *shogun*'s authority and bred political corruption. At the beginning of his tenure of office, Ienari, who followed Ieharu, appointed Matsu-daira Sadanobu (1758-1829) to a vital post and made him carry out the needed reforms.

Unfortunately, after Sadanobu's retirement, Ienari became more and more extravagant. As a result, the finances of the *bakufu* again fell into disarray. In the meantime, learning and the arts made rapid strides, notably during the Bunka and Bunsei eras (1804-1829). Among the masters of the graphic arts were the *ukiyo-e* painters— Katsushika Hokusai (1790-1849) and Utagawa Hiroshige (1797-1858). Other noted painters included Ike-no-Taiga (1723-1776), Maruyama Okyo (1733-1795), Shiba Kokan (1738-1818) and Tani Buncho (1763-1840), each of whom distinguished himself by his own peculiar style. As for Dutch (foreign) learning, its study had been launched by Aoki Kon-yo (1698-1769) during Yoshimune's time.

With the great progress of learning in the Edo period, the stream of national thought and sentiment grew broader and deeper. The branches of learning contributing the most to the growth and spread of this thought were national history and Japanese classics together with the study of Shinto. A monumental work of this period was the "Dai-Nihonshi" (A History of Great Japan, refer to p.556), the compilation of which was begun by Tokugawa Mitsukuni (1628-1700) —lord of the Tokugawa family branch ruling Hitachi Province (now, Ibaraki Prefecture).

Side by side with the spread of patriotic thought in domestic politics, earnest discussions and deliberations were carried on about pressing questions of national coast defense, which had been oc-casioned by the arrival of Russian and British vessels. In 1792 and again in 1804, Russia sent representatives to Japan to demand the opening of trade relations. Still blindly adhering to the traditional policy of isolation, the *bakufu* rejected the demand on both occasions.

As for the English, they attracted widespread attention here in the following manner: In 1808, when the Napoleonic wars were at their height in Europe, an English man-of-war in hot pursuit of a Dutch vessel (the two countries were then at war) suddenly sailed into Nagasaki. It left only after the crew had behaved in a most unruly fashion.

Earlier, during the Kansei era (1789-1800), Hayashi Shihei (1738-1793) wrote and published a book in which he urged the necessity of strengthening coastal defenses, and Matsudaira Sadanobu personally inspected the area around Edo Bay (Tokyo Bay). The *bakufu* paid special attention to the defense of the island of Ezo, as Hokkaido was then called. Kondo Juzo (1771-1829) went to the island of Etorofu and erected a national landmark there, while Mamiya Rinzo (1780-1844) not only explored the island of Sakhalin, but even set foot on the continent of Asia beyond the narrow straits. Military science and the art of gunnery introduced from the West were practiced more and more in earnest, as some of the feudal clans set about making serious military preparations for the defense of their coast.

Years of anxiety rolled on and passed into decades until 1853 when Commodore Perry of the United States Navy, in command of a squadron, came to Uraga and demanded Japan to open its doors to trade. It was as if the entire Japanese nation heard the loud clanging of bells announcing the dawning of a new era. In the same year, a Russian envoy by the name of Poutiatine came to Nagasaki to demand the opening of commercial relations.

The next year, 1854, the *bakufu* concluded a treaty of amity with the United States at Kanagawa (a part of the present city of Yokohama) and opened Shimoda (in Izu) and Hakodate (in Hokkaido) to American vessels. This pact is popularly known as the Treaty of Kanagawa. The *bakufu* next signed similar treaties with Great Britain, Russia and the Netherlands. Thus, the policy of seclusion pursued for more than two centuries was abandoned as Japan stepped forth to join the community of nations.

It should be remembered that what Japan had concluded with those Occidental countries were treaties of amity, of friendly relations. In 1858, therefore, it concluded a Treaty of Amity and Commerce with Townsend Harris, American consul general (refer to p.384), to make Kanagawa, Hyogo (now, Kobe), Nagasaki and Niigata new open ports. At the same time, Shimoda was closed. In the same year, Ii Naosuke (1815-1860), as *tairo* (highest official of the *bakufu* below the *shogun*), put his signature and seal on the provisional treaty without waiting for the sanction of the Imperial Court. He also concluded similar agreements with the Netherlands, Russia, Great Britain and France (refer to p.418).

By the time Emperor Meiji (1852-1912) ascended the throne in 1867, the *bakufu* had become so utterly effete that it no longer possessed any authority with which to carry on the government of the country. In April of that year, therefore, Tokugawa Yoshinobu, who then held the office of *shogun*, voluntarily relinquished the reins of government to the Imperial Court. Thus 265 years after Ieyasu's appointment to the office of *shogun*, the Edo Bakufu came to an end, bringing to a close the long period of government by the military class.

Meiji and Taisho Periods (1868-1926)

The Meiji Restoration ushered in the dawn of the modernization of Japan, paving the way for Japan's entry into the family of modern nations. In other words, the Restoration of 1868 forms a very significant landmark in the long history of the country.

But the governmental innovations consequent upon the Meiji Restoration were simply instituted along the lines of restoration of the time-honored government by the Emperor. In March 1868, Emperor Meiji issued his administrative principles, commonly called the Imperial Oath of Five Articles. The general policy of the government was thus firmly established. In July of the same year, Emperor Meiji visited Edo and changed its name to Tokyo. He returned to Kyoto for a while, but in the spring of the following year (1869) he settled in Tokyo, which became the capital of the country. Shortly after this, the *daimyo* throughout the country returned their status and fiefs to the Emperor. Thereupon, the feudal system was officially abolished and a new form of administrative government was set up. Feudalism gave place to the centralization of power as reform after reform was instituted, including the adoption of educational and military systems.

Things Western were introduced into the country by those Japanese who had studied abroad and also by foreigners who came to Japan. One outcome was the spread among the people of the ideas of liberty, equality and civil rights. Thoughtful Japanese began to entertain a craving for the adoption of a parliamentary system. For this purpose, all sorts of practical movements were started. The government, too, recognized the need to adopt an assembly system (the Diet). In 1881, an Imperial edict was issued that promised to put it into practice in ten years. Then in 1885, the administrative system that had been in use ever since the days of the Great Reform of Taika (645) was abolished and replaced by a modern cabinet system. Ito Hirobumi (1841-1909) was appointed as the first Prime Minister of Japan. The year 1888 saw the completion of the Japanese Constitution, the drafting of which had been under way since 1881. Once the Imperial approval had been obtained, it was promulgated on February 11 of the following year (1889). In 1890, the first Diet session was convened.

Chief among the important international events in the Meiji era were the two wars Japan fought—one with China (1894-1895) and the other with Russia (1904-1905). The cause of the Sino- Japanese War was the struggle between the two countries over their interests in Korea plus the rivalry for political power between the two factions—conservative and progressive—of the Korean government. The war broke out in July 1894. After significant military defeats, China requested peace and a treaty was signed in 1895. As a result, China ceded to Japan the Liaotung Peninsula and Formosa. However, Russia, Germany and France intervened and demanded that Japan return the peninsula. Japan had no choice but to accede.

Subsequently, Russia sent troops to Manchuria (now, the north-eastern district of China) and gradually made it clear that it had designs on Korean and Chinese territory—a manifestation of her long-cherished desire to secure an ice-free port in the Far East. Fearing that this might menace its peace, Japan started negotiations for the withdrawal of Russian troops from Manchuria. Russia, however, stood pat on its contentions. Great Britain, which had interests in China and India, also considered the Russian action as a menace. Accordingly, it concluded an alliance with Japan in 1902.

With the tacit understanding of Great Britain, Japan declared war on Russia in February 1904. After victories on land and sea, it concluded peace with Russia in 1905 through the mediation of President Theodore Roosevelt of the United States in the Treaty of Portsmouth.

The fact that Japan emerged victorious from these two wars was instrumental in elevating its international standing and accelerating the development of its capitalistic structure.

In the earlier decades of the Meiji era, the nation was busy acquiring new knowledge and skills from Occidental countries in the different fields of politics, economics and science. In due course, many people assimilated the imported knowledge to meet local needs and carry out research along original and creative lines of their own. Brilliant discoveries in medicine and surgery, notable inventions in the manufacture of arms and ammunition and other triumphs were achieved. The study of Japanese and Chinese classics, which for a time had been sadly neglected, was revived with energy. In the realm of literature, the latter half of the Meiji period produced a large number of celebrated novelists and *haiku* poets as well as astute critics and capable exponents of Western literature.

As for the fine arts, the necessity for preserving old works of art began to be strongly urged as early as the 12th or 13th year of the Meiji era, triggering a fast-spreading movement for an art revival. Master painters, both of the native and Western schools together with sculptors to match them in skill, appeared in large numbers. Architecture and the arts of dyeing, weaving, pottery and lacquerware also reflected Western influences. On the one hand, they preserved much of the antique allegiance of former periods, but on the other hand, they added new and refreshing features.

In July 1912, Emperor Meiji died and Emperor Taisho ascended the throne. Under the reign of the new Emperor, Japan's influence was further expanded. When World War I broke out in 1914, Japan sided with the allied powers as an ally of Great Britain. The Japanese forces saw action chiefly in the Pacific and Indian oceans, but they also assisted British and French forces in the Mediterranean. As one of the victor nations, the international position of Japan soared even higher. Japan was now one of the "Big Five" of the world, ranking third in naval power.

After the war, conferences were held and treaties signed with a view to securing world peace. At the Versailles Peace Conference in 1919, a new peace instrument was set up—the League of Nations. Accordingly, Japan became a member of the Council of the League. In 1921 a conference was held in Washington, and two treaties were concluded on that occasion—the Four-Power Pact pertaining to the Pacific Islands and the Nine-Power Treaty concerning China.

Showa and Heisei Periods (1926 –   )

Emperor Taisho died in 1926, and the late Emperor Hirohito acceded to the throne. Japan was now in Showa era. An antiwar pact was signed in Paris in 1928, and two years later the Naval Disarmament Conference was held in London. Then in 1932 another arms limitation conference took place, this time in Geneva. Japan took part in all these conferences and signed all the treaties involved.

Prior to the Geneva Conference, Japan clashed with China. In 1932, Japan took over control of Manchuria, setting up the state of "Man-chukuo" and thereby extending its influence in that part of Asia. In 1937, the clash of interests developed into an armed conflict between Japan and China.

This led to opposition from the United States and Great Britain and ultimately to the Pacific War (World War II). Japan was defeated and all Japanese territory was occupied by the Allied powers with the aim of instituting a large-scale reform of Japan and turning it into a truly democratic state. The people in general denounced all that remained of militarism.

The greatest undertaking in the democratization of Japan was the revision of the Constitution. A new Constitution was drawn up, and Emperor Showa renounced his mythical divinity. After seven years of occupational control by the Supreme Commander of the Allied Powers, Japan regained its independence in 1952. In 1956, it was accepted as a member of the United Nations.

Japan, thus, returned to the community of nations. With coopera-tion with the United Nations as its key foreign policy line, it gradu-ally elevated its position in international society.

In 1971, Japan signed an agreement on the Ryukyu Islands with the United States of America providing for an end to the island chain's postwar occupation rule by the U.S. Forces and its reversion to the homeland as the new prefecture of Okinawa.

Seeking an improvement in relations with other Asian nations, Japan concluded a series of treaties normalizing relations with the Republic of Korea in 1965, the People's Republic of Mongolia in 1972, the People's Republic of China in 1972 and with the Democratic Republic of Vietnam in 1973. Japan also established diplomatic relations with the German Democratic Republic in 1973, shortly before the two Germanies were admitted to the United Nations.

In the meantime, the Japanese economy had recovered from the blows of the war, and the speed of its economic reconstruction astonished the world. Beginning in 1960, Japan launched its so- called high economic growth policy, with technical innovations and invest- ment in new facilities advancing by leaps and bounds. As a result, Japan soon blossomed into one of the world's leading industrial nations. It switched to the IMF (International Monetary Fund) agreement's Article Eight status in 1964, thereby ending trade and exchange controls, then proceeded to join the OECD (Organization for Economic Cooperation and Development).

During the 1970s the Japanese economy was severely shaken by the so-called "dollar shock" that resulted from the flotation of the US dollar and then again by the "oil shock" that occurred with the outbreak of the third Middle East War and the ensuing dramatic increase in the price of petroleum. Due to Japan's heavy dependence on petroleum imports, this latter development was particularly severe. The result was a shift in the Japanese economy away from the period of high growth and into the country's worst postwar recession. After a few years of low economic growth, the economy eventually stabilized and entered a period of stable growth.

✓ The lives of the Japanese people changed significantly during this period. Household electrical appliances became much more common and private ownership of automobiles became widespread as the consumer revolution even penetrated agricultural areas. As the average Japanese life-span increased, society on a whole began to age and nuclear families became prominent. The appearance of personal computers and their increased adoption into every aspect of society created a computerized society.

In the midst of such social changes, the Japanese social conscious- ness showed a dramatic development. The revolution in attitudes held by and about women touched all parts of society. 1975, designat- ed as the International Year of Women, was a watershed year that saw widespread recognition of women's abilities in all areas of society.

During the 1980s, the revolution that was taking place in the woman's image and life-style fused with growing demands for sweep- ing changes in the people's life-styles on the whole. This movement saw a shift away from an emphasis on "quantity" to a recognition of the importance of "quality."

In the diplomatic field, 1978 was a monumental year as the Treaty of Peace and Friendship between Japan and People's Republic of China was signed. In recognition of Japan's status as an advanced industrial nation, the summit of the seven industrially advanced nations was held in Tokyo twice—in 1979 and again in 1986.

Thus becoming one of the most influential nations in the world, Japan has now turned its attention to the important task of finding a way to contribute to world peace and democracy in the fast-changing world situation.

In January 1989 Emperor Showa died after a reign of 63 years, thrusting Japan into a new period—the Heisei period.

V. Language

There have been many scholastic attempts to find a relationship between the Japanese language and other languages, including the Korean, Chinese, Ural-Altaic and Indo-European languages. However, the most widely accepted theory holds that the spoken Japanese language developed independently of all other languages although the written language is primarily based on Chinese *kanji* characters. As with many languages, Japanese can be separated into written and spoken language, with the difference between the two lying in verb endings, auxiliary verbs and postpositions. The written language is mainly used for official documents and publications.

One of the peculiarities of spoken Japanese is that it is further divided into recording and conversational styles. Nowadays, official documents, literary works, journals and newspapers are primarily written in the recording style. Depending on the situation, the conversational style can be used in an abrupt, plain, polite or very polite form. A further distinction lies in the spoken language of men and women, which can vary quite dramatically. Thus, the phrase "I am Japanese" may be rendered in more than 14 different ways with subtle but distinct differences in conversational form.

The language commonly spoken among the educated class in Tokyo has been adopted as standard Japanese and is used in schools throughout the nation under the direction of the Ministry of Education.

Written Characters and Pronunciation

Written Japanese makes use of two different syllabries—*katakana* and *hiragana*, each of which consists of 50 phonograms. Both are derived from *kanji* (Chinese characters), complex ideographic characters originally developed in China but used for written Japanese as well. *Katakana* was formed by taking one part of a *kanji* character and simplifying it. *Hiragana* was formed through the simplification of Chinese characters written in a cursive style. In the following tables these syllabries are given with transliterations into Roman characters according to the Hepburn system. Consonants are pronounced like their English equivalents and are usually followed by a vowel. Each vowel has only one sound, the approximate English equivalent of which is as follows: *a*—as in rather; *i*—as in pin; *u*—as in bull; *e*—as in met; *o*—as in November.

Although there is still some historical doubt, the invention of *katakana* is ascribed to Kibi-no-Makibi, a scholar-statesman who lived during the eighth century. It seems that the study of the Sanskrit alphabet, which was already under way at the time, is what led to the establishment of this simplified system of phonetic characters.

The Katakana Syllabary

ア *a*	イ *i*	ウ *u*	エ *e*	オ *o*	
カ *ka*	キ *ki*	ク *ku*	ケ *ke*	コ *ko*	
サ *sa*	シ *shi*	ス *su*	セ *se*	ソ *so*	
タ *ta*	チ *chi*	ツ *tsu*	テ *te*	ト *to*	
ナ *na*	ニ *ni*	ヌ *nu*	ネ *ne*	ノ *no*	
ハ *ha*	ヒ *hi*	フ *fu*	ヘ *he*	ホ *ho*	
マ *ma*	ミ *mi*	ム *mu*	メ *me*	モ *mo*	
ヤ *ya*	イ *i*	ユ *yu*	エ *e*	ヨ *yo*	
ラ *ra*	リ *ri*	ル *ru*	レ *re*	ロ *ro*	
ワ *wa*	イ *i*	ウ *u*	エ *e*	オ *o*	ン *n*

The Hiragana Syllabary

い *i*	ろ *ro*	は *ha*	に *ni*	ほ *ho*	へ *he*	と *to*
ち *chi*	り *ri*	ぬ *nu*	る *ru*	を *o*	わ *wa*	か *ka*
よ *yo*	た *ta*	れ *re*	そ *so*	つ *tsu*	ね *ne*	な *na*
ら *ra*	む *mu*	う *u*	い *i*	の *no*	お *o*	く *ku*
や *ya*	ま *ma*	け *ke*	ふ *fu*	こ *ko*	え *e*	て *te*
あ *a*	さ *sa*	き *ki*	ゆ *yu*	め *me*	み *mi*	し *shi*

え	ひ	も	せ	す	ん
e	*hi*	*mo*	*se*	*su*	*n*

Originally developed in the ninth century, this arrangement of the *hiragana* characters is called *iroha*. The *iroha* actually forms a poetic verse that Chamberlain translated as "All is transitory in this fleeting world. Let me escape from its illusions and vanities!"

When ハ (は) and ヘ (へ) are used as postpositions, they are pronounced *wa* and *e* instead of *ha* and *he*.

Katakana is mainly used for transcribing foreign words that have entered the Japanese language and for foreign names. It is also used when sending telegrams in Japanese. Books for children and compositions by young students are generally written in *hiragana*, with some *katakana* included. Chinese characters are generally used to express nouns and the stems of inflective words.

Most books and publications other than those for children are written with a large percentage of *hiragana* in combination with Chinese characters. The pronunciation, and sometimes the meaning, of the Chinese characters are often indicated in *hiragana*, printed either at the side of, or in parentheses following the Chinese characters.

When two dots are placed at the upper-right corner of a character, they change its pronunciation in the following way:

ka → が *ga*   *ki* → ぎ *gi*   *ku* → ぐ *gu*   *ke* → げ *ge*   *ko* → ご *go*

sa → ざ *za*   *shi* → じ *zi*   *su* → ず *zu*   *se* → ぜ *ze*   *so* → ぞ *zo*

ta → だ *da*   *chi* → ぢ *ji*   *tsu* → づ *zu*   *te* → で *de*   *to* → ど *do*

ha → ば *ba*   *hi* → び *bi*   *fu* → ぶ *bu*   *he* → べ *be*   *ho* → ぼ *bo*

These characters are called sonants, and although the above examples have been given for *hiragana*, the same rule applies for the equivalent *katakana* characters.

There are also half-sonants, in which case a small circle is placed at the upper-right corner of the letter instead of the two dots.

ha → ぱ *pa*   *hi* → ぴ *pi*   *fu* → ぷ *pu*   *he* → ぺ *pe*   *ho* → ぽ *po*

In addition to these changes, there are certain adaptations found principally in words derived from Chinese ideographic characters. They are formed by the combination of two characters but pronounced as one. Their sounds are as follows:

106

きゃ	きゅ	きょ	ぎゃ	ぎゅ	ぎょ	しゃ	しゅ	しょ
kya	*kyu*	*kyo*	*gya*	*gyu*	*gyo*	*sha*	*shu*	*sho*

じゃ	じゅ	じょ	ちゃ	ちゅ	ちょ	ひゃ	ひゅ	ひょ
ja	*ju*	*jo*	*cha*	*chu*	*cho*	*hya*	*hyu*	*hyo*

びゃ	びゅ	びょ	ぴゃ	ぴゅ	ぴょ	みゃ	みゅ	みょ
bya	*byu*	*byo*	*pya*	*pyu*	*pyo*	*mya*	*myu*	*myo*

にゃ	にゅ	にょ	りゃ	りゅ	りょ
nya	*nyu*	*nyo*	*rya*	*ryu*	*ryo*

There are also double consonants that cause a repetition of the following consonant. They are romanized, either by doubling the consonant such as in *Nikko*, *teppo* (gun), or by using t before such as in *matchi* (match).

Accent: The spoken Japanese language has a well-marked, rhythmical pitch accent. However, the exact tone of the accent changes greatly, depending on the contents of speech and the mood of the speaker. Sometimes accents placed on individual words shift when the words are used in conjunction with other words.

Sentence Word Order

As a rule, the genitive precedes the nominative in Japanese sentences. The attributive adjective precedes its noun (though a predicative adjective follows its noun), the noun precedes its preposition (hence it is called a postposition) and the explanatory or dependent clauses precede their principal clause. The main verb is found at the end of the sentence.

Example: "Please shut the door" in Japanese is "*To* (door) *o* (postposition denoting the accusative case) *shimete* (shut) *kudasai* (please)". "Beautiful flowers" in Japanese is "*kireina* (beautiful) *hana* (flowers)."

In Japanese the preposition follows the noun; hence, it is more properly called a "postposition." These postpositions, "*te,ni,o,ha*," are not independent words, but merely particles by which the case of nouns or pronouns is determined.

Nouns have no inflection to indicate singularity or plurality; e.g., "*kodomo*" means both child and children. When wishing to show the plural of a noun, an indicator such as *ra*, *tachi*, *gata* or *domo* are attached, as in *kodomo-ra* or *kodomo-tachi*, both meaning children. Generally, however, the plural distinction is not made, but is left to be understood from the context. In the case of pronouns, the distinction of number is more strictly indicated, as in *watakushi* (I), *watakushi-tachi* (we), *anata* (sing. you), *anata-gata* (pl. you) and *anohito* (he or she) and *anohito-tachi* (they).

Personal pronouns are very often omitted, being inferred from the context.

Japanese verbs have no person or number. Tense and mood are usually expressed by changing the final vowel or by auxiliary suffixes. As an example, the conjugation of the verb *motsu* (to have) is given below:

Affirmative	Present	*motsu*
	Future	*matsudaro*
	Past	*motta*
Negative	Present	*motanai* or *motanu*
	Future	*motanaidaro*
	Past	*motanakatta*
Imperative		*mote*
Gerund		*motte*
Conditional	Present	*motsunara*
	Future	*motsunara*
	Past	*motteitara*
Conjectural	Present	*motteirudaro*
	Future	*motsudaro*
	Past	*mottaro*

Inflection of Verbs: Japanese verbs are divided into two classes according to the changes that they undergo. (1) Verbs that do not undergo any change in the root; (2) those which undergo a change both in the root and in termination.

First Class. Verbs which undergo a change in termination only:

Aff. Present	Neg. Present	Future	Past	Gerund	Imp.
kiru (to put on clothing)	kinai	kirudaro	kita	kite	kiro
miru (to see)	minai	mirudaro	mita	mite	miro
taberu (to eat)	tabenai	taberudaro	tabeta	tabete	tabero

Second Class. Verbs which undergo a change both in the root and in termination:

Aff. Present	Neg. Present	Future	Past	Gerund	Imp.
suru (to do)	shinai	surudaro	shita	shite	shiro
kuru (to come)	konai	kurudaro	kita	kite	koi

Conditional Forms: The conditional forms of phrases are obtained by adding either *nara* or *ra* as a suffix to the verb. Thus, *Kimi mo aruku*

nara, boku mo aruko (If you walk, I will also walk) or *Hanaga saita-ra, mini yuko* (When the trees bloom, we shall go to see them).
Conjectural Forms: The conjectural form of the verb is obtained by suffixing the particle *daro*. Thus, the verb *aruku* (to walk) has the following conjectural forms:

	Present & Future	Past
Aff.	*aruku daro*	*aruita daro*
Neg.	*arukanai daro*	*arukanakatta daro*

Wish or petition is expressed by adding to verbs the particles *tai* (or *taku*) and *hoshii* (or *hoshiku*). For example, *mitai* (want to see) as in *Watakushi wa mitai* (I want to see) or *mitehoshii* (wish someone to see) as in *Watakushi wa anata ni mitehoshii* (I wish you to see).

To express a desire to let another do certain things, there is inserted between the root and the suffix the particle *se* or *sase*: *misasetai* (I want to let you or him see it).

Passive verbs are formed by suffixing the particles *rareru*, or simply *reru*, to the root: *mirareru* (to be seen), *mirarenai* (not to be seen), *taberareru* (to be eaten) and *taberarenai* (not to be eaten).
Honorific Forms: Japanese abounds in honorifics. They are divided into two classes: (1) those formed by the inflections of auxiliary verbs or auxiliary particles and (2) those in which special words are used. Both classes have so many varieties that it is impossible to list them in this brief survey.

Adjectives and Adverbs

Adjectives can be classified as follows:

(1) Those that end with the suffix *i* and can be used attributively without inflection, predicatively with or without inflection and with or without the aid of verbs: *takai* (high) or *hikui* (low). These adjectives become adverbs when the suffix is changed into *ku*: *takaku* (high) or *hikuku* (low).

(2) Those that are formed by adding the suffix *na* to nouns, used attributively without inflection and predicatively with the aid of auxiliary verbs: *shizukana* (quiet) or *akirakana* (clear). These adjectives also become adverbs if the suffix *na* is changed into another suffix *ni*: *shizukani* (quietly) or *akirakani* (clearly).

(3) Those that are formed by adding the suffix *no* to nouns, making up compound adjectives, and used attributively without inflection: *joto-no* (high-grade) or *hidari-no* (left).

(4) Those that are used only as attributive adjectives and without inflection: *iwayuru* (so-called) or *arayuru* (all). There are also some kinds of adverbs used in combination with corresponding words: *kesshite* (never), followed by a corresponding negative verb; e.g., *dekinai* (cannot do) or *moshi* (if), which is an adverb because it modifies the following conditional verb, as in *yokattara* (be good).

Auxiliary Particles or Postpositions

In Japanese the cases of nouns and the connections between the various words in a sentence are all shown by the use of particles called *te-ni-o-ha* (post-positions).

Auxiliary particles can roughly be classified as follows:

(1) Particles suffixed to nouns to indicate their case. The nominative case is indicated by *wa* or *ga*: *Watakushi wa nemuru* (I sleep) or *Kare ga okoru* (He gets angry). The dative case is indicated by *ni*: *Ano musume wa haha ni nite iru* (That girl resembles her mother). The accusative or objective case is indicated by *o*: *Kohii o ippai motte kite kudasai* (Bring me a cup of coffee, please).

(2) Particles that indicate place, method, time, etc. The particle *de* or *dewa* is used to indicate place, time, etc.: *Nikko de mimashita* (I saw it at Nikko); *Nippon dewa nanto iimasu ka* (What do they call it in Japan?); *Ichinichi de dekiru desho* (It can probably be finished in a day); *Kisha de mairimashita* (I came by train); *Take de dekita kago* (A basket made of bamboo); *Hyaku-en de kaimashita* (I bought it for ¥100), or *Byoki de arukenai* (I cannot walk because of sickness).

The particle *ni* or *niwa* is used to indicate place and time as well as person or thing: *Doko ni osumai desu ka* (Where do you live?); *Tokyo ni sunde imasu* (I live in Tokyo); *Myocho hachiji ni shuppatsu-shimasu* (I leave at eight o'clock tomorrow morning), or *Kono hako niwa hairimasen* (They cannot be packed in this box).

The particle *to* or *towa* is used to indicate companionship or connection: *Chichi to kimashita* (I came with my father) or *Taro to Jiro towa kyodai desu* (Taro and Jiro are brothers).

(3) Particles that indicate direction or the beginning or end of an era. The article *kara* or *yori* is used in the sense of "from," "since" or "after"; *Rondon kara* (from London); *Meiji Ishin yori* (since the Meiji Restoration), or *kore kara* (after this).

The particle *made* is used in the sense of "to" or "until": *Rondon kara Tokyo made* (from London to Tokyo) or *Tenki wa ban made daijobu desho* (The weather will stay good until tonight). *Made* is also used in the sense of "for" or "as": *Go-sanko made ni o-me ni kakemasu* (I present these merely for your personal reference).

The particle *e* indicates the points of the compass or general direction: *higashi e* (to the east), *nishi e* (to the west) or *Tokyo e yuku* (to go to Tokyo).

(4) The particle that is used in asking questions: The particle *ka* is added at the end of the sentence when questions are asked: *Kore desu ka* (Is this it?) or *Niwa ni ki ga takusan arimasu ka* (Have you many trees in your garden?). When a question opens with an interrogative word, the final *ka* may sometimes be omitted: *Ikura desu* (How much is it?).

Conjunctions

The Japanese language is rich in particles used as conjunctions.

(1) The particle *to* (and) is used to connect two nouns. Phrases are generally connected by *soshite*, which sometimes may be omitted: *Watakushi wa boshi to sutekki o kai, (soshite) tsuma wa yubiwa to kushi o kaimashita* (I bought a hat and a stick, and my wife a ring and a comb).

The particles *dano* and *ya* are used in almost the same sense as *to*, though it is sometimes inferred that other things may exist besides what is expressed by the nouns connected by these conjunctions: *Kiku dano bara dano ga kireini saite iru* (Chrysanthemums and roses are beautifully in bloom) or *Koko niwa shika ya saru ga takusan iru* (Many deer and monkeys are here).

(2) The particle *ka* is used in the sense of "or": *Kore ka are ka* (This or that) or *Noru ka soru ka* (Whether one succeeds or fails).

Aruiwa, *matawa* and *moshikuwa* are used in a similar sense, although with many variations.

(3) Particles used as adversatives in the sense of "but," "however" and "yet": *Ga* (denoting weak opposition), *keredomo* (stronger opposition) and *shikashi* or *shikashinagara* (strongest opposition); *Ryokan o sagashita ga mitsukaranakatta* (I looked for an inn, but could not find one), or *Nidome ni mitsuketa keredomo akibeya ga nakatta* (On a second attempt I found one, but there were no vacant rooms).

(4) Other particles are *shidai* (as soon as) and *kara* (as or because).

VI. Religion

Special Characteristics of the Japanese Religious Concept

Every powerful nation—that is, a nation powerful enough to form a national entity—has its own set of myths about its founding, and it is in these myths that one can find the key to the particular type of faith followed by the nation. In clarifying the nature of Japanese religions, therefore, an understanding of Japanese myths is of supreme importance since they constitute the original beliefs of the Japanese. For the time being, they may be referred to as primitive Shinto. Viewed from a purely scientific standpoint, "primitive Shinto" is nothing but an underdeveloped, simplistic set of religious beliefs. Emotionally, however, "primitive Shinto" is regarded as a pure and vitally important religion by the Japanese.

Devotion to primitive Shinto, however, has never prevented the Japanese people from delving deep into the intrinsic nature of religion itself. Based on a sense of superiority, national faith often verges on exclusivism. Contrary to this general rule, however, the Japanese people have, on the whole, been very receptive in absorbing different religions from foreign lands. Of course, there have been some instances where alien faiths faced strong opposition.

Thus, Japan is unique in the history of world religions, with several different faiths—one original and others borrowed—flourishing side by side with apparent equanimity. This religious "parallelism" may very well be beyond the easy understanding of Westerners, who are primarily devoted followers of monotheistic beliefs. Indeed, there are many scholars who claim that it is a sign of religious immaturity to hold more than two faiths. It is true that jumping from one religion to another on the slightest pretext is not exactly admirable, but there is a way of thinking in the Orient based on the idea that "two is one and one is two." This philosophical concept also applies to religion. There is always a way of tolerantly understanding one religion in terms of another.

Blessed from the start with this religious magnanimity, the Japanese people have steadily developed it, especially in regard to primitive Shinto. When a baby is born or on the occasion of *Shichi-go-san* (the festival celebrated by families with children of three, five or seven years of age, refer to p.36), a majority of the Japanese visit the shrine of their guardian god. When a death occurs in a family, on the other hand, a Buddhist priest is usually called in and the deceased is cremated and interred in a cemetery in the compounds of a Buddhist temple and never in the precincts of a Shinto shrine.

Some families have two different altars, one for Shinto gods and the other for deceased family members, set up inside their homes. This type of double-layered worshipping is practiced with no apparent sense of contradiction.

It was as early as the middle of the sixth century when Buddhism was first introduced to Japan that the peculiar relationship, or rather, coexistence, between Shinto and Buddhism came into being. In fact, the *Honji-suijaku* doctrine, which regards Shinto deities as manifestations of Buddhas and Bodhisattvas, long dominated the religious history of Japan. It is of particular scholastic interest that primitive Shinto as a national faith has been broad-minded enough to accommodate such a theory.

Japanese culture is based on three different religious philosophies: native Shinto, and imported Buddhism and Confucianism. It is interesting to note that the three religions, refusing to go their separate ways, have merged and produced a sort of "trinity." Although the union is an extension of a similar blend of Confucianism, Taoism and Buddhism that developed in China, it in no way diminishes the miracle of its practice in this country.

In Japan, Christianity was banned from the latter part of the 16th century. Even under the strict governmental ban, however, there was never a lack of believers who refused to trade their faith for personal safety. There were many who worshipped the Virgin Mary, or Maria as they called the mother of Christ, in some way or other that would not attract the attention of government officials. They made statues of Maria disguised as *Kannon*, the Buddhist Goddess of Mercy, statues thus known as *Maria-Kannon*. By replacing, in appearance only, the Virgin Mary with the Goddess of Mercy, in this way they avoided persecution by the government (refer to "hidden Christians" p.862 and 866).

More important, however, is the fact that the Japanese Christians in those days found it ethically permissible to substitute a Buddhist goddess for the Virgin Mary. The religious consciousness of the Japanese people is thus broad and all-embracing, so much so that even in the case of a monotheistic religion such as Christianity, the Japanese are apt to find a common denominator with other religions such as Buddhism.

It may sound contradictory to most foreigners to hear that Buddhism now has as many followers as Shinto and that believers in the two faiths largely overlap. It is not, however, correct to attribute this seeming paradox to a lack of purity in faith. It is also not entirely right to conclude that the Japanese people are believers in polytheism.

An old Japanese poet sang at a certain shrine: "I do not know which guardian god is here enshrined; Nevertheless I cannot help weeping for extreme gratitude."

It is a well-known fact that Buddhism strongly emphasizes the idea of self-effacement. Even in Shinto, the philosophy of self-negation is a major tenet. With the Japanese people, who are primarily believers in both Shinto and Buddhism, the idea of self-negation, or self-effacement, is considered more important than the actual objects of worship. It is not as important to identify the object of worship as it is to work oneself into the necessary state of mind for proper worshipping. Just as the above poem points out, one can be utterly oblivious of the identity of the object of worship. The important thing is to bring oneself to a state of mind where one can "weep for gratitude."

It is, of course, dangerous to make hasty generalizations about the religious temper of the Japanese people from this single poem. But this tiny verse seems to suggest the innate unwillingness of the Japanese people to be in any way restricted by their objects of worship. It is not that the Japanese are unprincipled in their faith, but that they carry their religious attitude to extremes. They force themselves into a state of self-effacement and then accept whatever comes their way as an object of worship.

There is an old Japanese proverb which goes: "Out of a sardine's head, a true faith." Of course, this does not mean that the object of worship could be something insignificant like a sardine's head. The ultimate meaning is that the attitude toward and the capacity for faith are far more important than the object of faith. Nourished by this tolerant philosophy, the Japanese people have always been very receptive to foreign religions. They accept Buddhist images with just as much respect as they do Shinto deities.

The religious consciousness of the Japanese people appears very simple, but actually it is extremely refined and complicated. It is neither polytheistic nor monotheistic. Based on the philosophy equating with many and vice versa, the religious consciousness of the Japanese people does not find it difficult to embrace one and all types of faiths. This unique Japanese mentality may suggest the possibility of mutual understanding among the various religions in modern times.

Shinto

Now, let us consider Shinto as a religion in the true sense of the word—and not as a folk myth. Strictly speaking, Shinto today is one of many forms of religion practiced in Japan. But is it entirely correct to treat Shinto simply as "another" religion in Japan's case? There are a variety of "new religions," many of which originated in primitive Shinto. Some of these Shinto beliefs started out as easily definable sects known as "Sectarian Shinto."

In contrast, what is known as Jinja Shinto transcended the bounds of a sect from the start. It is so called because it is symbolized by the *jinja*, or shrine, structure. Formerly, it was called State Shinto or the National Shinto Faith. Once a powerful national cult officially sponsored by the government, Jinja Shinto is no longer government-supported in accordance with the present Constitution of Japan enforced after World War II.

It is undeniable, however, that Jinja Shinto—at least the way of thinking inherent in it—is still deeply rooted in the minds of the Japanese and transcends all other sectarian beliefs. It is out of a common belief based on national sentiment—and not out of Shinto belief as a sectarian faith—that the Japanese people pay homage to such Shinto shrines as the Grand Shrines at Ise, Yasukuni Shrine and Meiji Shrine in Tokyo.

Although the concept of *ujiko* (shrine parishioners) and *danka* (Buddhist parishioners) is declining among the Japanese people today, few would completely refrain from going to either shrines or temples to pay homage.

The reason why Sectarian Shinto, divided as it is into separate sects, maintains a certain degree of influence among the Japanese people is because it uses the "National Shinto Faith" as a springboard, gradually introducing its believers to an appreciation of the finer points. Incorporation by the Sectarian Shinto group of the systems and structures developed by many schools of Buddhism also provides the much-needed semblance of familiarity. Although every sect actually forms a separate religion, it is not as exclusive as some other religions. To exaggerate somewhat, Sectarian Shinto is a midway point between the "National Shinto Faith" and Buddhism—the two most widely held religious beliefs in Japan.

The leaders of Jinja Shinto are quite unwilling to have their belief ranked on the same level as Sectarian Shinto. They would like to project themselves as the practitioners of the common belief of the Japanese people based on national sentiment. It is very difficult, however, to position Jinja Shinto in a precise relationship to other Japanese religious beliefs.

But in a manner of speaking, the essential characteristic of Japanese religion is the overlapping of one religion with another without any sense of contradiction.

Up to now, we have studied the present position of Shinto among the Japanese people. When was it, then, that Shinto coalesced into a philosophical system in the true sense of the word? Although the exact time is beyond the scope of this discussion, available data points to the Kamakura period (1192-1333). Developed from a humble origin, Shinto began to assume a philosophical form in the Kamakura period when it started treating problems of the mind. According to Shinto theory, a pure and clear mind is nothing but *kami* (deity); or to put it more simply, the mind is *kami*. By the way, it is undeniable that at the very core of Shinto philosophy, there are layers of teachings simply extracted or synthesized from Buddhism and Confucianism.

In the Shinto pantheon, there is a variety of "gods"—the creators, the moon, stars, mountains, rivers, seas, fire, animals, vegetables and many more. Originally, these gods were all considered to be external existences exerting their domineering influence on humans from outside. Later, however, they came to "reside" within the mind of the people. Although not as systematic as some other religious theories, Shinto philosophy has reached the apex of its refinement.

It was during the 15th to 17th centuries that a number of Shinto schools, notably Yoshida Shinto and Yoshikawa Shinto, made their appearance, stressing the "mind" as the nucleus of their philosophies. Thus, Shinto finally attained its own philosophy.

The newly developed Shinto philosophy, however, became the object of attack by opposing Shinto camps. These attacks were instigated primarily by Suika-Shinto, which tried to purge all external philosophies such as Confucianism and Buddhism, and Fukko-Shinto, which advocated a return to the days of mythology as well as the exclusion of all intellectual concepts from the practice of Shinto. And for a time, these ultra-nationalistic schools won the day as Shinto became a powerful weapon of nationalistic political factions.

When Japan opened its doors to foreign intercourse after hundreds of years of seclusion, however, highly emotional ultra-nationalism visibly retreated from the forefront in Shinto as well as in all other intellectual fields. It gave way to a kind of Shinto equipped with at least a certain degree of level-headed philosophy.

Thus, Sectarian Shinto has always had a certain number of followers because of the particular teachings that developed during the Meiji period (1868–1912). Jinja Shinto, on the contrary, has little philosophy of its own to offer. Since government support was completely cut off through the enforcement of the Present Constitution after World War II, it is now functioning only with the backing of religious sentiment of the people.

According to the 1988 "Shukyo Nenkan" (Religious Yearbook) published by the Cultural Agency, there were 81,385 *jinja* (shrines) belonging to Jinja Shinto, or nonsectarian Shinto, with 102,422 priests.

Sectarian Shinto consists of about 160 sects. Some of the oldest of these are Fusokyo, Izumo Oyashirokyo, Konkokyo, Kurozumikyo, Misogikyo, Ontakekyo, Shinto Taikyo, Jikkokyo, Shinto Shuseiha, Shinto Taiseikyo and Tenrikyo.

Worship in Shinto consists of obeisances, offerings and prayers. Obeisance takes the form of a humble bow lasting a minute or two. The offerings presented before the altar are primarily food and drink. Cloth was formerly added to these, but eventually a symbolic offering came into use, consisting of strips of paper representing lengths of cloth. These offerings are attached to a wand or twig from an evergreen *sakaki* tree and placed before the altar. The offerings, according to Shinto belief, are no less important as spiritual nourishment to the enshrined deities than the shrine structure serving as their permanent, sacred abode.

In the regular ritual, the presentation of offerings follows the formal *norito* prayers, the purpose of which is to appeal to the deities by vividly addressing them. Great stress, therefore, is placed on the way that the prayers are presented rather than on their contents. To make them as impressive as possible, the words of the prayers were originally given the highest sublimity and solemnity that archaic Japanese possessed.

Purification is essential before worship and is achieved by three principal methods—*harai* (exorcism), *misogi* (cleansing) and *imi* (abstention). Exorcism is performed by a priest with the purpose of removing uncleanliness caused by an offense against the gods. It consists chiefly of the presentation of offerings, after which the priest waves a wand (*gohei*, or *nusa*) tipped with the strips of paper described earlier over the person to be purified. He also chants words of purification in a manner not unlike the custom in Roman Catholic churches.

The *misogi* is a cleansing rite intended to remove accidental defilement acquired by contact with unclean things such as might be caused by death or disease. It is effected by ablutions, usually performed by the mere sprinkling of water or salt. A number of practices common today are vestiges, or even complete survivals, of this ancient custom. On the left side of the pathway near the shrine oratory, there is usually some water for worshippers to use to clean their hands and mouth before worshipping.

Perhaps the most interesting method of purification, however, is *imi*, or abstention. Exorcism and lustration confer purity by removing uncleanliness, whereas abstention is a method of acquiring a positive purity by avoiding the source of pollution. It was, therefore, the duty of priests rather than of laymen to practice the necessary austerities, which consist chiefly in observing certain prohibitions.

Formerly, Shinto priests scarcely ever performed the funeral services, the dead being given over to the care of Buddhism. But Shinto funeral services have now become more common. Marriages were formerly not celebrated with religious rites, whether Buddhist or Shintoist. Today, it is fashionable, however, to have the wedding ceremony performed at a Shinto shrine, and sometimes at a Buddhist temple, or even a Christian church.

According to the 1988 Religious Yearbook, the total number of adherents of all sects of Shinto in Japan is 112,203,139.

Buddhism

It was in the middle of the sixth century that Buddhism was first introduced to Japan. Opinions were divided at the time on how to treat this new foreign religion. Of the powerful families then at the helm of the government, the Soga family advocated the acceptance of Buddhism, while the Mononobe family firmly opposed it.

As Buddhism entered Japan with the stream of scholastic and cultural achievements of China, its acceptance meant the introduction of a highly developed culture. The view of Buddhism as a vehicle of culture was too important for Japan to pass over. Those who advocated its acceptance were naturally the farsighted liberals eager to absorb the highly advanced culture currently flowering in China. Those who opposed Buddhism, on the other hand, maintained that Buddha was a foreign god, incompatible with the native deities of the land.

As Buddhism came to play an increasingly important role in a variety of cultural fields in Japan, the gap between the "foreign god" and its native counterparts gradually narrowed. Finally, through repeated modifications, Buddha came to possess characteristics closely resembling those of the Shinto deities.

From the Nara period through the Heian period, Buddhism in Japan developed as a kind of national cult heavily supported by the Court. As a "religion to keep the country in safety," it came to be accepted as a native belief rather than a foreign faith. For example, Emperor Shomu (reigned 724-749) believed that Buddhism was a "guardian faith of the state," as expounded in the *Konkomyo-Saisho-o-Gyo* sutra. In the ancient capital of Nara, many national ceremonies were carried out in accordance with Buddhist teachings. Later in the Heian period, two celebrated Buddhist priests, Saicho (also known as Dengyo-Daishi, 767-822) and Kukai (also known as Kobo-Daishi, 774 -835), preached that Buddhism was a "religion to keep the country in safety."

Similarly, Prince Shotoku (574-622, refer to p.85), who preceded Emperor Shomu, exhorted the nation in his Constitution of Seventeen Articles to "sincerely revere the Three Treasures—Buddha, Dharma and Samgha, which are the final refuge of all creatures and the supreme objects of faith in all countries. Who in any age dare fail to offer homage to these Three Treasures?" Buddhism was thus accepted as a religion containing universal truth for any age or country.

Prince Shotoku himself was a serious scholar of Buddhism, as is evident from the excellent commentaries he wrote on Buddhist sutras. He expounded the superiority of Buddhism and even went so far as to use the new religion as the basis for governmental policies. Buddhism played an especially important part in the Taika Reform in 645 by which the reins of government were restored to the Emperor from the current ruling clans.

According to the "Nihonshoki" (Chronicles of Japan), Emperor Kotoku (reigned 645-655) set "great store by Buddhist ways and slighted the ways of Shinto." In fact, he issued a decree establishing Buddhism as the legitimate religion of the nation.

It was also about this time that the Pure Land Buddhist belief originated. Moreover, at the time of Emperor Saimei (reigned 655-661), who succeeded Emperor Kotoku, the *Bon* Festival began to be widely observed. Other Buddhist practices such as *hosho* (freeing captive creatures) and *sessho-kindan* (prohibition of killing) also became popular. The construction of a variety of large temples in the city of Nara from the time of Prince Shotoku to the end of the eighth century also provides evidence of the popularity of Buddhism at the time. Moreover, in direct proportion to the growth in the number of temples, Buddhism steadily permeated every stratum of society, finally assuming the form of a national cult participated in by people from all walks of life, from the Emperor down to the common people.

In short, Prince Shotoku's duty was to shape the nation into a powerful political unity. Under the circumstances, he had to be basically nationalistic. But in his earnest attempts to introduce culture from China, he was equally cosmopolitan. He showed an exceptional willingness to absorb foreign culture, as revealed by his introduction of both a Buddhist school then flourishing in Kokuli, Korea, as well as new studies from Sui in China. Prince Shotoku's dual attitude was reflected in the character of Buddhism as it developed in the Japan of the times.

It may be no exaggeration to say that Buddhism in Japan in the period lasting from the 7 to the 12th centuries was indeed a religion that kept the country safe. And yet, it had an aspect of universality as "the supreme purpose of faith in all countries." This dual characteristic of Buddhism greatly contributed to the fact that Japan in this period avoided a closed-door policy, absorbing as much foreign culture as possible.

There is very little in Japanese culture that is not tinged with Buddhist influence. The culture and arts of the Kamakura and Higashiyama periods offer good examples. Its influence, particularly that of the Zen Buddhist sect, is noteworthy in many fields of Japanese culture in the latter part of the 15th century, or the Higashiyama period in Japanese art history. It is not too much to say that Buddhism has virtually fostered the religious concepts as well as the cultural life of the Japanese people. Although originally a foreign religion and culture, Buddhism has completely embedded itself in Japanese soil and succeeded in creating a unique culture for its adopted country.

It was during the Kamakura period (1192-1333) that Buddhism in Japan, while maintaining close relations with its counterparts in Tang, Sung and Yuan China, steadily began to formulate its own doctrines and take root in the hearts of the Japanese people. In this period, four important Buddhist sects made their debut—Jodo founded by Honen, Jodo-Shinshu founded by Shinran, Zen expounded by Eisai and Dogen, and Hokke (also called Nichiren) founded by Nichiren. Thus, Buddhism spread to the furthest corners of the country.

The Kamakura period was a time of great difficulties for the nation, plagued as it was by internal disturbances and the Mongolian attempts at invasion in 1274 and 1281 (refer to p.91). Reduced to a state of desperation, the people longed for a new salvation—in the form of Buddhism.

It is often pointed out that Japanese Buddhism in the Kamakura period was more practical than theoretical, which was precisely what was required in that turbulent period. The simplicity and ease with which Buddhism was explained, with a promise of salvation not only for the elite but also for ordinary people, also greatly contributed to the rapid popularization of the religion. If Buddhism in the Nara and Heian periods was a state religion, in the Kamakura period it was a people's religion.

Buddhism, however, was unable to escape the usual ways followed by all religions. As soon as it acquired a great following among the nation, it was quickly divided into a number of different sects. These various sects became more concerned about their own management than in preaching and propagating their religious faith. Ceremonies and formalities became an end in themselves, while spreading the Buddhist faith became a matter of secondary importance.

Just as water in a puddle becomes stagnant and finally turns putrid, Buddhism in the Edo period (1603–1867) began to show signs of degradation. In the Edo period, the common people were required to register at a temple as Buddhists. Accordingly, they became regular donors to temples, or in other words, *danna* or *danka*—corresponding to parishioners. Thus, the parishioner system was established in the Edo period.

When viewed from the aspect of religious faith, however, the people and their temples were not so closely bound as one might suppose. As a matter of course, cries began to be raised against Buddhism, with some Shinto believers and nationalistic scholars maintaining that Buddhism was a heresy imported from overseas. It is true that there was a Shinto group that advocated a harmonious marriage of Shinto and Buddhism, but this group was not convincing enough to stem Shinto's overwhelming onslaught against Buddhism.

Thus, Buddhism, once a powerful state religion officially advocated by Prince Shotoku and the one-time spiritual pillar of the Japanese people in times of national crises, was openly attacked as "heresy." Antagonism toward Buddhism reached its peak at the time of the Meiji Restoration, when it was officially denounced as heresy by the government. Time seemed to have regressed to the sixth century when Buddhism was first introduced to Japan.

Wild as the storm of antagonism was, Buddhism eventually survived the crisis, chiefly because of the sanity of the Japanese people. At heart, people were aware of the importance of foreign culture and were unable to tolerate for long the Shintoists' spiteful attack on Buddhism. The government ban on Buddhism, however, had one good point—it served as a powerful stimulant for various Buddhist sects to do some serious soul-searching. Having lost what had been given them in the Edo period, Buddhist sects were no longer able to enjoy easy living. As a result, they were forced to work hard to propagate their doctrines.

Today, most of the Japanese people are said to profess a belief in Buddhism. Various criticisms notwithstanding, there is no denying that strenuous efforts on the part of Buddhist leaders restored Buddhism to the nation's good graces after the severe trials it underwent at the time of the Meiji Restoration.

The true aim of the governmental ban on Buddhism at the time of the Meiji Restoration is said to have been the clear delineation of the line dividing Buddhism and Shinto. As the two religions gradually grew closer after the former's introduction to Japan, a random mixing of the two religions often occurred. It was inevitable that the unraveling of this mixture would be demanded sooner or later. It was the government's view that although coexistence of two religions may be permitted, the random mixing of the two should never be allowed.

Although the Japanese people today believe in both Buddhism and Shinto without any qualms, it is not because they are mixing the two. The separation of Buddhism and Shinto served to clarify the relationship between the two religions. Buddhism in Japan has followed a unique path. Developed and patronized by the Japanese people on an equal footing with Shinto, it is not the same Buddhism as practiced in India or China.

As has already been stated, Buddhism was officially introduced into Japan in the middle of the sixth century when the King of Paikche (on the Korean Peninsula) presented sutras and images of Buddha to the Imperial Court of Japan. These presents were soon followed by priests and nuns as well as by temple architects and sculptors. Half a century later, during the reign of Empress-Regnant Suiko (reigned 592–628), Buddhism obtained a firm footing at the Court and in the country under the patronage of Prince-Regent Shotoku.

The form of Buddhism thus established in Japan came through China and is known as the *Mahayana*, or "Great Vehicle" (*Daijo Bukkyo* in Japanese). *Maha* means "great" and *yana* "vehicle," the spiritual vehicle by means of which one may attain enlightenment and emancipation.

Buddhism as brought to Japan was an advanced development of this religion, demonstrated artistically in ceremonies and supported by a system of idealistic philosophy. At first, there were no sects, although many appeared as the religion developed.

In the Nara period, the "Six Sects of the Southern Capital (Nara)" came into being—Sanron, Jojitsu, Kusha, Ritsu, Hosso and Kegon. The first three are now extinct. Teachers belonging to these sects wrote many commentaries on the sutras, and it is worthy of note that they were all products of learned scholarship. This shows how eagerly Japanese intellectuals pursued the study of Buddhism, which to them was not only a new religion and philosophy, but also a new science, a new culture and an inexhaustible mine of artistic inspiration.

Thus far, the main features of Buddhism in Japan had remained Chinese, the influence of the national genius having had little effect on it. The Heian period (794–1185) saw the emergence of two great priests—Saicho, or Dengyo-Daishi (767–822), the first exponent of the Tendai doctrines of Buddhism in Japan, and Kukai, or Kobo-Daishi (774–835), who introduced the Shingon doctrines of Buddhism into Japan. They gave a strong national bent to the imported religion, chiefly through the application of the doctrine of *Honji-suijaku*. According to this doctrine, Shinto deities are regarded as various manifestations of Buddhas and Bodhisattvas, as described above.

Buddhism now became all-powerful with two great rival centers. One was the monastery northeast of Kyoto on Mt. Hiei—the seat of the Tendai sect, whose doctrines were based on pantheistic realism. The other monastery was on Mt. Koya, south of Osaka, where the esoteric philosophy of the Shingon sect with its complex symbolism was taught. These two monasteries became the fountainheads of Buddhist learning.

With the growth of its power, however, Buddhism became secularized and corrupt, giving rise to four new sects in the 13th century aimed at its purification. All four have remained powerful to the present day. They are the Zen, Jodo, Jodo-Shinshu (or Shinshu) and Hokke (also called Nichiren) sects.

The Zen sect, brought into Japan from China by Eisai (1141–1215) and Dogen (1200–1253), "seeks salvation by meditation and the teaching of emptiness." This sect found adherents among the powerful leaders and *samurai* of the *shogun's* government in Kamakura. In *zen*, each believer must work out his own salvation through austere discipline, both physical and mental, and thus develop the measure of willpower and self-control needed by a true *samurai*. A marked development of this is seen in *bushido* (the way of the *samurai*), which was greatly influenced by *zen* principles.

The Jodo and Jodo-Shinshu sects were founded respectively by Honen (1133–1212) and Shinran (1173–1262), Honen's disciple. Essentially one in doctrine, both teach that the only way to salvation lies in absolute trust in the all-saving power of Amida Buddha (Amitabha) —a doctrine generally called *tariki-hongan* (salvation through absolute faith in another power).

The two sects, however, have some important differences. The Jodo sect emphasizes repetition of the formula *Namu Amida-Butsu* (Namo' mitabhabuddhaya), or "Glory to Amitabha Buddha," which is regarded as a meritorious deed on the part of the believer. On the other hand, the Shinshu sect regards faith in Amida Buddha as the all-sufficient and only essential thing, the repetition of the formula being considered only as the expression of a thankful heart.

Another important difference is that the Shinshu sect does not recognize the principle of the celibacy of the clergy as well as all other ascetic practices. Furthermore, the Shinshu sect is more logical in its observances, with its adherents believing in Amitabha Buddha alone. Although they worship before the founder's image as the revealer of the Amitabha doctrine, the sect has discarded all other images. Needless to say, this sect stands entirely aloof from the self-power Buddhist practices, which keep the priests of the Shingon and Nichiren sects so busily occupied.

The Nichiren sect, founded by Nichiren (1222-1282), bases its teaching on the *Hokekyo* (Lotus Sutra). As a result, the sect is also called Hokke-shu. While the initiated regard the study of the *Hokekyo* as essential to attain enlightenment, ordinary believers consider that the only requirement consists in the repetition of the *daimoku*, or formula *Namu Myohorenge-kyo* (Glory to the Sutra of the Lotus of Truth). This is chanted in loud tones, often in groups, to the accompaniment of drums. Indeed, the Shinshu and the Nichiren sects are the most demotic Japanese Buddhist sects.

The leading sects of Buddhism in Japan are:

Hosso: Brought by Dosho from China in 655. There are two main temples of this sect—Kofukuji and Yakushiji, both in Nara.

Jishu: Established by Ippen in 1226, the head temple is known as Yugyoji and is located in Fujisawa near Kamakura.

Jodo: Honen is the founder. Chion-in in Kyoto is the head temple of the most flourishing branch.

Kegon: Roben established this sect in 740. The head temple is Todaiji in Nara.

Nichiren: Founded by Nichiren, this sect is divided into many branches, the largest and most influential of which is Nichiren, bearing the original name. The Nichiren head temple is called Kuonji and located in Minobu, Yamanashi Prefecture.

Ritsu: This sect was introduced into Japan by Chien Chen, a Chinese priest, in 754. Toshodaiji at Nara is the head temple.

Shingon: Kobo-Daishi is the founder. It is divided into two main branches—Kogi and Shingi, which are subdivided into numerous smaller divisions. The most celebrated temples of this sect are Kongobuji on Mt.Koya; Toji, Daigoji Sambo-in and Chishaku-in in Kyoto, and Hase Temple in Hase, south of Nara.

Shinshu (or Jodo-Shinshu): Founded by Shinran, it is divided into many branches, the most influential of which are the Otani and Honganji schools, both in Kyoto. The former has more than 9,500 temples, while the latter has about 10,400.

Tendai: Founded by Dengyo-Daishi. There are three branches, with Enryakuji, Saikyoji and Onjoji (Miidera Temple) serving as the head temple for each branch. The first two are located in Sakamoto and the third in Otsu—all near Kyoto.

Yuzunembutsu: Founded by Ryonin in 1117. The head temple is Dainembutsuji and is located in Osaka.

Zen: This sect has three main branches—Rinzai, Soto and Obaku.

The largest temple of the Rinzai branch is Myoshinji in Kyoto. Soto has two main temples—Eiheiji near Fukui and Sojiji in Tsurumi, Yokohama. The head temple of the Obaku branch is Mampukuji in Uji, south of Kyoto.

With the end of World War II, many new Buddhist religions that had been active in the prewar years saw a dramatic increase in the number of adherents. Some of the most popular ones are Reiyukai, Soka Gakkai and Rissho Koseikai.

According to the 1988 Religious Yearbook, the total number of adherents of all sects of Buddhism in Japan is 93,395,913.

Christianity

Christianity was first introduced into Japan in 1549 when Francis de Xavier, accompanied by two Spanish Jesuits, landed at Kagoshima. From that time until 1639—the year missionaries were expelled, Roman Catholic missionaries were active in Japan. During that period, it is claimed that 200,000 Japanese were converted to Christianity, including famous *daimyo* (feudal lords), generals and cultivated ladies of high rank. Favored at first by Oda Nobunaga (1534 –1582), Christian missionaries were later placed under a ban by Toyotomi Hideyoshi (1536–1598). Finally, they were all ordered to leave the country.

When the Tokugawa Shogunate was established, still stricter measures were adopted, especially following the Shimabara Rebellion in 1637 (refer to p.96). Christianity, however, was never entirely eradicated in certain parts of Kyushu, as is proved by the remarkable fact that within a month after the erection of a Roman Catholic Church at Nagasaki in 1865, there occurred the memorable scene known as "The Finding of the Christians." Thousands of Christians from the village of Urakami (now, a part of Nagasaki) and its vicinity, who had secretly kept the faith transmitted to them by their forbears through successive generations for about 225 years, openly confessed their religion. In 1914, a Roman Catholic Church with accommodations for 6,000 people was established at Urakami. The church was destroyed by the second atomic bomb in August 1945.

When the Tokugawa Shogunate collapsed in 1867, a program of great reforms—political, social and otherwise—was adopted. The doors were also thrown open to Christian teaching. In 1873, missionaries were officially permitted to establish schools, publish religious tracts and preach their doctrines in all the seaports open for foreign trade. In April of the same year (1873), exiled Christians were permitted to return to their homes and were free to entertain any religious belief they chose. In the preceding year, a Christian church was established in Yokohama, marking the beginning of the Union Church. In the following year, a sister church was organized at Tsukiji, Tokyo—the first Christian church in the metropolis.

The vernacular translation of the Bible was undertaken early in the

Meiji period, with the New Testament being completed in 1879 and the Old Testament in 1886. The chief translators were S.R. Brown, G.F. Verbeck, D.C. Greene, R.S. Maclay and J.C. Hepburn—all American missionaries. Japanese assistants included Matsuyama Takayoshi, Okuno Masatsuna, Uemura Masahisa, Ibuka Kajinosuke, Takahashi Goro and others.

Between 1885 and 1889 when the country was swept by a great tide of reforms inspired from the West, Christianity made phenomenal progress. Later, it suffered from a nationalistic reaction. However, largely through native leadership, Christian churches became filled with the growing self-consciousness of the nation.

The Greek Orthodox Church in Japan traces its beginning to the arrival in 1861 of Father Nicolai (Ioan Kasatkin) as chaplain to the Russian Consulate at Hakodate. For half a century, or until his death, he was the center of a great Christian movement. He was assisted by a devoted band of Japanese clergy.

According to the 1988 Religious Yearbook, Japan has 8,695 churches and 1,422,303 adherents of Christianity.

VII. Social System

●Government and the People

Emperor and Imperial Family

The Emperor is a symbol of the State, with sovereignty residing with the people. Article 4 of the Japanese Constitution stipulates that the Emperor shall not hold powers related to government. He merely performs ceremonial functions such as the appointment of the Prime Minister—as designated by the Diet, and of the Chief Justice of the Supreme Court—as designated by the Cabinet. With the advice and approval of the Cabinet, he also performs the dissolution of the House of Representatives, promulgation of laws, treaties, etc.

Crown Prince Akihito became the 125th Emperor on the death of Emperor Showa on January 7, 1989.

The Emperor was born on December 23, 1933. Preceded by four older sisters, the arrival of the long awaited Crown Prince was celebrated throughout the land. Crown Prince Akihito entered Gakushuin (School of Peers) Middle School in 1946, the year after World War II had ended. The widow Mrs. E.G. Vining, came from America to tutor the Crown Prince in English that year. During the four years she spent with him, she taught him the ideals of democracy as well as English.

Crown Prince Akihito was married to Miss Shoda Michiko on April 10, 1959. As Miss Shoda Michiko was the first commoner to marry into the Imperial Family, the story of their romance was a popular topic among the public.

Blessed with a family of two boys and one girl, the Emperor took Mrs. Vining's counsel to live with his family to heart, a major break with tradition. When not busy with official duties, he also enjoys doing marine research, including a study of the classification of the spiny-finned fishes known as goby.

Empress Michiko was born as the oldest daughter of Shoda Eizaburo and Fumiko. Her father was the president of the Nisshin Flour Milling Company. Her many hobbies include music, sports, painting and writing poetry. In addition, she has a keen sense of fashion that is widely acclaimed, having been included on the 1984 international list of best-dressed women.

Crown Prince Naruhito was born on February 23, 1960. He spent two years from June 1983 studying transportation on the Thames River during the 18th century at Merton College in Oxford University. Scaling peaks as a member of the Japan Mountain Climbing Association is his favorite pastime, although he also enjoys skiing, skating, tennis, horseback riding and a variety of other sports. In addition, he is interested in music and is proficient on the viola.

Prince Fumihito was born on November 30, 1965. The prince was chairman of the Natural Culture Research Society at Gakushuin University and married fellow-member Kawashima Kiko, the daughter of a professor at Gakushuin University. The wedding took place in June 1990. Beginning in September 1988, he spent two years studying at Oxford University. He is an avid marine researcher, specializing in examining the large group of scaleless fishes popularly called catfish.

The only daughter of the Imperial Couple, Princess Sayako, was born on April 18, 1969. An ardent dog lover, the princess was able to fulfill a long-held dream to visit a seeing-eye dog training center on her first trip abroad to England in 1984. Sayako has been studying traditional dance since entering the junior high school of Gakushuin.

Political and Juridical Systems

The Constitution recognizes the respective independence of the legislative, executive and judicial branches. The National Diet represents the legislative, the Cabinet represents the executive and the Courts represent the judicial.

It is to be noted, however, that no clear distinction is made in Japan between the legislative and the executive branches as is done in the United States. The people have the right to elect the members of the National Diet, which is the legislative body and represents the most important source of power among the three in a constitutional state. They also have the right to screen the justices of the Supreme Court. The Prime Minister is designated by the National Diet and must himself be a member of the Diet.

Any Japanese citizen 20 years of age or over, whether male or female, has the right to vote in National Diet elections, prefectural elections and all other local elections.

House of Representatives and House of Councilors (Legislative Body)

Electoral Process, Number of Members, Term in Office : The electoral process and number of members for each House is set forth in the Public Office Election Law. Today, there are 512 members of the House of Representatives (Lower House) and 252 in the House of Councilors (Upper House).

Representatives remain in office for four years unless the House is dissolved while Councilors serve for six years (with half the members standing for election every three years but with no dissolution of the Upper House). No one can be a member of both Houses at the same time.

Both Houses must resolve or approve, in principle, all legislative measures as well as the national budget, the ratification of treaties, etc. In case the two Houses do not see eye to eye on bills concerning the budget or treaty ratification, the Constitution stipulates that the decision of the House of Representatives takes precedence over that of the House of Councilors. Furthermore, the Constitution stipulates that a concurring vote of two-thirds or more of all the members of each House is required to enact amendments to the Constitution. Furthermore, Constitutional amendments must be approved by a popular vote.

Political Parties: As of Februaly 1990, the Liberal-Democratic Party, the Japan Socialist Party, the Komeito, the Japan Communist Party and the Democratic Socialist Party are the five major political bodies in Japan.

The strength of each of these parties and others in both Houses of the Diet is indicated below.

Seats Held by Each Political Party

As of Februaly 1990

	House of Representatives	House of Councilors
Liberal Democratic Party	285	110
Japan Socialist Party	139	73
Komeito	46	21
Japan Communist Party	16	14
Japan Democratic Socialist Party	14	10
United Socialist Democratic Party	5	0
Rengo	0	12
Other Parties	0	8
Independents	7	4
Total	512	252

Cabinet (Executive Body)

The Cabinet is comprised of the Prime Minister and 20 Cabinet Ministers. The Prime Minister has the right to appoint or dismiss a Cabinet Minister. The following ministries and agencies come under jurisdiction of the Cabinet:

Ministry of Justice
Ministry of Foreign Affairs
Ministry of Finance
Ministry of Education
Ministry of Health and Welfare
Ministry of Agriculture, Forestry and Fisheries
Ministry of International Trade and Industry
Ministry of Transport
Ministry of Posts and Telecommunications
Ministry of Labor
Ministry of Construction

Ministry of Home Affairs
General Affairs Agency
Defense Agency
Science and Technology Agency
National Land Agency
Hokkaido Development Agency
Economic Planning Agency
Environment Agency
Okinawa Development Agency

Each of these ministries and agencies is headed by a state minister. In addition, the chief cabinet secretary and the director-general of the Prime Minister's Office are included in the Cabinet. Though not a state minister, the chief of the Legislative Bureau is also an important member.

The Court System (Judicial Body)

The judicial power or jurisdiction belongs exclusively to and is exercised by the Supreme Court together with the lower courts (the High Court, the District Court, the Family Court and the Summary Court). In the Supreme Court, there are 15 judges headed by the Chief Justice of the Supreme Court, who is designated by the Cabinet and appointed by the Emperor. The other 14 judges are appointed by the Cabinet, but they are subject to examination by the voters at general elections following their appointment. Furthermore, they must pass examination by the people every ten years, even though they have been approved by the voters previously.

The lower court judges, who are appointed by the Cabinet, hold office for ten years, but they can be reappointed when their tenure expires. The retirement system stipulates that when judges of the Supreme Court and Summary Court reach 70 years of age, they must retire, while judges of the High Court and the District Court must retire at 65. The status of an incumbent judge is guaranteed by the government.

There is also the Impeachment Court, which is composed of members of the House of Representatives and the House of Councilors. If a judge is found negligent in his duties or disgraces his position or status, he is subject to trial and impeachment by this court.

The various public prosecutors' offices in charge of prosecution have been established in correlation with the various law courts. They are the Supreme Public Prosecutor's Office, which corresponds to the Supreme Court, the High Public Prosecutor's Office—High Court, the District Public Prosecutor's Office—District Court, and the Local Public Prosecutor's Office, which corresponds to the Summary Court.

Local Autonomy

The Constitution provides for a system of local autonomy under the supervision of the Ministry of Home Affairs, a central government organization. The Japanese local self-governing body is broadly classified into administrative divisions—*to*, *do*, *fu* and *ken*.

To means metropolitan area; namely Tokyo-to.

Do means district; there is presently only one *do* (Hokkai-do).

Fu means urban area; there are two *fu* (Osaka-fu and Kyoto-fu).

Ken means prefecture; there are now 43 *ken*.

These administrative units are subdivided into cities, towns and villages. It can be said in this connection that one of the most striking features of postwar Japanese local autonomy is the rapid and extensive merger of cities, towns and villages. This is taking place under a law actually calling for such mergers.

The heads of local self-governing bodies, including the governor of the *to*, *do*, *fu* and *ken*, the mayor of the city, the headman of a town or village and also local assembly members are elected by the voters living in their respective administrative divisions.

The local assembly, which operates on the basis of a single-chamber system, is authorized to enact, amend or abrogate ordinances or regulations. The residents of an administrative division have the right to demand that any ordinance or regulation be revised or abolished, provided that they can secure the signatures of one-fiftieth or more of the total number of residents. When a specified quota of residents' signatures is filled, it is in order to demand the dissolution of a local assembly, the dismissal of an assembly member or to hold a local election on a specific issue. The people also have the right to recall the head of an administrative division.

The administrative affairs of all local self-governing bodies are undertaken by local public service personnel.

International Relationship

Postwar Japanese independence was recognized at the San Francisco Peace Conference, which took place in San Francisco in September 1951. At this conference, 56 of the allied nations that were at war with Japan, signed the peace treaty. In subsequent years, Japan has concluded separate peace treaties or established de facto diplomatic relations with several other countries.

Relationship With United Nations: Although Japan could not join the United Nations immediately after regaining independence, it engaged in various activities in cooperation with such U.N. organizations as UNICEF and ECAFE. In 1956, Japan re-established diplomatic relations with the USSR. With this move lending momentum, Japan officially joined the United Nations in December of the same year as the 80th member. The increasing economic power of Japan has given greater importance to its role and position on the international scene. With a policy of omnidirectional diplomacy, Japan presently has diplomatic relations with 169 countries, spreading good will in many areas. (As of June 1990)

Relationship With the U.S.: Japan's friendship with America has been the basis of its diplomacy and this support has been consistent since the end of World War II. This influence is not simply in political and economic spheres, but in national security, culture and sports as well.

This relationship has undergone a change in recent years. America, the world's economic power as the key currency nation, has switched from being a creditor nation to a debtor nation, while Japan has begun to assume America's former role, rapidly expanding to take over some 40% of the international financial market. This has led to American demands for burden sharing in the field of economy.

Demands for an open market such as the removal of restrictions on American corporations participating in public works projects and the import liberalization of rice, oranges, beef and other products have been made with increasing force. Japan is now working hard to solve these problems and maintain its friendly relations with the USA.

Relationship With Europe: Europe is planning to unify as a 320-million-people market with the reorganization of the E.C. in 1992, making it increasingly likely that the relationship between Japan as an influential member of the Western market and Europe will become more intimate. Furthermore, the last part of the 1980s saw a major reorganization of Europe, with the collapse of socialist and communist economic systems and the spread of capitalism and a market-based economy stemming from the economic stagnation that the former systems has experienced for many years. West Germany and East Germany were reorganized as Germany in October 1990. With the rise in economic strength in reorganized Europe, the role that Japan is capable of playing in contributing to the stabilization of these economies continues to grow.

Relationship With Asia: The democratization of the Asia region has been steadily progressing though there are some problems in some countries. Besides an increase in exports by NIES and ASEAN nations to advanced countries, economic and talent exchanges have also occurred.

There are areas in the Asia region, however, where tensions still exist. The countries in Indochina, the People's Republic of China and Democratic People's Republic of Korea are, all in all, not necessarily in an economically favorable condition, but Japan must develop its plans sincerely and carefully to get and maintain relations with these nations.

As is seen in the recent relationship between the U.S. and USSR, the world is said to have entered an age of dialogue, but economic differences constitute the main barrier for the peace and stability. In this sense, the role of financially strong Japan is unquestionably great.

Self-Defense Forces

Japan has renounced war as a means of executing its sovereign right, and, at the same time, has abolished military power as an instrument for settling conflicts between nations. The Self-Defense Forces are maintained in order to defend Japan against direct and indirect aggression for the purpose of preserving the peace and independence of this country, to maintain the national security and, when necessary, to take charge of maintaining public order. It consists of the Ground, Maritime and Air Self-Defense Forces.

People

The total population of Japan in 1989 according to the Management and Coordination Agency was 122,335,313.

The population breaks down to approximately 60,200,209 males and 62,135,104 females.

The average life expectancy has greatly increased, from 46.9 years for males and 49.6 years for females in 1936 to 75.5 years for males and 81.3 years for females in 1988. The latter statistics are according to the Ministry of Health and Welfare.

The increase of single-person households due to unmarried singles, separations through work situations and divorces has started to produce great changes in the traditional family. The aging of the population in a significantly larger proportion and the increase of elderly single households have become a major problem. According to population projections in 1986, by 2010 the total population of Japan will be 135,820,000, of which almost one in four (23.6%) will be over 65 years of age. Although this is the natural consequence of a constant striving to live longer, problems such as the aging labor force and the insufficiency of young labor as well as the increase of homes with bedridden elderly foreshadow a grim future. These problems must be conquered through appropriate and well-planned countermeasures.

Statistics (1988)

Average Household Savings	¥8,513,000
Average Monthly Working Hours	179.9 hrs.
Average Monthly Overtime	15.7 hrs.
Average Life span	
Men	75.5 yrs.
Women	81.3 yrs.
Average Starting Salary	
Men	¥153,100
Women	¥125,800
Average Age at Marriage	
Men	28.5

```
              Women              25.8
Annual Number of Marriages (1989)   708,000
Average Monthly Salary
              Gross          ¥481,250
              Net            ¥405,938
```

●Economy

Japanese GNP

The scale of a nation's economic activity can be measured by its GNP (gross national product). Needless to say, a nation's GNP is the total sum of goods and services annually produced by the people.

According to the latest data, the Japanese GNP in current prices was ¥391,298.6 billion in 1989 (calendar year), a 6.5% increase over the previous year's level. GNP expressed in current prices is called nominal GNP, and nominal GNP per capita in 1989 was a little more than ¥3,180,000—a 6.1% increase over the previous year's figure. This growth rate was smaller than that of the GNP as a whole (6.5%).

Real GNP, which is calculated by subtracting from the nominal GNP the portion inflated by increased prices, was ¥347,059.9 billion (calculated on the basis of prices in the 1989 calendar year) in 1989— a 4.9% increase over the previous year's level.

A comparison with the GNP of other countries is necessary to understand the size of the Japanese GNP. In particular, a comparison of the per-capita GNP of various countries is important because the size of the population differs from country to country. Shown in Tables 1 and 2 is a comparison of the Japanese GNP with that of other industrialized countries over the past several years and in 1988, which is the latest year for which data on international comparisons of GNP is available. As seen in these tables, Japan's GNP is among the highest in the world. This is one of the reasons why Japan is regarded as one of the richest countries in the world.

Table 1 Shares of GNP among the G7 Countries

	1965	1980	1988
Japan	5.4%	10.6%	16.3%
USA	42.0	26.4	30.7
U.K.	6.0	5.4	4.6
West Germany	7.0	8.3	7.1
France	6.0	6.6	5.7
Italy	3.6	4.0	4.8
Canada	3.1	2.6	2.8

Table 2 GNP Per Capita in Major Countries

(Unit: U.S. dollar)

	1975	1980	1988	
			GNP	National Income
Japan	4,475	9,068	23,316	16,730※
USA	7,401	11,995	19,813	17,729
U.K.	4,254	9,584	14,590	10,787
West Germany	6,767	13,273	19,741	17,314
France	6,502	12,413	16,999	—
Italy	3,452	8,063	—	6,805
Canada	7,309	10,782	18,873	13,984
Switzerland	8,739	16,558	29,676	26,769
Korea	589	1,583	4,025	3,615

※ The figure of 1987

National income is calculated by deducting the depreciation expenses of production facilities from the GNP. Table 2 shows a comparison of national income per capita among developed countries.

Japan's External Assets

Both GNP and national income represent the size of the wealth produced by a nation's annual economic activities. That is, they indicate the size of the wealth flow. However, not only flow but stock is important to examine the size of the wealth that can be used by people.

Among the various stock indexes, considerable attention is paid to that of overseas assets. These external assets are credit (assets) that a country has in relation with other countries. Net external assets are determined by deducting overseas debt (liabilities) from overseas assets.

Japan's net external assets stood first in the world at the end of 1985. They amounted to $129.8 billion, a 1.75 times increase over the previous year's level, far surpassing the U.K., which ranked second ($90 billion), and Saudi Arabia, which ranked third ($80 billion). By contrast, the United States became a debtor nation for the first time that same year. The U.S.'net external assets, which had ranked first until 1983, decreased to $28.3 billion in 1984, and finally the U.S. incurred a net debt of $111.9 billion by the end of 1985.

With its net external assets increasing annually since then, Japan has ranked first for five consecutive years, reaching $293.2 billion at the end of 1989. However, the growth rate was very small—only a 0.5% increase over the previous year's level. One of the reasons for that was that Japan's external debt increased by $119.1 billion because purchases by foreign investors of Japanese corporate bonds, which were issued overseas by Japanese companies to raise funds, increased by 46.7% compared with purchases made at the end of the previous year.

Although Japan came to rank first in net external assets in 1985, it had been standing behind the United Kingdom and the United States, which had begun their global activities much earlier than Japan, in terms of gross external assets. However, Japan became first with its gross external assets of $1,469.3 billion at the end of 1988, surpassing those of the U.K., which marked $1,395.1 billion. As a result, Japan had become No.1 in the world in terms of assets as well as credit (both net and gross).

Of course, it can be pointed out that the Japanese economy still has certain vulnerabilities. As for external investment by the U.S. and European countries, for instance, direct investment such as investment in plant projects exceeds investment in securities. In Japan, however, securities investments exceed direct investment, although securities whose appraised values are likely to fluctuate are not always sound assets. However, the impression of "a rich Japan" has spread domestically as well as internationally because of the large scale of its external assets.

Japan's Key to Success

In 1945 World War II ended with Japan on the losing side. Severe air raids devastated the whole of Japan. As a result, its production facilities, which the country had built up through the process of modernization since the Meiji Restoration, were heavily damaged. The "Pauley Interim Report," which was announced by the U.S. occupation forces on December 7, 1945, said that the Japanese standards of living and production would be restored but kept at a level no higher than that of 1926 to 1930. The image of "reconstruction" that Japan had immediately after the war was not to be an economic power but to become a country that could take pride in itself as a "nation with a high level of culture," even though it meant that the country would not recover its former economic level.

But how did Japan actually reconstruct itself ? As the Japanese government declared in its "Economic White Paper" of 1955 when 10 years had passed since the end of the war: "Japan is no longer in the postwar period." It had regained the economic level it had before the war (1935-1936). There is no doubt that Japan was largely helped in the reconstruction of its economy by the increase in demand resulting from the so-called "Korean special procurement boom" caused by the outbreak of the Korean War in 1950.

Japan then entered the "high economic growth era of the 1960s." Strictly speaking, this era did not totally coincide with the 1960s, which is usually used to refer to the era, but lasted for 15 years from

1959 to 1973. During this period, Japan's industrial structure underwent a transition. Before that, the Japanese economy was mainly dependent on light industry as it had been in the prewar period, but it carried out a transition to heavy chemical industry during this period. In particular, consumer electronics along with the steel and automotive industries laid the foundation as Japan's key industries, improving their competitiveness as time went on. Passing West Germany in 1968, Japan ranked second after the U.S. in terms of the size of its GNP among the capitalist countries. This was mainly due to the high growth rate of its economy over those 15 years, averaging nearly 12% a year.

Why was Japan so successful during this period? There are several reasons.

First, the democratization promoted by postwar reforms injected new vitality into Japanese society. For example, an agrarian reform boosted the farmers' incentive to produce, and laborers felt a surge of enthusiasm for their work through the approval of a series of laborers' rights, including the right to organize. The economy was also activated through the elevation of the status of women. Moreover, the break up of the *zaibatsu* (financial conglomerates) provided companies with new business opportunities and encouraged competition.

Second, the production facilities, which were heavily damaged during the war, were completely replaced through the introduction of the latest, highly innovative technology from the U.S. and Europe. As a result, Japanese productivity made rapid progress. New demand was stimulated along with the development of new industries, including the consumer electronics and automotive industries.

Third, based on the people's high rate of savings, financial institutions were willing and able to finance a company's capital investment. The main purpose of the government's monetary policy, which was called "growth finance," was to supply companies with funds for capital investment. The companies, which had belonged to a *zaibatsu*, started reorganizing as a group. Financing by a major bank to companies within the group played an important role in the ability of the companies to raise funds for capital investment.

Fourth, Japan tried to improve its self-defense capacity through the establishment of the Self-Defense Force. However, the percentage of the defense budget was very small at that time, with the lion's share of funds, manpower and resources being allocated to meet private demand.

The End of High Growth Era

This high economic growth era ended in 1973. Many people believe that this is because oil prices quickly quadrupled due to the first energy crisis of November 1973, but this is not correct. Before that, the exchange rate between the *yen* and the dollar, which had remained unchanged (360 *yen* to the dollar) since 1949, collapsed due to what is called the "Nixon shock" in August 1971, triggering an increase in the value of the *yen*. The Japanese economy took a turn for the better after experiencing a recession caused by the strong *yen*, but was soon struck by a high rate of inflation. Inflation accelerated from the end of 1972 to 1973 so that the rate of increase in consumer prices had already exceeded 20% before the energy crisis. But the boom caused by the strong *yen* was on the verge of collapse before the energy crisis broke out.

Certainly, the energy crisis had considerable impact on the Japanese economy. Since oil prices rapidly inflated, the demand for other products and materials shrunk. As a result, Japan experienced a negative economic growth rate in 1974 for the first time since the war. Although the growth rate rose and reached 2.5% in 1975, it remained at about 5% for the last four years of the 1970s. In 1980 the growth rate fell to 4% because of the second energy crisis in 1979.

Economic Friction and the Yen Appreciation in 1980s

Growth rate fluctuations and recession

The trend in the Japanese economy in the 1980s is indicated in the fluctuation of the real economic growth rate (refer to Table 3). The economy showed a low growth rate of about 3% for three years from 1981 to 1983. The growth rate then rose and remained around 5% for two years from 1984 to 1985, but it decreased to 2.5% in 1986. And after reaching a peak of 5.7% in 1988, it stayed at nearly 5%.

Table 3 Japanese Real Economic Growth Rate in the 1980s

(%)

Year	1980	81	82	83	84	85	86	87	88	89
Growth rate	4.3	3.7	3.1	3.2	5.1	4.9	2.5	4.6	5.7	4.9

The fluctuation of the economic growth rate clearly describes a drama of the Japanese economy in the 1980s. Briefly speaking, Japan made a big effort to expand exports to recover the growth rate, which dropped to about 3% as a result of the second energy crisis. This effort brought about an increase in the *yen* value. Japan suffered from a year-long recession because the strong *yen* caused a slump in exports, as had been the case in the past. However, the import prices of raw materials decreased and the Japanese economy took a turn for the better. A strong *yen* also played an important role in enhancing the appraised value of "Japan Money," thrusting Japan into the position of an economic power with large assets.

Strong yen and consumer prices

Economic growth is completely dependent upon an increase in demand. That is, the economic growth rate is equal to the rate of increase in demand. Demand consists of the difference between domestic demand and foreign demand (which is determined by subtracting imports from exports). The percentage of the Japanese economy depending upon foreign demand is smaller than that of other developed countries, but foreign demand increased rapidly from 1983 to 1986 (refer to Tables 4 and 5), causing very severe economic friction between Japan and the U.S. Seven developed nations agreed to accelerate the appreciation of the *yen* at the Group of Seven (G7) meeting in September 1985, expecting that the *yen* hike would have the effect of checking the increase of Japanese exports.

Table 4   Ratio of Foreign Demand to the Aggregate Demand in Japan (Nominal values, calendar year)

(%)

Year	1983	84	85	86	87	88
Ratio	1.9	2.9	3.8	4.4	3.8	3.5

Table 5   Growth Rate of Domestic Demand and Foreign Demand Compared with the Previous Year (Nominal, calendar year)

(%)

Year	1983	84	85	86	87	88	89
Domestic demand	2.9	5.3	5.4	3.7	4.7	7.4	7.2
Foreign demand	151.5	63.4	36.8	22.0	-10.4	-21.0	-18.5
GNP	4.0	6.4	6.4	4.4	4.1	5.1	5.2

This effect became apparent at last from the end of 1987 to the beginning of 1988 when the *yen* rate reached the highest level (121 *yen* to the dollar) in history. Since Japan also tried to expand its imports, its trade surplus shrank in 1988 and 1989, causing the *yen* to weaken against the dollar. However, the *yen* has been getting strong again since the summer of 1990, partly because the difference in real interest rates between Japan and the United States dissipated.

The *yen* hike played an important role in remarkably strengthening Japan Money. For example, Japanese tourists who go on an overseas trip with a strong *yen* have rapidly increased, reaching nearly 10 million a year. In addition, the very low rate of increase in consumer prices in the late 1980s was attributable to the *yen* appreciation. However, since Japanese companies had money enough to spare due to the rise in the the *yen*, land prices continued to rapidly increase.

Structural Impediments Initiative (SII) Talks with the USA.

Although Japan's trade surplus is decreasing, there is still a large trade imbalance between Japan and the U.S. (a surplus for Japan and a deficit for the U.S.). The SII talks were held between Japan and the U.S. from May 1989 to June 1990 based on President Bush's proposal that both Japan and the U.S. should demonstrate initiatives to remove structural impediments that are one of obstacles to achieving a trade balance between the two countries. During the talks, Japan promised many things, including the improvement of Japanese trade practices, public investment amounting to ¥430 trillion over the next 10 years and the conversion of farmland to residential land within controlled urban areas. Needless to say, all of them will be the conditions that restrict the management of the Japanese economy.

Prospects in 1990s

One of the subjects for the Japanese economy is how to cope with the ongoing movement toward internationalization. Because of the *yen* hike, Japanese laborers receive the highest wages in the world if converted into dollars, while land prices are a hundred times as high as those in the U.S. Under such circumstances, more and more Japanese companies are expanding their activities in foreign countries. In some cases they are being favorably received by local people, but in others some friction over investments may be caused. The question is often asked if Japanese-style management methods can be applied to foreign businesses. And some people are afraid of the "hollowing out" of Japanese industry. Also questioned is the impact over the opening of the Japanese rice market, as requested in the GATT Uruguay Round.

However, capital investment continues to be active in Japan at present, and most economists agree that the Japanese economy will continue to grow at an annual rate of 4 or 5% unless social unrest over the oil supply is caused by the Persian Gulf crisis.

Foreign Laborers

Attracted by the image of a "rich Japan," many foreigners (people from other parts of Asia, in particular) have recently started coming to Japan to work. Japanese companies are plagued by a labor shortage because the Japanese economy has kept growing and expanding for such a long time. However, current Japanese law does not authorize the employment of foreigners except for those who have special expertise or professional skill such as lawyers, engineers or artists. However, the opinion is now being expressed that regulations for the employment of foreign laborers should be relaxed. In any case, it is obvious that Japan is faced with the problem of how to deal with foreign laborers to maintain a steady economic growth in the future. It can also be said that this is one of the problems related to the internationalization of Japan.

●Education

History

Education in Japan is of high quality and widely available. In modern times, it has twice undergone important reforms: first, the introduction in 1872 of a modern, entirely new, educational system and second, a thoroughgoing reform carried out after World War II. Designed to cope with the present democratic system, the latter reform was based on the concept of equal opportunity in education.

Schools before 1872: Historically, Japan has a long tradition of institutionalized education. The initiation of modern schooling under the new educational system in 1872 was a truly epoch-making step in the annals of education in Japan, but quite a number of schools were already in existence. In fact, the existence of schools of a sort can be traced as far back as the Muromachi period (1336–1573). In the Edo period (1603–1867), these schools developed further to form the rudiments of a school system.

In the Edo period, feudal society was based upon four distinct classes—the ruling *samurai*, farmers, artisans and merchants. Strict distinctions were enforced, especially between the *samurai* class and the common people making up the three lower classes. Education of the former and the latter developed along basically independent lines.

The country was made up of a number of semiautonomous districts controlled by *daimyo* (feudal lords) families. These districts were called *han*, and schools called *hanko* were set up for the training of *samurai*. The Tokugawa Shogunate and the *han* supported the *hanko*, which taught literary and military arts suited to the *samurai* ruling class.

At the same time, an institution designed to give the common people a minimal education was provided by the *terakoya* (temple schools). These schools offered simple educational facilities where mainly reading, writing and calculation by abacus were taught. The *terakoya* originated in the late feudal period when Buddhist temples were educational as well as religious institutions, gradually developing after the middle of the Edo period. By the end of the period, they were not only flourishing in such large cities as Edo (now, Tokyo) and Osaka, but also in small provincial cities and even in remote farming and fishing villages. In short, they could be found throughout the country.

While the *hanko* and *terakoya* typified the schools of the Edo period, there were several other educational institutions as well. One of them was the *gogaku* (country schools). Some of these were set up for the ruling class and similar to the *hanko*, while others were designed for the common people and similar to the *terakoya*.

A third type allowed the sons of both *samurai* and commoners to study side by side. This latter type of *gogaku*, however, differed from the *terakoya* in that it was protected and supervised by the shogunate and the *han*.

There were also *shijuku*, or private schools. Usually set up in the homes of teachers, these schools specialized in such subjects as Chinese classics, calligraphy, the abacus, Japanese classics and Western learning. Since the shogunate regarded Confucianism as central to education, *kangakujuku* (state-run schools), which stressed Confucian learning in Chinese, flourished throughout the Edo period. Other *shijuku* offered the common people instruction in such things as calligraphy or the abacus, becoming widely established before the end of the period. The *shijuku* and *terakoya* paved the way for the opening of elementary schools throughout the country shortly after the promulgation of the new system in 1872.

Education after 1872: The Meiji Restoration of 1868 brought great political, economic and social reforms. Immediately after the Restoration, the Meiji government started to work out measures for educational reform. On August 3, 1872, it promulgated a new educational system by Cabinet decree that formed the basis of the modern educational system in Japan.

The school system was basically divided into three stages—elementary school, middle school and university. Elementary school was an eight-year course divided into ordinary and upper levels, each consisting of four years. Normal schools were established for the training of elementary school teachers. In 1886 the four-year ordinary elementary school course was made compulsory, and over the next decade the four units of schooling—elementary school, middle school, university and normal school—were clarified by legislation. Middle school was divided into two stages—ordinary and upper.

In the decade after 1897, various schools aimed at providing secondary education for women as well as business education and advanced vocational education were systematized in quick succession, completing a comprehensive system of modern education.

In 1907 the period of compulsory schooling was extended by two years, making ordinary elementary school a six-year course and upper elementary school a two-year course. From this time until the reform of the educational system after World War II, the basic school system remained unchanged. The University Edict of 1918 authorized the establishment of private and municipal universities and colleges, and in 1926 the Kindergarten Edict was promulgated.

Elementary school teaching rules served as a standard for educational content when the school system was established. After the School Edict of 1886, simple guidelines titled "Subjects of Study and Their Extent" were laid down for elementary and middle schools.

A system of approval for textbooks was adopted, but after 1897 the texts were compiled by the government. The use of such government-written textbooks continued until the post-World War II educational reforms.

Education after World War II: In 1947, two years after the end of World War II, the educational system was altered to the so-called single-track "6-3-3-4" school system. Elementary school had been an eight-year course since 1872, but under this new system it was reduced to six years. The two-year, upper elementary school course was incorporated into the three-year, junior high school, while the three kinds of secondary schools—middle school, girls' school and vocational school—were all reorganized into a three-year, high school. As a rule, most were co-educational.

Existing universities with their preparatory departments, higher schools, higher vocational schools, higher normal schools, women's higher normal schools, normal schools and young men's normal schools were all reorganized into four-year universities that were generally co-educational. Graduate schools were provided for those who desired to continue their studies. (For a variety of reasons, two- and three-year junior colleges were authorized in 1949, while technical colleges were established in 1962.)

With all these changes, the reorganization of the entire educational system was completed, forming the system that is still in force today.

Present State of Education

Educational opportunities are available throughout life, from childhood to old age, in a variety of forms—in the home, in school and in society.

The quality of school education under the 6-3-3-4 single-track system adopted in 1947 is quite high and is available on a nation-wide basis. Meanwhile, in line with the recognition of the need for lifelong education, there has been a marked extension of various forms of social education.

A. Preschool Education: The principal facilities for children are kindergartens and nursery schools. Kindergartens, under the supervision of educational administrative agencies of national and local authorities, are designed to afford children a good environment conducive to healthy mental and physical growth. Set up for children from three to six years old, they offer one-year, two-year and three-year courses.

Nursery schools, on the other hand, are under the supervision of national and local welfare administrative agencies. They are designed to provide daily care on behalf of the parents for babies and small children up to five years old. Thus, kindergarten and nursery school differ in function, role and supervision, but guidance and instruction of children three years old and over—even in nursery school—are based on kindergarten education instructions. In reality, therefore, the two systems are complementary.

With the growing interest of parents in the care and education of their children in recent years, the number of children enrolled in kindergartens and nursery schools has increased markedly. In 1989, 63.2% of five-year-olds were enrolled in kindergarten. This figure has altered somewhat over the past ten years as increasing numbers of children are enrolled in nursery school. Combined with the 31.2% of five-year-olds enrolled in nursery schools, the total percentage of five-year-olds enrolled in all types of preschool educational facilities topped 94.5% in the same year.

B. Compulsory Education: Compulsory education begins at the age of six and extends over nine years, breaking down into six years of elementary school and three years of junior high school.

Enrollment at the level of compulsory education has always been quite high, even before World War II. It was 41.4% in 1880, only a few years after the introduction of the modern educational system (refer to p.140), reaching 99% in 1920 and 99.9% in 1968.

C. High School Education: High school offers full-time, part-time and correspondence courses. The full-time course takes three years to complete, while part-time and correspondence courses each require four years or more. Although part-time courses are available both in the daytime and at night, the majority of the courses are offered at night.

High school can be broadly divided into two types: general education and vocational education in areas such as agriculture, business and industry. Enrollment in high school education immediately after the introduction of the new school system in 1950 was 42.5%, but it has risen steadily since then, reaching 94.5% in 1988. Particularly striking is the rise in the enrollment of female students. Whereas in 1950 the enrollment ratio of male students was 48% and of female students 36.7%, the enrollment ratios in 1988 switched to 93.4% for male students and 95.7% for female students.

D. Special Education: Complete schooling from the elementary to the high school level is provided for children and students requiring special education because of mental or physical handicaps.

In addition to schools for the blind and deaf, there are special schools for the mentally retarded, physically handicapped and physically weak children.

Furthermore, special classes for the mentally and physically handicapped are created as occasion demands in ordinary elementary and junior high schools. As of 1989, a total of 93,812 students were enrolled in special education classes in elementary, junior high and high schools.

E. Higher Education: Higher education is provided by universities, junior colleges and technical colleges. Moreover, a number of universities have graduate schools.

Universities offer higher education to high school graduates or those who have attained an education equal to or higher than that of the high school graduate. The normal course of study requires four years, but in medicine and dentistry it is six years.

A bachelor's degree is awarded to those who have completed four years or more of study at a university and have passed the required examinations. Junior colleges accept high school graduates or equally qualified students for a two- or three-year course of study in preparation for vocations or ordinary life.

Attendance at universities and junior colleges rose dramatically during the intensive economic growth of the 1960s. As of 1990, 36.3% of high school graduates attended universities (including junior colleges), a number maintained over the preceding ten years. Particularly prominent is the increase in the number of entrants into junior colleges, an increase closely related to the rapid rise in the number of female entrants. In 1990 the number of female entrants accounted for 30.2% of the total number of university entrants and 92.5% of the total number of junior college entrants.

This rapid increase in enrollment in universities and junior colleges has been made possible by the establishment of new universities as well as by the creation and expansion of departments and courses in established universities. In 1990 the number of universities totals 507 and junior colleges 593—both approximately 1.1 times more than the figures for 1980. Technical colleges are five-year institutions (five years and six months in mercantile technical colleges), providing technical education for junior high school graduates or those with equivalent qualifications. Industrial technical colleges were established in 1962 to meet the quantitative and qualitative shortage of technicians caused by technological developments. Graduate schools are organized separately from undergraduate faculties, and include master's and doctor's degree courses. A master's degree is conferred upon those who have completed two or more years of graduate study, have acquired the necessary credits and have won acceptance of their master's degree thesis. A doctor's degree is awarded to those who have completed five or more years of graduate study (four years or more in medical or dental research), have acquired the necessary credits and have won approval of their doctorate thesis.

The graduate school system was established in 1974 with the Standards for the Establishment of Graduate Schools, an ordinance enacted by the Ministry of Education. In 1990, universities with graduate schools totaled 303—94 national, 23 public and 186 private universities, accounting for 59.8% of all 507 universities.

Classified by field of study, engineering degrees topped all others with 45.9% of the total number of master's degrees granted, followed by physics, agriculture and humanities in that order. The fields of medicine, dentistry and pharmacology held the majority of doctorate degrees with 41.6% of the total, followed by degrees in the natural sciences. Relatively few degrees were awarded in the humanities and social sciences.

Special Training Schools and Other Miscellaneous Schools: Other institutions have been established to provide the education necessary for actual working and living situations or improving the academic level. Courses cover such a wide range of subjects as accounting, bookkeeping, secretarial skills, cooking, cosmetology, data processing, nursing, dental hygiene, foreign languages, tea ceremony, flower arranging, calligraphy, test preparation and tutorials. Special training school courses are required to be longer than one year, to have more than 40 persons per class and to provide a systematic education. The curriculum is divided by the academic level of entrants into three courses: advanced course, specialized course and general course. As for entrance qualifications, completion of a junior high school education is required for the first and completion of a high school education for the second. No particular qualification is required for the third, which is open to the general public.   The largest of these three curriculums is the specialized course—77.2% of all the students in 1990. Specialized training schools have grown rapidly to meet the diversified demands of a changing society, with 1.3 times more schools and 1.8 times more students than there were in 1980.

A breakdown of students by subject shows that the largest segment is aspirants to industrial-related fields with 22.2%, followed by medical-related fields (20.8%) and culture and education (19.3%). The ratio of female students to male students is 52% to 48%.

As for other miscellaneous schools, a year or longer, as a rule, is required for graduation, but if the curriculum is simple, graduation can be completed between three months and a year. There are no regulations concerning class size or entrance requirements and general educational methods are adopted.

In terms of the number of students by course, the preparatory schools lead with 33.6%, followed by driving and language schools (the figure, as of 1990). The male to female ratio is about even in all courses except preparatory schools, where male enrollment is significantly higher.

The number of high school graduates entering these special training schools or miscellaneous schools to learn a technical skill or obtain some kind of qualification directly connected to a vocation has been on the increase. In 1990, a total of 5.5% of high school graduates entered one of these institutions. Lifelong education courses are also available for adults.

School Education Statistics

Type of School	Number of Schools	Number of Teachers (Full Time)	Number of Students
Kindergartens	15,076	100,935	2,008,069
Elementary Schools	24,827	444,203	9,373,195
Junior High Schools	11,275	286,061	5,369,157
High Schools	5,504	285,915	5,623,135
Schools for the Blind	70	3,381	5,599
Schools for the Deaf	108	4,605	8,169
Schools for the Handicapped	769	36,811	79,729
Technical Colleges	62	4,000	52,930
Junior Colleges	593	20,489	479,390
Universities and Colleges	507	123,838	2,133,277
Graduate Schools	303	50,591	90,238
Special Training Schools	3,301	31,724	791,462
Miscellaneous Schools	3,438	19,310	425,625
CORRESPONDENCE:			
High Schools	84	1,840	166,986
Junior Colleges	9	22	32,367
Universities	13	77	135,176

F. Nonschool Education: In addition to the educational activities provided in the regular schools mentioned above, various educational and training activities are conducted in the home, place of business and elsewhere. Because of the increasing demand for lifelong education, special emphasis has been placed on providing education and training in institutions other than schools.

(a) Social education in Japan is defined as "organized educational activities made available mainly to youths and adults (including physical culture and recreational activities), except those conducted as part of the regular school curriculum." Various physical education, sports and cultural activities, classes and lectures are sponsored by national and local government bodies as well as socio-educational organizations.

Following are the major facilities for social education: Civic centers play an important role in local communities by sponsoring youth classes, cultural activities, and physical culture and recreational meetings in cities, towns and villages. As of 1987, a total of 91.1% of the nation's cities had civic centers.

Youth houses are public facilities where youths and youth leaders may live together while undergoing collective training. At present, there are 14 national and 267 public youth houses situated throughout the country. They provide working youths with convenient facilities for social education, since there is no lodging charge at a national youth house and only a nominal charge at a public one.

Libraries: As of 1988, there were 1,805 libraries in Japan. The breakdown is as follows:

National (National Diet Library) 1
Metropolitan and Prefectural 68
Municipal 1,221
Town and Village 483
Private 30
Others 2

Traveling libraries operate in remote areas.

Museums, Zoos, Botanical Gardens, etc.: As facilities for social education, museums (including science, history and art museums), aquariums, zoological and botanical gardens play an important role. As of 1987, such facilities totaled 737.

The number of libraries and museums increased 2.2 times from 1967 to 1987.

Social-Physical Education Facilities: A large number of gyms, athletic stadiums, swimming pools, baseball fields, and tennis and volleyball courts are provided by national and local government organs, business corporations and private organizations. By 1987 there were 34,405 social gymnastic facilities established by local public bodies— an increase of 40% over the previous five years and 7.4 times the number of twenty years ago. In addition to these facilities, private and corporate physical education facilities are open to the public along with school physical education facilities.

(b) The Ministry of Education has provided subsidies to social education courses and lectures sponsored by local autonomous bodies in order to promote a society in which people can continue their education throughout their lives. Different courses are offered to meet the needs of various groups of people such as young people, women and elderly people. On the other hand, cultural seminars held by private enterprises in urban areas better reflect the needs of the day than the above courses and lectures, and have been on the increase.

Social Education Facilities As of May 1987

Civic Centers 17,440
Libraries 1,802
Museums:
    General 100
    Science 83
    History 224
    Art 223
    Outdoor 8
Zoos 35

Botanical Gardens	20
Zoological and Botanical Gardens	8
Aquariums	36

Children's and Youth Education Facilities   As of 1987

Youth Houses (dormitory type)	267
Youth Houses (non-dormitory type)	160
Children's Cultural Centers	45
Children's Nature Houses	246
Others	335
Total	1,053

Educational Content and Textbooks

Development of the Curriculum in Elementary, Junior High and High Schools: Education in Japan aims at "the full development of the personality and the nature of a healthy people, sound in mind and body, who will love truth and justice, esteem individuality, respect labor, have a deep sense of responsibility and be imbued with the spirit of independence, capable of building a peaceful state and society."

In order to maintain nationwide educational standards and universalize public education in Japan so as to achieve this fundamental goal, the central government under the School Education Law and its enforcement ordinance prescribes the subjects to be taught and the hours of instruction. The government also publishes curriculum standards for compliance by each school. These latter standards are determined by the Minister of Education on the basis of the deliberations and recommendations submitted by the Council for Curriculum, which is composed of teachers, researchers, and other learned and experienced persons.

On the basis of curriculum standards prescribed by national, prefectural and municipal governments, each school works out its own curriculum in consideration of actual conditions within the school and the community as well as the physical and mental development levels and personalities of the pupils.

The standard course of study prescribed by the central government is revised about every ten years to cope with changes in society. The latest revisions have been in force since 1980 for elementary school, since 1981 for junior high school and since 1982 for high school.

Eight subjects are taught in elementary school: Japanese, social studies, arithmetic, science, music, arts and crafts, home economics and physical education. There are eight required subjects in junior high school: Japanese, social studies, mathematics, science, music, fine arts, health and physical education, and industrial arts and home economics. Electives include foreign language, music, fine arts, health and physical education and industrial arts and home economics. In addition, there are separate curriculum areas such as moral education and special activities. The usual high school curriculum provides instruction in Japanese, social studies, mathematics, science, health and physical education, art, home economics and foreign languages.

In curriculums emphasizing vocational training, such subjects as agriculture, fishery, industry, business, home economics, public welfare, merchant marine skills, foreign language, fine arts and music are also offered.

The Ordinance for Enforcement of the School Education Law and curriculum standards prescribe a minimum number of 240 school days a year for elementary and junior high school. A minimum of 35 weeks (34 for the first grade of elementary school) of instruction in each course plus morals and special activities is also prescribed.

The standard total of teaching hours is relatively balanced among three groups of subjects—literary subjects, science- related subjects, and subjects related to the arts and physical education. It should be noted that more teaching hours are allocated to subjects related to music, fine arts and physical education in Japan than in other major countries.

Textbooks: Textbooks are the principal study material. The law stipulates that elementary, junior high and high schools must use textbooks. Since 1948, a system has been in effect for accrediting books privately written or compiled for use as textbooks. Accreditation or authorization are done by the Minister of Education on the basis of recommendations made by the Research Council for Textbook Authorization, which is composed of teachers and other learned and experienced persons.

The adoption of textbooks is the responsibility of the boards of education of public schools or principals of national or private schools. But, in practice, the same series of textbooks is adopted for broad areas for public elementary and junior high schools where more than one board of education is responsible.

Textbooks for compulsory education are provided free of charge, the expense being borne by the central government.

Teachers

Training of Teachers: The system of teacher training is an open one. Anyone who has acquired the necessary credits, as provided in the Educational Personnel Certification Law, in a university with courses approved by the Minister of Education as suitable for teacher certification is awarded a teaching certificate. Actually, national teachers' colleges or faculties, of which there is one in each prefecture, play a major role in training teachers for elementary and junior high schools, especially the former. Elementary and junior high school teacher certificates (first class) are, in principle, awarded to four-year university graduates, while second-class certificates are awarded to junior college graduates. In the case of high schools, first- class certificates are awarded to those who have completed an additional year of study after university or to those who have taken a master's degree. Four-year university graduates, however, receive second-class certificates.

Employment and Compensation: Competent prefectural boards of education appoint or dismiss teachers in public elementary and junior high schools (run in most cases by city, town and village authorities) and public high schools (run in most cases by prefectural authorities).

However, the appointment and dismissal of teachers in kindergartens and full-time high schools run by city, town and village authorities are the business of the city, town and village boards of education concerned.

There are four salary tables for teaching staffs in national and public schools—universities and junior colleges, technical colleges, high schools, and junior high and elementary schools plus kindergartens, respectively. Grades and steps in the salary tables are based on the degree of complexity, difficulty and responsibility of the teaching duties as well as on academic background, type of teaching certificate and years of teaching experience. Kindergarten, elementary, junior high and high school salary tables have three standard grades —for principals, teachers and assistant teachers. Technical college tables have five grades—for principals, professors, assistant professors, lecturers and assistants. University and junior college tables have five grades—for professors, assistant professors, lecturers, assistants and nonteaching staff members.

As a rule, half of the salary of teachers in public elementary and junior high schools is defrayed by prefectural government funds, the remaining half coming from the national treasury. There is almost no difference in salary levels in public schools anywhere in the country regarding position, academic background and length of service.

Some Further Facts: The proportion of women teachers has increased remarkably, accounting in 1990 for 58.3% of the total in elementary schools, 36.4% in junior high schools and 20.5% in high schools. But the proportion of women principals newly appointed in 1988 is still very low, no more than 3% in either of the elementary, or junior high and high schools.

The average number of full-time teachers per class is 1.4 in elementary schools and 1.9 in junior high schools, while the number of pupils per teacher is 21.2 in elementary schools and 18.8 in junior high schools. However, in practice, the number of pupils in a class in elementary and junior high schools is affected by local population density. The national average in 1990 was 29.7 in elementary schools and 35.2 in junior high schools, but in heavily populated areas many classes reach the legal maximum of 40.

VIII. Traditional Japan

●Literature

Origins of Japanese Literature

Japanese literature in written form began around the sixth or seventh century. Myths and traditions have been preserved in the "Kojiki" (Record of Ancient Matters, 712) and "Nihonshoki", or "Nihongi" (Chronicles of Japan, 720)—the oldest books in Japan. These, together with the legends recorded in the "Fudoki" (Records of Local Surveys, the first geographical book, 713) and the "Norito" (Shinto liturgies, compiled in the tenth century), prove the existence of an oral literature handed down by word of mouth before being recorded in written form. It is supposed that the period of such oral literature was quite long. Most early written literature, as referred to above, dates from the time that the capital was set up at Nara (710).

All ancient literature was written in Chinese characters. The "Kojiki" and "Nihonshoki" are largely written through the use of expressions adopted from the Chinese classics. The "Man-yo-shu", the first Japanese anthology of lyrics, consists of poems composed in classical Japanese without the use of Chinese words. The poems were set down in Chinese ideographs (used phonetically) called *man-yo-gana*. In this sense, the age was characterized by the exclusive use of Chinese ideographs. With the exception of such works as the "Man-yo-shu" and "Kaifuso"—a collection of Chinese poems by Japanese writers, ancient literature can be found in historical, geographical and religious books, full of both lyrical as well as epical elements and marked by simplicity and boldness.

Japanese myths as recorded in ancient literature are especially unified and cohesive, but comparatively wanting in episodes. The simplest resolve themselves into a prototype in which the son of the deity descends to the land which he is destined to reign over. The main legend concerns the family of deities in the Takamagahara who descended from Amaterasu-Omikami, unified the country and passed on the throne to their descendants.

It is interspersed with hero myths centered around Emperor Jimmu and Prince Yamato-Takeru-no-Mikoto as well as with the love tales of Prince Okuninushi-no-Mikoto and others. More than 110 songs in the "Kojiki" and over 130 in the "Nihonshoki" and other ancient poems are pregnant with romantic lyricism. In the literature of this period, however, the name of the poet mattered little since the literature was transmitted orally. It was when poetry developed as individual written works of art for appreciation through reading that the

"Man-yo-shu" blossomed as the flower of ancient Japanese literature.

"Man-yo-shu" and Ancient Lyrics

The "Man-yo-shu" consists of 20 books containing over 4,500 poems in all. It was not an anthology compiled by a few individuals within a limited period of time, but had a number of compilers extending over many years until at last the collection developed into its present form. The last and most prominent compiler was Otomo-no-Yakamochi. The most recent date of the poems is 759, or about 450 years later than the oldest pieces in the anthology. On the whole, the forms of *tanka* (short poem, ⟨5-7-5-7⟩-7) and *choka* (long poem, ⟨5-7-5-7⟩×n-7) were established early in the anthology. The Japanese songs consist exclusively of melodies with five- and seven-syllable lines because these are essentially the number of syllables that best agree with the phonetics of the Japanese language, although their form may have been partly influenced by the Chinese quatrains of 5 and 7 characters.

The representative poets of the "Man-yo-shu" are Kakinomoto-no-Hitomaro, Takechi-no-Kurohito, Yamabe-no-Akahito, Otomo-no-Tabito, Takahashi Mushimaro, Yamanoue-no-Okura, and Otomo-no-Yakamochi. Of these, Hitomaro excelled in both long and short poems as well as in *sedoka* (5-7-7, 5-7-7), contributing masterpieces of nature and love poems in a style marked by grandeur and sublimity. Indeed, he is regarded as a Japanese poet of the highest order.

Most of the representative poets, including Hitomaro, were government officials. The "Man-yo-shu" also includes *azumauta*—folk songs of the people living in eastern Japan—and verses composed by *sakimori*, or frontier guards, who were sent to the Province of Tsukushi (on the northern tip of Kyushu, 500 km from Nara—then the capital of Japan), where they had to perform military duties. The *azumauta* poems concerned the life and ingenuous affection of the common people in the provinces.

All this gives the "Man-yo-shu" a variety lacking in later anthologies. But the "Nihon Ryoiki" (822)—the first collection of Buddhist legends—probably reflects the actual state of plebeian life in olden times better than any other work of ancient literature.

One of the distinctive features of the "Man-yo-shu" is the way in which its poems effectively convey abstract feelings and subtle, elusive moods through concrete, natural phenomena. Such ornamental devices as *makura-kotoba* (lit. pillow-word) and *joshi* (introductory verses) do not remain merely ornamental. By alluding to the subtle aspects of the inner life, they combine life with nature by means of sensation and emotion. The poems depicting natural scenery are not merely nature poems, but are permeated with lyricism and affect the unity of observation and sensation.

Classical Literature in the Heian Period

Emperor Kammu moved the capital to Kyoto in 794, and the following 400 years—from the 9th to the 12th century—were regarded as the age of aristocratic culture. The poetry in the early part of the period and the prose in the middle span set patterns followed for a long time in their respective phases. Their grammar, which also set a standard for later ages, was considered as classic.

The civilization of ancient Japan developed under the influence of Chinese culture, which it largely adopted. Early in this period, the study of Chinese poetic versification continued to be the rage, as it was in the previous period. Japanese men used Chinese poetry and prose as a means to convey their thoughts. *Tanka* or *waka*, of which such fine specimens were recorded in the "Man-yo-shu", declined from the end of the eighth century, leaving a vacuum. Their only use during these years was in the exchange of gifts among women of the upper classes. These forms were also preserved as *utai* pieces for recitation among the populace.

Worthy of note is the development of the Japanese phonetic symbols known as *kana* letters. As the *man-yo-gana* were Chinese ideographs and difficult to write, they were simplified into a running or cursive style for the sake of convenience. As a result, a set of symbols called *hiragana* was invented by the middle of the ninth century. Another set of phonetic signs known as *katakana* is also a series of simplified forms of *man-yo-gana*. At first, they were used by students in marking marginal notes when they attended lectures on Buddhist works and other books. Although they were originally derived from Chinese ideographs, these Japanese letters were devised for the express purpose of writing Japanese sounds.

From the end of the ninth century to the beginning of the tenth century, a tendency arose to create a new culture by harmonizing Japanese culture with alien cultures. Coupled with the invention of Japanese letters, this movement made possible the production of anthologies and narratives, with the "Kokin-Wakashu" (A Collection of Japanese Poems, Ancient and Modern) as the forerunner. It coincided with the rise of a pure Japanese style in other aspects of culture such as architecture and the fine arts.

The compilation of the "Kokin-Wakashu" under the Imperial command, which took place after 905, was a notable event in the cultural history of Japan. It was the first anthology to be compiled after the "Man-yo-shu" and contains poems extending over about a century and a half. Among the representative poets in this collection may be mentioned the six celebrated poets—Ariwara-no-Narihira, Ono-no-Komachi, Priest Henjo, Priest Kisen, Otomo-no-Kuronushi and Bun-ya-no-Yasuhide. It was compiled by Ki-no-Tsurayuki and others. (Tsurayuki, who was also the author of "Tosa Nikki"—the first diary-style novel—left a notable mark on the history of prose.)

In the "Kokin-Wakashu", the poetic style was idealistic, attempting to produce an artistic effect through an appeal to the intellect. It is written in graceful, refined language with a curvilinear rhythm. This manner of composition set the pattern for later poets and established the poetic style of the verses in the eight anthologies compiled by Imperial command. The latest anthology was "Shin-Kokinshu" (New Collection of Japanese Poems, Ancient and Modern—compiled around 1205). It represented the style of court poetry in which aristocratic life was best reflected.

Growth of Narratives: Narratives developed by two processes. In one, the narrative consisted of expanded forewords to poems (explanations of the circumstances attending the composition of the poems) called *uta-monogatari* (tales based on poems). In the other, orally transmitted legends and traditions were set down in *kana* letters in a process called *tsukuri-monogatari* (tales of fiction). "Ise Monogatari" is the oldest work of the former type, while "Taketori Monogatari" is the oldest of the latter.

Although "Taketori Monogatari" is a romantic tale, there gradually appeared similar but more realistic narratives such as the "Utsubo Monogatari" and "Ochikubo Monogatari." Eventually, the early 11th century witnessed the advent of "Genji Monogatari," which combines the above two types in the most profound sense. At any rate, it is a matter for wonder in the history of world literature that such purely prose tales appeared as early as the tenth century.

Women Authors: The Heian period (794-1185) brought about the rise of the aristocracy and the advancement of the arts. Aristocratic culture, otherwise known as Heian culture from the name of the capital, was predominantly feminine in character. *Miyabi* (urbanity, or urban manners) and *monono-aware* (aesthetic awareness and sensitivity) were the ideals of the age and the standard of worth. Socially, the aristocracy contributed to making life refined and elegant, and establishing a unique style permeated with subtle sensation and emotion. But for all this, responsible women emerged to take the lead in the creation of culture. Accordingly, many talented artists appeared among the female members of the aristocracy.

Under the patronage and encouragement of the Imperial House, they took part in competitions for the composition of poems and narratives. These contests were called *uta-awase* (poetical tournaments) and *monogatari-awase* (narrative tournaments), respectively. Some of the talented women who thrived in this atmosphere were the poetess Izumi-Shikibu, narrative writer Murasaki-Shikibu, essayist Sei-Shonagon and writers known only as the Daughter of Sugawara Takasue and the Mother of Fujiwara Michitsuna. The former is well-known as the author of "Sarashina Nikki" (Diary), while the latter is known for the "Kagero Nikki."

Two Great Classical Prose Works: The most notable prose creations are the novel "Genji Monogatari" by Murasaki-Shikibu and the

"Makura-no-Soshi" (Pillow Book) essays by Sei-Shonagon, both of which are presumed to have been written in the early 11th century. The latter is an accumulation of beautiful, fragmentary pieces revealing keen insight and close observation, while the former is a monumental work—a conglomeration of every aspect of aristocratic court life compressed in the refined analysis of emotions.

"Makura-no-Soshi" is unrivaled by any other work of Japanese literature in regard to the delicate and refreshing beauty of the authoress' sensibility. On the other hand, as a comprehensive narrative the "Genji Monogatari" remains unsurpassed in this country. Not only was the Japanese novel unable to shake itself free from the influence of "Genji Monogatari" for several centuries, but even today it is regarded as a classic example of the Japanese novel. It was translated into English by Arthur Waley and Edward Seidensticker, among others, and has been favorably received in other European countries as well.

Many noteworthy narratives were produced after "Genji Monogatari," including "Sagoromo Monogatari." It is noteworthy that the oldest collection of short stories—the "Tsutsumi-Chunagon Monogatari"—had already been compiled around the middle of the 11th century. It includes ten short pieces depicting various phases of human life replete with novel conceptions and clear-cut themes.

It must also be remembered that as historical novels, "Eiga Monogatari" and "Okagami" opened up a new field in literature. The "Konjaku Monogatarishu" is a collection of legends presenting a close-up picture of the life of the common people as well as the *samurai* (warriors). It also tells of the Buddhist faith and the strong, ardent spirit of the new age. The life and sentiment of the common people were also reflected in the "Ryojin Hisho," a collection of songs and ballads.

Growth of Medieval Literature

Shin-Kokinshu: From about the middle of the 12th century, the influence of the aristocrats gave way to the rising *samurai* class. The social structure was, in fact, renewed under the leadership of the *samurai*. But in the field of culture, the *samurai* class remained on a lower level of creativity. The aristocrats, priests and recluses, who were neither priests nor laymen, still held sway in the world of letters. Buddhism, the religion that had exerted a powerful influence in the previous age, continued to hold a dominant position in thought and literature, still prescribing the character of creative output. In this period, one new Buddhist sect after another arose, producing such distinguished literaly priests as Honen, Shinran, Nichiren and Dogen, all of whose writings are important works of Buddhist literature.

In regard to poetry, the "Shin-Kokinshu" was compiled in 1205. The poems in this anthology revealed a new symbolistic style exquisitely elaborate in their rhetoric, constructing a dream world removed from real life. Among the more notable poets in the anthology were Fujiwara-no-Shunzei (1114-1204), Priest Saigyo (1118-1190), Fujiwara-no-Teika (1162-1241) and Princess Shikishi-Naishinno. Teika wrote a number of critiques on *waka* poems and was a leader in this sphere. Besides, Minamoto-no-Sanetomo (1192-1219), the third Kamakura Shogun, left his own collection of *waka* poems—the "Kinkaishu," which contains many excellent lyrics rich in individuality. However, poetry after the "Shin-Kokinshu" reached an impasse and was doomed to decline.

The representative prose works of medieval literature were war narratives, while drama consisted of *noh* and *kyogen* (comic sketches). In addition, books of essays as well as *renga* (linked verse), a derivative form of *uta*, should be mentioned.

War Narratives and Essays: The "gunki-monogatari" (war narratives) were recited to the accompaniment of the *biwa* (lute) and other musical instruments. Unlike ordinary *monogatari* (narratives), whose audience was chiefly limited to the aristocratic class, the war narratives were aimed at a larger circle of readers and listeners. They marked the advent of a new form of literature because a sense of political consciousness was introduced into the works. The rise and fall and activities of armies—groups rather than individuals—constituted their subject matter. Moreover, they were epics that attained a narrative unity through the development of historical facts rather than by emotions.

With "Hogen Monogatari" and "Heiji Monogatari" as the forerunners, this aspect of literature reached its consummation in the "Heike Monogatari" (1223-1240), followed by the "Gempei Josuiki" (popularly known as "Gempei Seisuiki") and the "Taiheiki." The latter derived its subject matter from the disturbances in the Namboku period (era of the Northern and Southern Dynasties, 1336-1392. refer to p.92). These were followed by the "Gikeiki" and "Soga Monogatari", two variations of war narratives that have as their respective heroes the tragic general Minamoto-no-Yoshitsune and the Soga brothers—devoted sons who revenged themselves upon their father's murderer. (Refer to p.474). Both Yoshitsune and the Soga brothers gained popularity as national heroes and their exploits have often been used as the themes of novels and plays in later ages.

Of the essays, the "Hojoki" by Kamo-no-Chomei (d. 1216) is the most famous. Chomei was a typical hermit of the age who led a solitary life in the recesses of the mountains quietly contemplating social conditions and the mutability of human life. The author of the "Tsurezure-gusa," Priest Kenko (1282-1350), was also a recluse. At first sight, this work would seem to be a jumble of desultory thoughts, but actually it is as many-sided and complex as human life itself, showing a deep understanding of humanity. It is an excellent book of essays often mentioned in comparison with the "Makura-no-Soshi." Refer to p.156.

Noh Plays and Kyogen (Comic Sketches): The texts of *noh* plays are *yokyoku* or *utai*. *Noh* traces its remote origin to the popular plays of the Tang Dynasty in China. When introduced into Japan, these Chinese plays consisted primarily of juggling and acrobatics, but from about the middle of the 14th century realistic mimicry became their main feature.

Kanze Kan-ami (1333-1384) established the foundation for *noh* plays as an art, while his son Zeami (1363-1443) brought them to fruition. Zeami attached great importance to mastering mimicry. However, in consideration of the tastes and inclinations of the upper classes who patronized *noh* plays, he restricted mimicry to music, dancing and artistic agility.

The highest principle of *noh* plays lies in *yugen* (subtlety), which is akin to the graceful beauty of the ladies and noblemen of the Court. *Noh* is a musical drama accompanied by *utai* (chanted texts), orchestra and dancing. *Utai* includes a *jikata* (chorus) and *serifu*—lines delivered by the *shite* (the principal actor) and *waki* (the secondary actor), alone or in duets, trios, etc. The music in *noh* is performed by the *hayashi* (*noh* orchestra) using the following instruments: the *fue* (flute), *ko-tsuzumi* (small drum), *o-tsuzumi* (medium-sized drum) and *taiko* (large drum).

Five plays are performed in a day, most of which are lively pieces. The first is a *kami-mono* (god piece), the second—*shura-mono* (fighting piece, also known as *otoko-mono* or male piece), the third—*katsura-mono* (wig piece, popularly known as *onna-mono* or female piece), the fourth—*kurui-mono* (frenzy piece) and the fifth—*kiri-noh* (closing piece).

The repertory of *noh* plays actually performed today includes more than 250 plays. There is a fixed type in their construction. Rather than attempting realism, they aim at luring the audience into an atmosphere of fantasy and displaying the picturesqueness of changing scenes. Involving as little movement as possible on the part of actors, these extremely formalized plays try to create as much significance and sentiment as possible.

The *kyogen* is a farcical, realistic form of drama, light and optimistic, reflecting everyday life and social conditions. Presented as an interlude between *noh* plays, the repertory numbers 300 at present. *Kyogen* are characterized by the healthy, carefree spirit of the common people. Refer to "Nohgaku and Noh-Kyogen" in p.164-168

Renga and Haikai: The beginning of *renga* was the composition of a single poem by two persons. The practice soon gained wide popularity as it enabled a number of people to freely enjoy the pleasure of collective, creative activity. It was hailed in the Middle Ages as a new type of recreational art. Nijo Yoshimoto (1320-1388), *kampaku* (supreme adviser to the Emperor), took a special interest in *renga* and compiled the "Tsukubashu" (1356), a collection of *renga* in 20 books. After that, *renga* rose in the public's estimation and became popular throughout the land, producing such poets as Shinkei (1406-1475) and Sogi (1421-1502). *Renga* consists of a long series of verses of 5-7-5 syllables each and short ones of 7-7 syllables. Possessing an independent meaning, each verse develops in accordance with the preceding one. The essential point in the progress of the series lies in the relation of *tsukeai* (attaching), or the appreciation of the previous line, and the composition of a new verse in continuation of the one before. However, the *hokku* (initial verse) alone contains a *kireji* (a particle used in completing the meaning of a verse). For that reason, it constitutes a world complete in itself and is thus distinguished from the *hiraku* (the other ordinary verses). In due course, the *hokku* developed as a separate form of poetry.

Haikai originally meant comicality. The *renga* in the *haikai* style grew into a separate poetic form toward the end of the medieval period. Because of the tendency of *gekokujo* (the lower dominating the upper) to gradually become more pronounced in society, the common people were able to gain more ground. This resulted in an increased desire for colloquialism and laughter in literature. The "Inu-Tsukubashu," compiled by Yamazaki Sokan (1464-1553) and marked by a strong plebeian character, is regarded as the direct progenitor of the *haikai* literature of later times.

Modern Literature and the "Renaissance"

The persistent civil disturbances in the 13th century came to an end toward the close of the 16th century when a new type of culture arose. From that time to the middle of the 19th century, a rigid system of feudalism was in force under the leadership of the *samurai* class. *Bushido* (the way of the warrior) and Confucianism constituted the moral backbone of the governing class. However, since Confucian ethics rejected polite literature, it was the *chonin* (townspeople) who became patrons of the arts in modern times. This period is accordingly referred to as the period of *chonin* literature.

Literature in modern times may be roughly divided into two periods. The first half is the period of *Kamigata* (Kyoto-Osaka area) literature, culminating in the Genroku era (1688-1704). The latter half—the period of Edo literature—culminated in the Meiwa and An-ei eras (1764-1781), with most of the writers coming from Edo (now, Tokyo).

Throughout both periods, the setting is located most frequently in the gay quarters and many of the characters are courtesans. This is partly because the ideals and goals of the *chonin* lay in the accumulation of wealth and the enjoyment of life. It is also due to the fact that the courtesans, who could give free rein to their individuality and sentiment, provided literature with more interesting subjects than women of gentle birth. The latter, wanting in individuality, were compelled by Confucian morality to live in a state of subjection to the sterner male sex. Moreover, the gay quarters in those days functioned, so to speak, in the same way as fashionable society, and even persons of high social standing could frequent it without suffering a reflection on their honor.

Literature flourished remarkably early in modern times, partly due to considerable improvements in the art of printing, making possible the production of books in larger quantities and their sale at lower prices. At the same time, a tendency arose in the fields of arts and science to disfavor the traditional methods of the Medieval Ages and revive classical learning while promoting the freedom and independence of academic pursuits at one's own discretion. This period is comparable to the Renaissance in European history.

Haikai (Haiku) and Basho: In the world of literary arts, it was *haikai* that gave expression to a sense of modernism earlier than the other forms of literature, becoming the most important form of poetry in the period under review. Early in this period, the view that *haikai* was of a lower order than *renga* had still not been entirely eliminated.

But a new school known as *Danrin-fu* was founded by Nishiyama Soin (1605–1682). While directly attempting to reflect sentiment, at the same time, it aimed at accepting all phenomena in real life as the subject matter of poetry. Therein fully evolved the popularity inherent in *haikai*, but it could by no means produce work of a high poetical value.

It was Matsuo Basho (1644–1694) who exerted himself, with ultimate success, to assimilate the traditional concepts of medieval literature and give them a popularity and freedom, thus elevating *haikai* to essentially the same level as *renga* and Chinese poetry. He tried to penetrate the realm of *yuga* (elegance) through assimilation with nature and by seeking after never-failing freshness in an effort to avoid adherence to traditional beauty. The collection of *hokku* or *haiku* by Basho and his disciples, called the *Shichibushu*, is prized as the sacred book of *haikai*. Among his disciples were the *Juttetsu* (Ten Great Disciples), who were the most prominent and celebrated *haiku* poets of their time.

Modern Literature in Edo Period

Saikaku: Toward the end of the Middle Ages, a collection of rather vulgar short stories, entitled the "Otogi-Zoshi," was published, while early in modern times a kind of prose literature called "Kana-Zoshi" came into being. Some of the stories in such books were popular adaptations of classics, while others were aimed at providing moral instruction.

These were followed by "Koshoku Ichidai Otoko" (1682) from the pen of Ihara Saikaku (1642–1693). Discovering a new beauty in real life and personal experiences, he produced masterpieces of *koshokumono* (amorous stories) in which he portrayed contemporary society while analyzing the sexual impulses of man. He also wrote other significant works such as "Seken Munazanyo" (1692)—tragicomedies in the lives of the *chonin* class where money was regarded as all-important. It is especially noteworthy that such acute observations on the relationship between money and life were made as early as the 17th century.

Joruri, Kabuki and Chikamatsu: The *joruri* as herein referred to is a recitative accompanied by the manipulation of puppets and the performance of *samisen* (or, *shamisen*) Music. In this field, Chikamatsu Monzaemon (1653-1724) produced truly valuable examples of dramatic verse. The *joruri* is enjoyable both when seen or heard since it depicts a world of fantasy as a musical spectacle. Besides writing *jidaimono*, the historical plays hitherto in vogue, Chikamatsu also created the *sewamono*—realistic dramas of contemporary life. A dramatic poet fascinating the readers with his ornate, virile style, he is regarded as the Shakespeare of Japan. He was also a prominent *kabuki* dramatist.

Singing and dancing are important factors in *kabuki* plays. It is said that *kabuki* originated in the dance-plays accompanied by the *samisen*—the new musical instrument of the day—performed in Kyoto about 1603 by Okuni, an attendant at Izumo Taisha Shrine.

The art gradually developed, and in the Genroku era (1688-1704) such great actors as Ichikawa Danjuro, who started the *aragoto* (a play with a superhuman hero or a fierce deity in the leading part), flourished in Edo. The *Kamigata* (Kyoto-Osaka area) boasted Sakata Tojuro and other actors, who won fame in realistic dramas. In the early days of *kabuki*, the actors were also playwrights, but later playwriting was left in the hands of creative artists. Chikamatsu wrote about 40 plays for Sakata Tojuro and other *kabuki* actors.

Later, *joruri* and *kabuki* were brought closer together, with fewer and fewer differences between them. Of course, puppet plays were performed just as frequently, with more and more improvements in the manner of presentation and greater complexity in the plots. Such monumental works as "Sugawara Denju Tenaraikagami" (1746) and "Kanadehon Chushingura" were produced by Takeda Izumo (1691-1756), who was regarded as the greatest playwright after Chikamatsu.

Literature in the Edo Period: After the Tokugawa Shogunate was established in Edo, peace reigned over the land for the next two-and-a-half centuries. Partly because of this and partly because the feudal system became flexible, the age lost its spirit of liveliness. Averting friction with the realities of life, literature began to deal with the phases of life free from the pressures of the times, striving to discover *warai* (comedy) and *asobi* (amusement). Thus, literature in the Edo period degenerated into *gesaku* (writing for fun or pleasure), losing its strong craving for life.

(I) **Novels**: A great variety of novels appeared. Most were written in a light vein merely aimed at finding flaws in society and human nature while delineating the weaknesses of man. They included *kibyoshi* (the yellow book), a kind of "nonsensical" literature featuring pictures; *sharebon*, which devoted its pages exclusively to descriptions of special scenes in the gay quarters, and *kobanashibon*, which is a collection of humorous short shorts. They all contain short stories treating life in a light vein in pursuit of laughter.

In contrast to these, "Ugetsu Monogatari" and "Harusame Monogatari" by Ueda Akinari (1734-1809) are collections of short pieces with backbone, so to speak. Pervaded with classical taste, they truly deserve the name of short story. As a writer of mysterious short stories, Akinari is peerless.

The historical novel, whose subject matter is likewise derived from the past, is called *yomihon* (story book). Santo Kyoden (1761-1816) and Takizawa Bakin (1767-1848) are the most celebrated authors of this kind of novel. Especially well-read in Chinese literature and endowed with the rare power of conceiving plots, Bakin wrote the voluminous work, "Nanso Satomi Hakkenden" (1814-1841). Full of variety, it was the longest novel that had ever been produced up to the advent of the 1868 Meiji Restoration. But it cannot be denied that besides being excessively fictionalized and artificial, his work attaches too much importance to moralizing.

In contrast to *yomihon*, the *ninjobon*, is based on real life and chiefly treats amorous dalliances between men and women. A representative work of this genre is "Shunshoku Umegoyomi" by Tamenaga Shunsui (1790-1843). Its worth as a literary work of art may not be high, but in its form as a novel it shows some measure of advance. Its method of describing situations while stressing dialogue and its attitude of seeking the keynote of social life and human nature exerted not a little influence on the novels of the Meiji and later eras.

Lastly, the *kokkeibon* (comical book) aimed directly at humor. The typical works are "Tokaidochu Hizakurige" (1802-1809) by Jippensha-Ikku (1765-1831), "Ukiyoburo" (1809-1812) and "Ukiyodoko" (1811-1812) by Shikitei-Samba (1776-1822). In the former, rather than using natural humor, the author seeks to deliberately tickle his readers by means of exaggeration. A unique aspect of the book is that it took the form of a guide to travelers on the Tokaido Highway. In the latter two works, the writer dexterously reveals the commonplace manners of everyday life and the external features of the language.

(II) **Poetry**: Just as various new forms were developed in the novel, new styles came into being in the realm of poetry and flourished in their own inimitable way. In regard to *haikai*, Yosa Buson (1716-1783) became the foremost of the *haikai* poets after Basho. An eminent artist of the *nanga* school of painting, he excelled in giving reality a sense of beauty in a classical atmosphere. After Buson, the unique poet Kobayashi Issa (1763-1827) enlivened *haiku* poetry by boldly using colloquialisms.

However, the forms of poetry that gave a fresh spirit to the age were *senryu* and *kyoka*. The *senryu* is a thoroughgoing, popular kind of literature. Like the *hokku*, it consists of 17 syllables, but it need not contain the seasonal word essential to *haikai*. Deriving its favorite themes from human affairs, the *senryu* is a kind of genre poetry, or human-nature poetry that endeavors to view things from a comically cynical standpoint in flaunting evil. Almost all the noted *senryu* verses are to be found in the "Yanagidaru" (1765-1791)—a collection published in 24 volumes.

The *kyoka* is a 31-syllable poem marked chiefly by witticism, satire, word play and humor, taking pleasure in an intellectual interest not found in *senryu*. The representative *kyoka* poet was Ota Shokusanjin (1749-1823).

(III) Kabuki and Kabuki Dramatists: While the *joruri* reached a deadlock, *kabuki* in the Edo period climbed to the zenith of prosperity. Successive generations of noted actors like Ichikawa Danjuro and Onoe Kikugoro were the object of adulation by the populace.

Among the *kabuki* dramatists were such excellent talents as Tsuru-ya Namboku IV (1755-1829) and Kawatake Mokuami (1816-1893). Namboku was a master at creating cruel murder scenes and abnormal love scenes, reproducing the world of decadence on the stage. Mokuami, who also displayed uncommon skill in portraying degenerate characters such as burglars, effected a rational rearrangement in *kabuki* drama. The burglars in Mokuami's dramas, however, are not thoroughgoing villains because they do not arouse antagonistic feelings in the audience. In other words, Mokuami portrayed his rogues to give his audience the impression that his antiheroes are constantly bothered by their consciences, with the paradoxical result that the audience feels a sense of sympathy and tolerance for them.

●Drama

The origin of the theater in Japan can be traced back to the beginning of the seventh century when a form of stage art called *gigaku* was introduced from China. Many things—from Buddhist doctrines to musical instruments—were imported at the time. A little later came *bugaku* and *sangaku*, of which more will be said later.

Patronized by the ruling class of the time, both *gigaku* and *bugaku* became very popular. The only data available on *gigaku* has been obtained from notes handed down by priests in some of the larger temples. It was a sort of comical dance drama, apparently performed at religious services in Buddhist temples. The only traces of *gigaku* that remain today are the 200 or so *gigaku* masks preserved at certain temples.

Bugaku was a dance drama performed to the accompaniment of *gigaku*. Adapted to suit Japanese tastes after its introduction, *bugaku* became a representative form of court entertainment in the Nara (710

-784) and Heian (794-1185) periods. Today, it is still preserved and patronized primarily by the Imperial Household Agency. It is performed at Imperial ceremonies and presented to the public at least once a year. It is also performed at some of the larger Shinto shrines and Buddhist temples.

Sangaku was simpler than the other two aforementioned forms of ancient dance drama. It was a generic term for public entertainment, including comic mimicry, acrobatics, juggling and puppetry.

Apart from these imported forms of entertainment, there was also a native dramatic performance. Mention is made of this in the oldest historical records in Japan—the "Kojiki" and the "Nihonshoki," (sometimes called "Nihongi"). Two of the most noteworthy legends recorded in these books refer to indigenous performances. One of them tells the following tale:

The Sun Goddess, called Amaterasu-Omikami, became angry at the outrageous conduct of her brother Susano-o-no-Mikoto and hid herself in the Cave of Heaven, thereby plunging the whole world into complete darkness. To alleviate her anger, a goddess named Amenouzume-no-Mikoto was persuaded into performing a comic dance in front of the cave, much to the merriment of the gods. Attracted by the hilarity outside, the Sun Goddess came out of the cave to see what was happening. Lo and behold, there was light again outside. This legendary dance was often performed to help departed souls rest in peace. It was the prototype of *kagura*, which is performed today at shrine festivals.

The other legend concerns the origin of the mime dance. Two brothers quarreled and the younger emerged victorious. The defeated brother was required to entertain the winner by moving his limbs frantically about in imitation of a drowning man. This legend is said to be the oldest record of a dance called the *hayato-mai*. It may have been performed to celebrate a victory, or as a mime dance. Thus, the primitive entertainment of Japan took the form of religious rites performed for the repose of the souls of the departed, in celebration of a victory or as a prayer for a rich harvest. These primitive forms of Japanese entertainment blended with imported forms as time passed, eventually giving birth to stage art centuries later.

Nohgaku and Noh-kyogen

The Heian period (794-1185) was a glorious age for the nobility. During this period, *bugaku* was nurtured under their patronage. In 1192, Minamoto-no-Yoritomo established a shogunate military government in Kamakura and a military age began. In the realm of theatrical entertainment, the *dengaku* and *sarugaku* became popular among the masses as well as the warrior class.

The *dengaku* may be regarded as a form of art consisting of the acrobatic stunts of the *gigaku* and *sangaku* as well as a primitive dance performed in times of rice-planting or in supplication to the gods for a rich harvest. The *sarugaku*, which is a derivation of the world *sangaku*, is based on the *sangaku*. Accordingly, both *dengaku* and *sarugaku* have common traits, although the former came into fashion a little before the latter. Both had performers who belonged exclusively to them and both were performed at shrine festivals.

Etymologically, the word *noh* comes from *geino* (the art of public performance or accomplishment) and *saino* (talent). The original terms used were *dengaku-no-noh* or *sarugaku-no-noh* (talent for performing *dengaku* or *sarugaku*, as the case may be). As time passed, the actors of both *dengaku* and *sarugaku* formed troupes and guilds, with the *sarugaku* gradually developing as these troupes competed to perfect their art.

Special mention must be made of Kan-ami (1333-1384), a talented *sarugaku* actor who organized a troupe named *Kanzeza*. He considerably improved the *sarugaku-no-noh* by introducing a kind of dance called *kuse-mai* in which he performed as he chanted the history of a temple or the life of a noted priest in the form of an epic. In 1374, Kan-ami came to the attention of then *shogun* Ashikaga Yoshimitsu (1358-1408), who became his patron.

Kan-ami's son, Zeami, followed in his father's path. Before long, this art became known simply as *noh*, developing as a dance drama of a very high level of excellence. The *noh* repertoire of today consists of more than 200 dramas, the majority of which are attributed to Zeami. He was not only a distinguished *noh* performer and writer of *noh* texts, but also wrote excellent monographs on contemporary theaters called Kadensho and Nohsakusho—the first and best of their kind in Japan.

Zeami was followed by such *noh* actors and playwrights as Komparu Zenchiku and Kanze Kojiro. In comparing Zeami's works such as "Hagoromo" and "Yuya" with those of his successors, including "Ataka" and "Momijigari," one finds a marked change in emphasis from mere chanting and dancing to more dramatic aspects.

Noh plays are divided into five categories. These categories are usually numbered, although sometimes they are classified by the characters of the *shite* actors, or protagonists, of the dramas. They are:

First category: *kami-mono* (god pieces), or *waki-noh* such as "Takasago" and "Yoro"

Second category: *otoko-mono* (men's pieces), or *shura-mono* (fighting pieces) such as "Tamura"

Third category: *onna-mono* (women's pieces), or *katsura-mono* (wig pieces) such as "Matsukaze"

Fourth category: *kyoran-mono* (mentally deranged pieces), *genzai-mono* (mundane pieces), *yubu-mono* (ecstatic pieces) and *shunen-mono* (revenge pieces)—all known collectively as *kyoran-mono* (frenzied-women pieces), or *kurui-mono* (frenzy pieces) such as "Sumidagawa"

Fifth category: *oni-mono* (demon pieces) or *kichiku-mono* (ghost pieces), popularly called *kiri-noh* (closing pieces) such as "Kurama Tengu."

Most of these *noh* plays are known as *fukushiki-noh*, or double *shite* pieces, in which the *shite* (principal actor) exits halfway through the play only to enter again as an entirely different character. In "Takasago," for example, the *shite* in the first part of the play portrays an old man, while in the latter part he becomes the god of the Sumiyoshi Myojin Shrine. In a *noh* play of this type, the same performer plays the parts of both the first and second *shite*.

All *shogun* after Yoshimitsu, were enthusiastic followers and patrons of *noh* drama. Toyotomi Hideyoshi (1536-1598) was not only a patron, he also acted in *noh* pieces himself. He even wrote and produced a *noh* play in which he himself was the hero. A change occurred in the Edo period (1603-1867) when the common people were prohibited from giving *noh* performances. As a result, *noh* drama became the exclusive pastime of the *samurai* class. Accordingly, it was no longer included among everyday theatricals, but was elevated to the dignity of classic drama.

When the Tokugawa Shogunate government was overthrown in 1867, *noh* players lost their traditional protectors and were forced to survive by giving lessons to *noh* enthusiasts among the upper class. They also took steps to become independent professionals, but the majority of their audiences was composed of their own disciples. Even today, most *noh* fans consist of those who take lessons themselves in this stage art. In Tokyo, *noh* performances are held on Saturdays and Sundays, while in most other urban areas *noh* plays are only staged on special occasions.

Apart from the staging of *noh* plays, however, the *utai* (chanting of *noh* texts) became quite popular among the Japanese people at large. In the past, there were many followers and groups throughout the country who were active in *utai*.

In olden days when *noh* was as much the drama of daily life as Shakespearean plays were in Elizabethan England, there were several schools that flourished. In the Edo period, however, the number of schools was reduced to five—Kanze, Hosho, Kongo, Komparu and Kita. In 1922, yet another school named Umewaka developed from the Kanze school, although it was short-lived. Today, there are still only the five *noh* schools mentioned above. The different schools have slightly varied styles of chanting and dancing as well as their own texts.

The *noh* stage has its own unique features. The stage proper is 5.5 sq.m with four pillars and a wall at the back. To the right of the stage—as the audience faces it—is the *Jiutai-za* (place for the chorus). The orchestra—in front of the wall—is located in the *Atoza*, while to the left is a passage known as the *Hashigakari*. This corridor is not only the passage through which the actors enter and exit, but also serves as part of the stage.

The *Hashigakari* is separated by a curtain from a room called the *Kagami-no-Ma* (Mirror Room). This room is so called because when the actor has finished his make-up, he sits before a large mirror to make a final check of his appearance. The entire wall at the back of the stage is paneled with a large pine tree painted on the panels. The painted paneling is the only form of stage scenery used in *noh* plays. There is no stage setting except for a prop called *tsukuri-mono*, which is used from time to time in some performances, but this small prop is more symbolic than realistic.

Both stage and corridor are neatly roofed, making the *noh* theater a sort of "house within a house." The audience is seated at a lower level than the stage and corridor.

The *noh* orchestra consists of a *taiko* (large drum), *o-tsuzumi* (medim-size drum), *ko-tsuzumi* (small drum) and *fue* (flute). The players are seated in the order mentioned from left to right as seen by the audience. The *noh* chorus is made up of about eight chanters.

As the chorus chants the prelude, the first actor appears on stage —or rather in the corridor—from behind the *age-maku* (entrance curtain). (The stage itself does not have a curtain). *Noh* performers include a *shite* (principal actor) playing the leading part, *waki* (secondary actor), *tsure* (associates) and *kyogen-kata* (*noh* comedians). The performance of a *noh* piece centers around the *shite*, although the *waki* plays a useful part in "drawing out" the *shite*. In some plays, the *shite* and *waki* are aided by assistant performers, or *tsure*.

It is during the interlude or in pieces requiring a more realistic performance that *kyogen-kata* act their parts. The actors in all of the five schools of *noh* play exclusively either *shite* or *tsure* roles. Each school also has its own chorus, but the *waki* and *kyogen-kata* are experts who do not belong to any of the schools.

In *noh*, adult actors usually play the parts of children. However, a *kokata* (child actor) is sometimes used instead to express cuteness or pathos to the audience. Sometimes a *kokata* also takes the part of grown-up characters in order to emphasize the *shite's* acting and, at the same time, to avoid excessive realism.

Generally, only the *shite* actor is masked. *Shite-zure*, or assistants of the *shite*, also wear masks, but only when they represent female characters. (The word *tsure* changes euphonically to *zure* when combined with another word as in *shite-zure*.) Even the *shite* is not masked when playing a character in a worldly or realistic drama. No other actors are masked. Since the days of Zeami, both mask and costumes styles have remained more or less conventional, except that they have gradually become more gorgeous. The *noh* costumes and masks used today are valued as works of exquisite craftsmanship, some of which date back several hundred years.

Noh is essentially an extremely restricted stage art—symbolic, static and solemn, yet elegant and graceful. As already pointed out, the reason for this is that it attained full maturity as a reflection of the aesthetic tastes and feelings of upper-class warriors during the Edo period. In this sense, *noh* has much in common with *zen*, *chanoyu* (tea ceremony), temple architecture and Japanese landscape gardening, all of which developed during the Middle Ages.

Noh-kyogen, or *kyogen* for short, also developed from *sarugaku*. The operatic element of *sarugaku* developed into *noh*, while the conversational element formed the nucleus of *kyogen*. Being of the same derivation, *noh* and *kyogen* cannot be considered separately. As previously noted, *kyogen-kata* are not properly *noh* actors. In *fukushiki-noh* (noh drama where the *shite* takes two different parts—one in the first half of the play and the other in the latter half), a *kyogen* actor enters the stage when the *shite* exits after his first part. His function is to explain the development of the situation in a performance known as *ai-kyogen*, or an interlude.

Besides *ai-kyogen*, an independent *kyogen* piece was formerly given as a comic interlude between *noh* plays. Nearly 300 independent *kyogen* pieces have been handed down since the 15th century—all written in dialogue form, with many topical allusions presented in a satirical vein and spoken in the everyday language of the times. These comic plays are said to have appeared in book form in the 17th century for the first time. Until then, they were transmitted orally. It is, therefore, quite possible that there was considerable extemporaneous dialogue thrown in. What is known for certain is that *kyogen* were usually written by more than one playwright.

As might be expected, *kyogen* plays were often looked on as a farcical adjunct to, and of less literary or histrionic value than *noh*. But recently, its realism—the direct opposite of the symbolism of *noh* —as well as its dialogue content have begun to attract the attention of dramatic critics.

Today, two schools of *kyogen* exist: the Okura and Izumi schools. *Kyogen* is presented on the same stage as *noh*. *Kyogen* actors corresponding to the *shite* of *noh* plays are sometimes called *omo*, while those corresponding to the *waki* are known as *omo-ado*, or *ado* for short. Masks are used in only a few *kyogen* pieces. Unlike *noh* plays, normal garments—clearly those of the common people—are worn instead of the gorgeous costumes used in *noh*.

Sometimes, *noh* and *kyogen* performances are presented on a stage temporarily adapted from the stage of a regular theater.

The principal stages where *noh* and *kyogen* are generally performed are listed below:

Ginza Nohgakudo; 6-5-15 Ginza, Chuo-ku, Tokyo ☎ (03) 3571-3872
Kanze Nohgakudo; 1-16-4 Shoto, Shibuya-ku, Tokyo
☎ (03) 3469-5241
Kita Nohgakudo; 4-6-9 Kami-Osaki, Shinagawa-ku, Tokyo
☎ (03) 3491-7773

Hosho Nohgakudo; 1-5-9 Hongo, Bunkyo-ku, Tokyo
☎ (03) 3811-4843
Umewaka Nohgakudo; 2-6-14 Higashi-Nakano, Nakano-ku, Tokyo
☎ (03) 3363-7748
Kongo Nohgakudo; Shijo-agaru, Muromachi-dori, Nakagyo-ku, Kyoto
☎ (075) 221-3049
Kyoto Kanze Kaikan; 44 Enshojicho, Okazaki, Sakyo-ku, Kyoto
☎ (075) 771-6114

Puppet Plays

The war between the Genji (Mimamoto Clan) and the Heike (Taira Clan) in the 12th century, sometimes compared to the War of the Roses, is one of the landmarks in Japanese history. Naturally, there are many episodes and legendary romances about this war, including the fictitious love affairs of Minamoto-no-Yoshitsune—a historical figure whose military prowess helped gain eventual victory for his clan. At the same time, however, he incurred the jealousy and enmity of his elder brother Yoritomo, the leader of the Minamotos. The story goes that to keep from falling into the clutches of his brother's troops while in flight from the capital, Yoshitsune fell in love with a maiden named Joruri.

Set to ballad music and chanted by a minstrel to the accompaniment of a *biwa* (Japanese lute), this romance caught the fancy of the people of the time. This style of reciting ballads came to be known as *joruri*. Later, the *samisen* (or *shamisen*), a three-stringed instrument introduced to Japan from the Ryukyus (the Luchu Islands) around the year 1560, replaced the *biwa*. Around 1600, the puppet element of the *sangaku* was added to the *joruri*, thereby creating a sort of composite art now known as puppet drama. This new form of theatrical entertainment gained great popularity, not only in the Kyoto and Osaka areas, but also in Edo (the present Tokyo).

Puppet drama entered its golden age at the beginning of the 18th century when the master dramatist Chikamatsu Monzaemon (1653-1724) and the brilliant *joruri* reciter Takemoto Gidayu (1651-1714) brought this form of stage art to new heights of excellence. Besides Chikamatsu, the leading playwrights of puppet drama were Ki-no-Kaion (1663-1742), Namiki Sosuke (also called Namiki Senryu (1695-1751)) and Chikamatsu Hanji (1728-1786).

Perhaps the most famous puppet plays that have been handed down are "Sugawara Denju Tenaraikagami," "Yoshitsune Sembonzakura" and "Kanadehon Chushingura" (or "Chushingura" for short, the Revenge of the Forty-Seven Loyal *Samurai*, refer to p.382)—all written jointly by Takeda Izumo, Miyoshi Shoraku and Namiki Sosuke between 1746 and 1748. These three masterpieces are also among the most popular *kabuki* plays—the sister drama of the puppet show (to be mentioned later). Especially noteworthy is the last-named play, "Chushingura," which was the most frequently staged of any *kabuki* play.

This is a brief synopsis of the play: Subjected to a deliberate insult, the lord of a castle and a man of probity violates the law. He is forced to commit *seppuku*, or ritual suicide, after which his property is confiscated. His vassals, determined to avenge their erstwhile master, disperse and dissemble, pretending to turn into drunken vagabonds. After a year of patience and hardship, they finally succeed in locating and slaying the wrongdoer. As punishment, they are all ordered to commit *seppuku*, which they do. Based on an historical event, the play has several heart-rending scenes of inward strife between love and duty—the leitmotif of both puppet drama and *kabuki*.

At first, each puppet was manipulated by one man, who operated it by putting his hand under its skirt. This method of operating puppets continued until a skillful manipulator named Yoshida Bunzaburo (d. 1760) improved the mechanism of puppets to indicate various kinds of expressions. As a result, three men are necessary to operate each puppet. The main operator was in charge of the body and the right hand, one of the two assistants managed the left hand and the other worked both legs. (As puppets representing women do not have legs, the second assistant handles the *kimono* skirts for female puppets.) This method of three-man manipulation is still practiced today.

At first, puppet shows were staged only at the Takemotoza Theater in Osaka, where Takemoto-Gidayu and other *joruri* chanters performed. But soon after, when a rival theater called Toyotakeza was built, the two theaters vied with each other to attract audiences.

With the death in 1751 of Namiki Sosuke, one of the most prominent puppet playwrights, puppet drama began to decline, never again to be restored to its former grandeur. It did not die out, however. The puppet theater in its old form still exists today under the name of *Bunraku*, named after Uemura-Bunrakuken who did much to preserve its traditions in the latter half of the 18th century.

Today the Bunraku Kyokai, established through the efforts of the Ministry of Education, the prefectural and municipal governments of Osaka and NHK (Japan Broadcasting Corporation), plays an important roll of preserving and promoting the development of the traditional art of *bunraku*. In Osaka, the plays are given at the National Bunraku Theater and in Tokyo at the National Theater.

Near the front of the stage and extending across it stands a long panel about 45 cm high, behind which the puppets are operated. The panel functions not only as a device to conceal the lower part of the operators' bodies, but also sometimes as a part of the stage scenery. The chief operator wears a pair of *geta* (wooden clogs) about 31 cm high so that he can hold the puppet on a level with his chest. The puppets are about two-thirds life size. Each one is so devised that the head can be detached from the body. There are about 70 varieties of puppet heads, since different heads and costumes are required for different roles.

Joruri reciters are called *tayu*. The *tayu* and the *samisen* player sit on a revolving dais on the right side of the stage (as seen by the audience) and face out diagonally. The National Bunraku Theater in Nippombashi, Osaka, is the only theater in Japan especially built for staging puppet plays.

Apart from the aforementioned *bunraku* puppets, there are marionette-type puppets dating from the end of the Edo period. About 50 cm tall, they are manipulated by strings from above. These marionettes are not so popular today, but are still performed by some groups. The plays are much the same as those in the *bunraku* repertoire. Some classical *kabuki* dramas are also staged by these marionette performers.

Finally, finger-operated puppets were introduced into Japan from the West. Various kinds of puppet shows are given on a noncommercial basis in regional areas, operated either by a single man or a three-man group. Such puppet performances are given by farmers at festivals, constituting a form of folk art. Typical representatives are Awaji and Awa puppets, slightly larger than *bunraku* puppets.

Kabuki

During the days of peace established by the Tokugawa Shogunate government (1603–1867), the townspeople prospered. Women, who had remained in the background during the preceding period of wars and disturbances, began to become active. Among the words in current usage about that time was the verb *kabuku*, meaning "to deviate from normal manners and customs, to do something considered absurd."

In 1603, a girl in the service of the Izumo Taisha Shrine, intending to raise funds for the repair of the shrine, donned a singular garb and performed a series of novel dances within the precincts of the Kitano Shrine in Kyoto. Dressed like a man, with a cross dangling from her neck and a sword in one hand, Okuni, as this maiden was named, exuded a magnetic charm. Sometimes presenting a dancing interpretation of a man surreptitiously meeting his sweetheart and sometimes enacting a short farce with clowns, Okuni and her troupe gradually caught the fancy not only of the townsfolk, but also of the *daimyo* (feudal lord). Dubbed *Kabuki Odori*, her entertaining style of dancing proved a great hit and is regarded as the origin of *kabuki*.

Okuni and her troupe had their imitative rivals. Since prostitutes were used to mimic Okuni, it was not long before this theater began to violate public morals. As a result, the Tokugawa Shogunate government banned the performance of *kabuki* dances by women, a move that rapidly spurred the development of performances by handsome youths. Unfortunately, the resultant use of juvenile actors stimulated the evil of sodomy, which had become an unwholesome practice among some warriors and members of the clergy. After the ban, *kabuki* dances gradually began to appeal to the townspeople. However, the Shogunate government again took drastic action against it in 1651.

In 1653, government permission to present *kabuki* dancing was finally obtained on condition that adult men instead of youths did the acting and, when necessary, played the part of women. More importance was now attached to the dramatic element and various wigs used to portray women and boys were devised.

Initially, however, *kabuki* was little more than a one-act dramatic sketch with a bit of humor or satire thrown in. As time went on, however, plays of more than one act began to be produced, requiring the first use of a curtain.

The development of *kabuki* reached its zenith around the year 1700, coinciding with the period when the Tokugawa administration was well consolidated. It was a time when first-rate masters in various fields of artistic endeavor flourished, including the novelist Ihara Saikaku, the *haiku* poet Matsuo Basho, the dramatist Chikamatsu Monzaemon and the decorative artist Ogata Korin.

Chief among the *kabuki* actors of those days were Sakata Tojuro (1647-1709) and Yoshizawa Ayame (1673-1729) in the Osaka-Kyoto area, and Ichikawa Danjuro I (1660-1704) and Nakamura Shichisaburo (1662-1708) in Edo (now, Tokyo). As previously stated, Chikamatsu and other playwrights of the time devoted themselves not so much to *kabuki* as to the puppet play. The prosperity of puppet drama lasted for half a century or so before it began to decline, as already pointed out, with the death of the playwright Namiki Sosuke.

Namiki Shozo (1730-1773), who followed Namiki Sosuke, is said to have played a valuable part in the development and blossoming of *kabuki*. Shozo was an Osaka puppet dramatist who diverted his efforts and energy to *kabuki*, producing play after play. He deserves the credit for having devised a revolving stage and what is called in *kabuki* parlance—*seri*, a section of the stage floor so devised as to enable an actor to gradually appear on the stage from below or disappear from the stage downwards.

Today, the revolving stage plays an indispensable part in Japanese scenic effects for it enables the audience to watch two scenes taking place concurrently as the stage turns slowly around. The gradual appearance of an actor by means of the *seri* onto the stage floor may be considered as effective as a close-up on the screen. The *seri* is also sometimes used to raise the level of a stage house to show the downstairs portion, a device designed to render stage settings less complicated.

No *kabuki* theater is complete without the *hanamichi*, an aisle leading from behind the audience directly onto the stage on the left-hand side (looking from the audience). The *hanamichi*, which was already in use in the days of Shozo, is considered part of the stage. Actors often enter and exit along this aisle, and part of the action takes place on it. One great advantage of the *hanamichi* is that its proximity to the audience helps to create an intimate feeling.

About this time, culture began to take root in Edo, the political center of the country. From about 1760 on, Edo was considered the center of *kabuki*. Warriors began to be treated in *kabuki*, which by then was separated into two definite categories—historical plays with a complicated plot and realistic dramas with townspeople portrayed as the heroes and heroines. With the development of *samisen* music, *kabuki* dancing was gradually elevated to an art form. Chief among the *kabuki* dramatists of the time were Namiki Gohei (1747-1808) and Horikoshi Nisoji. The principal actors were Nakamura Utaemon I (1714-1791) and Segawa Kikunojo (1693-1749).

Tiring of unending tranquility under the Tokugawa administration, the public began to seek a strong spiritual stimulus. With the advent of the 19th century, dramatists reflecting this trend came to the fore. Perhaps the most representative writer of this movement was Tsuru-ya Namboku IV (1755-1829), whose claim to fame rests with his masterpiece—"Tokaido Yotsuya Kaidan," or simply "Yotsuya Kaidan."

Reduced to poverty, a *ronin*, or masterless *samurai*, frequents the entertainment quarters with what little money his plain-looking but chaste wife has collected by pawning her clothes. Meanwhile, the only daughter of a rich family falls in love with this *ronin*. Regarding his homely wife with contempt, he poisons her. The ghost of his murdered wife relentlessly haunts him until he is finally driven insane. Full of gruesome scenes showing the dreadful effects that the poison has wrought on the features of the woman and her skeleton, this play is considered the most grotesque and thrilling of any ghost *kabuki* drama. Powerfully stimulating plays like this were very popular with the public. In fact, some *kabuki* plays were so erotic that at one time there was talk of banning *kabuki* again.

The Tokugawa Shogunate government consistently took restrictive measures against *kabuki*. For example, it was prohibited to stage any play with topical allusions. When incidents occurring during the Edo period were dramatized, they had to be treated as events of pre-Edo days, including the necessary changes in proper names. Moreover, all Edo place names had to be substituted by those of Kamakura locations, the site of the Minamoto Shogunate government.

Despite such restrictions, it was not difficult for the audience to realize that the plays were dramatizations of events in their own time. As may be expected, *kabuki* plays of the Edo period were the greatest source of entertainment for the general public, who regarded them as plays of contemporary life.

Kabuki actors of the day were dubbed *kawara-kojiki* (beggars on a dry riverbed, since the plays were first shown in a hut built on a dry riverbed of the Kamo River in Kyoto). Indeed, *kabuki* actors were considered as being on a lower level than the common people. Nevertheless, they had great popularity and it was not unusual for the designs of the *kimono* worn by actors to dictate the fashions of the day.

Even after the Meiji Restoration (1868), *kabuki* continued to enjoy its former popularity for some time. However, the attitude of the government toward it completely changed. Following the example of Western countries, the government protected and nurtured *kabuki*, utilizing it as a means of educating the people. Ichikawa Danjuro IX (1838-1903), a noted actor of the time, was quick to cooperate with the government. Unlike his predecessors in the Edo period, he positively presented plays that were faithful to historical facts.

In the meantime, plays tinged with Western culture and customs began to be staged. Most of these plays were written by Kawatake Mokuami (1816-1893) and his disciples. Attached as they were to the theater, these playwrights had received no formal education. As a result, they were unable to make full use of new materials that otherwise would have provided them with good motifs. It was the dramatists of the following generation, including Okamoto Kido (1872 -1939) and Mayama Seika (1878-1948), who wrote and produced *kabuki* plays representative of the new age.

In Tokyo, *kabuki* plays are staged for 25 days a month throughout most of the year, from about 11 a.m. until 9 p.m. (intermission 3 : 30 p.m.-4 : 30 p.m.) The pieces presented include new plays by present-day dramatists as well as time-honored classics. Sometimes, the same plays are staged two or three times a year in different programs. Since classical plays, or costume plays, are usually quite long, the general practice is to stage only a portion of one without any explanation of what has taken place before or what is to take place afterwards.

After all is said and done, the beauty of *kabuki* consists in its acting. This explains why *kabuki* is characterized by such traditional techniques as *dammari* and *mie*. *Dammari* is a silent show, or pantomime, in which several actors perform without uttering a single word. *Mie* means a pose or posture, and refers to the practice of players to assume a dramatic stance and remain still for a moment to display a dramatic feeling.

Kumadori is another technical *kabuki* word that refers to the special make-up style often used by an actor playing the role of a masculine character, called an *aragoto*. Many devices have been developed to appeal to the auditory sense. Sometimes rhyming words are modulated with effect, while at other times the audience is entertained with what is called *tsurane*. This is a manner of elocution in which the principal actor in a play speaks his part, long and loud.

Kabuki is a stage art in which everything is contrived so as to allow the actors to show their skill to their best advantage. In addition to its musical, picture-like fascination, *kabuki* has a dancing charm that may well be called the leitmotif of a *kabuki* performance. All traditional *kabuki* plays are marked by specific, time-honored methods of acting that have been conventionalized through a long series of improvements. Bizarre and fantastic as they may sometimes seem, *kabuki* methods nevertheless offer convincing evidence that they are the ultimate expression of that which can be physically arranged.

The principal *kabuki* theaters are listed below:

Kabukiza Theater: 4-12-15, Ginza, Chuo-ku, Tokyo
☎ (03) 3541-3131

Meijiza Theater: 2-31-1, Hamacho, Nihombashi, Chuo-ku, Tokyo
☎ (03) 3660-3939

Kokuritsu Gekijo (National Theater of Japan): 4-1 Hayabusacho, Chiyoda-ku, Tokyo   ☎ (03) 3265-7411

Shimbashi Embujo Theater: 6-18-2, Ginza, Chuo-ku, Tokyo
☎ (03) 3541-2211

National Bunraku Theater: 1-12-10, Nippombashi, Chuo-ku, Osaka
☎ (06) 212-2531

Minamiza Theater: Shijo-Ohashi Higashizume, Higashiyama-ku, Kyoto   ☎ (075) 561-1155

●Japanese Music

The "Kojiki" (Record of Ancient Matters) and the "Nihonshoki" or "Nihongi" (Chronicles of Japan, refer to p.152) contain a considerable amount of primitive Japanese poetry, which was either chanted or sung. What form the music took, however, is unknown. Three songs from these collections are still sung or chanted at the Imperial Court as well as at some Shinto shrines. They are the *kume-uta*—a military song supposedly sung by Emperor Jimmu (refer to p.84) on his expedition to the ancient state of Yamato (the present Nara district) the *Yamato-uta*—a folk song of Yamato Province and the *Azuma-asobi*— a folk song of the eastern provinces.

Since these songs were revised in the Middle Ages, however, the present version does not truly represent the original primitive form. Nevertheless, enough has been preserved to show that the modulation to which these songs were set was entirely different from that of modern Japanese folk songs.

Only three musical instruments are known to have been used in ancient times—the *fue* (flute), the *koto* (a horizontal harp or zither) and the *tsuzumi* (hand-drum). The *fue* is short with six holes and is still used for playing religious music. The *koto* was called *Yamato-goto*, or *wagon*. Another type was the *so-no-koto*, which differed from the *wagon* in the simplicity of its construction and the number of its strings. The *wagon* had six strings and a narrow case, while the *so-no-koto* had 13 strings strung on a broad case. The *wagon* was fashioned from a board—1.9 m long and 13 to 20 cm wide, upon which were stretched six strings, each resting on a bridge. It was played with a long, slender plectrum held in the right hand. It is impossible to say what form the *tsuzumi* took since the oldest drums now extant were imported from abroad during the Middle Ages.

Later, a *hichiriki* (a type of flageolet, or flute) was imported from China and added to these three instruments. It is to the accompaniment of these four instruments that Emperor Jimmu's song of victory is now sung. It is noteworthy that the song was accompanied by dancing since it was customary for dancers wearing military costumes and carrying long swords to perform to it.

According to historical records, the importation of Korean music and musical instruments began around the middle of the fifth century. These included the *Kudara-goto* (Korean harp), two examples of which can be seen in the Shosoin Repository in Nara. The *Kudara-goto*, somewhat like the European harp, is held upright and played with both hands. In the early seventh century, Korean music (probably derived from Indian or Chinese music) called *gigaku* was introduced into Japan. Some aspects of the *gigaku* are still extant in the "Lion" and "Goblin" dances performed in various parts of the country.

Indian music seems to have reached Japan along with Buddhism around the middle of the eighth century. Eight ancient compositions are still extant, derived for the most part from the Buddhist drama of India. It is worthy of note that no musical instruments came directly from India.

The first direct importation of Chinese music dates from the middle of the seventh century, continuing down to the middle of the ninth century, during which time Chinese culture was in vogue. But Chinese music later began to be replaced by Japanese adaptations, some of which were sung to an orchestra composed of five or eight instruments—three wind instruments, two string instruments and three percussion instruments.

The wind instruments were harmonized and reduced in number in accompanying songs. A string instrument shaped like a mandolin, called a *biwa* in Japanese, was one of the instruments used. It is supposed to be of Indian origin and is so called because it resembles the shape of a *biwa* (loquat).

There are three kinds of drums. The *da-daiko* is 7.3 m high, approximately 1.8 m in diameter and is covered with hide. It is no longer used in ordinary orchestras, but reserved for Court ceremonies. For ordinary occasions, there is the *tsuri-daiko* (hanging drum), 1.2 m high and covered with leather. The *ninai-daiko* (portable drum) is carried on a 2.4-m-long pole by two men and beat while the bearers are walking. This tradition continues on the day before the start of the six annual *sumo* tournaments.

Dancing accompanied the performances. For the most part, the dancers wore masks depicting different characters with fantastic expressions. Some of the dances were of a military nature, notably the *taihei-raku* in which the dancers wore military costumes and flourished swords and halberds.

Gagaku, which includes the *taihei-raku* and *manzai-raku*, is now performed at Imperial Court ceremonies as well as at Shinto and Buddhist rituals. It is believed to be the combined result of musical influences from Korea, India and China during the ninth century. Since *gagaku* was originally the music of the Court, the Japanese people themselves rarely had the opportunity to enjoy it. It has recently become customary to have public performances of this music as well as the dancing two or three times a year so that music lovers may appreciate them.

The 13th century witnessed the further development of the *biwa* because it was believed that songs which the instrument accompanied encouraged martial spirit. It was to the accompaniment of the newly developed *heike-biwa* that the famous "Heike Monogatari," a dramatic narrative depicting the tragic fall of the Heike family (refer to p.89), was chanted. In the late Edo period, special encouragement was given to performances on the *biwa* by the Shimazu family in Satsuma Province (now, Kagoshima Prefecture). Thus, the instrument came to be known as the *Satsuma-biwa*.

Another form of the *biwa* originated in Chikuzen Province (now, Fukuoka Prefecture) in the latter part of the Meiji period (1868–1912). Called the *Chikuzen-biwa*, it is chiefly played by women.

The *shakuhachi*, a type of flute, found its way into Japan around the end of the sixth century from India by way of China. In India, it had five finger holes, but these were increased to six in China. The additional hole was retained in Japan, while the instrument was lengthened to make the pitch match with other instruments. Even with these improvements, however, its tone was too low to be played in harmony with other instruments and it fell into disuse. The *shakuhachi* most commonly used now is about 50 cm long.

With the development of *noh* drama in the 14th century, a great impetus was given to the development of Japanese music. *Sarugaku*, from which *noh* originated (refer to p.168), was a form of interlude introduced during a Shinto festival to entertain the deities. It was a simple form of comedy which later developed into *kyogen*, the comic interlude now performed between *noh* dramas. *Sarugaku* was also taken up by Buddhist priests and developed into a serious type of play dramatizing Buddhist doctrines.

The *koto*, mentioned previously, appears to have been brought to Japan 1,200 years ago from China, which, in turn, received it from the West. The original six strings have now been increased to 13, and the instrument has been improved in many ways. It still retains a following among all classes, particularly women, although it has lost some of its former popularity. Further improvements have been attempted by specialists in recent years. Miyagi Michio (1894–1956), a masterful *koto* player and an authority on *koto* music despite the fact that he was blind, organized an orchestra made of *koto*, *shakuhachi* and *samisen* (or *shamisen*). He attained a fair amount of success and composed some fine *koto* concertos.

The *samisen*, although popularly regarded as a pure Japanese instrument, was imported from south China about 400 years ago by way of the Ryukyu (Luchu) Islands (now, Okinawa Prefecture). In the Ryukyus, the skin used to cover the drum upon which the strings are strung, was originally taken from large snakes. But in Japan the skins of cats and dogs are used for this purpose. It was in 1560 that the Ryukyu instrument was first brought to Japan on a trading boat, and it appears to have become an immediate hit. As an innovation, it was played with a large plectrum similar to that used for the *biwa*.

As the instrument used for accompanying popular ballads called *joruri* (refer to p.161), the *samisen* soon grew in popularity, rivaling the *biwa* as an instrument for accompanying tales of ancient love and bravery. The ballad, in turn, developed into a drama in which puppets were used as the actors, while a chorus chanted the story to the accompaniment of the instrument.

In 1690, one of the greatest exponents of *joruri*, Takemoto Gidayu (1651-1714), succeeded in founding a new school. He introduced new rhythms to the chant and was fortunate enough to obtain Japan's greatest dramatist, Chikamatsu Monzaemon (1653-1724), as his coadjutor. The term *gidayu* thus came to replace *joruri* to a certain extent, although the former is actually only a subdivision of the latter. This school has continued to flourish throughout the country centered on Osaka.

The *samisen* also came to be used in ordinary theater as the instrument for accompanying the *ko-uta* (short songs) introduced in plays. The first use of the *samisen* in *kabuki* was in Edo in the middle of the 17th century. It was such a success that the songs were made longer and longer until they assumed the proportions of *naga-uta* (ballads). To these also must be added a group of songs known as *ha-uta*, an improved form of which has been given the name of *utazawa*.

It seems probable, however, that the *samisen* vogue has had its day, and that the subtle distinctions between the different styles of songs and tunes no longer attract interest as before. Much of the loss of popularity can be traced to the introduction of many musical instruments from the West together with the varied forms of Western music. With its modes and complicated harmony, Western music has opened up fresh vistas of musical thought and occasioned increasing dissatisfaction with Japanese music. Demands are accordingly being made for reforms, and to a certain extent Japanese music has already been influenced by music from the West.

●Fine Arts

The beginnings of Japanese fine arts can be traced back 1,500 or 1,600 years, from which time they have steadily developed down to the present day. There are many reasons to account for this remarkable continuity. One is that the country abounds in natural beauty, conducive to the growth of art and an artistic temperament. The Japanese are also imaginative by nature, a characteristic that stimulates the creation of works of art. But the most important cause of all is the patronage given to the fine arts by the Imperial House, which has not only prevented their decline, but has truly encouraged their growth. The protection of the arts was one of the duties relegated to the military class in the Middle Ages by the Imperial House, and the warrior chiefs did not fail in fulfilling their duty.

The Japanese fine arts have at various times been modified by foreign influences. First, the Chinese fine arts (including those of Korea) gained prestige. In turn, they brought in their train the influence of Indian, Persian and even Grecian and Roman fine arts. The introduction of the Indian fine arts resulted from the spread of Buddhism into China. This is also true of Persian and the ancient Western fine arts. Since the early 19th century, the Japanese fine arts were gradually influenced by those of Western Europe.

While the influence of the Chinese fine arts was considerable and cannot be overlooked in any discussion of the subject, as time went on the Japanese fine arts began to develop their own unique characteristics. At the beginning of the Heian period, these peculiarities may be said to have combined to the point where Japanese fine arts could be distinguished from the fine arts of other nations.

About the same time, a parallel development in literature occurred as a manifestation of the national character, and this, in turn, brought a reaction in the fine arts. Henceforth, the Japanese arts became independent of religion, to which they had been closely interrelated.

The following periods in the development of the Japanese fine arts are generally recognized (not necessarily corresponding to those in history):

1. Archaic period, prior to introduction of Buddhism (552 A.D.)
2. Asuka period (552-645)
3. Nara period (645-794)
4. Early Heian period (794-897)
5. Late Heian period (897-1185)
6. Kamakura period (1185-1392)
7. Muromachi period (1392-1573)
8. Momoyama period (1573-1615)
9. Edo period (1615-1867)
10. Meiji period (1868-1912)
11. Taisho period (1912-1926)

12. Showa period (1926-1989)
13. Heisei period (1989-   )

The period previous to the introduction of Buddhism covers prehistoric as well as protohistoric times. Even then, native art was guided by inspirations drawn from the Asian continent. Progress was so rapid that the highly developed arts of the continent were readily accepted and assimilated during the following Asuka period.

In the Asuka period, Buddhist influence on the fine arts was strongly marked. Great progress was made in architecture, sculpture, painting and allied arts. The best examples are to be found in the Horyuji Temple near Nara. The fine arts of the period came chiefly from Korea, but their style can be traced to the Northern and Southern Dynasties of China.

The Nara period is generally divided into the Hakuho (645-709) and Tempyo (710-794) periods. In the Hakuho period, the Chinese arts of the Sui and early T'ang Dynasties were imported directly from China instead of coming via Korea. In the Tempyo period, Kegon-kyo (Avatamaska Sutra) Buddhism was introduced. Since its doctrines tended to encourage the growth of an idealistic art, it wrought considerable influence. It was also during this period that the arts of the Kai-yuan and the Tien-pao periods of the T'ang Dynasty of China were introduced to Japan.

The early Heian period began with the establishment of Heiankyo (now, Kyoto) as the capital in 794. During this period, esoteric Buddhism (Guhyayana) was introduced from China by such noted Japanese priests as Kukai (Kobo-Daishi) and Saicho (Dengyo-Daishi). A style of art derived from the doctrines of esoteric Buddhism came into vogue. Thereafter, painting and sculpture became a regular part of the study of Buddhism. At the same time, Chinese literature, law and politics were introduced into Japan, exercising an influence on the fine arts.

In the late Heian period, the national consciousness began to awake, manifesting itself in the fine arts as well as in literature—all of which began to display unique characteristics. The applied arts also made remarkable progress, partly because of the adoption of new designs and plans that the progress of painting brought within reach. In religion, the doctrines of esoteric Buddhism were no longer in favor, giving way to the Jodo doctrine, which was forcibly expounded by Eshin (942-1017).

The Kamakura period began with the overthrow of the Tairas in 1185 by the Minamotos, who founded a Shogunate at Kamakura in 1192. The cultivation of the arts was in the hands of the Kyoto Court nobles, who were encouraged by the military administration at Kamakura.

In the succeeding Muromachi period, the Ashikaga family established its Shogunate government in Kyoto. Among the Ashikaga Shogun, Yoshimasa (1435-1490) is celebrated as a patron of the arts.

It was he who encouraged the cult of the tea ceremony, helping it to develop into a refined social entertainment, with which the arts of incense burning and flower-arranging were closely connected. Zen Buddhism became popular in the Kamakura period, with the result that toward the close of this period, the simplicity and refinement characteristic of the faith had affected the arts of the country.

The Momoyama period, although short, was pregnant with new issues. Oda Nobunaga and Toyotomi Hideyoshi endeavored to promote a new and vigorous civilization through their military policies. The results were fresh and bold, bringing the elimination of religion as the motif of art. At the same time, however, there were some noteworthy attempts to revive the old style of the Heian period.

The Edo period covers the time of the Tokugawa Shogunate government at Edo (the present Tokyo). During the early years of this period, the various Tokugawa Shogun were very assiduous in persuading scholars and artists to migrate from Kyoto to Edo, making Edo a rival art center to Kyoto. Almost every branch of the fine arts showed great activity. Besides architecture and painting, the applied arts like lacquerwork, metalwork, ceramics and weaving all made striking developments.

The art of the Ming and Ch'ing Dynasties of China also exerted considerable influence on painting, as shown in the development of the *nanga* school, which includes the *bunjinga* school. The influence of the Western fine arts also became noticeable after the middle of this period, owing to the study of Dutch books, particularly those on the art of painting.

The modern period commenced with the Meiji Restoration in 1868 when the Shogunate was abolished and power returned to the Emperor. Edo was renamed Tokyo and made the national capital that same year.

Painting

Characteristics of Japanese Painting

Whereas in the West, painting in oil colors has received the largest amount of attention, in Japan interest has been chiefly directed to painting in water colors. The water color dissolves in liquid glue as in the case of *sumi*-ink, which is made of vegetable lampblack mixed with glue. Pictures done entirely in *sumi*-ink are called *sumi-e*, but often the pigment is used side by side with various colors.

In figure painting, Western art strives to bring out the beauty of the human form. Oriental artists, on the other hand, try to portray figures by putting greater stress on action than on form itself, especially when the object is to depict something superhuman such as a Buddha or a god. Oriental art generally excels in pictorializing action rather than form, a trend most evident in Japanese paintings, especially in the *sumi-e* of the Muromachi period and the *nanga* productions of the Edo period.

Japanese landscape painting dates back to the Heian period when many charming scenes were produced on the folding screens of the palaces. This type of art, therefore, may be said to antedate that of Europe where all the great works of landscape painting have been produced within the last two centuries. Oriental landscape painting takes a broader view than that favored by artists in the West where the field of vision is purposely narrowed. For its guiding principle, it has three distant views—"high and distant," "distant and profound" and "flat but distant." Mountains soaring high into the clouds and a mist in the distance as well as scenes characterized by vastness and profundity are favored. This naturally presents a completely different appearance to the paintings.

From the point of view of art or technique, there is a striking difference between Oriental and Occidental painting. Whereas in the West the artist uses a model in his studio, painting from nature is unusual in the East, both in figure and landscape painting. It is true that the Japanese artist sketches from nature, but this is merely for purposes of reference in preparing the real work. As a rule, the Japanese artist draws freely from his imagination and memory.

Finally, whatever the object painted, Japanese art endeavors to convey a sense of action or movement. This is accomplished by the manner in which the strokes are made.

Religious Paintings in the Early Period

Prior to the introduction of Buddhism, there was little development in the art of painting in Japan. It was from China through Korea that Japan received its first great inspiration in art along with its first lessons in Buddhism. Accordingly, early efforts in art were of a religious nature. The pictures painted on the doors and panels of the *Tamamushi-no-Zushi* (Golden Beetle Miniature Shrine, refer to p.729) in the Treasure Hall of the Horyuji Temple near Nara are the finest examples of the early paintings of the Asuka period. They were inspired by the introduction of Buddhism. (The shrine received its name because it is decorated with the iridescent wing-sheaths of a beautiful beetle called *tamamushi*, arranged under openwork fittings of gilt bronze on the edges of the pedestal.) The mural paintings representing the Buddhist paradise in the Main Hall of the Horyuji Temple, are unique examples of the style developed in the early Nara period, closely resembling the style then prevailing in Central Asia. Refer to p.727 (Unfortunately, they were damaged in the fire of January 26, 1949. The walls containing the pictures were removed and are currently housed in a new hall especially constructed for them.)

In the Tempyo period (710-794), painting made a remarkable advance under the cultural influence of the T'ang Dynasty in China. The figure of *Kisshoten*, or Goddess of Beauty, of the Yakushiji

Temple and the painting on a folding screen known as "Lady Under a Tree," preserved in the Shosoin Repository at Nara, are good examples of Tempyo period paintings.

Heian period

Japanese painting entered a period of great development in the Heian period. One reason was due to the growth of esoteric Buddhism, which, for purposes of invocation, made use of Mandalas of the Holy Worlds as well as pictures of Buddhist divinities and other religious paintings. The sect thus attached special importance to painting. Furthermore, the new doctrine of *Amida* (Jodo Buddhism), propagated by the priest Eshin, came to the fore in the Heian period, producing a profound effect on the art of painting.

Among the Buddhist paintings of this period, those representing the Buddha Amitabha and his Bodhsattvas coming down from heaven to welcome the faithful are the most important. There is an excellent work of this kind, attributed to Eshin, at the Daien-in Temple of the Kongobuji Temple on Mt.Koya near Osaka.

A notable development of the period was the progress made by secular art as distinguished from religious painting. This may be seen in the *nise-e*, or portraits, and in the *emakimono* (picture scrolls illustrating stories). One of the most celebrated of the latter is the series by Takayoshi that illustrate "Genji Monogatari," a novel written by the celebrated authoress of the Heian period, Murasaki-Shikibu.

Besides the growing demand for landscape paintings in the Heian period, many scenes from nature were also painted on the sliding doors of the Imperial Palace and folding screens.

The decline of Chinese influence during the period should also be noted, with the development of Japanese art culminating during the Kamakura period in the creation of *Yamato-e*. This is the painting in pure Japanese style in contrast to *Kara-e*, or Chinese-style painting.

Kamakura and Muromachi Periods

The Kamakura period may be regarded as an extension of the Heian period, except that the technique became more polished and refined. Both the secular and religious paintings of this period show an improvement in artistic quality as the Japanese style gradually attained perfection.

At this point, however, a new style of Chinese art—the style of the Sung and Yuan Dynasties—began to influence Japanese art. Since the result was a still-wider separation between the *Yamato-e* and *Kara-e* schools, the paintings of the two schools may be distinguished at a glance. As a rule, the paintings of the *Yamato-e* school are characterized by exquisitely fine detail and bright pigmentation. The Chinese school, characterized by the influence of the Sung-Yuan paintings, grew with the spread of the doctrines of Zen Buddhism. It also used color, but placed more emphasis on black-and-white art, differing from that of the *Yamato-e* school by putting more stress on the gradation of color.

The middle of the Kamakura period had already witnessed the rise of the Chinese style. In the Muromachi period, it was flourishing side by side with the Tosa school, which was producing such great masters as Yukimitsu, Yukihiro and Mitsunobu. But Mitsunobu (1434 -1525) was the last of the masters of *Yamato-e* for soon after his demise it began to decline.

Two priests, Mincho and Josetsu, were important in popularizing Chinese art during the Muromachi period. It was Shubun, another priest and a pupil of Josetsu, who brought the Chinese style to perfection, however. Sesshu (refer to p.767), his pupil, continued the tradition. After him came a long line of artists, the most noted being the painters of the Kano school. This school, founded by Masanobu —a retainer of the Ashikaga Shogun, claimed to be the direct descendant of the *Yamato-e* masters. It maintained its prosperity throughout the Muromachi and Edo periods.

Modern Schools of Painting

Of the ancient arts of Japan, there was hardly one which was not derived from religious influences. After the Momoyama period, however, religion ceased to exercise its former influence. With a clear distinction being drawn between religious culture and general civilization, art grew entirely independent of religion. This was also the case with architecture, but painting developed more freely and created many schools. Here is a general survey of the art of painting developed during the Momoyama period and continuing throughout the Edo period, according to the principal schools:

Beginning with the Kano school, revolutionary changes were effected in its style and technique by Eitoku (1543-1590). Under the patronage of Nobunaga and Hideyoshi, he created the wall and screen paintings of the Azuchi and Osaka castles on a far larger scale than was formerly attempted. Sanraku (1559-1635), a pupil of Eitoku, followed in the foot steps of his master, striving to bring the new style to perfection.

When the Tokugawa Shogunate was established in Edo, it strove to transplant the arts of Kyoto there, inviting the leaders of the Kano school to take up residence in the new capital. One of those invited was Tan-yu (1602-1674). Although he lacked Eitoku's breadth and scope, nevertheless he was very successful in blending the Japanese and Chinese styles of painting. Tan-yu's descendants were appointed official painters to the Tokugawa Shogunate and continued to hold this position through the Edo period down to the Restoration in 1868.

The Tosa school went into eclipse with the fall of the Ashikaga family, but it was revived in the Momoyama period. It achieved distinction at the beginning of the Edo period under the leadership of

Mitsuoki (1617-1691), but after him the Tosa school scarcely produced any painters of note. Toward the close of the Edo period, artists appeared who endeavored to return to the old *Yamato-e* style, independent of the traditional Tosa school. The leader of this movement was Okada Tamechika (1823-1864), who worked out a more or less new style by immersing himself in ancient methods.

The Sotatsu and Korin school originated with Hon-ami Koetsu (1558-1637), who, while following the old style of the Heian period, added charm and elegance to it. Other artists of this school were Tawaraya Sotatsu and Ogata Korin (1658-1716), both of whom rose to fame in the Genroku era (1688-1704). This was the most prosperous period under the Tokugawa administration, as luxury and extravagance reached a high point and the entire nation enjoyed some measure of wealth. Korin entered into the spirit of the times, throwing his heart and soul into the creation of beautiful works of great ornamental value. Thus, he helped to bring the decorative techniques of the Sotatsu and Korin school to their highest point.

The Maruyama school was founded by Maruyama Okyo (1733-1795), whose pictures are not only very true to nature, but also have great decorative value. He appears to have been the first to apply to Japanese painting the principles of perspective as developed in the West.

The Shijo school, a branch of the Maruyama school, was started by Matsumura Goshun (1752-1811). He first studied under Yosa Buson of the *nanga* school, but later received instructions in technique from Okyo. In fact, his works are regarded as even more elegant than Okyo's.

The *nanga* school of painting, introduced from China, came into prominence after the middle of the Edo period. In Chinese painting, there was a broad distinction between the Northern and Southern schools, the former being characterized by vigor and the latter by softness. The *nanga* (lit. Southern-pictures) school, as the name denotes, was the Southern. Although it had acquired distinction in China since ancient times, it was only introduced into Japan in the 18th century. The artists who followed this style and converted it into an independent school of Japanese painting were Ike-no-Taiga or Taigado, (1723-1776) and Yosa Buson (1716-1783).

Besides being a great admirer of the work of Ni Yun-lin, Taiga was also influenced by the paintings of I Fu-Chiu, who came to Japan in the Kyoho era (1716-1735). Taiga chiefly favored landscape painting done with a very slight use of color. Buson, a famous *haiku* poet, followed nature very closely in his landscape paintings. Although Chinese in form and style, his pictures often astonished observers with their natural appearance. In this respect, he surpassed Taiga, his intimate friend.

Toward the close of the Edo period, a galaxy of painters appeared, the most noted of whom were Tanomura Chikuden (1777-1835) and

Watanabe Kazan (1793-1841, refer to p.596). Chikuden, a man of lofty sentiment, is noted for the high tone of his work, while Kazan—a learned scholar of Confucian literature who had also studied foreign affairs through Dutch literature—is also famous for the originality of his ideas and the ease of his style. Chikuden was most gifted in landscape painting in the style of the *nanga* school, while Kazan not only excelled in landscape painting, but also in figures, flowers and birds.

The *ukiyo-e* school first made its appearance in the early part of the 17th century. Meaning "Floating World," *ukiyo* was originally a Buddhist term contrasting the floating secular world with the reality of the spiritual. During the Edo period, it came to mean the world of pleasure and pictures in the school. It is somewhat different from the so-called genre pictures, which had been in vogue much earlier. Principally, it is the work of artists of the *Yamato-e* school, who were fond of painting historic scenes. The genre pictures were intended for the appreciation of the upper strata of society—not for the masses.

The *ukiyo-e* school, on the other hand, aimed at appealing to the masses, portraying beautiful women, erotic scenes and actors. At first, the works appeared as illustrations for books, but later independent prints were produced. Indeed, it was in the creation of prints that the *ukiyo-e* school chiefly devoted its labors, and, in fact, there was not a single painter of this school who was not so engaged.

Iwasa Matabei (1578-1650) is popularly considered as the father of the *ukiyo-e* school, although the genre pictures that he painted were not intended for the lower classes. It is, therefore, improper to call him an *ukiyo-e* painter. Actually, it is difficult to select any single individual as the originator of *ukiyo-e*. But Hishikawa Moronobu, who flourished in the Genroku era (1688-1704), was the first great master to contribute to the development of the *ukiyo-e* school. Most of Moronobu's pictures were drawn for wood-block engravings, but he also left some excellent paintings. An examination of the latter makes it clear that he must have first studied the Tosa and Kano styles before working out his own style.

As technical skill progressed, *ukiyo-e* grew more popular, especially in Edo. Suzuki Harunobu (1725-1770) produced *Azuma-Nishiki-e*, a portraits of beautiful women in polychrome prints. He was followed by such great artists as Kitagawa Utamaro (1753-1806), Toshusai-Sharaku (? - ?), Utagawa Toyokuni (1769-1825), Katsushika Hokusai (1760-1849) and Utagawa Hiroshige (1797-1858)—all of whom achieved tremendous popularity.

Color Prints

The origin of Japanese *hanga* (wood-block prints), though not exactly known, may be traced as far back as the Nara period. It must, however, be attributed to the great efforts of the *ukiyo-e* painters that such prints attained real merit as works of art. Color prints made from drawings of the *ukiyo-e* school depicted scenes in everyday life and portraits of contemporary actors and favorite beauties. At first, they were not seriously received by artistic circles, being sold largely to the common people.

The Japanese color prints in the Edo period were produced with the cooperation of three different artists—a painter, an engraver and a printer. The process of making color prints in the Edo period was as follows: The artist first draws the picture in black and white; this is known as the *shita-e*, or "foundation picture." It is drawn on translucent paper, which is pasted face down on a block of wood, usually cherry. The block is sawed with the grain—not across it as is done in Europe—and then scraped until every detail of the design becomes clearly visible. After the thin, remaining layer is oiled, the engraving work begins. The borders of the outline are incised first with a knife, then the spaces between the lines of the drawing are excavated by means of chisels.

In printing, the color is applied with a brush and the impression is made by hand pressure assisted by a kind of pad. The beauty of the print depends on the skill with which the pressure is applied. Gradations of tone and color may be produced from a single block. In fact, considerable artistic feeling can be expressed during the printing operation. Uninked blocks for embossing a portion of the design were used as early as 1730. The effects resulting from two or more blocks were obtained in some cases by preparing a single block with different-colored ink or with different shades of the same color. The tones of sky and water were graded in the same manner. The superfluity of color, where lighter shades were required, was removed by wiping the inked block with a cloth. The usual method of obtaining color effects, however, was done with the use of several blocks, with the number corresponding to the number of colors to be produced. The ordinary size of color prints is 36 cm by 20 cm as blocks of a larger size were inclined to warp.

Many artists have made Japan's color prints famous. Shunsho, Sharaku and Toyokuni are well known for their portraits of actors; Harunobu, Kiyonaga, Eishi, Utamaro and Toyokuni for their pictures of beautiful women. In landscapes, Hokusai and Hiroshige produced superior works. Hokusai's views of Mt.Fuji are favorites with foreign collectors as are his series of Chinese poets and their poems—ten tall prints in which figures and landscape are combined in a very attractive manner.

Hiroshige's views of scenes along the Tokaido Highway and Edo, and especially the masterpieces—the 53 stages on the Tokaido Highway—are also well known. Prints of birds and flowers, often with a few lines of poetry, are also very popular. Truly, Hiroshige's exquisite works are deservedly famous.

Sculpture

The art of sculpture in Japan prior to the Meiji period was mostly confined to the carving of Buddhist images, although images of national deities and portrait statuary were occasionally produced.

The first historic reference to sculpture in Japan was in regard to the work of Shiba-Tatto, a Chinese sculptor who came to Japan in 522 A.D. His son Tasuna and his grandson Tori were the master artists of their day. Many of the sculptures of the time are attributed to Tori, including the gilt bronze figures of Buddha and his two attendants in the Horyuji Temple near Nara. The inscription on the back of the halo attached to the main figure states that it was cast by Tori in 623 A.D. Excellent examples of images in gilt bronze are preserved in the Imperial Household collection. Known as the "Forty-eight Buddhist Images," they are representative examples of the sculpture of the day.

The powerful influence which Buddhism had begun to exercise is shown by the specimens of sculpture in the Nara period that have come down to the present. Foremost among the excellent works of the period is the colossal figure of Buddha (in a sitting posture) at Todaiji Temple at Nara. Known as the Nara *Daibutsu*, it was cast by order of Emperor Shomu and completed in 749. It is the largest cast statue ever produced in Japan, measuring 16.2 m in height. Kuninaka-muraji Kimimaro was the artist mainly responsible for this bronze work.

The supremacy of esoteric Buddhism in the Heian period stimulated the production of Buddhist images of a symbolical, mythical character. The best examples are to be seen at Muroji Temple near Nara and Kongobuji Temple on Mt. Koya. About the time that Buddhism began to be nationalized through the efforts of the priest Eshin in the late Heian period, a Buddhist sculptor with a new technique appeared on the scene named Jocho (d. 1057). Some of Jocho's masterpieces are still preserved, the most noteworthy of which are the images of *Amida* at the Hokaiji and Byodo-in temples in Kyoto.

Japanese sculpture made fair growth in the Nara and Heian periods, but attained its highest technical development in the Kamakura period when it freed itself from Chinese influences. The age produced many great sculptors, including Unkei, Kaikei and Tankei, who were the most influential. The two wooden statues of *Kongo-rikishi* (Deva Kings) in the portal of *Nandaimon* Gate of Todaiji Temple (refer to p.715) are said to be the joint creations of Unkei and Kaikei. The sitting image of *Senju-Kannon* at Rengeo-in (Sanjusan-gendo) Temple in Kyoto is Tankei's work.

Considerable progress was also made in the art of casting bronze images. The Great Buddha, or *Daibutsu*, of the Kotoku-in Temple at Kamakura (refer to p.431) is, among others, eloquent proof of this advance. Cast in the Kencho era (1249-1255), it is about 13 m high, including the pedestal.

The Kamakura period may be regarded as the golden age of the art of sculpture in Japan, with practically no further development being made later. The Muromachi period that followed witnessed the rise of the Zen sect of Buddhism, which does not attach as much importance to the production of sacred images as the other sects. It was natural, therefore, that religious sculpture should fall into decay, a trend that continued into the Momoyama and Edo periods when the only activity in the form of sculptural art was the carving of masks for *noh* drama.

However, the decline of religious sculpture after the Muromachi period was compensated to some extent by the rise of decorative sculpture for architectural purposes. The handsome palaces built in the period brought into being what was known as "temple carving," which included the carving of human figures, birds, animal, flowers, etc. in the form of pictorial designs.

Although the carving of images made no progress during the Edo period, architectural carving was developed along with various minor arts such as metal, pottery and lacquerwork—applications of sculptural art that are strictly a modern phenomenon. In the modern period, too, French influence has been conspicuous, especially in plaster-modeling and casting.

Sculptural art during the Edo period was in the hands of mere craftsmen and not of artists in the strict sense of the term. With the advent of the Meiji period, a turning point was reached in the history of Japanese sculpture as a result of the introduction of Western-style techniques, the invitation of talented Western artists and various other factors.

Handicrafts

Metalwork

Metalwork seems to have been the first of the handicrafts in which any skill was developed, judging by the specimens which have come down to the present time from the earliest period. One of these specimens is the grand banner made of gilt bronze, which formerly belonged to Horyuji Temple but is now a part of the collection of the Imperial Household. Designed for hanging from the ceiling, it is about 7 m (23 ft) in length, with the top forming a canopy from which draperies and pendants are hung. The metal fittings of the canopy are of excellent design and delicate workmanship.

Amakuni, who flourished in the Taiho era (701-704), is often regarded as the pioneer sword smith of Japan. His outstanding work was a sword he forged for Emperor Mommu (683-707).

The Shosoin Repository at Nara is a veritable treasure house for this period, containing as it does more than a thousand articles presented to Todaiji Temple in 756 A.D. Most of the items were the property of Emperor Shomu, including swords, mirrors, dress, ornaments, musical instruments and weapons of war.

In the Heian period (794–1185), marked progress was made in the development of handicrafts, especially in metal and lacquerware. The metal fittings in the *Konjikido* (Main Hall) of Chusonji Temple in Iwate Prefecture and of the sutra casket presented by the Taira family to Itsukushima Shrine at Miyajima are excellent specimens of the work of this period.

From that time to the Kamakura period, the military spirit ensured continual progress in the manufacture of armor and swords. Myochin, the most celebrated of the armor-makers, lived in Kyoto around the middle of the 12th century. From his genius sprang a long line of Myochin smiths lasting for ten generations. Since the sword was regarded as the soul of the *samurai*, sword smiths took the foremost place in the ranks of craftsmen. Their number must have been considerable, seeing that the names of those recorded alone amount to over 20,000. The most famous craftsmen were Yoshimitsu, Masamune and Yoshihiro.

There was notable development in metalwork in the 15th century. Goto Yujo (1440–1512), who was a page of the eighth Ashikaga Shogun Yoshimasa, introduced a new era in the art of metal engraving by founding the Goto school. In its field, it is as famous as the Kano school is in painting. The art of making swordguards was also elevated to a specialty, the Munetada family standing foremost among the noted craftsmen.

Remarkable development was also made in casting owing to the popularity of the tea ceremony. The articles produced were chiefly iron kettles, but many of them were designed by such masters as Sesshu and Tosa Mitsunobu. In this work, the Ashiya family of Fukuoka Prefecture, Kyushu, was highly regarded. Good work was also done at Temmyo in Sano in the present Tochigi Prefecture.

During the Edo period (1615–1868), remarkable development was registered in every branch of handicraft arts due to the increased demand throughout the country. It was during this period that a popular style called *machibori*, used for the decoration of metalware as distinct from sword decoration, was created by Yokoya Somin (1670–1733) and other masters of the art.

Among the Kyoto artists of this period, Ichinomiya Nagatsune (1722–1786) must be regarded as the best in his special line of metal engraving. Among others of note, Goto Ichijo (1791–1876) revived the classic style modified by the pictorial method. The master casters of this period were Kanaya Gorosaburo, who worked in Kyoto early in the 18th century, and Murata Seimin (1761-1837), a master of wax modeling.

Among later developments was inlay, of which there are several styles.

Lacquerware

The production of lacquerware in Japan dates from very ancient times, having been introduced from China in the early years of intercourse with that country (seventh century). By the 11th century, the production of gold lacquer was being encouraged by the demands of the upper classes. In the 13th century, improvements were made in lacquer mixing as well as in the art of gold and silver inlay. A new style of polished lacquerware had also been created. It was known as *Negoro-nuri* after the Negoroji Temple in Wakayama Prefecture where it was first made. A rustic style of carving and lacquering called *Kamakura-bori* had also developed. Rough designs were first carved in bold relief and then lacquered black and red.

The 14th and 15th centuries brought further improvements in the art, especially in gold lacquering and raised gold lacquerwork. Nashiji lacquerware made by sprinkling gold dust to produce the dotted appearance of a Japanese pear skin also came into favor. In fact, the art attained such a high level by the middle of the 15th century that Chinese lacquer artists were being sent over to Japan to learn the secrets of the local artisans. It is recorded that gold lacquerware was especially preferred by the Chinese court whenever the *shogun* sent gifts.

Among the noted lacquer artists of this period, mention must first be made of Koami Michinaga (1410–1478), personal attendant to Shogun Yoshimasa. He is known for his outstanding work in *takamaki-e* (raised and polished work). Such famous painters as Tosa Mitsunobu (1434–1525), Noami (1397–1471), Soami (d. 1525) and others supplied him with designs. Igarashi Shinsai was another noted lacquer artist who flourished in the time of Shogun Yoshimasa.

Further progress was made from the latter Muromachi to the Momoyama periods, chiefly because of the patronage extended to the art by the *shogun*. Such noted Kyoto lacquer artists as Koami, Choho, Kyui and others were invited to make their homes in Edo (now, Tokyo). Kyui was the founder of a long line of lacquer artisans who were patronized by the *shogun*. He himself was in the service of the third Tokugawa Shogun, Iemitsu. Koami Nagashige (1599–1651) served both at the Kyoto Court and at that of the *shogun*, producing works characterized by refinement of tone. Ogata Korin (1658–1716) and his master Hon-ami Koetsu (1558–1637), both previously mentioned as painters, also produced lacquerware of unique artistic design. Koetsu's activity as an artist covers a very wide sphere as he was well versed in calligraphy and painting as well as ceramic and lacquerwork. Korin, another talented artist like his teacher Koetsu, founded a unique type of design popularly known as *Korin-moyo* (Korin design). His lacquerwork is characterized by mother-of-pearl inlay.

The development of the art was greatly encouraged by the observance of the tea ceremony and incense-burning, which were in vogue about that time. Small, highly decorated *inro* (medicine boxes) became popular among the *samurai* and merchants, also serving to stimulate interest in the art.

The fame of Kaga Province (now, Ishikawa Prefecture) for the production of lacquerware dates from the middle of the 16th century, when Igarashi Doho, originally in the service of Shogun Yoshimasa, was invited by the lord of Kaga to settle in his domain. He and his son Kisaburo thus founded the Kaga style of lacquerware. Tokyo, Kyoto and Kanazawa are still, as in the past, the principal centers for the production of high-grade lacquerware. Next come Takamatsu and Nagoya. Inexpensive ware for daily use is made in Fukushima, Ishikawa, Toyama, Wakayama and other prefectures.

Ceramics

Specimens of the oldest glazed pottery in Japan are found among the eighth century treasures in the Shosoin Repository in Nara. The origin of what is truly worthy of being called ceramic art, however, is generally regarded to have been in the beginning of the 13th century, when an artisan named Kato Shirozaemon (1169–1249)—also known as Toshiro (refer to p.581)—introduced Chinese ceramic techniques. After his return from China, he established a ceramic kiln at Seto in Owari Province (now, Aichi Prefecture), where he produced the first Chinese-style pottery in Japan. Thereafter, from the Kamakura to Muromachi periods, Seto thrived as the center of ceramic production in this country. As a result, the term *setomono* (Seto ware) has become a popular synonym for pottery.

The progress of the art received encouragement in the 16th century through the popularity of the tea ceremony. As all the utensils used in the ceremony were supposed to represent the finest efforts of the artists, there was keen competition in providing porcelain suitable for the occasion. New kilns were established in various parts of the country. The one in Arita, established in 1598, deserves special mention. It was built by Lee-San P'ing, a Korean potter, who came over from Korea that year.

In the Edo period, the art of ceramic ware developed to a very high level, independent of Chinese influence. Almost every province came to have a kiln, each with its own unique type of products. Among the most noted examples are *Arita-yaki* of Saga Prefecture, *Kyo-yaki* of Kyoto and *Kutani-yaki* of Ishikawa Prefecture.

Cloisonné Ware

The origin of *shippo* (cloisonné ware) remains unknown, but it can be traced to very olden times as specimens are preserved in the Shosoin Repository at Nara. It is chiefly made at Nagoya, but is also produced in Kyoto, Tokyo and Yokohama. The discovery of new cloisonné methods in 1880 by Namikawa Sosuke (1847–1910) of

Tokyo led to a sudden demand for the ware. Later developments included the use of silver bodies in place of copper, the production of ware with transparent designs in the French style and the use of gold chloride for the production of reddish monochromes.

Glassware

The first glass objects in Japan were produced around the fourth and fifth century. The manufactured objects, however, were secondary produce made from sheet glass imported from China. The sheet glass was melted and made into necklace beads, bracelets and similar items. Beads were manufactured in great quantities during the Nara period from the early to late eighth century, but they were used more often for decorating Buddhist icons, ritual objects and sanctuaries than as personal ornaments. They are also found among *chindangu* —valuables buried for the purpose of consecrating the building site of a Buddhist sanctuary or pagoda. The set of *chindangu* found under the Great Buddha Hall of the Todaiji Temple in Nara contains numerous glass beads together with those of jadeite, amber and rock crystal, indicating that glass was valued as highly as precious and semiprecious materials.

The Shosoin Repository in Nara, built during the eighth century, houses innumerable art treasures. They include a cut-glass bowl brought from Persia through China, glass stemcups from China as well as small, native glass products such as fish-shaped pendants and scaled foot rules used as ornaments to be worn at the waist. The art of glassmaking, however, gradually declined after the ninth century.

It was probably during the early 17th century that the production of glassware was renewed. Japan had contacts with Europe for the first time in 1543. The first glass items from Europe reached Japan in 1549, when the Jesuit missionary Francisco de Xavier presented Ouchi Yoshitaka, a *daimyo* (feudal lord), with a mirror, telescope and other gifts. Not long after the importation of European glass, glass-making methods were introduced to Nagasaki around the beginning of the 17th century. In the early 18th century, glass also began to be produced in Osaka.

Splendid examples of cut glass were turned out at Kagoshima in Kyushu during the second half of the 19th century. Satsuma glass originated in 1846 at a laboratory of medicines and chemicals established by the Shimazu family, which ruled this district. In 1855, Shimazu Nariakira, lord of the Satsuma clan, expanded the glass factory and encouraged its activity.

Cut glassware known as *Satsuma kiriko* was produced at this factory. At the factory were more than 10 kilns of various types, with more than 120 craftsmen working there. The quality of *Satsuma kiriko* was such that a Dutch visitor to the factory recommended it as "worthy enough to be displayed at an exhibition in Europe." The manufacture of *Satsuma kiriko* declined after the death of Nariakira, but about that time a fine cut glassware known as *Edo kiriko* was already being produced in Edo (the present Tokyo). A government glass factory was established in 1873 at Shinagawa, Tokyo, and other post-Restoration factories were soon able to produce tableware lamps and bottles, although sheet glass was not produced until early 20th century.

Netsuke

The carving of ornamental *netsuke* was practiced throughout the Tokugawa regime. *Netsuke* is a kind of toggle by which purses, pouches, *inro* (medicine boxes), etc. are suspended from the girdle. There was a great demand by the merchants for ornaments that would vie with the ornamental sword guards of the *daimyo* and *samurai*. *Netsuke* date from the latter part of the Momoyama period, but it was not until the latter part of the 17th century that *netsuke* ornamentation reached the dignity of a special art. However, the international campaign against trading in ivory and Japan's ban on ivory imports, the material from which *netsuke* are made, have placed the future of this traditional craft in jeopardy.

●Architecture

Ancient Japanese Architecture

Japan's architecture has developed almost entirely in wood as befits a country extensively covered with forests. As a result of fires and the ravages of war, however, ancient wooden structures are now few and far between. Nevertheless, through the practice of replacing structures thus destroyed with exact replicas of the original, it is possible to reconstruct primitive Japanese architecture and follow the course of its development.

As a rule, Japanese architecture is characterized by simplicity, regularity and refinement. Even solidly constructed castles, some fine examples of which have escaped the ravages of time, are distinguished by lightness and airiness—a tribute to the skill of their architects.

While the Japanese developed a primitive architecture, they owe much to China for modifying and influencing it. As in so many other instances, religion has played a leading part. It was through the construction of places of worship that native Japanese architecture progressed. Moreover, further advances were achieved through the design of buildings constructed for the study of Buddhism, which was introduced from China. In fact, the influence of Buddhism on Japan cannot be overestimated in any respect, and certainly not in the field of architecture, which has twice—in the seventh and eighth centuries and again in the 13th century—drawn direct inspiration from the neighboring continent.

Prior to the Introduction of Buddhism

A general idea of ancient Japanese architecture before the introduction of Buddhism may be obtained from Shinto shrines, the finest
examples of which are the Ise Jingu Shrine at Ise and the Izumo
Taisha Shrine at Taisha Town near Matsue. Although they have
been reconstructed many times, their primitive form has been preserved. The Izumo Taisha Shrine's Main Hall is a square wooden
structure with four corner pillars, between which are side pillars.
Two of the side pillars are high enough to support the ridgepole.
There is a thick pillar in the center.

A notable feature of the building is the crossed ends of the rafters
used to support the ridgepole. These crosspieces are called *chigi*. As
improved methods of construction were developed, they came to be
regarded merely as ornaments, especially since the ends were embellished with carvings. The roof is thatched. To keep the thatch in
position, two poles are laid lengthwise on it. Short, cigar-shaped logs
called *katsuogi* are placed crosswise and secured to the thatch to keep
the poles from moving.

The facade of the building is at the gabled ends, with the entrance
placed to one side rather than in the center. Unlike the Izumo Taisha
Shrine, the Ise Jingu Shrine is oblong in shape. The facade in this
case is at the side, while the entrance is in the middle.

The Izumo Taisha Shrine is shaped like an ancient dwelling house
and is supposed to have originally been the house of Okuninushi-no-
Mikoto, to whose spirit the shrine is dedicated. This is not the case
with the Ise Jingu Shrine, however, which was first built as, and in the
form of, a shrine. The shrine structures do not have quite as grand
a scale as the main building of the Izumo Taisha Shrine, but there is
something profound and awe-inspiring about them. This impression
is heightened all the more because of its location in the depths of a
forest. Accessory structures to these shrines include a kind of
beamed pylon called a *torii* (Shinto gate) and wooden fences.

After the Introduction of Buddhism

Although Chinese architecture did have some influence on native
Japanese architecture before the arrival of Buddhism, it was only in
the sixth century with the construction of Buddhist temples that this
influence became conspicuous. Temple architecture developed as
early as the reign of Empress-Regnant Suiko (reigned 592–628) and
made further progress with the encouragement of Prince-Regent
Shotoku (574–622, refer to p.85). It was during this period that the
Horyuji Temple was built near Nara. Part of the original structure
still stands, and is thought to be the oldest wooden structure in the
world.

The chief features of the temples built in this period may be summarized as follows. The main structures were located in an enclosure surrounded by a double fence. They included a *goju-no-to* (five-story pagoda) in which sacred relics were kept; the *kondo* (gold hall or main hall), which housed the image of the Buddha to whom the temple was dedicated; the *kodo* (sermon hall), a short distance behind; the *kyozo* (scripture house), standing to the left of the sermon hall, and the *shoro* (belfry) to the right of the main hall. All these structures were connected with each other by a continuous corridor that circumscribed the grounds in the shape of a square.

A similar arrangement of buildings can be seen in the Shitennoji Temple at Osaka. These buildings have stone foundations, tile roofs and a red-painted exterior. The pillars have a defined entasis and stand on granite bases of rough stone flattened on their upper surfaces. The hipped roofs of the Main Hall and the inner gate as well as the projection of the eaves and *kaerumata* (the special form of forked support used between the timbers) are distinctive features of old Japanese Buddhist temple architecture. This, in turn, was undoubtedly modeled on the style of the architecture of the Northern and Southern Dynasties of China that was introduced into Japan by way of Korea. *Sanju-no-To* (Three-Story Pagoda) of Hokkeji Temple, not far from Horyuji Temple, also dates from this period.

When the nation's capital was relocated in Nara in the latter half of the seventh century, a new age of architecture developed. Many magnificent palaces and mansions were erected, although hardly any traces of them remain today. The main relic of the period is *Sanju-no-To* (Three-Story Pagoda) of the Yakushiji Temple at Nara, a beautifully proportioned structure revealing advances in design compared to the Horyuji pagoda. The Main Hall of the Toshodaiji Temple near Nara is another example of the architctural art of the time and represented, in turn, an advance over the architectural design of the Pagoda of the Yakushiji Temple.

In the early Heian period (ninth century), the arrangement of the temple buildings underwent a great change, caused by the doctrines of esoteric Buddhism and leading to the construction of temples on such sites as Mt. Hiei near Kyoto and Mt. Koya in Wakayama Prefecture. This greatly increased the freedom of choice in the location of the different structures, although the structures themselves showed no great change in form.

In domestic architecture, there was a tendency to adhere to the old style. Even the Imperial palaces retained their original simplicity, the roofs being either thatched or boarded. With the establishment of the capital at Nara, however, splendid palaces imitating the Chinese Imperial palaces began to be built. The Sermon Hall of the Toshodaiji Temple is said to have formed part of the Imperial palace at one time. Apparently, palace architecture of the day did not differ much from that of temples. In the early Heian period, there was a tendency to adhere more to Japanese architectural styles with their simplicity of form and ornamentation.

The mansions of the nobility were plain wooden buildings constructed in the *shinden-zukuri* style, with the main buildings and the *shinden* (sleeping mansion) standing at the center and the other structures grouped around it. Corridors connected the various buildings.

In view of the advances made in the architecture of palaces and mansions, it was only natural that there was a parallel development in the architecture of shrines. The Sumiyoshi Shrine of Osaka, the Kasuga Taisha Shrine of Nara, the Kamikamo and Shimokamo Shrines of Kyoto and the Usa (Hachimangu) Shrine near Beppu in Kyushu are examples of the changes that took place. They are vivid proof of the influence of Buddhist architecture introduced from China.

The simple *torii* and fences of the older shrines were amplified by two-story gates and winding corridors—integral parts of Buddhist temples. The Itsukushima Shrine on Miyajima Island near Hiroshima illustrates the changes brought about in shrine architecture by the influence of Buddhism. It should be noted, however, that the character of the main structures was strictly preserved.

At the same time, temple architecture became more refined and tasteful. A fine example is the *Goju-no-To* (Five-Story Pagoda) of Daigoji Temple in Kyoto, revealing a major advance in the beauty of its proportions. The *Ho-odo*, or Phoenix Hall, of Byodo-in Temple at Uji in the southern suburbs of Kyoto is also a fine example of temple architecture of the late Heian period (11th century). Built in the form of a central hall with wings extending on either side, it vaguely resembles a phoenix. The wings terminate in towers, while a corridor at the rear of the Main Hall represents the tail of the bird. The line of the roof and the eaves is graceful, and the structure blends in well with its surroundings.

Kamakura to Nambokucho Periods (1192-1392)

This period saw further developments in religious architecture through the introduction of a new style from China. This is evident in the restoration of the Todaiji Temple at Nara, the original of which was destroyed by fire. The temple as reconstructed, however, is not preserved in its original form today. The *Nandaimon* (Great South Gate) was unquestionably part of the first reconstruction, but the Belfry and the Main Hall appear to be of a later date, although modeled after the original structures.

The architecture has been described as Indian in style, but this is due to a misunderstanding of the term used. It merely refers to one style of temple architecture popular under the Sung Dynasty of China as compared with another style introduced with Zen Buddhism. This latter style also originated in China and may be seen in the *Shariden* (Relic Hall) of the Engakuji Temple at Kamakura. Built in 1279, the hall remained intact until 1923, when it was badly damaged by the Great Kanto Earthquake, although it has since been restored. Built of plain wood with a thatched roof, it is the period's only extant building. The Zen temples of the time were probably built by Chinese, mostly in this style.

Zen Buddhism was in great favor during the Kamakura period, when a large number of Zen temples were constructed. An outstanding example of this style can be seen in the *Kaisando* (Founder's Hall) of the Eihoji Temple in Gifu Prefecture, which was built in 1352. The structure is made of plain wood and is not very large, but it includes all the features of the *Shariden* (Relic Hall) of the Engakuji Temple at Kamakura.

Muromachi Period (1336–1573)

The development and progress of architecture during this period can be seen in shrines and family dwellings. The division of shrine architecture into several styles had already taken place following the introduction of Buddhist ideas.

At first, these differences extended only to details, but later they even appeared in the ground plan. A mixture of shrine and temple styles is best seen in the Main Hall of the Kibitsu Shrine near Okayama City in Okayama Prefecture. Built between the years 1390 and 1402, the hall is divided into four sections, each of which is on a higher level than the preceeding one. The Oratory or Hall of Worship is in front of the Main Hall and is connected to it. It was one of the very few shrines built in the temple style. Refer to p.767

A few remarkable examples of Japanese architecture of the period remain intact. The *Ginkaku* (Silver Pavilion) in Kyoto was built by the eighth Ashikga Shogun, Yoshimasa, in 1483 in imitation of the *Kinkaku* (Gold Pavilion), which was constructed by the third Shogun, Yoshimitsu, in 1397. These structures were built partly as dwellings and partly as temples in a blending of the old style with the new.

Near the Silver Pavilion is the *Togudo*, a devotional hall with a tearoom attached to it that seems to have undergone some modification since its construction. It is an example of the mountain villas of the time that were patterned after the priests' quarters of Zen temples. This devotional hall is the only remaining structure of this particular style, and although it has not remained in its original state, a general outline of the style of this kind of building of that period can be seen.

Azuchi-Momoyama Period (1573–1598)

In the early part of this period there was considerable activity in artistic fields, especially in the remarkable development of domestic architecture. It is closely associated with the military architecture of the time, which manifested itself in castle construction. Such strongholds had previously been built in places difficult to approach, with the natural features of the countryside being used to increase their impregnability.

In the Muromachi period, a tendency had already developed to build such castles in open places where they could be used both as forts as well as mansions for the feudal lords. Their appearance, standing on high stoneworks with copper-rust roofs and white walls soaring high into the sky, is inexpressably sublime. The succession of ornamental gables projecting upward and outward creates a very special kind of harmony.

A citadel built in 1576 by Oda Nobunaga (refer to p.93) at Azuchi on Lake Biwa was the first of these castles. It was seven stories high. Historical records indicate that great efforts were made to decorate the exterior as well as the interior. Oda's example was followed by Toyotomi Hideyoshi, who built the Fushimi and Osaka castles. Both were later partially or entirely destroyed. The principal example of the citadels of this period still extant is that of Himeji.

Situated within their forts, the mansions of the feudal lords were proportionally splendid in appearance. As stated previously, the domestic architecture of the nobility was borrowed from Zen Buddhist temples. Immediately after this style was applied to the castles of the feudal lords, however, it lost its simplicity and took on great splendor. Mansions in this style included an upper room, with a *tokonoma* (alcove) and a number of anterooms separated from it by sliding screen doors. The floors of all the rooms were furnished with closely fitting mats, while the screens were covered with translucent paper.

The feudal lords added to the splendor of the style by maintaining the loftiness of the rooms and adding to their decorations. Many palatial structures, said to be relics of Fushimi Castle built by Hideyoshi, are still preserved. One is the building that now forms the *Shoin* (Study Hall) of the Nishi-Honganji Temple of Kyoto. Nijo Castle in Kyoto is also a relic of the days of Hideyoshi. All these structures were profusely decorated with paintings, some in black and white but done mostly in various colors on a gold background. Besides the embellishment of the walls and ceilings, the transoms were ornamented with delicate carvings. There was also profuse use of metal fittings.

Such palatial buildings were naturally provided with handsome surroundings. The gates were ornamented with Chinese-style painted carvings, a good example of which is the gate of the Nishi-Honganji Temple in Kyoto—a relic of Fushimi Castle.

In contrast to these gorgeous palaces were the humble cottages in which it was customary to hold the tea ceremony. Such cottages, extreme in their simplicity, reflected the dual nature of the military aristocrats of the time—simplicity on the one hand and gorgeousness on the other. In the grounds of the Nishi-Honganji Temple in Kyoto is an edifice called *Hiunkaku*, which was originally located in the garden of Hideyoshi's Jurakudai mansion. It provides eloquent proof of the simplicity of some of the palace structures. A model of simplicity, a cottage in the Katsura Imperial Villa grounds on the outskirts of Kyoto was built under the supervision of Kobori Enshu (1579–1647, refer to p.205), renowned master of the tea ceremony.

Edo Period (1603–1867)

The practice of building a luxurious and imposing mansion side by side with a structure of exquisite simplicity continued throughout the 17th, 18th and 19th centuries.

Since domestic architecture underwent such diverse changes, it was only natural that religious architecture should also experience new developments. Shrines were greatly developed under the influence of Toyotomi Hideyoshi, with the individual structures being brought together under one roof instead of being separated. The Osaki Hachiman Shrine at Sendai and the Kitano Shrine in Kyoto, both built in 1607, are examples of this development. The Hall of Worship and the Main Hall as well as their connecting gallery were all brought together under one roof.

Inside and out, the structures are embellished with colored carvings, creating an appearance of great richness and beauty that resembles the Founder's Hall of the Eihoji Temple in Gifu Prefecture. The Kitano Shrine is on a still-larger scale with a number of supplementary halls, and its roof ridges are very complicated. Quite a number of shrines of this kind have been built since the early Edo period, with the Toshogu Shrine of Nikko being regarded as the most beautiful.

The style of architecture of Buddhist temples has similarly changed significantly, including a loss of some elegance. The development of ornamentation has followed the same course as shrines and domestic architecture. Examples of the Buddhist architecture of the early Edo period are the entrance hall of the Zuiganji Temple near Sendai, the Main Hall and *Goju-no-To* (Five-Story Pagoda) of the Toji Temple, the Two-Story Gate of the Nanzenji Temple and the Main Hall of the Seisuiji Temple (Kiyomizu-dera)—all in Kyoto. The Assembly Hall of the Enryakuji Temple on Mt. Hiei, the Main Hall of the Zenkoji Temple at Nagano and the Hall of Buddha of the Zuiryuji Temple at Gifu also belong to this group of temple buildings. Among the examples constructed since the Meiji Restoration in 1868 is the *Amida* Hall of the Higashi-Honganji Temple in Kyoto.

Modern Architecture after Meiji Restoration

Introduction of Western Architecture

The Meiji Restoration of 1868 brought about a complete change in every aspect of Japanese culture and architecture was no exception. When Japan opened its doors to foreign countries, Western-style architecture began to be vigorously imported. At first, it was transplanted to Japanese soil mainly at the hands of carpenters engaged in putting up Western-style buildings under the direction of foreign architects.

Compromises between Japanese and Western styles, or what might be called quasi-Western structures, marked the beginning of Western architecture in post-Restoration Japan. Apart from this, the Meiji government commissioned foreign architects to design and build government and public offices in typical Western styles.

Chief among them were the Osaka Mint built in 1871 by T. Waters, an English architect, and Shimbashi Station in Tokyo built in 1872 by R.T. Bridgens, an American architect. Besides these two, several architects invited from France, Italy and other countries took an active part in construction. At that time, the dawn of modern architecture in Europe was beginning to give way to the golden age of eclecticism. It was only natural that the works of those architects were eloquent expressions of either classicism, romanticism or eclecticism. A Briton by the name of J. Condor was the most noteworthy of the foreign architects of the time, wielding considerable influence on Western-style architecture in Japan. Engaged as an instructor in architecture at Tokyo Imperial University (now, Tokyo University), he was the first foreigner to provide Japanese students with a regular architectural education. He directed the construction of the Imperial Household Museum (built in 1882) in Tokyo—the predecessor of the Tokyo National Museum (the present building dates from 1937). He was also responsible for the Rokumeikan (built in 1883), another Tokyo building that was used as a sort of social clubhouse.

The year 1879 saw the first group of graduates in architecture from Tokyo Imperial University—a total of four: Tatsuno Kingo, Katayama Tokuma, Sone Tatsuzo and Sadachi Shichijiro. Several years later, regular Western-style buildings went up one after another. Tatsuno was responsible for the main office of the Bank of Japan (built in 1896), Katayama for several Mitsubishi office buildings (built in 1894) and Sadachi for postal and telegraph offices of various regions (built in 1887). These were products of imported eclecticism—the prevalent architectural trend in Europe at the time, but they had nothing in common with the traditional architecture of Japan.

A reaction against this European trend in architecture soon followed. It took the form of nostalgia for and reappreciation of traditional Japanese-style architecture. In 1889 a Chair of Japanese Architecture was established at the college, later called the Engineering College. Kigo Seikei was engaged as a lecturer, immediately followed by the appointment of Ito Chuta and Sekino Tadashi to the staff. An academic system was thus set up to encourage the study of traditional architecture. In the construction of the Nippon Kangyo Bank in Tokyo by Takeda Goichi (in 1899), for example, elements of Japanese-style architecture found expression.

Creation of New Materials and Methods

Meanwhile, eclecticism in architecture ended in Europe, giving way to a new movement in 1894 known as "L'art Nouveau." This new mode was immediately introduced into Japan by Tsukamoto Yasushi. The Secession movement in architecture that came in the wake of "L' art Nouveau" was also brought to these shores. Stores designed in this new style appeared on the Ginza, providing the most attractive shopping section in Tokyo. Despite what might be suggested by the term, the secession style as it was introduced into Japan did not involve a separation from the past architectural tradition, but the adoption of a new style.

New building materials such as steel, cement and glass were adopted by Japanese architects more promptly than might be expected. In 1909, Sano Toshitaka, a trailblazer in the construction of steel-frame buildings in Japan, put up a three-story, steel-frame building for Maruzen Co., Ltd. in Tokyo. Then in 1913 an airport building was constructed with a steel frame in Tokorozawa, a western suburb of Tokyo.

World War I (1914–1918) stimulated an economic boom in Japan. Riding on the crest of this wave, regular ferroconcrete office buildings seven to eight stories high sprang up here and there. Chief among them were the Kaijo Building (built in 1918) in Tokyo, designed by Sone-Chujo Architects and Engineers, Inc., the Marunouchi Building (built in 1923) in Tokyo designed by Mitsubishi Real Estate Co., Ltd., and the Dojima Building (built in 1923) in Osaka, designed by Takenaka Komuten General Contractor Co., Ltd.

In 1916, famed American architect Frank Lloyd Wright came to Japan and supervised the construction of the Imperial Hotel, which was completed in 1921. Besides the hotel, Wright designed several other buildings, exerting as beneficial an influence in the field of architecture in Japan as Condor had done a few decades before.

Then came the disastrous earthquake and fire of 1923, which devastated the greater part of the Tokyo and Yokohama area. The majority of Tokyo's wooden buildings were damaged by the earthquake, while the fires that followed destroyed almost all of them as well as many others that had survived the violent shock. The stability of ferroconcrete buildings during an earthquake was recognized, especially since the newly built Imperial Hotel was practically untouched. Consequently, great importance was attached to the method of designing based on an accurate calculation of strength and the consideration of other safety factors in buildings.

About 20 years after the start of the Secession movement in Europe, a new movement was started in Japan, too, in 1920, when a group of young architects broke with the style of the past.

Most of the buildings erected during that period, however, were products of European eclecticism. Designed in the classic style were such buildings as the Mitsukoshi Gofukuten Building (built in 1914) by Yokokawa Tamisuke, Tokyo Station Building (built in 1914) by Tatsuno Kingo and other architects, the main office of Mitsubishi Bank (built in 1922) by Sakurai Kotaro and the National Diet Building (built in 1936) by Okuma Kiho. Representative of the neo-Gothic style of the time were the auditorium of Tokyo University (built in 1925) by Uchida Yoshikazu (also known as Uchida Shozo) and the auditorium of Waseda University (built in 1927) by Sato Koichi.

A sort of revival of traditional Japanese architecture asserted itself in the 1880s among Japanese architects. However, the revival movement did not go farther than the fusion of elements from Buddhist and Shinto construction into modern architecture. Among the more notable edifices coming under this category are the Kabukiza Theater in Tokyo (built in 1924) by Okada Shin-ichiro and the Okura Shukokan Museum of Tokyo (1927), built by Ito Chuta.

Apart from the effort to adopt some of the outward features of traditional Japanese architecture, a new movement got under way headed by Horiguchi Sutemi and Murano Togo. These architects sought to apply the essence of Japanese art to modern Western-style architecture. They found the real spirit of modern architecture in the sort of practical simplicity evident in the structure of a *chashitsu*, or tea-ceremony room.

●Gardens

Landscape gardening is an art that has developed in Japan since olden times. Its origins may be traced to the reign of the Empress-Regnant Suiko (554–628), when according to the "Nihonshoki" (Chronicles of Japan compiled in 720, refer to p.152), well-designed gardens with artificial hills and ornamental ponds already existed in Japan.

The aim of the art is to create a scenic composition on a plot of land much as an artist composes a landscape on a canvas. For this purpose, rocks, trees and running water are naturally arranged so as to leave no trace of artificiality. The traditional features of such a garden include an island set in a lake or pool and connected with the mainland by bridges. Curiously shaped boulders and rocks are carefully arranged as well as a stone lantern, with all the elements placed in such a way as to give, even to a garden of limited size, something of the sweep of a vast landscape.

When the national capital was transferred from Nara to Kyoto in 794, a garden called Shinsen-en (Sacred-Fountain Garden) was laid out in the capital on an immense scale, although only a small portion of it still remains. The most typical gardens in the Heian period (794 –1185) were those attached to *shinden* (sleeping mansion)-*zukuri* architecture. In these gardens, to the south of the building was an open space, south of which a narrow pond extended from east to west. The water of the pond was supplied from north of the building site by a *yarimizu*, or artificial stream, which the stream was usually divided into two channels—one emptying directly into the pond and the other coursing down a hill as a waterfall. The nobility of the day enjoyed themselves on the pond, which was large enough so that they could relax on a colorfully decorated boat while musicians provided entertainment.

With the introduction of Zen Buddhism during the Kamakura period (1192–1333), the principles of religion were applied to the traditional rules guiding the construction of landscape gardens. The gardens designed in this period were not as decorative as those of the Heian period, but were more tranquil and substantial. The Zuisenji Temple garden in Kamakura offers visitors an example of the gardens of this period.

It was during this period that two famous books on gardens were written—one the "Emposho" (Book of Gardens) by the priest Zoen and the other the "Sakuteiki" (Book of Garden Planning) by Fujiwara-no-Nagatsune. Both books are regarded as authoritative even today. In laying out a garden during in this period, a designer made skillful use of the available natural features. This tendency was developed further in the Muromachi period (1336–1573) and probably culminated in the Higashiyama period (about 1480–1490).

A typical example is the garden of Jishoji Temple in Kyoto, in which the original features are preserved in their entirety. The Jishoji Temple, incidentally, is popularly known as Ginkakuji (Silver Pavilion Temple) because the *Ginkaku* (Silver Pavilion) stands in its garden. Quite a number of gardens can be found representing the style of the period, including those of the Tenryuji, Rokuonji and Tojiin temples in Kyoto. (Rokuonji Temple is popularly called the Kinkakuji, or Gold Pavilion Temple, after the Gold Pavilion standing in the garden.)

Another type of garden in the Muromachi period worthy of note is the *hiraniwa* (flat garden). This garden is characterized by the absence of a hill or pond, containing only stones and trees arranged on a flat piece of ground.

In the Muromachi period (1336–1573), the development of both hill and flat gardens progressed, but in the succeeding Azuchi-Momoyama period (1573–1598), popular tastes in garden design changed. In that period, the heroic spirit of the age found expression in the grand scale of architecture. This change in architectural style naturally had its influence on gardens, which were modified to meet the new requirements in taste.

The general tone of landscape gardening was transformed at one stroke from a sense of tranquility strongly savoring of Zen Buddhism to one of color and vigor. As a result, large stones and plants with bold outlines such as the cycad became the dominant decorative features. A typical garden of this description can be seen in the precincts of Nishi-Honganji Temple in Kyoto.

The popularity of the tea ceremony also influenced landscape gardening since the garden had to be arranged to include a *sukiya* (tea-ceremony house). Several such gardens have been preserved to the present day. Among the famous garden designers in this period, the names of Soami, Mon-ami and Zen-ami deserve special mention. One of the greatest designers, however, was Sen-no-Rikyu (1521–1591) — the well-known master of the tea ceremony, who was responsible for creating the garden of the Chishaku-in Temple of Kyoto as well as a number of others.

In the Edo period (1603–1867) a noticeable change took place. The actual designing and execution of the work of constructing gardens passed very gradually from the hands of the tea masters and priests to professional gardeners, who dealt in the raw materials.

At the beginning of the period, the work of Kobori Enshu (1579–1647), a master of the tea ceremony, was outstanding. The celebrated garden of the Katsura Imperial Villa of Kyoto is the finest example of his work. It is said that he undertook the project on condition that no time limit be set for its completion, no fixed sum be set on expenses and no interference be made in his work. This masterpiece of landscape gardening can still be seen in an excellent state of preservation.

Kobori Enshu also designed the garden of the *Koho-an* of Daitokuji Temple as well as those of Kodaiji, Nanzenji and Chion-in temples. Other famous Kyoto gardens of the period worthy of mention include those of Nijo Castle and the Shugaku-in Palace as well as the garden of Hompoji Temple laid out by Hon-ami Koetsu.

Gradually, the center of activity shifted from Kyoto to Edo (now, Tokyo). Later, a new possibility was shown in the art through the utilization of the natural scenery surrounding a garden in forming the composition. The garden at the Hamarikyu was so laid out that a way to the sea was opened to create a lagoon and preserve the view of Mt. Fuji seen beyond Shinagawa Bay. Utility also began to affect the construction of gardens as, for example, the duck pond at the aforementioned Hamarikyu and the cultivation in the Kairaku-en Garden at Mito of reeds for use in making arrows and plums for consumption purposes.

Not only did the *daimyo* (feudal lords) make the gardens attached to their mansions in Edo works of art, but they also constructed gardens of great beauty at their country estates, surpassing even the *shogun*'s own garden in Edo. Among these may be noted Kenroku-en in Kanazawa, Ritsurin Koen Garden in Takamatsu and Koraku-en in Okayama, all of which are still in a good state of preservation.

Although the Meiji Restoration in 1868 doomed some of these celebrated gardens to neglect, many have been preserved in their original form. Among those in Tokyo are Kiyosumi-en at Fukagawa,

Rikugi-en at Komagome and Koraku-en at Koishikawa.

Types of Gardens: The gardens of Japan have long been classified into two general types: the *tsukiyama* (hill garden) and the *hiraniwa* (flat garden). The former features hills and ponds, while the latter is characterized by a flat area without hills or ponds. For many centuries, the main garden on the southern side of a mansion was invariably done in the hill style, while the flat style was largely reserved for smaller gardens tucked away in cramped places. The two styles thus developed side by side, but with the introduction of the tea ceremony and the inclusion of *chashitsu* (tea-ceremony room), the flat style made great progress.

Each of these styles had three forms: *shin*, *gyo* and *so* (elaborate, intermediate and abbreviated), representing the formal, the semiformal and the informal. Just as in the case of the hill and flat styles, however, there were infinite gradations among all three forms.

The hill garden features a hill usually combined with a pond and a stream. Examples of this style include the Shukkei-en at Hiroshima, Rakuraku-en (also called Hakkei-en) at Hikone and Suizenji Garden at Kumamoto. The garden at the Kyu Shibarikyu (Former Shiba Detached Palace) in Tokyo is an example of a garden built around a lagoon.

In a flat garden, stones, trees, stone lanterns, water basins and wells form the important decorative elements. The scenic features of the sea, a lake or a pond are taken as models. The most famous example of a flat garden is at Ryoanji Temple in Kyoto, where, enclosed by a low wall on three sides, 15 rocks of varying sizes are arranged on a flat piece of ground covered with white sand. There is not a single tree or shrub. The trees outside the walls and the distant view serve as a background.

Another famous flat garden is that of Shinju-an Temple in the compound of Daitokuji Temple in Kyoto. In this garden, 15 rocks are set up in groups of seven, five, and three in a narrow strip of ground bordered on the far side by a low hedge, which once served to connect the garden with the avenue of pine trees at Kamo several miles away. The garden takes in a lovely view of distant Mt. Hiei as its background. The garden of Daisen-in Temple, also situated in the compound of Daitokuji Temple, is another well-known example.

The *chaniwa* (garden attached to the tea-ceremony house) should also be mentioned briefly. In reality, it represents the path leading up to the *chashitsu* (tea-ceremony room), where the tea ceremony is performed. Thus, it is a separate part of the garden and generally partitioned off from the rest. The aim of the designer of the *chaniwa* was to create a feeling of loneliness and detachment from the world, as suggested by such poetic conceptions as "a solitary cottage on the seabeach in the waning light of an autumn eve," or "a pale evening moon, a bit of the sea, through a cluster of trees."

Care was taken to invest such gardens with an air of solitude by cultivating moss on the ground and stones, thus providing the necessary patina. It should be noted that the path to the *chashitsu* is always curved so as to conceal the entrance until the instant it is reached, a result also obtained by planting clumps of trees to cut off the entrance from view. This principle is followed in traditional Japanese homes of any pretension, provided there is sufficient ground in front of the house.

An offshoot of landscape gardening, only on a smaller scale, is the *hako-niwa* (box-garden). It may sometimes be seen at the entrance to a workshop or similar place in a crowded city. A miniature pond, often stocked with goldfish, tiny rocks, trees, etc., make up what may well be described as a toy garden. There is also the *bonkei*, or tray garden—a miniature garden created with mud, peat, varied-colored sand and other materials. *Bonseki*—the art of creating landscapes with stones and sand on black lacquered trays as a form of decoration, and *bonsai*—the cultivation of miniature trees, may both be included as other aspects of the art of gardening.

Principal gardens in Tokyo and Kyoto are as follows:

Tokyo

※	Akasaka-Rikyu Garden	Moto-Akasaka 2-chome, Minato-ku
	Shiba-Rikyu Onshi Garden	Shiba Kaigan 1-chome, Minato-ku
	Tokaiji Garden	Kita-Shinagawa 3-chome, Shinagawa-ku
	Hama-Rikyu Onshi Garden	Hama-Rikyu Teien, Chuo-ku
	Korakuen Garden	Koraku 1-chome, Bunkyo-ku
	Rikugien Park	Hon-Komagome 6-chome, Bunkyo-ku
	Chinzanso Garden	Sekiguchi 2-chome, Bunkyo-ku
△	Dembo-in Garden	Asakusa 2-chome, Taito-ku
	Kiyosumi Garden	Kiyosumi-cho 3-chome, Koto-ku

Kyoto

※	Kyoto Imperial Palace Garden	Kyoto Gyoen, Kamigyo-ku
※	Sento Palace Garden	Kyoto Gyoen, Kamigyo-ku
	Daitokuji Hojo and East Garden	Murasakino Daitokuji-cho, Kita-ku
△	Shinjuan Garden	Murasakino Daitokuji-cho, Kita-ku
	Daisen-in Garden	Murasakino Daitokuji-cho, Kita-ku
△	Koho-an Garden	Murasakino Daitokuji-cho, Kita-ku
	Koto-in Garden	Murasakino Daitokuji-cho, Kita-ku
△	Gyokurin-in Garden	Murasakino Daitokuji-cho, Kita-ku
△	Juko-in Garden	Murasakino Daitokuji-cho, Kita-ku
△	Ryuko-in Garden	Murasakino Daitokuji-cho, Kita-ku
△	Hoshun-in Garden	Murasakino Daitokuji-cho, Kita-ku
	Rokuonji (Gold Pavilion)	Kinkakuji-cho, Kita-ku Garden
	Toji-in Garden	Tojiinkita-machi, Kita-ku
	Hompoji Garden	Hompojimae-cho, Kamigyo-ku
△	Omote-Senke's and Ura	Ogawadori-Teranouch, Kamigyo-ku

Senke's Garden	
※ Kan-Kyuan Tea Garden	Mushanokoji, Kamigyo-ku
※ Shokokuji Kaisando Garden	Imadegawa-dori-Karasuma, Kamigyo-ku
※ Shugaku-in Imperial Villa	Shugakuin, Sakyo-ku
Jishoji (Silver Pavilion)	Ginkakuji-cho, Sakyo-ku Garden
※ Murin-an Garden	Nanzenji Kusakawa-cho, Sakyo-ku
Nanzenji Hojo Garden	Nanzenji Fukuchi-cho, Sakyo-ku
Nanzen-in Garden	Nanzenji Fukuchi-cho, Sakyo-ku
Konchi-in Garden	Nanzenji Fukuchi-cho, Sakyo-ku
Tenju-an Garden	Nanzenji Fukuchi-cho, Sakyo-ku
Shisendo Garden	Ichijoji Monguchi-cho, Sakyo-ku
Manshu-in Garden	Ichijoji Teranouchi-machi, Sakyo-ku
△ Saiho-in Tea Garden	Kurodani-cho, Sakyo-ku
Seifuso Garden	Tanaka Sekiden-cho, Sakyo-ku
※ Katsura Imperial Villa Garden	Katsura Shimizu-cho, Ukyo-ku
Osawa Pond, Garden	Saga Osawa-cho, Ukyo-ku surrounding
Tenryuji Garden	Saga Tenryuji-Susukinobaba-cho Ukyo-ku
※ Saihoji Garden	Matsuo Jingatani-cho, Ukyo-ku
Ninnaji Garden	Omuro-Ouchi, Ukyo-ku
Myoshinji Garden	Hanazono Myoshinji-cho, Ukyo-ku
△ Gyokuho-in Garden	Hanazono Myoshinji-cho, Ukyo-ku
△ Tokai-an Garden	Hanazono Myoshinji-cho, Ukyo-ku
△ Reiun-in Garden	Hanazono Myoshinji-cho, Ukyo-ku
Taizo-in Garden	Hanazono Myoshinji-cho, Ukyo-ku
Keishun-in Garden	Hanazono Myoshinji-cho, Ukyo-ku
Ryoanji Garden	Ryoanji Goryonoshita-cho, Ukyo-ku
Shinsen-en Garden	Monzen-cho, Nakagyo-ku
Nijo Castle Ninomaru Garden	Nijo-Horikawa, Nakagyo-ku
※ Honganji Daisho-in Garden	Honganji-Monzen-cho, Shimogyo-ku
△ Tekisui-en Garden	Honganji-Monzen-cho, Shimogyo-ku
Shosei-en Garden	Higashi-Tamamizu-cho, Shimogyo-ku
Chion-in Garden	Hayashishita-cho, Higashiyama-ku
Chishaku-in Garden	Higashi-Kawara-cho, Higashiyama-ku
Myoho-in Garden (only in early November)	Myohoin-Maekawa-cho, Higashiyama-ku
△ Joju-in Garden (KiyomizuTemple)	Kiyomizu 1-chome, Higashiyama-ku
Shoren-in Garden	Awadaguchi Sanjobo-cho, Higashiyama-ku
※ Entoku-in Garden	Shimokawara-cho, Higashiyama-ku

208

Kodaiji Garden	Shimokawara-cho, Higashiyama-ku
Daigo Sambo-in Garden	Daigo Higashioji-cho, Fushimi-ku
Kanjuji Garden	Yamashina Kanjuji Niodo-cho, Higashiyama-ku
Byodo-in Garden	Renge, Uji, Uji City

Notes

※　permission required in advance

△　not open to the public

●Tea Ceremony, Flower Arrangement and Incense Burning

Tea Ceremony

Chanoyu, the tea ceremony, is an aesthetic cult practiced in cultured circles in Japan, where it is regarded as an artistic discipline for the attainment of enlightenment and mental composure. In contrast to the drinking of coffee, which has little significance beyond the enjoyment of taste and aroma, the tea ceremony is "a religion of the art of living." One learns to appreciate an artistic atmosphere through the medium of the indescribably delicate aroma of powdered tea.

Originally, tea was used more as a medicine than as a beverage. The tea plant, native to southern China, was from very early times highly prized for its power to relieve fatigue, delight the soul, strengthen the will and repair the eyesight. Taoists considered it an important ingredient in the elixir of immortality, while Buddhists made extensive use of it to prevent drowsiness during their long hours of meditation.

Buddhists of the southern Zen sect, who adopted many Taoist doctrines, formulated an elaborate tea ritual. The monks gathered before the image of Buddha and drank tea out of a single bowl with all the formality of a holy sacrament. It was this Zen ritual that finally developed into the tea ceremony of Japan in the 15th century. History, however, indicates that the drinking of tea was already known in Japan during the reign of Emperor Shomu (reigned 724–749), who was said to have invited 100 Buddhist monks to the Imperial Palace for tea.

It is probable that in olden times tea was one of the most precious items imported from China. The leaves were probably imported into Japan by ambassadors to the Tang Court of China and prepared in the prevailing fashion. In 805, a priest named Saicho brought back some green-tea seeds from China, where he had studied for a few years, and planted them on Mt. Hiei near Kyoto.

Many tea gardens are mentioned in literature in the succeeding centuries. Meanwhile, the beverage grew in popularity among the aristocracy and priesthood. By the 15th century, under the patronage of Yoshimasa, the eighth Ashikaga Shogun, the tea ceremony was fully formulated and turned into an independent, secular performance. It should be noted that tea became something more than simply an idealized form of refreshment—it was a means by which purity and refinement could be worshipped.

The *sukiya*, or teahouse, consists of the *chashitsu* (tearoom) designed to accommodate not more than five guests; a *mizuya* (service room), where the tea utensils are washed and arranged before being brought in; a *yoritsuki* (waiting room), where the guests wait until they receive a summons to enter the tearoom, and the *roji* (garden path) connecting the *yoritsuki* with the tearoom.

The tearoom is about 2.7 sq.m, with a special entrance for the host and another for the guests. The latter entrance, called *nijiriguchi*, is so small that guests must crawl in on their hands and knees—high and low ranks alike. Smaller rooms are not uncommon, and in nearly every case, the uninitiated are disappointed with the unimpressive appearance of the exterior and interior of the tearoom. Its simplicity and purity are in emulation of a Zen monastery, with the aim of making it a sanctuary from the vexations of the outside world.

The size of the room is four and a half *tatami* (straw mats, each measuring 90 cm by 180 cm). The half mat fills the space in the center of the room. At one corner of this half mat, a square hearth is fitted into the floor to allow for a brazier on which an iron kettle is placed. The host sits next to the hearth with all the utensils for making the tea arranged at his side. The utensils consist of the *chawan* (tea bowl), *chaire* (tea caddy), *chasen* (bamboo whisk) and *chashaku* (bamboo spoon). These articles, which the guests are permitted to closely inspect after the tea is served, are often valuable objects of art.

There are many ways of holding the tea ceremony, varying in accordance with the occasion and the season as well as the school of the host. Each school uses different utensils in a different manner. Powdered tea is often served informally without invitation, and the host may or may not provide a meal. Among the many schools of the tea ceremony now in existence, Ura-Senke, Omote-Senke and Musha-koji are the most popular.

The following is a description of a representative form of the ceremony:

The guests, five in number, assemble one by one in the *yoritsuki*, or waiting room—a small room generally of only three mats in which they are expected to register their appreciation of the various, tastefully arranged articles. Indifference is a deadly sin. Moreover, the host will be greatly disappointed if his guests fail to appreciate his kindness since he is anxious to satisfy them in every way. In due time, the host enters, makes a deep bow and retraces his steps to the tearoom without a word to the guests. This silent salutation is understood to mean that the host is ready to receive the guests in the tearoom.

The *shokyaku* (principal guest), who is qualified for his role, heads the procession to the tearoom, holding the same position of responsibility until the serving and drinking are over. This usually takes about two hours (more than three hours is required for the entire ceremony). In going to the tearoom, the guests must proceed along a *roji*, or garden path, only about 6 m long. It is so arranged, however, as to sever all connection with the outside world in order to create an atmosphere conducive to the tranquil state of mind so vital to an appreciation of the ceremony in the tearoom.

Rocks, trees and stone lanterns are tastefully arranged to form a harmonious combination of nature and art. Before the guests enter the tearoom, they wash their hands and rinse their mouth at a stone basin filled with fresh water. The principal guest is the first to begin the ritual of purification and to enter the room.

The guests, who each follow a prescribed order, kneel in turn on the mat in front of the *tokonoma* (alcove) and respectfully inspect the *kakemono* (hanging scroll). The next thing to be examined is the tiny incense-holder located on a side shelf. When its contents have been emptied into the hearth in honor of the guests, the leader will ask the host for permission to inspect it. A small square piece of silk, called a *fukusa*, is always used as a means of protection when placing the incense-holder on the *tatami* or when holding it for examination.

A repast called *kaiseki* forms an important part of the ceremony and is prepared with the greatest care. It is served on individual trays. Since there are not as many courses as served in the conventional Japanese dinner, etiquette requires that the guests leave none of the dishes unfinished. A unique aspect of the repast is the custom requiring the host to bring everything in personally. The tearoom is accessible only to the host while the ceremony is being conducted lest the peace and tranquility of the occasion be disturbed by intruders. Although he enters from time to time, he does not eat with his guests.

There are elaborate rules of etiquette for eating this meal. When it is over, the guests put all the empty dishes and bowls on the trays, and the host removes them one by one to the adjoining room. When sweets are served, the first sitting closes. At the host's suggestion, the guests retire to the waiting room or to some other appointed place where a bench is provided. This ritual is referred to as *nakadachi*, or intermediate retirement.

The *gozairi*, or second sitting, is the real tea ceremony. The guests are summoned by gentle strokes on a gong or a thick board hung near the tearoom. Five or seven strokes are usually sounded to signal that the host is ready to serve the *koicha*, or "thick tea." The purification ritual is repeated and the guests enter the tearoom in the same order as for the first session. On entering, with the principal guest in the lead, they find that the hanging scroll has been replaced by some flowers arranged in the alcove.

The *koicha* is prepared from powdered tea. Two or three spoonfuls are put in a cup-like bowl, hot water is poured on it and the tea then beaten to a creamy froth with a bamboo whisk. When the preparation is ready, the host places the bowl in front of the principal guest. With a bow to his fellow guests, the latter holds it in the palm of his left hand, steadies it with his right and takes a sip. After complimenting the host on its excellent flavor, consistency and so on, he takes two or more sips before he passes it on to the second guest. The bowl is thus passed around until every guest has tasted it.

The prescribed etiquette insists that the spot of the bowl from which each guest has taken a sip must be wiped clean with *kaishi* (a piece of white paper) before it is passed on. The principal guest must also not forget to ask the host for the privilege of closely inspecting the tea bowl for an appreciation of its qualities, according to the rules of etiquette. When the last guest finishes, he hands the bowl to the leader, who returns it to the host. The tea caddy and spoon are also passed around for appreciation, and with that the ceremony ends.

It is usual for *usucha* (thin tea) to be served following this, either in the same room or in another, but with less formality. Two bowls are usually provided. Each guest is expected to empty his bowl and return it to the host, who rinses it out prior to making tea in it for the next guest.

Hours have elapsed since the guests first assembled in the waiting room, but they are neither tired nor bored. The guests are not strangers to each other, for the host has been careful in his selection with a view to creating an atmosphere of warm congeniality. Topics of conversation are many and varied since *chanoyu* is practically related to every aspect of art, including garden landscaping and flower arrangement. Finally, with a salutation to their host, the guests depart. Etiquette requires that they should convey their thanks to the host on the following day, either in person or by letter.

Among the famous *sukiya* (teahouses) still standing are the *Togudo* (registered as a National Treasure) of the Ginkakuji Temple in Kyoto, designed by Shuko in the 15th century—the "Father of the Tea Ceremony"; the *Shokintei* of the Katsura Imperial Villa in Kyoto, designed by Kobori Enshu (1579-1647, refer to p.205), one of the greatest of the tea-masters; the *Koho-an* and the *Shinju-an* of the Daitokuji Temple in Kyoto; the *Myoki-an* (registered as a National Treasure) in Kyoto, originally the residence of Sen-no-Rikyu (1521-1591)—another great tea-master, and the *Rokuso-an* in the National Museum in Tokyo.

Flower Arrangement

The art of arranging flowers, known as *ikebana* or *kado*, is an expression of the Japanese aesthetic. Although historians dispute the origin of the art, it is agreed that the institution has reached its present stage of development purely as a native art in this country independent of all outside influences. It is popularly believed that the small tearoom in the *Ginkaku* (Silver Pavilion) of the Jishoji Temple (Ginkakuji Temple) in Kyoto, built toward the end of the 15th century by Yoshimasa, the eighth Shogun of the Ashikaga family, is the birthplace of Japan's floral art.

The art of flower arrangement gained social recognition under the patronage of the different Ashikaga Shogun of the late 15th century. And later, during the Edo period, many schools sprang up, rivaling each other in popular favor.

The styles of flower arranging may be divided into two main categories—formal and natural. To the formal belongs the style known as *rikka*, or standing style, from which sprang a more popular form called the *ten-chi-jin*, or "heaven-earth-man." The natural style is known as *nageire*, or the thrown-in style. The *bunjin-ike*, an offspring of the nageire school, was developed by the *bunjin* (literati) class during the 18th century.

There are three fundamental principles followed in the arrange-ment of flowers in the formal style, regardless of the form the arrangement may take or the school to which the arranger may belong. They are the leading principle (heaven), the subordinate principle (earth) and the reconciling principle (man). Any flower arrangement that does not embody these three principles is consid-ered barren and dead.

If a single plant or branch is used, the main part shooting upwards represents heaven, a twig on the right bent sideways in a V-shape denotes man and the lowest twig or branch on the left with the end slightly bent to point upwards signifies earth. Three separate plants or branches—not necessarily of the same kind—are often used to represent these three elements.

Another important point consists in regarding the flowers from three different aspects: the nature of the flower, the location in which it is to be placed and the shape of the vase.

In decorating the alcove with flowers, one must arrange them so as not to hide the *kakemono* (scroll painting). If the scroll depicts mountain scenery, flowers that grow in marshes or by river banks should be selected, but if the *kakemono* shows flowering plants, then flowering branches should be chosen for the vase.

For wedding feasts, flowers are arranged to appear as natural as possible. The combination of pine, bamboo and plum—called *sho-chiku-bai* in Japanese and representing constancy, prosperity and purity—are regarded as most auspicious on such occasions. Weak-stemmed flowers that easily fall apart are not generally used.

Beginners in the art of flower arrangement are usually first taught to arrange *haran* (a long-leafed variety of orchid). Their training is considered complete when they have been initiated into the secrets of arranging flowers that are regarded as the most difficult to display to advantage. The arrangement of a single blossom of *botan* (tree peony), or of *shakuyaku* (Japanese peony) is regarded as extremely

213

difficult and only possible by those masters of the art.

Today, there are more than 20 well-known schools of *ikebana*, plus innumerable offshoots and branches of these schools. Of these, some of the principal schools are the Adachi-shiki, Enshu-ryu, Ikenobo, Ko-ryu, Kuwabara-senkei, Kyofu-ryu, Misho-ryu, Nakayama-Bunpo-kai, Ohara-ryu, Saga-ryu and Sogetsu-ryu.

Incense Burning

The burning of incense, known as *kodo*, is regarded as the cultivation of mental composure by developing a refined sense of smell in the same way that the tea ceremony and flower arrangement gratify the pleasures of taste and sight, respectively. Formerly a favorite pastime of the aristocracy, incense burning gradually fell into disuse. However, it still has its votaries.

It is accompanied by ceremonies similar to the tea ceremony. Although the origin of incense burning remains unknown, history records that a fragrant piece of wood that washed ashore on Awaji Island near Kobe was presented to Empress-Regnant Suiko (reigned 592–628).

Later, during Emperor Shomu's reign (eighth century, refer to p.86), incense is said to have been sent to the Emperor from Central Asia and donated to the Todaiji Temple at Nara. It is one of the treasures currently being kept in the Shosoin Repository at Nara. In later years, various kinds of incense were sent from Central Asia, Korea and China, but the mixed incense called *awase-ko*, introduced from China in the tenth century, is the foundation for the incense burning practice of the present day.

The burning of incense has, of course, always been associated with Buddhism, but in the 15th century the secular and recreative use of incense became popular and has continued up to the present. In the secular sense, it serves to scent the air of a parlor when a guest is expected or to impart a sweet perfume to clothing or accessories prior to their use. Very often in time of war, *samurai* (warriors) were in the habit of burning incense in their helmets when preparing to go to the front in order to maintain their calm as well as their sense of beauty, even on the battlefield.

In its recreative use, incense is used to test the accuracy of one's sense of smell. The host of a party is chosen to burn the incense, while the guests sit around in a half circle. Sometimes participants are divided into two sides. A censer filled with burning incense is then circulated among the guests, each of whom must guess the scent. Their guesses are written down and the score is added up at the end of the game.

●Bonkei, Bonseki and Bonsai

Bonkei and Bonseki

Bonkei and *bonseki*, words generally translated as "tray land-scape," represent the art of creating a scenic view on a tray. Products of this art, often enjoyed as a hobby by the old and young alike, form a part of interior decoration, usually as an ornament in the *tokonoma* (alcove).

Bonkei differs from *bonseki* in the materials and techniques applied. *Bonkei* represents various kinds of three-dimensional scenery in miniature created with such materials as earth, sand, gravel, moss and natural or artificial plants. Spatulas, brushes, sieves and spoons are the tools. The size of the tray used for this purpose is about 30 to 90 cm by 15 to 45 cm, and from 2.5 to 5 cm deep.

Dark brown peat is used to form the major portion of *bonkei* scenery. The peat is usually coated with a solution of clay and water. A lake, sea or river is expressed by sand. Real or artificial trees and grass are also used to create scenery. Sometimes, miniature houses, bridges and other structures as well as artificial human figures and animals are used to add a sense of realism. Then again, brown or green paint is sometimes applied to the tiny mounds to represent hills or mountains. As often as not, real moss is used to cover the ground. To indicate an expanse of water, sand is sometimes mixed with a blue pigment, while waterfalls and waves are similarly represented by the use of white clay or white paint. Places noted for their scenic beauty in Japan, including typical mountain and seaside scenery, supply most of the motifs to *bonkei* artists. Sometimes, famous scenes in foreign countries are adopted as models.

Bonseki trays are usually lacquered and sometimes bordered by a low rim measuring about 45 cm by 23 cm. They are either rectangu-lar or oval. Scenery is represented on this kind of tray by an inge-nious arrangement of various-sized natural stones (sometimes only by a single stone) and white sand. As in *bonkei*, spoons and sieves are used. Feathers, tiny brooms and chopsticks are indispensable in making this kind of tray landscape.

Sand used for this purpose may be classified into nine kinds in accordance with the size of the grain. Different landscapes are represented by the varied use of these kinds of sand. The black color of the tray and the stones are contrasted with the white sand, con-stituting the usual color scheme of the *bonseki*—a simple but elegant effect typical of a Japanese *sumi*-ink painting. The same materials —stone and sand—may be used over and over again. Used sand is sifted and reclassified for further use.

Materials as well as tools when not in use are sorted and stored away in a small chest of drawers. In addition to the materials mentioned above, tiny bridges, boats, pagodas, *torii* (gateways to shrines), houses, figures, etc., often made of ivory or copper, are sometimes used to add charm to *bonseki* scenery, as in *bonkei*. Sites well known for their scenic beauty are often used as models in *bonseki*, too. Landscapes characterized by seasonal changes as well as those noted for their vivid sunrises and sunsets are also typical of *bonseki*.

Apart from *bonseki* proper, there is a group called *bonga* (lit. tray-picture). As its name suggests, a picture is portrayed in sand, so to speak, on a black-lacquered board. The tools and techniques are much the same as those used in *bonseki*, the only difference being that no stones are used in *bonga*.

In point of technique, *bonga* may be divided into three types: those made just like *bonseki* except for the omission of stones, those which are a pictorial representation in sand and those combining the elements of the first two.

As ornaments, *bonga* are sometimes laid flat like most *bonseki*, and sometimes they are hung on the wall or displayed in the *tokonoma* (alcove). In the latter case, several devices are used to prevent the sand from falling off the board. One way is to mix arabic gum powder with the white sand. When heated, the arabic gum melts and makes the sand adhesive.

The origin of tray landscape is generally considered to date back to the 14th or 15th century. In some of the illustrated books of the time, pictures have been found showing what may well be regarded as the beginning of *bonkei* and *bonseki*—drawings of a shallow wooden box filled with undulating soil planted with little trees and small stones scattered all around. Another picture shows a pot containing stones, while one drawing depicts a wooden plank with a cone-shaped stone set on it and sand spread around.

It seems that in ancient times, the Japanese customarily placed a stone or a small pile of earth on a tray to symbolize the sacred, imaginary mountain—*Shumisen*—which, Buddhism teaches, is the center of the world, and *Horai*—the sacred mountain of the Taoists where hermits live in eternal youth.

This is the origin of tray landscapes. As time rolled on, however, the religious motif gradually gave place to a love of nature, and people began to enjoy creating tray landscapes as ornaments. This sort of elegant pastime was eventually elevated to the dignity of an art almost on a level with that of landscape gardening, *sumi*-ink landscape painting, flower arrangement and the tea ceremony.

After the middle of the 19th century, the art of making tray landscapes became more popular than ever before. As a result, several schools of this art were founded. Today, there are some ten *bonkei* schools and a few less in *bonseki*.

Bonsai

The art of raising miniature potted trees, called *bonsai* in Japanese, is one of the many arts that have been perfected in Japan.

In many countries of the world, various kinds of plants are potted for the appreciation of their pretty flowers and foliage. But miniature potted trees as trained and nurtured in Japan are unique in that they show clear signs of annual growth and create the impression that they are part of a natural forest with its seasonal changes. Indeed, the word *bonsai* has attained international currency.

The tradition of appreciating the beauty of nature as revealed in *bonsai* may be traced back more than 1,000 years to the Heian period of Japanese history as one of the *emakimono* (picture scrolls), now owned by the Imperial Household, depicted examples of this art. Though it has undergone many changes of fortune, the art of *bonsai* has been preserved to this day and is still a vital art.

Some *bonsai* that are firmly rooted have powerful trunks and gnarled boughs; others have graceful branches and lovely foliage. And still others bear fruit. *Bonsai* and *haiku*, miniature 17-syllable poems, have much in common for *bonsai* artists create beautiful poetry in miniature potted trees.

Bonsai may be defined as a tree or trees cultivated through nanization, or artificial dwarfing, in a small, tray-like vessel so as to be admired for the effect it is intended to produce. The purpose of this effect is to create an aesthetic sentiment by suggesting a piece of scenery. In other words, *bonsai* are designed to suggest trees growing in all possible environments—giant trees, tall and upright, trees hanging over a cliff, gnarled old trees whose growth has been stunted by winds and snowstorms, trees leaning to one side due to the wind blowing constantly in the same direction, a grove of trees in a field, trees growing among rocks as on a pine-clad islet, etc.

In other words, *bonsai* are intended to make one feel as though he were actually looking at the trees in the very fields or mountains where they flourish. So-called potted plants are appreciated merely for the verdure of their leaves and the splendor of their flowers, whereas *bonsai* evokes an appreciation of the beautiful by its suggestion of an entire landscape.

As might be expected, *bonsai* artists take great pains in the training and care of their trees. Sometimes they go to the fields or mountains in search of tiny stunted trees for training in pots. Or they may begin by raising seedlings in small pots, and, as the trees grow, transplant them to larger pots. There are cases where layerage is practiced on the branches of an aged tree by a special technique. Cutting and grafting are also resorted to frequently.

Some *bonsai* are said to be several hundred years old. Their long life is attributed to the painstaking care taken from generation to generation in replacing old earth with new and in root-pruning.

Simply to plant a tree in a small pot and thereby check its growth is not all that is required of *bonsai* culture. Care must also be taken to see that the trees to be trained for *bonsai* are provided with sufficient nourishment to induce vigorous growth and that all the branches that have grown too long are cut off to foster the thicker growth of smaller branches. Thus, individual as well as groups of trees are created that not only proportionally compare in luxuriance to the giant trees in a forest, but are also capable of stimulating the imagination of lovers of natural beauty.

●Dress

Socially, the Meiji Restoration of 1868 brought great changes. Age-old Court ceremonials were considerably modified or entirely replaced by European forms. Exceptions included the rituals concerned with the enthronement of the Emperor, the Crown Prince's marriage and Shinto services in the Imperial Palace sanctuary. The Emperor and the Empress now appear in Court in European dress, as do Court officials and ladies as well as the general public. On special occasions, a Court dress called *keiko* is worn by the ladies.

Western clothes are worn extensively by the ordinary Japanese, but on special occasions traditional dress is sometimes worn.
This consists of the following:

Kimono: Regarded as the traditional Japanese dress, it is a loose garment reaching to the ankles. The left part is folded in front over the right part and held snugly in place around the body by an *obi* (described later). The sleeves are wide and of varied sizes. When the *kimono* is hung up, the vertical length of the sleeves is usually about one-third of the entire length of the *kimono*. In girls' formal *kimono*, they are sometimes almost double the usual sleeve length and are called *furisode* (swing sleeves).

The *kimono* consists of four parts: the sleeves (*sode*), the body (*migoro*), the gussets (*okumi*) and the neckband (*eri*). The cutting of a *kimono* from the original material is done in straight lines in disregard of the curves of the human body. The form of the *kimono* is said to have been developed in the eighth century, and since then there has been no fundamental change in the basic form. The only changes have been minor such as in the length or width of the sleeves and the width of the neckband. Thus, the only real changes in the style of a *kimono* have largely taken place in the dyeing methods and patterns.

Generally worn unlined in summer and lined during the rest of the year, the *kimono* is made of different materials designed in various patterns. Besides the ordinary house *kimono*, there are fine-patterned, striped and spotted *kimono* for outdoor wear, traveling, attending the theater, etc.

The crested garments for women's use are designed in every imaginable variety. Some called *somoyo* have designs all over, from the shoulder to the sleeves and the skirt, while others called *susomoyo* have the design across the hem. These garments are worn at ceremonies or on other formal occasions, corresponding to the evening dress of European women. They differ, however, in that they are not necessarily worn only in the evening but at any time of the day. For mourning, a plain black garment with the family crest (left undyed) is worn. Women's informal full dress is called *homongi* (visiting dress), which is widely worn for social occasions. It is made of dyed (in one color), exquisitely patterned cloth, with an attractive, multicolored design running across the skirt. Men's formal dress consists of a silk, double-layer *kimono* with five crests (left undyed), a *haori* and a *hakama*. The latter two garments are worn over the *kimono*. There is no men's visiting dress corresponding to the women's *homongi*.

Haori: This is a kind of cloak falling a little below the knee and loosely fastened in front by means of braided cords. It is only worn over the *kimono* and never without it, although the *kimono* may be worn without the *haori*. Accordingly, its sleeves are patterned after those of the *kimono*. It is made either of black material with three or five family crests, or of a patterned material without a crest. The *haori* designed for winter wear is made of a thick, heavy material with lining. For summer use, it is very thin and light, being made of such native silk products as *sha* or *ro* and usually without lining.

Although an ordinary *haori* may be either crested or uncrested, those designed for ceremonial use must have three or five family crests—one high up on the center of the back and one at the back of the upper section of each sleeve. When five crests are used, one at the front of each sleeve is added.

The crests may be printed or embroidered, but those for ceremonial *haori* are invariably printed. There are over 300 family crests now in use, but if different varieties are counted, there are more than 3,000. The braided cords used to fasten the *haori* in front may be of any color, except those for ceremonial wear, which are of pure white silk.

Obi: This is the sash that holds the *kimono* together, for the garment has no buttons or other means of fastening. A woman's *obi* is about 60 cm wide, folded double lengthwise and is about 380 cm long. For formal dress, it is made of elegant, heavy silk material, and is wound round the waist twice and tied behind.

Although the *kimono* and *obi* are two different items of apparel, in use they are really one and inseparable. When one speaks, therefore, of the *kimono*, he usually includes the *obi* in his conception. As in the case of the *kimono*, there are also various unwritten laws governing the color and design of *obi* for different occasions. Men's *obi* are only ten cm wide and somewhat shorter than those of women. For ordinary wear, moreover, men use an *obi* made of some soft material like silk crepe.

Hakama: This is a wide, divided skirt made of a thick silk such as *Sendai-hira* or *Gosen-hira*. Though *hakama* are worn less frequently these days, they are still often worn by men for such ceremonies as marriages, funerals and ancestral rites.

Dogi: This is a short undergarment made of wadded silk worn in winter to keep the chest and back warm. It is made of wadded silk.

Hadagi and Naga-juban (Undergarments): The *kimono* is worn with two undergarments: *hadagi*—a cotton gauze undershirt worn next to the skin to protect the other garments and *naga-juban*—a sort of under-kimono, traditionally made of silk but recently more often made of polyester. A replaceable collar is sewn onto the *naga-juban* and is visible when the *kimono* is worn.

Tabi (Socks): These are made of cotton cloth or silk. Tabi for women are generally white, while those for men are dark blue, except for formal occasions when white *tabi* are worn. The tip of the *tabi* is split into two unequal parts, the smaller section containing the big toe and the larger one holding the other toes. Thus, the front strap of the sandal or clog can be inserted between these two parts. The *tabi* is fastened on the inner side of the foot by small metal clasps or hooks called *kohaze*.

Different materials are used for the cover, lining and sole of *tabi*. In *tabi* used for ceremonial occasions, the cover is made of a silk material such as *habutae* or *ayaginu* (figured silk), while in *tabi* designed for general use it is made of a plain material. For the *tabi* lining, different materials are used, depending on whether the *tabi* is used in summer or winter. For the sole, such fabrics as drill are used.

Hakimono: This is the general name for the various kinds of foot-gear, including *geta* (clogs), *setta* (leather-soled sandals) and *zori* (strapless sandals easily slipped on and off). *Geta* are generally made of *kiri* (paulownia) wood.

Hairdressing: Women usually wear their hair up (if it is long enough) when dressed in *kimono*. Very traditional styles have been abandoned because in addition to very long hair, the application of camellia oil is necessary. Wigs are worn on special occasions such as weddings.

Headgear: In olden days, neither men nor women wore anything on their heads, either inside or outside the house. There were some exceptions, however. Farmers and petty traders for instance, wore *sugegasa*—large hats made of sedge. In rainy weather, upper-class Japanese carried heavy umbrellas made of folding bamboo frames covered with oiled paper. Moreover, women shaded themselves from the sun by means of light, paper parasols. Today, foreign-style umbrellas are used, though Japanese-style umbrellas are still seen on occasion, carried chiefly by women when dressed in *kimono* and by *sumo* wrestlers. European-style caps and hats commonly used by men in pre-war days, even when attired in Japanese dress, are not so popular now, except as part of some student uniforms and for boys with baseball caps. Women, however, never wear hats except when attired in Western dress.

Ancient Styles

Before the changes brought about by the Meiji Restoration, the Court nobility, or *kuge*, of Kyoto had one style of ceremonial dress, while the military nobles of Edo had another. So also with people of different classes—*samurai* (warriors), priests, physicians, farmers, artisans and merchants. Each class wore its own distinguishing dress.

The Emperor wore an *uwagi* (outer garment) with long sleeves and wide cuffs reaching almost to his ankles. This was worn over one or more undergarments plus a kind of trousers that came to the ankles. The outer garment was tightly tied at the waist by a belt and was worn either with *osode* or *kosode* (long or short sleeves), which were white or creamy and made of the finest silk.

The sword was worn at the left side, attached to the waist by silk cords. The Imperial headgear, called *gyokan*, was made of lacquered silk gauze. Close-fitting and flat on top, it had a thin, stiff piece of material rising from the back. During enthronement ceremonies, or when attending the function called *Daijo-e* (Great Food-Offering to the Imperial Ancestors at the Court), the Emperor wore a crown set with jewels. The ministers wore a garment called *konaoshi* of a reddish brown color and similar to the Imperial garment. The rest of the Court nobles were distinguished by robes of different colors—red, scarlet, deep green, light blue, etc.—in accordance with their rank.

The *shogun*, on the other hand, on ceremonial occasions wore *hitatare*, which came down over the feet and trailed behind, giving the impression of a person walking on his knees. The trousers were tied over the outer garment at the waist. His headgear, called *eboshi* (a kind of high, brimless hat), was held in place by two cords tied under the chin. It is similar to the hat worn today by *sumo* referees. The top of the *eboshi* was bent to one side, to the right for the *shogun* and to the left when worn by other military nobility. The sword was worn at the left side of the waist.

For full dress, the ordinary *samurai* class wore *kataginu* and *hambakama*. This combination was known as "*kamishimo* (ceremonial dress)". *Kataginu*, or "shoulder-dress," was a kind of coat worn over the outer garment, covering the back down to the waist and draping over the shoulders, where it was folded in horizontal pleats. In front, it came down to the waist in two narrow pieces over the neckband. *Hambakama* (half-*hakama* or trousers) looked like a divided skirt reaching to the ankles. It is pleated and very full. The *haori* completed the full dress prescribed by custom for the common people. *Haori* and *hakama* constituted the ordinary visiting dress of the *samurai*.

Women's full Dress in Pre-Meiji Days

In the Court at Kyoto and the shogun's castle at Edo, women wore a garment called *kouchigi* with a scarlet petticoat, letting their hair hang down their backs. The consort of the *shogun* wore an *itsutsu-ginu* (five-fold coat) in winter and *uchiginu*, or unlined coat, in summer. Over the coat, she wore a loose-flowing gown of ornate embroidery called *uchikake*. Among the ordinary upper classes, a black silk gown stamped with the family crest was considered full dress. This was tied with a large *obi* at the waist, while underwear consisted of a white *habutae* gown.

●Budo (Martial Arts) and Traditional Sports

Traditional games and martial arts existed in Japan before the Meiji period, but there was no concept of modern sports before this period. *Takagari, kemari, yabusame* and *sumo* were all enjoyed by the aristocracy.

Takagari, or falconry, was introduced to Japan from China in the fifth century and reached the peak of its popularity in the early Tokugawa period in the 17th century.

Kemari is a type of Japanese football, also introduced from China in the middle seventh century. The object is for the players to keep the deerskin ball in the air as long as possible by kicking it from one to another.

Yabusame, or archery on horseback, has its origins in the late seventh century. Performed as a ceremony by courtiers or Imperial guards, it became an annual event at the festival of Tsurugaoka Hachimangu Shrine in Kamakura in 1266. In fact, it is still performed today.

With the rise of the military class in the late 12th century, *bujutsu*, or martial arts such as *kenjutsu* (fencing), *iaijutsu* (fast sword drawing), *jujutsu* (unarmed combat), *kyujutsu* (archery), *sojutsu* (spearmanship), *bajutsu* (horsemanship) and *suijutsu* (swimming), was developed by the *bushi* or *samurai* (warriors). *Bujutsu* led to the development of numerous martial traditions in the late 15th century that were gradually standardized into styles or schools and systematized during the peaceful reign of the Tokugawa Shogunate government.

Interest in some of these arts declined with the modernization of Japanese society right after the Meiji Restoration in 1868, but it revived with the nationalism evoked by the Sino-Japanese War in 1894-1895.

In 1895, the martial arts were centralized by a national organization called "Dai Nippon Butoku Kai" (the Greater Japan Martial Arts Association) and were adopted into the educational system in 1911.

In 1926 a revision was made in the appellation of certain Japanese martial arts. The revision reflected a change in the philosophy of the practitioners of these disciplines. Two examples are the change of *kenjutsu* to *kendo* (Japanese-style fencing) and the change of *jujutsu* to *judo*. Although the suffixes *jutsu* and *do* are both derived from the original meaning of way, *jutsu* indicates the training in a technique or method, while *do* includes this as well as a broader meaning that encompasses a philosophical and spiritual discipline. They were practiced at schools on a limited scale side by side with modern sports.

Because of their militaristic character, however, they were banned by Occupation authorities after World War II, but beginning in 1950 the ban was lifted and they were given a new start as sports rather than martial arts.

In 1964 *judo* was added to the Tokyo Olympic Games, and in 1970 the first World Kendo Tournament was held in Tokyo at the Nippon Budokan Hall (Japan Martial Arts Hall). The World Union of *Karatedo* Organizations was also formed and held its first World Championships in Tokyo in 1970.

Budo was derived from *bujutsu*, or martial arts, which was the accomplishment of the *samurai*, who mastered at least one or two of these arts—both for self-defense and aggressiveness on the battle-field. Some of the major ones are as follows.

Judo

Judo is the modern adaptation of *jujutsu*, which developed from *sumo* as the art of grappling with one's enemy and defeating him on the battlefield. Although a weapon was not generally used in *jujutsu*, sometimes the art was employed to disarm an enemy. There were many techniques in *jujutsu* such as hitting, jabbing and kicking—executed from a specific distance—as well as throwing, holding, strangling and dislocating—utilized when grappling with the enemy. *Jujutsu* together with *kenjutsu* became a major martial art in the Edo period (1603-1867), branching out into many rival schools.

Of these schools, the Tenshin Shin-yo and the Kito schools are the most famous. In fact, they were the fountainhead of the *Kodokan judo* of today. It should also be noted that *aiki-jujutsu* of the Daito school developed into *aikido* as practiced today.

Kano Jigoro (1860-1938), after mastering these two *jujutsu* schools, modified and coordinated them. In 1882 he organized modern *judo* and called it *Kodokan judo* after his first training *dojo* (training hall). He abolished the narrow-minded ethical aims of the old *jujutsu* schools and introduced a broad, new educational idea. He also formulated a scientific training system based on modern athletic principles. More specifically, Kano divided *judo* techniques into three major sections, namely: (1) the art of attacking the vital points, (2) the art of throwing one's opponent and (3) the art of grappling on the mat. Thus, he made it possible to use both the art of throwing and the art of mat-grappling in *randori* (free-style training). In this way, *judo* became a modern sport in every sense of the word. Comparable to any other modern sport, it gradually spread throughout the world. The International Judo Federation was established in 1952 and the number of its member nations reached 152 (As of September 1990).

The first International Judo Championships were held in Tokyo in May 1956. Finally, it was officially designated an Olympic sport in the 18th Olympic Games held in Tokyo in 1964. Indeed, it has become a very popular sport in recent years, both in Japan and abroad.

Judo training has three phases—*kata* (form), *randori* (free-style training) and competition. In practicing *kata*, one studies the theory and method of *judo* techniques. In free-style training, one learns the application of the techniques by freely using them against an opponent. In a *judo* match, the contestant who scores the most points by effectively applying *judo* techniques against his opponent is judged the victor. In a *judo* match, attacking the vital points as well as bending and twisting the joints are banned.

The grade-ranking system (*dan* and *kyu*) has been instituted to classify *judoka* (players) according to the degree of their mastery of judo. There are five *kyu* starting with the lowest rank of fifth *kyu* up to first *kyu*, which is the top rank in the *kyu* class. *Dan*, which is higher than *kyu*, starts with the lowest rank of first *dan* and ends with the top rank of tenth *dan*. To indicate the general ranks of *kyu* and *dan*, different colored belts are used. Namely, a white belt indicates that the wearer is fourth *kyu* or lower and a reddish brown belt—first, second or third *kyu*. A black belt indicates any rank between first and fifth *dan*, a red-and-white belt—sixth to eighth *dan* and a red belt —ninth or tenth *dan*. It must be mentioned in this connection, however, that even the holder of sixth or higher *dan* can also wear a black belt.

Kodokan Judo Hall is mecca for *judo* aspirants, and gives instruction to foreigners. The address is 1-16 Kasuga, Bunkyo-ku, Tokyo. ☎ (03) 3811-7154.

Judo and *kendo* are also taught at Budo Gakuen, which is located at Nippon Budokan Hall, 2-3 Kitanomaru-Koen, Chiyoda-ku, Tokyo. ☎ (03) 3216-5143.

Aikido

Aiki-jujutsu of the Daito school, one of the old schools of *jujutsu*, is regarded as the origin of *aikido*. *Aiki-jujutsu* was founded by Minamoto-no-Yoshimitsu (1045-1127). After being handed down in the Minamoto family for generations, it was finally taken over by the Takeda family in Kai Province (now, Yamanashi Prefecture). The secret of the art was later assumed by the Takeda family in the Aizu District in the present Fukushima Prefecture. Ueshiba Morihei (1883 -1970), who learned the art from Takeda Sokaku—the seventh generation of the Takeda family in Aizu, developed *aikido* in its present form by adding the salient points of the Kito and Yagyu schools of *jujutsu* to the art of *aiki-jujutsu*. *Aikido* is performed without any weapons, as a rule, but one may be used if an opponent is armed.

The practice of *aikido* was originally only for the purpose of learning *kata* (form). It was not a sport, but strictly a martial art based on traditional *jujutsu*. Tomiki Kenji (1900-1979), a disciple of Ueshiba Morihei, classified and coordinated the techniques of *aikido*, formulating a free-style method. Thus, he succeeded in reorganizing it as a modern, noncompetitive sport.

In *judo*, a technique is executed, as a rule, while the two contestants are holding each other's collars and sleeves. In *aikido*, the two contestants remain apart from each other, never giving the opponent a chance to get a hold. The purpose of *aikido* is to throw one's opponent to the floor or attack his weak point by applying a pain hold in order to throw him or pin him down. The reason why it is highly recommended as an art of self-defense is because *aikido* has made it possible to practice the art of attacking the vital points or bending and twisting one's opponent's limbs—both powerful tricks of traditional *jujutsu*.

Aikido well serves the aim of maintaining and increasing physical fitness because it helps to improve the flexibility of the joints and promote smooth physical movement. One can, therefore, practice *aikido* no matter how old one is because it is not necessary to depend too much on muscular strength. *Aikido* is becoming increasingly popular, both in Japan and abroad. It is expected that the day will come when *aikido* will spread like *judo* throughout the world, even though there is no such thing as competitive *aikido* or *aikido* tournaments, as is the case of the other martial arts.

Karatedo (or simply Karate)

This is the art of hitting or jabbing one's opponent with one's fist or kicking him off his feet. It rules out the use of a weapon. The history of *karatedo* is very old, developing over a long time from the Tang Dynasty through the Sung Dynasty to the Ming Dynasty in China. Later, it was introduced to Okinawa from China, gradually becoming a unique combative art.

It was in 1922 that Funakoshi Gichin (1870-1957) introduced *karate* to Japan. Under the influence of the indigenous martial arts and also through scientific modification, it has made remarkable progress in Japan. It has developed into several schools, among which Shotokan, Goju, Shito and Wado are the most famous. Many other schools subsequently developed from these four main schools. In recent years, *karate* has rapidly found its way into several foreign countries. At present, about 30 countries, including the United States, Britain, Germany and Italy, have taken up *karatedo*. Moreover, the number of *karate* enthusiasts in these countries is expected to grow steadily from year to year.

Karate training includes the fundamentals, *kata*, basic *kumite* and free *kumite*. In basic training, one is required to repeatedly practice punches, jabs and kicks as well as defensive blocks. For this purpose, a bundle of straw is used as a dummy. When one is well trained in basic *karatedo*, it is not difficult to break at a single stroke between 10 to 15 Japanese roof slates or five boards 1.5 cm thick laid atop one another.

Kata (form) is devised on the basis of these fundamental motions so that they may resemble as much as possible the motion of an actual fight. They are devised in such a way that one man can go through the motions of counterattacking an imaginary enemy who may be attacking him from all possible directions.

The basic *kumite* is an applied form of *kata* to be practiced by two people. One becomes the attacker, punching and kicking in accordance with regular forms, while the other becomes the defender and tries to block or dodge the attack. He may even counterattack. Free-style *kumite* does not set any restrictions on either offensive or defensive motions. In other words, one can freely use any technique that one has learned in basic *kata* and basic *kumite*. There is one strict rule, however, in free-style *kumite*—whether it is a punch or a kick, one must stop one or two inches short of his opponent's body. Only when one has fully qualified as a holder of a *dan* degree, can he practice all the powerful techniques of *karatedo* with safety.

Kendo

Kendo is Japanese-style fencing. Originating from *kenjutsu* as one of the most important Japanese martial arts, it is based on the use of the sword. It attained a high degree of development when the *bushi* rose to power in the Kamakura period in the 12th century. It was battle-tested and perfected during the succession of internal wars from the middle of the 14th century. Though the establishment of the Tokugawa Shogunate government in 1603 ushered in a long reign of peace, the *samurai* were always encouraged to master *kenjutsu*.

Moreover, *kenjutsu* was even regarded as a form of practical ethics based on Confucianism and Buddhism—the most important bases of morality in those days. As a result, a great many masters of *kenjutsu* emerged in this period and established more than 200 schools, of which about 50 still survive. *Kenjutsu* later developed into *kendo* following the modernization of some of its techniques. (refer to p.223)

The Meiji Restoration gave rise to a transitional period from *kenjutsu* to *kendo* because at this time the *samurai* class was abolished together with the custom of carrying a sword. Having thus lost its original significance, *kenjutsu* gradually took on a new meaning as *kendo*—a modern sport.

The end of World War II in 1945 brought about the second transitional period in the history of *kendo*. The original type of *kendo*, which had played an important part in fostering the militaristic spirit in education, had to go. As a result, *kendo* was reborn as a sport in 1952 after having renounced its martial character. The All-Japan Kendo Federation was established in October of the same year. The new sport is now coming into its own both in school and social athletic programs.

A *kendo* match is played by two opponents wearing protective equipment and wielding a bamboo sword. The match is won by effectively hitting three specified parts of the body—*men* (head), *do* (trunk) or *kote* (wrist)—or jabbing the throat—*tsuki*, and by scoring the first two out of three points.

The protectors consist of a face guard like one used for Western fencing, a breastplate to cover the trunk, gauntlets to protect the arms and hands, and a skirt of padded cloth to guard the groin.

The bamboo sword is made of four strips of bamboo, which should be less than 118 cm long and weigh more than 485 gr. for adult fencers. A correct, effective hit is made with the top third of the sword.

As in other traditional sports, there are ten ranks from *shodan* (first grade) to *judan* (tenth grade), awarded in accordance with the degree of the skill and knowledge of the practitioner. In addition, a title of *renshi*, *kyoshi* or *hanshi* is given anyone who holds the fifth or higher grade and has contributed to the development of the *kendo* world.

Naginata

This is a Japanese-style halberd adopted as a weapon at the beginning of the 13th century. It is a sword with an extremely long handle. It became the favorite weapon of the warrior monks, who were called upon in medieval times to defend the wealth and property of the large Buddhist temples. Actually, it was generally used by low-class *samurai*.

The *Naginata* also became the woman's favorite weapon for self-defense in the Edo period (1603-1867). Naturally, the blade was shortened and the handle was often beautifully decorated with gold or silver lacquer. In fact, the art of *naginata* was very popular in the Edo period and many *naginata* schools were set up. After the Meiji period (1868-1912), the art of *naginata* became a martial art exclusively for women. Later, it was adopted in some school athletic programs after an appropriate set of rules had been introduced.

Iaijutsu

This art of quickly drawing the sword dates back to around 1600. In the subsequent centuries, many schools of *iaijutsu* were founded, of which the most influential were Hasegawa, Katayama and Tamiya. This branch of the Japanese martial arts was practiced by the *samurai* along with *kenjutsu*. It enabled the *samurai* to draw his sword in any emergency and instantly counter an enemy attack from any direction.

Kyudo

Kyudo from *kyujutsu* is archery, which has its own history in the use of unusually long bows and arrows. From the feudal period, two main schools of Japanese archery developed—Ogasawara and Heki. *Yabusame*, or horseback archery, performed even today at Tsuruga-oka Hachimangu Shrine in Kamakura and other places, originated during the Kamakura period (1192–1333).

Kyudo made a new start in the postwar years as a sport. By and large, the founding of the Japan Kyudo Federation in 1949 was the primary impetus of the reorientation of *kyudo*. The bow is made of wood and bamboo glued together, with a length of about 2.21 m. The arrow consists of a bamboo shaft, three feathers and an arrowhead. In a contest, the number of arrows hitting the target decides the winner, with each contestant usually shooting 10 to 20 arrows.

Sumo

Sumo, or Japanese-style wrestling, is believed to have originated in Japan. History records that the first match was performed before the Emperor in 200 A.D., although the origins of *sumo* go back even further to the time of Emperor Jimmu and before.

Professional *rikishi* (*sumo* wrestlers) are all "giants," usually weighing from 90 to 240 kg. Some 750 to 800 wrestlers are divided into six divisions: *jonokuchi, jonidan, sandamme, makushita, juryo* and *makunouchi* (bottom to top). The highest rank in the *makunouchi* division is called *yokozuna*, or grand champion. The next positions are, in order, *ozeki* (champion), *sekiwake* (junior champion), *komusubi* (second junior champion), all of which are called by the general name of *sanyaku* or "the first three rankings," and *maegashira* (ordinary wrestlers).

The wrestlers live and train in dormitory-gymnasiums called *heya*, or stables. Each of the 44 stables is run by a former wrestler, usually of a high rank, who is assisted by coaches and trainers—also ex-wrestlers. Apprentice wrestlers enter a stable as young as 15, reach their peak strength in their mid-20s and retire in their early-30s or earlier. In recent years, many foreign-born *sumo* wrestlers have appeared on the scene. The first to win a tournament was Hawaiian wrestler Takamiyama in 1972, followed by Konishiki in 1989, also from Hawaii and the only foreign-born *rikishi* ever to attain the second-highest rank of *ozeki*.

A series of six annual, 15-day tournaments is held—in January, May and September at the Ryogoku Kokugikan Sumo Arena in Tokyo, in March at Osaka, in July at Nagoya and in November at Fukuoka. The win-loss records made in each tournament determine the wrestler's rank and salary in the following tourney, except for *yokozuna*, which is a permanent rank. The tourney winner is awarded a champion's flag, several trophies, a monetary prize of ¥5 million and the engraving of his name on the trophy given in the name of the Emperor. Between tournaments, *sumo* wrestlers tour the country, competing in local matches.

This is how it is performed by professionals in the two top divisions: First, two *rikishi* wearing only a silk sash called a *mawashi* enter a ring of hard-packed clay measuring 4.55 m in diameter and set up on a square mound about 75 cm high. A symbolic, Shinto-style roof is suspended from the ceiling of the stadium over the ring. They confront each other in accordance with a traditional squatting, stamping ritual, after which the referee announces the names of the wrestlers. Meanwhile, the players rinse their mouths with "power water" kept in basins beside the ring and toss salt on the clay as an act of purification. Next, the players face each other, squatting and touching the clay with their clenched fists in psychological preparation for the bout. They begin after about four minutes of the preliminary ritual. This *shikiri* preliminary corresponding to the "on your mark, get-set" in Western athletics can be tedious for those who lack adequate knowledge of *sumo*, but it is extremely absorbing to *sumo* fans since the initial attack is a source of increasing tension and excitement to them. In former days, the *shikiri* sometimes went on and on, not uncommonly as long as 30 or 40 minutes.

The issue is decided when any part of a wrestler's body except the bottoms of his feet touches the ground, or when he steps out or is forced out of the ring. There are some 70 different thrusting, pushing, throwing, lifting, tripping, pulling and forcing techniques at their disposal. If a protest is raised against the decision of the referee by any of the five judges or waiting wrestlers seated around the ring, the judges get together in the ring to settle the matter. They can confirm or reverse the referee's decision, or call for a rematch.

Before the bouts of the wrestlers of the *makunouchi* and *juryo* divisions, a spectacular ceremony called the *dohyo-iri* (ring entry) is held in which all the wrestlers of these divisions wearing richly embroidered, ankle-length "aprons" parade onto the ring, then clap their hands and lift their aprons in accordance with a time-honored *sumo* ritual.

The *yokozuna* wrestler does not participate in the ceremony mentioned above because he has a special ceremony to perform independently of the rest. This ceremony is known as the *yokozuna dohyo-iri*. In observing the function, he wears *yokozuna*, the snow-white sacred hawser over his ornamental apron. When dressed, he is ushered into the ring heralded by a wrestler of high rank and followed by another in the capacity of guard and swordbearer. The latter two wrestlers are also imposingly decked out in decorative aprons matching that of the *yokozuna*.

The ceremony performed by the *yokozuna* is symbolic of prayer and oath-taking as well as a demonstration of the basic form of wrestling and the spiritual power with which *sumo* is to be presented. They are represented by the performance of three formalities, namely: *chiri-chozu* (a form of courteous greeting), the basic wrestling techniques in three motions with the hands, and the motions of feet which are symbolic of dispelling evil spirits and defilement to clear the way to victory.

Nihon Sumo Kyokai (Japan Sumo Association) is at Ryogoku Kokugikan Sumo Arena, 1-3-28 Yokoami, Taito-ku, Tokyo. ☎ (03) 3623-5111.

IX. Modern Japan

●Japanese Society

Shattered by the defeat in World War II, Japan managed to achieve a miraculous economic recovery and growth after the war. In particular, the nation's plan to double its national income in the 1960s led Japan to become one of the world's economic superpowers, although business experienced several ups and downs along the way.

This economic growth has given the Japanese a material affluence, and, at the same time, it has dramatically changed the social mechanisms of the country, affording an opportunity for the Japanese to review their way of life and the meaning of living.

For example, advanced medical technology and an improvement in the welfare system made possible by the economic prosperity have markedly prolonged the average life span of the Japanese. But this has posed a new problem of how the Japanese should cope with an aging society.

On the other hand, the expansion of the economy has increased the number of female workers and encouraged many housewives to get a job outside the home. This is forcing the husbands to share the household duties more than ever before, and requiring couples to review the traditional husband-wife relationship. In addition, since they have obtained most of what they want, they are now paying more attention to the spiritual aspects of life than to the materialistic side. Generally speaking, during the period of rapid economic growth, people found pleasure in purchasing various "things." Those who had experienced the postwar austerity were happy when they purchased their first electric refrigerator or TV set. As they became richer, they sought more luxurious things such as expensive audio equipment and passenger cars. It may be said that the TV commercial message "To be big is nice," which was once popular, represented the general sentiment of the Japanese in those days.

The first oil shock of 1973 reminded the Japanese that natural resources are not limitless, and urged them to reflect on the single-minded pursuit of material affluence. On the other hand, the world-wide environmental disruption caused by over-industrialization is beginning to have a significant effect on their daily life. Thus, the mode of living of the Japanese is undergoing change through the interaction of the severe international economic and political situations as well as through alterations in domestic social conditions such as the shift toward an aging society.

Some of the characteristic features of Japanese life are described in the following sections.

231

Sophistication of Consumer Spending

1) Because of its strong economy, which has been attracting the attention of the world, Japan's national income has been steadily rising year by year. As income has climbed, so has consumer spending. In recent years, consumer spending for such durable goods as home electric appliances has been proportionately decreasing, while spending on traveling, dining out and other services as well as for nondurable goods (food, etc.) has been increasing. With respect to durable goods, more and more consumers are seeking higher quality. On the whole, consumer spending has become increasingly sophisticated and diversified. Probably this can best be illustrated by passenger cars and overseas travel.

The strong domestic demand for automobiles is one of the major factors in Japan's economic prosperity. Recently, the demand for cars with larger displacement has been increasing. The growth of imported cars is also impressive. According to a survey conducted by Japan Automobile Importers' Association, imported cars sold during 1988 accounted for 33.1% of the total number of new passenger cars with a displacement exceeding 2 liters. The average age and average annual income of those who purchased an imported car for the first time in that year was 37 and ¥11,200,000, respectively. In contrast, those who replaced their imported car with a new imported car during the same period showed an average age of 41 and an average annual income of ¥13,900,000. The implication is that the number of people buying imported cars is expanding.

2) The number of Japanese traveling abroad has been rapidly increasing. It nearly doubled from approximately 4,950,000 in 1985 to about 9,660,000 in 1989, heralding an age in which 10,000,000 Japanese annually cross the seas (Table 1).

Table 1   Change in Number of Japanese Traveling Abroad

Year \ Purpose	Total	Sightseeing	Business	Other
1985	4,948,366 (100.0) (106.2)	4,024,051 (81.3) (105.4)	762,793 (15.4) (110.4)	161,522 (3.3) (106.3)
1986	5,516,193 (100.0) (111.5)	4,506,186 (81.7) (112.0)	824,224 (14.9) (108.1)	185,783 (3.4) (115.0)
1987	6,829,338 (100.0) (123.8)	5,641,610 (82.6) (125.2)	958,266 (14.0) (116.3)	229,462 (3.4) (123.5)
1988	8,426,867 (100.0) (123.4)	7,028,001 (83.4) (124.6)	1,120,230 (13.3) (116.9)	278,636 (3.3) (121.4)
1989	9,662,752 (100.0) (114.7)	8,106,523 (83.9) (115.3)	1,224,480 (12.7) (109.3)	331,749 (3.4) (119.1)

Note: Figures in brackets indicate percentages of total,
and figures in parentheses indicate percentages
of the previous year's figure.
Source: White Paper on Tourism

In each of the five years, more than 80% of those who traveled abroad were tourists. In 1989 alone, as many as 8,100,000 Japanese went on a sightseeing trip abroad. The overseas travelers in 1989 are broken down by sex into 597,000 males and 369,000 females. However, for the past decade, female travelers have surpassed male travelers in the annual rate of growth. With respect to female travelers, the age group of 20 to 29 years accounts for 41% of the total in marked contrast to the fact that nearly one half of the male travelers are in their 30s or 40s. (Fig. 1).

Fig. 1 Breakdown of Japanese Overseas Travelers by Sex and by Age Group (1989)

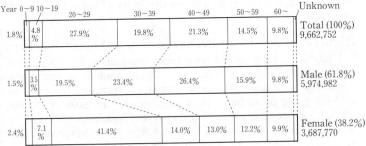

Year	0~9	10~19	20~29	30~39	40~49	50~59	60~	Unknown	
	1.8%	4.8%	27.9%	19.8%	21.3%	14.5%	9.8%		Total (100%) 9,662,752
	1.5%	3.5%	19.5%	23.4%	26.4%	15.9%	9.8%		Male (61.8%) 5,974,982
	2.4%	7.1%	41.4%	14.0%	13.0%	12.2%	9.9%		Female (38.2%) 3,687,770

Note : Figures in brackets indicate percentages of total, and figures in parentheses indicate percentages of the previous year's figure.
Source : White paper on tourism

These figures suggest that enthusiasm for traveling abroad has been constantly spreading among young women, contributing a great deal to the steady increase of Japanese going abroad.

3) Nevertheless, it is not that the life of the Japanese is characterized solely by the above-mentioned favorable conditions—continuing expansion of the economy and consumer spending. Among other things, the aggravation of the housing shortage in metropolitan areas has become a serious problem concerned with national life.

The rise in land prices, which began in the Tokyo Metropolis a few years ago, has spread to the entire metropolitan area and further to such big cities as Osaka and Nagoya, and is now rapidly reaching smaller cities and towns. The price of land in the Tokyo Metropolis, which had begun to increase in 1985, continued to skyrocket until it calmed down somewhat in 1988. According to official land prices periodically announced by the government, the average price of land in Tokyo more than tripled in only three years, from ¥296,800 per square meter in 1985 to ¥951,300 per square meter in 1988. As a result, the number of housing starts in Tokyo declined from about 35,000 in 1980 to some 23,500 in 1988. Instead, housing starts increased in Saitama, Chiba, and Kanagawa—the prefectures adjoining the Tokyo Metropolis.

According to the "Economic White Paper" for 1989, the cost of buying a lot in Tokyo and building a house on it is estimated to be as much as ¥80 million, while the cost of buying a condominium in Tokyo is ¥60 million per apartment. These costs are much more than the average worker can afford. Such being the case, the number of those who can afford to buy a house in Tokyo has been constantly decreasing so that a growing number of people working in Tokyo have to seek a house outside Tokyo.

The sharp rise in land prices is largely attributable to the fact that much of the surplus funds made available by continued prosperity and low interest rates was invested in real estate. Though there are at last signs of the increase in land prices leveling off in 1990, it will remain difficult for most people working in big cities to buy a house near their workplace.

High-Level Academic Background and Women Workers

1) Many years have passed since Japan was said to have become a society with a high academic level. Throughout the postwar economic recovery and subsequent economic expansion, the ratio of students going on to high school continued to increase. In recent years, it has been more than 90%. In the past decade, the ratio of high school graduates who went on to college or junior college was 35% to 37%; that is, one out of three high school graduates goes on to a higher educational institution (Table 2).

Table 2 Ratio of Students Going on to College/Junior College

	Male	Female	Total
1980	41.3	33.3	37.4
1981	40.5	33.0	36.9
1982	39.8	32.7	36.3
1983	37.9	32.2	35.1
1984	38.3	32.8	35.6
1985	40.6	34.5	37.6
1986	35.9	33.5	34.7
1987	37.1	35.1	36.1
1988	37.2	36.2	36.7
1989	35.8	36.8	36.3

Source: Ministry of Education "Basic School Survey"

The increase in the number of people with a high-level academic background contributed to the high rate of economic growth after the war. At the same time, however, it has intensified the competition among students preparing themselves for an entrance examination to a school of higher learning. As a result, it has become necessary for educationists to give priority to a curriculum adapted to entrance examinations for schools of higher learning. Besides, the number of elementary school children and junior high school students receiving extra lessons at a supplementary school has been increasing year by year. According to a survey conducted by the Ministry of Education, the number of elementary school children attending a supplementary school increased from 1,300,000 (12% of the total) in 1976 to 1,800,000 (16.5%) in 1985. Similarly, the number of junior high school students attending a supplementary school increased from 1,800,000 (38.0% of the total) in 1976 to 2,700,000 (44.5%) in 1985.

Recently, the school educational system and the examination system for entrance into a school of higher learning have become hot issues, with some critics pointing out that they have caused the creativity and originality of young people to deteriorate.
2) Females with a higher academic background have also been proportionately increasing. In some measure, this accounts for the recent marked increase in the number of working females.

According to 1988 labor statistics, woman workers numbered 24,080,000, nearly 50% of the total number of employable females of 15 years and over. In other words, one out of two females in Japan is engaged in some form of work.

Though the proportion of working females seems appreciably high, many problems still remain to be solved.

For example, let us look at how the average husband and wife, both holding jobs, spend their time in their daily life (Fig. 2 and Fig. 3).

Fig. 2 How Working Husbands and Wives Spend Their Time (weekday)

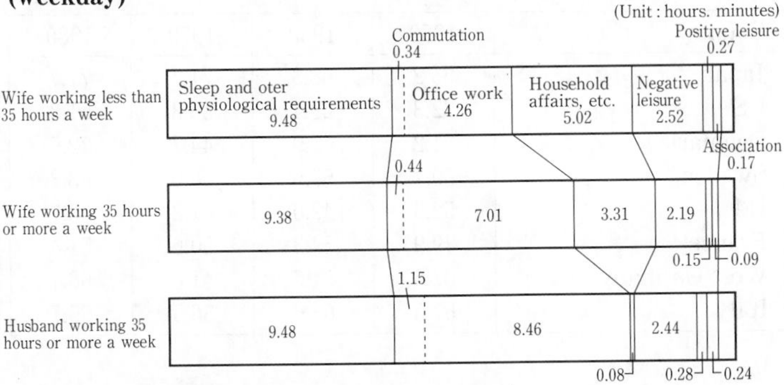

(Unit : hours. minutes)

Note : Husband and wife of nuclear family.
Source : "Actual Condition of Female Labor"(1989), Women's Bureau, Ministry of Labor

Fig. 3 How Working Husbands and Wives Spend Their Time (Holiday)

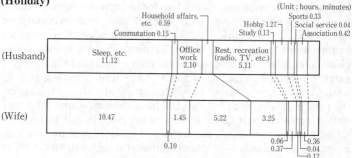

(Unit : hours. minutes)

Note : 1. Husband and wife of nuclear family.
2. Both husband and wife work more than 35 hours a week.

While the wife working 35 hours or more a week spends 3 hours and 31 minutes a day on household affairs, the husband spares only 8 minutes for his chores. This suggests that the husband spends much more time on "positive leisure" than his wife does.

This situation is the same on holidays. The wife spends 5 hours and 22 minutes on domestic chores vs. 59 minutes spent by the husband. Thus, the time the wife can set aside for rest and recreation is only about 60% of what her husband can spend.

In addition, the wife has to take care of their children and aged parents. In Japan, as far as the typical family is concerned, it will not be in the near future that both the husband and wife equally share the burden of household affairs.

Table 3 Changes in the proportions of unmarried females between 20 and 24 in industrialized countries

Country	1950	1960	1970	1980
Japan	55.2	68.3	71.7	77.7
USA	32.3	28.4	36.3	51.3
Denmark	51.2	45.9	44.7	72.5
Sweden	59.7	57.5	60.0	83.3
U.K.	52.5	42.0	41.2	53.7
France	49.9	54.3	50.6	51.4
West-Germany	67.6	54.6	41.6	60.1
Italy	67.5	65.6	56.5	55.7

Note: Some of the figures shown for a particular year are those for the year before or after that year.
Source: United Nations "Demographic Yearbook"

3) One of the characteristic features of Japanese society is the tendency for both males and females to marry late, although this may not be directly related to the increase in the number of females who are working.

According to a survey conducted by the Ministry of Health and Welfare, in the 16 years from 1972 to 1988 the average age of first marriage rose from 26.7 to 28.5 for males and from 24.2 to 25.8 for females. The proportion of unmarried females between the ages of 20 and 24 in Japan is considerably higher than in most industrialized countries (Table 3).

Some attribute the tendency toward late marriages to an imbalance in the number of marriageable males and females. However, it is the more predominant view that the prime cause is that society with a high level of academic achievement has rapidly developed since 1965.

4) The declining birthrate as well as late marriages have become serious social problems.

Since the "second baby boom" in the mid-1960s, the birth-rate in Japan has been steadily decreasing. The number of births, which was 2,700,000 in 1949, dropped below 2,000,000 in 1975 and was estimated at 1,240,000 in 1989.

Generally speaking, females between 25 and 29 are the most fertile. The declining birthrate is partly attributable to a relatively small proportion of females of this age group. The tendency of late marriage as mentioned above is related to the declining birthrate. Other factors that should not be overlooked are the economic and mental burden of child rearing, the difficulty in rearing a child while working outside the home and the unsatisfactory housing shortage.

In any case, with the arrival of an aging society near at hand, it has been pointed out that the problem of a declining birthrate will become more serious in the near future.

Arrival of Aging Society

1) In 1947 the average life of a Japanese was 50.1 years for a male and 54 for a female. In 1988 it reached the world's highest level: 75.5 years for a male and 81.3 for a female.

With the growth of the average age, the age of the population has been rapidly increasing. The percentage of people of 65 years and over to the total Japanese population (ratio of aged people), which had been approximately 5% until around 1955, reached 11.6% in October 1990. Though this is still lower than the levels in the United States and Europe, it is estimated that the ratio of aged people in Japan to the total population will become 16.3% by the year 2000— comparable to the projected figures for the U.S. and Europe—and exceed 23% by the year 2020 to emerge as one of the world's most aged societies.

2) From the viewpoint of each individual man, the average of his remaining life—that is, how many years he or she can live from hence

237

forward—is more important than the average of his total life span.

At present, the average remaining life of people 60 years of age is 19.94 years for males and 24 years for females. It might be interesting to note that at the time these people were born (from 1926–1930) the age groups which could expect the same number of remaining years were 48 year old males and 47-year-old females. In other words, it follows that men in their 40s about 60 years ago and men in their 60s of today are the "same age" physically.

Viewed in this way, it might be said that Japan's aging society will be one in which those aged people who are "as young as" the people who were in their 40s in the early 20th century account for a high percentage.

3) According to a survey conducted in 1988 of the aged people of 65 years and over, those who were living with their children accounted for 61.9%, while 24.2% were living with their spouse alone and 10.4% were living all alone. However, the ratio of aged people living with their children has been declining year by year. The above-mentioned ratio of 61.9% for 1988 is 19.7 percentage points less than the ratio in 1960 (81.6%). Besides, according to the results of surveys conducted in the last five years, the parent generation (in their 60s) and child generation (in their 30s and 40s) who wish to live together have been proportionately decreasing.

This situation can be clearly understood when we look at the household configuration of aged people (Fig. 4).

Fig. 4 Change in Household Configuration Involving Aged Members (65 years and over)

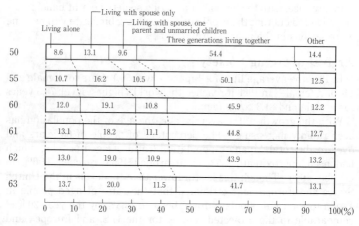

The number of households in which three generations of people live together has been decreasing year by year, while the number of households in which aged people live with their spouse alone or all alone have been increasing.

4) The arrival of an aging society poses many other problems in Japan such as the securing of jobs for those aged people who wish to or must work longer than they are expected to.

Conclusion

As described so far, Japan has grown markedly on the base of its economic prosperity. This, in turn, has presented new problems and challenges. In a sense, it might be said that the advent of an aging society involves all those problems and challenges.

Besides, the future course of events will definitely be different from the process of the postwar economic recovery and economic expansion. In the future, it will become much more important for Japan as a member of international society to endeavor to develop itself in close cooperation with other countries around the world.

●Mass Media

Newspapers

Brief History of Modern Japanese Newspaper

In 1870, the Yokohama Mainichi Shimbun (Yokohama Daily News), printed with lead type, was published daily, making it the predecessor of modern Japanese newspapers. The emergence of this newspaper subsequently gave rise to many others in rapid succession both in Tokyo and Osaka.

With the rapid development of the modern Japanese political system, newspapers acquired large circulations.

Furthermore, the wars with China (1894–1895) and Russia (1904–1905), kept national feelings running high. Pandering to this sentiment, newspapers grew in popularity throughout the country during the 45 years of the Meiji period.

In the meantime, newspapers emphasizing political topics developed in Tokyo, the center of Japanese politics, while newspapers primarily devoting themselves to news reporting without any special political leaning thrived in Osaka where commerce was of vital importance. Osaka is the birthplace of both the Asahi Shimbun and the Mainichi Shimbun, both of which developed by doing business on a commercial basis.

At the beginning of the Taisho period in 1912, these two newspapers simultaneously made inroads into Tokyo and gradually but firmly established themselves, outrivaling the politically inclined newspapers then existing in Tokyo. These two newspapers both followed an independent, nonpartisan policy in competing with each other in the objective reporting of news. Thus, they were largely responsible for formulating the general characteristics of the Japanese newspapers of today.

In 1931, about 1,200 daily newspapers and some 7,700 weeklies and semimonthlies were published in Japan.

But as the internal situation intensified during the years between the outbreak of the China Incident (1937) and World War II (1941), government control of the press tightened. As a result, many newspapers were either abolished or forced to merge by government order until there were only 55 newspapers left in the country—five in Tokyo, four in Osaka and one in each of the 46 prefectures.

Soon after World War II ended, freedom of the press was restored with the abolishment of all the laws that had kept it in check. When Japanese press circles established the Japan Newspaper Publishers and Editors Association, practically every newspaper in Japan became a member. While the primary objective of the association is to uphold freedom of the press, its members have agreed to abide by the ethical rules stipulated in "The Canons of Journalism," which it adopted.

Newspaper Today

There are 125 daily newspapers in Japan, most of which publish both morning and evening editions. If the morning and evening editions are counted separately, as is usually done in Western countries, there are a total of 67,380,000 copies published daily in Japan. With this figure, Japan ranks second after the Soviet Union, which has the world's largest daily newspaper circulation amounting to 116,096,000 copies (source: the World Statistical Yearbook, 1987, published by the United Nations). USA ranks third with 63,263,000 copies and People's Republic of China is forth with 30,000,000 copies.

Furthermore, in terms of circulation per one thousand population, Japan ranks first with 562 copies. East Germany comes second with 550 copies, USSR ranks third with 422, followed by the Great Britain with 414 copies, West Germany with 350 copies and the USA with 268 copies.

Out of the 142 daily newspapers, 35 are published in Tokyo and 18 in Osaka, which means that 30% of Japan's daily papers is published in these major cities.

Among these papers, the five national dailies—Asahi, Mainichi, Yomiuri, Sankei and Nihon Keizai—are all published in both Tokyo and Osaka, but sold and circulated throughout Japan. Besides these five, which enjoy the largest circulations, there are three others that have a wide regional distribution—the Chunichi, the Hokkaido and the Nishi-Nippon, published respectively in Nagoya, Sapporo and Fukuoka. Then, there are the local newspapers published on a prefectural level.

The Asahi, Yomiuri and Mainichi are the Big Three newspapers of Japan. As of November 1989, the Yomiuri Shimbun was publishing 9,671,914 copies of its morning edition and 4,821,871 of its evening edition (total 14,493,875), the Asahi was publishing 8,086,434 copies of its morning edition and 4,973,422 copies of its evening edition, (total 12,879,856 copies) and the Mainichi a total of 6,305,388 daily copies. While the Chunichi had a total of 2,960,959 daily copies, the Hokkaido totaled 1,913,035 daily copies and the Nishi-Nippon 1,026,244 copies. The circulation of the Soviet newspaper Pravda was only 10,700,000 copies, giving the Yomiuri the largest circulation in the world.

Chart: Newspaper Circulation and Readership by Country

(As of 1984)

	Number of Newspapers	Circulation (Unit:1,000)	Circulation per 1,000 persons
Japan	125	67,380	562
USSR	724	116,096	422
USA	1,687	63,263	268
People's Republic of China	60	30,000	29
Great Britain	108	23,206	414
East Germany	39	9,199	550
India	1,334	14,847	21
France	101	11,598	212
Mexico	312	9,252	120
West Germany	—	21,362	350
Poland	45	7,887	214
Brazil	314	7,599	57

Source: UNESCO Culture Statistics Yearbook (1988)

In addition to the general newspapers mentioned above, seven sports newspapers and three evening newspapers (not including the Asahi Evening News) are published in the Tokyo area. These evening papers are Yukan Fuji, Nikkan Gendai and Naigai Times. The sports newspapers reflect a common interest in stories about personalities and athletes. The evening papers cultivate readership through their respective analyses of current events, trying to maintain a faithful readership and attract floating readers.

Moreover, unlike newspapers in other countries, Japanese newspapers without exception publish their dailies on Sundays, too. However, there are no evening editions on Sundays and national holidays. The home delivery system must also be mentioned when discussing newspapers in Japan.

New Technology

In 1988, the Asahi, the Yomiuri and the Mainichi, nationally distributed newspapers, expanded from 24 to 28 pages and began construction of new printing plants located throughout the Tokyo metropolitan area in order to make up for the insufficient capacity of their head offices. The new factories were equipped with the latest offset cylinder presses with multicolor printing capability. In this manner, the last edition can now be sent to areas with an increasing population while using the color-printing capabilities on the extra pages.

This decentralization of printing facilities can be seen not only in the Tokyo metropolitan area, but in the Osaka-Kyoto district as well.

This increase in offset printing facilities was due to added color printing capability for the 1988 Seoul Olympics; consequently, sports newspapers now contain more color. Many newspapers have now added a total CTS (Computer Type-Setting System) with a full output function and factory automation to complement it.

By using the personal computer communication, Chunichi and the Asahi began a data-bank service in 1986, inaugurating the expansion of the newspapers business activities. The Yomiuri has commenced on-line service over Hitachi and three other networks of an article data base called "YOMIDAS" into which most articles of the last issues of the Yomiuri morning and evening editions published by the Tokyo Head Office and all articles of the Home and Economic News are input.

Mainichi puts out the business newsletter "Big Management" through NTTPC communications as well as "Mainichi Article News" over Nikkei News Telecon. Japan Industrial Newspaper has also begun a Special Information Data Base Service of industrial news.

Asahi, the pioneer of data-base services, offers "HIASK" over Nikkei News Telecon as well as a personal computer on-line edition of news of the evening edition published by the Tokyo Head Office. The Daily Industrial News also offers "NK-MEDIA," on-line industrial news over "PC VAN" run by Nippon Electric Company.

An electronic library (EL) service in which all the articles are electronically filed as an image so they can be easily cross-referenced and a clip service called "Morning Review" for business are also offered.

Of the 19 companies offering electronic news services, eight use digital transmission, four use a combination of digital and analog transmission and more than half are converting to digital transmission. Asahi prints a satellite-transmitted edition in New York and San Francisco, while Yomiuri does the same in New York and Los Angeles.

Labor

In contrast with Europe and America where one joins a certain labor union according to one's type of work, in Japan the employees of each newspaper are considered one unit regardless of their type of work. These units constitute the Japan Federation of Press Workers' Union, which, in turn, belongs to the Japanese Trade Union Confederation (generally called "Rengo").

Foreign Correspondents

At present, a total of about 400 correspondents are stationed in Tokyo, and AP, UPI, AFP, Reuter, TASS and other important foreign news agencies, newspapers and news magazines maintain branches in Tokyo. Many of them are engaged in news-gathering activities in Asian countries with Tokyo as their home base. They gather at the Foreign Correspondents' Club of Japan in Yurakucho, Tokyo, which has such facilities as a lounge, a bar, a dining room and club rooms.

Special Overseas Correspondents and English Dailies: Japanese newspaper companies and news agencies in 1989 had about 170 correspondents stationed at various cities throughout the world. Now, the Kyodo News Service, Asahi, Mainichi and Yomiuri each keep a staff of 30 to 50 correspondents overseas. English-language newspapers published in Japan include The Japan Times, The Asahi Evening News, The Mainichi Daily News, The Daily Yomiuri and Nikkei Economic Journal.

Radio and TV Services

Radio broadcasts began in Japan on March 22, 1925. There were only 3,500 contracted receivers at that time. A little more than a year later, the government set up a national public broadcasting system called NHK (Nihon Hoso Kyokai, or Japan Broadcasting Corporation). Private stations began broadcasting in 1951 and commercial broadcasts started to be put on the air, ushering in the golden age of radio.

The first television broadcast in Japan occurred in February 1953 under the auspices of NHK, but it was not until six months later in August that actual programming was launched by NTV (Nippon Television Network Corp.). This inaugurated both public and private television services as well as the co-existence of television and radio.

At the start, the competition between NHK and NTV was intense. The 1960s saw the growing proliferation of television sets in the homes of the general public. Color broadcasts began in 1960 and by 1987 color TV sets had penetrated 99% of Japanese households.

The technological advances made in the 1970s brought astonishing breakthroughs in the development of telecast technology. Multimode sound (bilingual and stereo) broadcasts began in 1982, while 1985 brought University of the Air and close-captioned broadcasts.

Broadcasting via Satellite

When NHK initiated 24-hr., satellite broadcasting in 1987 less than 150,000 households had receivers. Encouraged by the satellite telecast of the Seoul Olympics, however, some 1.15 million households were enjoying satellite broadcasts by the end of November 1988, marking a larger increase than expected. The number of households receiving satellite broadcasts has increased probably because of lower receiver prices and the popularity of the broadcast content: world news, sports and entertainment, especially music.

High Vision

High-Definition Television (HDTV, also known as "High Vision" in Japan) has recently attracted attention in connection with the increasing use of satellite transmissions. The Ministry of Posts and Telecommunications and NHK have been developing HDTV with a highly defined screen with 1,125 scanning lines, four times as many pixels, a 9:16-wide screen and a presence created through a 30°visual angle as well as high-quality, CD-comparable sound with a digital system. This system will make use of the BS-3 communications satellite placed in orbit in 1990.

In response to the lead taken by the Ministry of Posts and Telecommunications and NHK, commercial television is developing EDTV (Extended-Definition Television). The advantage of EDTV is that it is compatible with the NTSC system currently in use. On the other hand, HDTV offers even higher quality images and sound. Only future developments will indicate which system will eventually be adopted.

Commercial FM Broadcasts

Between 1969 and 1970, NHK began nationwide FM radio broadcasts, while commercial broadcasts began in Tokyo, Nagoya, Osaka and Fukuoka.

As of 1990, there were 47 medium-wave, one short-wave and 35 FM stations, or a total of 83 stations in the commercial radio sector. As for TV, there are 48 VHF stations and 61 UHF stations, or a total of 109 television stations, although there are 153 (this figure as of 1989) member companies in the National Association of Commercial Broadcasters in Japan. There are also 10 commercial, close-captioned broadcasting stations.

International Broadcasts (Radio Japan)

NHK's Radio Japan broadcasts over shortwave are the only international broadcasts being made from Japan. As of 1990, broadcasts were aired for a total of 44.5 hrs. a day in 21 languages all over the world. In remote areas difficult to reach from Japan, local broadcast facilities are used for relay broadcasts: 12 hrs. a day from Gabon to Europe, the Middle East and Africa, 4 hrs. a day from Canada to the eastern part of North America and 6 hrs. a day from French Guiana to Central and South America.

New Media Trend

1987 was the inaugural year of CATV as the first multi-channel business cable television, or urban-type CATV station. It was founded as the Tama Cable Network in Ome City, Tokyo, followed by other stations one after another all over the country.

As of 1990, there were 90 multi-channel CATV companies with 61 facilities, with an overall total of 47,337 CATV systems. Also, in the same year, 6,172,278 contracted households received cable transmissions, a 6.9% increase over the previous year's figure. This figure is 18.6% of the total NHK viewers for the same period and is increasing at a rate of about 1% per year.

Presently under development by the Ministry of Posts and Telecommunications, the space cable network plan will supply diverse programs to nationwide CATV stations via commercial communications satellites when realized. As a result, increased attention has been placed recently on the potential for the future development of the CATV market by both the government and private sectors.

Books, Magazines and Periodicals

Recent years in Japan have seen a dramatic shift away from serious reading towards an emphasis on visual media, with the majority of published material being centered on light novels, comic books and easily accessible material. This has led to an overall decline in the industry as publishing houses report decreased profits and focus on lower-priced works of a nature more in tune with general trends.

In the early 1970s, the total publishing sales value in Japan amounted ¥500 billion, but even in 1988 this figure had still not reached ¥2 trillion.

The growth of gross sales value in 1981 hit its lowest level since the end of World War II with 1.9%, improving slightly the following year with 4.3%. In 1983, however, it decreased yet again to 3.4%.

The second-lowest growth rate after the low point in 1981 came three years later in 1984 with a dismal 2.6%, and it was not until 1985 that an upward trend was noted with 6.3%. However, this again dropped to 3.3% in 1986, then recovered somewhat to 4.6% in 1987.

The estimated actual sales value for books in 1987 was ¥63,636,740,000, while that for magazines was ¥1,116,992,120,000 — a total of ¥1,180,628,860,000.

This growth in 1987 was due to the appearance of a few million-sellers and the "audio book," a book recorded onto a cassette tape.

In 1987 Shinchosha released the works of five prominent modern authors recorded by actors onto 60- and 90-minute tapes under the name "Cassette-Book Library Series." This broke the ice and many other publishers of all sizes entered the cassette-book market. A number of bookstores have recently added popular cassette-book corners.

Although originally restricted to literary works, the field has expanded to include business, religion, history and a variety of other subjects. It can be predicted that each publisher will eventually enter the cassette-book market with works from their own catalogs.

The concept of an audio book was at first a little hard for the Japanese public to accept, but the profusion of "walkmans" (portable headphone stereo sets) among the younger generation symbolically indicates great potential for this market.

More than 200 titles were offered for sale in 1987, with a shipment value of ¥2.5 billion.

The latest trend in the publishing industry is the expansion of the comic sector. Many themes heretofore believed inappropriate to the comic format have been laid out in story form. The three-volume "Comic Introduction to Economics" released in 1987 sold a total of 1.25 million copies.

While continuing with the traditional policy of focusing on cooking and housekeeping issues, women's magazines have come to reflect societal changes and the role of modern women by offering a range of information that extends to many areas.

The 1980s also brought a boom in photo news magazines. Although already on the decline, it will leave a mark on the history of the publishing industry.

Another publishing industry trend is the diversification of distribution channels. Examples include increasing numbers of bookstores outside of urban areas, competition through home delivery and an increase in book corners in convenience stores. In conjunction with what is now called the New Media Age, the publishing market is also being transformed at a rapid tempo.

One significant change that is underway involves the distribution system for published matter. Traditionally, publishing houses dealt through agents to deliver their publications to bookstores, which, in turn, made them available to readers. However, this network has been disrupted by diversification in consumer needs and an increased demand for direct purchasing routes to bypass the former complicated system.

Bookstores are appearing more frequently in suburbs in reflection of the motorization of society, with more and more bookstores offering a wide range of services, including paperbacks, magazines and comic books as well as the rental of videos and CDs (compact discs).

Electronic publication is another current phenomenon. The computer industry has also developed CDs, which contain vast amounts of information. The necessary data can be accessed by personal computer. These CDs are a mere 12 cm in diameter and yet contain an entire year of newspapers. Since the "All New Dictionary of Science and Technology" appeared as the first CD-ROM publication (published by Sanshusha) in 1985, language dictionaries and information data bases of all sorts have appeared.

Electronic publications will continue to expand in the future. The Japan Electronic Publications Association was formed in 1986 to promote the growing industry.

Books: In 1987 the growth of the sales value of books surpassed that of magazines. Several million-sellers as well as a number of titles with sales over 500,000 contributed significantly to a growth in the sale of hard covers.

A total of 38,303 new books were published in 1988, not including reissues (from Publishers Yearbook).

Breakdown of New Books by Subject (1988)

Subject	Titles	% of Total
General	1,558	4.1
Philosophy	1,755	4.6
History	2,526	6.6
Social Science	9,036	23.6
Natural Science	2,884	7.5
Technology	3,535	9.2
Industry	1,679	4.4
Art	3,112	8.1
Language	796	2.1
Literature	7,898	20.6
Juvenile	2,910	7.6
Reference	614	1.6
Total	38,303	100.0

In an ordinary year, new books appear most frequently in April, followed by March—the month when the school year begins.

The average price of a new book in 1988 was ¥2,496, a ¥47 increase from the ¥2,449 average of the previous year. General, technology, art and reference works have slightly decreased in price, but there has been an increase in the prices of books on all other subjects.

Magazines: Magazines flourished through the mid-1980s, but the recent trend has been a decrease in magazine sales and a corresponding increase in book sales. The number of new magazines appearing has vastly decreased, while the circulation and sales value of existing monthly and weekly magazines has also dulled.

The approximate total circulation of monthly magazines in 1989 was 2,354,690,000 copies and that of weekly magazines was 1,946,300,000 copies, or a total of 4,310,000,000 copies.

There were an estimated 3,864 different magazines on the general market, which break down as follows (refer to the next page):

The return rate of unsold copies of periodic magazines often offers a problem—an estimated 20.7% for both monthlies and weeklies in 1989.

During the same year, 151 new magazines were founded while 88 failed. (All figures are from the 1990 Publishers Yearbook, Shuppan News Sha.)

Numbers of Magazines by Subject (1989)

Subject	Number
Books and newspapers	94
General	91
Philosophy	32
Religion	85
History and Geography	104
Politics	64
Current Events	66
Law	44
Economics, Finance, Statistics	226
Social Issues	106
Labor	57
Education	204
Manners and Customs	12
Natural Science	54
Medicine, Hygiene, Pharmacology	311
Engineering and Manufacturing	477
Home, Clothing, Beauty, Cooking	149
Agriculture, Livestock, Forestry, Industry	96
Commerce	101
Transportation, Communication	106
Art	96
Music and Dance	96
Drama and Film	50
Gymnastics and Sports	234
Hobbies and Leisure	51
Japanese Language	11
English Language	16
Other Foreign Languages	6
Literature	88
Poetry	19
Tanka	34
Haiku	46
Reading Matter	339
Women, General	69
Young Adult	3
Juvenile	197
Study and Test Aids	34
Total	3,864

●Manners and Customs

A high value is accorded in Japanese society to the concepts of *wa* (concord), *giri* (sense of obligation), *ninjo* (humanity), *makoto* (good faith) and *ishin-denshin* (tacit understanding). These ideas are, in a way, the key to an understanding of the Japanese people.

Among others, *giri* and *ninjo* are especially highly esteemed in traditional Japanese society. A person who had a sense of obligation and humanity is extolled as a "man of character." These are considered desirable traits expected of all members of society to ensure peaceful living.

Valuing concord above individual initiative within a group—the Japanese have found that their emphasis on group consciousness has sometimes worked against them in the past on the international scene. Nevertheless, it has contributed enormously to the present-day economic prosperity of Japan. Recently, there is even a movement in the United States and Europe to learn a lesson from the unique community consciousness of the Japanese, especially within business organizations.

Placing too much emphasis on concord within a group, however, can create an atmosphere in which expressing an opposing opinion is discouraged. In some cases, those who express a minority or dissenting opinion are ostracized. In such a conformist atmosphere, each member of a group tends to become afraid of holding opinions that differ from those of the other members and prefer being the same as the others rather than expressing his own individual opinion.

Consequently, it is said that the Japanese people can fully display their ability as a group, but not as individuals. This characteristic is better explained by the above-mentioned group consciousness of the Japanese.

These unique traits of the Japanese people appear in various forms in various phases of their social life. Concrete examples are given in the following sections.

Within Organization

Ringi

In Japanese companies of considerable size, decisions are often made by a collective procedure. The most popular collective procedure of decision-making is the one called *ringi*.

Ringi is the procedure taken by the originator of a plan to obtain the required sanction by circulating the draft of the plan through the appropriate layers of management (group leader, section chief, manager and so on). When the plan involves any other department, the originator also seeks the sanction of that department. The person who makes the final decision may be the president or the director in charge of the plan in question or a manager of lower rank, depending on the importance of the proposed plan. In any case, the draft must be approved by all the different management levels before it reaches the final decision-maker. This is the unique characteristic of the *ringi* system.

Nemawashi

Needless to say, there is the possibility of the draft being modified or even rejected along the way. Actually, however, that possibility is almost nil because it is common practice that before preparing the draft, the originator obtains the informal approval of the persons concerned by listening to their opinions of the plan and explaining the grounds for proposing it to them. This behind-the-scenes tactic is called *nemawashi*, a unique decision-making procedure followed by many Japanese companies.

Nemawashi is also used when deciding on something at a conference. For the above reason, it is rare that a plan presented at a conference is turned down after *nemawashi* has been carried out.

This method has the advantage of allowing many different levels of employees to participate in the decision-making process. On the other hand, it has the disadvantage of making it difficult to determine where the responsibility lies, especially when something goes wrong.

Compared with the so-called top-down method in which each of the different levels of management makes a decision on its own responsibility, the making of decisions by *nemawashi* seems a truly Japanese style that highly values concord (*wa*).

However, when this method (*nemawashi*) is always used, the intrinsic advantage of a conference—that is, the possibility of detecting and correcting defects in the original plan and of finding better solutions —can be lost. In this context, an increasing number of companies are reviewing their decision-making procedures and reconsidering their delegation of authority to the lower ranks.

Paternalism

Paternalism based on the lifelong employment system is another characteristic of Japanese companies.

Paternalism is the practice of regarding the entire company as a family and dealing with all its employees as the family members in the same boat. Typical examples of this are the provision of a company apartment house in which dozens of employee households live together (needless to say, the house rent is largely borne by the company), the holding of an athletic meet in which not only the employees but also their families participate and the sponsoring of pleasure trips planned by individual departments. All these are intended to strengthen the employee's sense of belonging to the company. In bygone days when the Japanese people were not so rich as today, the benefits mentioned above were primarily intended to promote the employee's welfare.

Today, however, as the lifelong employment system itself is being critically reviewed in the course of the growth of Japan's economy, such paternalistic activities are being phased out, except for those which are still needed from an economical viewpoint such as the provision of a company apartment house.

Consensus

Many of the Americans and Europeans who have talked with Japanese say perplexedly that the Japanese simply say "yes," even when they apparently do not think so. In Japan it is considered desirable for any matter to be decided unanimously. Because esprit de corps is always demanded within the same organization, there is a strong tendency to obtain a consensus among the persons concerned.

My-and-your attitudes

Many Japanese like to discriminate "my" from "your." For example, they call the company to which they belong "my company." Sometimes, those who are very amicable within their group show a cold indifference to "outsiders." When this attitude goes too far, "my company" becomes the only world for them, alienating them from the outside world or causing friction with outsiders. This can result in their becoming unsociable.

In Society and at Home

Greetings

A Japanese day begins with the morning greeting *ohayo gozaimasu* (good morning). By exchanging this greeting, they praise each other for getting up early in the morning, confirm that they belong to the same community and start the day's work with a fresh feeling.

Similarly, at the end of a day's work or after some cooperative job, Japanese exchange the greeting *otsukaresamadeshita* with each other, thus showing appreciation for their associate's effort. This is a custom that has the same nuance as the morning greeting *ohayo gozaimasu*.

Festivals

The Japanese are very fond of festivals. In Japan various festivals are held in every season of the year. In many cases on the occasion of a festival, the members of each town association (when it is held in a town) or the people living in the village community (when it is held in a fishing or farming village) decorate the streets and roads, carry a sacred palanquin through the streets and drink *sake* together. At individual homes, the family members celebrate the occasion by eating special dishes and chatting with their relatives and neighbors.

According to traditional belief, it is considered that God visits every festival and returns after the festival is over. Thus, the belief that the relationship between God and man could be deepened by appreciating the offerings made to God together is still inherent in present-day festivals. A sense of union springs from this belief and community consciousness is formed.

Thus, in Japan, God is regarded as a familiar existence, not an awesome one. This probably explains why Japanese like to visit shrines or temples so frequently.

Mid-year gifts and year-end gifts

There is a time-honored custom in Japan of making a mid-year gift in July and a year-end gift in December. According to this custom, people present a gift as a token of thanks to those from whom they have received assistance on various occasions. Originally, this custom was a religious one. The offering of a mid-year gift was one of the Buddhist events whereby the Buddhists held a memorial service for the departed souls of their ancestors and prayed for the longevity of their parents. Similarly, the presentation of a year-end gift was originally intended to give thanks to spiritual deities at the end of the year.

In that context, the custom represents the warmheartedness of the Japanese. Recently, however, the custom has lost its religious color. Instead, it is now generally regarded as an opportunity for businessmen to send gifts to their superiors and their customers.

Returning to one's native place

In Japan an exodus of people occurs three times a year—the New Year's vacation, consecutive holidays known as "Golden Week" from late April to early May and the *Bon* holidays in August, each lasting a week or so. On each occasion, all transport facilities are crowded with passengers and the expressways are jammed with vehicles, sometimes in a chain extending over several thousand meters.

Many of those who migrate from the cities during the New Year's vacation or *Bon* holidays return to their native place. Despite the formidable traffic congestion, they return to their home for a family reunion with their parents, brothers, sisters and relatives. One reason for this human outflow during these two periods is that they allow for a relatively long vacation. Another and more important reason is probably that New Year's and *Bon* hold a special meaning for the Japanese. For the Japanese, some of whom believe in God and profess the Buddhist faith and not a few of whom are atheists or agnostics, remembering their native place and meeting their old friends there twice a year may be a revelation of their religious feeling.

At the same time, however, it is certain that the exodus is partly attributable to the group consciousness of the Japanese—doing the same things as others do. Many Japanese consider it unbearable to stay at home when others are going out, feeling that they are being left out of the game.

Souvenirs

Formerly, Japanese made a journey to visit a shrine or temple on behalf of the community to which they belonged. Therefore, they were obliged to bring back the miraculous virtue given by the god to the community and share it with the community members. "Sembetsu" (a parting gift) given to such a representative traveler by his community was a token of his solidarity with the community, implying that he was supposed to bring back a souvenir in return for the gift.

This idea of *sembetsu* has been handed down to present-day Japan. The shopping spree of Japanese tourists overseas, which is sometimes frowned on by foreigners, is partly attributable to the fact that the tourists feel unconsciously that they have to bring back some souvenirs in return for the *sembetsu* they received when leaving Japan.

Omens

Though many Japanese do not seriously believe in omens, they normally choose "taian" (a lucky day) for their memorable events such as a wedding ceremony, the opening of a new shop and the ground-breaking for a new home. "Taian" and "butsumetsu" (an unlucky day) come from "on-yodo" transmitted to Japan from China many years ago. On-yodo is a method of divination based on the assumption that all activities in the natural world are governed by the prosperity and decay of Trees, Fire, Metals, Water and Earth.

In addition, not a few Japanese believe in "yakudoshi" (the critical age of a person when he or she is supposed to suffer misfortune), also transmitted from China to Japan. There is probably good reason for their belief. "Taiyaku" (the most critical age, which is said to be 33 for females and 42 for males) corresponds to the period during which people of the appropriate age are most susceptible to geriatric diseases and physical disorders.

The Japanese believe in the law of cause and effect as something different from superstitions, thereby feeling relieved and pleased.

●Entertainments

Theater

In addition to the traditional Japanese arts of *kabuki* and *noh*, a variety of modern theater, including dramas, comedies, avant-garde and Japanese versions of popular foreign productions, has gained popularity.

Shimpa Theater

The origins of *shimpa*, a new school of drama, can be traced back to the year 1888 when Sudo Sadanori, a *soshi* (political activist), presented a propaganda play in Osaka to help advance the cause of the democratic rights movement. In the following years, Kawakami

Otojiro (1864-1911) and his wife Sadayakko (1872-1946), who earned great popularity in Europe and America when she performed there in 1893 and 1899, were inspired by this new form of theater that was open to participation by anyone and did not have the constraints of the hereditary and family systems that govern *kabuki* and other traditional arts. At first, this new form of theater was given the name "soshi drama." However, as it gained popularity, this new genre earned the name *shimpa* (new school) in direct contrast with traditional *kabuki* theater.

At the beginning of the 20th century, the themes of most *shimpa* plays shifted to family tragedies. Works by popular contemporary authors such as "Konjiki Yasha (The Golden Demon)" by Ozaki Koyo, "Taki no Shiraito (White Thread of the Waterfall)" by Izumi Kyoka and "Hototogisu (The Cuckoo)" by Tokutomi Roka were dramatized. These works are still popular as representative examples of this genre. The work of contemporary actors, including Kitamura Rokuro (1871-1961) and Ii Yoho (1871-1933), helped introduce the golden age of *shimpa*.

The great development in modern theater in Japan that followed the cultural blossoming after the Meiji Restoration in 1868 was fortunately able to grow on the firm foundation of traditional Japanese theater. In early *shimpa*, we can find many acting and directing techniques that share common traits with *kabuki*. In particular, at first in *shimpa* there were male actors who played only female roles, a convention similar to that of the *oyama* found in *kabuki*. However, as *shimpa* developed along an independent course, these vestiges of the old school of drama ceased to exist and the genre moved away from *kabuki*. Hanayagi Shotaro (1894-1965) was the last great *shimpa oyama*. It was right about the time that *shimpa* began to move away from the influences of traditional theater that Mizutani Yaeko (1905-1979) made her appearance. She used her beautiful figure and great talent to establish the role of women in *shimpa*.

Although *shimpa* began to lose popularity around the beginning of the Showa period (1926-1989), it regained its audience in the 1930s when adaptations of literary pieces by Kawaguchi Matsutaro were staged. At present, *shimpa* still maintains a stable following and boasts a fine offering of talented actors and actresses.

Shingeki

After the Meiji Restoration, another new school of drama called *shingeki* (new drama) appeared. Compared to the traditional Japanese dramatic arts of *kabuki* and *noh* as well as the new theater of *shimpa*, this new school was based on modern ideas and was greatly influenced by the West.

In 1906, Tsubouchi Shoyo (1859-1935), a scholar of English literature who devoted his life to the complete translations of all of Shakespeare's works, formed the Bungei Kyokai (Artistic Association). Three years later, director Osanai Kaoru (1881-1928) and *kabuki* actor Ichikawa Sadanji II (1880-1940) formed the Jiyu Gekijo (Free Theater). These two organizations formed the base from which the first period in the history of *shingeki* developed. This period continued until the devastation wrought by the Great Kanto Earthquake of 1923. During this period, Tsubouchi devoted himself to training actors at the Association's research institute. Actress Matsui Sumako was one of his disciples. At the same time, the Free Theater used *kabuki* actors in productions of tragedies by Henrik Ibsen and the Russian novelist Maxim Gorky. The great Japanese writer Tanizaki Jun-ichiro was influenced by this new school of drama and was active during this period. The ideas evident in the naturalism and moralism that these people introduced from the West had a great impact on the younger generation of that time as well as on those active in cultural events.

The Tsukiji Shogekijo, the Mecca of *shingeki*, was built in 1924. Directors Hijikata Yoshi (1898-1959) and Osanai Kaoru were the central figures at this time and worked during their early days with actor Senda Koreya and actresses Yamamoto Yasue and Sugimura Haruko, who are still in the forefront of *shingeki* activity today. This group led *shingeki* towards realism and contributed much to its development. In the year 1929, the theater group divided because of differences in artistic ideals as well as for financial reasons. Many important *shingeki* troupes remained active until 1940, when the chaos of the war led to a dramatic decline in *shingeki*. In 1945, this theater was destroyed by air raids as the curtain closed on the second period in the history of *shingeki*.

The activity in *shingeki* that began after World War II was the start of the third period, which has continued down to the present day. *Shingeki* enjoyed a revival in its popularity after the war that lasted roughly until 1952. During this period, Mishima Yukio, Abe Kobo, Kinoshita Junji and other important playwrights appeared on the scene and propelled *shingeki* to its peak. Since then, *shingeki* has had its ups and downs in popularity, but it remains as an example of a modern tradition in Japanese performing arts.

There are currently four central theater groups active in *shingeki*. The Bungakuza (Literary Theater), the oldest remaining Japanese *shingeki* group, was established in 1937 and still maintains a strong position. The Haiyuza (Actors' Theater) was established in 1944 with the support of Senda Koreya, who was the first to introduce the ideas of Bertolt Brecht to Japan. The Haiyuza operates its own theater in Tokyo at Roppongi. The Gekidan Mingei (Folkart Theater) was established in 1950 and holds performances in a variety of genres throughout Japan. The Seinenza (Youth Theater) was established in 1954 and emphasizes creative theater. Over the years, many great Japanese actors have been trained by these theater groups.

Developments in Theater Since Shingeki

In the 1960s, underground theater, called *angura* (a corruption of the English word "underground"), appeared in Japan. This movement can best be compared with American off-off-Broadway theater. Kara Juro's Jokyo Gekijo (Theater of the Times), Suzuki Tadashi's Waseda Shogekijo and Terayama Shuji's Tenjo Sajiki (Upper Gallery) were representative of the theater groups led by young directors and playwrights that sprang up during this period. Their lack of funds forced these groups to perform in cafes, underground theaters and other small spaces. However, they turned this constraint to their advantage by boldly experimenting and expanding the realms of theater beyond what had been performed until then. As they experimented with anti-realist and anti-*shingeki* theater, they advanced the development of smaller, more varied theater and presented pieces that prompted a new investigation of all aspects of theater. In 1967, Kara began his practice of presenting performances inside a red tent that he put up in parks and shrines in Shinjuku, Tokyo. In this format, he continued to pursue experimental ideas in theater. In 1970, Sato Makoto followed suit with his black tent performances. The anarchic energy behind the creative forces that these two have promoted in their modern theaters was of an unparalleled level.

After the appearance of Tsuka Kohei, the standard bearer of modern Japanese theater during the 1970s, they began to receive critical recognition from the media and play an important role in shaping the future of Japanese culture and customs. When the movement entered the 1980s, it seemed to be losing its core of rebellion and uniqueness that had maintained it. However, thanks to the efforts of Noda Hideki's Yume-no-Yuminsha (People's Dream Playland) and Watanabe Eriko's Gekidan 300 (Theater 300), the small theater movement has gained the support of the next generation and climbed to new heights.

Ninagawa Yukio, whose direction of Shakespearean plays has earned him critical acclaim in Europe, staged "Romeo and Julliet" in 1949, marking the start of his brilliant career as a director. Ninagawa and others active at this time have been working hard to establish a practical commercial base for directors, playwrights, novelists and actors in Japan.

Under the leadership of director Asari Keita, the Gekidan Shiki (Four Seasons Theater) was established in 1953, later capturing the top position in the Japanese musical theater world with renditions of such fine Broadway hit musicals as "Cats" and "Phantom of the Opera" performed in large theaters and tents.

Established in 1914, The Takarazuka Revue is an all-girl theater troupe that has captured a unique place in Japanese theater. This troupe's repertoire ranges from musical renditions of such great Western classics as "Gone With the Wind" and "War and Peace" to classic Japanese period dramas. The Takarazuka Revue holds regularly scheduled performances at its birthplace of Takarazuka near Osaka as well as in Tokyo. It has also gained critical acclaim from abroad with performances in Europe and America.

Recently, there have been many performances of original productions of foreign musicals in Tokyo, including such famous ones as "My Fair Lady" starring Rex Harrison Jr. These performances are given in Japan with the original cast and have been quite popular. Due to the language barrier, however, audiences have shown even greater enthusiasm for the Japanese versions of these productions. In 1987 and 1988, a large-scale production of "Les Miserables" was organized in Japan. The combination of a foreign director working with Japanese singers proved to be a great success.

Principal Theaters

National theaters have been established for presentations of most traditional performing arts, including *kabuki*, *bunraku* and *shimpa*. In addition, the Kokuritsu Nohgakudo (National Noh Theater) and Ginza Nohgakudo Hall are used solely for presentations of *noh* and *kyogen*, the Kanze Kaikan Hall in Kyoto presents *noh* performances and the National Bunraku Theater in Osaka presents *bunraku*. The most famous of the theaters presenting *kabuki* performances are the Kabukiza in Ginza, which boasts advanced facilities and is used for presenting even the most complicated *kabuki* productions and the Minamiza in Kyoto (under reconstruction due for completion in October 1991). Performances are held from November, beginning with the all-star cast show, until the end of the season the following September.

Two daily performances are given at the Kabukiza, beginning at 11:00 a.m. and again at 4:30 p.m. Each performance lasts for approximately five hours and consists of three or four different acts, with a 15–30-minute intermission between each act. Explanations of the performance are available in English in the form of cassette players and earphones that are used while watching the show. Admission ranges from ¥2,000 to ¥14,000 for the best seats, which are traditional Japanese seats on *tatami* mats. It is possible to pay admission for only one act (¥500– 900, with the admission price depending on the play and the act to be seen). For those who want to stay longer, they only need pay the remaining fee. *Kabuki* performances are also held at the Shimbashi Embujo in Ginza and the Meijiza in Nihombashi.

A wide repertoire ranging from *shingeki* to Japanese period dramas is offered by many theaters, including the Teikoku Gekijo (Imperial Theater), Nissei Gekijo, the Tokyo Takarazuka Kagekijo—all in Hibiya—and the Shinjuku Koma Gekijo. Performances are usually held over a one- or two-month period for each presentation.

In addition to the above-mentioned theaters, small theater groups following in the tradition of the small-theater movement, offer performances at the Jiyu Gekijo (Free Theater) as well as under tents pitched in fields and parks for a few days. They strive to create a greater sense of intimacy between the players and their audiences.

Due to overcrowding in urban areas, Japanese theaters are rarely located in independent structures, often occupying one or more floors of large buildings. In the suburban areas around urban centers, more and more theater halls are being built so that theatergoers can enjoy a natural, wide-open environment. During the 1980s, many major private enterprises constructed large, fully equipped and technologically advanced theater halls as a means of improving their public image and furthering the goals of urban planning.

Music

After a period of stagnation during World War II, Western music regained its popularity when the war ended. The recognition of music as a legitimate part of the normal educational curriculum led to an increase in specialty instruction in music. The Tokyo Academy of Music, the only national school of music in Japan during the prewar days, was reorganized in 1949 as the Music Faculty of Tokyo University of Arts, which is still the center of musical instruction and performances in Japan and has trained many noted musicians. Mayuzumi Toshiro (1929-), Akutagawa Yasushi (1925-1988) and Dan Ikuma (1924-) are representative of the important composers who were trained here and brought a new style to Japanese music after World War II.

Since most of the Japanese who were active in Western music before World War II received their specialized training abroad, it was common for them to bring the style of the nation where they studied back to Japan just as they learned it. However, after the reforms that followed World War II, specialized training became available in Japan and more creative, individual works rich in artistic expression inspired by their creator's experiences abroad appeared and received critical acclaim abroad as well. In addition to the above three composers, musicians who played an important role in the postwar period include Yashiro Akio (1929-1976), Miyoshi Akira (1933-), Takemitsu Toru (1930-), Mamiya Michio (1929-), Takahashi Yuji (1938-) and Moroi Makoto (1930-).

In particular, the compositions of Takemitsu Toru, who makes use of ultramodern compositional methods as well as his meticulously refined Japanese sensitivity, have been widely praised at his many appearances both in Japan and abroad.

It was also after World War II that private, individual musical instruction for performers became common practice outside of the general musical instruction offered at schools. The Children's Music Classroom, an intensive training program in music for children aged five-seven, was organized after the war by cellist Saito Hideo (1902 -1974), pianist Iguchi Motonari (1908-1983) and music critic Yoshida

Hidekazu (1913–   ). Many musicians currently active internationally in music received training and developed under this method. Some examples are conductors Ozawa Seiji (1935–   ) and Akiyama Kazuyoshi (1941–   ), violinists Fujikawa Mayumi (1946–   ) and Shiokawa Yuko (1946–   ), cellists Tsutsumi Go (1942–   ), Yasuda Ken-ichiro (1944–   ) and Fujiwara Mari (1949–   ) and pianist Uchida Mitsuko (1948–   ).

In 1987 Ozawa Seiji organized many of these musicians into the Saito Kinen (Memorial) Orchestra, which earned wide acclaim during a tour of Europe. In 1990 the orchestra performed at the Salzburg Festival.

The Children's Music Classroom exerted a great influence on postwar Japanese musical instruction and developed into the present Toho Gakuen School of Music.

Furthermore, the original violin performance instructional method developed by Suzuki Shinichi (1898–1990), known as the Suzuki Method, emphasizes musical instruction at an early age. The aim of this method is to instruct children of an early age in a rational method so that they will develop with an instinctive knowledge of musical instruments. Once it was proven to be effective, it spread rapidly and is currently gaining acceptance in Europe and America as well. In addition, there are many networks of Music Classrooms sponsored in large cities by the makers of musical instruments. The number of people playing musical instruments has continued to grow steadily.

Soon after World War II finished, the Japan Music Competition was established as a forum for young performers. It is sponsored annually by the Mainichi Shimbun-sha and NHK (Japan Broadcasting Corporation). The young musicians whose talent won them recognition in this competition are currently supporting the growth of Japanese classical music.

NHK (Japan Broadcasting Corporation) sponsors the annual National School Music Competition, which is open to all junior high and senior high school brass ensembles. The steady rise in the quality of entrants that this competition attracts is reflective of the steady increase in the level of musical instruction offered in schools. At present, musical instruction is actively pursued in almost every class throughout Japan. Many junior high and high schools have orchestras, and at most general universities there are clubs in which student members participate in orchestras.

This great increase in musical instruction has led to a level of musical appreciation in Japan roughly equal to that found in Europe and the United States. Most major cities in Japan currently boast professional orchestras. In Tokyo alone, there are eight professional orchestras that give regularly scheduled performances: NHK Symphony Orchestra, Tokyo Symphony Orchestra, Tokyo Philharmonic Symphony Orchestra, Japan Philharmonic Symphony Orchestra, Tokyo Metropolitan Symphony Orchestra, Yomiuri Nippon Symphony Orchestra, New-Japan Philharmonic Orchestra and the New Star Japan Orchestra. Kyoto boasts the Kyoto Municipal Symphony Orchestra, Sapporo has the Sapporo Symphony Orchestra, Takasaki houses the Gumma Symphony Orchestra, Nagoya has the Nagoya Philharmonic Orchestra and the Osaka Philharmonic Symphony Orchestra is based in Osaka. Except for some of the orchestras active in Tokyo, however, the environment facing professional orchestras in Japan is generally severe, it will be difficult for them to improve the level of their performances remarkably without governmental support.

There has been a remarkable increase in the number of foreign performers and orchestra groups that have been attracted to Japan since its period of high economic growth in the latter half of the 1960s. This tendency has greatly increased in recent years, and concerts by nearly all of the world's leading orchestras and musicians can be heard in Tokyo and Osaka. The level of public interest in performances by foreign musicians in Japan has reached a high level. At the same time, the level of interest in Japanese musicians has increased considerably.

Compared to instrumental and orchestral performances, the area of Western music that has not seen great amount of development in Japan has been opera. Although there are many groups active in opera, including the Fujiwara Opera Group active since before World War II, the Nagato Miho Opera Group formed in 1945, the Nikikai, the Tokyo Indoor Opera House and the Kansai Opera Group, the lack of a facility for exclusive use as an opera house makes performances difficult to arrange. Furthermore, since a great deal of funding is required to put on a performance, there is relatively little activity in this area. In order to overcome these problems, the Second National Theater is being constructed as a permanent opera house. On the other hand, there are many performances in Japan by foreign opera groups. This began after the war when NHK (Japan Broadcasting Corporation) invited a combined Italian opera group on several occasions. Now, performances are held on a regular basis by such famous opera troupes as the Vienna National Opera House, the Milano Scala Theater, the Metropolitan Opera House and the Berlin Deutsch Opera. These performances are produced on a massive scale with orchestras, choruses, sets and entire troupes brought over to Japan to ensure that the production in this country equals that of the groups' original setting.

The spread of musical education was not restricted to classical. Popular music showed conspicuous growth, too. Since the 1970s there has been a steady increase in the number of rock groups formed by young musicians and supported by their young fans. Large concerts given at concert halls attract huge crowds, while less famous groups perform at the many "livehouses" (small live-music halls) located in urban entertainment districts.

Records and CDs

Recorded music has played an important role in popularizing Western music in Japan. Both before and after World War II, a large part of the support that has sustained the level of music appreciation in Japan has been provided by records. In the post-war period, Japan experienced great development in the electronics industry, which led to a progression from SPs to LPs and from monophonic to stereo. The level of audio equipment remarkably developed so that over 80% of all households in Japan were equipped with an audio system by the year 1980, reflecting the enthusiasm of young record listeners.

The annual levels of production of recorded music has increased steadily. In 1956, a total of 14,938,226 records were produced. By 1972, this figure had increased more than ten times to 152,049,903, making Japan the second largest record market after the United States. Only 10–15% of this total were classical records, with the rest being popular music, a tendency that has continued until the recent advent of CDs.

Japanese technology was responsible for the success in applying digital technology to the recording process. Compact disks (CD) were developed and commercialized in 1980 based on this technology. During the initial year or two after CDs reached the market, their prices were relatively high and their rate of distribution remained low. However, due to the high quality of their recorded sound and their ease of use, by 1987 CD sales outpaced sales of LP records, and in 1989 CD sales accounted for over 95% of the market share of recorded music with LPs being quickly phased out. Japan has the highest rate of distribution of CDs in the world.

The high quality of laser disks (LD) has made them popular among movie and music lovers. Although only 10% of all households in Japan presently possess an LD unit, cost reductions resulting from electronic innovations are expected to greatly increase their popularity and rate of distribution.

Principal Concert Halls

Tokyo

Tokyo Metropolitan Festival Hall	(03)-3828-2111
NHK Hall	(03)-3465-1751
Suntory Hall	(03)-3505-1001
Orchard Hall	(03)-3477-3244
Casals Hall	(03)-3294-1229

Osaka

Festival Hall	(06)-231-2221
The Symphony Hall	(06)-453-1010

Film

It can be said that Westerners did not discover Japanese movies until "Rashomon" appeared in 1950, but their actual beginning took place much earlier—more than 40 years before, in fact. The first small film studio was established in Tokyo in 1904, but it was not until 1912 that Nikkatsu, a large production company, was incorporated. At that time, Japan was making every effort to catch up with the economically and socially advanced countries of the West in order to build up a modern capitalist system by introducing Western culture and industrial techniques into the social and economic fabric of Japanese society.

So when the movie industry was transplanted from France and America in those days, it very soon took root and acclimatized itself in Japanese soil, rapidly developing into a big, modern industry. Those who chose to cast their lot with the Japanese movie industry were diligent, enterprising businessmen who did not hesitate to adopt the latest, up-to-date cinematographic equipment and techniques of the most advanced countries. They readily introduced into Japan talkies, technicolor, wide screens and, more recently, 70-mm movies, all of which they instantly adapted for use in their own films.

After World War II, Japan imported many American and European films and also produced a great number of its own films in such a diverse range of genre as comedies, romances, suspense stories, action films, violent films, science fiction, horror films, period dramas, modern stories and musicals. Many Japanese films have earned wide critical acclaim in foreign countries as well at home. The following are some of the more internationally well-known Japanese films: "Rashomon" (1950, directed by Kurosawa Akira), "The Life of Oharu" (1952, directed by Mizoguchi Kenji), "Tokyo Story" (1953, directed by Ozu Yasujiro), "The Gates of Hell" (1954, directed by Kinugasa Teinosuke), "Woman in the Dunes" (1964, directed by Teshigawara Hiroshi) and "L'empire de la Passion" (1978, directed by Oshima Nagisa).

The Japanese film industry was at its peak around the year 1958. In that year, over 1,127 million tickets were sold at movie theaters around the country. However, as television became more popular, the number of people going to movies began to decrease. In 1961, a total of 863 million tickets were sold and in the following three years, this number dropped dramatically until in 1964 only 431 million tickets were sold—less than half the figure for 1961. The year of 1964 marked the beginning of a recession in the Japanese film industry.

The 1970s

In 1971 Daiei Motion Picture Co., Ltd. (1941-1971) went bankrupt. In the same year, Nikkatsu Film Productions (established in 1912) withdrew from the action film genre under which it had developed and began full-scale production of pornographic films. This left only three large Japanese film companies: Shochiku (1924-   ), Toho (1936-   ) and Toei (1951-   ). In 1975 foreign films outpaced Japanese films in the Japanese marketplace for the first time.

In 1976 the number of tickets sold at movie theaters in Japan dropped to 166 million. Until that year, the three large film production companies virtually dominated the production and distribution of all Japanese films under the system developed in the early years of the Japanese film industry of production companies supported by their own actors and actresses, production staffs and studios. However, this bottom-heavy structure resulted in excessive labor costs and one by one studios disappeared to cover their companies' debts. This brought to an end the period marked by the relative ease with which these companies had been able to produce films.

It was a young producer named Kadokawa Haruki (President of Kadokawa Publishing Co., Ltd.) who broke away from this closed structure under the old system and revolutionized the Japanese film industry when he began producing films in 1976. In the following years, many corporations in fields unrelated to cinema began to become active in the production side of films. Some examples are Sanrio Co., Ltd. (toy manufacturer), the Fuji Sankei Group (broadcasting and journalism) and Marugen Co., Ltd. (real estate). These firms rented studios and hired productions staff directly from the large film production companies, then combined these with aspects from independent productions to make films that they financed on their own.

It was the infusion of corporate capital that gave the Japanese film industry the wherewithal to break out of the hard times that had befallen it. Director Sato Junya's "Proof of the Man" produced in 1977 by Kadokawa Haruki Films Inc. was a big hit. This achievement opened the way for talented young directors working in the 8mm format to make films with the support of corporate capital. Until then, they could only hope to become a director after at least ten years as an assistant in one of the large production companies.

In 1978 Oshima Nagisa, who had gained recognition for the films he had made at Shochiku that were being hailed as "Shochiku Nouvelle Vague (New Wave)," was awarded the prize for the best director at Cannes for his film "L'empire de la Passion." In 1979 Kurosawa Akira came out of his ten-year layoff from films and began working on the production of "Kagemusha."

The 1980s

From the beginning of the 1980s, the work of young, new directors helped reactivate the Japanese film industry. In 1982 Directors' Company and Film Workers and similar organizations were formed by film directors, who revealed great ambition in the films that they produced. In 1983 director Imamura Shohei's "The Ballad of Narayama" (refer to "Obasute" p.518)won the Grand Prix at Cannes in the same year that saw the production of Fuji Television's "Antarctica." This film, directed by Kurahara Koreyoshi, set a new record of ¥5,600 million in distribution revenue.

In 1985 the First Tokyo International Film Festival was held. This was also the year in which Kurosawa Akira released his grand production, "Ran" and was awarded the Order of Culture from the Japanese government—the first film personality to be so honored in Japan. In 1986 Shinoda Masahiro's "Yari-no-Gonza" was selected for the Silver Bear Prize at the Berlin Film Festival, and the following year Kumai Kei's "The Sea and Poison" won the same award. In 1988 Feature Film Enterprises, a film production investment organization, was established through the efforts of a diverse group of corporations.

1989 saw the emergence of many new directors from former comedians, actors, stage directors and others. The films released by this new school of directors are quite different from all previous Japanese films. This year also saw Sony and other large corporations become involved in the film industry in Hollywood.

In this way the number of films produced every year in Japan has steadily increased as the directors, producers and production staff refine their techniques. However, given the current market conditions in Japan, it is still publicity that attracts crowds to theaters so that it is difficult to fill large theaters for films made by new and relatively unknown directors. This explains why a glance at the movie section on any particular day will reveal an offering of many so-called "idol films" featuring popular singers and other entertainers as well as the never-ending flow of animal films. There are also, of course, the large-scale, large-budget, epic films (supported by lavish publicity budgets) that also do quite well at the box office. At present, there are still quite a few successful films that reflect the sensitivity of their directors.

During the first half of the 1980s, video recorders became quite popular in the average household. At present, there is a tremendous boom in the video rental business, with more than 15,000 video rental stores doing business throughout Japan—almost double the number of film theaters that flourished in Japan at the height of the film industry. This clearly indicates that many more people prefer to watch films on their own television screen rather than at a theater. As a result, there has been a rapid decrease in the number of small movie theaters and classic film theaters, both of which have been replaced by small art theaters whose programs are selected by the owners themselves. Corporations outside the film industry also have used this medium to enter the film market and show films, that do not receive general distribution, in small, fashionably decorated theaters that they operate.

Such developments have placed film theaters in an extremely precarious situation. However, the popularity of video films has resulted in a benefit for production companies. A few months after their release, films are re-released publicly on video, giving the production side two means of recovering their costs and turning a profit.

Since a variety of companies engaging in completely different fields of activities began to enter the Japanese film industry in 1976, there has been a gradual recovery and increase in activity in all areas of the cinema. At present, there are over 350 film directors active in Japan. Unlike Kurosawa Akira, Oshima Nagisa and Ozu Yasujiro, most are still relatively unknown abroad. Yamada Yoji, the director of the "It's Tough to be a Man" series that began in 1969 and turned out its 41st film in 1989 with "Tora-san Goes to Vienna," has brought a sensitive, comic touch to his films. In addition to this series, Yamada has also made "The Yellow Handkerchiefs of Happiness" and other heart-warming films. Fukasaku Kenji, another unique director, earned acclaim with the dynamic characters in his gangster series "Jingi Naki Tatakai" (Battle Without Honor and Humanity) that he began in 1973 and his 1982 production of "Fall Guy." Obayashi Nobuhiko, known as Japan's Spielberg, also earned great popularity among young fans with his "Sayonara Me" in 1982 and "The Discarnates" in 1988. Among the new directors that have earned some recognition abroad are Morita Yoshimitsu for his 1983 work "Family Game" and Itami Juzo for his 1987 film "A Taxing Woman" as well as several other of his films that have been shown overseas. Indeed, there are many fine young directors who have gained a following in Japan but have yet to be discovered abroad.

An area in which the Japanese film industry demonstrates unique talent and creativity is animation films. Although the majority of animations are made for young viewers, many films find an older and more sophisticated audience as well. The level of artistic design and direction evident in Japanese animations of recent years has earned wide acclaim both in and out of Japan. In particular, the animations of Miyazaki Hayao gained popularity among children and adults alike during the last half of the 1980s. His latest film, "Kiki's Delivery Service," was well received outside of Japan as well.

●Food and Drink

The Japanese diet includes a wide variety of food—noodles and bread as well as rice, beef and chicken as well as fish. Rice is, of course, the traditional staple food and is generally eaten at daily meals. Popular dishes include *suimono* (clear soup), *hitashimono* (boiled vegetables with a thin dressing), *nimono* (fish or vegetables cooked in soy sauce), *tempura* (fried seafood or vegetables), *yakimono* (broiled food), *sunomono* (fish, shellfish, or vegetables served with vinegar), *nabemono* (food served in the pot in which it is cooked like *sukiyaki*), *kabayaki* (grilled eel), *sashimi* (slices of raw fish) and *tsukemono* (pickles).

In addition to these traditional Japanese foods, there are many popular foods that have been introduced to Japan from abroad and changed to suit Japanese tastes, resulting in the creation of new and unique dishes. Two well-known examples of this are *ramen* (Chinese noodles) and curry rice. Both are popular dishes served at restaurants all over Japan. Hamburgers are another popular dish among young people who frequent the many fast food chain restaurants in Japan.

Still, in spite of the popularity of these foods, most home cooking is still based on rice, *miso* soup and other traditional foods and modern versions thereof, particular for dinner meals.

Since Japan is a maritime country surrounded by warm seas and containing many lakes and rivers in the mountainous regions, it abounds in unlimited varieties of fish that differ according to the season and the district. Most traditional Japanese dishes use fish as an ingredient. However, due to a decrease in the stocks of natural fish in the waters in and around Japan, and the extension of the fishery conservation zone to 200 miles off its coasts, the total catches of recent years have drastically decreased, causing an increasing dependence on imports. On the other hand, the Westernization of the Japanese life style has led to reduced consumption of fish, and many homes enjoy meat as frequently as their Western counterparts.

Dishes

Sukiyaki: Along with *tempura*, *Sukiyaki* is one of the typical Japanese dishes that usually appeal most to the foreign visitor's taste. It is prepared by cooking thinly sliced beef with such vegetables as *negi* (spring onions), *shungiku* (edible chrysanthemum leaves), mushrooms and *tofu* (bean card) in a pan over a brazier. It is flavored with soy sauce and *mirin* (sweetened *sake*). Chicken or pork may be served in a similar style.

Tempura: It is cooked by frying the ingredients in deep fat, usually fresh vegetable oil, after being coated with a batter made of egg, water and wheat flour. Among the delicious materials used are prawns, shellfish and eggplant. *Tempura* is eaten hot and dipped in specially prepared soy sauce and grated *daikon* radish.

Sushi: The *sushi* maker takes half a handful of boiled rice that has been cooled and seasoned with slightly sweetened vinegar, molds it into a small oblong and places a thin slice of raw fish filet on top. Shrimp, squid and sweet fried eggs are also used instead of fish. In other kinds of *sushi*, a flat piece of seaweed called *nori* is used to wrap and roll up a small handful of boiled rice with a slice of green cucumber or sweetened Japanese gourd peel inside.

Shabu-Shabu: The guests dip tender, thin-sliced beef and vegetables in boiling soup stock at their table and eat them after letting them cook for a few minutes. The soup is eaten with noodles after the meat and vegetables are finished.

Teppanyaki: Tender beef, seafood and fresh vegetables are cooked on a griddle set in the center of the table in front of the guests. The food is cooked according to the tastes of the guests, with the beef being cut by the cook into bite-sized morsels.

Yakitori: Chicken barbecued on a bamboo skewer

Tonkatsu: Fried breaded pork cutlet, is one of the most popular Western foods in Japan, and has now become thoroughly Japanized.

Kabayaki: Eels dipped in soy sauce and broiled.

Suimono: Clear soup with fish, chicken or egg and vegetables

Chawan-mushi: Steamed egg custard, with chicken and vegetables

Nizakana: Fish boiled in soy sauce

Yakizakana: Grilled fish

In addition to the above, *soba*, *udon* and other kinds of noodles are typical daily fare.

Soba are thin, brownish noodles made from a mixture of *soba-ko* (buckwheat flour) and wheat flour. *Udon*, which is made from wheat flour only, is similar in color to spaghetti but it is softer and wider. Some *soba* dishes such as *mori-soba* are served cold together with a side dish of soy-based broth into which the *soba* is dipped before being eaten. Other *soba* dishes and most *udon* dishes consist of a bowl of noodles in hot broth together with various other ingredients such as vegetables, eggs, *aburaage* (deep-fried *tofu*) or meat. The broth is made from soy sauce, *mirin* (sweetend *sake*), sugar and stock.

Beverages

Japanese green tea taken without milk or sugar, and black tea taken with milk and sugar or lemon are obtainable almost anywhere. Beer and soft drinks can also be procured almost anywhere as well as *sake*—the national drink distilled from rice and drunk either warm or cold and undiluted. Canned coffee, juice, cola and nearly every kind of drink, both domestic and imported, can be found in the many vending machines and 24-hr. "convenience stores" throughout the city.

Generally, Japanese cakes are of two classes—*higashi* (dried cake) and *namagashi* (undried cake). Among the *namagashi*, made of bean jam for the most part, *yokan* is popular among the Japanese. It is made of refined bean jam in gelatin form.

Alcoholic Drinks: *Sake*, a sort of rice wine, is the representative drink of Japan. Nada, located near Kobe, is famous throughout Japan for the *sake* produced there. Many local districts are proud of the *sake* they produce, with tastes varying depending on the climate and ingredients used. The consumption of beer and wine has increased greatly in recent years and due to the reduction of the tax and price of imported whiskey, Scotch Whiskey from the United Kingdom has changed from a luxury item to a common drink.

TRAVEL INFORMATION

Section I. Hokkaido

Hokkaido is the northernmost of the four main islands of Japan. Surrounded by three oceans and two straits, it is separated from Honshu (the largest of the four main islands) on the southwest by the Tsugaru Straits and from Sakhalin in the north by the Soya Straits, then bounded by the Japan Sea in the west, the Okhotsk Sea in the northeast and the Pacific Ocean in the southeast. The Habomai Island Chain lies off the eastern tip of the Nemuro Peninsula, consisting of Suisho, Yuri, Akiyuri, Shibotsu and Taraku islands plus adjoining reefs. Further to the northeast lies Shikotan Island, while Kunashiri and Etorofu lie abreast. Historically, the Habomai Island Chain, Shikotan, Kunashiri and Etorofu have been developed as part of Hokkaido.

Hokkaido, second in area only to Honshu, covers 83,520.09 sq. km — 22% of the total area of Japan. In spite of this fact, only 5,646,376 people live here, a mere 4.7% of the total population of Japan. There may be few residents, but countless numbers of visitors flock to Hokkaido continuously throughout the year to see the conical volcanoes, beautiful canyons, long stretches of fertile land, evergreen forests, and crystal-clear lakes and rivers. Magnificent natural beauty that can no longer be seen anywhere else in Japan is preserved here. It is this natural beauty that makes Hokkaido one of the most popular tourist attractions in Japan.

CLIMATE

Hokkaido lies on almost the same latitude as central Europe. In general, the winters are severe and the summers are cool and pleasant. Spring comes generally one to two months later than in the rest of Japan, and even in mid-summer the temperature averages only about 22°C. Autumn also visits here sooner than in other regions, and it is immediately followed by a long winter. The climate of this island varies greatly by district because of the influence of its topography as well as the cold and warm currents. For example, during winter, Sapporo and the rest of western Hokkaido are influenced by the seasonal winds from the northwest (or west), causing heavy snowfall and regularly cloudy skies, while Obihiro and the rest of the east have good weather about one-third of the time during winter.

PARKS

Towering mountains, smoldering volcanoes, deep valleys, caldera lakes surrounded by primeval forests and vast plains—the natural landscape of Hokkaido is mysterious and magnificent. There are numerous beautiful parks on the island to preserve this beauty for everyone's enjoyment.

There are six national parks: Shikotsu-Toya, Daisetsuzan (Mt. Daisetsu), Akan, Kushiro-Shitsugen (Marshlands), Shiretoko and

Rishiri-Rebun-Sarobetsu. Each one is laid out on a grand scale with volcanoes, lakes or marshlands. The parks containing clusters of volcanoes have hot springs in the vicinity, with many coming to bathe in the mineral waters. Jozankei, Noboribetsu and Akan are just such places.

There are four quasi-national parks: Onuma, Niseko–Shakotan–Otaru-Kaigan (Coast), Hidaka-Sammyaku (Mountains)–Erimo and Abashiri. These parks also have impressive natural formations. There are another 14 prefectural parks in Hokkaido, each boasting magnificent natural beauty so attractive to many tourists throughout the year.

HISTORY

People from Honshu penetrated Ezo (the present Hokkaido) for the first time around the beginning of the 13th century. These "mainland-ers" obtained power and severely oppressed the indigenous race, the Ainus. Finally, the Ainu eastern chieftain Koshamain staged an insurrection in 1457, but Takeda Nobuhiro suppressed and subjugated the rebel force, bringing the island under a central authority. In 1593, Kakizaki Yoshihiro, the great-great-grandson of Takeda Nobuhiro, was appointed lord of Ezo by Toyotomi Hideyoshi, the military ruler of the country. Kakizaki later changed his family name to Matsumae and built a castle on the site of the present city of Matsumae. The castle town became the political and economic center of Ezo, serving as a gateway from Honshu. When the treaty of peace and amity was signed between Japan and the USA in 1854, Hakodate was fixed as one of the open ports.

The Meiji Restoration (refer to p.99) did not come about peace-fully. Enomoto Takeaki led troops of the former Shogunate during these disturbances, but was defeated by the new government army at Goryokaku in Hakodate in 1869. The Meiji Government then as-signed a Commissioner of Colonization for Hokkaido and changed the name from Ezo to Hokkaido. Sapporo was established as the prefectural capital, and the Hokkaido Government Office was erect-ed here in 1886. Development progressed steadily after this, including the opening of the Aomori-Hakodate Ferry in 1908. With an eye to the overall development of Hokkaido, the Hokkaido Development Law was enacted in 1950, calling for the establishment of the Hok-kaido Development Agency in Tokyo and its bureau in Sapporo. With the launching of the Five-Year Development Plan in 1952 and then the mapping-out of a second 5-Year Plan, the development of Hokkaido has progressed by leaps and bounds. Sapporo was selected as the site for the 11th Winter Olympics in 1972. The world's longest ocean-floor tunnel opened under the Tsugaru Straits in 1988, bringing Hokkaido one step closer to Honshu.

POPULATION AND ADMINISTRATION

The population of Hokkaido is 5,646,376, the sixth most populous prefecture in Japan. However, the population density is the lowest in the country—a sparse 67.6 people per sq.km compared to the national average of 323.8. The Hokkaido Prefectural Government Office is located in Sapporo. The island is divided into 14 districts—Abashiri, Hidaka, Hiyama, Iburi, Ishikari, Kamikawa, Kushiro, Nemuro, Oshima, Rumoi, Shiribeshi, Sorachi, Soya and Tokachi—each having a district office. There are 32 cities, including Sapporo, Asahikawa, Hakodate, Otaru, etc.

INDUSTRIES

It is no exaggeration to say that Hokkaido's industry is dependent on its wide open spaces and abundant natural resources. The main industries are agriculture, fishery, forestry and mining. In Hokkaido, once called the Coal Kingdom, coal output has been declining year by year and many mines are now being shut down.

Hokkaido is cool and dry, and since nearly all of its arable land consists of volcanic ashes or peat bogs, the agricultural industry centers around dryland farming. The cultivation of beans, sugar beets and potatoes flourishes on the Tokachi Plain. The use of the latest agricultural techniques for large-scale farming has led to an extremely high production ratio. Moreover, Hokkaido is Japan's largest stockbreeding region, accounting for one-third of all the dairy cattle in the country. It is famous for producing butter, cheese and other processed milk products. Thoroughbred horses are raised in the Hidaka region.

The fishing industry here boasts the best catches in Japan. Herring, salmon, trout and crab, formerly the main haul, have been replaced by walleye pollack. Scallop cultivation and sea tangle harvesting also thrive. Moreover, the marine product processing industry is especially active, even surpassing the fishing industry in terms of production value.

Forestry centers around paper pulp and plywood that is produced from broad-leafed trees grown only in Hokkaido.

Since the temperature and topography resemble parts of Europe, beer and whiskey production also flourish.

SPECIALTIES AND CRAFTS

Ainu Crafts: Decorative trays, teaspoons, wooden bowls, hangers and other carved household goods are made by the Ainu people. Many of the carved patterns are charms against evil spirits, requests for protection and other religious motifs. Walnut, yew and other woods are carved directly on with a knife called *makiri*, with no rough sketch to work from.

Carved Wooden Bears: The Ainu people worship bears as messengers from God. During the rituals of *Iomante* (the Bear Festival), the men wear a crown of woven grapevines called sanpe, with a mask representing a bear tied onto it. This is the origin of the carved wooden bears.

Asshi Weave: Asshi is the Ainu word for a kind of tall, deciduous elm called *ohyo*. The light brown bark is boiled, made into thread and woven on a loom (in which the warp threads are wrapped around the body). It is operated from a sitting position. This fabric has been used in the daily life of the Ainu since ancient times. There is an abundant variety of types, which are made into tablecloths, belts, bags, boxes and many other items.

Wine: Beginning with Tokachi wine from Ikeda-cho Town, there are many vineyard districts in Hokkaido such as Otaru and Furano, each one working zealously to elevate the standard of quality. No wonder Hokkaido is acclaimed by wine lovers for the variety of its available products. The superb dry red, white and rosé wines of Tokachi have won many awards in international competitions.

Others: Seafoods—scallops, salmon, smelt, kelp, crab, sea urchin, squid and other processed marine products. Vegetables—potatoes, corn, asparagus, etc. Dairy products—ice cream, white chocolate, butter, cheese, etc.

TRANSPORTATION

Transportation to Hokkaido

By Air: JAL, ANA and JAS maintain regular flight service from Honshu and Kyushu. There are 13 airports in Hokkaido; Chitose, Asahikawa, Hakodate, Obihiro, Kushiro, Memambetsu (Abashiri) and Wakkanai (except in winter) are conveniently connected with Honshu by direct flights.

By Rail: Honshu and Hokkaido are also connected by railway via the Seikan Tunnel. This is an ocean-floor tunnel 53.9 km long, completed in 1988. The JR sleeper limited express, well known for its luxurious facilities, connects Ueno Station in Tokyo with Sapporo in about 16 hrs. Also from Osaka, the luxurious sleeper limited express is available for Sapporo. If you take the fastest train on the JR Tohoku Shinkansen from Tokyo, you can reach Sapporo within 11 hrs. by transferring to a limited express train at Morioka and Hakodate.

By Sea: There are a number of long-distance ferries operating between Hokkaido and locations all around Honshu. The travel times and company names for services operating out of Tokyo are as follows:

Tokyo – Tomakomai   30 hrs.
(Nihon Enkai Ferry)
Tokyo – Kushiro   33 hrs. 30 min.
(Kinkai Yusen)

Transportation within Hokkaido

Air: JAS, ANA and ANK connect the major cities. From Sapporo, for example, (Chitose or Okadama Airport), there are flights to Wakkanai, Hakodate, Memambetsu, Mombetsu, Nakashibetsu and Kushiro, and from Wakkanai, planes fly to Rishiri and Rebun islands.

Rail: JR limited- and ordinary-express trains connect the major cities of Hokkaido, with Sapporo as the hub. The travel times from Sapporo to other major cities are as follows (by limited express):

Hakodate   3 hrs. 45 min.   (287 km)

Tomakomai	50 min.	(72 km)
Asahikawa	1 hrs. 40 min.	(137 km)
Obihiro	2 hrs. 50 min.	(221 km)
Kushiro	4 hrs. 50 min.	(349 km)
Kitami	4 hrs. 30 min.	(322 km)
Abashiri	5 hrs. 20 min.	(375 km)
Wakkanai	5 hrs. 50 min.	(397 km) ※by express

Express trains with sleepers are also available at night from Sapporo east to Abashiri and Kushiro and north to Wakkanai.

Bus: There are many places in Hokkaido where buses are more convenient than trains. In recent years, some local JR lines have been replaced by bus service. Be careful when making travel plans as some of the bus routes to sightseeing areas are suspended in winter.

Roads: Hokkaido, with its abundant land and sparse population, offers the best driving conditions in Japan. During the summer, young people come by car and motorcycle to enjoy touring and camping. Snowfall is heavy in many areas, but the snow-removal facilities are excellent so that it causes little hindrance to travel along highways and main trunk roads.

ANNUAL EVENTS

Kanchu Misogi (Mid-winter Purification): January 17. Dating from 1831, this festival is in supplication for big catches of fish and abundant harvests. It is held at Samegawa Shrine in Kikonai Town. Carefully selected youths bear the object of worship into the frigid, rough winter ocean for purification.

Okhotsk Ryuhyo Matsuri (Okhotsk Ice Floe Festival): Early February. The ocean ice from the northern Okhotsk Sea breaks up and is carried by the wind and tidal currents to the northeastern coastline of Hokkaido. The ice floes are of various sizes and are quite beautiful. Many come to gaze at their glistening forms. The highlight of the festival held in Abashiri is the parade in which large chunks of ice are dragged through the streets on sleds. The ice sculptures are worth seeing, too.

Sapporo Yuki Matsuri (Sapporo Snow Festival): February 5-11 (when the last day falls on Saturday or Sunday, 6-12). More than 200 enormous snow and ice sculptures are constructed at O-dori Promenade Park and Makomanai in Sapporo. They are created by corporations and individuals, all competing for prizes. There are many participants from abroad, too. It is the biggest annual event in Sapporo.

Shiraoi Iomante: First Saturday and Sunday in February. This is a solemn Ainu festival in which a bear, captured alive, is returned to the country of the gods.

Lilac Matsuri: Late May. Held in the O-dori Promenade in Sapporo for three days, it ends on the last Sunday in May. Lilac is the official plant of Sapporo. There are two kinds of flowers: white and purple. Countless lilacs adorn the city during the festival.

Hokkaido Jingu Matsuri (also called the *Sapporo Matsuri*): June 14-16. It is held in homage to the deity of the city. During the festival period, portable shrines and floats parade through the city.

Hokkai Soran Matsuri: Early July. It is a festival of Yoichi Town. The marine procession of portable shrines and a large parade involving more than a thousand people are the highlights.

Hokkai Heso (Navel) Matsuri: July 28-29. This festival is held in Furano City, known as the navel of Hokkaido because of its location. It is said that drawing a picture on one's belly and dancing along while picking up rice cakes will give one strength.

Showa Shinzan Matsuri (Mt. Showa-Shinzan Fire Festival): First Saturday and Sunday in August. The 1943 eruption of Mt. Showa Shinzan is re-enacted through fireworks. The gigantic bursts of fireworks illuminate the summer evening sky.

Noboribetsu Jigoku (Hell) Matsuri: Last Friday and Saturday in August. The "devil" symbolic of the hot spring in Jigokudani, jumps out of the "hell" and performs a wild dance.

Kiku Matsuri (Chrysanthemum Festival): Late October-Early November. The display of thousands of chrysanthemums are the main attraction at this festival in Sapporo City.

TRAVEL ADVICE

The travel season in Hokkaido begins when spring finally arrives in early May. Cherry and plum trees, azaleas, lilacs and the rest of the spring flowers all bloom at once. Since there is no rainy season, June is generally refreshing, and the green of the brand new leaves is dazzling. This time of year and late September-early October, when salmon, scallops, corn and all the other Hokkaido specialties are in season, are the best seasons for sightseeing. The autumn leaves of early October cannot be overlooked either. The greatest number of people visit Hokkaido in July, August and early February when the annual Snow Festival is held in Sapporo, so reservations at these times are absolutely necessary. Up until about ten years ago, there were few visitors to Hokkaido during winter, but trips to the *Sapporo Yuki Matsuri* and the ice floes at Abashiri, Mombetsu and Wakkanai are now gaining in popularity. To the skier, Hokkaido is a paradise, with many package tours available from Tokyo and Osaka.

Area 1. Sapporo and Vicinity

Sapporo 2/4-5 ☎ 011

The site of the Hokkaido Prefectural Government, Sapporo is the political, economic and educational center of Hokkaido. With a population of 1,608,585, it is the fifth-largest city in Japan. The city is located at the southwest edge of the Ishikari Plain, occupying almost the entire valley of the Toyohira River (a tributary of the Ishikari River). It also covers an area of 1,118 sq.km, with most of the city situated on the alluvial fan of the Toyohira River. The name of the city is said to have come from the Ainu words "sato poro petsu," meaning "a long dry river" (indicating the Toyohira River). Sapporo was developed through urban planning. Construction to make Sapporo the capital of Hokkaido began from the time when the Commissioner of Colonization was stationed here in 1869. The city is regularly laid out, with boulevards intersecting each other at right angles.

The 105 m-wide, 3.8 km-long road that runs east to west is called O-dori Promenade (Main Street). It divides the city into north and south, while the Sosei River, a tributary of the Toyohira River, runs south to north and divides the city from east to west. All the straight streets dividing the city like a chessboard have names based on this design. For example, a street running east to west with O-dori Promenade as the cardinal point would be called Minami-Ichijo (South 1st St.) or Kita-Sanjo (North 3rd St.). Conversely, streets running north to south with the Sosei River as the cardinal point would be called Higashi 1-chome (East 1st Ave.) or Nishi 3-chome (West 3rd Ave.). The block south of Sapporo Station and west of the Sosei River is the administrative district centered around the Hokkaido Prefectural Government Office. It has a long history as the base of development in Hokkaido. A modern shopping district stretches to the south of O-dori Promenade, with fashionable shops lining both sides of the street. It is always bustling with crowds of people. As one continues south, movie theaters, restaurants, bars and coffee shops increase, finally evolving into a flourishing entertainment district.

The most prominent features on the outskirts of the city are Shikotsu-Toya National Park and Jozankei Hot Springs. There are also several good ski resorts among the many high hills.

TRANSPORTATION

Buses: The bus lines center around the JR Sapporo Station and radiate outward through the city. Buses to Jozankei and Lake Shikotsu leave from the bus terminal in front of the JR Sapporo Station, and most of the intra-city lines leave from the central O-dori Bus Terminal on O-dori Promenade. Regular sightseeing buses leave from the bus terminal in front of the JR Sapporo Station. There are many different routes, including the "Akashiya (acacia) Course" and the "Suzuran (lily of the valley) Course," that take in the famous landmarks of Sapporo. These pleasure trips are all run by the Sapporo Municipal Bureau of Transportation and require reservations.

Subways: The Namboku Line (14.3 km), the Tozai Line (17.3 km) and the Toho Line (8.1 km) pierce the heart of the city and intersect at O-dori Station.

Streetcars: Only one line is still running but many city residents as well as tourists still depend on it.

A 1-day pass for buses, subways and streetcars is available.

Refer to the supplement for details regarding the "i" **System Information Center** in Sapporo.

PLACES OF INTEREST

Hokkaido University 4 : 500 m northwest of the JR Sapporo Station, about 10 min. on foot. The campus is so large that even the students taking classes here everyday are not familiar with all of it. It started as Sapporo School of Agriculture in 1876, but now contains 12 different faculties. The long, poplar-lined avenue that runs through the campus and leads to the university farm is a Sapporo landmark. On the Faculty of Agriculture campus, there is a bust of the first dean of the Sapporo School of Agriculture, Dr. William S. Clark (1826-1886) of Massachusetts, USA. He only taught here for one year, but he left his students with a deep impression of his Christian frontier spirit. His parting words, "Boys, be ambitious!" live on in the hearts of students today.

Hokkaido University Botanical Gardens 4 : 10 min. on foot from west of Sapporo Station. Located roughly at the center of the city, the gardens cover an area of 134,000 sq.m. The spacious grounds house plants collected from all over the world. The university museum, also found here, contains precious displays of stuffed brown bears, cranes, squirrels and other animals.

Clock Tower Building 5 : About 700 m south of Sapporo Station, it can be reached on foot in about 10 min. The building was constructed in 1878 as the military exercise hall for the Sapporo School of Agriculture. The clock tower was added in 1881, and the chimes of the American-made clock have been musically ringing the hour ever since. Today, the building serves as a historical museum with about 400 exhibits.

O-dori Park 4-5 : About 700 m south of Sapporo Station, 10 min. on foot from the station. This is the 105-m-wide, 3.8-km-long green belt that forms the center of O-dori Promenade. The 147.2-m-tall Sapporo TV tower stands at the east end. Inside the park, there are lawns bordered by flower beds, fountains and various sculptures. It also serves as the grounds for annual events held every season.

Former Head Office of Hokkaido Prefectural Government 5 : 7 min. on foot, southwest of Sapporo Station. This building was erected in 1888 as the head office of the Commissioner of Colonization. The brick, neo-baroque structure has been restored to its original state and is designated as an Important Cultural Property. Inside are pictures and materials that document the history of Hokkaido. It also serves as archives.

Yukijirushi Dairy Products Company Museum: 15 min. by bus from Sapporo Station, it is located on the grounds of the Yukijirushi Dairy Naebo Factory. The odd, hexagonal building with the snowflake motif was erected in 1976 to commemorate the 50th anniversary of the founding of Yukijirushi (Snow Brand) Dairies. The museum contains dairy product manufacturing machines (used since the company was founded) and exhibits of the history of dairy farming and milk products. One can also observe the dairy product manufacturing process and sample their ice cream and milk. Reservations necessary. ☎ (011)704-2329

Sapporo Beer Garden 5 : 10 min. by bus from Sapporo Station, about 1.5 km to the east. The garden contains a brewery, a beer museum and a "Mongolian" (mutton) barbecue restaurant. The beer museum is in a 19th-century brick building that was used as a brewery from 1888 to 1965. The exhibits tell the history and science of beer brewing. A 3.8-m-diameter pot imported from Germany and 19th-century Sapporo Beer posters highlight the exhibits. It is also possible to tour the factory. Reservations are necessary. ☎ (011) 731-4368 The restaurant here is one of the "must" tourist spots in Hokkaido.

Nijo Market 5 : 10 min. to the north-east on foot from Susukino Subway Station. Walk down Tanuki-koji and cross the Sosei River. Fish mongers, grocers, department stores—about 70 shops with their goods displayed—offer a colorful spectacle, with the multitudes of shoppers and tourists creating an uproar all day long.

Tanuki-koji and Susukino 5 : The arcade, 400 m south of O-dori Park between Minami Nijo and Sanjo, is called Tanuki-koji (Badger Alley). This shopping district has a history dating from the Meiji period. Today, appealing restaurants serving local cooking, souvenir shops and clothing stores make a colorful array. It is also known among local residents as the consumate amusement area. Susukino is to the night what Tanuki-koji is to the day. There are more than 4,000 bars, cabarets and clubs with their brilliant neon lights brightening the sky at night. Near Susukino Subway Station.

Ramen Yokocho (Chinese Noodle Alley) 5 : More than 15 *ramen* restaurants line the narrow alley next to New Susukino Bldg., east of Susukino Subway Station. Each bowl of noodles seems to taste better than the last. This area has become one of the most popular spots in Sapporo.

Sapporo Underground Shopping Center 5 : With O-dori Promenade serving again as the cardinal point, Aurora Town stretches east and west, while Pole Town extends north and south, encompassing about 150 shops. It flourishes as one of the main shopping areas for Sapporo residents.

Nakajima Park 5 : 2 km south of the JR Sapporo Station. This Japanese garden houses several structures designated as Important Cultural Properties. Hassoan is a tea house that was constructed in the early 17th century by the famed landscaper Kobori Enshu. The name means eight-window hermitage, and accordingly, it has eight windows. The purely Japanese atmosphere has been retained today with gables, copper tile and *tatami*-mat floor. There is also the

Hoheikan, a Western-style structure erected in 1879 by the Commissioner of Colonization. The two-story wooden building was originally erected on O-dori Promenade, but since it was not used very much, it was moved here in 1957. The exotic building is now used as a wedding hall and is popular with young couples for the foreign atmosphere it provides. The park also contains a variety of leisure facilities, including "Children's World," a rose garden and a winter sports museum. Near Nakajima-Koen Subway Station.

Hokkaido Shrine 4 : About 4 km west of Sapporo Station, 5 min. on foot from Maruyama Koen Subway Station. The shrine was built for a guardian deity in conjunction with colonization. However, the main building was destroyed by fire in 1974, and the present one is a reconstruction erected in 1978. The grounds contain cherry trees, pines and cypresses that were planted when the shrine was first built. The cherry trees create a beautiful scene when they bloom. The famous *Hokkaido Jingu Matsuri* festival occurs here in mid-June, when the portable shrines and floats fill the streets.

Maruyama Park 4 : About 4 km west of Sapporo Station and 5 min. on foot from Maruyama Koen Subway Station. It is about 600,000 sq. m in area and is famous for its cherry blossoms in spring. Known as a sports center, the park also contains a baseball field, tennis courts and an ice-skating rink where world championships are held. To the southwest lie the 70 m class Miyanomori and the 90 m class Okurayama Ski Jumps, where ski jump competitions are held. The area around Maruyama Park is blanketed with a thick, primeval forest with 390 different kinds of trees and has been designated as a Natural Monument.

Mt. Moiwa 4 : Alt. 531 m. Located 6 km southwest of central Sapporo, or 15 min. by bus from Maruyama Koen Subway Station to the ropeway station at its foot. The summit commands a panoramic view of Sapporo City, the Ishikari Plain, Mt. Tarumae and the view even extends as far as Mt. Daisetsu. The mountainside contains a primeval forest, an algae park and a ranch, among other things. As a result, the mountain has become popular as a nice place to enjoy a day trip.

Historical Village of Hokkaido: 50 min. by bus from Sapporo Station, 15 km to the east. This village contains some 30 restored Meiji and Taisho period buildings brought from various places around Hokkaido, including the former Sapporo Station Building, the former Otaru Newspaper Office and the former Urakawa Municipal Office. The village is a part of the Hokkaido Prefectural Nopporo Forest Park and covers an area of 542,000 sq. m. The buildings are surrounded by imposing greenery. The village is divided into an urban section, a rural village, a fishing village and a mountain village, reproducing the life styles of the colonial days. The most popular is the moving exhibit—the horse-drawn streetcar.

Makomanai Park Outdoor Arena: Opened in 1972 as the main ice-skating rink for Asia's first winter Olympics. Since the grounds also contain an indoor skating rink, one can enjoy ice skating all year round. The area around it is Makomanai Park, a favorite place for local residents to relax. Near Makomanai Subway Station.

Hitsuji-ga-Oka: About 11 km southeast of Sapporo Station, or about 40 min. by bus. A series of gently rolling hills are peaked by a grassy plain where sheep graze freely. The observation deck provides a sweeping view of Sapporo that is particularly breathtaking at night. There is a 2-m-tall bronze statue of William Clark that is often the object of souvenir photographs by tourists. Hunger pangs can be satisfied at a restaurant serving "Mongolian" barbecue, a Hokkaido specialty.

Jozankei Spas 2 : About 30 km from central Sapporo, it takes around 50 min. by bus from Sapporo Station. Deluxe *ryokan*, or Japanese-style inns and hotels line the banks of the upper reaches of Toyohira River. The spring waters are hot (70-90°C) and are said to be efficacious against nervous and gastroenteric disorders. The mineral spring water bubbling up from the river bed is surrounded by inns, souvenir shops and traditional restaurants. Many skiers at the Sapporo International Ski Grounds spend the night here.

Ski Grounds in the Sapporo Area

Sapporo International Ski Grounds: 1 hr. 30 min. by bus from the JR Sapporo Station, roughly between Jozankei and Otaru. This large ski ground opened in December 1978 on the northeast face of Asaridake Peak, 1,281 m in altitude. It is a popular day trip for Sapporo residents. There are four ski courses that cover beginning to advanced skiers and eight sky-cabin lifts that can carry 4-6 people. Naturally, the snow quality is good and the atmosphere attracts the younger set. The season is from late November to mid-May.

Makomanai Ski Grounds: 15 min. by bus from Makomanai Subway Station. There are courses for skiers of all levels of accomplishment, three lifts and facilities for night skiing.

Teine Olympia: 50 min. by bus from Sapporo Station. 11 ski lifts leave from the western foot of Mt. Teine (alt. 1,023 m). There are six courses to choose from, and nighttime facilities are provided. The ski season is from December through April. When there is no snow, an amusement park, go-carts, archery, golf, and other athletic and leisure facilities take over.

Teine Highland Ski Grounds: On the northeastern slope of Mt. Teine. The grounds cover an area of 400,000 sq.m. There are five lifts and ropeways and seven courses, including the grand slalom course used in the Olympics. Skiers particularly appreciate the spectacular view of Sapporo, Ishikari Plain, the Japan Sea and the Daisetsu Mountain Chain from the summit.

Mt. Moiwa Ski Grounds: 20 min. by bus from Sapporo Station. The variety of slopes on the south face of Mt. Moiwa appeal to everyone, from the rawest beginner to the most seasoned skier. There are five lifts as well as night facilities, and skiing is possible from mid-December to late March.

Area 2. Niseko-Shakotan-Otaru Kaigan (Coast) Quasi-National Park

A natural park that extends to the west of Otaru, the lush beauty of the forest-covered mountains and the wild sea form a landscape of spectacular contrast. The spa at the foot of the mountain is an ideal base for mountain climbing and skiing in the Niseko Mountain Chain, while the beautiful beaches, fantastic crags and the strangely shaped boulders of the Shakotan Peninsula and Otaru Coast offer fascinating views of nature on a grand scale. The Shakotan Peninsula sticks out like a lump on western Otaru. At one time, it was the best place in Hokkaido to catch herring. The winding shoreline is a continuation of the extraordinary sea-eroded cliffs. The contrast of the dark blue ocean and the towering crags is a breathtaking sight. The myriad precipices and undulations hinder passage, and there is as yet no road that circles the peninsula. For this reason, sightseeing is divided into east and west Shakotan. Yoichi on the Hakodate Main Line is the gateway to the former and Iwanai to the latter. It is relatively easier to get around in east Shakotan, and many come for the day from Sapporo to look at the beautiful ocean called Shakotan Blue.

Otaru ②☎0134

About 35 min. from Sapporo by rapid train on the Hakodate Main Line, or 55 min. by bus. Otaru is the first port city on the northwest coast of Hokkaido with a population of 166,522 on 244.7 sq. km of area. The name is derived from the Ainu words "ota oru nai" (river on a sandy beach). The city flourished during the late 19th and early 20th centuries as a center for herring fishing. After the Meiji Government selected Otaru for development, it prospered as a major port for unloading commodities, receiving the nickname "the Wall Street of Hokkaido." Although it lost its economic momentum after World War II, it remains a major center for commerce and industry. Since the city is on the side of a hill and has many steep slopes, it is sometimes called "hill town." There are many classical stone build-ings in the town, lining the streets with the ghosts of its past glory.

PLACES OF INTEREST

Otaru Canal: 10 min. on foot from Otaru Station, down the hill towards the port. The area around the 20 to 40 m-wide, 1,300 m-long canal is covered with stone warehouses from the Meiji and Taisho periods. The famous former Otaru Warehouse, with fabulous dolphin-like fish ornaments on the roof, now houses the Otaru Municipal Museum, where the peak of the city's prosperity is recalled. A cobblestone promenade constructed with 600,000 pieces of granite runs along the canal. It is lighted by 31 gas street lights, re-creating the 19th-century atmosphere of a port city with their soft glow.

Temiya Cavern: 2 km northeast of Otaru Station and under a cliff alongside the coastal road in Temiya Park. Faint symbols carved on the inner walls of the cave can barely be discerned. They were discovered in 1865, and the argument as to whether they are ancient or modern has been going on ever since.

Kitaichi Glass No. 3 Annex: 1.5 km east of Otaru Station, 5 min. by bus. It has been known for its lamps and hand-blown glassware since mid-Meiji period. The storefront was originally a stone warehouse and has enough space for a gallery to display lamps and glasswork from all over the world—300 different kinds of lamps from five countries in the north hall and as many as 4,000 glassware in Kitaichi Hall. There is also a coffee shop. It takes about 1 hr. to see everything.

Otaru Park: 1.2 km south of Otaru Station, or 5 min. by bus. The area forms a plateau, providing an extensive view of Otaru, the port and the ocean beyond. The grounds contain a multi-purpose gymnasium, a public auditorium, a civil assembly hall, baseball fields, a library, a playground and much more, making it a favorite place where local residents can relax. In the spring, about 6,000 azaleas burst into full bloom, drawing large crowds with their beauty.

Shukutsu Marine Park: About 7 km to the north of Otaru, or 25 min. by bus. This seaside park provides a view of the rugged landscape of the Shakotan Peninsula, designated as a quasi-national park. It contains one of the top aquariums in Japan, the Nishin Mansion (home of a herring fisherman built at the end of the 19th century), and all the facilities for enjoying water skiing, yachting and other marine sports.

Asarigawa Spa: 8 km southwest of Otaru Station, or about 30 min. by bus; a deserted area facing the Asari River. The spa opened in 1954, but its history is short. Since the area is quiet, however, many come to convalesce here. There is golf in the summer and skiing in the winter. The waters are said to be efficacious for treating rheumatism, anemia and gastroenteric disorders.

The Oshoro Area: Shioya, Ranshima and many other excellent places to swim in the ocean can be found along National Highway 5 from Otaru to Yoichi, and the shoreline view makes a pleasant drive. Some of the highlights include the towering cliffs and wild scenery of the Oshoro Shore, the Oshoro Stone Circle and the Fugoppe Cave where ancient pictographs are inscribed on the walls.

Shakotan Peninsula and Niseko Mountain Chain Area

Yoichi 2 : 20 km west of Otaru. With a population of 25,709, the town was founded on the eastern neck of the Shakotan Peninsula and

developed along the mouth of the Yoichi River. The main industries
are turbot and cod fishing as well as grape and apple cultivation, the
latter being regarded as a Hokkaido specialty. There is a Nikka
Whisky factory that offers tours.

Shakotan Town: Located on the very tip of the Shakotan Peninsula,
it prospered during the golden age of herring fishing that lasted until
the 1920s. It has now 4,319 residents on 237.9 sq. km of area. The
mysterious curves of the winding shoreline attract many tourists.
Since the inland area is dominated by the towering peaks of Mt.
Yobetsu and Mt. Shakotan, agriculture is virtually non-existent.
Alaskan pollack, sea urchin and other varieties of inshore fishing is
the main industry.

Cape Kamui 2 : The cape juts out from the northwest edge of the
Shakotan Peninsula. In the heyday of shipping, it was known, along
with Capes Motsuta and Ofuyu, as one of the three most dangerous
shorelines in Hokkaido. The ships would lower their sails and offer
straw figures and sacred *sake* to the sea god for protection against
evil and for safe passage. Until 1856, women were forbidden to sail
through here. On the tip of the 80-m-high cape stands the Cape Kamui
Lighthouse, and when its light shines on the legendary boulder, called
Kamui-Iwa (Rock), it presents a mystical sight. Sightseers also enjoy
viewing the Nenbutsu Tunnel and the towering rocks of Mizunashi.

Iwanai 2 : Located in the heart of the Niseko-Shakotan-Otaru
Kaigan (Coast) Quasi-National Park. Once the waters were rich in
herring, but with their disappearance, the fishing and processing of
Alaskan pollack, salmon and trout have become the major industries.
Iwanai is also famous as the first place where asparagus was cultivated in Japan and today canned asparagus is a specialty of Iwanai.
30 min. by bus from the JR Kozawa Station.

Raiden Coast: The southwest coast of Iwanai. Many amateur fishermen and campers come to enjoy the wild, rough beauty of the coastal
scenery.

Kutchan 2 : 93 km or about 2 hrs. 10 min. by rapid train from
Sapporo. It is situated at the junction of the national highway that
runs between Niseko-Shakotan-Otaru Kaigan (Coast) Quasi-National
Park and Shikotsu-Toya National Park. It is known as the starting
point for the ascent of Mt. Yotei. Specialties of the city are potatoes,
oats and beans.

Mt. Yotei 2 : Alt. 1,898 m. One of the Shiribeshi volcano group, it
has a rounded peak that resembles the crest of Mt. Fuji, so it is also
called Ezo(Hokkaido)-Fuji. From the summit, one can see the Pacific
Ocean and the Mt. Showa Shinzan volcano cluster. The mountainside
is covered with Ezo cherry trees, potentilla, Chinese bellflower, and
some 260 other varieties of alpine flora. It would be hard to decide
which is more spectacular—the blossoms of summer or the changing
leaves of autumn. The summit contains an ovular crater called "the
caldron," and there is a 13,000 sq. m crescent-shaped volcanic lake in

the western foothills. This peak is a favorite with mountain climbers, with the most popular trail to the summit taking 4 hrs. from Kutchan.
Kombu Spa: 15 min. by bus from Niseko Station on the JR Hakodate Main Line. Momijidani, Aoyama, Koikawa and the rest of the hot springs included in this spa are located between Niseko-Annupuri and Chise-Nupuri, each offering a quiet retreat for the enjoyment of nature.
Niseko-Annupuri: Alt. 1,308 m. Its triangular peak is the highest of the Niseko Mountain Chain. Mt. Yotei, Lake Toya, Shakotan and the Japan Sea can all be viewed from the top. Above 900 m, the face of the mountain is covered with bamboo grass and other high-altitude alpine flora. It is covered with snowdrifts more than 3 m deep—much to the joy of skiers. In the summer, many families come to climb the mountain, lodging at Niseko Goshiki Spa. The climbing distance is about 2 km and should take about 1 hr. 30 min to cover.
Niseko Goshiki Spa: 35 min. by bus from Niseko Station. Alt. 560 m. The hot river that flows from the rocks of Iwao-Nupuri has been drawn off to create a spa. The water temperature is 80°C and is effective for neuralgia, rheumatism and female ailments. It is also popular as a base from which to go hiking, mountain climbing and skiing in the Niseko Mountain Chain.
Oshamambe 2 : 1 hr. 20 min. from Hakodate by limited express, it serves as a junction for the JR Muroran Main Line and Hakodate Main Line. The town stretches narrowly along Uchiura Bay and is surrounded by mountains—Mt. Shamambe to the north, Mt. Osha-mambe and Mt. Bozu to the south. The main industries are dairy farming and the manufacture of wood products. Turbot and surf clams were once the main products of the fishing industry, but they have not been flourishing lately. Presently, scallops make up 70% of the catch. Oshamambe is also known throughout the country as the source for a kind of crab called *kegani*. Gift shops selling this type of crab line National Highway 5.

Area 3. Hakodate and Southern Hokkaido

Hakodate 2 ☎0138

Facing Honshu at Aomori across by the Tsugaru Straits, Hakodate serves as the southern gateway to Hokkaido. The 347.9 sq.km city is home to a population of 309,484, making it the third-largest city in Hokkaido after Sapporo and Asahikawa. Founded in 1454 when the Kono Clan built a castle in the foothills of what is now called Mt. Hakodate, it was named after the shape of the castle, *hakodate*, meaning box-shaped castle. Prosperity came to the town in 1859 with the signing of a commercial treaty with the USA. Like Yokohama and Nagasaki, Hakodate was opened as one of Japan's first trading ports. Subsequently, it became the center of politics and economics in place of Matsumae and Esashi, which had held this position for the previous 250 years. In former times, Hakodate had served as the main gateway to Hokkaido through the ferry that connects it with Aomori, but with the coming of the age of flight, this role has been taken over by Sapporo. Today, the city is popular with tourists for its exotic atmosphere as an international port city. Fishing and shipbuilding, the main industries, are foundering so that the economic strength of the city is not what it once was. However, the opening of the Seikan (Aomori-Hakodate) Tunnel might change its fortunes once again.

Refer to the supplement for details regarding the "i" **System Information Center** in Hakodate.

PLACES OF INTEREST
Mt. Hakodate: Alt. 335 m. Located southwest of Hakodate City, jutting out into the Tsugaru Straits. Offering a sweeping view of the city and its port, the mountain peak is the perfect vantage point from which to gaze at the night lights, which are said to be particularly beautiful in Hakodate. There are also monuments to pioneering geologist Ino Tadataka, the first man to make an accurate map of Japan, and English zoologist Thomas Wright Blakiston. The mountainside is a botanist's dream with more than 600 different kinds of plants, including the Hokkaido specialty— *Hakodate Shinobu Goke* (moss).

Hakodate Port: Located at the northeastern tip of Mt. Hakodate, in the southeastern corner of Hakodate Bay. Some of the many sights in the area include the Kanamori Warehouses and the monument to Takataya Kahei, a shipper active in the late Edo period in Japan's northern sea area. An excursion boat circles the port.

Hakodate Park: About 3 km southwest from Hakodate Station. It can be reached by a 10 min. stroll from the Aoyagicho Streetcar Stop. The park sprawls over an area of 50,000 sq. m on the southeastern slopes of Mt. Hakodate. It contains 1,000 cherry trees, and tourists flock to the area when the blossoms reach their peak in May. Scattered among the trees are a museum, a library, flower beds, playgrounds and a zoo for small animals.

Hakodate Museum: Located inside Hakodate Park. Arts and crafts, native and archaeological artifacts and documents—some 350 items —are on display here. Fishing gear and other objects of daily life from the Ainu as well as stone implements, earthenware, figurines and ancient money excavated from sites around Hakodate are among the exhibits.

Halistos Greek Orthodox Church: 2 km west of Hakodate Station, or about 10 min. on foot from Jujigai Streetcar Stop on the east face of Mt. Hakodate. The green-roofed, white-walled church with a cross mounted on its high steeple was originally established in 1859 as a chapel for the Russian consulate, becoming the first Greek Orthodox Church in Japan in 1872. The present majestic, Byzantine-style church structure dates from 1916. The illuminated church is a beautiful sight at night. The bell now hanging in Nicolai Cathedral in Kanda, Tokyo, was moved from this church in 1928.

Motomachi: This is a district on the bluff of the northeastern face of Mt. Hakodate where the Halistos Church and other brick- and- wood, Western-style mansions built during the Meiji period can be seen. The poplar-lined streets and cobblestones create an exotic atmosphere on this hill overlooking the port, making it a perfect place to take a walk. The road to the Foreigners Cemetery is lined on both sides with stylish restaurants and coffee shops.

Foreigners Cemetery: 3.5 km from Hakodate Station, on top of a small hill that overlooks the ships sailing in and out of port. The rusty crosses and strangely shaped gravestones on the green lawn form a peaceful scene. The oldest graves belong to two American sailors who fell ill and died during Admiral Perry's mission in 1854.

Former Hakodate Public Hall: 15 min. on foot from Suehiro-cho Streetcar Stop. Completed in 1910, this two-story wooden building is representative of the Western-style architecture of the Meiji period. Designated as an Important Cultural Property in 1974, it consists of a main building and an annex. The main building is constructed with the symmetry characteristic of English colonial architecture, creating an atmosphere of bygone days popular with tourists.

Goryokaku: 4 km east of Hakodate Station, or 15 min. by bus. Goryokaku was built to cope with the defense of Ezo over an eight-year-period from 1857, later becoming Japan's first Western-style fortress. It was named for its shape of a five-pointed star. During the Battle of Hakodate in 1869, Enomoto Takeaki made his last, futile stand for the Tokugawa Shogunate against the Meiji Restoration here. The 250,000 sq. m grounds with their 30 m-wide outer moat have been turned into a park. There is a 60 m-high watchtower by the entrance gate called Goryokaku Tower. The first floor is a historical museum, while the second and third floors contain a restaurant, a coffee shop and gift shops. It affords a panoramic view of the fort, Mt. Hakodate and the city. Relics of the battle are displayed, and it is for this historical inheritance that it has been made an Important Cultural Property. There are lots of cherry trees and wisteria, which attract crowds when they are in bloom.

Cape Tachimachi: 4 km southwest of Hakodate Station, on the southeastern edge of Mt. Hakodate. Tachimachi is a transposition of the Ainu word piushi which means "a place on the rocks where you wait for fish and catch them with a spear." Standing on the rough, rocky surface of the cliff, one can gaze out over the Pacific Ocean. Disappearing into the distance immediately in front are the rolling peaks of the Tsugaru mountains on the right, and the Omorihama coastline and Yunokawa Spa are clearly visible on the left.

Yunokawa Spa ⬚2⬚: The region where the Matsukura River empties into the Tsugaru Straits, 6 km to the southeast of Hakodate Station, or 30 min. by streetcar. The hot springs were discovered 300 years ago, making this one of the oldest spas in Hokkaido. From the squid season of summer through the fall, the fire lures of the fishermen can be seen from the windows of the inns, providing a memorable scene for any traveler. The waters are said to be efficacious for neuralgia, gastroenteric disorders, rheumatism and female ailments.

Trappistines Convent: 10 km southeast of Hakodate Station, or 10 min. on foot from the Torapisuchinu Bus Stop. It was founded in 1898 by eight Catholic sisters from France and is managed by the Trappist Order. About 70 sisters reside here today as devout followers of the precepts of Benedict. The general public is not allowed to enter the convent, but the front garden, with its statues of St. Mary and St. Michael, and the museum can be viewed. The candy and cookies made here are regarded as Hokkaido specialties. They can be purchased here or in gift shops in the city.

Mt. Esan ⬚2⬚: Alt. 618 m. 1 hr. 50 min. by bus from the Hakodate Bus Center. Mt. Esan is an active, conic-tholoide volcano on the eastern edge of the Kameda Peninsula. The view of smoke curling up from the lava cliffs is intriguing. It takes about 1 hr. 50 min. to climb to the top, where one can look out over Shimokita Peninsula, the Hidaka Mountain Chain, Mt. Yotei and Mt. Komagatake. The area around the mouth of the volcano is covered with cliff orchids and moorwart (a total of 113 families and 633 species of alpine plants flourish here), but the blossoming of the azaleas in early June is said to be especially beautiful. Mt. Esan, the Hiura Coast, Cape Choshi and Cape Esan form a picturesque landscape with rocky columns rising from the ocean, jagged reefs and sea-eroded cliffs. This is a highlight of Esan Prefectural Park.

Shikabe Spa: 1 hr. 45 min. from Hakodate Bus Center, along National Highway 5, there are eight inns and public baths. The hot springs were discovered in 1632, and are good for anemia and gastroenteric disorders. The geyser that spouts a 10–15 m stream of hot water every 5 min. is quite a sight to see, but the relaxed atmosphere is what really brings people here.

Onuma Quasi-National Park ⬚2⬚

Covering an area of 88.5 sq. km, it includes three lakes (Onuma, Konuma and Junsainuma) dammed by the volcanic eruptions of Mt. Komagatake. The park has an established reputation for the beauty of the fresh new leaves of spring and an abundance of wild birds. Many families come to enjoy this aspect of outdoor nature on their holidays. Cycling can be enjoyed from the time when the skunk cabbage blooms in the spring through the fall, while skating can be enjoyed during the winter.

Lake Onuma: The largest of the three lakes. It has an area of 5.1 sq.

km and a circumference of 24 km, and is 13.6 m at the deepest point. The 33 little inlets along the shoreline and the 81 islands floating in the middle comprise a beautiful landscape. The silver firs, pines, maples and other unique trees and plants growing around the lake shore add a special Japanese touch to the scene. There are bridges leading to the islands, providing a peaceful setting for a leisurely stroll.

Lake Konuma: The lake has an area of 3.8 sq. km and a circumference of 16.3 km. A total of 31 tiny islands are sprinkled around the lake, with lots of bogwood about. From December to March, the winter landscape is complemented by swans that descend on the area around Tsukimi Bridge, located on the border with Onuma.

Lake Junsainuma: Located to the northwest of Lake Konuma, with Mt. Higure as a barrier between them. Tiny, wild water lilies grow on the water, brightening the deep purple surface of the lake in summer. Although it embraces 14 islets, this is the smallest of the three lakes.

Mt. Komagatake 2 : One of the highest peaks in Hokkaido, this 1,131 m high active volcano has become a symbol of Onuma Quasi-National Park. This is actually a collective name for 3 mountain peaks—Mt. Saharadake, Mt. Kengamine and Mt. Sumidamori, with smoke still drifting up from each of their mouths. Because frequent eruptions have created fissures in the peak, it looks different from every angle. From the summit, one can look out over all of Onuma Quasi-National Park and across the Tsugaru Straits to the Shimokita Peninsula. Above the 600 m altitude point, mountain azaleas, selaginella, moorwart and other alpine plants grow in abundance.

Trappist Monastery: 25 min. on foot from Oshima-Tobetsu Station on the JR Esashi Line. Like the Yunokawa Convent, this was the first Trappist Monastery. It was founded in 1896 by Okada Furie, a naturalized Frenchman. The monks lead self-sufficient lives, selling the butter and cheese they produce on the open market. Since the front of the main building has been reconstructed in recent years, sightseers can glimpse inside it.

Esashi 2 : 75 km to the west on National Highways 227 and 228 from Hakodate and about 2 hrs. by bus. Located along the west coast of the Oshima Peninsula, this town was once famous for herring fishing. The Japanese mainlanders settled here from the earliest days, and the Matsumae culture began to develop from around the time Takeda Nobuhiro unified the area in 1457. There are many buildings and festivals that recall this rich heritage, but the folk song "Esashi Oiwake" is particularly famous.

Okushiri Island 2 : A 143-sq. km island lying 61 km off the coast of Esashi. Most of the population of 5,000 live around the ports of Okushiri and Aonae, and are engaged in fishing for squid and trout. The ruins of a castle wall remain from what is said to have been the fortress of Takeda Nobuhiro for a time. Today, a ferry runs to the island from Esashi Port (2 hrs. 5 min.) and Setana Port (1 hr. 50 min.), while an airplane flies from Hakodate (40 min., 1-2 flights per day). **Matsumae** 2 : 100 km to the southwest on National Highway 228 from Hakodate, or about 1 hr. 30 min. by bus from Kikonai Station on the JR Esashi Line. Since the town served as the cradle of *samurai* culture in Hokkaido, it is sometimes called the "Kamakura of Hokkaido." For 400 years it flourished as the local political, economic and cultural center, but after the Meiji Restoration, influence over the area gradually shifted to Hakodate. Today it is known chiefly as a charming former castle town. The castle began with a structure completed by Matsumae Yoshihiro between 1600-1606, but it was rebuilt as a true fortress for the defense of the northern area in 1854. This secure castle, which covers 400 m from east to west and 300 m from north to south, has 16 gates and 7 batteries. Because the inner citadel gate, old front gate and many other sections retain their original form, it has been designated an Important Cultural Property. Inside the donjon, which was restored in 1961, is a museum containing cultural assets related to the Matsumae Clan and the Ainus.

Seikan (Aomori-Hakodate) Tunnel 2 : The tunnel went into service on March 13, 1988, connecting Honshu and Hokkaido by train. Of the total length of 53.9 km, 23 km runs under the bottom of the Tsugaru Straits. It used to take 3 hrs. 50 min. by ferry to cross over from Aomori to Hakodate. However, a new route through the tunnel has reduced the time to 2 hrs. 30 min. There are two underwater stations along the tunnel: Yoshioka Kaitei (Ocean Floor) Station and Tappi Kaitei Station.

Seikan Tunnel Museum: Two cylindrical buildings lie abreast of the tunnel entrance. A model of the Tsugaru Straits as well as data on the geological features and construction of the straits-tunnel are preserved and exhibited inside. A projection room and a hall are on the second floor.

Area 4. Shikotsu-Toya National Park

The topography of this national park, which extends to the southwest of Sapporo, was formed by numerous volcanoes. The hot springs and caldera lakes attract more tourists than anyplace else in Hokkaido. The park includes the Mt. Yotei, Mt. Tarumae, Mt. Usu and Mt. Showa Shinzan volcanic group, the Shikotsu, Toya, Kuttara and Okotampe lake group, and the Jozankei, Toya, Bankei and Noboribetsu hot-springs group. It was designated as a national park in 1949 and covers an area of 983.3 sq. km.

Lake Toya Area

Nakayama Pass: 45 km southwest of Sapporo, or about 1 hr. 30 min.

by bus. Located in the middle of National Highway 230, which bisects Shikotsu-Toya National Park, it has an altitude of 836 m. The pass has long been famous for the magnificent view it provides, including Mt. Yotei and the Muine Range. The view is so inspiring that the regular sightseeing buses often make a rest stop here. Stores and restaurants fill the white birch forest around the pass, and nearby are the sports training facilities of the Nakayama Toge Kemmin Center.

Rusutsu Plateau Country Land: 10 min. by bus from the Kimobetsu Bus Stop. This extensive leisure land is located along National Highway 230 at the base of Mt. Yotei. Attractions include 60 rides and games to enjoy, a 40 m freefall, a water slide, an aqua-coaster, tennis courts, etc.

Rusutsu Plateau Ski Grounds: Constructed on the eastern face of Mt. Sorioi (alt. 715 m) opposite Mt. Yotei. There is a gondola, 9 lifts and 11 ski courses. National Highway 230 runs right by, offering easy accessibility that attracts many skiers. During the winter, a bus runs directly from Sapporo.

Lake Toya 2 : About 2 hrs. 40 min. from Sapporo by bus, 105 km along National Highway 230. This is Japan's third-largest caldera lake, covering an area of 70 sq. km, a circumference of 45.5 km and a depth of 179.2 m. The many eruptions of the Shiribeshi volcano spewed forth several piles of pumice stone, some of which collapsed and dammed the water to form the lake. For this reason, a volcanic cone rises from the middle of the lake, forming Nakanoshima Island in the center. Nakanoshima Island actually consists of four small islands, which are covered with thick forests in which over 100 Ezo-deer roam. There are also wild Ezo-rabbits in the Lake Toya area. An excursion boat cruises the ice-free lake.

Toya-ko Spa: Adjoining Lake Toya. The spa boasts the third largest quantity of hot water in Japan as well as the most *ryokan* (Japanese-style inns) and gift shops of all the spas in Hokkaido. The view of Mt. Usu and Mt. Showa Shinzan at the rear and Mt. Yotei directly in front is beautiful enough to rank as one of the three best views in Hokkaido. The hot springs were discovered in 1917, with the water temperatures ranging from about 55-60°C. The waters are said to be efficacious against chronic muscular rheumatism and gastroenteric disorders. The inn-lined streets of the town are usually bustling, providing accommodations for more than 7,000 guests. For three days in late August, the *Toya Kosui Matsuri* (Lake Toya Festival) is held and includes such events as setting lanterns adrift on the water, fireworks and boat races.

Volcanic Science Museum: The museum contains data on the August 1977 eruption of Mt. Usu and data on Lake Toya. The sound-and-light show portraying the huge eruption of Mt. Usu and the reenactment of an earthquake are popular with visitors.

Mt. Showa Shinzan 2 : 15 min. by bus from Toya-ko Spa, 5 km away. The altitude is 407 m. Smoke still spouts from the yellowish-brown peak with its unique, instantly recognizable shape. The mountain was created as a result of hundreds of eruptions since 1943 and has been designated as a Natural Monument. The mountain has stopped growing for the present, but scorching gas escapes through fissures in the belonite lava and the fumarole.

Nearby is a bear ranch and a botanical garden containing some 700 kinds of plants from South Africa, India and other tropical regions that are cultivated by utilizing volcanic heat.

Mt. Usu 2 : A 732 m-high active volcano to the west of Mt. Showa Shinzan, this mountain is conoid. The upper portion has subsided into a 1.5 km diameter caldera, from which rises Usu Shinzan (New Mt. Usu) at the center and Greater Usu and Lesser Usu straddling it on each side. Since the mountain is a valuable resource for volcanologists, its name is famous around the world. A ropeway (seats 106) takes only 6 min. to run from the foot to the peak, where one can enjoy the majestic panorama of Lake Toya and Uchiura Bay.

Sobetsu Spa: 10 min. by bus from Toya-ko Spa, 4 km away. Known for its tranquil atmosphere, the spa is located on the south bank of Lake Toya, with Mt. Usu and Mt. Showa Shinzan forming a backdrop. The mineral waters, which have temperatures ranging between 67–91°C, are effective for external lesions, rheumatism and hives. This is an ideal area for a family trip.

Orofure Pass 2 : 20 km from Sobetsu. The 930-m-high pass lies in the middle of the ridge that cuts off Sobetsu Town from Noboribetsu City. The observation platform provides a view of Lake Toya, Mt. Showa Shinzan, Mt. Yotei, Lake Kuttara, the Pacific Ocean and many other scenic masterpieces of nature. The passage to Mt. Orofure makes a perfect hiking course, with 1 hr. 30 min. required for a round trip.

Zenkoji Temple: 1.4 km northwest of Usu Station on the JR Muroran Main Line. The Tokugawa Shogunate constructed it in 1804 as one of three government temples in Ezo (the present Hokkaido) for the enlightenment and colonization of the native islanders. The other two are the Toju-in Temple at Samani in the Hidaka district and the Kokutaiji Temple at Akkeshi in the Kushiro district.

Usu Local Museum: Located on the grounds of Zenkoji Temple. The *Maria* (Mary) *Kannon*, which was secretly worshipped by followers of Christianity during the period of oppression of the Shogunate, is preserved here. The statue was carved into a lantern and serves as a valuable reminder of the onerous circumstances of those days. The image of Gautama in this collection was made with the same technique as that of *Shaka-Nyorai* in the Seiryoji Temple in Kyoto (a National Treasure), and this one is a valuable historical relic as well.

Muroran 2 ☎0143: 1 hr. 43 min. by JR limited express on the JR Muroran Main Line or 103 km on the Do-o Expressway from Sapporo. The city covers an area of 81.6 sq. km and has a population of 126,882. Spreading along the Etomo Peninsula facing Uchiura Bay, it is Hokkaido's foremost industrial port city. All of the flat ground in the city is occupied by factory buildings, while the residences of its citizens are concentrated in the hilly sections. The name Muroran comes from the Ainu word morueran (gentle slopes). The following eight famous sights are located along the coast facing the vast open sea.

1. The night lights of Muroran
2. The cliffs called *Kin Byobu* and *Gin Byobu* (Gold Screen and Silver Screen)
3. The beauty of Cape Chikyu
4. Daikoku Island, where black lilies bloom
5. The view from Mt. Sokuryo
6. The view of Cape Etomo
7. The view of the open sea from Masuichi Beach
8. The magnificent landscape at Tokkarisho

Many sightseers make the rounds of these scenic places.

Cape Chikyu 2 : 15 min. by bus from Muroran Station and then a 40 min. walk. The cape juts out at the southernmost tip of Etomo Peninsula. An observation platform has been erected on a 147-m-high cliff. A hiking trail has been laid out from the town to this cape.

Noboribetsu 2 : 1 hr. 15 min. from Sapporo by the JR limited express, or 97 km along the Do-o Expressway. It is home to one of Japan's most famous spas. The city sprawls across large tracts of trees, lakes and marshes, capes and many other features of natural beauty. The town is divided into four areas—Horobetsu, Nobori-betsu, Washibetsu and Noboribetsu spas. Recently, it has come to serve as a bedroom community for Muroran.

Noboribetsu Spa 2 : 7 km north of Noboribetsu Station. This typical Japanese spa is located on a 200-m-high mountain and is surrounded by primeval forests. One reason the resort is so famous is because there are 11 different kinds of springs. Bathers can select the spring that best suits their purpose. The mineral waters, with temperatures ranging from 45-98°C, are said to be especially effica-cious against nervous afflictions. All of the *ryokan* have bathing facilities, but those of the Dai-ichi Takimotokan are unsurpassed. The bath is 5,000 sq. m and includes a hot waterfall plus a water slide.

Shihorei Peak: A position along the ropeway will work its way up to the peak in 10 min. from the spa. It is also called Mt. Kuma (bear mountain), with more than 180 brown bears grazing freely on a bear ranch at the top. From the observation platform at an altitude of 549 m, one can view Lake Kuttara, Mt. Tarumae, the Pacific Ocean and Mt. Komagatake. At the peak, an Ainu village of the early Meiji period, *Yukara-no-Sato*, has been reconstructed. Daily goods from Ainu life, Asshi cloth and carved wooden bears are manufactured and sold in the reed huts.

Jigokudani (Hell Valley): 5 min. on foot to the northeast of the spa. The explosive crater valley is 450 m in diameter, with an area of 100,000 sq. m and completely circled by a 10-m-high, russet-colored precipice. Steam and scalding water gush out from countless fumaroles of all sizes, creating a truly hellish scene. The entire site can be viewed from the observation platform to the west of the entrance, but if one would like to look more closely, the nature trail north of the entrance is ideal for this purpose. It is possible to fully take in the strange landscape at each of the 11 points along the way, but all off-trail areas are prohibited. It takes about 40 min. to cover the whole course.

Noboribetsu Primeval Forest: This is the 4 sq. km forest that covers the area from Jigokudani to Oyunuma. One of the larger alpine forests in southern Hokkaido, it is home for oaks, *katsura*, magnolias, mountain ash, kalopanax and many other trees growing here.

Karles Spa: 8 km northwest of Noboribetsu Spa. The clear radium waters that bubble up from the bed of the Chitose River are said to be similar to those in Karlesbade, Czechoslovakia. Hence, the name. The water temperatures range from 50-62°C and are said to be beneficial for spinal cord ailments.

Lake Kuttara: A typical volcanic lake, 3.5 km east of Noboribetsu Spa. Situated at an altitude of 258 m, the lake has an area of 5 sq. km and a depth of up to 147.5 m. Surrounded by primeval forest, the lake is quite mysterious because swamp waters flow in but no river flows out. The waters are clear to a depth of 19 m, surpassed in its clarity only by Lake Mashu.

Shiraoi ☐2 : From ancient times, Ainu settled at this oasis of greenery, which is wedged between the industrial zones of Muroran and Tomakomai. The first Japanese mainlanders came to live in this place when the Sendai Clan built an encampment here in 1855. Today, this quiet provincial town has a population of 23,870.

Shiraoi Poroto Kotan: This model Ainu village was reconstructed along the shores of Lake Poroto, a beautiful body of water surrounded by flowers and trees. A 16-m-tall statue of the village headman stands at the entrance to greet visitors. Along with the Museum of Ainu Culture, reed *chise* (house), *nusa* (altar) and *pu* (storehouse) are scattered about. The museum contains Ainu clothing, treasures and the tools of daily living as well as three-dimensional displays of hunting methods and ceremonies. In addition, the life-style and culture are explained inside the *chise*, while the *Iomante-rimuse* (dance to send off the bear) is performed in the plaza, much to the acclaim of the visitors. A large gift shop market, the Shiraoi Mingeikaikan, can also be found here.

Sendai Clan Encampment Site: 20 min. on foot from Shiraoi Station. In 1855, the Shogunate ordered the Sendai Clan to defend the southern and eastern parts of Ezo, including the islands of Kunashiri and Etorofu. The clan erected projecting encampments in 4 places, with the Shiraoi camp serving as the headquarters. The breastworks and moats remain in their original state, while the barracks have been restored. A museum is also located nearby.

Lake Shikotsu Area

Chitose ☐2☐ ☎0123: Pop. 77,306. 41 km to the southeast of Sapporo and south of the Ishikari Plain. The city is broad from east to west, with the JR Chitose Line and National Highway 36 running parallel through the center. The city has become an aerial gateway to Hokkaido and is also known for housing a Self-Defense Force base. It is the entrance to Lake Shikotsu and other tourist spots. In addition to the JR, limousine buses run between the airport and the principal hotels in Sapporo.

Lake Shikotsu ☐2☐: Located on the western edge of Chitose, this caldera lake has an area of 77.3 sq. km, a circumference of 40.9 km and a maximum depth of 360 m. It is the deepest lake in Japan after Lake Tazawa in Akita Prefecture. Its brightness contrasts with the primitive yet tranquil surroundings. More than anywhere else in Hokkaido, brown bears and many other woodland animals prowl about. The inns clustered around the lake offer a magnificent view of the peaks of Mt. Eniwa and Mt. Tarumae, while the excursion boat that cruises around the lake is convenient for sightseeing. *Shikotsu Kosui Matsuri* (Lake Shikotsu Festival) is held on the second Saturday and Sunday in July.

Mt. Eniwa ☐2☐: A 1,320-m-high active, conic volcano on the northwest shore of Lake Shikotsu. This peak first attracted notice when it became the site of the downhill race in the Sapporo Olympics in February 1972. There are many cracks in the upper regions, from which puffs of smoke rise into the sky.

Lake Okotampe: 55 min. by bus from Sapporo Station and 14 km from the shores of Lake Shikotsu. A solitary lake in the northwest foothills of Mt. Eniwadake, its ancient waters have a circumference of 5 km and a depth of 20.5 m at the deepest point. The pale green waters only cover an area of 400,000 sq. m, but like Lake Shinonome and Lake Onneto, this is one of the three "mysterious lakes" of Hokkaido.

Tomakomai ☐2☐ ☎0144: Pop. 158,635. 50 min. by the JR limited express from Sapporo, or 64 km along the Do-o Expressway. The city began to rapidly develop when the Oji Paper Company opened its Tomakomai factory in 1910, and today it is known as the site of most of Japan's paper manufacturing. The lush forests in the foothills of Mt. Tarumae, the clear currents of the Tomakomai River and the opening of the Muroran Main Line are what made it possible for Tomakomai to become the nation's "Paper Capital." The factories are concentrated around the harbor area, while the commercial district lies to the south of the station.

Mt. Tarumae: Alt. 1,041 m. This triple volcano has erupted more than 20 times since 1667. The dome of dark lava that formed from a particularly massive eruption in 1909 is well known. The mountain can be seen from the banks of Lake Shikotsu and other nearby locations, but the view from the window of the JR Muroran Main Line train is especially magnificent.

Lake Utonai: 12 km from Tomakomai along National Highway 36. Located in the rugged Yufutsu Plains, this salt-water lake has a circumference of 17 km. Known as a playground for migratory birds, numerous swans can be seen here, from mid-November until the snow thaws. There is a wild bird observation center on the lake shore. In the winter, the lake is an excellent place for ice skating.

Area 5. Along Hidaka Coast

The Hidaka Coast runs along the Pacific from Tomakomai to Cape Erimo. It is blessed with relatively warm temperatures, and the pasturing of race horses is done on a large scale. The JR Hidaka Main Line and National Highways 235 and 336 run along the coast, hemmed in by the Hidaka Mountain Range. The dashing forms of thoroughbred horses galloping across a field, the stripes in the sand made by seaweed drying in the sun and other scenic aspects of the fishing villages can be enjoyed from the train window.

Nibutani Ainu Culture Museum: 30 min. by bus from Tomikawa Station on the JR Hidaka Line. The Biratoricho area, located along the Sarukawa River, is said to have been the cradle of Ainu culture, and kotan (villages) of all sizes were once scattered throughout the region. The museum contains more than 1,000 specimens of some 300 different kinds of traditional Ainu tools and artifacts.

Yoshitsune Shrine: This shrine is believed to have been erected in 1799 by famed Ezo explorer Kondo Juzo (1771-1829) to enshrine Minamoto-no-Yoshitsune (1159-1189), the younger brother of Minamoto-no-Yoritomo, founder of the Kamakura Shogunate Government. Legend has it that Yoshitsune came to live here to escape his predicament in Hiraizumi and eventually gained the respect of the local Ainu. Today, the surrounding area has been turned into Yoshitsune Park, which is an ideal place to relax during the cherry blossom season in spring and the changing of the leaves in autumn.

Hidaka Kentucky Farm 2 : 10 min. by car from Tomikawa Station, along the eastern part of the lower reaches of the Sarukawa River. This vast, 1.25 sq. km leisure land offers a bridle path, tennis courts, an archery range and other sports facilities as well as lodges and other accommodations.

Hidaka-Sammyaku (Mountains) - Erimo Quasi-National Park 3 : Established in 1981, the park covers an area of 1,034.5 sq. km. It centers around the Hidaka Mountain Range, which serves as the habitat for many kinds of alpine plants, butterflies and wild animals.

The southern edge extends to the scenic landscape of Cape Erimo.
Samani ⬛3⬛ : The final stop on the JR Hidaka Main Line and the front door to the Hidaka-Sammyaku - Erimo Quasi-National Park. The town played a major role in Hokkaido's history, with one of Ezo's three main Buddhist temples, Toju-in, erected here at the end of the Edo period. Business formerly flourished around the port, but today the train-station area has become the economic center. The town contains Cape Enrumu, Kannonyama Park and many other places of natural beauty. With an altitude of 811 m, Mt. Apoi is 8 min. by bus from Samani Station. The mountain is a fairly easy climb (6.1 km to the summit, 3 hrs.) compared to the steepness of the rest of the Hidaka Range and offers a favorite hike for local residents. Although the altitude of the mountain is quite low, a wide variety of rare alpine plants grow there. In fact, more than 800 species have been introduced to the academic world. The cluster of alpine plants around the peak has been designated as a Special Natural Monument.

Hidaka Yabakei Gorge ⬛3⬛ : 8 km east of Samani Station, or 35 min. by bus. Bordered by the wild waves of the roaring ocean, the sheer cliff face extends for 8 km. This site of dynamic, haunting beauty was named for its resemblance to Yabakei Gorge in Kyushu, although in terms of untamed wilderness, it is in some ways superior to the original.

Cape Erimo ⬛3⬛ : 1 hr. 10 min. by bus from Samani Station, the cape constitutes the southern tip of the Hidaka Mountains and forms the center of the quasi-national park. Jutting out into the Pacific, the cape presents a majestic seascape formed by 60 m high cliffs and a variety of fantastic reefs and rocks extending several kilometers out to sea. Constantly exposed to strong winds and bereft of vegetation, the cape is quite desolate. The sea off the cape is where cold and warm currents meet. In summer, it is blanketed by a dense fog, often with little or no visibility, so that the sea here has been regarded as perilous since olden times. At the tip of the cape stands a lighthouse established in 1889.

Golden Road ⬛3⬛ : The 33-km-long National Highway 366 between Shoya and Hiro-o has been named Golden Road because of the excessive cost of constructing the highway along the coast with its long stretch of sheer cliffs. Construction began in 1928 and took seven years to complete, but the need for such a road had actually been advocated since the Edo period, with Kondo Juzo (1771-1829)— a noted Ezo explorer—one of its strongest proponent. For this reason, there is a Kondo Juzo Excavation Memorial, and one tunnel has been named the Juzo Tunnel. The road is exciting to drive along, with the wild waves crashing directly below. On rough days, the Pacific Ocean waves send their spray across the road.

Fumbe Falls: The 21 m high, 48 m wide falls cascade beside the Golden Road. Since the water source is underground, it never dries up, turning into a column of ice during the winter. It can be seen from the right-side windows of the bus heading toward Erimo.

Area 6. Sapporo to Asahikawa and Daisetsuzan National Park

Ebetsu 2 : 25 km along National Highway 12 from Sapporo. Located in the center of the Ishikari Plain, this city of 92,316 people flourished as a colony from 1878, but today it is being developed as a satellite city of Sapporo. The town contains dairies, ceramics factories, colleges and other educational institutions as well as residential districts.

Nopporo Primeval Forest: A part of the prefectural Nopporo Natural Park, the forest sprawls among Ebetsu, Hiroshima and Sapporo. Covering an area of 20 sq. km, some 17 km from Sapporo Station, the forest contains a mixture of more than 400 species of coniferous and broad-leaved trees. The path through the dense forest is perfect for bird watching.

Iwamizawa 2 ☎0126: Pop. 83,753. Located in the eastern part of the Ishikari Plain, it is an important transportation center in Hokkaido. 28 min. by limited express from Sapporo, or 32 km along the Do-o Expressway. Rice cultivation and other forms of agriculture thrive in the area around the city, including large crops of onions, cabbages and other vegetables. There is also a natural park that includes a primeval forest and a sports facility.

Yubari 2 ☎01235: Pop. 24,982. 1 hr. 5 min. from Sapporo to Shin-Yubari Station by limited express on the JR Chitose and Sekisho lines, thence 30 min. by local train. Located in the mountains along the Yubari River, the town developed around coal mining. Formerly, the best coal ore in the country was mined here, but the industry has fallen on hard times, with only a quarter of the boom town's peak population remaining. In order to escape the mining ghost town image, the town has been developed as a "historical coal town" centered around a coal museum. A ski resort and other tourist facilities are also being developed. Yubari melon is a famous speciality of this area.

Mikasa 2 : Adjoining the eastern part of Iwamizawa, it was one of the first towns to begin mining in the Ishikari coal fields. Mining operations continue here and there, but the output is decreasing year by year.

Sunagawa 2 ☎01255: Pop. 24,375. 51 min. by limited express from Sapporo on the JR Hakodate Main line. A small but modern industrial city conveniently connected to the rest of Hokkaido by rail. Chemical fertilizer manufacturing and lumbering are the main industries, but recently, the concrete and automotive industries have been gaining prominence. The city offers a Children's World, Hokko Park and many scenic spots for tourists.

Takikawa ☐2 ☎0125: Pop. 50,818. 57 min. by limited express from Sapporo Station. This town stands at the junction of the JR Hako-date Main Line and Nemuro Main Line, or 81 km from Sapporo along the Do-o Expressway. Located at the confluence of the Ishikari River and the Sorachi River, the city is known as the center of a granary district. The main agricultural products are rice, apples and onions. Stock breeding also flourishes here, boasting the nation's largest crossbreeding production of wild and domestic duck. Blessed with ascending air currents, an area near the city is popular as a flight center for glider pilots.

Rumoi ☐2 ☎01644: Pop. 33,454. Located on the coast of the Japan Sea, Rumoi serves as the political and economic center of northwestern Hokkaido. It has flourished around the port and bay area since it was first established as a trading center in 1634. Many marine products are brought into the harbor and their processing is a thriving industry.

Yagishiri Island ☐2 : 25 km northwest of the coast of Haboro, this tiny island has a circumference of only 12 km. It takes 1 hr. 10 min. to get here by boat from Haboro. Fishery is the main industry followed by farming. At the center of the island is a primeval forest of *onko* (yew), sheep pastures and plains, where a profusion of evening primroses and lilies of the valley bloom. A local history museum near the port features exhibits explaining the history and culture of the island. Swimming and camping are possible along the south coast.

Teuri Island ☐2 : Situated 4 km west of Yagishiri Island, or 1 hr. 30 min. from Haboro by boat. Ever since it was opened as a fishing port in 1786, fishing has been the main industry. Residences are concentrated along the eastern shore, but the hilly central region is a wilderness. The western coast is full of reefs and cliffs, where murres and other sea birds nest, leading to its designation as a Natural Monument.

Asahikawa ☐2 ☎0166

Pop. 361,742. 1 hr. 33 min. by the JR limited express from Sapporo, located in central Hokkaido. Second in size only to Sapporo in Hokkaido, the city is the economic and cultural center of the central region. Founded by troops of *tondenhei* (peasant soldiers), it flourished after the Sino-Japanese War (1894-1895) due to the expansion of the rear guard and continued as a sort of northern military capital until 1945. Today, both commerce and industry thrive here, and modern buildings line the streets. A pedestrian mall, called Heiwa-dori (Peace Street), extending straight out from the station is packed with department stores and famous specialty shops. Although pulp and other lumber industries are the main sources of income, the city is famous for the large volume of furniture produced here. There are also many *sake* breweries.

Because Asahikawa is ideally situated for continuing on to northern or eastern Hokkaido, it has developed as the center of a transportation network that includes the JR Hakodate Main Line, Soya Main Line, Sekihoku Main Line and Furano Line. The Asahikawa Airport is also located directly outside the city and can be reached by a direct flight from Tokyo. Moreover, the Do-o Expressway from Sapporo was extended to Asahikawa in 1990.

PLACES OF INTEREST

Tokiwa Park: This is a 6-sq.-km city park located near the Asahi Bridge spanning the Ishikari River. 15 min. on foot, or 7 min. by bus from JR Asahikawa Station. The park centers around Chidorigaike Pond, where rowboats can be rented; but it also has a youth science museum with a planetarium, a library, a prefectural art museum and more. The colorful flower beds, poplar-lined promenade and other scenes of natural beauty make it a perfect place for a stroll.

Kaguraoka Park: 5 min. by bus from Asahikawa Station with an additional 10 min. walk. This park contains lush lawns, huge, old trees and other beautiful verdure. Mt. Daisetsu can be seen from the observation platform. Kamikawa Shrine, where the guardian deity of the Kamikawa region is enshrined, has stood here since the days of colonization.

Foreign Tree Species Specimen Forest: 10 min. by bus from Asahikawa and an additional 5 min. walk brings one to Hokkaido's oldest cultivation nursery for foreign-tree species. Established in 1898, it covers an area of 18,000 sq. m set aside for nursing the growth of trees and shrubs. At present, there are 40 different kinds of pine trees alone.

Arashiyama Natural Park: 7 km northwest of Asahikawa Station, or 25 min. by bus. This park is a preserve for wild birds and squirrels, and also offers a panoramic view of the Daisetsu Mountain Chain as well as the city. The foothills contain the Hoppo Wild Grass Park, where samples of several different kinds of northern grasses are grown. The Ainu Culture Forest occupies a 20,000 sq. m corner of the park. Various aspects of village life have been reconstructed in the forest, including *chashi* (forts), *chise* (reed houses), *setsu* (bear corrals), *pu* (food storehouses), etc., in an effort to preserve and communicate Ainu culture. The museum exhibits daily and ceremonial items, allowing the tourist to get a real feel for what life in a *kotan* (Ainu village) was once like.

Yukara Weaving Craft Museum: 4 km from Asahikawa Station, or 15 min. by bus. Erected on a plateau overlooking the city streets, the graceful facade reminds one of a monastery. Inside are examples of handwoven *yukara* pongee silk. There is also a dye room, a spinning room and a weaving room, where one can watch cloth being woven.

Kamui Kotan: 17 km from Asahikawa Station along National Highway 12, or 25 min. by bus, it lies in a canyon that connects the Kamikawa Basin with the Ishikari Plain. Kamui Kotan means the

Abode of God's in the Ainu language, and early every October the people of Ainu descent gather at the Kotan Festival to pray for the safety of the waterway. The swift currents of the Ishikari River dashing through the fantastically shaped rocks are one of the most magnificent sights in central Hokkaido. Nearby are cave dwellings, a stone circle and many other sights that will interest the tourist.

Daisetsuzan National Park [3]

Covering an area of 2,308.9 sq. km, the park was established in December 1934. This alpine park, called the "Roof of Hokkaido," boasts the imposing Mt. Daisetsu as its core. Many rare plants and animals can be found here. The seasonal beauty of Sounkyo Gorge and Tenninkyo Gorge is breathtaking, especially the pale greens of spring and the red tints of autumn. Besides the many hot springs bubbling forth all over the area, Mt. Tokachidake, Lake Nukabira and Lake Shikaribetsu are all located within the precincts of the park.

Mt. Daisetsu [3] : This actually indicates the chain of mountains that runs along the northern side of Daisetsuzan National Park. There are nearly 20 peaks, all in the 2,000 m class, including the highest Mt. Asahi (alt. 2,290 m), followed in order by Mt. Hakuun (alt. 2,230 m), Mt. Akadake (alt. 2,078 m), Mt. Ryoun (alt. 2,125 m), Mt. Pippudake (alt. 2,197 m), Mt. Kumagatake (alt. 2,210 m), Mt. Kurodake (alt. 1,984 m) and Mt. Hokkai (alt. 2,149 m). The mountains are home to mouse hares (said to be remnants of the Ice Age), brown bears, Ezo deer, alpine butterflies, and many other rare animals and insects. There is also a myriad of plant species (especially alpine plants). Snow glitters on the mountain tip, even on the hottest days of summer. Although snow starts to fall from late September, the ski season is not until around mid-December. When the snow finally begins to melt in late May, the mountainside becomes cloaked in green. Hot springs bubble up here and there in the primeval forest that covers the foothills. It is the perfect place to relax and enjoy nature.

Daisetsu National Highway: This is the name for the section of National Highway 39 that runs from Asahikawa to Abashiri and covers the distance between Kamikawa and Rubeshibe. The 90-km-long, 6-m-wide paved road runs across the northern part of Daisetsuzan National Park. It is one of the most famous scenic drives in Hokkaido because both sides of the road offer a continuous panorama of spectacular scenery like Sounkyo Gorge and Sekihoku Pass.

Sounkyo Gorge [3] : Starting from near the source of the Ishikari River, the gorge drops to a depth of 150 m and extends for 20 km. Solidified lava and ash rise up into incredible columnar joints, while many waterfalls rush down the sides. The mysterious landscape inspires one with the grandeur of nature. Sounkyo Spa is located right in the middle of the gorge, while 7 km farther up are the beautiful gorges called Obako and Kobako.

Sounkyo Spa: 1 hr. 55 min. by express bus from Asahikawa Station. It serves as the starting point from which to explore the beauty of the gorge and climb the Daisetsu Mountain Chain. It was discovered between 1854–1860 and is the oldest hot springs resort in the area. The water temperatures range from 51–93°C and are efficacious against rheumatism and anemia. There are many deluxe inns to stay at, with accommodations for more than 6,000 guests. In one corner of the town is the Sounkyo Gorge Museum, where the ecosystem of Mt. Daisetsu with its flora and fauna are explained through models and specimens. There is also a ropeway station for Mt. Kurodake. The town bustles with tourists throughout the year.

Mt. Kurodake ⃞3 : Alt. 1,984 m. This majestic mountain is shaped like a pyramid. From the fifth station from Sounkyo Spa and its observation platform, one can proceed on to the flower-covered fields of the seventh station by lift. This is high enough to taste the sweet alpine air, but the view from the summit is exceptional, allowing one to cool off in mid-summer by gazing across the perpetually snowy fields and valleys.

Sekihoku Pass: Alt. 1,046 m. This is the highest point on the Daisetsu National Highway and comes right between Kamikawa and Rube- shibe. It is possible to see the nearby peaks of Mt. Muridake and Mt. Mukasan as a sea of foliage undulates below, but on clear days, one can even pick out Mt. O-Akan and Mt. Me-Akan. There are souvenir shops and restaurants here, and buses stop for a break to allow the passengers to look at the view.

Tenninkyo Spa ⃞3 : 39 km from Asahikawa, at the foot of the 2,290-m-high Mt. Asahi—an active volcano, which is the highest peak in Hokkaido. Like Sounkyo Spa, this is a starting point for climbing Mt. Daisetsu. The surroundings are desolate, while the inns seem to cling to the sides of the canyon. The mineral waters somehow seem untouched by man. Hagoromo (Feather Robe) Falls is a 10-min. walk from the spa. The 270-m drop makes this the second-longest falls in Japan. Vast quantities of water crash into the sheer walls and spray out and down, presenting a splendid sight. This is said to resemble the feather robe of a legendary angel; hence, the name of the falls— Hagoromo. Shikishima-no-Taki Falls, called the "Niagara of Hok- kaido," is also located nearby.

Asahidake Spa: 45 km from Asahikawa, or 1 hr. 30 min. by bus, and halfway up Mt. Asahi at an altitude of 1,050 m. It has long been a favorite base for mountain climbers. The spa is surrounded by plateaus, offering glimpses of the dignified peaks of Mt. Asahi between the coniferous trees. Since there is a ropeway to Tennyoga- hara Plateau and Sugatami-no-Ike Pond near the mountain top, one has a chance to look out over the profusion of blooming alpine plants. The slope along the ropeway in the primeval forest becomes a ski ground from the time the trees are frosted in glittering ice in the winter until the spring thaw. One can enjoy the beautiful scenery

301

while skiing down to the spa-resort town.

Shirogane Spa ⬛3️⃣ : 21 km from Biei Station on the JR Furano Line, at the foot of Mt. Tokachi. This spa has long been a favorite base for climbing Mt. Tokachi and skiing. Surrounded by a lovely forest of white birches, the spa has a rustic atmosphere that is popular with families. With temperatures ranging from 46–57°C, the mineral waters are good for gastroenteric disorders. Nearby, the Shirohige-no-Taki Falls, formed by deposits of hot-spring water, are a beautiful sight on the Biei River, adding to the charm of the spa town.

Mt. Tokachi ⬛3️⃣ : This mountain towers above the southwestern edge of Daisetsuzan National Park. An active, conical volcano with an altitude of 2,077 m, it has erupted repeatedly and still seems constantly on the verge of bursting forth again. Mt. Daisetsu, Mt. O-Akan, Mt. Ashibetsu, Mt. Yubari and Mt. Yotei can all be seen from the peak. The west face is a popular ski ground.

Furano ⬛2️⃣ ☎0167: Pop. 27,208. 2 hrs. 12 min. from Sapporo by express on the JR Hakodate and Nemuro main lines. This is the junction for the JR Nemuro Main Line and Furano Line. Lying in the southern part of the Furano Basin, it is an economic and transportation center. Since it is situated almost exactly in the middle of Hokkaido, it is sometimes called the "navel of Hokkaido." The Sorachi River runs through the town, and because the land is fertile, agriculture is thriving with such produce as potatoes, beans, beets and asparagus. Recently, the cultivation of lavenders has been on the rise, for which Furano has become famous. Many come to see the lavender blossoms covering the fields in a purple carpet from mid to late July.

Lavender Forest: 7 km northwest of the city. This is a resort area managed by the city. The hotel, Highland Furano, has tennis courts and other sports facilities as well as hot springs. There is also a 16,000-sq.-m field of lavenders and a 3-km-long walking path that passes through the trees and around the pond. From the middle of July to early August this area is popular among tourists who travel from all over the country to see the magnificent "purple carpet" that is created when the lavenders bloom.

Furano Ski Grounds: Directly in front of Mt. Tokachi and the Daisetsu Mountain Chain, the ski grounds run down the eastern face of Mt. Kitanomine (alt. 1,209 m). Covering 1,670,000 sq.m, this is one of the largest ski areas in Hokkaido. It is known throughout the world as one of the sites of the World Cup Alpine Ski Series, and all kinds of skiers gather here. During the ski season, the special "Furano Express" runs from both Sapporo and Chitose Kuko (Airport) stations.

Tomamu ⬛2️⃣ : A plateau spreading out in the foothills of Mt. Tomamu (alt. 1,239 m), situated northeast of Tomamu Station on the JR Sekisho Line. It has been developed as a large-scale ski resort patterned after that of Aspen, Colorado, in the USA. The 36-story hotel, condominiums and other accommodations as well as a golf course, tennis courts, wild bird sanctuary and a nature trail are all laid out so as not to disturb the harmony of nature. In the winter, the Tomamu Ski Grounds are popular. The non-stop limited express trains run from both Sapporo and Chitose Kuko stations during the ski season. The world-class slopes combined with excellent transportation and lodging facilities attract skiers from all over the country.

Karikachi Plateau Sahoro Ski Grounds: Located on the eastern face of Mt. Sahorodake, which is a 1,059-m-high peak at the eastern end of the Daisetsu Mountain Chain. The slopes are bowl-shaped so that no matter which one you descend, you end up on the central slope in front of the hotel. There are 15 different trails, with each one bringing out the characteristics of the surrounding forest. Japan's first Mediterranean Club vacation village, Club Med Sahoro, is located here.

Area 7. Obihiro to Kushiro and Nemuro

Obihiro ③ ☎0155

2 hrs. 50 min. from Sapporo by limited express via Chitose, Sekisho and Nemuro Main Lines, the city has a population of 166,288. Situated in the center of the Tokachi Plain, the city was modeled after Washington D.C., with broad avenues systematically laid out. As the city is located in the middle of one of the most fertile regions in Hokkaido, it is not only the seat of local government, but it also serves as a major industrial center.

PLACES OF INTEREST

Midorigaoka Park: A massive 420,000 sq. m park located 3 km southwest of the city. It contains the Obihiro Hyakunen Kinenkan, which is a museum commemorating the centenary of the city's founding in 1886. Besides many other scenic attractions in the park, there is also a memorial to adventurer Uemura Naomi (b. 1941), who conquered the highest peaks on five continents alone, crossed the North Pole by dog sled and finally disappeared in the harsh Alaskan winter on Mt. McKinley. The park is famous, too, for a 400-m-long bench that can seat 1,282 persons.

Manabe Gardens: 10 min. by bus from Obihiro Station, laid out along the Sanai River, this is one of the few promenade-type Japanese gardens in Hokkaido. Covering an area of 10,000 sq. m, it has a large pond (where red carp regally swim), man-made hills, a 13-story pagoda, a tea house and other beautiful sights along the leisurely promenade.

Tokachigawa Spa: 12 km northeast of Obihiro Station, or 25 min. by bus. Many stay here because it is conveniently located between the Lake Akan and Mt. Daisetsu regions. It is fully equipped with leisure

303

facilities, too. Located nearby are the Tokachigaoka Observation Platform, a cycling terminal and Tokachigaoka Park, which features the world's largest floral clock—18 m in diameter.

Lake Shikaribetsu ③ : Located in the southern portion of Daisetsu-zan National Park, the lake can be reached in 1 hr. 50 min. by bus from Obihiro Station. Extending from north to south at an altitude of 810 m, the long, caldera lake has an area of 3.5 sq. km, a circumference of about 16 km and a maximum depth of 108 m. Volcanic eruptions have made the lake shore irregular, with the primeval forest hanging right over the water's edge. The reflection of Mt. Tembo on the rippling lake is exquisite. The rare *oshorokoma* (a kind of salmon) swim the waters. Two inns with hot springs are located along the banks, while an excursion boat sails around the lake.

Lake Nukabira ③ : 1 hr. 45 min. by bus from Obihiro Station. This is an artificial lake made by damming the Otofuke River and Nuka-bira River. Surrounded by a primeval forest, the lake is stocked with rainbow trout and *wakasagi* (a kind of smelt) for those who want to rent a boat and go fishing. The waters of Nukabira Spa on the shore of the lake are efficacious against nervous and gastroenteric disorders and abrasions.

Ikeda ③ : Situated in the eastern portion of the Tokachi Plain. Spanning 372 sq. km, the town has a population of 10,524. Around this rural town are extensive grape vineyards, from which the famous Tokachi wine is produced. A 10 min. walk from the station brings one to an ancient-looking castle, the Wine Palace. The production of Tokachi wine can be observed here. On the third floor is a municipally run steak and wine restaurant.

Kushiro ③ ☎0154

4 hrs. 50 min. from Sapporo by limited express via Chitose, Sekisho and Nemuro Main Lines, or 40 min. by airplane to Kushiro Airport. Situated at the mouth of the Kushiro River, it is the largest city in eastern Hokkaido, with a population of 208,854. Because Kushiro is blessed with a natural port that never freezes over, it boasts the largest catches of fish in Hokkaido. In addition to fishery, other major industries include food processing, paper manufacturing and coal mining. The city serves as the gateway to such major scenic attractions as Akan, Akkeshi, Nemuro and Shiretoko. The Kushiro-Shitsugen (Marshlands) National Park with a sanctuary for cranes also stretches in and around the city.

PLACES OF INTEREST

Lake Harutori: A long narrow lake southeast of the city, 15 min. by bus from Kushiro Station. The Kushiro Municipal Museum and Harutori Park are located in the immediate vicinity, while the lake itself offers boating. The *hifuna* (scarlet crucian carp) swimming in the lake have been designated as a Natural Monument.

Tanchozuru (Crane) Natural Park: 40 min. by bus from Kushiro Station, or 20 km northwest of the city. This is a sanctuary for the Japanese crane, which have been designated as a Special Natural Monument. Besides the more than 20 cranes that live inside the fence, many wild cranes come to feed here in the winter as well.

Kushiro-Shitsugen (Marshland) 3 : 30 min. by bus from Kushiro Station, Japan's largest marshlands (210 sq.km) spread out beyond the northern edge of the city. This is the habitat of Japanese cranes as well as northern salamanders, long-tailed rose finches, white-faced dragonflies, the *ito* fish (a kind of freshwater salmon) and many other species of fauna. It was designated as the country's 28th National Park in 1987. Centered around the reed and grasslands and the alder grove, some 700 plant species (such as Ezo day lilies) grow here, with botanists often coming to study at this marshland park. Tourists can gaze out over the magnificent landscape from the observation platform.

Lake Toro: 10 min. on foot from Toro Station on the JR Semmo Main Line. The 22 km in circumference inland-sea lake is located in the middle of the marshlands. In former times, pekampe, a kind of wheat that served as a staple in the Ainu diet, was grown here. Evidence of Ainu *chasi* (fortress) and cave dwellings have been found on the lake shore. Campgrounds and the Shibecha Local Museum are also located here.

Akkeshi 3 : 45 km from Kushiro Station on National Highway 44. The town is divided from north to south by Lake Akkeshi, but it was joined in 1972 when the Akkeshi Ohashi Bridge was completed. Fishery is the main industry on both sides of the town, with its oysters being particularly famous. Lake Akkeshi covers an area of 32 sq. km, has a circumference of 30 km and is 11 m deep at its greatest depth. Oysters and *asari* (shortneck clams) are cultivated in the lake's unique mixture of ocean and fresh water. There are more than 80 *kakijima*, islands composed of natural oyster shells upon which Akkeshi grass and other plants grow. South of the lake is Cape Aikappu, the site of the Hokkaido University Marine Biologic Experiment Museum and Aquarium.

Kiritappu-Shitsugen (Marshlands) 3 : About 50 min. to the east of Akkeshi Station by bus, flat marshlands spread out as far as the eye can see, with hundreds of wild grasses blooming in profusion with the change of season. It has been designated as a Natural Monument. Seals cavort in the nearby ocean.

Nemuro 3 ☎01532: 2 hrs. 10 min. or 136 km from Kushiro by the JR rapid train. With a population of 38,352, Nemuro is Hokkaido's easternmost city. Covering the entire Nemuro Peninsula, the port city has an area of 519 sq. km. Some 90% of the industry comes from the salmon, trout, squid, saury, crab, seaweed and cod that are caught or processed in Nemuro Port, Hanasaki Port, Habomai Port or

Ochiishi Port, but the region is especially famous for the Hanasaki crab (June–December). The amusement quarter has many wholesalers, gift shops, bars and restaurants serving local cuisine.

Cape Nosappu 3 : 45 min. by bus from Nemuro Station to the light house and then a 3 min. walk from there, it is a cape at the tip of the Nemuro Peninsula. The Nosappu Lighthouse, the oldest in Hokkaido, was erected in 1872 on the right side of the cape. On the left is the Bokyo-no-Ie (Homesick House) and the Hoppokan (Northern House), both of which exhibit data on the northern territories. The massive, 97 m-high observation tower, completed in 1987, offers a panoramic view. 3.7 km across the Goyomai Channel floats the nearest of the Habomai Islands—Kaigara Island. From early February to late March, ice floes float by the cape.

Lake Furen 3 : At the neck of the Nemuro Peninsula is a lake with a circumference of 96 km. The lake water travels through a 300 m-wide channel to Nemuro Bay. The lake is famous for the great flocks of swans that converge on it around the end of October.

Notsuke Peninsula 3 : Located between the Nemuro Peninsula and Shiretoko Peninsula, it is shaped like the curved back of a shrimp and thrusts out 28 km into the Nemuro Straits. Most of the peninsula consists of grassy fields and marshes. Killed by inrushing sea water and winds, the dead fir trees—some fallen and others still standing, create an eerie and desolate landscape. This forest of deadwood is known as *todowara*. During the summer, shrimp-trawlers glide over Odaito Swamp while in the winter come the swans and ice floes.

Area 8. Akan National Park

Kussharo and Akan—Enfolded in ancient primeval forests, these two large caldera lakes are the focal points of the Akan National Park. Common excursion entrances include Bihoro, Kushiro, Obihiro, Kawayu and Teshikaga, but the most popular course is to enter from Bihoro and leave via Kushiro and Obihiro, or the reverse. This is a tourist location of the scale one would expect of Hokkaido. A sightseeing bus leaves from the Memambetsu (Abashiri) Airport for Lake Akan and travels via JR Bihoro Station, Bihoro Pass and Kawayu Spa. From Lake Akan, a bus is available to Kushiro, and in late July and mid-August, to Obihiro.

Teshikaga 3 : 1 hr. 27 min. from Kushiro on the JR Semmo Main Line. The entire town is a tourist town affiliated with Akan National Park. Located in the immediate vicinity of Lakes Kussharo and Mashu, the town also has hot springs to bathe in.

Lake Kussharo 3 : 2 hrs. 20 min. on a regular sightseeing bus from the JR Mashu Station, or a distance of 15 km. This enormous, freshwater, crater lake is located in the northwestern part of the Kussharo caldera. It has an area of 79.7 sq. km, a circumference of

58 km and a maximum depth of 117.5 m, making it the largest lake in Akan National Park. Many small rivers and streams flow into the lake, but they flow out together as the Kushiro River. The double-conical volcano rises from Nakanoshima Island in the middle of Lake Kussharo, while Cape Wakoto juts out from the south bank. With Sunayu, Ikenoyu, Nibushi, Kawayu, Wakoto and other hot springs clustered around the lake, tourists come to bathe in them throughout the year.

Kawayu Spa 3 : 10 min. by bus from Kawayu Onsen Station, this spa is located in the northern part of Teshikaga. The original name was Seseku Petsu, which means "hot river," and, in fact, hot water gushes out of the hot springs and pours into Lake Kussharo. The waters are efficacious for rheumatism, diabetes and dermatological disorders. There are about 30 lodging facilities at the spa, which is surrounded by a forest of coniferous trees. One can watch the volcanic smoke drifting up from Atosanupuri (Mt. Io).

Atosanupuri (Mt. Io) 3 : 5 min. by bus from Kawayu Onsen Station to the foot of the mountain. This is an active volcano (alt. 510 m) that formed in the center of the Kussharo caldera. It is part of the Atosanupuri Volcano Chain and is covered from base to peak with countless fumaroles of all sizes that rumble and spout sulfur, some of which has crystallized and collected around the fumaroles. Dense growths of creeping pines and alpine orchids are nearby, while a huge grove of white Ezo azaleas and sparse clumps of white beech grow in the volcanic ash zone. There is a 2-km-long (about 30 min.) nature trail from Kawayu Spa to this area.

Lake Mashu 3 : 20 min. by bus from Mashu Station. This mysterious lake, called God's Lake, is one of the clearest lakes in the world. 200-m-tall caldera cliff walls surround the lake, while Mt. Kamui-Nupuri, God's Mountain, towers over the east bank. The area tends to be enclosed by dense fog, and like the famous song, "The Fog of Lake Mashu," says, there are days when nothing can be seen but the milky whiteness of the mist. For use on clear days, there is an observation platform on the west bank with a superb view of an island called Kamuishu floating gently on the indigo waters of the lake. The comma-shaped lake, with neither inlet nor outlet, is famous because the water level never changes. The lake is stocked with rainbow trout and steelheads. It has an area of 19.6 sq. km, a circumference of 21 km and a maximum depth of 211.5 m, with clarity down to about 25 m.

Mashu Spa: 10 min. on foot from Mashu Station, this hot-springs area looks over the Kushiro River flowing through Teshikaga. Since it is easy to reach and convenient for sightseeing tours to Lakes Akan and Mashu, it is usually bustling with tourists. The mineral waters, with temperatures ranging from 30–99°C, are efficacious against chronic articular rheumatism, neuralgia and gout. The large quantities of water produced here from the 45 separate water sources have permitted the construction of several hot-spring pools.

Trans-Akan Road: This is the road that connects the two largest attractions of Akan National Park: Lake Akan and Lake Mashu. It is part of National Highway 241, which runs through Teshikaga and Obihiro, the distance from Teshikaga to Lake Akan being 42 km. Growing on both sides of the road is a coniferous forest of silver firs and pines as well as dense growths of white beech and mountain ash —the kind of natural beauty that can be seen only in the northern regions. En route is the observation platform, Sokodai, from which one can command a magnificent view of Mt. Me-Akan and Mt. O-Akan as well as Lakes Penketo and Panketo.

Penketo and Panketo: Penketo is an Ainu word for "upper lake" while Panketo means "lower lake". These two lakes were originally part of Lake Akan, but were separated by an eruption of Mt. O-Akan. They can best be seen from Sokodai, where their mysterious waters can be glimpsed through the deep green sea of trees.

Mt. O-Akandake ③ : This conical, dormant volcano towers over the eastern edge of Lake Akan, facing Mt. Me-Akan across the lake. The mountain reaches an altitude of 1,370 m and can be climbed in 4 hrs. from Takiguchi, although the descent takes only a little over 3 hrs. From the foothills to around the 500 m altitude range, the face of the mountain is covered by a mixture of pines, silver firs, oaks, white beeches and other trees. From here to an altitude of 1,000 m, this changes to a forest of pines and other coniferous trees. Then up to an altitude of 1,200 m, groves of birch appear, giving way to clumps of creeping pine in the next 100 m. For the rest of the way up, one encounters fields of cliff orchids, cowberrys and other alpine flowers.

Lake Akan ③ : Enfolded within the skirts of Mt. O-Akan and Me-Akan is a diamond-shaped lake with an area of 13 sq. km, a circumference of 31 km and a maximum depth of 44.8 m. The inlets and outlets to the lake are quite complex, with many small streams flowing in from all directions and flowing out as the Akan River. The lake contains several islets and a forest with a mixture of silver firs, pines and birches growing around it. The scene becomes quite beautiful when the leaves take on their autumn tints. Lake Akan is particularly famous for *marimo*, a kind of alga (called aegagrophila), which grows sponge-like balls. But today, these alga balls grow only in the inlets of the lake. *Kokanee*, believed by the Ainu to be God's fish, swim the lake waters together with pond smelt. The pleasure boat that circles the lake makes a stop at Churuimoshiri (an island at the mouth of a river), where *marimo*, or aegagrophila, can be observed in water troughs.

Marimo was first discovered in Japan in Lake Akan in 1896. It is a type of alga also found in freshwater lakes in Europe and North America that produces spherical, dark green growths averaging 6-8 cm in diameter. It can be quite beautiful and has been designated as a Special Natural Monument.

Akan Kohan Spa: This spa is located on the southern shore of Lake Akan. Inns and gift shops are concentrated between National Highway 241 and the lake shore, a section that becomes especially lively with tourists during the summer. The water temperature ranges from 45–80℃ and is soothing to rheumatism. There are nearly 40 hotels and inns. An excursion boat also leaves from here.

Ainu Kotan: 10 min. on foot from the Akan-Kohan Bus Stop, on the western edge of the spa town. This is an Ainu village for tourists. Both sides of the street are crammed with Ainu folk craft shops selling Nipopo dolls, Ainu folkcraft and carved wooden bears as the most popular items. Carving demonstrations are given, showing how the wood items are crafted. Performances of Ainu folk dances can be enjoyed at the adjoining Ainu Tourist Center.

Akan Kohan Visitor's Center: 10 min. on foot from Akan-Kohan Bus Stop. The hall displays animals that can be seen along the nature trails as well as exhibits and explanations using photographs and models representing the topography, geological features and climate of Lake Akan. Also on view are the types of *marimo* and fish that inhabit the lake.

Akan-Shitakara Region Natural Recreation Village: 40 min. by bus from Akan-Kohan Bus Stop. Spreading around a Japanese crane preserve, this large zone contains a recreational farm where one can enjoy inspecting the cultivation of vegetable, rice and other crops, a mine and a railway museum displaying an old, wooden Western-style station building and a steam engine as well as a crane observation center and camp grounds. During the winter, one can watch at close quarters the cranes dancing on the ice-covered fields.

Area 9. Abashiri and Shiretoko

Kitami 3 ☎0157: 185 km or about 3 hrs. by limited express on the Sekihoku Main Line from Asahikawa. Located at the center of the Kitami Basin, this city has a population of 106,187. It was founded by just two platoons of colonization troops of *tondenhei* (farm soldiers) in 1897, but today it is known as a cargo collection center for agricultural goods and lumber. Since the city is also famous for mint production, there is a mint museum and gift shops selling many unusual mint confections. In terms of tourism, Kitami serves as a relay station for Mt. Daisetsu.

Onneyu Spa 3 : 20 min. by bus from Rubeshibe Station, or 30 km to the west of Kitami, along National Highway 39. Typical of the hot springs in the Kitami region, the clear water of the Muka River meanders among the shops and inns. Each of the 13 lodging places has its own hot-spring source, with water temperatures ranging from 42–52℃. The waters are said to be efficacious against nervous disorders and dermatological diseases. The Neneyama Ski Grounds are also located nearby, and it is only a 5-min. walk to the place where Ezo purple azaleas, a Natural Monument, grow in profusion (early to mid-May).

Abashiri ③ ☎0152

The city, with a population of 42,877, is located in the center of Abashiri Quasi-National Park. It faces the Okhotsk Sea and is hemmed in on the outskirts by Lake Notoro, Lake Abashiri, Lake Mokoto and Lake Tofutsu. In terms of industries, Abashiri Port is the base for northern fishing operations, so fishing is the mainstay along with the thriving business of processing marine products. There are also facilities for mink and silver-fox fur production, with 15% of the mink production in Hokkaido being done here.

Moyoro Shell Mound: 5 min. by bus from the JR Abashiri Station. The remains of the aborigines of the Abashiri region, the Moyoros, are found here. There are 28 cave dwellings covered by trees and weeds on the flat ground near the mouth of the Abashiri River. Artifacts from these people were found at depths ranging 30 cm–3 m. One can see them just as they were discovered at the nearby Moyoro Shell Mound Museum.

Abashiri Prison Museum: 15 min. by bus from Abashiri Station and an additional 5-min. walk. Abashiri Prison was built in 1891, when convicts were dispatched here to construct roads through the unexplored territory, but today it is the only prison museum in Japan. The original gate, cells, baths and re-education center of the prison have been reconstructed on this site and can be seen along with handcuffs, ball and chains, and many other exhibits reflecting the daily life and hard labor of the prisoners.

Okhotsk Ice Floe Museum: 15 min. by bus from Abashiri Station will take one to the peak of Mt. Tento (alt. 207 m), known throughout the area for the wonderful view it provides. The red brick building on the observation platform is the Okhotsk Ice Floe Museum. The exhibits are arranged around the theme of ice floes, their creation and science, accompanied by easy-to-understand explanations. The Ice Floe Experience Room, where one can see an actual ice floe, is especially popular with visitors.

Lake Abashiri: 10 min. by bus from Abashiri Station. This salt-water lake is located at the west end of the city and extends over to Memambetsu. It has an area of 34 sq. km, a circumference of 42 km and a maximum depth of 16.1 m. The Yobito Peninsula juts out from the center of the east coast, while the Abashiri River flows in from the southern shore to create a delta, then flows out of the back of the lake and into the Okhotsk Sea. There are many campgrounds around the lake, and many go boating on it, too. In winter, ice fishing for *wakasagi* (a kind of smelt) on the lake is famous. Along the southeast shore is a swamp where many plants grow that have been designated as a Natural Monument.

Lake Notoro 3 : Located north of Lake Abashiri, this round lagoon with an area of 58 sq. km and a 35-km-long shoreline is open to the Okhotsk Sea at the north end. Misaki Road extends to Cape Notoro along the lake's east coast, while the Okhotsk National Highway runs from the south coast to the west. The sand dunes and pastures spread out gently, and are covered with coral grass that turns a beautiful deep red in the autumn. The sand bars, with their natural flower gardens, present a landscape unique to Okhotsk.

Lake Saroma 3 : 1 hr. 10 min. by bus from Abashiri Station, or 42 km down National Highway 238. The largest lagoon in Hokkaido, this lake has an area of 151.7 sq. km, a circumference of 90 km and a maximum depth of 19.6 m. It is mostly separated from the Okhotsk Sea by a thin 20-km-long sand bar and is connected to the ocean only by a small mouth. Since the waters are salty, it has many fish that are usually found in the open sea. Oysters and scallops are also cultivated in the lagoon.

Lake Tofutsu 3 : This long, thin lake has an area of 9.3 sq. km and a 31-km-long shoreline and lies alongside the Okhotsk Sea to the southeast of Abashiri. Since it is connected to the ocean around Kitahama on the northeast bank, the water contains some salt. The JR Semmo Main Line and National Highway 244 run parallel along the sand bar on the northern shore, while horses and cows graze peacefully in the wide pastures on the southern bank. Swans descend on the lake in November before it freezes and again in April when it melts. The main tourist attraction in the area is the Koshimizu Natural Flower Garden, the largest of its kind in Hokkaido. It is best seen from late June through July.

Shiretoko Peninsula 3

This peninsula juts out about 63 km off the northeast end of Hokkaido. Designated as a National Park in 1964, it became known with the wilderness boom, and since then the number of tourists has rapidly increased. However, there are no roads circumventing the peninsula, while the railways only go as far as Shari at the western neck. Mt. Shiretoko, Mt. Io, Mt. Rausu and the other mountains in the Chishima Volcano Range form the backbone. The forest-covered bases, caved in by the ocean, create a stretch of sheer cliff for 15 km along the east coast and another for 30 km along the west coast. Utoro in the west and Rausu in the east are the two jumping-off places for sightseeing. An excursion boat (a 3-hr. 45-min. trip) leaves from Utoro and affords a view of the unexplored cape of the peninsula from the sea. With the completion of the Trans-Shiretoko Highway that connects Rausu and Utoro, sightseeing has become quite convenient.

Oronko Rock: 55 min. by bus from Shari Station. The rocky mountain on the east side of Utoro Port has a steep stone flight of 170 steps that lead to the top. From here, one can look out over the clear,

blue, port waters to the town and the Shiretoko Mountain Range.
Shiretoko Five Lakes 3 : 1 hr.10 min. by bus from Shari Station.
These 5 lakes at the foot of the Shiretoko Mountains were formed
through the damming of the river by volcanic eruptions. Since all of
them are small, the trail that circumnavigates them is only 2.4 km
long, or about an hour's walk. Ivy, mountain sumac and volcanic ash
mix with the silver firs and pines in the largely coniferous forest that
surrounds the lakes, while yellow Nemuro pond lilies, bog myrtle and
the like grow on the lakes themselves. The area is also known for its
abundance of birds and sometimes even a fox or two can be seen here.
Kamuiwakka Falls: 1 hr. 45 min. by bus from Shari Station via the
Shiretoko Trail (from June to mid-October). Because the falls are a
mixture of sulfurous hot-spring and river waters, they are also called
Yunotaki (Hot-Water Falls). The falls have a 32-m drop and a width
of 2 m.
Oshinkoshin Falls: 40 min. by bus from Shari Station. They are also
called "Twin Falls" since part way down it splits into two cascades.
About 300 m towards Utoro, there is a splendid view of the Okhotsk
Sea and the Shiretoko Mountain Range from the top of Oshinkoshin
Hill.

Area 10. Northern Hokkaido

Nayoro 2 ☎01654: Lying at the confluence of the Teshio and
Nayoro rivers, the town has a population of 31,598. The food-
processing industry has developed with the aid of abundant, high-
quality water in the area. Agriculture largely consists of medicinal
plants, which grow well in the northern regions. In the winter, one
can ski among trees glittering with ice at the Nayoro-Piyashiri Ski
Grounds. 1 hr. 10 min. from Asahikawa by express on the JR Soya
Main Line.
Shibetsu 2 : 50 min. by express on the JR Soya Main Line from
Asahikawa, or 55 km along National Highway 40. Established in
1899, this city was the last location developed by the policy of
utilizing colonization troops. It spreads out along the Teshio River
and its tributaries, with rice paddies providing the main source of
agriculture. There are also sugar refineries, lumberyards and other
agricultural-related industries. The construction of a road that cuts
across from the Okhotsk Sea to the Japan Sea has made Shibetsu a
convenient sightseeing location.
Sarobetsu Natural Flower Garden 2 : Located at the central part
of the vast Sarobetsu Plain, which is 8 km wide from east to west and
27 km long from north to south, this garden is situated along the
highway that connects the JR Toyotomi Station and Wakasakanai.
One can look across the seemingly endless plain and see the line of the
horizon in the north. As is appropriate for the large, northernmost

marshlands, there is a combination of alpine and marshland plants growing in profusion, their blossoms running rampant from early spring to late autumn. In June and July especially, cotton grass and Ezo day lily blooms fill the fields with color. This area is a part of the Rishiri-Rebun-Sarobetsu National Park.

Wakkanai 2 ☎0162: Pop. 49,299. 4 hrs. 20 min. by express from Asahikawa on the JR Soya Main Line—a distance of 260 km. Divided from Sakhalin by the Soya Straits, the city serves as a sort of international border. Wakkanai and its vicinity were originally a place where the Ainu lived. The area was established as a trading district with a duty station directly controlled by the Matsumae Clan in 1684-1688. There was another population surge during the Meiji period, when Wakkanai became a herring fishing center. However, the spotlight really shone here after the Russo-Japanese War (1904-1905), when the southern part of Sakhalin came into Japan's possession. A ferry was opened between Wakkanai and Sakhalin (in 1906), making this the sole gateway. Also, a railway was opened from Asahikawa in 1922. The town boomed overnight, continuing to prosper until the end of World War II (when Sakhalin was lost to the Soviet Union). It has been gradually declining ever since. It is now reviving as a fishing town, however, and as the economic and cultural center of the north. Crab, sea urchin, seaweed and other marine delicacies are unloaded on Wakkanai's docks. Wakkanai Park, a 15-min. walk from Wakkanai Station, is a municipal park located on a hill behind the city. On clear days, one can see Sakhalin across the ocean. There is also a ropeway to a Children's World of rides and games.

Cape Soya 2 : 55 min. by bus from Wakkanai Station or 35 km along National Highway 238. This is the northernmost cape in Hokkaido mainland. Along the coast, with its blooms of sweet brier and Ezo day lilies, stands a monument shaped like the North Star— the northernmost monument in Japan. From here, one can look across the Soya Straits and see Sakhalin. Among the hills are open-grazing ranches for beef cattle. One can visit the Cape Soya Lighthouse and an old naval watchtower used during the days of the Russo-Japanese War. A bronze statue of Mamiya Rinzo (1780-1844, refer to p.98), known for his explorations of the northern ocean, stands at the tip of the cape.

Rishiri Island 2 : 52 km to the northwest of Wakkanai. This is a volcanic island with a 68 km circumference. Mt. Rishiri (alt. 1,721 m), sometimes called Rishiri-Fuji, towers at the center of the island, which has been designated as Rishiri-Rebun-Sarobetsu National Park. Since there is little flat land on the island, most residents make their living through fishing. Specialties include Rishiri sea tangle and sea urchin as well as such delicacies as octopus, squid and Atka mackerel. There is a ferry (taking about 1 hr.30 min.) and regular flight service (taking 20 min.) from Wakkanai.

Rebun Island [2] : Situated about 10 km north of Rishiri Island, this is Japan's northernmost island. The island is long and narrow from north to south and is nearly all hills, so there are alpine plants no matter where you look. Most of the population is concentrated along the east coast, where they make their living by offshore fishing. Sea urchin and abalone are harvested in particularly great quantities. You can get to the island by ferry (in 2 hrs. and 10 min.) or airplane from Wakkanai (taking 20 min.). The 20 km from Cape Sukoton to Motoji Coast is perfect for hiking (taking about 8 hrs.). This island is also part of Rishiri-Rebun-Sarobetsu National Park.

Section II. Northeastern Honshu
(Tohoku District)

Northeastern Honshu is called the Tohoku (Northeastern) or Ou District. It is composed of six prefectures: Aomori, Iwate, Akita, Yamagata, Miyagi and Fukushima. The city of Sendai in Miyagi Prefecture serves as the Tohoku regional center.

The Tohoku District was once called "Michinoku" (Innermost Country) because of the rough, mountainous terrain, severe climate and difficult access to natural resources. However, this inaccessibility has also been instrumental in preserving the great natural beauty of the area, making it a fascinating place to visit. Indeed, Tohoku is rich in scenic locations, including three national parks (Towada-Hachimantai, Rikuchu Kaigan (Coast) and Bandai-Asahi), eight quasi-national parks and many hot springs. Travelers to this district are invariably captivated by the simple manners and customs of the local people as well as by the unique cultural heritage as expressed in numerous traditional folk dances, songs and festivals.

The Ou Mountain Chain, running up the center parallel to the coastline, forms the backbone of the district, stretching 500 km all the way to Kanto. The Ou Mountain Chain and the Nasu Volcano Chain partially overlap, forming many hot springs and scenic spots such as Lake Towada, Hachimantai Plateau, Mt. Zao and Bandai Plateau. On the east side of the mountains lies the Pacific seaboard, while on the west side is the Japan Sea coast.

The Tohoku region is devoid of extensive plains, but large cities have risen along the coast and in river basins. There is a marked difference in climate between the eastern and western halves, while the valleys in between the mountains have their own unique climate. As the many excellent ski resorts indicate, Tohoku is characterized by cold, snowy winters.

Though much effort has been expended on the economic development of the Tohoku District, its progress still lags behind that of the Kanto and Kansai districts. However, transportation facilities such as railways and expressways have steadily improved in recent years. The 535.3-km stretch between Ueno (Tokyo) and Morioka (Iwate Prefecture) can now be covered in less than three hours on the Tohoku Shinkansen. The Tohoku Expressway runs approximately 700 km from Tokyo to Aomori, shortening the distance between cities and making economical sightseeing a reality.

Modern industry is developing, but the production of lacquerware, copper and iron household utensils, traditional textiles, toys and many other traditional folkcrafts items continues unabated. Although Tohoku is a one-crop district, it is the leading rice producer of Japan. The Sanriku region on the Pacific coast is known for the abundance of fish catches. Other industries in the district include

315

fruit cultivation, stock and dairy farming, and forestry.

Area 1. Aomori Prefecture

Aomori 6 ☎0177

Pop. 291,576. The capital of Aomori Prefecture, the northernmost prefecture on Honshu. The Aomori Plain lies adjacent to Mutsu Bay. The city can be reached from Tokyo in 1 hr.10 min. by plane, or about 5 hrs. by taking the JR Tohoku Shinkansen train from Ueno (Tokyo) and transferring at Morioka to a limited express train on the JR Tohoku Main Line—a distance of 740 km.

Bordered on the north by Mutsu Bay, the city covers nearly all of the plain and spreads to the south over part of the Hakkoda Mountains. Because it faces Hakodate on Hokkaido across the Tsugaru Straits, it serves as the gateway to Hokkaido for both rail and sea traffic. The opening of the Seikan (Aomori-Hakodate) ocean-floor Tunnel has enhanced the city's importance as a transportation center. Over the years, it has developed commercially as a commodity distribution center and has become the political as well as the economic center of this prefecture. There are many hot springs that can be used as a base for sightseeing trips to nearby scenic attractions such as Mt. Hakkoda, Lake Towada, and the Shimokita and Tsugaru peninsulas. The *Nebuta Matsuri* Festival in summer is famous throughout Japan.

HISTORY

Aomori developed as a port town under the second lord of the Tsugaru Clan, Nobuhira, in 1624. It is said that the name Aomori was taken from the beautiful green (*ao*) of the pine forest (*mori*). The city was selected as the prefectural capital soon after the Meiji Restoration in 1868. The Aomori-Hakodate ferry service was inaugurated in 1873, followed by the inauguration of the railway form Tokyo in 1891. Thus, it had already developed as a transportation center by the early years of this century.

INDUSTRIES

As a trading region for materials and resources, the economy of this area is quite active. The cypress forests in this prefecture are of the best quality found anywhere in Japan, and the lumber that they supply is used equally for furniture and processed wooden goods. The area is also noted for the high quality of its processed marine products industry, while the apple orchards found within the cities and the surrounding areas are among the best in Japan.

TRANSPORTATION

The JR Tohoku and Ou main lines, National Highways 4 and 7, and the Tohoku Expressway traverse the whole of Tohoku, converging in Aomori. The JR Tsugaru Straits Line passes through the Seikan Tunnel, linking Aomori with Hakodate in Hokkaido by rail, while automobiles can cross over to Hakodate by ferry. Aomori is also the main route for sightseeing in Towada, where the JR Towada Bus Line originates.

ANNUAL EVENTS

Nebuta (August 2-7): One of the four great festivals of Tohoku, like *Tanabata* in Sendai, *Kanto* in Akita and *Hanagasa Matsuri* in Yamagata. It has been designated as an Important Intangible Folk Cultural Property. The *Nebuta Matsuri* Festival is said to have originated when Sakanoue-no-Tamuramaro (758-811) subjugated local rebels by devising *nebuta* (giant figures representing men, animals and birds) to mislead the enemy. (Refer to p.327) During the festival, these *nebuta* are carried or pulled through the main streets on carriages. This same festival is held from August 1 - 7 at Hirosaki (pronounced *neputa* here) in the same prefecture.

PLACES OF INTEREST

Places of interest in the city include the Munakata Shiko Memorial Hall where works of this famous wood-block printer (1903-1975) are exhibited, spacious Gappo Park along Aomori Bay and the fish market in front of the JR Aomori Station. The unusual, 13-story, triangular "Aspamu" building introduces the sights and industries of Aomori. It also houses restaurants and offers local specialties for sale. From the observation lounge, a panoramic view of Mutsu Bay and the Hakkoda Mountains can be enjoyed.

Asamushi Spa 6 : 25 min. from Aomori by local train on the JR Tohoku Main Line or 45 min. by bus. Located in the eastern part of the city, the spa lies on the western neck of the Natsudomari Peninsula. Regarded as one of the leading spa resorts in Tohoku, it provides an excellent view of Mutsu Bay. The plentiful hot waters are efficacious for digestive-tract disorders and nervous illnesses. About 500 m north of the spa town is the Asamushi Aquarium, containing some 5,200 fish of 450 species, including those from tropical, temperate and frigid zones. Every mid-November, large swans from Siberia migrate for the winter to Kominato on the opposite side of the Natsudomari Peninsula from Asamushi and stay until late March. They have been designated as a Special Natural Monument.

Hakkoda Mountains 6 : 1 hr. by bus from Aomori Station to Ropeway-mae Bus Stop. These dormant volcanoes, which stand in the middle of Aomori Prefecture between Aomori and Lake Towada, act as the northern pillar of the Ou Mountains. The mountains can be broadly divided into northern and southern ranges. Odake, with an altitude of 1,585 m (the highest of the 10 peaks, all in the 1,500-m class), is in the northern half of the volcanic chain, while Mt. Kushigamine, with an altitude of 1,517 m, is the central peak in the southern half. Except for the taller peaks, the foothills are sprinkled with lakes and marshes, hot springs and other spectacular features of natural beauty. The green leaves of spring and the tinted ones of autumn are especially beautiful. The area is also famous as a mecca for spring and summer skiing (May-July).

Sukayu Spa [6] : 1 hr.25 min. by bus from Aomori Station. Located at an altitude of 900 m on the face of Mt. Odake, the spa has long been known for the curative powers of its mineral waters. It is the first hot springs designated as a National Recuperative Spa. Nearby is Jigokudani, where sulfurous gas and hot water are belched from the ground. A collection of 300 different kinds of alpine plants at the Tohoku University Botanical Garden is also close-by. The waters of the spa are quite acidic, making them effective for nervous disorders. Sukayu Spa is famous for a gigantic bath called *Sennimburo* (Bath of 1,000 People).

Lake Towada and Vicinity

Towada-Hachimantai National Park [6-7] : The park extends over three prefectures—Aomori, Akita and Iwate—and as the name indicates, it is divided into the Towada and Hachimantai sections. Consisting of the Hakkoda Volcano Chain and Lake Towada, the former is characterized by the harmonious beauty of the landscape. The Oirase River, which flows from Lake Towada, the new, green leaves of spring and the autumn colors on the plateaus around the foothills of the Hakkoda Mountains are exquisite. The Hachimantai region has luxuriant, coniferous forests and marshes, with Mt. Iwate, sometimes called "Nambu Fuji," at the center. Nambu is the former name of parts of Iwate and Aomori prefectures and was so named because the Nambu Clan once dominated this region. The park covers an area of 854.1 sq.km.

Routes to Lake Towada

1. Aomori Route: Aomori – Sukayu Spa – Mt. Yakeyama – Neno-kuchi – Lake Towada. 3 hrs. 10 min. by bus.

2. Morioka/Odate Route: Morioka/Odate – Oyu Spa – Hakka Pass – Lake Towada. 2 hrs. 15 min. by bus from Morioka, 2 hrs. 6 min. from Odate.

3. Hirosaki Route: Hirosaki – Kuroishi – Takinosawa – Neno-kuchi. 2 hrs. 10 min. by bus.

4. Misawa/Hachinohe Route: Misawa/Hachinohe – Towada City – Mt. Yakeyama – Nenokuchi – Lake Towada. 2 hrs. 16 min. by bus from Misawa, 2 hrs. 30 min. from Hachinohe.

Lake Towada [6] : 44 km in circumference and an area of 59.8 sq.km. Situated to the south of the Hakkoda volcanoes and on the border between Aomori and Akita prefectures, this is a double caldera lake. It extends 10 km from east to west and 8 km from north to south. Except for the Nakayama and Ogura peninsulas, both of which jut out from the south bank, the lake is nearly circular. Clear to a depth of 14-15 m, the 327-m-deep lake is the third-deepest crater lake in Japan. Around the lake are caldera sommas of about the same height, all of which slope sharply down to the water. The highest point is the 1,011-m-high Mt. Ohanabe on the north bank of the lake.

The outer face of the rim is covered with forest, contrasting with the starkly bare lake side. The two peninsulas divide the lake into four parts: *Higashi-no-Umi* (East Lake), *Naka-no-Umi* (Central Lake), *Nishi-no-Umi* (West Lake), and *Kita-no-Umi* (North Lake).

Excursion Boats: Playing an important part for sightseeing in the Lake Towada vicinity, the boats provide a view of the lake unobtainable from the lake shore. The main route goes from Lake Towada (Yasumiya) to Nenokuchi, passing the Nakayama and Ogura peninsulas. Boats leave frequently for this 1-hr. trip.

Somma Observation Platforms: Many observation platforms have been erected on the mountains, which have an altitude difference of 300 m more or less. The four mountains listed below are the most well-known.

Mt. Ohanabe: 30 min. by bus from the Nenokuchi Bus Stop with an altitude of 1,011 m. Offering the best northern view of the lake, it is one of the few places where one can obtain a view over the rim of the volcano.

Mt. Towada: 1 hr.50 min. on foot from Nenokuchi or 1 hr.40 min. on foot from Utarube. Lake Towada lies at one's feet, while the Hakkoda Mountains, Mt. Iwate and the Hachimantai area can be seen in the distance.

Kankodai: 5 min. by bus from Lake Towada Bus Stop. It stands at the neck of the Ogura Peninsula along National Highway 103. There is a good view of the Central Lake from here, with the cliffs of the Ogura Peninsula to the right and Nakayama Peninsula on the left.

Hakka Pass ⑥ : 15 min. by bus from Lake Towada Bus Stop. The pass is located in the southern portion of the Towada caldera. The West Lake and the two peninsulas spread out magnificently, with a view of the Hakkoda Mountain Chain in the distance. This is perhaps the best of the observation platforms in the area.

Oirase River ⑥ : As the only river flowing out of Lake Towada, it runs north from its source in Nenokuchi in the northeastern section and empties into the Pacific at Hachinohe in northern Aomori Prefecture—a total length of 67 km. During the 14 km from the lake to Mt. Yakeyama, it goes through innumerable changes amidst the dense forest, dislaying all the beauty of a typical mountain stream. Both sides of the river are pressed in by exposed lava rocks formed by eruptions of the Towada volcano, forming myriads of waterfalls in the process. Moreover, the whole area is covered with a forest of broad-leafed trees, beautifying the surroundings in the spring with their greenery and in the fall with their flaming colors. Since National Highway 102 connecting Hirosaki and Towada City runs right by the river, the beauty of the area can be enjoyed from the bus.

Yasumiya: 3 hrs. 10 min. by bus from Aomori to Lake Towada Bus Stop. Regarded as the largest tourist district around Lake Towada, it is situated at the neck of the Nakayama Peninsula. The quiet beauty of the lake contrasts with the bustle around the souvenir shops, the Towada Science Museum and the Towada Aquarium.

Statues of Two Girls by the Lake: 15 min. on foot from Lake Towada Bus Stop. The statue, which might be said to be a symbol of the lake, stands among the trees along the bank. This bronze statue of two nude girls facing each other was created in 1953 by Takamura Kotaro (1883–1956), a famous sculptor and poet.

Nenokuchi: 2 hrs. 45 min. from the JR Aomori Station by bus. It is located on the northeastern shore of the lake by the outlet of the Oirase River. Included in the routes from Aomori, Misawa and Hirosaki, it also serves as the gateway for Lake Towada as well as the terminal for excursion boats.

Tsuta Spa 6 : 1 hr.50 min. by bus from Aomori Station. The hot springs are located near the foothills of the Hakkoda Mountains, the valley of the Tsuta River, the swamps and many of the other beauties of nature. It was a favorite spot of Omachi Keigetsu, a literary figure of the Meiji period, who introduced the beauty of Lake Towada and the Oirase River in his works. His grave and a bronze likeness stand here. With temperatures ranging from 42-47℃, the spa waters are efficacious against feminine afflictions and gastrointestinal disorders.

Shimokita Peninsula 6 : The northernmost peninsula on Honshu juts into the ocean in the shape of an axe. It has been designated as a quasi-national park. It enfolds Mutsu Bay and faces the Tsugaru Peninsula, separated from Hokkaido by the Tsugaru Straits. The rugged nature and rustic people here are appropriate to this desolate northern tip of Honshu. Seaside beauty at places like Hotokegaura Beach, Cape Shiriya and Cape Oma, hot springs like Yagen and Shimoburo, and Mt. Osorezan, which is well-known for its eerie sight, are just some of the attractions.

The gateway to the peninsula is Noheji Station on the JR Tohoku Main Line. Since the area lacks any convenient form of transportation, it takes 2-3 days to see the whole peninsula.

Mutsu 6 ☎0175: Pop. 49,914. This is the northernmost city on Honshu. It plays a central role on the Shimokita Peninsula as a transportation junction for the entire peninsula. A bus network covers all the areas of interest for the sightseer, with the JR Shimokita, Ominato and Shimokita Kotsu Line Tanabu stations as the points of departure.

Mt. Osorezan 6 : 40 min. by bus from Tanabu Station. Located more or less at the center of the Shimokita Peninsula, this is a generic name for several mountains (including the 828-m-high Mt. Otsukushi) and the valley they enclose. The valley is at the bottom of a 4-km-diameter caldera and contains Lake Usorisan. The spirits of the dead are said to gather here. Osorezan-Bodaiji Temple on the northern coast of Lake Usorisan is in the middle of this gathering ground for lost souls. This temple is said to have been founded by the famous priest Ennin, also known as Jikaku-Daishi (794–864). The main festival of the temple is held every July 20–24. During this festival, worshippers come to the temple to talk to the spirits of the departed through mediums called *itako* because it is believed that the dead gather here during this period. Four hot springs bubble forth on the extensive temple grounds, while fumaroles and geysers erupt around the lake. The surrounding scenery is stark and nearly bare of vegetation, reminding one of a traditional vision of hell.

Yagen Spa ⑥ : 20 min. by bus from Ohata Station on the Shimokita Kotsu Line. It is located in a 10-km-deep valley near the upper reaches of the Ohata River, which empties into the Tsugaru Straits. The dense primeval forest of white cedars appears almost a like fairyland.

Hachinohe ⑥ ☎0178: Pop. 242,900. An industrial town on the southeastern Pacific coast of Aomori. Hachinohe can be reached in 4 hrs. 50 min. by taking the Tohoku Shinkansen to Morioka from Ueno (Tokyo) and transferring to the limited express on the JR Tohoku Main Line—a distance of 644 km. A leisurely trip by car can be made by turning onto the branch route from the Tohoku Expressway. The city spreads along the coast from east to west. The cement, chemical, and steel industries are thriving, but it also boasts some of the largest fish catches in the whole country.

Kabushima ⑥ : East of Hachinohe. Once an island, the area is famous for black-tailed gulls (a Natural Monument) and serves as the gateway to the Tanesashi coast, which is famous for the beauty of its white sand and coral reefs. Thousands of these gulls build nests here in February. A couple of months after the eggs are hatched from May to June, the parents and grown chicks head south in late August.

Misawa ⑥ ☎0176: Pop. 42,206. 1 hr.10 min. from Tokyo by air. It is a little south of the base of the Shimokita Peninsula along the Pacific coast. Bordered on the northwest by Lake Ogawara, it is the eastern gateway to Lake Towada. The Sabishiro Coast in the suburbs of the city is where the American fliers landed upon completing the first non-stop, trans-Pacific flight in October 1931. A memorial stands here to commemorate the success of their courageous attempt. A U.S. Air Force base is also located here.

Tsugaru Peninsula ⑥

Stretching 35–40 km from east to west, this peninsula divides the Japan Sea and Mutsu Bay, and, like the Shimokita Peninsula, is part of the northernmost portion of Honshu. Blizzards sweep across this wild land through most of the winter, and there are parts that remain undisturbed by man. Cape Tappi at the tip of the peninsula is the Honshu gateway to Seikan Tunnel, linking it to Hokkaido via the JR Tsugaru Straits Line.

Seikan Tunnel and the JR Tsugaru Straits Line ⑥ : A 53.9-km-long tunnel. It serves as Honshu's rail connection with Hokkaido, with some 23 km of the total length running under the seabed of the

Tsugaru Straits. Construction began in 1964, but various difficulties delayed its completion until 21 years later in 1985.

The JR Tsugaru Straits Line began operation in March 1988, connecting Honshu and Hokkaido by rail in 2 hrs. 30 min. Until then, it took 3 hrs. 50 min. by ferry from Aomori to Hakodate. The world's first ocean-floor stations, Tappi Kaitei Station and Yoshioka Kaitei Station, are located along this line.

Cape Tappi 6 : 1 hr.30 min. from Aomori to Miumaya on the JR Tsugaru Line, with an additional bus ride of 40 min. Located at the tip of the peninsula, it is separated from Cape Shirakami on Hokkaido by only 20 km. Caves of all sizes, created by reefs and erosion from the waves, shape the precipitous cliffs with a wild beauty, making the cape a major sightseeing destination.

Goshogawara 6 ☎0173: Pop. 51,320. About 1 hr.30 min. from Aomori by local train on the JR Ou Main Line via Kawabe. It is the economic and cultural center for the west central part of the Tsugaru Peninsula. It is also a major transportation point for the region and the starting point for the Tsugaru Railways.

Lake Jusanko 6 : 1 hr.15 min. by bus from Goshogawara Station. Located on the west coast of the Tsugaru Peninsula, the lake is 7 km from east to west and 5 km from north to south, with a channel connecting the northwest end to the Japan Sea. The Iwaki River carries in sediment so that the deepest point only goes down 2 m. Both fresh water and salt water fish live here, while swans fly in for their winter migration.

Kamegaoka 6 : 35 min. by bus from Goshogawara Station. The area is noted for the 4,000-year-old relics of the Jomon era found here. Unusual figures and earthernware of the type known as Kamegaoka have been excavated. These artifacts are of special interest to the archaeologist.

Fukaura Coast 6 : Located in the central Tsugaru coastal region. The town of Fukaura has long been known as a safe port for ships running into trouble at sea. The coast is lined with sea-eroded cliffs and reefs, creating a breathtaking scene. It has been designated as a quasi-national park. An excursion boat cruises the shore during the tourist season.

Tsugaru Plain

Hirosaki 6 ☎ 0172: Pop. 175,797. Ranking as the second-largest city in Aomori Prefecture, it is reached in about 50 min. by local train on the JR Ou Main Line from Aomori. The city has a history of about 300 years as the castle town of the Tsugaru Clan, and remains a vibrant commercial and cultural center. With the main activity centered around apple cultivation, the whole city bustles with pickers during the harvest season. Tsugaru folk songs and Tsugaru lacquerware and other folkcraft items are also produced in abundance. It is the western gateway to Lake Towada. The *Neputa Matsuri* Festival,

like that of Aomori, is enthusiastically celebrated every August 1-7.
Hirosaki Park, a 20 min.-walk from Hirosaki Station, marks the sight
of an old castle. The main building of the castle was built in 1611, and
several buildings still standing recall this past. Known for its cherry
trees, the park serves as a place where city residents can relax. 1.5
km west of the station is Saisho-in Temple, famous for a five-story
pagoda erected in 1667. The pagoda is 31 m tall and took 10 years to
complete. It has been designated as an Important Cultural Property.

Mt. Iwaki 6 : Alt. 1,625 m. A dormant volcano rising northwest of
Hirosaki. Since the uniquely shaped conical peak resembles Mt. Fuji,
it has been given the name Tsugaru-Fuji. Its religious significance for
the people of the Tsugaru Plain area dates back to ancient times.
Iwakiyama and Takateru shrines stand near the starting point for the
ascent, with the inner sanctuary of Iwakiyama Shrine gracing the
peak. During its long history as a sacred mountain, many trails to the
summit have been carved out. The Tsugaru-Iwaki Skyline ropeway,
however, goes 1,247 m up the face. If one takes the lift, the peak can
be reached with just a 30-min. walk.

Iwakiyama Shrine: 40 min. by bus from Hirosaki Bus Terminal near
Hirosaki Station. It is believed that the shrine was built during the
Hoki era (770–781). Most of the buildings now standing date from the
17th century and are so elaborately decorated that the shrine is often
called the "Nikko of Tohoku." A festival is held annually around
September 20.

Owani Spa 6 : 14 min. from Hirosaki Station by the JR local train
or 30 min. from Chuo-Hirosaki Station on the Konan Railways. It is
located along the Hirakawa River where the hot springs have a long
history. The water temperatures ranging from 60–80℃ are efficacious for back and nervous ailments. The surrounding area is famous
for apples as well as for its excellent ski grounds.

Kuroishi 6 ☎0172: Pop. 40,743. 30 min. from Hirosaki Station on
the Konan Railways. Situated in the southeast part of the Tsugaru
Plain as the most fertile region in Aomori Prefecture, the town is the
distribution center for rice and apples grown here. The Aseishi River,
a tributary of the Iwaki River, flows through the southern part of
town, while National Highway 102 running beside it is the western
gateway to Lake Towada. It takes about 1 hr. 40 min. to reach
Nenokuchi. Nuruyu, Ochiai and Itadome hot springs are located
along National Highway 102, while spas such as Aoni and Kiriake are
scattered about the mountains through which this highway passes.
This area is called the Kuroishi hot-springs region, with many visitors
using the spas as bases from which to enjoy the sights of Lake
Towada.

Area 2. Iwate Prefecture

Morioka 7/12-① ☎0196

Pop. 231,713. Serving as the prefectural capital, the city is situated roughly in the middle of the region. It takes about 3 hrs. 20 min. to get here from Ueno (Tokyo) on the JR Tohoku Shinkansen—a distance of 536 km. The Kitakami, Shizukuishi and Nakatsu rivers flow through the heart of the city. Mt. Iwate (alt. 2,039 m) towers at the northwestern edge of this tranquil city rich in verdure. Formerly a castle town of the Nambu family, the city contains vestiges of this past that can be seen in the remains of Morioka Castle as well as in the houses along the streets. Traditional specialties are textiles and ironware so famous that iron kettles are known as *Nambu-tetsubin* (Nambu iron kettles).

Chagu-Chagu Umakko Festival is held every June 15 to pray for the healthy growth of horses. Brightly costumed boys and girls parade through the city on horses decorated with colorful ornaments.

A major transportation center, Morioka is the terminal station on the JR Tohoku Shinkansen. The Tohoku Expressway also passes through and buses leave from here for Lake Towada, Hachimantai Plateau, the Rikuchu Coast and Lake Tazawa.

PLACES OF INTEREST

Iwate Park 12-① : 20 min. on foot from the JR Morioka Station. Located in the center of the city on the site of the former castle of the Nambu family. There is a monument inscribed with a poem by Ishikawa Takuboku (1886–1912), a well-known poet who spent his youth in Morioka.

Ishiwari-zakura 12-① : A unique cherry tree, which has been designated as a Natural Monument, grows on the premises of the Morioka District Court and stands 1.7 m tall. Since it grows from the fissure of a gigantic granite boulder 22 m around, it is named *Ishiwari-zakura*, which means "rock-splitting cherry tree." The tree, which has a trunk with a girth of 3.9 m, is about 330 years old.

Tsunagi Spa 7 : 30 min. by bus from Morioka Station. This tranquil hot-springs resort along the Shizukuishi River attracts visitors from throughout the area. It has many modern, well-equipped *ryokan* or Japanese-style inns.

Oshuku Spa 7 : 55 min. from Morioka Station by bus. The ancient resort is situated even further west in the mountains than Tsunagi Spa.

Koiwai Farm 7 : 12 km northwest of Morioka. This large farm spreads over 26 sq.km at the foot of Mt. Iwate. Nine hundred head of Holstein cattle as well as chickens are raised here. Archery and riding in horse-drawn carriages as well as on horse-back can be enjoyed on the farm, which is open to the public.

Mt. Iwate ⑦ : Alt. 2,039 m. This dormant volcano towers over the northwestern end of Morioka. It is named Nambu-Fuji because it resembles Mt. Fuji. Visible from anywhere on the plain below and long regarded as a symbol of the area, the mountain consists of two volcanic groups—East Iwate and West Iwate. The tallest peak of East Iwate is Mt. Yakushi.

Hanamaki ⑦ ☎0198: Pop. 70,143. 3 hrs. 7 min. from Ueno (Tokyo) to Shin-Hanamaki on the JR Tohoku Shinkansen—a distance of 500 km. Located between Morioka and Ichinoseki, it is enriched by tourism and agriculture. It is also a place that has many memories associated with the famous poet Miyazawa Kenji (1896-1933) and sculptor poet Takamura Kotaro (1883-1956, refer to p.320). Hanamaki Spa along a tributary of the Kitakami River is the perfect hotsprings resort area for a family outing since it is equipped with the most up-to-date facilities for sports and other forms of recreation and amusement, including excellent ski slopes. The cherry trees along the Daigawa River and around the spa resort are a famous sight. Several other mountain spas such as Dai, Shidodaira, Namari and Osawa are all nearby.

Hachimantai Plateau (Iwate Area) ⑦

A part of the Towada-Hachimantai National Park. The vast plateau is northwest of Morioka, and straddles Iwate and Akita prefectures. The plateau extends over Mt. Chausu (alt. 1,578 m) on the east, Mt. Mokkodake (alt. 1,578 m) on the south, Mt. Yakeyama (alt. 1,366 m) on the west and other peaks, while just about in the center rises the summit of Hachimantai Plateau at an altitude of 1,614 m. The curve from the base to the summit is so gentle that it seems like a plateau. Remnants of volcanic activity long past are evident not only in the steam and smoke, but also in the rumbling sounds and boiling mud here and there on the plateau. For sightseeing, the "Aspite Line" (a toll road) passes near the peak. The rustic spas scattered around the base, the most popular of which are Tamagawa, Toshichi, Fukenoyu and Goshogake, serve as headquarters for visiting the area. On clear days, one can see as far as the Pacific Ocean from the peak.

The best season for visiting Hachimantai is between July and September. In mid-July the alpine plants burst into bloom, in August the weather is stable and in mid-September the leaves start changing colors. Skiing can be enjoyed from December to June.

Routes to Hachimantai

1. Iwate Prefecture Route: Morioka Station – the summit of Hachimantai, 1 hr.57 min. by bus.
2. Akita Prefecture Route: Rikuchu-Hanawa Station on the JR Hanawa Line – the summit of Hachimantai, 1 hr.36 min. by bus.
3. Aomori Prefecture Route: Lake Towada – the summit of Hachimantai, 2 hrs. 40 min. by bus.

Hachimantai Onsenkyo (Spas Area): 1 hr.30 min. by bus from Morioka Station. A large resort area spreading along the base of the magnificent ridge of Mt. Iwate, it is surrounded by a prefectural forest, the natural recreation village and other lush greenery. Skiing, tennis, golf and cycling are some of the sports that can be enjoyed here.

Ichinoseki 7 ☎0191: Pop. 61,172. 2 hrs. 40 min. from Ueno (Tokyo) on the JR Tohoku Shinkansen—a distance of 442 km. It takes 35 min. from Sendai. In the Edo period Ichinoseki was the castle town of the Tamura family, who served the Date Clan of Sendai. Today, it is a central commercial and timber market. In addition it serves as a base for sightseeing at Chusonji Temple in Hiraizumi, Mt. Kurikoma and other places of interest in the area. It is also the southern entrance to the Rikuchu Coast.

Gembikei Gorge 7 : 20 min. from Ichinoseki Station by bus. A magnificent 2-km-long gorge full of countless, fantastically shaped rocks, waterfalls and deep pools.

Mt. Kurikoma 7 : Alt. 1,627 m. Located in the center of the Ou Mountains, this dormant volcano straddling Iwate, Akita and Miyagi prefectures has been designated as a quasi-national park. Sukawa Spa at the northern base of the mountain can be reached by bus from Ichinoseki in 1 hr.40 min. A 4-km walk from the spa to the peak takes about 1 hr.30 min. The mountain is thickly blanketed with greenery, with many alpine plants growing near the summit. A magnificent view of many of the main mountains in the Tohoku District can be obtained form the peak.

Geibikei Gorge 7 : 45 min. by bus from Ichinoseki Station. It is noted for the fantastic rock formations on the sheer walls of the cliffs overlooking the limpid Satetsu River, a tributary of the Kitakami River. Odd-looking rocks and steep cliffs tower 30–100 m on both banks of the river. The excursion boat offers the best view.

Hiraizumi 7 : 9 min. by local train on the JR Tohoku Main Line, or 22 min. by bus from Ichinoseki Station. Chusonji Temple and Motsuji Temple recall the time when the town prospered under the total control of the Fujiwara family for a hundred years from about 1090.

Chusonji Temple 7 : 5 min. by bus from Hiraizumi. There is also a direct bus service from Ichinoseki via Hiraizumi that takes 26 min. Founded in 1105 by the Fujiwara family, it greatly expanded over the next 21 years. At one time, there were more than 40 buildings on the precincts, but most of them have burned down. Today, the only original buildings are *Konjikido* (lit. Golden Hall) and the *Kyozo* (Sutra Library).

    Konjikido Hall (Golden Hall): A rather small structure only 5.5 m square. In spite of its size, the splendor of the interior decoration is known throughout Japan. *Konjikido* derived its name from the fact that its exterior walls were originally covered in gold leaf. The inner chamber contains three altars and the mummified remains of Kiyo-hira, Motohira and Hidehira (lords of the Fujiwara family for three generation). The main pillars and rafters are lacquered and inlaid with mother-of-pearl, while each pillar is decorated with Buddhist religious scenes. The artistic merit of the hall, which has been designated as a National Treasure, lies primarily in the elaborate decoration rather than in the construction.

Kyozo (Sutra Library): Erected in 1108. It was originally a two-story structure, but the upper level was destroyed by fire in 1337. This building is also only 5.5 m square. Many sutras were once stored here, but they are now housed at the *Sankozo* (Treasure Hall). The inner chamber contains an altar enshrining *Monju-Bosatsu-Shishi*, the Bodhisattva of wisdom or intellect.

Sankozo (Treasure Hall): Immediately in front of *Konjikido*. This is a modern structure built to preserve the cultural properties and works of art remaining at Chusonji Temple. The burial effects of the three generations of Fujiwara as well as Buddhist altar fittings, statues of Buddha and other objects of value have been moved here from other parts of the temple. More than 3,000 objects are stored here.

Motsuji Temple: 7 min. on foot from Hiraizumi Station. The temple was founded some 850 years ago. It flourished under the patronage of the Fujiwara family, surpassing even Chusonji Temple, but all of the original buildings were destroyed by repeated fires. Oizumigaike Pond at the center of the garden is an excellent example of a Jodo-type garden.

Former Site of Takadate Mansion: 15 min. on foot from Hiraizumi Station. On a hill east of Chusonji Temple next to the Kitakami River, a hall was built by the Fujiwara family for Minamoto-no-Yoshitsune (1159–1189), the younger brother of Minamoto-no-Yoritomo—founder of the Kamakura Shogunate. After the elder brother Yoritomo established his government, the brothers quarreled, and Yoshitsune fled to Hiraizumi seeking the protection of the Fujiwara family. Yoritomo pursued with an army and set fire to the building, leading to a tragic end for Yoshitsune. The remains of the hall were washed away by the river, but the hill still offers an excellent vantage point of the Kitakami River as well as the small, reed-thatched *Gikeido* Hall and a Treasure House that often provoke tears from visitors.

Takkoku-no-Iwaya: 20 min. by bus from Hiraizumi Station. There is a cavern about 6 km southwest of the station near the border of Ichinoseki City. Sakanoue-no-Tamuramaro (758–811), sent by Emperor Kammu as the *Sei-i-Taishogun* (refer to p.90) to suppress a rebellion (refer to p.317), built a little temple to honor *Bishamonten*, the Buddhist guardian god of warriors, in this cave. There were 108 figures of the god in *Bishamon* Hall, but the temple was destroyed by an accidental fire in 1946 so that the present structures now date from

1961. On the face of a boulder forming a sheer precipice near the cave was a 17-m-high carving of *Dainichi-Nyorai*, a Buddhist Deity, but now only faint traces remain. It is believed to have been carved at the end of the 11th century.

Mizusawa ☎ 0197 ⬜7️⃣: Pop. 57,511. 30 min. by local train from Ichinoseki Station on the JR Tohoku Main Line. The economic center for the surrounding towns and villages, the city is known as the location of the International Latitude Observatory. In Mizusawa Park, 800 m southwest of the station, stands a monument to Takano Choei (1804-1850). This eminent scholar was born here, studied Dutch medical science under Philipp Franz van Siebold (1796-1866) and pioneered the introduction of modern medicine to Japan.

Rikuchu Kaigan (Coast) National Park ⬜7️⃣

This long, thin region stretching along the eastern coast of Tohoku and facing the Pacific has been designated as a National Park. The park has a total area of 123.5 sq.km and extends 210 km from the northern part of Iwate Prefecture to the northern part of Miyagi Prefecture. Miyako at the center divides the park into two regions. In the north there are terraced slopes averaging a height of about 150 m, while in the south there is a typical ria-type coastline with many inlets, sea-eroded grottoes, cliffs and stone columns. Also not to be overlooked in this national park are the numerous rare plants and animals that are found here, many of which are protected as Natural Monuments. The park's layers of exposed cretaceous strata make it of special interest to the geologist.

Ofunato ⬜7️⃣ ☎0192: Pop. 38,501. 2 hrs. 25 min. by rapid train from Ichinoseki on the JR Ofunato Line, along Ofunato Bay. For many years this has been a fishery center for the district, but recently there has been a noticeable development of cement and other industries. The nearby Pacific coast abounds in scenic wonders and is part of the Rikuchu Kaigan (Coast) National Park.

Goishi Coast ⬜7️⃣: 40 min. by bus from the JR Sakari Station. It is located at the south end of Ofunato Bay on the tip of Matsusaki Peninsula where many camellia and *kaki* (persimmon) trees grow. The coast is lined with cliffs, grottoes, tunnels and other fantastic natural forms. An excursion boat available along the coast provides an excellent view.

Kamaishi ⬜7️⃣ ☎0193: Pop. 54,805. 1 hr.40 min. by express from the JR Tohoku Shinkansen Shin-Hanamaki Station. Centrally located in eastern Iwate Prefecture, it is known for its modern steel industry. Although massive smoke stacks and factories have customarily crowded the area in front of the station, many of these steel factories have been closing down recently. Instead, the city has been developing as a fishing town as well as one of the leading trading ports on the Sanriku Coast.

Miyako ⬜7️⃣ ☎0193: Pop. 59,526. 2 hrs. 30 min. from Morioka and 1 hr.15 min. from Kamaishi on the JR Yamada Line. Known as a base for deep-sea fishing, the town has long flourished as the largest fishing port north of Kamaishi on the Pacific coast. It is also the base for sightseeing trips to Jodogahama Beach, Cape Kitayamazaki and other sites of natural beauty along the Rikuchu Coast that provide some of the major scenic attractions of the Rikuchu Kaigan (Coast) National Park.

Jodogahama Beach [7] : 20 min. by bus from Miyako Station. Situated on the north side of Mt. Usuki, which juts out into Ofunato Bay, the beach is considered one of the most beautiful sites on the Rikuchu Coast. The deep green of the red pines on pure white boulder clusters (which are lined up like the teeth of a saw) are reflected in the ocean, creating a sight of unimaginable beauty.

Ryusendo Cave [7] : 2 hrs. 40 min. from Morioka Station by bus. It is a large stalactite grotto 2.5 km long, where a clear underground stream forms deep pools and currents. The underground lake with its emerald-colored water is especially famous. Transparent down to a depth of 41.5 m, it is said to be one of the clearest body of water in the world.

Cape Kitayamazaki [7] : 15 min. by bus from Tanohata Station on the Sanriku Railways. This is another prominent sight along the Rikuchu Coast, with vertical cliffs 200 m high extending over a distance of 8 km. There is a nature trail for viewing the appealing coastal beauty at close range.

Kuji [7] ☎0194: Pop. 39,556. 2 hrs. from Hachinohe on the JR Hachinohe Line—a distance of 65 km. Once a castle town, it is the northern gateway to Rikuchu Kaigan (Coast) National Park and the home of *Kokuji-yaki*, a traditional type of pottery.

Area 3. Akita Prefecture

Akita [7/12-②] ☎0188

Pop. 295,677, the capital of Akita Prefecture. The city is situated in the middle of the prefecture on the Akita Plain, which lies along the coast of the Japan Sea. It can be reached by plane in 1 hr. from Tokyo or 4 hrs. 40 min. from Ueno (Tokyo) by taking the JR Tohoku Shinkansen to Morioka and transferring to the JR Tazawako Line— a distance of 663 km. A commercial city with an agricultural background, Akita once flourished as the castle town of the Satake Clan, but in recent years it has become increasingly industrial. The Akita Bayside Industrial Complex has opened alongside Akita Bay, and a steam-generated electrical plant, a paper manufacturing factory, refineries and other industries operate here. It is the transportation axis for the Oga Peninsula and Lake Tazawa. The area is also known for such culinary specialties as *kiritampo*, a sort of grilled rice cake, and *shottsuru-nabe*, a type of stew containing a seasoning made by pickling *hatahata* (sand fish) in salt.

Akita is representative of a modern distribution market on the Japan Sea coast in the Tohoku District, with very little atmosphere of a castle town remaining. Heading west on Hirokoji-dori Street from Akita Station leads one to the shopping district, while a walk down Kawabata-dori Street, which parallels the Asahi River, will take one to an amusement district with many restaurants and bars. **Senshu Park**, a 5-min. walk from Akita Station, was once the site of the castle belonging to the Satake family. Akita Hachiman Shrine on the park grounds is dedicated to the lords of the Satake Clan. The park also contains a library and an art museum, making it a favorite recreation spot for city residents. The **Hirano Masakichi Art Museum** at the park entrance includes a number of works by Leonard Tsuguji Fujita. People come to the park in spring to enjoy the beautiful azaleas and cherry blossoms.

ANNUAL EVENT

Kanto: One of the four largest festivals in the Tohoku District. A *kanto* is a long pole with paper lanterns hung from horizontal bamboo ribs. From August 4–7, youths balance these *kanto* on their foreheads, shoulders and hips. Using their hands for balance, they compete in showing off their skill, with some of the best able to balance as many as 50 lanterns each. The festival is held to pray for good harvests.

PLACES OF INTEREST

Oga Peninsula 7

Northwest of Akita. The peninsula has been designated as a quasi-national park. It projects 28 km into the Japan Sea and measures 20 km from north to south at its broadest point. At the eastern base of the peninsula is Hachirogata, flanked by Mt. Kampuzan (alt. 355 m) on the west. Further southwest in the northern foothills of Mt. Honzan (alt. 715 m) are three mysterious lakes called Ichinomegata, Ninomegata and Sannomegata. Steep cliffs close off the western coast, while the northern and southern coasts have gentler, sea-eroded slopes. The peninsula is criss-crossed by sight-seeing highways such as the "Kampuzan Panorama Line," making it a convenient place for a drive.

Mt. Kampuzan 7 : 1 hr.10 min. from Akita Station by bus. Located at the center of the neck of the Oga Peninsula, the entire mountain is cloaked in luxuriant grass, making it an excellent picnic ground. The "Kampuzan Panorama Line" runs right to the summit.

Oga Spa: 1 hr.50 min. by bus from Akita Station. Located on the north coast of the peninsula, it is a base for sightseeing on the Oga Peninsula. Hotels and *ryokan* or Japanese-style inns have been built so that the Japan Sea spreads out in front, while Mt. Kampuzan towers behind.

Cape Nyudozaki 7 : The cape at the very tip of the Oga Peninsula. The gentle, grass-covered plain runs into sheer, 30-m-high cliffs that drop off to the Japan Sea. Glass-bottomed excursion boats skirt the cape.

Hachibodai Plateau: 15 min. by bus from Cape Nyudozaki, 30 min. on foot from Oga Spa. This fairly high mountain has an excellent observation deck that looks over the perfectly round crater lakes — Ichinomegata and Ninomegata—as well as Mt. Kampuzan, Cape Nyudozaki and the Ou Mountains in the distance.

Namahage: On New Year's Eve, a unique annual event is observed throughout the Oga Peninsula. On this day, groups of young men disguised as ogres (called *namahage*) roam from door to door. They are courteously received by the master of the house in formal dress. First, they pay their respects to the family shrine inside the house, then they chase after the children and newlywed wives shouting in rough voices: "Any brats around here who don't listen to what their parents say ?" On leaving the youths are treated to *sake* and *mochi* (rice cakes). The origin of the word *namahage* is as follows: *Nama* is a spot that appears on the skin when one sits warming by the fire too long. These spots are considered to be signs of laziness. *Hage* is a verb meaning "to strip off." Hence the word *namahage*, or "strip off the sign of laziness," is a reprimand to sluggards.

Noshiro 6 ☎0185: Pop. 57,604. 50 min. from Akita by limited express on the JR Ou Main Line to Higashi-Noshiro, with an additional 15-min. bus ride. It is the third-largest city in Akita Prefecture following Akita and Odate. Situated at the mouth of the Yoneshiro River, it is known as a center for the processing and shipment of timber cut and sent from the cedar forests in the upper reaches of the Yoneshiro River. A special kind of lacquerware called *Shunkei-nuri* made in the city is characterized by a light orange color through which the grain of the wood is clearly visible.

Odate 6 ☎0186: Pop. 69,503. About 1 hr.30 min. from Akita by limited express on the Ou Main Line. The second-largest city in Akita Prefecture, it is the marketing center for lumber from nearby forests. Objects made of bent cedar are the speciality here. It is also the home of the famous Akita dog. Odate is a junction on the JR Hanawa Line and the southern gateway to Lake Towada.

Hachimantai Plateau (Akita Area) 7

Fukenoyu Spa: 1 hr.15 min. by bus from Rikuchu-Hanawa Station on the JR Hanawa Line. Situated on the plateau at an altitude of 1,100 m, it is also known as *Kodakara-no-yu* (spa good for women wishing to have a baby). The water temperature ranges from 89–93℃.

Goshogake Spa: 1 hr.5 min. from Rikuchu-Hanawa Station by bus along the "Aspite Line," a toll road. It is known for the boiling masses of mud called *jigoku*, or hell, filling the sky with their sulfurous smoke. Nearby, a 2-km-long nature study trail passes by muddy volcanoes and hot-water swamps. The springs are 85–90℃.

Tamagawa Spa 7 : 1 hr.15 min. by bus from the JR Rikuchu-Hanawa Station. It boasts the greatest water output in the Tohoku District, and a hot-springs research center is located here. Situated in the western foothills of Mt. Yakeyama, the spa is often used as a base by mountain climbers. A trail runs by the spa town where one can see a giant cauldron bubbling forth 9,000 lit. of 99℃ water per minute, more than 100 vents emitting rumbling sounds and steam, and other magnificent scenery.

Yuze Spa 7 : 300 m west of the JR Yuze Station, along the Yone-shiro River. There is so much hot water here that it even gushes up from the bed of the river. Featuring good hotels and *ryokan*, Yuze Spa makes a convenient starting point for visiting Towada-Hachimantai National Park.

Mine Land Osarizawa: 30 min. by bus from Rikuchu-Hanawa Station. A ruin of the oldest mine in Japan, Osarizawa Mine, has been transformed into a sightseeing spot. A 1.8-km-long former gallery displaying electrically operated mannequins and old tools tells how mines in the Edo period operated.

Lake Tazawa and Vicinity 7

Lake Tazawa 7 : 1 hr.10 min. by limited express on the JR Tazawa-ko Line from Akita, getting off at Tazawako, with an additional 15-min. bus ride. With a depth of 423.4 m, this is the deepest lake in Japan. It has a circumference of 20 km and an area of 26 sq.km, and offers a good view of Mt. Komagatake. The best times to visit the area are in spring when the trees are sprouting new leaves and autumn when the leaves change colors.

Mt. Komagatake 7 : Alt. 1,637 m. A conoid volcano that erupted as recently as 1970 and towers over Lake Tazawa in the northeast. Although it is the largest mountain in Akita Prefecture, it is compara-tively easy to climb since a bus goes up to the eighth station. The summit is a treasure trove of alpine plants, with so many species growing here that it has been designated as a Natural Monument. The summit offers a fine view of the beautiful surroundings. Ta-zawako Ski Grounds are on the western face.

Tazawako Plateau: 40 min. by bus from Tazawako Station. This is a rugged plateau with an altitude of 700 m, including the northwest foothills of Mt. Komagatake. The view of Lake Tazawa from here is especially magnificent. The ski facilities here are set up for night skiing.

Kakunodate 7 : About 1 hr. from Akita or from Morioka by limited express on the JR Tazawako Line. Located in the northern part of the Yokote Basin, the beautiful town is sometimes called the "Little Kyoto of Tohoku." It was a castle town, first under the Ashina family and then under the Satakes. One can still see the rows of old houses of former *samurai* that have been designated as a historic district for their architectural value. Kakunodate has also long been famous for its beautiful cherry trees.

Southern Akita Prefecture

Yokote ☐7☐ ☎0182: Pop. 42,406. About 1 hr. from Akita by limited express on the JR Ou Main Line. From Ueno (Tokyo) it can be reached in 5 hrs. 20 min. by taking the JR Tohoku Shinkansen to Fukushima and transferring to a limited express on the JR Ou Main Line—a distance of 504 km. During the feudal period, this was also a castle town of the Satake Clan. Today, it is the region's cultural, economic and commercial center. Yokote is known for its heavy snowfall in winter.

Kamakura: An annual event unique to this snowy area occurs throughout the city of Yokote on Saturday and Sunday in the middle of February. On these two days, children build igloo-like snow huts called *kamakura* alongside the streets of the city. Inside, altars enshrining the god of water are set up, before which flowers and food are placed. Sitting around fires inside these snow huts, the children talk and play or treat passersby to *amazake*, a sweet, slightly alcoholic beverage made from rice. At night the lights of the fires are reflected in the snow, transforming the city into a veritable fairyland.

Yuzawa ☐7☐ ☎0183: Pop. 36,591. 1 hr. 20 min. from Akita by limited express on the JR Ou Main Line. From Ueno (Tokyo) it can be reached in 4 hrs. 57 min. by the JR Tohoku Shinkansen, with a transfer at Fukushima. Once a castle town of the Satake Clan, it is now known as a *sake*-producing center. The wood industry also flourishes here.

Inukko Matsuri (Dog Festival): Held on February 15-16. Children build small shrines of snow, placing *inukko* (puppy), crane and tortoise figures made of rice flour inside to prevent misfortune. Painted red or blue and glittering in the cradle light, these floury creatures create a scene of phenomenal beauty.

Mt. Chokai ☐7☐: Alt. 2,236 m. Towering over the border between Akita and Yamagata prefectures, the cone-shaped volcano is the main peak in the Chokai Volcano Chain. It has been designated as a quasi-national park. Since it is the most majestic mountain in the Tohoku District, it is called Dewa-Fuji or Akita-Fuji because of its resemblance to the original. The extensive view from the summit of Mt. Iwaki in the north takes in the Azuma and Asahi mountain chains to the south, Mt. Kurikoma to the east and Sado Island in the Japan Sea to the southwest. Kisagataguchi and Fukuraguchi in Yamagata Prefecture, located along the toll road called the Chokai Blue Line, are the bases for mountain climbing.

Area 4. Yamagata Prefecture

Yamagata 8/13-① ☎0236

Pop. 243,951. The capital of Yamagata Prefecture is situated in the southeastern part of the Yamagata Basin. It can be reached by plane from Tokyo in 55 min. or in 3 hrs. 10 min. by taking the JR Tohoku Shinkansen from Ueno (Tokyo) to Fukushima and transferring to a limited express on the JR Ou Main Line—a distance of 363 km. As the commercial and agricultural center of the region, Yamagata boasts a commercial district lined with modern buildings. Once the castle town of the Mogami family, the city still reveals traces of this past. Casting is the main industry, while fruit, cherries and grapes in particular, are the local speciality. This is the western gateway to Mt. Zao and an important transportation point, with buses leaving here for all sightseeing locations.

ANNUAL EVENT

Hanagasa Matsuri Festival: One of the four largest festivals in the Tohoku District. It is held from August 6-8. From dusk until about 10:00 p.m., large groups of people wearing brightly decorated coolie hats and *yukata* (cotton *kimono*) dance through the streets in a lively spectacle that attracts a large number of sightseers.

Refer to the supplement for details regarding the "i" **System Information Center** in Yamagata.

PLACES OF INTEREST

Kajo Park 13-① : 10 min. on foot from Yamagata Station. It was originally the site of Yamagata Castle—home of the Mogami family, but all that now remains are the moats and some stone walls. The park contains a baseball stadium, a variety of athletic fields, a prefectural museum and a public hall. The cherry blossoms are also famous.

Kaminoyama Spa 8 : About 15 min. from Yamagata Station on the JR Ou Main Line. The city of Kaminoyama was once the castle town of the Matsudaira family, but today it flourishes as the starting point for sightseeing trips to Mt. Zao. The many modern hotels and *ryokan* or Japanese-style inns make it easy to enjoy oneself. The "Zao Echo Line", a toll road, goes to Mt. Zao.

Tsukioka Park: 10 min. on foot from Kaminoyama Station. Situated on the site of the former Kaminoyama Castle, on a plateau, the park offers a nice view of the Zao mountain. The park contains a ferro-concrete castle reproduction constructed in 1982.

Risshakuji Temple 8 : Generally known as Yamadera, it is reached in 15 min. by rapid train on the JR Senzan Line or 45 min. by bus from Yamagata Station. Located in the northern part of Yamagata, this is the largest Tendai-sect temple in northern Japan and is believed to have been founded by the priest Ennin (794–864) in 860. The many temple buildings are scattered all over the mountain, linked together by steep stone steps. It takes 2–3 hours on foot to see all the temples.

Tendo 8 ☎0236: Pop. 56,556. 30 min. from Yamagata on the JR Ou Main Line. Situated just north of Yamagata, the city is famous for the production of *shogi* (Japanese chess) pieces. In fact, more than 90% of all the *shogi* pieces in Japan are made here. It is also known for the cultivation of cherries, grapes and many other kinds of fruit. Tendo Spa is 1 km east of Tendo Station in the middle of the rural district. It is one of the most prominent hot-springs resorts in Yamagata. Appropriate for hot springs in a *shogi* town, many signs on *ryokan* or Japanese-style inns and baths are shaped like *shogi* pieces and *shogi* can be played in the bath. Many other unique sights abound as well.

Higashine Spa 8 : 35 min. from Yamagata by local train on the JR Ou Main Line. The rustic atmosphere of the spa town stems from its rural setting. In the school yard of Higashine Elementary School near the spa is a 28-m-tall zelkova tree measuring 16 m at the base that is more than 1,000 years old. It has been designated as a Special Natural Monument.

Sagae 8 ☎0237: Pop. 42,369. 30 min. from Yamagata on the JR Aterazawa Line. The city lies 14 km northwest of Yamagata and receives a great deal of snow during the harsh winters. It has long been a place where *sake* and rice are produced and is known throughout the country as the No. 1 grower of cherries. Sagae Spa in the city serves as the gateway for the ascent of Mt. Gassan and the Asahi Mountain Chain.

Asahi Mountain Chain: Located along the border between Yamagata Prefecture and Niigata Prefecture. Mt. Oasahi (alt. 1,870 m) is the highest peak in the chain, which extends 60 km from north to south and 30 km from east to west. Ranging in height from 1,600–1,800 m, the peaks radiate outward from Mt. Oasahi. The slopes are gentle, but because the gorges are steep, it is called the Tohoku Alps. Alpine plants and squirrels, weasels, flying squirrels, monkeys, bears, antelopes and many other small animals have their habitat here.

Zao Quasi-National Park (Yamagata Area)

Mt. Zao 8 : At the center of the 400.89-sq.-km Zao Quasi-National Park. The peak is popular with mountain climbers and skiers. Mt. Zao is a congregation of volcanoes, including Mt. Kumanodake (alt. 1,840 m) as the highest. There are many sightseeing roads and ropeways or lifts that make ascent easy. The winter offers skiing and the beauty of ice frozen on trees, spring brings the beauty of new leaves, summer features mountain climbing and viewing alpine plants and autumn sets the mountain ablaze with the changing colors of the leaves. In short, Mt. Zao can be enjoyed anytime throughout the year.

The many spas around the foot of the mountain are attractive, too.

The four gateways to Mt. Zao are Yamagata Station and Kaminoyama Station on the JR Ou Main Line in Yamagata Prefecture, and Sendai Station and Shiroishi-Zao Station on the Tohoku Shinkansen in Miyagi Prefecture.

Zao Spa 8 : 40 min. by bus from Yamagata Station. It is a favorite haunt for skiers on nearby Mt. Zao. *Ryokan* or Japanese-style inns line the main streets of the town, while on the edge of the town is a large outdoor bath that accommodates 150 people at a time. The air of the spa town is filled with the smell of sulfur.

Zao Ski Ground: Known as one of the largest ski resorts in Japan, it is also famous for the beauty of the ice frozen on the trees. Located on the northwest face of Mt. Jizodake in the Zao mountains, the ski grounds consist of 11 slopes ranging in altitude from 850–1,700 m. Zao spa serves as a base for skiers and is well equipped with ropeways and lifts.

Zao Echo Line: A mountain road 26 km long. It crosses Mt. Kattadake and links Kaminoyama Spa in Yamagata Prefecture with Togatta Spa in Miyagi Prefecture. The highest point is on Katta Peak. On the Miyagi side (refer to p.347), it runs past rugged volcanoes, while on the Yamagata side it passes refreshing greenery and reveals the Asahi Mountain chain and Mt. Gassan as well.

Okama: A 330-m-in-diameter crater lake that is embraced by Mt. Kumano, Mt. Kattadake and Mt. Goshiki. Surrounded by rough walls formed through volcanic eruptions, the lake has deep, emerald-green water that creates a mystical atmosphere. The high alkaline content of the water, however, prevents anything from living in it.

Shinjo 8 ☎0233: Pop. 42,780. About 55 min. from Yamagata by limited express on the JR Ou Main Line. In the 17th century, Shinjo became the castle town of the Tozawa family and flourished as a key point in the Mogami River transportation system. Today, it is the industrial, economic and cultural center of northern Yamagata Prefecture and remains an important transportation point. Mogami Park, 15 min. on foot from Shinjo Station, is where Shinjo Castle once stood. The park contains the Tozawa and Gokoku shrines. City residents come here to relax.

Mogamikyo Gorge 8 : 25 min. by the JR local train from Shinjo to Furukuchi. The 16 km of the 229-km-long Mogami River that extends from Furukuchi to Kiyokawa is a ravine. With a cedar forest pressing against the water's edge, the river is broken up by numerous waterfalls. Since National Highway 47 runs along the river, one can see it from the car window. However, the best way to view the area is to take the excursion boat down the river. The excursion boat goes from Furukuchi to Kusanagi Spa in 1 hr.

Ginzan Spa 8 : A quiet mountain spa in the eastern part of Obanazawa (50 km north of Yamagata). It flourished during the Edo period as a production center for safflowers, a valuable ingredient in dyes and lip color. Three or four old-fashioned wooden inns, enfolded in steam, line both banks of the Ginzan River, which empties into the Mogami River. The snow-covered winter scene is truly magnificent.

Shonai Region and Dewa Sanzan (Three Mountains)

Sakata ⑧ ☎0234: Pop. 101,522. 4 hrs. 10 min. from Ueno (Tokyo) by taking the Joetsu Shinkansen to Niigata and transferring to a limited express on the JR Uetsu Main Line—a distance of 486 km. Situated at the mouth of the Mogami River, Sakata is the second-largest city in Yamagata prefecture. The port here originally developed as a distribution center for rice and commodities, including grain. Today, it has become a major industrial port handling chemicals, food and steel. Sakata not only ranks as the largest industrial city in Yamagata Prefecture, it is also a famous squid-fishing region.

Homma Museum of Art is 500 m northwest of Sakata Station. The mansion of the Homma family, famous for its wealth, has been opened to the public as a museum. Many rare books, antiques and pictures are on display. The house is enclosed by a beautiful garden called Kakumu-en in which stones and fountains have been artfully arranged. Situated on a hill overlooking the commercial district in Sakata and 10 min. from Sakata Station by bus, Hiyoriyama Park commands an extensive view of the Japan Sea and the surrounding area. Many monuments to renowned poets have been erected here and there, while a reproduction of a ship active during the Edo period sits on the pond.

Tobishima Island ⑧ : 2 hrs. by boat from Sakata Port. With several other islands grouped around it, the main island of Tobishima Honto is 40 km northwest of Sakata by sea. The black-tailed gulls on Honto are protected as a Natural Monument. The maze of caves formed by the constant pounding of the waves is a major scenic attraction.

Tsuruoka ⑧ ☎0235: Pop. 100,162. About 40 min. from Sakata by local train on the JR Uetsu Main Line. Formerly the castle town of the Sakai family, today it is a distribution center for the rice harvested in the area. The main industries of the city are agricultural equipment, silk textiles, canned foods, liquor (*sake*) brewing and glass.

Tsuruoka Park, in the center of the city was the site of Tsurugaoka Castle. Shonai Shrine, dedicated to the lords of the clan, stands amid pine and cedar trees. The park is a famous cherry-blossom site, with more than 400 trees growing here. Chido Museum to the west of the park, a onetime retreat for the lords, contains historical buildings and folk objects.

Yunohama Spa ⑧ : 40 min. by bus from Tsuruoka. Situated on the Shonai Beach along the Japan Sea, it includes many modern *ryokan* that boast the best facilities in the Shonai area. Ocean swimming, camping and golf can all be enjoyed nearby.

Atsumi Spa ⑧ : 6 min. by bus from Atsumi-Onsen Station on the JR

Uetsu Main Line. It is located at the foot of Mt. Atsumi, 2 km up from where the Atsumi River empties into the Japan Sea. The venerable spa is surrounded by an air of serenity. Visitors can enjoy the rich, local color of the early morning market near Kumano Shrine.

Mt. Gassan 〔8〕 : 1 hr.30 min. from Tsuruoka by bus, getting off at the eighth station on Mt. Gassan. From here, it is a 2-hr. hike to the top of the mountain, which has an altitude of 1,984 m. Mt. Gassan is the main peak of Dewa Sanzan, a chain of three sacred mountains extending southeast from Tsuruoka. The mountain is shaped like a sleeping cow, and since the snow stays on the ground until as late as July, off-season skiing can be enjoyed. Gassan Shrine, an ancient religious training ground, stand on the summit, which offers an extensive view of the Japan Sea and Mt. Chokai. Black lilies and many other alpine plants grow in abundance on Midagahara Plain by the eighth station.

Mt. Yudono 〔8〕 : 1 hr.20 min. by bus from Tsuruoka with an altitude of 1,504 m. Located to the southwest of Mt. Gassan, it is considered to be the inner shrine of the three sacred mountains of Dewa Sanzan.

Mt. Haguro 〔8〕 : 55 min. by bus from Tsuruoka with an altitude of 419 m. The lowest of the Dewa-Sanzan group, it is situated at the northern base of Mt. Gassan. The entire mountain is contained within the precincts of Dewa-Sanzan Shrine. A promenade of giant cedar trees continues for 2 km from the base to the top.

Yonezawa Area

Yonezawa 〔9〕 ☎0238: Pop. 93,009. 2 hrs. 30 min. from Ueno (Tokyo) on the JR Tohoku Shinkansen, transferring at Fukushima to a limited express on the JR Ou Main Line—a distance of 316 km. It is situated at the center of the Yonezawa Basin, to the west of the Ou Mountain Chain and in the southern part of Yamagata Prefecture. It was once the castle town of the Uesugi family, which ruled the area from 1601 to the Meiji Restoration in 1868. The most famous member of the family is Uesugi Kenshin (1530–1578), one of the most powerful lords of his day in Echigo Province (now, Niigata Prefecture). He is known historically for his one-on-one battle with Takeda Shingen (1521–1573), the famous lord of Kai Province (now, Yamanashi Prefecture).

Matsugasaki Park: 10 min. by bus from Yonezawa Station. The Uesugi family castle once stood here, but today only moats and stone walls remain. Uesugi Shrine in the park is dedicated to Uesugi Kenshin. Close by is Matsuzaki Shrine, dedicated to another illustrious member of the Uesugi family, Harunori (1751–1822), who established the silk-weaving industry in the city as part of a policy to bring prosperity to the province. This tradition continues today in the famous *Yonezawa-ori* silks.

Onogawa Spa 〔9〕 : 30 min. by bus from the JR Yonezawa Station. A tranquil, mountain hot-springs resort set against the hills and overlooking the Odaru River.

Shirabu Spa ⑨ : 50 min. by bus from the JR Yonezawa Station. Situated 900 m up the northern slope of Mt. Nishi-Azuma and along the Odaru River, it serves as a base for ascending Mt. Nishi-Azuma. There is a tropical botanical garden nearby.

Tengendai Plateau ⑨ : Situated 1,300 m up the face of Mt. Nishi-Azuma. It can be reached in 4 min. by ropeway from Shirabu Spa. This summer resort area is a good place for hiking. In winter, it is converted into a ski grounds, which can be enjoyed from early December to mid-May. The ski area is complete with lifts and ropetows.

Akayu Spa ⑧ : 5 min. by bus from the JR Akayu Station. This venerable spa town spreads out to the east of the station. Grapes and cherries are cultivated in the nearby Lake Hakuryu district, and picking grapes can be enjoyed when they are in season.

Area 5. Miyagi Prefecture

Sendai 8/10-11 ☎022

Pop. 878,632. The capital of Miyagi Prefecture is located in the southeastern part of the prefecture, facing the Pacific coast. Ranked as the largest city in the Tohoku District, it is the economic, cultural, and political center there. It can be reached from Ueno (Tokyo) on the JR Tohoku Shinkansen in 1 hr. 50 min., or 352 km. Sendai originally developed as the castle town of Date Masamune (1567-1636), who built his castle in 1600 on a plateau in the western part of the city. The city was nearly burned to the ground during World War II, but has been rebuilt and developed as a modern city with a well-planned network of roads, broad avenues and tall buildings. Also known as the "Forest Capital," the city is blessed with the greenery of trees luxuriantly blanketing the surrounding hills. Scenic spots such as Matsushima, Mt. Zao and Kinkazan Island are all located nearby.

HISTORY

Sendai is closely associated with the *daimyo* (feudal lord) of the district, Date Masamune. Regarded as the strongest *daimyo* in the Tohoku District during his day, he was trusted by Toyotomi Hideyoshi, who placed all the *daimyo* in the country under his rule as was also done by Tokugawa Ieyasu who, after Hideyoshi's death, established the shogunate in Edo (now, Tokyo). The fief that Masamune left at his death was the largest north of Edo. Masamune is also remembered in connection with Christianity. When the second Tokugawa Shogun, Hidetada, began persecuting Christian converts in the country, Masamune obtained the release of Franciscian padre F. Luis Sotelo (1574-1624) and tried to learn about the outside world from him, even giving Sotelo permission to preach Christianity in his territory.   Masamune also sent one of his retainers, Hasekura Tsunenaga, as his ambassador to Spain and Rome.

INDUSTRIES

Sendai is mainly a commercial and consumer center, but wholesale and financial dealings as well as other tertiary industries also thrive. The main industrial products are rubber, iron and steel as well as food, woodwork and electrical appliances. Besides the production of *sake* and beer, lacquerware is also important.   Traditional Date culture still flourishes in the crafting of objects from 5-million-year-old petrified trees called *Umoregi* as well as *Sendai-tansu*, chests decorated with elaborate ironwork and carved lacquerware called *tsuishu*.

TRANSPORTATION

Sendai is a relay station for the JR Tohoku Shinkansen and Tohoku Main Line. It is also serviced by the JR Joban Line for Ueno (Tokyo), Senzan Line for Yamagata, and the Senseki Line for Matsushima and Ishinomaki. The Sendai Airport is 40 min. by bus from the city, linking it with Sapporo, Nagoya, Komatsu, Osaka, Fukuoka and Okinawa. One can drive to Sendai directly from Tokyo on the Tohoku Expressway in about 5 hrs. 30 min.

Inner-City Transportation: Buses are available covering the city as well as nearby tourist areas.   A subway also runs under the city. Regular sightseeing buses (in Japanese only) not only circle the city, but they also offer routes to Matsushima , Ojika Peninsula, Kinkazan Island and Zao along the "Zao Echo Line".

ANNUAL EVENTS

Tanabata Matsuri (Star Festival): Held from August 6-8. The city's most famous festival is celebrated on an especially large scale. During the festival period, bamboo branches decorated with strips of colored paper, paper streamers and other glittering material of fanciful design are set up in front of every house. With shops along the main streets competing against each other in the lavishness of their displays, this colorful, gay spectacle invariably attracts large crowds of sightseers.

Donto Matsuri (Fire Festival): Held on January 14 at the Osaki Hachiman Shrine in the city. New Year's decorations are brought from all over the city and burnt to pray for the happiness and safety of the year.

Refer to the supplement for details regarding the "i" **System Information Center** in Sendai.

PLACES OF INTEREST

Former Site of Sendai Castle ⏹10 : 20 min. by bus from Sendai Station. It is located on top of a hill overlooking all of Sendai and the Pacific Ocean in the distance. Built in 1603 by Date Masamune, Sendai Castle (commonly called *Aobajo*, lit. Green-leaf Castle) was used as the residence of Masamune and his descendants for the next

270 years. The buildings were destroyed by fire so all that remains today are stone walls, earthworks, a reconstructed turret and moats. A statue of Masamune riding a horse stands on the former site of the donjon. The Sendai Municipal Museum in the park offers exhibits of data on the history of the Date Clan as well as displays of artworks and crafts.

Nishi Koen Park 10 : 2 km west of Sendai Station. The former residential quarters of the Date clansmen have been opened to the public as a park. The municipal auditorium, a library and an astronomical observatory also stand here.

Zuihoden Mausoleum 10 : Located to the east of the former site of *Aobajo* Castle on a hill overlooking the Hirose River. Zuihoden Mausoleum, the tomb of Lord Masamune, has stone steps leading to the entrance that are lined with massive cedars, recalling the grandeur of the Date family. Regarded as a fine example of ornate, Momoyama-style architecture, it was destroyed in 1945, but has been reconstructed.

Wild Flower Garden 10 : 18 min. by bus from Sendai Station. Called Yaso-en, this botanical garden covers 95,000 sq.m. Some 1,000 species of wild flowers decorate the garden with beautiful colors throughout the year.

Hasekura Tsunenaga's Tomb 10 : Near the JR Kita-Sendai Station on the precincts of Komyoji Temple. A small, five-story pagoda stands here together with a monument to the Catholic missionary, Sotelo, who accompanied Hasekura to Spain.

Hasekura Tsunenaga (1571-1622) was ordered by Masamune to visit various foreign countries on a tour of investigation. A small, deep-sea craft modeled after an English ship wrecked off the coast of Uraga was built for transport and named the Date-maru, which was the first Japanese-manned craft to cross the Pacific. Hasekura set sail on September 15, 1613, with a company of 150, arriving first at Luzon and then sailing across to Acapulco by January 25, 1614.

There, the party became the guests of the Spanish government and thus continued their voyage on a Spanish ship. Sailing from San Juan de Ulua on the east coast of Mexico in June 1614, Hasekura visited Cuba and proceeded to Seville, arriving in October of the same year. When the party arrived at Madrid in December, they were received by Philip III. In February 1615, Hasekura was baptized and received the Christian name of Philip Francisco. After being welcomed by the president of the Swiss Republic in Geneva, he made a ceremonial entry into Rome in October 1615. He and his retinue were received by Pope Paul V in November and were entertained as the Pope's guests.

Hasekura spent the next two years in southern Europe, observing the situation there before leaving Spain early in 1618 for Mexico with a letter from the Pope and a portrait of him. From Mexico the Japanese ship conveyed him to Luzon and finally back to Japan where he arrived in August 1620, having spent seven years carrying out his mission. A portrait of Hasekura wearing a cloak, hakama and two swords is preserved in the Vatican. Hasekura maintained his faith in

Christianity until his death.

Osaki Hachiman Shrine ☐10☐ : 15 min. by bus from Sendai Station. The main shrine, erected in 1607 by Date Masamune, is famed for its beauty, which is of such superior artistic merit that it has been designated as a National Treasure. Like Zuiganji Temple at Matsushima, the ornately decorated building is typical of Momoyama-period architecture.

Sakunami Spa ☐8☐ : 1 hr.10 min. by bus from Sendai Station. Set along the Hirose River, the spa is surrounded with pre-eminent natural beauty enhanced by the verdure of spring and the changing leaves of autumn. The waters are said to be efficacious against ailments of the digestive system. The spa is not only a favorite holiday resort for the people of Sendai—something like a home away from home, but *Kokeshi* dolls are also made here.

Akiu Spa ☐8☐ : 50 min. by bus from Sendai Station. Located on the upper reaches of the Natori River, the tranquil spa is surrounded by lush greenery. The waters are good for gastroenteric ailments. 14 km up the Natori River are the Akiu Great Falls, which plunge 55 m, stretching across 4.5 m. A 15-min. walk away from the spa is Rairaikyo Gorge, which is famed for the beauty of its fresh green leaves in spring and the colored ones in autumn.

Tagajo Castle ☐8☐ : 40 min. by bus from Sendai Station and a 5-min. walk from the bus stop. Located in Tagajo, a city established during the Nara period and flourishing as the heart of the Tohoku District, the castle was said to have been erected in 724. The outer walls, measuring 873 m from east to west and 1,090 m from north to south, contained inner fortifications of 105 m from east to west and 120 m from north to south.

Shiogama ☐8☐ ☎022: Pop. 62,076. 16 km northeast of Sendai. Located on the southwestern shore of Matsushima Bay, it is a picturesque spot overlooking the large and small islands in the bay. The third largest fishing port in Japan and active throughout the year, Shiogama Port is a base for excursions to Matsushima, with boat tours leaving from here.

Minato Matsuri (Port Festival): Held on August 5. More than 100 ships fill the port, with every ship decked out in multicolored streamers and banners. The pageant of these colorful ships circling Matsushima Bay for five hrs. is a magnificent spectacle.

Shiogama Shrine: 10 min. on foot from Hon-Shiogama Station on the JR Senseki Line. Standing on a summit thickly wooded with cedar groves, the shrine offers an excellent view of the sea. The shrine is very popular since the god enshrined here is closely related to salt, and protects seafarers and expectant mothers.

Matsushima ☐10-Ⓐ☐

The name, meaning "Pine Island," is derived from the many pine-covered islands in the bay. Matsushima is regarded as one of the three most famous scenic locations in Japan. The other two are Amanohasidate on the Japan Sea coast north of Kyoto and Miyajima Island in Hiroshima Bay. There are more than 260 islands of all sizes scattered about Matsushima Bay, offering an endless variety of scenic delights. Most of the islands were formed by the strata of volcanic tuff and some white sandstone, which is the most abundant type of stone found on the mainland. Some islands are mere pinnacles, others appear like battlements and some tower above the rest. Although many are uninhabited, some of these islands have caves, tunnels, and archways eroded by waves. Pine trees cling to the scanty soil in all sorts of fantastic positions. With the clusters of pine-clad islands harmonizing with the sea to create a breathtaking scene, the view is outstanding in any kind of weather—sunshine, rain or snow— and either at dawn or in the moonlight.

TRANSPORTATION

Matsushima has two bases for sightseeing: Hon-Shiogama (26 min. from Sendai Station) and Matsushima-Kaigan (Coast) Station (39 min. from Sendai Station) on the JR Senseki Line.

Excursion Boats: Departures from Shiogama Port (5 min. on foot from Hon-Shiogama Station) and Matsushima-Kaigan Wharf (3 min. on foot from Matsushima-Kaigan Station). Three different companies offer various courses, with the most popular tour leaving from Shiogama, circling Matsushima Bay and arriving at Matsushima Coast in 1 hr.

Sightseeing buses: Seven courses covering Sendai and Matsushima, all of which leave from Sendai Station.

How to Get Around: Take an excursion boat available from Shiogama that circles the harbor and arrives at the Matsushima Coast. From here, cross over to Fukuurajima Island and see Godaido Temple, Zuiganji Temple, Kanrantei Villa and the aquarium, then head toward Oshima Island. Continue on to Mt. Sokanzan and look over the bay. Return to the Matsushima Coast. Although one could also follow this same course in the opposite direction, this is the most common route. The three main sights—Kanrantei Villa, Godaido Temple and Zuiganji Temple—can be covered on foot in 1 hr.30 min.

PLACES OF INTEREST

There are four famous observation platforms from which the pine-clad islands of Matsushima can be seen from different angles: Mt. Otakamori in the east, Mt. Ogidani in the west, Mt. Tamonzan in the south and Mt. Tomiyama in the north. These points are celebrated as the "Four Great Views" of Matsushima.

Kanrantei Villa: 2 min. on foot from Matsushima-Kaigan Station. Situated on top of a rocky cliff immediately west of Matsushima-Kaigan Wharf, this tea-ceremony house was removed from Fushimi Castle in Kyoto and presented as a gift from Toyotomi Hideyoshi to Date Masamune at the end of the 16th century. The sliding doors are the work of Kano Sanraku (1559–1635), one of the foremost artists of his time. The garden contains the Matsushima Museum, which displays the military equipment and household effects of the Date family as well as shells and other local objects.

Godaido Temple: 5 min. on foot from Matsushima-Kaigan Station. Situated on a small, pine-cloaked islet north of Kanrantei Villa, it is accessible by two short bridges. The temple contains images of the five deities who conquer evil and lead to truth. The islet often appears in pictures as a symbol of Matsushima.

Zuiganji Temple: 5 min. on foot from Matsushima-Kaigan Station. Situated immediately west of Godaido Temple, it was founded in 828 and belongs to the Myoshinji school of the Rinzai sect of Buddhism. The present buildings were reconstructed in 1604 at the order of Date Masamune. *Chumon* Gate, *Onarimon* (Gate for the Emperor), the Main Hall, the residential building and the gallery are all excellent examples of Momoyama-style architecture and have been made National Treasures or Important Cultural Properties because of their artistic merit.

An avenue of cedars leads to the temple past many caves dug out of the rocks. These caves, some of which even have two floors, are said to have been used in former times by priests who sat here in religious meditation. Just inside the temple entrance to the left is Hosshin-Muso Cave, a large grotto that was used for meditation by priest Hosshin-Muso, who had traveled to Sung-Dynasty China in the 13th century.

The sliding doors in the Main Hall were painted by masters of the Kano school. The most beautiful and interesting room is the Peacock Room, which contains a wooden, seated statue of Masamune in armor. One eye is missing because he lost it as a result of the smallpox. There is also a wooden statue of Makabe Heishiro (Hosshin-Muso's name as a layman).

Mt. Ogidani ⌐10-Ⓐ⌐: 30 min. on foot from Matsushima-Kaigan Station. One of the four recommended places to see in Matsushima, it is located 400 m up the mountain off the west side of National Highway 45. From here, one can obtain a magnificent view of the islands scattered over the inland sea.

Mt. Sokanzan ⌐10-Ⓐ⌐: 15 min. on foot from Matsushima-Kaigan Station. It faces Mt. Ogidani across National Highway 45. From the summit, one can see everything from Mt. Otakamori to Shiogama and nearly all of Matsushima.

Oshima Island: Located 5 min. on foot southwest from Matsushima-Kaigan Station, this beautiful island with steep cliffs is connected to the mainland by Togetsukyo Bridge. Caves chiseled out of the rocks on the island contain carved Buddhist images and were once used by priests as retreats.

Fukuurajima Island: 15 min. on foot from Matsushima-Kaigan Station. Situated southeast of Godaido Temple, it is connected by the

252-m-long Fukuurabashi Bridge. The island has been turned into a natural botanical garden where camellia and 250 other species of plants grow wild. There is a promenade around the island that can be covered in 30 min.

Mt. Tomiyama 10-Ⓐ : 10 min. by train on the JR Senseki Line from Matsushima-Kaigan Station. It is a 30-min. walk from Rikuzen-Tomiyama Station. Mt. Tomiyama is one of the four best places to see Matsushima, with a view from the peak that is especially spectacular. The *Tomiyama-Kannon* (the Goddess of Mercy) is enshrined here.

Mt. Otakamori 10-Ⓐ : 1 hr. by boat from Matsushima-Kaigan or 1 hr. 10 min. by boat from Shiogama Port. The mountain is located on Miyato Island, the largest island in Matsushima. Of the four best places to see Matsushima, this is the only one that offers a complete, 360-degree view.

Mt. Tamonzan 10-Ⓐ : 30 min. by bus from Hon-Shiogama Station and an additional 10 min. on foot. Located on the northern edge of the Shichigahama Peninsula, it is another of the four best places to see Matsushima. Bishamondo Temple stands on the summit, which offers a splendid view of Matsushima Bay.

Ojika Peninsula and Kinkazan Island 8

The peninsula projects southeast into the Pacific from Mangoku-ura in Ishinomaki. The bay and cape have a jagged, ria-type coastline of unsurpassed beauty. The "Ojika Cobalt Line" toll road, which passes up the center of the peninsula, makes an excellent drive. Enoshima island, where black-tailed gulls wheel over the rocks, lies off the east coast, while Kinkazan Island is located off the very tip of the Peninsula.

Ishinomaki 8 ☎0225: Pop. 122,770. 55 min. by rapid train on the JR Senseki Line from Sendai. This flourishing port is at the mouth of the Kitakami River, which flows 249 km from north to south, making it the longest river in the Tohoku District and the fourth longest in Japan. Before the introduction of the railway, Ishinomaki was the only port available for shipping rice produced in the Sendai area. It was once the largest port on the Pacific coast in Tohoku and is still a key port for deep-sea and coastal fishing off of the Sanriku region. The main industries are marine products and paper production. It also serves as the gateway to Kinkazan Island.

The JR Ishinomaki Station is also the entrance to the Ojika Peninsula and the Minami(Southern)-Sanriku area, with sightseeing buses for the Minami-Sanriku-Kinkazan Quasi-National Park leaving from here.

Onagawa 8 : 25 min. from Ishinomaki Station on the JR Ishinomaki Line. Facing Onagawa Bay on the Ojika Peninsula, the town is another base for deep-sea and coastal fishing. Tohoku University has a marine laboratory here.

Kinkazan Island 8 : 2 hrs. from Ishinomaki Port or 30 min. from Onagawa Port by ferry. Ayukawa, which is accessible in 1 hr. 30 min. by bus from Ishinomaki Station, has a ferry to the island that takes 25 min. Located off the southern tip of Ojika Peninsula and separated only by the 1-km-wide Kinkazan Channel, an island is situated here, measuring 4 km from east to west and 5 km from north to south. Kinka translates literally to "Gold Flower," a name apparently suggested by the sparkling mica in the rocks of the island. Mt. Kinkazan (alt. 445 m) towers over the center of the island, which is densely wooded with the primeval forest left in its natural state. Wild deer, monkeys and many kinds of birds have their habitat here. Along with Mt. Osorezan and the Dewa-Sanzan mountains, it was once one of the three sacred places in the old Ou provinces (the present Tohoku District), with women prohibited from setting foot on the island.

Koganeyama Shrine: 15 min. on foot from Kinkazan Pier. Built on the western face of Mt. Kinkazan, the shrine is dedicated to the two Shinto deities of wealth and good fortune. A 2-km-long path leads from the rear of the shrine to the summit where the inner hall, Owadatsumi Shrine, stands. From here, the view is truly magnificent, with the Pacific Ocean disappearing into the horizon on the east, and Matsushima and the distant green mountains visible to the west.

The 54-m-tall Kinkazan Lighthouse stands on the southern coast of the island.

Kesennuma 8 ☎0226: Pop. 66,404. 1 hr.40 min. from Ichinoseki Station on the JR Ofunato Line. Together with Shiogama and Ishinomaki, it is one of the three largest fishing ports in Miyagi Prefecture. The city is situated on the shores of Kesennuma Bay, which is known for its beautiful seascape and as the base for sightseeing in the southern part of the Rikuchu Coast. It is also a junction for the JR Ofunato and Kesennuma lines.

Narugo Spas Area 8

This area includes all the spas scattered about the Arao River basin, including Kawatabi, Higashi(East)-Narugo, Narugo and Naka-yamadaira as well as spas in the Onikobe Spas Area such as Kamita-ki, Todoroki and Fukiage.

Narugo Spa 8 : About 1 hr.40 min. by local train on the JR Rikuu-To Line from Sendai to Narugo via Kogota or about 1 hr. from Furukawa on the JR Tohoku Shinkansen. Regarded as one of the three most famous spas in the Ou old provinces, this resort lies at the center of the Narugo Spas Area. The streets are filled with deluxe hotels and inns, gift shops and *kokeshi* doll factories—all wrapped in steam from the spa. The spa originated in 837 with an eruption of the Narugo volcano. With temperatures ranging 35–100℃, the mineral waters are good for rheumatism, female complaints and skin diseases. Ski grounds are located in the nearby mountains. It is also the home of Narugo *kokeshi* dolls. A 30-min. walk from the spa brings one to the entrance to Narugokyo Gorge where there is an exhibition hall called the Nihon Kokeshi-kan that contains nearly 5,000 *kokeshi* dolls.

Narugokyo Gorge: 2 km west of Narugo Station. The gorge extends 2.5 km from Otani Bridge to the entrance of Nakayamadaira Plateau. Both sides of the meandering promenade are lined with sheer cliffs and fantastically shaped rocks such as the "Screen Boulder" and the "Lion Boulder." Many come here to see the fresh greenery of spring or the bright colors of autumn.

Nakayamadaira Spa: 15 min. on foot from the JR Nakayamadaira Station. This resort is located at the western end of the Narugo Spas Area in the foothills of 420-m-high Mt. Kuromori beside the clear waters of the Otani River. It is a popular place to escape the summer heat or to enjoy the autumnal tints.

Higashi-Narugo Spa: Right next to the JR Higashi-Narugo Station. Once the resort of the lords of the Date Clan, the quiet spa along the Arao River consists of four different springs.

Fukiage Spa: 30 min. by bus from Narugo Station. Situated on the Fukiage Plateau, the spring is famous for the geyser here. Every 30 min. or so scalding water of more than 100℃ spurts several meters into the air accompanied by a loud, roaring sound.

Zao Quasi-National Park (Miyagi Area) 8-9

Shiroishi 9 ☎0224: Pop. 42,381. 2 hrs. 10 min. from Ueno (Tokyo) to Shiroishi-Zao on the JR Tohoku Shinkansen—a distance of 307 km. Situated between Fukushima and Sendai, the city spreads over the southern part of the Shiroishi Basin southeast of Mt. Zao. The former castle town has retained many vestiges of its past. The main products are Japanese-style paper and a thin noodle called *umen*. It serves as the southern entrance to Mt. Zao, with many buses leaving in the direction of the "Zao Echo Line."

Togatta Spa 8 : 50 min. by bus from the JR Shiroishi-Zao Station. Located in the eastern foothills of Mt. Zao, the spa offers an inspiring view of the imposing mountain. For folkcraft lovers, Togatta is the home of the Togatta kokeshi doll. Ski grounds are located nearby. An entrance to the Zao Echo Line is also here at the spa resort.

Aone Spa 8 : 1 hr. by bus from Shiroishi-Zao Station. This venerable spa is situated 5 km northwest of Togatta Spa on a plateau with an altitude of 500 m. The view that spreads out to the east includes the distant Pacific Ocean and Kinkazan Island.

Obara Spa 9 : 25 min. by bus from Shiroishi-Zao Station. It is situated on the gorge overlooking the upper reaches of the Shiroishi River, with inns lining the cliffs along the river banks. 5 km further up the river is a sheer, 2-km-long stretch of quartz trachyte cliffs called *Zaimoku Iwa* (Timber Rocks), which have been designated as a Natural Monument.

Kamasaki Spa ⑧ : 35 min. from Shiroishi-Zao Station by bus. The water here is efficacious against cuts, making this ancient spa famous for its curative properties. *Yajiro kokeshi*, one type of tradional *kokeshi* dolls, is produced nearby.

Area 6. Fukushima Prefecture

Fukushima 9/13-② ☎0245

Pop. 272,993. The capital of Fukushima Prefecture and can be reached in 1 hr. 40 min. from Ueno (Tokyo) on the Tohoku Shinkansen — a distance of 273 km. Fukushima is the political, economic, cultural and educational center as well as a major transportation point for the Tohoku District. Silk thread and textiles were once the only major industry, but after World War II the cultivation of peaches, apples, pears and other fruit has increased. Accordingly, the food processing industry is also thriving. Outside the city are many hot springs such as Iizaka, Tsuchiyu and Takayu that often serve as bases for the ascent of Mt. Azuma.

Fukushima Perfecture consists of three areas — Nakadori, Hamadori and Aizu, and Fukushima City is included in Nakadori Area.

Shinobuyama Park 13-② : North of Fukushima. Lying in the foothills of Mt. Shinobu, long known as a sacred mountain, the park is famous for cherry trees.

Mochizuri Kannon Temple: 20 min. by bus from Fukushima Station to Mochizuri Bus Stop with an additional 10-min. walk. The temple is famous for the Mochizuri Stone, which is featured in the traditional "Hyakunin-Isshu" (refer to p.32) card game. Composed of granite, it stands 3 m tall and 2 m across. In ancient times, flowers were placed on the stone and cloth was rubbed against the flowers to dye it. Legend has it that when green wheat stalks are rubbed against the stone, the figure of one's beloved appears.

Iizaka Spa ⑨ : 25 min. by Fukushima Kotsu Electric Railway or 30 min. by bus from Fukushima Station. It is 9.8 km north of Fukushima. Known as the largest spa resort in southern Tohoku, Iizaka is located along the Surikami River, a tributary of the Abukuma River, with many inns and hotels lining the banks and fronting on the river. The Anabara and Tennoji spas are located 2 km upstream from Iizaka Spa.

Nakadori Area

Mt. Ryozen ⑨ : 1 hr.10 min. by bus from Fukushima Station. Located about 20 km to the east of Fukushima, the 823-m-high mountain is famed as the former site of a fortress built by loyalist Kitabatake Akiie (1318–1338). The west side is covered with rock formations such as *Tengu* (goblin) Rock and *Fudo* (a fierce Buddhist deity) Rock scattered eerily about. From the summit, there is an imposing view of the Pacific to the east and Kinkazan Island to the northeast.

Nihommatsu ⑨ ☎0243: Pop. 35,120. About 20 km south of Fukushima. The Abukuma River flows to the east of the city, while Mt. Adatara towers to the west. Formerly a castle town, it is famous for its silk reeling, textile and timber industries.

Adatara Mountain Chain: A chain of volcanoes that extends 9 km from north to south in the Bandai-Asahi National Park. The main peak, Mt. Adatara (alt. 1,709 m), is surrounded by Mt. Kimen, Mt. Minowa, Mt. Tetsuzan and others. Mt. Bandai and Mt. Zao can be seen over the mountain ridge. Many people are attracted to the spas around the foothills, with Dake and Shiozawa spas often serving as gateways to the mountains.

Dake Spa: 25 min. by bus from Nihommatsu Station. It is located at an altitude of 570 m on the slope of the eastern foothills of Mt. Adatara. The spa lies amidst desolate surroundings, but ski grounds and a golf course are located nearby. It serves as one starting point for the ascent of the Adatara Mountain Chain. Okudake Spa is 30 min. by bus from here. The lift, which runs from early May to early October, takes one to within a 1-hr. 30-min. hike of the top of Mt. Adatara.

Hamadori Area

Iwaki ⑨ ☎0246: Pop. 357,844. The city faces the Pacific in the southeastern part of Fukushima Prefecture. With an area of 1,230 sq. km, it boasts the largest land area of any city in Japan. It takes about 2 hrs. 10 min. from Ueno (Tokyo) to Taira by limited express on the JR Joban Line—a distance of 216 km. The Taira district in the center of the city was once a famous coal-mining section, but the town has shed this part of its past and become a modern, commercial district with new educational facilities.

Yumoto Spa: 10 min. on foot from the JR Yumoto Station which can be reached in 2 hrs. by limited express from Ueno (Tokyo). The spa uses water that bubbled out during mining excavations. It is the best known of the many spa resorts along the Joban Line. 3 km inland is an enormous amusement center called the Spa Resort Hawaiians, which uses the abundant hot-spring water. Housed in a 6,600-sq.-m glass dome, the center features such lively shows as Tahitian dances as well as hula and flamenco throughout the day and well into the night. There is a hot-spring pool or bath for every taste.

Nakoso ⑨ : Located 189 km from Tokyo, the city is celebrated for the fortress barrier that once stood here to guard against invasion by northern tribes. Originally, the barrier was close to the shore, but changes in the elevation of the coast have resulted in the site now lying some distance inland. The barrier is located 2.2 km south of the JR Nakoso Station.

Soma ⑨ ☎0244: Pop. 39,478.   About 3 hrs. 40 min. from Ueno (Tokyo) by limited express on the JR Joban Line—a distance of 313 km.   It is the political and economic center of the area.   Once the castle town of the Soma family, it is now flourishing with business and agricultural enterprises.   Soma Port in the northern part of the city is developing into a modern industrial area.   The Matsukawaura Lagoon is located in the eastern part of town.   Called "Little Matsushima," the lake is long from north to south, with many beautiful, pine-covered islands lying in the middle.   It is also noted as a good nursery for seaweed and the source of tasty seafood.   Serving as the economic center of the region, Haramachi (pop. 48,985) ranks with Soma and is famed for its annual horse festival called *Nomaoi* (Wild Horse Chase).

Nomaoi: A festival from July 23–25 on a moor in the southern suburbs (10 min. by bus from Haranomachi Station on the JR Joban Line). The main attraction is the competition to catch shrine flags on the 24th.   Dressed in the *samurai* costumes of feudal days, the participants, all on horseback, gather for the ceremony at Hibarigahara. They vie until sunset for a shrine flag shot into the air with fireworks, with the first to get the flag winning a prize. On the 25th, the festivities move to nearby Kodaka Shrine, where some ten men dressed in *samurai* costumes chase bare-backed horses into an enclosure, while other men in white robes catch them with their bare-hands as an offering to God.

Aizu Area

Aizu-Wakamatsu ⑨ ☎0242: Pop. 117,415.   The central city in the Aizu area, located in the western part of Fukushima Prefecture towards the northeastern part of the Aizu Basin.   It takes about 2 hrs. 30 min. from Ueno (Tokyo) on the JR Tohoku Shinkansen, transferring at Koriyama to the JR Ban-etsu-Sai Line—a distance of 292 km. For 700 years Aizu-Wakamatsu was a castle town called Aizu.   Its strategic position made it the strongest castle in southern Tohoku District.   The land was granted to Hoshina Masayuki (1611–1672), son of the second Tokugawa Shogun, Hidetada.   During the Meiji Restoration of 1868, Aizu Clan stood in favor of the Tokugawa Shogunate and fought a fierce battle of resistance for nearly a month, but they were beaten in the end.

Aizu-Wakamatsu has been thriving as a business center in this area from feudal days, and many high-tech companies are developing here today.   Traditional specialties are lacquerware, wooden goods, *sake*, rice and persimmons.   The lacquerware produced here as *Aizu-nuri* is made in the same way as it was in the 17th century.   *Sake* brewing also flourishes, with more than 20 factories producing the rice wine in the city.   There are many historical relics to see and hot springs to relax in.   Regular sightseeing buses leave for the Bandai-Azuma region from here.

Tsurugajo Castle (Wakamatsu Castle) [9] : 15 min. by bus from Aizu-Wakamatsu Station. The castle was first built in 1384 by Ashina Naomori. After passing through various hands, it was destroyed (except for some stonewalls and moats) in the battle with the Imperial forces in 1868. The donjon now standing was reconstructed in 1965 and houses a museum. From the observation platform on the top floor, there is a good view of the city and the Higashiyama area.

Iimori Hill: 10 min. by bus from Aizu-Wakamatsu Station. Here lie the tombs of the *Byakkotai* (White Tiger Band), a group of youths aged 15–17 who swore to protect the castle with their lives from the Imperial troops in the conflict of 1868. When they saw flames rising from the castle, the 19 members realized that the castle had fallen into the hands of the enemy and hastened to carry out their vow by taking their own lives, although one of them was revived afterwards. Their 19 tombstones and those of 31 others who died in battle are located here. Almost 5,000 objects are on display in the nearby Byakkotai Memorial Hall.

Aizu Matsuri Festival is held from September 22–24. A colorful *samurai* procession parades through the streets of the city, recalling the historical events that occurred at Tsuruga Castle and Iimori Hill.

Oyaku-en Garden: A 17,000-sq.-m garden with ponds and streams, through which visitors may walk. It was redesigned at the order of the second lord of the Clan at the end of the 17th century. Previously, it was a medicinal garden from which the name is derived (*yaku*= medicine). Even today, there are some 300 species of medicinal plants growing here. There is a nice view of the mountains from the tea house here.

Aizu Samurai Residence: A reproduction of the 35-room residence of a leading retainer of the Aizu Clan. On the grounds are a magistrate's office, a rice refinery and other important buildings of the Aizu Clan.

Refer to the supplement for details regarding the "i" **System Information Center** in Aizu-Wakamatsu.

Higashiyama Spa [9] : 20 min. by bus from Aizu-Wakamatsu Station. The spa is set in the mountains along the Yukawa River about 5 km southeast of Aizu-Wakamatsu. It is the most popular hot-spring resort in this district, with *ryokan* or Japanese-style inns lining both sides of the Yukawa River and many bridges in between, imparting a unique atmosphere to the area. Mt. Seaburi, towering 823 m to the rear of the town, is a hill on top of a plateau that extends 6 km from north to south. On top is an observation platform with a superb view of Mt. Bandai and Lake Inawashiro.

Kitakata [9] ☎0241: Pop. 37,279. Situated in the northern part of the Aizu Basin. 20 min. by train from Aizu-Wakamatsu on the JR Ban-etsu-Sai Line. Sometimes called the "Kurashiki of Tohoku," this atmospheric town has long been known as a place where rice, *sake*, *miso*, soy sauce and other foodstuffs are produced, with many old-fashioned warehouses still standing in the city center. *Kitakata ramen* (Chinese noodles) is also famous.

Ashinomaki Spa 9 : 45 min. by bus from Aizu-Wakamatsu Station. Located about 16 km south of Aizu-Wakamatsu along the Okawa Gorge, this spa has a magnificent view. It lies at the center of the prefectural park, Okawa Rhine.

Enzoji Temple 9 : About 1 hr. from Aizu-Wakamatsu on the JR Tadami Line and 5 min. on foot after getting off at Aizu-Yanaizu Station. Established in 807, the temple has a main hall at the top of the approach of stone steps that is an ornate reconstruction dating from 1830. It contains a statue of *Fukuman-Kokuzo-Bosatsu*, one of the three most celebrated such images in Japan. The *Hadaka-Mairi* (lit. praying in the nude) Festival held here each January 7 is the most famous in the region and features young men dressed only in loin-cloths who struggle among themselves to be the first to climb a thick rope to the top.

Tadami 9 : 2 hrs. 40 min. from Aizu-Wakamatsu on the JR Tadami Line. The town is located along the upper reaches of the Tadami River on the western edge of Fukushima Prefecture. This is one of the snowiest regions in Japan, and 4 m of snowfall in one year is not unusual. The Tadami River begins at Oze Marsh in Nikko National Park and flows 137 km to Kitakata on the western edge of Fuku-shima Prefecture. Along the upper and middle portions of the river are numerous dams for some of Japan's leading hydroelectric plants.

Bandai Plateau and Azuma Mountain Chain 9

Included in the 1,895.82-sq.-km Bandai-Asahi National Park. The national park is composed of four sections: the Lake Inawashiro area; Mt. Bandai, the Iide Mountain Chain and the Asahi Mountain Chain; the Azuma Mountain Chain, and the Mt. Gassan, Mt. Haguro and Mt. Yudono area.

Mt. Bandai was created by an eruption of Ura (Backside)-Bandai. At the same time, Lake Hibara, Lake Akimoto, Goshikinuma Marshes, and many other lakes and marshes were created on the Bandai Plateau in an incredible array of natural beauty. The Iide Mountain Chain and Asahi Mountain Chain, sometimes called the "Tohoku Alps," also reveal the majesty of nature. The Azuma Mountains contain many active volcanoes offering a magnificent spectacle.

Inawashiro 9 : 40 min. on the JR rapid train from Koriyama. It is enclosed by Bandai-Azuma to the north and the Adatara mountains in the east, while the southern part of town faces Lake Inawashiro. It is a base for sightseeing in the Bandai-Azuma area.

Noguchi Hideyo Memorial Hall: 10 min. by bus from Inawashiro Station. It is a memorial to the great work of Noguchi Hideyo (1876 –1928) and the home he grew up in. Noguchi joined the Rockefeller Laboratory in New York and researched the causes of syphilis and rabies. He also discovered the parasite that causes yellow fever and is famous for supplying the blood serum for it. However, the doctor caught yellow fever himself and died in Africa in 1928.

Lake Inawashiro 9 : Located almost in the center of Fukushima Prefecture. The lake has an area of 103.9 sq.km and a circumference of 49 km, making it the fourth-largest freshwater lake in Japan. It lies on a 514-m-high plateau, with the north shore spreading open slightly and the mountains pressing right up against the banks. The waters of the Nibbashi River, which flow out from the northwest edge of the lake, are used for irrigation and hydroelectricity. The lake water is also carried to the Koriyama Basin via a series of canals to provide water for the entire region. Lake Inawashiro is believed to have been created when eruptions of the Bandai mountains spewed lava and ash, damming up small streams. The lake has only a few fish—crucian carp, carp, dace and similar types. Flocks of swans make their habitat here during winter.

Inawashiro Ski Resort: 20 min. by bus from Inawashiro Station on the JR Ban-etsu-Sai Line. The vast ski grounds are located on the southern face of Mt. Bandai at an altitude of 600 m. Everyone from the rawest beginner to the most advanced skier can enjoy rushing down the slopes with an excellent view of Lake Inawashiro below. Lifts are provided for the many skiers who come here.

Nakanosawa Spa: 30 min. by bus from Inawashiro Station. Lying on a 750-m-high plateau, this spa in the western foothills of the Adatara Mountain Chain has long been enjoyed by visitors. It serves as a base for skiing and climbing in the nearby Adatara mountains.

Numajiri Spa: On a plateau with an altitude of 880 m. It is located further back up in the mountains than Nakanosawa Spa.

Mt. Bandai 9 : The most famous peak in the Aizu region, towering over the Inawashiro Basin to the north. The south side reveals a beautiful volcanic-cone shape with a long base, but the north face is somewhat jagged from the pits and craters left by eruptions. The peaks include Mt. Dai (Great)-Bandai (the highest at 1,819 m), Mt. Akahani and Mt. Kushigamine. Bandai Plateau is in the northern foothills. The most interesting trail to the top is from Nekoma-Happodai on the Bandai Gold Line, which can be covered in about a 2 hr. -hike. There is another interesting route from the Inawashiro Ski Resort.

The eruption of Mt. Bandai on July 15, 1888, blew off the northern half of both Mt. Ko(Little)-Bandai and Mt. Kushigamine, causing great destruction. Before the eruption, there were several pools in a depression called Numanotaira that marked the site of the ancient crater. Sulfur was obtained from a small elevation in the middle. However, the entire depression was filled in and covered over with rocks from the 1888 eruption. It was preceded in the early morning by a terrific rumbling resembling distant thunder accompanied by a tremendous earthquake. This was followed by the eruption of

Ko-Bandai. A great column of black smoke rose from the peak and darkened the sky, while a "rainfall" of ashes blotted out the sun. More than 10 explosions occurred during the eruption, in the course of which the greater part of the peak was destroyed. Enormous amounts of matter were ejected, and tumbled down the slopes over some 70 sq.km, burying several villages along the way. Altogether, 461 people were killed. The finer particles such as silica, which were blown up by the explosions, were carried as far as the Pacific coast. These explosions were not accompanied by an ejection of lava, but were evidently caused by steam pressure generated underground. The catastrophe wrought a complete change in the topography of the area. The northern slopes, which had previously been covered with dense growths of trees and vegetation, were reduced to a barren desert of rocks and stones, while the damming of the Hibara and Nagase Rivers resulted in the formation of new lakes.

Bandai Kogen (Plateau) 9 : 30 min. by bus from the JR Inawashiro Station to Bandai-Kogen Bus Stop. The plateau, formed by the eruption of 1888, is located 800 m up the northern foothills of Mt. Bandai. There are more than 100 lakes and marshes of all sizes, including the three Bandai Lakes (Hibara, Akimoto and Onogawa) and the Goshikinuma Marshes. The area is known for the many wild birds found here. The center of the plateau forms the south shore of Lake Hibara near the Bandai-Kogen Bus Stop.

Lake Hibara 9 : Right next to the Bandai-Kogen Bus Stop. With a circumference of 38 km, it is the largest of the Bandai Plateau lakes. The rough, jagged shoreline and several islands lying in the middle create a picturesque scene. There are many camping grounds along the shore, while excursion boats leave from docks along the banks.

Lake Akimoto 9 : 20 min. by bus from Inawashiro Station. With a circumference of 12.5 km, the lake is elongated from east to west in the eastern part of the Bandai Plateau. Created by the eruption of 1888, Mt. Shirabu towers over the eastern sector where the autumn leaves are especially beautiful.

Lake Onogawa: 25 min. by bus from Inawashiro Station, with an additional 10-min. walk from Onogawako-iriguchi Bus Stop. Lying west of Lake Akimoto, this is the smallest of the three Bandai Lakes with a circumference of 8.3 km. The shoreline is rich in variety, while several small islands clad in green lie in the middle. The "Bandai-Azuma Lake Line", a sightseeing road that runs along the south bank, offers a nice view of the area.

Goshikinuma Marshes: 25 min. from Inawashiro Station by bus, getting off at Goshikinuma-iriguchi Bus Stop. The large and small marshes strewn about the hills between Lake Hibara and Lake Akimoto have been given the common name, Goshikinuma Marshes. The marshes contain waters of a variety of colors, including cobalt blue, emerald and orange, and they all lie tranquilly amidst the forest.

The largest marsh is Bishamonnuma (5 min. on foot from Goshikinuma-iriguchi Bus Stop) where the reflection of Mt. Bandai on the water is quite beautiful. Goshikinuma-iriguchi Bus Stop and Bandai-Kogen Bus Stop are connected by a scenic trail that makes a pleasant 1-hr. hike.

Bandai-Azuma Lake Line: A 13.1-km-long toll road that runs from Bandai Plateau along lakes Onogawa and Akimoto and connects with National Highway 115. Sanko (Three Lakes) Paradise along the way provides a view of the three Bandai lakes. Beautiful groves of larch grow alongside the highway.

Bandai Gold Line: A 17.6-km-long toll road that starts at Bandai Plateau and heads west to the southwest foothills of Mt. Bandai via Nekoma-Happodai Plateau. One of the gateways for ascending Mt. Bandai, Nekoma-Happodai is located at an altitude of 1,194 m, offering a magnificent view of Lake Inawashiro as well as the lakes and marshes of Ura-Bandai.

Tsuchiyu Pass: Located in the northern foothills of Mt. Adatara along the highway between Fukushima and Inawashiro. The rest house in the pass is known for its fine view of Mt. Bandai, Mt. Azuma and Mt. Adatara. Many bus routes such as the Fukushima Station – Bandai Plateau or Inawashiro routes go through the pass.

Tsuchiyu Spa ⑨ : 40 min. by bus from Fukushima Station. The spa is situated on the face of Mt. Azuma-Kofuji (Little Fuji) along the Arakawa River. Besides serving as a popular gateway to Bandai and Azuma, it is also the home of the *Tsuchiyu kokeshi* doll.

Azuma Mountain Chain: Part of the Bandai-Azuma National Park. The Azuma Mountain Chain extends from the western part of Fukushima Prefecture to the border of Yamagata Prefecture. The mountains are grouped into two volcanic zones: Higashi (East)-Azuma and Nishi (West)-Azuma. The Okura River runs between the two zones from north to south. The tallest peak in the Higashi-Azuma group is Mt. Higashi-Azuma (alt. 1,975 m), which forms a triangle with Mt. Issaikyo (alt. 1,949 m) and Mt. Azuma-Kofuji (alt. 1,705 m) with its beautiful conoid peak.

The Higashi-Azuma volcanic zone is still active, with major eruptions having occurred in 1893 and 1950. Although the upper portions of the peaks are largely bare of trees, in some places on the eastern slope a kind of rhododendron grows, while Yajidaira at the western foot is noted for its alpine plants. The principal peak in the Nishi-Azuma volcanic zone is Mt. Nishi-Azuma (alt. 2,035 m). Mt. Higashi-Daiten (alt. 1,928 m) rises to the east of this peak, while Mt. Nishi-Daiten (alt. 1,982 m) is on the west.

Mountain spas such as Nuruyu, Takayu and Goshiki lie scattered about the foot of the peaks in the Higashi-Azuma zone.

Bandai-Azuma Skyline: A 29-km-long toll road that goes from Takayu Spa on the northeastern face of Mt. Azuma-Kofuji to Tsuchiyu Pass along the Higashi-Azuma mountains, passing Jododaira near the top of Mt. Azuma-Kofuji en route. The scenery along the road varies, alternating between such contrasts as beautiful groves of beeches and bleak volcanic zones, but magnificent views can also be obtained.

Jododaira: 1 hr.10 min. from Fukushima Station or 1 hr.20 min. from Bandai-Kogen Station by bus. This flatland is located 1,580 m up the mountain and is enclosed by Mt. Issaikyo and Mt. Azuma-Kofuji. Mt. Issaikyo is covered with gravel from an eruption, resulting in a desolate scene. There is a rest house here, and the regular sightseeing bus makes a 30-min. rest stop here. From the Jododaira Bus Stop, it is a mere 10-min. walk to the top of Mt. Azuma-Kofuji. Mt. Issaikyo is a 2-hr. hike from the same place.

Takayu Spa: 40 min. by bus from Fukushima Station. Also called Shinobu-Takayu, the spa is located on the northeast face of Mt. Higashi-Azuma at an altitude of 750 m and offers a wonderful view of the entire Fukushima Plain. The Azuma Ski Grounds and a golf course are located nearby.

Nuruyu Spa: 25 min. by bus from Fukushima Station and an additional 35 min. by the inn's micro-bus. It is a secluded mountain spa on the eastern slope of Mt. Azuma-Kofuji at an altitude of 910 m, offering waters that are efficacious against eye ailments.

Koriyama ⑨ ☎0249: Pop. 305,689. 1 hr.20 min. from Ueno (Tokyo) on the JR Tohoku Shinkansen—a distance of 227 km. The city's location in central Fukushima Prefecture makes it an important transportation center. Sprawling over 729 sq.km, the city did not really begin to develop until the latter half of the 19th century when the water from Lake Inawashiro began being used for irrigation and hydroelectricity, allowing for the growth of significant textile and chemical industries. With offices of many of the largest companies located here, it is one of the leading commercial and industrial capitals in the prefecture.

Kaiseizan Park: 15 min. by bus from Koriyama Station. Located on a plain 3 km west of the station, the park centers around Lake Isuzu, with some 2,000 cherry trees growing along the banks. The baseball stadium and pool make it a favorite place for city residents to relax. The park also contains Kaiseizan Daijingu Shrine.

Bandai-Atami Spa ⑨: 20 min. on the JR Ban-etsu-Sai Line or 50 min. by bus from Koriyama Station. The spa is located in the foothills northwest of Koriyama, with hotels and inns lining the Gohyaku River (a tributary of the Abukuma River) and National Highway 49. 1 km up the river from the spa is the Gohyakugawa Ravine to which one can make a round trip on foot in just 30 min. to enjoy the verdure in spring or the bright colors in autumn.

Miharu ⑨: A small town in a valley 10 km northeast of Koriyama. Meaning "Three Springs," the name is derived from the abundant plum, cherry and peach trees that bloom in succession. The many old temples and storehouses here recall days gone by. It is also famous as the place where dolls and toy horses called *Miharu-goma* are made. More than 1,500 years old, the Miharu Waterfall Cherry tree on a hill 4 km south of the center of the city is a massive example of a drooping cherry tree, measuring 9.5 m around and 13 m tall. When in bloom, it is said to resemble a cherry blossom cascade—hence, the name. It is protected as a Natural Monument and is a major landmark in Miharu.

Abukuma Cave ⑨ : 50 min. from Koriyama to Kammata on the JR Ban-etsu-To Line. This stalactite grotto was discovered in 1969. The interior is a mixture of horizontal and vertical passageways in a three-dimensional layout. Entrance is permitted only as far as 600 m, a section that is equipped with lights, ladders and walkways. This incredible natural wonder was carved out of limestone by underground rivers over 60 million years ago.

Sukagawa ⑨ ☎0248: Pop. 60,485. 12 min. from Koriyama on the JR Tohoku Main Line. It is a major city of the Sukagawa Besin, which is situated along the middle of the Abukuma River in central Fukushima Prefecture. It is famous for the large peony garden—a 30-min. bus ride from the station. The garden covers an area of 100,000 sq. m and contains several hundred bushes that are over 200 years old. In all, there are some 290 species and 4,000 bushes. The roses, azaleas, irises and other flowers that grow here add a touch of different colors, revealing sensuous blooms for about a month starting from late April.

Shirakawa ⑨ ☎0248: Pop. 45,332. 1 hr.25 min. to Shin-Shirakawa from Ueno (Tokyo) on the JR Tohoku Shinkansen—a distance of 186 km. There is also a Shirakawa Station on the JR Tohoku Main Line, and at present, the city is centered around this station. Famed for the Shirakawa Barrier first established in the seventh century, the city served as the front door to the Tohoku District. The town developed along the Abukuma River. In the past, it was a castle town of the Komine family and later the Niwa and Matsudaira families, always fulfilling a central function in the region. Even today, Shirakawa Station is the hub of a bus network, and the city is also the center of southern Fukushima Prefecture. The city still has many landmarks and historical sites. The main industries are glass, embroidery and liquor brewing.

Former Site of Komine Castle ⑨ : 7 min. on foot from Shirakawa Station on the JR Tohoku Main Line. Constructed in 1340 as a strategic location for the Tohoku District, the castle was destroyed in fighting with the Imperial troops in 1868. Today, with only stone-walls and moats remaining, the site has been carefully preserved as Shiroyama Park.

Nanko Park ⑨ : 5 min. by bus from Shin-Shirakawa Station on the JR Tohoku Shinkansen. The park has a lake named Nanko (South Lake) with a circumference of 2.5 km that was originally built as an irrigation reservoir for feudal lord Matsudaira Sadanobu (1758-1824, refer to p.97). Cherry, plum, pine and other trees line the banks. Nanko Shrine standing in the northeastern part of the park is dedicated to Sadanobu, a patron of scholarship.

Kashi Kogen (Plateau) ⑨ : 45 min. by bus from Shirakawa Station. The northernmost plateau in Nikko National Park. Many primeval forest zones remain in the area, making it a treasure-trove of wild birds. It is popular as a place where one can enjoy oneself throughout the year by hiking, skiing or simply escaping the summer heat.

Kashi Spa ⑨ : There is only one *ryokan* or Japanese-style inn at this hot spring in the upper reaches of the Abukuma River. The waters are 45℃ and effective against healing skin diseases, rheumatism and nervous ailments. Located 4 km west of the Kashi-Kogen Bus Stop, it can be reached on foot in 1 hr, but the inn will pick up travelers with a micro bus.

Shin (New)-Kashi Spa: 45 min. by bus from Shirakawa Station. It is situated at an altitude of 800 m in the foothills of Mt. Kashi. The spa waters are taken from the abundant flow at Kashi Spa. The tranquil inns are surrounded by primeval beech groves, with golf courses and ski slopes located nearby.

Section III. East Central Honshu
(Kanto District)

Honshu is the largest of the four main islands of Japan. The east central part contains eleven different prefectures as well as Tokyo at the center of the Pacific coast, the international port of Yokohama, the ancient capital of Kamakura in Kanagawa Prefecture, Mt. Fuji in Shizuoka and Yamanashi prefectures, Nikko in Tochigi Prefecture and Japan's biggest rice producing area—Niigata Prefecture—on the Japan Sea. Each of them is blessed with its own particular cultural tradition and natural scenery.

The heart of east central Honshu is the Kanto District, the most active area in Japan. It contains Tokyo, the capital of Japan, where national administrative organizations and Japan's most prominent corporations are highly concentrated. It also includes the following six prefectures: Kanagawa, Chiba, Saitama, Gumma, Tochigi and Ibaraki, each of which is closely related to Tokyo in a variety of ways.

The Kanto Plain, the most extensive flatland in Japan, is located in the center of the Kanto District. It is bordered by mountain ranges on the north and west, and by the Pacific Ocean on the east and south. The Kanto Plain is intersected by a number of fairly long rivers, including the Nakagawa River, Tone River, Arakawa River, Tama River and Sagami River, all of which empty into the Pacific Ocean or Tokyo Bay.

With Tokyo Bay as the southern border, the Kanto Plain is elongated between the embrace of the Boso and Miura peninsulas. Tokyo Port is located at the innermost part of the bay, Yokohama Port is at the center of the west shore and Yokosuka Port is on the west shore at the mouth of the bay. The Izu Island Chain dots the southern offing of the bay like stepping stones, while the Ogasawara Island Chain lies even further south. All of these islands are under the administration of the Tokyo Metropolitan Government.

The Kanto District began its development somewhat later than the Kyushu and Kinki (Nara, Kyoto, Osaka) areas, starting in the latter half of the 12th century. With the establishment of the Tokugawa Shogunate in Edo (now, Tokyo) in 1603, construction of a network of roads and reclamation works progressed rapidly, eventually resulting in the most densely populated area in Japan.

Today, Tokyo has grown to prominence on a global scale, both in terms of size and international influence, and this prosperity has naturally affected the Kanto District and the entire East Central Honshu region as well. Each area is tied to Tokyo with a extensive network of expressways and railways.

Area 1. Tokyo and Vicinity

Tokyo is a gigantic city that sprawls over an area of 2,166.26 sq. km and has a population of 11,654,574. It stretches within a narrow range of 80 km from east to west. Twenty-three *ku* (wards) covering the old city area occupy the east end. The old city area contains many historical remains, the most conspicuous of which are the ancient walls, gates and moats of the Imperial Palace (the former Edo Castle).

The city, a unique amalgamation of the tranquil past and the boisterous present, has in the past 30 years become steadily bigger, busier and more crowded. Larger, higher and more stylish buildings have mushroomed, completely changing the skyline as well as the appearance of the streets.

Tokyo is the center of national administration, education, culture and economy as well as a thriving industrial city. As an international city, it ranks foremost in Asia, and most nations have diplomatic envoys here. Tokyo also has far more foreign businesses than any other city in Japan. There are 217,295 residents (based on June 1990 findings) of other nationalities in Tokyo, most of whom are business-men. It is regularly selected as a location for international confer-ences and since it is representative of Japan, Tokyo is popular as a center for tourism. The number of visitors to Japan has been steadily increasing, reaching 2,985,764 in 1989. Few of these visitors bypass Tokyo on their trips.

The capital of Japan is the city where East and West blend most harmoniously. The modern conveniences, to say nothing of the modern transportation network, allow visitors to Tokyo to relax. The transportation network extends from the center of Tokyo to many local areas. The services and facilities offered at the hotels measure up to the highest world standards. On the other hand, since Tokyo was the cultural center of Japan for nearly three centuries during the Edo period (1603-1867), it has maintained many cultural assets of bygone days such as *kabuki* and *noh* drama, *sumo*, pictur-esque gardens, culinary delights and colorful festivals, to cite only a few.

HISTORY

Tokyo was formerly called Edo. For 265 years, it served as the base for the Tokugawa Shogunate, but when it toppled and was replaced with the Emperor in the Meiji Restoration of 1868, the capital was moved here from Kyoto and renamed Tokyo (lit. Eastern Capital). The name was selected in contradistinction to Kyoto, also known as Saikyo (lit. Western Capital).

In Kyoto the attendants of the Emperor, many of whom were aristocrats related by marriage to the Imperial Family, held the real administrative power and flourished culturally during the Heian period (794–1185). On the other hand, the Tokyo area was merely countryside. There was a local administrative office in what is now Fuchu City, but the area around it was sparsely inhabited. Other than the areas reclaimed as manors for the aristocracy, however, the vast majority of land was rough wilderness.

When government by aristocracy began to crumble, the local *samurai* clans gained power. The Taira, one of these clans, eventually took control of the government. The powerful families in Kanto held their ground and transformed themselves into *samurai* clans. Early in the 12th century, an affiliate of a powerful family from Chichibu (a mountainous region in western Saitama Prefecture) constructed a small castle in a corner of the plateau where the Imperial Palace now stands. The lord named himself after the area, Edo, and the castle became a small controlling power in the region.

National power was finally snatched away from the Tairas by the Minamoto Clan in 1185. Minamoto-no-Yoritomo, the chief of the clan, established the shogunate in Kamakura in 1192. The Edo Clan continued on as local authorities, but in 1457 Ota Dokan, a high-ranking retainer of Uesugi Sadamasa (a major figure in the Kamakura Shogunate Government), came into possession of the area and had a full-scale castle built. This is said to have been the beginning of Tokyo.

In the 400 or so years since the end of the Heian period, there were short lulls of peace, but in general it was a period of infighting between *samurai* clans, with the management and ownership of Edo changing hands frequently. The first man to unify the entire country was Toyotomi Hideyoshi (1536–1598) in 1590. At this time, Hideyoshi gave one of his senior statesmen, Tokugawa Ieyasu (1542–1616), the eight provinces of Kanto in exchange for his former domain Mikawa and Suruga provinces (now, eastern Aichi Prefecture and central and western Shizuoka Prefecture). Ieyasu selected Edo as his base from which to rule, restored the dilapidated castle and promoted the growth of the castle town. Nominally, Ieyasu was just one of many lords under Hideyoshi, but in reality he was already then nearly as powerful as Hideyoshi.

After Hideyoshi's death, the lords divided into two opposing factions—the Toyotomi faction and the Tokugawa faction. The Tokugawa faction was able to grasp the leadership in the power struggle, and Ieyasu established the shogunate in Edo, receiving the title of *shogun* from the Emperor in 1603. Kyoto continued to be called the capital, but in actuality the capital was now Edo. The aristocracy lost the power it used to have so that the role of the Imperial Court was restricted only to automatically confirming each successive generation of the Tokugawa family as *shogun*, conferring an honorary position on members of the *shogun's* family or *daimyo* (landed feudal lords subordinate to the *shogun*) and holding traditional Imperial Court events.

The city of Edo grew by leaps and bounds. Shops lined the streets in the center of town, giving birth to the unique merchant culture exemplified by *kabuki* and *ukiyo-e*. In 1731 the population numbered more than 562,000. By 1787 this had swollen to 1,368,000, making it the largest city in the world during the 18th century.

One of the fundamental policies of the Tokugawa Shogunate was isolationism, but in June 1853 Admiral Matthew Perry's ships from America arrived at Uraga (eastern end of the Miura Peninsula, Kanagawa Prefecture) and broke up this conservative tradition. This became a catalyst for anti-Tokugawa groups in Kyoto and other western districts in Japan, bringing the groups that had been fomenting discontent against the Shogunate to the surface. By 1868 Tokugawa Shogun had abandoned the reins of power, and the Meiji Restoration Government was established in its place.

Edo was renamed Tokyo and Edo Castle was taken over by the Emperor. The surrounding villages were incorporated into the former castle town, and the nation's capital, Tokyo Prefecture, was born. In 1888 the City of Tokyo was inaugurated, with 15 *ku* (wards) centered around the old city, while Tokyo Prefecture consisted of one city and six counties. In 1893 three counties were incorporated from Kanagawa Prefecture, thus setting the present limits of Tokyo City. The population at the time was 1.8 million (1.27 million in the central wards alone.)

A factory town was formed in the region east of the Sumida River as well as a commercial center to the west, while even further along the shores of the bay up to Kawasaki City in Kanagawa Prefecture a modern, large-scale industrial zone quickly sprang up. After much of the center of the city was destroyed by a huge earthquake in 1923, a totally new city was born. The rural communities had become impoverished, while the city area was flourishing economically, resulting in a massive influx of people to Tokyo City and a mushrooming population. By 1932 the population had reached 5.88 million, and in 1941 when World War II had reared its ugly head it was 6.78 million. During the middle of the war in 1943, Tokyo City and Tokyo Prefecture were unified to become the new Tokyo Metropolis, but much of the ward section (old Tokyo City) was destroyed or burned down during World War II from air raids, which also caused many deaths. When the war ended in 1945, the population had shrunk dramatically to 2.78 million.

Tokyo's revival after the war was nothing less than remarkable. The streets were soon cleared and new buildings erected, and within ten years the final vestiges of war damage had disappeared. Activity increased in manufacturing, distribution of goods, services, education, culture and all other areas as the population began to explode again. In 1964 the 18th Olympic Games were held in Tokyo, and to Japan this was proof to the world that the city had completed her recovery from war-time devastation.

The so-called "growth-intensive" economics in Japan began in 1960, with the activization and expansion of Tokyo following soon thereafter. The population passed 10 million in 1962, and the city budget surpassed ¥1 trillion in 1969. Today, the rapid growth of high-tech industries and a healthy trade surplus have turned Tokyo into a financial and economic center equivalent to New York that operates 24 hrs. a day. This situation is reflected in tourism, which decreased slightly due to the high *yen* but is now increasing again. In 1989, there were 2.99 million visitors from abroad (up 24% from the previous year) and 805,000 business-related visits (up 20%).

As a result of the high concentration of governmental organizations, private enterprises and universities in the metropolitan area, Tokyo has grown at an excessive pace. This has led to congested traffic with insufficient office and construction space, skyrocketing land and rental costs, relocation of residential areas farther and farther away from the city and intense discomfort for commuters. In order to solve some of these problems, Shinjuku has been developed as a new business district with its cluster of super-skyscrapers, including the new Tokyo Metropolitan Government Office scheduled to open in 1991, while businesses and universities are moving or planning to move their main quarters to the suburbs and other prefectures. Relocation of national administrative offices is under serious consideration as well, with some having already moved. However, even this is not enough. In fact, it might be more realistic to say that the city is just managing to keep up with the rapidly deteriorating situation. Recently, effective waterfront development centered on the reclamation of land from the sea in the bay area has created some hope. In short, the Tokyo of today is a combination of the dreams of tomorrow and the difficulties of the present.

GOVERNMENT

The Tokyo Metropolis, governed by an elected governor along with the 128 members of the Tokyo Metropolitan Assembly, is comprised of 23 *ku* (wards), 26 cities, seven towns and eight villages. Two of the towns and seven of the villages are located on the Seven Isles of Izu and Ogasawara Islands. The 23 wards cover a total area of 599.73 sq.km.

The 26 cities are all concentrated in the western portion. Some have factories of large companies, others offer a variety of universities, while still others are concentrating their efforts on attracting tourism. Still, what they all have in common is that they serve as bedroom communities for commuters to Tokyo. This is a result of the burgeoning population of the 23 wards and skyrocketing land prices, which have pushed the residential areas further outside the city proper. This has also affected the five towns and one village in western Tokyo, with many people even locating their homes in neighboring prefectures.

CLIMATE

Tokyo is a year-round tourist mecca. Each season has its own attractions. Spring, known for the beautiful cherry blossoms, and autumn with its good weather are considered the ideal times to visit Tokyo. The summer in Tokyo is hot and humid, while the winter can be fairly cold with a very occasional snowfall. But in general the climate of Tokyo is mild throughout the year.

Climate of Tokyo: Averages for 1951-1980

	Jan.	Feb.	Mar.	Apr.	May	Jun.	Jul.	Aug.	Sep.	Oct.	Nov.	Dec.	Av.
Average Temperature °C	4.7	5.4	8.4	13.9	18.4	21.5	25.2	26.7	22.9	17.3	12.3	7.4	15.3
Average Precipitation mm	54	63	102	128	148	181	125	137	193	181	93	56	146

TRANSPORTATION FROM THE AIRPORT

All international flights arrive at the New Tokyo International Airport (Narita), except those of China Airlines. Their flights land at the Tokyo International Airport (Haneda). Both airports offer a variety of transportation facilities to the city center.

From New Tokyo International Airpot (Narita)

Buses: A limousine bus runs to the Tokyo City Air Terminal (TCAT), taking 70-90 min. It is 15-20 min. from there to Tokyo Station (additional fare required). There are also buses directly to the JR Tokyo Station, Ginza/Shiba, Shinagawa, Akasaka, Shinjuku and Ikebukuro. Except for the bus to TCAT or Tokyo Station, they stop in front of major hotels in each of these areas. It takes about 1 hr.40 min. to Ginza/Shiba and Shinagawa and 2 hrs. to the other locations.

Taxis: About 60-90 min. to the city center via the expressway. Fare will be about 7 or 8 times that of the limousine bus (including tolls).

Keisei Electric Railway: The Skyliner (limited-express train) runs from Narita-Kuko (Airport) Station to Keisei-Ueno Station in 1 hr. and the regular limited express in 1 hr.15 min. A special fare is required for the Skyliner. Keisei-Ueno Station is close to the JR Ueno Station, only a couple of minutes on foot.

JR Railways: JR runs buses from Narita Airport to the JR Narita Station (25 min), from which trains leave for Tokyo and Ueno. A rapid train on the Sobu Main Line will arrive at Tokyo Station in 1 hr.20 min. and the limited express in 1 hr.

From Tokyo International Airport (Haneda)

Buses: Limousine buses run to Shinjuku and Akasaka, stopping at major hotels in each area. It takes about 1 hr. to Shinjuku and 50 min. to Akasaka.

Monorail: The monorail takes about 15 min. from Haneda Airport to Hamamatsucho Monorail Station. At Hamamatsucho Station, one can transfer to the JR Yamanote or Keihin-Tohoku Line.

Taxis: About 30 min. to the city center from Haneda Airport. A cab is also available from Hamamatsucho Station.

INTRA-CITY TRANSPORTATION

The fastest, most convenient and most economical method of transportation is by train, both railway and subway. The subways of Tokyo (and all of Japan, where available) are well lighted, clean and safe.

How to buy a ticket: Automatic ticket-vending machines are located near the ticket gate at railway and subway stations. A station map with the fare for each destination is hung directly above the vending machines. If one cannot read the Japanese characters on the map, it is best to purchase the cheapest ticket and pay the additional fare, if need be, at the destination station. There are ticket vending machines that take ¥1,000 bills and ¥500 coins, but most of them require ¥100, ¥50, or ¥10 coins. Place the coins in the machine and push the button indicating the correct fare. The ticket will appear in the receptacle at the bottom along with any necessary change.

A ticket should be bought before getting on the train each time and handed to the man at the gate when getting off. If one loses the ticket while riding or decides to go some place farther than the original destination, go to the fare-adjustment window (or to the ticket gate if there is none). One must pay any additional fare for the greater distance, but no part of the fare is returned if one gets off closer. When one transfers to a line run by a different company, you must buy another ticket at the transfer station. To overcome this inconvenience, there are some automatic vending machines that sell through tickets.

Special Discount Tickets in the Tokyo Area

● One-day train pass

The holder of this pass is eligible for unlimited travel for one day on all JR lines within the boundaries of the map below.

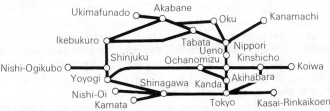

● One-day subway pass

This pass allows unlimited travel for one day on all Eidan Subway Lines. See map page 23.

● Tokyo Free Pass

This one-day free pass entitles the holder to free passage on JR (within the range of One-day train pass), Eidan Subway, Toei (municipal) Subway, Toden (municipal tram) and Toei buses (excluding double-decker buses between Ueno and Asakusa)

Rush Hours: On weekdays from 7 a.m. to 9 a.m. and 5 p.m. to 7 p.m. At these times, the city's trains, subways and buses are so packed with commuters and students that it is sometimes all but impossible to get on. It is best to avoid these hours if possible. Taxis are available, but the roads are often just as crowded.

JR Railways: There are a total of 15 lines managed by JR in the city, but for most sightseeing jaunts, one will only need to use four of these —Yamanote, Chuo, Sobu and Keihin-Tohoku lines. The cars of each line are painted with a color that represents that line.

Other Railways: Many other railways run from main stations on the JR Yamanote Line to other areas, even extending to other prefectures. There are seven companies other than JR that manage railway lines: Tokyu Line, Odakyu Electric Railway (Odakyu Line), Keio-Teito Electric Railway (Keio Line), Seibu Railway (Seibu Line), Tobu Railway (Tobu Line), Keisei Electric Railway (Keisei Line) and Keihin Electric Express Railway (Keikyu Line). Most of them connect residential areas to the city for commuters and students. However, there are also some famous sightseeing locations along these lines. For example, the Odakyu Line, which leaves from Shinjuku, offers Odawara, Hakone and Enoshima, while Chichibu is located along the Seibu-Ikebukuro Line, departing from Ikebukuro. There is no JR station in Asakusa, but the Tobu Nikko Line leaves from here for Nikko.

Subways: Tokyo has an extensive subway network connecting most inner districts and sub-centers. It is fast, clean and safe, and possibly the most convenient and economical way of getting around Tokyo. The Teito Rapid Transit Authority operates seven lines (called "Eidan" Line) and the Metropolitan Government operates three lines (called "Toei" Line). As many as two to five lines intersect at the main stations, and since one can freely change lines, Eidan to Eidan and Toei to Toei, it is possible to go to the station that is closest to one's destination. They come at 3-7 min. -intervals. Each line is symbolized by a color and the trains themselves are marked with it. Circles of each color are also used to indicate the direction for transfering to another line, and subway maps are indicated with these colors. The subway maps printed in the guides of Tokyo (available at hotels and JNTO Tourist Information Centers) also use the same colors to make them easy to understand.

Buses: Though there is a dense network of buses covering the city, bad traffic conditions usually slow them down, and the routes are complicated; thus, they are not really recommended for tourists.

Taxis: There are many taxis found cruising the streets and lined up in front of hotels and main stations waiting for customers. Most taxis in Tokyo are medium-sized, four-to five-passenger cars, and the rear doors are opened automatically by the driver. The fare meter is attached to the front dashboard where the customer can see it. Since fares are calculated by both time and distance, if one asks the cab to wait, it can be quite expensive. After 11 p.m., the fare increases by 30%. As of August 1990, the basic fare is ¥540 for the first 2 km and ¥80–90 for each additional 355 m. No tipping is required. In Tokyo it becomes very difficult to catch a cab after 11 p.m.

TRAVEL ADVICE

Here is some information useful for arranging a sightseeing plan if one has only a limited amount of time.

Historical Structures and Old Shrines and Temples: Some of the most popular sights with tourists are the Imperial Palace (formerly Edo Castle), the Akasaka Detached Palace and the National Diet Building. Although not a historical structure, Tokyo Tower is also a famous landmark. Some of the more famous old shrines and temples include Asakusa-Kannon (Sensoji) Temple, Ueno Toshogu Shrine, Meiji Shrine and Zojoji Temple. The Asakusa-Kannon Temple is especially well known.

Historical Japanese Gardens: The Imperial Palace East Garden, Rikugi-en Garden and the Hama Rikyu Garden are popular. The Suijo Bus (a regular excursion boat along the Sumida River) calls at the Hama Rikyu Garden. Shinjuku Gyoen Garden, where the funeral service of Emperor Showa was held, is an exquisite example of the perfectly harmonious blending of Japanese and Western styles.

Fine Arts and Performing Arts: *Kabuki* is regularly performed at the Kabukiza Theater and the National Theater. The regular sight-seeing bus "Kabuki Night Tour" includes English explanations over earphones during the performance. The National Noh Theater is one of seven *noh* theaters giving regular performances. The historical development of the fine arts and crafts can be seen at the Tokyo National Museum. Other interesting museums include the Ota Memorial Museum of Art (*ukiyo-e*), the Nezu Institute of Fine Arts (ancient Chinese and Japanese art), the Japan Folk Crafts Museum, Pentax Gallery (photography) and the Japanese Sword Museum.

Amusement Parks and Zoos: Tokyo Disneyland is first on the list of popularity. The most famous zoos are Ueno Zoo, Tama Zoological Park and the Sunshine International Aquarium.

Popular Entertainment Areas: Ginza is refined and sophisticated. Shinjuku, Shibuya and Ikebukuro bustle unpretentiously; Akasaka, Roppongi and Harajuku are chic, and Ueno and Asakusa retain a plebeian feel.

Shopping: The popular entertainment areas are also shopping areas. However, low prices for electric goods can be found in Akihabara; cameras and watches at Shinjuku and Ikebukuro, and clothing in Yokoyamacho. Brand-new products are sold 20–30% below normal market price. Ueno *Ameya-yokocho* (Abbr. *Ameyoko*) is also famous for its low prices of food, watches, apparel and imported items. Kanda, the student district (sometimes called Japan's "Latin Quarter"), is known as a bookstore (especially used books) district. However, in recent years, the streets have become crowded with ski, tennis and other sports-goods discount shops. In addition to these, many department stores are scattered through the downtown Tokyo areas. Although the price is not necessarily low compared with the above-mentioned discount shops, they offer a wide variety of goods with good quality.

Antique Markets

Togo Shrine: Held on the first and fourth Sundays of the month but canceled in case of rain. Near Harajuku Station on the JR Yamanote Line.

Nogi Shrine: Held on the second Sunday of each month and canceled in case of rain. Near Nogizaka Subway Station on the Chiyoda Line.

Setagaya Boro-ichi: Held on December 15–16 and January 15–16, with a 400-year history. Near Setagaya Station on the Tokyu Setagaya Line.

Heiwajima Komingu Kotto-sai: A large-scale (over 250 shops), antique fair at the Tokyo Ryutsu Center, Heiwajima, held four times a year. 15 min. by monorail from Hamamatsucho Station on the JR Yamanote or Keihin-Tohoku Line.

For more information, contact the Tokyo Flea Market Committee ☎ 03-3950-0871.

Sample Tours of Tokyo: Starting from Tokyo Station.

One-Day Course: Walk along the moat of the Imperial Palace to the National Diet Building. Use the subway to get to Asakusa and Ueno. Sensoji Temple, Ueno Toshogu Shrine and the Tokyo National Museum are on the route. From Ueno, take the JR Yamanote Line to one of the shopping districts, Ikebukuro or Shinjuku.

Three-Day Course: <Day 1> From the Imperial Palace, walk along the moat to the National Diet Building and the Imperial Palace East Garden. Exit the garden from *Otemon* Gate and take the subway to Shinjuku. Look up at the skyscrapers and stroll along the busy streets, then take the JR Yamanote Line to Ikebukuro to see the Sunshine 60 Building and its surroundings. <Day 2> Take the JR Yamanote Line to Ueno. After visiting the many famous places in Ueno Park, take the subway to Asakusa. See Sensoji Temple and then get on the Suijo Bus (Sightseeing Boat) on the Sumida River to the Hama Rikyu Garden. Walk to Ginza from Shimbashi or take the subway to Akasaka-mitsuke. (If *kabuki* is being performed, return to your hotel from Asakusa and participate in the Kabuki Night Tour. Advance reservations required.) <Day 3> Take the JR Yamanote Line to Hamamatsucho. After seeing Zojoji Temple and Tokyo Tower, take the JR Yamanote Line from Hamamatsucho to

Harajuku. Visit Meiji Jingu Shrine and the Ota Memorial Museum of Art, then look around Harajuku. Take the JR Yamanote Line to whichever shopping district that appeals the most such as Shibuya, Shinjuku or Ikebukuro.

Short Trips from Tokyo: Many well-known places are within easy access by non-stop bus or train for those who wish to make side trips from Tokyo. Some of the more popular places include Nikko, Kamakura, Hakone, Mt. Fuji and the Fuji Five Lakes District. If one does not wish to see too much, a day trip is easily possible; or, if one stays the night, there is time to look around more carefully. One or two-day package tours to these places are offered by leading travel agencies.

Regular Sightseeing Bus Tours: There are various sightseeing bus tours for foreign travelers, operated by the travel agencies listed below. All tours are accompanied by English-speaking guides and offer pick-up service at major hotels in central Tokyo. Detailed information is available at hotel desks or at the offices of the following travel agencies or bus companies:

Japan Amenity Travel (hereafter Amenity)   ☎ 03-3573-1417
Hankyu Express International (hereafter Hankyu)
   ☎ 03-3459-9080
Hato Bus   ☎ 03-3435-6081
Japan Gray Line (hereafter G Line)   ☎ 03-3433-5745
JTB (Japan Travel Bureau) Sunrise Center   ☎ 03-3276-7777
For bus tours under operation, refer to the Supplement.

ANNUAL EVENTS

The traditions of folk life and religion in Japan have been preserved through the many annual events. Here, we will introduce some of these events. By participating, it will be possible to see another aspect of the modern metropolis, Tokyo. (Dates of events are subject to change.)

New Year Celebration: December 31–January 1. Most Japanese are busy on Dec. 31 cleaning their homes and cooking *osechi ryori* (traditional New Year's dishes) in preparation to greet the New Year. Late in the evening, many Japanese go to shrines and temples to pray for happiness throughout the coming year. Meiji Jingu Shrine and Asakusa-Kannon (Sensoji) Temple are especially popular.

New Year's Greetings with the Imperial Family: January 2. The public may enter the grounds of the Imperial Palace and exchange New Year's greetings with the Emperor, Empress and their Family.

Dezomeshiki: January 6. A New Year's Parade by the Tokyo Fire Defense Agency through Harumi Plaza in Chuo Ward.

First Sumo Tournament: 15 days from early January at the Ryogoku Kokugikan *Sumo* Arena.

Setsubun: Around February 3. According to the lunar calendar, this is the day in which winter changes to spring. At temples such as Gokokuji Temple, Ikegami-Hommonji Temple, Asakusa-Kannon

Temple and Okunitama Shrine (Fuchu City), sumo wrestlers, actors/actresses, and other celebrated personalities throw beans from the stage to drive away evil spirits. This custom attracts sizable crowds.

Asakusa-Kannon Jigenhoyoe: March 18 at Asakusa-Kannon Temple. Since this is the day on which it is believed that *Kannon* (the Goddess of Mercy) appears in Asakusa to spread happiness, it is the busiest day of the year for Sensoji Temple. A parade of boys and girls dressed in traditional costumes as well as the Golden Dragon Dance and other beautiful dance performances can be seen.

Hana Matsuri: April 8. The celebration of Sakyamuni's (Buddha's) birthday. Images of Sakyamuni as a child are worshipped in small, flower-bedecked halls. The *Hana Matsuri* at Gokokuji Temple is particularly famous.

Cherry Blossom Viewing: Early to mid-April at various locations. Famous sites for cherry-blossom viewing are usually packed. Yasukuni Shrine, Chidorigafuchi Park, Ueno Park, Sumida Park, Hama Rikyu Garden and Shinjuku Gyoen Garden are only a few of the many well-known sites in Tokyo.

Tsutsuji Matsuri: Late April at Nezu Shrine. This event celebrates the blossoming of the azaleas that carpet the expansive shrine precincts. The tea ceremony, *nodate*, is performed outdoors.

Kurayami Matsuri: May 5 at Okunitama Shrine in Fuchu. In the evening, a parade of countless portable shrines led by enormous drums livens the city streets.

Summer Sumo Tournament: 15 days from early to mid-May at Ryogoku Kokugikan *Sumo* Arena.

Sanja Matsuri: Mid-May at Asakusa Shrine. It is regarded as the largest festival in Tokyo, with more than 100 portable shrines carried about while festival music and dances are performed. Three gigantic shrines are brought out on the last day, enhancing the festive atmosphere.

Kanda Matsuri: Mid-May on even-numbered years at Kanda-Myojin Shrine. Known as one of the Three Great Festivals of Edo (now, Tokyo), large portable shrines are carried at a lively pace through the streets.

Sanno Matsuri: June 10-16 on odd-years at Hie Shrine. Also known as one of the Three Great Festivals of Edo, this festival features an old-fashioned parade centered around portable shrines ornamented with phoenixes on top.

Torigoe Jinja Taisai: Second Sunday in June at Torigoe Shrine. The festival includes Tokyo's largest *mikoshi*, or portable shrine, which is sometimes called the *Sen-gan Mikoshi* (1,000 *kan*, 1 *kan*=8.27 lbs. *Kan* changes euphonically to gan when combined with other words). The shrine is carried through the street by brave souls.

Asagao Ichi: July 6-8 at Iriya-Kishibojin Shrine. Here, a market consisting of more than 100 stands selling morning glories, the flower that represents summer in Japan, is considered to be quite famous.

Hozuki Ichi: July 9-10 at Asakusa-Kannon Temple. This is known as the day on which *Kannon* blesses people with special happiness, with stands selling ground cherries crowding the busy temple grounds and wind chimes attached to the pots filling the air with their beautiful ringing.

Fireworks: Late July over the Sumida River. This summer night festival has succeeded the tradition of the river carnival at Ryogoku of the Edo period in which incredible displays of colorful fireworks are sent up in ceaseless bursts of color.

Tokyo Takigi Noh: Early August at Hie Shrine. Beginning at dusk, *noh* is performed outdoors by torchlight, creating a mysterious spectacle of great beauty. (*Takigi noh* is also performed at Gokokuji Temple during this period as well as at Kinuta Park in Setagaya Ward, Koganei Park in Koganei City and Shinjuku Gyoen Garden in October.)

Fukagawa Matsuri: Mid-August at Tomioka Hachimangu Shrine. Also noted as one of the Three Great Festivals of Edo occurring only once every three years, it features a procession of 50 portable shrines. A dance performed by beautiful *geisha*, attracts people from the entire Fukagawa area.

Autumn Sumo Tournament: 15 days from early to mid-September at Ryogoku Kokugikan *Sumo* Arena.

Dai-Ginza Matsuri: Early October, centering around Chuo-dori Street in Ginza. A big parade, bargain sales, outdoor art exhibits and a music festival are just a few of the many events. However, the beautiful "Sound and Light Parade" that passes through the streets at night is the highlight of this colorful festival. Folk entertainment from all over the country is also performed.

Kiku Matsuri: Mid-October-early November. Exhibits and competitions of chrysanthemums are held at Asakusa-Kannon Temple, Yasukuni Shrine, Hibiya Park, Shinjuku-Gyoen Garden and many other locations.

Art Exhibition: October-November at the Tokyo Metropolitan Museum of Fine Art (in Ueno Park). Exhibitions by Japan's leading art groups are held during this period.

Shichigosan: November 15 at all shrines. Dressed in traditional *kimono*, children—3-and 5-year-old boys as well as 3-and 7-year-old girls—are taken to a shrine where their parents pray for their health.

Tori-no-Ichi Fair: November at Otori shrines. On the days of the cock (*tori*) according to the lunar calendar, it is the custom to pray at Otori Shrines for prosperity in business and family safety. Worshippers buy a decorative rake called *kumade*, which is believed to bring prosperity. There are Otori shrines all over the city, but the Otori Shrine in Asakusa is the most well known.

Gishisai: December 14 at Sengakuji Temple. A festival of mourning is held for the 47 loyal *samurai* (made famous by the *kabuki* play "Chushingura"), who were buried at Sengakuji Temple. (refer to p.382).

Toshi-no-Ichi: Mid-late December. Markets mainly selling articles to be used in New Year celebrations are set up. At Asakusa-Kannon Temple, there is also a *hagoita* (originally a battledore, but now a decoration) market during this period.

JNTO's Tourist Information Center (TIC): Kotani Bldg., 1-6-6 Yurakucho, Chiyoda-ku, Tokyo ☎ 03-3502-1461

PLACES OF INTEREST (Within 23 Wards of Tokyo)

Chiyoda Ward

In former times, Edo Castle was also called Chiyoda Castle. This was the origin of the name of the ward, the area of which consists of what were once the castle grounds. The grounds of the Imperial Palace were the inner fortifications for Chiyoda Castle, south of which is now the nucleus of the central government. The backbone of the economic system is concentrated to the east, making this ward truly the heart of Japan.

Marunouchi ⌷31⌷: The district on the west side of the JR Tokyo Station, up to the moats of the Imperial Palace. Marunouchi, which means "within the castle compound," was so-named because it was once enclosed by the earthworks that surrounded the castle. Today, it is a leading office district in Japan, and many companies have head offices here. It is the business center that moves the Japanese economy.

Tokyo Station ⌷30-31⌷: Some 3,000 trains, both JR and subway, carrying about 700,000 passengers daily, pass through this central Tokyo Station. The station building on the Marunouchi side (the west side) was originally completed in 1914. Although the steel-reinforced brick and stone building was damaged during the war, it was restored in 1954. The beauty of the renaissance-style building is regarded with deep affection by city residents. The new building on the opposite side (the Yaesu Exit), which was completed after 1956, contains the Daimaru Department Store and a subterranean shopping center. The Tokyo Disneyland ticket center and a bus terminal are near the North Exit on the Yaesu Side, while the bus stop for Tokyo City Air Terminal (TCAT) and Narita Airport is located at the South Exit.

Tokyo Central Post Office ⌷31⌷: Founded in 1871. Moved to this location in 1903, the post office handles some 5 million items of mail daily. All mail in Tokyo passes through this post office.

Tokyo Metropolitan Government Office ⌷31⌷: Completed in 1957 according to the design of internationally renowned architect Tange Kenzo. A statue of Ota Dokan, who first erected Edo Castle (1457), stands in front of the main entrance. It is planned to relocate the office to Shinjuku in 1991. Near the JR Yurakucho or Tokyo stations or the subway.

Teikoku Theater ⌷31⌷: Equipped with the latest stage technology.

Musicals and all other kinds of theatrical performances and shows are held at this leading Tokyo theater. When it first opened its doors in 1911, many new-style dramas of those days were staged here. The present building was reconstructed in 1966. Near the JR Yurakucho Station on the Yamanote or Keihin-Tohoku Line or Yurakucho and Hibiya subway stations.

Idemitsu Museum of Arts 31 : Located on the ninth floor of the building containing the Teikoku Theater. The museum houses a collection of Eastern Art collected by successful entrepreneur Idemitsu Sazo. (10:00 a.m.-5: 00 p.m.; Closed Mondays).

Otemachi 30 : This district adjoins Marunouchi on the north. It was named after the zone that extends from the front of the main gate to the inner citadel of Edo Castle, *Otemon* Gate. Otemachi is second in importance to Marunouchi as a large-scale business district. Near Otemachi Subway Station.

Communications Museum 30 : This museum houses exhibits of mail and other forms of communication. There are 200,000 stamps from all over the world and a postal-related library of 24,000 volumes. (9:00 a.m.-4:00 p.m.; Closed Mondays)

Yomiuri Shimbun (Newspaper) Tokyo Head Office 30 : Regarded as one of the three largest newspapers in Japan, Yomiuri Shimbun was first published in 1874. (The other two are Asahi and Mainichi.) A tour (1 hr.) is available, but reservations must be made in advance. (☎ 03-3242-1111)

Meteorological Agency 30 : Included as part of the Ministry of Transport, meteorological observations and weather predictions are made here through a large computer. Near Takebashi Subway Station.

Mainichi Shimbun Tokyo Head Office 28 : Published in 1872 as Tokyo Nichi Nichi Shimbun, it was Tokyo's first daily newspaper. It was renamed Mainichi Shimbun in 1943 and is now one of the three largest newspapers in Japan. Near Takebashi Subway Station.

The Imperial Palace 28-29 : The residence of Emperor since 1869. Until then, it served as the home of the Tokugawa Shogun as Edo Castle, and the palace grounds today are the former inner fortifications of the castle. First erected in 1457 by Ota Dokan, Edo Castle was rebuilt and expanded in 1606 by Tokugawa Ieyasu. The entire construction project took 30 years to complete, spanning three generations of Tokugawa Shogun. It was an enormous castle that more or less covered what is Chiyoda Ward today. Since the time when the last Tokugawa shogun left the castle with the Meiji Restoration in 1868 and the Emperor took up residence here, the outer fortifications were gradually demolished, creating the heart of Tokyo and setting the scale for the present Imperial Palace. Since many of the buildings were destroyed by fire and earthquakes as well as warfare during this time, all that remains of the original castle is a few towers, castle gates, stone walls and the moats. The palace grounds contain the residences of the Imperial Family, several buildings for official duties and the reception rooms for the guests of state as well as the Imperial Household Agency and the Imperial Palace Security Police. The general public is only allowed into the East Garden. However, on January 2 for the New Year Greetings, and on December 23 for the Emperor's Birthday, access is allowed as far as *Chowaden* Hall where the Imperial Couple and their Family can be seen. The Imperial Palace is nevertheless still beautiful just seen from the outside. In fact, the shape of the double iron bridge, Nijubashi, is loved throughout Japan. The view seen from Miyakezaka looking over the moats, the stone walls and the area around it has been praised by English poet Edmund Branden as one of the most beautiful in the world. Near Hibiya, Nijubashi-mae, Takebashi, Otemachi and Sakuradamon subway stations.

Imperial Palace Plaza ⌷29⌷ : Commonly known as the *Kokyo-mae Hiroba* (lit. Plaza in front of the Imperial Palace), it comprises the spacious plaza and the moats between the office buildings of Marunouchi and the east side of the Imperial Palace. A heavily traveled road runs through the middle, but the space on either side is covered with lawn and pine groves, offering a nice place to relax in the busy city. Located on the north side is a fountain commemorating the marriage of the present Emperor and Empress, while to the south stands a bronze statue of a 14th-century *samurai* loyal to the Emperor, Kusunoki Masashige. Near Otemachi or Nijubashi-mae subway stations.

Imperial Palace East Garden ⌷28⌷ : Formerly located in the heart of Edo Castle. Much of the original landscaping remains, covering 210,000 sq.m, and making up about one-third of the entire palace grounds. It is hard to believe that these tranquilly beautiful Japanese-and Western-style gardens are in the middle of the city. One can enter either from *Hirakawa* Gate, *Otemon* Gate or *Kitahanebashi* Gate. (9:00 a.m.–4:00 p.m. Entrance only opens until 3:00 p.m.; Closed Mondays, Fridays and over the New Year's Holidays) For *Hirakawa* Gate and *Kitahanebashi* Gate, get off at Takebashi Subway Station. Otemachi Subway Station is convenient for *Otemon* Gate.

Kitanomaru Park ⌷28⌷ : It was the site of the Northern Citadel (*Kitanomaru*) of Edo Castle. The moat-enclosed, sunlit park used to be part of the Imperial Palace grounds, but it was opened to the public in 1969 to commemorate the 60th birthday of Emperor Showa. In addition to the Nippon Budokan and other facilities on the east side, a dense forest is on the west. Near Kudanshita or Takebashi subway stations.

Nippon Budokan ⌷28⌷ : In Kitanomaru Park. Erected as a demonstration hall for *judo* and other martial arts during the 1964 Olympics. The massive octagonal structure with a bronze-tiled roof was modeled after the venerable *Yumedono* Hall at Horyuji Temple in

Nara.　Sports events, concerts and assemblies of all sorts are held here.

Science Museum　28 : In Kitanomaru Park.　The structure housing the largest general science museum in Japan is shaped like a hand with the fingers extended.　Models, machines and other exhibitions cover themes ranging from space science to agriculture.　(9:00 a.m.-4:50 p.m.; Daily)

National Museum of Modern Art, Tokyo　28 : In Kitanomaru Park.　The museum was established to propagate and educate the public about modern art. 20th century paintings, prints, sculptures and other artworks are collected and displayed here.　(10:00 a.m.-5:00 p.m.; Closed Mondays)

National Archives　28 : In Kitanomaru Park.　All the official documents since the Meiji period (1868-1912) are preserved for applicants to read.　(9:30 a.m.-5:00 p.m.; Closed Sundays and national holidays)

Craft Galley; National Museum of Modern Art, Tokyo　28 : In Kitanomaru Park.　Traditional crafts produced in the 20th century and modern works are on display.　The building was originally the headquarters of the Imperial Guard, but is now an Important Cultural Property.　(10:00 a.m.-5: 00 p.m.; Closed Mondays)

Chidorigafuchi Park　28 : Famed for its cherry trees.　The 800-m-long promenade is lined with them.　Boats can be rented along the edge of the moat. The National Cemetery for the Unknown Soldiers of World War II adjoins the southwest edge.　A memorial service is held for them every spring and autumn, and lighted lanterns are set adrift on the moat at Chidorigafuchi on the night of July 13.　Near Kudanshita Subway Station.

Yasukuni Shrine　28 : Dedicated to the some 2.5 million servicemen who gave their lives for their country from the Meiji Restoration through World War II.　Beyond the largest *torii* gate in Japan spanning the approach is a bronze statue of Omura Masujiro, minister of military affairs in the new Imperial Government after the Meiji Restoration.　In spring the cherry blossoms are very beautiful here. Near Kudanshita Subway Station.

Yurakucho　31 : The busy commercial district joining Marunouchi to the south centers around the JR Yurakucho Station.　Since the Hibiya theater district, where Takarazuka and many other theaters stand, is also nearby, the area bustles at night, too.　Yurakucho and Hibiya subway stations are also located here.

Yurakucho Center Building　31 : Commonly known as Yurakucho Marion.　It is a twin building connected by a passageway that contains two department stores and five movie theaters. On the outer wall to the south is a massive clock from which mechanical figures appear to chime in the hour.

Tokyo Kotsu Kaikan　31 : A 15-story building containing the offices of domestic and overseas travel agencies as well as the information office of the National Vacation Villages. The head office of the Japan National Tourist Organization (JNTO) is here. On the top floor is a revolving restaurant with an excellent view of the area.

Hibiya Park 33 : Opened in 1903 as the first Western park in Tokyo. The park contains Hibiya Public Hall and Hibiya Library as well as a large fountain in the middle surrounded by flower beds, an outdoor music hall, ponds and tennis courts. Near Hibiya or Kasumigaseki subway stations.

Kasumigaseki 33 : The district stretching off the west end of Yurakucho with Hibiya Park in between. Some 30 central government offices are concentrated here and in Nagatacho, the area immediately west. It is the heart of administration and justice in Japan. Near Kasumigaseki Subway Station.

National Diet 33 : Hall of Japan's parliamentary government. The massive building, which took 17 years to complete (construction ending in 1936), has 12,500 sq.m of floor space and extends 206 m across the front. It stands 21 m tall, while its central tower rises 65. 5 m. Near Kokkaigijido-mae or Nagatacho subway stations.

Hie Shrine 32 : This shrine was honored by generations of Tokugawa Shogun as the home of the guardian god of Edo Castle. Accordingly, it was the largest shrine in Edo. Although the imposing Main Shrine fell victim to incendiary bombing during World War II, it was rebuilt in 1962. Near Akasaka-mitsuke or Akasaka subway stations.

National Diet Library 29 : Japan's only national library. There are many data rooms divided by such topics as national administration, cultural exchange, etc. Newspapers, magazines, books and maps as well as Braille books, records, films and all other domestic publications are stored here.

National Theater 29 : Founded in 1966 to preserve ancient Japanese performing arts, cultivate traditional artists and provide a forum for research and study. It has a large and small hall with the best stage equipment available. The National Entertainment Hall next door is for vaudeville-like entertainment of days gone by. Near Hanzomon Subway Station.

Yotsuya 32 : Named after Yotsuya Gate, which once stood on the outer moat of Edo Castle. The JR Yotsuya Station stands on the filled moat. However, part of the moat is still brimming with water to the north of the station. In the neighborhood are Sophia University, St. Ignacious Church (established 1949) and Sotobori Park with its beautiful cherry trees in spring.

Ochanomizu 26 : This area was named after the clear water (*mizu*) that bubbled forth here and was used to make tea (*ocha*) for the Tokugawa Shogun. There are many universities and schools in this student district. Jimbocho, the district famous for second-hand books, is down the hill from the JR Ochanomizu Station. Near Ochanomizu Station on the JR Chuo Line or the subway, or Shin-

Ochanomizu Subway Station.

Nicolai-do (Orthodox Church in Japan) 26 : The Japan Halistos Church. Designed in 1891 by Greek Orthodox priest Kasatkin Nicolai, it is usually called Nicolai Cathedral. The central dome is 38 m high in this exquisite Byzantine-type structure.

Transportation Museum: Containing the first Japanese steam locomotive, a royal coach of the Meiji period, a Shinkansen car, etc, this museum is especially popular with railroad fans. It also houses exhibits and data covering the entire range of transportation from rail, sea and air to automobiles. Near the JR Akihabara or Kanda stations.

Akihabara Electric-Appliance Store District 26 : Some 1,000 electric-appliance stores line both sides of a 1-km stretch of road where shoppers can find everything from batteries, household electric goods, audio-video equipment, radio components, personal computers and electric equipment parts to clocks, watches and other electrically powered items. They are sold for 20–30% off the retail price and less if you bargain. Many shops provide a duty-free service corner for foreign visitors.

Kanda-Myojin Shrine: An ancient shrine founded in 730. During the Edo period, it rivaled Hie Shrine in importance. The Main Shrine, gaily painted in vermilion, is a 1934 reconstruction. Near Ochanomizu Station on JR or the subway, or Shin-Ochanomizu Subway Station.

Chuo Ward

Much of this district was created through ocean reclamation during the Edo period. It developed as a commercial district. Today, the northeast end is full of clothing wholesalers, the stretch from Nihombashi to Ginza is covered with banks and shops of all sizes and Kabutocho has many securities firms.

Nihombashi 30 : Nihombashi Bridge spans the Nihombashi River, and this name eventually came to represent the entire district. The bridge was built in 1603, and in the next year when the five main routes leading out of Edo were designated as Five Major National Highways by Tokugawa Ieyasu, this bridge served as the starting point for all of them. Originally an arched, wooden bridge, it still serves even today as the starting point for major roads like National Highway 1. The "0 mile" marker for the Japan National Highway is inlaid in the center of the bridge. The present bridge was constructed in 1911 in the Renaissance style and was once famed for its beauty. The expressway running above it, however, has detracted a great deal from the view. Near Nihombashi or Mitsukoshi-mae subway stations.

It was here at Muromachi Itchome (part of which was formerly called *Anjincho*), a back street near Nihombashi Bridge, that William Adams, the English pilot, lived in the 17th century. To mark the site

377

of his former home, the principal residents of the street erected a monument on July 28, 1930, that reads as follows: "In memory of William Adams, known as Miura Anjin, the first Englishman to settle in Japan, coming as pilot on board the Charity in 1600, who resided in a mansion built on this spot, who instructed Ieyasu, the first Tokugawa Shogun, on gunnery, geography, mathematics, etc., rendering valuable service in foreign affairs, and who married a Japanese lady, Miss Magome, and died on May 16, 1620, at the age of 45 years." The Japanese word *anjin* means "pilot," and the street was once called by his Japanese name. Adams and his Japanese wife are buried near Yokosuka in Miura Peninsula, where he had an estate. Refer to p.441.

Bank of Japan 30 : The central bank of Japan. It not only handles the country's stores of gold and issues bills, but also functions as a central mechanism of economic and financial activity. Constructed in 1896, the solemn granite building of neo-baroque style is located on the site of the gold mint of the Edo period. Near Mitsukoshi-mae Subway Station.

Mitsukoshi Department Store 30 : This famous department store first opened its doors here in 1673 as a dry-goods store called "Echigoya."

Suitengu Shrine: Well known for its power to provide safe childbirth and prevent casualties at sea, it attracts many pregnant women, who come here to pray. Near Ningyocho Subway Station.

Tokyo City Air Terminal (TCAT) 26 : Located along Metropolitan Expressway 6 at the Hakozaki Interchange. The limousine bus for Narita Airport leaves from here. The airline check-in counters are on the first floor, restaurants, shops and waiting rooms fill the second, and on the third floor are duty-free shops, the arrival lobby and the point of departure. Near Ningyocho Subway Station.

Tokyo Stock Exchange 30 : The area between Kabutocho and Kayabacho. It is the Wall Street of Japan where more than 120 securities firms of all sizes are gathered around the Tokyo Stock Exchange in the middle. On an average day, some 220,000 transactions occur in which 400 million stocks change hands. Near Kayabacho Subway Station.

Yamatane Museum of Art 31 : On the eighth and ninth floors of the Yamatane Building in Nihombashi-Kabutocho. Masterpieces of modern and contemporary Japanese art are on display. In addition to the relaxing exhibit halls, there is a research library and a tea room. (10:30 a.m.–5:00 p.m.; Closed Mondays)

Bridgestone Museum of Art 31 : On the second floor of the Bridgestone Building. A large marble statue of the "Goddess of Victory" by Rouf stands at the entrance. The collection centers around famous painters and sculptors of the Impressionist and Ecole de Paris schools. There are also recent Japanese artists among the revolving display of 250–300 works. (10:00 a.m.–5:00 p.m.; Closed

Mondays) Near Tokyo Station, or Kyobashi Subway Station.

Ginza 35-② : One of Japan's leading shopping districts. Ginza-Chuo-dori, the main street, runs north to south from Kyobashi through Ginza-Itchome to Hatchome to the Shimbashi shopping district. This street is generally called Ginza-dori Street. On Sundays and holidays, it is blocked off from automobile traffic and opened to pedestrians. Shops cram the many bustling back streets along both sides. Here in Ginza are numerous showrooms, boutiques and department stores as well as famous establishments such as Mikimoto, restaurants serving cuisine from all over the world, coffee shops, bars and other places of amusement. Ginza is also one of the world's leading art-gallery districts, containing some 250 to 300 establishments. At night, the gay neon signs light up the sky, while the store windows are brightly illuminated. The streets are filled with throngs of people strolling, shopping or on their way to dinner in the Ginza area. Near Ginza Subway Station.

Tokyo Central Museum of Art 35-② : An art gallery on the fifth floor of the Ginza Boeki Building in Ginza-Nichome. Exhibits center around modern artists of all nationalities. On the eighth floor, some 2,000 works by major Japanese artists are displayed on slides. (10:00 a.m.–6:00 p.m.; Daily) Near Ginza-Itchome Subway Station.

Ginza-Yonchome 35-② : Located at the intersection of Harumi-dori Street, which leads from Hibiya to Tsukiji and Harumi, and Ginza-dori Street. This area marks the heart of Ginza with the glass-plated, cylindrical San-ai Dream Center, Wako store with the antique clock on top, Mitsukoshi Department Store and Ginza Core Building with its glass elevator all clustered around it. The night view of Ginza is especially beautiful here.

Sony Building 35-② : Filled with boutiques and high-quality restaurants in addition to the Sony showroom. Each floor is divided into four perfectly square sections, with a floor level 90 cm higher than the previous one arranged along a spiral staircase to form a three-dimensional promenade.

Riccar Art Museum 35-② : A *ukiyo-e* and print museum on the seventh floor of the Riccar Building. Utamaro, Hokusai and other famous print artists from all over the world are included in the 5,000 work collection. (11:00 am.–6:00 p.m.; Closed Mondays) Near Ginza Subway Station or the JR Yurakucho Station.

Kabukiza 35-② : Originally opening its doors as a *kabuki* hall in 1889, it is now the most popular theater for *kabuki* plays and other stage performances. The present edifice is a 1924 construction that was repaired in 1951. A runway called *hanamichi* (lit. flower-way) leads to the 27-m-wide stage, which contains a revolving stage 18 m in diameter. It has a seating capacity of 1,906. Near Higashi-Ginza Subway Station.

Shimbashi Embujo 35 : Erected in 1925 as a rehearsal hall for the *geisha* of Shimbashi, it is now a popular theater for dramatic performances. The Azuma Odori, a *geisha* dance recital held in spring and autumn, is famous. Near Higashi-Ginza Subway Station.

Asahi Shimbun Tokyo Head Office: One of the three largest newspapers in the country, ranking with Yomiuri and Mainichi. Asahi was established in Osaka in 1879 and branched into Tokyo in 1888. Tours are available three times per day, except on Sundays and national holidays. (☎ 03-3545-0366 for reservations.) Near Tsukiji Subway Station.

Tsukiji Honganji Temple: A branch of the Nishi-Honganji Temple of Kyoto. The Indian-style stone building, measuring 87 m across, 56 m deep, and 33 m high, was reconstructed in 1934 after the previous building was destroyed in fires from the great earthquake of 1923. The temple was originally founded in 1617.

Tokyo Central Wholesale Market 27 : Marine products, meat, eggs, vegetables, fruit and other raw foodstuffs are sold here. Fish is the main item in terms of both volume and value. The market covers an area of 210,000 sq.m. There is a pier where 3,000-ton-class ships can dock and an enormous refrigerator, which always holds enough to supply the entire city for ten days. It is one of the largest such markets in the world.

Hama Rikyu Garden 27 : Once a villa of the sixth Tokugawa Shogun, Ienobu. Serving as a detached palace for the Imperial Family since the Meiji period, it was given to the City of Tokyo in 1946 and opened to the public as a park. It covers an area of 247,500 sq.m, with a circular promenade around a lovely tidal pond. The vestiges of a garden belonging to a *daimyo* (feudal lord) of the Edo period are well preserved. (9:00 a.m.–4.30 p.m.; Closed Mondays) Near the JR Shimbashi Station. Refer to p.205

Tokyo International Trade Center 27 : The main exhibition space for international product samples. The East Hall, the most well known of the five halls, is a domed design 31 m tall and 121 m in diameter, enclosing a space of 10,000 sq.m in which not a single column is used. Although a wide variety of exhibitions have been held here, the Japan Convention Center was constructed in Makuhari City in Chiba Prefecture in 1989. Commonly known as Makuhari Messe, this fully-equipped center is now used for many events formerly held at the Tokyo International Trade Center, including the Motor Show. A bus runs from the JR Tokyo Station via Ginza Subway Station.

Tokyo Port 27 : A top-ranking, international trading port, it developed around the mouth of the Sumida River. The rapid growth through reclamation of land along the outer edges of the port has led to the construction of a succession of large docks. Passenger liners and ferries for the Izu Seven Islands and Ogasawara Island leave from Takeshiba Pier near the JR Hamamatsucho Station. Leisure facilities that developed in conjunction with the growth of the port have become a new recreation area for city residents. One of the remaining fortifications built in the bay by the Tokugawa Shogunate in preparation for a possible attack by the "Black Ships (foreign ships)" has been turned into the Metropolitan Marine Park. The Ship Science Museum stands along the strip of land between the fortification and the shore. Shaped like a ship, the museum contains general data on the ocean and ships. The observation platform where the mast should have been provides a splendid view of Tokyo Port. Ariake-Tennis-no-Mori Park, an artificial beach and the Tokyo Sports Center are located nearby. (Ship Science Museum—10:00 a.m. –5:00 p.m.; Daily.) A bus runs from the JR Shinagawa Station or Monzennakacho Subway Station.

Minato Ward

During the Edo period, the block from Akasaka to Toranomon was a *samurai* residential district, while the area from Azabu to Mita and Takanawa was full of temples and shrines. Akasaka today is a prominent amusement district ranking with Roppongi and Aoyama in popularity among international visitors. Azabu has become an expensive residential district where many embassies are located. The southeastern section is a part of the Keihin (Tokyo–Yokohama) Industrial Zone.

Shimbashi 35 : With the JR Shimbashi Station at its heart, it borders Ginza-Hatchome to the northeast. The section to the west of the station is commonly called Karasumori and has long been known as the entertainment district of the commoner. Countless bars and restaurants, both large and small, fill the area.

Matsuoka Museum of Art: On the eighth floor of the Matsuoka-Tamuracho Building. The collection includes Chinese ceramics of the 14th-17th centuries, ancient Indian, Pakistani and Grecian art, and Japanese paintings from the 15th century through the present. (10:00 a.m.–5:00 p.m.; Closed Mondays) Near Onarimon Subway Station.

The Okura Shukokan Museum 33 : Located on the land adjoining Hotel Okura. The collection includes ancient art from Japan, China, India, Thailand and other East Asian countries. (10: 00 a.m.–4:00 p.m.; Closed Mondays) Near Kamiyacho or Toranomon subway stations.

World Trade Center Building 33-Ⓐ : There are three underground floors and 40 above ground in this 152-m-tall super-highrise. This is where the mechanisms of trade, both domestic and foreign, are concentrated. The 40th floor holds an observation platform, while the 38th and 39th floors house restaurants. Near the JR Hamamatsucho Station.

Zojoji Temple 33-Ⓐ : Many buildings fill the spacious temple grounds. It originated when Tokugawa Ieyasu moved the temple here from Kojimachi (in Chiyoda Ward) in 1590 to serve as the family temple. It then prospered under the patronage of the Tokugawa family. Most of the buildings standing today are postwar reconstructions, but *Sammon* Gate, the only old structure left intact, tells of the former glory. Enormous mausoleums containing several generations of Shogun's remains also stood here, but they were destroyed by incendiary bombing during World War II. Today, only the gates of the mausoleums of the second Shogun Hidetada and the seventh, Ietsugu, remain. The temple is surrounded by Shiba Park, which contains a swimming pool and a golf driving range. Near Shiba-Koen or Onarimon Subway Station.

Tokyo Tower $\boxed{33\text{-}\circledA}$: The general broadcast transmission tower that towers over the back of Zojoji Temple. It is 333 m tall, the fourth tallest tower in the world. At 150 m is an observation platform, while the special observation platform is at 250 m. In the daytime, one can look over the Kanto Plain as far as Mt. Fuji, while at night it commands a view of the spectacular Tokyo city lights. (9:00 a.m.–8:00 p.m., until 9:00 p.m. during August.) The lower part of the steel tower contains the Tokyo Tower Building, which has an aquarium on the first floor, shops on the second, a wax museum on the third, the Modern Science Museum on the fourth, and television transmission rooms on the fifth. Near Onarimon or Kamiyacho subway stations.

Keio Gijuku University: The university's origins lie in the school of Western learning founded by Meiji-period philosopher and educator Fukuzawa Yukichi (seen on the ¥10,000 bill) in 1858. School buildings were first erected at the present location in 1871, and like Waseda University (in Shinjuku Ward), it is one of the top private universities in Japan. Some of the historic, original buildings still remain among the clusters of modern structures. Near the JR Tamachi Station.

Sengakuji Temple: This temple contains the graves of the 47 *samurai* and their lord, Asano Naganori, famed through the *Kabuki* play "Chushingura." Every December 14, a memorial ceremony is held in their honor. Artifacts from the 47 *samurai* and other articles are on display in the Hall of the Loyal Retainers. Near Sengakuji Subway Station.

Revenge of the 47 Samurai: This took place in March 1701. It began when the fifth Tokugawa Shogun, Tsunayoshi, ordered Kira Yoshinaka, Asano Naganori and one other *daimyo* to provide entertainment for the Imperial messengers who would come from Kyoto. Kira was familiar with this kind of entertainment, and Asano was placed in the position of being taught the conventions and etiquette and serving as assistant. Unfortunately, however, the two did not get along very well. (According to the *kabuki* play, Kira was angered because he felt Asano's gift of gratitude for his instruction was insufficient, prompting him to insult Asano.) However, Asano was fairly quick-tempered, and on the day the messengers were to arrive at Edo Castle, Asano drew his sword upon Kira and wounded him. (There are too many explanations as to the relationship between Kira and Asano and to the circumstances and real causes leading up to the sword wound to guess at the correct one.) Since the drawing of a sword in Edo Castle was strictly prohibited, Asano was ordered to commit ritual suicide at once, and his fief in Ako in Harima Province (now, the southwest portion of Hyogo Prefecture) as well as his castle were confiscated by the shogun. Kira, on the other hand, did not even receive a slap on the wrist. Many citizens criticized the government for the unfair decision, including *daimyo* (feudal lords) and scholars because it was customary to punish both parties in a fight. Those connected with the Asano Clan lost their homes and status and were scattered to the wind. However, 47 of his retainers decided that by killing Kira they would avenge their lord, Asano Naganori, at the same time righting the unfair decision of the Shogunate. The leader was Oishi Kuranosuke, Asano's chief retainer, and his 46 followers were of all ages and ranks. These 47 loyal *samurai* attacked Kira's mansion in Honjo (now, Sumida Ward, north of Ryogoku Kokugikan *Sumo* Arena) on December 14,1702, and accomplished their mission. The public unanimously applauded them, but the Shogunate ordered them to commit ritual suicide for conspiracy. (Since there were conflicting opinions within the Shogunate, this decision was delayed.) On February 4, 1703, Oishi and his followers committed ritual suicide, and their remains were buried at Sengakuji Temple alongside Lord Asano's. However, of the 47, one low-ranking *samurai* named Terasaka Kichiemon disappeared before the attack on Kira's mansion. It is said that this was commanded by Oishi as part of a certain secret mission, but no one really knows. He was later buried at Sengakuji Temple. Refer to p.170

Tozenji Temple: This temple is famous because it was used by British envoy Sir Rutherford Alcock and his retinue in 1859, becoming the quarters for the first British Legation in Japan. The entrance hall and inner parlor of the legation still remain. In 1861 fourteen fanatic *samurai* advocating the expulsion of foreigners attacked the legation, and the marks of this can still be found in the entrance hall. Near Sengakuji Subway Station.

Hatakeyama Memorial Hall: An art museum, once the retreat of Shimazu Shigehide, former lord of the Satsuma (now, Kagoshima Prefecture) Clan. It is set in the middle of a beautiful garden. The exhibits center around tea ceremony utensils and ancient eastern art. (10:00 a.m.–5:00 p.m.; Closed Mondays) Near Takanawadai Subway Station.

Institute for Nature Study, National Science Museum 27 : Formerly an Imperial estate, it was opened to the public as a nature study park in 1949. The 200,000-sq.-m park is covered with natural forest, hills, marshes and ponds, including some 800 species of plants and 100 species of animals living in their wild state. (9:00 a.m.–5:00 p. m.; Closed Mondays) Near Meguro Station on the JR Yamanote or Tokyu Mekama Line.

Tokyo Metropolitan Teien (Garden) Art Museum: Set in the former residence of Prince Asaka. The museum opened in 1933 and is famous for the Art Deco architecture and the beauty of the garden. (10:00 a.m.–6:00 p.m.; Closed second and fourth Wednesdays) Near Meguro Station.

Zempukuji Temple: The site of the first American legation to Japan after the commercial treaty was signed between Japan and America in 1858. A memorial to the first minister, Townsend Harris, stands on the grounds. All of the buildings were burned through incendiary bombing during World War II, but the many historical materials that were preserved can be found in the temple buildings. A bus is available from the JR Shibuya Station.

Townsend Harris: Appointed consul to Japan in August 1855 on the recommendation of Commodore Perry after years of commercial voyaging among the Pacific islands and in the Far East. In July of the following year, he arrived at Shimoda on the Izu Peninsula which had been designated as the site of the first American consulate. His primary mission was to conclude a treaty providing for the residence of an American Minister in Edo, free trade with the Japanese and the opening of additional ports. In November 1857 he was permitted to go to Edo from Shimoda to open negotiations. After a tentative agreement was reached, Harris returned to Shimoda in March of the next year. In April 1858 he went back to Edo to receive the Shogunate's reply. When no reply forthcoming, he returned to Shimoda in June and in July signed the treaty at Kanagawa (now, Yokohama). The United States Senate approved his appointment as Minister to Japan in January 1859, and on July 7, he established the American Legation in Edo at Zempukuji Temple. Here he remained until his retirement in 1861. Harris died on February 25,1878, and was buried in Greenwood Cemetery, Brooklyn, New York.

Prince Arisugawa Memorial Park ⎡27⎤: Once the possession of Prince Arisugawa, he donated it to the City of Tokyo. Opening to the public as a memorial park in 1934, the tranquil park covers an area of 36,300 sq.m, with clear streams flowing into ponds. Near Hiro-o Subway Station.

Pentax Gallery ⎡27⎤: A camera museum containing cameras and lenses from Japan and the rest of the world as well as other related items in the collection totaling some 3,400 pieces. There is truly an abundant variety, from the oldest to the newest. (10:00 a.m.–5:00 p.m.; Closed Sundays and national holidays) Near Roppongi Subway Station.

Roppongi ⎡34⎤: A nighttime amusement area where young people and performing artists can often be found. Clustered around the Roppongi intersection are buildings full of various kinds of entertainment facilities, *yakitori* bars, hostess bars, supper clubs, deluxe restaurants serving international cuisine and discos. The streets are crowded with young merry makers well into the night. Many of the night spots can be found around Roppongi Subway Station.

ARK Hills ⎡34⎤: A group of tall office buildings and cultural facilities that were completed in 1986. Apartment buildings and a hotel can also be found in this futuristic complex. The offices are designed with state-of-the-art technology, allowing them to be used on a 24-hour basis. In addition to the TV studios, there is Suntory Hall, designed for performances of classical music with a large pipe organ. Near Toranomon or Kamiyacho subway stations.

Akasaka 32 : The area that joins Roppongi to the north. There are many night clubs as well as high-class, traditional Japanese and other restaurants serving major political and financial figures. However, there are also some comparatively inexpensive bars and restaurants, making Akasaka a popular international entertainment district. It is an attractive and stylish area, located near Akasaka-mitsuke or Akasaka subway stations.

Hitotsugi-dori Street 32 : A 600-m-long stretch that goes from Aoyama-dori Street to TBS (Tokyo Broadcasting System Inc.). Bars, hostess clubs, coffee shops and discos abound, attracting large crowds at night.

Suntory Museum of Art 32 : On the 11th floor of the Tokyo Suntory Building, standing at the corner of Akasaka-mitsuke square. A collection of ancient Japanese art centering around paintings portraying customs, clothing, furniture, eating utensils and other articles used in daily life are on display. Since there are some 2,000 pieces in the collection, they are displayed by rotating them seven or eight times a year. Near Akasaka-mitsuke Subway Station.

Toyokawa Inari Shrine 32 : The god enshrined here is popular since the deity is said to provide commercial prosperity and happiness. The steady, daily stream of worshippers has been nearly continuous since the Edo period. It is a branch of the temple of the same name in Toyokawa, Aichi Prefecture. Near Akasaka-mitsuke Subway Station.

Akasaka Detached Palace 32 : The state lodging facilities utilized by Queen Elizabeth, the President of the United States and other foreign dignitaries. During the Edo period, a mansion of the Kii (now, Wakayama Prefecture) Tokugawa family stood here. It was converted into the site of the Akasaka Detached Palace in 1871, with construction completed in 1909. Designed in the pure neo-baroque style, the structure has a luxurious facade that was modeled after Buckingham Palace, while the plush interior resembles Versailles. The Palace can be found near Yotsuya Station on the JR Chuo Line and the subway.

Aoyama-dori Street 32 : The wide avenue that leads from Akasaka-mitsuke to Shibuya. It is lined with modern buildings, boutiques, cafes, famous restaurants and other fashionable establishments.

Aoyama Cemetery 34 : Southwest of Meiji Shrine Outer Garden. Many of Japan's distinguished personalities, including leaders of the Meiji Restoration, are buried here, with the first graves dating from 1872. It is known as a beautiful spot for cherry-blossom viewing in spring. Near Nogizaka or Gaien-mae subway stations.

Nezu Institute of Fine Arts 34 : A collection of some 10,000 works of ancient Eastern art. Besides the many superb pieces, the beauty of the garden surrounding the building is well known, too. (9:30 a.m.–4:30 p.m.; Closed Mondays) Many antique shops are congregated in this area. The road from Minami-Aoyama-Yonchome to Nishi-Azabu is called Antique Street. Near Omotesando Subway Station.

Meiji Shrine Outer Garden (Jingu-Gaien) 38-Ⓐ : The outer garden of Meiji Shrine, built in Harajuku (in Shibuya Ward) in 1915. Today, it is a park with many sports and cultural facilities, sprawling across 486,000 sq.m and straddling three wards—Minato, Shinjuku and Shibuya. The main facilities include the Prince Chichibu Rugby Stadium; Jingu Baseball Stadium, where the games of the Tokyo Six-University League are held and which also serves as the home stadium for the Yakult Swallows pro-baseball team; the track and field that served as the main venue for the 1964 Olympics; a gymnasium and an indoor swimming pool; the Meiji Jingu Pool, and the Memorial Picture Gallery where 80 large paintings portray the main events in the lives of the Meiji Imperial Couple. Near Shinanomachi Station on the JR Chuo Line or Gaien-mae Subway Station.

Shinjuku Ward

This ward is adjacent to the west end of Chiyoda Ward and is almost in the center of the 23 wards that make up metropolitan Tokyo. During the Edo period, one of the gateways to the castle town, it flourished as a lodging place for travelers along the old Koshukaido Highway. The west and east commercial districts divided by the JR Shinjuku Station make up one of the most energetic districts in Tokyo. Eating establishments, department stores and one of the city's main amusement areas, Kabukicho, fill the east side. West of the station is the "subcenter of Tokyo"—the super-skyscraper cluster where vast numbers of businessmen are swallowed up every day.

Shinjuku Station 36-37 : The largest station in Japan, averaging some 2.5 million passengers a day on JR, other suburban railways (Odakyu, Keio) and subways. The station building, called "My City," has two floors underground and eight above that house some 250 stores selling fashionable clothing, interior goods, all kinds of foodstuffs, etc. In fact, there is almost nothing that cannot be found here. Many large department stores are clustered around the station. Shinjuku Station is both a hub of the Tokyo transportation system and a large shopping zone. There are many famous discount shops selling cameras, audio/video equipment, personal computers and watches near the station.

New City Subcenter (Super-skyscraper Cluster) 36 : Developed after the completion of the Keio Plaza Hotel in 1971 broke the ice. Today, there are 12 super-skyscrapers and more underway. The 560,000-sq.-m area contains tall, beautiful buildings of the latest designs, including eminent hotels, but for the most part they are utilized as business offices for some of the most prominent firms in Japan. The Tokyo Metropolitan Government Office is to be moved here in 1991, making it even more of a city center. At present, the tallest building is the 224-m-high Shinjuku Mitsui Building, but surely an even taller one will appear someday. The area is near Shinjuku Station.

Kabukicho ⌗37⌗: An amusement district 100 m north of Shinjuku Station. Contained in the 90,000-sq.-m district are the Koma Gekijo (a theater for stage shows), 14 movie theaters, restaurants, bars, recreation establishments and coffee shops, making the scintilating name Kabukicho more than appropriate. Seibu-Shinjuku Station is at the west end of the district, while the eastend marked the by Hana-zono Shrine, famed for the *Tori-no-Ichi* fair in November.

Shinjuku Gyoen Garden ⌗26⌗: One of the largest parks in the city, with an area totaling some 580,000 sq.m. It would probably take at least 3 hrs. to walk around the vast expanse. In 1901 it was used by the Imperial Family for formal garden parties and the like, and was not opened to the public until it was turned into a state-managed park in 1949. The park contains some 1,900 cherry trees of 65 species, attracting vast crowds to view their blossoms in spring. Some of the features of the park include the French-style garden designed by Professor Henri Martine of the Versaille School of Landscape Gardening, the exquisite beds of chrysanthemums in the Japanese garden, and the hothouse with 670 kinds of orchids plus many other tropical and subtropical plants. One completely forgets the bustling commercial district outside the boundaries of such beautiful natural surroundings. Two Imperial funerals have been held here, the most recent being the one for the late Emperor Showa in February 1989, in which 164 countries, the E.C. and 27 international organizations were represented. (9:00 a.m.–4:30 p.m.; Closed Mondays) Near Shinjuku Gyoen-mae Subway Station.

Waseda University: Founded in 1882 by Meiji-period politician Okuma Shigenobu as Tokyo College. It became a university in 1902, and today some 43,000 students study in the eight faculties and graduate school. It ranks with Keio Gijuku University as one of the most prestigious private universities in Japan. Near Waseda Subway Station.

Arakawa Metropolitan Streetcar Line: The sole remaining streetcar line in Tokyo. Running the 12.2-km-long route between Waseda and Minowabashi (Arakawa Ward), cars depart every 2–5 min. Since the leisurely pace makes a nice change from the usual hustle and bustle of the city, many residents enjoy the ride and subsequent stroll through the *shitamachi* (downtown) area.

Bunkyo Ward

There are many hills in this region, which is the home for Tokyo University, Ochanomizu Women's University and many other famous universities and schools. During the Edo period, many feudal lords had mansions here, the vestiges of which are still visible. Several ancient shrines are located here as well.

Koishikawa Koraku-en Garden ⟨26⟩: Originally the mansion of the Mito family, one of the three most powerful branches of the Tokugawa family and directly related to the Shogun. The 69,500-sq.-m garden is representative of the garden of a feudal lord during the Edo period. (9:00 a.m.–5:00 p.m.; Daily) Near Suidobashi Station on the JR Chuo Line or the subway.

Tokyo Dome Stadium ⟨26⟩: Popularly called the "Big Egg" because of its oval shape, it is the home stadium for the Yomiuri Giants and the Nippon Ham Fighters, both pro-baseball teams. Completed in the spring of 1988, it is Japan's first covered stadium (air-dome type), and many regular-season games are held here. In addition to baseball, the Dome is used for other sports events, concerts and shows of all kinds. Koraku-en Amusement Park, a skating rink, bowling alley, and many other types of sports and leisure facilities are located near by. Since it is the only such amusement center in the city, the area is always bustling with young people. Near Koraku-en Subway Station or Suidobashi Station on JR or the subway.

Kodokan Judo Hall: An internationally famous *judo* training center where athletes of all nationalities can be seen practicing this traditional martial art. Near Koraku-en or Kasuga subway stations.

Koishikawa Botanical Garden ⟨26⟩: Affiliated with the science department of Tokyo University. Some 1,500 species of plants are cultivated in the 160,000-sq.-m garden where a variety of flowers bloom each season. Some 500 kinds of tropical and subtropical plants have been collected in the hothouse. (9:00 a.m.–4:30 p.m.; Closed Mondays) Near Myogadani or Hakusan subway stations.

Tokyo St. Mary's Cathedral: An ultra-modern Roman Catholic Church, the facade of which is made of stainless steel. The building is a harmonious combination of straight and curved lines, forming a large cross when viewed from above. The beauty of the resonance of the church pipe organ is famous. Facing the cathedral is Chinzanso Restaurant, well known for its beautiful Japanese garden—a popular site for weddings, receptions and parties. The cathedral can be found near Gokokuji Subway Station.

Gokokuji Temple ⟨26⟩: Founded in 1681 by the fifth Tokugawa Shogun, Tsunayoshi, at the request of his mother. It received the patronage of successive generations of Tokugawa Shogun, becoming one of the most prominent temples in Edo. Remnants of this glorious past can be found in the *Hondo* (Main Hall) and *Gekkoden* (Study Hall). It is also famed for its many superb tea houses. The graves of several historical figures are located behind the Main Hall. Near Gokokuji Subway Station.

Rikugi-en Garden ⟨26⟩: Entrusted by the fifth Tokugawa Shogun, Tsunayoshi, Yanagisawa Yoshiyasu (1658–1714), a statesman of unparalleled importance, began construction in 1695 of this garden project that took more than seven years to complete. It fell into the hands of Iwasaki Yataro, founder of the Mitsubishi-*zaibatsu* (financial conglomerate), during the Meiji period. It was donated to the City of Tokyo in 1938 and opened as a public park. A pond and artificial hills are artistically arranged in the 86,517-sq.-m garden, which is traversed by a path winding through a dense groves of trees. (9:00 a.m. -4:00 p.m.; Closed Mondays) Near Komagome Station on the JR Yamanote Line.

Toyo Bunko Library (The Oriental Library): Based on a collection of some 35,000 volumes compiled by English journalist and traveler George Ernest Morrison during his stay in Beijing and later purchased by the Iwasaki family, who opened the library to the public in 1924. It includes books in every Western language, Chinese books, Korean books, Tibetan books and more, amounting to a present total of about 700,000 volumes. Located near Komagome Station on the JR Yamanote Line, it has been made a branch of the National Diet Library.

Nezu Shrine: Founded in 1706 by the fifth Tokugawa Shogun, Tsunayoshi. The Main Shrine, designed in the Gongenzukuri-style of architecture, was partially destroyed during World War II. It was repaired immediately, however, and retains the same solemn dignity of days gone by. The azaleas that cover the grounds bloom in May, creating a riot of color. Near Nezu Subway Station.

Tokyo University [26]: The most prominent national university in Japan. Founded in 1869, it has a total enrollment of some 20,000 students, including those in the graduate school. During the Edo period, this was the site of the mansion of the Maeda family, lord of Kaga province (now, Ishikawa Prefecture). The front gate, known as *Akamon* (Red Gate), is still standing. Near Hongo-Sanchome Subway Station.

Yushima Tenjin (Yushima Shrine) [37]: An ancient shrine said to have been originally established in 1355 to sanctify Sugawara Michizane (845-903), the greatest scholor of his day. Refer to p.843. Although it was restored by Ota Dokan in 1478, the present main shrine dates from only 1870. But it still possesses a composed, dignified air. The precincts have long been famous for their plum blossoms, with a white plum blossom festival being held every late February-early March. Near Yushima Subway Station.

Yushima Seido (Sacred Hall at Yushima): A large shrine dedicated to Confucius (a Chinese philosopher and founder of Confucianism, who lived from 551 B.C.-479 B.C.) and built by the fifth Tokugawa Shogun, Tsunayoshi. It was then made into a government school called Shoheiko, which educated bureaucrats through the Edo period. The hall contains figures of Confucius and three other great Chinese sages said to have been brought over from China by Zhū Zhī-yú (a Chinese scholar in the 17th century). After repeated fires, the present reconstructed building only dates back to 1923. Near Ochanomizu Station on JR or the subway, or Shin-Ochanomizu Subway Station.

Taito Ward

This area best retains the atmosphere of old Tokyo. In terms of sightseeing, there is Ueno, which developed as a temple town around Kan-eiji Temple, and the amusement district in Asakusa, which sprang up around Asakusa-Kannon Temple (Sensoji Temple). These two areas and their surroundings contain several small and medium-sized enterprises, with many traditional craftsmen continuing to pursue their artistry here. These people are apparently what comprises the unique vitality of the *shitamachi*, or downtown, area.

Ueno-Hirokoji [37]: The main street of Ueno. This wide avenue goes from the south entrance (Shinobazu Entrance) of the JR Ueno Station, passes in front of Keisei Ueno Station, and heads towards Okachimachi and Akihabara. It is lined with shops, restaurants, discount stores and department stores of all kinds, while the back alleys are crammed with places to eat and drink. Under the JR elevated tracks between Ueno Station and Okachimachi Station, there is a famous discount market called *Ameya Yokocho* or generally abbreviatd as *Ameyoko*. This is so named because soon after World War II, when all the people were hungry, many small candy shops (*ameya*) appeared along the alley (*yokocho*) of this area. Later, a wide variety of imported goods, which were very difficult to obtain in those days, were sold here at reasonable prices so that it became a very popular shopping area in Tokyo. Here, many of the shops sell food, clothing, accessories and other goods at low prices. Near JR Ueno or Okachimachi Station and Ueno-Hirokoji Subway Station.

Shitamachi Museum [37]: West of Keisei Ueno Station and along the bank of Shinobazu Pond. Fascinating displays on the everyday life-style of the *shitamachi* (downtown) dweller in the early 20th century fill the exhibition space. (9:30 a.m.–4:30 p.m.; Closed Mondays)

Shinobazu Pond [37]: 2 km in circumference. It constitutes the remains of what formerly was an inlet, with the red-painted Bentendo Temple standing in the center and connected to the east bank by a bridge. The north part of the pond constitutes Ueno Zoo's Aquatic Branch, which is linked to the rest of the zoo by monorail. On the west bank is a boat rental dock, while at the south edge is a bandstand that has been built over the water. In summer, evening events are held, enlivening the area by attracting many spectators.

Ueno Park [36-37]: Japan's largest city park. The 531,855-sq.-m space was opened to the public in 1924. During the Edo period, the entire park was contained within the precincts of Kan-eiji Temple and was once full of temple buildings. During the Meiji Restoration of 1868, however, there was a fierce battle between the Imperialist troops and Shogunate supporters here, resulting in the destruction of most of the temple buildings. But there are many cultural facilities, including the various buildings of Kan-eiji Temple and Toshogu

Shrine, that escaped destruction in the park. Since there have been numerous cherry trees here for centuries, it is one of the favorite places in Tokyo for viewing them in spring. Near the JR Ueno Station or the subway.

Bronze Statue of Saigo Takamori 37 : A representation of Saigo Takamori, the popular patriot from Kagoshima Prefecture (in Kyushu). In 1868 he advanced the Imperial forces to Edo, but after negotiations with Katsu Kaishu, an important retainer of the Tokugawa Shogun, he succeeded in having Edo Castle surrendered without a battle. As a result, the city was saved from the ravages of war. This statue was erected in his honor in 1892.

Kan-eiji Kiyomizudo Temple 37 : A hall erected by the founder of Kan-eiji Temple, the priest Tenkai, in imitation of Kiyomizu Temple in Kyoto in 1631. It stands in front of Shinobazu Pond, and inside the stage-like construction is enshrined a *Senju-Kannon* (One Thousand-Armed *Kannon*).

Ueno-no-Mori Art Museum (Ueno Royal Museum) 37 : Inaugurated in 1887 as the exhibition hall of the Japan Art Association. Assuming its present name in 1972, it provides space for all kinds of exhibitions by various art associations. (10:00 a.m.–5:00 p.m.; Daily)

Tokyo Bunka Kaikan (Tokyo Metropolitan Festival Hall) 37 : A concert hall opened in 1961 to commemorate the 500th anniversary since the founding of Tokyo.

National Museum of Western Art, Tokyo 37 : Constructed in 1959 to house the Matsukata collection returned by the French Government after World War II. The building was designed by French architect Le Corbusier. In the front garden stand "The Thinker," "Citizen of Carre," " Gate of Hell" and three other works by Rodin. The first floor contains sculptures, especially the works of Rodin, while the second floor exhibits French Impressionist painting. The collection consists of 80 pieces of sculpture and 460 paintings, largely from 19th-century France. (9:30 a.m.–5:00 p.m.; Closed Mondays)

National Science Museum 37 : The exhibition space is divided into five themes displaying specimens, models and hands-on equipment for the purpose of spreading knowledge about natural science and applied engineering. (9:00 a.m.–4:30 p.m.; Closed Mondays)

Tokyo National Museum 36 : This most prominent of Japanese museums offers, in addition to the permanent collection of 87,500 objects, significant exhibitions culled from ancient temples and shrines as well as private collectors all over the country.

The main hall, directly facing the front gate, has 25 rooms containing ancient Japanese sculpture, textiles, metalwork, armor and swords, ceramics, paintings, lacquerware, calligraphy and other traditional objects exhibited according to type.

Hyokeikan, the building to the left of the main hall, is itself an Important Cultural Property. Constructed in 1908 to commemorate the marriage of Emperor Taisho (grandfather of the present

Emperor), it contains nine rooms exhibiting ancient Japanese artifacts by period.

Toyo-kan (The Gallery of Oriental Antiquities) to the right of the
main hall has ten exhibition galleries featuring ancient art and
artifacts from Asian countries other than Japan.

The Horyuji Treasure House in back of the *Hyokeikan* houses 318
ancient objects presented to the Imperial Family in 1878 by Horyuji
Temple. They date mainly from the Hakuho period (645-710), but
they can be viewed only on fair Thursdays.

In addition, the following are located behind the main hall: the
Kujokan, a building that originally stood in the Kyoto Gyoen (Imperial Park) and retains the paintings on the sliding doors by Kano
Sanraku (1559-1635); the *Okyokan*, which was erected as a study in
1742 and still contains the paintings on the sliding doors by Maruyama Okyo (1733-1795, refer to p.185); the *Azekura*-style scripture
house of the Kamakura period (1192-1333), and three tea houses as
well as a beautiful Japanese garden. (9:00 a.m.-4:30 p.m.; Closed
Mondays)

Kan-eiji Temple ☐36☐ : Erected in 1625 by Priest Tenkai in order to
pray for Edo Castle so that it would not be attacked by enemies or
fall upon misfortune. When the fifth Tokugawa Shogun, Tsunayoshi,
had the *Komponchudo* Hall built, there were 36 halls and towers and
36 subsidiary temples on the vast grounds. It received the protection
of the Tokugawa Shogunate throughout the Edo period and consequently flourished. After most of the buildings were burned down in
the civil war in 1868, a good part of the grounds were later made into
Ueno Park.

Tokyo University of Arts ☐36☐ : A national university founded in
1949 by combining the Tokyo School of Music, founded in 1897, and
the Tokyo School of Fine Art. The school contains an art data room
possessing many National Treasures and Important Cultural Properties that is open to the public. (10:00 a.m.-4:00 p.m. Until 12:30 p.m.
on Saturdays.; Closed Sundays, national holidays, and school vaca-
tions)

Tokyo Metropolitan Art Museum ☐37☐ : Constructed in 1926. Since
then, prestigious art exhibits of all kinds, such as the *Nitten* and
Nikaten group exhibits, are held more than 200 times a year here.
The present building is a large-scale series of galleries completed in
1975 and now ranks as one of the world's leading art galleries. (9:00
a.m.-5:00 p.m.; Closed Mondays)

Ueno Zoo ☐37☐ : Oldest zoo in Japan; founded in 1882. Covering an
area of 136,823 sq.m, the zoo houses some 10,000 animals of 900
species from all over the world, including the most popular of them
all—the Giant Panda. The Shinobazu Pond Annex is connected to the
main park by monorail and a pedestrian overpass. Raised here in
Japan's No.1 aquarium are large flocks of aquatic birds that gather
on the pond as well as fresh-water fish, salt-water fish, sea tortoises

and porpoises. (9:30 a.m.–4:30 p.m.; Closed Mondays)

Toshogu Shrine 37 : In Nikko (Tochigi Prefecture), is perhaps the most famous of the Toshogu shrines dedicated to Tokugawa Ieyasu, founder of the Tokugawa Shogunate. Since shrines of this name were also constructed in all major areas, this particular Toshogu Shrine is just one of them. The shrine was set up on these grounds in 1627, but the main shrine built in 1651 and now standing here is a redecoration by the third Shogun, Iemitsu. It is a magnificent building elaborately ornamented in gold, with 50 massive, stone lanterns erected by the Tokugawa family and various *daimyo* (feudal lords) that are particularly eye-catching. The Kan-eiji Temple's Five-Story Pagoda, immediately east of Toshogu Shrine, is covered entirely in lacquer and stands 36.4 m high. Constructed in 1639, it is representative of the architecture of the early Edo period.

Daimyo Clock Museum 36 : This museum houses exhibits of Japanese clocks made by clock artisans under the orders of various *daimyo* (feudal lords) during the Edo period. There are a total of about 200 clocks, many of which are quite rare. (10:00 a.m.–4:00 p.m.; Closed Mondays) Near Nezu Subway Station.

Iriya Kishibojin (Shingenji Temple): A popular temple among the residents of the city. The famous Morning Glory Market is held here every July. Near the JR Uguisudani Station.

Otori Shrine: Known for the *Tori-no-Ichi* (Cock Fairs) held here each November. It is also a popular place to worship. Near Minowa Subway Station.

Asakusa 36 : An active area, especially around the Asakusa-Kannon Temple, since the Edo period. While Ginza, Shinjuku, Shibuya and Ikebukuro are flourishing as new centers of activity, Asakusa like Ueno retains much of the *shitamachi* or downtown atmosphere of the Edo period. Lowbrow restaurants and stores line the streets, bustling energetically throughout the year. Moreover, many traditional festivals and fairs add spice to the everyday hustle and bustle. It is around Asakusa Subway Station.

Asakusa-Kannon Temple (Sensoji Temple) 36 : The oldest temple in Tokyo. It was founded in the early years of the seventh century, but most of the temple was badly damaged by bombing during World War II, except for the *Nitemmon* Gate and Demboin main quarters. Nearly all of the present buildings were reconstructed, however. *Kaminarimon* Gate, facing Asakusa-dori Street, has a massive 100-kg, 3.3-m-tall lantern, suspended in the middle, with images of the gods of the wind and thunder on the right and left, respectively. A promenade section called Nakamise-dori is basically both sides of the narrow, paved entrance way to the temple crammed with tiny food and souvenir shops, many of which have been in business since the Edo period. *Kaminari okoshi* (puffed rice confection), *ningyo yaki* (doll-shaped cakes filled with sweet bean paste), and Edo toys and sundries—the things reminiscent of a different age—are popular with visitors. continuing down Nakamise-dori, one comes to *Hozomon* Gate, with statues of Deva Kings standing guard on each side. Just beyond and to the left is the Goju-no-To (Five-Story Pagoda), and in front of that on the inner left side is Demboin Temple, which was built in 1777 and served as the main priests quarters. The temple is surrounded by a beautiful garden created by famous, early Edo-period landscape gardener Kobori Enshu. Continuing through *Hozomon* Gate brings one to the Main Hall. Enshrined here is an image of *Sho*(Holy)-*Kannon*, the Goddess of Mercy, which is strictly concealed from view. Visitors gather the smoke from the large incense burner that stands in front of the Main Hall in their hands and rub it on their skin in the belief that it purifies the body and cures illnesses. Erected in 1618 by the second Tokugawa Shogun, Hidetada, *Nitemmon* Gate is to the right of the Main Hall. Statues of the Deva kings stand on either side.

Asakusa Shrine ⬜36 : The Main Shrine is beautifully carved with elaborate ornamentation, typifying early Edo-period shrine architecture. Erected by order of the third Tokugawa Shogun, Iemitsu, and renovated in 1963, it is popularly called *Sanja-sama* (Three Shrines). The *Sanja* Festival, one of the largest in Tokyo, is held here every May.

Sumida River ⬜26-27 : A tributary of the Arakawa River, this river originates in the Chichibu mountains in the western part of Saitama Prefecture. The Sumida River branches off at the lower reaches of the Arakawa River and empties into Tokyo Bay. Since it is the largest river running through the city area of Tokyo, it was once called *Okawa* (Big River). Of the 28 bridges that span the river, 13 of them have some special structural characteristics and are thus called "The 13 Bridges of the Sumida River." The one in the Asakusa area called Azumabashi Bridge is the point of departure for the *Suijo* Bus (sightseeing boat) leaves for the Hama Rikyu Garden (at the mouth of the river) and Hinode Pier near Hamamatsucho Station on the JR Yamanote or Keihin-Tohoku Line. The trip takes 35 min.

Sumida and Koto Wards

Covering an area called the Koto Delta, these two wards are lowlands enclosed by the Sumida River to the west and the Arakawa River to the east. Koto Ward, in the southern part of the delta, consists almost entirely of land filled in during the Edo period. Old shrines, temples and historical landmarks are found in great concentration in both wards along the Sumida River, but the rest of the two wards contains many medium-and small-sized factories. The section of Koto Ward facing the ocean has been developed as part of the nation's "Waterfront Project," with many tall buildings revitalizing the area. Moreover, many new attractions such as the Ariake Tennis Coliseum and the Yumenoshima Tropical Plant Dome have been built.

Mukojima Hyakka-en Garden 26 : A famous, old garden lands-caped in 1804. It contains many varieties of flowering plants, so arranged that some are in bloom during every season. The blossoms of the bush clover in early autumn are particularly famous. Insect-listening, moon viewing and other refined events are held here. (9:00 a.m.–5:00 p.m.; Closed Mondays) Near Higashi-Mukojima Station on the Tobu Isesaki Line.

Ryogoku Kokugikan Sumo Arena 26 : The home of the Japan *Sumo* Association, seating 11,500. Tournaments are held here three out of six times a year—in January, May and September. It is installed with the latest equipment so that a touch of the button changes the arrangement of the facilities, allowing wrestling, *judo* and other sports events as well as a wide variety of shows and concerts to be held here as well. The hall contains a *sumo* museum that displays exhibits on *sumo* from the Edo period to the present. Near the Ryogoku Station on the JR Sobu Line.

Kiyosumi Garden 26 : Covering an area of 50,000 sq.m, this is one of the most prominent gardens in the city. It is particularly famous for the rocks gathered here from all over Japan. (9:00 a.m.–4: 30 p.m.; Daily) Near Morishita Subway Station.

Tomioka Hachimangu Shrine 27 : Founded in 1627. The shrine was destroyed by repeated fires, but was reconstructed each time. It is famous for the monument enscribed with the names of top *sumo* wrestlers throughout history as well as the *Fukagawa Matsuri* Festi-val, which is celebrated only once every three years. Near Monzen-nakacho Subway Station.

Kameido Temmangu Shrine 26 : Dedicated to the great scholar Sugawara Michizane (845–903), who is popularly called *Tenjinsama*. Founded in 1662, it was held in special reverence by the Tokugawa Shogun. It is noted for its wisteria, which usually bloom in late April, decorating the banks of the pond on the grounds. *Fuji Matsuri* (Wisteria Festival) is held at this time. Near Kameido Station on the JR Sobu Line.

Shinagawa, Ota and Meguro Wards

The area along the coast of Shinagawa and Ota wards is a freight terminal and part of the Keihin (Tokyo-Yokohama) Industrial Dis-trict. With the rapid reclamation of land through land fills, the Tokyo Bay Tunnel was constructed between here and the section of reclaimed land in Koto Ward. The western portion of Shinagawa and Ota wards (both separated from the eastern portion of the two wards by the JR Tokaido and Keihin-Tohoku line tracks) and Meguro Ward did not begin to develop as a residential district until the early years of this century. Today, this area is one of the most fashionable residential districts in Tokyo.

Tokyo International Airport (Haneda Airport) 25 : Opened in 1931. It took on its present name in 1952, serving as the aerial gateway to Japan. Since the opening of the New Tokyo International Airport (Narita Airport) in 1978, it has served mainly domestic flights. There is a monorail service from the JR Hamamatsucho Station.

Hommonji Temple ⟨24⟩: Founded in 1274 by Nichiren (founder of the Nichiren sect, one of the most prominent Buddhist sects in Japan), supposedly at the request of Kamakura-period *samurai* Ikegami Munenaka. It was formerly one of the largest temples in the Kanto area, with more than ten halls and pagodas. Except for the *Somon* (Main Gate), *Goju-no-To* (Five-Story Pagoda) and a few other structures, it was nearly completely destroyed in air raids in 1945. Most of the buildings now standing are reconstructions. Nichiren died at this temple in 1282 and a mourning ceremony called the *Oeshiki* is held every October 11-13. A procession is held with followers carrying a long pole with artificial flowers and many lanterns hung in a circular pattern (called a *manto*). At the same time, large, ornamented drums are sounded and sutras are read. Near Ikegami Station on the Tokyu Ikegami Line.

Meguro Fudo (Ryusenji Temple) ⟨27⟩: One of five temples set up by the founder of Kan-eiji Temple, the priest Tenkai. Dedicated to *Fudo*, God of Fire with various colored eyes, to protect Edo Castle, the five temples can be found in various locations around Edo. This temple flourished under the protection of the Tokugawa Shogunate during the Edo period and is still a popular place of worship.

A 3-minute walk to the north from here brings one to Gohyaku Rakanji Temple. The *Gohyaku Rakan* are 500 disciples of Buddha who attained Nirvana, with statues of all *Gohyaku Rakan* standing in the middle of the Main Hall. The statues are said to date from the founding of the temple in the late 17th century. It is commonly believed that everyone resembles one of the *Rakan*. Near Fudo-mae Station on the Tokyu Ikegami Line.

Japan Folk Craft Museum ⟨27⟩: A folkcraft and folk article museum founded by eminent art critic and avid folk craft researcher Yanagi Muneyoshi. Only a portion of this collection of some 12,000 pieces is on display. The main building is constructed of stones from Oya in Tochigi Prefecture in the style of a Japanese storehouse, while the main gate to the west annex is from a mansion of the Edo period. (10:00 a.m.-5:00 p.m.; Closed Mondays) Near Komaba-Todaimae Station on the Keio Inokashira Line.

Nearby are the Museum of Modern Japanese Literature and the Tokyo Metropolitan Museum of Modern Japanese Literature, which displays data and books on Japanese literature.

Shibuya and Setagaya Wards

The part of Shibuya Ward enclosed by the JR Yamanote loop line and the section around Shibuya and Harajuku stations is an immensely active shopping and amusement district. The atmosphere is different from that of Ginza, Akasaka or Roppongi and even Shinju-ku or Ikebukuro. The western part of the ward is a residential district, which is joined to Setagaya Ward—the largest ward in Tokyo composed solely of residential housing. In short, it is one of the leading residential areas in Tokyo.

Shibuya 39 : Shibuya Station is a bus and train terminal connecting the suburbs to the city center. Many roads also radiate from the station. The area west and northwest of the station has long been an amusement district, with Dogenzaka Hill, Tokyu Honten-dori Street (with many specialty restaurants) and Spain-dori Street (where young people gather everyday) creating a festival-like atmosphere. There are buildings with shops and restaurants offering fashion and gour-met experiences as well as supplies for the Sunday carpenter. Filling out the area are department stores, restaurants, boutiques and coffee shops. East of the station is Miyamasuzaka-dori Street, which heads toward Aoyama and Akasaka. The many office buildings around here give this eastern sector a more tranquil atmosphere than the rest of the area. All this can be found around Shibuya Station on the JR Yamanote Line, or Tokyu Toyoko, Tokyu Shintamagwa, Keio Ino-kashira lines, or the subway.

Tokyu Bunka Kaikan, the eight-story building connected to Shibuya Station by a bridge, contains four movie theaters, stores and restaurants as well as a planetarium on the eighth floor.

Northwest of Shibuya Station on the way to Yoyogi Park are two unique museums called the Tobacco and Salt Museum and the Tokyo Electrical Energy Museum.

Kodomo-no-Shiro (National Children's Castle) 39 : A unique facility with music studios, a modeling studio, a computer room, pool and theater all designed for children. It also contains a hotel, restau-rants and conference rooms used for a wide variety of purposes. (1:00 p.m.-5:30 p.m. and from 10:00 a.m. on Sundays and national holidays.; Closed Mondays) Near Omotesando Subway Station.

NHK Broadcasting Center 39 : The head office of NHK (Nihon Hoso Kyokai, or Japan Broadcasting Corporation), which was com-pleted in 1973. The 23-story building contains 22 TV studios, 23 radio studios and eight recording studios. An average of 1,600 programs are produced here a week and broadcast over the nation-wide net-work to TV sets and radios in homes all over Japan. International broadcasts are made to 18 regions in 21 languages. The adjacent NHK Hall is six stories above ground and two below, and can seat 4,000 people. It houses one of the largest pipe organs in the world. The multi-purpose hall is used for concerts, shows and plays of all sorts. (Tours offered April–September 10:00 a.m.–6:00 p.m. October –March 10: 00 a.m.–4:00 p.m.; Closed every fourth Monday)

Tokyo Metropolitan Yoyogi Park 27 : The Olympic Village for the 1964 Games. The 540,000-sq.-m grounds contain a wild bird sanctuary, a playground, a children's cycling course and a promenade. A grove of trees brought and planted by athletes from more than thirty countries grows among the native greenery. Near Yoyogi-Koen Subway Station.

Yoyogi National Stadium $\boxed{38}$: An indoor stadium constructed for the Tokyo Olympics. Its unique construction is famous. When there are no events, it is open to the public, becoming a skating rink in winter. There is a pool in the main stadium, while indoor ball games are held in the annex. Near Harajuku Station on the JR Yamanote Line and Meiji-Jingu-mae Subway Station.

Meiji Shrine $\boxed{26}$: Dedicated to Emperor Meiji (1852–1912) and his Empress (1850–1914). Their mausoleums are in Fushimi in Kyoto. It is unusual to erect a separate shrine for the Emperor and Empress; however, the illustrious achievements of Emperor Meiji so deeply impressed the nation that immediately after his death proposals came forth simultaneously from all over the country to erect a shrine to perpetuate his memory. Upon completion of the shrine in 1920, a grand dedication ceremony was held on an unprecedented scale. The original shrine was in pure Shinto style of dignified simplicity. The *Honden* (Main Shrine), *Haiden* (Oratory) and some other structures were destroyed in 1945, but they were restored to their former magnificence in 1958. The large *torii* gates at the various entrances to the grounds are made of cypress wood more than 1,700 years old from Mt. Ari in Taiwan. The *torii* gate standing at the point where the southern and northern approaches meet is one of the largest wooden *torii* gates in Japan. It is about 12 m high, with pillars 1.2 m in diameter. Behind the shrine is the reinforced-concrete Treasure House in which many articles used by Emperor Meiji are exhibited, including the six-horse carriage in which the Emperor rode at the time of the promulgation of the Imperial Constitution in 1889. Covering an area of 723,000 sq.m, the Inner Garden has many trees and shrubs donated in honor of the Emperor from people all over the country. The area to the left of the southern approach was formerly an Imperial Household garden that Emperor Meiji and his Empress visited many times to enjoy the numerous species of iris growing here. The Iris Garden, with more than 100 varieties, is still the finest of its kind in Tokyo. The water lilies in the south pond, flowering at the same time as the irises, provide a beautiful display in late June or early July. The garden is open to the public throughout the year. Near Harajuku Station on the JR Yamanote Line and Meiji-Jingumae Subway Station.

Ota Memorial Museum of Art $\boxed{38}$: Specializing in *ukiyo-e* wood-block prints, this museum's collection has many fine works, including paintings and prints by famous *ukiyo-e* artists of the Edo period such as Sharaku and Hiroshige. (10:30 a.m.–5: 30 p.m.; Closed Mondays and from the 25th to the end of the month)

Harajuku $\boxed{38}$: The area to the south of the JR Harajuku Station that is invariably crowded with young people. It is intersected by

Meiji-dori Street and beautiful Omotesando Street, with zelkova trees lining both sides of the latter street from Meiji Shrine to Aoyama-dori Street. Packed with chic shops and boutiques that offer the latest fashion arrivals, the district is so fashionable that it is sometimes called "the Tokyo Champs-Elysees." Near Harajuku Station on the JR Yamanote Line or Omotesando and Meiji-Jingumae subway stations.

National Noh Theater: The only national theater in Japan built exclusively for *noh* and *kyogen* (a kind of farce) performances, which are held on a regular basis by all schools of *noh* and *kyogen*. Near Sendagaya Station on the JR Chuo Line.

Japanese Sword Museum: This unique museum specializes in Japanese swords and accessories with high artistic merit. There are more than 30 National Treasures and numerous Important Cultural Properties and Important Art Objects among the swords on display. (9:00 a.m.–4:00 p.m.; Closed Mondays) Near Sangubashi Station on the Odakyu Line.

Tokyo Islamic Mosque: Founded in 1938 by Turkish residents in Tokyo. The top of the massive dome and the minaret in the front are decorated with the symbol of Islam, the crescent moon. Near Higashi-Kitazawa Station on the Odakyu Line.

Metropolitan Komazawa Olympic Park 24 : One of the main venues for the 1964 Tokyo Olympics. Many trees cover the 410,000-sq.-m park, with a big flower clock indicating the changes of season as well as the time with its blossoms. The 51-m-tall Olympic Memorial Tower stands in the central plaza. Near Komazawa-Daigaku Station on the Tokyu Shintamagawa Line.

Goto Art Museum 24 : This museum's collection of ancient Eastern art includes many National Treasures and Important Cultural Properties. The displays change every month or two, with special exhibitions held every spring and autumn. The beautiful garden is open to the public. (9:30 a.m.–4:30 p.m.; Closed Mondays) Near Kaminoge Station on the Tokyu Oimachi Line.

Toshima, Nakano, Suginami, Nerima and Itabashi Wards

All five of these wards are essentially residential districts. There are schools, small-and medium-sized factories, small amusement areas around the stations, old shrines and temples and historical landmarks, but overall they are clearly residential areas. However, the Ikebukuro area in Toshima Ward is an exception. Formerly, it was a bar district like Ueno or Shinjuku, but since the 1970 it has rapidly been transforming itself into a new kind of entertainment area.

Ikebukuro 26 : The number of passengers using the JR Ikebukuro Station exceeds a million a day. The shops around the station account for some of this enormous wave of humanity. The area around the East Exit is a large shopping district with three department stores, an underground shopping park, camera discount shops and other speciality shops, restaurants and movie theaters.

The east section contains one of Tokyo's most famous modern landmarks, Sunshine City. In addition to the department stores and large buildings by the West Exit, a busy bar and restaurant district fills the back streets, but since a spacious park and Rikkyo University also stand here, it is more subdued than the East Exit. The Ikebukuro area is one of the main entertainment districts in Tokyo, but it still retains a common, residential air. Ikebukuro Station is on the JR Yamanote or Saikyo lines, Tobu Tojo or Seibu Ikebukuro lines and the subways.

Sunshine City ☐26☐: Futuristic urban space composed of a skyscraper and a super skyscraper, completed in 1978. The core of the "City" is the 60-story Sunshine 60 Building. From its observation platform at the top, one can look over nearly the entire Kanto area. Next to Sunshine 60 is the World Import Mart, a 53-m-tall, 11-story building, and the 65-m-tall, 12-story Bunka Kaikan. As Japan's first general import center, the World Import Mart and its many specialty stores display and sell products imported from all over the world. The main attractions, however, are on the tenth floor—the planetarium and international aquarium, which are constructed on a scale rarely seen in Japan. The World Import Mart and Sunshine 60 are connected by a shopping and restaurant promenade called *Alpa* (the first basement floor through the third floor above ground). The plaza, with a fountain, and the artificial garden are beautiful. Bunka Kaikan, to the east of the Sunshine 60, contains the Ancient Orient Museum on the seventh floor and the Sunshine Theater in which *kabuki*, musicals and other events are performed on the fourth floor. The museum displays a collection of some 3,000 ancient artifacts and treasures unearthed from civilizations of the ancient Orient. Behind Sunshine 60 stands the 129-m-tall, 37-story Sunshine City Prince Hotel. An 84-m-long moving sidewalk at the entrance of Sunshine City carries visitors to the shopping promenade. (Sunshine Planetarium: 11:00 a.m.–5:30 p.m.; Daily; Sunshine International Aquarium: 10:00 a.m.–6: 00 p.m.; Daily; Ancient Orient Museum: 10:00 a.m.–5: 00 p.m.; Closed Mondays) Near JR, Tobu and Seibu Ikebukuro Station or Higashi-Ikebukuro Subway Station.

Rikkyo University: Approximately 12,000 students study at this university, which was originally Saint Paul's School. Founded in 1874 by Anglican missionary Channing Moore Williams in Tsukiji, it is located about 10 min. on foot to the west of Ikebukuro Station.

Mejiro ☐26☐: A quiet residential district in the area around Mejiro Station on the JR Yamanote Line, next to Ikebukuro. Gakushuin University, formerly a place of learning for the Imperial Family and the nobility, and Japan Women's University, established in 1901, are located here as well.

Kishibojin Temple [26]: Dedicated to *Kishibojin*, a goddess who protects children. This temple was established in 1537, although the present buildings, of particularly magnificent construction, were erected in 1666. *Susuki mimizuku* (owls made of pampas grass) sold in the shops on the temple grounds and in front of the gate are one of the few traditional crafts still produced in Tokyo. Near Mejiro Station on the JR Yamanote Line.

Nakano Sun Plaza [26]: Constructed in 1973 to promote the welfare of working young people, this center contains study halls, international conference rooms, a hotel, wedding halls and other facilities. What brings young people to the Plaza on a regular basis, however, are the concerts held here. The white, 92-m-high skyscraper has 21 floors above ground and 2 below. The basement floors are occupied by a swimming pool, a bowling alley and a gymnasium. Near Nakano Station on the JR Chuo Line.

Tetsugakudo Park [26]: Established in 1906 by philosopher and educator Inoue Enryo (1858-1919) as a temple of spiritual cultivation. It was donated to the City of Tokyo in 1944 and turned into a park. Buildings include the hexagonal *Rokkendai*, which is dedicated to six wise men from Japan, China and India, and *Shiseido*—the small temple dedicated to Confucius, Sakyamuni (Buddha), Socrates and Kant. Near Araiyakushi-mae Station on the Seibu Shinjuku Line.

Myohoji Temple: This famous Nichiren-sect temple was founded in the early 17th century. Although the remaining temple buildings are reconstructions built in 1812, they are known for their incredible decorations and carvings. Near Higashi-Koenji Subway Station.

Rissho Koseikai Daiseido Cathedral: This enormous cathedral, which belongs to the prominent religious group Rissho Koseikai, was modeled after the large tower of the Mahabodi Temple in India. Not only are the ornaments on top of the pinnacle towers are of pure gold, but the image of Sakyamuni worshipped in the temple is also covered in gold. Near Honancho Subway Station.

Toshima-en [24]: One of the most popular amusement parks in Tokyo. Many come to enjoy the thrill-packed rides or the many different kinds of swimming pools. Near Toshima-en Station on the Seibu Ikebukuro Line.

Koganji Temple (Togenuki Jizo): The *jizo* is widely worshipped in Japan as the Buddha of salvation, and the *Togenuki Jizo* at Koganji Temple has been among the most famous since the Edo period. *Toge*, or thorn, is said to represent the suffering of the body and soul, and many come each day to have the thorn removed (*nuki*). The temple has a widespread popularity that rivals that of the Asakusa-Kannon Temple. Worshippers fill the grounds on the 4th, 14th, and 24th of each month in particular. Near Sugamo Station on the JR Yamanote Line or the subway.

Kita, Arakawa, Adachi, Katsushika and Edogawa Wards

These five wards occupy the northeastern portion of Tokyo. While there are some large residential districts in this area, most of the wards have a high concentration of factories.

Furukawa Gardens: The site of the former residence of Furukawa Ichibei (1832–1903), once known as the copper king. It is famous because the building and Western garden were designed by English architect Josiah Condor (1852–1920), who had a tremendous influence on Western architecture in Japan. It is not possible to enter the Western-style building, but its facade and the harmony between the purely Japanese-style garden and the Western-style garden is masterfully accomplished. It becomes especially beautiful when the azaleas bloom in early May. (9:00 a.m.–4:30 p.m.; Closed Mondays) Near Kami-Nakazato Station on the JR Keihin-Tohoku Line.

Asukayama Park ⎡24⎤: A famous site for cherry-blossom viewing since the Edo period. It has even been represented in an *ukiyo-e* print by Hiroshige. Just when the cherry blossoms fall, the azaleas burst into bloom, providing another landmark with their beauty. Near Oji Station on the JR Keihin-Tohoku Line.

Paper Museum: Exhibits explaining the history and manufacturing methods of Western and Japanese paper, paper goods, paper arts and crafts and other paper-related items are on display. (9:30 a.m.–4:30 p.m.; Closed Mondays and national holidays) Near Oji Station on the JR Keihin-Tohoku Line.

Nishiarai Daishi (Sojiji Temple): Established in 826 when Kobo Daishi (774–835), founder of the the *Shingon* sect, made a pilgrimage to the Kanto District. Like the Kawasaki Daishi Temple (Heigenji Temple) in Kawasaki City, this is one of the most famous Shingon-sect temples in the Kanto region. Located near Daishi-mae Station on the Tobu Daishi Line, it is also famous for its beautiful peonies.

Horikiri Iris Garden ⎡25⎤: The garden began in the early 19th century when a local farmer started cultivating many different kinds of irises. The garden has been famous ever since their beauty became known to the people of Edo. Today, there are 6,000 flowering irises of some 200 different species. The best time to see them is in mid-June. (9:00 a.m.–4:30 p.m.; Closed Mondays. Daily during May and June) Near Horikiri Shobu-en Station on the Keisei Line.

Shibamata Taishakuten (Daikyoji Temple) ⎡25⎤: Founded in 1629. The grounds are filled with dignified buildings. The wood carving decorating the *Haiden* (Oratory) and *Naiden* (Inner Hall) are famous, as is the Suikei-⋅n Garden. Along the temple gate road, which has retained vestiges of the past, there are many shops selling the local specialty—*kusa dango* (a mugwort-flavored dumpling)—and restaurants offering river-fish cuisine. The "jumping monkey" toys sold here are a traditional folk craft. The town around the temple is well known throughout Japan as the location of the popular movie series "Torasan" (refer to p.265), an episode of which has been produced every year since 1969. Near Shibamata Station on the Keisei Kanamachi Line.

Mizumoto Park 25 : A large water park covering a total area of 1.52 sq.km. There are waterfalls, currents and ponds as well as a promenade around the water. A total of 50,000 irises grow in the Iris Garden, creating an incredible sight in mid-June. A bus is available from Kanamachi Station on the JR Joban Line.

PLACES OF INTEREST (in the Vicinity of Tokyo)

Along JR Chuo Line and Keio Line

The station on the JR Chuo Line following Nishi-Ogikubo, the western edge of the 23 wards, is Kichijoji (in Musashino City). From here and west along the train tracks to Takao (in Hachioji City), there are many places of interest, making it an excellent area for excursions. The Keio Line runs roughly parallel with and to the south of the Chuo Line. The many limited expresses (Shinjuku–Keio-Hachioji), expresses (Shinjuku–Takaosanguchi) and local trains make the Keio Line convenient for excursions.

Kichijoji 24 : 15 min. from Shinjuku by rapid train on the JR Chuo Line and 17 min. from Shibuya by express train on the Keio Inokashira Line. It is the largest shopping and restaurant district on the Chuo Line west of Nakano, with the area around the north exit becoming especially lively at times with its many fashionable shops. The market of the past around Kichijoji Station has been preserved, thus providing a unique atmosphere not found in other shopping districts.

Inokashira Park 24 : The beautiful park spreading out to the southwest of Kichijoji Station. On the park's 280,000 sq.m is a pond formed by natural springs and a dense growth of trees. One can enjoy boating on the pond among the many aquatic birds. Since the banks are lined with cherry trees, it is a popular place to view cherry blossoms in spring. 25 min. from Shibuya Station on the Keio Inokashira Line.

International Christian University: Opened in 1953 to educate young people from all over the world in developing an international and democratic outlook based on the spirit of Christianity. Boasting the spacious campus, ICU includes a graduate school in Education and Education Administration. It can be reached by bus from Mitaka or Musashi-Sakai stations on the JR Chuo Line.

Jindaiji Temple 24 : Founded in 733, making it the second oldest temple in Tokyo after Asakusa-Kannon Temple. It is famed for its noble figure of Sakyamuni in *Shakado* Hall, an image believed to have been created in the early eighth century. The many trees on the grounds provide a refreshing change from the city. The *Jindaiji soba* (buckwheat noodles) sold around the temple is famous as is the *daruma-ichi* held March 3-4. Dharma (Chinese; ?-528) was a priest who founded the Zen sect. Pronounced *daruma* in Japanese, the *ichi*, or market, sells round, papier-mâché dolls representing Dharma in the seated position of *zen* meditation (called *zazen* in Japan). The temple can be reached by bus from Tsutsujigaoka or Chofu Station on the Keio Line or from Mitaka or Kichijoji Station on the JR Chuo Line.

Jindai Botanical Garden 24 : A spacious, 250,000-sq.-m park adjoining Jindaiji Temple. Some 100,000 grasses, trees and shrubs of 3,000 species are grown here, with some plants always in bloom regardless of the season. Besides the garden's sapling and seed market, the roses here are especially famous and attract large crowds during the May-June blossoming season. (9:30 a.m.-4:00 p.m.; Closed Mondays)

Keio Hyakkaen: A famous iris garden, this 20,000-sq.-m occupies about half of the entire Japanese garden. As many as 400 different kinds of irises burst into bloom during April-July. (9:00 a.m.-5:00 p.m.; Closed Wednesdays) Near Keio Tamagawa Station on the Keio Sagamihara Line, 24 min. by rapid train from Shinjuku.

Koganei Park: A 570,000-sq.-m park. It is thick with lawns and mixed groves of trees, yet contains many different kinds of facilities, the most prominent of which is the Musashino Kyodokan. This splendid building was used for the festivities celebrating the 2,600th-anniversary of Imperial reign in 1940. The hall contains archaeological, historical and folk data for the area displayed in chronological order. (9:00 a.m.-4:30 p.m.; Closed Mondays) Among the trees of Koganei Park are some 2,000 cherry trees, attracting large crowds of revellers when they bloom in early April. The park can be reached by bus from Musashi-Koganei Station on the JR Chuo Line.

Okunitama Shrine: Founded in the late seventh century when the six shrines of what was then the Province of Musashino were combined into one. The present shrine buildings are late 17th-century reconstructions, but their venerable dignity recall the days when the shrine flourished under the patronage of the lords of the province. The famous *Kurayami Matsuri* (lit. Dark Festival) held here in May is said to have its origins in the seventh-century shrine festival. Near Fuchu Station on the Keio Line, 20 min. by limited express from Shinjuku.

Takahata Fudoson (Kongoji Temple) 41 : An ancient temple said to have been founded before the eighth century. Together with Narita Fudo in Chiba Prefecture and Oyama Fudo in Kanagawa Prefecture, it is said to be one of the three great *Fudo* (the God of Fire) temples on the Kanto Plain. The miniature mountain on the precincts, which is covered with cherry trees, harmonizes beautifully with the *Niomon* Gate and *Goju-no-To* (Five-Story Pagoda) when the trees are in bloom. Near Takahata Fudo Station on the Keio Line, 30 min. by limited express from Shinjuku.

Tama Zoological Park 41 : Located on rolling hills. All kinds of animals are kept in close-to-natural conditions among the densely growing trees of the 470,000-sq.-m park. Some of the attractions are the popular koala house, lion park and insect house. (9:30 a.m.–5:00 p.m.; Closed Mondays) Near Tama Dobutsu-Koen Station on the Keio-Dobutsuen Line, 37 min. by express from Shinjuku.

Tachikawa 41 ☎0425: Pop. 150,601. 35 min. by rapid train from Shinjuku on the JR Chuo Line. This western suburb of Tokyo is known for the U.S. military base that was located here for some 30 years after the end of World War II. Today, it is the transportation and commercial center of the Tama region.

Showa Memorial Park: A sports and leisure park set up on the former site of the U.S. military base that once stood here. The 180,000-sq.-m grounds also contain a plaza where concerts are held, attracting many people here on their days off. (9:30 a.m.–5:00 p.m.; Closed Mondays) Near the JR Tachikawa Station.

Hachioji 41 ☎0426: Pop. 432,731. About 45 km west of Tokyo. A post-station on the old Koshukaido Highway during the Edo period (1603–1867), it flourished as a silk-weaving center during the Meiji period. Even today, there are more stores here handling *kimono* than in other areas. Recently, many universities have moved here, transforming Hachioji into a university town. About 40 min. from Shinjuku by the JR Chuo Line or the Keio Line.

Tama Mausoleum and Musashino Mausoleum 40 : The entrance to the mausoleums is located along a stretch of the Koshukaido Highway lined with gingko trees. The gravel approach is a refreshing place surrounded with cedar groves. The Tama Mausoleum enshrines the remains of the grandfather of the present Emperor, Emperor Taisho. Next to it, to the east, is the Tama East Mausoleum enshrining Empress Teimei, his Consort. Immediately northeast of them is the Musashino Mausoleum where Emperor Showa, father of the present Emperor, who passed away in January 1989, is entombed. It can be reached by bus from Takao Station on the JR Chuo Line or the Keio Takao Line.

Mt. Takao 40 : The ancient temple *Yakuo-in*, founded in 744, stands on the mountain peak. The entire mountain is believed to be sacred, and for that reason the natural attributes of the mountain have been completely preserved, making it a popular picnic spot for city dwellers. Next to Takaosanguchi, the station where the cable car leaves for the mountain top, is the Takao Natural Science Museum, which exhibits models and samples explaining the flora and fauna as well as the topography of the area. An observation platform, Yaso-en (Wild Grass Park) and Saru-en (Monkye Park) are located on the summit. Near Takaosanguchi Station on the Keio Takao Line, 53 min. by limited express from Shinjuku Station.

Along JR Ome and Itsukaichi Lines

The JR Ome Line leaves from the JR Tachikawa Station and heads toward Okutama Town in the mountains. There are many public housing complexes and new housing developments along the tracks, but once the train passes Ome Station, the mountains close in on both sides, creating a zone of beautiful gorges. On the way from Tachikawa on the Ome Line is a station called Haijima, which forms a junction with the JR Itsukaichi Line. This train runs through gentle farmland, finally arriving at Itsukaichi. The mountains separating each of the three towns of Itsukaichi, Okutama and Ome are part of the Chichibu-Tama National Park — the largest natural space in the Tokyo area.

Chichibu-Tama National Park ☐40☐ : The park straddles Tokyo as well as the three prefectures of Yamanashi, Saitama and Nagano. The central part of the Kanto mountain region has many peaks covered with primeval forests. Spreading over an area of 1,216 sq. km, it offers thrills for the mountain climber with peaks that are over 2,000 m in altitude and profusely ornamented with sub-alpine flowers, many beautiful gorges, mysterious stalactite caves and a wide variety of wild life. The mountain area also includes a village where the old ways of life, traditions, customs and festivals are still retained.

Akikawa Valley ☐40☐ : A large valley up the river from Ajiro Bridge in Itsukaichi. It is divided into northern and southern sections. The river in this valley is not only gentle enough that children can play in it, but fishing and camping are possible, too. It can be reached by bus from Itsukaichi Station on the JR Itsukaichi Line.

Yoshino Plum Groves ☐40☐ : A onetime local specialty of the area was *Omejima*, a striped fabric dyed with plum roots. It was for this reason many plum trees were planted here. The blossoming in March is the best time to enjoy the trees and their rich fragrance. Near Hinatawada Station on the JR Ome Line.

Mitake Gorge ☐40☐ : It stretches for about 4 km from near Sawai Station to near the JR Mitake Station. Promenades along both banks provide a comfortable trail along which to enjoy the scenery. In addition to the fishing in the gorge river, canoe practice and competitive events are often held here.

Mitake Shrine ☐40☐ : Founded during the early eighth century by the priest Gyoki (668–749), who was famous for building the Great Buddha at Todaiji Temple in Nara. It was said that the shrine was built on land dedicated to *Zaogongen*, a deity who kept away devils. After the 12th century, it flourished as the central place of worship for believers in this god. The small but beautiful shrine building stands at the top of Mt. Mitake. (alt. 1,070 m). There are many lodging facilities for pilgrims around the approach and near the peak, which can be reached by cable car. These lodging houses are rich with the special atmosphere only found in buildings from another age.

Formerly the possessions of Mitake Shrine, a famous suit of armor and many other National Treasures and Important Cultural Properties are on display in the treasure house. A bus from Mitake Station on the JR Ome Line arrives at the cable car station in 10 min.

Lake Okutama 40 : Constructed in 1957 as a reservoir to supply drinking water to Tokyo. Enclosed by mountains higher than 1,000 m in altitude, the lake possesses a beauty that makes it hard to believe it is artificial. More than 10,000 cherry trees grow along its banks making it famous as the best place to view mid-April cherry blossoms among the sites of natural beauty in Tokyo. 20 min. by bus from Okutama Station on the JR Ome Line.

Along Seibu Railway

The Seibu Railway lines (Ikebukuro Line and Shinjuku Line) run from Tokyo to the southwestern part of Saitama Prefecture. These lines are mostly used by commuters, but there are quite a few attractive tourist spots and places to go in the area. The Kan-etsu Expressway also passes through this area.

Tokorozawa 41 ☎0429: Pop. 292,418. Located about 30 km from Tokyo at the junction of the Seibu Shinjuku and Ikebukuro lines, this is one of the most important cities on the Seibu Railway. It is also the distribution center of the famed green tea produced in the vicinity, known as "Sayama Tea." Lake Tama and Lake Sayama, southwest of Tokorozawa, are both man-made reservoirs with a combined capacity of more than 34 million m^3, which is enough water to support the 12 million people of Tokyo for one week. There are several wooded areas in the vicinity as well as many cherry trees and azaleas, making it particularly lovely in spring and autumn. In the area from the southeastern shore of Lake Sayama to the northern shore of Lake Tama, there are over 20,000 cherry trees. It is one of the most popular spots for viewing cherry blossoms in and around Tokyo. (Near Seibukyujo-mae Station on the Seibu Yamaguchi Line.) The 165,000-sq.-m area around here houses Seibu-en Recreation Park, which offers various amusement and leisure facilities; UNESCO Village composed of model houses representing the architecture of 41 countries; Seibu Stadium, the home grounds of the Seibu Lions baseball team, and an indoor, artificial ski slope.

Hanno 41 ☎0429: Pop. 70,362. Situated in the hilly, southern part of Saitama Prefecture. It is a commercial town active in the lumber, furniture and textile industries. The Naguri River, originating in the Chichibu Mountain Chain further northwest, flows through Hanno, lending a special beauty to the city. It becomes the Iruma River after passing through Hanno. The Seibu Ikebukuro Line goes 33.1 km beyond Hanno to Seibu-Chichibu in the Chichibu Basin. This region has many places of interest and fine scenery that attract hikers and anglers. Shomaru Pass (alt. 766 m), Mt. Izu (851 m) and Mt. Tenran (195 m) are some of the local scenic attractions.

Kawagoe ⬜41⬜ ☎0492: Pop. 293,690. Located 40 km northwest of Tokyo, Kawagoe is an historic town noted for the Buddhist Kita-in Temple, founded by Ennin (also known as Jikaku-Daishi, 794-864) in 830. It is affiliated with the Tendai sect. Six of the present buildings were either moved here from the castle in Edo (now, Tokyo) or constructed by Iemitsu (1604-1651), the third Tokugawa Shogun, and are registered as Important Cultural Properties. On display in the temple precincts are images of *Gohyaku Rakan* (Buddhist monks who have attained Nirvana). The quaint spectacle of these moss-covered, stone figures will appeal to tourists looking for unique and fantastic images. The temple is a 5-min. walk from the JR Kawagoe Station. Toshogu Shrine, just south of Kita-in Temple, is dedicated to Tokugawa Ieyasu (1542-1616), founder of the Tokugawa Shogunate. Erected during the early part of the 17th century, the gorgeous, vermilion-colored structures are registered as Important Cultural Properties.

Along Tobu Tojo and Ogose Lines

The Tobu Railway operates the Tojo Line between Ikebukuro in Tokyo and Yorii, a town northwest of Saitama Prefecture. The Tobu Ogose Line branches off at Sakado Station. Popular scenic attractions along these lines include the following:

Heirinji Temple: This is a Buddhist temple of the Rinzai sect. The temple stands in a thickly wooded section in Nobidome, about 4 km southwest of Asaka Station, or 5 km south of Shiki Station, both on the Tojo Line. Buses are available from both stations. It was founded in 1375 in the present Iwatsuki City, northeast of Omiya, and was removed to its present site in 1663 by Matsudaira Terutsuna (1620-1671), a *daimyo* (feudal lord) of Kawagoe at that time. The temple edifices, mellowed by time and weather, stand quietly in the approximately 100,000-sq.-m compound. A clear stream of water drawn from the Tamagawa Aqueduct through an irrigation ditch completed in 1655 by Matsudaira Nobutsuna (1596-1662)—Terutsuna's father, flows around the temple's inner landscape garden.

Ogose Plum Grove: This grove is well worth a visit during early March, when the plum blossoms are in full bloom. A 3.5-km bus ride west from Ogose Station will bring one here. Picturesquely situated on the Oppe River in a 12,000-sq.-m area, the grove has almost 1,000 trees, including some over 400 years old.

Along JR Keihin-Tohoku Line

The north bound JR Keihin-Tohoku Line enters Saitama Prefecture after crossing the Arakawa River and terminates at Omiya Station. Along this line are Kawaguchi and Warabi, well known for their casting, machinery and metal industries; Urawa, the administrative center of Saitama Prefecture, and Omiya, the most industrialized area in the prefecture. These and other surrounding cities serve as bedroom communities for people working in Tokyo. The JR Saikyo Line connecting Omiya and Shinjuku runs more or less parallel to the Keihin-Tohoku Line. The Tohoku Expressway, which is connected with the Tokyo Metropolitan Expressway, also runs through the area.

Kawaguchi [41] ☎0482: Pop. 426,761. This city is located between Tokyo (south across the Arakawa River) and Urawa (north). The Toda Rowing Course is situated 3.5 km west of the city along the north embankment of the Arakawa River. It is the sole, still-water course in Japan and was the site for the rowing competition of the Tokyo Olympics in 1964. It is located near Toda-Koen Station on the JR Saikyo Line. Angyo, in the eastern part of Kawaguchi, is known for producing cultivated saplings for gardening. With a horticulture industry dating back to the Edo period (1603–1867), the area is presently active in the cultivation of ornamental plants and flowers as well as *bonsai* (miniature potted trees, refer to p.217). The Saitama Prefecture Botanical Promotion Center, located in the central part of the city, exhibits approximately 600 cultured varieties and 3,000 species of garden plants.

Urawa [41] ☎048: Pop. 400,946. Urawa serves as the capital of Saitama Prefecture and lies within easy reach of Tokyo (25 km and 40 min. from Tokyo Station). It has developed as the center of administrative as well as cultural activities in Saitama Prefecture, providing a residential district as well.

Omiya [41] ☎048: Pop. 390,021. Omiya is one of the most active cities in Saitama Prefecture. Around the JR Omiya Station are some large department stores as well as fashionable shops. Both the JR Tohoku and Joetsu Shinkansen make regular stops at Omiya. Looking across the street from the west side of the station, one may see a few tall buildings, including "Sonic City" and "Jack Omiya." This area is rapidly being transformed into a new mecca for business and shopping activity. In the suburbs is a well-established, large-scale industrial area involved in producing machinery, food stuffs, chemicals, pharmaceuticals and textiles. Furthermore, as a satellite city of Tokyo, the area is becoming a large, residential district. The origin of Omiya goes back to a group of dwellings centered around the present-day Hikawa Shrine, which is said to date from some 1,600 years ago. It is one of the most sacred *Shinto* shrines in the former Musashi Province, which included present-day Tokyo (Metropolis), Saitama Prefecture and eastern Kanagawa Prefecture. The name Omiya itself means "large shrine." Located 1.5 km northeast of Omiya Station, Hikawa Shrine is a time-honored shrine dating back to the fourth century. Its premises cover approximately 100,000 sq.m, with the approach to the shrine extending over 2 km. Rows of aged *keyaki* (zelkova) and cedars grow thick among impressive shrine edifices. A popular annual festival, the *Daito-sai*, is celebrated on December 10, attracting enormous crowds. At the festival, the approach is filled with stalls selling *kumade* (lit. bear claws—ornamental bamboo rakes) to well-wishers. North of the shrine is Omiya Park, equipped with sports facilities in an area of 345,000 sq.m. The park is well known for its beautiful cherry blossoms in spring. Located north of the park, the Omiya Bonsai Village consists of 12 *bonsai* (miniature potted tree) gardens exhibiting pine, plum, and azaleas as well as other trees and plants arranged in different styles for sale. They are open from 9:00 a.m. to 4:00 p.m. and are closed on the first and third Thursdays of every month. Located near Omiya-Koen Station on the Tobu Noda Line.

Along JR Joban Line

The JR Joban Line is a long-distance line that connects Ueno in Tokyo with Sendai via the seaside route—a distance of 367 km. The section included within the metropolitan area on this line lies between Ueno and Toride (Ibaraki Prefecture) and extends for 40 km. The nearby Joban Expressway enhances the access to this area. The major cities of Matsudo, Kashiwa and Abiko still maintain their unique traditional systems of commerce and industry, but recently they have been transformed into bedroom communities of Tokyo.

Matsudo 41 ☎0473: Pop. 445,605. Located 18 km from Ueno. Lying on the east bank of the Edo River, Matsudo is a suburban residential area of Tokyo. It is also connected by the Shin-Keisei Electric Railway with Keisei-Tsudanuma on the Keisei Electric Railway.

Kashiwa 41 ☎0471: Pop. 295,974. About 30 km from Ueno. Adjacent to Matsudo on the northeast, Kashiwa serves as a junction for the JR Joban Line and the Tobu Noda Line heading for Omiya (43 km) and Funabashi (19.9 km). Like Matsudo, it has grown as a residential area for commuters to Tokyo since the 1970s.

Noda 41 ☎0471: Pop. 110,605. Located 15 km from Kashiwa on the Tobu Noda Line, Noda flourishes as a commercial and industrial town along the Edo River. It is especially noted as Japan's largest *shoyu*, or soy sauce, production center. Shimizu Park, located 500 m west of Shimizu-Koen Station, boasts an extensive recreation area rich in cherry blossoms, azaleas and other seasonally flowering trees and plants.

Abiko 41 ☎ 0471: Pop. 118,386. Located 34 km from Ueno. The JR Narita Line branches off here to go to the city of Narita, 33 km distant. A short, 800-m stroll south of the station will take one to Lake Teganuma, a narrow strip of water about 10 sq.km in area and 34 km in circumference. Excursion boats are available and fishing is permitted.

Along Tobu Isesaki Line

The Tobu Isesaki Line connecting the main cities of western Gumma Prefecture with Asakusa in Tokyo plays an important role in both tourism and industrial activities. Kasukabe (Saitama Prefecture) and Tatebayashi (Gumma Prefecture) are among the major cities along this line.

Kasukabe 41 ☎ 048: Pop. 183,787. Located 36 km from Asakusa in Tokyo, Kasukabe is highly noted for the beautiful wisteria vines growing in nearby Ushijima, which is about 6 min. away by bus (2.4 km) from Kasukabe Station. The base of the centuries-old trunks are about 9 m in circumference and cover a trelliswork area of 540 sq.m. These gorgeous, violet-colored flowers, dangling like grapes more than 2 m, are usually at their best around early May. The site is designated as a Special Natural Monument.

Tobu Zoo and Playland 41 : The complex is four times as large as Tokyo's Ueno Zoo and is divided into three zones: The east side, complete with various recreational facilities including ponds; the central zoo portion, and the western zone with a pasture land and a bird sanctuary. The zoo has some 5,000 animals, ranging widely among various species. Located near Tobu Dobutsu-koen Station, which is 48 min. by semi-express from Asakusa.

Tatebayashi 41 ☎0276: Pop. 76,172. This city developed in the flatland between the Tone and Watarase rivers in southeast Gumma Prefecture. Tateyama Castle was constructed here at the end of the Muromachi period (1336–1573), spurring the growth of a castle town. In addition to the food and textile industries, automobile production has flourished in recent years. Tatebayashi silk pongee boasts a long tradition.

Morinji Temple 41 : Near the Morinji-mae Station on the Tobu Isesaki Line. Among this temple's treasures is the "Bunbuku Chagama" (Good Luck Tea Kettle). According to legend, this is the celebrated Dancing Raccoon Kettle from the following Japanese tale:

Long, long ago at a temple called Morinji, there was an old teakettle. One day when the temple priest was about to boil water for his tea, the kettle suddenly sprouted the head and tail of a raccoon. The priest, thunderstruck, called in his novices to witness the sight. While they were staring in amazement, the kettle jumped up and began flying around the room. But they finally managed to capture this mischievous kettle. The priest sold the troublesome kettle to a tinker, who trudged home with it. That night he was awakened by a strange sound and saw the kettle covered with fur, walking about on four legs. This happened continuously until the tinker showed the teakettle to a friend, who said: "This is certainly a lucky teakettle. You should show it for money." The tinker, taking this as good advice, set up an exhibition and soon became rich beyond all expectation. Needless to say, the kettle later became a precious temple treasure.

Tsutsujigaoka Park (Azalea Garden of Hanayama): 4 km from Tatebayashi Station (75 km from Asakusa). Covering 16,000 sq. m of land, this park has more than 10,000 bushes of various species in the garden. Some are over 200 years old, with most of them being brought down from the mountains of Nikko. The flowers bloom

411

between mid-April and mid-May. Buses run from the station to the park in 15 min.

Tokyo to Chiba

The most rapidly expanding area around Tokyo is found along the Tokyo Bay coastline from the cities of Ichikawa to Chiba in Chiba Prefecture, located east of Tokyo. The western part of this region is called the Keiyo (Tokyo–Chiba) Industrial Area. The eastern part is being developed on a large tract of reclaimed land as residential areas, man-made beaches, parks, sports centers and industrial areas. There are plans to modernize and expand the present facilities at Chiba Port at the eastern end of the region. Goi and Ichihara, heavy industrial zones, form a border. The JR Keiyo Line, which began full-scale operations in April 1990, was originally planned as a freight line, but it has now become a vital means of transportation between central Tokyo and this area. Trains leave from the underground platform at Tokyo Station for Soga near Chiba Port, covering a distance of 43 km. The line runs almost parallel to the Sobu Line between Ochanomizu in Tokyo and Chiba. The JR Sobu Rapid Line (a 40-km route between Tokyo and Chiba), the Tozai Subway Line (connecting Nishi-Funabashi with central Tokyo) and the Keisei Electric Railway (from Ueno to a number of cities in Chiba) provide transportation for the great number of residents living in this region, the majority of whom commute to central Tokyo. The Keiyo Expressway and the Higashi-Kanto Expressway are also convenient since they connect to the Tokyo Metropolitan Expressway.

Tokyo Disneyland ⌐25/35⌐ : The first Disney theme park outside the USA opened in 1983. Like Disneyland in California and Disneyworld in Florida, the spacious grounds are divided into five themelands, each with their own rides and spectacular shows. (8:00 a.m.–8:00 p.m. or 10:00 a.m.–6:00 p.m.; Daily from March to October. Closed Tuesdays and some Wednesdays from November through February, irregularly.) A direct bus service is available from the Yaesu North Exit of the JR Tokyo Station, or Urayasu Station on the Tozai Subway Line. Or, the JR Keiyo Line is available from Tokyo underground station to Maihama, with an additional 5 min.-walk to Tokyo Disneyland. Deluxe hotels and a concert hall (Tokyo Bay NK Hall) have sprung up in the area around Disneyland, transforming it into a large, new resort area. Increasing popularity of Tokyo Disneyland is evidenced by the great number of visitors not only from all over Japan but from adjacent countries overseas whose number is growing every year.

Ichikawa ⌐41⌐ ☎0473: Pop. 418,759. Located 16 km from Tokyo Station on the JR Sobu Rapid Line, it is an industrial city with a number of educational institutes. It is also a residential city adjacent to Tokyo. The wooded bluff on the left bank of the Edo river, known as Konodai, is about 1.5 km north of Konodai Station on the Keisei

Electric Railway, or 2.5 km northwest of the JR Ichikawa Station (buses are available from both stations). It is known as the site of the former provincial government of Shimosa (now, northern Chiba Prefecture and part of Ibaraki Prefecture) as well as the scene of battles in 1564 between the Satomi and Hojo clans. Mama, adjoining the southeastern part of the city, was often referred to in old Japanese poems and is known as a good residential area. Guhoji Temple, located on the wooded hill at Mama, belongs to the Nichiren sect of Buddhism. It has a pair of black *Nio* images (Deva Kings) standing at the two-story gate, said to be the works of Unkei—a prominent sculptor in the early part of the Kamakura period (1192–1333).

Hokekyoji Temple: Headquarters of the Nakayama-Myoshu sect of Buddhism. This temple can be reached from Shimosa-Nakayama Station, which is 30 min. by the JR Sobu Line from Ochanomizu in Tokyo. It was founded by Nichiren (1222–1282) in 1253 and contains some National Treasures in the form of documents handwritten by Nichiren himself. The temple premises, which cover 45,000 sq.m, contain many valuable structures.

Funabashi 41 ☎0474: Pop. 521,519. 24 km from Tokyo Station on the JR Sobu Rapid Line. Funabashi near Ichikawa is an industrial and residential area on Tokyo Bay. As the city expands, the population also increases, turning it into a satellite city of Tokyo. This expansion includes "LaLaport"—a large-scale shopping center with a wide range of facilities such as a hotel, theater, tennis courts and a drive-in movie theater as well as the Nakayama Race Track. Ocean parks are also being constructed on the reclaimed land.

Narashino 41 ☎0474: Pop. 145,304. Located 27 km east of Tokyo's Ochanomizu Station. Tsudanuma is the center of this newly developed residential town for commuters working in Tokyo. Many railroads are concentrated in this area west of Chiba, making it a convenient center of transportation. A 3-min. walk from Yatsu Station on the Keisei Electric Railway will bring one to the Yatsu Rose Garden, which features approximately 6,300 varieties of colorful roses that bloom between mid-May and mid-June.

Chiba 21/22-① ☎0472

Pop. 809,128. Reached in 45 min. from Tokyo Station by the JR Sobu Rapid Line. This is the largest city in Chiba Prefecture and the seat of the Prefectural Government. Chiba not only thrives as the prefecture's administrative, economic and cultural center, but it is also a distribution center for local products. At the same time, the city is one of the satellite cities around Tokyo and includes the Keiyo (Tokyo–Chiba) Industrial Area, with active petrochemical refineries as well as metal, chemical and electric power generation industries. Furthermore, now that Chiba Port is under construction, the city itself has begun emphasizing its identification as a port city. Within the Chiba Central Port area, there are many facilities and recreational centers. One example is the Chiba Port Park. With a total area of 250,000 sq.m, this park has 125-m-high Port Tower, Chiba Prefectural Museum, an outdoor stage and man-made links. The "Nippon Convention Center" (popularly called Makuhari Messe) also opened in Makuhari in 1989. This large-scale, four-story building has a 55,000-sq.-m exhibition hall, a multi-purpose hall with a seating capacity of 9,000, and other convention and meeting facilities. The convention center is surrounded by a "World Business Garden" as well as ultra-modern office buildings, hotels and shopping centers. Adjacent to it the modern Chiba Marine Stadium (a baseball stadium), comparable in facilities to that of the U.S. Major League, has also been constructed.

Area 2. Yokohama and Vicinity

Kawasaki and Yokohama are located along the west side of Tokyo Bay and are referred to together with Tokyo as the Keihin (Tokyo – Yokohama) Industrial Area. This, of course, is one of the nation's most important industrial zones. In addition, these cities comprise one of the most developed areas among major cities in Japan with a high population density.

Kawasaki ⬚41⬚ ☎044: Pop. 1,127,952. This city stretches east and west in a narrow belt along the south bank of the Tama River, midway between Tokyo and Yokohama. Its eastern portion facing Tokyo Bay is right in the middle of the Keihin Industrial Area, host to a great many factories. Various steel and petrochemical plants can be found along the coast, while the inland region is well established with plants involved in high-tech electronics and the electrical industry. The administrative center of the city is located further inland, with the western portion of the city being considered as a residential community for Tokyo professionals. The JR Kawasaki Station is located toward the eastern edge of the city in a commercial district with many shops and restaurants as well as movie theaters. To get here, it takes 25 min. on the JR Keihin-Tohoku Line from Tokyo Station or 13 min. by limited express on the Keihin Electric Express Railway (generally called Keikyu) from Shinagawa.

Kawasaki-Daishi: This is another, popular name for Heigenji Temple. It is dedicated to Kobo-Daishi (also known as Kukai, 774–835), the great founder and priest of the Shingon sect of Buddhism. This temple was founded in the 12th century and stands as one of the most famous temples in the Kanto District. The temple hosts many well-wishers, especially during the first three days of the New Year, putting it in constant competition with Meiji Shrine in Tokyo. Its Main Hall, reconstructed after World War II, stands with divine magnificence over all who view it.

Mukogaoka Park: Located on a hill, affording a bird's-eye view of the Tama River. Mukogaoka Park is an extensive recreation area full of trees and shrubs. In its vicinity, one can find the Nihon Minka-en Open Air Museum of Japanese Traditional Houses, which exhibits 20 old houses transplanted from east Japan, each of which represents the architecture of a different district. The houses contain everyday furnishings of the period they represent, allowing a look into a Japanese farmhouse of the past. Since the houses are naturally set in a wooded area, a genuine touch of traditional life-style is experienced. Near Mukogaoka-yuen Station on the Odakyu Line.

Yomiuri Land: Yomiuri Land is a comprehensive recreation park situated on a section of Tama Hills. Its total area is spread across 600,000 sq.m and offers such attractions as a unique, underwater ballet theater, an aquarium containing fish representing more than

360 species, coelacanth and manatee, and various other sporting and recreational facilities. For those who like nature, the rose garden and plum grove provide an ideal setting for an enjoyable visit. The park is closed on Tuesdays. To get here from Tokyo, take the Odakyu Line at Shinjuku and get off at Yomiurirand-mae and then catch a bus, or take the Keio-Sagamihara Line, also at Shinjuku, to Keio-Yomiurirand.

Yokohama 41/46-47 ☎045

Located at the center of the west side of Tokyo Bay, Yokohama is one of Japan's two largest trading ports together with Kobe. It has rapidly developed as a port town ever since foreign trade opened in 1859. As a result of voluminous import and export activities, Yokohama plays an important role as a part of the Keihin Industrial Area with Tokyo and Kawasaki. In 1988 the approximate volume of exports through Yokohama Port amounted to ¥5.9 trillion and imports to ¥2.5 trillion.

The Negishi Coastal Industrial Area lies along Negishi Bay, just 5 km south of the city center, with advanced, heavy and chemical industries involved in petroleum refinery, shipbuilding, electric-power generation and other industries. Near the north end of Yokohama Port lies an extensive area where a shipbuilding yard was formerly located. A new city development plan to construct the Minato Mirai 21 ("MM21" for short) is in progress here and is due for completion in the year 2000. (refer to p.420)

Yokohama had a population of 3,152,742 as of February 1,1989. Thus, this is the second-largest city in Japan after Tokyo as far as population is concerned. The city is administratively divided into 16 wards. The central part of the port facilities are within Naka Ward, which also includes the Kanagawa Prefectural Government Offices, Yokohama Municipal Offices and the offices of various other governmental organs as well as banks and branch offices of large companies. Nishi Ward, situated north of Naka Ward, contains Yokohama Station, various department stores and numerous office buildings. Moving northeast from here along the shoreline, one will pass through Kanagawa and Tsurumi wards, finally reaching Kawasaki. Along the coast in these wards are several piers, warehouses and large plants.

The other regions not mentioned above, including the districts around the city, are rapidly being developed as residential areas, with many suburbanites commuting to Tokyo.

Yokohama is also known as one of the first cities in Japan to receive various aspects of Western civilization—newspapers, telephones, railroads, beer brewing and ice cream making to mention but a few. With this background as a gateway to Japan, the city has a nuance that is a bit different from that of Tokyo. Seeking this subtle difference in the atmosphere of Yokohama, many visitors come from nearby cities included in the greater Tokyo region.

HISTORY

Yokohama was first opened to foreign residents in 1859 when it was a mere fishing village. Five years earlier, Commodore Matthew C. Perry of the U.S. Navy landed here to induce Japan to sign a treaty of peace and amity with the United States of America. A portion of the foreshore was then set apart as a foreign settlement and leased to foreigners.

At first Yokohama was divided into two districts—Kangai (outside the boundary) district and Kannai (inside the boundary) district. Facing the harbor, Kannai served as the foreign quarter for the town. On a range of low hills south of the town was a district known to foreigners as the Bluff (Yamatemachi) and to the northwest was another hilly district known as Noge.

Yokohama was organized as a municipality in 1889 after its population had grown to 121,000. Two years prior to that, the water-supply system was completed, and later, in 1896, the port was greatly improved. The boundaries of the city were gradually extended as it experienced a corresponding increase in population.

Unfortunately, the city has been hit by catastrophes twice in the 20th century. The first resulted from the Great Kanto Earthquake of 1923 and the second from air raids in May 1945. After World War II, however, the city was quickly rehabilitated, and in 1989 the Yokohama Exposition was held in commemoration of the municipality's 100th anniversary, attracting more than 13 million visitors.

TRANSPORTATION

From Narita or Haneda: If one plans to go directly from the New Tokyo International Airport at Narita to Yokohama, take the limousine bus for Yokohama City Air Terminal (YCAT). The 2-hr. bus ride will take one straight to YCAT, which is near the east exit of Yokohama Station. From the Tokyo International Airport at Haneda, take the bus that goes directly to the east exit of the JR Yokohama Station.

From Tokyo: To get to Yokohama from Tokyo on JR, it takes 35 min. on the Keihin-Tohoku Line, 25 min. on the Tokaido Main Line and 31 min. on the Yokosuka Line. For those using the Keikyu Line, it takes 20 min. from Shinagawa on the limited express. The Tokyu Toyoko Line from Shibuya (in Tokyo) takes 30 min. by the express train. The JR Shinkansen only stops at Shin-Yokohama Station, which is connected by the JR Yokohama Line (13 min.) and the subway (12 min.) to Yokohama Station.

Transportation within the city: The JR Keihin-Tohoku Line (west of Sakuragicho, it is called Negishi Line) runs through the city, covering most of the points of interest. The "Blue Line" double-decker buses run by the municipality leave Kannai Station to take tourists around to various points of interest. Passengers may get on and get off freely around the port and other places. They run every 20–30 min. Another interesting mode of transport is the "Sea Bass" boat (leaves every 20 min.; the duration is 15 min.) that takes one from the east exit of Yokohama Station to Yamashita Park by crossing Yokohama Port. Excursion Boat: There are two excursion tours leaving Yamashita Park—the "Marine Shuttle" (1-hr. 30-min. ride) and the "Akai Kutsu" (40-min. ride).

ANNUAL EVENTS

Shunsetsu: Late January–early February. Held in Chinatown, this festival celebrates the Chinese New Year based on the lunar calendar and is very lively. The popping of firecrackers echo through the town accompanied by magnificent dragon and lion dances.

International Ladies Ekiden (Long-distance Relay Race): Fourth Sunday in February. First-class runners from around the world participated in this very popular event.

International Costume Parade: May 3. This parade is the highlight of the Yokohama Port Festival held from May 3 to July 20. Led by Miss Yokohama, it leaves Yamashita Park and includes numerous citizen groups and foreign residents dressed in unique costumes.

Anniversary Bazaar of the Opening of Yokohama Port: During the week of June 2. This event is held at Yokohama Park. Many outdoor vendors offer their wares to park visitors. June 2 is the day when Yokohama Port opened.

Yokohama Dontaku: First Saturday and Sunday in June in Yokohama and Yamashita parks. Parade participants are dressed in costumes symbolizing the Meiji period and are accompanied by a brass band.

International Fireworks Display: July 20. This is the final event of the Yokohama Port Festival. Various types of fireworks illuminate the sky, painting the night with dazzling colors. At Yamashita Park.

Yokohama Takigi Noh: July 27. Using Yokohama Port as an evening background, an elaborate and sophisticated *noh* performance, lighted with burning wood, takes place on an outdoor stage.

Yokohama Hommoku Jazz Festival: The last Sunday in August. The outdoor concert goes on for approximately 8 hrs. at the Hommoku Municipal Park Baseball Field.

Osannomiya Autumn Festival: Early or mid-September. The climax is a parade of large portable shrines riding on floats through the city. At Hie Shrine.

Yokohama Carnival: Late September. This is an autumn festival taking place around the west exit of the JR Yokohama Station. A colorful parade of portable shrines, various floats and marching bands pass through the city.

Festival to Celebrate the China Nation Founding Day: October 1. A parade showing various Chinese traditional performances marches through the area, with firecrackers popping in the background. In Chinatown.

Yokohama Festival: Mid-October. This is a local festival held at

Yamashita Park with a variety of attractions such as a float parade, cutter race, walking rallies, etc.

Whistles of New Year's Eve: All the ships docked in the port simultaneously blow their whistles on the night of December 31 to bid farewell to the old year and greet the new one. Chinatown celebrates the evening with a lot of firecrackers.

Refer to the supplement for details regarding the "i" **System Information Center** in Yokohama.

PLACES OF INTEREST

Sojiji Temple: It was originally founded in Noto (Ishikawa Prefecture) as the head temple of the Soto sect of Zen Buddhism, but after being ravaged by a fire, it was rebuilt in 1911 at the present site. It is a 5-min. walk west from Tsurumi Station on the JR Keihin-Tohoku Line. There are some 30 large structures in the compound, which extends over 495,000 sq.m. Anyone entering the grounds is sure to be astounded. The Main Hall, constructed of ferroconcrete, covers an area of approximately 6,600 sq.m and is 39 m high.

Hongakuji Temple: In June 1859 Townsend Harris (1804-1878), the first American Consul General to Japan, moved his office from Gyokusenji Temple in Shimoda on the Izu Peninsula to this temple in order to establish the first American Consulate General. Unfortunately, all of the temple's prewar structures, except the front gate, were reduced to ashes during World War II. It is located about 600 m north of Yokohama Station.

Yokohama Station 46 : Yokohama's main station. The JR Tokaido Main Line, Yokosuka Line, Keihin-Tohoku Line and Yokohama Line stop here. It is also for the Keikyu Line, Tokyu Toyoko Line, Sagami Railway and Yokohama Municipal Subway. The west exit of the station bustles with fashionable stores such as Takashimaya and Mitsukoshi department stores, JOINUS and Okadaya More's and the station building named CIAL as well as several movie theaters and hotels. At the east exit are a number of buildings, including Sogo (a department store with the largest shopping space in Japan); LUMINE fashion building, and Yokohama Sky Building, which has a rotating restaurant on the roof overlooking the city. In addition, a large-scale, underground shopping mall with boutiques and food stores below the west exit is called "the Diamond," while its counterpart beneath the east exit is "Porta."

Kamonyama Park 46 : Located on a hill overlooking Yokohama Port, about 10 min. on foot from Sakuragicho Station on JR and Tokyu Toyoko Line. This park was opened in 1914 dedicated to Ii Kamon-no-Kami (Court rank) Naosuke (1815-1860), Chief Minister of the Tokugawa Shogun during the latter part of the Edo period, who signed the Treaty of Amity and Commerce with the U.S and four other countries (refer to p.98). As a result, Yokohama Port was opened to these five countries. Besides his bronze statue standing in

419

the center of the park overlooking the port, a culture center containing a music hall and library has been added to the park grounds.

Iseyama Kotaijingu Shrine 46 : Set on a hill next to Kamonyama Park, the Shinto shrine has been worshipped as the tutelar deity of Yokohama citizens. The architecture used in the main hall is that of the *Shimmei-zukuri* (*Shimmei* style). The shrine, which is also noted for its cherry blossoms, has a simple and beautiful structure.

Nogeyama Park: Situated on a small hill and covering approximately 90,000 sq.m in area, the park is noted for its cherry blossoms in spring. Nogeyama Zoo covers one-third of the park. The shopping area at the foot of the hill has a cordial, inviting atmosphere. A 10-min. walk from Hinode Station on the Keikyu Line.

Minato Mirai 21 (MM21) 46 : The waterfront area between Kannai and Yokohama stations is being transformed into a new city center for Yokohama. *Minato* refers to the port, *Mirai* means future and 21 represents the 21st century. The approximate 1.86 sq.km of land located in front of Sakuragicho Station, consists of the back lot of a shipping dock and other reclaimed land. The plan is to develop a new city with an estimated daytime population of 190,000 by constructing high-rise office buildings, convention centers, international conference halls, hotels and residential buildings.

Yokohama Maritime Museum 46 : Located within the grounds of MM21. This is a port and ship museum that serves as the home port for the sleek sailing vessel Nippon Maru. Built as a training ship, the all-white ship is referred to as the "Swan of the Pacific Ocean" or "Noble Lady of the Ocean" because of its graceful figure in full sail. The sailing ship is a four-masted barque type constructed in 1930, and has been highly regarded throughout the latter history of Japanese shipbuilding. Thus, instead of dismantling such a sea-going masterpiece, it was placed on exhibit here.

Yokohama Museum of Art 46 : Located within the confines of MM21, the museum opened its doors in 1989. Modern and contemporary masterpieces of the world are on exhibit here in this museum. Besides displays that include paintings, sculptures and photographs, the museum includes a children's workshop corner and an information center.

Isezakicho 46 : One of the most popular shopping and dining areas in Yokohama. The shopping mall consists of approximately 500 shops and stretches 1.5 km from its entrance near Kannai Station. The back-street area off the main street is noted as a famous nightspot and is lively with game centers, bars and cabarets.

Bashamichi 46 : The red-brick road runs toward the port from the JR Kannai Station. It is the oldest shopping street in Yokohama, and one can sense its history in many of the restaurants, tea houses, Western goods shops and Japanese confectionery shops located here. The street itself has a very attractive appearance.

Kanagawa Prefectural Museum 46 : The museum has displays on the nature and history of Kanagawa Prefecture. The museum building was built in 1904 as the head office of the Yokohama Specie Bank (the predecessor of Bank of Tokyo) and is designated as an Important Cultural Property for its architectural importance. Closed on Mondays and the day following a national holiday.

Yokohama Park 46 : Located east of the JR Kannai Station, the park was originally laid out in 1877 as the first Western-style park thrown open to the Japanese. Yokohama Stadium, home of professional baseball's Yokohama Taiyo Whales Team, is located here. In 1934 the visiting All-American Baseball Team played their first game here with the All-Japanese Team. In commemoration of the event, plaques in memory of Babe Ruth and Lou Gehrig, star players of the time, decorate the left and right wings of the pole.

Nihon-o-dori Street: A scenic street running from Yokohama Park to the port, lined with rows of ginkgo trees. In addition to numerous office buildings and banks, the Prefectural Government Offices and Courthouse stand along Nihon-o-dori Street.

Port-Opening Memorial Hall 46 : Built in 1918 to commemorate the 50th anniversary of the opening of Yokohama Port, this red-brick, Neo-Renaissance-style clock tower is presently used as a public hall.

Yokohama Archives of History: Housed in the reconstructed former British Consulate building, this museum's exhibits, references and storage total as many as 140,000 pieces, including photographs, *ukiyo-e* (woodblock prints) and Yokohama newspapers. Closed on Mondays.

Silk Center 46 : Situated at the entrance to the O-Sambashi (large pier). The Silk Museum is located on the second and third floors of the Silk Center. This unique museum exhibits the process of raising silkworms and producing silk, references on the history of silk and its extravagant use. The various silk products on exhibit are all sure to attract the interest of the visitor.

Yokohama Port 46 : An international port that covers a water surface area of 7.8 sq.km. Yamashita Park lies alongside the port. To the left is the O-Sambashi (also called Minami Sambashi—the South Pier), measuring 450 m in length and 49.5 m in width. The South Pier is capable of receiving several large vessels docked alongside. Central Pier is northwest of South Pier, while Yamashita Pier is to the southwest. There are several other docking facilities beyond Central and Yamashita piers surrounded by docks, warehouses and enormous cranes. The Yokohama Bay Bridge spans the port as part of the Tokyo Metropolitan Expressway, measuring 860 m in length and 55 m in height.

Yamashita Park 46 : The park stretches over 1,000 m of land between the South and Yamashita piers, with a total area of 74,000 sq. m. Built in 1930, it has long been a recreational retreat for both local residents and tourists, and is a frequent site of festivals and public events. Trees and flowers cover the entire area, and a statue called the "Guardian of Water"—presented in 1960 by the city of San Diego, California, USA. (Yokohama's sister city)—stands in the fountain in the center of the park. The "Water Tower of India," presented by the Indian traders association, is also part of the fountain.

Hikawa Maru [47]: Moored near the shoreline in front of Yamashita Park. It was a one-time passenger liner that sailed the Pacific Ocean, plying between Japan and North America from 1930 to 1960. The beautiful "Queen of the Pacific Ocean" weighs 11,625 tons and measures 163.3 m in length and 20.1 m in width. Docked permanently now and open to the public, it offers a restaurant, coffee shop and a banquet room on board.

Yokohama Doll Museum [47]: Located near the Marine Tower. This museum of fantasia exhibits over 4,000 dolls from 95 countries. The museum is located on the second and third floors of a fantastically shaped building next to the Marine Tower (see below), while a doll shop is on the first floor. The fourth floor is occupied by a multi-purpose theater.

Marine Tower [47]: Completed in 1961 to commemorate the centennial anniversary of the opening of Yokohama Port. This tower, decagonal in shape and 106 m in height, is one of the highest, land-based lighthouses in the world. It is complete with restaurants and souvenir shops as well as an observatory that offers a panoramic view of the city, port and Tokyo Bay. Take the elevator 100 m up to the observatory.

Yokohama Chinatown [46]: 500 m southwest of Yamashita Park. This is one of Japan's most famous dining and shopping districts. The aroma of delightful cuisine fills the air from more than 100 exclusive restaurants specializing in Canton, Peking, Shanghai and Szechuan style cooking. Shopping can be enjoyed in the various shops selling Chinese confectioneries, clothing, cooking ingredients, sundry goods and herbal medicines. A 7-min. walk from Ishikawacho Station on the JR Negishi Line.

Motomachi Shopping Street [47]: Located in proximity to Chinatown on the other side of the O-oka River, this street is a shopper's paradise in Yokohama and is lined with many chic and fashionable clothing shops, interior goods stores, accessory shops, famous restaurants, coffee shops and bakeries.

The Yamate area is located in a hilly region behind Motomachi. Many Christian churches and missionary schools of historical importance can be found among the remains of the foreign settlement, which developed when the port first opened. Now, it is known as one of Yokohama's exclusive residential areas, offering a beautiful view of the harbor. By walking through the area, one will find the Kanagawa Museum of Modern Literature, Yamate Museum and Iwasaki Museum.

Minato-no-mieru-oka Park (Harbor-View Park) [47]: "Minato-no-mieru-oka Park" literally means a harbor-view-hill park. This hilltop park commands a spectacular view of the port of Yokohama that is especially beautiful at night. The park was originally the site of the British troop garrison when Yokohama was one of the first ports opened to the outside world in 1859. The adjoining land, formerly called *Fransu-yama* or French Hill where French troops had their barracks, is now a part of the park. A 20-min. walk from the JR Ishikawacho Station or a 10-min. bus ride from Sakuragicho Station.

Negishi Forest Park 47 : The park was opened in 1977 on the site where Japan's first Western-style, horse racing track used to be. Visitors can watch different breeds of horses and enjoy pony rides here. Also in the park is the Negishi Equine Museum, which exhibits items related to horses in general and the role played by horses in Japanese history in particular. A 10-min. bus ride from Negishi Station on the JR Negishi Line.

Sankei-en Garden 47 : Originally built and owned as a residence by the late Hara Tomitaro (1808-1939), one of the wealthiest silk merchants in Yokohama and an ardent art collector. The garden landscaped on Hommoku Hill covers a total area of 170,000 sq.m and is beautifully provided with large and small ponds as well as seasonal plants and flowers. This garden is especially noted for its historical architecture set amid natural scenery for added effect. These structures include a temple, hall, pagoda, villa, tea house and farmhouse— all dating back to a period between the 14th and 18th centuries and registered as Important Cultural Properties. Notable structures include the *Rinshunkaku*, which is the only remaining example of villa-style architecture in the 17th century belonging to the Tokugawa branch family of Kii (now, Wakayama Prefecture); the *Choshukaku*, the tea house also built in the 17th century and moved from the gardens of Nijo Castle in Kyoto; the Three-Story Pagoda from Tomyoji Temple in Kyoto, which dates back to the beginning of the 14th century, and the Yanohara Residence brought from Shogawa Village in Gifu Prefecture. The beautiful garden is a product of perfect harmony between nature and man-made structures. A 6-min. bus ride from the JR Negishi Station.

Hasseiden (Hall of the Eight Sages) 47 : Built in 1933 at Hommoku Seaside Park near the Sankei-en Garden by the late Adachi Kenzo (1864-1948), a prominent political figure of the past. This is an octagonal, ferroconcrete sanctuary that houses life-size statues of the "Eight Sages of the World"—Sakyamuni, Confucius, Socrates, Christ, Prince Shotoku (594-622), Saint Kobo (774-835), Saint Shinran (1173-1262) and Saint Nichiren (1222-1282). At the center of these statues is a large mirror symbolizing the universe, an image expressed by the hall's founder.

Yokohama Port Symbol Tower 47 : An observatory that stands on the northeast corner of Hommoku Pier and sends signals to ships entering and leaving Yokohama Port. A large, stainless steel model of a scallop shell standing in the precincts is the landmark. The tower commands a fine view of the harbor and sea. It can be reached by bus from Ishikawacho Station on the JR Negishi Line.

Gumyoji Temple: Believed to be the oldest Buddhist temple in Yokohama, Gumyoji Temple is situated on a hill adjacent to Gumyoji Station on the Keikyu Line—also a few minutes walk from Gumyoji Subway Station. Belonging to the Shingon sect of Buddhism, the temple is dedicated to the Eleven-Headed *Kannon*—the Goddess of Mercy. Standing 1.8 m high, the wooden image was carved in the ninth century and is listed among Japan's Important Cultural Properties.

British Commonwealth War Cemetery: This is situated at Karibacho in Hodogaya Ward, 4.8 km south of Hodogaya Station on the JR Yokosuka Line. Buses are available from the station. There are more than 2,000 British Commonwealth citizens buried in this 73,000-sq.-m graveyard.

Yokohama Dreamland: This is an extensive amusement park, with the Hakone and Tanzawa mountains dominating the background. Houses from around the world stand amid the beautiful flower beds. Among its many attractions are the shuttle loop, a pool and various other amusement facilities plus a hotel. A 20-min. bus ride from Totsuka Station or Ofuna Station on the Tokaido Main Line.

Taya Caves 48 : Situated on a hillside behind the Josenji Temple at Tayacho. These caves are located 2.4 km northwest of Ofuna Station, from where buses are available. Originally excavated 750 years ago by the Hojo family in order to hide their treasures, the caves were later enlarged during the Edo period (1603–1867) by a group of the Shingon-sect Buddhists. Members of this sect were said to have performed their mystic religious practices in the caves. The total length of the caves is 1.5 km, the height is 2 m and the width 1 m. Visitors may explore the caves guided by a temple priest (1 hr. required). On the walls and ceilings are innumerable Buddhist images and Sanskrit characters carved with great skill and painstaking care by unknown artists.

Shomyoji Temple 41 : This is a Buddhist temple of the Shingon-Ritsu sect founded in the 1260s by Hojo Sanetoki (1224–1276). A member of the ruling family headquartered at Kamakura, Sanetoki later changed the family name from Hojo to Kanezawa. His tomb is on the hillside behind the temple. The object of worship housed in the main hall is the 1.7-m-tall, wooden statue of *Miroku-Bosatsu* (Maitreya), carved in 1276. This image and the bronze bell in front of the main hall, which was cast in 1269 and recast in 1301, are both Important Cultural Properties along with many other items in the temple. 500 m east of Kanazawa-Bunko Station on the Keihin Electric Express Railway (Keikyu).

Within the boundaries of the temple area stands the famous Kanazawa Bunko (library), which was founded by Hojo Sanetoki in 1275. The library previously contained thousands of volumes collected by the succeeding heads of the Kanesawa family and was open to the public. But after the downfall of the Hojo family of Kamakura in 1333, it was utterly neglected and the books were either scattered or lost. The present library, under the management of the Kanagawa Prefectural Government, was housed in a two-story ferroconcrete building in 1930, bringing together whatever books and documents were left from the old library. It is now open to the public. The first floor is used for the main office, stacks and reading rooms, while the second floor houses a museum, where many treasures of the Shomyoji Temple are displayed. Among the volumes contained in the present library are more than 20,000 rare books and 7,000 ancient documents, including a variorum edition of the Chinese classic "Monzen," which is a National Treasure, and a copy of the "Issaikyo" (a complete collection of Buddhist Scriptures), published in China during the Sung Dynasty.

Area 3. Kamakura, Enoshima and Miura Peninsula

The Miura Peninsula is a small projection south of Yokohama facing the eastern Boso Peninsula. The Uraga Straits, the narrow channel between the Miura and Boso Peninsulas, serves as the gateway to Tokyo Bay. Yokosuka, long home to a naval base, overlooks the Uraga Straits.

The city of Kamakura lies on the western neck of the Miura Peninsula. It became the capital of the first feudal government, the Kamakura Shogunate, which ruled the nation from 1192 to 1333. Sagami Bay lies between Kamakura and the open sea. The Miura Peninsula in the east and the Izu Peninsula to the west gently embrace the waters of this bay, forming a graceful semi-circle.

Enoshima, a famous tourist attraction, is a beach resort immediately west of Kamakura, while Zushi and Hayama, also famous seaside resorts, lie along the southern shoreline.

Miura is located further south, with its Misaki Port famous for landing tuna. On the opposite bank, Jogashima Island, a popular picnic spot, is linked to Miura by the Jogashima Ohashi Bridge.

The Miura Peninsula shoreline is rich with variation and blessed with warm weather all year long due to the ocean current. The transportation system is well developed, making it a popular recreational area for Tokyo and Yokohama residents. Many visitors not only come to see the old capital of Kamakura, but also to enjoy ocean sports such as fishing, surfing and sailing during the summer.

TRANSPORTATION
Rail: The JR Yokosuka Line runs from Tokyo Station to Kurihama (Yokosuka City) in 10-min. intervals. The main stations used for sightseeing are Ofuna, Kita-Kamakura, Kamakura, Zushi and Yoko-

suka. To tour Enoshima, get on the Shonan Monorail at Ofuna or take the Enoshima Electric Railway (commonly called Enoden) from Kamakura. The Shonan Line, popular name of a portion of the JR Tokaido Main Line, leaves Tokyo Station in approximately 10-min. intervals. (Shonan indicates the areas along Sagami Bay, including Kamakura, Zushi, Hayama, Oiso, etc.) The JR Yokosuka Line branches off at Ofuna and heads for Kamakura. Enoshima is accessible also from Fujisawa Station on the JR Shonan Line, by the Odakyu Enoshima Line or the Enoden.

The Keihin Electric Express Railway (commonly called Keikyu) leaving Shinagawa in Tokyo is a good means of transportation for the Miura Peninsula. Its rapid-limited express train connects Tokyo and Misakiguchi (Miura City) in 1 hr.

Odakyu Enoshima Line trains depart from Shinjuku in Tokyo or Katase-Enoshima in intervals ranging from 10–30 min. The trains of Enoshima Electric Railways, running part of the way along the streets, depart from Fujisawa or Kamakura in roughly 12-min. intervals in either direction. Since there are several stops on the line, the street cars are convenient for sightseeing in western Kamakura.

Road: The main roads of the Miura Peninsula include National Highway 134, running parallel to the western shoreline (along Sagami Bay); the Yokohama-Yokosuka Expressway, running through the central portion, and National Highway 16, running along the eastern shoreline (along Tokyo Bay). The excellent roads and scenic beauty of the surrounding areas attract many visitors, making the roads very congested on weekends and holidays. It will probably be easier to take the train when visiting the old capital of Kamakura.

PLACES OF INTEREST

Ofuna 48-49 : 18 km from Yokohama. Ofuna is an important junction on the JR Tokaido Main Line since the JR Yokosuka Line for Kurihama (via Kamakura, Zushi and Yokosuka) branches off to the southwest from this point. Near the station is the Ofuna Studio of Shochiku Co., one of the largest motion picture companies in Japan. On a low hill west of the station stands a concrete, 25-m-tall image of *Kannon*, the Goddess of Mercy, completed in 1960.

About a 15-min. walk from Ofuna Station is the Kanagawa Prefectural Ofuna Botanical Garden. Covering an area of 89,000 sq.m, it was laid out in 1962 on the site of an agricultural experimental station. The garden is designed to give guidance for flower cultivation in the prefecture, to open and expand the market for flowers and plants, and to hold floral exhibitions from time to time. Among the numerous seasonal flowers are 1,000 peonies of hundreds of species that bloom from mid-to late May. With grassy plots, greenhouses, resting places and a pond with a fountain, the garden provides an ideal picnic place. It is open to the public, but closed on Mondays and the day after national holidays.

Fujisawa 48 ☎0466: Pop. 341,303. 52 km from Tokyo Station, around 50 min. on the JR Tokaido Main Line; 55.6 km from Shinjuku, Tokyo, within 1 hr. by express on the Odakyu-Enoshima Line. This city lies west of Kamakura, while seaside resorts such as Kugenuma, Enoshima and Katase are situated to the south. Regarded as a satellite city of Tokyo, it used to be a market for farm products from the Sagami Plain to the north. Nearly 1 km northeast of Fujisawa Station is Yugyoji Temple, officially called Shojokoji Temple. It was founded in 1325 as the central headquarters of the Jishu sect of Buddhism, whose itinerant priests are expected to perform pious services throughout the land according to the precedent set by Saint Ippen (1239-1289). Hence, the name "Yugyoji" (Peripatetic Preachers' Temple).

On stepping into the precincts, the visitor will first notice a huge ginkgo tree overshadowing the spacious grounds as well as the imposing Main Hall beyond. On the left of the hall is a belfry in which is hung an old temple bell cast in 1356, while on the right just inside the back gate is an ancient stone monument 1.5 m high. This monument was erected in 1418 to commemorate the souls of the people and animals that died in the Kanto District during the civil war between the Uesugi and Ashikaga families from 1416 to 1417.

Shaded by a pine grove, the beach at Fujisawa, known as Kugenuma, is now a quiet residential area.

Katase and Enoshima ⎡48⎤ : Situated about 4 km from Fujisawa Station, these two seaside resorts are linked by a bridge. The beach east of the Katase River is called Katase-Higashihama, while the area west of the river is known as Katase-Nishihama. The latter is next to Kugenuma.

Near the west end of Katase Bridge is a large parking lot, next to which is Enoshima Marineland. Opened in 1957, it features dolphin shows and a whale museum. Across the street from Marineland stands the two-story Enoshima Aquarium, with a corridor connecting the basements of these two establishments. The first floor is laid out as an aquarium to show marine life in a natural setting, while the second floor is a specimen gallery.

West of Marineland along the shore are the Enoshima Marine Zoo (marine animals) and the Pool Garden—complete with bathing facilities. Boats and yachts may also be rented here. These establishments are grouped into an area called "Seaside Palace," while the beach is named "Shonan Seacoast Park."

Ryukoji Temple ⎡48⎤ : 100 m northeast of Enoshima Station on the Enoden Line. This is a sanctuary of the Nichiren sect of Buddhism. Saint Nichiren (1222-1282), founder of the sect, attacked in polemics other older Buddhist sects so ruthlessly that he was on the verge of being executed by decapitation in 1271 by the Kamakura Shogunate. Miraculously, however, he was saved from execution when, as legend goes, the executioner's sword was broken by a thunderbolt. Between 1278 and 1288, his six disciples celebrated his deliverance by erecting a memorial on the spot chosen for the execution in front of the temple. At that time, Katase was an execution ground, and it was at this spot that the envoys sent in 1275 by Kublai Khan with a demand for tribute were beheaded. *Oeshiki*, the annual festival of Ryukoji Temple, takes place on September 10-13.

Enoshima Island 48 : A beautiful wooded islet, 180,000 sq. m in area. It is connected with Katase beach by a 600-m-long concrete bridge called Bentembashi, with separate paths for pedestrians and vehicles. On the islet is a street flanked by a line of inns and souvenir shops solidly up to Enoshima Shrine, which is dedicated to three female Shinto deities. The approach consists of about 300 stone steps, but now there is a 106-m-long, outdoor escalator that terminates under the observation tower of the Enoshima Botanical Garden at the center of this small island.

Before the Meiji Restoration (1868), Enoshima Shrine was a Buddhist temple built by an eminent priest named Mongaku in 1182. The structure was established at the request of Minamoto-no-Yoritomo (1147-1199), founder of the Kamakura Shogunate, and contains a nude image of *Benten*—the Indian Goddess of Music and Beauty and one of the Seven Gods of Prosperity.

Enoshima Botanical Garden 48 : Spreading over 18,000 sq. m in area, it consists of a garden of tropical plants, a small zoo, a playground and an observation tower, which stands 54 m high and is 114 m above sea level. The observation platform at the top of the tower offers a fine view of Mt. Fuji and Oshima Island with its smoking volcano. The top of the tower is also used as a lighthouse.

Going down the hill on the southwestern side, the visitor comes to a scenic spot called *Chigogafuchi*. Proceeding to the east from here, one will find a cave called Oiwaya—once noted for the presence of a nude image of *Benten* placed at the far end. Since the cave has been blocked off by rock slides, chances are slim that it will be reopened to visitors anytime soon. However, the *Benten* image was transferred to the oratory in Enoshima Shrine.

Shonan Harbor 48 : Constructed in 1964 on the east coast of scenic Enoshima Island to protect Katase beach from erosion by waves and to develop the district for tourism as well as fishing. The port includes a yacht harbor that was used in the 1964 Tokyo Olympic Games.

Farther east along the coast from Katase to Kamakura at Koshigoe is a Buddhist temple called Mampukuji. Koshigoe is now a part of Kamakura. The temple is known as the spot where Minamoto-no-Yoshitsune (1159-1189), a younger brother of Yoritomo, stayed in 1185. Suspected of harboring rebellious plots and prevented by his brother from entering Kamakura, Yoshitsune wrote letters of allegiance to Yoritomo that are known as the "Koshigoe Appeal."

Kamakura 49 ☎0467

Pop. 176,682. Located 51 km by rail from Tokyo. Kamakura is a noted tourist attraction of the same stature as the other historical capitals, Kyoto and Nara. The city is surrounded on three sides by mountains abundant with greenery and contains many old shrines and temples. Since the Meiji period, the area has become an exclusive residential area, serving as home to many wealthy entrepreneurs, politicians, writers, painters and artists. Since Tokyo and Yokohama are only a short distance away by rail, the hills have been residential-ized and turned into a bedroom community for Tokyo.

TRANSPORTATION

On the JR Yokosuka Line, it is 51 km from Tokyo Station to Kamakura, taking 1 hr. If one takes the Odakyu Electric Railway Enoshima Line from Shinjuku in Tokyo, a transfer should be made to the Enoshima Electric Railway (Enoden) at Fujisawa Station for Kamakura. During the New Year's holidays and the spring and autumn festivals, the city is closed to automotive traffic. Driving is not advisable since traffic is congested, even under normal conditions.

HISTORY

Kamakura, which had been nothing more than a remote fishing and farming village, was settled by Minamoto family in early 12th cen-tury, and Minamoto-no-Yoritomo set up his headquarters here in 1180. Yoritomo was successful in overcoming the Tairas in 1185, receiving the title of *shogun* from the Imperial Court in 1192. Kamakura then became his capital. Yoritomo's son, Yoriie (1182–1204), succeeded him as *shogun*, but the power had fallen into the hands of the Hojo Clan, of which Yoritomo's wife Masako was a member. The third Shogun, Sanetomo (1192–1219), was the second son of Yoritomo. With his death, direct lineage to Yoritomo was extinguished, and although no battles were fought, the Hojo Clan assumed total control as the regent of the Kamakura Shogunate government. Imperial courtiers and princes were sent from Kyoto to retain the position of *shogun* in name only.

The entrenchment of the Hojo Clan in 1224 brought stability to Kamakura. The *samurai* government, based on the principles of *zen*, led to the development of a new culture quite different from that of Kyoto. Many of the famous temples and cultural properties still remaining in Kamakura date from this period.

The government of the Hojo Clan continued for over a hundred years until increasing autocracy triggered a revolt by the local *samurai* and their clans, finally toppling under the Ashikaga, Nitta and other anti-Hojo clans in 1333. The Kamakura period thus refers to the era between 1192, when Yoritomo established the shogunate in Kamakura, and 1333, when the Hojo Clan was overthrown.

The temples and shrines of Kamakura received continued support and so remained a vital force, but the city atrophied. By the Edo period (1603–1867), Kamakura was reduced to a poor village surviving on farming and fishery, and commerce with those visiting the temples and shrines.

ANNUAL EVENTS

Hatsumode (First Shrine Visit): January 1. The most popular shrine in Kamakura for this important ritual is Tsurugaoka Hachimangu Shrine. Many women dressed in beautiful *kimono* can be glimpsed praying to the strains of music of the *Kagura*, a sacred dance performed in the *Maidono* (Dance Hall).

Setsubun (Bean-throwing Festival): February 3 or 4. Held at the Tsurugaoka Hachimangu Shrine, Kamakuragu Shrine and Kenchoji Temple.

Hanami (Cherry-Blossom Viewing): Held in early April at Kenchoji Temple, Kosokuji Temple, Hanzobo Temple, Kamakuragu Shrine, Kuzuharagaoka Hill, Mt. Kamakura and other locations. The old capital decorated with beautiful cherry blossoms is at its most beautiful at this time of year.

Kamakura Festival: A total of eight days from the first Sunday in April. This is the largest festival in Kamakura, with a variety of events taking place all over the city. Tsurugaoka Hachimangu Shrine serves as the center of the festival, with highlights such as the *Shizuka-no-Mai*, an elegant dance named after the famous Lady Shizuka (refer to p.434), *Yabusame* (archery on horseback) and *nodate* (outdoor tea ceremony) taking place here. Other shrines and temples offer special exhibitions of their treasures at this time.

Fireworks Festival: Early August at Kamakura Beach. The brilliant colors of the spectacular fireworks are reflected in the sea.

Tsurugaoka Hachimangu Shrine Festival: September 14–16. It is noted for the *Shinkosai*, an ancient procession on the 15th, and *Yabusame* on the 16th. *Yabusame* has been a tradition since the time of Minamoto-no-Yoritomo. A mounted archer shoots at three targets while galloping by them at full speed.

Menkake Gyoretsu (Procession of Masks): September 18 at Goryo Shrine. A humorous parade passes through the city by ten people in traditional costumes wearing grotesque, outrageous, sad and other masks of various expressions.

Takigi-Noh (Torchlight Noh): September 21–22 at Kamakuragu Shrine. Top performers from various dance schools perform *noh* on an outdoor stage. The performance starts in the evening, with torchlight adding a mystical beauty.

Tsurugaoka Hachimangu Memorial Festival: December 16. After the main ceremony, the *Hatcho-mai* dance and other old religious arts are performed. The torchlight creates a spectral air.

Refer to the supplement for details regarding the "i" **System Information Center** in Kamakura.

PLACES OF INTEREST

The important tourist attractions in Kamakura may be divided into two groups: those to the east of the JR Yokosuka Line, including Tsurugaoka Hachimangu Shrine, the Modern Art Gallery, Tomb of Yoritomo, Kamakuragu Shrine, and the Buddhist temples of Kenchoji and Engakuji, and those to the west of the line, including the Kamakura Daibutsu (Great Buddha), Hase Kannon Temple, and the beaches of Yuigahama and Shichirigahama. Of the 65 Buddhist temples and 19 Shinto shrines in Kamakura, those mentioned above are probably of greatest interest to visitors.

Kamakura Daibutsu (Great Buddha) 49 : A seated bronze figure of Amitabha is located on the precincts of the Jodo sect Kotoku-in Temple about 400 m north of Hase Station on the Enoshima Electric Railway, also called Enoden (1.7 km southwest of Kamakura). It can also be reached in 8 min. by bus from Kamakura Station. Before it was damaged by a storm in 1369 and finally carried away by tidal waves in 1495, the image was originally enclosed in a large hall. Since then, however, the figure has remained in the open. Many of the foundation stones that once supported the pillars of the edifice may still be seen in their original positions. The bronze *Daibutsu* is 13.3 m tall, the circumference at the base is 29.4 m and the length of the face is 2.3 m. The silver boss on the forehead weighs 13.6 kg, while the image itself is 121-odd tons. One can reach the interior shoulder level by a staircase inside the Buddha.

The image is believed to have been cast in 1252 by Ono Goroemon or Tanji Hisatomo, both leading casters of the time. Since it is generally considered to be a very fine specimen of the art of casting, it has been singled out by the government as a National Treasure. The position of the hands, which are laid on the lap with the palms and thumbs touching, represents the Buddhist sign for steadfast faith. The expression on the face, with its half-closed eyes, admirably depicts the perfect repose and passionless calm that is the root idea of the Buddhist doctrine. Although the biggest bronze image of the Great Buddha is located in Nara (refer to p.716), the one in Kamakura is nevertheless one of the largest in Japan.

Hase Kannon 49 : This Jodo-sect Buddhist temple near the *Daibutsu* is celebrated for its eleven-headed gilt statue of *Kannon*, the Goddess of Mercy. Standing 9.2 m high in the main hall of the temple, the statue is one of the tallest wooden images in Japan. It is said to have been carved in 721 by priest Tokudo from half of a mighty camphor tree log and is a duplicate of the *Kannon* image at Hase Temple, south of Nara, which was supposedly carved from the other half of the same log by the same priest.

Designated as an Important Cultural Property, the temple bell in the precincts was cast in 1264 and is the third oldest Kamakura temple bell. From the grounds, one may obtain an excellent view of the seacoast extending from Yuigahama Beach to Hayama.

Kosokuji Temple 49 : It is a small temple located about a 5-min. walk from the north of Hase Kannon. Although the precincts are not very spacious, the beautiful flowers like those in Zuisenji Temple to the east are highly acclaimed. The sight of the blooms on the massive *kaido* or aronia tree in late April deserves special mention. Plums, peonies, irises, azaleas, ginger and sasanquas also color the grounds with their uninterrupted beauty all year round.

Gokurakuji Temple 48 : On the main road from Kamakura to Katase in front of Gokurakuji Station on the Enoden, 2.4 km southwest of Kamakura Station, 8 min. on foot. Founded in 1259 by Hojo Shigetoki (1198-1261) together with a priest named Ninsho (1217-1303) as the first abbot, the temple was unfortunately destroyed several times by fire and earthquake. Its original stateliness is gone, but it still possesses many Important Cultural Properties, including a wooden statue of Sakyamuni (chief object of worship). On the temple grounds are the tombs of the founder and the first abbot. The Gokurakuji Temple belongs to the Shingon-Ritsu sect of Buddhism.

Inamuragasaki Point 48 : A little to the southwest of Gokurakuji Temple, with Yuigahama Beach on the east and Shichirigahama Beach on the west. Today, the point forms a cliff rising sheer from the sea, but in olden times a strip of sand appeared at the bottom of the cliff at low tide, permitting an approach to Kamakura from the west. It was a strategic spot for the defense of Kamakura when it was the seat of the Shogunate.

In 1333, Nitta Yoshisada (1301-1338), a loyalist army general fighting for the Emperor in Kyoto, is said to have thrown a golden sword into the sea from the cliff with a prayer to the sea-god that the tide would recede and make way for his army at the bottom of the cliff to march on Kamakura. History relates that the waters miraculously receded, resulting in a complete rout of the enemy led by Regent Hojo Takatoki (1303-1333) and a glorious victory for the loyalists. The highlands on the western part of the point have been turned into a park, offering a panoramic view of Shichirigahama Beach extending toward the west.

Shichirigahama Beach 48 : The name given to a 4-km-long stretch of beach from Inamuragasaki Point to Koyurugisaki Point at Koshigoe. It is celebrated for its exquisite view of Enoshima Island and the distant Mt. Fuji. Since the ocean is rough here, swimming is prohibited, but recently it has become a popular spot for surfing and sailing. Near Enoden Inamuragasaki or Shichirigahama Station.

Yuigahama Beach 49 : Located 1.4 km south of Kamakura Station, 8 min. by bus, and along a crescent that extends for about 2 km. It is considered to be one of the finest, most popular swimming resorts around Tokyo because of its sandy beach and shallow waters. Various events are held on the beach during summer, one of the most popular of which is the annual Fireworks Festival in August. Needless to say, the event attracts a huge crowd of people.

During the days of the Kamakura Shogunate, the beach was only used for riding and archery by Minamoto-no-Yoritomo (1147-1199), founder of the Shogunate, and his successors. Presently, the road is lined on both sides with drive-ins and restaurants, and stays busy all year round with young speed maniacs driving motorcycles and colorful sports cars up and down the road. The beach continues south toward Zaimokuza Beach on the other side of the Namerikawa River. Near Enoden Yuigahama Station.

Komyoji Temple [49] : An imposing Buddhist temple of the Jodo sect in the hills behind Zaimokuza Beach. The spacious precincts contain many magnificent halls. Founded by the fourth Regent, Hojo Tsunetoki, it began as a small temple, but it was raised to its present scale when it was relocated to this site in 1243. It continued to prosper through the benevolence of the Tokugawa Shogunate. The temple is not only noted for the tombs of the Naito family, a lord during the Edo period, but also for its stone-lanterns.

Wakamiya-Oji (Avenue) [49] : The 1.8-km-long main approach, leading from Yuigahama Beach south to Tsurugaoka Hachimangu Shrine. At the southern end of the avenue is a big stone *torii* (shrine gate) erected in 1618 (about 10 m high, an Important Cultural Property). After passing through the second *torii*, the road runs straight as an arrow to the third *torii*. For about 500 m between the second and third *torii*, this section of the avenue, which is somewhat elevated and flanked with cherry trees and azaleas, is called "Dankazura." In olden times, this main road measured 9.1 m in width at the first *torii* and 2.7 m in width at the third *torii* at the northern end—a principle of perspective that is said to have been used to make the avenue appear longer than it actually was. The Wakamiya-Oji area, especially the western section (called Komachi-dori Street), is a bustling commercial district full of coffee shops, restaurants, antique shops and bars. Here, tourists can buy a fine local product called *Kamakura-bori* (articles chiseled in hardwood and repeatedly lacquered in black and then vermilion), which is prized for its artistic value and durability.

Tsurugaoka Hachimangu Shrine (49-Ⓐ): A "must" for tourists visiting Kamakura. Located 700 m northeast of the station, it may be reached by walking along Wakamiya-Oji, an avenue shaded by cherry trees. Founded in 1063 on another site by Minamoto-no-Yoriyoshi (998-1075), it was moved in 1191 to its present location by Shogun Yoritomo, although the existing buildings only date from 1828. The shrine is dedicated to Emperor Ojin, (reigned 270-310), Empress Jingu (his mother) and *Himekami*. (a goddess in the myth)

The gigantic ginkgo tree to the left of the stone steps, some 7 m in girth and 30 m in height, marks the spot where the third Kamakura Shogun, Sanetomo, was assassinated in 1219 by his nephew Kugyo.

Kugyo, the chief priest of Tsurugaoka Hachimangu Shrine, had hidden himself behind the trunk of the tree, awaiting the Sanetomo's return from a visit to the shrine. When the original gingko tree died, the present one was planted on the spot. During the subsequent centuries, it has grown to its present enormous size. In the colonnade enclosing the bright vermilion oratory and main edifice, several ancient swords, suits of armor, masks and other objects are on display, many of which are listed as either National Treasures or Important Cultural Properties. The annual festival of the shrine is celebrated on September 14-16, when *mikoshi*, or portable shrines, are carried through the streets. A demonstration of *Yabusame*, the gallant feat of archery by horsemen in the hunting attire of warriors of the Kamakura period, can be seen in the compound on September 16.

One of the minor shrines on the grounds, called *Wakamiya* (Junior Shrine), is located to the right of the stone steps. The structure, which dates back to 1624, is dedicated to Emperor Nintoku (d. 399), son of Emperor Ojin, and three other deities.

Wakamiya is associated with Lady Shizuka, a celebrated dancer and mistress of Yoshitsune (1159-1189), a younger brother of Yoritomo.

After Yoshitsune's flight to northern Japan to escape the murderous designs of his brother, Shizuka was taken to Kamakura and questioned about her lover's whereabouts. While here, she was compelled to dance at the colonnade of this shrine to entertain Yoritomo and his wife. This story has become a favorite theme with Japanese story-tellers and artists.

Farther to the right is the *Shirahatasha* (White Flag Shrine), erected in memory of Yoritomo and Sanetomo, and so called because the banner of the Minamoto Clan was white.

Kamakura Municipal Museum: Located between *Shirahatasha* and the lotus ponds. This ferroconcrete structure was built in 1928 in the style of the Shoso-in, the eighth-century treasure house of Todaiji Temple at Nara. It houses more than 40 Important Cultural Properties as well as many other art and historical objects, preserved chiefly from the Kamakura and Muromachi periods (1192-1573). Most of the sculptures, paintings, masks, industrial art works and ancient documents have been collected for display from private owners as well as from shrines and temples located in the city and its environs.

The three-story Kanagawa Prefectural Modern Art Gallery is to the left as one enters the shrine grounds. It is located on the grounds of the Tsurugaoka Hachimangu Shrine and contains approximately 3,500 Japanese paintings, sculptures and woodblock prints from the Meiji period onward. Temporary exhibitions are held in this building, while regular exhibitions are shown in the new building, which is located northwest of the exit of the Hachimangu Shrine compound. Closed on Mondays and the day following a national holiday.

Tomb of Minamoto-no-Yoritomo 49 : The tomb of Yoritomo, the first Kamakura Shogun, is located about 500 m northeast of Tsuru-gaoka Hachimangu Shrine. Overlooking the site of Yoritomo's castle, it is marked by a small, moss-covered stone pagoda, 2 m high, surrounded by a stone wall and shaded by trees.

Kamakuragu Shrine 49 : 1.8 km northeast of Kamakura Station, 10 min. by bus. It was erected by Imperial order in 1869 and is dedicated to Prince Morinaga (1308-1335), the third son of Emperor Godaigo (1288-1339).

Prince Morinaga was taken prisoner by the Ashikaga forces after his unsuccessful attempt to restore power to the rightful Emperor. He was confined in a stone cave at the back of the present shrine, where in 1335 at the age of 27 he was assassinated by order of Ashikaga Tadayoshi (1306-1352). The latter was a brother of Taka-uji (the first Ashikaga Shogun), who was fleeing from Kamakura at that time because of the storming of the town by Hojo Tokiyuki (d. 1353), a son of the last Regent Hojo Takatoki.

The prince's tomb is in an arbor on a hill called Richikozan, 300 m east of the shrine, and is reached by climbing some 170 stone steps. The annual festival of the shrine is held on August 20, the date on which the prince was killed. *Takigi-Noh* (Torchlight *Noh*), staged in the compound on September 21 and 22, is very famous. The *shishi-gashira* (lion's head) sold at the shrine is a popular good-luck charm.

Kakuonji Temple 49 : Located 700 m north of the Kamakuragu Shrine, this temple is affiliated with the Sen-yuji school of the Shin-gon sect of Buddhism. It was founded in 1218 by Hojo Yoshitoki (1163 -1224), the second Regent. As the chief object of worship, it contains a seated wooden trio of *Yakushi-Nyorai* and two attendant *Bosatsu* plus a wooden statue of *Jizo-Bosatsu*, generally called the *Kuro* (black) *Jizo* and believed to possess the power to prevent fires. Both are Important Cultural Properties and attract thousands of pilgrims. On the hill at the back of the temple are numerous stone caves, popularly known as *yagura*, which, judging from the human bones and tomb-stones found here, must have been used as burial sites.

Zuisenji Temple 49 : A Buddhist temple of the Rinzai sect belong-ing to the Engakuji school, about 1 km east of Kamakuragu Shrine in a quiet, secluded spot surrounded by hills. Founded in 1327 by Muso-Kokushi Soseki (1275-1351), a distinguished Zen priest, it was later restored by Ashikaga Motouji (1304-1367), brother of the second Ashikaga Shogun—then governor-general of the Kanto District. In 1387 the temple was named by Emperor Gokameyama as second in importance among the ten large Rinzai-sect temples in the Kanto District. Enshrined in the founder's hall is a wooden image of the priest Soseki, an Important Cultural Property. It is 1.2 m high and shows the priest sitting in a chair. His noble mien is well reproduced, and the figure is considered to be an excellent example of the work of the Muromachi period (1336-1573).

Laid out by its founder using stones, water and evergreens in beautiful harmony, the temple garden is considered one of the typical specimens of the gardens created under the influence of *zen* philosophy in the late Kamakura period (1192-1333). The temple is known as the "temple of flowers" because an abundance of plums, narcissuses, cherry trees, peonies, bellflowers and various other species of flowers and plants decorate the temple through all four seasons. The plum blossoms (February to early March), narcissuses (late January to mid-February) and the colored autumn leaves (mid-November to early December) are famous for being the most beautiful in Kamakura. One can enjoy a fine view of Kamakura from the Henkai-Ichirantei Arbor at the top of the hill behind the temple.

Samponji Temple (Sugimotodera) 49 : A Buddhist temple belonging to the Tendai sect about 1.4 km east of Tsurugaoka Hachimangu Shrine. The temple is said to have been founded in the eighth century, long before the establishment of the Kamakura Shogunate. The three wooden statues of the Eleven-Headed *Kannon* are the chief objects of interest in the thatched main hall. Because two of them are regarded by experts as works of the Heian period (794-1185), they have been designated as Important Cultural Properties.

This temple has been the starting point for pilgrimages to the 33 *Kannon* temples in the Kanto District since olden days, and is popularly known by the name of *Okura-no-Kannon* (Goddess of Mercy at Okura).

Jomyoji Temple 49 : A Rinzai-sect temple affiliated with Kenchoji Temple, situated about 350 m east of Samponji Temple or 2.4 km east of Kamakura Station (15 min. by bus). Founded in 1188 by Ashikaga Yoshikane (d. 1199), it was once ranked fifth among the Five Great Zen Temples of Kamakura.

Kamakura Gozan (Five Great Zen Temples of Kamakura): Of the many temples in Kamakura that are of the Rinzai Zen sect, five of them were placed under the special protection of the shogunate and given a ranking. In order, they were: Kenchoji Temple, Engakuji Temple, Jufukuji Temple, Jochiji Temple and Jomyoji Temple.

Hokokuji Temple 49 : Located 5 min. by foot south of Jomyoji Temple. Hokokuji Temple belongs to the Kenchoji school of the Rinzai sect. It was constructed during the 13th century, but it was totally destroyed by a fire in 1890 and again by the Great Kanto Earthquake and fire of 1923. The present buildings are all new. However, the old bamboo garden with a tea ceremony house among the green stalks is famous.

Myohoji Temple 49 : The most famous Buddhist priest during the Kamakura period was Nichiren (1222-1282), the founder of the Nichiren sect of Buddhism. This is the area in which he first preached his doctrines upon his arrival in Kamakura from Awa Province (now, a part of Chiba Prefecture) in 1253. His outspoken proslytizing methods created antagonism among other sects and schools, and eventually his temple was set on fire. Nichiei, Nichiren's disciple, rebuilt the temple in 1357 with many large halls and towers on spacious grounds. The stone steps extending from the *Niomon* Gate to the *Hokkedo* Hall are covered with beautiful moss, becoming famous over the centuries as the "Mossy Stone Steps." In May the stone steps are surrounded with white-fringed irises, creating a contrast of special beauty.

Nichiren (1222-1282) was born in Kominato on the southeast coast of the Boso Peninsula and entered the Buddhist priesthood when he was 15. He studied for over three years at the Buddhist monastery on Mt. Hiei near Kyoto, then returned to his native place and began preaching new doctrines. When this led to his expulsion, he went to Matsubagayatsu, Kamakura, and built a hermitage where he passed his days in devotion and preaching on the public thoroughfares. He also spent part of this time in writing his tracts, "On the True Defense of the State" and "On Public Peace." His vehemence and intolerance finally offended the authorities, who exiled him to Ito on the Izu Peninsula. On his release, he returned to Kamakura again and continued to spread his religious propaganda in spite of all obstacles. Once, he was on the point of being executed by the authorities, and another time he was exiled to Sado Island in the Japan Sea. Finally, after a stormy career of over 40 years, he died at the age of 60 at Ikegami (now, in Tokyo), where Ikegami Honmonji Temple—one of the headquarters of the Nichiren sect—now stands (refer to p.396). His remains were interred at Kuonji Temple in Minobu to the west of Mt. Fuji.

Nichiren-sect Temples: Southwest of Kamakura Station is Hongaku-ji Temple, dating from 1436. The tomb of Goro Masamune, the celebrated swordsmith of the 13th to 14th centuries, is located in its precincts. Myohonji Temple at Hikigayatsu, which is not far from here, was founded by Hiki Yoshimoto, who later became a priest named Nichigaku—a disciple of Nichiren. Myohoji and Ankokuronji, other temples of the same sect at Matsubagayatsu, are around 1.1 km southeast of Kamakura Station. Ankokuronji Temple, founded in 1274, marks the site of Nichiren's original hermitage. Coming from his native village in Awa Province (now, a part of Chiba Prefecture) in 1253, Nichiren lived in a stone cave at Matsubagayatsu from 1257 to 1260, during which time he wrote his famous tract entitled the "Rissho Ankokuron" (Establish the Right Law and Save Our Country). A copy of this treatise made by Nichiro, one of his chief disciples, is the temple's most treasured possession. Nichiro's grave is also in the temple precincts.

Zeniarai Benten (Money-washing Shrine) 49 : Located at Sasuke, about 1 km northwest of Kamakura Station. This very popular shrine is dedicated to *Benten*, also known as *Benzaiten* (Goddess of Beauty and Good Fortune). People from far and near believe that whatever money they wash at the shrine on the days of the "snake" (one of the 12 Oriental Zodiac Signs) with spring water in the cave on the shrine grounds, they will see it doubled or even tripled later on. A spectacular sight is a tunnel leading to the cave formed by wooden *torii* gates that have been consecrated to the deity by followers appreciative of the goddess' blessing.

Jufukuji Temple 49 : Located 500 m north of Kamakura Station, this is a Rinzai-sect temple. Founded in 1200 by Masako (1156–1225), wife of Minamoto-no-Yoritomo, it originally ranked third among the Five Great Zen Temples of Kamakura. But the reconstructed main hall is now the only existing edifice. It contains a wooden statue of *Jizo* (an Important Cultural Property), the chief object of worship and the guardian god of children. Tombs said to be those of Masako and the third Shogun Sanetomo (1192–1219), her second son, are found in the cemetery caves on the hillside behind the temple.

Eishoji Temple 49 : A little north of Jufukuji Temple. This nunnery of the Jodo sect was founded in 1636 by Lady Eisho, mistress of Tokugawa Ieyasu (1542–1616), who was the founder of the Tokugawa Shogunate. The temple was built on the site of the home of Ota Dokan (1432–1486), a feudal lord who built his castle at Edo (Tokyo) and settled there. Lady Eisho was his great-great-granddaughter. It is the only nunnery remaining in Kamakura. The Kamakura-period halls convey an impression of purity appropriate for a nunnery. The temple is noted for its beautiful plum groves and camellias.

Engakuji Temple 49 : Located close to Kita-Kamakura Station, or 2.4 km northwest of Kamakura Station (10 min. by bus). The headquarters of the Engakuji school of the Rinzai sect of Buddhism, this temple was founded in 1282 by Hojo Tokimune (1251–1284), then the Regent. A priest named Mugaku-Sogen (1226–1286), or Bukko Zenji, came from China during the Sung Dynasty and became its first abbot. It once ranked second among the Five Great Zen Temples of Kamakura, but the Great Kanto Earthquake of 1923 destroyed a number of its buildings. The Shariden (Hall of Holy Relics of Gautama Buddha), a National Treasure, was built in 1285 by Hojo Sadatoki, Tokimune's son. It contains what is said to be a tooth of Buddha brought from China. The bronze bell, a National Treasure, was cast in 1301 and is the largest in Kamakura, measuring almost 2.6 m high and over 1.4 m across. The belfry is on a hill to the right as one enters the two-story gate. The mausoleum of Tokimune, the founder, is beyond the Shariden at the back of the main temple. The temple contains a large number of art objects and ancient documents that have been designated as Important Cultural Properties.

Tokeiji Temple 49 : Located about 300 m southeast of Kita-Kamakura Station is a fine temple belonging to the Engakuji school of the Rinzai sect of Buddhism. A nunnery up to the latter part of the 19th century, it was known as *Enkiridera* (Divorce Temple) due to the fact that it was a place of refuge provided under the divorce law promulgated by Regent Hojo Sadatoki (1271–1311) for wives ill-treated by their husbands or mothers-in-law. The widow of the former Regent, Tokimune, founded the temple in 1285 and she became the first prioress of the nunnery. Its main hall and the wooden statue of *Sho*(Holy)-*Kannon* enshrined therein are Important Cultural Properties. The temple is also known for the lovely flowers that bloom each season and beautify the site. It is especially beautiful here when the plum trees blossom.

Jochiji Temple 49 : This Buddhist temple of the Rinzai sect nestles in a tall cypress grove about 500 m southeast of Kita-Kamakura Station between the Kenchoji and Engakuji temples. It was founded in 1283 by the Regent Hojo Morotoki, Tokimune's nephew, and is ranked fourth among the Five Great Zen Temples of Kamakura. During the Great Kanto Earthquake of 1923, the temple collapsed and now has little to show for its former splendor. The seated wooden image of *Jizo*, the guardian of children, is said to be the work of Unkei (1148-1223), a master-sculptor of the early part of the Kamakura period (1192-1333). Perhaps because it is the only sculpture that the temple boasts of, it is listed as an Important Cultural Property. A mossy spring beside the temple gate is numbered among the "Ten Clear Wells" of Kamakura. Since Kamakura is located near the seashore, well water in the area generally tastes salty. Clear, fresh water in the spring near the temple gate was regarded as one of the most important sources of drinking water in olden days.

Meigetsu-in 49 : Referred to as *Ajisaidera* (Hydrangea Temple) since the approach is lined with several thousand hydrangeas, presenting a beautiful sight when the flowers all burst into bloom at the same time in mid-June. After Hojo Tokiyori (1227-1263) had originally built a temple called Saimyoji on this location, his son built this temple here later on as part of Zenkoji Temple. The temple temporarily declined, but it was revived in the mid-14th century through the efforts of Uesugi Norikata (1324-1394), a powerful governor-general of the Kanto District. It is noted for its beautiful hydrangeas, narcissuses, *boke* or Japanese quinces, *suzuran* or lilies of the valley and various other flowers.

Kenchoji Temple 49 : The headquarters of the Kenchoji School of the Rinzai sect of Buddhism and the foremost of the Five Great Zen Temples of Kamakura. It stands in a grove of magnificent Japanese cedars, 650 m north of Tsurugaoka Hachimangu Shrine. The temple is located 1.5 km north of Kamakura Station (6 min. by bus) and 1.2 km southeast of the JR Kita-Kamakura Station (4 min. by bus). The temple was founded in 1253 by the Regent Hojo Tokiyori (1227-1263) for Rankei-Doryu (1213-1278), a Chinese priest also known as Daigaku-Zenji, whose tomb is on the hillside at the back of the temple. Daigaku-Zenji was one of the many Chinese priests who took refuge in Japan on the fall of the Sung Dynasty (960-1279) and found the Hojo regents to be protectors and patrons. These priests repaid their patrons by providing information on the state of affairs in China and by negotiating with the member of the mission sent to Japan by Kublai Khan (1215-1294), founder of the Yuan Dynasty in China. The original buildings were destroyed by fire in 1415, while the reconstructed buildings were ravaged during subsequent civil wars. Under the protection of the Tokugawas, however, the famous priest Takuan (1573–1645) did much to retrieve the temple's former fortunes. The temple has a bronze bell that was cast in 1255 (the second oldest among the Kamakura temple bells and a National Treasure) and many Important Cultural Properties. These include the main hall and a Chinese-style gate (both built in 1646), the tombstone of Daigaku-Zenji, and a wooden image of Hojo Tokiyori that is on display in the Main Hall and regarded as a masterpiece of the Kamakura period.

On the same hillside as that of Daigaku-Zenji is the tomb of Kawamura Zuiken (1618–1700), the leading figure in the field of civil engineering in the early part of the Edo period (1603–1867). His biography is inscribed in Japanese on the stone tablet beside his tomb.

Hanzobo Temple ⬚49⬚: Constructed in 1890 by the chief abbot of Kenchoji Temple to serve as a guardian of the mountain. It is dedicated to the god, Hanzobo Daigongen, who appears as half-priest, half-layman. The eleven grotesque images of *Tengu* (a long-nosed goblin) standing on the cliffs in the temple precincts are a famous landmark. The cherry trees lining the road from here to Kenchoji Temple provide a scenic place for hiking during cherry blossom season.

Miura Peninsula

Zushi ⬚45⬚ ☎0468: Pop. 57,948. 3.9 km southeast of Kamakura, 5 min. by the JR Yokosuka Line (20 min. by bus), this popular seaside resort lies on the west side of the Miura Peninsula. Because of its mild climate and convenient access to Tokyo and Yokohama, it has become a residential area for many commuters as well as for many well-to-do people; big companies also maintain villas here.

The Keihin Electric Express Railway (Keikyu), running from Shinagawa in Tokyo to Uraga, branches off at Kanazawa-hakkei for Keihin-Zushi (6.1 km, 9 min.). Located 1.3 km east of Jimmuji Station on this line is an old Buddhist temple of the same name belonging to the Tendai sect. Jimmuji Temple is noted for the lovely view of Sagami Bay from the hill at the rear. Along the shoreline road from Zushi to neighboring Hayama are many stylish coffee shops, high-class restaurants and traditional Japanese restaurants that attract gourmets.

Hayama ⬚45⬚: Located around 4.5 km south of Zushi Station (15 min. by bus). This beach resort commands a more magnificent view of Mt. Fuji than Zushi does.

Hayama Marina ⬚45⬚: A summer resort center at Abuzuri. At the north end of the town are a yachting harbor, a swimming pool and other recreational facilities. There is also a resort hotel of the same name. An Imperial Villa is situated along the rocky shores among verdant pines at Isshiki in the southern part of town. All along this side of Chojagasaki point on the south edge of town are good beaches for swimming and surfing.

Hayama Park: A few minutes walk south from the Hayama-Koen Bus Stop will bring the visitor to a lovely, 1,700-sq.-m enclosure along the beach shaded by a pine grove. It was once the riding ground of the adjoining Imperial Villa, but it was transferred to Kanagawa Prefecture and opened to the public as a prefectural park in 1951.

Yokosuka [45]: ☎0468: Pop. 433,109. This city grew in importance soon after Commodore Perry visited Uraga in 1853. Yokosuka's quick development resulted from the efforts of Oguri Kozukenosuke (1827-1868), a minister of the Tokugawa Shogunate who worked in cooperation with a French naval shipbuilder named Léon Welnie (1834-1908) to build a steel refinery in the area. This success sparked construction of a naval shipyard that eventually led to the establishment of a naval port here. Further development of naval facilities continued until the end of World War II in 1945. After 1945 military industries disappeared and non-military industries expanded significantly in the local area. However, due to the presence of a naval base of the U.S. Seventh Fleet and the Japanese Maritime Self-Defense Force (which are located on former Japanese naval facility sites), the area has retained its naval image.

Among the many hills in Yokosuka, Ogusu Hill (alt. 242 m), the highest on the peninsula, is located within the city limits. On the boundary with Zushi stands Mt. Takatori (alt. 139 m), which is famous as a training ground for rock climbers. Although Yokosuka's climate is quite mild, the city is cooler in summer and warmer in winter than the Tokyo-Yokohama district. Yokosuka can be reached from Tokyo (1 hr.15 min.) and Yokohama (40 min.) on the JR Yokosuka Line. The Keikyu Line runs from Shinagawa (Tokyo) to Yokohama and on to Uraga (55.5 km) in the southeastern part of Yokosuka, branching off at Horinouchi to Misakiguchi.

Rinkai (Seaside) Park: Located on the other side of Yokosuka Station, the park commands a fine view of the bustling port, where many vessels are constantly arriving and departing. There are statues of Oguri Kozukenosuke and Léon Welnie in the park.

Tsukayama Park [45]: Located about 1 km southwest of Anjinzuka Station on the Keikyu Line, this park is noted for the tombs of William Adams, the first Englishman to set foot in Japan, and his Japanese wife. The tombs stand on a hill called Tsukayama and can be reached after a short climb from the station. The park offers a lovely view of the surrounding area, which is also noted for its cherry blossoms in spring.

William Adams (1564-1620) was born at Gillingham in Kent, England. A shipwright, skipper and operator of his own trade house, Adams joined a Netherlands trading company in June 1598 and set sail for the East as the chief pilot of one of the five ships comprising a merchant fleet. After the fleet encountered a severe storm in the Atlantic Ocean, Adams' ship was the only one to cross the Pacific, finally drifting off the shores of Bungo (now, known as

Oita Prefecture), in Kyushu on April 19, 1600. After reaching Japan, Adams was more fortunate. He won the confidence of Ieyasu, the first Tokugawa Shogun, and taught him gunnery, shipbuilding, mathematics, navigation, etc. He later married a Japanese woman and adopted the Japanese name Miura Anjin after the Miura district, where he had been given a fief by Ieyasu. He died at Hirado in Kyushu on May 16, 1620, during a visit to the British factory there. Later, the ashes of Adams and his wife were buried at Tsukayama, a part of the estate given to him by Ieyasu. A memorial service is held annually on April 14 before the tombs, a rite usually attended by the governor of Kanagawa Prefecture, the mayor of Yokosuka and members of the British Embassy.

Mikasa Park ⬚45⬚ : Located about 1 km east of Yokosuka Station (3 min. by bus and then a 5-min. walk), this park lies on the Inaokacho coast on the other side of Yokosuka Bay. It is the resting place of the former Japanese battleship Mikasa, which was the flagship of the Japanese Combined Fleet commanded by Admiral Togo Heihachiro (1847-1934) during the Russo-Japanese War (1904-1905). It is now preserved as a memorial ship on a concrete foundation after having been completely restored in May 1961. The Mikasa was built in March 1900 at the Vickers Co. shipyard in England and was decommissioned from the Japanese Navy in 1923 because of restrictions placed on the total tonnage of Japanese battleships imposed at the Washington Conference. Part of its middle deck serves as an exhibition room where numerous relics of Admiral Togo and the flagship are on display. Mikasa Park is also a 15-min. walk from Yokosuka-chuo Station on the Keihin Electric Express Railway.

Sarushima Isle: This tiny islet of about 1 km in circumference lies off Mikasa Park (10 min. by ferry). Until 1945 it was a "secret islet" fortified with shore batteries. Now, however, it is a natural park that is popular with swimmers and surfers as well as with campers and anglers. More than 80 species of subtropical plants grow on the islet.

Yokosuka City Museum: Located in the center of the city in Chuo Park, this museum consists of two buildings. The hall of natural sciences features exhibits on topography, plants, animals and marine life of the Miura Peninsula. Since many of the marine life specimens on exhibit are quite rare, they will probably be of interest to visitors. The hall of anthropology next door houses exhibits on the history of the Miura Peninsula as far back as 20,000 years ago.

Kinugasayama Park ⬚45⬚ : This park is situated 1 km south of Kinugasa Station on the JR Yokosuka Line (10 min. on foot) or about 5 km south of Yokosuka Station (15 min. by bus) on a hill near the ruins of a castle of the same name. The Miura family, who ruled the local district, held this stronghold until it was destroyed in 1180 by Hatakeyama Shigetada (1164-1205). The latter was a brave general who later served under the banner of Minamoto-no-Yoritomo, founder of the Kamakura Shogunate. Commanding a fine view of the Miura Peninsula, the park is especially noted for its cherry trees, which blossom in early April.

Cape Kannonzaki [45] : Located 4.9 km east of Uraga Station on the Keikyu Line (15 min. by bus), the cape lies at the southeastern tip of the Miura Peninsula. Well known for its ocean views, it faces Futtsu Point on the west shore of the Boso Peninsula across the 5.6-km Uraga Straits leading to Tokyo Bay. The white octagonal lighthouse, erected on the cape in 1869, is the oldest Western-style lighthouse in Japan. Although the lighthouse was demolished by the Great Kanto Earthquake in 1923, it was reconstructed in 1925. Towering 15 m high, its beam is visible 37 km out at sea. The Kannonzaki Nature Museum is located 10 min. on foot south of the lighthouse.

Uraga [45] : Located 6.6 km from Yokosuka-chuo Station on the Keikyu Line. Lying at the eastern end of the Miura Peninsula, this commercial port is the south terminal of the railway's main line running from Shinagawa, Tokyo. (61.2 km, 1 hr.) In the days of the Tokugawa Shogunate (1603-1867), Uraga was an anchoring place for barges awaiting inspection before being allowed to enter Tokyo Bay.

In 1846, Commodore Biddle arrived at this port with two warships and a letter from the President of the United States to the Emperor of Japan, proposing the opening of the country to American commerce and relations (A Danish research ship called here the same year). The proposal was rejected, but seven years later, Commodore Perry's fleet arrived in Uraga with another letter from the President of the United States. This time the letter was formally received and acknowledged at Kurihama, near Uraga. Now a part of Yokosuka City, the town is known for the dockyard of Uraga Dock Co. located here.

Kurihama [45] : Located 3.8 km southwest of Uraga Station (15 min. by bus), this area is part of Yokosuka City as well as the terminal station of the JR Yokosuka Line (8 km southeast of Yokosuka Station, 11 min.). The Kurihama Line of the Keikyu branching off the main line at Horinouchi passes through here and extends as far as Misakiguchi. A ferry service run by the Tokyo Wan (Bay) Ferry Co. is available between Kurihama and Kanaya, Chiba Prefecture, on the other side of Tokyo Bay (travel time: 35 min.).

Kurihama is noted as the place where Commodore Matthew Calbraith Perry (1794-1858) of the American Navy formally handed a letter from the President of the United States to the Tokugawa Shogun's representatives in 1853, demanding the opening of some Japanese ports to American commerce and diplomatic relations. Standing on the shore of Kurihama Port 1.5 km southeast of Kurihama Station is a monument erected in 1901 in memory of that historical moment. The ceremony was attended by Rear Admiral Rogers, a grandson of Commodore Perry. The following words are engraved on the back of the monument: "This monument commemorates the first arrival of Commodore Perry, Ambassador from the United States of America, who landed at this place on July 14, 1853. Erected July 14, 1901, by America's Friend Association." There is also another inscription in Japanese written by Ito Hirobumi (1841–1909), a famous Japanese statesman of the Meiji period. The Black Ship Festival is held here each year on July 14 to commemorate Perry's visit.

Miura 45 ☎0468: Pop. 52,116. Situated at the southern tip of the Miura Peninsula, the city has developed around the local fishing industry. One can go to Misaki, its port, by taking a rapid-limited express on the Keikyu Line from Shinagawa (Tokyo) to Misakiguchi Station. The 65.7-km ride takes 1 hr. and 15 min. The city center can be reached by bus in 20 min. Misaki is a base for the deep-sea fishing industry, with the local catch amounting to 64,259 tons, worth a cash value of ¥62 billion (as of 1989). The majority of the catch is tuna, which accounts for 70% of the total.

Jogashima Island 45 : About 500 m off the Misaki Port, an elongated islet 1.8 km in length and some 4 km in circumference. The islet is connected to Misaki by the Jogashima Ohashi Bridge, which is 575 m long, 11 m wide and 21 m above sea level. Most of the activity on the islet is centered around the lighthouse on the western side where a bus terminal, souvenir shops and *ryokan* or Japanese-style inns can be found. Offering a fine view of Misaki Port, the islet also serves as a breakwater for the port. The southern side of the islet, which faces the Pacific Ocean, is composed of a series of sheer cliffs formed from erosion by waves. The area is popular with anglers and swimmers. The highlands located in the center of the islet are designated as a natural park and command a magnificent view of the sea. A youth hostel is located in the park. From Misaki pleasure boats are available for a 40-min. excursion around Jogashima Island to Aburatsubo.

Aburatsubo 45 : Located north of Misaki, this is one of the many tiny bays that lie along the west coast of Miura City. It is 15 min. by bus from Misakiguchi Station. The waters inside this inlet are blue, clear and of an oily smoothness; hence, the name literally means "oil pot." The deep recess of Aburatsubo, named Aburatsubo Marina, not only provides safe anchorage for yachts and boats, but is also a good area for fishing. At the mouth of Aburatsubo, an aquarium belonging to the Misaki Marine Biological Station, University of Tokyo is open to academic visitors only. Aburatsubo Marine Park, located at the tip of a small peninsula, covers an area of approximately 40,000 sq.m and offers displays of fish and dolphins. An aquarium called "Fishland" contains about 40 separate fish tanks with many different species of marine life. A donut-shaped tank measuring about 80 m in diameter should be of special interest to visitors since it contains approximately 3,000 fish of many species, including porgies, yellowtail and sharks. Other attractions include an "educational tank," "photography tank" and a tank for large, fresh-water fish as well as shows focusing on fish habits and other events that include feeding sessions by divers. Another facility is equipped with a water stage where dolphins and seals perform in a synchronized swimming show with rhythmical music and spotlights.

Miura Beach 45 : This stretch of shoreline is composed of beaches facing the Urga Straits and extends approximately 5 km long. Due to the local currents, the water is very clear and the area is quite popular in summer. The beaches are near Miura-Kaigan Station on the Keikyu Line.

Area 4. Along the Tokaido Highway

From Shonan District toward Hamamatsu

In the past, the Tokaido Highway connected Tokyo and Kyoto. As a means to consolidate its political power, the Tokugawa Shogunate built and maintained several routes that led from Tokyo to other areas. Among them, the Tokaido was regarded as the most important route. This road has played a major role in the political, cultural and economic development of Japan.

The JR Tokaido Main Line and Tokaido Shinkansen are the main railroads serving these areas. Other JR lines and railway companies provide transportation service from their major stations. National Highway 1 and the Tomei Expressway, linking Tokyo and Nagoya, also run through this area.

Many large plants of major Japanese industrial companies have been constructed along the railways and highways that developed along this historical road. This has, in turn, helped to stimulate the growth of smaller industrial cities throughout Japan. The area that surrounds the Tokaido Main Line is the industrial heart of Japan, including the long belt of cities that extends from Tokyo to Osaka.

Chigasaki 44 : ☎0467: Pop. 197,336. Located 59 km from Tokyo, this city faces Sagami Bay east of Hiratsuka. Blessed with a temperate climate, it was once famous as a health resort, but it has since developed into a satellite city around Tokyo and Yokohama. The shoreline has many sandy beaches that attract crowds of visitors in summer. The JR Sagami Line runs from Chigasaki to Hashimoto (near Hachioji, Tokyo) via Atsugi (34 km).

Samukawa Shrine 45 : 20 min. by bus from the JR Chigasaki Station. As the main shrine of Sagami Province (now, Kanagawa Prefecture), it was patronized by many generations of *samurai* families, extending from Minamoto-no-Yoritomo to the Tokugawa Clan. Respected as a guardian shrine of the local area, it has gained many followers.

The shrine was initially founded in 727, but the current structure was completed in 1932. The main hall and 21 other structures stand on the shrine grounds, which cover 47,000 sq.m.

Atsugi 45 ☎0462: Pop. 185,920. This city is located 45 min. from Shinjuku (Tokyo) by express on the Odakyu Line. Since the Sagami

River (the largest river in Kanagawa Prefecture) converges with several other rivers and flows through the center of the city, Atsugi developed as a terminal for river cargo during the Edo period. An industrial complex is now being built in the northern part of the city that will eventually become the site for many advanced industrial plants. Rail and road transportation networks linking the area with other districts are also rapidly expanding to meet its industrial needs. To the west of the city stand the Tanzawa mountains, popular for the hot springs in Iiyama, Nanasawa and Kotakuji. Its short distance from the city makes this area a popular resort.

Mt. Oyama ‍ 44 ‍ : Located in the southeastern portion of the Tanzawa mountains, the pyramid-shaped peak of Mt. Oyama with an altitude of 1,252 m is noted for the Afuri Shrine that was established here for mountain worshippers long ago. Also known as "Afurisan" (rainy mountain), it is said to have wrought a miracle to cause local rainfall. The main compound of the Afuri Shrine is located at the summit of Mt. Oyama. The lower compounds are lower down on the mountain at an altitude of 700 m. The shrine can be reached by cable car. The peak offers visitors a magnificent view of Sagami Bay, Oshima Island, Miura Peninsula, Boso Peninsula and even Mt. Fuji and the mountains of Hakone. Oyama Fudo (Daisanji Temple), founded in the middle of the eighth century, is situated near the lower compounds. After getting off the cable car, one can find a small temple town with many *tofu* (bean curd) restaurants and souvenir shops selling local specialties. It can be reached in 25 min. by bus from the Odakyu Isehara Station.

Tanzawa Mountain Chain ‍ 44 ‍ : This range sprawls across Kanagawa, Shizuoka and Yamanashi prefectures, extending 40 km from east to west and 30 km from north to south. Designated as Tanzawa-Oyama Quasi-National Park, the park contains many connected mountains with rugged peaks of about 1,500 m as well as deep valleys and woods filled with wild deer, bears and other animals. The natural setting attracts many hikers from the Tokyo and Yokohama areas. The hike can be challenging for veteran climbers, but since some areas are simple enough for children, it is also a perfect spot for a family outing. The area offers seasonal beauty throughout the year, but it is especially beautiful in early summer and in autumn when the changing of the colors is breathtaking. In June the mountains are covered with azaleas. The area is divided into East Tanzawa, West Tanzawa, Rear Tanzawa and Front Tanzawa. Most of the hikers head for Front Tanzawa because of the magnificent views to be found here and the ease of the climb. To get to Front Tanzawa, take the Odakyu Line to Hadano, which is the entrance to the area.

Hiratsuka ‍ 44 ‍ ☎0463: Pop. 238,689. Located 64 km from Tokyo, this city is situated on Sagami Bay in the central-southern portion of Kanagawa Prefecture. It developed as the Seventh Stage from Edo along the old Tokaido Highway during the Edo period. The network of roads that connect it with Atsugi, Isehara and Hadano helped this area prosper as a trading center. It has continued to develop as a trade and commercial center, typified by the busy area around the station that is crowded with merchandise. One of the most prosperous commercial sectors in the Shonan district (the shoreline district ranging from Zushi to Odawara), Hiratsuka is especially noted for the *Tanabata* Festival held annually for a five-day period beginning on July 7.

Oiso 44 : Pop. 31,879. Located 68 km from Tokyo, 1 hr.10 min. by train, this city is known as a summer beach resort. On the western outskirts of the town, there is a magnificent recreation center called Oiso Long Beach. It offers bathers a wave pool, a current pool with a 600-m-long circuit, a competition-size pool, and six other assorted pools as well as three hotels, six restaurants and a golf course.

On the bluff northeast of the town is an observation platform (alt. 181 m) called Shonandaira. It is about 1.7 km, or 30 min. on foot, from the JR Oiso Station, but it can be reached by car as well. A resthouse awaits those who make it to the top along with a fine view of Mt. Fuji, the Hakone mountains, Mt. Oyama and Sagami Bay.

Kozu 44 : Located 78 km from Tokyo, 1 hr.30 min. by train. It is the junction for the JR Gotemba Line (61 km, connecting Kozu with Numazu on the JR Tokaido Main Line). About 4 km north of Kozu is the little village of Soga. In the 12th century, two brothers—Soga Juro and Goro—lived here and gained widespread fame for avenging the death of their father (refer to p.474).

This hilly district of Soga is covered with a grove of *ume*, or plum trees, which burst into fragrant white or pink blossoms in February.

Odawara 44 ☎0465: Pop. 190,218. Odawara is located 40 min. by the "Kodama" on the JR Tokaido Shinkansen from Tokyo Station or 1 hr.10 min. by limited express on the Odakyu Line from Shinjuku (Tokyo). It serves as a gateway to the famous scenic, hot-springs resort of Hakone, with bus and train service available to different parts of the resort.

Historically, Odawara is known as the castle town of the Hojo Clan, which exercised extensive control over the Kanto Plain toward the end of the 15th century. Situated at the eastern foot of the Hakone mountains, Odawara flourished as a stage during the Edo period in an area that was the most dangerous place to pass on the old Tokaido Highway. At present, Odawara is a commercial and industrial city where food, chemical and various other industries thrive.

A four-story donjon restored in 1960 stands on the site of the old Odawara Castle, 400 m south of the station. It can be seen from the window of passing Tokaido Main Line trains. On display inside the donjon are various historical materials remaining from the old castle town. The ancient site contains many blossoming plum and cherry trees, azaleas and wisteria as well as a children's amusement park with a small zoo. The Hotoku Ninomiya Shrine, dedicated to Ninomiya Sontoku (1787–1856), a thinker and authority on agronomy, is located near the entrance to the castle grounds.

Saijoji Temple (Doryoson) ⬚44⬚: One of the largest temples of the Soto sect of Zen Buddhism in Japan, this temple is situated in the northeastern part of thickly wooded Mt. Myojin (alt. 1,169 m). An image of an eleven-headed *Kannon* is enshrined in the main hall of the temple. A hall dedicated to Doryoson, a priest who contributed to the construction of the temple, contains a statue of *Tengu* (long-nosed goblin). According to legend, Doryoson was transformed into the statue when he died. The temple is 15 min. by bus from Daiyuzan Station, the terminal station on the Daiyuzan Line (between Odawara and Daiyuzan, 9.6 km, 20 min.) of the Izu-Hakone Railway.

The section between Odawara and Atami offers one of the most scenic views along the Tokaido Main Line. There is a fine view of the sea, hills and fields covered with groves of mandarin orange, persimmon and plum trees. A convenient, two-lane road runs closely along the shoreline of Sagami Bay (Manazuru Highway and Atami Beach Line), offering a pleasant view of the ocean.

Cape Manazuru ⬚44⬚: This cape protrudes approximately 3 km into Sagami Bay. Besides a reef that continues from the cape to the water's surface, about 500 m farther out stands an enormous rock called *Mitsuishi* (three rocks). At the edge of the cape is the Tomyo Hill area designated as a natural park. It contains many subtropical chinquapin and camphor trees, and is known as a good fishing and diving spot. The cape can be reached in 20 min. by bus from the JR Manazuru Station.

Yugawara Spa ⬚44⬚: 15 min. by bus from Yugawara Station (100 km from Tokyo and 1 hr.25 min. by the JR limited express). Attractively situated on the Fujiki River, the spa is surrounded by mountains on three sides and the sea on the southeastern side. All of the *ryokan* in the area have private hot-spring baths. With water temperature ranging 38–92°C, the hot springs are believed to be efficacious for the treatment of cuts, bruises, burns, gastroenteric trouble, piles and gynecological diseases. Man-yo Park in the hot-springs town contains approximately 85 species of Man-yo plants (plants that are sung about in the "Man-yo-shu"—the oldest anthology of *waka* poetry. refer to p.153). Two waterfalls, called *Fudo-no-Taki* and *Godan-no-Taki*, are among the local sights.

From Oku-Yugawara, the innermost part of the spa, a winding mountain road named the "Tsubaki (Camellia) Line" leads 20.1 km up to Hakonemachi on Lake Ashi, 723 m above sea level. The road also cuts through Taikanzan-Fujimi Pass, which commands a magnificent view of Mt. Fuji. Lake Ashi can be seen in the foreground and the Pacific Ocean on the other side, with Hatsushima Island and the volcanic island of Oshima visible in the distance. On the western side of the pass the peak of Mt. Taikan soars to an altitude 1,011 m. The

"Yugawara Parkway," a toll road, also runs from Oku-Yugawara for a distance of 5.8 km to Kurakake Pass on the Hakone-Atami Drive.
Atami ⬚51 ☎0557: Pop. 48,332. Located 105 km from Tokyo at the northeastern neck of the Izu Peninsula, 55 min. by the "Kodama" on the JR Tokaido Shinkansen. Serving as the entrance to the peninsula, Atami is one of the most flourishing and popular spa resorts in Japan because of its superb shoreline and mild climate. The name "Atami," meaning "hot sea," dates back at least to the Nara period (710–784). During the Tokugawa period, it was common practice to present water taken from around Atami to the *shogun* at Edo Castle.

Modern Atami serves as a bustling resort area, with many large hotels stretching from the shoreline to the mountains. In addition, many souvenir shops, bars and restaurants are scattered through the city, helping to make it a popular site for corporate recreational facilities and plush senior citizens' homes. Atami is also famed for its magnificent night skyline, known as the "Million-Dollar View." With an average temperature of 61°C, the mineral water is known to be efficacious for the treatment of rheumatism, neuralgia, dermatitis, trauma and gynecological diseases.

Izusan Spa ⬚51 : Located 2 km northeast of Atami Station, 7 min. by bus. Not only is this spa noted for its saline hot springs, but the entire area is also known for its ancient hot springs dating back to the Kamakura Shogunate. According to legend, this was the site where Minamoto-no-Yoritomo (1147–1199), founder of the Kamakura Shogunate, first met his future wife Masako of the Hojo family. It is a quiet area located near Atami and affords a magnificent view of the ocean.

On the hill northwest of the spa is the Izusan Shrine, which dates back to the early part of the ninth century. Along with Hakone Shrine at Moto-Hakone, it is regarded as one of the two most popular Shinto centers in the Hakone-Atami district.

MOA Museum, located on a hill overlooking Atami Station, exhibits many ancient Japanese paintings, crafts, potteries and Buddhist images designated as National Treasures and Important Cultural Properties. It also exhibits pieces by modern Western artists, including Claude Monet and Henry Moore. Other museum attractions include a *noh* stage and a circular hall where light, images and sound are combined into interesting displays. Places certain to be of interest to all visitors are the restored "Golden Tearoom" of Toyotomi Hideyoshi (1536–1598), a powerful general who unified medieval Japan, and the house of Ogata Korin (1658–1716), a famous painter of the mid-Edo period.

The MOA Museum offers visitors a combination of fine arts, a beautiful garden and a panoramic view of Sagami Bay. Closed on Thursdays.
Atami Plum Garden: Located 3 km southwest of Atami Station along a road that leads to the Tanna Tunnels, this grove of nearly 1,300

plum trees is magnificent when in bloom from late December until early March. A Plum Festival is held here every year from January 15 to February 15.

Kinomiya Shrine: Near Kinomiya Station on the JR Ito Line and along the way to the Plum Garden. This shrine boasts one of the largest camphor trees in Japan. About 2,000 years old and 20 m round at its base, the tree has been designated as a Natural Monument. Not far from Kinomiya Station is the popular residence of the Tsubouchi Shoyo (1859-1935), the most noted Shakespearian scholar this country has ever produced. This house is known as Soshisha.

Atami Koraku-en: This extensive recreation area is located on Cape Uomi, south of the spa area. It has a show hall that can seat 3,000 people, a bowling alley, and an amusement park with a large Ferris wheel, pool, hotel and various other recreational facilities. Nearby, a ropeway leading to an observatory on Cape Uomi commands a panoramic view of Sagami Bay.

Nishikigaura ⌷51⌷: Located 2.5 km south of Atami Station, this picturesque strip of coastline extends south for about 2 km from Cape Uomi. The larger of two rocks that jut out from the cape is called Kabuto-Iwa (helmet rock), while the other one is known as Eboshi-Iwa because it resembles an *eboshi* (a tall, brimless hat worn by people of high rank in ancient times and still worn today by *sumo* referees).

A road running along Nishikigaura, in a section cut out along the cliffs many meters above the sea, provides a magnificent view, especially of coastal scenery and Oshima Island.

Hatsushima Island ⌷51⌷: Located 10 km off the southeast coast of Atami, this island can be reached in 40 min. from Atami Port or 25 min. from Ito Port. The island (about 3 km in circumference) is popular with young campers and anglers in summer. Hatsushima Vacation Land, situated in the eastern part of the island, offers many recreational facilities.

Mishima ⌷51⌷ ☎0559: Pop. 104,048. 121 km from Tokyo, 1 hr.5 min. by the JR Tokaido Shinkansen. Serving as an entrance to the Izu Peninsula, this city is the terminal station on the Izu-Hakone Railway that goes to Shuzenji via Izu-Nagaoka. Bus lines also run to Shimoda near the southern tip of the peninsula or to hot-spring resorts in Hakone.

About 1 km southeast of the station stands Mishima Shrine, held in veneration by warriors during the Kamakura period (1192-1333). Just south of the station is a park called Rakuju-en, which was once a villa of the Korean royal family of Lee. The source of the garden pond, Obama-ike, is thawing snow from Mt. Fuji.

Numazu ⌷51⌷ ☎0559: Pop. 211,868. 127 km from Tokyo, 6 min. by local train from Mishima on the Tokaido Main Line. This city is situated at the mouth of the Kano River, which is fed by water flowing from the mountains of the Izu Peninsula. At Numazu the JR

Gotemba Line branches off to Kozu from the Tokaido Main Line. Running over the steep mountain region, it is a local auxiliary line of the Tokaido Main Line . The Numazu Interchange on the Tomei Expressway is the entrance to the Izu Peninsula.

High-speed boat service is available to such points as Heda, Toi, Dogashima and Matsuzaki on the west coast of the Izu Peninsula. Because of its balmy climate, Numazu is noted as both a summer and winter resort. A former Imperial Villa located on the outskirts of the city has been open to the public as the Numazu Goyotei Memorail Park since 1969.

Sembon-Matsubara (Beach of a Thousand Pines) 51 : A scenic spot on Suruga Bay about 1.5 km southwest of Numazu Station (bus is available). Many gnarled old pines growing near the seashore are said to have been planted by a highly virtuous Buddhist priest named Zoyo during the 16th century. The entire vicinity has been designated as Sembonhama Park. The beach is ideal for swimming during summer.

Mt. Kanuki: Altitude 193 m, 2 km south of the JR Numazu Station. A scenic road runs to the mountain summit, from where one can survey the entire neighboring district.

Fuji 51 ☎0545: Pop. 221,189. Located 147 km from Tokyo, 1 hr.13 min. by the "Kodama" on the JR Tokaido Shinkansen to Shin-Fuji. The JR Tokaido Main Line also has Fuji Station, which is connected by bus with Shin-Fuji Station in 10 min. Fuji is the junction for the JR Minobu Line, which skirts the western base of Mt. Fuji and leads to Kofu (89 km) on the JR Chuo Main Line via Fujinomiya and Minobu. The latter two cities are noted as great Japanese Buddhist centers. Fuji is well known for its paper industry that developed with the abundance of water resources provided by the thawing snow of Mt. Fuji. The seashore southeast of the station, called Tagonoura, has been celebrated for its fine view of Mt. Fuji since olden days.

On the coast is Tagonoura Port, the southern entrance to the industrial district comprising of Fuji, Fujinomiya and the neighboring towns. Fuji is one of the departure points for the sightseeing buses that circle Mt. Fuji and the Five Lakes lying at its base. Sightseeing buses depart from Shin-Fuji Station on the JR Tokaido Shinkansen.

Shimizu 51 ☎0543: Pop. 242,625. 169 km from Tokyo or 12 km from Shizuoka. Situated on the innermost shore of Suruga Bay, this city developed as a port city in ancient times. The present Shimizu Port, a busy international trading port, is also rapidly developing as a base for deep-sea and inshore fishing industries. Other noted industries include canning, shipbuilding and fuel-oil production.

Seikenji Temple: Situated 1 km west of Okitsu Station on the JR Tokaido Main Line. Founded in 572, this temple belongs to the Rinzai sect of Zen Buddhism. It is celebrated for its fine view of Shimizu Port and a pine grove at Miho. Behind the temple's main hall and study is a lovely landscape garden laid out in the middle part of the Edo period. In the garden is a 170-year-old stone-image of *Gohyaku-Rakan*, or 500-*Arhat*. *Arhat* is a Sanskrit word that means "saint."

Miho-no-Matsubara ⎡51⎤: This area projects into the sea in a northeasterly direction from the east of Kunozan Hill, forming a natural breakwater for the port of Shimizu. On clear days, one can see Mt. Fuji from this 3.2-km stretch of white sand lined with a green avenue of old pine trees. Popularly known as Miho-no-Matsubara (Pine Groves of Miho), it has been a favorite theme for Japanese poets and artists since ancient times. The seashore is 8.3 km (around 25 min.) from Shimizu by bus.

In the pine groves of Miho is a tree called *Hagoromo-no-Matsu* (The Pine Tree of the Feathery Robe). A legend described in an ancient *noh* play tells how a fisherman named Hakuryo succeeded in making a goddess dance to heavenly music in exchange for the return of a magic robe that she had left hanging on a pine tree. Covering 12 sq. km of land, the Miho area is surrounded by the heavenly pine groves. There is a social education center open to the general public that houses the Marine Science Museum Tokai University and Human Science Museum Tokai University. Miho Culture Land, including Miniature Land, which presents exhibits of many famous sights from around the world and the stages of the old Tokaido Highway in miniature, and a Natural History Museum with its House of Dinosaurs are also located in the area.

Ryugeji Temple: Located 4.5 km south of Shimizu Station, 15 min. by bus. The temple stands at the northern foot of Udo Hill next to Nihondaira Plateau, which commands a sweeping view of Suruga Bay. The temple, on the other hand, is noted for its fine view of the pine grove of Miho and Mt. Fuji. A *sotetsu* or cycad (Cycas revoluta, sometimes translated as a Japanese fern palm) said to be 1,100 years old is growing in the temple precincts. Measuring 5.2 m around at its base and 3.7 m in height, it has been designated as a Natural Monument.

Shizuoka ⎡51/54-①⎤ ☎054

Pop. 470,356. Situated on the delta of the Abe River, this city is located 181 km from Tokyo, 1 hr.30 min. by the "Kodama" on the JR Tokaido Shinkansen. Not only is the city the central part of the prefecture housing the Shizuoka Prefectural Government Office, it is also the center of local politics, economy and culture. As a commercial and industrial center, the city boasts many branch offices of large companies with headquarters in Tokyo and Osaka. Traditional markets also play an important role here, including the wood industry and furniture industry, the latter usually ranking first or second in Japan. The city is famous for its local production of lacquerware and lacquered *geta* (wooden clogs). Shizuoka is also the number-one producer of tea , with 60% of all the tea in Japan being produced here.

Travellers are familiar with the famous "green" sight that can be seen from the Shinkansen. Other noted products include mandarin oranges, strawberries, *shiitake* (a species of brown mushrooms) and preserved *wasabi* (a kind of horseradish).

During the Tokugawa Shogunate (1603-1867), Shizuoka was a castle town called Sumpu. Strategically important as a western outpost of Edo (now, Tokyo), it prospered because it also served as the 20th stage along the old Tokaido Highway. Ieyasu, founder of the Tokugawa Shogunate government, often praised the scenic and healthy environment of this locality and did much to enhance it.

During the 75 years of his life, Ieyasu spent more than 25 years living in this city in his "Castle of the Floating Isle." Encircled by deep moats, its ruins, still remain in the center of the northern half of the city. Ancient stone walls serve as a reminder of the castle's past glory. The former castle site is now a park equipped with various sports facilities. Although times have changed, Shizuoka continues to be an important transportation center.

Shizuhatayama Hill 54-①: This small, verdure-covered hill in the northern outskirts of Shizuoka is located about 1.5 km from the station. Because a large number of cherry trees grow on its sunny side, the hill is a popular site during the cherry-blossom season, which is usually the first week of April.

Sengen Shrine 54-①: Located at the southern foot of the hill, the shrine is well worth a visit. The present shrine buildings were rebuilt from 1804 to 1865. Murals painted by artists of the Kano school decorate the ceiling of the oratory. At the rear of the oratory, three flights of stone steps lead to a park, from which one can view Shizuoka City and the surrounding countryside. The annual festival of the shrine, held April 1-5, is the most colorful event in Shizuoka, attracting large crowds.

Constructed in 1536 by Imagawa Yoshimoto, Rinzaiji Temple behind the Sengen Shrine is another celebrated religious center. There is a kind of dignified beauty about the ritualistically severe atmosphere of the grounds. The present strcuture was rebuilt by Ieyasu during the latter part of the 16th century. The garden is famous for its splendor, but unfortunately it is not open to the public.

Toro 51: About 2.5 km south of Shizuoka Station (about 20 min. by bus), sandwiched between Kunozan Hill on the east and the lower reaches of the Abe River on the west. As the site of an excavated hamlet that flourished some 1,700-1,800 years ago, the village contains some rare relics of immense historical value, throwing light on the mode of life led by people in those ancient times. The relics were accidentally found in an area of about 165,000 sq.m. in January 1943 when a factory was being built. Excavations then continued until August 1950.

The zone containing the relics consists of three parts—a residential area, rice paddies and forest land. Altogether, 12 foundations of the ruined dwellings, oval in shape, were unearthed with their original outlines perfectly preserved. Several others were found partly damaged, however. The largest dwelling is 12 m long and 11 m wide. Several buildings with raised floors, three pillars and a ladder were unearthed and are presumed to be the relics of storehouses.

Many articles of daily use were also discovered, including agricultural implements and kitchen utensils as well as bronze bracelets, rings and glass beads, apparently worn by local maidens of that period. Most of the articles are shown as exhibits at the Toro Museum on the same site. The whole area where these remains were found is now protected by the government as a Place of Historical Importance.

Kunozan Hill 51 : Alt. 219 m. 10 km southeast of Shizuoka Station, about 35 min. by bus; 10 km southwest of Shimizu Station, about 30 min. by bus. Comprising the southwestern end of Udo Hill (alt. 307 m), its south side is formed by a long, straight line of tall cliffs facing Suruga Bay.

Since it is protected from the north wind by a range of hills and is exposed to the sun, the hill is in a position where the thermometer rarely drops below 4°C in winter or rises above 30°C in summer. As a result, it is suitable for the cultivation of vegetables and strawberries, particularly for the winter market. Every possible inch of the foothills is utilized for what is called *Ishigaki* (stonewall) cultivation of strawberries.

The farmers build stonewalls on the hillside against the sun. Strawberries are planted between the walls of stone, although concrete blocks are used today instead of stones. The stone in absorbing the heat of the sun in the daytime and radiating it throughout the night onto the plants helps the strawberries ripen far ahead of the season.

Kunozan Hill is also known for the Toshogu Shrine, the main structures of which have been designated as Important Cultural Properties. The shrine was built in 1617 by Hidetada, the second Tokugawa Shogun, in honor of Ieyasu (1542-1616)—his father and founder of the Tokugawa Shogunate. Ieyasu's remains were interred on this hill before being moved to the mausoleum in Nikko. A long flight of 1,159 stone steps with 16 zigzags leads to the shrine atop Kunozan Hill. Elaborately decorated in the *Gongen* style, it contains many priceless pieces of art, including swords, one of which has been designated as a National Treasure.

A little way down from Toshogu Shrine (about 5 min. on foot) is an aerial ropeway running northward up to the Nihondaira Plateau (6 min.). Located on the northern side of Udo Hill and separated from Kunozan Hill by a valley, the plateau is also accessible from Shimizu and Shizuoka by bus via the "Nihondaira Parkway." Nihondaira Plateau, covered with tea plantations, commands a fine view of Mt. Fuji to the northeast, while to the south, it presents a grand view of

Kunozan Hill and the blue waters of the Pacific. To the east, the pine groves of Miho and the port of Shimizu come into view. Thus, the visitor can enjoy a panoramic, 360-degree, view.

Shizuoka Prefectural Art Museum: Located to the north of Nihondaira Plateau, the museum can be reached in 10 min. on the Shizuoka Railway from Shin-Shizuoka Station. The museum contains a broad range of exhibits by Japanese artists from the Edo period to the present, while Monet, Corot, Pissarro, Goya, Munch, Braque and Picasso are just a few of the Western artists whose works are also on display. A path lined with magnificent statues amidst a grove of trees leads to the museum, which was completed in 1985. The museum is closed on Mondays.

Togeppo Saiokuji Temple ☐51☐ : Surrounded by bamboo groves and trees, this quiet Rinzai-sect Zen temple was founded in 1504 by Socho (1448–1532), a famous *renga* (linked-verse, refer to p.158) poet. The gardens, supposedly modeled after Ginkakuji Temple (Silver Pavilion) in Kyoto, are renowned for their solemn beauty. The entire grounds, including the gardens, have been designated as a Historical Site and Place of Scenic Beauty. The temple, located southwest of Shizuoka Station, is about 25 min. away by bus.

Umegashima Hot Springs ☐50☐ : Located about 2 hrs. north of Shizuoka Station by bus on the mountains (alt. 1,000 m) above the upper reaches of the Abe River. This spa area is famed for its beautiful summer greenery and autumn leaves. The temperature during the summer rarely tops 25°C, making it an excellent retreat from the summer heat.

Yaizu ☐51☐ ☎054: Pop. 112,320. Adjoining the southwestern edge of Shizuoka. Yaizu Port is noted as a deep-sea fishery base for tuna and bonito. The marine-products processing industry is also active.

The Yaizu Fish Center located right beside the Yaizu Interchange of the Tomei Expressway, is an extensive market that covers a total area of 26,000 sq.m. The wholesale market for fresh fish and processed goods is open to the public. A specialty and souvenir corner (sampling available) and a large cafeteria offering a fresh-fish menu are popular attractions. Closed Wednesdays.

Shimada ☐51☐ ☎0547: Pop. 74,500. Situated 208 km from Tokyo, 25 min. by train from Shizuoka. Situated on the eastern bank of the Oi River facing Kanaya on the opposite bank, the city is known as a trading center for the timber brought down from the forests growing along the upper reaches of the Oi River.

Since there was neither a bridge nor a ferry between any of these towns in feudal times, travelers had to ford the stream or be carried across, either on the shoulders of professional carriers or in a sort of sedan chair called *rendai*, which was transported on the carriers' shoulders. Crossing this river was considered to be one of the most dangerous parts of the journey on the old Tokaido Highway since the river was often flooded, seriously hindering traffic.

Utagawa Hiroshige (1797–1858, refer to p.187) skillfully depicts this river scene in one of his *ukiyo-e* masterpieces. Known as *rendai-watashi*, which literally means carrying by a *rendai* across the river, this traditional river scene is revived every year for one day between the end of July and the beginning of August.

Makinohara Tableland ⌷51⌷: An upland stretching south of Kanaya, the area is noted for its extensive tea plantations. The Makinohara plantations occupy about one-sixth of Shizuoka Prefecture's total tea-producing area of 1,209 sq.km.

Backed by the graceful, snow-capped Mt. Fuji and alive with scores of women tea pickers (their hair covered with white towels), these large tea plantations present an unforgettable picture in early summer. Geologically, Makinohara is an elevated delta formed by deposits from the Oi River. Because one can gain an impressive view of the plains below from this extensive tableland, it is popular with hikers. The JR Tokaido Shinkansen tunnels through this tableland. Occupying a part of the vast tea plantation, Makinohara Park contains a statue of a priest named Eisai (1141–1215), who introduced tea from China to Japan. A tea festival is held biannually in early May along with various enjoyable events.

Kanaya ⌷51⌷: Pop. 22,359. Here is a station of the Tokaido Main Line as well as a starting station of the Oigawa Railway (65 km), which runs north on the banks of the Oi River to Ikawa via Senzu. The railway is popular among railway buffs because they can ride on a train pulled by a steam locomotive to Senzu, where a matchbox-like train carries them further to Ikawa, chugging through the forest en route. A magnificent view of Sessokyo Gorge can be seen from the window of the mountain liner. Sumatakyo Spa on the outskirts of the Southern Japan Alps is a popular summer retreat visited by many tourists during autumn when the leaves change colors.

Omaezaki Point ⌷51⌷: Stretching to the south of Makinohara Tableland, this is the southernmost tip of Shizuoka Prefecture. Sandwiched on the east by Suruga Bay and on the west by the Enshu-nada Sea, it is a noted cape town located about 1 hr.20 min. from Shizuoka Station by express bus. The shoreline is rich with sandy beaches and coral reefs, attracting many fishermen and shell diggers. Omaezaki Lighthouse on the tip of the plateau stands 54 m high above sea level, offering a magnificent view of the area that includes Mt. Fuji. The western side of the point is lined with the Nan-en Sandhills, which continue approximately 30 km to the mouth of the Tenryu River. The area is famed for producing muskmelon and *suika* or watermelon. Local windsurfers crowd the area for enjoyment, but during the international competitions held in early May world-famous surfers come to compete in the championship events.

Kakegawa ⌷57⌷ ☎0537: Pop. 72,099. Formerly a stage on the old 53-stage Tokaido Highway. Presently, it is the junction for the 67. 9-km-long Tenryu-Hamanako Line leading to Shinjohara on the

Tokaido Main Line via the northern shore of the Hamana Lagoon. A market for locally produced tea as well as factories for auto parts and musical instruments are located here.

Fukuroi 57 ☎0538: Pop. 52,333. Situated 58 km from Shizuoka or 19 km from Hamamatsu. Farming, including tea and melon cultivation, once flourished, but today the musical instrument and construction-equipment industries are being developed. Located 4 km north, 10 min. by bus from the station, Kasuisai Temple is one of the celebrated old temples of the Soto sect of Zen Buddhism. Famed for its flowers, the peonies that bloom from mid-April to early May are especially beautiful.

Iwata 57 ☎0538: Pop. 82,602. Situated east of the estuary of the Tenryu River. The town is both an agricultural and industrial center. Cotton textiles such as velveteen and corduroy are a major industry, comprising 98% of the share in Japan. About 1.5 km north of the station is the site of the ancient Totomi Kokubunji Temple, designated as a Special Place of Historical Importance. Totomi is the name of an old province that once occupied the western half of the present Shizuoka Prefecture.

Area 5. Fuji-Hakone-Izu National Park

The Fuji-Hakone-Izu National Park covers 1,223.5 sq.km and stretches over Shizuoka, Yamanashi, and Kanagawa prefectures and Tokyo. It is comprised of four regions, each with its own unique characteristics: the famous Mt. Fuji and the Five Lakes in the Mt. Fuji region, the complex volcanic topography and hot springs of the Hakone region, the richly varied coastline and diversified hot springs of the Izu region, and the Black Current and volcanic islands of the Izu Islands region. These regions are typical tourist attractions in Japan. Seven Islands of Izu will be introduced in Area 13 since they are located in the Tokyo area.

Mt. Fuji and Environs

Mt. Fuji, the highest and most beautiful mountain in Japan, has been portrayed in poetry and paintings since olden times. Once, this conical mountain was regarded as a god and was worshipped by many followers. Witnesses of the various eruptions in the past have left documentation of the frightening sight. Today, with many visitors enjoying the challenging hike to the top or the magnificent view, this area is crowded throughout the year. The well-developed mountain routes allow even senior citizens and children to reach the summit without undue effort. The foothills contain the beautiful Five Lakes, primeval forests, bucolic mountain villages and historical sites as well as large-scale leisure and accommodation facilities. From Tokyo or Yokohama, a trip to the Five Lakes or other scenic spots at Mt. Fuji's base may be made in a single day. Those desirous of touring the district at their leisure, however, will find it more conve-nient to spend one or two nights at one of the hotels in the lake district.

TRANSPORTATION

The northern foot of the mountain (Yamanashi Prefecture side) can be reached by taking the Fuji Kyuko (Fujikyu) Line from Otsuki Station (88 km from Shinjuku in Tokyo on the JR Chuo Main Line). To climb the mountain (the climbing season is limited to two months from July 1 to August 31), take a bus from the Fujikyu Kawaguchiko Station to a point midway up the mountain (*go-gome* or fifth station). Use the Chuo Expressway and get off at the Kawaguchiko Inter-change (110 km from Tokyo) when driving. There is also a highway bus that goes to lakes Kawaguchi, Yamanaka, Shoji and Motosu from Shinjuku, Tokyo.

The southern foot of the mountain (Shizuoka Prefecture side) can be reached by taking the JR Gotemba Line, Minobu Line or Tokaido Shinkansen. Bus service is available from Gotemba Station on the JR Gotemba Line, Fujinomiya Station on the JR Minobu Line part way up the mountain (new fifth station), Shin-Fuji Station on the JR Tokaido Shinkansen and Mishima Station, also on the JR Tokaido Shinkansen and the Tokaido Main Line. Except for the bus from Mishima, all these buses run only in July and August. Drivers can reach here by taking the Tomei Expressway and getting off at either Gotemba Interchange (85 km from Tokyo) or Fuji Interchange (125 km from Tokyo).

Mt. Fuji 53

Alt. 3,776 m. Rising on the borders of Shizuoka and Yamanashi prefectures, it is the highest and most popular mountain in Japan. The monarch of the Fuji Volcanic Chain (refer to p.72), Mt. Fuji is considered to be one of the most beautiful conical volcanoes in the world. The base of Mt. Fuji, which forms an almost perfect circle, stretches 35 to 40 km from east to west and the same distance from north to south. Many explanations have been given as to the origin of its name, one of which is that it is derived from the Ainu word for "fire."

The volcano has not been active for more than 250 years, but apparently there was a time when smoke rising from its crater was a familiar feature of the landscape. There are 18 different eruptions on record, the most destructive ones having occurred in 800, 864 and 1707. The eruption in 1707 blanketed Edo (now, Tokyo) 100 km distant with a layer of ashes 5 cm deep. Now only a few, faint clouds of steam rising at 80°C from one isolated section on the summit remain as a reminder of the mountain's former activity.

Mt. Fuji has been a favorite subject matter for poets and artists through the ages in Japan. Indeed, they have tried to outdo each other in best depicting the beauty and charm of this matchless mountain.

Yamabe-no-Akahito, one of the greatest of the "Man-yo-shu" poets (refer to p.153) in the early part of the eighth century, wrote the following 31-syllable poem about Mt. Fuji:

Tago-no-ura yu	"As slow I pace on Tago's shore
Uchiidete mireba	Fair Fuji I descry;
Mashiro nizo	Her peerless peak aloft doth soar,
Fuji no takane ni	Snow-crowned against the sky."
Yuki wa furi keru	

Ota Dokan (1432-1486), a lord of Edo who built his castle-fortress near the swampy shore of Edo Bay under Fuji's eternal gaze, was an ardent lover of Fuji, whose poems have come down to us through five centuries. His 31-syllable poem is also still very popular:

Waga io wa	"The high crown of Fuji
Matsubara tsuzuki	Looks in at the window
Umi chikaku	Of my house near the sea
Fuji no takane o	on Edo Bay
Nokiba ni zo miru	Afore the pine-clad moor."

Matsuo Basho (1644-1694), the greatest master of *haiku*, or 17-syllable poem (refer to p.160), was inspired to write the following verse on Fuji while standing on the shore of Lake Kawaguchi and gazing at the mountain across the water. Because of the mist, it seemed to change shape every minute.

Kumo kiri no	"On Kawaguchi's shore I muse,
Shibashi bankei o	While Fuji through the changing mist
Tsukushi keri	Presents myriad of views."

Katsushika Hokusai (1760-1849), a well-known *ukiyo-e* artist, painted Fuji in nearly all its moods in his famous series of color prints known as "Fuji Hyakkei", or the Hundred Views of Fuji.

Since ancient times, Mt. Fuji has been regarded as a sacred mountain by the Japanese. Up to the Meiji Restoration (1868), Japanese women were not allowed to climb the mountain. The mountain is now climbed every year by upwards of 300,000 people, including many women, who find special accommodations at different stages along the trails.

The first foreigner to make the ascent was Sir Rutherford Alcock, first British minister, on July 26, 1860. The first European woman to reach the summit (in 1867) was Lady Parkes, wife of the British minister plenipotentiary and envoy extraordinary to the Tokugawa Shogunate government in Edo (now, Tokyo).

Among the more notable foreigners associated with Mt. Fuji is the late Dr. Frederick Starr (1858-1933), an anthropologist and professor of Chicago University. He first visited Japan in 1904, returning 15 times over a period of 30 years. He climbed Mt. Fuji five times, dressed like a native pilgrim in white tunic and *kyahan* (gaiters), straw sandals and sunshade, and crying "Rokkon Shojo" (May our senses be purified!) and "Oyama wa seiten" (May the weather on the mountain be good!).

He died in Tokyo in 1933, but his love for Mt. Fuji lives on in the form of a monument erected to his memory in full view of Mt. Fuji. His words are inscribed on it, as follows: "Fuji bare and naked in a blaze of sunshine is beautiful; Fuji with its summit wrapped in cloud and mist is more beautiful; Fuji blotted out by the fog until but a hint of line is left is most beautiful." The monument stands a short distance above Sengen Shrine at Subashiri, the starting point of the Subashiri Trail to the summit of Mt. Fuji.

Geologists believe that Mt. Fuji is a Quaternary formation. In other words, it is said that in the Glacial period at the beginning of the Quaternary period—about 600,000 years ago—two mountains were thrust upward from the earth's surface one after another on the present site of Mt. Fuji with an interval between. About 300,000 years after that, an immense quantity of lava poured forth from the same location and spread over these mountains, forming the outer crust and giving Mt. Fuji its present shape.

The crater on the summit of the mountain is nearly circular in shape, with a diameter of about 800 m. The bottom is level, lying 220 m below Kengamine—the highest peak in the southwestern ridge of the crater. At one time, there seems to have been a lake at the bottom. The crater, known as *Nai-in* (Sanctuary), is regarded with special reverence. Eight peaks form part of the crater ridge: Kengamine, Hakusan (or Shaka), Kusushi, Dainichi (or Asahi), Izu, Joju (or Seishigadake), Komagatake and Mishimadake.

From the peak of Kengamine, two paths circle the crater (popularly called *Ohachi-Meguri*). One path skirts the edge and the other crosses over the eight peaks. The first is an easy trail about 3.5 km long, taking 1 hr.20 min., while the latter is steep and somewhat longer. At the foot of Hakusan Peak—a huge rock on the northwestern side of the crater, there is an icy cold spring called Kimmeisui (Gold-Sparkling Water). North of Koma Peak are Gimmeisui (Silver-Sparkling Water) and Sengen Shrine.

Near the top of Kengamine Peak, a meteorologist named Nonaka Itaru and his wife made some observations in the winter of 1895. A concrete building of the Meteorological Observatory currently stands near the site of the stone hut in which they lived. The annual mean temperature on the summit is -6°C. The mean temperature in January, the coldest month of the year, is -20°C, while that in August, the hottest month, is 6°C. The annual mean atmospheric pressure on the summit is 638 millibars.

During the climbing season, a post office is kept open near Sengen Shrine. At the summit of the mountain, a climber may enjoy *goraiko*, the name given to the ever-changing phenomenon of the sunrise. As soon as the dark eastern sky becomes purple, it grows brighter and brighter till at last a streak of clouds rises like a dragon, then presently it changes color into that of molten copper. In an instant, it assumes the shape of a red-hot iron ball, and finally the scarlet sun floats up, adding incessantly to its dazzling radiance.

To the northwest, Mt. Yatsugatake and Mts. Hodaka and Shirouma of the Northern Japan Alps are seen above the vast sea of clouds. The Boso and Miura peninsulas, the Seven Islands of Izu and the Izu Peninsula stretch from east to southeast with the Pacific Ocean forming the background.

Vegetation: Mt. Fuji is said to be a veritable storehouse of plants. Almost 2,000 species of plants grow on the hillside. They reveal a fairly distinct vertical distribution according to altitude and other environmental factors.

Like other high mountains in central Japan, Mt. Fuji may be divided into the following three sections: (1) The Montane Belt (about 1,000 m in height) containing a variety of trees. Typical among them are larches, red pines, prickly firs, beeches, *daimyo* oaks, *keyaki* (zelkovas), oaks, maples and cherries. (2) The Broad-Leaved Tree Belt (about 1,500 m in height) containing vegetation consisting mainly of deciduous, broad-leaved trees. Typical trees are beeches, oaks, white birches, alders and mountain ash. (3) The Acerose Tree Belt (from about 1,500 m up to about 2,300 m) consists mainly of acerose trees, with several species of deciduous, broad-leaved trees, and shrubs. Typical varieties are silver firs, larches, hemlocks, northern hemlocks, short-leaved pines and Hondo spruces.

When one enters the Alpine Belt from about 2,300 m above sea level (around the fifth or sixth station on the trails), the vegetation becomes very scanty except for some low shrubs and short, creeping forms of the Japanese larch. Near the summit, or around the eighth station, the growth of mosses becomes conspicuous.

Time to Visit: Mt. Fuji is covered with snow from the base to the peak in winter, and even in the middle of summer, the snow never entirely disappears from the summit. The mountain is officially opened to climbers on July 1 and closed on August 31. There are climbers all the year round, but the one-month period from mid-July to mid-August is considered the best time to climb Mt. Fuji. Indeed, during that time, every trail is crowded with long lines of hikers extending from the base to the summit. When the mountain is officially closed to climbers, practically all the stone shelters built at various stations along different trails are closed. As a result, accommodations and food are not always readily available.

Trails: The six popular routes are as follows. The Kawaguchiko and Fujinomiya trails are convenient since one can drive to the fifth station. The Gotemba and Subashiri trails are popularly taken as a descending path. The Yoshida and Shoji trails are not taken frequently as they progress in a round-about manner. All the trails are divided, from the starting point to the summit, into ten sections (each of which is called *go*) of unequal distances. At the end of each section, a station has been set up; e.g., *ichi-gome* (first station), *ni-gome* (second station), etc.

At most of these stations, there is a stone signpost, and in many cases, a stone shelter. Although the size of the shelter varies, they can all accommodate climbers, with the charges for lodging and meals differing each year.

The usual precautions for ordinary mountain climbing are advisable.

Ascent: Although the ten sections into which the trails are divided vary greatly according to the different route, the approximate length of each trail is from 15 to 25 km. The total time required for climbing each trail ranges from 5 to 9 hrs. for the ascent if one takes the buses that run up to the fifth station, and 3 to 5 hrs. for the descent. Climbers generally start early in the afternoon, reaching the seventh or eighth station before dark. They spend the night in one of the stone shelters and climb to the summit early the following morning.

After making a circuit of the crater in the morning, they begin the descent about noon and reach the base by late afternoon. In recent years, however, many climbers have taken to starting late in the afternoon—4 p.m. or 5 p.m.—climbing during the night to reach the summit in time for sunrise, called *goraiko*, as previously explained. They usually explore the crater in the morning and descend in the afternoon. This method of climbing has become quite popular lately for several reasons: to escape the heat, to see the sunrise, to save time, etc.

Kawaguchiko Trail: Via the Fuji Toll Road-Subaru Line (Kawaguchiko Station-29.5 km, 1 hr. by bus-the fifth station(*go-gome*)-7.5 km, 5 hrs. on foot-the summit). The tourist driving along the toll road can enjoy a panoramic view of the Fuji Five Lakes, the surrounding mountains, the Southern Japan Alps and Suruga Bay. It joins the Yoshida Trail at the sixth station.

Yoshida Trail: (Fuji-Yoshida Station-1.4 km, 5 min. by bus-Fuji Sengen Shrine-9 km, 2 hrs. 50 min. on foot-Umagaeshi-10.8 km, 6 hrs. 20 min. ascent on foot-the summit). This is the former main route for climbing Mt. Fuji.

Subashiri Trail: (Gotemba Station-1 hr.15 min. by bus-Komitake, the new fifth station-8.1 km, 5 hrs. 30 min. on foot-the summit). Komitake Shrine (alt. 2,000 m) is the starting point of this route. The trail joins the Yoshida Trail at the eighth station (alt. 3,350 m), a junction known as *Oyukiai* (Great Meeting Spot). A sturdy stone shelter stands here. It takes 2 hrs. 30 min. to reach the new fifth station from the summit by descending another route, the steep *Sunabashiri* (sand-sliding) route—a section that is covered with volcanic sand.

Gotemba Trail: (JR Gotemba Station-13 km, 45 min. by bus-the new fifth station-11 km, 6 hrs. 20 min. on foot-the summit). As this trail above the new fifth station (alt. 1,402 m) is rocky and hard on the feet, it is mainly used for descent. It takes about 1 hr. to hike down from the summit to the seventh station. The 7 km between the seventh station and the new fifth station is a section called *Suna-bashiri*. One can easily descend this section in only 35 min. Hoei Peak (alt. 2,702 m) rises about 1 km south of the fifth station on this trail. It was formed by the last eruption of Mt. Fuji, which occurred in 1707.

Fujinomiya Trail: (JR Fujinomiya Station–1 hr.45 min. by bus via Fujisan Skyline–new fifth station, alt. 2,380 m–5.4 km and 4 hrs. 10 min. on foot–the summit). This trail has been regarded since olden times as the "front entrance" to Mt. Fuji, while the Yoshida Trail is referred to as the "rear entrance." It is a convenient trail for climbers from the Kansai region. The trail is better known for its variety of vegetation as well as its panoramic view of the extensive skirts of Mt. Fuji, Suruga Bay, Izu Peninsula and even the Enshu-nada Sea. The Munatsuki-Hatcho, the steepest part of the path, begins after the eighth station and leads to the *Okuno-in* (Inner Shrine) of Sengen Shrine at the summit. It takes 4 hrs. 10 min. to cover the 5.4 km of the ascent.

Shoji Trail: Beginning at Akaike on Lake Shoji (15.5 km), the route runs partway through the shade of the virgin Aokigahara Forest, which provides shelter from the summer sun. A large lava tunnel called Fuji Fuketsu (Lava Cave) with a floor of solid ice and numerous icicles is in the thick forest about 5 km uphill from Akaike. The tunnel begins at the northern foot of Mt. Omuro (alt. 1,447 m)—one of the big parasitic cones on Mt. Fuji.

Refer to the supplement for details regarding the "i" **System Information Center** in Fuji-Yoshida.

Fuji-Yoshida ⬛50⬛ ☎0555: Pop. 55,999. About 1 hr. by limited express on the JR Chuo Main Line from Shinjuku in Tokyo to Otsuki, transferring to the Fujikyu line, with an additional 45-min. ride. The express bus arrives here in 1 hr.45 min. from Shinjuku Station via the Chuo Expressway.

The city is a center for bus services to the outskirts of Mt. Fuji. A bus line leads to Gotemba via Lake Yamanaka, another to Kofu via Lake Kawaguchi and a third to Fujinomiya via Lake Kawaguchi, Lake Shoji, Lake Motosu and Shiraito Falls. The city's traditional industry is the manufacture and marketing of textiles, especially silk known as *Kaiki*—the silk of Kai Province (now, Yamanashi Prefecture). Presently, high-tech industries such as semi-conductors are expanding.

The city is noted for the Fire Festival of Sengen Shrine, held on August 26 toward the official close of the Mt. Fuji climbing season (August 31). On the evening of the festival day, dozens of bonfires, each nearly 7 m high and 1 m in diameter, are lighted at different places throughout the city. Keepers of the mountain shelters along the Yoshida Trail also join in the celebration by lighting bonfires at their respective posts.

Young men carry a 1,125-kg, vermilion-lacquered portable shrine shaped like Mt. Fuji through the streets. Legend has it that whenever Mt. Fuji erupted in olden days, the explosion always occurred on the northeastern side of the mountain. Fearing the further wrath of the gods of the mountain, people in the district took to praying for more peaceful days. As a result, today the festival has become a semi-official closing ceremony of the annual climbing season.

Fujikyu Highland: An extensive amusement park located near the exit of the Chuo Expressway between Fuji-Yoshida and Lake Kawaguchi. For the enjoyment of both children and adults, the premises are equipped with over 60 kinds of rides and attractions, a large stage, accommodations and restaurants. The main attraction of this park is the extensive skating center that is open from October to March.

Lake Kawaguchi 50 : 17.4 km in circumference, 5.6 sq.km in area and 831 m above sea level. Like Lake Yamanaka, it is a favorite summer resort. Kawaguchiko Station on the southeastern shore of Lake Kawaguchi is the gateway to the lake district and the terminal of the Fujikyu Line.

Kawaguchiko Station is 26.7 km, or about 50 min. from Otsuki on the Chuo Main Line. It can be reached in 1 hr.50 min., either by limited express train from Shinjuku, Tokyo, with a transfer at Otsuki, or 1 hr.45 min. by express bus from Shinjuku Station via the Chuo Expressway.

The scenic beauty of this lake is enhanced by the small, thickly wooded islet called Unoshima (Cormorant Isle), on which there is a shrine dedicated to *Benten*—goddess of fortune and music. The leaves of maple and other deciduous trees on the islet present a brilliant spectacle when they change color in autumn. Lake Kawaguchi is also noted for a fine view of Mt. Fuji from its northern shore, where the majestic peak may be seen both in its natural form and as an inverted image on the surface of the placid lake waters.

The lake and surrounding district form an ideal summer retreat, where visitors can find good camping sites and enjoy boating, water skiing, tennis and fishing. In winter the district offers a skating rink as well as fishing for *wakasagi* (a kind of smelt) through holes cut in the ice.

The southeastern shore of Lake Kawaguchi in the Funatsu district (1 km northwest of Kawaguchiko Station) is more populated than any other area of the Fuji Five Lakes. The bustling town of Kawaguchiko with hotels, *ryokan*, restaurants and souvenir shops forms the center of the district.

A superb view of Mt. Fuji and the lake can be obtained here from an observation tower atop Mt. Tenjo (alt. 1,104 m) soaring up from the eastern shore. A ropeway is available from the lakeshore near

Kawaguchiko Station to the summit, while excursion boats offer trips around the lake (40 min.). The lake festival takes place on August 5.

There are two museums near the lake. One is the Yamanashi Prefectural Fuji Visitors Center containing materials on the natural history of Mt. Fuji. It is located near the toll-gate of the 29.5-km-long "Fuji Subaru Line", which leads to the fifth station on Mt. Fuji. The other is the Fuji Museum in front of the Fuji Lake Hotel at Funatsu. It has exhibits relating to the people and natural surroundings of the Fuji Five Lakes district, including the Amano Collection, noted for its erotica.

Mt. Mitsutoge 50 : Alt. 1,786 m. Rising northeast of Lake Kawaguchi, this is the most popular mountain on the periphery of Mt. Fuji. To ascend the mountain, take a bus at Kawaguchiko Station (running only on Sundays and national holidays from late April to early November) bound for the Mitsutoge climbers trail as far as the gateway to the mountain, which takes 25 min. From there, it is a 2-hr. 30-min. hike to the summit. The most popular course takes 4 hrs. 50 min. in which one climbs from Fujikyu Mistutoge Station, then via the summit descends to Lake Kawaguchi.

Lake Yamanaka 50 : About 20 km from Gotemba Station to Asahigaoka on the southern shore, 40 min. by bus and 12 km from Fuji-Yoshida to Asahigaoka, 25 min. by bus. Lake Yamanaka has the highest altitude (981 m) and the largest area (6.4 sq.km) of the Five Lakes. Situated on the northeastern slope of Mt. Fuji, the lake has become a favorite summer resort (average temperature in August is 20℃). Hotels, villas and clubhouses belonging to various colleges and organizations have risen all along its shoreline together with other buildings.

Since this is the most popular of the Five Lakes with the younger generation, many stylish pensions and restaurants are available. There are also fine tennis courts and various water sports facilities. During the cold season in January and February, *wakasagi* (a kind of smelt) can be caught in the lake through a small hole cut through the ice. The lake is stocked with various species of fish, including *wakasagi*, carp and eels.

The extensive forest bordering the lake includes many cherry trees, which are in full bloom in early May. The forest is also noted for its many varieties of singing birds. Asahigaoka on the southern shore of Lake Yamanaka is the busiest section of the district with its hotels and souvenir shops. Buses arrive here from many nearby places, while excursion boats making a circuit of the lake (30 min.) start from here.

The waters of the Katsura River running near Fuji (or Oshino) Spa offer excellent trout fishing, both in summer and autumn. The spa is located about 1 km east of a point midway between Fuji-Yoshida and Lake Yamanaka. Another point of interest is Oshino Village, known for eight ponds called "Oshino Hakkai" (Eight Seas of Oshino). It includes a beautiful view of a farming village dotted with traditional Japanese farmhouses.

Lake Saiko 50 : 2.1 sq.km in area. Lying west of Lake Kawaguchi, it can be reached in about 25 min. by bus from Kawaguchiko Station. The lake is also known as Lake Nishi-no-Umi (Western Lake), while Higashi-no-Umi (Eastern Lake) was the old name of Lake Kawaguchi. Nestled in a dense forest lining the southwestern shore are the lodging villages of Nemba and Saiko. It is also known as a good place to fish for silver carp and *wakasagi* (a kind of smelt).

Some of the scenic spots in the vicinity include the following: *Jukai* (Sea of Trees) of Aokigahara is the name given to the extensive forest region extending 16 km in circumference, mainly between lakes Saiko and Shoji. People are warned against getting lost in this forest because magnetic lava in the area prevents a compass from working properly. South of Lake Saiko is a hill known as *Koyodai* (Maple Hill), which commands a view of the entire forest.

Tree Molds at Narusawa: An eruption of Mt. Fuji in 864 caused lava to flow over a grove of trees, which eventually disappeared and left a complex network of holes in the cave walls. The caves are protected as Special Natural Monuments.

Fugaku Fuketsu (Lava Cave): Southwest of Koyodai and near Fuketsu Bus Stop (40 min. from Kawaguchiko Station) is a lava cave covered with numerous icicles and lava stalactites. A similar cave called Narusawa Hyoketsu (Ice Cave) is located along the Tokai Natural Trail in the *jukai*. In the Forest of Aokigahara are several large lava caves that were formed when molten lava from the volcano was forced out by inner pressure, leaving cavities behind.

Lake Shoji 50 : Located 40 min. from Kawaguchiko Station, or 1 hr. 25 min. from Fujinomiya Station by bus. It is secluded on three sides by wooded mountains, which open toward the southeast facing Mt. Fuji. It is one of the most beautiful, though the smallest (750,000 sq.m in area), of the Five Lakes. Between April and November, this area is well known for silver carp fishing. On the lake, skating and fishing for *wakasagi* (a kind of smelt) through holes cut in the ice are popular winter pastimes. This is the starting point of the Shoji Trail leading to the top of Mt. Fuji.

The principal attraction here is the hike to Panorama-dai Plateau (alt. 1,328 m). Rising between Lake Shoji and Lake Motosu, the plateau offers a magnificent view of Mt. Fuji over the "Sea of Trees" clustered in front. The summit is 2.5 km from the Panoramadai-shita Bus Stop on the northwestern shore of Lake Shoji, or a 1-hr. 20-min. hike.

Lake Motosu 50 : 50 min. from Kawaguchiko Station and 1 hr.15 min. from Fujinomiya Station by bus. It is the westernmost of the Five Lakes and the deepest. Because of its great depth (126 m), Lake Motosu does not freeze over, even in mid-winter. The beauty of its deep blue water offers a pleasant surprise to visitors. Souvenir shops line the vicinity of the bus stop on the eastern shore, and except for a camping site and the adolescent sports center located on the southeastern shore, the lake area stays very quiet.

Fujinomiya ☐51☐ ☎0544: Pop. 116,853. 20 min. by the JR Minobu Line from Fuji Station on the Tokaido Main Line. It was once one of the main points of departure for climbing Mt. Fuji and also served as a base for a trip to the Fuji Five Lakes at the northern foot of Mt. Fuji, but this role has gradually shifted to Shin-Fuji Station on the JR Tokaido Shinkansen. Bus service is available from the city to Shiraito Falls.

Sengen Shrine ☐51☐: Standing about 1 km northwest of Fujinomiya Station, it is the head shrine of the various Sengen shrines on Mt. Fuji, all of which are dedicated to Konohana-Sakuyahime-no-Mikoto—the goddess of the mountain. The Main Hall was built in 1604 and has been designated as an Important Cultural Property.

Taisekiji Temple ☐51☐: Located in Kamijo, 30 min. by bus from Fujinomiya Station, this temple was founded in 1290 by priest Nikko (1246–1333). He was one of the leading disciples of Saint Nichiren (1222–1282, refer to p.437), the founder of the Nichiren sect of Buddhism. The *Sho-Hondo* building, 66 m high and uniquely modern with a suspension-roof, is one of the largest, single-floor religious structures in the world. With a seating capacity of 6,000 people, it was completed in October 1972 as a "sanctuary for world peace" and the headquarters of the Nichiren-Shoshu sect of Soka Gakkai—one of the largest religious organizations. The Fuji Art Museum, located within the grounds, exhibits a wide variety of art, including classical Japanese painting, classical Chinese pottery, paintings by the Impressionists and various other masterpieces.

Shiraito (White Thread) Falls ☐50☐: Located midway between Lake Motosu in the north and Fujinomiya in the south. A bus covers the 13-km distance from the latter point in 35 min. On the upper reaches of the Shiba River are famous waterfalls resembling countless white threads dangling over a cliff that is 26 m high and 130 m wide. Just across the road east of the falls is another waterfall called *Otodome-no-Taki*.

Asagiri Plateau ☐50☐: A massive plateau extending approximately 15 sq. km along Fujinomiya Highway, running from south to north between the Shiraito Falls at the foot of Mt. Fuji and the border of Yamanashi Prefecture. It can be reached by bus for Fuji-Yoshida from Shin-Fuji Station on the JR Tokaido Shinkansen, taking about 40 min. to the Asagiri Bus Stop. The Asagiri Plateau is formed from volcanic rock from Mt. Fuji and covered with tall, coarse grasses but few trees.

This area not only consists of many dairy farms, but various recreational facilities can also be found here. In the southern portion at a tourist spot called Makaino Bokuju (Pasture), one can go horseback riding or milk cows. Furthermore, there is a vast natural park named Kachosammyaku (lit. Flowers-Birds' Mountains) complete with a botanical garden, a wild bird park, restaurants and a cycling course. Lake Tanuki (35 min. by bus from Shin-Fuji Station) is just the place to enjoy camping, boating and fishing. Moreover, it is noted for its beautiful azaleas. In the central portion of the area is the Fuji Trout Farm, which offers trout fishing and trout dishes, and Mochiya Amusement Park, which is equipped with a variety of recreational facilities. In the northern portion, Asagiri Green Park (45 min. by bus from Shin-Fuji Station) offers a golf course, tennis courts, a skating arena and other outdoor sports facilities.

Gotemba ⬜51⬜ ☎0550: Pop. 76,957. Situated on the JR Gotemba Line between Kozu and Numazu, Gotemba can be reached from Shinjuku (Tokyo) in about 1 hr.45 min. by direct express on the Odakyu Electric Railway. The express train runs through to the JR Gotemba Line. A highway bus leaving from Tokyo Station arrives in about 1 hr. 30 min. via the Tomei Expressway.

From Gotemba, bus service is available to Sengoku in Hakone via Otome Pass (alt. 1,000 m), to Lake Yamanaka and Lake Kawaguchi, and farther northwest to Kofu. There is also a regular sightseeing bus service (in Japanese) that makes a circuit of scenic spots around the base of Mt. Fuji in 8 hrs. 10 min. It makes the following tour: Mishima (9:40 a.m.)–Gotemba (10:20 a.m.)–Lake Yamanaka (Cruise)–Fuji Sengen Shrine–Mt. Fuji Fifth Station (Lunch)–Fugaku Fuketsu (Lava Cave)–Asagiri Plateau–Shiraito Falls–Shin-Fuji (5:25 p.m.)–Mishima (6: 15 p.m.).

Gotemba City and its vicinity offers various sports and amusement facilities such as Gotemba Family Land, Nippon Land "How Amusement Park," the Fuji Safari Park and Fuji Speedway where international motor races are held.

Hakone and Vicinity ⬜51⬜

A popular, year-round resort for those of all nationalities because of its abundance of hot-spring resorts, beautiful scenery and salubrious climate. Its easy accessibility from Tokyo by rail and a web of good roads plus plentiful tourist facilities in the district also add to its attraction.

TOPOGRAPHY

The Hakone district lies within the crater of an extinct volcano about 40 km in circumference. It includes many hot springs and a mountain lake called Ashi, also known as Lake Hakone in English. The principal mountains lying within the crater are Mt. Kamiyama (alt. 1,438 m), Mt. Komagatake (alt. 1,327 m) and Mt. Futago (alt. 1,091 m).

All the mountain peaks show traces of ancient as well as more recent eruptions since there are double crater ridges. Two rivers drain the district—the Hayakawa, the northern outlet of Lake Ashi, and the Sukumo, which rises at the foot of Mt. Kurakake (alt. 1,004 m). There are 17 communities under the administration of Hakone-machi within the limits of the crater, including Yumoto, Miyanoshita, Miyagino, Gora, Sengokuhara, Moto-Hakone and Hakonemachi proper.

Evidence of past volcanic activity may be observed at Owakudani (Valley of Greater Boiling) as well as at several other places in the district. Owakudani, also called Ojigoku ("Big Hell"), is located near Owakudani Station on the 4-km-long Hakone Ropeway running between Sounzan and Togendai. The entire gorge reeks of sulfurous fumes pouring forth from crevices in the rocks or from the bare earth, sometimes with great force. Clouds of steam constantly hover over this inferno. In many places, steam will spurt out if a stick is thrust through the thin crust of earth covering the boiling caldron below.

At some places, boiling hot-spring water bubbles out of the ground, much of which is channeled into tanks and piped to distant places. Near the top of the mountain are a number of solfataras, which send out never-ending clouds of sulfurous steam, while blobs of grayish matter boil ceaselessly in the ground. Sightseers should keep to the beaten track through this weird and desolate region.   In clear weather, a fine view may be obtained from the hill overlooking this weird scene. A similar phenomenon can be observed at Yunohana-zawa near Ashinoyu.

HOT SPRINGS

There are 12 hot-spring resorts in the Hakone district, known since olden times as the "Twelve Spas of Hakone"—Yumoto, Tonosawa, Miyanoshita, Dogashima, Sokokura, Kowakidani, Kiga, Gora, Ubako, Sengokuhara, Ashinoyu and Yunohanazawa. Two additional spas, Ohiradai and Ashinoko, have been developed later. Yumoto has the longest history, but Miyanoshita, Gora and Kowakidani are the most popular spas today, especially among foreigners.

TRANSPORTATION

Hakone is best reached from Tokyo or Yokohama by train via Odawara (Tokyo–Odawara is 84 km, 40 min. by the JR Tokaido Shinkansen). The Odakyu Electric Railway also runs between Shinjuku in Tokyo and Hakone-Yumoto via Odawara (1 hr.20 min. by limited express).

From Odawara the Hakone Tozan Railway runs along the deep, intervening gorge to the Hakone resorts, including Yumoto, Tonosawa, Miyanoshita, Kowakidani and Gora (Odawara–Gora 15 km , 50 min.). Gora is connected by a cable car with Sounzan (Gora–Sounzan 1.2 km, 9 min.), and the 4-km-long Hakone Ropeway connects Sounzan with Togendai on the north shore of Lake Ashi via Owakudani and Ubako in 33 min.

In addition, a 13.8-km-long stretch of the Hakone Bypass Toll Road, running along the old Tokaido Highway, links Odawara and Hakonemachi on the southern shore of Lake Ashi. The 13.8-km-long Hakone Turnpike also runs from Odawara to Mt. Taikanzan, where it joins the Yugawara-Hakone Highway ("Camellia Line") leading to Hakonemachi. Drivers along this turnpike on a fine day can obtain a view of the blue waters of Sagami Bay and picturesque Enoshima Island at close range as well as the Boso Peninsula in the distance. Togendai, on the northern shore of Lake Ashi, can also be reached in about 2 hrs. 10 min. by express bus from Shinjuku Station in Tokyo via the Tomei Expressway.

Bus Service in Hakone: The Hakone district has a well-developed network of bus routes. Almost all places of interest in the district can be reached by bus from the cities lying on the outskirts: Odawara, Yugawara, Atami, Mishima and Gotemba.

As Odawara, Atami and Mishima are on the JR Tokaido Shinkansen, tourists from the Tokyo-Yokohama or Osaka-Kobe areas may make a bus tour of the Hakone district after detraining at any of these three stations. They can also return by any of these routes. Though a tour can be made in one day, staying overnight at a spa in the Hakone district is a more leisurely, enjoyable way to visit the area.

PLACES OF INTEREST

Hakone-Yumoto 　51　: Located 6 km west of Odawara, about 15 min. by bus or train, it is one of the oldest towns and spa resorts in the Hakone district, as well as the terminal of the Odakyu Electric Railway running from Shinjuku in Tokyo and passing through Odawara. It is situated about 100 m above sea level at the confluence of the Hayakawa and Sukumo rivers in the eastern foothills of the Hakone mountains. The simple, thermal hot springs contain very few traces of minerals, but are efficacious against neuralgia, rheumatism, gynecological disorders and chronic diseases of the digestive organs. The temperature ranges 35-74°C.

The chief places of interest in the neighborhood are Sounji Temple of the Rinzai sect of Zen Buddhism and two waterfalls called Tamadare and Hatsuhana. The temple was established by a will left by Hojo Soun (1432-1519), one of the most important lords of his time. His portrait on silk is kept in the temple as one of the nation's Important Cultural Properties. This temple was once the largest in eastern Japan and the headquarters of Toyotomi Hideyoshi—a great general and statesman in the latter 16th century—while he was besieging Odawara in 1590. With the downfall of the Hojo Clan, however, the temple was allowed to go to ruin and now only a few buildings remain. The tombs of the five lords of the Hojo family stand in the grounds.

Daimyo Gyoretsu (Feudal Lord Procession): The most famous tourist attraction in Hakone. In the procession, about 120 local residents colorfully costumed as a lord and his retainers parade through the resort district just as the ancient warriors did on the path leading from the various provinces to Edo (now, Tokyo) in olden days. The parade is annually held on November 3, but the date is subject to change. The procession moves at a very slow pace from Sounji Temple to Moto-Hakone in the morning and returns to Sounji Temple in the afternoon.

Hatajuku: A village located about midway along the section of the old Tokaido Highway running from Hakone-Yumoto to Moto-Hakone. It is noted for the crafting of *Hakone-zaiku*, which is a combination of inlay, mosaic and marquetry wares. Besides showing demonstrations of the production process, the Hatajuku-Yosegi-Kaikan (Woodcraft Hall) also displays and sells examples of this unique folkcraft.

Tonosawa Spa: About 1 km up the valley along the road to Miyanoshita from Yumoto, beautifully situated on the Hayakawa River. The temperature of the simple thermal spring ranges 43–64℃.

Amida Temple: Founded early in the 17th century and dedicated to *Amida* Buddha, the buildings stand 2 km (30-min. walk) from Tonosawa Spa on the slopes of Mt. Tonomine (alt. 556 m). A splendid view of the surrounding country may be enjoyed from the summit.

Ohiradai Spa: Midway between Yumoto and Miyanoshita. The spa consists of weak, common-salt springs (75℃), considered efficacious for the treatment of neuralgia, rheumatism and skin diseases.

Miyanoshita ⬚51⬚: Located 12 km west of Odawara, 35 min. by the Hakone Tozan Railway or 30 min. by bus, this is one of the key transportation centers of Hakone. With an altitude of about 400 m above sea level, it is generally cool, even in summer. The medicinal value of its hot springs (weak common-salt) is well known for the treatment of chronic diseases of the digestive organs, neuralgia, rheumatism, gout and gynecological disorders.

Good roads radiate in every direction from Miyanoshita, affording delightful walks and drives among the hills and valleys of this picturesque district. They also lead to various places of interest in the area.

Among the interesting hikes in the vicinity of Miyanoshita are: (1) Mt. Sengen (alt. 802 m), which rises behind the Fujiya Hotel—the oldest hotel (opened in 1878) in the Hakone district. The extensive view from the summit of Mt. Sengen, which can be climbed in about 1 hr., gives a good idea of the geography of the Hakone area. The downhill trail to the west leads to *Chisuji-no-Taki* Falls near Kowakidani. (2) Dogashima is about 500 m, or 10 min., from Miyanoshita. A trail along the side of a ravine leads to picturesque cascades. (3) Opposite the Fujiya Hotel rises a high, grassy hill known as Mt. Myojo (alt. 924 m). It can be climbed by way of Dogashima Spa in about 1 hr.30 min.

The Daimonji-yaki Festival: It takes place every year on Mt. Myojo on August 16 after the fashion of the raging bon-fires on Mt. Nyoigadake in Kyoto on the same night. On this night, many torches are burned on the hillside, lighting up against the night sky the huge outline of the Chinese character *dai* meaning "large." The crossbar of the ideograph measures as long as 108 m.

Dogashima Spa: Situated a little below Miyanoshita (10 min. on foot) in a very secluded spot on the banks of the Hayakawa River. Visitors to the *ryokan* here are carried from Miyanoshita by the private cable car or ropeway run by the respective *ryokan* for their exclusive use. The river offers some refreshing scenery, including many rapids and small waterfalls. The hot springs are of the common-salt type (temperature ranges 52–61℃), efficacious for the treatment of stomach diseases, rheumatism and neuralgia.

Sokokura Spa: About 500 m northwest of Miyanoshita Station. The hot springs have the same content and medicinal value as the one at Miyanoshita. It is also noted for its many historical associations. A memorial dedicated to Nitta Yoshinori (d. 1403), a loyalist general, is among the famous relics in Kozan Park. Another is the stone bath-house said to have been utilized by Toyotomi Hideyoshi (1536–1598) for soldiers wounded in his war against the Hojo Clan of Odawara.

Kowakidani (Valley of Lesser Boiling): Also called *Kojigoku* or "Little Hell," the area can be reached in 7 min. by bus from Miyano-shita. The place derives its name from the sulfur fumes that come from a cave in the vicinity. With temperatures ranging from 47–90℃, the hot-spring water is efficacious against neuralgia, anemia, dermatitis, etc.

The nearby hills and valleys are known for their cherry trees and azaleas. The view from Kowakidani of the Hayakawa Valley and the surrounding mountains is one of the finest in the vicinity.

Kowaki-en: A vast resort center sprawling over some 1 sq.km of land. It contains *ryokan*, hotels and recreational facilities such as a spa hotel, jungle restaurants, Utopia Polynesia with sixteen open-air baths surrounded by woods, a bowling alley, heated pool, tropical botanical garden and much more.

Chokoku-no-Mori (Sculpture Wood): 5 min. from Kowakidani on the Hakone Tozan Railway. Disembark at Chokoku-no-Mori Station. Also called the Hakone Open-Air Museum, it features many modern works of sculpture exhibited outdoors.

Kiga: 1 km northwest of Miyanoshita, on the western bank of the Hayakawa River. There are several simple, thermal and common-salt hot springs (temperature ranges from 38–91℃), which are efficacious for the treatment of neuralgia, rheumatism and dermatitis. A stone tablet was erected here by the villagers in honor of a French general, who often visited Kiga in the early years of the Meiji period (1868–1912). About 1 km farther on, where the road crosses the river, is Miyagino. Beyond the bridge is a path running along the hillside above the river and leading back to Miyanoshita via Dogashima.

Gora ⬜51⬜ : Located 3 km from Miyanoshita, 12 min. by the Hakone Tozan Railway; 15 km from Odawara, about 50 min. also by the Hakone Tozan Railway. Lying at an altitude of some 600 m on the eastern slopes of Mt. Soun, it commands an extensive view that includes the upper stretches of the Hayakawa River, Mt. Myojin (alt. 1,169 m) and Mt. Myojo (924 m) as well as other distant Hakone peaks and even affords a glimpse of the Pacific Ocean. Gora is the terminal of the Hakone Tozan Railway from Odawara as well as for a cable car to Sounzan.

The hot-spring water here is piped from Owakudani, a spa that can be reached by taking a cable car and then a ropeway, or by bus via Sounzan. The saline sulfur water (temperature 35-95℃) has thera-peutic effects for rheumatism, paralysis, dermatitis and gynecological disorders.

There are many cherry trees along the cable car line as well as in the vicinity of Gora Park, which is also noted for its azaleas. The Hakone Museum of Art, which stands on a hill overlooking the park, displays ancient Japanese porcelain.

From Sounzan the terminal of the cable car from Gora, the Hakone Ropeway runs to Togendai, near Kojiri, on the northern extremity of Lake Ashi. Extending for a distance of 4,035 m (33 min.), it is the longest of its kind in Japan, stopping twice midway—Owakudani and Ubako. At Owakudani Station a revolving observation platform not only affords a panoramic view of the Hakone district, it also permits a close look at the fumes rising from Owakudani Valley and a marvelous view of Mt. Fuji on clear days. From the station to most of the solfataras in the neighborhood, it is about 10 min. on foot. From Togendai ferryboats ply across the lake to Moto-Hakone and Hakonemachi on the southern shore.

Ubako: The most secluded spa of all the hot-spring resorts in this district, it nestles at an altitude of 900 m at the foot of a slope northwest of Owakudani. The hot springs here, with a big, naturally rocky pool, are of the simple thermal type (temperature is around 45℃). The mineral water is reputedly helpful in the treatment of neuralgia and rheumatic diseases. Ubako is located on the regular bus line from Kowakidani via Owakudani to Kojiri, near Togendai, on the northern shore of Lake Ashi. From Kojiri, however, ferryboat services are also available to Moto-Hakone and Hakonemachi via Hakone-en.

Sengokuhara: Located 6 km from Miyanoshita, 15 min. by bus, in the northern part of the Hakone Spas Area. This popular resort consists of five spas—Motoyu, Kamiyu, Shimoyu, Hyoseki and Sengoku. The hot water, piped from Owakudani (temperature ranges between 20-75℃), is reportedly good for the treatment of anemia, rheumatism, dermatitis, etc.

West of this resort lies a vast plain called Sengokuhara or Sengoku-bara, which is overgrown with *susuki* or pampas grass (Miscanthus sinensis) and clusters of marshy plants. It is bordered on the south by Lake Ashi, and on the north and west by a range of three mountains —Kintoki (alt. 1,213 m), Nagao (alt. 1,144 m) and Maru (alt. 1,154 m), all three of which form part of the outer crater wall.

Among the many species of marshy plants growing here, the irises that bloom in mid-July are especially noted for their beauty. To protect these plants from extinction, most of the marsh is closed to the public, but the Hakone Botanical Garden of Wetlands is open to tourists and ordinary plant lovers. The garden covers 30,000 sq.m and contains irises and 870 other species of plants for a total of 100,000 marsh plants. Most of these plants bloom between May and August, presenting visitors with a beautiful view.

Otome Toll Road, 15.6 km long, connects Sengokuhara with Gotemba, passing under Otome Pass (alt. 1,000 m) through a tunnel. The pass is noted for its inspiring view of Mt. Fuji. Nagao Pass (alt. 903 m), located to the southwest of Otome Pass between Hakone and Gotemba, is noted as a spot with a beautiful view of Mt. Fuji.

Ashinoyu: Located 6 km from Miyanoshita, 10 min. by bus, at an altitude of 900 m above sea level on the eastern slope of Mt. Komagatake (alt. 1,327 m). Two hot springs, both containing sulfur and especially efficacious against rheumatic ailments, constitute its main attraction. Skating can be enjoyed here in winter. Ashinoyu is a good starting point for climbing Mt. Komagatake, Mt. Futago and Mt. Kamiyama.

Yunohanazawa: 2 km from Ashinoyu, on the road to Mt. Kamiyama from Ashinoyu. Situated at an altitude of 940 m on the slopes of Mt. Komagatake, it is the highest of the hot-spring resorts in the Hakone district. A golf course lies on the outskirts.

Mt. Komagatake 51 : Two transportation modes are available; from the southeastern base, Komagatake-noboriguchi Station (a 720-m-long cable car, 5 min.); from the southwestern base, Hakone-en on the shore of Lake Ashi (a 1,783-m-long ropeway, 8 min.). An artificial ski ground called Komagatake Snowland operates on the summit in winter. The view from the summit takes in Mt. Fuji, Lake Ashi, Mt. Futago and the distant mountains of the Izu Peninsula.

Soga Brothers: About 500 m beyond Ashinoyu along the main bus route to Moto-Hakone are three small, moss-covered stone monuments erected in memory of the Soga Brothers—Goro and Juro—and Toragozen, the mistress of Juro. The Soga Brothers are famous for vindicating their father's honor in the latter part of the 12th century.

According to the story, their father, Kawazu Sukeyasu, was treacherously slain by a kinsman named Kudo Suketsune, a high-ranking vassal of Minamoto-no-Yoritomo (founder of the Kamakura Shogunate). Their mother married again, and their stepfather sent Goro, the younger of the two, to Hakone Shrine (also known as Hakone Gongen) on the shores of Lake Ashi to become a priest. Goro, however, ran away from the shrine to join his brother, who had decided to avenge their father's death.

Patiently awaiting their opportunity for 17 long years after the death of their father, they finally saw their chance and killed Kudo while he was attending Yoritomo on a hunting expedition in the foothills of Mt. Fuji. Juro, who was then 26 years old, was killed by one of Kudo's retainers and Goro was captured.

Later, Goro was condemned to death and executed. Toragozen, who aided the brothers in their revenge, became a nun after their death.

Moto-Hakone 44 : Located on the southeastern shore of Lake Ashi, this is the most prosperous town in the lake area. It can be reached from Odawara in 55 min. by bus via Miyanoshita. There are also bus lines to Moto-Hakone from Yugawara, Atami, Mishima and Numazu.

Ferryboats are available to Hakonemachi on the southern shore, to Hakone-en on the eastern shore, and to Kojiri and Togendai on the northern shore. As thermal waters are piped from Yunohanazawa Spa, most *ryokan* at Moto-Hakone have hot-spring baths. It is also referred to as Ashinoko Spa. Hakone Shrine is not far from the bus terminal.

Kosui Matsuri (Lake Festival) is held on July 31. Ceremonial rites are observed on boats in the middle of the lake by priests and parishioners of the shrine. Parishioners and visitors from neighboring districts set afloat thousands of lighted lanterns from the shore in a service offered to the nine-headed dragon that is believed to be the guardian of the lake.

Hakone Shrine 44 : Popularly called Hakone Gongen. The shrine is about 500 m from the Moto-Hakone Bus Stop along the eastern shore of Lake Ashi. It is tucked away in the densely wooded hillside at the southern foot of Mt. Komagatake. Said to have been founded by Saint Mangan in 757, it was once one of the largest shrines in central Japan. The three Shinto deities to which it is dedicated are Ninigi-no-Mikoto, Konohana-Sakuya-Hime-no-Mikoto and Hikohohodemi-no-Mikoto.

The shrine is widely known as the place where Minamoto-no-Yoritomo took refuge after his defeat at Ishibashiyama near Odawara. He fought here in 1180 against the Taira Clan in an attempt to regain the power of his forefathers in Kyoto.

A treasure house where many old relics are preserved stands beside the main hall of the shrine. Among them are such priceless treasures as a picture scroll depicting the origin of Hakone Shrine, a wooden image of Saint Mangan—founder of the shrine and the sword which Soga Goro (refer to p.474) is said to have used in avenging the death of his father in the latter part of the 12th century.

Hakone-en 44 : On the eastern shore of Lake Ashi (15 min. from Moto-Hakone or Kojiri by ferryboat or bus) is an all-round recreation center with a large camping ground and an "International Village." The camping ground contains one hundred cottages, a big dining hall, an aquarium, four tennis courts, a swimming pool and a harbor for yachts and powerboats.

From here to the summit of Mt. Komagatake, it is about 7 min. by ropeway (1,783 m in length). The International Village is laid out on an excellent site, with many houses constructed in the typical architectural styles of various countries.

Hakone Jumoku-en (Hakone Arboretum): About a 20-min. walk either from Hakone-en or Kojiri. Covering 536,000 sq.m and containing some 450 varieties of natural plants native to Hakone, the park is an ideal place for taking a walk and enjoying nature.

Hakonemachi: 1.5 km from Moto-Hakone, 5 min. by bus, along a winding road from Moto-Hakone, parallel to the old Tokaido Highway. Lined with huge old cedars, the road also passes the site of the former Hakone Barrier. Formerly one of the largest and most important post stations on the old Tokaido Highway, this area is now a popular summer resort. Bathing, boating and water-skiing on the lake and hiking are the typical leisure activities here.

From here, roads radiate to several cities and spas on the JR Tokaido Main Line. To Odawara it is 1 hr. by bus along the Hakone Bypass—a 13.8-km toll road running along the valley of the Sukumo River. To Yugawara it is 1 hr. by bus via Yugawara Pass (Mt. Taikan). To Atami it is 50 min. by bus via Hakone Pass (alt. 849 m), Jukkoku Pass and Atami Pass. To Mishima it is a 50-min. bus trip via Hakone Pass.

One of the most popular roads in the area is the "Ashinoko (Lake Ashi) Skyline Drive." This is an 11.7-km toll road leading from Hakone Pass to Kojiri on the northern shore of Lake Ashi by way of the mountain ridges rising on the western shore of Lake Ashi and Umijiri Pass (alt. 855 m). This road affords splendid views of the lake and Mt. Fuji, Sagami and Suruga bays, and the Southern Japan Alps in the distance as it runs northwest over Yamabushi Pass (1,034 m) and winds along the western side of Mt. Mikuni (1,102 m). From Umijiri Pass the road extends farther to Nagao Pass and is called the "Hakone Skyline." The other road is the "Hakone Turnpike", which runs for 13.8 km from Yugawara Pass (Mt. Taikan) to Odawara, following the mountain ridges south of the Hakone Bypass.

Hakone Barrier: Hakone was the site of one of the historic barriers that separated different sections of the country in feudal times. At such barriers, all travelers had to present their passports to officials in guardhouses and give the reason for their journey.

The Hakone Barrier was very important because it commanded the main road between the two capitals—Edo (now, Tokyo) and Kyoto. It was established in 1619 by the Tokugawa Shogunate a little to the north of Hakonemachi, between the lake and the mountains. The Barrier was removed in 1869, but a monument marks the spot where it once stood. The exact replica of the Barrier Guardhouse was built on a plot opposite the old site. The Hakone Checkpoint Exhibition Hall is near the site of the Barrier Gate. In it are displayed the historical materials mainly connected with the Barrier, including weapons, armor, old documents and other things showing the life and the customs of the people of the Edo period (1603–1867).

Lake Ashi 51 : 725 m above sea level. The area of the lake is 6.8 sq.km, with a circumference of 18 km and a depth of 40.6 m at the

476

deepest point. At its northern end, an outlet flows into the Hayakawa River, which runs underground for a distance and then bubbles up to the surface like a spring, finally ending its short, rapid course in Sagami Bay at Odawara.

Angling is one of the most popular pastimes enjoyed at the lake, which abounds with black bass and trout. In winter large flocks of mandarin ducks migrate from the north down to the lake. Lake Ashi is also famous for the Sakasa-Fuji (inverted reflection of Mt. Fuji), which can be seen on a clear, calm day, especially at daybreak. The best place to view this phenomenon is near the wooden *torii* (gate) and images of *Jizo*, the guardian deity of children, along the road between Moto-Hakone and Hakonemachi.

Ferryboats crisscross Lake Ashi, connecting five main points along the shore: Hakonemachi, Moto-Hakone, Hakone-en, Kojiri and Togendai. It is a 10-min. ride between Hakonemachi and Moto-Hakone, and a 40-min. trip between Moto-Hakone and Kojiri. Large excursion ships modeled after medieval European pirate and mer-chant ships, twin-fuselage ships are available.

One of the most noted maple-viewing spots in the Hakone district is along the eastern shore of Lake Ashi. The flame-tinted leaves of the maple and other deciduous trees are best viewed from a boat on the lake. Small pleasure boats and yachts may be hired at the ferry stations of Moto-Hakone, Hakonemachi, Hakone-en and Kojiri.

Izu Peninsula 51

Noted for its hot springs, the name was originally *Yu-Izu* (*yu* = hot water, *izu* = gush out). This land mass lies south of the Hakone district between the Sagami-nada Sea on the east and Suruga Bay on the west.

The Amagi mountains, practically an extension of the Hakone mountain range, stretch far down the peninsula. The highest peak is Mt. Amagi (alt. 1,406 m), where wild boar and other game are to be found. The Kano River has its sources in this mountain, flowing north through the extensive area of the peninsula and emptying into Suruga Bay at Numazu.

Owing to its historic associations as well as its hot springs and seaside resorts, its wealth of natural beauty and its accessibility, the Izu Peninsula is a popular tourist area all year round. Its mild climate also adds to its appeal, causing plum trees to burst into bloom two months ahead of those in Tokyo.

There are several historic spots on the peninsula such as Ito, where William Adams (known as Miura Anjin—his Japanese name, refer to p.441), the first Englishman to set foot in Japan in 1600, built what was probably Japan's first ocean-going vessel. Then there is Shimoda, where Townsend Harris, the first representative of the United States to Japan, resided for nearly 15 months. On September 4, 1856, he hoisted the first American flag seen in Japan.

TRANSPORTATION

Rail: The Izu Peninsula can be approached either from the Tokyo or Osaka area. From the Tokyo area, limited express trains offer frequent service on the JR Tokaido Main Line running either to Izukyu-Shimoda on the Izukyu Line or to Shuzenji on the Izu-Hakone Railway. One can also take the JR Tokaido Shinkansen to Atami or Mishima, transferring to the Izukyu Line or the Izu-Hakone Railway, respectively. Atami is the east and Mishima is the west entrance to the Izu Peninsula. From the Osaka area, the JR Tokaido Shinkansen is recommended as the best and perhaps only way to approach the area. In addition some limited express trains on the Tokaido Main Line run directly between Shinjuku, Ikebukuro (both in Tokyo), and Izukyu-Shimoda or Shuzenji.

Important points on the peninsula can also be reached by car or bus from Tokyo and Yokohama as well as from Hakone and the Fuji Five Lakes region. Coastal, high-speed boats run between Numazu and Matsuzaki, touching at Toi and Dogashima.

Roads: A network of roads extends through the peninsula. The cross-country route on National Highway 136 and National Highway 414 runs longitudinally from Mishima to Shimoda at the southern tip of the peninsula via Amagi Pass. Many spas are located en route, including Nagaoka, Ohito, Shuzenji, Yoshina, Yugashima, Yugano and Rendaiji. Perhaps the most refreshing excursion is the drive along the coast on either side of the peninsula. The eastern coastal route on National Highway 135 runs from Atami Spa to Shimoda, touching at several noted seaside, hot-spring resorts, including Ito, Atagawa and Imaihama.

A 42-km toll road called "Izu Skyline" extends from Atami Pass (alt. 617 m) to Amagi Kogen (Plateau). It runs at an altitude of 500 –700 m along the ridges of the mountains that form the backbone of the Izu Peninsula. The parkway, with four interchanges at Atami Pass, Kameishi Pass, Hiekawa and Amagi Kogen, is accessible from Hakone, Atami, Ito or Shuzenji. A motorist driving south along this route can enjoy a picturesque view of Hatsushima and Izu-Oshima Island on the left, contrasting beautifully with the blue sea. On the right, one will be able to enjoy the celebrated sight of Suruga Bay, with the snow-capped cone of Mt. Fuji rising in the north.

At Kameishi Pass a road branches east down to Usami Station on the JR Ito Line and west to Ohito, a popular hot-spring resort.

Along the western coast travelers can glimpse the ever-changing view of Mt. Fuji from different points on the way (mainly on National Highway 136) when the weather is clear. The drive through the coastal sections, extending from Numazu to Mito and from Toi to Matsuzaki, is delightful. From Kumomi near Matsuzaki, the Minami (South)-Izu Road (12.2 km), popularly known as the Margaret Line, leads the driver to Cape Iro on the southernmost tip of the Izu Peninsula.

East Izu

Ajiro ⬛51⬛ : Located between Atami and Ito on the JR Ito Line, it is one of the best-known fishing ports on the peninsula. Ajiro Spa, sometimes called Minami-Atami (Southern Atami) Spa, consists of saline hot springs.

Ito ⬛51⬛ :☎0557: Pop. 72,839. 122 km from Tokyo. This is the second-largest spa resort on the peninsula after Atami and can be reached from Tokyo via Atami in 2 hrs. by the JR limited express. The spa town spreads out around the Matsukawa River flowing through the center of the city. Sagami Bay and Hatsushima Island lie in front, while the Amagi mountains, covered with mandarin orange groves, soar at the rear. The scenic beauty and abundant hot springs attract many visitors. The area offers with tennis courts, golf courses and marine sport facilities as well as villas and pensions, a popular accommodation choice with the younger generation. The local products of Ito include mandarin oranges, mushrooms, camellia oil and marine products.

History: Ito is noted as the place to which Minamoto-no-Yoritomo (1147-1199) was banished by the powerful Taira Clan in 1160. On a hill behind the town is the tomb of Ito Sukechika, a local feudal lord at the time of Yoritomo. Yoritomo seduced Sukechika's daughter Yaehime, but he escaped her father's vengeance with the aid of her brother.

When Yoritomo subsequently rose to power, Sukechika fell into his hands. In gratitude for the help he had received from Sukechika's son, Yoritomo expressed his wish to retain Sukechika in his position as a feudal lord. Sukechika, however, refused to receive favors at the hands of his enemy and committed suicide. Local superstition still associates the spirits of Yoritomo and Yaehime with *Otonashi-no-mori*, a thick grove of old trees surrounding a small shrine in the town where the lovers used to meet.

Refer to the supplement for details regarding the "i" **System Information Center** in Ito.

Butsugenji Temple: A Nichiren sect Buddhist temple located on a small hill a little southeast of Ito Station. Among its treasures is a picture of paradise painted by Saint Nichiren, who was exiled to the temple for a short time (1261-1263).

Adams Monument: 2 km southeast of Ito Station, at the mouth of the Okawa River. It was erected in August 1947 in memory of William Adams (1564-1620), who is called Miura Anjin by the Japanese (refer to p.441). After setting up a shipyard on the site where the monument now stands, the English pilot built Japan's first European-style, ocean-going vessels. He is said to have constructed two vessels (one of 80 tons and the other of 120 tons) between the years 1605 and 1610. The William Adams Festival is held here between the 6 and 10 of

August in commemoration of his services to Japan.

Next to the Adams Monument stands a stone tablet with a poetic epigraph on William Adams written in July 1948 by Edmund Blunden, a well-known English poet, to express his pleasure on visiting the tomb of the famous English maritime engineer.

From Ito the Izukyu Line runs to Izukyu-Shimoda for a distance of 45.7 km along the eastern coast, passing en route such spas as Atagawa, Inatori and Imaihama. Buses run west from here to Shuzenji, the best-known inland spa on the peninsula (1 hr.), and south to Shimoda (2 hrs.). Steamship service to Izu-Oshima Island is available and takes 1 hr.20 min. It takes approximately 50 min. by speedboat.

Kawana ⌐51⌐: 10 min. from Ito on the Izukyu Line. It is noted for its excellent golf links, regarded as the best in the Orient, and the Kawana Hotel. The hotel has two 18-hole courses—*Fuji* (6,691 yards) and *Oshima* (5,705 yards).

Lake Ippeki ⌐51⌐: Lying 5.5 km south of Ito, 25 min. by bus, the lake contains 12 islets on its mirror-like surface. Surrounded by low hills, it has a circumference of 4 km. Boating and fishing for hatchery-bred carp and crucian carp can be enjoyed. On the shore stands the Ikeda Museum of 20th-Century Art, which exhibits Impressionist paintings and works by Piccasso, Matisse, Bonnard, etc.

At the northeastern foot of Mt. Omuro is the Izu Cactus Park, covering 200,000 sq.m; 35 min. by bus from Ito Station. About 5,000 varieties of cacti and other tropical plants from Mexico, Argentina, Texas (USA) and other areas have been planted in the garden, which also contains a zoo, an observation platform and other tourist attractions.

Jogasaki Beach ⌐51⌐: Located to the south of Kawana, the jagged coastline was formed by waves eroding the lava platform that runs out into the Sagami-nada Sea. Cliffs with a height of several decameters extend over approximately 9 km, offering the most magnificent view of Izu Peninsula on the east coast. Two hiking courses also offer visitors views of coastal landscapes full of variety. Since the establishment of the Izu Marine Park, the area has been noted as a base for scuba diving and various other marine sports.

Atagawa Spa ⌐51⌐: 24.3 km, or 30 min. from Ito by the Izukyu Line. One of the five most popular spas in Izu, it contains many souvenir shops and recreation facilities as well as a cluster of high-rise hotels. The gush of the hot springs is so common that the sound of spurting water can occasionally be heard, while clouds of steam drift over the city. All the *ryokan* compete in offering the most elaborate open-air bath, each presenting a fine view of the Izu Islands in the distance. In front of the station is the Atagawa Tropical and Alligator Garden, which makes use of the thermal waters of the spa. North of Atagawa lies Hokkawa Spa, while to the south is Katase Spa.

Inatori Spa ⌐51⌐: This comparatively new spa developed in 1956 when weak, common-salt springs with a temperature of 57℃ gushed forth. The spa is also the largest fishing port in eastern Izu, providing an abundance of fresh seafood for the culinary enjoyment of visitors. It only takes 40 min. by speedboat to go to Izu-Oshima Island, an area known for its good fishing. The Izu Bio Park, a large safari-type park, is located in the northwestern mountains and covers an area of 1.5 sq.km.

Imaihama Spa 51 : Located along the main bus route from Ito and Shimoda or on the Izukyu Line, the resort is situated on a picturesque beach of white sand and green pines. It is popular with swimmers and campers in summer. Mineral water is piped in from the Mine Spa.

Yatsu Spa: 15 min. on foot from Kawazu Station on the Izukyu Line. Using the heat produced by the abundant hot springs, irises are widely cultivated in this area. In the grounds of Kinomiya Shrine at the spa is an enormous camphor-tree, which has been designated as a Natural Monument.

Mine: Located 2 km from Kawazu Station, the spring water is utilized in greenhouses for cultivating irises and other flowers. Mine is also noted for its 800-year-old *sotetsu* or cycad plant with four trunks, which is also designated as a Natural Monument.

Other spas in the southeastern part of the peninsula include Yugano, Odaru and Nanadaru on the Kawazu River.

South Izu

Shirahama Beach 51 : Situated 3 km northeast of Shimoda (10 min. by bus), it extends almost 700 m along the shoreline. The contrast between the fine white sand and deep-blue water is incredibly beautiful, a sight considered to be the most inspiring on the peninsula. In summer the young people swimming and surfing in the water create a lively scene.

Shimoda 51 : ☎0558: Pop. 30,454. 45.7 km from Ito 1 hr.5 min. by the Izu Kyuko Railway (Izukyu), or 2 hrs. 50 min. from Tokyo by the JR limited express. It is a port town and fishing base at the southern tip of the peninsula. Situated on Shimoda Bay and partly enclosed by a range of hills, Shimoda is the most important port on the Izu Peninsula. From Shimoda regular steamship service is available to the Izu Islands.

Shimoda is famous as the place where Townsend Harris (1804-1878), the first American diplomatic representative to Japan, resided for more than a year from September 3, 1856.

Under the treaty with Japan concluded by Commodore Matthew Perry of the United States Navy at Yokohama (Kanagawa Prefecture) on March 31, 1854, the port of Shimoda was opened to American shipping. Although Harris hoisted the American flag at the port—"the first consular flag ever seen in this Empire," as he records in his diary—he quickly discovered that Shimoda was useless as a trading port. Refusing to deliver his credentials through the local governor, he sought permission to proceed to Edo (now, Tokyo) and present them himself. This was at first refused, but finally after repeated negotiations, the Japanese officials consented. Harris entered Edo on November 30, 1857, to become the first foreign diplomatic representative received by Japan. His diplomatic ability and tact led to the conclusion of a commercial treaty—the first ever made between Japan and a Western nation—on July 29, 1858. By the terms of this treaty, Yokohama instead of Shimoda was opened to foreign trade the following year.

Harris took up residence in Shimoda at **Gyokusenji Temple** in Kakisaki Village about 2 km east of the town along the harbor road. For many years, the temple was left in a state of disrepair, but on the initiative of the late American Ambassador Edgar A. Bancroft and the late Viscount Shibusawa, it was restored. Most of the financial backing came from the America-Japan Society, of which the late Prince Tokugawa Iesato was president.

At a ceremony on October 1, 1927 marking the restoration, a granite tablet was unveiled on which this passage from Harris' diary is engraved:

"Thursday, September 4, 1856. Slept very little from excitement and mosquitoes; the latter enormous in size. Men on shore to put up my flagstaff. Heavy lot. Slow work. Spar falls, breaks crosstrees, fortunately no one hurt. At last get a reinforcement from the ship, flagstaff erected. Men form a ring around it, and, half past two p.m. of this day, I hoist the first Consular flag ever seen in this Empire. Grave reflections. Ominous of change. Undoubted beginning of the end. Query,—if for the real good of Japan ?"

Underneath is the following inscription:

"In memory of Townsend Harris, American Consul-General, who by the Treaty of Yedo, July 29, 1858, opened Japan to the world, and on this spot, September 4, 1856, raised the first Consular flag in this Empire and here resided until November 23, 1857. Erected by Viscount E. Shibusawa, Edgar A. Bancroft and Henry M. Wolf of Chicago. September 4, 1927."

On the back of the tablet is an inscription in Japanese, in which the late Viscount Shibusawa paid a glowing tribute to the memory of Townsend Harris. The tablet stands on the exact spot where the flagpole once stood.

In the temple a framed portrait of Townsend Harris hangs above a glass case containing the following momentos of Harris' residence here: two American silver dollars, a chipped wine glass, a blackened pipe and two cigars—items found between the walls when the temple was being repaired.

During the repairs, the hole in the wall through which a stovepipe was placed while Harris lived here and the original crossbeams— brown and smoky from the heat of the stove—were left untouched. A faded photograph of Commodore Perry and a photograph of Ambassador Bancroft are also among the relics in the temple. But the temple's more valuable display is an eight-volume diary in Japanese kept by the elders of the village detailing Harris' daily life.

On a terrace to the left of the temple are three gravestones of members of Perry's fleet—an assistant surgeon, a sailor and a marine. Two similar stones are nearby, for a fireman and a marine who died some years later. To the right of the temple are the gravestones of three Russian sailors of the vessel Diana who lost their lives in a tidal wave that overwhelmed Shimoda when the Russian frigate was anchored in the port.

Commemorating the first landing of Commodore Perry from his American "Black Ships," an annual festival called *Kurofune Matsuri*, or the Black Ship Festival, is celebrated at Kurofune Square in Shimoda for three days in the middle of May. Begun in 1934, the event has now become one of the major festivities in this part of the country.

Bentenjima Island: Facing Gyokusenji Temple is a tiny islet called Bentenjima on which there is a little temple dedicated to *Benten*— goddess of music and fortune. It was from this islet that Yoshida Shoin (1830–1859), a famous loyalist, rowed out with a companion one stormy night in March 1854 to one of Commodore Perry's ships and pleaded in vain to be taken to America. Since it was still a capital offense at that time for a Japanese to go to a foreign country, Yoshida and his companion both eventually suffered the extreme penalty. This story is known to the West through Robert Louis Stevenson's short sketch on Yoshida's life. Refer to p.805

Ryosenji Temple: Located in the western quarter of Shimoda, the temple is famous because Commodore Perry and Daigaku-no-kami Hayashi, the representative of the Tokugawa Shogunate government, arranged a supplementary treaty in its Main Hall after the conclusion of the Kanagawa Treaty. The supplementary treaty was signed on May 25, 1854.

Zushu-Shimoda Folk Museum: Boasting a beautiful white facade, it contains data on the opening of Japan to the West, and relics of Commodore Matthew Perry, Townsend Harris, Yoshida Shoin, Evfimii Putyatin and other major figures of the day—a total of some 800 exhibits.

Shimoda Aquarium: Located at Wakanoura Beach, which is noted for its scenic promenade running along Shimoda Bay. The main attraction is a circular aquarium called Perry. It is 21 m in diameter, weighs 1,000 t. and floats on the sea. Shows featuring dolphins, seals and various kinds of fish are presented.

Cape Tsumeki 51 : Located on the southeastern tip of Suzaki Peninsula, the cape is noted for its unmanned white lighthouse and clusters of beautiful wild narcissi. It can be reached in 15 min. by bus from Shimoda. The fields of narcissus, containing some 1.5 million plants, covers the entire cape right up to the foot of the lighthouse.

They bloom from the end of December into January. The Imperial Shimoda Villa is located immediately northwest of this beautiful cape.

Mt. Buzan: A hilly mountain located to the east of Shimoda Station. It is also called Mt. Nesugata (sleeping posture) because the mountain resembles a sleeping woman when seen from the Shimoda Highway. Ropeway service is available to the top of the mountain, where a watchtower for *Kurofune* or "Black Ships" was placed at the end of the Edo period. This mountain commands a fine view of Shimoda City, Shimoda Port, Suzaki Peninsula and the Izu Islands.

Rendaiji Spa 51 : Situated west of Rendaiji Station on the Izukyu Line, the spa is more than 1,300 years old. There is an abundant flow of simple thermal water, some of which is piped to Shimoda.

Shimogamo Spa 51 : 10 km southwest of Shimoda, 25 min. by bus. There are numerous saline hot springs of high temperature (50℃) at this southernmost spa on the peninsula. Melons and tropical plants are grown in greenhouses heated with hot-spring water.

Cape Iro 51 : 40 min. by bus from Shimoda to Irozaki Bus Stop, the closest to the cape. It projects into the sea like a crane's beak at the outermost point of the Izu Peninsula. Bus service is available as far as Irozaki, located 1.5 km from the cape, a 20-min. walk. Situated south of Irozaki near a ridge of hills, a group of fantastically shaped rocks protrude above the surface of the sea. Jungle Park, a botanical garden with tropical plants of different varieties, is located nearby.

Perched high on the cliff are an observation tower, a meteorological station and a lighthouse. Halfway down is the Iro Shrine, where mariners worship the enshrined deity. Just below the shrine, the cliff drops nearly 50 m almost perpendicularly into the sea, where raging waves crash against its sides. A good view of the Izu Islands can be obtained from the cape. Taking a boat from Shimoda is the best way to view the romantic scenery of the coast (40 min.).

Cape Hagachi 51 : 40 min. by bus or 45 min. by boat from Matsuzaki. It can also be reached from Shimoda in 1 hr.30 min. by bus. The cape consists of steep, rocky cliffs soaring 250 m above the sea. The adjacent coast to the north of Hagachi forms wall-like cliffs more than 500 m high. This craggy cape is inhabited by about 250 wild monkeys. Sightseeing boats for Cape Hagachi take approximately 25 min. for a round trip.

Central Izu

Hatake Spa 51 : 30 min. by bus from Mishima Station on the JR Tokaido Shinkansen or Tokaido Main Line. Situated in a quiet place in the open basin of the Kano River, the spa offers a view of Mt. Fuji to the north soaring high over Mt. Ashitaka. On a small hill about 500 m east of Hatake Spa are more than 100 caves said to be the abodes of cave dwellers in ancient times.

Nirayama 51 ☎0559: Pop. 17,569. 18 min. from Mishima by the

Izu-Hakone Railway. This little spa town is located about 1 km southwest of Nirayama Station. It can also be reached via the "Izu Fujimi Parkway," a 11.3-km-toll road that connects with Kurodake on the "Izu Skyline Drive." It has many historical landmarks, including a reverberatory (2 km east of Izu-Nagaoka Station on the Izu-Hakone Railway, 3 min. by bus). Construction was started in 1853 by order of the Tokugawa Shogunate under the direction of Egawa Tarozaemon (1801-1855). He was the chief administrator of Izu Province (now, part of Shizuoka Prefecture) and studied Western gunnery in the late Edo period under Takashima Shuhan (1798-1866), who is often referred to as the father of modern gunnery in Japan. The old building remains almost as it was in bygone days. Tarozaemon's son, Hidetoshi, made hundreds of guns here for the Shogunate government after his father's death.

Egawa's Old House: 1.5 km east of Nirayama Station. Egawa Tarozaemon was born here. It is perhaps the oldest, existing, private house in Japan, dating back 700 years.

Hirugakojima: 1 km east of Nirayama Station, this is known as the place of exile of Minamoto-no-Yoritomo (1147-1199). After 20 years of hardship and privation here, he finally defeated the enemy—the Taira Clan—and established his Shogunate government in Kamakura in 1192. A stone monument stands on a little hill in memory of Yoritomo.

Nirayama Castle: 1 km east of Nirayama Station on a little pine-clad hill. The castle was once an important stronghold of the Hojo Clan. With Odawara as its headquarters, the clan prospered during the 15th century, but now only the moat and the outer wall of the inner citadel remain.

Izu-Nagaoka Spa 51 : ☎0559: Pop. 14,556. The spa is located 3 km southwest of Izu-Nagaoka Station, 5 min. by bus. The station is 11.4 km, or 20 min. by train, from Mishima—a popular resort with a mild climate and a number of simple thermal springs beneficial in the treatment of rheumatism and neuralgia. The abundance of luxurious *ryokan* complete with beautiful Japanese gardens, golf courses, and strawberry and orange picking events attract many visitors. South of the spa is an 1,800-m-long ropeway running from the southern foot to the summit of Mt. Katsuragi (alt. 452 m). An amusement park, "Izu-Nagaoka Eightland," is on the summit, which commands a fine view of Mt. Fuji and Suruga Bay.

Ohito Spa 51 : Situated on a small hill near Ohito Station on the Izu-Hakone Railway. The hill commands a grand view of Mt. Fuji and the Hakone mountains across the clear waters of the Kano River. Because of its scenic charm and abundant hot springs, Ohito is a very popular resort area. Fishermen come to this *ayu* (sweetfish) mecca to try their skill as soon as the sweetfish season opens in June. The 19.2-km-long Usami-Ohito Road connects Usami on the east coast with Ohito via Kameishi Pass on the "Izu Skyline Drive."

Shuzenji Spa 51 ☎0558: Pop. 17,851. 35 min. from Mishima, disembarking at Shuzenji Station—terminal of the Izu-Hakone Railway, or 2 hrs. and 15 min. on a direct limited express from Tokyo. It has been known as a resort since the ninth century. Together with Atami and Ito, it constitutes one of the three most popular spas on the Izu Peninsula. The hot-spring resort, 3 km southwest of Shuzenji Station (7 min. by bus), snuggles serenely in the picturesque valley of the Katsura River—a tributary of the Kano River, with Mt. Daruma (alt. 982 m) rising to the west. There are a large number of saline hot springs (temperatures ranging 37-74℃), which are efficacious for the treatment of gastric and dermatological diseases. The most remarkable is *Tokko-no-yu* Hot Spring in the bed of the Katsura River. A long mountain road runs from here to Shimoda (2 hrs. by bus) at the southeastern tip of the peninsula, crossing through Amagi Pass en route.

Shuzenji Temple: Situated on a small hill in the center of the town. Said to have been founded in the Daido era (806-810) by Kobo-Daishi or Saint Kobo, the temple is associated with two tragic events that happened toward the end of the 12th century in the Kamakura Shogunate. First, the imprisonment and subsequent murder by Minamoto-no-Yoritomo (1147-1199), founder of the Kamakura Shogunate, of his younger brother Noriyori (1156-1193). Secondly, the assassination of Yoritomo's son, Yoriie (1182-1204), by Hojo Tokimasa (1138-1215), father of Yoritomo's wife, Masako, who usurped the political power of the Minamoto Shogunate.

Noriyori's tomb is on the temple-side of the river, while Yoriie's tomb stands on the opposite bank. There is an old temple near the latter tomb called Shigetsuden, said to have been erected by Yoritomo's wife in memory of her murdered son. The setting of the popular *kabuki* drama entitled "Shuzenji Monogatari" by Okamoto Kido (1872-1939), based on the tragic story of Yoriie and a mask maker, is laid at the hot-spring resort.

Shuzenji Natural Park: 10 min. by bus from Shuzenji Spa, on the bus route to Mt. Daruma and Cape Heda. The 400,000-sq.-m park remains in its natural state, with flowers of spectacular beauty blooming throughout the year. In particular, approximately 3,000 plum trees put forth sweet-smelling flowers through the end of January into February, 5,000 rhododendrons are in flower in mid-April and 1,000,000 irises of 300 species bloom in early June. Needless to say, they are a major attraction.

Funabara Spa: 10 km south of Shuzenji Station, 20 min. by bus and 20 km east of Toi, 30 min. by bus, along National Highway 136. The spa is attractively situated on the northern skirts of the Amagi mountains. Here and in the surrounding mountains boar hunting has become a popular winter sport.

Yoshina Spa: 11 km south of Shuzenji Station, 20 min. by bus, in a secluded area at the northwestern base of the Amagi mountains on the Yoshina River. The mineral water of the hot-spring at Yoshina, said to be the oldest of its kind on the Izu Peninsula, has long been regarded as a boon to women, especially barren women. Tsukigase and Sagasawa spas are located in the neighborhood with a serene, comfortable atmosphere perfectly suited for family trips. *Ayu* (sweet-fish) in summer and boar in winter are famous culinary delights.

Yugashima Spa 51 : Located approximately in the middle of Izu Peninsula where the Kano and Nekko rivers join. This secluded area is surrounded by dense woods and embraced by the foothills of Mt. Amagi, with *ryokan* or Japanese-style inns lining the clear stream flowing through the valley. They are constructed in a variety of styles in this restful, recuperative spa town. The new leaves of spring and colors of autumn reflected in the river add a seasonal beauty to the area. It can be reached from Shuzenji Station in 35 min. by bus.

About 2.3 km south of the spa is the 25-m-high Joren Falls. Buses from Shuzenji to Shimoda pass near the waterfalls. *Wasabi*, a special product of Amagi that is similar to horseradish, is cultivated along the stream flowing from the basin of the waterfalls. The upper part of the stream, an excellent place for trout fishing, is known as the Amagi International Trout Fishing Spot.

Showa Forest: Covering an area of some 16 sq.km, this natural park centers around the Amagi Pass. Because of its primeval nature, it has been designated as a National Recreation Forest. Swimming and camping are some of the attractions besides enjoying the variation in view of Hatcho Pond, Joren Falls and the Kawazu Seven Falls. Showa Forest Hall, standing in the park, contains the Izu Modern Literature Museum, the Forest Museum, a restaurant and other facilities.

The hike to Hatcho Pond is an interesting activity. Situated near the highest part of Mt. Amagi at an altitude of 1,125 m, it is an about a 2-hr., 8-km hike uphill from Amagi Pass (alt. 800 m). The area is well known for its colorful autumn leaves. Nature students will be interested in a species of green frogs found in the vicinity of the pond that lay their eggs on the branches of trees during the summer months.

Mt. Amagi 51 : Alt. 1,406 m. Occupying the central part of the peninsula, the peaks consist of a group of dormant volcanoes. These volcanoes include Banzaburo (alt. 1,406 m), Banjiro (alt. 1,300 m), Hoki (alt. 1,024 m), etc.—all rising east of Amagi Pass. From Shuzenji to Amagi Pass by bus, it takes 45 min., and from Shimoda, 1 hr.15 min. The mountains are of post-Tertiary and pre-Quaternary geological formation, originating with the subterranean eruption of a newly created volcano.

The area is covered with a luxuriant primeval forest famed for its excellent timber. Since the mountain is also alive with wild boar, deer, rabbits and gamebirds, it has an irresistible attraction for hunters. The boar-hunting season lasts from November 1 through

February 15. In spring the mountain cherries bloom, towards early summer the mountain is covered with fresh verdure and multicolored azaleas, while in autumn the gorgeous hues of the leaves create a brilliant scene.

Many waterfalls can be seen along the 5-km descent of the Kawazu River between Amagi Pass and Yugano. Odaru Falls, Deaidaru Falls, Kanidaru Falls, Shokeidaru Falls, Hebidaru Falls, Ebidaru Falls and Kamadaru Falls are known as the Kawazu Nanadaru (Seven Falls). A hiking trail leading to these waterfalls runs beside the Kawazu River. Many unique open-air baths are situated around the basin of Odaru Falls, which cascades down 27 m.

Yugano Spa: 6 km (15 min. by bus) northwest of Kawazu Shore and 36 km (1 hr.20 min. by bus) from Shuzenji Temple. The spa is situated off the lower part of the winding bus road going south from Amagi Pass. It is a serene and secluded spa facing Kawazu Valley in the upper reaches of the Kawazu River. The rural air and simple life were introduced in the famous novel, "Izu-no-Odoriko" (The Dancing Girl of Izu) by a Nobel-prize laureate, Kawabata Yasunari.

West Izu

Mito ⬚51⬚: A noted scenic spot on the western coast of the peninsula, Mito is located 4 km west of Izu-Nagaoka Spa and can be reached in 10 min. by bus. Izu-Mito Sea Paradise on the beach features dolphins and giant turtles, which swim within an area enclosed by nets attached to the tips of projecting rocks. From the beach, peerless Mt. Fuji can be seen rising in all its majesty to the north.

The road from Numazu to Mito (35 min. by bus) follows the picturesque shores of Uchiura and Enoura bays, also presenting an impressive view of Mt. Fuji across the water. Since the waters of both bays abound in various kinds of marine life such as sea bream, horse mackerel and flatfish, fishing attracts many sportsmen. Excursion boats travel from Numazu to Izu-Mito Seaside Paradise and Cape Ose (for the latter, only in summer)—a beautiful cape covered with pine trees and blessed with a magnificent view of Mt. Fuji.

Heda ⬚51⬚ ☎0558: Pop. 5,029. Noted as a good fishing port as well as the best swimming area in West Izu, the town can be reached in 55 min. by bus from Shuzenji Station, or 30 min. by high-speed boat from Numazu.

Toi ⬚51⬚ ☎0558: Pop. 6,045. Located 31 km southwest of Shuzenji via Funabara Pass, 50 min. by bus; 45 min. by high-speed boat from Numazu. Regarded as one of the best hot-spring resorts on the west coast, it is a popular summer resort with a good beach. In the mountain behind the spa, there is a small gold mine that was discovered 400 years ago. The 26.5-km bus ride (50 min.) down the coast from Toi south to Matsuzaki offers some beautiful seascapes and a fine view of Mt. Fuji along the way.

Dogashima ⬚51⬚: Located near the center of the west coast of the peninsula, it can be reached in 42 min. by bus from Toi or 1 hr.5 min. by high-speed boat from Numazu. It is interesting for its fantastic rock formations and caves caused by wave erosion, a phenomenon that can be observed in various places along the western coast from Dogashima to Shimoda. They are believed to have been the abodes of cave dwellers in ancient times. The excursion boat touring around the caves of Dogashima takes 20 min.

Matsuzaki ⌞51⌟ ☎0558: Pop. 9,632. It can be reached in 50 min. by bus from Shimoda, 1 hr.40 min. by bus from Shuzenji and 1 hr. 15 min. by high-speed boat from Numazu. Situated on the southern portion of the west coast of Izu, it faces Suruga Bay. This town prospered around Matsuzaki Port, a deep-sea fishing base since ancient times. It now plays a major role in the economy, transportation and tourism of West Izu. Besides such noted products as *katsuobushi* or dried bonito and agar-agar, fruit cultivation thrives due to the genial climate. Kiwi fruit, strawberry and mandarin orange picking can be enjoyed. Hot springs bubble forth in the town where resort hotels and other facilities are ready to welcome tourists.

Osawa, an old spa in the reaches of the Nakagawa River, is situated to the east of Matsuzaki, while lodging villages like Iwachi, Ishibu and Kumomi lie along the cove of the west coast where both hot springs and swimming can be enjoyed.

Area 6. Kofu to Matsumoto
Along JR Chuo Main Line

The region along the JR Chuo Main Line containing the two cities of Kofu and Matsumoto is located in the mountainous, central part of Japan's Main Island of Honshu. The jagged mountain ranges in this region are called Japan Alps after the Alps in Europe, and the surrounding mountains are just as steep. However, the presence of beautiful lakes and highlands as well as colorful plants, alpine flowers and trees highlight the rugged peaks. The climate generally remains cool, making it a pleasant spot to visit during the hot summer. These desirable natural features attract numerous visitors to the area, which has well-developed resort facilities.

TRANSPORTATION
Rail: The JR Chuo Main Line connects Shinjuku in Tokyo and Matsumoto via Kofu. This line also extends from Matsumoto to Nagoya via the Kiso region. Along the way to Matsumoto, the line branches out into the Fuji Kyuko Railway (Otsuki to Kawaguchiko), the JR Minobu Line (Kofu to Fuji on the Tokaido Main Line), the JR Koumi Line (Kobuchizawa to Komoro on the Shin-etsu Main Line) and the JR Iida Line (Tatsuno to Toyohashi on the Tokaido Main Line). Matsumoto is the terminal station of the Matsumoto Electric Railway Line (to Shin-Shimajima), the JR Oito Line (to Itoigawa on

the Hokuriku Main Line) and also the station on the JR Shinonoi Line
(to Nagano on the Shin-etsu Main Line).

Road: The Chuo Expressway runs parallel to the JR Chuo Main Line.
Long-distance bus services are available from Tokyo (most of them
from Shinjuku) to Kofu, Kamisuwa, Okaya, Matsumoto, Ina,
Komagane and Iida.

Kofu and Vicinity

Katsunuma 　50　: About 2 hrs. from Shinjuku on JR. The hilly area
east of Kofu has been noted for its grape production since the Edo
period, with Katsunuma situated at the center of this region. The
production of grapes in this area is one of the largest in Japan at
present. From early August to late October, many of the vineyards
are open to the public for picking grapes (admission required).
Needless to say, the wine-producing industry is very active and many
wineries scattered through the town allow visitors to observe, taste
and buy the delicious local wines. The municipal Budo-no-Oka
(Grape Hill) Center is complete with a wine store, a restaurant that
serves locally produced wine, a barbecue restaurant and an exhibition
focusing on the history of grapes and wine.

Enzan 　50　 ☎0553: Pop. 27,150. Located north of Katsunuma, on
the northeastern tip of the Kofu Basin. It is noted as a former lodging
stage along the Ome-Kaido Highway. Before the railroad or automobile was introduced, Ome-Kaido was the main trading route connecting Tokyo and the Kofu Basin area. Besides its many ancient shrines
and temples, the city is well known as one of the bases for climbing
Mt. Dai-bosatsu-rei (alt. 2,057 m). The mountain is famous for its
magnificent view of Mt. Fuji.

Erinji Temple 　50　: Founded in 1330 by the famous Zen Buddhist
priest Muso-Kokushi (1275-1351). It is the final resting place of
Takeda Shingen (1521-1573), a powerful feudal lord dominating
Koshu (now, Yamanashi Prefecture), Shinshu (now, Nagano Prefecture) and a part of the Kanto District during the Age of Civil Wars.
Some of his belongings are exhibited in the treasure house. The
beautiful gardens laid out by Muso-Kokushi should be of interest to
visitors.

Nishizawa Valley 　50　: 1 hr. by bus, from Enzan Station on the JR
Chuo Main Line to the Nishizawakeikoku-Iriguchi Bus Stop. This is
the source of the Fuefuki River, which flows through the Kofu Basin.
Sparkling clean water rushes past granite boulders to form a scene of
great natural beauty highlighted by Nanatsugama-Godan Falls. The
rhododendrons blooming in June and the red leaves of mid-October
show off the valley at its best.

Kofu 　50/54-②　 ☎ 0552

Pop. 198,976. 1 hr. 40 min. by limited express from Shinjuku in
Tokyo. Located in the middle of the Kofu Basin, this is the seat of

the Yamanashi Prefectural Government as well as the center of transportation and commerce. Fruit has been cultivated in the area since olden times, but today the gem-cutting and precision-machinery industries are also prosperous.

Historically, Kofu is famed as the headquarters of Takeda Shingen (1521-1573), with many artifacts, relics and temples centered around his life remaining. Many tourists visit Kofu, partly to observe the historical sights here and partly to visit other nearby locations.

Refer to the supplement for details regarding the "i" **System Information Center** in Kofu.

Maizuru Park 54-② : Adjacent to Kofu Station on the southeastern side, the park offers a panoramic view of the city. It was named after the castle that once stood here, the shape of which resembled a dancing crane (*maizuru*). Today, it is known as a place to enjoy cherry blossoms.

Zenkoji Temple 54-② : Situated 2 km east of Kofu Station. This temple originated sometime between 1558-1570 when Takeda Shingen brought an image of Amitabha from Shinano Zenkoji Temple in Nagano and erected a large monestary patterned after the original Zenkoji Temple. The present two-story gate and Main Hall, rebuilt in 1796, are considered to be among the most prominent examples of 18th century architecture in eastern Japan. The gold and copper Amitabha and five other statues are designated as Important Cultural Properties.

Takeda Shrine 54-② : A shrine dedicated to Takeda Shingen. Founded in 1917, for sixty years it stood on the site of Tsutsuji-ga-saki Mansion, the headquarters for three generations of the Takeda family: Nobutora, Shingen and Katsuyori. But only the moats, stone walls and earthworks have survived. The Shingen Festival held by the Shrine in early April is one of the largest festivals in Kofu.

Yamanashi Prefectural Art Museum: Famous for works such as "The Sower" and "Return of the Flock" by Millet. It also has works of Corot, Courbet, Turner and Moore. Closed on Mondays.

Yumura Spa 50 : Located at the entrance to the beautiful Shosenkyo Gorge, the town is provided with many large, well-equipped *ryokan* or Japanese-style inns. With temperatures ranging 42-52°C, the hot springs are efficacious against neuralgia, gout and trauma. 15 min. by bus from Kofu Station.

Shosenkyo Gorge (Mitake Shosenkyo) 50 : North of Kofu along the Arakawa River. The upper reaches of the river stretch for a distance of over 4 km. The gorge is noted for its varied scenic beauty, including enormous rocks and swift, fresh currents. The 1 km from Takishita to Senga Falls via Ishimon (Stone Gate) Rock is especially magnificent. Each season offers a unique beauty, but the coloring of the leaves in mid-October is regarded as the best. An additional 3 km upstream is Oku (Inner)-Shosenkyo Gorge, also known as Itajiki-

Keikoku. Here, natural beauty to satisfy the most discriminating taste can be found.

Shimobe Spa ⬚50 : 1.5 km east of the the JR Shimobe Station on the JR Minobu Line. This spa is known as the place that Takeda Shingen visited to heal his wound from a sword duel with a rival warrior Uesugi Kenshin. Shingen fought many battles and a large number of his soldiers were wounded in battle. So he secretly chose several hot springs for the treatment of wounds and illnesses. These spas were called *Shingen-no-Kakushiyu* (Shingen's Secret Spas), and Shimobe Spa was one of them. Serenely situated along the river flowing through the valley, the many *ryokan* are utilized by travelers when visiting Kuonji Temple or the Fuji Five Lakes.

Kuonji Temple ⬚50 : Situated halfway up Mt. Minobu (alt. 1,153 m), the foundation of the temple dates back to 1274. It is the general headquarters of the Nichiren sect of Buddhism. Founded by Saint Nichiren (1222-1282, refer to p.437), the sect currently has more than 10 million followers. Scores of magnificent temple buildings stand in its precincts. Covering an area of 8 sq.km, the precincts are densely forested with ancient cedars.

The principal buildings include the *Soshido* (Founder's Hall), *Hondo* (Main Hall), *Shinkotsudo* (Hall of the Remains) and *Ihaido* (Hall of the Posthumous Tablets). There are also a belfry and a museum where many valuable objects are preserved.

This group of the temple buildings is called *Hon-in* (Main Sanctuary). The *Hon-in* stands on the southern side of Mt. Minobu and is reached by ascending 287 stone steps from Minobusan—the terminal of the bus line, 15 min. from Minobu Station on the JR Minobu Line. Minobu Station is about 1 hr. by express, either from Kofu on the Chuo Main Line or Fuji on the Tokaido Main Line.

Oku-no-in(Inner Sanctuary): Situated on a terrace on the summit of Mt. Minobu. The grounds are reached in 7 min. by the 1,665-m-long ropeway extending from the *Hon-in*. The summit commands a panoramic view of the surrounding country, including the Fuji River to the east and Mt. Shichimen (alt. 1,982 m) to the southwest.

Nirasaki ⬚50 ☎0551: Pop. 28,729. 13 km northwest of Kofu on the JR Chuo Main Line. Situated on the northwestern tip of the Kofu Basin, it was a station on the old Shinshu Highway and prospered as an important point of transportation. Nirasaki is also a base for climbing Okuchichibu mountains and the Southern Japan Alps.

Masutomi Spa ⬚50 : About 28 km northeast of Nirasaki and approximately 1 hr. by bus. Its thermal springs produce one of Japan's strongest emanations of radium, efficacious for treating neuralgia and gastric troubles. With Masutomi as a base, the peaks of Mt. Mizukaki (alt. 2,230 m), Mt. Kimpu (alt. 2,598 m) and the Shosenkyo Gorge may be explored.

Yashajin Pass ⬚50 : Alt. 1,770 m. 1 hr. 20 min. by bus from Kofu and a 50-min. walk from Tozanguchi Bus Stop. One of the passes leading to a climbing route in the Southern Japan Alps. The pass commands a fine view of Mt. Kitadake (alt. 3,192 m), the nation's second-highest mountain after Mt. Fuji, and other surrounding mountains. Mountain climbers can enjoy a magnificent view at the pass. Mt. Kitadake and the two neighboring high peaks above and the Hakuho Valley below also offer splendid views, but even this is surpassed when the slopes are ablaze with colored leaves in late October.

Minami Alps (Southern Japan Alps) National Park 50

Sprawling over an area of 357.98 sq.km, the park features the magnificent alpine scenery of the Akaishi Mountain Chain soaring southeast of the Northern Japan Alps. The range is confined on the east by the Fuji River and its tributary, the Kamanashi River, and on the west by the Tenryu River, which flows out of Lake Suwa. Major peaks of this mountain group from north to south include Mt. Kai-Koma (alt. 2,966 m), Mt. Senjo (alt. 3,033 m), Mt. Kitadake (alt. 3,192 m), Mt Shiomi (alt. 3,047 m), Mt. Arakawa (alt. 3,083 m), Mt. Akaishi (alt. 3,120 m) and Mt. Hijiri (alt. 3,013 m). The park is noted for the beauty of its gorges, valleys, rivers, waterfalls, granite cliffs, primeval forests and patches of alpine flora. To climb the Southern Japan Alps mountains from the Kofu side, get on a bus from Kofu Station and go to Hirokawara Bus Stop, a 2-hr. 5-min. trip. The buses are operated between early June and early November every year.

Mt. Amari 50: It has an altitude of 1,672 m, with the slope rising southwest of Nirasaki. As the northernmost peak of the Akaishi Mountain Chain, it is situated about 20 km from Nirasaki Station on the JR Chuo Main Line. The summit can be reached by car via Sawara Pond in 50 min. Azaleas blooming on the peak are a beautiful sight in mid-June.

Kobuchizawa 50: About 2 hrs. from Shinjuku (Tokyo) by limited express. The town serves as the junction of the JR Koumi Line, which winds along the eastern skirts of Mt. Yatsugatake to Komoro (79 km) on the JR Shin-etsu Main Line. The Koumi Line is noted for the magnificent plateau scenery visible from the train window. Nobeyama on this line is a railway station with the highest altitude of all JR stations, standing 1,346 m above sea level.

Mt. Yatsugatake: A generic name for eight peaks, including Aka-dake (alt. 2,899 m), which is the highest. The foothills form a number of plateaus, while the sides of the mountain are covered with forests of evergreen trees. The mountain can be climbed from Kobuchizawa and Chino on the Chuo Main Line or Kiyosato and Matsubarako on the Koumi Line.

Mt. Akadake 50: Towering 10 km northwest of Kiyosato Station on the JR Koumi Line and located about 20 km east of Chino Station on the JR Chuo Main Line. From Chino to the summit via Minoto-guchi, it is 40 min. by bus and then about 5 hrs. on foot. There is a hut on the summit. At the top of Mt. Akadake, one can view such mountains as Mt. Fuji, Mt. Kai-Koma and Mt. Kitadake to the south, and Mt. Tateshina and Mt. Asama to the north. Mountaineers are fond of successively tackling a number of the Yatsugatake peaks, starting from a base such as Lake Matsubara in the north and ending at Kiyosato or Kobuchizawa in the south.

Kiyosato Plateau 50 : The eastern slope of Mt. Yatsugatake, with the JR Kiyosato Station at the center. The plateau contains Utsukushi-no-Mori (lit. Beautiful Woodland, 15 min. by bus from Kiyosato Station). It is noted for its azaleas and lilies of the valley, which begin blooming in mid-June. A people's lodge and the Kiyosato Educational Experiment Project are located here. Among the buildings in the Kiyosato Educational Experiment Project is Seisenryo Hall, established in 1938 by Dr. Paul Rush of Kentucky, USA, as a model Christian village.

Around Kiyosato Station, there are many colorful souvenir shops and restaurants as well as fantastically made pensions, all of which hold a special appeal for the increasing number of young women travelers.

Lake Matsubara 53 : Located about 2 km, about 10 min. by bus from Matsubarako Station on the JR Koumi Line. The lake has a circumference of 2 km and is 1,123 m above sea level. Lying at the northeastern foot of Mt. Yatsugatake, the lake provides a good skating rink in winter and excellent camping grounds on its shore in summer. There are a number of smaller lakes in the neighborhood.

Suwa and Tateshina

Chino 53 ☎0266: Pop. 49,147. 2 hrs. 20 min. by limited express from Shinjuku (Tokyo). This city is located in the southeastern plateau area of Nagano Prefecture, ranging in elevation from 800-2,500 m and spreading out from the eastern slope of Mt. Yatsugatake to the edge of the Suwa Basin. The quantity of agar-agar produced here is the largest in Japan, while the production of *sake*, soy sauce, *miso* and precision machinery is also flourishing. The city is the main gateway for visits to the Tateshina Plateau and Lake Shirakaba.

Venus Line 52 : A 75.2-km-long scenic motorway constructed between Chino and the Utsukushigahara Plateau via the Tateshina Plateau, Lake Shirakaba and Mt. Kirigamine. Ranging over altitudes between 800 m and 2,000 m as it runs up and down along the plateau, it makes a pleasant drive. The woodland, lakes, marshlands and alpine plants seen from the window comprise a scene of great natural beauty.

Tateshina Plateau 53 : A plateau spreading from the southern foot of the conically shaped Mt. Tateshina (alt. 2,530 m) to the western foothills of the North Yatsugatake mountains at an altitude of 1,200-1,500 m. Known as a resort area since the beginning of the 20th century, today it is one of the very popular places favored by the

Japanese people, offering accommodations as well as recreational and sporting facilities. Tateshina Spa at the center of the plateau has many *ryokan* and hotels scattered among the white birch and larch woodlands stretching from the edge of Lake Tateshina to Pool-daira Plateau. Soaking in hot-spring pools and golfing can be enjoyed as well as fishing and boating (and skating in winter) on the lake. Around the lakeshore is the Marie Laurencin Museum, exhibiting more than 250 works created by this French artist (1885–1956). The museum, which was opened in 1983 to commemorate the 100th year since her birth, can be reached in 25 min by bus from the JR Chino Station.

Lake Shirakaba 53 : The lake is 347,100 sq.m, its circumference is about 6 km and it lies at an altitude of 1,420 m. This man-made lake, narrow from east to west, is especially popular with young people as there are a number of luxurious hotels, *ryokan*, villas, multipurpose recreational centers and sports facilities. At Higashi Shirakabako on the eastern side of Lake Shirakaba is a bus terminal where buses leave for Kirigamine. In winter ice skating can be enjoyed on the lake, which is about 50 min. from Chino Station by bus.

Kurumayama Plateau: This plateau of Mt. Kurumayama (alt. 1,925 m) is known for its abundant marsh plants and *nikko kisuge* or day lilies. Moreover, the plateau is a favorite place for hang-gliding enthusiasts. The lift takes one to the summit where a superb view of the Northern and Southern Japan Alps mountains, Mt. Fuji and Mt. Asama can be obtained. The eastern slope of the mountain is ideal for skiing in winter.

Shirakaba Plateau: Located at the northern foot of Mt. Tateshina. It includes Lake Megami, which possesses a mysterious beauty, especially in the mornings and evenings, the vast Tateshina Pasture and Gosensui Natural Park, famous for its beautiful scenery made up of springs, woodlands and marsh plants. Skiing and skating are popular in winter.

Suwa 53 ☎0266: Pop. 52,060. 2 hrs. 15 min. by limited express from Shinjuku in Tokyo to Kami-Suwa. The city occupies a large part of Suwa Basin on the southeastern shore of Lake Suwa, and extends to Mt. Kirigamine in the north and the Akaishi Mountain Chain in the south. The production of watches, optical lenses and precision machinery in this city is one of the largest in Japan. The eastern city line adjoins Chino, which is situated approximately halfway on the Chuo Expressway (total distance 360 km) between Tokyo and Nagoya.

Lake Suwa 53 : 14.5 sq.km in area and 17 km in circumference. The lake is located at an altitude of 759 m and has an average depth of 4.1 m. The rivers flowing into the south of the lake supply nutrients, and since the lake is so shallow, it is one of the most nutritious lakes in Japan. Needless to say, fish and shellfish cultivation flourishes. In fact, the area has long been known for its fishery production. The Tenryu River is the only outlet of the lake, with a sluice controlling the flow. The Kami-Suwa Spa area on the eastern shore is popular with tourists, offering an abundant flow of thermal spring water as well as an amusement park, aquarium, iris garden and *karin* or Chinese quince-lined road. An excursion boat departs from the eastern shore. The fireworks held each August 15 are another noted tourist attraction. When it gets colder (usually around the end of January through February), strange phenomena such as the *O-Miwatari* (God Crossing) and *O-Hikari* (Great Light) can be seen over the lake.

O-Miwatari (God Crossing): The ice on the lake cracks when the temperature suddenly drops at night in winter. Then, the water in the cracks immediately freezes. When the temperature goes up the next morning and causes the ice to expand, the cracked part is pressed in from both sides, swelling up in a great thunderclap to form a kind of ridge nearly 1 m high and sometimes extending for a few kilometers. This phenomenon is called "O-Miwatari." According to an old belief, the god of Suwa Shrine crosses the lake on this elevated ice road to meet the goddess of *Shimosha* (the Lower Shrine) at Shimo-Suwa. Local residents used to predict the annual harvest by the way the ridge was formed or broken.

Suwa Shrine [53]: Known for its great number of followers throughout Japan. Although the present structures were rebuilt in the 18th century, the origin of this shrine is quite old and many original ceremonies from the past remain. The god enshrined was originally worshipped as the god of hunting, but as farming began to take over, it became the god of agriculture.

In the 12th century when the warrior class was gaining power, the god was worshipped as a God of war, a religious custom that was widespread in Japan. Accordingly, some 10,000 branch shrines were constructed around the country, although no other shrine has followed suit. Suwa Shrine is divided into *Kamisha* (Upper Shrine) and the *Shimosha* (Lower Shrine), and each is made up of two lesser shrines. *Kamisha* consists of *Hommiya* in Suwa City and *Maemiya* in Chino City, while *Shimosha* includes *Akimiya* and *Harumiya* (both in Shimo-Suwa Town). Designed in accordance with time-honored architectural traditions, all the structures are regarded as valuable and magnificent, with the ornamental carvings being especially noted for their beauty.

The *On-Bashira* Festival held every six years at this shrine is known for its spectacular scale and exciting ceremonies.

Kirigamine Plateau [52]: 50 min. by bus from the JR Kami-Suwa Station, at altitudes between 1,600 m and 1,800 m. The grassland of this serenely beautiful plateau extends for 10 km from east to west and 15 km from north to south. Various plants and flowers cover the plateau with their color in summer. Summer sports include both gliding and hang-gliding, while winter sports focus on skiing. Many species of marsh plants are found in Yashima Marshland and Odoriba Marshland within the boundaries of the plateau.

Shimo-Suwa Spa: The area around the spa flourished as a stage town for centuries, and *honjin* or the inn appointed by the shogunate government for high-ranking officials of the Edo period still remains. The tranquil atmosphere is quite different from that of Kami-Suwa Spa.

Okaya ☐53☐ ☎0266: Pop. 60,238. An industrial city on the western shore of Lake Suwa, it is bordered on the west by Shimo-Suwa and on the north by Matsumoto. With industrialization following the same pattern as in Suwa City and Shimo-Suwa Town, Okaya became the foremost silk-reeling town in the late 19th and early 20th centuries. The city recovered after World War II with the precision-machinery industry. Okaya is the terminal for trains on the JR Iida Line leading to Toyohashi on the JR Tokaido Main Line. En route, the line passes such cities as Ina (pop. 59,448), Komagane (32,311) and Iida (92,050). The Iida Line runs along the Tenryu River as far as Sakuma Dam (refer to p.598), passing scenic Tenryukyo Gorge along the way.

Tenryukyo Gorge ☐53☐: Located in the middle reaches of the Tenryu River near Iida. The river is overhung with cliffs more than 100 m high covered with a dense growth of old pines.

Shooting the Tenryu Rapids: Excursion boats that shoot the rapids are available for viewing the beautiful scenery of the gorge. Shooting the rapids begins at Benten (10 min. by bus from Iida Bus Center) and ends at the disembarkation point at Tenryukyo. The 8-km distance is covered in 1 hr. Excursion boats may be available at Tokimata on the route near the JR Tokimata Station. From here, it is 3 km, or 30 min. to Tenryukyo.

The granite cliffs, marked by vertical fissures, can be seen near the disembarkation point. They constitute the most picturesque sight on the excursion down the river. The best time to make this trip is in summer when cool breezes can be enjoyed or in autumn when maple leaves are at their best along the banks of the river.

Shiojiri ☐52☐ ☎0263: Pop. 56,630. About 2 hrs. 40 min. from Shinjuku (Tokyo), or about 2 hrs. from Nagoya by limited express. Adjacent to Matsumoto in the south, the city is an important junction of the JR Chuo Main Line and the Shinonoi Line. Located at the junction of the old Nakasendo Highway and Hokkoku-nishi Highway, the area once prospered as a stage town in the Edo period, with traces of this past still visible in Seba and Motoya.

Matsumoto ☐52☐ ☎ 0263

Pop. 194,604. About 2 hrs. 50 min. from Shinjuku and 2 hrs. 10 min. from Nagoya by limited express. As the central city in the Matsumoto Basin, it serves as the gateway to the Chubu-Sangaku (Japan Alps) National Park and Utsukushigahara Plateau in the east.

Matsumoto is connected with Itoigawa on the Japan Sea by the

106-km-long JR Oito Line, which runs north along the eastern foot of the Hida Mountain Chain in the Chubu-Sangaku (Japan Alps) National Park. Along the Oito Line there are a number of towns and villages such as Omachi and Hakuba that are the bases for climbing the peaks of the Hida Mountain Chain. From Matsumoto to Nagano, it is about 50 min. by limited express on the JR Shinonoi Line.

As the economic and transportation center of the basin of the same name, Matsumoto has prospered since the beginning of the 20th century from sericulture and the spinning industries. More recently the food, textile and machine industries have developed in the city. Both Matsumoto Castle and Shinshu University are in the city, while Asama Spa is in the suburbs.

Matsumoto Castle 52 : 1 km northeast of the JR Matsumoto Station. The moats and stone walls are the remnants of the original structure built in 1504. The imposing six-story donjon, designated as a National Treasure, is connected by corridors with a small keep on the northern side. Within the compound of the inner moat is a museum displaying mementos of the castle as well as numerous folkloric material connected with the city and the surrounding Matsumoto Basin. The top floor of the donjon offers a panoramic view of Matsumoto and the Northern Japan Alps.

Asama Spa 52 : 4 km northeast of the JR Matsumoto Station, 20 min. by bus. It is situated at the western foot of the Utsukushigahara Plateau.

Utsukushigahara Plateau 52 : 1 hr.10 min. by bus from Matsumoto Bus Terminal. This 5-sq.-km plateau situated at an altitude of 2,000 m has a commanding view of nearly all the mountains in Nagano and Yamanashi prefectures. The plateau is also well known for the variety of beautiful flowers that bloom here from May to August. *Renge-tsutsuji* or lotus-azaleas flowering in late June are especially famous. Ogato at 2,034 m is the highest point on the plateau, with steep cliffs forming its south side. Looking out over these cliffs, one can see Sanjiro Ranch just below and the Northern Japan Alps in the distance.

The Utsukushigahara Openair Museum is near the terminal of the Utsukushigahara toll road (popularly called "Venus Line") from Kirigamine, 2,000 m above sea level on the east side of Mt. Uchifuse. The 100,000-sq.-m, outdoor sculpture garden can be reached in 1 hr. 25 min. by bus from the Matsumoto Bus Terminal.

Japan Alps

The name Japan Alps is given to the volcanic ranges extending from north to south through the central and widest part of Honshu. The Japan Alps consist of three lofty ridges called the Southern Japan Alps, Central Japan Alps and the Northern Japan Alps. Except for Mt. Fuji, Japan's highest mountain, almost all of the tallest mountains in Japan are included in these ranges. The Japan Alps are thus appropriately called the "Roof of Japan."

The term "Japan Alps" was first used in 1881 in the book "Japan Guide" written by William Gowland, an English mining engineer connected with the Osaka Mint. It was later used by the Rev. Walter Weston (1861-1940) in his work "Mountaineering and Exploration in the Japanese Alps" (1896), in which he compares the Hida Mountain Chain with their European prototype in ruggedness, variety of alpine flora, and bird and animal life. Later, however, the term "Japan Alps" came to be applied to a wider range of mountains. In addition to the Hida Mountain Chain (Northern Japan Alps), they now include the Kiso Mountain Chain (Central Japan Alps) and the Akaishi Mountain Chain (Southern Japan Alps).

Chubu-Sangaku (Japan Alps) National Park ⌷52⌷

Chubu-Sangaku (Midland Mountains), or Japan Alps National Park, is composed of almost all of the peaks in the Hida Mountain Chain. Regarded as Japan's foremost mountain park, it sprawls over four prefectures: Nagano, Gifu, Toyama and Niigata—a total area of 1,698.98 sq.km. The major peaks in the park are from south to north —Mt. Norikura, Mt. Yakedake (an active volcano), Mt. Hotaka, Mt. Yarigatake, Mt. Tateyama (refer to p.614) and Mt. Shirouma. All of these peaks average 3,000 m in altitude. A luxuriant growth of alpine plants in addition to snow grouse and antelopes can be seen on the peaks. Truly, the park is a mecca for mountaineers. Kamikochi is the most popular place from which to start exploring the Japan Alps National Park.

In the park, hot springs bubble up at various places, including Shirahone, Nakanoyu, Nakabusa, Tateyama and Kanetsuri, where mountain climbers can soak and relax to get rid of their fatigue. The Kurobe River runs north between the mountains of Sirouma and Tateyama before flowing into the Japan Sea. Located on the upper reaches of the Kurobe River, the fourth Kurobe Dam (popularly called Kuroyon Dam), was completed in 1963 after seven years of work to generate electric power.

The Kamikochi Valley lies along the upper reaches of the Azusa River surrounded by lofty peaks. The lower reaches of the river, where it enters the Matsumoto Basin, comprise the Saikawa River— a tributary of the Shinano River. The valley can be reached in 2 hrs. from Matsumoto to Shin-Shimashima by the Matsumoto Electric Railway and then by the connecting bus. Kamikochi, situated 1,500 m above sea level, has many well-appointed inns and camping areas in addition to a fine Western-style hotel. Indeed, it is the best-developed base for climbing the peaks in the national park.

Taisho Pond was created in 1915 by the eruption of Mt. Yakedake (alt. 2,455 m), the only active volcano in the Hida Mountain Chain. Lava and mud spewed out of the mountain, blocking the course of the Azusa River.

Kappa Bridge, a suspension bridge over the crystal-clear waters of the Azusa River is located 2 km upstream from Taisho Pond and commands a fine view of Mt. Hodaka (alt. 3,190 m) to the north. Halfway between Kappa Bridge and Taisho Pond on the right banks of the Azusa River is a bust of the Rev. Walter Weston (1888–1915), who introduced the Northern Japan Alps to the world.

Mt. Norikura 52 : With an altitude of 3,026 m, this conical volcano soaring at the southern tip of the national park has many tarns near its summit. Its eastern slopes can be used for skiing as late as June. Since a bus is available to a point near the summit, it is the easiest peak to reach in the Northern Japan Alps mountains. The Norikura Skyline is a 14.4-km toll road, extending from Hirayu Pass to the bus terminal in Norikura Tatamidaira (alt. 2,702 m). Visitors will see alpine plants and snow-covered mountainsides on the way.

It is a 2-hr. 30-min. bus ride from Kamikochi to Norikura Lodge via Nakanoyu Spa, Hirayu Spa and Hirayu Pass. From the lodge to the summit, it is 3 km, or approximately a 1-hr. 30-min. hike. Norikura Lodge can also be reached by bus (1 hr. 35 min.) from Takayama Station on the JR Takayama Main Line via Hirayu Pass. Shirahone Spa (55 min. by bus from Shin-Shimashima Bus Terminal on the Matsumoto Electric Railway) is situatd on the northeastern side of Mt. Norikura. The route runs part of the way along the road leading to Kamikochi.

Mt. Hotaka 52 : With an altitude of 3,190 m, this is the third-highest mountain in Japan after Mt. Fuji (alt. 3,766 m) and Mt. Kitadake (alt. 3,192 m) in the Akaishi Mountain Chain (the Southern Japan Alps). It is the general name given to five peaks—Mae(Front)-, Nishi(West)-, Oku(Inner)-, and Kita(North)-Hotaka plus Kara-sawadake, among which Oku-Hotaka is the highest. The ascent is usually made from Kamikochi. From here, a climb of 8 km (around 6 hrs. 30 min.) up the steep valley of Dakesawa brings one to the summit of Mae-Hotaka. It takes another 1 hr. 30 min. to reach the summit of Oku-Hotaka, 2 km northwest of Mae-Hotaka.

The successive tackling of a number of peaks from Oku-Hotaka northward to Mt. Yarigatake (alt. 3,180 m) is perhaps the most arduous and dangerous mountaineering trek next to that from Nishi-Hotaka to Oku-Hotaka. The summit of Mt. Yarigadake can also be reached by going upstream along the Azusa River from Kamikochi. Since the summit is shaped like a spear, the mountain was named Yari, which literally means a spear.

Omachi 52 ☎0261: Pop. 31,833. 36 km from Matsumoto to Shinano-Omachi on the JR Oito Line. The Omachi Alpine Museum, where various materials and data on the Northern Japan Alps are displayed, is located in the city, which is also one of the main bases for climbers of the Northern Japan Alps.

Omachi is the base on the Nagano Prefecture side for exploring the Tateyama-Kurobe Alpine Route. To get to Kuroyon Dam (refer to p.

499), take a bus from Shinano-Omachi Station to Ogisawa (40 min.), then transfer to a trolleybus that passes through a 5.4-km-long tunnel bored through a mountain range. North of Omachi on the western side of the JR Oito Line lie three lakes: Kizaki, Nakatsuna and Aoki. **Happo-one** 52 : A ridge extending to the east of Mt. Karamatsu (alt. 2,696 m). Situated south of Mt. Shirouma, it is well known for having a number of large ski slopes at its eastern tip. The skiing area is provided with a 2,000-m-long aerial cablecar as well as a number of chair lifts and rope tows. The skiing season here extends from December to April.

There are many ski courses such as the Happo-one Ski Course, as well as pensions and lodging facilities along the JR Oito Line.

Mt. Shirouma 52 : With an altitude of 2,932 m, the peak soars over the northern sector of the national park. One can climb the mountain from the JR Hakuba Station via Hosono. It takes 1 hr. by bus to reach the Sarukura Lodge, and from here to the summit it is 7.5 km, or approximately a 6-hr. 30-min. hike. En route one passes through a 2-km-long snow valley and the *Ohana-batake*—a large flatland carpeted with alpine flora in July and August. The *Ohana-batake* has been made a Special Natural Monument, with its large variety of alpine flowers creating a beautiful sight. Near the summit are two lodges equipped with accommodation facilities.

From the summit, innumerable peaks are visible to the east, of which Mt. Myoko (alt. 2,454 m) and Mt. Togakushi (alt. 1,904 m) are the most prominent. To the north, the Japan Sea can be seen on a clear day, to the southwest are the lofty ridges of Tsurugi (alt. 2,998 m) and Tateyama (alt. 3,015 m) beyond Kurobe Gorge, while to the southeast Mt. Fuji lifts its majestic head in the distance.

Area 7. Tokyo to Niigata
Along JR Joetsu Line

This route extends to the central portion of Niigata Prefecture via a long tunnel cutting through the Mikuni Mountain Chain, which proudly stands in the northeastern sector of the Kanto Plain. The Mikuni Mountain Chain southwest of Shimizu Pass have been designated as the Jo-Shin-Etsu Kogen (Plateau) National Park, which is known for its beautiful mountains, plateaus and marshlands, while the southern portion adjacent to Gumma Prefecture contains many excellent hot springs. The central portion of Niigata Prefecture is noted as one of the major rice producers, with orderly plots of carefully tended rice paddies filling the landscape. Agriculture flourishes here as well as commerce and industry. Sado Island lies off the coast of Niigata, the terminal station of the JR Joestu Line. Noted for its scenic beauty and traditional entertainment, it is the fifth largest of the Japanese islands.

TRANSPORTATION

Rail: Trains on the JR Joetsu Line departing from Ueno Station in Tokyo runs through the center of Gumma and Niigata prefectures before arriving at Niigata. On the way, the JR Joetsu Line meets the Shin-etsu Main Line at Nagaoka. Running almost parallel to the JR Joetsu Line, which has no direct train from Tokyo to Niigata, the JR Joetsu Shinkansen goes directly to Niigata, arriving in a minimum amount of time. Many lines branch from the JR Joetsu Line between Tokyo and Niigata, but those that lead to tourist attractions include Chichibu Railway (Kumagaya to Mitsumineguchi), the JR Ryomo Line (Shin-Maebashi to Oyama), the JR Agatsuma Line (Shibukawa to Omae), the JR Iiyama Line (Echigo-Kawaguchi to Toyono), the JR Yahiko Line (Higashisanjo to Yahiko) and the JR Echigo Line connecting Niigata and Kashiwazaki along the coast of the Japan Sea.

Roads: The Kan-etsu Expressway connecting Tokyo and Nagaoka is widely used when touring around the Takasaki area. It is also connected at Nagaoka to the Hokuriku Expressway, which starts from Niigata, links the major cities in the Hokuriku district such as Toyama and Kanazawa, and runs to the Meishin Expressway as far as Kyoto and Osaka. A long-distance bus runs on the Kan-etsu Expressway and connects Ikebukuro in Tokyo with Nagaoka and Niigata.

Kumagaya ☐20☐ ☎0485: Pop. 147,292. Located in the center of the northern portion of Saitama Prefecture, the city is an important transportation point. It prospered as a lodging and market town of the old Nakasendo Highway during the Edo period, but it has now developed into an industrial satellite city of Tokyo. It is located 36 min., and 62 km, from Ueno (Tokyo) on the JR Joetsu Shinkansen.

Nagatoro ☐52-53☐: 31.6 km from Kumagaya, 50 min. by the Chichibu Railway. This outstanding tourist spot is situated on the upper reaches of the Sumida River, which is known here as the Arakawa River. Celebrated for its scenic beauty and the unusual formation of the rocks (crystalline schists) that form its banks for a distance of 1 km, this river is a popular place for picnics, especially in spring during the cherry-blossom season and in autumn when the leaves change color. In summer, boating and angling for *ayu* (sweetfish) can be enjoyed. Mt. Hodo (alt. 497 m), whose summit can be reached by an 800-m-long ropeway, and a local folk museum are located nearby. An observation platform has been erected atop Mt. Hodo.

Nagatoro can also be reached from Ikebukuro in Tokyo via the Tobu Tojo Line to Yorii, connecting there with the Chichibu Railway —a total distance of 87.9 km. The trip takes 2 hrs. 10 min.

Chichibu ☐53☐ ☎0494: Pop. 61,463. Situated 12.5 km south of Nagatoro. It is the site of the ancient Chichibu Shrine, where the famous *kagura* (sacred dance) is performed on December 3 as well as on other festival days. At the December 3 festival, known as *Chichibu-yomatsuri* (Night Festival), elaborate floats are drawn along the street and spectacular displays of fireworks are staged. The town is a center for the manufacture of silk fabrics called *Chichibu-meisen* as well as for the production of cement.

Chichibu is conveniently reached from Ikebukuro, Tokyo, on the Seibu Chichibu Line by limited express, which covers the distance of 76.9 km in about 1 hr. 30 min.

Mitsumine Shrine: Situated on the summit of Mt. Mitsumine (alt. 1,101 m). Regarded as one of the most celebrated Shinto centers in this district, it contains some excellent carvings and art treasures. For the climb, bus service is available from Mitsumineguchi—the terminal of the Chichibu Railway (56.8 km, 1 hr. 40 min. from Kumagaya)—to Owa at the eastern foot of the mountain. The trip takes only 15 min. A 1,900-m-long ropeway is available from Owa to the summit.

The hike from Mt. Mitsumine to Okutama by way of Mt. Kumotori (alt. 2,017 m), south of the former mountain, is a popular route with mountaineers. Lake Chichibu lies at the northwestern foot of Mt. Mitsumine.

Extending 5.9 km from Lake Chichibu to the Treasure House of Mitsumine Shrine, the Mitsumine Toll Road provides many good scenic views en route. This district is part of the Chichibu-Tama National Park.

Oku-Chichibu: The Chichibu Mountain Chain straddles Tokyo as well as Saitama, Yamanashi and Nagano prefectures to the west of the Chichibu Basin. Major peaks such as Mt. Kumotori to the east, Mt. Mizugaki to the west, Mt. Ryokami to the north and Mt. Okusenjo to the south are all connected to one another. Known for its deep woodland and scenic valleys, the area offers some superb views from peaks ranging from 2,200 m to 2,600 m high. But it is impossible to climb these mountains without proper climbing gear and prior knowledge of the route.

Takasaki 52 ☎0273: Pop. 235,071. Located 105 km from Ueno (Tokyo), 47 min. by the JR Joetsu Shinkansen, in the south-central portion of Gumma Prefecture. A leading commercial and industrial city in the northern Kanto region, the city has developed the machinery, metal and chemical industries in addition to the conventional industries. Upon approaching Takasaki by train, one can see the magnificent statue that serves as the symbol of the city—the *Takasaki Byakui Daikannon* (Goddess of Mercy in White). Erected in 1936, it stands approximately 42 m high on a rise to the southwest. A section of Mt. Kannon, where the figure stands, contains a large amusement park. From here a nature promenade goes to Darumaji Temple, which is famed for the *Daruma-Ichi* or the good luck *daruma* doll market held annually in early January. Takasaki especially bustles with many visitors at this time.

Maebashi 18/52 ☎0272

Pop. 282,102. About 1 hr.30 min., 115 km, by limited express from Ueno (Tokyo), transferring at Takasaki to a local train. Maebashi, the capital of Gumma Prefecture, has developed into a diversified industrial city through municipal efforts to attract factories. The city has a long history as is obvious from the abundance of tumuli and other historical sites as well as old religious edifices such as Kozuke-Sosha Shrine the mid-sixth century. Shikishima Park in the northwestern part of the city is noted for its cherry blossoms, azaleas and rose garden as well as the Silk Reeling Memorial Museum.

Mt. Akagi 52 : Northeast of Maebashi, 1 hr.15 min. by bus from the JR Maebashi Station. The main peak of Mt. Kurobi, which has an altitude of 1,828 m, and Mt. Akagi each have serene crater lakes called Ono and Kono, respectively. The latter mountain is covered with a beautiful blanket of trees. Kakumambuchi Marsh and Mt. Jizodake with a ropeway by the crater lake, an arboretum and pastures fill the area, which bustles with visitors and mountain climbers throughout the year. Besides the many varieties of alpine flora at Kakumambushi, azaleas brighten the area between June and July. Lakes Ono and Kono freeze over in winter, making them perfect for ice-skating.

Shibukawa 52 ☎0279: Pop. 47,553. Situated approximately in the center of Gumma Prefecture, the city is adjacent to the northeastern edge of Maebashi. Serving as an important transportation center where the JR Joetsu Line and Agatsuma Line meet, it bustles with many people visiting the Ikaho Spa and Lake Haruna.

Ikaho 52 ☎0279: Pop. 4,416. One of the most celebrated of Japan's spas. It is located 30 min. from Shibukawa Station and 1 hr. 15 min. from Takasaki Station by bus. Built on a series of terraces on the northeastern slope of Mt. Haruna at an elevation of about 700 m, Ikaho consists almost entirely of *ryokan* and shops catering to the needs of tourists. The hot springs have temperatures ranging from 45 -66°C, and are believed to be especially efficacious for treating gastric ailments.

From the neighboring hillsides, which are covered with wild flowers from June to September, one can obtain beautiful, wide-ranging views of the surrounding countryside.

The best view is from Ikaho Highland, which overlooks the neighboring area.

Mt. Haruna 52 : Facing Mt. Akagi to the east across the city of Shibukawa, Mt. Haruna is actually the general term for a number of peaks, including Mt. Kamon (alt. 1,449 m)—the highest, Haruna-Fuji (alt. 1,391 m) and Mt. Eboshi (alt. 1,365 m). Lake Haruna lies between Haruna-Fuji on the east and Mt. Kamon on the west. An aerial ropeway is available (3 min.) from the lakeshore to the summit of the conical peak of Haruna-Fuji.

Lake Haruna 52 : 1,084 m above sea level, 4.8 km in circumference. Formed by the crater of an extinct volcano, the clear lake is abundant with *wakasagi* (a kind of smelt), trout and carp. The outflow from the lake forms Benten Falls, which is about 3 km northwest of Ikaho. In winter when the lake freezes over, skating and *wakasagi* fishing through a hole cut in the ice can be enjoyed. Celebrated for its azaleas in spring, the lake shore provides ideal camping grounds with many bungalows in summer. The Haruna Kogen (Plateau) Youth Hostel is situated on the eastern shore.

Haruna Shrine 52 : About 2 km southeast from Lake Haruna. This ancient Shinto shrine stands amid precipitous rocks and aged Japanese cedars on the southwestern side of Mt. Haruna. A gate with some fine carvings of dragons stands along the paved approach. Behind it rises a huge, halberd-shaped rock, while at the rear of the main shrine is another precipitous rock, the top of which resembles a man's head. The buildings are decorated with many artistic carvings.

Nakanojo: Pop. 19,727. Situated on the JR Agatsuma Line, it is the gateway to Sawatari Spa and Shima Spa, which can be reached in 30 min. and 45 min., respectively, by bus from the station. The Agatsuma Line follows the course of the Agatsuma River, a tributary of the Tone River. The lower reaches of the Agatsuma River, about a 3.5-km stretch downstream from the JR Kawarayu Station, are celebrated for the crimson-colored cliffs on either side. This section is called the Agatsuma Gorge.

Shima Spa: As one of the three most famous spas in Gumma Prefecture along with Ikaho and Kusatsu, it was designated as the first National Health Spa in 1954. Since this serene spa has no amusement facilities, the forests and valleys here have a special beauty. The temperature of the hot spring is 43–82°C, and efficacious against gastroenteric disorders neuralgia and rheumatism.

Kawarayu Spa: Situated on a cliff rising above the Agatsuma River, the spa can be reached in 15 min. on foot from the JR Kawarayu Station. The thermal waters of the spa are said to be efficacious for the treatment of digestive ailments and rheumatism.

Kusatsu 52 ☎0279: Pop. 8,512. Located in the northwestern portion of Gumma Prefecture, the town is on a plateau near the border between Gumma and Nagano prefectures. Known through the folk song, "Kusatsu, such a nice place, should be visited at least once," this noted spa town handles 2.5 million visitors annually.

The hot-spring resort is in a small basin at the eastern base of Mt. Shirane, which has an altitude of 1,200 m. The mineral waters have been known throughout Japan for their therapeutic value since ancient times. Kusatsu Spa in the east and Arima Spa in the west are equally admired as being among the best spas in Japan, both said capable of healing any disease other than love sickness. *Jikan-yu* (time baths) in the very hot water is an enjoyable custom.

The main public bath, called *Netsunoyu* (heat bath), is located in the town square. Its water is so hot that bathers submit to a sort of military discipline, with a "bathmaster" directing operations. The first stage consists of an operation called *yumomi* in which the temperature is reduced by stirring up the water with long boards, while the bathers rock from side to side chanting in unison. At the bathmaster's command, the bathers—who frequently number as many as 200—enter the water, remaining absolutely motionless for 3 to 4 min. Any movement, of course, would only make the heat of the bath doubly trying to the bathers. At intervals of a minute or so, the master announces how much longer they must stay in the water, and in response all the bathers answer in chorus. Thus, the bathmaster will say: "If you are all ready—enter the water." Once they are in, he declares: "Three minutes more," then "Only two minutes left," and then "Just a little longer" and finally, "Get out of the water s-l-o-w-l-y." Needless to say, this last order is obeyed instantly.

A version of the *yumomi* (mixing of the water) has been adapted as a dance named "momi-odori," which is presented four times a day.

The waters of Kusatsu have long been celebrated for their health-restoring properties. Indeed, many prominent people have visited the spa and testified to their efficacy against rheumatism, gout, chronic dermatitis and similar ailments. Minamoto-no-Yoritomo, founder of the Kamakura Shogunate, was especially prominent in spreading the fame of the hot spring in the 12th century. During the Edo period, the eighth Shogun Yoshimune, ordered hot-spring water transported in barrels to the Edo Castle for his bath. The mineral waters were also popular among the citizens of Edo.

In 1878, moreover, the spa was visited by a German doctor, Erwin von Bältz (1849–1913), who proclaimed the spa's curative qualities to the world.

Kusatsu is a neat little town surrounded by pine and larch forests. More than 150 *ryokan* are arrayed around the square in the center of town, an area that is called *Yuba* (Hot Water Field) and is fenced off on three sides by stone walls. It is full of steam from the boiling water gushing out of the earth. The water here is processed to collect the sulfur deposits, which are called *yunohana* or hot-spring flowers.

Recently, the *ryokan* have been getting larger and higher, and as the spa town fills up, condominium-type hotels are advancing on the surrounding greenery. There are also many pensions, which are popular among the younger generation. The area is popular as a sports resort complete with skiing, tennis, golf and other sporting facilities.

Routes to Kusatsu: The easiest access is from the JR Naganohara Station, 30 min. by bus. Naganohara is 43 km from Shibukawa and takes about 45 min. by limited express or about 2 hrs. 30 min. from Ueno (Tokyo) by limited express. From Karuizawa on the Shin-etsu Main Line, Kusatsu can be reached by bus in 2 hrs. 30 min. Except in winter, it can also be reached from Yudanaka (the terminal of the 33.

3-km-long Nagano Electric Railway originating from Nagano Station on the JR Shin-etsu Main Line) in 1 hr. 45 min. by bus via the Shiga Heights route.

The Shiga-Kusatsu Kogen Highway runs from Kusatsu to Shiga Heights. A 41.5 km, highway and one of the highest (averaging 2,000 m above sea level) in Japan, it crosses the central part of the Jo-Shin-Etsu Kogen National Park. Driving along the highway, one can enjoy such grand sights as the Nikko mountains and the Northern Japan Alps.

Several interesting places in the vicinity afford pleasant walks: *Sai-no-Kawara* (the Styx Riverbed), devastated by the emission of sulfurous gas; *Koridani* (Frozen Valley), iced up all year round; *Sesshogawara*, the site of some curiously shaped rocks; Osen Falls, and Mt. Shirane.

Mt. Shirane 52 : Alt. 2,171 m. This mountain is called Kusatsu-Shirane to distinguish it from Mt. Nikko-Shirane (alt. 2,578 m) and another larger Mt. Shirane of 3,192 m in altitude, the second-highest peak in the Southern Japan Alps. As an active volcano, it has erupted four times during the past few decades. The surrounding woods present a desolate appearance, with trees scarred by the effect of recent eruptions.

The mountain has three craters, with dense vapors rising from the central one, which is called *Yugama* (Hot-Water Caldron). A 2,396-m-long aerial ropeway extends from *Sesshogawara* at the upper section of the Kusatsu Ski Grounds to the summit. Since the close observation of the craters is dangerous, one is only permitted to proceed to the look-out point well back from the rim of the craters. The ropeway is used by skiers in winter.

Manza Spa 52 : The town nestles between Mt. Shirane and Mt. Manza (alt. 1,994 m). The area surrounding the spa provides good ski grounds, which lie at an altitude of nearly 2,000 m and contain an abundant supply of powdery snow. Manza Spa can be reached by bus from Manza-Kazawaguchi Station on the JR Agatsuma Line in 50 min. and from Naka-Karuizawa on the JR Shin-etsu Main Line in 1 hr.50 min.

North of Naganohara are Hanashiki Spa (30 min by bus) and the artificial Lake Nozori (1 hr.50 min. by bus), while to the west are Lake Tashiro and Shin-Kazawa Spa.

Shin-Kazawa: 30 min. from Manza-Kazawaguchi Station and 1 hr.10 min. from Komoro Station on the JR Shin-etsu Main Line—both routes by bus. Situated at an altitude of 1,300 m on the slopes of Mt. Asama (alt. 2,568 m) and Azumaya (alt. 2,354 m), Shin-Kazawa is a good ski resort in winter and a health retreat in summer. Kazawa, 4 km from Shin-Kazawa, offers similar attractions, with the National Vacation Village lying between them.

Numata 52 ☎0278: Pop. 47,611. 147 km from Ueno (Tokyo). About 2 hrs. 5 min. by limited express on the JR Joetsu Line, Numata lies on a plateau overlooking the valley of the Katashina, Usune and Tone rivers. At Numata Park in the city, an ancient merchant house is preserved and open to the public. Typical of the merchant houses in the Edo period, it is about 250 years old and is believed to be the oldest in eastern Japan. It is registered as an Important Cultural Property.

The city serves as the gateway to the Nikko National Park. From Numata to Lake Marunuma and Lake Sugenuma, it is 2 hrs. by bus. From the lake, a toll road leads to Nikko-Yumoto in the interior of the Nikko district via the Konsei Tunnel.

Along the way from Numata to Lake Sugenuma, a road branches off at Kamata in a northernly direction toward Oshimizu (Numata-Oshimizu, 1 hr.50 min. by bus). This area contains the old Oikami Spa and Katashina Spa, popular with skiers. From Oshimizu, it is about 8 km, or a 3-hrs. 30-min. hike to Ozenuma—a scenic mountain lake in Nikko National Park. For detailed information on Lake Ozenuma, refer to p.553.

Sarugakyo Spa: 35 min. by bus from Jomo-kogen Station on the JR Joetsu Shinkansen. Regarded as the most highly developed spa resort in the region, with modern hotels and *ryokan* or Japanese-style inns, the hot springs lie on a plateau on the northern shore of Lake Akaya along the southeastern foothills of Mt. Mikuni (alt. 1,636 m) on the border of Gumma and Niigata prefectures. The Sarugakyo-Mikuni Spas Area refers to five historical, recuperative spas: Okudaira, Yujuku, Kawafuru, Hoshi and Sarugakyo.

Minakami 52 ☎0278: Pop. 7,633. About 2 hrs. 20 min. from Ueno in Tokyo by limited express on the JR Joetsu Line, or a 140 km distance by way of the Kan-etsu Expressway. Situated on the northern tip of Gumma Prefecture, the area bustles throughout the year due to its many tourist attractions such as Mt. Tanigawa and other peaks, ski grounds, a pair of artificial lakes called Fujiwara and Dogen and an area containing six different spas: Minakami, Tanigawa, Oana, Yubiso, Takaragawa and Yunokoya. Located near Minakami Station on the JR Joetsu Line, the Minakami Spa area is filled with many luxurious hotels and *ryokan*, while the Tone River running between them creates an attractive view. To the north, one can see Mt. Tanigawa, a popular site among climbers. Takaragawa Spa, which can be reached in 40 min. by bus from Minakami Station, is noted for its enormous, open-air bath gushing up from the Takara River, a branch of the Tone River. It is also known as a spot for enjoying the beautiful autumn leaves when they change color.

Mt. Tanigawa 53 : This central peak of the Tanigawa Mountain Chain is a part of the Jo-Shin-Etsu Kogen (Plateau) National Park. Although it isn't very high with an altitude of only 1,963 m, the steep valleys thrill mountaineers. The rock wall called Ichi-no-kurasawa is highly noted as one of the three best spots for rock climbing along with Mt. Tsurugi and Mt. Hodaka in the Northern Japan Alps.

This mountain is also known as the "Devil's Mountain" since the unstable climate causes many disasters. As the name might suggest, the area is characterized by rugged beauty. Ordinary tourists can get to the Tenjindaira, the observatory on Mt. Tanigawa, via a ropeway. Near the JR Doai or Tsuchitaru Station.

Major Border Tunnels: Four huge tunnels run under the Tanigawa mountains and across the border between Gumma and Niigata prefectures. Completed in 1931, Shimizu Tunnel is a loop-shaped tunnel that extends for 9,702 m and consists of   two sections — one between Yubiso and Doai on the Gumma side, and the other between Tsuchitaru and Echigo-Nakazato on the Niigata side. Today, it is used exclusively for trains bound for Ueno on the JR Joetsu Line, but for the first 36 years after its completion, trains going in both directions between Tokyo and Niigata travelled alternatively on a single set of tracks.

Shin-Shimizu Tunnel, used exclusively by trains bound for Niigata, was constructed in 1967. The total length of this straight tunnel measures 13,490 m, with Yubiso and Doai stations located within the tunnel. Completed in 1981, the Dai-Shimizu Tunnel is used only by the JR Joetsu Shinkansen. Equipped with double-tracks and measuring 22,228 m in length, the Dai-Shimizu Tunnel is the second-longest tunnel in the world following the Seikan Tunnel between Honshu and Hokkaido. The 19,000-m-long Kan-etsu Tunnel was completed in 1985 for the Kan-etsu Expressway.

Yuzawa ⬚52⬚ ☎0257: Pop. 9,632. 1 hr.15 min. from Ueno (Tokyo) via the JR Joetsu Shinkansen. The town is located at the southernmost tip of Niigata Prefecture along the southern border of Gumma Prefecture around Mikuni Pass and Mt. Tanigawa. In addition to hot springs, ski courses such as Yuzawa-onsen, Nakazato, Iwappara and Naeba as well as the Ishiuchi Ski Course in Shiozawa with their abundant snow also attract crowds in winter.

This spa area is famous among the Japanese as the setting for the novel "Yukiguni" (Snow Country) by Nobel Prize laureate, Kawabata Yasunari (1899–1972). The town retains nothing of the rustic appearance described in the 1936 novel and has instead become a major tourist spot with high-rise hotels and resort condominiums.

Naeba Ski Course: Located in the Joetsu district, which is known as the mecca for skiing because of its excellent facilities as well as the quality and amount of snow. The many slopes lying below the summit of Mt. Takenoko (alt. 1,790 m) are considered among the best in Japan. In fact, the World Cup and various other international competitions are held here.

Koide ⬚17⬚: This is the gateway to Oyu Spa, about a 30-min. bus ride to the east, and to Tochiomata Spa—5 min. further southeast. Inland of Tochiomata Spa lies the 157-m-high Oku-Tadami Dam. It was built for a hydroelectric power station by making use of the water from the Tadami River, a tributary of the Agano River, which runs along the boundary of Niigata and Fukushima prefectures.

Echigo-Kawaguchi ⎡17⎤ : 245 km from Ueno (Tokyo). This is the junction of the JR Iiyama Line (97 km) leading to Toyono on the JR Shin-etsu Main Line. Noted for the production of lily bulbs, the town is located at the junction of the Uono and Shinano rivers, where boat rides as well as fishing ponds stocked with *ayu* or sweetfish are available.

Tokamachi ⎡17⎤ ☎0257: Pop. 46,962. 22 km from Echigo-Kawaguchi on the JR Iiyama Line. Known as a major producer of silk textiles, the area receives the heaviest snowfall in Niigata Prefecture. The *Tokamachi Yuki Matsuri* (Snow Festival) held annually on the second Friday, Saturday and Sunday in February attracts many visitors. The snow carnival and art exhibition are very beautiful, while the *kimono* fashion show held on a snow stage is gorgeous.

Ojiya ⎡16⎤ : ☎ 0258: Pop. 44,110. Situated north of Tokamachi and south of Nagaoka, the area is known for such products as the luxurious silk *Ojiyachijimi* and colored carp, sometimes called swimming jewels. The *Ojiyachijimi* weaving process can be seen at the Municipal Industrial Hall. The famous *Shinano Funakudari* excursion boat departs from the eastside of neighboring Kawaguchi Town and can take one to Ojiya in 1 hr.30 min.

Nagaoka ⎡16⎤ ☎ 0258: Pop. 182,808. Situated approximately in the middle of Niigata Prefecture. After Niigata, this is the largest commercial and industrial city in the prefecture. About 1 hr.35 min. from Ueno on the JR Joetsu Shinkansen, the city is an important transportation center because not only do the JR Joetsu and Shin-etsu Main Line form a junction here, but the Kan-etsu Expressway (245 km from Tokyo) and Hokuriku Expressway also meet here in addition to National Highways 8 and 17. There are five spas in the city as well as Yukyuzan Park, a famous place for viewing cherry blos soms, and the Nagaoka Museum of Science, which displays archaeological artifacts such as earthernware marked by flames dating back to 3,000 B.C.

Kashiwazaki ⎡16⎤ ☎0257: Pop. 87,184. An important transportation point in central Niigata. The northeastern edge of the city is adjacent to Nagaoka and can be reached from the latter city in about 40 min. by local train on the JR Shin-etsu Main Line. From Niigata, it is 2 hrs. 10 min. on the JR Echigo Line or 1 hr.14 min. by limited express on the JR Shin-etsu main Line. A 36-km-long Shoreline extending from the north to northwestern edge of the city contains the Shojodo Cave, eroded by the pounding of the waves, as well as various summer recreational areas such as the Kujiranami swimming area and the Kashiwazaki citizens retreat.

To the southwest, one can see the famous conical-shaped Mt. Yoneyama (alt. 993 m), a popular subject of local songs. The panoramic view of Sado Island from the summit is magnificent.

Izumozaki: 25 km northeast from Kashiwazaki on the JR Echigo

Line. The city prospered as the landing spot for gold produced on Sado Island on its way to Edo (now, Tokyo) during the Edo period. Along with Kashiwazaki and Niitsu, this region has been known since olden days for producing petroleum. The first machine for boring petroleum wells appeared here only fairly recently. Today, the area has been turned into the Petroleum Industry Memorial Park, which houses the Petroleum Memorial Museum with exhibitions on the history of petroleum. The Museum as well as the Ryokando attract many visitors. The latter is a house that memorializes Ryokan (1758 –1831), who was born nearby, became a priest and later gained fame as a scholar, poet and calligraphist.

Tsubame ⌷16⌷ ☎0256: Pop. 44,672. Situated between Niigata and Nagaoka. Like Sanjo and Yoshida, the city has been known for its hardware and cutlery industries since ancient times. In addition to spoons, knives and forks, the production of kitchenware and agricultural machinery as well as golf clubs has flourished recently. Tsubame-Sanjo Station of the JR Joetsu Shinkansen and the Hokuriku Expressway Sanjo-Tsubame Interchange are on the border with Sanjo.

Sanjo ⌷16⌷ ☎0256: Pop. 86,540. The city specializes in the production of hardware and printed cotton fabrics. Higashi(East)-Sanjo is the junction for the JR Yahiko Line (26 km), which runs from Higashi-Sanjo to Yahiko and stops at Tsubame and Yoshida.

Yahiko Shrine: 1 km northwest of the JR Yahiko Station. It stands at the eastern foot of Mt. Yahiko (alt. 638 m) amid a setting of superb Japanese cedars. The annual lantern festival held on July 25 features a procession that night of more than 20 large lanterns decorated with artificial flowers.

A 1-km-long ropeway extends from a place near the shrine to the summit of the mountain. The mountains surrounding Mt. Yahiko are part of the Sado-Yahiko-Yoneyama Quasi-National Park. Yahiko may also be reached from Niigata by bus in 1 hr. 20 min.

Shirone ⌷16⌷ ☎025: Pop. 35,620. The city is celebrated for its 300-year-old kite-flying festival. Called *tako-age* and held in early June, it consists of two groups competing with each other on either side of the Nakanokuchi River. Measuring 7 m in length and 6 m in width, and made with specially treated strings, the kites are maneuvered so that the strings cut the opponents' kite strings. Similar kite-flying contests also take place at Sanjo and Kamo in Niigata Prefecture in early June.

Niitsu ⌷16⌷ ☎0250: Pop. 64,766. Located 316 km from Ueno (Tokyo), it can be reached in 2 hrs. 30 min by the JR Joetsu Shinkansen, transferring at Nagaoka to a limited express on the JR Shin-etsu Main Line. It is the junction for the Uetsu Main Line to Akita (272 km) and the Ban-etsu-Sai Line to Koriyama (177 km). The city specializes in the production of oil and natural gas, although the industry no longer thrives as before. Noted as a bedroom community of Niigata, Niitsu is also celebrated for its large cultivation of tulips and hyacinths.

Niigata 16/18-19 ☎025

Pop. 472,068. Situated in the delta region at the mouth of the Shinano River. Serving as the capital of Niigata Prefecture, the city plays a central role in the politics, economics, education and culture of the prefecture. Niigata Port was one of the five trading ports opened by the treaties between the Tokugawa Shogunate and five Western countries in 1858. Since then, it has developed as the largest trading port on the Japan Sea side, while industry has thrived as well. The recent advance of heavy and chemical industries in the east harbor area has brought even more prosperity to the city. A large fire in 1955 and an earthquake in 1964 devastated the city, but recovery has transformed it into a modern urban area. The central part of the city consists of Honcho-dori Street, Furumachi-dori Street and Nishihori-dori Street, which are reached by crossing the Bandai Bridge over the Shinano River from the JR Niigata Station.

Niigata can be reached from Ueno (Tokyo) in 1 hr.50 min. (334 km) on the Joetsu Shinkansen. It is approximately 300 km away from Tokyo via the Kan-etsu and Hokuriku expressways, and can be reached in 5 hrs. by the express bus. By air, it is directly connected with Osaka, Nagoya, Sapporo and Sendai.

Refer to the supplement for details regarding the "i" **System Information Center** in Niigata.

PLACES OF INTEREST
Niigata Prefectural Government Memorial Hall (former Prefectural Assembly Hall) 18 : Erected in 1883, this structure, with its combination of Eastern and Western styles of architecture, served as the center of administration for the prefecture for some 50 years. The facade of this wooden, two-story building resembles the parliament building in England. It is Japan's only remaining prefectural assembly hall building from the early part of the Meiji period.
Niigata Folk Museum (the former Niigata Customs House): Construction began after Niigata Port was opened to the West in 1858 and was completed in 1869. The building is a synthesis of Japanese and Western architecture, offering a wide variety of exhibits on the history of Niigata as a port town.
Northern Culture Museum, Niigata Branch 18 : The former villa of Ito Bunkichi, a well-to-do landowner. Located in Yokogoshi Village to the south of Niigata, this villa is featured by magnificent construction and a beautiful Japanese garden.
Japan Sea Tower 18 : A rotating observatory located in the pine groves at Yoriihama. It offers a panoramic view of Niigata City, Mt. Yahiko, Sado Island and the Niigata Plain. Inside are exhibitions presented by Niigata's sister cities, Galveston, Texas, in the USA and

Khabarovsk in the USSR.

Terao Central Park: Noted for a large tulip garden. The sight of the many species of tulips blooming in mid-April is spectacular.

Sado Island 16

An island situated 35 km off the west coast of Niigata City. It measures approximately 59 km from north to south and 31 km at the widest point from east to west, with a total area of 857 sq. km. The island is shaped like the letter "H" lying on its side, with Ryotsu and Mano bays as the east and west inlets respectively. Kuninaka Plain is in the middle of the island, while the rest of the area is covered with mountains. Due to the warm current, the climate is so mild that it rarely snows during winter. Although agriculture, fishery and food processing are active, tourism is the main industry. Visitors are attracted by the ruggedly beautiful beaches, many historical sites and rich folk tradition. The tourist season extends from mid-April to early November. Since there are no railways, the main transportation method is by bus.

Routes to Sado Island: It takes 25 min. by air (non-regular service), 1 hr. by jet-foil or 2 hrs. 20 min. by ferry to go from Niigata to Ryotsu. It takes 2 hrs. by ferry to get to Akadomari from Teradomari and 2 hrs. 30 min. from Naoetsu to Ogi.

Ryotsu 16 ☎02592: Pop. 20,283. Formerly known as Ebisu, the town consists of two sections: the northern area called Ebisumachi and the southern part called Minatomachi. It serves as the main entrance to the island as well as a port of refuge for Niigata from September to April, when strong winds are likely to prevail. Ryotsu is situated on the northern shore of Lake Kamo.

Lake Kamo 16 : About 17 km in circumference. It is connected with the sea by a narrow inlet. With Mt. Kimpoku (alt. 1,173 m) towering to the north, the ever-placid surface of the lake serves as a huge looking-glass to mirror these majestic peaks. Oyster cultivation is a thriving industry here.

Sado Island was well known as a place of exile in feudal times. Among the most exalted of these exiles was Emperor Juntoku (1197 –1242), who was defeated by the Regent Hojo Yoshitoki in an attempt to overthrow the Kamakura Shogunate. One of the points of interest is the site of Kuroki-no-Gosho (Unhewn-Timber Palace) at Izumi. Located about 10 km southwest of Ryotsu, it served as the abode for the unlucky Emperor for 22 years. Other tourist spots include his mausoleum at Mano on the western coast and the nearby Mano Shrine.

Myosenji Temple 16 : Situated close to Mano Shrine, it contains the tomb of Hino Suketomo. A courtier of Emperor Godaigo (1288–1339), he was also exiled here and subsequently executed by the governor. Another celebrated exile was Saint Nichiren, who lived on the island from 1271 until 1274. He lived in a hut at the entrance to the Komponji Temple for six months. Later, he was allowed to move to another place, a site now occupied by Myoshoji Temple. Here, his house was restored and protected by a shelter and is now a place of pilgrimage for his followers.

Aikawa [16] : Pop. 11,645. 1 hr.15 min. by bus from Ryotsu. The town has been famous for its gold mine since gold was discovered in 1601. Worked by prison labor during the Edo period, the mine became Imperial property at the time of the Meiji Restoration (1868). The gold veins have almost been exhausted. A kind of pottery made with red clay from the mine called *Mumyoi-yaki* is made at Aikawa.

Senkaku Bay [16] : Lying to the north of Aikawa, the bay boasts of fantastic rock formations among the cliffs formed by the rough waves of the Japan Sea. Excursion boats for viewing the rocks can be hired at Tassha, 15 min. by bus from Aikawa. A walkway runs along the cliffs, from which a beautiful view, quite different from that seen from the sea, can be enjoyed.

The west coast of the island from Senkaku Bay to Cape Hajiki on the northern tip of the island is called Soto-Kaifu (Outer Coast) and consists of a series of natural marvels in the form of cliffs. The east coast southward from Cape Hajiki is called Uchi-Kaifu (Inner Coast).

Compared to the serene and scenic Uchi-Kaifu, Soto-Kaifu abounds with peculiar rocks, reefs and cliffs, and is one of the main tourist attractions of Sado Island. Cape Hajiki, a steep cliff where a white lighthouse stands, and Futatsugame and Onogame—two enormous boulders to the west—make up one of the most beautiful sights in Soto-Kaifu. Magnificent Onogame is a single sheet of stone 167 m tall, with a protruding peak that is a sharp, sheer cliff. A superb panoramic view of Soto-Kaifu is available from the summit. From May to June, the peninsula area around Onogame is covered with the blooms of *kibana-kanzo* or yellow-day lilies.

Besides Mt. Yahiko on the mainland, Sado-Yahiko-Yoneyama Quasi-National Park occupies a large portion of Sado Island. It includes Mt. Kimpoku, Senkaku Bay and Soto-Kaifu as well as Lake Kamo and its vicinity. The southern tip of the island, including the port town of Ogi, is also part of the park.

Regular sightseeing bus service making the rounds of the tourist attractions on Sado Island is available from Ryotsu and Ogi. The tour takes 4–8 hrs.

Area 8. Takasaki to Naoetsu Along JR Shinetsu Main Line

Takasaki, which is on the route from Tokyo to Niigata, is the starting point for the 328-km JR Shin-etsu Main Line. But there is no train running between Ueno (Tokyo) and Niigata via the Shin-etsu Main Line. A majority of the long-distance trains running on this line make Nagano, Myoko-Kogen, Naoetsu or Kanazawa their destination. For information concerning the routes from Tokyo to Takasaki, refer to Area 7.

PLACES OF INTEREST

Annaka 52 ☎0273: Pop. 45,847. An old castle town located 10.6 km west of Takasaki, 14 min. by train. Niijima Jo (1843-1890), the founder of Doshisha University—the first Protestant university in Japan—was born here. In the suburbs of Annaka is the Akima Plum Grove, which is the largest of its kind in the Kanto District, with more than 30,000 plum trees growing in an area covering 500,000 sq.m.

Isobe: Located 17.6 km west of Takasaki, it can be reached in 20 min. by train. The city is known for its cold mineral spring, although the water is heated for bathing. For many years, those suffering from digestive disorders and neuralgia have come here for the therapeutic baths. The mineral water is also used in making a thin wafer that is sold at the spa.

Mt. Myogi 52 : This is the general term given to three mountains —Hakuun (alt. 1,081 m), rising in the northeast; Kinkei (alt. 856 m), situated in the southeast; and Kondo (alt. 1,104 m) to the west. All these mountains are marked by sheer cliffs and steep slopes, with huge rocks jutting up here and there. Some of these rocks are called by such names as Taiho-Iwa (Cannon Rock) and Rosoku-Iwa (Candle Rock) because of their shape. Geologists explain that Myogi is probably the remnant of a very old volcano and that the serrated form of its rocky peaks and pinnacles was largely caused by erosion.

The climb up Mt. Myogi usually starts from the town of Myogi at the eastern foot of Mt. Hakuun, where the time-honored Myogi Shrine stands in a thickly wooded grove of cedars. The town can be reached by bus from the JR Matsuida Station in 10 min. The beauty of Mt. Myogi can be fully appreciated by driving along the "Myogi Maple Line" (14.7 km).

Gumma Safari World: The 700,000-sq.-m area is divided into seven zones and a bird park. Approximately 1,600 animals of 60 species of ferocious beasts such as lions, tigers, elephants and rhinoceroses roam freely around the park. Birds are also uncaged. Near Joshu-Tomioka Station on the Joshin Electric Railway.

Karuizawa 52 ☎0267: Pop. 15,549. Located 146 km northwest of Ueno Station in Tokyo, it takes 1 hr. 52 min. by the JR limited express. Situated on the southeastern slopes of Mt. Asama on a plateau rising at an altitude of 900-1,000 m, Karuizawa is known as an international summer resort. The area was initially introduced as a villa area for foreign residents in 1886 by venerable Archdeacon A. C. Shaw, an English missionary. Karuizawa was originally established with plush resort hotels and villas belonging to the upper class and celebrities such as writers, poets, painters and entertainers. But today the area is crowded with the younger generation, and there are many new hotels, pensions, lodges and various sports and recreational facilities for them. Thus, this area has changed considerably from the past when it was known as an exclusive resort area.

The original Karuizawa, referred to as Kyu(Old)-Karuizawa, is north of the JR Karuizawa Station. The main street running through the center of the town is called "Karuizawa-Ginza" and is lined with many branches of boutiques and famous restaurants from Tokyo and Osaka as well as souvenir shops.

Attractions of the area include St. Paul's Catholic Church (a symbol of Karuizawa), tennis courts famed as the place where the romance of Emperor Akihito and Empress Michiko originated, Nihon Seiko-kai Church (the oldest church in Karuizawa) on the grounds of the villa of A.C. Shaw and the former Mikasa Hotel, which has been designated as an Important Cultural Property.

By climbing up to the Usui Pass observation platform east along the border of Nagano and Gumma prefectures, a magnificent view of the north Kanto mountains can be enjoyed. Going north on the "Shiraito Highland Way" (a toll road), one will reach the famous Shiraito Falls.

The area west of Kyu-Karuizawa is referred to as Naka(Middle)-Karuizawa. It is a recreational zone containing the Karuizawa Skate Center (with some of the best facilities in Japan) and various other sports facilities. Other points of interest include Takanawa Museum, exhibiting art by Man Ray, Paul Klee, Max Ernest and Jasper Jones; two spas—Hoshino and Shiotsubo; and Yacho-no-mori for bird watching.

The newly developed area to the south of the JR tracks is called Minami(South)-Karuizawa. It offers many sports and recreational facilities such as golf courses and tennis courts. The Peynet Museum, which exhibits works of Raymond Peynet (1908-), a French painter, is situated on the shores of Lake Shiozawa.

Mt. Asama 52 : Alt. 2,568 m. Smoke constantly billows from this active volcano on the border of Nagano and Gumma prefectures. So far, approximately 50 eruptions have been recorded, but the big eruption of 1783 is especially famous and responsible for the scenic Onioshidashi (Pushed-out Rocks by a Demon). This enormous stream of solidified lava measures 3 km from east to west, 12 km from north to south and has a thickness of 30 m. Asama Garden and Onioshi-dashi Garden are landmarks that can be reached by bus in about 35 to 50 min. from the JR Karuizawa Station or Naka-Karuizawa Station.

Komoro 52 ☎0267: Pop. 44,087. Located 165 km from Ueno (Tokyo), 2 hrs. 15 min. by limited express, it is the junction for the 79-km Koumi Line leading to Kobuchizawa on the JR Chuo Main Line. This railway line runs on the highest altitudes from north to south across the plateau (alt. 967 m to 1,375 m) on the eastern slopes of Mts. Tateshina and Yatsugatake and along part of the valley of the Chikuma River.

Kaiko-en Garden: Lying on the ruins of a castle, this garden is located 3 min. on foot from the JR Komoro Station. A grand view of the Chikuma River can be obtained from the top of the stone walls of the ruins. The garden is famous for its cherry blossoms in spring and crimson foliage in autumn.

Takamine Plateau 52 : This highland, located in the saddle between the mountains lying west of Mt. Asama, offers a magnificent view of Mt. Fuji and the Northern Japan Alps. It is noted for more than 1,200 varieties of alpine flora that bloom here in summer. The ski grounds open in winter. It can be reached in 50 min. by bus from Komoro Station.

Ueda 52 ☎0268: Pop. 117,987. 183 km from Ueno (Tokyo), about 2 hrs. 20 min. by limited express. Once a castle town, it is the central city for the Ueda Basin as well as the junction for the Bessho Line of the Ueda Kotsu Railway. Only three turrets of the former castle are now standing and are used as a museum for the display of ancient armor and weapons.

Rice, wheat, barley and vegetables are cultivated in the basin along the Chikuma River.

Bessho Spa 52 : This hot-spring resort near Ueda can be reached by the Ueda Kotsu bus or train (12 km, 30 min.). The spa is noted for the natural bathtub of rocks formed by the crevices, from which mineral water gushes. It is thought to be efficacious against rheumatism, neuralgia and dermatitis. It is considered worthwhile to visits some of the many old temples and shrines around the spa such as Kitamuki-Kannon Temple, Anrakuji Temple with its Hakkaku-Sanju-no-To (three-story octagonal pagoda, a National Treasure), Chuzenji Temple, Zenzanji Temple and Jorakuji Temple.

Sugadaira Plateau 52 : A basin-type plateau located at an altitude of 1,300 m. The area includes ski slopes, golf courses, villa areas, pastures and vegetable fields. During summer it is crowded with young people attending training camps for such sports as rugby. It can be reached in 1 hr.5 min. by bus from the JR Ueda Station.

Togura-Kamiyamada Spa 52 : Supplied by hot water gushing from the southern banks of the Chikuma River, this is the most modern and bustling spa area in Nagano Prefecture. The vicinity is active with the cultivation of apple orchards.

Shinonoi 52 : The junction for the JR Shinonoi Line (Shinonoi – Shiojiri, 68 km). It is situated near the famous battlefield of Kawana-kajima, where Uesugi Kenshin and Takeda Shingen clashed in the 16th century.

To secure the town, then an important strategical location, Uesugi Kenshin, the head of the clan in Echigo Province (now, Niigata Prefecture) and his archrival, Takeda Shingen of Kai Province (now, Yamanashi Prefecture) fought here five times on even terms. Both are still remembered as famed warriors, politicians and administrators.

Obasute 52 : 22 km south of Nagano, about 30 min. by train on the

JR Shinonoi Line, this town is located on the slopes of Mt. Kamuriki (alt. 1,252 m), where the tragic, 11th-century legend "Obasute" originated. Refer to "The Ballad of Narayama" p.263.

At that time the region was very poor and suffered from severe food shortages. A man was nagged by his wife everyday to abandon his aged mother in the mountain. Finally, the man decided to carry out his wife's wishes, but he could not free himself of his guilty conscience and ended up bringing his mother back home.

Obasute is also a notable place for moon-viewing. There are countless, terraced paddyfields on the mountainsides, and on the full moon night in September, one can enjoy the fine view of the moon reflected in the water of each paddy.

Nagano 52/55 ☎0262

Pop. 342,647. 221 km from Ueno (Tokyo), about 2 hrs. 45 min. by limited express on the JR Shin-etsu Main Line. It was formerly called Zenkoji after the famous temple of that name in the city. The station itself is shaped like a temple, thus symbolizing the original Buddhist character of the town. The name was changed when the city was made the capital of Nagano Prefecture.

This prefecture is centrally located on Honshu, the main island of Japan, and is called the Roof of Japan because the highest mountain range, the Japan Alps (11 peaks are over 3,000 m in height), lie on its eastern boundary. The whole area is over 2,000 m high with four national parks, lakes, highlands and hot springs.

The city thrives on commerce brought by the many tourists. Apricots and apples are among the chief products of the surrounding district.

The 71-km Nagano Electric Railway runs from Nagano to Yudanaka via Suzaka (pop. 53,526) and Nakano (pop. 41,356). From Suzaka, a railway line branches off to Yashiro on the Shin-etsu Main Line, while another line branches off from Nakano (Shinshu-Nakano Station) to Kijima.

Zenkoji Temple 52 : Regarded as one of the most popular Buddhist temples in Japan, it occupies an elevated site (59,000 sq.m) at the northern end of the city. It is about 2 km from the station and 10 min. by bus. Zenkoji-shita Station on the Nagano Electric Railway is closer to the temple. Founded in 642, the present *Hondo* (Main Hall) was reconstructed in 1707 and is registered as a National Treasure.

The chief statues worshipped, which are designated as Important Cultural Properties, are those of *Amida-Nyorai* and his followers— *Kannon* and *Seishi*. They are made of bronze and are believed to have been presented by a king of the Paikche Dynasty of Korea in 552. However, the statues were said to have suffered at the hands of Japanese iconoclasts opposed to the introduction of Buddhism. At one time, the images were consigned to flames and then thrown into a canal at Naniwa (Osaka). However, a man by the name of Honda

Yoshimitsu recovered the statues in 602 and carried them to his native village in Shinano Province (now, Nagano Prefecture), where he afterwards built a small temple for them.

For centuries the statues experienced many vicissitudes, but finally they were restored to Zenkoji Temple in 1598. The temple is named after the founder, whose name, Yoshimitsu, can also be read "Zenko". Images of the founder, his wife and his son are worshipped in the tabernacle along with the images of *Amida-Nyorai* and his followers.

The main statue is opened to public view every seven years. The next time is scheduled to be in the spring of 1991. Under the altar is a tunnel surrounding the temple. Since the statue cannot be seen, worshippers pass through the entire darkness of the tunnel (about 40 m long) groping their way and, if lucky, touch the "Key to Paradise," which is believed to promise them an easy passage into eternity.

The temple is uniquely administered by priests and priestesses of two different sects, Tendai and Jodo. The abbess' position is that of the highest priestess. When the temple gate is opened at dawn, the devotees wait on the approach road for the abbot or the abbess to bless them. About half an hour after dawn, the morning service is held, presided over by the abbot first and then the abbess. Hundreds of worshippers come from all over Japan to attend the morning service.

Jo-Shin-Etsu Kogen (Plateau) National Park ⬜52

Covering an area of 1,889.15 sq.km, the park consists of two parts —a district straddling Niigata, Gumma and Nagano prefectures, and another to the northwest extending over Niigata and Nagano prefectures. The former includes among its major landmarks Mt. Tanigawa (alt. 1,963 m) near the eastern extremity, the active volcano Shirane rising in the center to an altitude of 2,171 m, another active volcano, Mt. Asama (alt. 2,568 m), at the southern extremity, Shiga Heights and Sugadaira Plateau. The latter section includes Mts. Myoko (alt. 2,454 m), Kurohime (alt. 2,053 m), Togakushi (alt. 1,904 m) and Iizuna (alt. 1,917 m) within its limits.

The national park teems with hot springs. Since the park is quite easy to approach from the capital, it is popular with metropolitan residents for picnicking, camping, mountain climbing and skiing. Hot-spring baths and wildlife observation can also be enjoyed here.

Iizuna Plateau ⬜52 : A plateau located at an altitude between 1,000 and 1,300 m high on the southern foothills of Mt. Iizuna (alt. 1,917 m). It can be reached in 35 min. by bus from Nagano Station. Daizahoshi Pond is the center of many other attractions such as Lake Iizuna and ten other lakes as well as Ichinotorii Natural Park, where a profusion of alpine flowers grow. Worshipped in ancient times, Mt. Iizuna is noted as the birthplace of the *Iizuna* school of *ninja* arts. Iizuna Shrine and countless other small shrines show the remnants of *ninja* training.

Mt. Togakushi $\boxed{52}$: Alt. 1,904 m. Once an object of religious worship, the peak is frequently referred to in poetry. Togakushi Shrine in the heart of this mountainous region used to be a sacred place for priests practicing asceticism. It consists of three shrine buildings—*Hokosha*, *Chusha* and *Okusha*—that can be reached by bus from Nagano Station via a 12.4-km-long toll road called "Togakushi Bird Line." It requires 50 min. to reach Hokosha, 1 hr. to Chusha and 1 hr.5 min. to Okusha.

It is a 30-to 40-min. walk between *Hokosha* and *Chusha* (Middle Shrine), where there are a lot of inns once used as lodgings for pilgrims. From *Chusha* to *Okusha* (Inner Shrine), it is a 4-km, 50-min. hike up a slope. A bus also departs from Kurohime Station on the JR Shin-Etsu Main Line.

Mt. Togakushi is flanked by Mt. Iizuna (alt. 1,917 m) on the east and Mt. Kurohime (alt. 2,053 m) on the northeast. The plateau of Togakushi is well known for such singing birds as bush warblers, thrushes and cuckoos.

Soba (buckwheat noodles) served in a bamboo basket made by the farmers here should not be missed.

Kurohime $\boxed{52}$: 27 km north of Nagano, 35 min. by train on the JR Shin-etsu Main Line. This is the most convenient station to get to Lake Nojiri as well as Mts. Kurohime and Togakushi. The town was the home of Kobayashi Issa (1763–1827), a well known *haiku* poet, whose dwelling has been preserved at Kashiwabara.

The Kurohime Plateau is a double conoid volcano spreading around the eastern rim of Mt. Kurohime (alt. 2,053 m). It is also called the "Shinano-Fuji" because of its magnificent beauty. The plateau is especially well known for the superb view it affords of the surrounding area. Great quantities of snow accumulate during winter so that the mountain slopes make excellent ski grounds. One of the slopes is actually covered with about a million cosmoses gathered from all over the world. Graced with the blooms during summer and autumn, the plateau is a splendid sight. It takes 15 min. by bus from Kurohime Station to Kurohime Kogen (Plateau) Ski Grounds.

Lake Nojiri $\boxed{52}$: Standing at an altitude of 654 m, the lake is 4 km to the northeast and 12 min. by bus from Kurohime Station. It lies at the foot of Mts. Myoko and Kurohime and measures 16.5 km in circumference. The jagged shoreline of this beautiful lake has 48 promontories. The west shore is the tourist base, with recreational, camping, boating, yachting and water ski facilities concentrated here. The time required for a trip around the lake by sightseeing boat is 40 min.

Myoko Plateau $\boxed{52}$: A large plateau that spreads from the eastern to the southern base of Mt. Myoko (alt. 2,454 m), a tholoid-type volcano. The area can be enjoyed throughout the year—hiking in spring, relaxing at resorts in summer, viewing the colored leaves in autumn and skiing in winter. The closest station, Myoko-Kogen, is located 38 km north of Nagano, about 50 min. by local train, and 255 km from Ueno (Tokyo), 3 hrs. 30 min. by limited express.

Akakura Spa 52 : 6 km northwest of Myoko-Kogen Station, 15 min. by bus. It stands 785 m above sea level on the eastern slopes of Mt. Myoko and commands an extensive view of the surrounding area, including the Kubiki Plain to the north, the Japan Sea and even Sado Island in the distance. To the west soars Mt. Myoko together with Mts. Kurohime and Iizuna, while Lake Nojiri lies to the south. The spa is a splendid place for skiing in winter since there is plenty of snow and good skiing facilities are available.

Myoko Spa is 1 km, or 2 min. by bus, southwest of Myoko-Kogen Station, while Ikenotaira Spa is 5 km, or 10 min. by bus heading west. Both these hot springs are good places for skiing, with Shin-Akakura Spa situated between Myoko Kogen and Akakura Spa.

Hand-made utensils made of white birch, "*akebi*" vine and royal ferns are special products made here.

Mt. Myoko 52 : Alt. 2,454 m. Part of the Jo-Shin-Etsu Kogen (Plateau) National Park, it can be climbed in 6 hrs. from Akakura or Ikenotaira Spa. The road from Akakura forks to the right and left at the top of the village street, with the right branch going to Kita-Jigokudani (North Hell Valley) and the left fork leading to Minami-Jigokudani (South Hell Valley). The two roads meet again at a shrine (about 5 km by either route), just beyond which is a pond. From here to the summit (2 km), it is a steep climb, but hikers are aided by chains attached to rocks.

Mt. Myoko is an extinct volcano. The long, semi-oval ridge surrounding it includes Mt. Maeyama in front, Mt. Akakura to the south and Mt. Kanna to the north. At the summit stands a small temple dedicated to Amitabha Buddha and offering a view that includes Mts. Fuji and Asama, the Japan Sea and even Sado Island on a clear day.

Seki Spa 52 : This spa faces the clean Otakiri River about 8 km (20 min. by bus) southwest of Sekiyama Station, the one next to Myoko-Kogen Station.

Tsubame Spa: Situated 3 km farther inland, this sedate spa in a simple setting can be reached from Akakura Spa by bus in 15 min. Both spas are good ski areas, while Tsubame is also one of the starting points for climbing Mt. Myoko.

Sasagamine Plateau 52 : 50 min. from Myoko-Kogen Station by bus, it is situated halfway up Mt. Sasagamine (alt. 1,545 m) and is one of the entrances to Mt. Myoko. Lying at an altitude of 1,300 m, the plateau is a green-blanketed grassland full of pastures. It is adjacent to a National Vacation Village complete with camping and lodging facilities.

Yamada Spa 52 : 900 m above sea level at the northern foot of Mt. Shirane, 30 min. by bus from Suzaka Station, which is 25 min. from Nagano by the Nagano Electric Railway. It is a good summer retreat and ski center like Goshiki and Shichimi spas, which are in the neighborhood. *Kokeshi* dolls and wooden folkcraft articles are the souvenirs of Yamada Spa.

Yudanaka Spa 52 : 40 min. from Nagano by the Nagano Electric Railway. It also serves as the entrance to several hot-spring resorts in the vicinity as well as to Shiga Heights. Andai and Shibu spas, lying almost contiguous, are situated to the southeast, forming the most thriving resort area in the district. Shibu Spa can be reached in 5 min. by bus from Yudanaka Station.

Kambayashi Spa: 4 km, 15 min. by bus from Yudanaka Station. The area makes a fine summer resort, occupying the highest elevation (850 m) among the hot-spring resorts in the vicinity and commanding an excellent view. About 1.5 km west into the mountain from Kambayashi is Jigokudani Spa, where a 20-m-high jet of hot water and wild monkeys who come to bathe in the hot springs are the chief attractions.

Shiga Heights 52 : Regarded as the heart of the Jo-Shin-Etsu Kogen (Plateau) National Park, this plateau is situated on an eminence about 1,500 m above sea level. On the plateau are more than 70 lakes and ponds, with many white birch forests adding to the beauty of the scenery. The plateau is popular in all four seasons with hikers, campers, rowers, anglers and skiers.

Maruike, named after the pond in the area, is the central point (30 min. by bus from Yudanaka Station), serving as a junction to various plateaus in the surrounding area. There are several chic hotels and lodges here as well as such attractions as Biwaike Pond and Hasuike Pond near the bus terminal.

Shiga Nature Education Park, run by Shinshu University, is located in the marshland southeast of Maruike. It provides information about the characteristics and environment of the plateau. In the eastern part of the plateau is a group of ponds and swamps called *Shijuhachi-ike*, meaning 48 ponds. The mystical Lake Onuma, the largest on the plateau, along with Mt. Higashidate (alt. 1,994 m) to the north and Mt. Yokote (alt. 2,305 m) to the south provide the background for an enjoyable hiking trail.

Oku(Inner)-shiga Heights is 14 km along the Oku-Shiga Woodland Path, which extends north from Hasuike Pond and runs for 70 km. The plateau, which can be reached by bus in 1 hr.15 min. from Yudanaka, is the innermost resort area of Shiga Heights. The serene environment is popular with visitors. Chigoike Pond on the summit of Mt. Yakebitai (alt. 2,009 m) is noted for the large clusters of marsh plants that grow here.

The spas in Shiga Heights include Hoppo (50 min. by bus from Yudanaka) and Kawaragoya, both on the southwest slope of Mt. Higashidate, as well as Ishinoyu, Kidoike and Kumanoyu (46 min. by bus from Yudanaka) to the south of Maruike.

Shiga Heights contain a wide variety of accommodations, including deluxe resort hotels and a People's Lodge as well as dormitories and villas belonging to schools and companies. Needless to say, many visitors come here, especially during the winter ski season. This mecca for skiers offers about 20 ski slopes collectively referred to as the Shiga-Kogen Ski Grounds. It is one of the best-equipped ski resorts in Japan. The Shiga-Kusatsu Expressway (Shiga-Kusatsu Plateau Route) extends for 41 km from Kambayashi Spa to Kusatsu Spa in Gumma Prefecture via Shiga Heights. This refreshing, scenic route is full of superb mountain and plateau landscapes, but it is closed during winter.

The JR Iiyama Line running 108 km from Nagano to Echigo-Kawaguchi in Niigata Prefecture along the JR Joetsu Line via Iiyama and Tokamachi branches off from the Shin-etsu Main Line at Toyono.

Iiyama ☐52☐ ☎0269: Pop. 29,280. 50 min. from Nagano by train. Developed as a castle town, it is now a center of local politics, transportation and commerce. Mt. Madarao (alt. 1,382 m) on the western side borders Niigata Prefecture. The city produces *tatami* matting, paper, household Buddhist altars and ski equipment.

Nozawa Spa ☐52☐: 45 min. by bus from Iiyama Station on the JR Iiyama Line or in 30 min. by bus from Kijima Station—a terminus of the Nagano Electric Railway. It is said that the hot springs were discovered by a priest by the name of Gyoki (668–749), who devoted himself to a variety of social work in the eighth century. The spa gained popularity after being opened to the public by the feudal lord of Iiyama in the 17th century. Located at an altitude of 600 m, it boasts an abundance of *minshuku* or family-style inns to cater to visiting tourists and local rare delicacies such as *nozawanazuke* or salted *nozawana* greens. There are many ski grounds in the area along the Iiyama Line, which is known for having the heaviest snowfall in Japan. Nozawa-Onsen Ski Grounds was the birthplace of skiing in Japan and is a popular venue for ski competitions.

Mt. Madarao ☐52☐: Rising over the southwestern edge of Iiyama with an altitude of 1,382 m. Its plateau on the eastern base of the mountain attracts many young women with various sporting and recreational facilities such as ski slopes, tennis courts, a pool and more than 100 chic pensions. It can be reached in 40 min. by bus from Iiyama Station.

Joetsu ☐17☐ ☎0255: Pop. 128,932. The third-largest city in Niigata Prefecture came into existence when the two old cities of Takada and Naoetsu were combined in 1971.

Takada ☐17☐: Situated 290 km from Ueno (Tokyo), it can be reached in about 3 hrs. 50 min. by limited express. The area is noted for its heavy snowfall, with the eaves of the houses extending outward to an unusual length to keep the streets open.

Takada, which developed as a castle town, has a lot of historical places. The Takada Castle ruins, with the inner and outer moats still remaining, are 20 min. on foot from Takada Station. In spring the blossoms of some three thousand cherry trees reflect beautifully in the water.

Naoetsu ⬚17⬚: Situated on the coast of the Japan Sea, the city is also the junction for the JR Hokuriku Main Line. It can be reached from Ueno (Tokyo), in 4 hrs. and 5 min. (a distance of 296 km) by limited express or in 2 hrs. and 30 min. by taking the Joetsu Shinkansen to Nagaoka and changing to the limited express on the Shin-etsu Main Line.

The Shin-etsu Main Line branches off to the east at Naoetsu and runs along the beautiful seashore, touching en route at Kuroi, Saigata, Katamachi, Kakizaki and Yoneyama stations. Yoneyama is located at the foot of Mt. Yoneyama (alt. 993 m), where a barrier was formerly established by the lord of Takada.

The Japan Sea coast from Kuroi to Katamachi, a distance of about 10 km, is a center for natural gas, which is piped to Tokyo.

Area 9. Tokyo to Nasu and Shiobara
Along JR Tohoku Main Line

There is an active volcano called Mt. Nasudake in the northeast part of the Kanto District. Nasu Plateau, spreading over the southern foot of this mountain, and the Shiobara region in the southwestern valley are noted for their quality spas and a landscape that retains its beauty throughout the year. A part of Nikko National Park, it is one of the leading resort areas in the Kanto District. There are many attractive towns and cities with unique traditions along the JR Tohoku Main Line and other local lines heading toward this area.

TRANSPORTATION

Rail: The JR Tohoku Main Line or the JR Tohoku Shinkansen can be used to reach Nasu and Shiobara. The "Aoba" trains on the JR Tohoku Shinkansen stop Omiya, Oyama, Utsunomiya and Nasu-Shiobara stations. Branch lines include the JR Ryomo Line (Oyama to Shin-Maebashi), Watarase-Keikoku Railway (Kiryu on the JR Ryomo Line to Mato), JR Mito Line (Oyama to Tomobe) and the Mo-oka Railway (Shimotate on the JR Mito Line to Motegi). It is also possible to use the Tobu Railway originating in Asakusa, Tokyo, to go to the main cities on the JR Ryomo Line.

Road: The main roads are the Tohoku Expressway and National Highway 4. National Highway 50 parallels the JR Ryomo and Mito lines.

Along JR Tohoku Main Line

Oyama ⬚15⬚ ☎0285: Pop. 138,697. This city serves as a main transportation point on the southern edge of Tochigi Prefecture. The JR Oyama Station, 77 km from Ueno in Tokyo, is where passengers on the JR Tohoku Shinkansen (40 min. from Ueno) and on the Tohoku Main Line transfer to the Ryomo and Mito lines. The city has electrical, metal, machinery, and chemical industries, but recently it has been developed as a bedroom community of Tokyo.

Originally, this area prospered both as a lodging town on the old Nikkokaido Highway and a castle town under the Oyama family. The castle site has been converted into Shiroyama Park along with its beautiful cherry trees.

Utsunomiya 15/19 ☎0286

Pop. 418,921. 110 km from Ueno in Tokyo, 47 min. on the JR Tohoku Shinkansen. Serving as the capital of Tochigi Prefecture, the city lies in the center of the prefecture and is reputedly the most prosperous city in Northern Kanto District. The construction of plant complexes in recent years especially has spurred the rapid development of the area. A rich past has left the city with many historical sites, including old temples and ancient shrines.

A 27-m-high statue of the *Heiwa* (Peace) *Kannon*, which was completed in 1954 after six years of work, stands in front of Oyaji Temple—about 9 km northwest of the JR station, 25 min. by bus. The temple is said to have been founded by Kobo-Daishi (774–835) or Saint Kobo, who introduced the Shingon doctrines of Buddhism into Japan. Now belonging to the Tendai sect, the temple structure is built partly within a huge cavern, on the walls of which are nine Buddhist images elaborately carved in relief, including the 4-m-high *Senju Kannon* (Thousand-Handed *Kannon*), the chief object of worship. They seem to have been carved during the early part of the Heian period (794–1185) and are considered to be the oldest stone Buddhist images in Japan. They are all protected as Important Cultural Properties. The spot is also a Place of Historical Importance, while the vicinity is noted for its azaleas in spring and colored leaves in autumn.

The hills in this area are composed of Oya stones, named after Oyaji Temple. A kind of tuff, soft and easy to work with, the stone has been used for building fences and warehouses in the village. Other points of interest are a museum showing the history of Oya stones and how they are quarried as well as an underground quarry converted into a sightseeing attraction. The deepest portion of this mine goes down approximately 60 m to an impressive, spacious chamber.

Shiobara Spa 14

This famous spa has been enjoyed by many since the first hot springs (*Motoyu*) were discovered in 806.

Transportation: Nishi-Nasuno Station on the JR Tohoku Main Line serves as the entrance to Shiobara Spa. It can be reached in 2 hrs 15 min. (152 km) from Ueno (Tokyo) on a rapid train. The JR Tohoku Shinkansen arrives at Nasu-Shiobara Station. It takes 1 hr. 10 min.

(158 km) from Ueno. Bus service to Shiobara Spa is available from both stations, but buses from Nishi-Nasuno Station are more convenient. The spa can also be reached by bus running from Kinugawa Spa. When driving, take the Nishinasuno-Shiobara Interchange exit on the Tohoku Expressway.

The spas along the valley of the Hoki River were referred to as the Eleven Spas of Shiobara, but only the following seven remain today. Oami Spa, graced with beautiful waterfalls and cliffs, is located at the entrance of the spa area, 14 km northwest of Nishi-Nasuno Station and 30 min. by bus. Fukuwata Spa is known for a park containing the Shiobara Imperial Villa, a summer resort for the Imperial Family, and rocks of various shapes in the valley. It is located 2 km upriver from Oami Spa. Shiogama Spa is situated in the beautiful valley called *Shiki-no-Sato* (lit. Four-Season Village). It is located 1 km upriver from Fukuwata Spa. Tranquil Shionoyu Spa, featuring waterfalls, is located 1.5 km from Shiogama Spa. Hataori Spa, once a resort for the upperclass during the Meiji period, is 500 m upriver from Shiogama Spa. Monzen Spa is the center of administration in Shiobara Town and is adjacent to Hataori Spa. The most popular of the spas is Furumachi Spa, which is 45 min. by bus from Nishi-Nasuno Station. The aforementioned seven spas all lie along the Hoki River Gorge.

The 14-km-long Shiobara-keikoku (Gorge) Walkway connects Oami Spa and the Hako-no-mori Play Park in the Furumachi Spa area. The therapeutic effects and hot-spring quality differ somewhat among each of the seven spas, but the weak saline water has temperatures ranging 32–74°C. It is efficacious for the treatment of rheumatism, neuralgia, gastroenteric problems and dermatitis.

Arayu Spa (Oku-Shiobara Spa) and Motoyu Spa are deeper in the mountains. Both spas are very quiet and feature the beauty of new leaves in spring and colored ones in autumn. A scenic road called the "Nichien Momiji (Maple) Line" connects the Shiobara Spa area and Kinugawa Spa near Nikko.

While passing through mountains along the slopes of Mt. Takahara (alt. 1,795 m), one can obtain a magnificent view along the road, especially from early October into early November when the colors of the leaves set the mountainside ablaze.

Nasu Plateau 14

Transportation: Entry to Nasu can be made from either Kuroiso Station on the JR Tohoku Main Line (164 km from Ueno in Tokyo, about 2 hrs. 25 min. by rapid train) or Nasu-Shiobara Station on the JR Tohoku Shinkansen. Use the Nasu Interchange when driving on the Tohoku Expressway.

This vast plateau spreads under the southern base of Mt. Chausu (alt. 1,915 m), the main peak of the Nasu Volcano Chain, which continually belches great clouds of smoke.

Overlooking the Kanto Plain, the plateau contains many hot springs. Several large sporting and recreational facilities stand along the well-developed highways. This area is highly regarded as a Kanto mountain resort, with many private villas owned by affluent people or leading companies located here.

The eastern part of this plateau is known as the location of the Nasu Imperial Villa. To the south of the villa are the Nasu International Country Club and the Lake Rindo Family Bokujo (Pasture), either of which can be reached in 25 min. by bus from Kuroiso Station.

The pasture spreading along the shore of Lake Rindo is filled with various recreational and sporting facilities especially suited for families. Southwest of the Imperial Villa is Nasu Safari Park (20 min. by bus from Kuroiso Station) and Minamigaoka Bokujo (Ranch)—a tourist spot complete with accommodations and recreational sports facilities (35 min. by bus from Kuroiso Station)—as well as *minshuku* (family inns), rental villas, pensions and lodges at Nasu Kogen (Plateau) Villages.

To the west of the plateau, one can find the 500,000-sq.-m Nasu Highland Park (1 hr. by bus from Kuroiso Station) with sports facilities, an amusement park and a wild bird park. Another point of interest is the Nasu Royal Center, which includes in-door recreational facilities, a dinner theater, a museum and hotels. 40 min. by bus from Kuroiso Station.

Itamuro Spa, discovered some 900 years ago, is located in the valley to the southwest, 35 min. by bus from Kuroiso Station.

Nasu Spas Area 14 : There are six main spas situated at the eastern foot of Mt. Chausu. Except for Nasu-Yumoto, the hot-spring waters are plain, with temperatures ranging 40-76°C and efficacious against rheumatism, neuralgia, gastroenteric ailments and dermatitis.

Shin-Nasu Spa (30 min. by bus from Kuroiso) at the entrance of the spas area is not a large town. *Ryokan* or Japanese-style inns are scattered through the woods in this tranquil spot. In contrast, Nasu-Yumoto Spa, located 1 km to the northwest of Shin-Nasu Spa and 35 min. by bus from Kuroiso Station at an altitude of 900 m, is a bustling spa town serving as the center of the spas area. Found about 1,300 years ago, this hot spring has sulfurous waters.

Yuzen Shrine: Located near Nasu-Yumoto, this shrine is dedicated to two "healing" Shinto deities — Onamuchi-no-Mikoto and Sukunahikona-no-Mikoto—and is celebrated for the *Sesshoseki*, or Death Stone, which is kept within a wooden enclosure at the back of the shrine. The stone, of pyroxene andesite, is 8.5 sq.m wide and 1.5 m high and lies on a barren hillside popularly called *Sai-no-Kawara* (the Styx Riverbed). Steam billows up from the ground and there is a strong smell of hydrogen sulfide around the stone. The name Death Stone derives from the fact that a number of animals have died near it.

An old tale recounts a strange episode dating back to the 1140s to 1150s when a beautiful girl named Tamamo was a favorite of ex-Emperor Toba (1103–1156). One night when all the lights were extinguished, the body of Tamamo was seen glowing with light. When the ex-Emperor suddenly became ill, the Court diviner traced the illness to Tamamo's supernatural light and, by dint of prayer, forced the girl to reveal her true identity—a "nine-tailed fox." The fox was hunted and fled to Nasu, where it turned into a stone that killed everything that touched it. The stone was later exorcised by Genno, a Buddhist priest of the 13th to 14th centuries. At the touch of his wand, it split asunder, whereupon a woman appeared before the priest and thanked him.

Volcano Highway: A scenic toll road that runs from Nasu-Yumoto Spa around the eastern foot of Mt. Chausu. The view of Nasu Plateau from the Nasu Observation Platform on the way is majestic. Along this highway are 5 spas—Benten (50 min. by bus from Kuroiso), Omaru (600 m north of Benten Spa), Asahi (2 km east of Omaru Spa), Kita (600 m north of Asahi Spa) and Yawata (3 km north of Nasu-Yumoto Spa). All are small, with only one place of accommodation at each, but they are known for the scenic beauty that surrounds them throughout the year. A ropeway to the summit of Mt. Chausu is available near Omaru Spa. The 800 m from the ropeway summit station to the summit of Mt. Chausu can be climbed in 30 min.

Along Ryomo and Mito Lines

Tochigi ☐15☐ ☎0282: Pop. 86,306. 1 hr. 20 min. from Asakusa in Tokyo by rapid train on the Tobu Nikko Line and 12 min. or 11 km from Oyama on the JR Ryomo Line. The city was the seat of the Tochigi Prefectural Government from 1871 to 1884.

The dated facades of the buildings recalling the prosperity of the past attract many visitors, especially from Tokyo. Mt. Ohira, with some of the most beautiful cherry trees in the Northern Kanto District; Ohirasan Shrine, where exquisite hydrangeas blossom, and Kinchakusan Park, celebrated for its azaleas—all can be found in the suburbs of the city.

Sano ☐15☐ ☎0283: Pop. 82,893. 18 min. or 16 km from Tochigi by the JR Ryomo Line. Major industries include apparel assembly, wood-working, and plastics. Sosoji Temple (Sano-Yakuyoke-Daishi) is known throughout the Kanto District. Ganzan-Daishi (912–985), who is worshipped at this temple, has been considered a guardian against disaster since olden times.

Ashikaga ☐15☐ ☎0284: Pop. 168,195. Located on the southwestern edge of Tochigi Prefecture along the border with Gumma Prefecture. The Watarase River flows through the center of the city. The textile industry has flourished here since the 11th century and, along with the machinery and chemical industries, constitutes the city's most important industry today. The city is also noted as the home of the

Ashikaga family, who founded the Muromachi Shogunate (1336–1573) in Kyoto.

A shrine erected in 1668 and dedicated to Confucius as well as a library stand 600 m northwest of the station on the site of Ashikaga Gakko, an old classical school.

According to one tradition, the Ashikaga Gakko was founded in the ninth century by Ono-no-Takamura (802–852), one of the best poets of his time. It was restored in 1432 by a lord called Uesugi Norizane (1411–1466), who invited a Buddhist priest to take charge of the school and imported many classical books from China. Several of the old books still used and preserved in the school library are National Treasures or Important Cultural Properties; the site is designated as a Place of Historical Importance.

Bannaji Temple ⁣15⁣: Belonging to the Shingon sect (Buzan school), this Buddhist temple is situated opposite the site of the Ashikaga Gakko. It was established in the 1190s by Ashikaga Yoshikane (d. 1199) on the premises of his mansion and given his Buddhist name Banna. Yoshikane was a famous general under Minamoto-no-Yoritomo, the first Kamakura Shogun. Thereafter, it became the family temple of the Ashikagas. The Main Hall (called *Omido* or *Dainichido*), dedicated to *Dainichi-Nyorai*, and the Belfry are Important Cultural Properties.

Ota ⁣15⁣ ☎0276: Pop. 135,813. 15 min., or 8 km southwest of Ashikaga on the Tobu Isesaki Line. The automobile, electronics, machinery and textile industries flourish here. Ota is noted as the home of Nitta Yoshisada, the general who overthrew the Kamakura Shogunate in 1333.

Daiko-in Temple ⁣15⁣: About 2.5 km northwest of Ota Station. This imposing Jodo-sect Buddhist temple is popularly called Donryu after the name of its first abbot, Donryu (1556–1623). It is said Donryu guards the health of all infants. Konryuji Temple, about 500 m north of this temple, is where Nitta Yoshisada is entombed.

Kiryu ⁣15⁣ ☎0277: Pop. 128,674. 1 hr. 40 min. from Asakusa in Tokyo on the Tobu Kiryu Line direct express. Textiles have traditionally been a major product throughout the Northern Kanto District, but textiles here are especially noted, ranking with Nishijin textiles of Kyoto. Production still continues today although modern industries such as the machinery and metal industries are active as well. The Morihide Textile Museum Yukari provides a wide variety of information about Kiryu textiles.

Yabuzuka ⁣15⁣: 7 min. by the Tobu Kiryu Line from Shin-Kiryu. The city contains the 50,000-sq.-m Japan Snake Center, which exhibits 100,000 reptiles of 300 species collected from all over the world; the Mikazukimura, a typical village of the late Edo period, reproduced on a large hill, and the Historical Folk Museum with exhibitions of many relics and artifacts found around the vicinity. Yabuzuka Spa is another attraction in this popular tourist town.

Ashio ⌜15⌟: Approximately 42 km from Kiryu. The city prospered through mining for 360 years after a vein of copper was discovered in 1610. Closed in 1973, the mine was revived as a tourist attraction called Ashio Copper Mine Sightseeing and the area now bustles with many tourists who visit the abandoned mine.

Isesaki ⌜15⌟ ☎0270: Pop. 113,421. 15 min. by JR from Maebashi. The city is located southwest of Maebashi and north of Saitama Prefecture across the Tone River. It is famed for *Isesaki-Meisen*, a traditionally handcrafted textile. Recent years have stimulated the rapid development of the transportation machinery, food and electronics industries, but the wool textile industry is also active so that Isesaki remains a city of textiles. This is the terminal of the Tobu Isesaki Line originating at Asakusa Station in Tokyo. The entire 114.5-km distance is covered in 2 hrs. 30 min.

Yuki ⌜15⌟ ☎0296: Pop. 53,425. About 10 min. or 7 km from Oyama by the JR Mito Line. It is the home of the *Yuki-Tsumugi*—a traditional, hand-woven silk fabric, the weaving technique of which dates from the Muromachi period (1336–1573). Elaborately woven from hand-spun silk yarn, it is characterized by a very tasteful design and sober color. The actual weaving process can be seen at the Senshoku Shiryokan (Dye Museum).

Shimodate ⌜15⌟ ☎0296: Pop 65,534. About 20 min. or 17 km from Oyama by the JR Mito Line. It is the junction for the Mo-oka Railway, which runs 42 km northeast to Motegi via Mo-oka. Shimodate is also the starting point for the Joso Line of the Kanto Railway running southeast to Toride on the JR Joban Line (51.1 km). It is the largest commercial town along the JR Mito Line.

Mo-oka ⌜15⌟ ☎0285: Pop. 60,330. About 30 min. or 16.5 km from Shimodate by the Mo-oka Railway. It is the distribution center for agricultural products in this neighborhood. The cotton textile known as *Mo-oka-momen* was a specialty of the town until the end of the Meiji period. However, the western portion of the city has now been turned into an industrial park.

Mashiko ⌜15⌟: 25.2 km away from Shimodate by Mo-oka Railway. The city has long been known as the home of *Mashiko-yaki* (Mashiko ware). A kind of folk pottery, it is admired for its simplicity and fresh beauty. Firing of the kilns started in 1855. Today, about 200 kilns— large and small, in and around the town—annually turn out pottery worth some ¥2.4 to ¥2.5 billion. A noted potter, Hamada Shoji (1897 –1978), designated as an Intangible Cultural Property, introduced Mashiko ware throughout Japan by building a kiln in this town in 1924. Its worldwide reputation is also due to Bernard Leach (1887– 1979), an English potter who was given the Second Order of the Sacred Treasure for his contribution to this art.

The production process of *Mashiko-yaki* can be seen at the Tsuka-moto Pottery. Besides the Kyonan Center, which displays and sells a wide variety of ceramics, the area is full of pottery stores. From late

April to early May and from late October to early November, the city holds a big pottery sale every year. Mashiko Sankokan Museum, a 25-min. walk from Mashiko Station, is a handicraft museum on the premises of Hamada-Shoji's house. Exhibitions include pottery, metalwork, glass, textiles and woodwork from all over the world.

Motegi 15 : 42 km from Shimodate. Many farm products are marketed here, including *shiitake* (a species of brown mushrooms) and leaf tobacco.

Iwase 15 : This agricultural town is located in the Tsukuba Mountain Chain 30 km from Oyama, taking about 35 min. by the JR Mito Line. Tomiya Kannon (popularly known as Oyamadera), an old Buddhist temple of the Tendai sect, stands 2 km north of the station. Its three-story pagoda, dating from 1465, is an Important Cultural Property.

The town is also celebrated for its varieties of cherry trees. The 1-km-long approach (lined with old cherry trees) to Isobe Shrine—about 1.6 km northwest of Haguro Station on the JR Mito Line—has been designated as an Outstanding Scenic Place. Usually blooming from early to mid-April, they are known as the Sakuragawa cherries after the name of a stream formerly called Sakuragawa (Cherry River) flowing at the back of the shrine. It is said to be the scene of a noh play titled Sakuragawa.

Rakuhoji Temple, also known as Amabiki Kannon, is situated halfway up Mt. Amabiki (alt. 409 m) of the Tsukuba Mountain Chain. Said to have been founded in 586, this Shingon-sect temple has an extensive compound that measures 66,000 sq.m in area.

Inada 20 : Located 41 km from Oyama, taking about 50 min. by the JR Mito Line. This is the station for Sainenji Temple (popularly called the Inada Gobo), 1.5 km to the west. It is also the site of the hermitage where Saint Shinran (1173–1262), founder of the Jodo-Shinshu sect of Buddhism, stayed from 1217 to 1225. He completed the six-volume Kyogyo-Shinsho, the fundamental canon of the sect, here in 1224. Inada is part of Kasama (see below) and is known for the production of quality granite from the neighboring hills.

Kasama 20 ☎0296: Pop. 31,555. About 55 min. or 44 km from Oyama by the JR Mito Line. Once the castle town of the Makino family, it has developed as the shrine town of the popular Kasama Inari, standing 1.5 km north of the station. The shrine was established in dedication to Ukanomitama-no-Mikoto, a Shinto deity. The annual number of pilgrims to the shrine is said to exceed a million. The Chrysanthemum Festival held in the shrine precincts from mid-October till the end of November attracts large crowds of people from the surrounding districts.

Since the hills in the vicinity are composed of granite, good-quality clay the pottery can easily be obtained here. Indeed, the city has been a local center of the ceramic industry since 1772 and *Kasama-yaki* (Kasama ware) is a specialty here.

At Kataniwa, some 7 km northwest of Kasama Station, stands Ryogonji Temple of the Rinzai sect. Its front gate and a wooden statue of the Thousand-Handed *Kannon* housed in this temple are Important Cultural Properties. *Hime-haruzemi*, a rare species of cicada that breed on the temple grounds, are a Natural Monument.

Area 10. Nikko National Park

The park area sprawls over 1,406.98 sq.km, extends into Tochigi, Gumma, Fukushima and Niigata prefectures, and includes the Oku-Nikko (Inner Nikko) region as well as Nasu and Shiobara spas. For Shiobara and Nasu, refer to Area 9.

Besides its magnificent mountain scenery, complete with rivers, cascades, waterfalls, lakes and ancient trees, Nikko also has the finest handiwork of man in the mausoleum of Tokugawa Ieyasu (1542–1616), founder of the Tokugawa Shogunate, and that of his grandson Iemitsu. One scarcely knows which to admire more, the mausoleum themselves or the setting in which they are placed—a bold essay by Nature in landscape gardening. It is scarcely surprising, therefore, that foreign visitors should regard Nikko as by far the most interesting spot in Japan. The Japanese have a saying, "Never say *kekko* (magnificent) until you've seen Nikko," which is indicative of their own appreciation of one of the wonder spots of their land.

Nikko is also noted as having one of the richest deciduous forests in this country in addition to its beautiful highland acerose forests. Even the maples, which are especially attractive when tinted in autumn, are of diverse varieties. The greater part of this national park is composed of State forests. Indeed, this region has such a variety of flora, fauna, geographical and mineral wealth that it is like a vast natural museum.

Nikko is one of the most popular of the 28 national parks in Japan. Here is a region where tourists may spend their holidays, religious devotees may visit shrines and temples, and students of natural science or history may do research in their respective fields. In this great national park, there are facilities for camping, mountain climbing, sailing, angling, skiing and skating. The park possesses a number of splendid hot-spring resorts noted for their recuperative and curative effects. Moreover, Nikko may be enjoyed throughout the year for each of its four seasons has its own special attractions.

TRANSPORTATION

Rail: To get to Nikko, one can take the JR Tohoku Main Line or Tohoku Shinkansen, then change trains to the JR Nikko Line at Utsunomiya (a total of 150 km from Tokyo), but the Tobu Railway Nikko Line is more convenient since it is not necessary to change trains at all (total of 135.5 km from Asakusa, Tokyo. 1 hr.43 min. by limited express with comfortable accommodation). This line can also

be used to get to the Kinugawa area by changing lines at Shimoima-
ichi Station for the Tobu Railway Kinugawa Line. (Direct limited
expresses are also available.)

To get to Oze, convenient stations are Numata on the JR Joetsu
Line and Jomokogen on the JR Joetsu Shinkansen. Other possible
stations include Kinugawa-Onsen on the Tobu Railway Kinugawa
Line, Aizu-Kogen on the Yagan Railway Aizu Kinugawa Line and
Koide on the JR Joetsu Line. After getting off, take the bus for Oze
partway and then walk.

Road: To get to Nikko by car, take the Tohoku Expressway to
Utsunomiya. Then at the Utsunomiya Interchange, switch to the
Nikko-Utsunomiya Highway and get off at the Nikko Interchange
(150 km from Tokyo). To get to Kinugawa, get off the Nikko-
Utsunomiya Highway at the Imaichi Interchange and take National
Highway 121, which links Imaichi and Aizu-Wakamatsu.

To reach Kinugawa from Nikko, take National Highway 119
(linking Nikko and Utsunomiya) and then National Highway 121 at
Imaichi. Take National Highway 120 (linking Nikko and Numata) to
get to Oku-Nikko from Nikko. To get to Oze, take the Kan-etsu
Expressway and change to Highway 120 at the Numata Interchange.
Then, change to National Highway 401 at Kamata and head for
Oshimizu. National Highway 401 has branches at Tokura for
Hatomachi Toge (Pass) and Fujimishita. If one's first destination is
Ozenuma, head for Oshimizu, but if it is Ozegahara, head for Hato-
machi Toge or Fujimishita. Automobiles can only go as far as these
three points. After that, the rest of the way must be covered on foot.

Along JR Nikko Line

The JR Nikko Line branches off from the JR Tohoku Main Line at
Utsunomiya, and the following section covers this 41-km area:

Kanuma ⌷15⌷ ☎0289: Pop. 90,149. 124 km from Tokyo. The
beginning of another avenue of cedars that runs all the way to Nikko.
They can be seen from the train window. The chief products of this
town are wooden fittings, hemp yarn and rope, horticulture soil called
Kanuma-tsuchi and *satsuki-bonsai* (dwarf azalea trees).

Imaichi ⌷14⌷ ☎0288: Pop. 55,766. 144 km from Tokyo. It is the
meeting place of three old highways: from the south—the Reiheishi
Kaido (Kanuma Road), by which Imperial messengers used to travel
to the Nikko mausoleum; from the southeast—the Onari Kaido
(Nikko Highway), and from the north—the Aizu Road.

This is where one can find stately rows of ancient cedars on both
sides of the road leading to Nikko. Planting was begun in 1625 by
Matsudaira Masatsuna (1577-1648), *daimyo* of Kawagoe (now, in
Saitama Prefecture), as an offering to Toshogu Shrine. The trees and
their banks are now specially protected as a Natural Monument and
a Place of Historical Importance.

Nikko ⌷14⌷ ☎0288

Pop. 20,944.   The terminal of both the JR Nikko Line (Nikko Station) and the Tobu Railway (Tobu-Nikko Station). These stations are quite close to each other on the right bank of the Daiya River (a tributary of the Kinugawa River), along which the city stretches on rising ground to the northwest. Buses are available from the two stations to various points.

Nikko consists of two sections. The eastern section has a single, wide street leading from the stations to the Sacred Bridge over a distance of 1.7 km. This forms the older portion of the city. The western section beyond the bridge is called Nishimachi or Irimachi. The mausoleum and temples are located in this section.

Souvenirs of Nikko include lacquerware and wooden pieces such as hand-carved trays, the sleeping cat and the three monkeys. *Yuba*, made from soybeans (a dried, high-protein food), is a special product.

ANNUAL EVENTS

The Spring Festival of the Toshogu Shrine: May 17–18 and October 17.   The main event of the Spring Festival is the *Sennin Gyoretsu* (1,000-person procession), with various groups of people dressed in the costumes of *samurai*, priests and other figures of the Tokugawa period (1603–1867). On the morning of May 18, the spirits of Tokugawa Ieyasu, Toyotomi Hideyoshi and Minamoto-no-Yoritomo, each an important historical/military figure, are called forth and placed into their respective *mikoshi* (portable shrines), which are then taken in procession to *Otabisho* (Sojourning Hall). There, sacred music is played, offerings are made and a sacred dance called *Yaotome-no-mai* is performed. The performers are dressed in elaborate silk costumes and sing to the accompaniment of an orchestra composed of *komabue* (a kind of flute) and *hichiriki* (flageolets). After the service, the portable shrines are taken back to *Shin-yosha* (Sacred Palanquin House).

In addition, on May 17, *Yabusame* (horseback archery) is held to foster chivalry and valor. With horsemen dressed in the hunting attire of warriors of the Middle Ages (1192–1603), it takes place on the road connecting the Toshogu and Futarasan shrines.

Autumn Festival: October 17. It it conducted on a smaller scale than the Spring Festival, but the portable shrines are again carried to the *Otabisho*.

Gohan-shiki (Rice Ceremony): April 2.   The most popular rite of Rinnoji Temple in *Sambutsudo* (the Main Hall of the temple built in 1648). At the end of the ceremony, toys, vegetables and fruit are thrown to the crowd assembled in the grounds. In feudal times, the *daimyo* (feudal lords) who visited Nikko to pay homage at Toshogu Shrine were required to eat huge bowls of rice that were placed before them. Priests stood by with staffs to make sure the rice was eaten since it was regarded as a gift from the deity of the shrine and, therefore, not to be spurned. Eating the rice was thus a test of the lord's loyalty, and he had to submit to all the indignities heaped upon him by the priests on this occasion.

Tokonojinji: April 2. Another festival held on this night in *Sambutsu do*. This first includes the kindling of the *goma*, or holy fire of invocation, and then a dance by priests with their staffs and fans to the accompaniment of a song.

Ennen-no-mai (Longevity Dance): May 17. Comparable in importance with the *Gohan-shiki*, it is held in front of *Sambutsudo* and is performed by two priests clad in beautiful silk robes, wearing short swords and carrying fans. The dance is supposed to resemble the old *dengaku* dance of the Kamakura period (1192-1333).

Yayoi Matsuri of the Futarasan Shrine: April 13-17. The *Yayoi Matsuri* (March Festival) of the shrine is combined with the festivals of the subsidiary shrines, Hongu and Takino-o. On April 13 the *mikoshi* (portable shrines) of the three shrines are fitted up. On April 14 a Takino-o Shrine *mikoshi*, accompanied by priests and bands of men and women musicians and dancers, is carried in procession from Futarasan Shrine along the main road to Takino-o Shrine. Here, it remains till the 16th when it is taken back to its starting place via the *Gyojado* (Hall of Ascetic Practices). On the 17th, a ceremony is held in front of the three *mikoshi* placed in the Oratory. After the ceremony, the mikoshi are carried in a great procession to Hongu Shrine, where an ancient ceremony is performed before they are escorted back to Futarasan Shrine.

Tohai Matsuri: July 31-August 7. It consists of a visit to the Futarasan Inner Shrine on Mt. Nantai (alt. 2,484 m) by pilgrims, who must first cleanse their bodies by bathing in Lake Chuzenji. Formerly, women were not allowed to take part in this pilgrimage. The climb starts at Futarasan Chugushi Shrine, where the pilgrims assemble on the shores of the lake in the evening, heading for the top of the mountain as soon as the clock strikes midnight. They are clad in white and carry small lanterns and sticks. The objective of the early start is to see the sunrise on the summit. The distance is about 8 km, and although the upper part of the mountain is very steep, ordinary climbers can accomplish it in 4 hrs. Each climber has to pay a fee to the shrine. About 10,000 pilgrims make the ascent during the first week of August.

Waraku Odori: Friday and Saturday evening around August 7. Started in 1913 for the factory workers, it is a folk dance performed in the open space by the copper workers of the Furukawa Electric Co., Ltd. Shown to Emperor Taisho (grandfather of the present Emperor) during a summer visit here, it soon became popular. At present, tens of thousands of people participate in the festival.

Refer to the supplement for details regarding the "i" System Information Center in Nikko.

PLACES OF INTEREST IN NIKKO MAUSOLEUM

Tokugawa Ieyasu died in 1616 and was temporarily buried at Kunozan in Shizuoka Prefecture. The following year, his remains were transferred to Nikko and permanently interred here in accordance with instructions left by Ieyasu himself. In the same year, the Emperor conferred upon him the title Tosho Daigongen, or the "East Illuminating Incarnation of a Bodhisattva." It was not until 1634, however, that the construction of the mausoleum began. It was completed in 1636, 20 years after Ieyasu's death. It was the third Shogun, Iemitsu (1604-1651), the grandson of Ieyasu, who performed this act of piety. His example was followed by his successor Ietsuna, who provided for the maintenance of the shrine by granting it a domain. At the same time, an Imperial prince was invited to preside over the shrine, a custom that was followed until the fall of the Tokugawa Shogunate in 1868. The princes usually resided in Edo for political reasons and visited Nikko three times a year.

The shrine structures, many of which are designated as National Treasures, narrowly escaped destruction at the time of the Meiji Restoration (1868), when some of the Tokugawa troops took possession of the buildings and prepared to defend them. Fortunately, Itagaki Taisuke (1837-1919), a commander in the Imperial army and a leading statesman of his time, was able to persuade the Tokugawa adherents to evacuate the buildings, thereby saving the shrine structures.

No limit seems to have been set upon expenditures for the construction of the original mausoleum and shrine. The finest artists and most expert craftsmen were summoned to Nikko from all over the country at government expense. They were then organized into groups, which competed with one another in producing the finest work.

When the construction of the shrine was started, a type of architecture and decoration peculiar to the Edo period had not yet developed, and for the most part the style followed is that of the preceding Momoyama period (1573-1598). As 80% of the carpenters and artisans engaged in the work came from Kyoto or Nara, this was only natural. The mausoleum of Iemitsu and the adjacent structure, which were built about 17 years later, show traces of the transition to the Edo style.

The gorgeousness of the decorations is largely the result of the immense amount of gold leaf used in gilding. Altogether, it is said that 2,489,000 sheets were used, each of 25 sq. cm (a quantity which would cover 24,000 sq.m). It is estimated that the timber used in the building, if the pieces were laid end to end, would extend 530 km or somewhat more than the length of the Tokaido Main Line between Tokyo and Kyoto. Some 15,000 men worked on the buildings during the two years it took to erect them.

The buildings are constantly under repair. During the Tokugawa

Shogunate, it was the custom to repair them every 20 years, and since the repairs took ten years and the collection of material another ten years, the work was constantly in progress.

Information for Visitors to the Shrines and Temples

Visitors are required to pay a fee for admittance to Toshogu Shrine, Rinnoji Temple, the Treasure Museum, Futarasan Shrine and the *Oku-no-In* (Inner Precincts) containing the tomb of Ieyasu.

The shrines and temples are open, as follows:

8 a.m. to 5 p.m. between April and October

8 a.m. to 4 p.m. between November and March

The locations of the various shrines and temples are shown on the accompanying map 　19　. Six hrs. may be necessary for the visitor to inspect everything, but it is advisable to spread this over two days.

Sacred Bridge: An Important Cultural Property. Also called Mihashi or Shinkyo, it crosses the Daiya River parallel to the Nikko Bridge and is used only on ceremonial occasions. It has been partly opened to the public after 330 years, during which time entry by commoners was prohibited.

The bridge is 27 m long and 6 m wide and arches over the river in a graceful curve. Tradition has it that the bridge marks the spot where priest Shodo (735–817), founder of Futarasan Shrine on Lake Chuzenji, crossed the torrent on the backs of two huge serpents when seeking to reach the summit of Mt. Nantai. The bridge is lacquered red with gilt metal ornaments and rests on two huge stone supports shaped like a *torii* gate at each end.

The original bridge, built in 1636 for the use of the *shogun* and Imperial messengers on their visits to the shrines, was destroyed by floods in 1902. It was rebuilt in 1907.

The shrines are situated on the opposite side of the Daiya River on a hillside in the midst of a forest of ancient cedars. Just across Nikko Bridge is a monument erected by Matsudaira Masatsuna, who was one of the two commissioners charged with the construction of Ieyasu's shrine. Its inscription, dated April 17, 1648, states that he presented the cedars planted during the preceding 20 years to the Tosho Daigongen. The cedars are located in the precincts of the Nikko shrines and along the road from Yamasugebashi (now Sacred Bridge) past several villages in the neighboring provinces, extending for a total length of over 40 km.

It is popularly said that since Matsudaira Masatsuna could not afford to contribute expensive offerings to the shrines, he devised the less expensive but more tedious plan of planting avenues of cedars along the approaches to the shrines. The planting took more than 20 years and was not completed till 1651.

Fires and storms in places along the roads have caused gaps in the rows, but some 13,000 of the original trees are still standing, although exhaust fumes by passing cars are killing off a considerable number of the trees.

The wide flight of steps to the left of Matsudaira's monument passes the *Otabisho*, or Sojourning Hall, and leads to the shrines. The stone steps to the right, called Honguzaka Slope, lead to Hongu Shrine and Shihonryuji Temple.

Hongu Shrine: Popularly called Futarasan-Hongu, the shrine is entered by way of a stone *torii* gate, 4.3 m high. The first building is the *Haiden* (Oratory), and behind it is the *Honden* (Main Hall). Both are lacquered vermilion and decorated with carvings. The shrine was established in 790 by the priest Shodo and is one of the oldest in Nikko, but the present buildings date back only to the end of the 17th century when the shrine was rebuilt after being destroyed by fire.

Shihonryuji Temple: Located behind Hongu Shrine, the temple was founded in 766 by the priest Shodo. After the original building was burned down, it was replaced at the end of the 17th century by the present temple with a three-story pagoda. In the main hall is enshrined an image of the *Senju Kannon* or Thousand-Handed *Kannon* (in the center), with *Godaison* and an image of the founder, which he is believed to have carved, on the left and right, respectively.

Rinnoji Temple ⬜14⬜ : A Tendai-sect Buddhist temple. It is located on both sides of *Omotesando* (Main Approach), an avenue leading to Toshogu Shrine.

To the west of the *Kuromon* (Black Gate), which serves as the main gate, and across *Omotesando* is the *Hombo* (Abbot's Residence). General Ulysses S. Grant, the 18th President of the USA, stayed here for eight days when he visited Nikko in July 1879. East of the Black Gate is the *Goreiden* (Spirit Hall), where the tablets of the successive superiors, who were drawn from the Imperial Family, are enshrined. The hall is a superb specimen of the highest order of Buddhist art. A black-lacquered altar fills the entire inner portion of the central chamber. On the altar is a large reliquary, ablaze with gold leaf, while its doors are embossed with the Imperial crest. It contains the tablet of Prince Kitashirakawa, the last of the Imperial abbots of Nikko. The abbot's beautiful private garden, Shoyo-en, and the treasures in the hall can be viewed.

In front of the Main Hall, an aged cherry tree over 200 years old still bears blossoms of a prized yellow variety. Named *Kongo-zakura*, this tree is specially protected as a Natural Monument.

The main hall of Rinnoji Temple is called the *Sambutsudo* (Three Buddhas' Hall) because of the three gigantic gilt wooden images it contains. The Thousand-Handed *Kannon* (8.5 m high) is on the right, *Amida-Nyorai* in the center and *Bato Kannon* on the left. The *Bato Kannon*, with a horse's head on its forehead, is believed to be the incarnation of animal spirits and is thus worshipped as the guardian of animals. The hall also houses the portraits of priests Tenkai and Ryogen. Tenkai (1536-1643), who is generally known by the posthumous title of Jigen-Daishi, enjoyed the full confidence of Ieyasu and once presided over Rinnoji Temple. Ryogen (912-985), posthumously called Gansan-Daishi or Jie-Daishi, was, like Tenkai, a high priest of the Tendai sect. Erected in 1648, the *Sambutsudo* is the largest structure in Nikko, measuring over 32 m long, 25 m wide and nearly 26 m high. It is an Important Cultural Property. The original hall is said to have been established in 848 by a priest named Ennin (794 –864), who is generally known by the posthumous name of Jikaku-Daishi. The interior is constructed in the *Chudo-zukuri* style modeled after *Kompon Chudo* on Mt. Hiei near Kyoto. *Gohotendo* stands on the northern side of *Sambutsudo* and enshrines three Buddhist deities: *Daikokuten, Bishamonten* and *Benzaiten.*

On a nearby elevated site stands a bronze pillar about 13 m high called *Sorinto*, which was erected in 1643 by Tenkai to repel evil influences. It is similar in form to the one on Mt. Hiei. The top is decorated with 24 *Kinrei* (Golden Bells) and *Kinyoraku* (Golden Trinkets), while the bottom is used to store 1,000 sutras. The two *Itowappu Toro* (bronze lanterns) standing at the entrance of this tower were donated by silk yarn merchants in 1648.

Toshogu Shrine ⬚19⬚

After leaving Rinnoji Temple, it is only a couple of minutes' walk to Toshogu Shrine. The broad flight of ten stone steps is called the *Sennin Ishidan* (Thousand-Person Stone Steps) because in the early days the lower classes were not allowed to enter the temple, but were permitted to assemble on these steps for festivals. The stairs are designed so that the higher one climbs, the narrower the width and the lower the height of the steps to create a feeling of depth. The huge granite *torii* gate at the top of the steps stands 9 m high. The bronze tablet on the cross-stone is inscribed with the name of the shrine in the handwriting of Emperor Gomizuno-o (1596–1680), whose consort was a daughter of Hidetada, the second Tokugawa Shogun.

Goju-no-To (Five-Story Pagoda): The 35-m-high tower stands on the left of the *torii*. Its first-story architrave is decorated with the twelve zodiacal signs. There are black, lacquered doors on each side of every story, with the Tokugawa crest emblazoned on all above the first story. The present building dates from 1818.

Omotemon (Front Gate): Also called *Niomon*, or Deva Gate. 9 m in height, it stands at the top of a flight of stone steps. On the capitals of the front and inside pillars are carvings of chrysanthemums, and on those at the side are lion's heads, tree peonies and other designs. The lintels of the doorway and the projections from the central pillars bear the Tokugawa crest, while images of the two Deva Kings are set in the outside niches of the gate.

Within the gate, a path leads to the middle court. On the right are three Sacred Storehouses (*Sanjinko*), with the upper one showing two elephants carved in relief said to have been executed from drawings by Kano Tanyu (1602–1674). This was before any elephants had been brought to Japan. Since he drew the elephants based on written descriptions, the ears and tails appear different from real ones.

Shinkyusha: The stable for the accommodation of the sacred horse. Decorated with carvings of eight monkeys, it is the only nonlacquered structure in the precincts. In the second panel from the left is the celebrated simian trinity, referred to as "See no Evil, Speak no Evil, Hear no Evil," with one monkey shown covering his eyes, another his mouth and a third his ears. According to one legend, the carvings of monkeys will cure horse diseases. In front of the stable is a large *koyamaki* (umbrella pine), 25 m in height and 1.5 m in diameter, said to have been brought from Mt. Koya in Kii Province (now, Waka-yama Prefecture) and planted by Tokugawa Iemitsu. The font for holy water (*Suibansha*) is made of a solid block of granite. The second bronze *torii* gate is in front. *Kyozo* (Sutra Library) stands to the left. In it nearly 6,500 volumes of the Buddhist sutras are kept in a large octagonal, revolving bookcase 6 m high and 4.6 m in diameter. The rows of stone, bronze and iron lanterns in front of the upper storehouse and below the stone railing were presented by a great number of *daimyo* (feudal lords).

Ascending the front steps, the visitor will notice *Tobikomi-no-Shishi* (Leaping Lions) carved in the solid stones that serve as the main pillars of the stone balustrade. This spot forms the middle court. To the right is the *Shoro* (Belfry) and to the left the *Koro* (Drum Tower), both about 13 m high. Under a gigantic cedar near the belfry stands a bronze candelabrum, a present from the Netherlands. Nearby is a bell presented by the king of Korea. The bronze lantern across the way and the revolving lantern in front of the drum tower were also presented by the Netherlands in 1634. The crests of the Tokugawas on the lantern are upside-down, probably by mistake.

Honjido (Yakushido): One of the few edifices in the precincts with a Buddhist atmosphere. It was famous for the columns covered with metallic ornaments in the open portico for worshippers as well as for its huge *Naki-ryu* (Crying Dragon), a picture drawn in India ink by Kano Yasunobu (1607–1685) on the ceiling of the nave. Unfortunately, this edifice was destroyed by fire in 1961. It was called Naki-ryu because when visitors clapped their hands beneath it, the echoes made it seem as if the dragon had groaned. The reconstruction of this building was completed in 1968, with the present dragon painted by Katayama Nampu, a leading contemporary artist.

Yomeimon Gate: The Sunlight Gate at the top of the steps is the most elaborate gate in Japan. Named after one of the twelve gates of the Imperial Palace in Kyoto, this gate is designated as a National Treasure. All the art that attained such great perfection during this period was lavished on it. The gate is popularly called *Higurashi-no-Mon* (Twilight Gate), implying that one would like to continue look-ing at it until twilight falls. The characters on the tablet denoting the name of the shrine were written by Emperor Gomizuno-o. *Samurai* of humble rank were admitted only as far as this gate in those days, while higher-ranked *samurai* could proceed farther only by laying aside their swords.

The gate is a 12-columned, two-story structure, with *Irimoya* or "hip-gable" ends on the right and left and cuspid gables on the four sides. Its dimensions are: length 7 m, width 4.4 m and height 11.1 m. The brackets of the two stories are of the two-corbeled type, while male and female *kylins* (an imaginary animal in China of good omen) are carved on the beams under the gables. The rafter-ends of the upper story are decorated with dragons' heads and those at the four corners with the figures of dragons and clouds—all set in gold. The beam-ends of the upper story are also decorated with chiseled figures of dragons' heads with horses' legs and those in the lower story with lions' heads, both painted white. On the central beam in front of the second story is the figure of a white dragon. The balcony on the upper story is flanked by a railing depicting a group of Chinese children at play. All the brackets supporting the balcony are designed in the shape of tree peonies and lions, while between them are the carvings of a Chinese prince, sages and some immortals.

The drawings of two dragons decorate the ceiling of the porticos. The one nearer the entrance is known as the *Nobori-ryu*, or ascending dragon, originally drawn by Kano Tanyu (1602-1674), while the inner one is known as *Kudari-ryu*, or descending dragon, drawn by Kano Yasunobu (1613-1685). The columns, made of zelkova wood, are painted white and decorated with carvings of clouds and medallions of birds, beasts and flowers in bas-relief.

Two tigers are carved on one of the central columns, with the natural grain of the wood being cleverly used to represent the fur. They are called *Mokume-no-Tora* (Wood-grain Tigers). The patterns on one of the columns were purposely carved upside-down to dissipate the jealousy of evil spirits. This column is called *Sakasa-bashira* (Inverted Column) or *Mayoke-no-Hashira* (Evil-averting Column).

Yomeimon Gate is flanked by low fences and continued by galleries running east and west for over 223 m. The upper part of the front panels displays medallions of pines, bamboos, plums, phoenixes and pheasants, while the lower part depicts cranes, wild ducks and other waterfowl.

Shin-yosha (Sacred Palanquin House): Inside the gate to the west is a repository for the three *mikoshi* (portable shrines) used in the annual festival. The portable shrines are so heavy that several people are required to carry them. On the ceiling of this building are three large *tennyo* (heavenly maidens) painted by Kano Ryotaku, while the friezes depict flowers and birds painted in gorgeous colors.

Kaguraden (Sacred Dance Hall): East of the palanquin house is a slightly smaller building. The basket of flowers in the gilded panel at the right-hand corner was carved from a design by Kano Korenobu (1753-1808). The flowers are Japanese, but the basket is thought to have been copied from one used by early Dutch traders. This is the only carving in the precincts showing Western influence.

Upper Shrine Office: Opposite *Kaguraden* (Sacred Dance Hall). It was formerly used as *Gomado* (Incense Hall), where the holy fire of invocation was kindled during the recital of prayers. Carvings of carp and flowers cover the brackets, columns, friezes, etc.

Karamon (Chinese Gate): This National Treasure measures 3 m long and 2 m wide. On the ridge of the front gable is the bronze figure of a fabulous animal called *tsutsuga* that watches over all buildings at night, while dragons surround the ridges of the east and west gables. The pillars and doors are inlaid with carved ornaments of imported wood. On the right and left pillars in front are carved figures in relief of ascending and descending dragons, and on the borders of the doors are plums and bamboo in relief. The door panels are decorated with carvings of plums, chrysanthemums and tree peonies, the ceiling has a carved figure of a fairy playing a harp and the transom is sculptured with Chinese saints and immortals on all corners. The sculpture in the front part of the gate was made from a single tree and depicts 26 sages in three rows. The carving is designed so that all of the faces can be seen when viewed from the front.

To the right and left of the gate is the beautiful windowed wall (*sukibei*), also referred to as the *mizugaki* (sacred fence), enclosing *Haiden* (Oratory) and *Honden* (Main Hall). Between the gate and the oratory is a short, covered corridor, where visitors are requested to take off their shoes before entering the Oratory.

Haiden (Oratory): A National Treasure. The outer hall of the Main Hall, the Oratory and Main Hall are the chief edifices of the shrine. The roof of the Oratory is designed in the "hip-gable" style to the right and left, with a triangular dormer window in front. The five metaled steps of the open ante-hall lead into the Oratory, which is divided into three sections, including antechambers on the right and left. In the Oratory proper, the lacquered pillars are encased in metallic settings. The friezes over the lintel-pieces depict paulownia, bamboo, plums and pines together with phoenixes, pheasants and other birds. The coffered ceilings display dragons against a bluish back ground, while over the lintels are hung the portraits of 36 poets, painted by Tosa Mitsuoki (1617–1691), with their works indicated by the calligraphy of Emperor Gomizuno-o. At the back of the chamber is the sacred mirror, 80 cm in diameter, which is believed to represent the holy spirit of the deity.

The eastern antechamber was formerly reserved for the *shogun* and the three Tokugawa families of Owari, Kii and Mito. The panels consist of inlaid flowers of paulownia and Chinese phoenixes, while the friezes show flowers and birds arranged in a circular pattern.

The western antechamber was intended for the chief abbot of Rinnoji Temple, who was a member of the Imperial Family. The decoration of the panels and friezes is similar in style to that of the other chamber. The mats in the Oratory have special patterned borders.

Between *Haiden* and *Honden* is a passage chamber called the *Ishi-no-Ma* (Stone Room), with a matted floor resting on a stone pavement. The passage chamber is designated as a National Treasure.

Honden (Main Hall): A National Treasure. Measuring about 16 m long, 10 m wide, and 14 m high, it is approached by descending three copper-plated steps from *Haiden* to *Ishi-no-Ma* and then ascending five similar steps. The "hip-gable" roof has double rafters and double-corbeled brackets, and the ridgepole has crossed wooden beams at each end. Phoenixes are carved below the roof, while at the rafter-ends are the heads of tapirs, said to have the power of devouring bad dreams. The friezes and other parts are decorated as in the oratory. The paneled door in front is closed to ordinary visitors. The interior of the sanctum is divided into three apartments: *Gejin* (Outer Chamber); *Naijin* (Inner Chamber), and *Nai-Naijin* (Innermost Chamber). In the Innermost Chamber surrounded by specimens of art of the highest workmanship is the splendid, gold-lacquered shrine called the *Gokuden* (Sacred Palace), wherein are enshrined Tokugawa Ieyasu and associated deities Toyotomi Hideyoshi and Minamoto-no-Yoritomo.

From the terrace between *Yomeimon* and *Karamon* gates, the visitor proceeds through the decorated, vermilion-lacquered corridor of the enclosure. In the eastern open corridor is a gateway over which a small cat is carved. This is the famous *Nemuri-Neko* (Sleeping Cat), popularly said to be the work of Hidari-Jingoro, a noted sculptor.

Hidari means "Left-handed." It is said that he was so skillful and famous that his comrades became jealous of his craftsmanship and one of them cut off his right hand. Thereafter, he carved with his left hand. Hence, the name "Left-handed." He is a kind of legendary master sculptor. There are no rats in the shrine building because it is said the "Sleeping Cat" keeps all the rats and mice away.

A few steps after passing through this gate, one comes to *Saka-shitamon* Gate, which is decorated with fine carvings on the door-pillars, cross-beams and ceiling. The paved approach ascends more than 200 steps, and at the top is *Okusha* or Inner Precincts, at the entrance of which stands a bronze *torii* gate with a tablet. Alongside the *torii* gate are the *Akaganegura* (Copper Storehouse) and another oratory. Behind the oratory stands a gate called *Inukimon* (a bronze gate over 3.5 m high) cast in solid bronze, inside which is the *Hoto*, or the tomb of Tokugawa Ieyasu shaped like a small bronze pagoda, five m high and one m in diameter. The back of the door bears an inscription stating that when the stone tomb was damaged by a severe earthquake in 1683, it was replaced with a bronze tomb at the command of the *shogun*. The tomb is enclosed within a stone balustrade. In front of the tomb are a bronze flower vase shaped like a lotus flower and a bronze stork incense burner. A pair of bronze *komainu* (mythical dogs which it is popularly believed drive off evil spirits) sits in front of the gate.

In the days of the Tokugawa Shogunate, the sacred precincts inside *Sakashitamon* Gate were forbidden ground, even to the privileged class. Only on the occasion of a bicentennial festival was the section from the gate to the oratory accessible to the Imperial messenger, the deputy of the *shogun* and a few others participating in the ceremony.

Toshogu Shrine Treasure Hall: Walk out of Toshogu Shrine and turn left at the first path after passing through *Ichi-no-Torii* (First *Torii* Gate). Approximately 2,000 treasure items are stored in this hall, but only about 60 to 70 of them are exhibited at one time. Some valuable pieces include the five scrolls drawn by Kano Tan-yu depicting aspects in the life of Ieyasu (an Important Cultural Property), Ieyasu's armor (an Important Cultural Property) and the extravagant tools used to construct the Main Halls of Toshogu Shrine (National Treasures). In addition, portraits of the Tokugawa Shoguns, swords, arms, religious articles and information on the design of the shrine sculptures are other interesting exhibitions. To the left of the Treasure Hall is the stone *Karamon* (Chinese Gate) and the *torii* gate that once stood inside the *Okusha* (Inner Shrine).

Futarasan Shrine ⟨14⟩ : Situated a short way from Toshogu Shrine, it enshrines three Shinto deities: Onamuchi-no-Mikoto (popularly called Okuninushi-no-Mikoto), his consort Tagorihime-no-Mikoto and their son Ajisukitakahikone-no-Mikoto. These deities were revered for their virtues, which were responsible for bringing prosperity to the country. Since they all originated from Mt. Futara (the present Mt. Nantai), a shrine called Okumiya (Inner Shrine) was dedicated to them at its summit. For those who were not able to climb to the top of the mountain to pay homage to the deities, a shrine known as Chugushi (Middle Shrine) was built on the shores of Lake Chuzenji and another on the banks of the Daiya River called Honsha (Main Shrine). These three shrines make up Futarasan Shrine. It was founded in 790 by Priest Shodo. At the entrance is a bronze *torii* gate, 6.6 m high; on the right is *Haiden* (Oratory—an Important Cultural Property), behind which is a lacquered *Karamon* (Chinese Gate), and inside the gate stands *Honden* (Main Shrine—an Important Cultural Property). At the southwest corner of the fence enclosing the main shrine is an antique bronze lantern, 2.3 m high, called *Bake-doro* (Goblin Lantern). Legend has it that it used to assume the shape of a goblin at night, in which guise it was cut by a swordsman. Its scratches are still visible. Beside the oratory stands a large *koyamaki* (umbrella pine) said to have been planted by Saint Kobo. There is a three-trunked cedar, Oyako-Sugi (literally meaning Parent-and-Child Cedar), near the holy water basin containing water for purification—a natural curiosity regarded as divine. The *kagura*, a sacred Shinto dance performed on the ceremonial and festive occasions of a shrine, may be seen at this shrine for a fee.

After visiting Futarasan Shrine and descending the stone steps in front of the Oratory, the visitor will come to *Jogyodo* and *Hokkedo* halls of Rinnoji Temple. Popularly called *Futatsudo* (Twin Halls), both were founded in 848 in imitation of similar buildings on Mt. Hiei near Kyoto. Many images of Buddhist deities and saints were removed to these halls from the Nikko shrines when it was decided in 1871 to purge them of Buddhist elements.

By taking a path running 200 m south from the Twin Halls to *Jigendo* Hall of Rinnoji Temple on Daikoku Hill, the visitor will come to a small gate at the top of a flight of stone steps. *Amida* Hall, an Important Cultural Property, stands on the left inside the gate. To the right stands a Belfry and a Sutra Storehouse, both of which are Important Cultural Properties. *Haiden* (Oratory) is concealed by a stone fence in front. *Jigendo* was erected in honor of Tenkai (1536–1643), a trusted counselor of Ieyasu who was appointed chief abbot of the Nikko temples and whose tomb is at the rear of the Oratory. A massive, granite block 3.6 m high, this Important Cultural Property is guarded by six stone statues of *Rokubuten*, the Heavenly Kings. Tenkai was granted the posthumous title of Jigen-Daishi, for which the hall was named.

Go-oden: The mortuary shrine of Prince Kitashirakawa (1847–1895) was erected in 1896. The prince was the last of the prince abbots, a post he renounced in 1869. The small hall in which the prince's image is kept stands behind the Oratory. Finally, at the end of a flight of stone steps is his tomb, enclosed within a stone balustrade with a three-story stone stupa nearby. To the right are the tombs of the other 13 prince abbots of Nikko.

Iemitsu's Mausoleum: The mausoleum of Iemitsu (Taiyuimbyo) occupies a more elevated and retired site beyond Futarasan Shrine. Passing in front of the Twin Halls, one comes to the first gate (called *Niomon* or Deva Gate), with its pillars, rafters, architraves, etc., decorated with carvings and metal ornaments. Inside the gate on the left is a treasure house, while on the right is a massive granite font placed under a roof supported by 12 granite pillars. A dragon painted by Kano Yasunobu (1607–1685) is on the ceiling, while stone lanterns of every description are on all sides.

A flight of 21 stone steps leads to a second gate called *Nitemmon*, a two-story carved structure, with the images of two Buddhist deities (Komokuten and Jikokuten) set in the outside niches and those of the Gods of Wind and Thunder in the inside niches to stand guard over the gate. Ascending two flights of stone steps, one comes to the middle court, with a belfry on the right and a drum tower on the left. The third gate, standing in front, is called *Yashamon* because each of four *Yasha* (Buddhist demons) stands in the four niches. The profusely gilded gate is also known as *Botammon* (Peony Gate) from the carvings that decorate it. The fourth gate, called *Karamon*, or Chinese Gate, is decorated with low-relief carvings on a gold ground. The structures indicated above are all Important Cultural Properties. *Haiden* (Oratory), a National Treasure, lies inside the Chinese Gate. It is also very elaborately carved with flowers and birds in high relief on the friezes of the four sides. The interior covers an area of 63 tatami mats, and a gilt canopy hangs in the center. The two pairs of bronze flower vases and the pair of bronze stork candlesticks were presented by the three principal members of the Tokugawa family. There is also a pair of tortoise-shell lanterns presented by the Netherlands, while on the left are a display of musical instruments. In the passage on the way to *Honden* (Main Hall) are a number of low, gold-lacquered prayer desks, on which are boxes containing sutras. On the large panels in front and to the right and left are lions on a golden ground, the right one by Kano Tan-yu and the left by Kano Yasunobu, both distinguished artists of the Kano school.

Passing the *Ai-no-Ma* (Inner Shrine; a National Treasure), one comes to the Main Hall (a National Treasure) of Buddhist style with a "hip gabled-roof." Below the gables on the right and left are wave patterns, kylins, peonies and arabesques, while on the bargeboards a pair of dragons are carved. The rafter-ends form lions' heads carved out of a solid block. The interior is decorated so as to give prominence to its main object—a resplendently lacquered Buddhist shrine in which is seated the wooden figure of Iemitsu, about 1 m high. The shrine itself is 1.8 sq.m and over 3 m high. It is superbly decorated with paintings of animals, birds and flowers and stands on a lacquered dais.

On the way from the Main Hall leading to the Innermost Court, there is a small gate called *Kokamon*, which is distinguished from all the other gates because it is built in the Chinese style of the Ming Dynasty. It is a white plaster arch with rounded sides and stands out prominently in the midst of the intricate ornamentation of the other structures. The general public is prohibited from going beyond this gate.

Ascending the stone steps, one comes first to the Oratory of the sanctum, a small chapel in which the interior is painted wax-white. Its carvings, inlaid with metal ornaments, are beautifully colored. The tomb stands at the top of another flight of stone steps and is of bronze, in the same style as that of Ieyasu's. The gate (called *Inukimon*) in front of this innermost court is cast in solid bronze, with the Treasure Pagoda standing beside it. These three edifices (Oratory, *Inukuimon* Gate and Treasure Pagoda) are designated as Important Cultural Properties along with *Kokamon* Gate.

PLACES OF INTEREST AROUND THE MAUSOLEUM

Takino-o Shrine: Follow the avenue to the left of Nikko Bridge (near Sacred Bridge) and proceed along the right bank of the Inari River or ascend the pathway skirting the western side of Futarasan Shrine.

If the first route is taken, the visitor will pass *Kaizando* (Founder's Hall), dedicated to priest Shodo (737–817), founder of Futarasan Shrine. In the shrine is installed a wooden image of *Jizo-Bosatsu* (a Buddhist deity) attributed to Unkei, a great sculptor of the 13th century. The tabernacle in front of the image contains a statue of the priest surrounded by the figures of his ten disciples. Shodo's tomb is at the back of the hall, and near it are three small tombs of his disciples.

To the south of *Kaizando* is a small shrine called *Ubu-no-Miya* (Shrine of Parturition), or *Kyosha-do*. If a pregnant woman presents a votive offering in the shape of a Japanese chess piece, it is believed that an easy delivery will be assured. Farther along is a stone monument marking the spot where the horse on which Ieyasu rode in 1600 at the battle of Sekigahara was buried.

The precincts of the Takino-o Shrine are entered across a stone bridge called Go-obashi. To the right is the noted Shiraito-no-Taki (White Thread Falls). Ascending the stone steps, one passes through *Romon* (Tower Gate) to *Haiden* (Oratory), behind which is *Karamon* (Chinese Gate). *Honden* (Main Hall) lies beyond *Karamon*. These four structures are listed as Important Cultural Properties.

The stone *Un-dameshi-no-Torii* (Test-of-Luck Gate) in front of *Romon*, has a round hole in its upper part. It is believed that if anyone can throw three stones in succession through this hole while making a wish, their wish will be granted. To the west is *Sake-no-Izumi* or *Sake* Spring, where in former days (according to legend), a liquid bubbled up that tasted like *sake*. Close by, surrounded by a stone fence, there is a round stone called *Kodane-Ishi* (Child-giving Stone), which is worshipped by women who wish to bear children.

By taking the upper path from Go-o Bridge, one comes to *Gyojado*, which contains an image of En-no-Gyoja (also known as En-no-Ozunu), a Buddhist ascetic and miracle-worker who flourished in the seventh and eighth centuries. From *Gyojado* a cedar-lined path descends to Futarasan Shrine.

Kirifuri(Falling Mist)-no-Taki Cascade ⑭ : Located 4.8 km north of Nikko Bridge and about 10 min. by bus from Nikko Station. After crossing the Inari River and other small streams, one comes to a rotary observatory from which the cascade may be viewed. The cascade is 75 m high and divided into two stages. It ranks among the Three Noted Falls of Nikko, the other two being Kegon Falls and Urami-no-Taki (Back-view Cascade). A better view is offered from the observatory facing the front of the falls.

Nikko Botanical Garden : This is the grounds of the Tokyo University garden which cover an area of 13,170 sq.m, with the garden of the former Tamozawa Imperial Villa annexed to it. It contains about 2,300 varieties of plants, including many kinds of alpine flora from Nikko.

In the garden stands the Nikko Museum, which has on display

many materials concerning nature and culture in the Nikko National Park area, including the topography, geology, fauna and flora, history and the fine arts of the park.

Gammangafuchi : Located at the back of the Botanical Garden, there is a deep pool in the Daiya River to the south of the Tamozawa Bus Stop or east of the Hanaishicho Bus Stop. Looming over the pool is a huge rock on which a small image of *Fudo*, a Buddhist deity, is placed. Engraved on the rock are Sanskrit letters reading *Kamman*, popularly pronounced *Gamman*. On the right bank of the river are rows of images of *Jizo*, the Buddhist guardian deity of the souls of departed children. These images are called *Bake-Jizo* (Bewitching *Jizo*) because, according to popular superstition, nobody can count them correctly. Many of the original images have been washed away by floods, particularly by a devastating flood in 1902, leaving only 70 images.

Urami-no-Taki (Back-view Cascade): So called because it could formerly be viewed from the back. It is 6.5 km from Nikko Bridge and lies on the upper part of the Arasawa River. It is about 2 km northwest, 15 min. by bus or 40 min. on foot from Nikko Station. The cascade is about 30 m high and has a stone image of Fudo on one side. On the upper course of the Arasawa River, about 4 km from here, is Jigan Falls.

Kirifuri(Falling Mist) Kogen Plateau ⌷14⌷: It is located on the southern slope of Mt. Akanagi (alt. 2,010 m) about 20 min. by bus from Nikko Station. There are many falls and marshes as well as pastures and camping sites in the vicinity of the plateau. This area is known for the many species of *nikko kisuge* or day lilies that bloom here from early June to mid-July, especially the orange-yellow day lilies that cloak Kisugedaira in the first half of July.

By climbing the neighboring Mt. Maruyama (alt. 1,689 m), a magnificent view of the surrounding mountains can be enjoyed. The quality snow on the southern slope of this mountain attracts many skiers during winter.

Nikko to Chuzenji

19.2 km from the west side of Nikko Station to Lake Chuzenji via Irohazaka Driveway No. 2. Buses, which take 40 min., are available.

Irohazaka (Iroha Slope) ⌷14⌷ : This road connects Chuzenji Spa and Umagaeshi along National Highway 120 (500 m difference in altitude). Umagaeshi (lit. Horse Return) is so named because it was so steep for horses that they had to be sent back and travel was continued on foot. It is divided into Daini-Irohazaka (Iroha Driveway No. 2; 9,468 m long), which is used exclusively for ascent, and Daiichi-Irohazaka (Iroha Driveway No. 1; 6,486 m long), used exclusively for descent. Both roads are a continuous series of zigzag curves. Despite the transportational inconvenience, however, they are popular tourist attractions. This area is especially beautiful during autumn when the leaves change colors.

Daini-Irohazaka is noted for the view of Mt. Nantai (lit. Male Mountain) and Mt. Nyoho (lit. Female Mountain). Sometimes, wild monkeys can be seen roaming about. Along Daiichi-Irohazaka, Nyonin-do (Female Temple), Hannya-no-Taki (Falls of Wisdom) and Hoto-no-Taki (Hoto Waterfall) can be found. Nyonin-do is a temple for female pilgrims to Mt. Nantai. Since females were once prohibited from climbing to the summit of Mt. Nantai, they came to this temple to pray to the distant Mt. Nantai.

Akechidaira: 35 min. by bus from Nikko Station. Located at an altitude of 1,370 m, this plateau has a magnificent view. A ropeway is available to the observatory from the top of Daini-Irohazaka. From the observatory, Lake Chuzenji and Kegon Waterfall can be seen in front, while to the right are the ridges of Mt. Nantai and Mt. Nyoho.

Kegon Waterfall 14 : Created by the Daiya River, it drops off a 100-m stone face as it flows out of Lake Chuzenji. It is regarded as one of the three most beautiful waterfalls in Japan. Water gushes out in the middle of the stone wall producing several strings of falls. The depth of the fall basin is approximately 5 m. It is a 5-min. walk from Chuzenji Spa to the observatory, but an elevator is available from here to the fall basin.

Chanokidaira 14 : With an altitude of 1,600 m, this plateau is connected to the east shore of Lake Chuzenji. A ropeway is available from Chuzenji Spa. The Chanokidaira Kogen (Plateau) Botanical Garden features alpine plants in natural forests covering an area of approximately 70,000 sq.m. There is a Rock Garden inside allowing visitors to observe as many as 150 species of alpine plants that grow in the mountains and swamps of Nikko. Pathways pass through a grove of beech trees and azalea bushes. Magnificent views are available from three observation points—one in the middle of the Garden, one at the southern end and the other atop the ropeway station.

Lake Chuzenji 14 : Located at an altitude of 1,269 m and with a circumference of 21 km, the Lake covers a total area of 11.5 sq. km. The deepest point measures 161.5 m. Situated along the southern foot of Mt. Nantai (alt. 2,484 m), it is the largest of the lakes and ponds in Nikko National Park and is typical of high mountain-lakes in Japan.

The lake came into existence through an eruption of Mt. Nantai in which molten lava blocked the valleys of the Daiya River. Longer from east to west, the lake is straight along the northern shore but jagged along the south. Chuzenji Spa is located to the east of the Lake. Villas and campgrounds are scattered here and there around the lakeshore. In the water, one can enjoy trout fishing, various boating sports and water skiing. The autumn leaves from early to late October are among the most beautiful in the Kanto District.

Chuzenji Spa 14 : This is the only area around the lake developed with hotels, *ryokan* or Japanese-style inns and souvenir shops. Excursion boats depart from and boats dock by Ojiri Bridge, which spans the outlet of the Daiya River. The hot-spring water is piped from Yumoto Spa in Oku(Inner)-Nikko.

Utagahama Beach: Located along the lakeshore south of Chuzenji Spa. It has long been known as the most beautiful spot on Lake Chuzenji, providing a superb view of the lake and surrounding mountains from here. There are many luxurious villas belonging to French, British, Belgian and other embassies in the vicinity.

Chuzenji Temple: Also called Tachiki-Kannon, it stands on Utagahama Beach and belongs to the Rinnoji Temple. It is located on the road along the eastern shore of the lake leading to Hangetsu Pass, but may also be reached by boat. The main image, a *Senju Kannon* (Thousand-Handed Kannon), was carved by priest Shodo out of a *tachiki* (living tree-trunk), a hatchet having apparently been used to carve the lower parts. It stands about 5.5 m high, and the marks made by the chisel are still visible after a lapse of over a thousand years. The temple formerly stood on the western side of Chugushi Shrine, but it was washed away by the disastrous flood of 1902 and was then brought to its present site. Close to the temple stands a museum in which various antiquities are kept, including an iron staff and an hatchet said to have been used by Shodo. The statue and these two articles are designated as Important Cultural Properties.

On Teragasaki, or Hatcho-Dejima (a small headland to the southwest of Utagahama Beach, 45 min. on foot), is an old temple established in 848 and dedicated to *Yakushi-Nyorai*, a Buddhist deity. It is most easily reached by boat. The lakeshore here is noted for the beauty of the autumn leaves.

Chugushi Shrine: Located at the western end of Chuzenji Spa. A path leads from within the precincts to the summit of the mountain. There is a large bronze torii gate near the shore, with stone steps leading up to *Haiden* (Oratory). *Honden* (Main Shrine) is roofed with copper tile, while its pillars and walls are cinnabar-varnished. It is profusely ornamented with painted carvings. The two buildings are Important Cultural Properties. At the *Tohai Matsuri* (or Pilgrims' Festival) from July 31 to August 7, pilgrims are purified here by the priest before climbing the mountain.

Oku-Nikko (Inner Nikko)

Shobugahama Beach: Located on the northern shore of Lake Chuzenji, 10 min. by bus from Chuzenji-Spa. The beautiful sandy beach is popular as a base for camping and hiking during summer. Landmarks in the vicinity include the Fishery Agency Nikko Hatchery and Ryuzu-no-Taki (Dragon-Head Cascade).

Senjugahama Beach and Lake Sainoko: Senjugahama Beach is a stretch of sand surrounded by primeval forest on the western shore of Lake Chuzenji. Two camping sites are open during summer. Fly fishing in Lake Chuzenji began here. Approximately 50 min. on foot from here is the serene Lake Sainoko, surrounded by dense foliage.

Ryuzu-no-Taki (Dragon Head Cascade) 14 : North of Shobuga-hama Beach along National Highway 120. The cascade is a 300-m-long current created by the rapid flow of the Yukawa River from Senjogahara to Lake Chuzenji. The woodland in the vicinity is beautiful, especially when the Yashio azaleas bloom in May and the leaves change color in October.

Senjogahara 14 : A marshland plateau north of Lake Chuzenji that extends across the western foot of Mt. Nantai at an average altitude of 1,400 m. It was once a lake, but the profusion of plants gradually eroding the banks and the accumulation of sediment are slowly turning the area into a grassland. Featured by a wide-ranging variety of plant and tree species, the area takes on a special glory when the many alpine flowers and marsh plants bloom in succession between June and August.

Alpine flora and local scenery can be enjoyed by walking along the Senjogahara Hiking routes (5.6 km long) that starts at Shobugahama Beach, crosses Senjogahara and extends to the Yutaki Falls at the northern end of the marshland.

Odashirogahara: This grassland spreading west of Senjogahara is noted for its abundance of alpine flora. *Nikko-azami* or magenta thistle blooming in purple and reddish colors in July and August possesses a special beauty.

Kotoku Pasture: This 30,000-sq.-m pasture north of Senjogahara has a surrounding natural environment that is magnificent, taking on a special beauty during June when the pasture is ablaze with Zumi blossoms. Cross-country skiing is popular during winter. 20 min. by bus from Chuzenji Spa.

Nikko-Yumoto Spa 14 : About 30 km from Nikko Station and 13 km from Chuzenji Spa (1 hr.20 min. and 30 min. by bus, respectively).

Lying 1,800 m above sea level, the spa is surrounded by mountains on all sides except on the south, where it is open to Lake Yunoko. In summer the thermometer never rises over 27°C. In winter the frozen lake is an attraction to skaters and the snow-covered mountain slopes to skiers. Hiking around Lake Kirikomi and Lake Karikomi in the north and Mt. Shirane (alt. 2,578 m) in the west is also popular.

Lake Yunoko 14 : Measuring 1 km long and 500 m wide, this body of water is located at the western foot of Mt. Shirane and surrounded by forests. In recent years, it has become a popular trout-fishing spot where carp, gibel and other fish abound.

Konsei Pass 14 : Alt. 2,042 m. 5 km southwest of Nikko-Yumoto Spa. Although it is a steep climb part of the way, the summit of Mt. Konsei offers a fine view of the thickly wooded mountain slopes facing Nikko-Yumoto Spa, with Mt. Nantai and Mt. Omanago beyond, and Mt. Tsukuba in the distance rising 90 km southeast on the Kanto Plain. In 1965 a tunnel through the Konsei Pass was completed along with a toll road extending 8.2 km. The Konsei Tunnel, about 1,800 m above sea level, is 755 m long.

The descent on the other side is easy. After passing lakes Sugenuma and Marunuma (hot-springs baths available at the latter), the road follows the Katashina River past Shirane Spa, at the western foot of Mt. Shirane, to Kamata and then runs to Numata through scenery of great beauty.

Kinugawa Spa and Vicinity

Kinugawa Spa is situated in the final valley where the swift currents of the Kinugawa River flow out of the Nikko mountains. This makes it the entrance to the hot springs that are situated along the Kinu-gawa River such as Kawaji, Kawamata, Yunishigawa and Oku(Inner)-Kinugawa. It is a convenient base from which to sightsee in Nikko.

Kinugawa Spa ⌷14⌷: This old spa was discovered during the Edo period and is convenient to visit from Tokyo. This large-scale spa, one of the most prominent in the Kanto area, is 1 hr.55 min. from Asakusa, Tokyo, by limited express on the Tobu Railway.

Many large *ryokan* stand along the banks of the Kinugawa River in this bustling spa town. Some of the many landmarks in the area include Kurogane Bridge, famed for its beautiful night view, majestic valleys, autumn leaves around the Tenguiwa Observatory and the scenic Ryuokyo Gorge. A thrilling boat ride along the Kinugawa River is also an attraction.

To the south of Kinugawa Spa, 20 min. by bus, is Nikko Edo Village, an enjoyable 150,000-sq.-m facility that re-creates the life of the Edo period. Costumed employees and shows provide a taste of the culture and traditions of the time.

Kawaji Spa ⌷14⌷: Located 12 km north of Kinugawa Spa in the valley where the Ojika River joins the Kinugawa River. The moun-tains surrounding the modern, well-equipped *ryokan* of this spa town ensure a tranquil atmosphere. Landmarks such as Ryuokyo Gorge, Kawaji Dam and Lake Ikari can be reached by bus in 6 to 15 min.

Yunishigawa Spa ⌷14⌷: 1 hr.15 min. by bus from Kinugawa Spa. At the end of the 12th century, the Taira Clan was defeated by the Minamoto Clan, resulting in the establishment of the Kamakura Shogunate by Minamoto-no-Yoritomo. The remaining members of the Taira family dispersed throughout Japan, hiding in the mountains to save their lives. The Yunishigawa Spa area is said to have been one of these hiding places. The Yunishigawa Historical Museum and Heike (Taira Clan) Fugitive Museum exhibit many old *samurai* items, and articles corroborating the legend can be seen at these hiding places. It is also said that the Taira family actually found the hot springs itself.

Kawamata Spa ⌷14⌷: 1 hr.50 min. by bus from Kinugawa Spa close to the original flow of Kinugawa River. The fugitive Taira family is said to have also come here, with many historical sites and unique customs remaining as evidence of this. The hot springs are also famed for a geyser that spouts 15 m high every 45 min. Going further into the mountains, one will reach the Oku-Kinugawa Spas Area composed of Meotobuchi, Teshirozawa, Hatcho-no-Yu, Kaniyu and Nikkosawa hot springs. Each area has only one place of accommodation in the natural, serenely beautiful environment.

Oze 14 : A highland basin which lies in the western part of Nikko National Park, sprawling over the three prefectures of Gumma, Fukushima and Niigata. With altitudes ranging 1,400–1,600 m, it is surrounded by the Nasu Volcanic Mountains, including Mt. Hiuchi (alt. 2,356 m) and Mt. Shibutsu (alt. 2,228 m). The ponds of all sizes, swamps, marshland and primeval forests combine to create a beautiful scene. The area is noted for its rich variety of flora and fauna, especially the marsh plants. Its importance in biological study has resulted in its being strictly protected.

Ozenuma Swamp is located in the eastern part of the basin, while Chozo-goya hut on the eastern shore of the swamp is the center for sightseeing trips. The Visitor's Center (a small museum featuring the animals, plants and geology of the Oze district), camping sites, bungalows and an Environment Agency Office are all located here. Paths start here and go around the swamp, which is in danger of being buried beneath clusters of plants such as skunk cabbage, marsh marigolds and day lilies.

Ozegahara, west of the basin, is the most significant Oze marshland. It is divided into three regions: Shimotashiro, Nakatashiro and Kamitashiro, with Nakatashiro among the three especially containing many marsh plants of a wide variety of species.

Facilities such as camping sites, bungalows and offices of Gumma Prefecture and the Environment Agency can be found in these three regions. The Shimotashiro Intersection in the east and Yamanohana in the west are the main sightseeing points. Yamanohana also contains a botanical specimen garden. Visitors are supposed to walk on the wooden walkway, which was made partly to provide a comfortable walk but mainly to protect the plants. The best season to enjoy nature here is between June and September.

This area is accessible from Gumma, Fukushima, Niigata or Tochigi prefectures, but the most commonly used and convenient route is the 1-hr. 50-min. bus ride to Oshimizu on National Highway 120 from Numata Station on the JR Joetsu Line. Chozo-goya hut in Ozenuma is a 3-hr. (8 km) hike from Oshimizu.

Area 11. Along JR Joban Line

Here, we will describe the cities along the JR Joban Line (Ueno to Sendai) between Tsuchiura and Kita-Ibaragi. There may not be so many tourist attractions in this area, but the beautiful coastline, cherry-blossom viewing and various historical sites are worthy of mention. Moreover, the area is active as an academic center complete with Tsukuba Science City and the Tokai Branch of the Japan Atomic Energy Research Institute.

TRANSPORTATION

Rail: Most of the important places can be visited by taking the JR Joban Line, but for the Kashima-Itako area, popularly called Suigo (Water District), it is more convenient to take the limited express on the JR Kashima Line via the Sobu Main Line and Narita Line from Tokyo Station. The Kashima Line connects at Kashima-Jingu to the Kashima Rinkai Railway Oarai-Kashima Line that leads to Mito. Other railways in this area include the JR Suigun Line from Mito and the Ibaragi Kotsu Minato Line from Katsuta.

Road: National Highway 6 runs parallel to the JR Joban Line, but the Joban Expressway connecting the major cities from Tokyo to Iwaki may be more convenient. Long-distance buses running on this expressway depart from the Yaesu South Exit of Tokyo Station for Taira, Hitachi, Mito and Tsukuba. The Higashi(East)-Kanto Expressway runs to the Itako area.

PLACES OF INTEREST

Tsuchiura [20] ☎0298: Pop. 123,462. 66 km from Ueno (Tokyo). About 45 min. by limited express. Tsuchiura is situated on the western shore of Lake Kasumigaura in the south-central part of Ibaraki Prefecture. This is a satellite city of Tokyo and serves as the gateway to the Tsukuba Science City and the Lake Kasumigaura areas.

Kasumigaura [20]: The lake has a total area of 178 sq.km, a circumference of 138 km, and a maximum depth of 7 m. This freshwater lake is the second-largest lake in Japan after Lake Biwa. Many species of freshwater fish and wild birds can be found here.

The lake is full of *wakasagi* (a kind of smelt). Once, *wakasagi* were fished from boats with one big white sail, but now those boats are only for tourist trips from the end of July to the end of September.

At the southeastern extremity, the water flows through a canal into another lake called Kitaura (78.8 sq.km), which is connected with the Tone River.

Tsukuba [20] ☎0298: Pop. 133,311. This city borders the western edge of Tsuchiura, spreading south from the southwestern foot of Mt. Tsukuba. A bus runs to Tsukuba Center, the heart of the city, from Tsuchiura Station and Arakawaoki Station in about 25 min. A bus is also available from Tokyo Station to Tsukuba Center via the Joban Expressway, taking 1 hr. The current city limits were established in 1988 when the former Tsukuba Town was incorporated.

Tsukuba Science City was established for research and educational purposes. It covers an area of approximately 27 sq.km, although construction of new facilities is still underway. In addition to the

University of Tsukuba, which opened in 1974, the nearly 50 research facilities include the Tsukuba Space Center, Meteorological Research Institute, National Science Museum Tsukuba Botanical Gardens and other governmental research centers.

The Tsukuba Center Building in Tsukuba Center houses a variety of shops and restaurants, a hotel and an information room with video monitors and panels explaining all about the city. The Tsukuba Expo Center, originally a supplementary facility of the International Science Exposition held in 1985, utilizes video and other media to introduce the history of scientific technology and research achievements in Japan. Cosmic Hall, with the largest planetarium in the world, and Kodomo Park, with its enjoyable scientific facilities for children, are also here. For tours of the various research facilities, it is necessary to make an appointment at the information center. ☎ (0298)52-6789.

Mt. Tsukuba ⟨20⟩: Although the altitude is a mere 876 m, its beautiful form is conspicuous since it is the only protuberance on the plain. It has long received acclaim as being comparable to Mt. Fuji. The summit, consisting of Mt. Nantai and Mt. Nyotai, provides a magnificent view of the Kanto Plain. The top can be reached either by cable car from Tsukubasan Shrine at the southern foot of the mountain or by ropeway from Tsutsujigaoka at the southeastern foot. (Both Tsukubasan Shrine and Tsutsujigaoka are accessible from Tsuchiura Station, with one transfer at Tsukuba Bus Stop for the former.) Tsukubasan Shrine is dedicated to Izanagi-no-Mikoto and Izanami-no-Mikoto, an important god and goddess in Shinto mythology and the guardian gods of Mt. Tsukuba. The buildings are excellent examples of Japanese shrine architecture.

Mito ⟨20/22-②⟩ ☎0292

Pop. 230,310. Located 117.5 km from Ueno (Tokyo), 1 hr. 20 min. by JR limited express. The city was the seat of the Mito branch of the Tokugawa family and is now the administrative center of Ibaraki Prefecture. It is also the center of local transportation, with several railway and bus lines running to the neighboring districts.

Mito Castle once stood in the center of the city, but the castle buildings were nearly all destroyed during conflicts at the time of the Meiji Restoration in 1868 as well as by air raids in 1945.

The Mito fief was granted in 1609 to Tokugawa Yorifusa (1603–1661), the 11th son of Ieyasu (founder of the Tokugawa Shogunate), and thus it became one of the three main branches of the Tokugawa family along with Kii and Owari. The head of the Mito-Tokugawa family occupied the special position of vice-*shogun* but in consideration of this hereditary privilege, family members were barred from assuming the position of *shogun*.

Among the successive lords of the Mito family, Mitsukuni (1628–1700), the second lord, was the greatest. It was he who started in 1657 the laborious work of compiling "Dainihonshi" or "History of Great Japan" (397 volumes), a project that was completed in 1906.

From the main road, one can enter the former castle grounds at *Ninomaru* (the second citadel), from which a wide-ranging view of the adjacent countryside can be obtained. In *Sannomaru* (the third citadel) on the far side of the moat bridge (probably once a draw-bridge) is Mito Park, or Kodokan Park. The Kodokan 22-② , an educational institution established by Nariaki, the ninth lord of the Mito Clan (1800–1860), is located here. Only a few buildings remain, and together with the surrounding area, Kodokan is now a public park noted for its plum trees.

Behind the Kodokan are Kashima Shrine and Confucius Shrine dedicated to *Kashima-Myojin* and Confucius, respectively. They were both built by Nariaki, the former to commemorate contemporary military culture and the latter, civil culture.

Kairaku-en 22-② : About 3 km west of the station. This is one of the three most celebrated gardens in Japan, the other two being Kenroku-en in Kanazawa City and Koraku-en in Okayama City. It was designed by Nariaki as a retreat from the cares of office and completed in 1843, but it was turned into a public park in 1873.

The central part of the 110,000-sq.-m park is a plum grove containing 3,000 trees of some 100 species that bloom from late February through mid-March. The *Ume* (Plum) Festival is held during this period. Outdoor tea ceremonies, *koto* concerts and many other entertainments events are presented. A reproduction of the Kobuntei, a pavilion where Nariaki used to hold meetings with contemporary poets and compose poems, is located on the grounds.

Giretsukan 22-② : Located east of Kairaku-en and inside the Tokiwa Shrine compounds, this museum is dedicated to Tokugawa Mitsukuni and Nariaki. It houses relics, documents and personal belongings of these two lords as well as those of scholars and *samurai* retainers under the Mito-Tokugawas—all portraying the 300-year history of the clan.

Oarai Beach 20 : 11.6 km southeast of Mito on the Kashima Rinkai Railway. The northern half of the coast is a reef with a striking view, while the southern half is a shallow swimming beach. Nearby is the popular Oarai Aquarium with penguin and small fish shows as well as a seaside pool. Oarai Isosaki Shrine, founded in 856, has a marine museum and the Joyo Meiji Memorial Hall, which displays articles associated with Emperors Meiji and Taisho as well as with Mito *samurai* active during the Meiji Restoration.

Nakaminato, the biggest fishing base in Ibaragi Prefecture, lies across the Nakagawa River along the Ibaraki Kotsu Minato Line. The city is bordered by Ajigaura Beach, a spacious expanse of sand with a beautiful grove of pines.

Japan Atomic Energy Research Institute 20 : 3.1 km east of Tokai Station (136 km from Tokyo). The 3.46-sq.-km site lies amid a pine forest in Tokai Village facing the Pacific Ocean. It is the institution coordinating the use of atomic power for peaceful purposes in the country. The first successful nuclear reaction in Japan took place here in 1957.

The Ibaragi Atomic Energy Center has been set up for visitors. Panels and models are designed to impart a comprehensive understanding of atomic energy. Tour bus service is also available. Closed on Mondays. To make an appointment to tour the area, ☎ (0292) 82-3111.

Hitachi 20 ☎0294: Pop. 203,342. Located 153 km from Tokyo, or about 1 hr.30 min. by limited express on the JR Joban Line. The city borders Tokai Village to the south and the Pacific Ocean to the east. It is largely an industrial area where the major electric appliance maker, Hitachi, Ltd., operates together with its affiliate factories. Kawarago and other swimming areas in the city attract many visitors from Tokyo.

Kita-Ibaragi 20 ☎0293: Pop. 51,992. Located on the northeastern edge of Ibaragi Prefecture along the border of Fukushima Prefecture with the Pacific Ocean to the east. Until recently, it was the center of the Joban Minami (South)-Tanden Coal Mines, but since the last mine closed in 1971, electronics, machinery and other industries have been introduced in the Isohara district of Kita-Ibaragi City. Hiragata and Otsu ports, also in the same city, bustle with the fishery and marine-foods-processing industries. Otsuko on the JR Joban Line is the station for several seaside resorts. Izura, 5.7 km southeast of the station, 20 min. by bus, is noted for its picturesque scenery.

Along JR Suigun Line

The Suigun Line runs from Mito to Koriyama (143 km) on the JR Tohoku Main Line and Tohoku Shinkansen. From Kami-Sugaya (11 km from Mito), a 9.5 km-branch line runs to Hitachi-Ota.

Hitachi-Ota 20 : ☎ 0294: Pop. 38,070. 20 km from Mito. The city is the market for the large crop of tobacco grown in the neighboring districts.

On Zuiryusan Hill, 4.2 km north of Hitachi-Ota Station, is the cemetery of the Mito-Tokugawa family, containing the tombs of 13 lords of the clan. The arrangement of the tombs is similar to that of a Chinese cemetery, with the burial services of the Mito lords said to have been conducted according to Confucian rites. The cemetery covers practically the entire slope of a dense forest of aged pines and cedars and contains the tomb of Zhū Zhī-yú (1600–1682), an eminent Chinese scholar who became a naturalized Japanese.

Nishiyama, 2.5 km west of the JR Hitachi-Ota Station, is famous for its connection with Lord Mitsukuni of the Mito-Tokugawa family. He lived here in retirement after 1691. The Seizanso, his thatched cottage (rebuilt in 1819), stands in a dense grove of cedars, testifying to the humble manner in which he lived. A wooden statue of Mitsukuni is in a storehouse at the back of the main building.

Fukuroda [20] : 52 km from Mito. Fukuroda Spa, 1.2 km northeast of the station (5 min. by bus), and Fukuroda Falls, about an equal distance farther east, are the landmarks of the area. The falls are nearly 73 m wide, dropping from a height of 121 m in four tiers of cascades. The surrounding area is famous for its fresh spring verdure as well as its beautiful autumn leaves.

Konnyaku, a specialty, is a jelly made from the spherical, subterranean stem of the devils-tongue plant cultivated in the mountainous area. *Konnyaku* noodles, called *shirataki*, is one of the indispensable ingredients of *sukiyaki*.

Hitachi-Daigo [20] : Situated 56 km from Mito, the city lies along the Kuji River, which is noted for its *ayu* (sweetfish) fishing and hot springs. It is also the best place from which to climb Mt. Yamizo (alt. 1,022 m). On the summit is the ancient Yamizomine Shrine, while on the southeastern slope stands a Tendai-sect Buddhist Temple called Nichirinji. It is 50 min. by bus to the mountain and an additional 2-hr. 20-min. hike to the summit.

Area 12. Boso Peninsula

The Boso Peninsula [21] is the district to the southeast of Tokyo, stretching between Tokyo Bay on the west and the Pacific on the east, nearly corresponding to Chiba Prefecture.

The warm current referred to as the Kuroshio (black current), which flows along the outer-sea side of the peninsula, gives the area a mild climate. Spring flowers start blooming in January. The southern portion of the peninsula cultivates flowers, serving as a major supplier to the Tokyo metropolitan area.

For tourists the peninsula is famous for its wealth of historic sites, Shinto shrines and Buddhist temples plus a variety of beaches, all attracting a constant stream of visitors. There are two quasi-national parks—Suigo-Tsukuba and Minami-Boso—on the peninsula. Places of tourist interest include Narita, Sawara, Choshi, Kisarazu, Tateyama and many other cities and towns that serve as bases for side trips to the nearby scenic spots.

The industries on the peninsula range from the production of peanuts, vegetables, fruit, soy beans and dairy products to fishery, livestock breeding and natural gas extraction. As most of these products are sent to the capital, the peninsula is often called the "Kitchen of Tokyo." The Keiyo (Tokyo-Chiba) Industrial Zone, one of the largest in Japan, is located in western Chiba Prefecture at the back of Tokyo Bay.

TRANSPORTATION

Rail: The main railways for touring the peninsula are the JR Sobu Main Line, Sotobo Line and Uchibo Line, all of which depart from the underground platforms of Tokyo Station. Access to most of the tourist spots in the area is possible by using these lines and the JR Narita Line, which branches from Sobu Main Line at Sakura. Other lines include the JR Togane Line (Naruto to Oami), which connects with the Sobu Main Line, and the Sotobo Line in the middle of Kujukuri Beach; Kominato Railway (Goi to Kazusa-Nakano) and Isumi Railway (Kazusa-Nakano to Ohara) traversing the peninsula, and the JR Kururi Line (Kisarazu to Kazusa-Kameyama). The JR Kashima Line starts at Sawara on the JR Narita Line and heads for Itako and Kashima-Jingu in Ibaragi Prefecture.

Road: Chiba City, at the northeastern edge of the peninsula, serves as its entrance. From Tokyo there are two general routes to Chiba, either by the Keiyo Expressway or the Wangan (Bayshore) Expressway. These two expressways meet at Miyanoki Interchange in Chiba City. To go east from Chiba, take the Higashi(East)-Kanto Expressway, which extends to Itako in Ibaragi Prefecture. This expressway can also be used to go to the New Tokyo International Airport by taking the Narita Interchange. The whole peninsula is covered by a network of national highways, although the Chiba-Togane, Chiba-Sotobo and "Boso Skyline" toll roads are more convenient for touring.

Narita and the Suigo District

Sakura ⟨21⟩ ☎0434: Pop. 138,411. Situated 56 km from Tokyo Station, it is the junction of the Narita Line for Narita and Sawara. Sakura is 50 min. from Tokyo on the Sobu Main Line by limited express or 1 hr. from Keisei-Ueno in Tokyo on the Keisei Electric Railway by limited express. The National Museum of Japanese History stands on a rise that was once the site of the Sakura Castle. Located to the west of Keisei-Sakura Station, 15 min. on foot, the museum has four separate display rooms where one can see historical relics classified into 13 themes on various aspects of history from prehistoric and ancient to modern times as well as six themes on Japanese customs and life style. The collection totals 70,000 pieces, including some National Treasures and Important Cultural Properties. The museum is closed on Mondays.

Narita ⟨21⟩ ☎0476: Pop. 82,311. Located 69 km from Tokyo Station, about 1 hr. by limited express on the JR Narita Line or 54 min. from Keisei-Ueno in Tokyo by limited express on the Keisei Line. The city borders Ibaragi Prefecture to the north, separated by the currents of the Tone River. It grew up around Shinshoji Temple a long time ago, and more recently the New Tokyo International Airport, a gateway to Japan, has brought an increase of visitors from both at home and abroad.

Shinshoji Temple ⟨21⟩: About 800 m north of the JR Narita Station or Keisei-Narita Station (buses available). This Buddhist temple of the Shingon sect (Chizan school) is dedicated to *Fudo* (Acala), the God of Fire.

It was founded in connection with a rebellion started by Taira-no-Masakado in 939. The image of *Fudo*—alleged to have been carved by Kobo-Daishi (774–835), introducer of the Shingon doctrines—was sent by Emperor Sujaku from Jingoji Temple in Kyoto to Kozuga-hara (not far from Narita) in the custody of priest Kancho. Prayers were offered there until Masakado was killed and the rebellion crushed in 940. After that, the original temple to enshrine the image was erected in Kozugahara, but it was later moved to the present site in 1705.

The temple precincts, which cover almost 200 sq.km, are occupied by the *Niomon* Gate, Main Hall, Main Quarters, *Okuno-in Komyodo* (Hall of Enlightment), Buddha's Hall, the former Main Hall, a belfry and a Three-Story Pagoda along with a library, a museum and schools—all maintained under the auspices of the temple authorities. It took five years to construct the Main Hall, which was completed in 1968. It has a majestic appearance designed in the style of a traditional Buddhist temple, although built with the most advanced techniques. On the right side of the lower court is a sacred well, close to the hall of fasting for men, where pilgrims stay while they are practicing asceticism. Every morning in the dead of winter, ice-cold water is poured over their bodies. In a ritual called *Ohyakudo* (100 Times), they also walk 100 times around the Main Hall while reciting sutra with their beads and keeping tally with 100 white strings.

The temple attracts more than eleven million visitors every year, especially on New Year's Day (three million) and on the night of the *Setsubun* Festival (February 3 or 4, when the bean-throwing ceremony takes place) and also during the months of January, May and September.

Naritasan Park: The park is located behind the temple and covers 165 sq.km. Very attractively laid out, it has three ponds and many plum trees, cherry trees, peonies and wisteria.

New Tokyo International Airport (Narita Airport) 21 : This aerial entrance to Japan opened in 1978. However, only one of the three planned runways has been completed although the two remaining runways and other facilities are currently under construction. As of June 1990, a total of 51 airlines were utilizing Narita Airport, with an average of 315 international flights per day.

Toshoji Temple: Generally called Sogo Reido (Sacred Hall), it is 5 min. by Keisei Line from Keisei-Narita Station. This is the scene of the sacrifice made by Kiuchi Sogo (1612–1653), the headman of the village of Kozu more popularly known by the name of Sakura Sogo, for the sake of his fellow-villagers.

Sogo took the lead in presenting a petition to Shogun Tokugawa Ietsuna protesting against unjust acts committed by the local *daimyo* (feudal lord) in 389 villages in the *daimyo's* domain. Presentation of a petition directly to the *shogun* was a capital offense. Although the injustice was remedied and the oppressive exactions stopped, Sogo together with his wife and his four children were executed. To the left of their graves in Toshoji Temple is a sanctuary called Sogo Reido that was built in their memory. The tombstones were erected in 1752 (the 100th anniversary of the tragedy) by the descendants of the *daimyo* against whose unjust acts Sogo had petitioned. The old sanctuary was replaced by the present one in 1921.

Sawara 21 ☎0478: Pop. 50,523. 1 hr.30 min. (96 km) from Tokyo Station on the JR limited express or 89 km on the Higashi-Kanto Expressway. The city originally prospered as a commercial city when water transportation thrived along the Tone River, with houses in the central portion of the city now recalling the city's former glory. Sawara like Itako on the opposite bank of the Tone River, is a base for touring the Suigo (Water District).

In this city, Ino Tadataka (1745-1818) grew up to be Japan's foremost geographer and cartographer, and made a survey of the entire Japanese coastline, including Hokkaido. His surveying instruments are preserved at his former residence, which is designated as a Place of Historical Importance, 1 km southeast of the station.

Suigo-Tsukuba Quasi-National Park 20 : The park extends over Chiba and Ibaragi prefectures, including the lower course of the Tone River, the major part of Lake Kasumigaura, Itako, Kashima and Katori shrines, and the Choshi seacoast. The features of this park consist of picturesque lakes and rivers, seascapes at Cape Inubo, Byobugaura, the beach of Kashima, clusters of aquatic plants and the visits of migratory birds.

Sawara Municipal Aquatic Botanical Garden : Situated on reclaimed land between the Hitachi-Tone River and the Tone River, the largest in Japan in terms of the basin. A million irises of 250 species and other aquatic plants collected from all over the world are cultivated in the park, which covers 60,000 sq.m. Seasonal excursion boat service operates in June to provide a closer look.

Katozu Junikyo (Twelve Bridges): Junikyo refers to all the bridges crossing the narrow waterway, called Katozu, to the east of the Aquatic Botanical Garden. The best season to visit the Junikyo bridges is in May and June, when one can enjoy the scenic beauty highlighted by irises blooming on both banks of the waterway on an excursion boat operated by a boatwoman. Excursion boats depart from the JR Itako, Junikyo (Kashima Line) and Sawara (Narita Line) stations.

Katori Shrine 21 : About 4 km east of Sawara Station, 15 min. by bus. This is one of the oldest Shinto shrines in Japan, although the present sanctuary was reconstructed in 1700. It is dedicated to Futsunushi-no-Mikoto, a deity of martial valor. The precincts are overgrown with aged, sacred cedar. The approach leading to the shrine is lined with cherry trees that are called *Bijin-zakura* (Belle Cherries) because they were donated by local women. A magnificent view of the Tone River, including the sacred forest of Kashima Shrine and Mt. Tsukuba, can be obtained from the terrace behind the shrine. The Shrine Museum exhibits various ancient objects of art and documents regarding the shrine.

Kashima Shrine [20]: About 1 hr.50 min. (114 km) from Tokyo Station on a JR limited express. It is dedicated to Takemikazuchi-no-Mikoto, a deity of martial valor like the one worshipped at Katori Shrine. Although the present shrine buildings only date from 1604 and 1619, the custom of making pilgrimages to Katori, Kashima and Ikisu (near Kashima) shrines is an ancient one. The grounds are thickly wooded with magnificent cedars and pines. At the rear of the shrine is the celebrated *Kaname-Ishi* (Pivot Stone), which is believed to hold down the head of a monstrous subterranean catfish, popularly thought to be the cause of earthquakes. The stone is traditionally regarded as the reason for the absence of earthquakes in this district. Many suits of armor and swords, including one that is designated as a National Treasure, are stored in the shrine.

Southeast of the shrine are the Kashima Sand Dunes, one of the four largest dune areas in Japan, extending for 24 km along the Pacific coast from Kashima in the north to Hasaki in the south. To the north of the sand dunes is the Kashima Coastal Industrial Area, which was established in 1962. Centering around Kashima Port, it has developed into a large-scale industrial zone concentrating on the production of steel, petroleum and metal.

Choshi [21] ☎0479: Pop. 88,509. 2 hrs. (121 km) from Tokyo Station by limited express on the JR Sobu Main Line. The city is situated at the mouth of the Tone River and is one of the best fishing ports in Japan, serving as a base for deep-sea as well as inshore fishery. Halfbeak, sardine, mackerel, bonito and tunny are the main catches. Choshi is also noted for its production of soybeans. The Tone River is the third-longest river in Japan, running 322 km down the Kanto Plain and emptying into the Pacific at Choshi.

The city has many attractions such as Kawaguchi Shrine (known as the guardian of Choshi), the long-renowned Iinuma Kannon (Goddess of Mercy) Temple and the Choshi Ohashi Bridge extending 1,450 m across the mouth of the Tone River. By traveling 20 min. to the east on the Choshi Electric Railway that runs through the city, one will reach the mild sea breezes of Cape Inubo.

The cape (alt. 20 m), protruding towards the Pacific, is a tableland produced through erosion by the sea, with a white lighthouse on the tip. The Pacific Ocean stretching over the horizon and the wild waves dashing against the beach create a magnificent view. There is a path below the steep cliff allowing visitors to reach the shore, while Marine Park (an aquarium) stands near the lighthouse.

The Choshi Electric Railway terminates at Togawa. To the north stands a hill called Mt. Atago (alt. 73.6 m) on top of which is a white observatory with a wide-ranging view of the mouth of the Tone River to the north and the stretch of cliffs, called *Byobugaura*, to the west. These rugged cliffs extend some 9 km to Iioka Town.

Boso Peninsula

A circular trip around the Boso Peninsula may be made on the JR Uchibo and Sotobo lines by trains departing from Tokyo Station. Limited expresses leave more or less hourly. The JR Uchibo Line runs along Tokyo Bay, going to Tateyama and Chikura, and beyond to Awa-Kamogawa, while the JR Sotobo Line runs along the Pacific Coast of the peninsula to Awa-Kamogawa.

Goi 21 : Located 14 km south of Chiba, this is the junction for the Kominato Railway to Kazusa-Nakano (39.1 km) and the main station for Ichihara. Ichihara (☎ 0436, Pop. 251,121) is one of the centers of the rising Keiyo (Tokyo-Chiba) Industrial Zone. The shores of Tokyo Bay between Urayasu (about 20 km northwest of Chiba) and Kisarazu have been reclaimed and developed into a mammoth coastal industrial zone of the petrochemical, shipbuilding and steel industries. By traveling about 1 hr. from Goi on the Kominato Railway, one can reach the Yoro Gorge, which is noted for enjoyable camping, fishing and hot springs.

Kisarazu 21 ☎0438: Pop. 121,833. About 1 hr.5 min. (75 km) from Tokyo by limited express. This city can also be reached by ferry from Kawasaki in Kanagawa Prefecture on the opposite side of Tokyo Bay. (22 km, 1 hr.10 min.) A project is under way to construct a bridge over the bay connecting Kisarazu and Kawasaki. Kisarazu is the commercial center of the Uchibo district and a significant base in the southern portion of the Keiyo Industrial Zone. It has been known for *nori* or laver cultivation since olden times and is a popular spot for gathering shellfish.

Shojoji Temple stands 400 m west of the station. The name has been popularized by a children's song about an old *tanuki* (racoon-like animal) that is said to have died from pitting its drum-beating skill against that of the temple's priest.

Minami (Southern)-Boso Quasi-National Park 21 : Created in 1958, it covers the 190-km-long coastline of the peninsula in a semicircle between Cape Futtsu on Tokyo Bay, and Cape Taito (refer to p.568), which juts out into the Pacific Ocean. With an area of 56.7 sq. km, the peninsular park includes almost all of the typical places of scenic beauty such as beach and mountain resorts as well as historical sites. It is an ocean-side vacationland with such a mild climate throughout the year that the daffodils and rapeseed even bloom in the middle of winter.

Kimitsu 21 ☎0439: Pop. 88,171. Adjacent to Kisarazu in the south, many factories in the Keiyo Industrial Zone are located in the northwest of the city along Tokyo Bay. Their presence has stimulated the area's rapid urbanization. On the other hand, the Boso Hills in the inland section of the city have one of the largest rice yields in Chiba

Prefecture. Tourist attractions include such long-popular sightseeing spots as Mt. Kano and Jinyaji Temple as well as Lake Mishima and the Seiwa Prefectural Forest with its large arboretum.

Mt. Kano ⟨21⟩: Alt. 352 m. The peak can be reached in 30 min. by bus from Sanukimachi Station on the JR Uchibo Line. It is a favorite resort for holiday-makers, especially for picnicking families.

At Shiratori Shrine, a 10-min. walk from the summit, panoramic view of colorful ridges and many small valleys (called Kujukutani, or Ninety-nine Valleys) spreads out below. The summit is marked by the ancient Jinyaji Temple, said to have been founded by Prince Shotoku (574–622), but the present structures were built in the early part of the 16th and 18th centuries. In feudal days the temple prospered under the protection of military leaders from Minamoto-no-Yoritomo onward.

To the west of the summit is a pasture called Mother Bokujo, where about 200 head of dairy cows, beef cattle and sheep graze in the 2,500-sq.-km pasture. Surrounding the grassland are a lodge for accommodations, recreational facilities, a tennis court, a horse-riding course, natural trails, a barbecue restaurant, etc.

Futtsu ⟨21⟩ ☎0439: Pop. 55,942. Known for Cape Futtsu, a 5-km-long sandbank protruding into Tokyo Bay like a crane's beak. The city plays an important role as the southernmost base of the Keiyo Industrial Zone. Many people converge on this city as a jumping-off point for sightseeing in southern Boso.

Sanukimachi ⟨21⟩: Known for a 56-m-high ferroconcrete statue of *Kannon*, the Goddess of Mercy, erected on top of Mt. Otsubo (alt. 120 m) and commanding a bird's-eye view of Tokyo Bay. The mammoth statue has observation platforms inside its arms, shoulders and crown. With a 10,000-candle-power light fixed on the crown, the statue also functions as a lighthouse.

Mt. Nokogiri (Saw Mountain) ⟨21⟩: Alt. 329 m. This mountain, which takes its name from its serrated peaks, is famous for the old Buddhist temple Nihonji and rock caves with stone images of the Five Hundred Arhatz and other Buddhist images totaling 1,553 on the southern slopes.

Nihonji Temple ⟨21⟩: Reconstructed in 1969. The main image is a stone *Daibutsu* (Great Buddha) seated out of doors. At 31.05 m, it is the tallest image of Buddha in Japan.

Hama-Kanaya is the station from which the summit is reached. It is a 10-min. walk to the ropeway station and a 4-min. ride up. Near the railway station is Kanaya Port, which is connected in 35 min. by the Tokyo Bay Ferry with Kurihama Port in Yokosuka on the opposite side of Tokyo Bay (11.5 km).

Descending from Hama-Kanaya to the south along Tokyo Bay, one can find fine swimming beaches such as those at Hota, Katsuyama, Iwai and Tomiura. Of course, they are packed during summer.

Tateyama ⟨21⟩ ☎0470: Pop. 55,497. About 2 hrs. (129 km) from

Tokyo Station by limited express on the JR Uchibo Line. The city is situated on the southern tip of the Boso Peninsula and blessed with a mild climate. The west side faces Tateyama Bay next to the Uraga Straits, while the south side faces the Pacific Ocean across a beach named Heisaura. This tourist city offers a lighthouse at Cape Sunosaki, flower gardens along a seaside highway named "Daiichi (No. 1) Flower Line" between Cape Sunosaki and Shirahama Beach, bathing resorts in Tateyama Bay and Heisaura Beach, Nago-Kannon (Goddess of Mercy) Temple, Gake-no-Kannon Temple on Mt. Funagata and Awa Shrine. Shirahama Beach and Cape Nojima can be reached via Tateyama.

Nago-Funakata 21 : Next to Tateyama Station. Nago-Kannon and Gake-no-Kannon temples are landmarks. The former, 2 km east of the station, is an old temple built in 717, while the latter is a vermilion structure perched on the side of a cliff 2 km north of the station.

Tateyama Bay (Kagamigaura) 21 : The shallow waters are edged by an arching, sandy beach, the beauty of which makes this the busiest seaside resort in the Uchibo area. The bay has a total of six bathing beaches.

Nishizaki Beach is the southernmost bathing beach in Tateyama. The Tateyama National Vacation Village equipped with various recreational facilities is also here. Cape Sunosaki, about 3 km west of the Tateyama National Vacation Village, lies on the southwestern edge of the Boso Peninsula. On its tip stands a white lighthouse, offering a magnificent view ranging from the Izu Seven Islands and the Miura Peninsula to Mt. Fuji across an expanse of ocean.

The "Daiichi Flower Line" driveway, a 17.4-km-long coastal road, begins from the opposite side of the cape and heads for Shirahama on Cape Nojima. Many attractions can be found along the road. These include the Tateyama Family Park with large greenhouses and a flower-picking garden; Nambo Paradise, a large-scale recreation center containing a tropical botanical garden; the Tateyama Yacho-no-Mori(Wild Bird Forest) where bird-watching can be enjoyed, and the Shirahama Flower Park.

Shirahama 21 : 16 km south of Tateyama Station, 45 min. by bus. It is known for women divers (for top shells, ear shells and seaweed) and picturesque seascapes. A lighthouse stands on Cape Nojima, about 2 km from Shirahama Bus Stop. The shoreline from this cape to Cape Taito in the north for a distance of 70 km is generally referred to as Sotobo Beach. The inlets along the jagged coastline contain small but active fishing ports. The hills are covered with colorful blossoms in season.

Chikura 21 : About 2 hrs. 10 min. (140 km) from Tokyo Station by limited express on the JR Uchibo Line. This fishery town is located on the eastern edge of the peninsula. A scenic place noted for its beautiful sandy beach, it is crowded with many bathers in summer and has several *minshuku* (family inns) to accommodate them. Other attractions include Chikura Spa near the beach and Takabe Shrine, where the god of cooking is enshrined. The shrine is also famous for its cherry blossoms.

The "Daini (No. 2) Flower Line" driveway covers a distance of 5. 6 km from Chikura to Wada along the JR Uchibo Line. Futomi is the station for reaching a well-known islet called Niemonjima, where Minamoto-no-Yoritomo took refuge from his enemies. He remained hidden here under the protection of the Niemon family before he established the shogunate government in Kamakura in 1192. Yoritomo later rewarded Niemon by giving his family the island. Near the island's pier is the Futomi Flower Center, where many greenhouse flowers are cultivated. Since almost 90% of its arable land is allotted for flower cultivation, together with Wada and Emi, it makes up what is called the Flower Zone.

Kamogawa ⎡21⎤ ☎04709: Pop. 31,868. 133 km from Tokyo Station, about 2 hrs. 10 min. by limited express on the JR Sotobo Line. The JR station serving the city is named Awa-Kamogawa, which is the terminal of the JR Uchibo and Sotobo lines, whichever route, east or west, may be taken along the peninsula. It is a fishing and tourist center on the southeastern coast of the peninsula, with many people who tour along the coast stopping here. It is also popular as a villa and a retreat for those living in the Tokyo area.

Kyoninji Temple: 5 min. by bus from Awa-Kamogawa Station. Belonging to the Nichiren sect of Buddhism, it was founded in 1281 by priest Nichiryu. It is dedicated to Kyonin, Nichiren's chief disciple, who was killed here with Nichiryu's father in 1264, when the sect's founder Nichiren was attacked by a local lord named Tojo Kagenobu. The section of the coast where the town stands is called the "Matsushima of Kamogawa" because of its numerous pine-clad islets resembling Matsushima near Sendai in the Tohoku District (refer to p.342). Along Matsubara Beach is an oceanic leisure center called Kamogawa Sea World. It is equipped with recreational facilities and presents shows by killer whales, dolphins, sea lions and turtles.

Amatsu-Kominato: A town sandwiched between two cities, Kamogawa and Katsuura. Centered around two urban areas called Amatsu and Kominato, this town is known as the birthplace of Nichiren, the founder of the Nichiren sect of Buddhism. Refer to p.437. **Seichoji Temple** (Kiyosumi Temple) is located on Mt. Kiyosumi (alt. 383 m) to the north of Awa-Amatsu Station.

Nichiren served his novitiate here, and in 1253 he first uttered his holy invocation—*Nam-Myohorenge-kyo* ("Glory to the Sutra of the Lotus of the Supreme Law"). The temple is said to have been founded in 771, but the present main hall, dedicated to *Kokuzo-Bosatsu* (Akasa-garbha-bodhisattva), was erected in the late Edo period and given a vermilion coat of lacquer. On the grounds are a large bronze statue of Nichiren and a modern worshipper's hall equipped with a marble bath. The huge cedar in front of the main hall measures about 47 m in height, 17.5 m in girth, and is protected as a Natural Monument. Mt. Kiyosumi, a prefectural park, is used as an experimental plantation by the Agriculture Faculty of Tokyo University. The dense forests cover an area of some 22.5 sq.km. Nichiren was born as the son of a fisherman in 1222 in Kominato in the east end of the town.

Tanjoji Temple 21 : 5 min. by bus from Awa-Kominato Station. The temple was erected in 1276 to commemorate the birth of Nichiren and belongs to the Nichiren sect. The original temple built by his disciples, however, was destroyed by a tidal wave and fire, with the present structures dating from the Tempo era (1830-1844). The temple has spacious precincts but is especially crowded when worshippers come to celebrate Nichiren's birthday on February 16.

Tainoura 21 : Literally meaning the Bay for *Tai* (a kind of sea bream, often considered as an auspicious fish), this noted sea bream habitat has been specially protected for a long time, and the fish is designated as a Special Natural Monument. A large number of *tai*, some measuring as long as 1 m, can be seen from the sightseeing boat that starts from near the front gate of Tanjoji Temple. It is said that Saint Nichiren prohibited sea bream fishing in this bay. Mamembara Plateau is located to the northeast of Seichoji Temple (4 km, 1 hr.10 min. on foot) and is noted for some 200,000 hydrangeas that bloom in July.

Namekawa Island 21 : A recreation center where dancing by trained flamingos, a flight of 500 peacocks and other shows can be enjoyed. The 600,000-sq.-m site also has such facilities as a playground, a zoo, a big barbecue restaurant and swimming pools as well as accommodations. Close to Namegawa Island Station on the JR Sotobo Line.

Katsuura 21 ☎0470: Pop. 25,563. About 1 hr.40 min. (111 km) from Tokyo Station by limited express on the JR Sotobo Line. The city is equipped with good port facilities for offshore fishermen. A morning fair dating back some 400 years is held every morning except Wednesday in the center of the city. Some 2 km southwest of Katsuura is the Ubara sea area, which was the first Marine Park to be so designated in the Kanto District. There is a clean swimming beach here, while fishing can be enjoyed in the clear waters throughout the year. The Cape Myojin area, called Ubara-Risokyo, is a scenic place with a series of rugged cliffs sculpted by the waves. It has long been known as a villa area.

Onjuku 21 : Known for some 200 *ama* (women divers) and excellent sea bathing. The sandhills along the beach also offer sand skiing. On a hill at Cape Iwawada, 3 km east of the station, is a 17-m-high obelisk erected in 1928 to commemorate the landing of Don Rodrigo de Vivero (d. 1636, an ex-Governor of the Philippines) and his men, whose ship, the "San Francisco," was wrecked off the shore here in 1609 while returning to Spain.

Ohara ⬚21⬚: The junction for the Isumi Railway (27 km), which connects with the Kominato Railway at the Kazusa-Nakano terminal. The Yoro Valley is 20 min. by bus from the terminal. Ohara is a fishing town, but it also has swimming beaches. The *Hadaka* (Naked) Festival is held here on September 23 and 24. Fishermen march into the sea shouldering *mikoshi* (portable shrines) to petition the gods for a good catch.

Cape Taito ⬚21⬚: Located 3 km southeast of Taito Station on the JR Sotobo Line. The 66-km-long, curved stretch of sandy beach from Cape Taito to Cape Gyobu, southwest of Choshi, is called Kujukuri-hama or Kujukuri Beach (*Kujuku* literally means 99, while 1 *ri* is equal to about 3.9 km). Since Kujukurihama faces the open sea, the waves are rough at this beach, but in summer many not only come to enjoy the swimming, but also the fishing and surfing. The 17.3-km-long Kujukuri Toll Road runs along the coast, connecting Ichino-miyamachi and Kujukurimachi. On the Cape is a natural garden of various beach plants that grow in large clumps. The garden is a Natural Monument.

Kazusa-Ichinomiya ⬚21⬚: A popular summer and winter resort chiefly engaged in the cultivation of watermelons, tomatoes and melons. Tamasaki Shrine is noted for its annual *Hadaka-Matsuri*, which is celebrated on September 13. The main tourist points of Kujukuri Beach, north of Ichinomiya, include Shirako, noted for its tennis lodges; Shirasato, where seine fishing is enjoyed; Katakai where the Iwashi (Sardine) Museum stands; Hasunuma, complete with large-scale recreational facilities and a marine park; Yokoshiba, containing a Kiddy land; Asahi, noted for its hot springs, and Iioka, a fishing port. All of these areas have swimming beaches, accommodations and restaurants. Mobara, Oami, Togane and Naruto (see below) are the closest stations for reaching the above-mentioned locations.

Mobara ⬚21⬚ ☎0475: Pop. 80,700. 1 hr.3 min. (74 km) from Tokyo Station by limited express on the JR Sotobo Line. It is an industrial city with large chemical-fertilizer and electric-machinery factories operated by utilizing the natural gas produced in abundance in the city and its vicinity.

Oami ⬚21⬚: Located 63 km from Tokyo Station via the JR Sotobo Line, it is the junction for the JR Togane Line, running 14 km northeast to Naruto on the JR Sobu Main Line. Besides rice, the town produces *uchiwa* (round, nonfolding fans) and *sake*.

Togane ⬚21⬚ ☎0475: Pop. 42,309. Situated midway between Oami and Naruto. It is a commercial city noted for its cherry trees beside Lake Hakkaku and a grape vineyard, which is open to the public.

Naruto ⬚21⬚: The junction for the Sobu Main Line and the Togane Line, the area is famous for such carnivorous plants as *mosengoke* or sundews and *tanukimo* or bladderworts, which grow in large clumps in a marsh 1.5 km southeast of the station. These beautiful Natural Monuments bloom from early summer to early autumn, imparting an air of mystery with their strange means of nourishment.

Area 13. Seven Isles of Izu and Ogasa-wara Islands

Seven Isles of Izu

The Izu-Shichito (lit. Seven Isles of Izu) lie off the Izu Peninsula to the southeast, extending in a chain from near the entrance of Tokyo Bay toward the south for a distance of about 290 km. It consists of Oshima, Toshima, Niijima, Kozushima, Miyakejima, Mikurajima and Hachijojima, but sometimes it indicates all the islands in this are. Of all these islands, the most well-known one other than the above-mentioned seven islands is Shikinejima.

Administratively included in the Tokyo Metropolis, the islands are of volcanic origin and a continuation of the chain of volcanoes of which Mt. Fuji and the Hakone mountains are a part. Consequently, nearly 99% of the total area of the islands (28.730 sq.km) was incorporated in the Fuji-Hakone-Izu National Park in 1964.

Almost all of the islands afford places for swimming, surfing, fishing and camping. They can be reached either by boat from Tokyo, Yokohama, Atami, Ito, Inatori, or Shimoda on the Izu Peninsula or by air from Tokyo (Haneda Airport). It is more convenient to take the ferry to Oshima and Niijima, while it is better to fly to Miyakejima and Hachijojima. There are frequent boat departures to Oshima as well as flights to Hachijojima.

Oshima 44 ☎04992: Pop. 10,194. The island is 117 km southwest of Tokyo and 41 km east of Shimoda (Izu Peninsula). With an area of 91 sq.km, it is the largest island of the Izu-Shichito (Seven Isles) group. Okada in the northern part of the island can be reached in 7 hrs 30 min. (5 hrs. 50 min. in summer) from Takeshiba Pier in Tokyo. Motomachi is another port on the island and the center of island transportation as well as administration. It is 1 hr. 40 min. (1 hr. by speedboat) from Atami and 1 hr.20 min. (50 min. by speedboat) from Ito on the Izu Peninsula by the steamers of the Tokai Steamship Co., or 40 min. from Inatori by a speedboat of the same company. The distance between the two ports, Okada and Motomachi, is 7.7 km and can be covered in 20 min. by bus. A regular airline service is also available from Tokyo International Airport (Haneda) to Oshima Island, with several flights operated daily by Air Nippon. The distance is covered in 40 min.

The chief attraction of the island is Mt. Mihara, a typical truncated volcano. There was a major eruption in November 1986. The smoke from the volcano can be seen many miles out at sea, serving as a conspicuous landmark for navigators. Except for desert tracts on and around the volcano, the whole island is richly clothed with vegetation, and an exceptionally mild climate prevails all year round.

Although the island is part of the Tokyo Metropolis, its continuing isolation in the Pacific has permitted the development of many unique traditions and customs. For instance, the *anko* (or island girls) traditionally wear *kimono* made of dark cotton material splashed over with a white pattern, a peculiar headdress and white *tabi* (a kind of socks)—although today this is mainly for the benefit of tourists. They also carried their burdens on top of their heads. Since dairy farming is one of the chief occupations of the islanders, the milk yield is of high quality and abundant. The island is also noted for its production of camellia oil.

Mt. Mihara ⎡44⎤: Alt. 758 m. The summit can be ascended in 30 min. by bus, passing through Yuba from either Okada or Motomachi. A fine view of Mt. Fuji and other islands of the Izu group can be enjoyed from the summit.

Senzu ⎡44⎤: A 15-min. ride on the bus from Okada (9 km). This is the northern entrance to a natural park called Oshima Park, maintained by the Tokyo Metropolitan Government. It covers an area of some 5.46 sq.km and has a natural zoo, extensive camping grounds, a sand ski ground, lodges and other facilities for outdoor activities. The camellia garden of some 3,000 trees is of special beauty.

Gyoja Cave ⎡44⎤: The mouth gapes over the beauty of the seaside at the southern end of Oshima Park. It contains a stone image of a Buddhist ascetic named En-no-Ozunu (commonly called En-no-gyoja), who flourished in the seventh to eighth century.

Sakura-Kabu: The lower part of a huge *Oshima-zakura* cherry tree trunk said to be over 800 years old stands by the side of the road to Mt. Mihara from Oshima Park. This Special Natural Monument has a girth of about 8.5 m at eye level and a height of 13 m. It has 14 branches and begins to blossom in late March, attracting many visitors.

Other points of interest on Oshima Island are Kyodo Geinokan (lit. Museum of Provincial Arts; located halfway between Okada and Motomachi), where performances like the *Anko* Dance and the beating of *Gojinka-Daiko* Drums are performed twice a day; the Oshima Lighthouse at Cape Kazahaya, the light of which is visible from 50 km out at sea, and Habu Port, a fishing port located at the southern tip of the island (16.7 km, 40 min. by bus from Motomachi) on the former crater lake opening into the sea.

Sightseeing tours by bus include visits to Oshima Park, Mt. Mihara, Kyodo Geinokan, Habu Port, etc. The bus starts daily from either Motomachi or Okada, taking 5 hrs. 30 min. to 7 hrs.

Toshima ⎡45⎤: Located about 26 km southwest of Oshima, the island is accessible from Tokyo by ferry in 9 hrs. 10 min. via Oshima. (7 hrs.

in summer). From Oshima, it takes 1 hr.

This small island with a circumference of 8 km is noted for its camellia trees, which bloom from late February to early March. Fishing can be enjoyed in any area of the island as well as swimming at a certain section of Maehama Beach on the northern coast near the ferry port.

Niijima [44]: 10 hrs. 10 min. (7 hrs. 50 min. in summer) from Tokyo, 4 hrs. 30 min. from Shimoda, and 3 hrs. 40 min. from Atami (only in summer). As a mecca for marine sports such as surfing, wind surfing, diving, water skiing, parasailing and hang gliding, it is the most popular of the Izu islands with the young. Niijima has some good beaches for swimming such as Maehama on the west coast and Awaiura and Habushiura, both of which are located on the east coast. Habushiura is also popular with surfers. Wadahama, located on the west coast, offers good camping grounds.

Shikinejima [44]: Located approximately 6 km southwest of Niijima. The Island's land mass is said to have been separated from Niijima by a massive *tsunami* (tidal wave) about 300 years ago. It can be reached in about 10 hrs. 40 min. from Tokyo (8 hrs. 30 min. in summer) and 3 hrs. 40 min. from Shimoda.

It is a small island about 12 km in circumference. The complicated coastline with its rugged cliffs and reefs jutting in and out offers the most beautiful scenery of the Izu islands. Calm, sandy beaches are hidden between the wild cliffs, offering a perfect place to relax in summer. There are two hot springs, Ashitsuki Spa and Jinata Spa, both gushing from tidal pools in the rocks. Many visitors enjoy both sea and hot-spring bathing.

Kozushima [44]: Situated 11 hrs. 20 min. from Tokyo through Oshima, or 7 hrs. 50 min. by direct ferry (only in summer) and 2 hrs. 10 min. from Shimoda. On the east coast of Kozushima is a beautiful, white-sand beach called Tako-wan, where swimming and surfing can be enjoyed. For camping, Tako-wan and Nagahama beaches on the northwest coast and the beach at Sawajiri Bay on the west coast are popular. Both surfing and fishing are available here.

Miyakejima [44]: Connected with Tokyo by a 6-hr. 30-min. direct-ferry service, and 50 min. by air. Since the island is made up entirely of lava flow from Mt. Oyama (alt. 814 m) located in the center of Miyakejima, sand on the beaches here is black. The most recent eruption was in 1983. Swimming can be enjoyed along the northern coast of the island. Camping grounds are available at Okubohama on the north coast. The southern part of Miyakejima offers some good fishing places.

Mikurajima [45]: Accessible from Miyakejima in 1 hr., but no ferry service is available from Tokyo. Since no travel facilities such as taxis or buses are available on the island, tourists are expected to walk when visiting points of interest. Nature remains unspoiled here, with a chain of cliffs on the southern coast and a 100-m-high waterfall on the west coast providing the scenic highlights. The island has a population of about 250.

Hachijojima ☐44☐ : Pop. 9,767. This island lies about 290 km south of Tokyo. A little smaller than Oshima, it covers an area of 68 sq.km and can be reached by ferry from Tokyo in 10 hrs. 10 min. Air Nippon offers five daily round-trip flights, with a one-way flight taking 45 min.

The island has two extinct volcanoes—Mt. Nishi (or Hachijo-Fuji, alt. 854 m) in the northwest and Mt. Higashi (or Mt. Mihara, alt. 701 m) in the southeast. The island has long been noted for its *Kihachijo* fabrics, woven of silk and dyed with vegetation produced on the island. More recently, the raising of tropical plants has become the major occupation of the islanders.

A 6-hr. sightseeing tour by bus includes a visit to a botanical garden of subtropical plants and watching the making of *Kihachijo* as well as a performance of local arts at the Hattori House, which was once a residence of officials during the Edo period. The tour starts from the Hachijo Town Office at 9: 30 a.m. every day.

Ogasawara Islands

The Ogasawara Islands consist of about 30 islands, large and small, lying 900 km to 1,300 km southeast of Tokyo. Geographically, the Ogasawara Islands are classified into four major groups of islands— *Muko* (Groom), *Chichi* (Father), *Haha* (Mother) and *Kazan* (Volcano). The last is better known as Iwojima. This entire group of islands was reverted to Japan in 1968 as part of the treaty with the U.S. for the return of Okinawa and is now counted as part of the Tokyo Metropolis. The Ogasawara Islands were named after Ogasawara Sadayori, a lord of Nagano, who is said to have discovered the islands in 1593. In 1972 all of the islands were designated as the Ogasawara National Park. Facilities for tourists are still inadequate, but the pristine nature and tropical atmosphere make up for the inconvenience.

Chichijima (Father Island): Covering an area of 24.53 sq. km, it is the largest of the entire group of islands. The island is served weekly from Tokyo by a ferry, which takes 28 hrs. 30 min. There is no airlines service to this island. Fishing can be enjoyed almost anywhere along the coast. Swimming is best at Kohama Beach on the west coast, but no camping is allowed on the island. Chichijima is noted for its jagged coasts and its abundant, subtropical vegetation.

Hahajima (Mother Island): This slender island, 58 km in circumference and covering an area of 20.8 sq.km, is itself a fishing place. The island is also favored with many subtropical plants. The island can be reached from Chichijima by ferry in 2 hrs. 20 min, with service available three times a week.

Section IV. Central Honshu
(Chubu District)

Central Honshu comprises the major portion of the so-called Chubu (Central) District. This region abounds in high mountain ranges and large rivers that pour either into the Pacific Ocean or the Japan Sea. At this point, Japan's largest island, Honshu, is at its highest and broadest.

The region consists of three distinctive districts: the Central Highland District, the Tokai District and the Hokuriku District. The Central Highland District, forming the roof of Japan, strides over the three prefectures of Nagano, Yamanashi and most of Gifu. This district is marked by the Northern, Central and Southern Japan Alps running from north to south and also by a number of lofty volcanoes, including Mt. Fuji.

The district south of the Central Highland District is called the Tokai District and includes the prefectures of Shizuoka, Aichi and a part of Gifu. It faces the Pacific Ocean and includes the Izu Peninsula with a serpentine coastline in the east and the Ise region in the west. The district that runs along the Japan Sea coast is called the Hoku-riku District. From north to south are the prefectures of Niigata, Toyama, Ishikawa and Fukui.

The three districts also differ in climate as well as topography. The Tokai District is rainy in summer and warm in winter, making it especially suitable for agriculture. Due to its moderate climate, this district is said to be the most agreeable place to live in the entire Japanese Archipelago. The Hokuriku District is snowy in winter, while various basins in the Central Highland District have an inland climate with a wide range of temperatures that fluctuate drastically between the hottest and the coldest periods of the year. The mountainous areas in this district are densely wooded and offer superb scenery.

The pivotal point of the region is Nagoya, Japan's fourth largest city, which is often called Chukyo (Central Capital) because it is situated midway between Tokyo and Kyoto. Indeed, the Chubu District serves as the corridor linking the eastern and western parts of Honshu.

Administratively, the Chubu District is made up of nine prefectures —Aichi, Fukui, Gifu, Ishikawa, Nagano, Niigata, Shizuoka, Toyama and Yamanashi. In this book, however, this division is not followed. In this section on Central Honshu, Yamanashi is completely omitted, while the three prefectures of Niigata, Nagano and Shizuoka are only partially included. Instead, the northeastern part of Shiga and a large portion of Mie—prefectures that are included in the Kinki District— are touched upon here primarily for reasons of their accessibility from Nagoya.

Area 1. Nagoya and Vicinity

Nagoya 57/58-59 ☎052

Pop. 2,101,291. It is the capital of Aichi Prefecture. It prospered as a castle town around the Nagoya Castle and is now the core city of the Chukyo Industrial Zone, serving as a major center of industry, administration, culture and transportation.

To the south of the city is Ise Bay, while to the north is a flat expanse of land called the Nobi Plain. Admistratively, the city is divided into 16 sections, with the center extending from the section around Nagoya Station over to Sakae in Naka Ward. It is known for its orderly streets laid out like a checkerboard, highlighted by its famous 100-meter-wide road. This area is the business and commercial center of the city. To the south is a coastal industrial zone with a heavy-industry / chemical-industry complex centered around Nagoya Port, while to the east are groups of large housing complexes and parks.

TRANSPORTATION

Transportation to Nagoya

Air: 14 km north of Nagoya City is Nagoya Airport (in Komaki), connecting Nagoya with 17 cities in Japan. Regular international flights take off and land here as well. It takes 40 min. by bus between the airport and downtown Nagoya.

Railways: All the Tokaido Shinkansen trains running between Tokyo and Osaka stop at Nagoya. It takes 1 hr.51 min. from Tokyo (366 km) and 1 hr. from Osaka (190 km). Nagoya is a vital transportation hub of the Chubu District, serving as the junction for the JR Tokaido Shinkansen, the Tokaido Main Line, the Chuo Main Line and the Kansai Main Line. Other railways serving Nagoya include the Nagoya Railroad (commonly called Meitetsu for short), with a network covering Toyohashi, Shin-Gifu and the Chita Peninsula, and the Kinki Nippon Railway (commonly called Kintetsu for short), which connects Osaka, Ise and Kashikojima on the Shima Peninsula.

Bus: The Tomei (Tokyo-Nagoya) Expressway and the Meishin (Nagoya-Kobe) Expressway connect Nagoya with Tokyo and Osaka, respectively. Many bus services are available for nearby places of interest in the vicinity. There are also direct bus services to the Hokuriku District (Fukui and Kanazawa) and Shinshu District (Matsumoto and Iida).

Transportation within Nagoya

Subway and bus services together with the Nagoya Railroad (Meitetsu) are the major means of city transportation. There are three subway lines: the Higashiyama and Tsurumai lines running east and west, and the Meijo Line running north and south. The subways that provide frequent service and connect many places in the city are very convenient. City buses leave from the east entrance of Nagoya

Station and Sakae in the center of the city.
HISTORY
The origin of today's large, prosperous city of Nagoya dates back to the construction of an imposing castle (1610) by Tokugawa Ieyasu for his son Yoshinao. Prior to this, castles were built in this area by the powerful Imagawa and Oda families. After the Oda family moved to Kiyosu about 5 km away, the castle was abandoned. After Yoshinao came to Nagoya, the area developed into a castle town of the Owari Tokugawa family (one of the three Tokugawa branch families), and quickly became a prosperous commercial center as a result of the family's policy to foster and develop industry and agriculture.

After the Meiji Restoration (1868), the city underwent many vicissitudes. However, since the construction of the Tokaido Main Line and the Chuo Main Line, the city has become the center of this region, continuing its smooth development in commerce and industry as its population grew to 1 million. During World War II, Nagoya was turned into a military city, producing 60% of the nation's aircraft and suffering repeated air raids as a result. After the end of hostilities, the city moved quickly to reconstruct itself and laid the foundations for its postwar transformation into a modern city.

INDUSTRIES
Since Nagoya is the central city of the Chukyo (lit. Central Capital, another name for Nagoya) Industrial Zone, which ranks among the country's four leading industrial zones along with the Keihin (Tokyo -Yokohama), Hanshin (Osaka-Kobe) and Kita-Kyushu (Northern Kyushu) areas, it is noted for its wide variety of products. Today, it is a comprehensive industrial city, not only of heavy and chemical industries, but also of traditional light industries. Especially, the vicinity of Nagoya Port comprises a large-scale, waterfront industrial area on reclaimed land where some of the nation's largest steel mill complexes, automobile plants and petrochemical plants flourish. Both in the southwest and north of the city, new industrial complexes are in the process of construction. The city's main products include processing machinery, transportation equipment, metals, textiles, wood processing, foodstuffs and pottery for export as well as domestic consumption. Traditional products include cloisonne and Arimatsu tie-dyed fabrics.

ANNUAL EVENTS
Grand Festival of the Toshogu Shrine: April 16–17. A gala parade of gorgeous palanquins and floats in celebration of this festival.
Atsuta Matsuri: June 5. The annual festival of the Atsuta Shrine. A spectacular fireworks display, *noh* drama, local performing arts, *sumo* and *judo* bouts are staged. The *Kanto Makiwara*—a wooden frame topped with 365 lanterns representing each day of the year and forming a dome over which 12 lanterns representing the full moon of each month are hung in a straight line—is a truly impressive sight.

Nagoya Matsuri: Mid-October. This is the city's largest and most colorful festival, originating among commercial circles in olden times. The varied program includes a procession of men clad in ancient armor and gaily bedecked floats.

Refer to the supplement for details regarding the "i" **System Information Center** in Nagoya.

PLACES OF INTEREST IN NAGOYA

Nagoya Castle 58 : Located in the northwestern part of the city. This castle was built in 1610 by order of Tokugawa Ieyasu as a fortified residence for his son Yoshinao, founder of the Owari Toku-gawa family, whose descendants continued to reside here until the Meiji Restoration of 1868. Reduced to rubble during World War II, it was reconstructed in October 1959. It features a majestic five-story, ferroconcrete donjon, 48 m high and mounted with a new pair of golden *shachi* (a mythical fish). The rooms on the second, third and fourth floors are used to display art treasures that escaped the fire during the war, while the fifth floor serves as an observatory. The observatory is accessible by elevator and commands a panoramic view of the Nobi Plain and the Pacific Ocean. The three-corner turrets, the secondary citadel and stone walls, undamaged by World War II, are listed as Important Cultural Properties. The castle is the symbol of the city, providing one of its chief attractions.

Hisaya Odori Park 58 : Located in the central part of the city, this boulevard park runs north and south, is 1.8 km long, 100 m wide and has four lanes on each side. It is one of the few boulevards in Japan whose objective is to prevent disaster. Besides its plaza with trees, flowers and water, the median strip has a monument and a relief presented by friendship cities—Nanjing in China and Los Angeles in the United States.

Nagoya Television Tower 58 : Located near the middle of Hisaya Odori Park. Serving as the symbol of modern Nagoya, the silver-colored tower rises 180 m high, with its observatory at the 100-m level commanding a beautiful view. When the weather is fine, one can view Mikawa Bay, Chita Peninsula and the Central Japan Alps. At night, a splendid view of the metropolis may be enjoyed. Near Sakae Subway Station.

Hosho-in Temple (Osu Kannon) 58 : Popularly known in Nagoya as "Osu-no-Kannon-san," it corresponds to Asakusa-Kannon Temple in Tokyo. The street from Banshoji Temple, which is 500 m to the east of this temple, is surrounded by a flourishing environment simi-lar to the Nakamise approach to Asakusa Kannon Temple. The vermilion-colored Main Hall was rebuilt in 1970. The Osu Archives here are known for preserving many ancient documents designated as National Treasures and Important Cultural Properties. Near Osu Kannon Subway Station.

Tokugawa Art Museum 58 : It is located at Tokugawacho, Higashi

Ward, on the site of the former mansion of the feudal lord of the Owari Tokugawa family. Opened in 1935, it contains more than 10,000 paintings, swords, tea ceremony articles, dyed fabrics, craft items, etc., handed down through generations of the Owari Tokugawa family. The museum is known worldwide for its valuable cultural collection. Above all, the "Genji Monogatari Emaki" (Picture Scrolls of the Tale of Genji), painted in the 12th century, is a National Treasure as well as an important and representative work of Japanese picture scrolls. 15 min. by bus from Nagoya Station to Shindekicho Bus Stop.

Nakamura Park 58 : Located 2.5 km to the west of Nagoya Station. The park was laid out around Toyokuni Shrine, which was built in 1885 in memory of the birthplace of Toyotomi Hideyoshi, a famous Japanese warlord. Hideyoshi was born in this village and his birthplace is believed to be in the current bamboo grove near the shrine. Many people like to stroll through this Japanese-style park with its pond and spacious grounds that abound in many trees such as camphor trees. Near Nakamura-Koen Subway Station.

Nagoya Port 59 : Opened as a modern port in 1907 after improvement work. Now, it is the third most-important international trade port in Japan after Yokohama and Kobe. More than half of its trade revolves around international business. The export of cars and the import of petroleum rank highest on the list of trade items. On the port's Garden Pier is the Nagoya Maritime Museum and the Fuji Antarctic Museum, moored-ship museum using "Fuji," a well-known ship once used for the exploration of the South Pole—both attracting many visitors. The Central Pier is the place from which tour boats leave for cruises around the port, offering a comprehensive view of Nagoya Port.

Atsuta Shrine 59 : Near the JR Atsuta Station is Atsuta Shrine—the most important Shinto shrine in Japan next to the Ise Jingu Shrines (Ise Grand Shrines). Enshrined here is the *Kusanagi-no-Tsurugi* (Grass-Mowing Sword). Together with the Mirror at the Ise Jingu Shrines and the Jewels at the Imperial Palace, it constitutes the Three Regalia of the Emperor. The shrine's annual festival is held on June 5. Legend has it that when Prince Yamato-Takeru-no-Mikoto, son of the 12th Emperor Keiko, was starting on an expedition against the rebels in the eastern part of the country, he visited the Ise Jingu Shrines and was presented with a sword by Princess Yamato-Hime-no-Mikoto. In his expedition, he used the sword to mow down burning grass that the enemy had set aflame. The Prince left the sword hanging on a mulberry tree, whereupon it was secretly carried away by Princess Miyazu-Hime, his wife. It shone so brightly, however, that it set fire to a Japanese cedar, which fell burning into the fields from which, by popular etymology, the name Atsuta (Hot Fields) is derived. Near Jingu-mae Station on the Meitetsu Nagoya Main Line.

Shiratori Mound ⃞59 : Located 500 m northwest of Atsuta Shrine, it is a tumulus in which the remains of Prince Yamato-Takeru-no-Mikoto are said to have been buried after his death in Ise Province (now, Mie Prefecture). According to legend, he was transformed into a white bird (*shiratori*) after his death. This is one of the two ancient tombs in the vicinity, the other one being the Dampuzan Mound of Princess Yamato-Hime.

Tsuruma Park ⃞58 : A park designed by the same architect who laid out Hibiya Park in Tokyo, it blends Japanese and Western styles. In the western part is a French-style garden with a water fountain, a large flower bed, a rose garden and streets lined with Himalayan cedars. In the eastern part is a Japanese-style garden with a pond and Japanese irises. Flower festivals are held in spring, featuring cherry blossoms, azaleas, roses and Japanese irises. Since the park contains cultural and athletic facilities, people visit here seeking both relaxation and recreation.

Higashiyama Park ⃞58 : Located in the eastern part of the city, this is a park with a zoo, a botanical garden and plush greenery on all sides. It covers an area of about 850,000 sq.m, with a Japanese garden and a flower bed skillfully designed to topographically take advantage of the hills, ponds and wooded areas. There is also a large playground for children. The zoo contains 2,100 animals of 390 kinds, with an overpass connecting it with the extensive botanical garden. A large greenhouse with about 1,900 kinds of tropical plants is included in the garden. Outside are camellia, azalea and rose gardens, etc., which can be enjoyed through all four seasons. While strolling along pathways, one can enjoy looking at old Japanese architecture such as the house with a steeply pitched thatched roof of *"gassho-zukuri"* style in the Hida Mountain region and the typical gate of a *samurai* house.

Nittaiji Temple (Japan-Thailand Temple) ⃞58 : Located on a high hill in the northeast part of the city, it was erected in 1904 as a repository for Buddha's ashes and a golden image of Buddha presented by the King of Siam. The temple is maintained by the various sects of Buddhism by turns, as an international, non-sectarian temple. A 10-min. walk from Kakuozan Subway Station.

Heiwa Park ⃞58 : About 1.5 km north of Higashiyama Park. This is a public cemetery park laid out in a bright setting. The graves of several celebrated persons may also be found here, including Oda Nobunaga, a powerful war lord of the late 16th century who sought to unify the country. He was succeeded by Toyotomi Hideyoshi, who successfully brought the warring provinces together. In the park is a temple dedicated to *Senju-Kannon* (Thousand-Handed Goddess of Mercy)—a present from Taiwan. The park has an abundance of trees and is visited by many families on picnics. The place is known for its cherry blossoms. A 20-min. walk from the Hoshigaoka Subway Station.

Around Nagoya City

Ichinomiya ☐57☐ ☎0586: Pop. 259,763. Northwest of Nagoya City and 16 min. by the JR Tokaido Main Line from Nagoya. Located approximately in the central area of the Nobi Plain, it is known as a textile city. It now boasts the largest production of woolen fabrics in Japan, the most important industry here, as well as synthetic fiber and sewing industries.

Masumida Shrine ☐57☐: Standing about 700 m northeast of the JR Owari-Ichinomiya Station and covering an area of about 48,000 sq. m. In the large precincts are many old shrine buildings, which are quite deserving of its status as the most-revered shrine in this region since olden days.

Myokoji Temple ☐57☐: Situated south of the city of Ichinomiya, this is a very old temple founded in 1365 and revered by both Toyotomi Hideyoshi and Tokugawa Ieyasu. There are many ancient buildings such as the *Chokushimon* Gate (Gate for Imperial Messenger), which dates back to the foundation of the temple. The entire compound is encircled by thick shrubery. Stored in the Treasure House are many treasures such as ancient documents, images of Buddha and paintings.

Bisai ☐57☐ ☎0586: Pop. 56,047. Located to the west of the city of Ichinomiya, the city is known for its fabric industry (as is Ichinomiya city), especially for its woolen fabrics.

Tsushima ☐57☐ ☎0567: Pop. 59,162. Lying in the western sector of Aichi Prefecture, the city prospered as a shrine town of Tsushima Shrine. It is a 25-min. ride to Tsushima on the Meitetsu Tsushima Line from Shin-Nagoya. Tsushima Shrine is a 15-min. walk from Tsushima Station. It was originally built in 540 A.D. and revered by many people. It was the fashion in the Edo period to visit this shrine during a pilgrimage to Ise Jingu Shrine. The shrine was held in great reverence and protected by the Oda, Toyotomi and Tokugawa families. The shrine's famous annual festival (*Tsushima Tenno Matsuri*) is held on the fourth Saturday and Sunday in July.

Inuyama ☐57☐ ☎0568: Pop. 69.215. The city prospered as a castle town after Oda Nobuyasu, son of Oda Nobunaga, built a castle 40 km north of Nagoya in 1537. There are many tourist attractions such as Inuyama Castle, cormorant fishing, descent of the "Japan Rhine," Museum Meijimura and Little World of Man. The city is visited by many foreign tourists. It takes 27 min. by limited express on the Meitetsu Inuyama Line from Shin-Nagoya to Inuyama. Built on a cliff, Inuyama Castle commands right underneath it a view of the Kiso River. Although it is small, it is known as one of the finest castles in Japan, presenting a very striking appearance when it is illuminated at dark nights.

Japan Monkey Park: An amusement center with an area of about 560,000 sq.m. Located to the east of Inuyama Yuen Station, the park is divided into a northern and a southern part. The northern part includes amusement facilities and a natural botanical garden. In the southern part are monkeys, kangaroos, deer and other animals. The most prominent attraction is the Japan Monkey Center with about 1,000 monkeys of about 100 kinds from all over the world.

Japan Rhine 〔57〕: The part of the Kiso River from Inuyama upstream to Mino-Ota is named the Japan Rhine, covering a distance of about 13 km. It is so named because it resembles the Rhine River in Germany. For its descent, free bus service is available from Nihon Rain Imawatari Station on the Meitetsu Hiromi Line, 17 min. from Inuyama Station. The time required for the descent is from 1 hr. to 1 hr.20 min. One can enjoy a thrilling boat ride shooting the rapids, viewing strangely and marvelously shaped rocks and passing through almost still waters. Near the terminal of this exciting descent is Inuyama-bashi Bridge where cormorant fishing can be observed every night from June to September. The best time to watch is between 8:00 and 9:00 p.m.

Museum Meijimura 〔57〕: Located to the southeast of Inuyama. This open-air museum was constructed in 1965 to preserve architectural and cultural property from the Meiji period (1868-1912) and the Taisho period (1912-1926). On a large, hilly area of 1 sq.km are about 60 buildings that have been removed from their original site and reconstructed here in harmony with the scenic surroundings. In the village, visitors can ride on a train pulled by a locomotive that was used on the first railway line constructed in Japan between Shimbashi in Tokyo and Yokohama in the 1870s as well as an oldtime streetcar that once ran along the streets of Kyoto. There are Western-style buildings built early in the Meiji period and the former homes of Mori Ogai and Natsume Soseki, great authors that represent Japan, as well the facade and lobby of the old Imperial Hotel designed by Frank Lloyd Wright.

Little World of Man: In contrast to Museum Meijimura in which Japanese architecture is exhibited, it has a collection of 27 buildings from 17 countries around the world and exhibits about 6,000 folkcraft articles. Restored buildings are set up along circular promenades, showing in an easy-to-understand manner how the peoples of the world live. Visitors can enjoy trying on various types of folk costumes from different countries.

Komaki 〔57〕 ☎0568: Pop. 120,398. Located in the northern part of Aichi Prefecture, the city has developed as a residential satellite community of Nagoya. Komaki Interchange connecting the Tomei Expressway and Meishin Expressway, and Komaki Junction connecting the Tomei Expressway with the Chuo Expressway are in the western and eastern parts of the city, respectively. Thus Komaki serves as an important transportation center. In the southern part of the city is Nagoya Airport—the gateway of air travel in this region. Sixteen domestic cities and 13 overseas cities are served by regular flights.

Shinrin Park (Forest Park) 57 : A natural park with an area of 560,000 sq. m in the northeastern part of Nagoya and the northern hilly area of Owari-Asahi City. Within the natural park are a public park, a botanical garden, a golf course and grounds for various sports. Among others, the botanical garden is elaborately designed with a Japanese garden in the center and representative trees from various prefectures as a reminder of life in one's native place. This is also a good place to observe nature or take a walk. 1 hr. by the JR bus from Nagoya Station.

Seto 57 ☎0561: Pop. 123,373. A 30-min. express ride on Meitetsu Seto Line from Sakaemachi Station, Nagoya. The city is located in the northern part of Aichi Prefecture. As the word *setomono* (pottery) indicates, its production of pottery here is the largest in Japan. The main products are what they call "novelties" such as toys, ornaments, Japanese and Western dinnerware and electric appliances. These products are exported overseas. The *Setomono* Festival is held every year on the third Saturday and Sunday in September when street stands selling porcelain products can be found in every part of the city.

Seto Porcelain: Kato Shiro-Zaemon Kagemasa, simply called Toshiro, first established a kiln at Seto around the year 1200 and produced some primitive, unglazed ware. Tradition has it that he crossed over to China in 1223 with a priest named Dogen and studied the art of porcelain for four years. After his return to Japan, he traveled far and wide throughout the country in search of better clay. Failing to find any superior to that at Seto, he resumed his work here. He also brought some clay from China, from which he made porcelain known as *Toshiro-Karamono* (Chinaware of Toshiro). The ware made with Japanese clay after his return from China is known as Old Seto, which, together with *Toshiro-Karamono*, are very highly prized.

Komainu (a pair of carved, mythological, lion-like dogs usually found guarding the entrance of Shinto shrines) at the Fukagawa Shrine in the city are said to be among Toshiro's representative works. They are registered among the Important Cultural Properties. A monument made of china stands in Seto Park in memory of the famous potter, and the Suehiko Shrine, 600 m from the station, is dedicated to him. In the northern part of the city is the Kama Shrine, sacred to Kato Tamikichi—another famed potter who introduced the Kyushu method of making white porcelain to Seto in 1807.

Jokoji Temple 57 : 1 km east of the JR Jokoji Station on the Chuo Main Line. It is an old temple of the Rinzai sect built in 1336. In the quiet, wooded areas of Japanese cedars, one can still find the Main Hall, *Kaisando* (Founder's Hall), the belfry and the storage for Buddhist scriptures. It was originally the family temple of Tokugawa Yoshinao, the first lord of the Owari Tokugawa branch family. The Main Hall and the lord's mausoleum are registered among

Important Cultural Properties. Nearby is a pond on which one finds the *Rokkakudo* Hall and Jokoji Recreation Park. The place is known for its cherry blossoms.

Tajimi 57 ☎0572: Pop. 90,504. A 40-min. ride on the JR Chuo Line from Nagoya (36 km). Located in the southeastern part of Gifu Prefecture, it is known as a city of ceramics. In fact, the city was founded on the ceramics industry and has especially developed as the marketing center of *Mino-yaki* ceramics (*Tajimi-yaki* ceramics). The city has now transformed itself into a modern industrial city centered around family dinnerware. Station buildings with ceramic walls, bridges with ceramic ornaments and other ceramic-related attractions present a unique appearance not found at other places.

Eihoji Temple 57 : It is an old temple at the foot of Mt. Kokei, 2 km northeast of the JR Tajimi Station. The temple was founded by Muso-Kokushi in 1314, a celebrated priest of Zen Buddhism. Its *Kannondo* (Main Hall) and *Kaisando* (Founder's Hall) are both designated as National Treasures. The garden designed by Muso-Kokushi, known for his garden-making artistry, is famous. The temple is situated in a deep, winding valley by the side of a swift mountain stream and is noted for its romantic scenery.

Ena 57 ☎0573: Pop. 35,330. A 45-min. ride (68 km) by limited express from Nagoya on the JR Chuo Main Line. The city is located in the southeastern part of Gifu Prefecture. Large plants for such industries as paper pulp and watches have been established here in addition to the traditional wood-processing industry supplied from forests in the surrounding mountainous areas. This area is known for the famous Enakyo Gorge on the Kiso River, which runs through the northern part of the city.

Enakyo Gorge 56 : 15 min. by bus from Ena Station. It is a 12-km-long gorge created by an artificial lake fed by the Kiso River that runs through the northern part of Nakatsugawa City to the northern part of Ena City. Created in 1924, the lake is the result of the first power-generation dam in Japan. Cherry blossoms, azaleas, maple, etc., are conspicuously beautiful blooming among the large, fantastically shaped rocks on both sides of the gorge. All through the four seasons, many tourists visit here to look at the scenery from an excursion boat and an aerial cable car. A boat excursion takes about 30 min.

Enakyo Land: This recreational park is located north of Enakyo Gorge. From the same pier from which an Enakyo Gorge excursion boat starts, one can also take a ride in an aerial cable car. The park has 40 kinds of recreational facilities and is ideal for family outings.

Nakatsugawa 56 : A 50-min. ride (80 km) by limited express on the JR Chuo Main Line from Nagoya. It is located at the southeast corner of Gifu Prefecture. In olden times, the city was the gateway of the Kisoji Road of the old Nakasendo Highway that connected Tokyo and Kyoto and prospered as a stage. Now, plants for such industries as electrical appliances and paper pulp are found here so that the city is in the process of becoming an industrial city. There are also many scenic attractions such as plateaus, lakes and valleys.

Nenoue Plateau 57 : A 45-min. bus ride from Nakatsugawa Station. The altitude of this extensive plateau is 950 m. It contains excellent leisure facilities of a scale and variety unparalleled in the Chukyo District. Variety can also be enjoyed throughout the four seasons, including the viewing of cherry blossoms and azaleas in spring and the changing of the colors of leaves in autumn. Many visitors come here to enjoy hiking and driving. On the two lakes here, one can enjoy fishing *wakasagi* (a kind of smelt), rowing a boat, playing tennis and camping.

Mt. Ena 57 : It has an altitude of 2,190 m. Located to the southeast of Nakatsugawa City, this is the southernmost mountain of the Central Japan Alps. Ena Shrine is on the summit of Mt. Ena, which offers a view extending to the Northern Japan Alps, the Central Japan Alps and as far as Ise Bay. To reach the summit, it first takes 1 hr. by car from Nakatsugawa Station to Kuroisawa Plateau and then a hike of 3 hrs. 30 min.

Tsukechikyo Gorge 56 : A 1-hr. 5-min. ride by bus from Nakatsugawa Station. This is a gorge stretching along the Tsukechi River, a tributary of the Kiso River. It runs through a lush forest of Japanese cypress trees. Many waterfalls are found here as well as pleasant, natural promenades.

Kuwana ☎ 0594 57 : Pop. 95,575. Situated in the delta area where the Nagara River, Kiso River and Ibi River pour into Ise Bay, the city has prospered as a commercial port. During the Edo period, it was a castle town and the 42nd stage on the old 53-stage Tokaido Highway. Now, the city is a residential satellite community of Nagoya as well as a commercial and industrial city serving as an important center of the Hokusei (Northern Ise) industrial zone. The city is known for its casting and metal industries. A 30-min. ride on the JR Kansai Main Line (24 km) from Nagoya or a 20-min. ride on an express of the Kintetsu Nagoya Line.

Nagashima Spa 57 : A 45-min. ride from the Meitetsu Bus Center of Nagoya Station. This is a new hot-springs area sandwiched between the Kiso River and Nagara River. It has extensive recreational and amusement facilities as well as a large bathing facility where 2,000 people can take a bath at one time.

Sports Valley Tokai: One of the largest recreational resorts in this region, it is adjacent to Nagashima Spa. There are many recreational facilities such as an area for hang gliding, a motocross course, pools and tennis courts as well as various amusement facilities. It is especially popular with families and youngsters.

Tado Shrine 57 : 1.5 km to the west of Tado Station on the Kintetsu Yoro Line. From olden times, it has been called Kita(North) Ise Jingu Shrines in contrast to the Ise Jingu Shrines, and many people have visited here to worship. Founded in the fifth century, it is remarkable for its architectural beauty and picturesque surroundings. The shrine preserves 30 bronze mirrors, which are all designated as Important Cultural Properties. The great shrine festival held on May 4 and 5 features the ancient event of *Ageuma Shinji* (horseback racing up a cliff) dedicated to an abundant harvest.

Yunoyama Spa 57 : 1 hr.7 min. from Nagoya Station on a Kintetsu Nagoya line limited express, with a transfer at Kintetsu Yokkaichi Station to Kintetsu Yunoyama Line. It is a hot-springs resort surrounded on three sides by mountains at the foot of Mt. Gozaisho. The hot spring is an old one discovered in 718. Along the river are modern hotels and *ryokan* or Japanese-style inns. Cherry blossoms, azaleas, fresh verdure and red-colored maple leaves present a magnificent view. In Oishi Park upstream of the spa are several giant, fantastically shaped giant rocks set each above the other on the riverbed, some weighing as much as 800 tons. This is a good place for a walk.

Mt. Gozaisho 57 : This is the highest peak (alt. 1,212 m) in the Suzuka Mountain Chain, which is known for its abundance of flora and fauna. On the summit is the Gozaishodake Sancho (Summit) Park, a large recreational resort with bungalows, huts and youth hostels. A 20-min. ride in the aerial ropeway from Yunoyama Spa and then an 8-min. ride on a chair lift. The summit commands a magnificent view of Lake Biwa, Ise Bay and Mt. Fuji in the distance.

Yokkaichi 57 ☎0593: Pop. 269,832, 35 km southwest of Nagoya on Ise Bay. It is the largest industrial city in Mie Prefecture. In addition to petrochemical products, porcelain, machinery, and cotton and woolen fabrics are also produced here. Endowed with excellent port facilities and vast tracts of land for plants, the city forms the core of the northern Ise industrial complex. A 29-min. ride from Nagoya by limited express on the Kintetsu Nagoya Line.

Suzuka 57 : Located south of Yokkaichi. The city prospered as a stage on the old Tokaido Highway. Main products are textiles, transportation equipment, foodstuffs and paper. It has made remarkable progress as an industrial city.

Suzuka Circuit 57 : 15 min. by express on the Kintetsu Nagoya Line from Kintetsu Yokkaichi. Then, 15 min. by bus after getting off at Shirako Station. Located in a hilly area to the south of Suzuka City, Suzuka Circuit is a general recreation grounds centered around an international racing circuit but also includes playgrounds, swimming pools, an ice skating rink and a hotel. It is Japan's first internationally, officially recognized race course, with a total length of about 6 km. In fact, it is the representative racing circuit in Japan.

Kameyama 57 ☎05958: Pop. 37,356. 1-hr. ride (60 km) on the JR Kansai Main Line from Nagoya. The city was a castle town and a stage on the old Tokaido Highway. It prospered as an important transportation center connecting Edo (now, Tokyo) and Kyoto. Even today it is a major railways junction for Nagoya, Osaka and the Ise area. Old houses, relics of an old stage, are found everywhere. The city is known for the production of rice and tea, but artistic Christmas candles of varied colors are also produced here and exported overseas.

Area 2. Ise and Shima Peninsula

Tsu 57/60-② ☎ 0592

Pop. 150,421. 1 hr. by limited express on the JR Kansai Main Line from Nagoya (66 km), 50 min. by limited express on the Kintetsu Nagoya Line. Situated on Ise Bay, the city is the capital of Mie Prefecture. It was once a castle town of the Todo family, but is now developing as a modern city, playing a central role in the education, culture, administration and industry of Mie Prefecture.

Tsu Kairaku-en Park 60-② : 300 m southwest of Tsu Station. Once the villa of the Toda family, the park is filled with azaleas, Japanese wisteria and cherry trees and commands a sweeping view of Ise Bay. At the entrance is a prefectural museum.

Ruins of Tsu Castle 60-② : The Todo family lived in this fortified residential castle for 12 generations, but today only the ruins of Tsu Castle—part of the stone walls and moats—remain. In addition to the old ruins, there is a three-story corner turret rebuilt in 1958, while elsewhere in the compound are a Japanese-style garden and a Western-style garden.

Shitennoji Temple 60-② : It is said to have been founded by Prince Shotoku, but most of the old buildings were destroyed during World War II. In the modern ferroconcrete Main Hall are a wooden image of *Yakushi-Nyorai* and colored portraits of Prince Shotoku as well as Todo Takatora, a famous lord of this area, with his wife. These art objects are all designated as Important Cultural Properties.

Kannonji Temple 60-② : Located in the busy, central section of the city. It is dedicated to the sacred image of *Kannon* (the Goddess of Mercy), which, according to legend, was found in 709 in the net of a fisherman. Many people come to worship at this temple.

Senjuji Temple: 20 min. by bus from Tsu Station. The largest temple in Mie Prefecture, it was built in 1465. In the extensive precincts are the magnificent *Mieido* Hall and Main Hall as well as an unusual, four-story *Taikomon* Gate and a tea ceremony house called the *Anraku-an*. In the Treasure House in the precincts are a number of heirlooms, some of which are designated as National Treasures or Important Cultural Properties.

Matsusaka 57 ☎0598: Pop. 117,464. 1 hr.20 min. (86 km) by limited express of the JR Kisei Main Line from Nagoya and 1 hr. 10 min. by limited express of the Kintetsu Yamada Line. The city is located in the central part of Mie Prefecture, with the northeastern sector facing Ise Bay. Formerly a castle town of the Gamo family, it is now known for its textile industry, which dates back to the days of traditional Matsusaka cotton cloth, and for its high-quality beef known as "Matsusaka beef." The city also has a prosperous wooden products industry. It is also noted as the place where Moto-ori Norinaga, a great scholar in the middle of the Edo period, lived.

Matsusaka Park: This is the site of the old castle where now only stone walls remain. It is presently popular as a place of recreation and rest for the local inhabitants, with Japanese wisteria and cherry trees planted for their pleasure. The old residence of Moto-ori Norinaga (1730-1801) has been removed here. His personal belongings are on exhibit in this house along with his works and an old bell that he loved. Norinaga called his house *Suzu-no-ya* (House of Bell). Next to his house is Moto-ori Norinaga Memorial Hall. More than 10,000 pieces of materials connected with his life are kept here, including his self-portrait, his beloved bell and his medicine chest. Moto-ori Norinaga, a native of Matsusaka, was one of the great scholars who worked for the revival of Shintoism and helped to bring about the Imperial Restoration of 1868. The 44 volumes of his elaborate commentary on the "Kojiki" (Record of Ancient Matters, refer to p.152)—the most famous of his numerous works—form an excellent encyclopedia of ancient Japanese lore.

Okukahadakyo Gorge: 1 hr.50 min. by bus from Matsusaka Station and an additional 20 min. by car or a walk of 1 hr.30 min. after getting off at the Okukahada-so Bus Stop. It is located about 40 km southwest of Matsusaka. The name applies to the general area covering the upper stream of the Kushida River near the border of Nara Prefecture and its tributary, the Hachisu River. This gorge contains deep, primeval forests, fantastically shaped rocks and beautiful waterfalls on both sides of the two rivers. The gorge of the Hachisu River, also called Hachisukyo Gorge, especially has many waterfalls and cascades, and is also known for the autumnal colors of the leaves.

Ise-Shima National Park 77

This is a sea park centering around the coastline that juts out into Ise Bay in the eastern part of Mie Prefecture, covering a total area of 555.49 sq.km. This coastal area is a ria-type coastline created by repeated upheavals and subsidences, and presents a fine, varied view. The most magnificent is the scenery of the tranquil bays of Toba, Matoya, Ago and Gokasho—all dotted with several large and small islands. On the other hand, the rugged landscapes of the tablelands with cliffs eroded by the open seas (such as Cape Daio and Cape Anori) are a striking contrast to the serene scenery of the inland sea. The Ise Jingu Shrines here have a long history of nationwide veneration.

Ise 77 ☎0596: Pop. 105,594. 1 hr.25 min. by limited express from Nagoya, 1 hr.45 min. from Uehommachi Station in Osaka and 2 hrs. from Kyoto by limited express on the Kintetsu Yamada Line. It is the gateway to Ise-Shima National Park. The northern part is on Ise Bay, while to the south is the eastern end of the Kii mountains. This is the place where the Ise Jingu Shrines are located. Uji, where the Naiku Shrine is located, and Yamada, where the Geku Shrine is located, have merged to become Uji-Yamada City. Renamed later as Ise City, it prospers in commerce and the major industries of ship-building, textiles and machinery.

Ise Jingu Shrines ⟨77⟩: They consists of the Naiku (Inner-Shrine) and the Geku (Outer Shrine). They are connected by bus over the 5 km that separates them. The Naiku Shrine is dedicated to the Sun Goddess Amaterasu-Omikami, while the Geku Shrine is dedicated to Toyouke-Omikami, the Goddess of Farms, Harvest, Food and Seri-culture. These shrines are constructed of plain *hinoki* wood (Japanese cypress) obtained from the state forests in Kiso Mountain Chain. In form, they represent the archaic Japanese style that prevailed before the introduction of Chinese architecture, with the crossbeams on the roof and the wooden frames on top patterned after prehistoric Japanese structures. On such an auspicious occasion as New Year's Day, hundreds of thousands of people make a pilgrimage to the shrines to pray for good health and prosperity. Before the Meiji Restoration (1868), neither Buddhist priests nor nuns were permitted to enter the sacred precincts. Most Shinto shrines were influenced, more or less, by the Buddhist principles of the Ryobu-Shinto philosophy (adopted from both Shinto and Buddhist princi-ples). However, only at Ise and Izumo (refer to p.799), has Shinto succeeded over the centuries in keeping its traditions pure.

From very early times it has been the custom to replace the shrines every 20 years by erecting new ones on adjacent plots reserved for that purpose. The last such ceremony, called *Sengu-shiki* (Removal Rites), took place in October 1973. Among the regular annual festi-vals held by the shrines, the most important are *Kannamesai* in October, *Tsukinamisai* in June and December, and *Niinamesai* in November.

Geku (Outer Shrine) ⟨94-②⟩: A-5 min. walk from Iseshi Station or 15 min. by bus from the Naiku Shrine. It is situated in a magnificent grove of age-old Japanese cedars. The tradition is that this deity (Toyouke-Omikami), accompanying Prince Ninigi-no-Mikoto, came down to earth by order of Amaterasu-Omikami and was originally enshrined at Manai in Tamba Province (now, Kyoto Prefecture). In accordance with a revelation of Amaterasu-Omikami imparted to Emperor Yuryaku, however, the shrine was moved to its present location in 478.

In order to worship, the visitor first crosses the Hiyokebashi Bridge from the *Omote-Sando* Approach. To the visitor's right is a large Japanese camphor tree called *Kiyomori-no-Kusu*, which is about 800 years old and 10 m high. There is a story that when the famous general Taira-no-Kiyomori (1118-1181) visited the shrine as an Imperial messenger, his ornamental coronet got caught in a branch of the tree. He became so angry that he ordered the branch cut off. On the right after passing through the first *torii* gate, the visitor will find the *Anzaisho* (Imperial House of Sojourn) where the Emperor and Empress rest when they visit the shrine. Adjacent to it is a building called *Saikan*. Beyond the second *torii* gate the visitor will see the *Kaguraden* where sacred dances are performed. Adjacent to it are the *Kujoden*, the *Gojoden* and the *Haiden* (Hall of Worship) as well as the offices where *ofuda* (charms) are sold. The visitor then comes to the precincts of *Shogu* (Main Shrine), with its Main Hall (*Shoden*) enclosed by four fences. The outermost fence, called *itagaki*, is in the shape of an irregular rectangle. Besides the main entrance at the front, there are three other entrances—one on each of the other three sides. The fence is made of unvarnished Japanese cedar. The second fence, called *tono-tamagaki*, is composed of alternately long and short logs of Japanese cedar with horizontal rails. There is a thatched gateway at the south entrance closed with a white curtain. Only Imperial personages and Imperial messengers are permitted to proceed beyond this gate. The third fence is called *uchi-tamagaki*. Composed of a palisade of planks, it has another thatched gateway. The innermost fence, *mizu-gaki*, is also a wooden palisade with an entrance on the south side. Inside this fence is the *Shoden* (Main Hall), which measures 10.2 m in width, 5.8 m in depth and 6.1 m in height. The only shrine called *Yuiitsu Shimmei zukuri* (unique Shimmei style), the entire shrine is made of unpainted *hinoki* (Japanese cypress). It is magnificent with a thick, thatched roof.

Other buildings are the *Mikeden* on the east side of the Shrine (where food offerings are dedicated twice daily), the *Tohoden* and the *Saihoden* (which stand on both sides of the front gate of the innermost fence), the *Yojoden* (inside the gateway of the second fence) and the *Geheiden* (the opposite side of the *Mikeden*). There are a number of affiliated shrines, including Kaze-no-miya Shrine, dedicated to the Deity of Wind, who protects the crops from wind and rain.

Naiku (Inner Shrine) 95-① : 20 min. by bus from Iseshi Station and 15 min. by bus from Geku Shrine. It is located about 5 km southeast of Geku Shrine at the foot of Mt. Kamijiyama on the Isuzu River.

Naiku Shrine closely resembles Geku Shrine in its general arrangements. After crossing Ujibashi Bridge and then passing through the first *torii* gate, pilgrims customarily proceed to the banks of the Isuzu River where they wash their hands and rinse their mouths with its crystal-clear water. This is done in preparation for worshipping at the shrine. From the second *torii* gate, an avenue of centuries-old Japanese cedars leads up to the Shrine Office and *Kagura* Hall. Farther on are other buildings inside the fences surrounding the *Shoden* (Main Hall).

In the Naiku are enshrined the Mirror (*Yata-no-Kagami*), which is one of the *Sanshu-no-Jingi* (Three Sacred Treasures), the other two being the Sword and Jewels—all three constituting the Three Regalia of the Japanese Imperial Throne. Japanese mythology says that the Mirror was handed by Amaterasu-Omikami to Ninigi-no-Mikoto, her grandson, when the latter descended to reign on earth. According to the instructions of Amaterasu-Omikami, the Mirror was to be kept enshrined in the palace of the Emperor, and that was done until the sixth year of Emperor Suijin (92 B.C.). Then, about the third century, for fear that too close contact might possibly desecrate it, the Mirror was moved to Kasanui-no-Mura in Yamato Province (now, Nara Prefecture) and placed in a shrine. Eighty-eight years later, it was moved to its present site.

Visitors to the Ise Jingu Shrines should bear in mind that the general public is not permitted to proceed farther than the first fence. Moreover, courtesy calls for visitors to remove their hats and over-coats when standing before the shrines.

A traditional dance called the "Ise-ondo," performed by girls, can still be seen in the city. This centuries-old dance, which originated in the Edo period, is accompanied by special music played by an orchestra made up of a *shamisen*, *kokyu* (Chinese fiddle), etc. A sacred dance called *kagura* is also performed at the shrines in the halls set apart for this purpose. Before 1868 this dance was performed only among private circles, but from that year on private performances were prohibited and the dance has since been confined to the shrines. The dancing girls hold twigs of the sacred *sakaki* tree, their number and length of performance depending upon the amount of offering. The orchestra consists of a pair of *hyoshigi* (wooden clappers), *koto* (a string instrument resembling a zither), *fue* (flute), *sho* (bamboo flute for traditional Court music), *hichiriki* (flageolet), and *taiko* (drum).

Jingu Bunko: 7 min. by bus from Iseshi Station. The Bunko, built in 1906, is a library of the Jingu Shicho (the Board for Ise Shrines). It houses about 240,000 volumes of Japanese, Chinese and Western books on Shintoism.

Jingu Chokokan Museum: Near the Jingu Bunko. It is a white, two-story, ferroconcrete building. It exhibits, among others, shrine treasures, Shinto costumes, archaeological data, and sculpture and paintings by modern artists. In the central part of this building is a 1/20 model of the *Naiku Shogu* (Main Shrine).

Ise-Shima Skyline: It is a 16.3-km-long toll road running along the ridge of Mt. Asama and linking Naiku Shrine with Toba City—the gateway to Shima Peninsula. A view of the ria-type coastline of the Shima Peninsula as well as the Chita Peninsula in the distance spreads out below. Mt. Fuji can even be seen when the weather is fine.

Mt. Asama ☐77☐ : 25 min. by bus from Naiku Shrine. It stands to the east of Ise City at a height of 555 m. Known for its scenic view, the mountain has an observatory from which it is said 18 old provinces of the Tokai District can be seen. At the summit is a Buddhist temple called Kongoshoji that belongs to the Rinzai sect of Buddhism (20 min. by bus from Naiku Shrine). The date of its founding is unknown, but the temple is dedicated to an image of *Kokuzo-Bosatsu* (a Buddhist deity), reportedly carved by Kobo-Daishi (or Saint Kobo), in the Main Hall. Listed as Important Cultural Properties are the Main Hall plus a wooden image of *Uho-Doji* (a Shinto deity) and a portrait of Kuki Yoshitaka—a warlord from Shima Province (now, Mie Prefecture).

Futamigaura [77]: 10 min. by the JR Sangu Line or 25 min. by bus from Iseshi Station. This is the name of the coastline extending from Takashirohama at the mouth of the main stream of the Isuzu River to Tateishizaki, 5 km. to the east. It is also a *misogiba* (purification place) for the Ise Jingu Shrines, with two celebrated rocks—*Meoto-Iwa* (Wedded Rocks) at its east end. Visited by many bathers in summer, this shallow beach offers a view at sunrise that is famous for its solemnity. Under very favorable conditions, it occasionally includes a glimpse of Mt. Fuji.

Meoto-Iwa [77]: A 15-min. walk from Futami Bus Stop. *Meoto-Iwa* are the two large and small rocks at the east end of Futamigaura. According to Japanese mythology, they are likened to Izanagi-no-mikoto and Izanami-no-mikoto, the creators of the Japanese nation. The larger rock (9 m high), on which there is a *torii* gate, and the smaller one (4 m high) are joined by a large straw rope about 35 m long. The rope is replaced with great ceremony three times a year on May 5, September 5, and late December. During the April–September period, the sunrise can be seen between the two rocks.

Futami Plaza: A recreation center on the beach near the two rocks. It includes tropical plants, flamingos and Tropical Land with a cave aquarium. Demonstrations of *ama* (women divers) feeding fish and a comical performance of sea lions can also be enjoyed.

Toba [77] ☎0599: Pop. 28,424. 1 hr.30 min. from Nagoya, 1 hr.53 min. from Uehommachi Station in Osaka, 2 hrs. 18 min. from Kyoto by limited express on the Kintetsu Yamada Line, and 20 min. on the JR Sangu Line or 40 min. by bus from Iseshi Station. It is situated on Toba Bay in the northeastern part of Shima Peninsula. With a good, natural harbor, it has prospered as a port city since olden times. It is the starting point of sightseeing tours to the Ise-Shima region. Toba Bay, with its many large and small islands, offers some very picturesque scenery. The city has many recreational facilities such as an aquarium, Pearl Island, museum and observatory, and is visited by many people throughout the year as a marine tourism city. Toba is the terminal of the JR Sangu Line. The Kintetsu lines also offer travel convenience with their frequent direct connections with Nagoya, Kyoto and Osaka. Cape Irago and Toba are connected by high-speed boat in 35 min. There are 50-min. excursion boat tours in Toba Bay that include a visit to Dolphin Island and Pearl Island.

Hiyoriyama Hill: A little, 68-m-high hill at the rear of Toba Station. At the summit is a hexagon stone on which directions are carved with the date of May 2, 1819. The place commands a magnificent view of Toba Bay, with Chita Peninsula and Atsumi Peninsula in the distance.

Pearl Island 95-② : A 5-min. walk from Toba Station. It is a small island in Toba Bay where Mikimoto Kokichi first succeeded in producing a cultured pearl in 1893. The entire island forms a pearl museum. It is easily accessible from the mainland by a 65-m-long Pearl Bridge. On the island are the Mikimoto Pearl Museum, Mikimoto Kokichi Memorial Hall and the *Ama* (women divers) Museum. Visitors may watch *ama* diving and also buy pearls on the island.

Mikimoto Kokichi was born the son of a poor noodle-maker in Toba in 1858. When he was 33 years old, he saw tiny seeds of pearls sold at exorbitant prices in Yokohama, inspiring him to cultivate pearls in Ago Bay of Shima Peninsula. After many failures, he finally succeeded in 1893 in artificially producing the first semispherical pearl in an oyster. And then in 1905 he made the first perfectly spherical pearl at the present site of Pearl Island. Until he died in 1954 at the age of 96, he devoted himself to the culture of pearls.

Cultured pearls are produced by introducing an irritant inside the ovary of a live oyster, causing it to secrete the nacre of which a pearl is formed. It takes about seven years for pearls to fully develop by this method. Needless to say, Mikimoto pearls have achieved an international reputation.

Pearl Museum: It contains four exhibition rooms showing the era of natural pearls, the era of cultured pearls, the process of pearl culture, and the production and distribution of pearls. Many objects of art and crafts, tools, utensils and data are also exhibited here. In addition, there are necklaces decorated with natural Persian pearls and a five-story Mikimoto pagoda comprised of more than 10,000 pearls.

Toba Aquarium 95-② : A 5-min. walk from Toba Station. Located near Pearl Island, it has a hospital for fish and is one of the best-known aquariums in Japan. It keeps *sunameri*, the world's smallest whale, a dugong and rare sea otters in Mermaid Hall.

Dolphin Island: 10 min. by an excursion boat that cruises around Toba Bay from Toba Port. Dolphin Island, another name for Hinata Island in Toba Bay, is so-named because of its long, slender, dolphin-like shape. Fujimidai, 5 min. up by elevator from the pier, is said to be the best observation point in the Toba Bay area, commanding a splendid view of the scattered islands in Toba Bay as well as Atsumi Peninsula and Chita Peninsula in the distance. Near the pier is a place where shows featuring *ama*, dolphins and sea lions are presented every hour. A promenade encircles the island.

Sugashima Island 95-② : 18 min. by ship from Toba Port. 13 km in circumference, the island is known for its *Shirongo* Festival of *ama* and boxwood trees. In the middle of the island is 237-m-high Mt.

Oyama, which is entirely covered with boxwood trees. The hamlet in the northern part of the island is a fishing village, which has been known for its *ama* since olden times. The island's Shirahige Shrine holds the *Shirongo* Festival on July 11. This is a festival of the white-robed *ama*, who dive into the sea at the blast of a trumpet shell to compete for gathering *awabi* (abalone).

Shima 　77

Surrounded by the Enshu-nada Sea and Kumano-nada Sea, Shima is really a province of capes. It has a complex, ria-type coastline with quiet inlets such as Matoya Bay, Ago Bay, Gokasho Bay, etc., making a striking contrast with the rugged open sea. The starting points for tours in this region are Shima-Isobe and Ukata on the Kintetsu Shima Line. Limited express services directly connect Nagoya, Kyoto and Osaka with this region.

Matoya Bay 　77 : Located in the eastern part of Shima Peninsula. It is a typical ria-type inlet between Cape Sugazaki and Cape Anori. Oyster culture rafts form beautiful geometrical designs on the water surrounded by an intricate coastline. As if to serve as a door to the bay, Watakano Island in the center of the resort is located here.

Cape Anori 　77 : 20 min. by bus from Kintetsu Ukata Station. This is a cape that separates Matoya Bay from the Pacific Ocean. This place is known for its splendid view and a lighthouse built in 1882. Because strong winds prevent trees from growing here, the rugged, exposed and red-soil cliffs offer a barren view. At the bottom of the cape is Anori, which is a base for coastal fishing. A puppet show called *Anori Bunraku* is designated as an Intangible Cultural Asset. During the festival of Anori Shrine held on August 14 and 15 every year (lunar calendar), this puppet show is performed on a stage in an open place in the precincts.

Ago Bay 　77 : Located to the south of Shima Peninsula, it has a ria-type coastline with more than 60 large and small islands. The place is known as the site of the first pearl culture. On the quiet surface of the bay are countless pearl rafts. Also called Pearl Bay, it is known for its magnificent evening view. The starting point for sightseeing is Kashikojima Island where excursion boats are available.

Kashikojima Island 　77 : 2 hrs. 3 min. by limited express from Nagoya, 40 min. by limited express from Toba on the Kintetsu Shima Line. It takes 1 hr.25 min. by bus from Toba Station. This is the largest island in Ago Bay and is the sightseeing center of the Shima region. Since the shortest distance is only 20 m between the island and the mainland, which are connected together by bridges on the east and north coast, the island looks more like a part of the mainland. The island has many good hotels and *ryokan*, or Japanese-style inns, and is visited by many people.

Shima Marine Land: A 5-min. walk from Kashikojima Station. Designed after ammonite fossils, it includes an original marine museum and an aquarium. The water tanks, located left, right and above, are so designed that visitors tend to feel like they are under water. Performances by *ama* and the feeding of *mambo*, or sunfish, are held everyday. Kashikojima Sports Land near Kashikojima Bridge has facilities for tennis, archery and other sports.

Cape Daio 〔77〕: 20 min. by bus from Kintetsu Ukata Station and a 10-min. walk from Nagiri Bus Stop where the visitor gets off. This cape juts off the southeast end of Shima Peninsula, separating the Enshu-nada Sea from the Kumano-nada Sea. Because of strong winds, private houses are surrounded by high stone walls, creating a unique view. The sea off the coast has been known as a dangerous spot for the navigation of ships since olden times.

Wagu 〔77〕: 50 min. by bus from Ukata Station and 30 min. by boat from Kashikojima Port. *Ama* who work in this region live here, with many of their rest huts located along the beach. Oshima Island off the coast, reached in 10 min. by boat, is known for its groves of crinums.

Goza 〔77〕: 1 hr. by bus from Ukata Station, 25 min. by boat from Kashikojima Port and 15 min. from Hamajima Port. It is located at the tip of Maeshima Peninsula to the south of Ago Bay. This is a humble village where private houses are built with Mt. Kompira (alt. 119 m) in the background. The beautiful, white sandy beach is a good place for camping and swimming. The summit of Mt. Kompira commands a splendid view of peaceful, picturesque Ago Bay and the vast Pacific Ocean.

Hamajima 〔77〕: 25 min. by bus from Ukata Station and 15 min. by boat from Goza Port. Located in the southern part of Shima Peninsula to the west of Ago Bay, this town is a base for coastal and inshore fisheries. Cultured pearls are produced here, and taking advantage of the moderate climate, melons and vegetables are grown in greenhouses.

Nemu-no-Sato: 15 min. by bus from Ukata Station. Covering 2.3 sq. km, this large recreational area occupies about half of Osaki Peninsula, which juts out into Ago Bay. The grounds contain many facilities, with hotels at the center. There is a music camping ground with musical facilities, including a recording studio and an ensemble hall. Sports facilities include a golf course, tennis courts and a marina. In addition, there are a botanical garden, an orchard and a zoo laid out on a lawn. These facilities are connected to each other by roads and promenades. Flowering plants are found in profusion, while peacocks freely strut about. Various festivals and musical contests are held in the outdoor hall in the music camping ground.

Gokasho Bay 〔77〕: 50 min. by bus from Iseshi Station. This is a ria-type bay on Kumano-nada Sea to the west of Ago Bay. Since the climate is moderate and the water temperature is high, pearl rafts are concentrated here to avoid cold temperatures in winter. Although it has a ria-type coastline as does Ago Bay, the islands here are sparse. Rugged cliffs and caves, eroded by the sea, offer a magnificent view.

Area 3. Mikawa Bay and Coastal Area

Chita Peninsula and Atsumi Peninsula, which jut out into Ise Bay and the Enshu-nada Sea like the grasping pincers of a crab, Mikawa Bay, which is embraced by the two peninsulas, and the Oku(Inner)-Mikawa region inland along the JR Iida Line, refer to the area mentioned here. This is one of the best sightseeing regions in the Tokai District, with many scattered, large and small islands, numerous hot springs, beaches and roadways.

Chita Peninsula 57

This peninsula, the length of which is about 40 km from north to south, juts out between Ise Bay and Chita Bay. The northern part of the peninsula has many commercial and industrial cities, while the southern part takes advantage of its moderate climate in its development as a horticultural area. A toll road runs north and south through the central part of the peninsula, while trains of the Nagoya Railroad (Meitetsu) Lines run on both its east and west sides.

Chita 57 ☎0562: Pop. 74,517. 25 min. from Shin-Nagoya by express on the Meitetsu Tokoname Line, getting off at Asakura. The city is in the process of developing from a cotton-cloth-producing community to an industrial city. Shin-Maikohama Beach (about 400 m long), popular with many swimmers and surfers from Nagoya, lies to the southwest of the city.

Handa 57 ☎0569: Pop. 96,499. 35 min. from Shin-Nagoya by express on the Meitetsu Kowa Line. One may also reach here by the JR Tokaido Main Line via Obu Station in 45 min. Situated in the middle of Chita Peninsula, the city is known for its Chita cotton cloth turned out by a cotton-weaving industry that is still prosperous. It is also known for brewing *sake* and making soybean sauce.

Tokoname 57 ☎0569: Pop. 52,754. 45 min. from Shin-Nagoya by express on the Meitetsu Tokoname Line. It has a long history as a ceramics town extending back to the late 16th century. There are numerous square kiln chimneys all over the town.

Omidoji Temple (Noma-Daibo): 50 min. from Shin-Nagoya on the Meitetsu Chita Shinsen Line to Noma and then a 10-min. walk. This is an old temple founded in the second half of the seventh century. Yoshitomo, the father of Minamoto-no-Yoritomo (the founder of the Kamakura Shogunate), was killed here, and his grave can be found on the precincts. The present buildings were rebuilt or repaired in 1754. There are many buildings, including the Main Hall and the belfry.

Cape Morozaki 57 : 30 min. by bus from Kowa Station on the Meitetsu Kowa Line. It is located on the southern tip of the Chita Peninsula and faces Cape Irago of Atsumi Peninsula; in between is Shinojima Island, where ferries ply to the Irago and Toba regions. The cape serves as an inshore fishing base.

Shinojima Island $\boxed{57}$: 10 min. by boat from Morozaki Port. It is an island to the south of Morozaki Port with a circumference of 6.6 km. The splendid view from here is similar to that of Matsushima Island near Sendai. This island is a good place for sea bathing and fishing.

Mt. Sangane $\boxed{57}$: A mountain 320 m high located in the north, inland of Mikawa Bay. A highway (12.3 km) runs up to the summit of the mountain where a full view of Mikawa Bay can be observed from the rotating observatory.

Gamagori $\boxed{57}$ ☎0533: Pop. 85,894. A city on Mikawa Bay in the eastern part of Aichi Prefecture and 55 km from Nagoya. 39 min. by *shin-kaisoku*(new, rapid train) on the JR Tokaido Main Line. From Tokyo, take the Tokaido Shinkansen to Toyohashi and transfer to the Tokaido Main Line—a trip totaling about 3 hrs. It is a prosperous city, turning out such products as fabrics, textile rope and precision machinery, with mandarin oranges growing on the hilly areas. The city is a major tourist center in the Tokai District and the focal point of Mikawa Bay Quasi-National Park, attracting many tourists throughout the year.

Takeshima Island: This is a small island in Mikawa Bay to the southeast of Gamagori Station. The island is connected by a 417-m-long bridge to land near Gamagori Fantasy Hall. It has 238 kinds of temperate-zone plants—all designated as Natural Monuments.

Miya Spa $\boxed{57}$: 10 min. by bus from Gamagori Station. Situated to the south of Gamagori, it is a scenic place that commands a panoramic view of beautiful coastlines and Mikawa Bay. The mountainside and the southern area facing the sea are separated by National Highway 23. The spa offers a relaxed, leisurely atmosphere.

Katahara Spa: 20 min. by bus from Gamagori Station. This quiet spa at the foot of Mt. Sangane commands a view of scenic Mikawa Bay below. There are many well-equipped *ryokan*, some made of ferro-concrete in the style of Western hotels and some built as traditional, *Sukiya-zukuri* style inns.

Nishiura Spa $\boxed{57}$: 30 min. by bus from Gamagori Station. It is a new spa at the tip of the point jutting out into Mikawa Bay. On the hilly slopes are many modern *ryokan*, or Japanese-style inns, offering a view of the beautiful coastline. It serves as a base for sightseeing trips around Mikawa Bay, with speedboats connecting the area to Toba, Irago and Gamagori. Two small islands—Sarugashima and Usagishima—lie offshore. Sarugashima (lit. Monkey Island) is the popular name for Oki Island. It is so called because more than a hundred monkeys have formed a community here. Immediately north is Usagishima (lit. Rabbit Island) where some 400 rabbits roam freely. These islands are very popular with tourists.

Aichi Kodomo-no-Kuni (Children's World): A 5-min. walk from Kodomo-no-kuni Station on the Meitetsu Gamagori Line, near the neighboring stop of Nishiura. Run by Aichi Prefecture, it is a large-scale playground with an area of 1 sq.km. There are varied facilities such as go-carts, miniature cars and outdoor sports facilities as well as a mini-steam locomotive train that runs here.

Atsumi Peninsula 57

This is a peninsula extending about 47 km east to west. It stretches between the Pacific Ocean and Mikawa Bay and faces Chita Peninsula. The central sector consists of a range of mountains 200-300 m high. The Pacific side and the Mikawa Bay side have different characteristics. Horticulture thrives on the Pacific side where the climate is moderate, while on the Mikawa Bay side, the waters are calm and shallow, attracting many sea bathers to its beaches. The biggest tourist attraction on the peninsula is Cape Irago at the tip.

Tahara 57 : 35 min. by Toyohashi Railroad Atsumi Line from the JR and Meitetsu Toyohashi Station, getting off at Mikawa-Tahara Station. It is located in the central part of Atsumi Peninsula. This is the place where Watanabe Kazan (1793-1841) killed himself. Tahara was governed by the Tahara Clan during the Edo period, and Watanabe Kazan, a famed artist and scholar of Western learning, was a *samurai* in this clan. When he was punished by the Tokugawa Shogunate for his anti-isolationist views associated with Western learning, he committed suicide to avoid disgracing his lord. The area abounds in historical sites connected with him. These include a hall, where many materials related to him are exhibited, as well as his old residence.

Cape Irago 57 : 1 hr.30 min. by bus from Toyohashi Station. This cape is located not only at the farthest tip of Atsumi Peninsula, but it also lies at the southernmost extremity of Aichi Prefecture. Near the lighthouse at the end of the cape is a scenic place where poets Matsuo Basho—a master of *haiku*—and Kakinomoto-no-Hitomaro—one of the greatest poets in the "Man-yo-shu" (a collection of great poems dating from the late Nara period, refer to p.153)—composed poems in its praise. Irago is connected with Toba, Cape Morozaki, Gamagori and Nishiura Spa by ferry and speedboat.

Koijigahama Beach 57 : About a 1 km-long coastline to the east, from the vicinity of Cape-Irago Lighthouse. It is a white, sandy beach that forms a gentle arc. In summer lovely, warm-temperature plants such as *hamayu*, or crinums blossom, grow here.

Hii-no-Sekimon (Rock Gates): 1 km east of Koijigahama Beach. There are two caves beneath the cliff formed by the erosion of giant rocks by the sea. One sticks out from the ocean's surface and the other lies along the beach.

Atsumi Flower Center: 10 min. by bus from Cape Irago. Nestled in the windbreak woods facing the Pacific Ocean is a botanical garden that contains eleven large and small greenhouses. The large hothouses contain banana trees, bougainvillea, and other tropical and subtropical plants, while in the small ones are cacti and chrysanthemums, the blooms of which are regulated by longer periods of light through the utilization of electric illumination.

Okazaki ⬚57⬚ ☎0564: Pop. 296,429. 29 min. from Nagoya Station by *sin-kaisoku* (new, rapid train) on the JR Tokaido Main Line, getting off at Okazaki, or 40 min. from Shin-Nagoya by express (limited express also available) on the Meitetsu Nagoya Main Line, getting off at Higashi-Okazaki. The two stations are 10 min. apart by bus. Higashi-Okazaki Station is in the center of town, which is situated in the central part of Aichi Prefecture. The city is famous not only as the birthplace of Tokugawa Ieyasu, founder of the Tokugawa Shogunate, but also for its traditional industries such as cotton weaving, stone products and *miso* (soybean paste) industries. Today, the automobile-related, chemical and machinery industries are significant. Okazaki Park in the city, known for the beauty of its flowers, is the site of the castle headquarters of the Tokugawa family when it lived here in the mid-16th century. The donjon was restored in 1959 and is all that remains.

Toyota ⬚57⬚ ☎0565: Pop. 318,992. Take the Tsurumai Subway Line from Fushimi Station in Nagoya. It runs into the Meitetsu Toyota Line. This city is a well-known automobile industrial city located in the central part of Aichi Prefecture. The city has made tremendously rapid progress as an industrial center since the establishment of the present Toyota Motor Corporation here in 1937. Ninety percent of the city's industry is related to automobiles. The city's population is the third largest in Aichi prefecture. Many Toyota Motor-affiliated companies have been established one after another in nearby cities such as Kariya (pop. 116,273), Chiryu (pop. 51,905) and Anjo (pop. 137,070). Toyota and its vicinity now constitute an important industrial area in the Chubu (Central) Industrial Zone. Toyota Motor's production of automobiles, which began in 1938, is the largest in Japan. Today, the company has more than 200 affiliated companies in the Tokai and Kanto Districts and produces 3.6 million automobiles a year. Those who would like to visit the Toyota Motor plant should make reservations (☎ 0565-23-1567) three months in advance.

Kuragaike Park ⬚57⬚: 15 min. by bus from Toyotashi Station on the Meitetsu Toyota Line. Centering around a 70,000-sq.-m pond called Kuragaike are a dude ranch, botanical garden and swimming pool. Toyota Kuragaike Memorial Hall near the park has been exhibiting historical materials collected since the establishment of Toyota Motor as well as classic cars and the latest Toyota models.

Korankei Gorge ⬚57⬚: 40 min. by bus from Toyotashi Station. Known for its autumnal tints, it is the most scenic part of this region. The gorge is covered with maple leaves on both sides for about 1 km.

Toyohashi ⬚57⬚ ☎0532: Pop. 328,923. About 50 min. from Nagoya on either the JR Tokaido Main Line or Meitetsu Nagoya Main Line by JR *shin-kaisoku* (new, rapid train) and Meitetsu limited express, and 2 hrs. 30 min. by Tokaido Shinkansen from Tokyo Station (a distance of 294 km). The city's population is the second largest in Aichi

Prefecture. Its thriving industries are centered around spinning, wood and foodstuffs. Connected by means of the JR Shinkansen, Tokaido Main Line, Iida Line, Meitetsu Nagoya Main Line and Toyohashi Railway, the city is an important industrial, tourism and transportation center in the Mikawa region. Streetcars still run in the central part of the city.

Toyokawa ⬚57⬚ ☎05338: Pop. 109,786. 15 min. on the JR Iida Line from Toyohashi. In the Edo period, it was an active market town on the old Tokaido Highway. It owed its prosperity in the late Edo period to visitors coming to the Toyokawa Inari Shrine (formally Myogoji Temple). It is worshipped as the *Oinari-san* for business prosperity and good fortune, claiming millions of followers through-out Japan. Inside the precincts are about 90 buildings as well as a garden that is designated as a Place of Scenic Beauty.

Horaiji Temple ⬚57⬚: 1 hr.30 min. by bus from Toyohashi Station. Regarded as a famous temple of the Shingon sect, it is especially known for its *konohazuku*, or otus scops, which are considered to be sacred birds. The temple is situated on a mountainside of the thickly wooded Mt. Horaiji (alt. 684 m). It was originally constructed in the early eighth century, but it was not until 1974 that the Main Hall was rebuilt. From the bus stop to the Main Hall, it is a 1-hr. 20-min. walk up 1,425 stone steps. In the Japanese cedar grove to the east of the Main Hall is Toshogu Shrine dedicated to Tokugawa Ieyasu.

Yuya Spa ⬚57⬚: 1 hr. 10 min. on the JR Iida Line from Toyohashi. This is a hot-springs resort serving as a base for exploring the Oku-Mikawa region, including Horaiji Temple. Accommodation facilities line both sides of the Uzure River. Horaikyo Gorge, situated 2 km upstream from the spa, is known for its varied scenic view.

Mt. Chausu: 1 hr.30 min. on the JR Iida Line from Toyohashi and 1 hr. 10 min. by bus after getting off at Higashi-Sakae Station. Bordering on Nagano Prefecture, it is the highest mountain (alt. 1,415 m) in Aichi Prefecture. The 4-sq.-km Chausuyama Plateau on Mt. Chausu has an man-made lake, pastures and other attractive features that are unique in Aichi Prefecture.

Sakuma Dam ⬚57⬚: 1 hr.50 min. on the JR Iida Line from Toyohashi to Chubu-Tenryu. Completed in 1956, the massive dam was built by damming the Tenryu River where it runs through a deep, V-shaped valley. The progress of this tremendous task became the theme for many books and movies. One of the major dams in Japan, it towers 156 m high and spans 294 m.

Area 4. Hamana Lagoon and Vicinity

Hamamatsu and Hamana Lagoon

The western part of Shizuoka Prefecture is well known for the beauty of its vast expanse of Hamana Lagoon. Located midway between the Kanto District (Tokyo) and the Kansai District (Osaka), this central sector of the Tokai District is very conveniently situated in terms of transportation.

Hamamatsu ⟨57⟩ ☎0534: Pop. 525,975.　2 hrs. 5 min. from Tokyo Station (258 km) and 50 min. from Nagoya (109 km) by the JR Tokaido Shinkansen.　Situated just about halfway between Tokyo and Osaka, it is the most important city in this area, functioning as the transportation center served by the JR Tokaido Main Line, Shinkansen, National Highway 1 and Tomei Expressway.　When Tokugawa Ieyasu built Hamamatsu Castle (6 min. by bus from Hamamatsu Station) here in 1570, the city prospered as a castle town, laying the foundations for the present city.　Hamamatsu's three major industries are the musical instrument, motorcycle and weaving industries represented by such world-famous companies as Yamaha Corporation and Kawai Musical Instruments Mfg. Co. as well as Honda Motor Co. and Suzuki Motor Co..　It is also known for the culture of eels and *suppon* or snapping turtles.

Nakadajima Sand Dunes ⟨57⟩: Lying 30 min. by bus from Hamamatsu Station.　Facing the Pacific Ocean, the dunes are 4 km from east to west and 600 m from north to south.　Because of their very gentle undulation, delicate and beautiful wind-wrought patterns on the sands can be observed.　On Hamamatsu Festival days, May 3–May 5, famous kite-flying contests are held.

Hamana Lagoon ⟨57⟩: One of the largest lakes in Japan, located in the southwestern part of Shizuoka Prefecture.　With an area of 69.3 sq.km, it is the fourth largest lake in Japan.　The lake also has the third-largest perimeter in Japan of 92 km.　The long perimeter is due to its ria-type shoreline, with many capes shaped by the eroded valleys that subsided and formed a lagoon.　Although the mouth of the lagoon was once separated from the sea by a sand bar, an earthquake accompanied by tidal waves in 1498 opened a passage through the sand bar.　Both freshwater and seawater fish live in abundance in the lagoon.　The largest number of eels and snapping turtles as well as oysters and *nori*, or laver, are cultivated here.

Kanzanji Spa ⟨57⟩: 45 min. by bus from Hamamatsu Station.　This is a hot-springs resort located at the base of a peninsula jutting out into the northeastern part of Hamana Lagoon.　It was only in 1958 that hot water first started to flow out, but with the addition of many recreational facilities, Kanzanji Spa has become the largest place for accommodating the sightseers conversing on Hamana Lagoon.

Hamamatsu Flower Park: 7 min. by bus from Kanzanji Spa.　This is a very large park that requires a minimum of 1 hr. just to go around it.　There are greenhouses in which tropical flowers are grown as well as a Japanese garden, a Japanese iris garden, a rose garden and a peony garden, allowing visitors to enjoy flowers all year round.

Bentenjima Spa ⟨57⟩: 40 min. by bus from Hamamatsu Station. This spa flows out in Bentenjima Island, which is one of the reclaimed islands to protect Hamana Lagoon from the direct waves of the Pacific Ocean. The island is visited by many people who enjoy soaking in the hot-spring water, gathering shellfish at low tide and swimming in the sea.

Lake Inohana ⟨57⟩ : 1 hr.25 min. by bus from Hamamatsu Station, getting off at Mikkabi Bus Stop. It is located to the northwest of Hamana Lagoon and is connected with it through the 120-m-wide Seto Channel. Mandarine oranges are grown on the steep slopes of the shore of the lake, giving it the look of a mountaintop lake. Accommodation facilities are available in Seto. Excursion boats ply between Seto and Kanzanji (30 min.). Located at the junction of Lake Inohana and Hamana Lagoon, Seto and the surrounding area offer many good places for fishing.

Makayaji Temple ⟨57⟩ : Standing about 2 km to the north of Mikkabi town on the northern shore of Lake Inohana. This old temple built in 726 attracts many believers in *Kannon* (Goddess of Mercy) for protection against evil. The garden on the left side of the precincts is the oldest in Shizuoka Prefecture.

Ryotanji Temple: Located 20 km northwest of Hamamatsu, 50 min. by bus from Hamamatsu Station and a 15-min. walk after getting off at Jinguji Bus Stop. It is an old temple founded in 733. Designated as a Place of Scenic Beauty, the garden of the temple is the work of Kobori Enshu, a famous garden artist of the early Edo period.

Hokoji Temple ⟨57⟩ : Situated 27 km northwest of Hamamatsu, 1 hr. by bus from Hamamatsu Station and a 15-min. walk after getting off at Okuyama Bus Stop. It is the headquarters of the Hokoji school of the Rinzai sect and is a representative Zen temple in the Tokai District. It was founded in the late 14th century. Many believers visit this temple which enshrines the god of fire prevention. Scattered among the dense cedar grove on the spacious temple grounds are some thirty buildings, including *Shichison Bosatsu* Hall, an Important Cultural Property from the Oei era (1394–1427).

Area 5. Mino and Hida Region

Gifu Prefecture is located to the north of Nagoya. Its natural topography and climate have two contrasting aspects: the mountain province of Hida (now, also Gifu Prefecture) with a range of steep mountain ridges, and the river side region of Mino (now, Gifu Prefecture) with the three rivers of Kiso, Nagara and Ibi. Gifu Prefecture has varied and rich attractions for visitors. In addition to its natural affluence, this region is also endowed with the advantage of being an important traffic center dating back to olden times. It was said that "He who controlled the Province of Mino will control the whole country," and Mino often played important roles on the stage of history; in fact, many wars were fought here. Thus, there are many historical ruins, old castles and temples well deserving of a visit.

Gifu 57/61 ☎0582

Pop. 406,900. About 1 hr.50 min. from Tokyo to Nagoya by the Tokaido Shinkansen, transferring there to a rapid train on the Tokaido Main Line for another ride of 20 min. Located in the north part of Nobi Plain, the city is the capital of Gifu Prefecture. The Nagara River runs through the central part of the city, although a major portion of the city is situated on the left side of the river. With Mt. Kinka (alt. 329 m) in the background to the east, the whole city has a tranquil atmosphere. Located here are many historical sites such as Gifu Castle on Mt. Kinka as well as other ruins that will remind visitors of the vicissitudes in the lives of such famous feudal lords as Saito Dosan and Oda Nobunaga, who lived in a turbulent age. The city dates back to the 14th century when a castle was built on Mt. Kinka. Saito Dosan rebuilt the castle and also encouraged industry, laying the foundation for the present city. During the Edo period, the city prospered as a stage and commercial center of the old Naka-sendo Highway. Now, the city is known for its textile industry and flourishes as a trading center of ready-to-wear clothing. The city is an important traffic hub of the region with Gifu Station, which is for the JR Tokaido Main Line and Takayama Main Line, and is connected with Shin-Gifu Station of the Nagoya Railroad (Meitetsu). Meitetsu connects Gifu and Toyohashi via Nagoya, with some branch lines extending from Shin-Gifu Station.

PLACES OF INTEREST

Gifu Castle 61 : 15 min. by bus from Gifu Station to Gifukoen-mae Bus Stop and then a 3-min. ropeway ride. The castle is on the top of Mt. Kinka. Originally built during the Kamakura period (1192–1333), it was remodeled time after time by Saito Dosan and Oda Nobunaga and was reputed to be an impregnable fortress. After the decisive Battle of Sekigahara in 1600, the castle was abandoned. The present donjon was rebuilt in 1956. Inside are a local folklore museum and an observatory.

Nagaragawa Spa 61 : Lying at the foot of Mt. Kinka on the Nagara River. There are many *ryokan* on both sides of the river. This is a base for watching cormorant fishing and sightseeing in Gifu City.

Cormorant Fishing: It is held on the Nagara River from May 11 to October 15. Tame cormorants are used to catch *ayu*, a sweetfish that is common throughout the country and is highly praised for its flavor. The fishing takes place nightly, except during the full moon and when the water is excessively muddy after a heavy rain.

Cormorant fishing has a very ancient origin. It is first mentioned in a poem in the "Kojiki", the oldest record of ancient Japanese history compiled in 712. Another reference states that in the reign of Emperor Daigo (885–930), *ayu* caught by cormorants were sent as a present to the Imperial Court in Kyoto. At a later date, Minamoto-no-Yoritomo, founder of the Kamakura Shogunate, is reported to have partaken of two servings of *ayu* caught by cormorants in the Nagara River. The presentation of *ayu* to the Kamakura Shogun and the Ashikaga Shogun became a regular custom that was continued into the Tokugawa period. In 1890 three stretches of the river were selected as Imperial reserves and placed in charge of special fishermen.

A cormorant fishing boat is manned by three men. The master (called *usho*) at the bow, wearing antique ceremonial headgear, looks after 12 birds. The other two work as assistants steering the boat or attending to the decoy fire that is kept burning in an iron grate at the bow. Each cormorant wears a cord around the base of its neck to prevent it from swallowing the catch, except for very small fish. The boats usually go out in a flotilla of six, either before the moon rises or after the sun sets because on moonlit nights the fish are not attracted by the fires. Thin, 3.6-m-long leashes are used to control the birds. A bird generally captures 2 to 4 good-sized *ayu* every time it is put into the water. Under ideal conditions, it averages 40 to 50 fish a night. Cornering fish by the combined movement of a number of boats creates a lively, attractive scene. The fish, thus hard pressed, often jump ashore. The cormorants that are used stand about 60 cm high and weigh about 2-3 kg. They are caught with bird lime placed on the rocks, with the first birds captured being used as decoys for the others. It takes about two months to tame the birds as the first step and another three years to train them, after which they are allowed to swim together with trained cormorants to accustom them to the underwater fishing. A fleet of boats, gaily illuminated with paper lanterns, follow the fishing craft to allow sightseers to enjoy a close-up view of cormorant fishing. The boats accommodates 10-50 people and can be hired through hotels and *ryokan* or at the association office near the Nagara River for viewing cormorant fishing.

Gifu Park 61 : 15 min. by bus from Gifu Station. This wooded park is located at the west foot of Mt. Kinka and has an area of 200,000 sq. m. It is the former site of a mansion inhabited by Saito Dosan and Oda Nobunaga, the lords of Gifu Castle. In front of the ropeway station is a bronze statue of Count Itagaki Taisuke, an eminent leader of the Meiji Restoration and later a famous politician in the Meiji period. When the Count was addressing an audience in one of the buildings in the park, he was attacked by an assassin in 1885. It is said that the wounded Count cried out, "Itagaki may die, but liberty will never die." His words moved the people so deeply that the statue was built in memory of his ideal.

Nawa Insect Museum 61 : A short walk from the Gifukoen-mae Bus Stop. Opened in 1896 and now known worldwide, it is the largest and most famous private museum of its kind in Japan. It has more than 300,000 insect specimens, some of them dating back to 1879. The owner of the museum sometimes personally guides visitors from abroad.

Gifu Daibutsu 61 : A large image of Buddha in Shohoji Temple near the entrance of Gifu Park. The height of the image is 13.7 m, the length of the face is 3.6 m and the length of the ears is 2 m. It is made like a huge basket covered with paper on which sutras are written and then finished in lacquer. Shohoji Temple was built in 1683 and belongs to the Obaku school of the Zen sect.

Kakamigahara 57 ☎0583: Pop. 128,068. 20 min. from Shin-Gifu Station by the Meitetsu Kakamigahara Line. The city borders on the eastern part of Gifu City. In the Meiji period, a military training ground and air base were established here, causing the city to prosper along with those establishments. Now, an air base for the Self-Defense Air Force is located here and aircraft-related industries are thriving.

Hashima 57 ☎0583: Pop. 61,652. About 30 min. from Shin-Gifu Station on a Meitetsu Hashima Line and also served by the Tokaido Shinkansen at its Gifu-Hashima Station—the Line's only intermediate station in Gifu Prefecture. It lies in a flat land between the Kiso River and the Nagara River in the southwestern part of Gifu Prefecture. The city has been known for many years for *Mino-jima* fabrics and has a prosperous textile industry even now.

Ogaki 57 ☎0584: Pop. 146,907. About 30 min. from Nagoya by rapid train on the JR Tokaido Main Line. The city is the administrative, economic and cultural center of the southwestern part of Gifu Prefecture, or the northwestern part of the Nobi Plain. It has developed as a castle town since Ogaki Castle was built in 1535 by Miyakawa Yasusada, a local lord. Later, the castle belonged to the Toda family, and the city prospered as an important traffic center where the old Minoji Road and Nakasendo Highway met. Taking advantage of water traffic on the Ibi River and the Suimon River, Ogaki was very active as a trading center as well. It is often called a "Water City," and thanks to the rivers and pure, abundant underground water, the textile industry as well as the chemical and machinery industries have led the way in making it one of the prefecture's major industrial cities.

Ogaki Castle: A 7-min. walk from Ogaki Station. Ogaki used to be the gateway to the Kinki District. When the famous Battle of Sekigahara was fought in 1600, the castle was the headquarters of the Western anti-Tokugawa forces. The present castle was rebuilt in 1959. Inside the four-story castle are a local folklore museum, an industrial tourism hall, a science museum for children and an observatory.

Myojorinji Temple 57 : Standing at the summit of Mt. Kinsho to the northwest of the city. According to the legend, it was founded by the Imperial order of Empress Jito in 686. The temple is dedicated to

Kokuzo Bosatsu (Buddhist deity). The principal image enshrined here is one of the three largest of this deity in Japan and is avidly worshipped by many believers.

Yoro Park 57 : 20 min. by Kintetsu Yoro Line, getting off at Yoro Station with another 5 min. by bus. It is a natural park halfway up the Yoro mountain area located in the southwest part of Gifu Prefecture. There are many criss-crossing promenades with cherry and maple trees, and a famous waterfall called "Yoro-no-Taki" (Filial Piety Falls) with a height of 30 m and a breadth of about 4 m. It takes 20 min. from the Yoro-koen Bus Stop. This waterfall is known for a legend which says that the water of the falls turned into *sake* for the benefit of a woodcutter with unusual filial piety. Yoro Shrine, which is named after the legend, is located along the route to the falls.

Old Battle Field of Sekigahara 57 : 15 min. by the JR Tokaido Main Line from Ogaki to Sekigahara. This was the site of a decisive battle fought in 1600 between the forces of Tokugawa Ieyasu and his opponents led by Toyotomi Hideyori, young son of Hideyoshi—the powerful war lord who ruled over Japan until his death in 1598. Ieyasu was victorious and established a shogunate government (*bakufu*) that lasted more than two and a half centuries.

Sekigahara takes its name from the fact that in ancient times a barrier gate (*sekisho*) stood here. This barrier together with ones at Suzuka in the Ise Province (now, Mie Prefecture) and at Arachi in the Echizen Province (now, Fukui Prefecture) constituted the three principal barrier gates of feudal Japan where all travelers were stopped and strictly checked. A monument marks the place where the barrier stood 1.5 km west of Sekigahara Station. Nearby is Sekigahara War Land where the Battle of Sekigahara is reproduced with life-sized images in this large, 30,000-sq.-m, outdoor recreation facility.

Mt. Ibuki 57 : 50 min. by bus from Sekigahara Station to the summit of the mountain. The bus runs only in July and August. Mt. Ibuki, 1,377 m high, is located on the border between Gifu Prefecture and Shiga Prefecture. The mountain, which consists entirely of limestone, is a grassy plain with shrubs for the most part. It is a treasury of medicinal herbs. A road connects the summit with Sekigahara. There are gentle undulations at the summit and a 3-km-long promenade along the perimeter. The view from the summit is magnificent, with Nobi Plain and Lake Biwa below and the Japan Alps in the distance. Skiing attracts many people in winter.

Kegonji Temple 56 : About 1 hr. 20 min. by Meitetsu Tanigumi Line from Shin-Gifu Station transferring at Chusetsu and Kurono stations, then a 10-min. walk after getting off at Tanigumi Station. Kegonji Temple is the last leg of the 33-Temple Pilgrimage that traverses the old Western Provinces. Those who complete the pilgrimage and offer their final prayers at this temple are given a certificate in recognition of their faith and diligence. It is known by the familiar name of "Tanigumi-san." It is an old temple of the

Tendai sect founded in 798. Within its extensive precincts are large numbers of Japanese cedars, Japanese cypresses and cherry trees. Many temples and halls are found halfway up the mountain. The approach to *Niomon* Gate from Tanigumi Station is alternately lined with cherry and maple trees, attracting many visitors in spring and autumn.

Yokokuraji Temple [56] : 30 min. by bus from Tanigumi Station. Located to the west of Kegonji Temple, it is a Tendai sect temple said to have been founded by Dengyo-Daishi, or Saint Dengyo, in 801. In ancient times, the temple prospered with some 300 branch temples, but it declined in the Age of Civil Wars. The present buildings were constructed during the Kan-ei era (1624-1644). Facing a valley stream, the temple has stone walls around it like a rampart. In the precincts are buildings such as the Main Hall, a three-story pagoda, *Sharido* (where Buddha's ashes are kept) and *Niomon* Gate. Because of a vast number of treasures that belong to the temple, it is also called the "Shoso-in of Mino Province" after Shoso-in—the Repository of Todaiji Temple in Nara. Refer to p.717 for more information.

Mino-Kamo [56] ☎0574: Pop. 41,500. 42 min. from Nagoya by limited express on the JR Takayama Main Line, getting off at Mino-Ota Station (58 km). Located approximately in the central part of southern Gifu Prefecture, the city plays an important role in the Ota Basin where the Kiso River and the Hida River meet. The city once prospered as a stage on the old Nakasendo Highway and as a terminal for ferry boats operating on the Kiso River. Today, it is a sightseeing base for shooting the rapids of the Japan Rhine as well as an important transportation center for railway and motor traffic. Horticulture flourishes on the plateau north of the city.

Seki [56] ☎0575: Pop. 67,132. 55 min. by the Meitetsu Minomachi Line from Shin-Gifu, getting off at Shin-Seki. The city borders on the northeastern part of Gifu City. It is well known as a cutlery town on the basis of the tradition of Seki smiths dating back to the 13th century. It has thrived by making swords and agricultural tools, although the major products are now pocketknives, kitchen knives, scissors and dinnerware. Sales amount to ¥43 billion annually, about 30 % of which comes from exports.

Shin-Chokokuji Temple [56] : Located in the central area of the city. It is called the Horyuji Temple of Mino Province after the well-known temple of the same name in Nara. It has many treasures, including an image of *Juichimen* (Eleven-Headed) *Kannon* to whom it is dedicated, and a splendid garden.

Mino [56] ☎0575: Pop. 26,761. The terminal of the Meitetsu Minomachi Line, 1 hr. from Shin-Gifu Station. Located in the central part of the southern area of Gifu Prefecture, it is known for traditional *Minogami* paper. Although it developed as a castle town in olden times, it prospered as a trading center for paper and raw silk, utilizing transportation on the Nagara River. The city now has about

50 handmade paper manufacturers producing paper for *shoji* (sliding door) and art paper. Machine-processed paper produced here includes securities paper, cardboard, toilet paper and tissue paper.

Hachiman ⬛56⬛ : 1 hr. 15 min. by the Nagaragawa Railway from Mino-Ota Station on the JR Takayama Main Line, getting off at Gujo-Hachiman Station. This is a mountain town situated on the upper stream of the Nagara River in the central part of Gifu Prefecture. Regarded as the central town in this area, it constitutes part of an important traffic base connected with the Hida, Mino (now, both a part of Gifu Prefecture) and Echizen (now, Fukui Prefecture) regions. It is well known for the *Gujo Odori* (Dance) Festival held each year from early July to early September. Nearly 500,000 tourists visit here every summer.

Hachiman Castle ⬛56⬛ : Situated on top of Mt. Hachiman (alt. 354 m) north of the city. A fort was built in 1559, while the second and third citadels of the castle were built later in 1588, completing its construction as a full-fledged castle. The present castle was built in 1933 and modeled after Ogaki Castle. The antique look of the stone walls reminds the visitor of olden times. The summit of the mountain commands a view of the entire Hachiman town below.

Gero Spa ⬛56⬛ : 2 hrs. 5 min. (ll9 km) from Nagoya Station by limited express on the JR Takayama Main Line. Many *ryokan*, or Japanese-style inns, line both sides of the Masuda River, imparting a delightful atmosphere. Many tourists visit the spa, which is the best hot-springs resort in Gifu Prefecture and a base for exploring the Takayama and Oku(Inner) Hida regions.

Nigorigo Spa ⬛56⬛ : 2 hrs. by bus from Hida-Osaka Station on the JR Takayama Main Line. Located in the east-central part of Gifu Prefecture, the spa is built on the western slope of Mt. Ontake at an altitude of 1,800 m. It is the base for people who climb Mt. Ontake.

Mt. Ontake ⬛56⬛ : This isolated peak rises on the border between Nagano Prefecture and Gifu Prefecture. It is an active volcano (alt. 3,067 m) and has been worshipped as a sacred mountain from ancient times. On Tsurugamine Peak, the highest, is the inner sanctuary of the Ontake Shrine dedicated to the deity of the volcano. The history of the shrine dates back to the eighth century. Women have been allowed to climb this mountain since 1874. Mt. Fuji and the Northern Japan Alps can be seen from the summit, which offers an extensive, panoramic view. The first eruption ever recorded in the volcano's history occurred in October 1979 and even now the volcano emits some smoke.

Takayama ⬛56/68⬛ ☎0577

Pop. 64,238. 2 hrs. 45 min. (167 km) by limited express on the JR Takayama Main Line from Nagoya. It is the central city of the Hida Region in the northern part of Gifu Prefecture, nestled in the Central Japan Alps. The Kanamori family ruled this region from 1585. After the Kanamori family was transferred to Dewa Province (now, Yamagata and Akita prefectures) in 1692, it was placed under the direct rule of the Tokugawa Shogunate (*bakufu*)—such territories were called *Tenryo* (lit. heaven's domain)—until the end of the Edo period. The city of Takayama is located in the eastern part of the Takayama Basin and has developed along the Miyagawa River. It still maintains the atmosphere of an old castle town, especially in the Higashiyama-Teramachi area and Sammachi-suji Street with its projecting lattices. The city has several cultural constituents, including old merchant homes, many museums and a variety of historical relics. It is also known for the resplendent *Takayama Matsuri* (Festival) and traditional products of artisans. The flavor of old history and refined culture not only attracts Japanese, but also tourists from abroad.

Takayama Matsuri Festival is a representative event of the Hida Mountains region. Held annually on April 14 and 15 as well as on October 9 and 10, it is especially conspicuous because of the parade of gorgeously decorated, high-wheeled *yatai* (wagon floats). Because of their brilliance, they are called "Moving *Yomeimon* Gates" after the famous gate in Nikko. Traditional products are made here, including Hida *Shunkei-nuri*-style lacquerware and *Ichii-Itto*-style sculptures as well as wooden products such as fixtures and furniture.

Refer to the supplement for details regarding the "i" **System Information Center** in Takayama.

PLACES OF INTEREST

Takayama Jinya ⬛68 : An 8-min. walk from Takayama Station. It is the former administrative office of Hida Province (now, a part of Gifu Prefecture) under the Tokugawa Shogunate government. It was originally a villa of the Kanamori family, with the present building being rebuilt in 1816.

Sammachi-suji ⬛68 : A part of the city east of the Miyagawa River, which flows through the center of the city. This part of the city thrived as a commercial center, and many houses of rich merchants and townsmen once stood side by side. Many of these houses were built in the late Edo period and early Meiji period. Some of these old structures still remaining are presently used as tea houses, *ryokan* and buildings for dyers and *sake* brewers.

Takayama City Folklore Museum ⬛68 : 15 min. by bus from Takayama Station. Many archaeological materials and exhibits of this locality are displayed in a storehouse made entirely of Japanese cypress about 100 years ago.

Kusakabe Folkcraft Museum ⬛68 : A 15-min. walk from Takayama Station. This folkcraft museum, formerly the residence of the Kusakabe family, is designated as an Important Cultural Property. Rebuilt in 1879, the wooden structure has one main house and two storehouses. The splendid old residence was constructed by one of the powerful merchants who thrived under government patronage.

Yoshijima Family Residence ⟨68⟩ : Located next to Kusakabe Folk-craft Museum. This was the residence of the Yoshijima family, which was engaged in *sake* brewing for generations. Designated as an Important Cultural Property, it is a representative merchant family building that was rebuilt in 1908.

Hida Koshokan Museum ⟨68⟩ : An 18-min. walk from Takayama Station. Here, the visitor is able to see traditional works of crafts-manship being made such as *Shunkei-nuri* lacquerware, *Ichii-Itto* sculptures, *hinoki-gasa* (lit. Japanese-cypress hats) and woodwork.

Takayama Yatai Museum ⟨68⟩ : A 20-min. walk from Takayama Station. In a building modeled after the ancient *Azekura* style are four *yatai* (wagon floats) that are used for the Takayama Festival. Exquisite, delicate sculptures and *karakuri-ningyo* (mechanical mario-nette)—the works of well-known Hida craftsmanship—are displayed here. The visitor can have a close look at them while listening to the festival music played on tape in a combination aimed at creating a festive mood.

Ruins of Takayama Castle ⟨68⟩ : A 25-min. walk from Takayama Station. The ruins of Takayama Castle on Shiroyama Hill to the southeast of the city command a full view of the city. Since the castle was built in 1588, six generations of the the Kanamori family have lived here for a total of about 100 years. The castle was destroyed later; now, only the foundation stones of the donjon and the stone walls of the old castle remain. The site has been improved and is now called Shiroyama Park, serving as a place of recreation for the inhabitants of the city.

Shorenji Temple: 15 min. by bus from Takayama Station. It is a temple that was moved here in 1959 due to the construction of Miboro Dam 15 km south of Shirakawago village. Said to be the oldest main hall of the Shinshu sect, it was designed and built in 1504 in the *Shoin-zukuri* style, a very unique construction among Buddhist tem-ples. The Main Hall features a roof with a gentle slope.

Hida Minzokumura Folklore Village : About 10 min. by bus from Takayama Station. Located at the foot of Mt. Matsukura, southwest of the city, the village includes the Hida Folklore Museum, the Museum of Hida Mountains and the Hida-no-Sato Home. The village has a collection of traditional-style houses and various kinds of utensils showing the natural features and the lives of the people of the Hida region.

Oku(Inner)-Hida Onsen-kyo (Spas Area) ⟨56⟩

1 hr.25 min. by bus from Takayama Station. This is an area of hot springs scattered along the gorges of the Gamada River and the Takahara River, both of which flow to the west of the Hotaka Mountain Chain rising on the border between Gifu Prefecture and Nagano Prefecture. There are about 10 hotsprings here such as

Hirayu, Shin-Hirayu, Tochio and Shin-Hotaka, all of them serving as a base for climbers.

Hirayu Spa ⊡56⊡ : 1 hr. by bus from Takayama Station. Legend has it that this famous spa was discovered by vassals of Takeda Shingen, a famed warlord during the Age of Civil Wars. The spa claims to be efficacious for the treatment of cuts and bruises. It has developed as a hot spring for various kinds of cures and still maintains a rustic atmosphere. "Norikura Skyline" Highway runs from this spa, which is often used as a base for driving through Nagano and Gifu prefectures. Nearby is Hirayu Folklore Museum, which was a private house in the traditional *gassho-zukuri* style, featuring a thatched roof with a steep pitch before it was moved here to become a museum. Also, not far from here and deserving of a visit is the noted Hirayu Otaki Waterfall.

Shin-Hotaka Spa ⊡56⊡ : 1 hr.30 min. by bus from Takayama Station. This spa is the innermost hot spring in the Oku-Hida Spas Area. Included in this spa resort are a group of hotsprings scattered along the upper reaches of the Gamada River. This spa has a serene environment and commands a magnificent view of Mt. Yakedake (alt. 2,455 m), Mt. Nishi-Hotaka (alt. 2,909 m) and Mt. Yarigatake (alt. 3,180 m). The spa has been used for many years by people climbing these mountains, but a ropeway now carries people halfway up Mt. Nishi-Hotaka, offering an easy way to ascend the mountain.

Kamioka ⊡56⊡ : 1 hr.25 min. by bus from Takayama Station. It is a mining town located in the northernmost part of Gifu Prefecture next to Toyama Prefecture. The town has developed together with the Kamioka Mine, the largest producer of zinc and lead in Japan. To the northeast of the city is Kamioka Castle, which was restored in 1970. In the same compound are a museum displaying materials related to the Kamioka Mine and a folklore museum.

Area 6. Kisoji Road

Kiso Valley, known for Mt. Ontake and "Kiso-bushi" (an old folksong), is an area along the Kiso River between Torii Pass and Magome Pass in the southwestern part of Nagano Prefecture. The valley is surrounded by the Central Japan Alps to the east and Mt. Norikura and Mt. Ontake to the west. Except for a small, flat section of land along the river, the whole area is covered by forests. There was a road called the Nakasendo Highway running through this mountainous area, but now the JR Chuo Main Line and National Highway 19 parallel this road. The Kisoji Road is a part of the Nakasendo Highway, which is still reminiscent of the old highway.

Nakasendo Highway: One of the five major highways designated in the early Edo period. It starts at Nihombashi in Tokyo, and passes through stages such as Itabashi (Tokyo), Omiya (Saitama Prefecture),

Karuizawa (Nagano Prefecture) and Shimosuwa (Nagano Prefecture). It joins the Tokaido Highway at Kusatsu (Shiga Prefecture) and continues on to Kyoto. The total distance is about 129 *ri* (about 500 km). Many travelers, feudal lords and court nobles traveled this highway to and from Edo (now, Tokyo). Since the Nakasendo Highway is mostly mountainous, people had to undergo a toilsome journey when they traveled through the precipitous passes. Kisoji Road was very difficult to traverse, not only due to the steep mountains and thick forests, but also because people had to walk on crude stone pavements and plank roads.

Kiso Goboku (Five Trees): Kiso has long been known for its excellent forests, and the feudal lords who ruled this area imposed strict controls to preserve them. Even today, they remain as one of the best forests in Japan, supporting the economy of this area. The most important trees of the forests have been called *Kiso Goboku* (Five trees of Kiso) and include *hinoki* (Japanese cypress), *sawara* (sawara cypress), *nezuko* (Japanese arborvitae), *hiba* (hiba arborvitae) and *koyamaki* (Japanese parasol fir). Of these, it was said during the Edo period that "One *hinoki* is worth one neck." In short, a *hinoki* was protected since it was worth as much as a human life.

PLACES OF INTEREST

Kisoji Road had 11 stages along the old highway. From north to south, they are: Niekawa, Narai, Yabuhara, Miyanokoshi, Kiso-Fukushima, Agematsu, Suhara, Nojiri, Midono, Tsumago and Magome. If time permits, it would be a good idea to start from Niekawa and follow all the stages to the south in sequence. However, most people usually visit the area centering around Tsumago and Magome. A hiking trail called the Shinanoji Natural Promenade runs 9.3 km through Magome Pass between Tsumago and Magome, taking about 3 hrs to cover.

Narai ⟨56⟩: 2 hrs. 45 min. (222 km) by limited express on the Chuo Main Line from Shinjuku in Tokyo to Shiojiri. After changing to a local train there, it takes another 25 min. (21 km). As the 34th stage from Edo, it thrived during the Edo period. Even now, houses still remain along the old highway in the southwestern part of the town as reminders of the bygone days of this stage town. It is designated as a place in which a group of traditional houses are to be preserved.

Kiso-Fukushima ⟨56⟩: 30 min. (42 km) from Shiojiri by limited express on the JR Chuo Main Line and 1 hr.30 min. (133 km) by limited express on the Chuo Main Line from Nagoya. It is the center of administration and culture of the Kisoji Road region. To the east is Mt. Kiso-Komagatake (alt. 2,956 m), while to the west is Mt. Ontake. Houses are located on both sides of a valley of the Kiso River. A folklore museum displaying some 800 exhibits about Kisoji Road is situated 10 min. away by bus from the station.

Nezame-no-Toko ⟨63⟩: 5 min. by bus from Agematsu Station on the Chuo Main Line. It is a peculiar and extraordinary scenic area of granite rocks eroded by the torrent of the Kiso River. Rinsenji

Temple near the river commands the best view.

Tsumago 56 : 40 min. (34 km) from Kiso-Fukushima by local train and 1 hr. 10 min. (99 km) from Nagoya by limited express on the JR Chuo Main Line to Nagiso, then 10 min. by bus. The government has designated it as a place in which a group of old, traditional houses are to be preserved, including the surrounding natural scenery. There are rows of traditional, old houses, *minshuku* (private homes providing rooms and board), tiny teahouses and folkcraft shops, with paper-covered lamp stands and signboards combining to create a restful atmosphere. The Waki-Honjin Okuya, remains of the old *honjin*, and Kotokuji Temple are worth visiting.

Honjin is an officially appointed inn where feudal lords and other high-ranking officials or Court nobles lodged during the Edo period. *Waki-honjin* is a secondary one.

Magome 56 : 35 min. by bus from Nagiso Station. Designated as the southernmost stage on Kisoji Road, it is also well known as the birthplace of one of Japan's greatest authors, Shimazaki Toson (1872 -1943). This place appears in many of his works. Most of the old houses were destroyed by a fire in 1895, but some were restored on a steep, 600-m-long slope, old-style houses recalling memories of by-gone days.

Magome Waki-Honjin Historical Museum: Furniture, utensils and documents handed down in the Hachiya family are displayed here. For generations, the Hachiya family ran this secondary officially-appointed inn, with the exhibits showing what the stages of the Magome and Kiso valleys were like in olden times.

Central Japan Alps: A mountainous region in the southern part of Nagano Prefecture that separates the Kiso and Ina regions, extending about 20 km from east to west and about 100 km from north to south. It is so named because of its location between the Northern Japan Alps and Southern Japan Alps. There are 25 mountains with an altitude above 2,500 m, the highest of which is Mt. Komagatake (alt. 2.956 m), followed by Mt. Hoken (alt. 2,931 m) and Mt. Utsugi (alt. 2,864 m). The Central Japan Alps are thickly wooded with magnificent scenery.

Mt. Komagatake: This principal mountain of the Central Japan Alps is also called Kiso-Koma. The silhouette is rounded and presents a feminine appearance. It has long been an object of faith and worship with the inner hall of Komagatake Shrine at the summit. After a 50-min. bus ride from Komagane Station on the JR Iida Line to Shirabi-taira, the ropeway takes one in 8 min. to Senjojiki—right below the peak of Mt. Hoken and not far from Mt. Komagatake.

611

Area 7. Toyama Prefecture

Toyama Prefecture, the most northern prefecture among the three Hokuriku prefectures that face the Japan Sea in the Chubu District. Toyama is famous for the beauty of its mountains and gorges, the most impressive of which are the Tateyama Mountain Chain and Kurobe Gorge. Toyama Bay is known for its unique natural phenomena such as mirages and *maibotsurin* (sunken woods), and its abundant seafood. Houses built in the *gassho-zukuri* style in Gokayama nestle in the mountains along the border with Gifu Prefecture, offering one of the fascinating sights of this area.

Toyama 62/66 ☎0764

Pop. 316,719. Located in the middle of the Toyama Plain, it plays a central role in the administration and economy of Toyama Prefecture as its capital. Toyama Station is a main station along the JR Hokuriku Main Line and the starting point of the JR Takayama Main Line, which connects Toyama with Gifu en route to Nagoya. In and around the city are local trains of the Toyama-Chiho Railway. Toyama is also the starting point of the Tateyama-Kurobe Alpine Route. Toyama developed as the castle town of the Mizuno family in feudal days, and now the steel, machinery, chemical and paper pulp industries are flourishing due to the abundance of electrical power and the improvement of Toyama Port. Famous since olden times for producing pharmaceuticals, the area now has an annual turnover in medicinal products of more than ¥100 billion.

TRANSPORTATION

3 hrs. 45 min. (316 km) from Nagoya by limited express on the JR Tokaido and Hokuriku main lines; 3 hrs. 40 min. (327 km) from Osaka by limited express on the JR Hokuriku Main Line via the Kosei Line; 4 hrs. 10 min. (455 km) from Tokyo by the Joetsu Shinkansen changing trains at Nagaoka to a limited express on the Shin-etsu and Hokuriku main lines; 1 hr. by plane from Tokyo; 25 min. from Toyama Airport to the JR Toyama Station by bus; 6 hrs. 50 min. by long distance bus from Tokyo.

Refer to the supplement for details regarding the "i" **System Information Center** in Toyama.

PLACES OF INTEREST

Toyama-joshi (Toyama Castle Site) Park 66 : Located near the center of the city, about 1 km south of Toyama Station. Toyama Castle has been a historical symbol of the city since its construction in the first half of the 16th century. The present donjon was rebuilt in 1954. In the park area around this castle are an outdoor theater and a children's playground.

Kurehayama Park 66 : 15 min. by bus from Toyama Station. It is a hilly park 77 m above sea level, located west of the city. From this park, views can be commanded of the majestic Tateyama Mountain Chain soaring in the distance, the Jintsu River just below and as far as the Noto Peninsula to the north. It abounds in cherry trees, which attract many people during the middle of April when the blossoms are in full bloom.

Municipal Minzoku Mingei Mura (Folk Village) 66 : 10 min. by bus from Toyama Station. Located at the eastern foot of the Kurehayama Hill area, it exhibits folkcraft items as well as the tools and materials of traditional industries in the Hida and Toyama regions. The village has seven buildings, each of which was relocated here from various places around this area.

Yatsuo: About 25 min. from Toyama to Etchu Yatsuo by the JR Takayama Main Line. Situated in the center of Toyama Prefecture, it is known nationwide for its production of Japanese paper and its folksong, "Etchu-Owara-bushi." Each year from September 1-3, men and women of all ages wearing *kimono* and braided hats march through the town, singing and dancing lustily.

Tateyama Kurobe Alpine Route 66-67

This is a magnificent, mountain-sightseeing route winding its way from Tateyama Station of the local Toyama-Chiho Railway and passing through the center of the Northern Japan Alps to its terminus in Omachi in Nagano Prefecture. One can enjoy a superb view of 3,000-m-high class mountains from the convenience of a cable car, bus, ropeway and trolley bus. (Tateyama to Bijodaira by cable car; Bijodaira to Murodo by bus via Midagahara.)

Murodo, 2,450 m in altitude, is the highest point along this route. At Murodo change buses and proceed to Daikampo through the tunnel, which bores right under Mt. Tateyama. Take a 1,702-m-long, single-span ropeway to get to Kurobedaira, from where an underground cable car leads to Lake Kurobe. A trolley bus runs from here through the underground tunnel to Ogisawa, where one changes buses to reach Shinano-Omachi Station on the JR Oito Line. It is possible, of course, to follow this route in the reverse direction. During winter, however, this route is closed because of heavy snow. It is usually open from April 25 to November 30, subject to change depending on snow conditions.

TRAVEL TIME
Toyama Station-45 min. by the Toyama-Chiho Railway-Tateyama Station-7 min. by cable car-Bijodaira-35 min. by bus-Midagahara-20 min. by bus-Murodo-10 min. by bus-Daikampo-7 min. by ropeway-Kurobedaira-5 min. by cable car-Lake Kurobe-16 min. by trolley bus -Ogisawa-40 min. by bus-Shinano-Omachi Station

Bijodaira: The western end of Midagahara. Situated 950 m above sea level, the plateau is covered with a primeval forest abundant with Tateyama cedars, Japanese beech and hemlock. It commands a view of the Joganji River below.

Tateyama Kogen (Plateau) Parkline 66 : A scenic road threading through the moderate slope on the Midagahara plateau from Bijodaira to Murodo. On the way to Murodo is an observation point for viewing the 350-m-high Shomyo Falls, which has been designated as a Natural Monument.

Midagahara 66 : A plateau spreading along the western hills of Mt. Tateyama about 2,000 m above sea level. It is grassy as far as the eye can reach, turning into a vast expanse of alpine flowers between July and August. It takes approximately 1 hr. to walk around the promenade. Skiing can be enjoyed as late as June.

Mt. Tateyama 67 : Mt. Oyama (alt. 3,003 m), Mt. Bessan (alt. 2,885 m) and Mt. Jodosan (alt. 2,831 m) are collectively known as Mt. Tateyama. Along with Mt. Fuji and Mt. Hakusan, Tateyama is one of the three most sacred mountains in Japan and has been an object of religious worship since olden times. The Tateyama Mountain Chain comprises these three and eight other mountains, the highest of which is Mt. Onanji (alt. 3,015 m) which adjoins the ridges of Mt. Oyama. On the eastern side of the chain is the grand gorge of Kurobe and on the western side the beautiful Midagahara plateau.

Murododaira 66-67 : The plateau at the eastern end of Midagahara, 2,540 m above sea level, located just below the summit of Mt. Tateyama and facing the soaring Tateyama Mountain Chain. The area turns into a magnificent field of wild flowers in summer. A 20-min. walk from the bus station brings one to Mikurigaike, a mysterious-looking crater lake with a perimeter of 600 m. Within another 15-min. walk is Jigokudani Spa, known as the spring with the highest altitude in Japan—2,300 m above sea level. Throughout this area, the earth belches out gas, creating an infernal scene.

Daikampo 67 : 2,316 m above sea level, located on the eastern side of Mt. Tateyama at the opposite end of the Tateyama Tunnel from Murodo. From here, one can obtain a sweeping view of the majestic Ushiro (Rear)-Tateyama Mountain Chain, which towers like a huge folding screen.

Lake Kurobe 67 : An artificial lake created as a result of the construction of the fourth Kurobe Hydroelectric Power Plant (popularly known as "Kuroyon Dam"). The lake covers 3.49 sq.km and is 1,448 m above sea level. Kuroyon Dam is not only the highest arc-style dam in Japan, it is also one of the top-class dams in the world. It is 186 m high, 492 m long and stores about 200 million tons of water. The dam was completed in 1963 after seven years of difficult construction and at the sacrifice of many lives. Located between the Tateyama and Ushiro-Tateyama mountain chains, the lake's deep-blue water extends north and south. On the northern side of the dam are an observation platform and a resthouse from which one can view the entire dam. An excursion boat departs from the wharf on the left bank of the dam for a 40-min. cruise around the lake.

(For the Tateyama-Kurobe Alpine Route in Nagano Prefecture, refer to p.500).

Uozu 62 ☎0765: Pop. 49,535. 25 min. (26 km) by the JR local train from Toyama. Enveloped in a quiet atmosphere, the city faces Toyama Bay, with the Tateyama Mountain Chain soaring behind it. Located in the eastern part of the prefecture, it is the principal city of industry and commerce in Toyama Prefecture, but it has also been known for its woodcrafts and lacquerware since olden times.

About 700 m out in Toyama Bay, myarids of *hotaru-ika* or firefly squids can be seen. During the spawning season between April and May, the luminous bodies of the squids shine on the surface of the water like fireflies. This place is also famous for rare mirages that can be observed on nearby beaches on warm, clear, windless days between April and June, providing another interesting tourist attraction.

Unazuki Spa 62 : 1 hr.5 min. from Toyama and 30 min. from Uozu by limited express of Toyama-Chiho Railway. Flowing from the banks of the Kurobe River at the foot of the Northern Japan Alps Mountain Chain, Unazuki Spa is one of the most famous hot-spring resorts in the Hokuriku District. It serves as a base for exploring the beauty of the Kurobe Kyokoku (Gorge) as well as the starting point of the Kurobe Gorge Railroad.

Kurobe Gorge 62 : The Kurobe River originates between Mt. Washiba (alt. 2,924 m) and Mt. Mitsumata-renge (alt. 2,841 m) in the central part of the Northern Japan Alps region, and extends 86 km north to Toyama Bay. At Kurobe Gorge, a steep gorge along this river, one can see awe-inspiring precipitous cliffs running from Unazuki Spa to the upper stream as well as a number of hot springs. It is regarded as the most scenic gorge in Japan, with huge rock walls some 2,000 m high from the valley bottom to the mountain peak. The usual sightseeing course is to Keyakidaira from Unazuki by the Kurobe Gorge Railroad. Spend 1 hr. or so around Sarutobikyo Gorge and then return by train. The view of the gorge from the Kurobe Gorge Railroad is magnificent, extensive and rich in variety. The railroad generally operates from the beginning of May to the end of November. On the way are the Kuronagi and Kanetsuri spas, where open-air bath along the riverbed can be enjoyed amid the natural beauty of the gorge. Sarutobikyo Gorge is 15 min. on foot from Keyakidaira Station, the terminal of the railway line. Its name metaphorically implies that the valley is narrow enough for monkeys to jump across. The thick Japanese cedar forest that covers the gorge is typical of the views of the scenic Kurobe Gorge. From the observation platform, one can see a rapid stream washing the rock walls and creating a deep abyss in the valley below. This mysterious valley is designated as a Place of Scenic Beauty and a Natural Monument.

Takaoka 62 ☎0766: Pop. 177,368. 20 min. (19 km) by the JR Hokuriku Main Line from Toyama. Located in the northwest part of Toyama Prefecture, it is the center of the area in terms of transportation, economy and culture. Situated in the northern part of the city, Fushiki Port is one of the busiest trading ports on the Japan Sea, with modern metal and chemical factories standing abreast here. Traditional industries such as copper ware, textile printing and lacquerware flourish as well. This city has the historical background of being the provincial capital, with Kokubunji Temple (a state-established provincial temple) built here during the Nara period (eighth century). The prosperity of Takaoka began when the second Lord of the Maeda Clan, Toshinaga, built a castle here in 1609. Thanks to its long history, it abounds in historical relics and other remnants of a castle town worth seeing. Located on the tableland just outside the downtown area, the Takaoka Kojo (Old Castle) Park is 800 m northeast of Takaoka Station. Although this is the site of the Takaoka Castle, all that remains today are the outer moat and part of the stone walls. The huge, 210,000-sq.-m site is now an all-year-round recreation area for local residents with a historical museum, zoo, art museum and library. Takaoka Daibutsu (Great Buddha) is located in a narrow street near the Takaoka Old Castle Park. A large, wooden, gilt image of the Buddha was erected here in 1745, but was later destroyed by fire. The present image was made in 1933. Made from traditional Takaoka copper, it stands 15.4 m tall and is a symbol of the city. Zuiryuji Temple, a Buddhist temple of the Soto Zen sect, was founded by the Lord of the Kaga Clan, Maeda Toshitsune. Its *Somon* (Front Gate), *Sammon* (Main Gate), *Butsuden* (Sanctum) and *Hodo* (Lecture Hall) are lined up in a column and enclosed by corridors. The temple has many treasures.

Himi 62 ☎0766: Pop. ₍₎457. 30 min. by the JR Himi Line from Takaoka Station. Located on ᵗʰ᷆ eastern base of the Noto Peninsula, it is surrounded on both the north ᵃⁿᵈ south by hills. The fishery industry flourishes around the eastern pa᷆᷆ ᵒᶠ the city facing Toyama Bay. The area is famous for its tradition᷇ᵃˡ ᵇᵒᵈ of using a fixed shore net to fish for *buri*, a type of yellowtail.

Tonami 62 ☎0763: Pop. 36,977. 20 min. by the ᴶ from Takaoka. The city, situated south of Takaoka, pr᷆᷆ᵃⁿᵃ Line alluvial cone developed by the Shokawa River. The ᵇ᷆᷆ⁿ an Expressway passes through the northwestern part of the ᶜᵢ Tonami is famous for the cultivation of tulip bulbs, boasting the largest yield in Japan. A tulip fair is held from the end of April through the beginning of May.

Shogawakyo Gorge 62-63 : 1 hr.5 min. by bus from Takaoka Station. Created by the Shogawa River, which originates in Mt. Eboshi in the northern part of Gifu Prefecture, the gorge is an ideal place for drivers enjoying the spectacle of autumn colors.

Omaki Spa 63 : 1 hr. by bus from Takaoka Station, get off at

Shimohara Bus Stop and another 30 min. by boat to Omaki. Omaki Spa has an inn that serves as the starting point for sightseeing in the Gokayama area.

Gokayama ⬚63⬚: 1 hr.30 min. by bus from Takaoka Station, or 2 hrs. by bus from Kanazawa Station. This is a local area renowned as the home of *gassho-zukuri*, a style of architecture said to represent the most primitive form of Japanese residence. Consisting of a three- or four-story wooden house with a steep, thatched roof, this kind of house was inhabited together by several families totaling tens of people. The so-called "collective families system" functioned here. Such houses still remain here and there in the folds of the steep mountains. Typical *gassho* communities such as Ainokura and Suganuma—all of which are designated as Historical Sites—can be found in this area. Shirakawa-go on the Gifu Prefecture side is also known as a *gassho* community.

Area 8. Kanazawa and Ishikawa Prefecture

Ishikawa Prefecture, also known as old Kaga Province, is situated between Toyama Prefecture and Fukui Prefecture, and contains Kanazawa—the largest city in the Hokuriku District. This elegant old castle town of the powerful Kaga Clan is said to have maintained its ancient culture and tradition under the guardianship of the God-blessed "Hakusan" (lit. "white mountain"), which stands behind it. Kaga Onsen-kyo, an area that incorporates a series of spas from Yamanaka, Yamashiro and Awazu to Katayamazu, is one of the most famous hot-springs resort areas in the Hokuriku District. Many visitors to the Noto Peninsula visit these spas to enjoy their natural setting and relaxing baths.

Kanazawa ⬚62/64-65⬚ ☎0762

Pop. 425,310. It is the capital of Ishikawa Prefecture and the largest city in the Hokuriku District. Located in the center of the prefecture, it occupies one-sixth of the area of the entire prefecture. The downtown district is blessed with rich, green foliage and the clear streams of the Saikawa and Asano rivers. It still has old earthen walls and a row of houses with lattice doors everywhere as well as curved roads, T-shaped intersections and blind alleys—all reminiscent of the former castle town of the powerful feudal lord commonly referred to as "Kaga Hyakumangoku." (*Hyakuman* equals one million in the Japanese numeral system. *Koku* [sometimes pronounced *goku* when combined with other words] is a Japanese unit of measurement for crops, approximately equal to 5 bushels, and, in the feudal days, of the local yields and tributes thereof payable by the lords). With one million *koku* being the biggest of the yields, people here still boast of the honor since it implies the affluence of the district. In 1580 when Sakuma Morimasa built Oyama Castle (present Kanazawa Castle), Toyotomi Hideyoshi ordered Maeda Toshiie to occupy the castle three years after its completion. From that time on, the Maeda family ruled over the Hokuriku District as the most powerful clan in the area until the end of the Edo period. Kanazawa has prospered ever since as the center of administration, economy and culture in the district. In fact, it is the largest commercial city in the Hokuriku District. The traditional crafts, including *Kutani-yaki* (chinaware) and *Kaga Yuzen* (printed silk) have been representative products of Kanazawa since the Tokugawa Shogunate period. Its production of gold leaf accounts for 99% of the entire output in Japan. In addition, the production of textiles and textile machinery as well as *sake* and Japanese sweets is well known.

TRANSPORTATION

Transportation to Kanazawa

Trains: It is 4 hrs. 30 min. (623 km) from Tokyo via the JR Tokaido Shinkansen to Maibara, thence to Kanazawa by limited express on the JR Hokuriku Main Line; 4 hrs. 30 min. (515 km) from Ueno (Tokyo) to Nagaoka by the JR Joetsu Shinkansen, thence to Kanazawa by limited express on the JR Shin-etsu and Hokuriku main lines; 2 hrs. 55 min. (268 km) from Osaka by limited express on the JR Tokaido, Kosei and Hokuriku main lines; 3 hrs.(257 km) from Nagoya by limited express on the JR Tokaido and Hokuriku main lines.

By air: 1 hr. from Tokyo to Komatsu Airport. There are also flights from Fukuoka, Sapporo and Sendai. It takes 55 min. from Komatsu Airport to the JR Kanazawa Station by bus.

Buses: Besides the 4 hr.-trip from Nagoya by limited express bus, there are long-distance buses from Tokyo, Kyoto and other places.

Transportation within Kanazawa

There are the JR and Hokuriku-Tetsudo buses from one scenic point to another. The bus terminal is located in front of Kanazawa Station. The regular sightseeing bus services—"Kenroku-en Course," "Castle Town Course" and "Hyakuman-goku Course"—require reservations. Only Japanese-speaking guides are available.

TRADITIONAL INDUSTRIES

Kaga-Yuzen: Silk dyed with rich colors featuring gorgeous, picturesque patterns.

Kutani-yaki: Pottery, whose bright colors and elaborate designs are well known.

Ohi-yaki: Lightweight pottery with high heat insulation, featuring red, yellow and black glazes. Its tea ceremony ware is particularly famous.

Kimpaku (gold leaf): Used for Buddhist altar fittings, lacquerware, textiles and *Kutani-yaki* ware.

Kaga-Makie: Elegant and delicate designs in lacquer realized through the technique of sprinkling gold powder on the surface and sanding.

Kaga-Zogan: Inlaid gold or silver used as decoration for iron, copper and bronze ware.

Refer to the supplement for details regarding the "i" **System Information Center** in Kanazawa.

PLACES OF INTEREST

Oyama Shrine 64 : 5 min. by bus from Kanazawa Station and just north of Korimbo, the center of the city. *Shimmon* (God's gate), the main gate of the shrine, is in a unique mixture of Western and Japanese styles with three tiers. Remarkable for its stained-glass mosaic, the third tier enshrines Lord Maeda Toshiie, the founder of Kaga Clan.

Chuo(Central) Park 64 : 10 min. by bus from Kanazawa Station. Covering some 30,000 sq.m next to Korimbo (amusement area of the city), the park is place of recreation for Kanazawa residents. The red-brick Ishikawa Modern Literature Museum nearby presents various exhibits, including the personal articles and books of three famous, Kanazawa-born writers: Izumi Kyoka, Tokuda Shusei and Muro-o Saisei.

The Ruins of Kanazawa Castle 64 : 10 min. by bus from Kanazawa Station. Situated on the tableland between the Asano and Saikawa rivers, the castle was mostly destroyed by the conflagration of 1881. The only remaining part is Ishikawamon Gate and a small tenement house. This castle was inhabited by 14 generations of lords of the Maeda family and served as the base of the Kaga Clan after Maeda Toshiie moved here in 1583 and ruled the clan. Characterized by its lead-tile roof, the Ishikawamon Gate was rebuilt in 1788 and has been designated as an Important Cultural Property.

Kenroku-en Park 64 : Adjoining the castle grounds, it has been judged as one of the three most beautiful Japanese gardens along with Kairaku-en in Mito and Koraku-en in Okayama. With an area of 100,000 sq.m, it is the largest of the three. Kenroku means "Combining Six Features," indicating that the park has six prominent features —vastness, solemnity, careful arrangement, venerability, coolness and scenic charm. The park was built during the Empo era (1673–1681) by Maeda Tsunanori, lord at that time, and completed in its present form in 1837. It has three artificial hills and two ponds— Kasumigaike and Hisagoike. The water from the latter descends in a waterfall, while on the opposite shore stands a tea room called the *Yugaotei*. In the center of the grounds is Kasumigaike Pond with a perimeter of about 360 m. From a lookout platform in the corner of the adjoining Chitosedai, one is presented with a magnificent view of the city to the west, the Japan Sea in the distance, and Mt. Io and other mountains to the east. Near the Chitose Bridge is a cherry tree called *Kiku-zakura* (Chrysanthemum cherry tree) because its flowers have more than 300 petals like chrysanthemums. The noted stone lantern, known by the name of *Kotoji Toro*, stands on the northern shores of the pond. Besides cherry trees, there are azaleas, *kakitsubata* (rabbit-ear irises), *hagi* (Japanese bush clover) and maples. The ever-changing natural scenes as well as the artistic objects add poetic charm to each season. A feature that is especially well known is the beauty of *yukitsuri*, a pole from which ropes extend to support each branch of a tree in order to prevent the branches from breaking under the weight of the snow.

Seisonkaku 64 : Located in the southeast corner of Kenroku-en Park. This building was erected as the residence for the mother of the 13th lord, Maeda Nariyasu, in 1863. It is a lovely, two-story house, representative of the *Shoin*-style buildings constructed at the end of the Edo period, and is now designated as an Important Cultural Property. Within this structure, the Maeda family's heirlooms and art objects are on display. Located a short distance away are the Kanazawa Shrine, the Prefectural Art Museum, the Prefectural Museum for Traditional Products and Crafts and the Prefectural History Museum. The Prefectural Art Museum preserves and exhibits many celebrated pieces of Ko-Kutani (Old Kutani) ceramics and other art objects. Among the art pieces, the incense burner crafted by Nonomura Ninsei, a famous potter of the 17th century, is registered as a National Treasure.

The Prefectural Noh Theater: Located near Kenroku-en Park. It was built to preserve and promote the Kaga Hosho school of *noh* drama and traditional Japanese music. A regular monthly *noh* performance is held at the hall's theater, which can accommodate 400 people.

Myoryuji Temple (Ninja Temple) 65 : 15 min. by bus from Kanazawa Station. This interesting temple was erected in 1643 by the third Lord, Maeda Toshitsune. It is a four-story, seven-tiered complex structure with 29 stairs and 23 rooms. Because of its elaborate and mysterious design, including hidden rooms and doors as well as pitfalls, it is called the "Ninja Temple." It is said that this complicated construction indicates that the temple once served as a fortress. Prior reservations are necessary for a visit.

Nagamachi Samurai House District: Located in Nagamachi to the west of Korimbo in the center of the city. It is characteristic of a castle town, with its old *samurai* residences and earthen walls still remaining. In the middle of the site, one can visit Saihitsu-an and a Kaga-yuzen studio. The interior of the old Nomura family residence north of Saihitsu-an is open to visitors.

Utatsuyama Park 64 : 25 min. by bus from Kanazawa Station. This is a nature park sprawling over the entire area of Mt. Utatsu, which is 141 m above sea level and situated east of the center of the city. The peak commands a grand view of Mts. Hakusan and Tateyama as well as the Japan Sea. Within the park are monuments commemorating famous novelists born in the area, an amusement park called "Kanazawa Sunny Land," an aquarium and other points of interest.

Kahoku Lagoon 62 : 15 min. from Kanazawa Station by the Hokuriku Tetsudo Line, located in the northern part of Kanazawa City. The lagoon is also called "Lake Hasu (lotus)" because of the profusion of beautiful lotus flowers growing in the lake. Unfortunately, it has been reduced in size due to reclamation work, but it is still famous as a resting place for migratory birds such as *ko-hakucho* (small swan).

Yuwaku Spa 63 : 40 min. by bus from Kanazawa Station. Situated at the base of Mt. Io in the southeastern sector of Kanazawa, the spa is 400 m above sea level. Nearby are ski areas and a golf course as well as Lake Gyokusen, where boat rides can be enjoyed.

Edo Village 63 : 40 min. by bus from Kanazawa Station. Several Edo-period structures with historical ties to the Kaga Clan have been relocated to this 160,000-sq.-m site, which centers around the Korakuji Temple precincts above Yuwaku Spa. Some twenty buildings are arranged in accordance with the social system of the Edo period that separated the Japanese into four classes—*samurai*, farmers, artisans and merchants. The arrangement is intended to demonstrate the way each class of people lived in those days. Household effects are displayed in each of the buildings.

Shirayamahime Shrine 63 : 35 min. from Kanazawa (Nomachi Station) to Kaga-Ichinomiya by the Hokuriku Railway and then 10 min. to the shrine on foot. A much-celebrated shrine with an ancient history, it serves as the center for the Mt. Hakusan religion by functioning as the headquarters of 2,716 of Hakusan shrines in Japan. It enshrines *Okumiya* (Inner Sanctum) on the summit of Mt. Hakusan. The shrine treasures include a sword, which has been designated as a National Treasure, and many other objects of Important Cultural Properties.

Shishiku Plateau 63 : 25 min. on foot and by ropeway from Kaga-Ichinomiya Station. Although it is only 650 m above sea level, it commands a splendid view of the peaks of Mt. Hakusan and the Noto Peninsula as well as a sweeping panorama of the Kaga Plain. It is also a popular ski resort in winter.

Mt. Hakusan 63 : Along with Mt. Fuji and Mt. Tateyama, it is one of Japan's "Three Sacred Mountains." Extending over the borders of four prefectures—Ishikawa, Toyama, Gifu and Fukui, it is the main cone of the Hakusan volcanic zone. The mountain, whose peaks are covered with snow all year round, has been an object of religious worship since time immemorial. Of its three main peaks, Mt. Gozemmine—the highest—rises 2,702 m high, Mt. Onanjimine—the northwest peak—has an altitude of 2,684 m and Mt. Kengamine—the northeast peak—has an altitude of 2,677 m. Other, lesser peaks include Mt. Bessan (alt. 2,399 m) and Mt. Sannomine (alt. 2,128 m) to the south. Immense primeval forests cover the mountainsides, which abound in wild birds and alpine plants. The peak commands a picturesque view of a volcanic lake and fields of wild flowers spread out below. Mts. Norikura and Ontake appear in the east, the ranges of the Japan Alps are in the distance beyond the sea of clouds spreading from east to north, while the Kaga plain and the Japan Sea can be seen to the west. As Mt. Hakusan has a long history of religious pilgrimage, several trails have been developed from several different points, but the Ichinose trail starting from the base on the southwest side is the shortest and most popular. It is 7 km long and takes about 4 hrs. 30 min. to climb to Murodo.

Noto Peninsula 62

It comprises the northern half of Ishikawa Prefecture, casting itself out like a hook into the Japan Sea. The peninsula consists mostly of low hills, displaying a complex topography that is extremely lacking in level ground. While the west coast is eroded and rugged, the east coast is smoother but characterized by many indentations along the coastline. The coastline is worth seeing and can easily be approached by national highways that skirt around the peninsular coast and connect all the points of interest. The entire peninsula has been designated as Noto Hanto (Peninsula) Quasi-National Park.

Hakui 62 ☎0767: Pop. 28,510. 45 min. by express on the JR Nanao Line from Kanazawa. It is in the western part of the Noto Peninsula and serves as a starting point for a sightseeing drive around the peninsula coastline. The city radiates from the Hakui Shrine and is the commercial, economic and cultural center of the Noto region.

Hakui Shrine: Located in the center of the city, this ancient shrine is where the son of Emperor Suijin, Prince Iwatsukiwake-no-Mikoto, and his child are enshrined. The shrine's major annual event is *Karatoyama Shinji Sumo*, a *sumo* tournament held on September 25 that reputedly has been observed for 2,000 long years.

Chirihama: A sandy beach about 8 km long stretching to the south of Hakui Station. It is a beautiful beach with well-developed dunes and known for its exciting "*Nagisa* (Beach) Drive" that one can enjoy here.

Keta Shrine 62 : About 4 km to the north of Hakui Station, located on high ground facing the sea. Known as Noto-Ichinomiya Shrine, it has been the principal place of worship in this area since ancient times. The precise date of its initial establishment cannot be ascertained, but the present *Shimmon* (front gate), *Haiden* (Worship Hall) and the *Honden* (Main Shrine) were all built between the Muromachi period (1336-1573) and the beginning of the Edo period (1603-1867). Behind the shrine is a luxuriant virgin forest that has been designated as a Natural Monument and contains tall trees usually found in a warm climate along with *shii* or chinquapins and camellias.

Myojoji Temple 62 : 20 min. by bus from Hakui Station. Located on a hill in the northern part of the city, it is the headquarters of the Nichiren sect of Buddhism in this district, boasting the biggest temple in this area. It is said to have been built in 1293. The well-proportioned, Five-Story Pagoda surrounded by pine forests is an impressive sight. In addition to this pagoda, many other structures are registered as Important Cultural Properties.

Noto-Kongo 62 : A 30-km-long scenic coastline stretching from Fukura Port, 20 km north of Hakui, to Sekinohana. One of the highlights of sightseeings on the Noto Peninsula, it presents a rugged view of masculine beauty. The focus of interest is Gammon and Sekinohana. Gammon is a penetrated grotto, 6 m wide, 15 m tall and 60 m deep, created by erosion. On top is a thick growth of old pines. Around it are a flat rock bed called *Senjojiki* (the Space of One Thousand *Tatami* Mats) and Takanosu (Hawk's Nest), a rock towering 27 m high. For a view from the ocean, a sightseeing boat is available. Sekinohana is a beautiful karst with enormous jutting rocks pitted by numerous holes, resulting in a unique shoreline. Attractions such as *Zeniarai-no-Ike*, where it is believed that money washed in its waters will multiply, and a cave dedicated to *Benzaiten*, the goddess of music and good fortune, can be found here, with a path to guide one around the area. The imposing *Yasenodangai* cliff, which is frequently used as a setting in fiction and film, is popular with visitors. To get to Sekinohana, take a bus from the Hakui-chuo Bus Stop for 50 min. to Togi and then take another bus for 10 more minutes.

Sojiji Soin Temple 62 : 2 hrs. 30 min. by bus from Kanazawa Station to Monzen, or 1 hr.10 min. by bus from Togi; located in the center of town. Along with Eiheiji Temple in Fukui Prefecture, it was originally a headquarters of the Soto Zen sect. It was built in 1321 and placed under the protection of the Maeda family. It had 16,391 branch temples throughout the country in the Edo period as well as some 70 small and large halls within the pale of the temple. Unfortunately, most of the buildings in the temple precincts were destroyed by the fire of 1898. In the wake of this fire, the head temple moved to Tsurumi, Yokohama, in Kanagawa Prefecture, and consequently the Sojiji Temple here became Soin (original temple). Still, there are more than 20 halls left to remind visitors of the bygone days.

Cape Saruyama: 5 min. by bus from Monzen to Doge, and 1-hr. 30-min. walk after getting off the bus. A cape located at the northwest end of Noto Peninsula, it has a breathtaking cliff 200 m high, with a lighthouse perched on the edge of the cliff. A flight of 600 steps leads to the bottom.

Nanao 62 ☎0767: Pop. 50,027. 1 hr.10 min. (66 km) by express on the JR Nanao Line from Kanazawa. It has long been the hub of the Noto Peninsula. The former site of the Kokubunji Temple is to the south of the city. After the Meiji Restoration of 1868, the city developed as a port town for the Japan Sea lines and continues to play an important role in the import of lumber.

Wakura Spa ⟦62⟧ : 7 min. by bus from Wakura-Onsen Station, which is 1 hr.20 min. by express on the JR Nanao Line from Kanazawa. It is the largest hot-spring resort on the peninsula. It attracts many tourists as a base for sightseeing in the Noto region as well as a place for rest and recuperation. About 60 *ryokan* or Japanese-style inns equipped with modern facilities stand in a row and are supplied with abundant mineral water from the hot springs.

Noto-jima Island: 20 min. by bus from Wakura-Onsen Station. Located just offshore from Wakura Spa, it covers an area of 47.5 sq. km. On the island is Seaside Park with an aquarium as well as amusement facilities such as the Noto-jima Island Family Travel Village, which has a large recreation area for engaging in outdoor activities.

Wajima ⟦62⟧ ☎0768: Pop. 32,113. About 2 hrs. 20 min. by express on the JR Nanao Line from Kanazawa. Wajima is the center of the Oku(Inner)-Noto region on the outer coast of the Noto Peninsula. It was once prosperous as an important center of maritime transportation for commerce on the Japan Sea lines in the Edo period. The central district of the city straddles the mouth of the Kawarada River, while on the eastern side of the river is the commercial and industrial area, dominated by the production of famous *Wajima-nuri* lacquerware. The fishing industry flourishes on the western side. The sale of fresh fish and vegetables at the morning, open-air market on Hommachi Street attracts a lot of people. Wajima's traditional industry, *Wajima-nuri* lacquerware, is said to have begun a thousand years ago and accounts for one-third of the city's industry today. At the Wajima Lacquerware Hall, 15 min. on foot from the station, demonstrations of the processes of making lacquerware are given with explanations. Items are also offered for sale.

Shirayone Semmaida ⟦62⟧ : 25 min. by bus from Wajima Station. This unique farmland is situated east of Wajima on the sloping sides of mountains, whose skirts descends to the sea. The mountainsides are terraced with more than 2,000 small plots of rice fields, which together with the footpath banks form a beautiful pattern. Such a scene typifies the lack of level land in this area.

Kami-Tokikunike ⟦62⟧ : 40 min. by bus from Wajima Station. Situated along the Machino River a little inland from the Sosogi Coast, it is the house of a rich farmer, whose ancestor, Tokikuni—the son of Taira-no-Tokitada—a member of the eminent Taira Clan, was exiled here by the founder of the Kamakura Shogunate, Minamoto-no-Yoritomo. The present owner is the 25th direct descendent of Tokikuni. The somber-looking house was built in 1808 in the *Irimoya*-style, with a thatched roof and classical *Karahafu*-style entrance.

Shimo-Tokikunike ⟦62⟧ : 45 min. by bus from Wajima Station, 5 min. on foot from Kami-Tokikunike. The Tokikuni family was divided into two houses at the time of the 12th direct descendent. One of these houses is Shimo-Tokikunike, which is a 17th-century construction in the *Irimoya*-style and has been designated as an Important Cultural Property. The imposing structures show the power of the landed gentry of the day.

Sosogi Coast 62 : 40 min. by bus from Wajima Station. Situated 20 km to the northeast of Wajima, it is a stretch of scenic coast extending for about 2 km from the mouth of the Machino River. It is representative of the peninsula coastline of rhyolite eroded by the sea along its vertical and oblique joints. *Madoiwa*(Window Rock), the rock projecting into the sea, is a typical feature of the Sosogi Coast. During winter the wonderful phenomenon of bits of foam from the waves blowing in the air called *Nami-no-Hana* (flowers of the waves) can be seen. The coast is designated as a Place of Scenic Beauty and a Natural Monument.

Hekura Island 62 : 1 hr.50 min. by ship from Wajima Port. This small island (6 km in circumference), located 48 km north of Wajima, is famous as a place where *ama* (female divers) dive for abalone and seaweed.

Suzu 62 ☎0768: Pop. 25,983. 1 hr.50 min. from Kanazawa by express on the JR Nanao Line to Anamizu, thence 1 hr.40 min. by the Noto Tetsudo Line. It is situated on the tip of the Noto Peninsula, surrounded by the sea in three directions. Cape Rokko at the northeastern end of the Peninsula forms the borderline between the outer and inner inlets. Iidamachi at the inner inlet comprises the center of the city.

Cape Rokko 62 : 50 min. by bus from Noto-Iida Bus Terminal. Situated at the northeast end of the peninsula, it is characterized by a natural tableland of coastal terraces. A view can be commanded in every direction from a lighthouse at the tip of the cape. It is also valued as a unique place where both the sunrise and sunset can be seen.

Yoshigaura Spa 62 : 40 min. by bus from Noto-Iida Bus Terminal. It is a hot-spring resort known as a "lodge with a kerosene lamp," with one lodging located southeast of Cape Rokko. Behind the spa is a steep cliff, beyond which a reef stretches. It has been run for a century as a hydropathic establishment, but recently it has begun to attract many tourists.

Kihe-don 62 : 10 min. on foot from Iida Station on the Noto Railway. It is a historic museum that exhibits the folk objects of the Kihe family, who were engaged in salt manufacture and lacquer extraction.

Tsukumo Bay 62 : Near Tsukumowan-Ogi Station, which is 1 hr.10 min. from Anamizu via the Noto Railway. It is a small cove with a typical ria-type coast that constitutes the inner inlet. It was named Tsukumo (literary expression of the number ninety-nine) because there are so many indentations in the shoreline. In the middle of the bay is Horai Island covered with thick plants usually found in a warm climate. A sightseeing boat is available for a tour of the bay, departing from a wharf that is a 5-min. walk from the station.

Other Areas in Ishikawa Prefecture

Kaga 63 ☎07617: Pop. 68,861. Located at the southern tip of Ishikawa Prefecture. The city is active in textile and chain manufacturing, but it owes its fame to tourism centered around Yamashiro and Katayamazu spas, which comprise **Kaga Onsen-kyo** (Spas Area) along with Yamanaka and Awazu spas. Many historical ruins of the former castle town as well as the natural beauty of the Kaga Coast are worth seeing. The main station is the JR Kaga-Onsen Station.

Katayamazu Spa 63 : 10 min. by bus from Kaga-Onsen Station. This is a hot-spring resort by Shibayama Lagoon in the northern part of Kaga. The spring was discovered in 1653 in the lagoon. However, because of the difficulty of extracting hot water from the lagoon, the area was not developed as a spa until 1877 when a *ryokan* or a Japanese-style inn was opened. At present, there are approximately 30 *ryokan*, all of which are equipped with modern conveniences.

Yamashiro Spa 63 : 10 min. by bus from Kaga-Onsen Station, situated at the southern edge of Kaga Plain. It is one of the great spas in the Hokuriku District with a long history of 1,200 years. The quiet atmosphere reminds visitors of its prosperity during the Kaga Hyakuman-goku (refer to p.617) era.

Yamanaka Spa 63 : 25 min. by bus from Kaga-Onsen Station. It faces the clean mountain stream of the Daishoji River. Since it is surrounded by mountains in every direction, it is literally *yamanaka*, a Japanese word meaning "in the mountains." It has a long history commencing from the discovery of the hot spring about 1,300 years ago. The town was renovated after the conflagration of 1931 and today modern Japanese-style inns are lined up to serve visitors. The spa has attracted many literary people, including Matsuo Basho, the famous *haiku* poet of the Edo period. Yamanaka is proud of the beautiful Kakusenkei Gorge, particularly the stretch between the two bridges—Korogi and Kurotani.

Ioji Temple 63 : Located in the far western part of Yamanaka Spa. This old temple of the Shingon sect is dedicated to the *Yakushi-Nyorai*, which is worshipped as one of the three most revered *Yakushi-Nyorai* in Japan. It is said that this temple was founded 1,300 years ago by priest Gyoki. The temple has a statue of *Kongo-Doji*, which is designated as an Important Cultural Property.

Komatsu 63 ☎0761: Pop. 106,874. 20 min. from Kanazawa and 50 min. from Fukui, both via the JR Hokuriku Main Line. Komatsu Airport serves the Hokuriku District, including Kanazawa and Fukui. Komatsu is second only to Kanazawa as the leading commercial and industrial city in Ishikawa Prefecture. Maeda Toshitsune, lord of the Maeda Clan, encouraged the creation of new industries and the promotion of productivity in this area after building a castle here for his retirement in 1639. This new castle town eventually evolved as today's industrial city of Komatsu. With Komatsu Ltd. as the focal point, the silk textile and thread-plying industry as well as heavy industries are now quite prosperous here.

Awazu Spa 63 : 8 km south of Komatsu Station and 30 min. by bus. It is surrounded by mountains in all directions, except one in which it faces the Japan Sea in the distance. It was reportedly discovered in 718, making it the oldest spa in the Hokuriku District. Each *ryokan* here has its own characteristic garden. Yunokuni-no-Mori (Forest of Spa Province) is a local craft center dedicated to the display and preservation of the traditional industries of Ishikawa Prefecture. The manufacturing processes for *Kutani-yaki* porcelain, *Wajima-nuri* lacquerware, gold leaf, *Yuzen* textile, glass crafts and Japanese sweets are each demonstrated in different rooms. Of special interest is the area where visitors can try their hand at making a traditional craft.

Natadera Temple 63 : 30 min. by bus from Komatsu Station. The temple is situated in the west central part of the city, which spreads from north to south. History records that it was built by Taicho-Daishi in 717. Autumn at the temple is deservedly famous, with the tinted leaves and temple structures offering a harmonious contrast. The Main Hall, Three-Story Pagoda, Belfry, *Goma* (holy fire for invocation of the gods) Hall, Study Hall and kitchen are all registered as Important Cultural Properties.

Area 9. Fukui Prefecture

Fukui Prefecture is located at the western end of the Hokuriku District. Since it is the closest to the Kinai (the five old provinces around Kyoto, or the ancient capital of Japan), mainline culture promptly flowed into the area for centuries.

Many historical legacies remain to testify to these cultural influxes. The coastline from the Echizen Coast to Wakasa Bay, which has been designated as a quasi-national park, is full of natural beauty.

Fukui 63/67 ☎0776

Pop. 249,421. It is the prefectural capital, located in the middle of the Fukui Plain north of the prefecture. The city is divided into northern and southern parts by the Asuwa River. Administrative and economic activities are concentrated in the northern part, while recreational facilities for the city's residents such as Asuwayama and Yahatayama parks are located in the southern part. Fukui was once a flourishing castle town as well as a cultural and commercial center of the old Hokuriku Highway for a long time. Following a series of disasters, it has been transformed into a modern city. It is said that the prototype of the present city was established when Shibata Katsuie, a noted general, built a castle here in 1575. It developed into a castle town proper after Yuki Hideyasu, another feudal general, built a new castle and lived here as its lord in 1600. Its textile industry is so famous that Fukui is called "the textile kingdom." Indeed, the city is proud of its industry, one of the most prosperous in Japan.

TRANSPORTATION

2 hrs. 10 min. (180 km) by limited express on the JR Tokaido and Hokuriku main lines from Nagoya; 4 hrs. 10 min. (546 km) from Tokyo, first by the Tokaido Shinkansen to Nagoya, thence by limited express on the Tokaido and Hokuriku main lines; 2 hrs. 10 min. (191 km) from Osaka by limited express on the JR Tokaido, Kosei and Hokuriku main lines.

PLACES OF INTEREST

Ruins of Fukui Castle 67 : 300 m north of Fukui Station. Located in the middle of the government office section of town, these are the ruins of the castle that Yuki Hideyasu, the second son of Tokugawa Ieyasu, built in 1600. 600 m to the south are the ruins of another castle built by Shibata Katsuie in 1575. All that remain of either castle are the stone walls and moats.

Asuwayama Park 67 : 5 min. by bus from Fukui Station. Situated in the suburbs south of the city, the park covers the entire area of Mt. Asuwa, 100 m above sea level, and commands a sweeping view of the city. The park has a local history museum and a natural science museums as well as a 24-m-high Peace Tower with a dome, etc. on the mountain top, making it a favorite place of recreation for the residents of Fukui.

Ichijodani Ruins of Asakura Family (a feudal lord) 63 : 35 min. by bus from Fukui Station, 10 km to the southeast of the city. It is the place where the lords of the Asakura family fostered a unique culture for 103 years through five generations during the Age of Civil Wars until the Asakura Clan was destroyed by Oda Nobunaga in 1573. Discovered at the beginning of the Showa period, the ruins of the old castle are now designated as a Special Historical Site and well preserved as such. There is also a restored *samurai* residence, which is open to the public.

Maruoka Castle 63 : It is in Maruoka Town, northwest of the city. The donjon (an Important Cultural Property) on the hill is small, but it has become the symbol of the town. It is said to have been erected in 1576 by Shibata Katsutoyo, the adopted son of Shibata Katsuie. Old armor and documents are exhibited in the historical and folk museum inside the castle.

Yoshizaki Gobo Temple: 20 min. from Fukui to Awara-Onsen by the JR Hokuriku Main Line, thence 25 min. by bus. It is situated on the northeast shore of Lake Kitagata at the northern end of the Fukui

Plain. The whole area around the little hill, Mt. Yoshizaki, is a sacred place comprising many temple structures where Rennyo, the eighth head priest of the Honganji Temple of the Jodo-Shinshu sect, was engaged in missionary work for four years from 1471. However, the temple was destroyed by believers from other sects as well as by Oda Nobunaga, thus reducing the entire compound to ruins. At present, the western and eastern branch temples of the Honganji school stand side by side at the foot of Mt. Yoshizaki.

Awara Spa 63 : 15 min. by bus from Awara-Onsen Station. Located north of Fukui, it is known as the best spa in Fukui Prefecture. The spa was only discovered in 1883, but it has continually developed since then, thanks to its favorable location only 2 hrs. 30 min. from the Keihanshin (Kyoto-Osaka-Kobe) District and 20 min. from Fukui. The lack of beautiful scenery is well compensated by luxurious facilities, excellent service, hospitable spirit and magnificent gardens provided by *ryokan* or Japanese-style inns. Many visitors from abroad use it as a principal base for Hokuriku sightseeing.

Takidanji Temple 63 : 5 min. on foot from Mikuni Station, which is 25 min. from Fukui by the Keifuku Electric Railway. Located 500 m north of the station, this old temple is said to have been erected in 1381 and was protected by the lord of the province for generations. It possesses many cultural properties, among which the 1,700-sq.-m landscaped garden, reportedly created in the middle of the Edo period, is of special interest.

Tojimbo 63 : 30 min. by bus from Awara-Onsen Station, or 10 min. by bus from Mikuni Station. It is a unique beauty spot situated on the coast about 2 km northwest of Mikuni Port. The huge rock columns, with layered walls constantly washed by the rough waves of the Japan Sea, offer a fascinating natural scene. The rock walls are 50 m high and 40 m wide, and can be viewed either from the sea by a sightseeing boat or by walking on the boardwalk along the beach. A sweeping view can also be obtained from Tojimbo Tower's observation platform.

Eiheiji Temple 63 : About 16 km east of Fukui City. It is 30 min. from Fukui by the Keifuku Electric Railway. This much-revered temple is the headquarters of the Soto sect of Zen Buddhism, with some 15,000 branch temples throughout the country. It was erected in 1244 by the famous priest, Dogen (1200-1253). The temple precincts, spreading out at the bottom of the hill, cover 330,000 sq.m. Visitors will see *Chokushimon* (Gate for Imperial Messenger) at the front just inside the entrance and *Shidoden* (Worshipping Hall) on the left. *Sammon* (Main Gate), *Butsuden* (Buddhist Sanctum) and *Hatto* (Lecture Hall) stand in a straight line, with *Daiku-in* Hall (Priests' Residence) on the east and *Soto* Hall (Monastry) on the west of *Butsuden*. At the end of the corridor going east from *Sammon* Gate is the bathhouse, while at the western end is *Tosu* (Toilet). Structures are connected with each other by roofed corridors, forming what is called a *Shichido-Garan* (Seven-Hall Temple). Anyone can experience *sanro* (confinement for prayer) by staying at the temple and participating in the monastic life. By taking part in this formidable *zen* training, one can appreciate the strictness of the priest's life.

Ono ☐63☐ ☎0779: Pop. 42,130. About 1 hr. by the JR Etsumi-Hoku Line from Fukui. Occupying the northeastern part of Fukui Prefecture, it is one of the leading cities in the Okuetsu district. The city is profoundly reminiscent of an old but now-defunct castle town. A fine view of the Ono Basin and the Hakusan Mountain Chain can be enjoyed from the donjon restored on the summit of Mt. Kameyama in the western part of the city. Katsuyama (pop. 30,836), adjacent to Ono along the Kuzuryu River, is famous for its textile industry. It has several places worth seeing such as a 26-m-high Daibutsu (a great image of Buddha) erected in 1986 and modeled after the one at Todaiji Temple in Nara as well as the ruins of Heisenji Temple of the Tendai sect, which prospered in medieval times. Now Hakusan Shrine stands on the site.

Echizen Coast ☐63☐: 1 hr.10 min. by bus to the Echizen Coast (Sou Bus Stop) from Fukui Station. To get to Cape Echizen, get off the bus at Todaishita, one stop before the Echizen Coast (Sou Bus Stop). Located in the western part of Fukui Prefecture, this area is famous for its natural beauty, centered around coastal terraces, coral reefs and rough waves. Among them, Kochomon, eroded by wind and waves, is a great sight that deserves to be called a rock suspension bridge. National Highway 305 passes beneath Kochomon. In January and February, the entire area around the cape is covered with daffodils, offering a wonderful sight.

Sabae ☐63☐ ☎0778: Pop. 62,340. Located south of Fukui City, stretching both east and west. Sabae Station on the JR Hokuriku Main Line and Nishi-Sabae Station on the Fukui Railway are both located in the center of the city. It has flourished as a temple town surrounding Joshoji Temple, which was erected at the end of the 13th century. Although the main industries are textiles, it also produces frames for glasses, with Sabae accounting for 90% of the country's production of these frames.

Joshoji Temple ☐63☐: One of the representative temples in the old province of Echizen (now, Fukui Prefecture). Most of the current structures, however, were later restored during the Meiji period. Only *Kyozo* (Scripture House), *Shoro* (Belfry) and *Daishidomon* Gate were built in the Edo period. There is a fabulous sculpture of a dragon displayed in *Daishido* Hall, supposedly done by Hidari-Jingoro, a famous sculptor (refer to p.543).

Takefu ☐63☐ ☎0778: Pop. 68,943. 19 km from Fukui City, 20 min. by the JR Hokuriku Main Line. Originally developed as a farmland area, Takefu is a city in a basin, with the Hino River flowing through the middle of the city. In the Middle Ages, Takefu was a point of contact between the central government and the entire Hokuriku

District, and saw a power struggle for supremacy among competing clans. After the beginning of the Edo period, it became simply a quiet castle town. The main industry is textiles, but chemicals are also produced here. Traditional crafts, including cutlery, Japanese paper and *habutae* silk dolls, also continue to be active.

Rozan Park 63 : A 40,000-sq.-m civic park at the bottom of Mt. Murakuni, southwest of Takefu Station. With its 2,000 cherry trees, it is one of the prefecture's most famous flower-viewing places. It also commands a view of the city.

Echizen Ceramic Art Village: 35 min. by bus from Takefu Station. Located in Miyazaki Village adjacent to the northwest part of Takefu, it is a facility created to promote *Echizen-yaki* potteries, one of the six foremost ancient types of ceramic kilns in Japan. In compounds are artist studios and classrooms for the study of ceramic art as well as the Ceramic Art Hall where *Echizen-yaki* potteries and materials are exhibited.

Tsurugi Shrine 63 : 35 min. by bus from Takefu Station. It is an old shrine on a large, 40,000-sq.-m site in the center of Oda Town. It is said that the shrine was built in the third century when the sword of Prince Susano-o-no-Mikoto was enshrined here. The *bonsho*, a precious Buddhist bronze bell made in 770, is a registered National Treasure.

Tsuruga 63 ☎0770: Pop. 64,990. 1 hr.30 min. by limited express on the Hokuriku Main Line from Nagoya, 1 hr.20 min. (137 km) by limited express by the JR Tokaido, Kosei and Hokuriku main lines from Osaka. Situated in the southwest part of Fukui Prefecture, it faces Tsuruga Bay. The city boasts of having one of the main ports along the Japan Sea. Once used as an international port with direct lines to China, Korea and Siberia, the port is now busy with freighters importing lumber from Nakhodka and ferry boats going to Hokkaido. The city is becoming industrialized with the establishment of large factories of rayon, cement and nickel. Kehi Shrine stands in the center of the city, with a large, 11-m-high, vermilion-colored *torii* gate, an Important Cultural Property, towering as a prominent landmark. The shrine is known as Echizen-Ichinomiya, or the principal shrine in the old province of Echizen. The god enshrined here is believed to be the guardian of food supplies and safe voyages, attracting the area's religious reverence. Kehi-no-Matsubara is a park with beautiful, sandy beaches and a 1.5-km-long pine grove where some 50,000 Japanese red pines and Japanese black pines grow. There is also a children's playground here. During summer, the area is crowded with swimmers and campers.

Saifukuji Temple, located west of the city, is a noted temple in the Hokuriku District. It was built in 1368 with the aid of Shogun Ashikaga Yoshimitsu, with solemn temple edifices standing side by side within its extensive precincts. The garden in front of a study hall, constructed in the middle of the Edo period, is designated as a

Place of Scenic Beauty. Tsuruga Peninsula is a 40-min. bus ride from Tsuruga Station, getting off at Tateishi. Once called an isolated island of land, the peninsula juts out into the Japan Sea along the western coast of Tsuruga Bay. Development, however, is now evident in the form of two atomic power plants constructed here. There are also wonderful beaches along the coast and a sightseeing boat service is available from Tsuruga Port. Jogu Shrine, 25 min. by bus from Tsuruga Station, is an old shrine located in the east-central part of Tsuruga Peninsula. The main hall and a *torii* gate can be found in a pine grove. The dancing hall also stands in the precincts, facing the sea nearby. The Korean bell, which was reportedly brought from Korea when Toyotomi Hideyoshi launched his invasion here is designated as a National Treasure.

Mikata Five Lakes: Near Mihama Station, 25 min. by the JR Obama Line from Tsuruga. Surrounded by green mountains and filled with deep-blue water, they lie in the southwest part of Fukui Prefecture, looking out on Wakasa Bay. The most inland lake, Lake Mikata, has fresh water, while Lake Hiruga near the sea has salt water. However, the other three lakes—Kugushi, Suigetsu and Suga—have a mixture of both fresh and salt water. Thus, the composition of the water differs from one lake to another, although the lakes are connected with each other by streams, except for Lake Hiruga. There are sightseeing jet-boats available on every lake but Lake Hiruga.

Obama ⬜71 ☎0770: Pop. 34,211. It is 1 hr.5 min. from Tsuruga by the JR Obama Line. The city is situated in the southwest part of Fukui Prefecture. Popularly called "Nara by the Sea," this former castle town is dotted with many historical shrines and temples as well as a good, natural seaport, Obama Port. Fishing and the production of traditional craft, *Wakasa-nuri* lacquerware, flourish here. The hilly suburbs of Obama are full of temples with interesting structures and beautiful Buddhist images.

Jinguji Temple, situated to the southeast of Obama Station, is famous for Wakasa's "Water-Sending Ceremony" held every year on March 2. The water of Unose upstream of the Onyu River, which flows south of the temple, is said to pass underground to Nara to become the scented water of the Wakasa-i Well at *Nigatsudo* Hall of the Todaiji Temple. The water is used for the time-honored "Water-Drawing Ceremony" held there in March (Refer to p.719). Myotsuji Temple is an ancient temple, situated upstream along the Matsunaga River. Legend says that it was built in 806 by the *Sei-i-Tai-Shogun* (The Generalissimo for the Subjugation of Barbarians—the honorable title conferred by the Imperial Court on the highest-ranking warrior and also the formal appellation of *shogun*), Sakanoue-no-Tamuramaro. Long ago, the temple was prosperous enough to have 25 priests' lodges. Both the Main Hall and Three-Story Pagoda are designated as National Treasures. The pagoda, which was rebuilt in 1270, is 22 m high and has a simple, quiet appearance. Hagaji Temple is located at the base of Mt. Haga northeast of Obama. Historians tell us that Hagaji Temple was founded by the priest Gyoki at the command of Emperor Gensho (reigned 715-724), who wanted to pray for the peace and prosperity of the nation over which he reigned. The principal image, the *Juichimen* (Eleven-Headed)-*Kannon* standing statue, is a masterpiece created at the beginning of the Heian period (794-1185) and is designated as an Important Cultural Property.

Sotomo is situated at the tip of Uchitomi Peninsula projecting from the western side of Obama Bay. Sightseeing boats are available to enjoy the 6-km-long seacoast with its abundance of strange rocks and precipitous cliffs. The boarding spot is 3 km by bus from Obama Station. The granite mass, which has been eroded along its joints, has created a number of great caves, grottos and cliffs. The 50-min. sightseeing cruise is preferable. The mouths of the spectacular Omon and Komon caves should not be missed.

Section V. West Central Honshu
(Kansai District)

The Kinki District, also called Kansai, is the cradle of Japanese civilization as well as today's industrial and cultural center of west central Honshu. The core of this district is called the Keihanshin (Kyoto-Osaka-Kobe) area.

Kinki consists of six prefectures: Hyogo, Kyoto, Nara, Osaka, Shiga and Wakayama. However, in consideration of railway and other transportation conditions, part of Mie Prefecture is included, while part of Shiga Prefecture is omitted here and covered in Section IV.

Area 1. Osaka and Vicinity

Osaka 79-83 ☎06

Pop. 2,535,468. The capital of Osaka Prefecture and the second-largest city in Japan. Located at the center of the delta regions formed by the Yodo and Yamato rivers, the city is held back by Osaka Bay to the west but extends over the Osaka Plain to the east. The Yodo River flows into Osaka from the northeast, while the southern border of the city is formed by the Yamato River. Slightly to the east of the center is the Uemachi highland, which runs from north to south. Administratively, the city is divided into 24 wards.

Developed as an Imperial capital, a temple town and a castle town, Osaka is the nucleus of politics, economics and culture in western Japan. Like Tokyo, this vast metropolis has many faces. Although they formerly made up the backbone of the commercial prosperity that Osaka is famous for, the many canals that flowed through the city and the noted Happyakuya-Bashi (lit. "808" Bridges") that spanned them are gradually disappearing in the name of progress. While the look of the city has vastly changed, with skyscrapers and highways sprouting on the surface and subways and subterranean shopping centers burrowing underneath, the commercial energy has remained unchanged.

Osaka and Tokyo are separated by no more than 550 km, but the two cities are vastly different, not only in speech and cuisine, but also in behavior and ways of thinking. The historical difference between a political *samurai* town (Tokyo) and a commercial town of merchants (Osaka) created vast differences in the daily lives and customs of the people in east and west Japan. Interestingly enough, these differences are still in evidence today.

HISTORY

The area where Osaka now stands was once called Naniwa (Rapid Waves), presumably because of the difficulty ships had in anchoring here. The name is still used in a poetic sense. Since it was deemed a suitable site for a city by the fourth century, both Emperors Ojin and Nintoku are said to have built palaces on the hill where Osaka Castle now stands. Emperors Kotoku (597-654), Temmu (631-686) and Shomu (701-756) all had palaces in Naniwa where they entertained envoys from Korea. The palaces, located in what is now Hoenzaka in Chuo Ward, have all been designated as Historical Sites and are being excavated. It was in the 16th century under the leadership of Toyotomi Hideyoshi (1536-1598), renowned military ruler of Japan, that Osaka developed as a great commercial city. Hideyoshi had the merchants of Sakai (south of Osaka) and Fushimi (now, part of Kyoto) move to Naniwa and set up business here so that he could build the largest castle in Japan on the hill where the ancient palaces and, later, Honganji Temple had stood. After that, for the 265 years until the Tokugawa Shogunate was toppled, Osaka continued to develop as the distribution center for goods brought in from all over the country, and became a cultural center rivaling Kyoto. Osaka formed a municipal body with a population of 472,000 in 1889, but has since considerably expanded its area by absorbing outlying towns and villages. By 1940, the population had reached a peak of 3,252,000—nearly seven times the population of the city when it was first granted a charter. Since the end of World War II, Osaka has remarkably revitalized its position as the foremost industrial and commercial center in Japan. The shopping and amusement districts far surpass those before the war. The restaurants, hotels, night clubs, movie theaters and other facilities have increased in line with flourishing business activities and the construction of fashionable underground malls and skyscrapers.

INDUSTRIES

Osaka, once called the "Manchester of the Orient" because of its textile industry, is broadly divided into three industrial sectors. In the Yodo River area, chemicals, medicines, textiles and dyes are produced, while the Joto area in the east houses the machine industry and sundries manufacturers, and the seaside industrial zone in the west is mostly filled with shipbuilding, metals, chemicals and other heavy industries. Foodstuffs and printing are also significant industries. The traditional wholesalers maintain deep ties with industry. The city is composed of various specialized wholesale districts such as Doshomachi for medicines, Dobuike and Semba Center Building for textiles and Nippombashi for electric appliances. Mass communication industries such as broadcasting and newspapers are also active in Osaka. Even such traditional crafts as Naniwa tinware and Sakai knives are still manufactured.

TRANSPORTATION

Transportation to Osaka

Osaka is the transportation and communications center of the Kinki District.

By Rail: The JR Tokaido Shinkansen arrives from Tokyo in 3 hrs. (557 km). It is 1 hr. from Nagoya (187 km), 1 hr.40 min. from Hiroshima (339 km) and 3 hrs. from Fukuoka (621 km). In addition to the Shinkansen, the JR Tokaido Main Line and the Sanyo Main Line run east to west as trunk lines. From Nagoya, a Kinki Nippon Railway (Kintetsu) limited express will arrive in 2 hrs. 10 min.

By Long-Distance Bus: The comfortable buses are popular because they are well equipped, cost considerably less than the train, and, as they run on the highway, are a quick means of transportation. Routes include those from Tokyo, Yokohama, Nagano, Sendai, Niigata, Fukuoka, Kumamoto, Nagasaki, Kagoshima, etc.

By Air: Osaka has an international airport at Itami, located 15 km northwest of Osaka Station. It can be reached by non-stop bus in 30 min. Buses run to the airport from places including Umeda, Shin-Osaka, Namba and Abenobashi near Tennoji. Osaka can be reached by air from either Tokyo or Fukuoka in 1 hr. There are also direct, nationwide flights north to Sapporo and south to Kagoshima and Okinawa. The New Kansai International Airport is being constructed over the sea to the south of Osaka and is scheduled to open in 1994.

By Ship: Ships from Takamatsu, Tokushima and Kochi on Shikoku as well as Beppu, Hyuga in Kyushu and Naha in Okinawa call at either Osaka Port or Osaka-Nanko Port. The center of the city can be reached from Osaka Port by subway in 15 min. and from Osaka-Nanko Port in 30 min. by taking the computer-controlled Nanko Port Town Line and transferring to the subway. Travelers arriving in Kobe Port by ship can reach Osaka in 1 hr. via either the JR, Hankyu or Hanshin Electric Railway lines.

By Road: From Tokyo, take the Tomei and Meishin expressways and then enter the Hanshin Expressway at the Toyonaka Interchange. If coming from the western Honshu area, take the Chugoku Expressway and enter the Hanshin Expressway at the Ikeda Interchange. To reach the southern part of the city from the Nagoya area, take the Higashi Meihan Expressway and the Meihan National Highway, then enter the Nishi-Meihan Expressway.

Transportation in and around Osaka

The area in and around Osaka is covered with a network of trains and buses that make traveling quite convenient.

JR: The JR Osaka-Kanjo (Loop) Line circles the city center, running over 22 km, including Osaka, Kyobashi, Tsuruhashi and Tennoji stations. A complete circuit is made in 40 min. and includes junctions with other railways at many of the stations.

Subways: Managed by the Osaka Municipal Transportation Bureau, Osaka's six subway lines center around the Midosuji Line, which connects Esaka, Shin-Osaka, Umeda, Namba, Tennoji and Nakamozu. Some of the lines run partly along the same routes as other railway lines in the suburbs.

Other Railways: The following railways connect the city center with the suburban districts: Heading toward Kyoto are the JR Tokaido Main Line, the Hankyu Kyoto Line and the Keihan Main Line. Running between Osaka and Kobe are the JR Tokaido Main Line, the Hankyu Kobe Line and the Hanshin Main Line. For Nara, one can take the JR Kansai Main Line or the Kintetsu Nara Line from Namba Station. To get to southern Nara, there is the Kintetsu Osaka Line from Uehonmachi Station and the Minami-Osaka Line from Abenobashi Station. Heading toward southern Osaka/Wakayama are the JR Hanwa Line, the Nankai Main Line, the Nankai Koya Line and the Hankai Railway Hankai Line.

Note: JR Osaka Station and the Osaka terminal stations of the Hankyu and Hanshin railways are all in the Umeda area. Although these three stations are adjacent to each other, the JR Station is known as Osaka, while Hankyu and Hanshin stations are known as Umeda. The subway stop here is also called Umeda Station.

Buses: More than 100 routes are operated all over the city, but the buses are frequently caught in traffic.

Roads: Centering around the loop created by the Hanshin Express-way are many roads, including the Kobe Route to the west, the Ikeda and Moriguchi routes to the north, the Higashi-Osaka and Matsu-bara routes to the east, and the Sakai Route to the south. In addition, the Wangan (Bayside) Route runs along the coast of Osaka Bay from north to south and the Kinki Expressway runs inland from Suita heading south.

TRAVEL ADVICE

The average annual temperature in Osaka is 16.2℃, ranging from a low of 5.6℃ in January to a high of 28℃ in August. The summers are quite humid, but there is comparatively little rainfall and rarely any snow during winter.

Since the people of Osaka are *kuidaore*, or infatuated with eating, the city offers many different kinds of restaurants. The flourishing districts of Umeda and Sonezaki around the JR Osaka Station are called *Kita* (North Quarter), while that around Namba and Shin-saibashi is called *Minami* (South Quarter). The vicinity of Tennoji Station has another concentration of restaurants, while the Sonezaki Shinchi district near Umeda contains many high-quality clubs, bars and other expensive establishments.

Tours by the regular sightseeing buses operating in Osaka are only available in Japanese.

ANNUAL EVENTS

Although Osaka is a modern, thriving commercial and industrial city, it abounds in traditional festivals enjoyed from generation to generation in addition to many newer festivals. The following is a list of the most popular annual events.

Toka Ebisu: January 9-11. This festival of Imamiya Ebisu Shrine (Naniwa Ward) features a procession of *geisha* in exquisite *kimono* carried through the main streets in palanquins called *hoekago*.

Thousand of people come to pray for success in business during the coming year.

Doyadoya: January 14. This festival is held at Shitennoji Temple (Tennoji Ward) on the last day of the *Shusho-e* ritual, which is observed for the first two weeks of the new year. Two groups of nearly naked youths jostle each other for the amulets to keep away evil around the central pillar of Rokujido Hall while chanting "doya doya". Those who get one are believed to be assured good harvests of the year.

Hana Matsuri: April 8. The celebration of Buddha's birthday at Shitennoji and other temples.

Shoryo-e: April 22. Often called *Oshorai*, this Buddhist service is held at Shitennoji Temple to commemorate the demise of Prince Shotoku (574-622), who founded the temple. Classical court music and dances are performed on the stone stage in front of *Rokujido* Hall.

Otaue Shinji (Rice-Planting Festival): June 14. Held at Sumiyoshi Shrine (Sumiyoshi Ward). Rice seedlings are ceremoniously transplanted by maidens in traditional costumes to the accompaniment of folk songs for rice-planting. The Sumiyoshi and other local rustic dances are performed at the shrine.

Aizen Matsuri: June 30-July 2. There is a parade of *hoekago* like that of the Toka Ebisu festival. At Shoman-in Temple (Tennoji Ward).

Minato Matsuri (Port Festival): July 15-20. It is held in commemoration of the opening of Osaka Port for international trade in 1868.

Tenjin Matsuri: July 24-25. The festival of Temmangu Shrine (Kita Ward) and one of the three largest festivals in Japan. On the evening of the 25th, *Gozafune* (sacred ships) and other boats carry a portable shrine up the Dojima River. Flares and bonfires illuminate the waterway, both banks of which are crowded with spectators. Fireworks and other sideshows are arranged for their amusement.

Sumiyoshi Matsuri: July 30-August 1. This is the last of Osaka's gay summer festivals held at Sumiyoshi Shrine (Sumiyoshi Ward). Portable shrines are carried amid a happy clamor to the Yamato River and back.

National Inter-High School Baseball Tournament: Early August. The playoffs are held at Koshien Stadium in Nishinomiya for about 10 days.

Osaka Takigi Noh: August 11-12. Held at Ikutama Shrine (Tennoji Ward). *Noh* dramas are performed outdoors at night in the shrine precincts on a stage illuminated only by torches.

Osaka Matsuri: Early October. Held in the vicinity of Osaka Castle (Chuo Ward). A procession of *samurai* and other events are held to commemorate the exploits of Toyotomi Hideyoshi.

Midosuji Parade: Early October. A brass band and traditional performances from all over are held in the streets during this gay festival.

Shinno Festival: November 22-23. The festival of Sukunahikona

Shrine in Doshomachi (Chuo Ward), widely known as a town of medicine wholesalers. The shrine is dedicated to Shinno, the father of herb medicine, and Sukunahikona, the god of medicine. The festival originated in 1822 during a cholera outbreak when doctors distributed medicine among the public and *Hariko-no-Tora* (papier-mâché tigers), which are still passed out during the festival.

Refer to the supplement for details regarding the "i" **System Information Center** in Osaka.

PLACES OF INTEREST (within Osaka City)

Kita Ward

Osaka Station 80 : An average of 300,000 people pass through this front door to Osaka every day, making it one of the largest and busiest railway stations in Japan. It originated in 1874 when the Osaka-Kobe railway was completed. The 27-story-high station building, ACTY, contains the Daimaru Department Store and the Osaka Terminal Hotel. Umeda, the area around Osaka Station, is the city's business and amusement center, and is popularly known as *Kita* (North Quarter). Many department stores, office buildings, theaters and restaurants are located here. The station is the city's traffic hub —the terminal station for inter-urban railways, city buses and long-distance buses. The Umeda Underground Center is a huge, 17,000-sq.-m subterranean shopping center, popularly called "Whity Umeda." Filled with various stores and restaurants, it connects Osaka Station with other large buildings such as the Hankyu and Hanshin department stores. It also links up the Umeda, Higashi-Umeda and Nishi-Umeda subway stations as well as two interurban railway terminals: Hankyu and Hanshin. From here, journeys to Kyoto, Kobe, Takarazuka and many other neighboring cities and tourist attractions can be made.

Hankyu Sambangai Shopping Center occupies the four floors of the Hankyu Terminal Building, two of which are underground. An artificial river with a waterfall flows by the restaurants on the second basement floor. The first basement floor is filled with clothing and accessory shops, while the first floor is a vast book store. The concentration of fashionable, high-class boutiques on the fifth and sixth floors of the terminal building is called Hankyu Junanabangai. The Hankyu Grand Building, Hankyu Five and many other structures packed with places to satisfy sartorial and gourmet passions fill the area around the station. Hilton Plaza, right in front of Osaka Station, contains some 100 boutiques and restaurants of the most refined taste. It stands next to the 35-story Osaka Hilton International Hotel. Nearby is the cylindrical Osaka Marubiru Building with a hotel, boutiques and restaurants inside. Sonezaki Shinchi, 10 min. south of Osaka Station, is often called *Kita-no-Shinchi*. High-class bars, clubs and *ryotei* (Japanese-style restaurants) add color to

Osaka at night.

Midosuji Boulevard [81]: A 44-m-wide thoroughfare about 4 km long cuts through the central part of Osaka from Umeda in the north to Namba in the south. It is lined with beautiful ginkgo and plane trees as well as neat, modern buildings.

Nakanoshima [81]: The administrative center of Osaka is situated on a small island between the Dojima and Tosabori rivers—tributaries of the Yodo River. The area contains the Osaka Municipal Offices, the green-domed prefectural library constructed in 1904, the red-brick Central Public Hall completed in 1918, the Osaka Branch of the Bank of Japan constructed in 1903, the Asahi Shimbun (newspaper) Offices, the Osaka Grand Hotel, the Royal Hotel, the Osaka Festival Hall and the Osaka International Trade Center. The east end of the island is Nakanoshima Park—the oldest park in Osaka, having opened in 1891. Nearby are Yodoyabashi, Higobashi and Kitahama subway stations.

Museum of Oriental Ceramics, Osaka [81]: Located east of the Central Public Hall. Called Toyo Togei Bijutsukan, the museum houses the former Ataka collection of 965 pieces, including masterpieces of the Koryo and Ri dynasties of Korea. Natural light is utilized to show off the displays. National Treasures on display here include a bowl and celadon vase as well as many Important Cultural Properties.

Temmangu Shrine [81]: Located north of Nakanoshima Park, the shrine was founded in honor of Sugawara Michizane (845-903, refer to p.843) in 949. The present building was reconstructed in 1845. The festival of the shrine, *Tenjin Matsuri*, is held every July 24 and 25. It is one of the three largest festivals in Japan, ranking with the *Gion Matsuri* in Kyoto and the *Sanno Matsuri* of Tokyo. The main event of the festival is a boat procession on the Dojima River. 3 min. on foot from Minami Morimachi Subway Station on the Tanimachi and Sakaisuzi lines.

Ministry of Finance Mint [81]: Along the Yodo River, east of Temmangu Shrine. The mint was established in 1871 to unify the coinage system in Japan. Coins and medals of honor are still minted here. Thousands of Japanese coins from ancient times to the present as well as foreign coins are all on display in the museum. Since it is one of the best places for viewing double cherry blossoms, the area next to the river is opened to the public for about a week during cherry-blossom season. It is 12 min. on foot from Temmabashi Station on the Tanimachi Subway Line and Keihan Main Line.

Miyakojima Ward

Sakura-no-Miya Park [81]: A riverside park on the east bank of the Yodo River containing many sports facilities and a Japanese landscape garden. There is a fine view of Osaka Castle from the park. 15 min. on foot from Kyobashi Station on the Keihan and the JR Kanjo

(Loop) lines.

Fujita Museum of Art 81 : A collection of more than 5,000 pieces focusing on tea-ceremony articles and calligraphy, including many National Treasures and Important Cultural Properties. It is open to the public in spring and autumn. There is also a spacious garden. 12 min. on foot from Kyobashi Station.

Kanebo Textile Museum: 10 min. on foot from Miyakojima Subway Station on the Tanimachi Line. The collection includes textiles from all over the world, including Egyptian Copt texture as well as *noh* costumes and *kimono* (*kosode*). This museum is also only open to the public in spring and autumn.

Chuo Ward

Kitahama 81 : The vicinity of Kitahama Subway Station. Like the Kabutocho in Tokyo, this is the financial district of Osaka, with many securities firms concentrated here. The Osaka Securities Exchange was founded in 1878 as the Osaka Stock Exchange. An electronic sign tied into a computer displays the latest stock prices so that trading can be observed from the third-floor gallery.

Dobuike 81 : This area extends 800 m from north to south divided by Chuo-dori Street, and 500 m from east to west just inside of Dobuikesuji Street and Shinsaibasisuji Street. Some 1,500 textile wholesalers are concentrated in this district. This massive wholesale market partly includes the Semba Center Building, which stands under the elevated Hanshin Expressway. This two-story building is 930 m long and is made up of ten different wings. The basement, first and second floors of all the wings comprise the wholesale textile area. The basements of wings No. 2 and No.3 house wholesalers of imported goods. Hommachi and Sakaisuji-Hommachi subway stations are directly connected to the building.

Yugi Museum of Art 81 : 300 m south of Yodoyabashi Station on the Midosuji Subway Line and Keihan Main Line. The approximately 1,000-piece collection of tea bowls, hanging scrolls and other art objects, especially those related to the tea ceremony, contains eight Important Cultural Properties. Various parts of the collection are on public display four times a year.

Osaka Merchandise Mart Building 81 : The huge 22-story building with four basement floors was constructed in 1969. It was built to provide convenient and efficient space for the display of various kinds of merchandise by concentrating wholesalers here. Situated on the south bank of the Yodo River, it is one of the largest such showcases in the world. Near Temmabashi Station on either the subway or Keihan Main Line.

Osaka Castle 81 : The castle stands on the tableland formerly called Ishiyama in the eastern part of the city. Rennyo, a priest of the Jodo-Shinshu sect, founded a temple here in 1496. A castle was then built by the renowned military leader Toyotomi Hideyoshi (1536–

1598) and completed in 1585 after three years of construction. The castle is famed for its magnificent scale and the immense granite stones used for the walls. The castle was almost completely destroyed in 1615 by the Tokugawa Clan, which had fought the Toyotomi Clan for power. The Tokugawa Shogun had a larger donjon constructed on the site in 1630 as a sign of his prestige, but in 1665 it was struck by lightning and burned to the ground. The other buildings were nearly completely destroyed by incendiarism in 1868 by the retreating Tokugawa troops at the time of the Meiji Restoration. The present five-story donjon (eight stories inside) was constructed of ferro-concrete after the original in 1931. It towers 40 m high on a stone rampart (13 m high) and commands an extensive view of the city and its surroundings. It contains exhibits of historic interest in connection with the Toyotomi family and old Osaka. *Inui Yagura* (two-story tower; an Important Cultural Property), constructed in 1620, and other old buildings also remain. The castle grounds have been turned into a park containing the Osaka City Museum and Hokoku Shrine, which is dedicated to Hideyoshi and his family. At night, the entire castle is brilliantly illuminated. Near Osakajo-Koen Station on the JR Kanjo Line. Osaka-jo (Osaka Castle) Park is a forested area spreading east of the castle. The Osaka-jo International Culture and Sports Hall contains a 14,250-sq.-m hall with a capacity of 16,000 people. Indoor sports events and concerts are held in the hall. A rugby field and outdoor music pavilion can also be found here. The former site of Naniwa-no-Miya Palace is immediately south of Osaka Castle. Since it is believed that an ancient capital was once located here in the seventh and eighth centuries, excavations are under way to find them. The Osaka Municipal Central Gymnasium, southwest of Osaka Castle, was constructed in 1959 and can seat 10,000 persons. Many indoor sports events are held here.

West of Osaka Castle are the Prefectural Government Office, the Prefectural Police Headquarters, branches of several national government agencies, the NHK (Japan Broadcasting Corporation) Building and other private institutions.

Osaka Business Park (OBP) 81 : Situated north of Osaka Castle, it can be reached on foot in 5 min. from Kyobashi Station on the JR Osaka-Kanjo Line or Keihan Line. Covering 260,000 sq.m., the area was developed as a new "city center" to provide facilities for business and commercial services as well as culture and information services. New buildings are constantly springing up here. "Twin 21" is composed of the National Tower, MID Tower (both of which are 150-m-high, 38-story buildings) and the MID Theater. From the observation platform at the top of the MID Tower, one can look out over Osaka City all the way to Mt. Rokko and Awaji Island. The second floor of the National Tower contains Panasonic Square, a general electronic science museum run by Matsushita Electric Industrial Co., Ltd. In the Fujitsu Plaza OBP, one can freely operate OA and other types of new media.

Shinsaibashisuji Street [82]: A long, north–south road running parallel to and east of Midosuji Boulevard. The name is often taken to mean the southern part of the road, specifically the part from the pedestrian bridge called Shinsaibashi (over Nagabori-dori Street) to Ebisubashi Bridge over Dotombori Canal. This is the busiest shopping district in Osaka. Famous shops and fashionable buildings, including the Daimaru and Osaka Sogo department stores, Sony Tower and PARCO, line both sides of a 700-m-long section of the street. Suomachisuji Street, which intersects Shinsaibashisuji, is called European Village because it is filled with European-style cafes and shops selling imported European fashions. The area west of Midosuji Street, called American Village for its concentration of boutiques, used clothing shops and imported record stores, attracts young people and adds its special youthful energy to commercial Osaka. The closest subway station is Shinsaibashi on the Midosuji Line.

Manno Art Museum, Osaka [82]: Accessible 5 min. on foot from Shinsaibashi Subway Station, the museum has an 800-piece collection that consists of ceramics, painted scrolls, armor, and other old Japanese and Chinese objects of art. Open to the public in spring and autumn, the collection includes four National Treasures and twenty Important Cultural Properties.

Dotombori [82]: Running from east to west along the south bank of the Dotombori Canal, this district has been one of the busiest and most popular amusement quarters in Osaka for more than 350 years. Construction of the canal began in 1612 by Yasui Doton (d. 1615), after whom it was named. Many small theaters once stood here, but they have gradually been replaced by movie theaters and clusters of restaurant buildings appropriate to a city of *kuidaore* (refer to p.637). At night, the dazzling neon signs reflected on the canal waters add to the beauty and gaiety of the district. On the north side of the canal is Soemoncho, which is packed with cabarets and bars. The area called *Minami* (South Quarter) includes Dotombori at the center and the area from Shinsaibashisuji Street to Ebisubashisuji Street and all the way to Namba. Sennichimae and Namba, also included in the *Minami* area, are two of the most active areas in Osaka.

Ebisubashisuji Street: Extending south of Shinsaibashisuji Street from Ebisubashi Bridge to Namba is another amusement and shopping district ranking with Shinsaibashisuji Street. Many small shops and restaurants are located along this street.

Sennichimae [82]: Near Namba Station on the subway and the Kintetsu and Nankai railway lines. Adjoining Dotombori and Namba, this amusement quarter is now thronged with pleasure seekers in sharp contrast to more than a century ago when it was a desolate place with an execution ground, a crematory and a graveyard for executed criminals. Today, it is full of restaurants, theaters, movie houses and *pachinko* parlors. Hozenji Yokocho (Alley), with its many tiny eateries and the Mizukake Fudo Temple—a favorite religious attraction, is also well known. In a corner of Sennichimae stands Yoshimoto Hall. NGK Theater, located in the main hall on the second floor, is where *manzai* (stand-up comic duos) is performed in the daytime and shows from all over the world are featured at night. The basement contains a huge disco.

National Bunraku Theater 82 : The theater was established in 1984 to provide a place for the performance and preservation of data on *bunraku*, a traditional puppet-drama theater also known as *joruri*. The theater with a seating capacity of 731 persons and a small hall are not only used for puppet shows, but for the performance of dance and other traditional arts as well. Next to Nippombashi Subway Station on the Sakaisuji and Sennichimae lines.

Namba 82 : Another Osaka shopping district that includes Takashimaya Department Store, "Namba City" and Shin-Kabukiza Theater. From here, Nankai Line trains depart for Wakayama and Mt. Koya, while Kintetsu Line trains leave for Nara and Nagoya.

"Namba City" comprises the two basement floors as well as the first floor of the Nankai-Namba Station Building. It contains sporting goods, clothing and other fashionable specialty shops and restaurants. "Namba Pia" to the south is full of specialty shops popular with young people.

Shin (New)-Kabukiza Theater 82 : Situated along Midosuji Street, diagonally across from Takashimaya Department Store. This magnificent, five-story, ferro-concrete structure was built in the Momoyama-style for the presentation of *kabuki* plays. It is equipped with the latest facilities and has a seating capacity of about 2,000 persons. But *kabuki* is rarely performed now.

Minami Subterranean Center: Completed in 1971, this 800-m-long underground mall also known as Niji-no-machi (Rainbow town) connects Namba, Ebisubashisuji, Sennichimae and Nippombashisuji subway stations. Some 300 modern shops, coffee shops and restaurants fill the brightly illuminated, underground corridors broken up by plazas featuring uniquely arranged lights, fountains and plants.

Kozugu Shrine 83 : 7 min. on foot from Tanimachi Kyuchome Subway Station. This Shinto shrine is dedicated to the 16th Emperor, Nintoku, who is said to have held Court in Osaka. Today, it is a popular place for viewing plum blossoms and cherry blossoms at night.

Nishi and Naniwa Wards

Exhibition Hall of Osaka Science and Technology Center 80 : 5 min. on foot from Awaza Subway Station. Various kinds of industrial technology are simply explained through actual samples, models and panels from leading manufacturers. The museum stands next to Utsubo Park, a 100,000-sq.-m recreation area also offering a 2,000-

bush rose garden and tennis courts.

Denden Town: Located in an area extending from Sanchome to Gochome of Nippombashisuji Street, it is a 5-min. walk from Nippombashi Station on the subway or Kintetsu Line. Ranking with Akihabara in Tokyo, this electric discount district is crammed with some 200 shops of all sizes selling electric appliances at prices significantly below retail prices.

Osaka Prefectural Gymnasium 82 : 10 min. on foot from Namba Subway Station. Located west of Nankai-Namba Station, this is the Osaka arena for annual *sumo* tournaments in March. Other indoor sports events are held here as well. The Japan Crafts Hall is situated south of the gymnasium. The collection contains some 20,000 pieces, including ceramics, lacquerware, handmade textiles, paper and Okinawan folk craft.

Imamiya Ebisu Shrine 82 : Right next to the Nankai Imamiya-Ebisu Station. It is dedicated to the god of commercial prosperity, *Ebisu* (affectionately called *Ebessan* by Osaka residents). The present shrine was rebuilt with cypress wood in 1956. The main shrine festival is held from January 9-11, attracting more than a million people who come to buy *fukusasa*, a kind of bamboo grass that is said to bring prosperity.

Shin-Sekai 82 : A popular amusement quarter west of Tennoji Park. Modeled after Coney Island of New York in the USA, it contains restaurants, theaters and other places for enjoying oneself. Near Ebisumachi Subway Station on the Sakaisuji Line. Tsutenkaku is a steel tower erected in 1912 to serve as a symbol of Shin-Sekai. This structure was dismantled during World War II, and the present tower was constructed in 1956. The observation decks, 91 m and 103 m high, provide a panoramic view of Osaka.

Tennoji Ward

Tennoji 83 : Like Umeda in northern Osaka and Namba in the center, this is the landmark of southern Osaka. Located just on the border with neighboring Abeno Ward, it is sometimes known as Abeno. Kintetsu Department Store and many buildings offering various leisure facilities stand here. In terms of transportation, there is a concentration of railways going through the area. These include the JR Osaka-Kanjo (Loop) Line and JR trains bound for Wakayama, Shingu and Nara leaving from Tennoji Station as well as Kintetsu trains for Yoshino and Kawachi-Nagano leaving from Abenobashi Station. The Tennoji Subway Station and Nankai-Tennoji Station are also in this area.

Shitennoji Temple 83 : Familiarly known as Tennoji Temple, it is situated near Shitennoji-mae Subway Station on the Tanimachi Line and within walking distance of Tennoji Station. It was founded by Prince Shotoku (574-622) in 593, earlier than Horyuji Temple near Nara. The temple has been repeatedly destroyed by fire, however, and nothing remains of the original buildings. The *Hondo* (Main Hall), *Kodo* (Lecture Hall), *Goju-no-To* (Five-Story Pagoda), *Chumon* (Middle Gate), corridor and other structures were rebuilt in the Asuka-style after being destroyed by fire during World War II. The stone *torii* gate over the western approach was erected in 1294 and is considered the eastern gate to the Western Paradise in Buddhism. This stone *torii* and the few old buildings that have escaped the disasters wrought by history have been designated as Important Cultural Properties. At present, Shitennoji Temple is the headquarters of the Washu Buddhist sect, with its grounds covering 96,000 sq. m. The temple has a large number of valuable treasures, including swords said to have belonged to Prince Shotoku and a late Heian-period (794–1185) copy of the Lotus Sutra on a fan-shaped piece of paper decorated with superb paintings. They are National Treasures. There are also several other National Treasures and many Important Cultural Properties in the temple's possession.

The main festivals and ceremonies are the *Doyadoya* on January 14 (refer to p.638), the *Higan-e* rituals on the vernal and autumnal equinoxes, and *Shoryo-e* on April 22. (refer to p.638)

Tennoji Park [83]: Lying southwest of Shitennoji Temple. It was founded in 1909, making it the second-oldest park in Osaka. Covering an area of 250,000 sq.m., the park contains the Osaka Municipal Museum of Art, the Tennoji Zoo, the Tennoji Botanical Garden, a Japanese garden, and various other cultural and sports facilities. Chausuyama Hill, which is part of Tennoji Park, is a tumuli ground that was the site of the camp of Tokugawa Ieyasu—founder of Tokugawa Shogunate—during the famed siege of Osaka Castle in 1614. Keitaku-en Garden is situated on an eminence south of Chausuyama Hill. Founded in 1908, it is a typical Japanese promenade garden with a pond.

Ikukunitama Shrine [83]: Located near Tanimachi-Kyuchome Station on the Tanimachi Subway Line, it is dedicated to two Shinto deities—Ikushima and Tarushima. Reconstructed after World War II, the Main Hall has a complex roof of the Ikukunitama style. Torch-light performances of *Takigi noh* are held on August 11 and 12.

Sumiyoshi and Higashi-Sumiyoshi Wards

Sumiyoshi Shrine [79]: It is said to have been founded in the third century by Empress Jingu to enshrine three guardian gods for seafarers. In olden times, messengers leaving for T'ang Dynasty China would first stop here to pray for safe passage. The approach to the shrine is lined with many stone lanterns, while the arched bridge is said to have been donated by Toyotomi Hideyoshi and his consort Yodogimi in the Keicho era (1596–1615). The four main buildings are of the simple, Sumiyoshi architectural style. Reconstructed in 1808, they have been designated as National Treasures. The *Otaue Shinji* (Rice-Planting Festival) on June 14 and the *Sumiyoshi Matsuri* (Sum-

mer Festival) from July 30–August 1 are celebrated here. (refer to p.638). The shrine is close to Sumiyoshi-Toriimae Station on the Hankai Line or Sumiyoshi-Taisha Station on the Nankai Main Line.
Nagai Park: The park has a unique botanical garden that includes a roadside tree and hedge specimen garden, a track field where various official meets are held and the Osaka Museum of Natural History. The museum contains some 600,000 artifacts pertaining to topography, botany and other natural sciences as well as a life-sized model of the Naumann Elephant. Near Nagai Subway Station on the Midosuji Line.

Minato and Suminoe Wards

Modern Transportation Museum: In front of Bentencho Station on the JR Osaka-Kanjo (Loop) Line. It was established to provide information on the current condition and future prospects of transportation technology. Parts and miniatures of the Shinkansen super-express trains, explanations of how things move and linear motor cars are among the displays. A miniature train set is also operated in front of the JR Bentencho Station.

Osaka Port ⟨79⟩: When first opened to international ships in 1868, the port was located at the mouth of the Ajikawa River. Since the accumulation of earth and sand made that site unfit for accommodating large ships, the present 10-m-deep port was completed east of the old one. Today, it can accommodate 800,000-ton vessels and handles an annual average tonnage of 110 million tons. Benten Pier near the Ajikawa-Ohashi Bridge was completed in 1965 and is now the starting point for sightseeing boats plying the Inland Sea. Osaka Port is now the third-largest port in Japan following Yokohama and Kobe.

Osaka-Nanko (South Port) ⟨79⟩: A train is available to the Ferry Terminal on the computer-operated Nanko Port-Town Line (New Tram). Constructed on land reclaimed from the ocean, the port contains a six-berth ferry pier and a container pier. Domestic ferries as well as those bound for Shanghai and Pusan depart from here.

International Exhibition Center, Osaka: Commonly called "Intex Osaka," the hall can be reached in 10 min. on foot from Naka-Futo Station on the Nanko Port-Town Line. Of the seven display halls, Intex Plaza with a glass dome emitting natural light is the main one. Covering a total area of 128,900 sq.m., the building is equipped with a spiral escalator and other ultra-modern facilities.

PLACES OF INTEREST (in the Vicimity of Osaka)

Toyonaka, Mino-o, Takarazuka and Vicinity

The Hankyu Takarazuka Line forms a junction with the Hankyu Mino-o Line, while the JR Fukuchiyama Line also goes to Ikeda and Takarazuka.
Toyonaka ⟨78⟩ ☎06: Pop. 403,156. 20 min. from Umeda on the Hankyu Takarazuka Line. This residential suburb lying north of

Osaka contains Hattori Ryokuchi Park—a spacious prefectural park with lawns, ponds and flower beds—as well as the Open Air Museum of Old Japanese Farm Houses where old houses from all over Japan are on display.

Mino-o [78] ☎0727: Pop. 117,159. 40 min. from Umeda on the Hankyu Takarazuka Line. The city is the well-known holiday destination, including within its limits the 10-sq.-km Meiji-no-Mori (Meiji Woods) of Mino-o Quasi-National Park. The park is famed for the beauty of the fresh green leaves in spring and the colors of the maples in autumn. Ryuanji and Katsuoji temples, both very old, also stand in the park. The park is popular as an easily accessible place to relax away from Osaka.

Ikeda [78] ☎0727: Pop. 102,075. 25 min. from Umeda on the Hankyu Takarazuka Line. This is a residential suburb of Osaka. The Itsuo Art Museum, 10 min. on foot from Ikeda Station, offers a collection of some 5,000 pieces, including tea-ceremony articles, paintings by Yosa Buson (1716–1783) and other Important Cultural Properties.

Nose Myoken [78]: Founded around the year 1600, this famous Nichiren-sect Buddhist temple is located on top of Mt. Myoken (alt. 662 m). It is believed that worshipping here will bring good luck. One can reach the temple by cable car and connecting ropeway from Kurokawaguchi near Myokenguchi Station on the Nose Railway.

Takarazuka [78] ☎0797: Pop. 198,304. 40 min. from Umeda on the Hankyu Takarazuka Line, or 30 min. from Osaka Station on the JR Fukuchiyama Line. The city is popular as a hot-springs area that is convenient from Osaka. At Takarazuka Spa, many restaurants and *ryokan* line the banks of the Mukogawa River, which runs through the town. Takarazuka Family Land is a 150,000-sq.-m recreation center that features an amusement park, zoo and a botanical garden as well as a large opera house well known for plays and dances performed by an all-girl troupe.

Ibaraki, Takatsuki and Vicinity

The JR Tokaido Main Line and the Hankyu Kyoto Line run parallel between Osaka and Kyoto, while the Keihan Main Line runs slightly to the east. To get to the Senri district in Suita, one can take either the Kita-Osaka-Kyuko Line that extends from the Midosuji Subway Line or the Hankyu Senri Line.

Suita [78] ☎06: Pop. 340,148. Adjoining the north edge of Osaka City, this is basically a bedroom community for commuters to Osaka. Senri New Town, a new 12-sq.-km community straddling Toyonaka, began development in 1962 and now contains 40,000 residences. It is the first example of large-scale residential development in Japan.

Expo'70 Commemoration Park: The site of the 1970 World's Fair— "Expo '70." It reopened in 1972 as a memorial park to form the basis for a large cultural and recreational center. With a large area of 2.64 sq.km, it includes a Japanese garden where the various landscaping styles popular throughout history can be seen; a natural culture garden with ponds and streams; the National Museum of Ethnology, which researches and exhibits the folk cultures of the world; the Japan Folk Crafts Museum, Osaka; the National Museum of Art, Osaka, which specializes in modern art, and Expo Land with its massive ferris wheel and other amusement facilities. The park is 15 min. by bus from Senri-Chuo Station on the Kita-Osaka-Kyuko Line or the JR Ibaraki Station.

Ibaraki 78 ☎0726: Pop. 249,737. 14 min. from Osaka by the JR Tokaido Main Line. The town developed centuries ago as the castle town of Katagiri Katsumoto, a senior retainer of Toyotomi Hideyoshi. It also served as a post town for those heading west from Kyoto on the old Saigoku Highway. Today, factories for machines, electric appliances, food and other goods stand here.

Takatsuki 78 ☎0726: Pop. 355,030. Accessible in 20 min. from Osaka by *shin-kaisoku* (new, rapid train) on the JR Tokaido Main Line, this garden city is situated on the Yodo River. It is known as the place where Christian-convert *daimyo* (feudal lord) Takayama Ukon once ruled. It is also known for its many factories producing electric appliances, medicine, foodstuffs and other products. Settsu-kyo Gorge, north of the JR Takatsuki Station, is a good picnicking spot because there is a rapid stream as well as cherry trees that bloom in spring and other trees with their beautifully colored leaves in autumn.

Minase Shrine: Located about 10 min. on foot from Minase Station on the Hankyu Kyoto Line. It is dedicated to three Emperors: Gotoba, Tsuchimikado and Juntoku. The shrine marks the former site of the detached palace of Emperor Gotoba and was established in the 13th century. Dating from the 17th century, the shrine buildings are made of old wood from the palace, with the tea-ceremony house designated as an Important Cultural Property.

Hirakata 78 ☎0720: Pop. 387,211. 25 min. by express on the Keihan Main Line from Yodoyabashi in Osaka. Situated on the southeast bank of the Yodo River, this is a residential suburb of Osaka. The city includes the 170,000-sq.-m Hirakata Park, which is enjoyed for cherry-blossom and rose viewing as well as for the autumn chrysanthemum-doll show, which attracts many visitors.

Iwashimizu Hachimangu Shrine 78 : 4 min. by cable car from Keihan-Yawatashi Station. Founded in 859, this is one of the oldest Shinto shrines still existing in Japan. The *Honden* (Main Hall,) dedicated to Emperor Ojin and two deities, is richly decorated. Erected in 1634, the Main Hall, *Haiden* (Oratory) and other shrine buildings are Important Cultural Properties. In back of the Main Hall is a monument to Thomas Edison that was erected in April 1934 and commemorates his use of filaments made of bamboo from the groves at Iwashimizu that contributed to a successful electric light bulb in 1880.

Tennozan Hill [78]: Near the JR Yamazaki Station, 26 min. from Osaka by the JR Tokaido Main Line. The rise has an altitude of 270 m and provides an excellent view of the Osaka Plain. It was the scene of the 1582 battle between Toyotomi Hideyoshi and Akechi Mitsuhide (1528-1582) in which Mitsuhide was defeated and slain. Slightly before that, Mitsuhide had slain in a surprise attack both his own and Hideyoshi's lord, Oda Nobunaga (1534-1582)—military ruler of the nation—at Honnoji Temple in Kyoto. Myokian, adjacent to Yamazaki Station, was formerly a dwelling but has been converted into a Rinzai-sect Buddhist temple. It has two architectural treasures: a *Shoin*, which is the late 15th-century-style residence, and the tea-ceremony room *Taian* (a National Treasure) designed by Sen-no-Rikyu (1522-1591)—the master of tea ceremony. It is said to have been frequently visited by Hideyoshi. *Taian* is a National Treasure.

Hoshakuji Temple: Located halfway up Tennozan Hill. Said to have been founded by the priest Gyoki (668-749), this Shingon-sect Buddhist temple enshrines an image of the Eleven-Headed *Kannon*. The Three-Story Pagoda in the temple compound, believed to date from the Momoyama period (late 16th century), is an Important Cultural Property.

Muko [78] ☎075: Pop. 52,430. Situated southwest of the Kyoto Basin, 8 min. on foot from Nishi-Muko Station on the Hankyu Kyoto Line. This is the former site of Nagaoka Palace where Emperor Kammu ruled Nagaokakyo, the Imperial Capital established in 784. Nagaokakyo replaced Nara as the capital. Ten years later, Emperor Kammu moved the capital again to Kyoto. The spot where *Daigokuden* (the Great Hall of State) once stood has been made a historical-site park.

Kawachi Region

The Kintetsu Nara Line for Nara, the Kintetsu Osaka Line for Nagoya, the Kintetsu Minami-Osaka Line for Yoshino and its branch line, the Kawachi-Nagano Line, as well as the JR Kansai Main Line for Nara all run through this area, which forms the east and southeast portions of Osaka.

Higashi-Osaka [79] ☎0729: Pop. 501,546. The city's main station is Fuse, 10 min. by local train from Kintetsu Namba. Its easy access to central Osaka makes it a popular bedroom community. The Kongo-Ikoma Quasi-National Park in the eastern part of the city is a favorite holiday retreat for Osaka residents. The city's ancient Hiraoka Shrine is regarded as the source for Kasuga Shrine in Nara. The Hiraoka Plum Grove lines both sides of the path approaching the shrine, creating an exquisite sight when the trees blossom in spring. Located behind the shrine on the west slope of Mt. Ikoma, Hiraoka Park commands a panoramic view of the Kawachi and Osaka plains. Plums, wisteria, and azaleas beautify the park, with a hiking trail winding through them to Mt. Ikoma.

Kongo-Ikoma Quasi-National Park 79 : Covering 156.25 sq.km and straddling Osaka and Nara prefectures. The park has a vast mountain area. The north end is an excellent recreation area that includes Mt. Ikoma and Mt. Shigi, while the south part centering around Mt. Kongo (alt. 1,125 m) is popular with hikers and campers. The entire park is not only an ideal place for recreation, but it is also of interest to tourists because of its great natural beauty and many sites of historical interest. It can easily be reached from Osaka. A toll road called the Hanna Highway runs between Osaka and Nara, cutting through the north part of the park. The "Shigi-Ikoma Skyline" is a 18.6-km-long toll road that traverses the Ikoma mountains and branches off the Hanna Highway, heading south to Mt. Shigi and winding up on the east side of Mt. Ikoma and running the ridge via the Kuragari, Narukawa and Jusan passes. This highway affords drivers a splendid view of the entire surrounding area from 400–500 m above sea level. The entire distance can be covered in 30 min.

Fujiidera 79 ☎0729: Pop. 654,674. About 20 min. from Abenobashi in Osaka on the Kintetsu Minami-Osaka Line. As the region has long been inhabited, many ancient remains can still be found. It is also a bedroom community for Osaka. Fujiidera Temple, for which the city was named, was once said to have been founded in 725 by the priest Gyoki at the request of Emperor Shomu, but it is now believed to have been constructed by Lord Fujii, whose origins were in the Paikche Kingdom of Korea. The temple is famous for the dry-lacquered *Kannon* with 1,040 hands—a National Treasure created during the Tempyo period (729–749)—it can be viewed on the 18th of every month. Domyoji Temple, next to Domyoji Station on the Kintetsu Minami-Osaka Line, was founded in 594 to serve as the tutelary temple of the Haji family. It has strong ties to Sugawara Michizane, a great scholar-stateman, and is the setting for the famed *kabuki* play, "Sugawara Denju Tenarai Kagami." The main image, an Eleven-Headed *Kannon*, is a National Treasure. Domyoji Temmangu Shrine next door has many plum and cherry trees.

Habikino 79 ☎0729: Pop. 113,621. Since some of the earliest expatriates settled here, there are many ancient temples as well as shrines and tumuli. Although it has been residentially developed, the mountainous region adjoining neighboring Kashiwara is used to cultivate grapes. The Mausoleum of Emperor Ojin is on the hill to the west between Kintetsu Domyoji and Furuichi stations. With a length of 415 m, a height of 36 m, and extending 330 m across the front and 267 m across the back, this is the second largest tomb in Japan after that of Emperor Nintoku.

Konda Hachimangu Shrine is closely related to the mausoleum and has many cultural properties, including National Treasures. Many large tumuli can be found in what is called the Furuichi Tumuli Group. Eifukuji Temple is 10 min. by bus from Kishi Station on the Kintetsu Kawachi-Nagano Line. It was built to protect the grave of

Prince Shotoku (574–622), who made a significant contribution to Japanese history. Cloaked in an air of tranquillity, the grave site is in the inner precincts, one level higher than its surroundings. The present buildings were constructed by order of Toyotomi Hideyoshi's son, Hideyori. The *Niju-no-To* (Two-Story Pagoda) is an Important Cultural Property.

Tondabayashi ☐79☐ ☎0721: Pop. 106,337. The roots of this town are a *jinaimachi* (lit. temple town), a 5-min. walk from Tondabayashi Station on the Kintetsu Kawachi-Nagano Line. Built up around the Jodo-Shinshu-sect's Koshoji Betsuin Temple, the town flourished commercially, with many large, old houses with white walls, lattices and tiled roofs still remaining.

Kawachi-Nagano ☐79☐ ☎0721: Pop. 105,601. Located in the foothills of the Kongo and Izumi mountains, the city occupies the southeastern part of Osaka Prefecture and is the terminal station for the Kintetsu Kawachi-Nagano Line. Kanshinji Temple, 15 min. by bus from Kawachi-Nagano Station, is famed for its Kamakura-period *Kondo* (Main Hall; a National Treasure) and the many Buddhist images and art objects preserved here.

Sakai, Kishiwada and Vicinity

The Nankai Main Line, Koya Line, the JR Hanwa Line and Hankai Railway Hankai Line run through the area. The New Kansai Airport will open in 1994 on a man-made island in the ocean off this shoreline, so large-scale construction is currently under way.

Sakai ☐79☐ ☎0722: Pop. 806,212. 10 min. by express train from Namba on the Nankai Main Line. Ranked as the second largest city in Osaka Prefecture, Sakai lies south of Osaka across the Yamato River. It developed as a trading port and has been frequented by Chinese and other foreign vessels since the 15th century. By the 16th century, Sakai was prospering through the export of swords, armor, fans, and copper and sulfur produced here. When foreign trade was banned in the mid-17th century, the city began to decline, receiving a further blow when the course of the Yamato River changed in 1704, silting up the entrance to the port. Following the dredging of the port and the reclamation of 23 sq.km of land, however, Sakai is now a thriving industrial town producing and exporting iron and steel, petrochemicals, cutlery, bicycles, dyestuffs and other chemicals as well as farm and general machinery, textiles, and rugs and carpets.

Myokokuji Temple: Situated southeast of Myokokuji-mae Station on the Hankai Line. This Nichiren-sect temple is noted for its large Japanese fern palm—4.5 m tall and 17 m around the base. It is a Natural Monument.

Nanshuji Temple: Standing 200 m east of Goryo-mae Station on the Hankai Line. Founded in the 16th century, this famous Rinzai-sect temple is closely related to Sen-no-Rikyu, the man who perfected the tea ceremony. The garden is said to have been designed by his disciple, Furuta Oribe, around 1619. The *Butsuden* (Buddha Hall) is an Important Cultural Property, as are the main halls at Kaiezenji Temple (on the grounds of Nanshuji Temple) and nearby Daianji Temple. The latter temple is ornamented with particularly splendid religious paintings on sliding screens.

The Mausoleum of Emperor Nintoku: Located southwest of Mikuni-gaoka Station on the Nankai Koya Line, it can be reached in 20 min. from Namba. Regarded as the largest in the world, this keyhole-shaped grave is 486 m long, 35 m high in its highest place and covers an area of 465,000 sq.m. It is surrounded by a three-ringed moat. The adjoining area is the spacious Daisen Park, while nearby is the Mozu Tumuli Group containing the 363-m-long Mausoleum of Emperor Richu and many other massive burial mounds.

Izumi 79 ☎0725: Pop. 144,317. This was once the capital of Izumi Province (now, part of Osaka Prefecture). The cultivation of onions and other farm products, and the production of textiles are flourishing industries. The Kuboso Memorial Museum of Arts, southwest of the Izumi-Otsu Station on the JR Hanwa Line, contains many Chinese and Japanese paintings, calligraphy, bronze mirrors and other art objects that are National Treasures or Important Cultural Properties. The garden also contains a tea-ceremony house. Sefukuji Temple on the face of Mt. Masao is the fourth Station on the 33 Temple Pilgrimage in the Former Western Provinces. At the top of the stone stairs are several buildings and a nice view of the surrounding mountains.

Kishiwada 79 ☎0724: Pop. 187,605. This is a key city in the Senshu industrial region, with a thriving commercial sector. Kishiwada Castle, a 15-min. walk from the Nankai Kishiwada Station, has a donjon that was reconstructed in 1954 and a magnificent garden. Kumedaji Temple is said to have been established by priest Gyoki (668-749) and possesses many ancient treasures, while neighboring Kumeda Pond is said to have been built also by Gyoki to provide irrigation water for farming.

Nishinomiya, Ashiya and Vicinity

This region lies between Osaka and Kobe. It is divided by the JR Tokaido Main Line, with the Hankyu Kobe Line running north along the mountains and the Hanshin Main Line running south along the coastside.

Amagasaki 79 ☎06: Pop. 494,946. Accessible in 8 min. from Osaka on JR lines, the city is adjacent to Osaka. It is an important heavy and chemical industrial center, with iron and steel, machinery, metal goods and electric appliances being produced here. The shopping mall "Tsukashin" contains 250 specialty shops—divided into a restaurant street, fashion street, "Young Live Hall," a theater and art exhibition halls—as well as attractions such as musical fountains, all contributing to a pleasant atmosphere. It shows an interesting aspect of the residential town of Amagasaki.

Itami [78] ☎0727: Pop. 183,994. This industrial city north of Amagasaki can be reached from Osaka on the JR Fukuchiyama Line or from Umeda on the Hankyu Line via Hankyu Tsukaguchi in about 15 min. This is where the Osaka International Airport is located. Buses go to the airport from the Osaka, Kobe and Kyoto city areas. The New Kansai International Airport will be opened on a man-made island in Osaka Bay in 1994.

Nishinomiya [79] ☎0798: Pop. 411,455. Connected by the JR, Hanshin and Hankyu lines with Osaka (or Umeda) in 15–20 min. and situated west of Amagasaki, this is a famous *sake*-brewing center. The excellent water in the area has led to a high reputation for producing delicious *sake*, beer, whiskey, soft drinks and other beverages. Heavy industry thrives here as well. Nishinomiya is also famous as the home of Nishinomiya Shrine, known for its popular festival, *Toka Ebisu*, which takes place from January 9–11.

Koshien Stadium: 5 min. on foot from Hanshin Koshien Station. With a total area of 40,000 sq.m and a capacity of 70,000 persons, it is famous as the location of the Inter-High School Baseball Tournament held in March and August of every year. It is also the home stadium for the Hanshin Tigers of the Central Baseball League. Next to the stadium is Koshien-Hanshin Park, the most prominent amusement park in the area, containing a zoo, a winter ice-skating rink, a pool and much more. Many exhibitions and attractions are staged here.

Mt. Kabuto is a low rise of 309 m to the north of Nishinomiya. Kannoji Temple stands on the hillside. Also known as Kabutoyama-Daishi, it provides an excellent view of the Osaka Bay area. The cherry-tree blossoms and red-leafed maples are quite a sight. It can be reached by bus from the JR Nishinomiya Station in 25 min. and is a 20-min. walk from the bus stop to the top of the hill. Kabutoyama Shinrin (Forest) Park is a prefectural preserve, with many trees in the eastern foothills.

Nikawa Picnic Center: 40 min. on foot from Nikawa Station on the Hankyu Imazu Line. Lying at the northeastern foot of Mt. Kabuto, the picnic park is an ideal recreation area with a valley, crags, a pond and a path that offers a panoramic view of the surrounding area.

Ashiya [79] ☎0797: Pop. 86,420. About 20 km and 20 min. from Osaka on the JR, Hankyu and Hanshin lines. Blessed with a mild climate and a picturesque location at the foot of Mt. Rokko, this city is the best residential area in the Hanshin (Osaka–Kobe) district. The view of the surrounding area is magnificent. It is connected with Arima Spa in Kobe by a 10.6 km-long toll road called the Royu Highway. The Tekisui Art Museum, in Ashiya, is an 8-min. walk from Hankyu-Ashiyagawa Station. The bulk of the collection consists of ceramics, but it also includes calligraphy, dolls, battledores and a variety of other items.

Area 2. Kyoto

Kyoto ⎡78/86-87⎤ ☎075

Pop. 1,414,778. For more than 10 centuries, from 794 to 1868, Kyoto was the capital of Japan and the center of its civilization. Naturally, it is an important objective for the visitor to Japan. Brimming with historical and religious traditions and being the birthplace of the traditional arts and crafts that have won the admiration of the world, Kyoto retains a unique position among the great cities of the world. Nestled picturesquely among the surrounding mountains, it still exudes an old-world atmosphere. In spite of the signs of material progress, this ancient Buddhist center seems a place apart from the busy world, where the spirit of old Japan still prevails.

Imposing shrines, temples and palaces with elaborately designed gardens reflect the glory of Kyoto. In all, the city has over 200 Shinto shrines and some 1,500 Buddhist temples, including 30 of the latter that are the headquarters of various Buddhist sects. Kyoto is also a city of festivals, with colorful events filling the calendar in Kyoto from New Year's Day to the last day of the year.

However, Kyoto is no mere repository for Japan's traditional culture. Covering an area of 611 sq.km, it is the seventh largest city in Japan and an important industrial hub as well as the educational center of western Japan. It is also equipped with well-organized transportation facilities and hotel accommodations.

The expanded city of today still benefits from *Jyobo-sei* (the original checkerboard design of streets and avenues) laid out more than 1,100 years ago. The city is divided into nine administrative wards: Fushimi, Higashiyama, Kamigyo, Kita, Minami, Nakagyo, Sakyo, Shimogyo and Ukyo.

The climate in Kyoto is mild. The average temperature (in centigrade) of each season is: 13.7℃ in spring (April), 26.3℃ in summer (July), 17.0℃ in autumn (October) and 3.9℃ in winter (January).

TRANSPORTATION

Transportation to Kyoto

About 2 hrs. 40 min. (514 km) from Tokyo Station, 45 min. (148 km) from Nagoya or 3 hrs. 20 min. (663 km) from Fukuoka (Hakata) by the "Hikari" on the JR Shinkansen. A long-distance, night bus leaves from Tokyo, arriving in 8 hrs., while a bus from Nagoya takes 2 hrs. 40 min.

Transportation In and Around Kyoto

Railways: The JR Kyoto Station, Kawaramachi Station on Hankyu and Keihan-Sanjo Station on the Keihan Electric Railway are the main stations in Kyoto.

In addition to serving as a Shinkansen station, the JR Kyoto Station is connected to Osaka and Kobe by the Tokaido Main Line, Nara by the Nara Line and Kameoka by the San-in Main Line. The

Kinki Nippon Railway (Kintetsu) also runs a limited express to Nara. The municipal subway runs from Kyoto Station, going as far north as Kitaoji and as far south as Kintetsu Takeda, continuing through to the Kintetsu Line. The northern-bound subway goes right under Karasuma-dori Street, one of the main streets in Kyoto, making it especially convenient for sightseers. The Hankyu Kyoto Line runs from Kawaramachi Station to Umeda in Osaka. At Katsura Station along the way, a branch line heads for Arashiyama. From Demachi-yanagi Station, Keihan trains leave for Yodoyabashi in Osaka on the Main Line, from Keihan-Sanjo Station, trains leave for Uji on the Uji Line, and from Keishin-Sanjo Station, trains leave for Otsu on the Keishin Line. Trains of the Eizan Electric Railways also leave for Kurama and Yase from Demachi-yanagi Station. Keifuku Electric Railway connects Shijo-Omiya and Arashiyama.

Buses: Kyoto Municipal Bus, Kyoto Bus, Keihan Bus and several other bus companies cover the city with an extensive network of routes. The main terminals are at Kyoto, Sanjo-Keihan, Shijo-Kawaramachi, Shijo-Karasuma, Shijo-Omiya and Kita-Oji stations. Because of the many different routes involved, buses are somewhat difficult for the newcomer to use. However, in order to respond to the needs of foreign visitors, municipal buses in Kyoto have recorded English language announcements and maps in English.

Taxis: In addition to the front entrances of main hotels, railway stations and sightseeing locations, a taxi can easily be flagged down on the street. Or, if desired, one's hotel can make arrangements to hire out a special sightseeing taxi.

Roads: The most commonly used expressway interchanges are the Meishin Kyoto-Minami(South) Interchange and the Kyoto Higashi (East) Interchange. Since the many narrow roads winding through the ancient capital are frequently jammed with traffic, driving is not especially recommended for travelers.

Sightseeing buses: Bus tours for foreign tourists operated by major travel agents leave from in front of Kyoto's main hotels. (All buses are staffed with English-speaking guides; for details, refer to Supplement)

Travel Information

Japan National Tourist Organization's Kyoto Tourist Information Center (TIC): Kyoto Tower Building, Higashi-Shiokojicho, Shimo-gyo-ku. ☎ (075) 371-5649.

History

For centuries after the foundation of Japan, the capital shifted to a new place at the beginning of each reign. It was not until 694 that a permanent capital called Fujiwarakyo was established, but in 710 it was re-established in Heijokyo (now known as Nara). It continued there until 784, when the capital moved to Nagaoka on the southwestern outskirts of the present city of Kyoto. Again, it was shifted northeast to an area called Uda in 794, and it is here that the roots of the present-day Kyoto lie. It was first poetically described as Heiankyo (Capital of Peace), but later it came to be referred to simply as Miyako (Imperial Capital) or Kyoto (Capital City).

The new city was laid out in accordance with Chinese concepts and was completed in 805. There were nine wide boulevards running from east to west, beginning with Ichijo, or First Street, in the north, and ending with Kujo, or Ninth Street, in the south. These streets intersected another series of broad avenues, beginning with Kyogoku in the east and ending with Nishi-Kyogoku in the west. The city was surrounded by a low, earthen wall and ditch, and was pierced with 18 gates connected to the main thoroughfares.

The new city, thus started, did not escape calamity for long. In 960, the Imperial Palace, which was situated between Ichijo and Nijo, burned down for the first time, then suffered the same fate in 1177. In 1221, the area was dominated by the Kamakura Shogunate, and after 1336 it became the scene of a constant series of conflicts. Although there were short intervals of peace, from 1467 to 1477, the city was again ravaged by confrontations between the rival Yamana and Hosokawa forces, known as the Onin Rebellion. For the next hundred years, the Court was reduced to such a low state that when Oda Nobunaga entered with his forces in 1570, he found Kyoto in a deplorable state. One of his first projects was to rebuild the Imperial Palace, a work which was completed by his successor, Toyotomi Hideyoshi. Hideyoshi restored the temples, laid out the streets anew and brought back much of the glory of the old capital.

When the administration of the country was transferred to Edo (now, Tokyo) by the Tokugawa Shogunate, Kyoto lost much of its brilliance. However, it did manage to maintain its cultural superiority so that when the Meiji Restoration occurred in 1868, Kyoto continued to be called "the Capital." Even today, it maintains a different atmosphere from Tokyo, performing an especially important role in supporting the arts and academia.

INDUSTRIES

Kyoto is the center of Japan's traditional industries, but modern industries have also developed here.

Nishijin Silk Weaving: The production of silk in Kyoto dates back to the city's founding in 794, receiving the patronage of the Imperial Court. Later, Chinese artisans brought to Japan introduced improved techniques, which were quickly adopted by Kyoto weavers, who began to produce gauzes, brocades, damasks, satins and crepes. The civil strife of the 15th century prevented further development for a time, but silk weaving flourished under the peace brought by the Edo period (1603–1867).

Early in the 17th century, Chinese-style figured satins and Dutch-style patterned velvets were produced. By requiring that all silk fabrics used by the Imperial Court and the aristocracy be made at Nishijin, the Tokugawa Shogunate did much to foster the industry in this district. During the Meiji period, modern European techniques were introduced to the market, changing the face of the local textile market. The fabrics produced here are used for *obi* (sash), tablecloths, neckties and many other products. In recent years, woolen and synthetic fibers have been used as the basis for fabrics especially in making such products as shawls, scarfs, women's clothing and curtains.

Dyeing: Dyed fabrics known as *Yuzen-zome* or *Kyo-zome* are a Kyoto specialty in which a wide variety of patterns and colors are printed on silk fabrics in a complicated process. The "hand-painted" *Yuzen* process is said to have been invented by Miyazaki Yuzensai, an artist of the late 17th century. In the Meiji period, a mass-production method using paper stencils was developed, which in recent years some producers have mechanized almost completely. *Yuzen*-dyed scarfs, handkerchiefs and *kimono* are popular all over the world.

Embroidery: Introduced from China and Korea, embroidery was used to decorate Court robes, often in combination with printed designs. A major impetus was given to Japan on the opening of the country to foreign intercourse in 1854, when the beauty of these products attracted the attention of the outside world.

Ceramics: Porcelain produced in Kyoto is known as *Kyo-yaki*, of which *Kiyomizu-yaki* is the most famous for its elegance. It first gained national fame owing to the excellent workmanship of Nonomura Ninsei in the 17th century. Many improvements have since been made by other potters. These high-quality ceramics are used in the home as well as at tea ceremonies and other functions.

Kyoto Lacquerware: The gold or silver lacquerware called *maki-e*, decorated with designs produced by mixing metallic dust with lacquer, is especially renowned for its quality and elegance. Developed during the Azuchi-Momoyama period (1573–1598), this elaborate lacquerware was favored by the Imperial Court and the aristocracy, whose patronage encouraged the progress of the art. In the 17th century, a new development in the *maki-e* process was introduced through the mastery of Hon-ami Koetsu (1558–1637) and Ogata Korin (1658–1716), both of whom laid the foundations for today's refined and tasteful ware in those early days.

Dolls: Kyoto dolls, a prominent local handicraft, are the most graceful dolls made in Japan. Gosho, Fushimi and several other kinds of dolls are produced in the area.

Cloisonne: The cloisonne technique was introduced from China. The first cloisonne products were made in Japan during the Nara and Heian periods. The technique is used to fabricate such items as cigarette cases, jewelry boxes, vases and compacts, with much of the output being exported or sold as souvenirs.

Folding Fans: Kyoto produces about 90% of the folding fans made in Japan, some of which are made explicitly for export. Originally developed during the Heian period, fans not only provide the functional benefit of a cool breeze or used in dance and rituals, but they are also enjoyed simply for their artistic merit.

Among the many other traditional products of Kyoto are wood-block prints, damascene work, Buddhist altar fittings and bamboo-ware.

Machinery and Hardware: An electric machinery industry sprang up in Kyoto when the first hydroelectric power plant in Japan was completed in 1891. Products such as communications equipment, generators and transformers are manufactured here.

The development of the weaving and dyeing industries gave Kyoto a well-deserved reputation for the production of high-quality dyeing and spinning machinery. Some of the other machinery products include machine tools, medical equipment and precision apparatus—products that are highly valued both at home and abroad.

Kyoto's metal industry includes copper rolling, which boasts a 1,000-year history that dates back to the Heian period when the technology for producing copper Buddhist altar fittings was perfected. Today, the main products are copper bars, copper wire and copper plates for use as construction materials as well as in the production of electric appliances, rolling stock, ships and other goods.

Foods: The brewing of *sake* developed in the southern part of Kyoto in the Fushimi district, which is favored with excellent water. Besides being one of the major *sake*-brewing districts in Japan, Fushimi is also famous for its traditional cookies and pastries. Many of the confectioneries have been in business for hundreds of years.

Chemicals: The main products of the Kyoto chemical industry include plastics, glass, medicine, soap and dyes.

Other important industries in Kyoto include printing and paper processing as well as the production of furniture, religious articles and toys.

ANNUAL EVENTS

Okera Mairi: January 1. Held at Yasaka Shrine (Higashiyama Ward) from the night of December 31 to the morning of the new year. Many of the worshippers visit the shrine to bring home a flame from the sacred fire to use in cooking the first meal of the year, a custom that it is believed will help ward off illness during the coming year.

Toka Ebisu: January 8-12. Also called *Hatsu-Ebisu*, this is the 10th-day festival held at Ebisu Shrine (Higashiyama Ward) in honor of *Ebisu*, one of the Seven Gods of Fortune and the patron deity of commercial endeavor. Large numbers of people, especially merchants, visit this shrine dedicated to *Ebisu*.

Ho-onko: January 9-16. An annual memorial service held at Nishi-Honganji Temple (Shimogyo Ward) in honor of Saint Shinran (1173 -1262), founder of the Jodo-Shinshu sect of Buddhism.

Hadaka Odori (Naked Dance): January 14. A lively festival at Hokaiji Temple (Fushimi Ward). Two groups of boys and older youths, symbolically purified in both body and mind, gather naked except for a loincloth in front of Yakushido Hall. They raise their hands above their heads, pushing and shoving and using their backs while chanting "chorai, chorai, chorai!"

Yabiki Hajime (Toshiya): January 15. An archery contest in the outer corridor of Sanjusangendo Hall (Higashiyama Ward). In this contests, which originated in the 16th century, the winner is decided by the contestant who can shoot the most arrows from one end of the hall to the other end (120 m) in one day and night. Wasa Daihachiro, a *samurai* of Kii Province (now, Wakayama and a part of Mie prefectures), set the record in 1696 by shooting 13,053 arrows, of which 8,153 went the full length of the hall.

Hatsu-Kobo (Hakkobo): January 21. The memorial service for Kobo-Daishi (founder of the Shingon sect of Buddhism). It is the first fair of the year at Toji Temple. On the fair, the grounds are crowded with some 1,000 stalls, many of which sell antiques.

Setsubun: February 3 or 4. It marks the transition from winter to spring. On this day, most families perform the unique and traditional ceremony of throwing beans and shouting "*Fuku-wa-uchi, oni-wa-soto*" ("In with prosperity, out with the devils!") It is a symbolic invitation for good fortune to visit their house and rid it of any misfortune. Large-scale bean-throwing ceremonies are held at Yoshi-da Shrine (Sakyo Ward), Mibu Temple (Nakagyo Ward), Kurama Temple (Sakyo Ward) and Rozanji Temple (Kamigyo Ward).

Baikasai (Plum Blossom Festival): February 25. Held at Kitano Temmangu Shrine (Kamigyo Ward). *Nodate* (an open-air tea ceremony) and memorial rites for the shrine deity are held under the fragrant blossoms of the plum trees.

Spring doll festival: March 1–April 3. A collection of old Kyoto dolls is put on exhibition at Hokyoji Temple. A similar exhibit is held October 15–November 10.

Nehan-e: March 14–16. Buddhist services at Tofukuji Temple (Higashiyama Ward) and Seiryoji Temple (Ukyo Ward). At Tofukuji Temple, the *Nehanzu*, a picture scroll representing Buddha's entry into Nirvana, is put on public display. At Seiryoji Temple, a ceremony takes place in which three sacred torches are lighted in the memory of Gautama Buddha (Sakyamuni), who died on this day at the age of 79. These torch fires are said to forecast the condition of the rice crop.

Jusan Mairi (13-year-olds coming to worship): March 13–May 13. Held at Horinji Temple (Ukyo Ward). The temple is popularly known as "Kokuzosan," the name of the Buddhist deity (*Bosatsu*) enshrined here. It is believed that this deity brings wisdom and good fortune to children. Accordingly, it has become the custom for children to visit the shrine at 13 years of age. Girls, in particular, dress up in *kimono* for this occasion.

Miyako Odori: April 1–30. One of the Five Major Dances of Kyoto. Often called the Cherry Dance in English, it is performed at Gionkobu Kaburenjo Theater. The dance is very beautiful, consisting of a series of graceful movements accompanied by an orchestra of *samisen*, *fue* (flutes), drums and sometimes bells. The elegant stage scenery is changed with each new scene.

Yasurai Matsuri: Second Sunday in April A popular festival at the Imamiya Shrine (Kita Ward). Four demons (incarnations of misfortune and illness) dance around the *ujiko* (parishioners), who carry parasols decorated with flowers. Legend has it that in ancient times spring would bring a plague to Kyoto. It is believed that by standing under these parasols, designed to look like cherry blossom trees, misfortune can be prevented. It is hoped that life won't be brief like that of a cherry blossom (a symbol of short life). The festival is held to pacify the god of sickness, with ritual dances beginning at Imamiya Shrine at 3:00 p.m.

Gyoki-e: April 18–25. An annual memorial service performed in honor of Saint Honen (1133–1212), founder of the Jodo sect of Buddhism. A magnificent ceremony is held at Chion-in Temple (Higashiyama Ward).

Mibu-kyogen: April 21–29. Commonly known as "Mibusan-no-Kandenden." It is a performance of farcical pantomimes dating from the 13th century that are said to have originated in order to make Buddhist teachings easier to understand. Of the thirty, many humorous plays in the repertory, *Horaku-Wari*, or Plat–Breaking, is the most famous of the farces. The unusual gestures are accompanied by flutes and bells.

Yoshino-Tayu Hanakuyo (Flower Memorial Service): Third Sunday in April. Yoshino-Tayu was a famous *oiran* or "courtesan" of the Edo period, a woman of both wit and beauty who became the heroine of *kabuki*, *kyogen* and other forms of classical Japanese drama. "Tayu" women from Shimabara dress in the style of the original *oiran*, followed by others in a colorful procession starting at 11:00 a. m. from Koetsuji Temple to Joshoji Temple.

Matsuno-o Matsuri: First Sunday after April 20. Dedicated to the patron deity of *sake* brewing, it is held at Matsuno-o Shrine. Six portable shrines are carried across the Katsura River by boat.

Kamogawa Odori (Kamo River Dance): May 1–24. The dances and dance-plays, staged at the Kaburenjo Theater in Pontocho (Nakagyo Ward), are similar to the *Miyako Odori* of Gion.

Fujinomori Matsuri: May 5. This is an ancient, horse-running festival at Fujinomori Shrine (Fushimi Ward). A horse-racing ceremony is also held on the same day on the grounds of Kamigamo Shrine (Kita Ward). It is believed to have originated in 1093, when a horse-racing ceremony was performed for the gods to obtain peace and a good harvest.

Aoi Matsuri: May 15. Held at Kamigamo and Shimogamo shrines. It has become the custom on this day to offer the leaves of *aoi* (hollyhock) to the deities enshrined at both places. The origin of the festival can be traced back to the sixth century, when it was perform-ed to propitiate the shrine deities who, it was believed, had been stirring up great storms around the country. During the turmoil of the Muromachi period (1336-1573), the festival was not observed, but it was later revived during the Genroku period (1688-1703) and again in 1884.

During the festival, men clad in Heian period (794-1185) costumes re-enact an Imperial procession of those ancient times. Early in the morning on May 15, an Imperial messenger and his retinue in full Court costume assemble at the Kyoto Imperial Palace and parade to the shrines. The procession is accompanied by colorfully dressed guards, pages, halberd bearers and others who march in front of and behind a lavishly decorated Imperial chariot drawn by an ox.

Upon arrival at Shimogamo Shrine, a ceremony is performed. Another service is held at Kamigamo Shrine, where the procession disbands. It is one of the most famous events in the country and should not be missed by anyone with an interest in the old, traditional Japan.

Mifune Matsuri (Boat Festival): Third Sunday in May. The festival of Kurumazaki Shrine in Saga (Ukyo Ward). On this day, the serene atmosphere of the Heian period (794-1185) is vividly recreated on the Oi River. The Emperors and their courtiers often went to view the splendid scenery of Arashiyama here. Gaily decorated boats like those of ancient times float down the river, with music and dances, being performed on the two larger craft, the bowsprits of which are fashioned in the shape of a dragon and a phoenix, and beautiful dancers' fans being floated down the river.

Shinran-Shonin Kotan-e (Saint Shinran's Birthday): May 21. An impressive service is held at Nishi-Honganji Temple (Shimogyo Ward) to celebrate the birthday of Shinran (1173-1262), founder of the Jodo-Shinshu sect of Buddhism. Refer to p.673.

Takigi Noh (Noh Performances by Bonfire): June 1-2. Performed on the outdoor stage in front of the oratory at Heian Shrine. *Noh* plays are presented after dark under the stars, lighted only by the flames from wood bonfires. The enchanting atmosphere thus created adds to the mystic profundity of the *noh* play.

Takekiri-e (Bamboo-Cutting Ceremony): June 20. Held at Kurama Temple (Sakyo Ward). In this spectacular ceremony, conducted in front of the Main Hall, two groups of four priests dressed as warrior monks rush out with eight large bamboo poles representing serpents. They must cut the poles into three parts, and whichever side cuts the poles faster is guaranteed a good harvest.

Cormorant fishing: Mid-June to Late August. Demonstrated every evening on the Uji River. The birds are used to catch fish.

Gion Matsuri: July 1-29. One of the three largest festivals in Japan, held at Yasaka Shrine (Higashiyama Ward). It dates back to the ninth century when the head priest of the renowned Yasaka Shrine organized a procession of many people to escort the decorated shrine-wagons in order to appeal to the gods for protection from the pestilence that was then ravaging the city. On July 17, gorgeously decorated floats are paraded along the main streets to the accompaniment of flutes, drums, gongs and other musical instruments. It is called *Yamaboko-Junko*. There are two kinds of floats: The *yama*, which is carried by long poles on the shoulders of several men and decorated with legendary figures, and the *hoko*, a kind of ornamental tower. Set on four massive wooden wheels, the *hoko* is topped by a center mast 36 to 40 m high. The procession can be observed on the street anywhere along the route, but covered stands for spectators are provided on Oike-dori Street. The 16th is called *Yoiyama*, and in the evening *hoko* are decorated with many paper lanterns.

Onda Matsuri (Rice-Planting Festival): Third Sunday in July. Held at Matsuno-o Shrine (Ukyo Ward). Rice seedlings are planted by three maidens in colorful costumes. In former days, these seedlings were then carried home and re-planted to serve as charms against harmful insects.

Ceramics Market: August 7-10. Some 500 stalls are set up in the street offering the local *Kiyomizu-yaki* as well as various kinds of pottery from all over Japan. Everything from pottery for everyday use to the most expensive variety can be bought at comparatively low prices.

Matsuage: August 15. Held at Hanase (Sakyo Ward) from 9:00 p.m. Men throw lighted torches, attempting to set a bamboo basketful of firewood ablaze the top of a massive cypress pole (21 m high). When viewed from across the Kamikatsura River, the countless streaks of fire through the darkened sky create a scene of eerie beauty.

Daimonji Okuribi: August 16. Performed on Mt. Nyoigadake (Sakyo Ward) and other places. A spectacular bonfire is ignited on the hillside in the evening. The bonfire is laid out in the shape of the Chinese character *dai*, which means "large." Other characters are set afire in succession on four other hills surrounding the city. The event is held to send the souls of the dead, who return to heaven.

Jizo-Bon: August 22-24. A festival held in honor of *Jizo*, the Buddhist guardian deity of children, at every town in Kyoto.

Annual Festival of Iwashimizu Hachimangu Shrine: September 15. Historical-dress parades, dances and other events occur from 2:00 a.m. until evening.

Zuiki Matsuri: October 1-5. Decorated floats are paraded through the streets. The float carrying the portable shrine is made of *zuiki* (taro stems). At Kitano Temmangu Shrine (Kamigyo Ward).

Ushi Matsuri (Cow Festival): October 10. Held at Koryuji Temple in Uzumasa (Ukyo Ward). Around 7:00 p.m., the god *Madara* (protector from evil), accompanied by four Deva kings, musicians and many worshippers, appears astride a cow. After circling the area, the parade heads for *Yakushido* Hall, where the god begins reading

Buddhist sutras. The sutras are quite difficult and virtually incomprehensible to those present. However, at one point the god and four Deva kings suddenly flee into *Yakushido* Hall. This marks the end of this festival. The unique characteristics of this festival have earned it a reputation as one of Kyoto's three unique festivals.

Jidai Matsuri (The Festival of Eras): October 22. Held at Heian Shrine (Sakyo Ward). Commemorating the founding of Kyoto as the capital in 794, this festival features a unique procession of more than 2,000 people in groups wearing the costumes of each era for the last 1,100 years or so. One of the most popular events in Kyoto, the gorgeous historical parade extending more than a mile long starts from the Kyoto Imperial Palace and ends at Heian Shrine.

Kurama-no-Himatsuri (Great Fire Festival): October 22. A spectacular festival at Yuki Shrine (Sakyo Ward). Men dressed only in loincloths and *hanten* (a cotton jacket, a kind of *kimono*) parade through the streets carrying lighted torches around the portable shrine from 6:00 p.m. to midnight. The festival is in thanks for the gift of fire and accordingly the 160 houses in Kurama light bonfires. A procession of children and adults wearing only loincloths and headbands walk to the Main Shrine in the mountains from *Sammon* gate. Mt. Kurama is set ablaze with the light of the pine torches, creating an incredible sight.

Momiji Matsuri (Maple Festival): Second Sunday in November. People dressed in the costumes of the 10th century ride in boats and play the ancient music and games of the nobles of by gone days. At Arashiyama Park (Ukyo Ward).

Ho-onko: November 21-28. This memorial ceremony is held in recognition of the priest Shinran. It is held on different days at Higashi (East)-Honganji Temple and Bukkokuji Temple (both in Shimogyo Ward) and at Nishi (West)-Honganji Temple and other Jodo-Shinshu-Sect temples.

Ochatsubo Hokensai (Tea-Container Offering): November 26. Held at Kitano Temmangu Shrine in Kamigyo Ward. The famous general and statesman Toyotomi Hideyoshi held a grand tea ceremony here in 1587. In memory of this occasion, a procession of people dressed in old days costumes parade to the shrine, where they offer tea leaves picked during the year.

Kaomise (All-Star Kabuki Performances): About December 1-26. The top *kabuki* stars unite for a formal performance. The event originated in the 17th century when actors, playwrights and musicians renewed their contracts with the theater at this time of year and all the actors lined up on the stage. At the Minamiza Theater (Higashiyama Ward).

Shimai-Kobo (Final Service for Kobo-Daishi): December 21. Held at Toji Temple (Minami Ward). Like *Hatsu-Kobo*, this is the final memorial service of the year, with many stalls filling the temple grounds.

Shimai Tenjin (Final Offering to Tenjin): December 25. It is the festival of Tenjin (Sugawara Michizane), the patron god of scholars, at Kitano Temmangu Shrine (Kamigyo Ward). This is the last festival of the year. Many stalls open for business on the temple ground and people especially like to buy dried plums to eat with green tea on New Year's Day.

FLORAL CALENDAR

Plum Blossoms (Late February–Early March): Kyoto Gyoen (Imperial Park), Kitano Temmangu Shrine, Umenomiya Shrine, Nagaoka Temmangu Shrine and Zuishin-in Temple.

Cherry Blossoms (Late March–Early April): Maruyama Park, Kiyomizu Temple, Path of Philosophy, Kyoto Imperial Palace and Nanzenji Temple. (Mid-April): Hirano Shrine, Kamigamo Shrine, Daigoji Temple, Heian Shrine and Oharano Shrine. (Late April): Ninnaji Temple, Kuramadera Temple and Kibune Shrine.

Azaleas (Late April–May): Shisendo Temple, Shodenji Temple, Entsuji Temple and Keage area.

Rhododendrons (Late April–Early May): Zuishin-in Temple and Sanzen-in Temple

Peonys (Late April–Early May): Otokuni Temple

Wisteria (May): Byodo-in Temple, Kuramadera Temple and Nagaoka Temmangu Shrine

Blue Flags and Irises (May–June): Heian Shrine, Ota Shrine, Umenomiya Shrine and Tofukuji Temple.

Lotus Blossoms (June): Kanjuji Temple and Heian Shrine

Bush Clover (September): Kodaiji Temple, the Kyoto Imperial Palace, Kamigamo Shrine, Nashinoki Shrine and Nanzenji Temple.

Chrysanthemums (October): Nijo Castle, Maruyama Park and Daikakuji Temple.

Maple Leaves (Mid-Late October): Kurama-Kibune area and Nison-in Temple. (Early-Mid-November): Nanzenji Temple, Eikando Temple, Yoshimine Temple, Kozanji Temple, Jingoji Temple and Tofukuji Temple.

JNTO'S Tourist Information Center (TIC): 1st floor, Kyoto Tower Building, Higashi-Shiokojicho, Shimogyo-ku, Kyoto ☎ (075) 371-5649

PLACES OF INTEREST

Rakuchu

Rakuchu is the central urban district in the city of Kyoto. Its name dates from the 16th century, when Toyotomi Hideyoshi (1536–1598) ordered an earthwork defense built around the city. The area inside this earthwork was called Rakuchu and the area outside, Rakugai. Today, the Rakuchu district is no longer clearly defined so that only the name is left as a reminder of these former defenses. Although present-day Rakuchu is a progressive, modern district, much of its history has been preserved and the flavor of the old city carefully guarded.

Kyoto Gyoen: This park is protected by nine gates and tall walls occupying an area of about 650,000 sq.m between Teramachi-dori Street on the east and Karasuma-dori Street on the west. In former times, it was the part of the Imperial Palace that contained the residences of the Imperial princes as well as the high Court nobles. Today, it is open to the public as a people's park. Near Marutamachi Subway Station.

Kyoto Gosho (Kyoto Imperial Palace) [85]: Situated 3.5 km north of the JR Kyoto Station, the buildings have been repeatedly destroyed by fire so that the present structures only date from 1855. The original site of the palace built in 794 by Emperor Kammu was in the southwest part of the city. After the fire of 1788, the present site was selected, and a new palace, modeled after the old one, was completed in 1790. However, this, too, was destroyed by fire in 1854. The building now standing here has adopted the same style of elegant simplicity.

Kyoto Imperial Palace covers a site of some 110,000 sq.m and is open to the public except on second and fourth Saturdays, first, third and fifth Saturday afternoons, Sundays, national holidays and from December 25 to January 5. Visitors must first obtain permission from the Kyoto Office of the Imperial Household Agency. ☎ (075) 211-1215

Escorted by a palace guard (who is generally accompanied by an interpreter), visitors usually enter the palace grounds through *Seishomon* Gate on the west side, then proceed to *Mikurumayose* (Carriage Approach), once used by noblemen of higher rank. These noblemen were also allowed to pass through *Gishumon* Gate, south of *Seishomon* Gate, in an ox-drawn carriage. South of *Mikurumayose* is *Shodaibu-no-Ma*(Rooms for Dignitaries), which consists of three rooms that were used as waiting rooms for noblemen. After passing through *Shin*(New)-*Mikurumayose*—the entrance for the Emperor, visitors are led along a painted, covered corridor surrounding *Dantei* or *Nantei* (South Garden), a spacious white graveled courtyard. Looking beyond the courtyard, visitors can see the *Shishinden* through three gates: *Gekkamon* in the west, *Jomeimon* in the south and *Nikkamon* in the east. *Shishinden* (Ceremonial Hall), also called *Shishiiden* or *Gishikiden* was used for the most important functions of state—the coronation of the Emperor or the New Year's audience, for example. The hall faces south and measures 23 m by 33 m. The throne, called the *Takamikura* (a three-layered dais), is placed in the center. It is covered by an octagonal roof topped with a sculpture of a phoenix and draped with rich, silk fabric. The stands on each side are for the sacred treasures (sword and jewels). The *Michodai*, upon which the Empress sat, is 10% smaller than the *Takamikura* and is placed to the rear right of the throne.

On the east side of the front steps of the hall is a cherry tree called

Sakon-no-Sakura, while on the west side is a wild orange tree called *Ukon-no-Tachibana*. The names *Sakon* and *Ukon* were derived from the names for the archers and horsemen, respectively, posted in these positions in ancient times. The tablet above the entrance bears the three characters "*shi-shin-den*," (lit. Emperor's Hall). The panels inside the hall are covered with paintings of the Chinese sages by Kano Sukenobu, intended to represent the originals, which were created in 888 by Kose-no-Kanaoka (a painter active in the latter half of the ninth century) that were destroyed. Northwest of the *Shishin-den* is the *Seiryoden*, or "Serene and Cool Chamber," named for the stream drawn from Lake Biwa that runs under the steps. The design of the hall adheres closely to the original.

The hall is partitioned into several apartments. The main apartment contains a matted dais called *Michodai* where the Emperor sat on ceremonial occasions. It is covered with a silk canopy and red, white and black drapes. Stands for the Imperial regalia are arrayed on either side of the *Michodai*. Two wooden *komainu* (a pair of mythological, lion-like dogs usually found guarding the entrances of shinto shrines) stand on each side of the steps leading up to the dais.

Seiryoden, or *Seiroden*, is 18 m wide and 16 m deep. Built principally of cypress, it was originally intended to serve as the living room for the Emperor, but it was soon set aside for ceremonial use only. In one corner of the hall, the ground is cemented so that the Emperor could stand on the earth while worshipping his ancestors, as tradition required. The sliding screens in the hall are decorated with paintings by the Tosa school artists, with a Chinese or Japanese poem accompanying each one. The Imperial crest, a 16-petaled chrysanthemum, is in evidence everywhere.

Visitors are then led through the *Giyoden* Corridor to the *Oike-niwa*, or Pond Garden, so called because of the large pond taking up most of the garden. The pond embraces pine-clad islets and is paved with round stones on the western shore. In ancient times, the garden was outside the palace grounds, but it was included when the palace was reconstructed in the 17th century. *Kogosho* (Minor Palace) consists of three audience chambers used for small receptions. It burned down in 1954 but was reconstructed in 1958, with the paintings on the corridor doors and sliding screens restored to their original form. *Gogakumonjo* (Study Hall), with a *Shinden*-style exterior and a study hall-type interior, was used for monthly *waka* (31-syllable poem) parties.

Visitors are next led through the inner gate of *Otsune Goten* to the exit. *Otsune Goten* served as the residence of the Emperor from around the 17th century. Emperor Meiji, the great-grandfather of the present Emperor, resided here until 1868. The building and inner garden are opened to the public only on special occasions.

There are many other buildings of all sizes comprising the palace of the Empress, but they are not always shown to visitors. They stand amidst an extensive landscape garden.

Doshisha University 86 : Located north of the Kyoto Imperial Palace, this university includes the spirit of Christianity in its curriculum. It was founded in 1873 by Niijima Jo (1843-1890) and Yamamoto Kakuma (1828-1892) in cooperation with the American Board of Foreign Missions.

Shokokuji Temple 86 : North of the Imperial Palace and near Doshisha University. The temple ranks second among the five chief temples of the Rinzai sect. The Izumoji Temple of the Tendai sect originally stood on this site, but Ashikaga Yoshimitsu (1358-1408), the third Ashikaga Shogun, erected the Shokokuji Temple in 1392 by order of the Emperor. The original buildings and many of the treasures were almost totally destroyed by fire during the Age of Civil Wars in the 15th century. It was not until more than a century had elapsed that Toyotomi Hideyori (1593-1615), son of Hideyoshi, began reconstruction work on the Lecture Hall, while Tokugawa Ieyasu (1542-1616) had the main gate restored. However, the buildings were ravaged by fire yet again so that all the buildings except the Lecture Hall post-date the fire. Many temple treasures are on display in Shotenkaku, the temple treasure house. Near Imadegawa Subway Station.

Nishijin 86 : A silk-weaving district to the west of Horikawa-dori Street and north of Ichijo-dori Street. The name means "Western Camp" and dates from the fierce, internecine strife that raged through the city in the 15th century. The sound of looms can still be heard throughout the district today.

Nishijin Textile Center 86 : Located in Imadegawa-Omiya. The museum was established in 1915. In addition to the large display of Nishijin products, *kimono* are also shown and sold here.

Kitano Temmangu Shrine 86 : Popularly known as Kitano Tenjin. The shrine is situated in Kitano at the northwest corner of Kamigyo Ward, close to the Nishijin weaving district. It is dedicated to Sugawara Michizane, an eminent scholar-statesman, who was deified under the name of Tenjin. He was exiled to Kyushu where he died, but his death in 903 was followed by such severe earthquakes and thunderstorms in Kyoto that it was thought advisable to appease his spirit by erecting a shrine in his honor. Established in 947, it was the object of several Imperial visits.

The present buildings were constructed in 1607 by Toyotomi Hideyori. The *Honden* (Main Hall) and *Haiden* (Oratory) have both been designated as National Treasures, while the Middle Gate and Corridor are Important Cultural Properties. The cypress-shingled roofs were made according to a very complex plan that provides the buildings with an agreeable variety. The shrine is surrounded by an extensive grove that includes hundreds of plum trees, said to have been Michizane's favorite. Among the treasures of the shrine are nine picture-scrolls by Tosa Yukimitsu (14th century) and three others by

Tosa Mitsuoki (17th century) that describe the history of Kitano Shrine. The shrine is famous for *Baikasai* (Plum Blossom Festival) held on February 25, *Kitano Matsuri* (Kitano Festival) on August 4 and the *Zuiki Matsuri* (Taro Stem Festival) on October 1-5 (refer to p.663).

Hirano Shrine 86 : Located near Kitano Temmangu Shrine. The grounds contain four shrines rebuilt in the first half of the 17th century, each of which is an Important Cultural Property. The buildings are connected in pairs, an unusual feature that attracts the attention of students of architecture. The grounds are famous for the 40-odd species of cherry trees, some of which are extremely rare. For centuries, the viewing of these cherry blossoms at night has been a popular event known as *Hirano-no-Yozakura*.

Nijo Castle 85-① : West of Nijo-Horikawa, 10 min. on foot from Oike Subway Station. It was originally built in 1603 by Ieyasu, the first Tokugawa Shogun, to serve as his residence whenever he visited Kyoto. At the time of the Meiji Restoration in 1868, the castle was made the temporary seat of government, and it was from here that Emperor Meiji issued the edict abolishing the shogunate (the Restoration of the Imperial Rule).

During the time in which the castle was used as the Kyoto Prefectural Government Office (1871-1884), incredible damage was done to the priceless objects of art housed in the castle. When it was made an Imperial Villa in 1884, a great deal was done to restore the old splendor. It was placed under the jurisdiction of the Kyoto City Government in 1939.

The entire castle is a Historical Site, while the *Ninomaru* Wing (Great Audience Hall) is a National Treasure because of its splendid architectural beauty and gorgeous interior decoration.

The castle grounds, which cover an area of about 280,000 sq.m, are surrounded by stone walls with turrets at the corners and moats around the outside. Visitors are admitted at the *Higashi* (East)-*Otemon* Gate—a typical castle entrance. From this point, they can reach the *Karamon* Gate, which is designed in the *Shikyakumon* style. Decorated with beautiful wood carvings and exquisite metal work, it was once part of Fushimi Castle belonging to Toyotomi Hideyoshi. Inside the gate is a spacious courtyard planted with pine trees. After crossing the courtyard, visitors will reach the *Mikuruma-yose* (Carriage Approach). The *ramma*, or transom, shows tree peonies and phoenixes carved in wood. It is attributed to Hidari-Jingoro, a famous sculptor who also carved the *Nemuri-Neko* (sleeping cat) in the Nikko Toshogu Shrine (Refer to p.543).

The first building is the largest structure in Nijo Castle and contains numerous chambers. The remarkable paintings on the sliding screens are attributed to Kano Tan-yu (1602-1674) and other artists of the Kano school. The *Jodan-no-Ma*, or Main Chamber, is also known as *Chokushi-no-Ma* (Chamber for Imperial Messenger). It not only boasts some beautiful carvings on the shelves and *ramma*, but the ceiling is also coffered and highly ornamented. The *Ni-no-Ma* (Second Chamber) and the adjoining *Tozamurai-no-Ma* (Guard Chamber) contain some magnificent paintings of tigers and leopards slinking among some bamboo trees. When the wooden floor of the corridor is trod upon, it makes a squeaky noise; hence, its nickname—*uguisu-bari* (the floor that sounds like a bush warbler). It is one of the alarm devices designed to protect the inner chambers from intruders.

The second building, reached by a gallery from the first building, consists of three chambers of which the central one was used by the *daimyo* (feudal lords) attending the *shogun* on his visits to Kyoto.

The third building is composed of *Ohiroma* (Great Hall) and four other chambers. The Great Hall, the audience chamber of the *shogun*, has the raised seat where he sat far above the *daimyo*. The floor of the hall is made of large boards of zelkova wood, each measuring 5.5 m long and 18 cm thick. The shelves and transoms are highly decorated, while the sliding doors are painted with immense pine trees. On the ceiling are elaborate designs painted on a gold background.

The transom of the second chamber on the north side features an openwork carving of pine trees and peacocks attributed to Hidari-Jingoro made on a block of wood 35 cm thick. The last chamber, known as *Sotetsu-no-Ma* (Cycad Room), has cedar sliding doors painted with cycads.

The fourth building (*Kuroshoin*) has a chamber with wild geese and brown-eared bulbuls painted on the sliding doors. The shelves by the alcove show signs of early cloisonne work, while the wooden door on the east side of the *Tamari-no-Ma* (Waiting Room) is decorated with a painting, attributed to Kano Naonobu (1607–1650), showing a heron perched on the edge of a boat.

The fifth building, called *Shiroshoin*, contained the private apartments of the *shogun*. It is decorated with subdued, refined paintings of mountain scenery in black and white.

The Nijo Castle garden lies southwest of the *Ninomaru* Wing. The original garden was re-landscaped by Kobori Enshu (Refer to p.205).
Nijo Jin-ya ⬚87⬚: Originally the home of a wealthy merchant, this mansion was also used by *daimyo* on their visits to Kyoto because of its proximity to Nijo Castle. Included in the some twenty rooms are a tea-ceremony room and a *noh* theater. It is famous for its variety of secret contrivances, which were designed to protect the occupants from their enemies.

As this is now a private home, reservations are required. Inquire at JNTO's Kyoto Tourist Information Center (TIC). ☎ (075) 371-5649

Kawaramachi-dori Street ⬚87⬚: A 700-m-long stretch at the intersection of Shijo-dori Street, with Shijo Kawaramachi in the center. Lined with fashionable shops and restaurants, this street passes through the most prosperous commercial district in the city. Kiyamachi-dori Street runs to the east and Teramachi-dori Street to the west, and in the alleys behind these large streets are numerous bars and drinking establishments, making the district lively well into the night. 10 min. by bus from the JR Kyoto Station.

Pontocho 87 : An alley running between Sanjo and Shijo Bridges along the west bank of the Kamo River. Many bars, cabarets, restaurants, *ochaya* (tea houses where *geisha* parties are held) and other places of amusement are crowded on this narrow street. The celebrated cherry dance, called *Kamogawa Odori*, is held here annually at the Kaburenjo Theater.

Sanjo Ohashi Bridge 87 : Originally built in 1590 by order of Toyotomi Hideyoshi. The only original portions remaining in the present structure are the *giboshi* (bronze railing ornaments), which were presents from *daimyo* under Hideyoshi. The street leading from the Miyako Hotel across the Sanjo Ohashi Bridge to the west boundary of the city is an important thoroughfare called Sanjo-dori Street. In feudal days, all distances in and from Kyoto were measured from this bridge.

Shinkyogoku 87 : Located east of Teramachi. Known in English as the "Arcade," Kyoto's main entertainment district extends 500 m from Sanjo-dori Street to Shijo-dori Street. Countless restaurants, souvenir shops, movie theaters and a wide variety of other shops line the street. At night, the brightly lit street creates a lively sight.

Nishiki-no-Ichiba (Nishiki Market) 87 : Located on Nishiki-koji Alley, north of Shijo-dori Street. Extending 400 m from east to west, this food market is popularly known among local residents as the "Nishiki" market. More than 100 stores dealing in fresh fish, fruit and groceries crowd the arcade. The market is known for its abundance of high-quality food.

The Museum of Kyoto: The history of Kyoto is portrayed on panels and video tapes along with exhibits of traditional crafts. There is also a film library. One of the more unique displays is the reproduction of a narrow alley of *machiya*—the homes of commoners in olden days. The style and color of the houses vary, allowing one to imagine the Kyoto of days gone by. Souvenirs are actually sold from the shops along the alley by vendors speaking the traditional Kyoto dialect.

Rokkakudo (Hexagonal Hall) 87 : The popular name of Chohoji Temple. Situated east of Karasuma-dori Street between Rokkaku-dori Street and Sanjo-dori Street, the temple is said to have been founded in 587 by Prince Shotoku. In 1201, Shinran (1173–1262), founder of the Jodo-Shinshu sect of Buddhism, made a daily pilgrimage for 100 days to this temple from Mt. Hiei. When Ikenobo Senkei, the founder of the Ikenobo School of Flower Arrangement, was a priest here during the mid–15th century, he and his family lived in a house called *Ikenobo* behind the main hall.

Honnoji Temple 87 : Located in Teramachi-Oike, this is one of the main Nichiren-sect temples. It is well known as the temple where Oda Nobunaga was assassinated in 1582 by Akechi Mitsuhide, one of his generals. The actual temple where the assassination took place stood south of Rokkakudo, which is nearby. It was repeatedly destroyed by fire and eventually the buildings were moved here. A memorial to Nobunaga stands on the grounds.

Shijo-dori Street: A broad avenue running through the heart of the city from east to west. It attracts crowds with its many stores and banks lining both sides of the street. Daimaru, Fujii-Daimaru, Takashimaya, Hankyu—all the major department stores are here. Bars, restaurants and long-established souvenir shops can also be found in abundance.

Mibu Temple 87 : Located at the west end of Shijo-dori Street, this temple belongs to the Ritsu sect. Founded in 991, it is famous for a religious comedy performed here called *Mibu-kyogen* (refer to p.661)

Bukkoji Temple 87 : Located on Takakura-dori Street, south of Shijo-dori Street. The temple was founded in 1212 by the priest Shinran. Since the temple is the headquarters of the Bukkoji school of the Jodo-Shinshu sect, the Main Hall contains an image of Shinran, said to have been carved by the priest himself. The temple houses many other art treasures.

Kyoto Tower 87 : Soaring 131 m high in front of Kyoto Station, the tower was built on the roof of the nine-story Kyoto Tower Building. Besides two observation platforms as well as TV and FM broadcasting facilities, it is equipped with two elevators that travel from the roof of the Tower Building to the observation platforms.

The tower building itself has artificial hot-spring baths, a restaurant, a hotel, a department store, banks, offices and more. Japan National Tourist Organization maintains its Kyoto Tourist Information Center (Kyoto TIC for short) on the first floor and has information staffs that can speak English, French, Spanish, etc.

Higashi-Honganji Temple 87 : Located in Karasuma-Nijo near the JR Kyoto Station, this is the headquarters for the Otani school of the Jodo-Shinshu sect. All of the temple buildings, except for the *Hondo* (Main Hall) and *Daishido* (Founder's Hall), are closed to the general public, but those wishing to see the abbots villa must apply to the visitors division of the temple office. Founded in 1602, the temple was destroyed by repeated fires. The present buildings were completed in 1895 from contributions made by sect members from all over the country. Women devotees contributed their hair, which was made into 50 ropes, or hawsers, that were used in building the temple and are still preserved. Opposite the great, two-story gate in front of the temple is the Founder's Hall. It stands 38 m high and extends 76 m from north to south and 58 m from east to west. This large, double-roofed, elaborately decorated building is in the traditional *Irimoya*-style, and contains an image of Shinran said to have been carved by himself. Portraits of his successors as heads of the Otani school hang on both sides of the image. The massive pillars in the hall are made of zelkova wood.

Main Hall, situated south of the Founder's Hall, is connected to it by a corridor. The building is 29 m high and measures 52 m from north to south and 47 m from east to west. There are several other buildings, including a stage for the performance of *noh*. The *Choku-shimon* Gate (Gate for Imperial Messengers), also called *Kiku-no-Mon* (Chrysanthemum Gate), was moved here from Fushimi Castle but burned in 1911. This present gate is a reconstruction.

Among the many treasures of the temple is the "Kyogyo Shinsho", an exposition of the tenets of the Jodo-Shinshu sect written by Shinran himself in six volumes. Shinran first advocated his doctrines in these writings in 1224 when he was 51 years old. They are a National Treasure.

Shosei-en Garden 87 : Better known as Kikokutei, this was a villa of the abbot of Higashi-Honganji Temple. Situated east of the temple, it was formerly surrounded by a hedge of *kikoku* (trifoliate orange); hence, the name—Kikokutei (Kikoku Villa). It is said that part of Hideyoshi's Fushimi Castle was brought here. The famous landscape garden was designed in part by Ishikawa Jozan (1583-1672), a noted poet and scholar, and in part by Kobori Enshu, a master landscape architect.

Nishi-Honganji Temple 87 : The headquarters of the Honganji school of the Jodo-Shinshu sect, which originated here, is situated at Nishi-Rokujo, a 10-min. walk from the JR Kyoto Station. The temple is one of the best in Kyoto, often cited by art historians as the finest existing example of Buddhist architecture.

Shinran, also known as Kenshin-Daishi, was the founder of the Jodo-Shinshu sect of Buddhism. Born in 1173, he entered the priesthood when he was a boy, studying at the monastery on Mt. Hiei. Dissatisfied with the doctrines he had been taught, at the age of 28 he made a daily pilgrimage for 100 days to the *Kannon* at Rokkakudo Temple and became a disciple of Honen, founder of the Jodo sect, by divine direction. It was through Honen that Shinran was induced to inaugurate a married priesthood by wedding the daughter of a former Chief Minister of the Imperial Court.

Thus, the Jodo-Shinshu sect abandoned a celibate priesthood, abstinence from meat and other ascetic practices. It claims salvation by faith in Amitabha, who is invoked by the prayer formula—*Namu-Amida-Butsu*, or "Glory to Amitabha Buddha."

In 1602, Ieyasu (the first Tokugawa Shogun), fearing the growing power of the sect, sought to weaken it by giving a former abbot permission to found a new branch of the sect, which became known as the Otani school. Its chief temple is Higashi (East)-Honganji Temple in contrast to Nishi (West)-Honganji Temple—the headquarters of the original school.

The *Hondo*, or *Amidado* (Main Hall; an Important Cultural Property), was destroyed by fire and reconstructed in 1760. It enshrines an image of Amitabha carved by a sculptor of the Kasuga school. In the rooms to the right and left of the altar are portraits of Prince Shotoku (574–622) and Priest Honen (1133–1212). Every inch of the interior is elaborately decorated, especially the sliding screens, on which phoenixes and peacocks are painted on a gold background by a master of the Kano school.

The *Daishido* or *Goeido* (Founder's Hall; an Important Cultural Property) constructed in 1636, contains a seated effigy of the founder carved by Shinran himself at the age of 71 and given to his daughter, who was a nun. After his death and cremation, the image was varnished with lacquer mixed with his ashes and is, therefore, regarded with great veneration. The image was often threatened with destruction during the days when the sect was persecuted, but it was saved by disciples and believers.

To the right and left are portraits of successive abbots of the temple. A tablet written by the Emperor Meiji and bearing the characters "Kenshin" (lit. devotion) hangs over the entrance. The gate in front of the Founder's Hall, rebuilt in 1645, is regarded as one of the finest of its kind in Kyoto.

Shoin (study Hall; a National Treasure) is said to have been brought from Fushimi Castle in 1632, as was *Karamon*, a National Treasure in the *shikyakumon* (four-pillar gate) style. *Karamon*, the front gate of the Main Hall, is famous for its splendid carvings by Hidari-Jingoro. Most of the chambers in this large Study Hall are named after their principal decorations. Thus, the sliding screens and wall panels of *Suzume-no-Ma* (Sparrow Chamber) are decorated with bamboo and sparrows, the ceiling with flowers by Maruyama Ozui (1766–1829) and the cedar doors with monkeys and a flower basket by Kano Ryokei. *Gan-no-Ma* (Wild Geese Chamber) has fine, if somewhat faded, sliding screens painted with wild geese on a gold leaf background. The ceiling is decorated with flowers painted by Kano Ryokei. The sliding screens in *Kiku-no-Ma* (Chrysanthemum Chamber) are covered with gold-and-white chrysanthemums painted by Kaiho Yusetsu (1598–1677). The cedar doors were painted by Kano Hidenobu, with musk cats and cycads on one side, and horses and cypress trees on the other. The fans painted on the veranda are the work of Kano Koi (d. 1636) and Kaiho Yusetsu. *Ko-no-Ma* (Stork Chamber) was the abbot's audience chamber, and is the finest and largest of all of the chambers. Decorated with gorgeous paintings by Kano Tan-yu, Kano Ryokei and Maruyama Okyo (1733–1795), this is where Hideyoshi used to hold council. The carvings of wild geese on the transom are among the finest works by Hidari-Jingoro. *Shiro-shoin*, made up of *Shimei-no-Ma* (Purple Chamber) and two other rooms, is not as large as *Ko-no-Ma* (Stork Chamber), although it is said to have been one of the state halls in Fushimi Castle. The paintings are by Kano Koi and Kaiho Yusetsu, while those adorning the sliding screens in Kuroshoin (a National Treasure), next to *Shiroshoin*, are by Kano Eitoku. Admission to *Shoin* is permitted only on Saturday afternoons and Sundays (10: 00 a.m., 11:00 a.m., 1:30 p.m. and 2:30 p.m.). It is granted on application to the temple office by a reply postal card.

There are two *noh* stages. The one to the south of the *Ko-no-Ma* was a gift from the *shogun*, while that to the north was transferred from Fushimi Castle. The latter (a National Treasure) is considered to be the finest and oldest stage in Japan.

The *Hiunkaku* Pavilion (a National Treasure) stands alone in the southeast corner of the grounds. The three-story building, originally built in the 16th century on the grounds of the *Jurakudai* Mansion, contains Hideyoshi's tea-ceremony room, a bath and a rest chamber.

Shimabara: In its heyday, Shimabara, situated east of Nishi-Honganji Temple, was one of the foremost pleasure quarters in Japan, but now only two buildings retain its pre-modern atmosphere. A large gate stands over the entrance to the quarter.

Sumiya: A masterpiece of *ageya* architecture, this building has been designated as an Important Cultural Property. An *ageya* was an elegant restaurant where banquets and dinners were held. Representative of Edo-period merchant culture, the two-story building is roofed with tiles, copper plates and shingles, and consists of three main parts: the latticed exterior and entrance way, the huge, open kitchen and the interior rooms. It functioned as a meeting place and salon where famous artists, writers, *samurai* officials and other luminaries gathered.

Kyo-o-gokokuji Temple 87 : Popularly known as Toji, or East Temple, it is situated southwest of the JR Kyoto Station. Founded in 796 by Imperial Order, it was given in 823 to the priest Kukai, the founder of the Shingon sect, also known as Kobo-Daishi. The original buildings were for the most part destroyed during the Age of Civil Wars in the 15th century. The Main Hall, rebuilt in 1603 by Hideyori, son of Toyotomi Hideyoshi, is one of the largest existing Buddhist buildings of the Momoyama period. The Five-Story Pagoda, reconstructed by Iemitsu (the third Tokugawa Shogun) in 1644, is the highest, pre-modern pagoda in Japan at about 57 m. It can be seen from the train window on the JR Tokaido Main Line and Shinkansen.

The Treasure House contains an immense collection of ancient works of art, many of which have been designated as National Treasures or Important Cultural Properties. Of the various temple structures, the Five-Story Pagoda, *Kondo* (Main Hall), *Rengemon* Gate (built in 1191) and *Daishido* (Founder's Hall, built in 1380) are National Treasures. *Kodo* (Lecture Hall, built in 1598), *Kanjo-in* (Hall for Buddhist Confirmation Rites, built in 1634), *Hozo* (Storehouse, built in 1197) and five gates are all Important Cultural Properties. The Lecture Hall contains many Buddhist images that reflect the beliefs of Tantric Buddhism, many of which are National Treasures.

Higashiyama

A long narrow area also known as Rakuto, Higashiyama is sandwiched between the Kamo River, flowing north to south through the city and on to the Higashiyama Hills in the east. Made up of three districts, Higashiyama is crowded with countless temples and shrines. The area around Kiyomizu Temple is an excellent place for a stroll, as there are many famous buildings and streets full of souvenir stores. *Maiko*, or apprentice *geisha*, can be seen in the Gion entertainment district. The third district, between Nanzenji and Ginkakuji temples at the foot of the Higashiyama Hills, is also a nice place to take a walk.

Ginkakuji Temple [73]: Meaning Silver Pavilion, the temple is formally called Jishoji and stands at the northeast end of the city. It was originally built in 1482 by Ashikaga Yoshimasa, eighth *shogun* of the Muromachi (Ashikaga) Shogunate, as a country villa, but it was converted to a temple upon his death. The pavilion (a National Treasure) stands two stories high and has never actually been covered with silver, as the name would indicate. *Togudo* (a National Treasure), next to the Silver Pavilion, contains an effigy of Yoshimasa in the garb of a priest. In the northeast corner of the same building is a tiny tearoom of only four and a half *tatami* mats, and is said to be the oldest tearoom in Japan. A corridor leads from here to two rooms called *Roseitei*, which are reproductions of the rooms used by Yoshimasa for incense-burning parties. The garden, attributed to the landscape artist and painter Soami (d. 1525), is one of the most attractive in Kyoto.

Path of Philosophy: A 2-km-long promenade that extends from Ginkakuji-bashi Bridge in front of Ginkakuji Temple along the canal to Nyakuoji-bashi Bridge in front of Nyakuoji Shrine. It was so named because it was a favorite walking path used by the noted philosopher Nishida Kitaro while he was meditating. Cherry and camphor trees grow along the trail, and there is a rest house as well.

Honen-in Temple: Standing slightly off the Path of Philosopy, this modest temple at the foot of Mt. Nyoigadake is known for its quiet surroundings and attractive garden.

Mt. Nyoigadake [73] Really a hill rather than a mountain, it stands behind Eikando, a Buddhist temple. Mt. Nyoigadake is famous for the large bonfire that burns in the shape of the character *dai*, meaning large. It is set ablaze on the slope facing the city at the close of the *Bon* festival every August 16.

Zenrinji Temple [73]: Popularly called Eikando, this temple (located at the end of the Path of Philosopy) was reconstructed during the 15th century. The Main Hall contains an image of Amitabha called the *Mikaeri-no-Amida* (Backward-looking Amitabha) because the head of the image is turned halfway around to the left. Legend has it that as the priest Eikan was walking along chanting his prayers, he became aware that Amitabha was walking in front of him. Surprised, he stopped, and Amitabha turned around and said: "You're late." The temple is also famous for its red maple leaves.

Nanzenji Temple 73 : Situated in a pine grove east of Heian Shrine is the headquarters of the Nanzenji school of the Rinzai sect. Since it was founded in 1291, it has been ravaged by fire twice. However, some of the structures erected in the early 17th century still stand. Of the two gates standing before the Main Hall, *Sammon* Gate, nearest the temple, was erected in 1628 and is famous for its connection with a legend about the chivalrous robber Ishikawa Goemon, noted as a *kabuki* character. The ceiling is painted with angels and birds, believed to have been the works of famous painters of the Tosa and Kano schools.

Daihojo (a National Treasure), the superior's suite, was originally part of the *Seiryoden* in the Imperial Palace. *Daihojo* was donated to the temple when the palace was reconstructed in 1611. The paintings on the sliding screens are by artists of the Kano school. *Shohojo*, or the smaller superior's suite, was once part of Hideyoshi's Fushimi Castle. The painting of "Tigers in a Bamboo Grove" on gold leaf on the sliding screens is by Kano Tan-yu (1602–1674, refer to p.184). The lovely landscape garden, said to have been laid out in the early 17th century, is one of the most celebrated gardens in Kyoto.

There are 12 subordinate temples in the precincts. Nanzen-in, noted for serving as the temporary abode of Emperor Kameyama (1249–1305), has a landscape garden attached to the temple that was initially laid out in the 14th century. Tenju-an, another subordinate temple, contains the tombs of several eminent persons, including Daimyo-Kokushi (founder of Nanzenji Temple) and poet Hosokawa Yusai. The landscaping around Konchi-in, another subordinate temple, is said to have been designed by Kobori Enshu in 1632.

Murin-an Garden: Located near Nanzenji Temple, this mansion was once owned by Yamagata Aritomo, a noted general and statesman of the Meiji period. In addition to the Western-style building of the Meiji period, there is a traditional, Japanese tea-ceremony room and residential quarters. The garden creates a tranquil atmosphere with brooks, waterfalls and ponds, and Higashiyama Hills looming in the background. The villa is now owned by the Kyoto Municipal Office.

Kyoto University 86 : West of Ginkakuji Temple. Founded in 1897, this is the second-oldest as well as one of the largest national universities in Japan. Including those in graduate school, there are 15,000 students attending classes here.

Chionji Temple 86 : Located north of Kyoto University, the temple is popularly called Hyakumamben (One Million Times) because when an epidemic was raging in 1331, the presiding abbot held a service at which the prayer *Namu-Amida-Butsu* was recited a million times in succession. Founded by priest Honen (1133-1212), the temple includes among its treasures two scrolls (Important Cultural Properties) painted by Yen Hui (Ganki), a talented artist from Yuan-Dynasty China.

Shinnyodo ⬚86⬚ : Southwest of Ginkakuji Temple. This noted temple of the Jodo sect was moved here from Mt. Hiei about 900 years ago, but the present structures date back only about 250 years. *Juya* (Ten Nights), a religious service that takes place over ten nights, is held from the evening of November 5 to the morning of November 15.

Okazaki Park ⬚86⬚ : Opened as a public park in 1904. Covering about 100,000 sq.m along the canal flowing from Lake Biwa, the park contains the Kyoto Prefectural Library, a public hall, the Kyoto Municipal Museum of Art, the National Museum of Modern Art, a stadium and the Municipal Zoo.

The library was built in 1898 and houses some 160,000 volumes, including numerous books and documents from ancient times.

The Municipal Museum of Art was founded in 1933 and the modern art museum opened in 1963, but the zoo has been in operation since 1903. Many cherry and maple trees grow in the zoo, creating a scene of special beauty in spring and autumn.

Kyoto Municipal Museum of Traditional Industries ⬚87⬚ : Called Kyoto-shi Dento Sangyo Kaikan, it is a facility to introduce weaving, ceramics, lacquerware, bambooware, woodwork and other traditional arts of Kyoto. More than 20 different kinds of crafts are produced on the premises on various days. *Nishijin* weaving, the cutting of paper stencils for *Yuzen* dyeing, and inlay are demonstrated every day, while the craft products made here are sold as well. The basement contains reproductions of several *machiya* (town houses) formerly found in Kyoto.

Heian Shrine ⬚86⬚ : This famous shrine, located at the north end of Okazaki Park, is dedicated to Emperor Kammu, founder of the Heiankyo capital, Kyoto, and Emperor Komei—the last Emperor that reigned when Kyoto was the capital. The shrine was built in 1895 to commemorate the 1,100th anniversary of the foundation of Kyoto. It is composed of the East and West *Honden* (Main Halls), *Daigokuden* (Great Hall of State), two pagodas, *Otemmon* (Main Gate) and a large, ferro-concrete *torii* (Shinto gate). Except for the *torii*, these brightly colored buildings are replicas, on a reduced scale, of the first Imperial Palace built in 794.

Otemmon is a two-story gate painted bright crimson and roofed with blue tiles. The shrine festival is held on April 15, but there is another festival that has become one of Kyoto's most spectacular fetes: the *Jidai Matsuri*, held on October 22. (refer to p.664) The garden at the rear of the shrine is famous for its drooping cherry trees, maple trees, azaleas, irises and water lilies.

Kyoto Handicraft Center ⬚86⬚ : Located near Heian Shrine. Demonstrations show the manufacture of inlay work, cloisonne, woodblock prints, *kyo-ningyo* (doll), the painting of *Satsuma-yaki* (ceramic) and *obi* (sash). In addition to the items mentioned above, pearls as well as electric appliances for use abroad are sold here.

Chion-in Temple ⬚87⬚ : Located at the north end of Maruyama Park. Serving as the main headquarters of the Jodo sect, the temple was erected in 1234 by the priest Genchi, a disciple of Honen (1133-1212) —the founder of the sect. The ultimate aspiration of members of the sect is to be reborn in Jodo (the Pure Land)—the Western Paradise of Amitabha. Through faith and reliance in Amitabha, they may enjoy happiness after death in this land. To achieve this end, the followers of Amitabha recite, day and night, the prayer-formula *Namu-Amida-Butsu* as many times as possible.

One of the largest and most famous temples in Kyoto. The grounds cover an area of 145,000 sq.m. Fires repeatedly destroyed the temple buildings, but those still standing such as the *Sammon* Gate, *Hondo* (Main Hall) and *Hojo* (Superior's Quarters) date from the early 17th century. The best trees from the immense number felled in the Kiso forests were selected for the construction of this temple.

Sammon, a two-story gate standing 24 m high, is considered to be the most imposing temple gate in all Japan. The inscription on the tablet over the entrance was written by Emperor Reigen (reigned 1663 -1687).

The Main Hall is dedicated to Honen, and a statue that he made of himself is housed in a splendid *zushi* (a miniature shrine) behind the Main Hall.

The corridor behind the Main Hall leads to *Shuedo* (the Assembly Hall) and Superior's Quarters. It is constructed so that it emits the sound of a bush warbler at every step, a structural phenomenon attributed to the famous sculptor Hidari-Jingoro. (refer to p.543). The Assembly Hall is popularly known as the Hall of One Thousand Mats, although it actually has only 360 mats. Beyond this are the Superior's Quarters, which has sliding screens decorated with beautiful paintings by artists of the Kano school. The garden attached to the abbot's apartments is the landscape work of Kobori Enshu (1579 -1647, refer to p.205).

Kyozo (Sutra Library) southeast of the Main Hall, built in 1616, contains more than 5,600 volumes of the *Issaikyo* (a complete collection of Buddhist Sutras) printed in China during the Sung Dynasty. Among the other structures of importance are *Seishido*, situated on a hill northeast of the Sutra Library, the tomb of Honen and *Karamon* Gate (built in 1633). The temple possesses many objects of art, including 48 volumes of an illustrated biography of Honen (a National Treasure). Some of these objects are on display in the Treasure Hall.

Shoren-in ⬚87⬚ : Popularly called Awata Palace. Located north of Chion-in Temple, it is known for having been the residence of the head abbot of the Tendai sect, who, until the Imperial Restoration of 1868, held the rank of Imperial prince. The present buildings date from 1895. The sliding screens in the Main Hall are decorated with paintings by Kano Mitsunobu, Kano Motonobu, Sumiyoshi Gukei and other great artists. The garden, designed by Soami (d. 1525) and by kobori Enshu (d. 1647), both eminent landscape artists, is one of the finest landscape gardens in Kyoto.

Maruyama Park $\boxed{87}$: Regarded as the principal public park of Kyoto, this beautiful landscape garden is laid out at the foot of Higashiyama Hills at the east end of Shijo-dori Street. Several temples were once located here, but most of them were destroyed by fire. In 1886, the 97,000-sq.-m grounds were made a public park, one of the highlights of which is its cherry trees. When in bloom, they are illuminated at night, attracting thousands of visitors. Called *Gion-no-Yozakura*, or the Night Cherry Blossoms of Gion, it is one of Kyoto's most charming attractions.

Higashi-Otani $\boxed{87}$: Situated south of Maruyama Park. Founded in 1671, this is the burial place for the abbots of Higashi-Honganji Temple as well as for many believers. Halfway up the hill and enclosed by granite posts is a mortuary chapel dedicated to Shinran, founder of the Jodo-Shinshu sect.

Shogunzuka (General's Mound): Located on a hill behind Maruyama Park, this is where a giant, earthen statue of a warrior in full armor (2.4 m tall) is said to have been buried to symbolically protect the city. It is believed that when danger threatens the city, a loud clamor can be heard from the mound. The hill also offers a celebrated view of the city at night.

Yasaka Shrine $\boxed{87}$: Commonly called Gion Shrine, the grounds are located at the east end of Gion. The shrine is dedicated to the Shinto deities Susano-o-no-Mikoto, his wife, Inadahime-no-Mikoto, and their sons. According to an ancient document, the home of these deities was transferred here in 876 from Hiromine Shrine (now in Himeji City) in Harima Province (now, Hyogo Prefecture).

The present Main Shrine was erected in 1654 in an old residential style by order of the fourth Tokugawa Shogun, Ietsuna. The stone *torii* on the south side is 9.5 m high, making it one of the largest in Japan. Designed in the Gion-style, the Main Shrine is a single-story structure, with a half-hip and half-gable roof covered with cedar shingles. Among the chief treasures of the shrine are wooden *koma-inu* (a pair of lion-like dogs usually found guarding the entrances to Shinto shrines), attributed to the celebrated sculptor Unkei of the 12th and 13th centuries (Important Cultural Properties). The *Gion Matsuri* and *Okera Mairi* festivals of the shrine are among the most well known in Kyoto. (refer to p.659 and 662).

Kodaiji Temple $\boxed{87}$: Situated south of Higashi-Otani, the temple was built in 1606 by the widow of Toyotomi Hideyoshi in his memory. The temple has fallen victim to repeated fires, but the *Kaizando* (Founder's Hall) is in a splendid state of preservation, including its ornamental pillars and walls as well as its decorated ceilings by painters of the Tosa and Kano schools.

East of the Founder's Hall is the mortuary chapel, noted for its colorful lacquerwork, a process called *maki-e*. The Front Gate was brought from Fushimi Castle along with two tea-ceremony rooms that stand on the hill behind the chapel.

The landscape garden was designed by the famous Kobori Enshu and has been designated as a Historical Site as well as a Place of Scenic Beauty.

Sannen-zaka Hill and Ninen-zaka Hill 87 : The stone steps of Sannen-zaka (slope) link Kiyomizu-zaka and Ninen-zaka. Many of the shops are wooden, Edo-period structures that sell *Kiyomizu-yaki* ceramics, Kyoto delicacies and traditional souvenirs. Ninen-zaka is the street leading from Sannen-zaka to Kodaiji Temple.

Yasaka Pagoda 87 : Near Ninen-zaka Hill. The Five-Story Pagoda, standing 40 m high, was erected in 1440 by the sixth Ashikaga Shogun, Yoshinori.

Kiyomizu Temple 87 : Located southeast of Yasaka Pagoda on Otowa Hill. The grounds are surrounded by a dense grove of trees. The temple is dedicated to *Juichimen-Kannon* (Eleven-Headed *Kannon*), the image of which is an Important Cultural Property. It was established in 798, with the old *Shinden* Hall from the Imperial Palace at Nagaoka moved here to form the nucleus of the compound. The present temple structures were reconstructed in 1633 by order of the third Tokugawa Shogun, Iemitsu. The two-story west gate serves as the main gateway, with statues of the two Deva Kings standing in niches on either side. Nearby are a belfry and a three-story pagoda, while to the east are the *Kyozo* (Scripture Hall) and *Tamurado* (Founder's Hall). Near the Founder's Hall is *Asakura* Hall, erected by Asakura Sadakage (1473–1512), a devout believer. The Middle Gate is in the immediate vicinity.

The Main Hall (a National Treasure), standing on a cliff, has a wide, wooden veranda from which a panoramic view of Kyoto and its surrounding area can be enjoyed. It is rather breathtaking to look directly down into the deep valley below. "To jump from the balcony of Kiyomizu" is a Japanese expression for doing something daring.

North of the Main Hall is the residence of the superior, while the *Shakado* and *Amidado* are situated on another cliff east of the Main Hall. *Shakado* collapsed in a landslide after a heavy rainfall in July 1972, but it was reconstructed in 1975. At the foot of this latter cliff is Otowa Waterfall. Pious believers can be seen here praying to *Fudo-Myo-O*, who it is believed has the power to punish wicked beings. The three-story pagoda, standing on a hill on the opposite side of the valley, adds charm to the lovely scenery.

Nishi-Otani 87 : Located southwest of Kiyomizu Temple, this is a mortuary for the abbots of Nishi-Honganji Temple and a graveyard for many believers. It contains part of the remains of the saint Shinran, founder of the Jodo-Shinshu sect. A wooden image of

Amitabha stands in the Main Hall. In 1867, the old buildings were destroyed by fire but were rebuilt three years later. Surrounded by many venerable trees, the mortuary gives the area an atmosphere of great tranquillity.

Gion 87 : Situated on the east bank of the Kamo River across Shijo-Ohashi Bridge, this is one of the traditional entertainment districts of Kyoto. Near the river bank stands Minamiza Theater, with Kaburenjo Theater on one of the side streets of Hanami-koji alley. The *Miyako Odori* (Cherry Dance) is held annually at the Kaburenjo Theater in spring. Minamiza Theater, established in the early 17th century, is the oldest theater in Japan. Every December, *kabuki* performances with all-star casts are held here.

Gion Corner 87 : The Kyoto Visitors Club has set up Gion Corner (art theater) on the first floor of Yasaka Kaikan Hall in Gion so that foreign visitors may enjoy traditional Japanese arts. Here, one can enjoy the highlights of tea ceremony, flower arrangement, *bunraku* (puppet plays), *Kyomai* (Kyoto-style dance), *koto* music, *gagaku* (court music) and *kyogen* (classic farce). The show is performed twice a day, with tickets available at hotels and travel agencies as well as at the door. Information can be obtained from Gion Corner (☎ 075-561-1115), the Kyoto City Tourist Association (☎ 075-752-0225) or at the Kyoto TIC (☎ 075-371-5649).

Kenninji Temple 87 : Situated south of Gion, the temple was founded by the priest Eisai after his return from a second visit to Sung-Dynasty, China. It is the birthplace of the Rinzai sect of Buddhism as well as the headquarters of the Kenninji school. All the buildings were destroyed by fire, except for *Chokushimon* (Gate for Imperial Messenger), which is an original structure.

The other buildings, including the Main Hall, were rebuilt in 1763. The Superior's Quarters are said to have been built by the first Ashikaga Shogun, Takauji (1305-1358), at Ankokuji Temple in Aki Province (now, Hiroshima Prefecture) and later moved here.

There are many treasures at Kenninji Temple, including several scroll paintings by Kaiho Yusho (1533-1615) and a folding screen entitled "Fujin Raijin-Zu (Demons Creating Wind and Thunder)" by Tawaraya Sotatsu, a master artist of the early 17th century. Designated as a National Treasure, the screen is now exhibited at the Kyoto National Museum.

Rokuharamitsuji Temple 87 : Situated southeast of Kenninji Temple, the temple was founded in 963 by the priest Kuya (903-972). This eminent priest installed an image of the *Juichimen-Kannon* (Eleven-Headed *Kannon*) that he had carved in order to stop a pestilence then raging in Kyoto. Since the buildings were all destroyed by fire, the oldest structure now is the Main Hall, constructed in 1363. The temple contains many sculptures, including images of the Four Heavenly Guardians attributed to Unkei; a statue of Taira-no-Kiyomori (1118-1181), an early leader of the Taira Clan, and an image of Kuya emitting six figures of Amitabha from his mouth. All of these works are Important Cultural Properties.

Hokoji Temple [87]: Also called *Daibutsuden* (Hall of the Great Buddha), the temple is situated southwest of Nishi-Otani. In 1586, Toyotomi Hideyoshi ordered that it be constructed to enshrine the image of Buddha on the same grand scale as the one in Nara. The first Buddha was a seated wooden image 19.1 m tall, but both the hall and Buddha were destroyed in an earthquake in 1596. In 1612 and 1843, bronze images were made, but they fell victim to repeated fires. All that remain are the name "Daibutsuden" and a bell said to be one of the causes of the downfall of the Toyotomi family. Made of bronze and measuring 4.4 m high and 2.8 m in diameter, this large bell hangs in the belfry on the temple precincts. Hideyori, the son of Hideyoshi, had the temple rebuilt and the bell cast. The bell is historically famous for its inscription, which is made up of the words *koku-ka-an-ko*, meaning "Be in a State of Peace." Ieyasu (founder of the Tokugawa Shogunate), however, claimed that since the second and fourth characters (which are the Chinese readings for his name: *ka=Ie, ko=yasu*) are separated, the inscription amounted to an order to oppose him.

Hokoku Shrine [87]: Also called Toyokuni Shrine, it is located south of Hokoji Temple. The shrine is dedicated to Toyotomi Hideyoshi (1536-1598), whose tomb is on a hill called Amidagamine, east of the shrine. The shrine was originally erected in 1599 by order of Emperor Goyozei, but it fell into ruin during the Tokugawa period. Reconstruction commenced soon after the Meiji Restoration in 1868 and was completed ten years later. Besides a building that exhibits treasures, there is the *Karamon* Gate (a National Treasure), which once served as the gate to Hideyoshi's Fushimi Castle at Momoyama in southern Kyoto.

Kyoto National Museum [87]: Situated southeast of Hokoji Temple, the museum was erected in 1895 by the Imperial Household to provide a safe repository for art objects and other treasures belonging to Buddhist temples, Shinto shrines and certain individuals. The museum is divided into three departments: history, fine arts and crafts, with the 17 exhibition rooms displaying some 2,000 rare and valuable art works as well as historical and religious objects. The museum is closed Mondays (when Monday is a national holiday, it is closed on Tuesday) and from December 26 to January 3.

Myoho-in Temple [87]: This Tendai-sect temple stands across the street from the museum, although it was originally located in the precincts of Enryakuji Temple on Mt. Hiei. The two compartments of the reception hall, or *Ume-no-Ma* (Plum Chambers), are said to have been the rooms of the Empress Dowager Tofukumon-in at the Imperial Court. They are decorated with beautiful paintings by Kano Eitoku (1543-1590) and Kano Shoei (1519-1592). The temple is open to the public only for a week in early November.

Hokokubyo 87 : The tomb of Toyotomi Hideyoshi (1536–1598). Located on Amidagamine Hill east of the Hokoku Shrine, the tomb is reached by a flight of more than 500 stone steps. The tomb was neglected throughout the Tokugawa regime, but the mortuary shrine and a huge five-story pagoda were restored in 1897 to commemorate the 300th anniversary of Hideyoshi's death.

Chishaku-in Temple 87 : Situated south of Myoho-in, this is the headquarters of the Chizan school of the Shingon sect. Its subordinate temple, Shinshoji (popularly known as Narita-Fudo) in Narita is known throughout the country. Chishaku-in Temple was founded in Kii Province (now, Wakayama Prefecture), but it was transferred to its present site in 1598 by Tokugawa Ieyasu. Unfortunately, most of the old buildings were destroyed by a fire in 1947, but the magnificent sliding screens painted with cherry and maple trees by Hasegawa Tohaku (1539–1610) were saved. The garden was designed in the late 17th century, although some say it was designed by the great tea-ceremony master, Sen-no-Rikyu (1522–1591). It takes on a special beauty when the azaleas blossom in late May.

Sanjusangendo 87 : Located south of the museum, this is the popular name for Rengeo-in Temple, which is now affiliated with Myoho-in Temple. The name comes from the 33 (*Sanjusan*) spaces between the pillars in the elongated structure. Erected by order of ex-Emperor Goshirakawa in 1164, the original buildings were destroyed by fire in 1249 but rebuilt in 1266. It has been designated as a National Treasure. The principal image, a seated, wooden *Senju-Kannon* (Thousand-Handed *Kannon*; a National Treasure), is 3.3 m tall and was carved in 1254 by Tankei, son of the famous Unkei—an active sculptor of the 13th century. He was 82 years old when he made this image. *Kannon* is accompanied by 28 faithful followers (National Treasures) in addition to 1,001 smaller images of the same *Kannon*—all carved by Tankei and his assistants, and all designated as Important Cultural Properties. The once-elaborate decorations on the pillars and walls have almost entirely disappeared. In ancient days, there was an archery range behind the temple, and even now a *Toshiya* (Archery Contest) is held here every January. (refer to p.660). The large South Gate of Sanjusangendo was rebuilt in 1600.

Yogen-in Temple 87 : Located south of Sanjusangendo, this temple was established by Toyotomi Hideyoshi in 1594 to pray for the soul of Asai Nagamasa, who had been defeated in a battle with Oda Nobunaga. It is famous for the paintings of elephants and mythological lions on the cedar doors by master artist Tawaraya Sotatsu. When Fushimi Castle was on the point of capitulation to Toyotomi's forces, the defending *samurai* of Tokugawa committed *seppuku* (ritual suicide). In commemoration of their loyalty and devotion, the blood-stained floor planks were later used as ceiling boards in the corridor of the Main Hall. The blood stains can still be seen.

Rakuhoku

Also called Kitayama (Northern Mountains), Rakuhoku is north of central Kyoto. Believed since ancient times to be haunted by evil spirits, the steep mountains retain their air of mystery today. Rakuhoku is divided into four areas: Ichijoji and Shugaku-in located in the eastern urban areas; Kamigamo and Murasakino at the center; the outlying Rakuhoku area, including Kurama, Kibune and Ohara; and the mountainous area from Mt. Hiei to Lake Biwa in Shiga Prefecture. Although the places of interest in Rakuhoku are widely scattered over a large area, buses and trains provide easy access.

Daitokuji Temple 86 : Situated in the northern Murasakino district, this is one of the main temples of the Rinzai sect. It was founded in 1324 and was once famous for the magnificence of the buildings, although these structures were destroyed by fires in 1453 and 1468. As a result, all the present buildings post-date the latter year. *Chokushimon* (Gate for Imperial Messengers) was originally the south gate of Kyoto Imperial Palace, but it was given to the temple in 1640 by Empress Meisho. *Karamon* Gate (a National Treasure), with its splendid carvings, was brought here from Hideyoshi's Fushimi Castle. It is an excellent example of Azuchi-Momoyama-period (1573–1598) architectural art.

Sammon, the two-story main gate, was erected in 1589 by Sen-no-Rikyu (1522–1591), a master of the tea ceremony. The upper story contains images of Sakyamuni, Anan, Kayo and 16 arhats besides a statue of Rikyu made by himself. The placement of this statue here is said to be one of the reasons why Toyotomi Hideyoshi, a ruler of the feudal lords, ordered Rikyu to commit ritual suicide. The dragon on the ceiling of the lower story and the other painted decorations are the work of master Hasegawa Tohaku (1539–1610, the founder of Hasegawa school).

The *Butsuden*, or *Daiyuden* (Main Hall), built in 1665, contains images of Sakyamuni and his two disciples, Anan and Kayo, as well as Daito-Kokushi—the first abbot of the temple. The *Hatto* (Lecture Hall), rebuilt in 1636 at the rear of the Main Hall, has a distinctively Chinese architectural style. Northeast of the Lecture Hall is the *Hojo* (Superior's Residence; a National Treasure). The tablet contains an inscription bearing the characters for "Peerless Zen Temple" written by Emperor Godaigo. The paintings on the sliding screens are from the brush of Kano Tan-yu. The egrets and peasant with performing monkeys are especially admired. The garden was planned by famous landscaper Kobori Enshu.

Shinju-an, celebrated as the former residence of priest Ikkyu (1394–1481), contains a wooden statue of the priest and a tablet inscribed with his writing. The sliding screens were painted by Soga Dasoku (d. 1483). Application in advance is required to visit Shinju-an. Daisen-in, west of Shinju-an, contains paintings by Kano Motonobu

(1476–1559) on the sliding screens. The garden, designed by Kogaku-Soko (1465–1548)—the 77th abbot of the temple, is considered to be one of most artistically designed gardens in Japan. Refer to p.206

Ryugen-in, in front of the Gate for Imperial Messengers, is noted for its moss and tiny, white-sand and rock gardens. Zuiho-in, west of Ryugen-in, also has a beautiful garden. Koto-in contains a tea-ceremony room of exquisite simplicity. Koho-an, in the western portion of the precincts, has a tea-ceremony room designed by Kobori Enshu. The garden is also famous as being representative of Kobori's work. The tombstones of the Kobori family are in the southwest corner of the garden. Application for admittance must be made in advance.

Daitokuji Temple is full of priceless objects of art such as a portrait of *Kannon* with a crane and a monkey on each side (a National Treasure) by Mu Ch'i—a painter and priest from the Sung Dynasty, China in the late 13th century with the Japanese name of Mokkei, a painting of a dragon and tiger by the same artist, a manuscript written by Emperor Godaigo (a National Treasure), a small portrait of Sakyamuni in meditation by Soga-Dasoku and many examples of calligraphy by various priests.

Kamigamo Shrine ⟦72⟧: Located about 2 km north of Daitokuji Temple, this Shinto shrine is as famous as the Shimogamo Shrine. They were both founded at the same time, long before the foundation of the capital. Annual events at the shrine include a historic horse race on May 5 and the *Aoi Matsuri* on May 15. (refer to p.661).

Botanical Garden ⟦72⟧: Covering an area of 240,000 sq.m on the left bank of the Kamo River, the gardens were opened in 1924 to commemorate the coronation of Emperor Taisho. Various hothouses surround a large-domed greenhouse in the center.

Shimogamo Shrine ⟦86⟧: Located close to where the Kamo and Takano rivers meet, this shrine is celebrated for the *Aoi* Festival held annually on May 15. Together with its sister shrine, Kamigamo, it was founded long before Kyoto became the capital. It was partly rebuilt in 1628, but its Main Hall dates from 1863.

Shisendo Temple ⟦72⟧: Situated north of Ginkakuji Temple, this temple was founded in 1631 as a retreat by Ishikawa Jozan (1583–1672), a *samurai*, poet and scholar of the Edo period. In the Poet's Chamber, 36 portraits of Chinese poets adorn the walls.

A white-sand garden, lined with carefully pruned azaleas and surrounded by a forest, imparts a calm beauty each season, especially in autumn when the maple leaves turn crimson.

Manshu-in Temple ⟦72⟧: This temple originally stood on Mt. Hiei, but it was moved to its present location in 1656. It was always headed by an Imperial prince. The dry garden, with its stone bridges and islands, as well as the buildings were all designed by the son of the Imperial prince who had the Katsura Imperial Villa constructed. The Hasso Tea-ceremony Room, standing on the grounds was named for its eight windows.

Shugaku-in Imperial Villa [72]: A 30 min. walk from Shugakuin-mae Station on the Eizan Electric Railway. The villa is situated at the southwest foot of Mt. Hiei where Shugaku-in Temple once stood. It consists of three large gardens, each containing an annex called *Ochaya*. It was originally laid out by the Tokugawa Shogunate as a retreat for ex-Emperor Gomizuno-o. The grounds cover an area of 540,000 sq.m. The Upper and Lower Villas were completed in 1659, while the Middle Villa was built later for Princess Ake, daughter of the ex-Emperor. The villa was converted into a temple named Rinkyuji when the princess became a nun. In 1885, part of the temple was named the Middle Villa.

The three villas are somewhat separated from one another. The Lower Villa is approached from the front gate, with ordinary visitors using a small trap door opening in the large, polished bamboo door panel. Inside the gate, a path covered with fine pebbles leads to *Miyukimon*, a gate for the Emperor. After entering the garden through a side gate on the north side, visitors will come upon *Chumon*, the second gate. A path leads straight to the inner garden, to the left of which is an elegant porch at the top of a tiered ramp. The white paper screens seen at the porch make a beautiful contrast with the maroon colored walls of the building. Another garden path leads to the right, across a pond to *Jugetsukan*, a replica of the chamber used by ex-Emperor Gomizuno-o. There are two stone lanterns along the path: one shaped like a sleeve and the other of Korean-style. *Jugetsukan* contains four rooms laid out in an L-shape and surrounded by a veranda. Under the eaves hangs a tablet reading *Jugetsukan*, which is believed to have been written by ex-Emperor Gomizuno-o. The first room has 15 *tatami* mats of which three in a corner are raised and framed as the Emperor's seat. On the sliding door is a picture of the "Three Laughing Sages at Kokei." Next to the third room is a five-mat room with windows facing the pond. Seen from the window, the sleeve-shaped lantern accentuates the natural beauty of the garden.

From the east gate (back gate) of the Lower Villa, the visitor steps into a plaza with an unimpeded view of the mountain ranges far in the distance. The path, flanked by pine trees, branches off in two directions, the fork to the right leading to the Middle Villa and the one to the left leading to the Upper Villa. The Middle Villa covers about half of what was Rinkyuji Temple, which is on the left. Of the two buildings in the center connected with the villa, *Kyakuden* (Reception Hall) is the larger, while *Rakushiken* (House of Bliss) was originally part of Rinkyuji Temple. *Rakushiken* faces a pond on the south, and a veranda juts out from the room. It is decorated with many fine paintings, including one on a sliding door of the procession floats (*Yama* and *Hoko*) of the *Gion Matsuri* (festival) that is still used today. It is attributed to Sumiyoshi Gukei (1631-1705), as are the carp painted on both sides of one of the wooden doors. Legend has it that the carp escaped from the picture every night to swim in the pond until they were finally penned in by the nets added by Maruyama Okyo, a famous 18th-century artist. Rinkyuji Temple has a fine landscape garden with a pond, a narrow waterfall and a hill with an arbor on one side.

The Upper Villa has the largest and finest garden of the three. It is entered through the front gate, which stands at the end of an avenue of pines. Approaching the gate, one can see *Okarikomi* (Great Hedge) toward the left, with a four-tier mass of carefully pruned shrubs covering the slope—a magnificent sight. Turning to the right, one will come upon a stone lantern at the foot of the hill. On top of this hill is a small, two-room summer house known as *Rin-untei*, expressly built to provide an impressive panoramic view of the city and surrounding area.

Descending the steps again and crossing a bridge onto an islet, one comes upon another summer house called *Kyusuitei* (for which the characters on the tablet were written by ex-Emperor Gomizuno-o). On another island is an arbor, on the roof of which is a gilt bronze phoenix. If the visitor then walks along the western shore of the lake, he will return to the exit, having made a complete tour of the Upper Villa.

Shugaku-in Imperial Villa is closed on Saturday afternoons, Sundays, national holidays and December 25–January 5. Written permission to enter must be obtained in advance from the Kyoto Office of the Imperial Household Agency.

Kyoto International Conference Hall 72 : The six-story building has a total floor space of 27,885 sq.m and four wings. Completed in April 1966, the hall is located by Takaragaike Pond, west of Takaragaike Station on the Eizan Electric Railway. The building incorporates the best modern Japanese architectural techniques and is equipped with all the facilities needed to make an international conference a success. There are 14 conference halls, the largest of which can accommodate 2,000 people.

Entsuji Temple 72 : Located on a hill northwest of Takaragaike Pond. Once the villa of ex-Emperor Gomizuno-o, the grounds were later transformed into a convent. The rectangular, flat garden, partially covered with moss, is dotted with large stones. Beyond the clipped hedge that surrounds the garden, there is a nice view of Mt. Hiei. It is an excellent example of *shakkei* (lit. borrowed scenery)—the typical Japanese-garden style in which the surrounding landscape is included in the planning of the garden.

Mt. Kurama 72 : Alt. 750 m. Situated north of Kyoto, the mountain can easily be reached from Demachi-yanagi Station by the Eizan Electric Railway (30 min.) Kurama Temple, founded in 770 by priest Kantei, is situated halfway up the mountain. The original buildings were reduced to ashes by repeated fires, so that nothing remains to recall the once-grand temple. All the present buildings were reconstructed in 1872, except for the Main Hall, which was again destroyed by fire in 1945 and subsequently rebuilt.

Two famous events, the Bamboo-Cutting Ceremony and *Kurama-no-Himatsuri*, occur on Mt. Kurama (refer to p.662 and 664). Among the treasures of the temple is a painting of a demon by Kano Motonobu. About 1.6 km northwest of the Main Hall is a dale called Sojodani where legend has it that Ushiwakamaru, later known as Minamoto-no-Yoshitsune (1159-1189)—a famed general of Genji Clan, learned the art of fencing from a *tengu* (a long-nosed goblin).

Yase and Ohara: Two suburban districts at the western foot of Mt. Hiei. The women of the region are called *oharame* and are known for carrying heavy loads on their head. They also wear narrow *obi*, cover their heads with kerchiefs and wrap white, cotton cloth around their arms and legs.

Sanzen-in ⬚72⬚: An old temple of the Tendai sect at Ohara, about 5 km north of Yase-yuen Station—the terminal of the Eizan Electric Railway. It originated when the illustrious priest Saicho (767-822) built it on Mt. Hiei. In 860, the priest Joun rebuilt the temple buildings at the command of Emperor Seiwa and installed an image of *Yakushi-Nyorai*. The first Imperial abbot of the temple was the second prince of Emperor Horikawa, who took the name Saiun.

The Main Hall is called *Ojo-Gokurakuin*, or Hall of Paradise in Rebirth. Built in 1148, it contains lofty images of *Amida-Nyorai*, *Kannon* and *Seiji*. The other buildings were reconstructed from materials taken from the *Shishinden* (Ceremonial Hall) of the Imperial Palace during the Keicho era (1596-1615). One special feature of the Main Hall is its ceiling, which is shaped like the bottom of a boat and depicts flying angels and Bodhisattvas. The wall behind the main image is adorned with paintings of the Mandalas called *Kongokai* and *Taizokai* by priest Eshin (942-1017).

Jakko-in ⬚72⬚: This nunnery was built in perfect seclusion. A 25-min. walk to the west of Sanzen-in Temple, it is famed as the place where Empress Dowager Kenreimon-in, mother of the infant Emperor Antoku, became a nun in 1185. She spent the rest of her life here after her son met his fatal end with the rest of the Taira Clan at Dannoura (near Shimonoseki). Her tomb is on a hill behind the temple.

Mt. Hiei ⬚72⬚: Alt. 848 m. Soaring northeast of Kyoto, it can be reached from Kyoto in two ways: (1) Take the Eizan Electric Railway Line from Demachi-yanagi to Yase-yuen at the western foot of Mt. Hiei. Then, take the cable car from Yase-yuen Cable Station to the Hiei cable terminal and transfer to the ropeway leading to Shimeigatake Peak. (2) From the center of the city, it is about 1-hour's car ride to the mountain top. Passing through Kita-Shirakawa, the road winds up to Tanotani Pass. From here, the Mt. Hiei Toll Road (8.1 km long) extends to the summit via Yumemigaoka and Ipponsugi. Buses also go along the same route to the summit from the

JR Kyoto Station or Keihan-Sanjo Station on the Keihan Line.

Enryakuji Temple ☐72☐ : Located in a thick grove of cypress trees on the summit of Mt. Hiei. Enryakuji is one of the most important temples in the country, both from an historic as well as a religious standpoint. It was founded in 788 by the priest Saicho by order of Emperor Kammu. Saicho (767–822), also known as Dengyo-Daishi, was the eminent founder of the Tendai sect. The temple was located here to the northeast of Kyoto to protect the new capital from the evil spirits that were supposed to come from the northeast. However, it proved more of an affliction than a Heaven's blessing as the small monastery expanded and filled with turbulent warrior monks. Clad in armor, these monks made frequent raids on the city, sometimes even threatening the Imperial Palace. These troublesome monks were finally dispersed by Oda Nobunaga (1534–1582), who completely destroyed the temple buildings. Although Toyotomi Hideyoshi, one of Nobunaga's leading generals, restored the monastery and it was enlarged by Iemitsu—the third Tokugawa Shogun, the priests never again assumed such a war-like nature.

The principal buildings of Enryakuji Temple are *Kompon-Chudo* (Central Hall), *Kaidan-in* (Ordination Hall) and the Mausoleum of Dengyo-Daishi—all located at *Toto* (East Quarter). The Central Hall is a National Treasure, while the Ordination Hall is an Important Cultural Property. *Shakado* (Sakyamuni Hall) and the famous *Sorinto* Column (both Important Cultural Properties) are at *Saito* (West Quarter), while *Yokawa-Chudo* Hall and *Nyohoto* Pagoda are at Yokawa. The Central Hall contains many valuable treasures, including a statue of *Yakushi-Nyorai* (an Important Cultural Property) carved by Sachio. Near the Shimeigatake Parking Lot atop Mt. Hiei are a natural science museum, an amusement park and a revolving observation pavilion that offers a magnificent, panoramic view of Lake Biwa, Kyoto and the surrounding mountain ranges.

Rakusai

Rakusai is the area along the gently sloping hills to the west of central Kyoto. The tranquil atmosphere so attracted the aristocracy during the Heian period that they built their villas and temples here. Popular among sightseers for its beautiful natural scenery, it also provides a valuable historical link with the Kamakura-period temples. Rakusai can be divided into four areas: Hanazono and Uzumasa at the center, Arashiyama and Matsuo near the Katsura River, Sagano and Mt. Takao, and Nishiyama—the mountainous area in the southwest.

Kinkakuji Temple ☐86☐ : Known as the Gold Pavilion in English, it is situated at the foot of Kinugasa Hill, northwest of Hirano Shrine. A famous Muromachi-period (1336–1573) structure, it was originally designed to serve as the villa of a Court noble named Saionji Kintsune. It was greatly improved upon by its second owner, the third

Ashikaga Shogun Yoshimitsu (1358-1408), who retired here from the cares of state. Yoshimitsu had the Gold Pavilion built and the garden laid out in 1397. His son and successor, Yoshimochi, turned the villa into a Buddhist temple named Rokuonji in accordance with his father's wishes. Although the garden remains to attest to the refined and artistic life of the *shogun* five centuries ago, most of the buildings erected at that time were destroyed by repeated fires, culminating in the tragic loss of the treasured Gold Pavilion through arson in July 1950. An exact replica of the original was erected on the same spot in October 1955.

Visitors to Kinkakuji Temple first come to *Chumon* Gate. After passing along a path shaded by numerous tall pine and maple trees, they will come upon the garden. Beyond the pond rises the three-story Gold Pavilion topped by a bronze phoenix. The walls of the pavilion are completely covered with gold leaf. To the right of the path along the pond is the Main Hall. It houses the three Buddhist divinities of *Kannon*, *Benten* and *Taishakuten* as well as images of Ashikaga Yoshimitsu and Muso-Kokushi (a distinguished Zen priest, 1275-1351). The small court contains a 500-year-old pine tree shaped like a sailing ship. Up a zigzagging path beside the brook is an arbor called *Sekkatei*, built during the time of ex-Emperor Gomizuno-o but renovated in 1874. The post beside the alcove is made of nandin wood, while the shelves are made from bush clover wood. The stone lantern, basin and seat are said to have been brought from the *shogun*'s Muromachi Palace.

Toji-in Temple ⟨ 86 ⟩: A few minutes walk from Toji-in Station on the Keifuku Kitano Line. It was established in 1341 by Ashikaga Takauji (1305-1358), founder of the Ashikaga Shogunate. The present temple structures, however, were rebuilt in 1818. *Reiko-den* (Main Hall) contains statues of all the Ashikaga Shogun except for the fifth and tenth. The sliding screens were painted in India ink by the famous painter Kano Sanraku (1559-1635). The temple also has a beautiful garden and tea-ceremony room.

Myoshinji Temple ⟨ 86 ⟩: The headquarters of the Myoshinji school of the Rinzai sect are located near Myoshinji Station on the Keifuku Kitano Line. A massive temple with nearly 50 subordinate temples, it was founded in 1337 on the site of an Imperial Villa belonging to ex-Emperor Hanazono, but the present buildings are of a later date. The *Butsuden* (Buddha Hall) contains an image of *Sakyamuni*, while the ceiling of the *Hatto* (Lecture Hall) is decorated with a painting of a dragon by the eminent artist Kano Tan-yu. A bell with the oldest inscription in Japan (a National Treasure), cast in 698, hangs in a belfry west of the *Butsuden*. Gyokuho-in, located east of the Lecture Hall, is where ex-Emperor Hanazono studied Buddhism and houses his portrait. No Buddhist temple has so many subordinate temples rich in art objects as Myoshinji. Since Reiun-in, west of the priests' apartments, holds a large number of paintings by Kano Motonobu

(1476–1559), it is known as Motonobu Temple. Taizo-in has a garden said to have been designed by Kano Motonobu, Tenkyu-in is famous for paintings by Kano Sanraku and Keishun-in has a magnificent tea-ceremony hall and garden.

Ninnaji Temple 72 : Located near Omuro Station on the Keifuku Kitano Line, this is the headquarters of the Omuro school of the Shingon sect. It was formerly known as Omuro Palace. Construction began in 886 by order of Emperor Koko, but since he died before its completion, Emperor Uda had the remaining work completed two years later, becoming the first superior of the temple upon retirement.

From then until the Meiji Restoration in 1868, an Imperial prince had always served as the superior of the temple. Originally there were more than 60 *tatchu*, or subordinate temples, but frequent fires have greatly reduced their number, with the oldest remaining building dating from the first half of the 17th century. The Five-Story Pagoda (to the right as one enters the Middle Gate), standing about 33 m high, was constructed in 1637. At the end of the path leading from *Chumon* (Middle Gate) stands *Kondo* (Main Hall), whose main image is a wooden Amitabha (both the hall and the statue are National Treasures). *Kyodo* (Scripture Hall) is to the east, while *Miedo*, the former *Seiryoden* Hall where the priest Kobo Daishi is enshrined, is to the west. *Kondo* and *Miedo* were once part of *Shishinden* and *Seiryoden*, respectively, at the Kyoto Imperial Palace. Many National Treasures are included among the numerous objects in the treasure house. The temple grounds contain a thicket of cherry trees unique to this spot. These aged cherry trees, widely known as *Omuro-no-Sakura*, have short, thick trunks and eight petals. When they blossom from mid-to late April, thousands come to see this famous Ninnaji Temple landmark.

Ryoanji Temple 72 : Close to Ryoanji Station on the Keifuku Kitano Line, this is a Rinzai-sect Zen Buddhist temple. It was founded in 1450 by Hosokawa Katsumoto, a senior statesman of the Ashikaga Shogunate, whose tomb is on the temple grounds. The temple is famous for its rock garden, which consists only of stones and sand. It is regarded as a masterpiece by Soami, a master artist, who was greatly influenced by *zen* philosophy. Its utter simplicity might be difficult for the uninitiated to appreciate, but what appears to be nothing more than a flat space strewn with white sand and scattered with 15 oddly shaped stones somehow contains a stark beauty felt through the heart. Refer to p.206

Koryuji Temple 73 : Also known as Uzumasadera, this is a Shingon-sect Buddhist temple. It was founded in 622 by Hata Kawakatsu. The Hata family was part of a wave of immigrants who came to Japan from the Korean Peninsula. Hata was influential in the district and played a significant role in contributing to the development of Kyoto. It faces Uzumasa Station on the Keifuku Arashiyama Line. The *Kodo* (Lecture Hall; an Important Cultural Property) is the second-oldest structure in Kyoto, having been erected in 1165. The hall contains three National Treasures: the main image, a seated wooden figure of Buddha, and two gigantic, wooden statues of *Senju-Kannon* (Thousand-Handed *Kannon*) and *Fukukenjaku-Kannon* —all three older than the hall housing them.

Taishiden Hall, behind the Lecture Hall, contains a wooden statue that is a likeness of Prince Shotoku (574-622) that he is said to have carved himself at the age of 33. The present building dates from 1720. Located in the northwest corner of the grounds, Keigu-in (a National Treasure) offers great historical interest. Erected in 1251, it is a single-story, octagonal structure roofed with cypress bark. Popularly called *Hakkakudo*, it contains an image of Prince Shotoku at age 16 (also said to have been made by the prince himself), a statue of *Nyoirin Kannon* presented by a Korean king of the Paikche Dynasty and an image of Amitabha.

In the *Reihoden* (Treasure Museum) at the rear of *Taishiden*, various priceless Buddhist images are preserved, including a famous *Miroku-Bosatsu* carved in the Asuka period (592-628). The oldest sculpture in Kyoto (a National Treasure), it is said to have been brought from the Silla Dynasty in Korea. The very famous *Ushi Matsuri* festival is held here. (refer to p.663).

Toei-Uzumasa Eiga-mura (Movie Land): Located on the northern border of Koryuji Temple, this Edo-style land was constructed for the filming of historical movies. The magistrate's office, the lodging quarters and the other buildings recall a Japan of days gone by. It is sometimes possible to see the actual filming of *samurai* sword fights and the like. The miniature town facade made for filming is also interesting and video tapes of the best in Japanese cinema can be viewed in the Film Culture Hall.

Yuzen Cultural Hall 87 : This workshop for *Yuzen-zome*, a unique hand-painted method of dyeing silk fabric for *kimono*, is located 200 m east of Nishi-Kyogoku Station on the Hankyu Kyoto Line. The method was invented by Miyazaki Yuzensai around 1700, but in 1876 Hirose Jisuke devised a new method of stencil dyeing to mass-produce fabric. The silk fabric is decorated with stenciled patterns, steamed to set the colors for 30 min.-1 hr., and then rinsed in running water to wash out the excess dye. Visitors to the workshop can observe the process of *Yuzen* dyeing.

Arashiyama 73 : Popularly called Ranzan, this lovely place contains all the beauty of nature within its limited area. It can be reached by the Keifuku Arashiyama Line in 20 min. from Shijo-Omiya Station. The Oi River, locally called the Hozu River, runs around the foot of Arashiyama Hill, which can be approached from Arashiyama Station by crossing Togetsukyo Bridge. The beauty of the place lies in the varied vegetation on the hillside facing the river. Large pines are interspersed with innumerable cherry and maple trees, adding a colorful beauty to the scene. The cherry trees were transplanted from Yoshino in the latter part of the 13th century by order of ex-Emperor Kameyama, who at that time resided in the villa that is now the site of Rinsenji Temple near the bridge.

Crossing the bridge and climbing the hill, the visitor will arrive at Daihikaku, or Senkoji Temple, located picturesquely near the top. It contains an image of *Senju-Kannon* (Thousand-Handed *Kannon*)and a wooden statue of Suminokura Ryoi (1554–1614), a famous engineer who made the Oi River navigable as far as Tamba Province (now, part of Kyoto Prefecture) in 1606 by removing the rocks in the narrow gorge.

This is a popular place for boating, and on summer nights fishing is done with cormorants. The 2-hr., Hozu-River boat trip from Kameoka to Arashiyama is also popular.

Horinji Temple: Located on an eminence south of Arashiyama, this ancient temple is said to have been founded in 713. *Kokuzo*, the god of wisdom, is enshrined here. The temple is famous for the *Jusan Mairi* (13-year-olds coming to worship), March 13–May 13.

Matsuno-o Shrine $\boxed{73}$: Located south of Horinji Temple, this famous Shinto shrine dates from remote antiquity. It is dedicated to Oyamakui-no-Mikoto and his consort. The two important festivals held here, *Matsuno-o Matsuri* and *Onda Matsuri* (Rice-Planting Festival), are very famous. (refer to p.661 and 663)

Saihoji Temple $\boxed{73}$: Southwest of Matsuno-o Shrine, this is a temple of the Rinzai sect. Believed to have been founded in 731 by the priest Gyoki, it was reconstructed in 1339 by priest Muso-Kokushi (1275–1351). The garden, designed by Muso-Kokushi, is famed throughout the world for its unique feature. A typical example of a "promenade garden," it was designed to give the impression that the pond is geographically connected with the mountain off in the background. The entire garden is covered with nearly 100 species of green and yellow moss, some of which has grown to unusual denseness, leading to the name Kokedera (Moss Temple).

Katsura Imperial Villa $\boxed{73}$: Situated on the Katsura River, 4.8 km from the JR Kyoto Station, or near Katsura Station on the Hankyu Arashiyama Line. An outstanding example of Japanese architecture, the villa was built for Prince Toshihito (1579–1629), brother of Emperor Goyozei (1571–1617), who newly created the Hachijo family with the support of Toyotomi Hideyoshi. The villa and garden are situated in tranquil, beautiful surroundings with good views of Arashiyama and Kameyama Hills.

The garden is a typical "promenade garden," with several tea-ceremony houses overlooking a central pond. It is generally believed that the garden was designed by famous landscape architect Kobori Enshu, but there is no definite evidence to this effect. Rather, it is clear that the garden was laid out under the guidance of the prince and his son through the labors of Enshu's two brothers.

The work commenced in 1620 and was completed in 1624. One

characteristic of the garden is that it was planned so that no matter where the visitor stands, there is always a frontal view. In other words, there is never a rear view to hinder the enjoyment of the beautiful landscape.

One story has it that when Kobori Enshu was commissioned by the Tokugawa Shogunate to design this garden, he first made the *shogun* promise three things: first, to set no limit on expenditures; second, never to hurry the work, and third, not to allow anyone to see the garden before its completion. The villa came under the control of the Imperial Household Agency in 1883, and great pains have been taken since then to preserve the original structure. Visitors enter through *Miyukimon* Gate. Some portions of the main building, *Goten*, have been given special names. *Furushoin* has a veranda that is ideal for moon-viewing.

Nakashoin contains three apartments. The first is decorated with many valuable paintings by Kano Tan-yu, including a crow that is regarded as a masterpiece. The second apartment is noted for its painting of "Chikurin Shichiken" (Seven Recluses in a Bamboo Grove) by Kano Naonobu (1607–1650), while the third has a picture of pheasants in a snow-covered bamboo forest by Kano Yasunobu.

Miyukiden (Hall for Imperial Visits) is a simple structure built for visits by ex-Emperor Gomizuno-o and his consort. The painting on the wooden door is by Kano Tan-yu. "Kugi-Kakushi" (the fastenings used to conceal nails and bolts) represent narcissuses and are attributed to Kacho, a famous goldsmith. The long piece of timber forming the sill is believed to have been presented by Kato Kiyomasa (1562–1611, refer to p.864), a famous general under Toyotomi Hideyoshi. The shelves are all made from different kinds of rare wood, including red sandalwood, ebony and betel palm. The other rooms are marked by the same taste for simplicity.

Many buildings stand in the garden. The first one is *Gepparo*, situated on a hill in the northwest part of the garden. This building is simplicity itself, with a ceiling of reeds and a veranda of bamboo. On another hill is a grove of maples. *Shokintei* is at the opposite end of the grounds beyond a pond. It consists of several apartments, while the tablet under the east gable was written by Emperor Goyozei.

The house contains a famous tea-ceremony room that is so well lighted there is not a single dark corner to be found. *Shoiken* stands on the western part of the grounds and contains ten rooms. The oar-shaped catch of bronze on the outside of the sliding door facing the south veranda is nearly 1 m long and is also attributed to Kacho. In all, there are seven houses in the garden.

The villa is closed Saturday afternoons, Sundays, national holidays and December 25–January 5. Permission to enter must be obtained in advance from the Kyoto Office of the Imperial Household Agency.

Tenryuji Temple [73] : Located near Arashimaya Station on the

Keifuku Arashiyama Line, this is the headquarters of the Tenryuji school of the Rinzai sect. It was founded in memory of Emperor Godaigo in 1339 by the first Ashikaga Shogun, Takauji. The famous priest Soseki, also known as Muso-Kokushi, was the first superior. The temple was repeatedly ravaged by fires, but the present buildings date back about a hundred years.

The Main Hall, called *Tahoden* and situated in the center of the grounds, contains a memorial tablet of Emperor Godaigo. In the Lecture Hall to the right of the Main Hall are statues of Sakyamuni, *Monju* and *Fugen* Bodhisattvas. A noted landscape garden designed by Muso-Kokushi is located at the rear of the abbot's quarters.

Nison-in: Situated northwest of Tenryuji Temple, this is a temple of the Tendai sect. Although it was founded in the middle of the ninth century, the present structure dates from 1521. The Main Hall contains two standing images of Amitabha and Sakyamuni (Important Cultural Properties); hence, the name Nison-in, or Temple of Two Buddhas. Many maple trees growing in the precincts attract large crowds when they change color in autumn.

Seiryoji Temple: Located north of Arashiyama Station on the Keifuku Arashiyama Line, it is commonly called Syakado because of the 1.6-m-tall image of Sakyamuni (a National Treasure) in the Main Hall. This famed sandalwood image is believed to have been carved by Katsuma Bishu, a celebrated Hindi sculptor. It was reportedly brought to Japan in 987 through Cho-nen, a priest at Todaiji Temple in Nara. The form is so unique that it is called the Seiryoji-style *Sakyamuni* and can be seen on the eighth of each month.

An interesting festival at Seiryoji Temple is the *Saga-no-Otaimatsu* (Torchlights of Saga), which takes place on the night of March 15. It is held to forecast the condition of the rice crop.

Daikakuji Temple 73 : Situated 1.1 km north of Saga Station on the JR San-in Main Line, this was originally the detached palace of Emperor Saga, but was transformed into a temple by Emperor Junna, who appointed an Imperial prince as founder and abbot. The main images in the provisional Main Hall are wooden statues of the Five Vidyrajas attributed to Kukai (Kobo-Daishi)—all Important Cultural Properties. *Kyakuden* (Reception Hall) or *Shoshinden*, is also an Important Cultural Property. This was once the Imperial throne room for ex-Emperor Gouda. In the temple, there are many excellent paintings by Kano Motonobu (1476-1559), Kano Eitoku (1543-1590), Kano Sanraku (1559-1635), Kano Tan-yu (1602-1674), Ogata Korin (1658-1716) and Watanabe Shiko (1683-1755).

Mt. Atago 72 : 924 m in altitude. Located about 5 km northwest of Arashiyama. Atago Shrine on the summit is believed to offer protection against fire. Slightly below the shrine is a Buddhist temple called Tsukinowa-dera, or Getsurinji, which contains many Buddhist images. The "Arashiyama-Takao Parkway" is a two-lane toll road, 7 m wide and 10.7 km long, which was designed to give drivers a chance to view the scenic beauty of the Rakusai district (west of Kyoto). Running west from Arashiyama to Takao, the parkway permits the traveler to enjoy picturesque views of Sagano, Mt. Hiei, the streets of Kyoto, the rapids of the Hozu River and Mt. Atago, either at close range or from a distance. Besides the parkway's four observation platforms and five parking lots, regular bus service is also available.

Takao, Makino-o and Togano-o [72]: These three places lie close together along the ravine at the eastern foot of Mt. Atago, about 50 min. from the JR Kyoto Station by bus. They constitute the classic trio for viewing maples, which set the hillsides ablaze when they turn color in autumn. All of these trees are located on the west bank of the Kiyotaki River, a tributary of the Oi River. Jingoji Temple, an ancient temple at Takao, is reached by crossing the river. Founded in 781, it fell into ruin through neglect before it was reconstructed in the 12th century. The massive image of *Yakushi* in the Main Hall and the images of the five *Kokuzo* Bodhisattvas in *Tahoto* Pagoda are among the National Treasures here. A large bell cast in 875, bears an inscription by Fujiwara Toshiyuki (d.907), the famed calligrapher, and is one of the three most famous temple bells in Japan (a National Treasure).

Further upstream at Makino-o stands a temple called Saimyoji, which was reconstructed in 1699. Still farther up the Kiyotaki River, at Togano-o is Kozanji Temple. Among its possessions are six scrolls of an illustrated history of the Kegon sect by Fujiwara Nobuzane (1176-1265), four scrolls of animal caricatures by the priest Kakuyu, popularly known as Toba-Sojo (1053-1140), and a portrait of Myoe, an abbot of the temple—all National Treasures. The caricatures are on loan to the Tokyo National Museum.

Rakunan

Situated on the south side of the city, Rakunan is the area around the road linking Kyoto with Nara. From the earliest days of the city's history, the area has prospered and is famous for the many interesting shrines and temples scattered about. Although the places of interest are rather spread out, there are many important sites and structures dating back to the Heian period, including the spectacular Byodo-in Temple at Uji—once a resort for the wealthy and powerful of Kyoto. The district is also famous for its *sake* and tea production.

Sennyuji Temple: Standing 1.6 km southeast of Sanjusangendo, this was once the mortuary for the emperors in the six centuries following the reign of Emperor Shijo in the 13th century. All of the many Imperial mausoleums standing behind the temple as well as the temple itself were erected in 1668. There is a Yang-kouei-fei *Kannon*, said to resemble the beautiful Yang-kouei-fei (or Yokihi in Japanese) —the beloved of T'ang Dynasty Emperor Hsuan-Tsung, China.

Tofukuji Temple [73]: Located near Sennyuji Temple, this is the headquarters for the Tofukuji school of the Rinzai sect. Founded in 1236, it subsequently fell victim to repeated fires. The two-story *Sammon* (Main Gate), erected around 1380, has many Buddhist sculptures on the upper floor that are said to have been created by Jocho (d. 1057), a celebrated sculptor of the Heian period. The ceiling is decorated with exquisite paintings by Mincho (also called Chodensu, 1352-1431) and his disciple Kandensu.

The Main Hall was destroyed by fire in 1881 and rebuilt in 1934. The huge dragon painted by Domoto Insho (1891-1975) on the ceiling is acclaimed. The gorge between the Main Hall and the Founder's Hall is spanned by Tsutenkyo Bridge (lit. Bridge to Heaven). The cliffs are covered with beautiful maple trees. The Founder's Hall contains an image of the founder. There are incredible dry gardens around the abbot's apartments in the main temple as well as the subordinate temples Ryogin-an, Funda-in and others.

Many rare paintings by great artists such as Sesshu (1420-1506) and Mincho can be found at Tofukuji Temple. The most famous is a huge *kakemono* (scroll painting) by Mincho depicting "Sakyamuni's Entry into Nirvana." It is exhibited every March 15.

The scroll represents the dying Sakyamuni surrounded by men and animals, including a cat, not usually found in other paintings on this theme. It is said that while painting the picture, a cat always sat beside Mincho until one day he put it into the picture among the other animals. Strangely enough, the cat disappeared after that.

Fushimi 73 : When Toyotomi Hideyoshi (the first general to gain control over the feudal lords and unify the nation under his rule), constructed a castle here, the district assumed political importance; however, the area is now chiefly known for its *sake* brewing. Old-fashioned *sake*-production tools can be seen at the Okura Museum. Hideyoshi died in Fushimi Castle in 1598, and the magnificent structure was later demolished in 1623 by the Tokugawa Shogunate. Most of the sections of the castle as well as its furnishings were distributed among the temples of Kyoto.

Fushimi-Inari Shrine 73 : Located near the JR Inari Station on the Nara Line, this is one of the most famous Shinto shrines in Japan. Founded in 711, it is dedicated to several deities, principally Ukanomitama-no-Mikoto—the goddess of rice and other food. Except for the projecting section, the main shrine is roofed with cypress shingles and dates from 1499—a typical example of Momoyama-style architecture. The numerous red *torii* gates on the hill behind it were donated by faithful followers. Totaling more than 10,000, these *torii* form a vermilion tunnel about 4 km long. The stone figures of foxes, popularly believed to be the messengers of Inari Shrine, were also contributed by devotees.

Momoyama 73 : Meaning Peach Hill, the slope was named for the many peach trees that grew here. After the gorgeous Fushimi Castle founded by Toyotomi Hideyoshi was completely demolished in 1623, peach trees were planted around the site. Thus, this period is known as the Azuchi-Momoyama period (1573–1598), Azuchi indicating the site where Oda Nobunaga, Hideyoshi's lord, built Azuchi Castle as his base for ruling over the country. It lasted from the latter period of the Age of Civil Wars when Nobunaga gained power until the death of Toyotomi Hideyoshi. Ranking on a par with the Heian period, this period produced a variety of excellent art works noted for their ornate styles. Momoyama is located near Momoyama Station on the JR Nara Line and is the site of the mausoleum of Emperor Meiji and Empress Shoken, his consort.

Encircling the tombs are three stone fences. The inner fence has a bronze gate emblazoned with the Imperial crest. The characters on the granite lantern by the gate were written by Prince Kan-in and signify "Fushimi-Momoyama Mausoleum." The Imperial reserve at Momoyama covers an area of 1,210,000 sq.m, of which 20,000 sq.m are occupied by the mausoleum. The mausoleum of Empress Shoken is laid out in much the same style as that of the Emperor but on a smaller scale.

Emperor Kammu's Mausoleum ⬚73⬚: Located not far from Momoyama Station, this is the tomb of the Emperor who established Kyoto as the capital in 794.

Daigoji Temple ⬚73⬚: Located in the extreme southeast of Kyoto, this is a celebrated Shingon-sect temple. Founded in 874 by the priest Shobo who was of Imperial descent, it is one of two major headquarters for *Shugendo* (an ascetic practice) Buddhism and is accordingly highly revered by followers.

The temple is composed of the Upper Daigo and the Lower Daigo, each of which contains ancient structures. The five-story pagoda in the latter was constructed in 951 at the command of Emperor Murakami. Designated as a National Treasure, it is the oldest extant structure in Kyoto.

Sampo-in: Forming part of Daigoji Temple, this is the headquarters of the Daigo school of the Shingon sect. It was established in 1115 by Shokaku, the 14th abbot of Daigoji Temple. The present buildings, erected by order of Toyotomi Hideyoshi, contain several chambers decorated with beautiful paintings by Kano Sanraku (refer to p.184). The temple possesses an unrivaled collection of valuable pictures and calligraphy of historic interest. Two calligraphic scrolls have been designated as National Treasures. The landscape garden is one of the finest in Japan, with the huge cherry tree at the entrance attracting a crowd when it blooms in spring.

Hokaiji Temple: Located at Hino, south of Daigoji Temple, this temple belongs to the Buddhist Shingon sect. Both *Amidado* Hall and the main image, a famous wooden figure of Amitabha, are National Treasures. This latter excellent work was executed by Jocho (d. 1057, refer to p.188). Although some parts are scarcely visible, the mural paintings in the hall are also incomparable.

Kanjuji Temple [73] : Founded in 900, the Tokugawa Shogunate had the temple rebuilt in 1682. The most famous building is the *Shoin* (Study Hall) where the superb paintings on the sliding screens are attributed to Tosa Mitsuoki, a celebrated 17th-century artist. The beautiful garden, centered around a pond, has a "Kanjuji-style" stone lantern with a shade shaped like an open umbrella.

Zuishin-in Temple: The temple buildings date back to 1018, except for the Main Hall, which is a 1599 reconstruction. Legend has it that Ono-no-Komachi, the beautiful and talented poet of the Heian period, lived here. The well used for making up her face and the mound where she is said to have buried all the love letters from her admirers can be seen. The grounds of the temple, with plum and rhododendron trees growing in abundance, convey a feeling of serenity. It is a 15-min. walk from Kanjuji Temple.

Uji [73] : Pop. 173,027. Situated on the JR Nara Line, this is also the terminal for the Keihan Uji Line (17.3 km or 40 min. from Kyoto). This fashionable resort lies on the scenic banks of the Uji River in an area noted for its beautiful scenery, Buddhist temples, shrines and historic relics as well as for its top-quality green tea.

Mampukuji Temple [73] : Near Obaku Station on the JR Nara Line and Keihan Uji Line. Serving as the headquarters of the Obaku sect, the temple was completed in 1661 by Ingen (1592–1673), a famous Chinese priest of the Ming Dynasty. The temple structures, most of which are Important Cultural Properties, are designed in the Chinese style, which is quite different from the styles of other Buddhist temples in Japan.

It is worthy of note that the *Daiyuhoden* (Main Hall) was built of teakwood imported from Thailand. In *Hatto* (Lecture Hall), behind the Main Hall, are some 60,000 wood blocks that were used in printing the Obaku edition of the complete collection of Buddhist sutras in 7,334 volumes. They were printed here by the priest Tetsugen (1630–1682) from Higo Province (now, Kumamoto Prefecture) with the help of priest Ingen. Several of the temple's famous masterpieces painted by Ike-no-Taiga (1723–1776), an eminent artist, are on display in the Kyoto National Museum.

Byodo-in Temple [73] : Located east of the JR Uji Station, the temple stands on the banks of the Uji River. Originally a villa belonging to Fujiwara-no-Michinaga (966–1024), principal adviser to the Emperor, it was converted into a monastery in 1052. *Ho-odo* (Phoenix Hall), the original main hall, was built in 1053. Designated as a National Treasure, it still stands as an example of the finest religious architecture of the period when the Fujiwara family held a great deal of power.

The hall was designed to represent a phoenix, or *ho-o*—a mythological bird of Chinese origin—in the act of descending to earth, with the body represented by the central hall, the wings by the lateral corridors and the tail by the rear corridor. The overall effect is one of amazing architectural symmetry. A pair of bronze male and female phoenixes pose in flight atop the central hall.

The exterior of the hall was originally painted red and the interior was elaborately decorated. In fact, it is regarded as the zenith of the period's artistic excellence. Paintings on Buddhist subjects by Court painter Takuma Tamenari and others cover the doors, the panels on three sides and the walls behind the altar, although the colors have faded. The paintings on the door are reproductions.

The main image, Amitabha (a National Treasure) is attributed to Jocho (d. 1057), a noted Buddhist sculptor. This famous Amitabha is seated cross-legged on a lotus pedestal, his hands in his lap, his eyes half-open and slightly downcast, his eyebrows delicately drawn and with a noble nose of medium proportions. Overall, the figure creates an impression of perfect unity and harmony.

The ceiling is coffered and set with bronze mirrors, while the altar is inlaid with mother-of-pearl in designs of honeysuckle and other arabesques. The frieze around the upper part of the walls consists of 51 Bodhisattvas rising on clouds and playing music.

The graceful shape of the large bronze bell, which once hung in the belfry in the south elevation of the hall, has led it to be included as one of the three most famous temple bells in Japan. Although it has no inscription, its highly artistic designs of heavenly maidens and lions in relief on the surface suggest a Korean influence. Designated as a National Treasure, the bell is stored in the Treasure Hall along with the original phoenix as well as part of the frieze of Bodhisattvas and door murals.

Kannondo (Eleven-Headed Kannon Hall) is located north of Phoenix Hall. It is popularly called *Tsuridono* (Fishing Hall) because in the old days the waters of the Uji River ran underneath so that fishing could actually be enjoyed right inside the hall. Next to *Tsuridono* is a monument to Minamoto-no-Yorimasa (1104–1180), who killed himself here after he was defeated by troops of the Taira family. Because Yorimasa is said to have sat upon his open fan when committing suicide, the monument marking the spot of his death is surrounded by a fan-shaped stone fence. His tomb is inside the walls of Saisho-in, a subordinate temple behind Phoenix Hall.

On Tonoshima, an islet in the Uji River east of the temple grounds, stands a 13-story stone pagoda. It was erected in 1286 by the Buddhist priest Eison, also known as Kosho-Bosatsu (1201–1290), in order to prevent the killing of animals and to invoke the aid of the dragon king in the reconstruction of Uji Bridge. After being repeatedly ravaged by storms and floods, it lay in ruins for centuries until it was finally rediscovered in 1908 and rebuilt.

Agata Shrine: Standing close to Byodo-in, the shrine is dedicated to Konohana-Sakuyahime-no-Mikoto, the same goddess enshrined in Sengen Shrine in Fujinomiya at the foot of Mt. Fuji. The annual shrine festival is held in the darkness on the night of June 5—a unique and spectacular event known as the *Agata Matsuri*.

Hojo-in Temple: This temple of the Shingon-Ritsu sect also goes by the name of Hashi-dera, or Bridge Temple. Located at the north end of Uji Bridge, it contains a stone monument that gives an account of how the bridge first came to be constructed in 646. It is believed to be Japan's oldest stone monument with any sort of known history.

Uji Shrine: Situated a short distance from Hojo-in Temple, it is said to have been founded in 313 on the site of the residence of Prince Uji-no-Wakiiratsuko (d. 312). Dedicated to the prince, Emperor Nintoku (his eldest step-brother) and Emperor Ojin (his father), it consists of two separate shrines—the upper and lower.

Constructed in the early tenth century, the upper shrine buildings are said to be the oldest existing shrine buildings in Japan. Naturally, they have all been designated as National Treasures. There is a well with crystal-clear water that is numbered among the seven famous wells of Uji. The lower shrine, called Uji Shrine, has been designated as an Important Cultural Property as a fine example of Kamakura-period (1192-1333) architecture.

Koshoji Temple: Nestling cozily among the trees on the slope of Asahi Hill behind Uji Shrine, the temple was established in 1233. It was the first Soto-sect Buddhist temple built in Japan. The first abbot, priest Dogen (1200-1253), returned from Sung-Dynasty China and founded the new sect in Japan. He remained here for 11 years before moving on to Echizen Province (now, part of Fukui Prefecture), to build the famous Eiheiji Temple there. The present buildings were restored in 1649 after having lain in ruins for a long time.

The ancient sport of cormorant fishing is demonstrated every evening from mid-June to August 31 off Tonoshima, an islet in the Uji River.

Area 3. Tamba and Tango

The northwestern part of the Kinki District, is mountainous, with the northern portion facing the Japan Sea. The geographic features create beautiful landscapes here and there in this area, attracting many tourists from all over the country. Several feeders branch off the trunk line, the San-in Main Line. The main roads are National Highway 9 and the Maizuru Expressway.

Sasayama 70 : An old town of the Tamba District. It developed around Sasayama Castle, built by Tokugawa Ieyasu in 1609. High stone walls still remain at the castle site, which is also a popular place for viewing cherry blossoms. Sasayamaguchi Station can be reached in 1 hr.15 min. from Osaka by rapid train on the JR Fukuchiyma Line. The town is an additional 15-min. bus ride from the station, and about 70 km from Osaka on the Chugoku and Maizuru expressways.

"Unitopia Sasayama," 10 min. by car from Sasayamaguchi Station, has Carnival Show Case (flower botanical garden) with three climates (tropical, desert and alpine), a pool, tennis courts, fishing ponds, a lodge and camping facilities. The kilns for *Tamba-Tachikui-yaki* pottery are southwest of Sasayama in Konda. Denshukaikan Museum in "To-no-Sato", or Pottery's Village, displays superb old Tamba ware.

Fukuchiyama 70 ☎0773: Pop. 65,766. On JR it is 114 km from Osaka and 89 km from Kyoto. It is a junction on the San-in Main Line for the Fukuchiyama Line. The Maizuru Expressway is provided with the Fukuchiyama Interchange. Although Fukuchiyama developed as a castle town after the 16th century, it is now the commercial and industrial center of the Tamba District, concentrating on the manufacture of lumber and industrial machinery, the processing of food and the breeding of cattle.

Mt. Oe (alt. 833 m) is 25 km north of Fukuchiyama. It is familiar to every Japanese through its association with the legend described below.

The legend of the mountain originated around the year 990, when the caves of Mt. Oe were occupied by a bunch of bandits who committed such depredations that they were feared as the "Demons of Mt.Oe." Minamoto-no-Yorimitsu (948-1021), also known as Raiko, was dispatched to exterminate them. The adventures of Raiko and his followers also provide one of the most famous juvenile stories in Japan—the story of slaying of a monster called Shuten-doji.

Kameoka 71 ☎07712: Pop. 82,729. Situated about 20 km west of Kyoto, this ancient castle town is now an affluent rural city in the center of the Kameoka Basin along the middle reaches of the Hozu River. Farming and forestry are the most common industries in Kameoka, but it is also becoming a bedroom community for Kyoto. In addition, it is the starting point for shooting the rapids of the Hozu River to Arashiyama in Kyoto. Places worth visiting in the city include Yunohana Spa, Anaoji Temple, the 21st Station on the 33 Temple Pilgrimage in the Former Western Provinces and the ruins of Kameoka Castle, erected in 1579 by Akechi Mitsuhide.

Ayabe 70 ☎0773: Pop. 41,962. Situated 76 km from Kyoto, the town developed through the production of raw silk with many textile-related industries remaining today. Ayabe is located at the junction of the JR San-in Main Line and the JR Maizuru Line, with National Highway 27 passing by the city as well. Komyoji Temple on Mt. Kimio in the northeast part of the city is said to have been established in 599 by Prince Shotoku. Its *Niomon* Gate was built in 1248 and is a National Treasure.

Maizuru 70 ☎0773: Pop. 96,844. This old castle town faces Maizuru Bay, deeply indented in the northwest coast of Kyoto Prefecture. Blessed with a natural port on the coast of Japan Sea, it flourished as a naval station after the Meiji Restoration (1868) and today is a port for foreign trade. The scenic coast of Maizuru Bay, a part of Wakasawan (Bay) Quasi-National Park, has good fishing and swimming resorts. Shipyards, rolling-stock factories, chemical and glass factories and other plants are located in the city. It can be reached from Nishi-Maizuru on the JR Miyazu Line or from Higashi-Maizuru on the Obama Line. A long-distance ferry directly to Otaru in Hokkaido leaves from the port. Some of the local interesting sights include Matsuno-o Temple, the 29th Station on the 33 Temple Pilgrimage in the Former Western Provinces and Kongo-in Temple with a three-story pagoda—an Important Cultural Property.

Miyazu 70 ☎0772: Pop. 27,261. About 27 km from Nishi-Maizuru and some 30 km from Fukuchiyama on the Miyafuku Railway. Located in the innermost part of Miyazu Bay, scenic Amano-hashidate to the north attracts a large number of visitors all year round. The city is known as a prosperous fishing port and marine product processing center as well as for the production of Tango crepe.

Amanohashidate 70 : 2 hrs. 15 min. from Kyoto by limited express — a distance of 125 km, or 2 hrs. 30 min. from Osaka by limited express with a transfer at Fukuchiyama—a distance of 189 km. Famed since ancient times for its beautiful scenery, it is regarded as one of the three most scenic places in Japan along with Matsushima near Sendai and Miyajima in the Inland Sea and has been designated as a Special Place of Scenic Beauty by the government. The name, which means "Bridge of Heaven," was taken from the floating bridge of heaven upon which the god Izanagi-no-Mikoto and goddess Izanami-no-Mikoto of Japanese mythology stood while creating the islands of Japan. Actually, it is a 3.6-km-long sand bar varying in width from 15 to 150 m. Twisted pine trees of fantastic shapes grow upon it. It projects into Miyazu Bay, southwestward from Fuchu on the north coast of the bay to Monju on the opposite bank, forming a lagoon on its west side called Asoumi. It is divided into two parts on the Monju side and connected by a bridge. Most people take a 15-min. ferry to Ichinomiya from Monju because it affords an exceptionally good view of Amanohashidate and then take the cable car or lift to Kasamatsu Park. Here one can look diagonally across Amano-hashidate. Many people like to look at the scene upside-down from between their legs since it is supposed to make Amanohashidate look as if it were suspended in mid-air. Nariaiji Temple, another 6 min. by bus from the park, is the 28th Station on the 33 Temple Pilgrimage in the Former Western Provinces. Some of the best places from which to see Amanohashidate are Kasamatsu Park, Kunda Toge Pass in the east for a diagonal view, Ouchi Toge Pass in the west for a straight-forward view and Amanohashidate Viewland—6 min. on a lift from Amanohashidate Station on the Miyafuku Railway—for a side view.

Chionji Temple is right next to Monju wharf and is dedicated to one of the three most famous images of the Monju Bodhisattva in Japan (an Important Cultural Property), but it is not on public view. *Tahoto* Pagoda, constructed in 1500, is also an Important Cultural

Property.

The extensive peninsula spreading west of Miyazu Bay is called the Tango Peninsula. Its rugged coastline is covered with fishing villages, while many small islands dot the waters off the coast. It is a popular swimming area.

Area 4. Lake Biwa and Vicinity

East of Kyoto and across the mountains lies Japan's largest lake, Lake Biwa, brimming with fresh water. Shiga Prefecture, once called Omi Province, boasts a long history. The capital of Japan was transferred to Otsu, the current capital of the prefecture in 667. Scattered about the lush fields, gardens and mountain districts are many ancient shrines, temples and other cultural properties. A transportation network has been established around the lake, with roads and expressways as well as ferries that cross back and forth over the lake. The area has been designated as a quasi-national park.

Lake Biwa $\boxed{71}$: The largest lake in Japan, it was named because it is shaped like a *biwa*, or lute. The lake lies 85.6 m above sea level, has a circumference of 277 km, an area of 671.7 sq.km and a maximum depth of 103.8 m. Geologists believe that the lake was formed by a subsidence of the land 1.5 million years ago, when it was a much larger lake. The islets in the lake such as Chikubu, Take, Shiraishi and Okinoshima are composed of volcanic rock.

In accordance with the Chinese custom of the late 15th century, eight views around the lake (*Omi-Hakkei*) were selected as the most beautiful. From the north, they are "Evening Snow on Mt. Hira," "Flight of Wild Geese Descending on Katata," "Night Rain at Karasaki," "Evening Bell at Miidera Temple," "Breezes on a Fine Day at Awazu," "Evening Glow at Seta," "Autumn Moon at Ishiyama" and "Returning Sails at Yabase." In addition, *Biwako Hakkei*, or the eight best views of Lake Biwa, were selected in 1950 as the finest scenes of Biwako (Lake Biwa) Quasi-National Park. They are the "Panoramic View of Mt. Shizugatake," "Granite Cliffs of Kaizu-Osaki," " Placid View of Chikubu Island," "Ancient Castle of Hikone," "White Beach at Omatsuzaki," "Waterside Villages of Azuchi-Hachiman," "Thick Foliage on Mt. Hiei" and "Gentle Outflow of Seta-Ishiyama."

Koi (carp), *funa* (crucian carp), *ayu* (sweetfish) and many other types of aquatic life make their habitat in the lake. The freshwater clams are famous. Regular sightseeing boat and bus services are available daily from Hamaotsu in Otsu City to the many scenic spots on the lakeshore, including those mentioned above.

Otsu $\boxed{69}$ ☎0775: Pop. 241,257. A beautiful town on the southwest shore of Lake Biwa. It was the nation's capital for more than five years in the seventh century and has long flourished as a center for transportation across the lake. Today, Otsu is the capital of Shiga

Prefecture and an important sightseeing center. The city is also known for its modern industries such as nylon, polypropylene textiles, chemicals, electric appliances and precision machinery.

Otsu can be reached from Kyoto in 10 min. on the Tokaido Main Line—a distance of 10 km—or in 25 min. from Keishin-Sanjo Station (Kyoto) to Hamaotsu on the Keihan Keishin Line. The Meishin Expressway is served by the Otsu Interchange. Boats for lake excursions are boarded next to Hamaotsu Station.

Lake Biwa Culture Hall is 500 m east of Hamaotsu Station. Although the facade looks like a Japanese castle, the museum inside displays many artistic and archaeological National Treasures and Important Cultural Properties. The aquarium contains some 100 species of freshwater fish, focusing on those that live in Lake Biwa. The observation tower provides a sweeping view of Lake Biwa and the surrounding mountains.

Miidera Temple 69 : 5 min. by bus from Hamaotsu Station. Properly called Onjoji Temple, it is said to have been founded around 680 in memory of Emperor Kobun, son of Emperor Tenchi mentioned below. It is also the headquarters of the Tendai-Jimon sect. At the height of its prosperity, there were 850 buildings within the vast compound, with more than 60 still remaining. The temple also possesses many objects of historical and artistic value, several of which have been designated as National Treasures or Important Cultural Properties. *Kondo* (Main Hall), reconstructed in 1599, is also a National Treasure. The superbly constructed *Akaiya* (Hall at the Sacred Well) dating back to 1598, Two-Story Gate, Three-Story Pagoda and Belfry are all Important Cultural Properties. The old bell hanging in the Belfry in front of the Main Hall was chosen as one of the "Eight Views of Omi" (*Omi-Hakkei*) because it "tolls the knell of the parting day." *Kannondo* Hall is the 14th Station on the 33 Temple Pilgrimage in the Former Western Provinces and is dedicated to the *Nyoirin Kannon*. The view of Lake Biwa from the temple grounds is excellent.

Emman-in Temple 69 : Founded in 987, it is located north of *Niomon* Gate of Miidera Temple. *Shinden* (Emperor's Hall), an Important Cultural Property, is a large building constructed in 1647 through a contribution made by Emperor Meisho. The beautiful garden is full of enormous rocks and azalea bushes centered around a pond.

Otsu-e Art Museum: Standing in the precincts of Emman-in Temple. It contains some unique paintings called *Otsu-e* as well as works by the Edo-period artist Maruyama Okyo (1733–1795). One explanation for the origin of *Otsu-e* is that they were originally created by *ukiyo-e* artist Iwasa Matabei (1578–1650). Painted only with simple coloring, modern *Otsu-e* works are still done by the same traditional methods.

Omi Shrine 73 : Situated 400 m west of Omijingu-mae Station on the Keihan Ishiyama-Sakamoto Line. The shrine was established in

1940 in honor of Emperor Tenchi (626–671), who built a palace on this site in 667. There is a fine view of Lake Biwa from the precincts. Because Emperor Tenchi made Japan's first water clock named "Rokoku," the Clock Museum exhibits about 500 clocks from Japan and the rest of the world.

Hiyoshi Shrine ⬛71⬛: Since ancient times, it has enshrined the gods of Mt. Hiei and was later expanded to include the gods of Mt. Miwa in Nara and, furthermore, came to be worshipped as the tutelary shrine of Enryakuji Temple. The shrine was burned down in 1571 by Oda Nobunaga, but *Nishi-Honden* (West Main Hall) was reconstructed in 1586 and *Higashi-Honden* (East Main Hall) was completed in 1595. Created in what is called the "Hiyoshi" architectural style, both buildings are National Treasures. Many of the other structures are Important Cultural Properties. The three stone bridges also date from the 16th century, making them the oldest stone bridges still standing in Japan. *Sanno-matsuri* Festival celebrated three times a year is a gala fete that includes a gay parade of portable shrines and is particularly featured by continuous performances from April 12 to 15. The town where this shrine is located, Sakamoto, is also the temple town for Enryakuji Temple and many temples related to Enryakuji stand in the area. A cable car runs from Sakamoto Station on the Keihan Ishiyama-Sakamoto Line to Enryakuji Station near Enryakuji Temple.

Saikyoji Temple ⬛72⬛: Standing 1.5 km northwest of Sakamoto Station, it is the headquarters of the Tendai-Shinsei sect. Said to have been founded in the seventh century by Prince Shotoku, it was restored in 1486 by a priest named Shinsei. The large zelkova-wood *Hondo* (Main Hall; an Important Cultural Property), was constructed in 1739. Built in 1598, *Kyakuden* (Reception Hall; also an Important Cultural Property) is said to have been a part of Fushimi Castle and is decorated with paintings of the Kano school. The temple possesses many other treasures as well.

Shojuraigoji Temple ⬛72⬛: Located about 1 km northeast of Eizan Station on the JR Kosei Line. It was founded in 790 by saint Saicho, founder of the Tendai sect of Buddhism, and was restored in 1001 by Eshin. The Reception Hall, erected in 1641, is decorated with exquisite paintings by Kano Tan-yu, an eminent artist, and has been designated as an Important Cultural Property.

Ogoto Spa ⬛71⬛: Located southwest of Ogoto Station on the JR Kosei Line, facing the lake at the foot of Mt. Hiei. The spa boasts a long history as a curative mineral spring, but it also offers many recreational facilities.

Manganji Temple or Ukimido (Floating Temple) ⬛71⬛: In Katata, a northern part of Otsu, a little hall standing on the tip of a short bridge that projects over the lake, is popularly called *Ukimido* instead of its proper name of Manganji Temple. Said to have been founded in the tenth century to pray for safe travel on the lake, it lends the area a special atmosphere.

Gichuji Temple 69 : 8 min. on foot from the JR Zeze Station or the Keihan-Zeze Station. The small temple was founded in 1553. It is dedicated to Kiso Yoshinaka (1154–1184), a famed general of the Minamoto Clan. Next to Yoshinaka's grave is that of Matsuo Basho (1644–1694), Japan's greatest *haiku* poet. Basho was buried here at his own request.

Seta-no-karahashi Bridge: Once the route over the Seta River along the former principal road in Japan, the Tokaido Highway. In olden days, the bridge was an important strategic point and, when war broke out, it was frequently destroyed to defend the capital, Kyoto. The present structure was rebuilt in 1979, but it still maintains the old style. The view around the bridge in the evening, or "The Evening Glow at Seta," is one of the Eight Views of Omi. The Seta River that passes under the bridge and flows toward Osaka Bay is the sole river streaming out of Lake Biwa. At one point, it becomes the Uji River and then the Yodo River.

Ishiyamadera Temple 71 : A 5-min. walk from Ishiyamadera Station on the Keihan Ishiyama-Sakamoto Line. Belonging to the Toji school of the Shingon sect, it was founded in 749 by a famous priest of the Nara period, Roben, at the request of Emperor Shomu. It became popular to worship here during the Heian period. *Hondo* (Main Hall; a National Treasure), was built in 1096 and was supplemented by an outer section in 1602. In the big Main Hall, there is a small room named *Genji-no-ma* or "Prince Genji's Room," where Murasaki-Shikubu (987?–1014?), an eminent Court lady and author, is said to have written a part of her voluminous lifework "Genji Monogatari (Tale of Genji)." Graceful *Tahoto* (Two-Story Pagoda), donated by Minamoto-no-Yoritomo, founder of the Kamakura Shogunate, in 1194, is a National Treasure. The Belfry and many of the other edifices here are Important Cultural Properties. *Tsukimitei* (lit. Moon-Viewing Bower) not only has an excellent view of Seta-no-karahashi Bridge and the Seta River, but it is also a famed location for viewing the moon, as the name indicates.

Kusatsu 71 ☎0775: Pop. 91,091. Traditionally a lodging town south of Lake Biwa, it remains an important transportation point. The region is rich with fertile fields, among which quietly stand several shrines and temples containing National Treasures and Important Cultural Properties. The Shigaraki-Kogen Railway leaves from Kibukawa on the JR Kusatsu Line for Shigaraki, famous for its pottery.

Mt. Mikami 71 : Altitude of 432 m. Also called Omi-Fuji, it has a beautiful conical shape. Mikami Shrine in the western foothills is said to have been established by Fujiwara-no-Fuhito (659–720) at the command of the Emperor. *Hondo* (Main Hall) is a National Treasure, while *Romon* (Tower Gate) and *Haiden* (Oratory) are Important Cultural Properties.

Omi-Hachiman [71] ☎0748: Pop. 65,248. Situated on the southeast shore of Lake Biwa, facing Okinoshima Island. The town retains much of its Edo-period appearance, with some of these buildings open to the public.

Chomeiji Temple: 20 min. by bus from Omi-Hachiman Station on the JR Tokaido Main Line and up a flight of 808 stone stairs. Said to have been founded by Prince Shotoku (574-622), the present buildings date from 1524. Both the vermilion-painted Main Hall and the Three-Story Pagoda are Important Cultural Properties.

Azuchi [71]: The town where the famous Oda Nobunaga (1534-1582) built Azuchi Castle in 1579. It stood on Azuchiyama Hill, 1.5 km north of Azuchi Station on the JR Tokaido Main Line, and had a donjon that was 199 m high. The stone walls and the mausoleum of Nobunaga still remain today. Sokenji Temple was also erected by Nobunaga. A Three-Story Pagoda (an Important Cultural Property) towers over the grounds. A museum exhibiting archaeological arti-facts and other data about the prefecture stands on a hill named Omi Fudoki(Local History and Topography)-no-Oka southeast of the Azuchi Castle site.

Hikone [71] ☎0749: Pop. 97,127. 48 min. by *shin-kaisoku* (new, rapid train) from Kyoto on the JR Tokaido Main Line or 2 km from the Hikone Interchange on the Meishin Expressway. The town is famed for Hikone Castle, but spinning, machine manufacture and cement production are important industries today. Buddhist altar goods are also produced here.

Hikone Castle: Standing 1 km west of Hikone Station. It was completed in 1622 by Ii Naotsugu, the second lord of the Ii family. The donjon has three stories, rises 24 m and has white walls with beautifully variegated roofs. The castle is a National Treasure, while *Tembin Yagura* (turret) and the other buildings are Important Cultural Properties. The museum exhibits *noh* costumes, tea-ceremony utensils and other articles handed down by the Ii family. The cherry blossoms and maple leaves in the area are exquisite.

Genkyu-en, a garden laid out by the Ii family, is north of the castle. The lord of the castle at the end of the Edo period, Ii Naosuke (1815 -1860) was a *tairo*—the highest official of the Tokugawa Shogunate, but he was assassinated because he was the one who dared to decide opening of Japan to the West (refer to p.98).

Taga Shrine [71]: Situated southeast of Hikone, it can be reached in 10 min. on the Omi Railway from Hikone. The shrine is dedicated to the Shinto god Izanagi-no-Mikoto and goddess Izanami-no-Mikoto. It was once as popular a place of worship as Ise Jingu Shrines in Mie Prefecture. The solemn temple buildings were frequently ravaged by fire, with the present ones having been erected in 1932. The garden to the inner study is superb.

Koto-Sanzan (Three Temples on the East Side of Lake Biwa) [71]: It refers to the three temples southeast of Hikone on the east side of the Meishin Expressway: Saimyoji Temple, Kongorinji Temple and Hyakusaiji Temple. Saimyoji Temple has a magnificent garden as well as Main Hall and Three-Story Pagoda from the Kamakura period (1192–1333) that are both National Treasures. Kongorinji Temple also has an excellent garden and a Main Hall from the Kamakura period that is a National Treasure. The main hall of Hyakusaiji Temple is a tasteful structure erected in 1650. There is also a fine garden.

Nagahama ⬛71⬛ ☎0749: Pop. 55,351. It is situated on the east shore of Lake Biwa, 7.7 km, 15 min. from Maibara on the JR Hokuriku Main Line. Formerly the first fief of Toyotomi Hideyoshi (1536–1598), today it is a flourishing commercial and industrial city as well as a base for sightseeing trips to Chikubu Island and the northernmost district of the lake. Its products include silk crepe, diesel engines and polyethylene products.

Daitsuji Temple (Nagahama Betsuin): Located 500 m east of Naga-hama Station, it is a branch of Higashi-Honganji Temple of Kyoto. Standing at the rear of Toyotomi Park on the site of the former castle, the temple is an impressive edifice designed in the Momoyama style. The Main Hall and Visitors' Hall were constructed by Toyotomi Hideyoshi in 1586 in the Fushimi Castle compound and later moved here. They are both designated as Important Cultural Properties. The temple garden is also splendidly laid out in the Momoyama style.

Northern and Western Lake Biwa

An exhibition of *Bonbai*, or beautifully potted old plum trees, is held every year from January to March in the celebrated garden at Keiunkan Hall by Nagahama port. Around the lake are several temples, each with excellent Buddhist images; e.g., Koganji (or Dogenji) Temple with Eleven-Headed *Kannon*, a National Treasure. Towering 422 m above the north side of the lake, Mt. Shizugatake is a famous old battlefield. Take a bus from Kinomoto Station on the JR Hokuriku Main Line to O-oto and then a 3-min lift to reach the top, where one can obtain a panoramic view of the surrounding scenery. Lake Yogonoumi, with a circumference of 6.4 km, lies serenely in the northern foothills.

Chikubu Island ⬛71⬛: Measuring 2 km in circumference, this island lies in the northern part of the lake. It is the site of Hogonji Temple, dedicated to *Kannon* and *Benzaiten*—Goddess of Music, Speech, Wisdom and Money-making. The temple is said to have been found-ed more than 1,200 years ago by an eminent priest named Gyoki (668–749) by order of Emperor Shomu. Beside the temple stands a small shrine, Tsukubusuma, which is now a National Treasure. It is said that the materials for the magnificent buildings were originally part of Fushimi Castle. The island has high granite cliffs and is covered with dense thickets of bamboo, pine and cedar trees. Excursion boats to the island leave from Otsu, Hikone, Imazu, Iiura and Nagahama.

Mt. Hira ⬚71⬚ : The Hira mountains, the highest peak of which is Mt. Bunagatake (alt. 1,214 m), rise to the west of Lake Biwa. One can reach Kitahira Toge (Pass) on the slope of the peak from Hira Station on the JR Kosei Line (about 40 min. from Kyoto) by bus, chairlift and ropeway. It is necessary to hike for 1 hr.30 min. to reach the summit. The exquisite sight of the "Evening Snow on Mt. Hira" is one of the "Eight Views of Omi." The surrounding area is a popular resort for hiking and skiing, and the maple leaves in autumn are magnificent.

Omatsuzaki ⬚71⬚ : Also called Omi-Maiko, it is located southwest of Omi-Maiko Station on the JR Kosei Line (about 45 min. from Kyoto). The 1-km-long, crescent-shaped beach on Lake Biwa is suitable for swimming, camping and fishing. With Mt. Hira looming in the background, the "White Beach of Omatsuzaki" is popular with visitors as one of the "Eight Views of Lake Biwa."

Kaizu-Osaki ⬚71⬚ : 25 min. by bus from Omi-Imazu Station (1 hr.10 min. from Kyoto) on the JR Kosei Line. It is a picturesque, rocky place overlooking an abyss. The granite cliffs, covered with venerable pine trees, are a familiar scene on Lake Biwa. There is also a pleasant view of Chikubu Island. The "Oku(Inner)-Biwako Parkway" runs for about 19 km east on the peninsula across the cove, offering excellent lakeside scenery for a drive.

Area 5. Nara and Yamato Region

Nara ⬚76-77/90-91⬚ ☎0742

Pop.343,580. The capital of Nara Prefecture. Nara and its vicinity, a veritable repository of art objects, occupies what was once the northwest portion of Yamato Province (now, Nara Prefecture) and played an important part in early Japanese history. The region was the cradle of Japan's arts, crafts, literature and industries. Much can be learned about Japan's distant past from the many classic Shinto shrines and Buddhist temples still standing in Nara. These structures are situated amidst scenic surroundings, creating a tranquil, restful atmosphere.

In 710, the seat of government was moved here from a place 20 km south of Nara called Fujiwarakyo by Empress-Regnant Gemmyo and the new capital was set up on a grand scale. Called Heijokyo, it maintained this function through the reigns of seven emperors until 784, when Emperor Kammu moved the capital to Nagaoka, southwest of Kyoto. During these 74 years as the capital, Nara left an important mark on Japanese history.

TRANSPORTATION

Osaka and Nara are connected by the JR Kansai Main Line and the Nara Line of Kinki Nippon Railway (Kintetsu). There are direct trains from the JR Osaka Station via Tennoji, while Kintetsu runs from Namba in Osaka. By highway, one can take the Hanna National Highway across the col of Mt. Ikoma or the Nishi-Meihan Expressway via National Highway 24. Kyoto and Nara are connected by the Kintetsu Kyoto Line and the JR Nara Line. National Highway 24 runs from Kyoto for those who prefer to drive.

SPECIALTIES

Local products include *Nara-ningyo* (carved wooden dolls), writing brushes, india ink, deer horn products, lacquerware, *Nara-uchiwa* (rounded, non-folding fans) and *Kogaku* masks (used in traditional dances).

TRAVEL ADVICE

Kofukuji Temple, Nara Park (Deer Park), Todaiji Temple, Kasuga Taisha Shrine and other main attractions are within walking distance of the station. Buses also circle the city center and many taxis wait in front of the station. Yakushiji Temple and Toshodaiji Temple can be reached in 20 min. by bus. Kintetsu also runs to the nearest station, Nishinokyo, with a transfer at Saidaiji Station.

Refer to the supplement for details regarding the "i" **System Information Center** in Nara.

PLACES OF INTEREST

Nara Park 91 : Popularly called "Deer Park" because some 1,000 deer inhabit the area, it is the largest such park in Japan with an area of 5.25 sq.km. It is covered by a broad lawn on which groves of trees and plants, both natural and afforested, of many kinds grow, including huge cedars, oaks, andromedas and wisteria. Tame deer roam about picturesquely in twos and threes. Most of the classical structures from the ancient city are near Nara Park, which is immediately east of Kintetsu Nara Station. After passing through busy Sanjo-dori Street from the JR Nara Station, the visitor will see the famous Sarusawa Pond just to the south of the entrance.

Sarusawa Pond 90 : A 360 m-in-circumference pond lined with weeping willows. The *Goju-no-To* (Five-Story Pagoda) of Kofukuji Temple standing on a hill north of the lake is reflected on the water, presenting a beautiful sight. On nice days, many turtles basking along the edge of the pond in the noonday sun create an atmosphere of peaceful tranquility.

Kofukuji Temple 90 : Located north of Sarusawa Pond, this temple is the headquarters of the Hosso sect of Buddhism and one of the so-called "Seven Great Temples of Nara." It was originally called Yamashina Temple because it was founded at Yamashina, Kyoto, in 669 by the consort of Fujiwara-no-Kamatari (614–669), founder of the Fujiwara family, who died just before the temple was erected. In the temple, the consort placed images of Sakyamuni and the Four Heavenly Guardians that are said to have been made by special order of Kamatari while he was still alive. In 678, the Yamashina Temple was moved to a place in Umayasaka near present Asuka, south of Nara, and renamed Umayasaka Temple. When the center of government was moved to Nara in 710, the temple was again transferred to the new capital by the second son and heir of Kamatari, Fujiwara-no-Fuhito, who made it the tutelary temple of the Fujiwara family. Concurrent with the move, the name of the temple was changed to Kofukuji Temple, which means "Happiness-Producing Temple." Subsequently, it enjoyed great prosperity year after year, receiving the respect of both the Imperial Family and the public. At the height of its prosperity, Kofukuji Temple had as many as 175 buildings, but all of the original buildings were destroyed through the fires of war and had to be reconstructed.

Chukondo (Central Main Hall): Reconstructed in 1819 as a provisional edifice. It contains the wooden figures of Sakyamuni (the main image), *Yakuo-Bosatsu* (Buddha Yakuo), *Yakujo-Bosatsu* (Buddha Yakujo) and *Shitenno-Ritsuzo* (Four Heavenly Guardians)—all Important Cultural Properties.

Goju-no-To (Five-Story Pagoda): A National Treasure situated on the grounds of Kofukuji Temple. The second-highest pre-modern pagoda in Japan, it is probably the first object that attracts the attention of visitors to Nara. With a height of about 50 m, this imposing structure was first built in 730 in accordance with the wishes of Empress Komyo, the pious consort of Emperor Shomu. Destroyed by fire five times, it was reconstructed each time, following the original style in every detail (the present structure dating from 1426). It contains four Buddhas on the first story—*Amida-Nyorai* in the west, Sakyamuni in the south, *Yakushi-Nyorai* in the east and *Miroku-Bosatsu* (Maitreya Bodhisattva) in the north.

Tokondo Hall (a National Treasure): Situated immediately north of the Five-Story Pagoda. This temple was founded in 726 by Emperor Shomu as a place where he could pray for ex-Empress-Regnant Gensho's recovery from illness and for the peace of the state. It was repeatedly destroyed by fire before being rebuilt in 1415 along the same plan and elegance as the original. The main image of *Yakushi-Nyorai* (an Important Cultural Property), the god of medicine, stands on an earthen platform in the center of the hall, attended by *Nikko-Bosatsu* and *Gakko-Bosatsu*. There are also several statues of *Monju-Bosatsu*, Sakyamuni and other Buddhist gods.

Sanju-no-To (Three-Story Pagoda): Also a National Treasure, it is situated just above the stone steps northwest of Sarusawa Pond. This structure was originally erected in 1143 in accordance with the wishes of Taikemmonin, consort of Emperor Toba (1103-1156), but it was demolished by fire and reconstructed during the Kamakura period (1192-1333). Few pagodas are so well proportioned and graceful in shape. The interior of the first story was profusely decorated with paintings of the "Thousand Buddhas," although they are just barely visible now.

Nan-endo Hall: Located east of the Three-Story Pagoda, it is an octagonal hall containing as the main image a wooden statue of *Fukukensaku-Kannon*, which is believed to have been carved in 1188 by Kokei, father of Unkei—a famous sculptor of the 12th to 13th centuries. The figure is a National Treasure. The hall itself was established in 813 by Fujiwara-no-Fuyutsugu (775-826) to fulfill his father's dying wish. After repeated destruction by fire, the present hall, resembling Hokuendo in many respects, was erected in 1741. This is the ninth Station on the 33-Temple Pilgrimage in the Former Western Provinces. The bronze lantern in front of the hall dates from 816 and is an Important Cultural Property.

Hokuendo Hall: Standing north of the Three-Story Pagoda. It is another octagonal hall founded in 721 by Prince Nagayao, the Minister of the Right (the second-highest ranking office of the Imperial Court), at the command of Empress-Regnant Gensho. She wanted to pray for the peace of Fujiwara-no-Fuhito, who died in 720. The hall has been rebuilt four times. Dating from 1208 and designated as a National Treasure, the present structure displays a beautiful, bold simplicity. The principal image is a wooden, seated figure of *Miroku-Bosatsu*, which is 1.4 m high and said to be the work of a noted sculptor named Unkei. The image is a National Treasure. The hall also houses another National Treasure—a colored wooden statue of priest Seshin, but the statue of priest Muchaku, which formerly stood here to form a pair, has been moved to the Kokuhokan (Treasure House).

Kokuhokan: A ferroconcrete building with a floor space of 1,122 sq. m. Built on the precincts of Kofukuji Temple, it stores as many as 20,000 temple treasures including 63 national treasures and Important Cultural Properties. The hall contains a majority of the Buddhist images in the possession of the temple. Some of the most important of these are the *Hachibushu* (Eight Guardians), including *Ashura*, from the late Nara period (710-784); the *Judaideshi* (Ten Venerable Priests) of the same period; wooden statues of the *Junishinsho* (Twelve Divine Generals) from the Heian period (794-1185); *Kongo-Rikishi* (Deva Kings), said to have been carved by master sculptor Jokei in the Kamakura period, and figures of *Tentoki* and *Ryutoki*, said to have been created by Koben, the son of Unkei. All of these objects are National Treasures.

Nara National Museum 91 : Located east of Kofukuji Temple, the museum was established by the Imperial Household Department (now the Imperial Household Agency) in 1895. Because it is known for its superb collection of Buddhist art, it is an excellent place to discern its historical transitions, containing as it does many famous works from ancient shrines and temples in Nara as well as from other historical sites throughout the country.

Todaiji Temple (Great Eastern Temple) 91/93 : The main headquarters of the Kegon sect, this temple is well known for its principal image—the *Daibutsu* (Great Buddha), one of the largest bronze statues in the world. *Kegon*, or Avatamska in Sanskrit, literally means a garland or a bouquet of beautiful flowers. In the first week after having become the Enlightened One, or a Buddha, Sakyamuni sat down in profound meditation. Then in the second week, he preached the *Kegon* doctrine—the very beginning of all his teachings.

The construction of Todaiji Temple commenced at the command of Emperor Shomu (701-756) in 745 and was successfully completed in 752. Through successive generations, Todaiji Temple has enjoyed the supreme honor as the head of all the provincial temples as well as one of the "Seven Great Temples of Nara."

Nandaimon (Great South Gate): Designated as a National Treasure, the imposing front gate of Todaiji Temple is supported by 18 pillars, each measuring a little over 25 m high and 97 cm in diameter. It was constructed sometime during the late Nara period (710-784), but it was blown down by a typhoon in 962 and rebuilt in 1199. The exterior niches contain two wooden 8.4-m-tall figures of the *Kongo-Rikishi* (Deva Kings), the guardians of Buddhism. These statues are said to have been sculptured in 1203 by Unkei and Kaikei, another famous sculptor of the day, with the aid of 20 apprentices and were completed within only three months. Designated as National Treasures, these two statues are regarded as the ideal images for the *Kongo-Rikishi*, and perhaps nothing is comparable in terms of vigor and animation. In the rear niches are a pair of *komainu* (lion-like guardian dogs) measuring 1.8 m tall and resting on 1.3-m-high stone pedestals. It is believed they were carved in 1196 by Chinnakei (a Chinese craftsman from the Sung Dynasty) from stones brought from his native country. The *komainu* are Important Cultural Properties.

Daibutsuden (Hall of the Great Buddha): A National Treasure. The original was burned down in 1180 by Taira-no-Shigehira (1156-1185), son of Kiyomori, a powerful general of the Taira Clan. Kofukuji Temple also shared the same fate. Reconstruction was sponsored by the abbot Chogen (1121-1206), with the completion ceremony taking place in 1195. Emperor Gotoba (1180-1239), Shogun Minamoto-no-Yoritomo (1147-1199) and other dignitaries participated in the formalities. The Hall of the Great Buddha was again reduced to ashes in 1567 through the destructive force of internal strife, but it was restored again in 1709 by the priest Kokei. This is the Main Hall, or *Daibutsuden*, that one sees today. It measures 57 m across the front and has a depth of 50.5 m. The present total area is only two-thirds that of the original building, but it retains the same height of 47.5 m and is the largest ancient wooden structure in the world.

The first object attracting the attention of visitors entering the precincts of the Hall of the Great Buddha is the pair of gilt ornaments decorating both ends of the roof ridge. They are called *kutsugata* (shoe shape) or *shibi* (kite tail) because they are supposed to resemble these objects. In olden times, according to Chinese superstition, they were a charm against fire as well as the standard ornaments for the roof ridges of Buddhist temples and palaces.

Octagonal Bronze Lantern: A National Treasure. Standing 4.6 m high and set just in front of the Hall of the Great Buddha, it dates from later part of the Nara period (710-784). It is considered one of the finest works of its kind.

Daibutsu (Great Buddha): A National Treasure. The holiest object in Todaiji Temple, it is worshipped with the utmost reverence. The *Daibutsu* represents *Birushana-Butsu* (Vairocana), regarded as the original or spiritual body of Sakyamuni by the Kegon sect. In other words, *Birushana-Butsu* is the root and Sakyamuni is the branch. This enormous bronze casting was commissioned by Emperor Shomu at Shigaraki Palace, south of Lake Biwa, but the effort ended in failure. Work recommenced at Nara in 745 and was finally success-fully completed in 749. The casting was done in eight sections over three years. The figure is seated cross-legged on a tremendous bronze pedestal, the hands forming the mudra—a hand symbol re-presenting preaching. The right hand is a symbol that gives peace of mind, while the left assumes the symbol that grants wishes.

The statue is 16.2 m tall and has a face 5.3 m long by 3.2 m wide, eyes 1 m wide, a nose 50 cm high, a mouth 1.3 m wide, ears 2.6 m long, hands 2 m long and thumbs 1.6 m long. It is estimated that 437 tons of bronze, 75 kg of mercury, 130 kg of pure gold, 7 tons of vegetable wax, and vast amounts of charcoal and other materials were used to make the statue. The designer of the Great Buddha was Kuninaka-no-Kimimaro (d. 774), a Korean from the Paikche kingdom.

The dedication ceremony was held in 752 in the presence of Empress-Regnant Koken, her parents, ex-Emperor Shomu, his Empress Consort and all the court dignitaries as well as 10,000 priests and nuns. An earthquake in 855 shook off the head of the Great Buddha, but it was repaired in 861. This head and the right hand melted when the hall burned down in 1180, then in 1567, the head was lost again by fire. The present head is a 1692 restoration, while the body of the original statue has had to be repaired and partially replaced with new pieces of bronze since then.

The pedestal on which the Buddha sits is 20.7 m in circumference and is composed of 56 bronze lotus petals, each of which is 3 m high and is alternately turned upward and downward. Some of these petals are from the original construction. The pedestal is engraved with fine lines representing the *Rengezokai* (Padmalokadhatu), or Lotus-Flower World—a paradise believed to have been founded by Buddha Vairocana. The bronze pedestal rests on a massive stone foundation 2 m high.

A huge, gilt wooden halo decorated with the Sixteen Buddha incarnations is attached to the back of the Great Buddha. The exact date this halo was made is not known, but it is believed to date from the Genroku era (1688-1704).

Two large gilt wooden statues stand in front of the Great Buddha, the right one representing *Nyoirin-Kannon* and the left *Kokuzo-Bosatsu*. The former answers the prayers of believers, granting them good fortune through the miraculous power of a Cintamani, or Wishing Gem. The latter is believed to possess wisdom and happiness as vast as the air (*Koku*); hence, the name. These two fine statues were executed in the Genroku era, but the sculptor is unknown.

The *Komokuten* in the left corner behind the *Daibutsu* is a strange-looking wooden 5.5-m-tall statue of a figure trampling a demon under his feet. This excellent piece dates from 1797. As one of the Four Heavenly Guardians, *Komokuten* destroys all obstacles in the path of Buddhism and its devotees.

The model of the original Todaiji Temple on the right side of *Komokuten* shows the temple as it was at the time of its first construction. *Tamonten*, another of the Four Heavenly Guardians, is in the right corner behind the Great Buddha, with demon lying in agony under his sinewy feet. With an angry countenance he always watches the north, considered ominous in Japanese divination, to protect Buddhism and its believers.

Behind the Great Buddha to the right is a large pillar with a square hole at the bottom. According to superstition, anyone able to pass through the hole will be fortunate enough to enter paradise.

Kaidan-in Temple 93 : West of the *Daibutsuden*, this small temple is well known for its 1.6-m-tall clay images of the Four Heavenly Guardians (National Treasures). *Kaidan* refers to the terrace upon which Buddhist ordination is given. The original terrace was built in 754 in front of the *Daibutsuden* with soil brought from Mt. Wu Tai Shan in China by the Chinese priest Ganjin (688-763) at the command of the ex-Emperor Shomu. Ganjin is said to have given ordination to more than 500 Buddhists. Statues of Sakyamuni and *Taho-Nyorai* stand at the center of the temple, while the Four Heavenly Guardians protect each of the four corners. Clad in full armor, the guardians were once painted in profuse colors of which traces can still be seen. They carry weapons in their hands and trample demons under their heavy feet. Their furious faces, expressive eyebrows, sinewy muscles and iron limbs are most realistically executed. The temple was burned down several times, but the present structure is said to date from 1731.

Shosoin Treasure Repository 93 : Northwest of the *Daibutsuden*. This is a treasure house on stilts made of logs, with triangular cross sections piled up to form the walls in an architectural style called *Azekura*. Under the administration of the Imperial Household Agency today, it consists of three compartments in which art works of the late Nara period (710-784) such as jewels, glasses, musical instruments, silver objects, writing instruments, masks and mirrors are preserved. Many of these precious objects formerly belonged to

Emperor Shomu and were donated to Todaiji Temple on his death by his consort, Empress Komyo, and their daughter, Empress-Regnant Koken. Today, the treasures are preserved in two new ferroconcrete repositories and some of them are displayed annually at the museum in Nara Park from late October to early November.

Shoro (Belfry): Located east of the *Daibutsuden*, this structure dates from the 1200s. It contains one of the largest bells in Japan, measuring 3.9 m tall, 2.7 m in diameter and 24 cm thick, and weighing 26.3 t. Designated as a National Treasure, the bell was originally cast in 752, but it was badly damaged by a severe typhoon. It is believed the bell was recast in 1239.

Sangatsudo Temple 93 : Situated on a rise a little east of the *Shoro* (Belfry), this temple (a National Treasure) has a name meaning March Hall because yearly services of the Lotus Sutra are held every March by the lunar calendar. This temple is also called *Hokkedo* (Hall of the Lotus Sutra). Roben (689–773), who later became the first abbot of Todaiji Temple, founded it originally as Kinshoji Temple. The main section of the present temple was completed in 750, while the *Raido* (Chapel) was added in the mid-Kamakura period (1192–1333). The main image at *Sangatsudo* is the celebrated, dry-lacquer statue of *Fukukensaku-Kannon* (a National Treasure), which stands in the center of a platform surrounded by 14 other statues. It is believed *Fukukensaku-Kannon* spends the year alleviating the sufferings of all beings. The 3.6-m-high, dry-lacquer standing statue is three-eyed and eight-armed. The crown has a diameter of 61 cm, it is made of silver openwork and is ornamented with 20,000 pearls as well as agates, crystals and other jewels. Designated as National Treasures, the clay images of *Nikko-Bosatsu* (Surya-Prabha) and *Gakko-Bosatsu* (Candra-Prabha) flanking the *kannon* are so exquisite that they are regarded among the most prominent examples of late Nara-period (710–784) workmanship. Next to these two statues are 4-m-tall, dry-lacquer figures of *Bonten* (Brahma) and *Taishakuten* (Indra), which are also National Treasures. The Four Heavenly Guardians (dry-lacquer works; National Treasures) stand in the four corners of the hall. On each side of the front of the hall is a statue of one of the *Kongo-Rikishi* (Deva Kings; National Treasures), who guard the way with fierce expressions. There are two portable shrines in the rear corners behind the main image, the one on the right containing *Benzaiten* and the one on the left—*Kisshoten* (both of which are Important Cultural Properties). Among the cluster of other statues are the images of *Fudomyo-o* and *Jizo-Bosatsu* (Important Cultural Properties). Lastly, the 1.7-m-tall clay image representing a guardian of Buddhism, *Shitsukongoshin* (or Vajrapani; a National Treasure) is reverently enshrined in a miniature shrine behind *Fukukensaku-Kannon*. Except on December 16—the date of Roben's death, the statue is not open to view.

Nigatsudo Temple 93 : Located on an elevation diagonally behind

Sangatsudo, the temple is so named (*Nigatsudo* meaning February Hall) because an important religious rite called *Shunie* is held here every February by the lunar calendar. The temple was founded in 752 by the priest Jitchu, a disciple of Roben, and is noted for the *Dai* (Large)-*Kannon* and the *Sho* (Small)-*Kannon*—two historical images of the *Juichimen-Kannon* (Eleven-Headed *Kannon*). The latter is said to have been retrieved from Osaka Bay by Jitchu and is believed to be always warm to the touch. Both of these images are strictly hidden from public view so that their measurements are unknown. The temple building was burned down in 1667 but was rebuilt two years later. The *Shunie*, or *Omizutori* (Water-Drawing Ceremony), the most famous event at the temple, is celebrated from March 1 to 14 by the solar calendar, with the torchlight procession on the night of the 12th attracting a large number of spectators. The veranda provides a panoramic view of the *Daibutsuden* and its surroundings.

Tamukeyama Shrine ⬚93⬚ : Situated to the north of Wakakusa Hill, this is also known as Tamukeyama Hachiman Shrine and is dedicated to Emperor Ojin (reigned 270-310), his Empress and his parents. Originally dating from 749, it was destroyed by fire in 1642 and rebuilt by the priest Kokei in 1691.

The *Azekura* is an unusual kind of building, constructed with an elevated floor and triangular logs joined without nails. It is used as a repository for valuable objects. There are two *Azekura* just outside the front gate of Tamukeyama Shrine, the southern one belonging to the shrine and the northern one forming part of Todaiji Temple.

Kasuga Taisha Shrine ⬚91⬚ : Situated in the midst of verdant woods. Few shrines contain a greater atmosphere of peace and sanctity. The main hall of Kasuga Taisha Shrine, actually composed of four buildings, is constructed in the Kasuga architectural style and painted vermilion. These four buildings are respectively dedicated to Take-mikazuchi-no-Mikoto and Futsunushi-no-Mikoto—two brave generals in the Age of the Gods, Amenokoyane-no-Mikoto—the remotest ancestor of the Fujiwara family — and his consort, Himegami.

Kasuga Taisha Shrine was founded in 710 by Fujiwara-no-Fuhito and made the tutelary shrine of the Fujiwara family by his great-grandson, Nagate, in 768. The shrine has been reconstructed every 20 years, whether in need of repairs or not, along the lines of its original construction, with perhaps slight modifications in minor areas. The first *torii* gate stands at the end of Sanjo-dori Street, which runs east of the JR Nara Station. The second *torii* stands a short distance beyond, the eastward road from which is lined on both sides with stone lanterns. Twice a year, during the *Mantoro* festivals (February 3 or 4 and August 15), some 3,000 lanterns are lit at night. Passing through the south gate, visitors come to spacious grounds containing an old, floorless structure called *Heiden* dating from 1650 that once served as the offering hall. The *Naoraiden* (Reception Hall) on the left is of the same date, and various ceremonies are performed here.

The Main Hall of Kasuga Taisha Shrine stands solemnly on the rise behind the *Heiden*. Surrounded by an impressive gallery, the Main Hall is composed of four buildings, all National Treasures. The *Utsushidono* (Transfer Hall) is behind a large cedar growing in the left corner of the main hall. Divine images are temporarily transferred here during repairs to the Main Hall. The passageway connecting the *Utsushidono* and the Main Hall is said to have been executed by the famous sculptor Hidari-Jingoro (refer to p.543) and is an Important Cultural Property.

The *Yadorigi*, composed of seven species, blooms to the north of the *Utsushidono*. Six different kinds of trees and bushes—wisteria, camellia, nandin, cherry, maple, and elder—are grafted to the trunk of an evergreen tree called *isu* (distylium racemosum), creating a botanical wonder.

As the official festival of the shrine held on March 13, the Kasuga Festival is famous for the elegant dance offered to the gods.

Kasuga Wakamiya Shrine 91 : The shrine lies south of the Kasuga Taisha Shrine Main Hall, a couple of minutes on foot from the *Nammon* (South Gate). It is dedicated to the Shinto deity Ameno-Oshikumone-no-Mikoto, son of Amenokoyane-no-Mikoto. Architecturally, it is of the Kasuga-style, with the present structure dating from 1863. There are numerous stone lanterns along both sides of the road leading to the shrine. The road ends in front of a low, elongated building divided into three sections, the south section serving as the *Kaguraden* (Sacred Dance Hall). The date of construction is recorded as 1613.

The *kagura* (a sacred dance) is performed in the Sacred Dance Hall by maidens called *miko*. Clad in white vestments with long red culottes, each holds a branch of the sacred *sakaki* tree, a fan and tiny bells. The orchestra for the *kagura* consists of flutes, *hyoshigi* (wooden clappers), *koto* (a sort of zither), *sho* (a free-reed mouth organ or a kind of panpipe), *hichiriki* (a kind of flageolet) and drums.

The annual celebration, *On-Matsuri*, held from December 16 to 17 in honor of the Kasuga Wakamiya Shrine, is the largest festival in Nara. In addition to the mysterious rites at the shrine, it is famous for the historical costume procession with clothing representing each period. There is a deer park near the second *torii* gate of Kasuga Taisha Shrine, with more than 1,000 tame deer, believed to be divine messengers, usually roaming about Nara Park and the precincts of the shrines and temples. The sight in the evening as they gather in the park is quite unique. Every year around mid-October, their horns are cut—a popular event called *tsunokiri*.

Nara Dreamland 74 : This is a large amusement park modeled after the American Disneyland that covers 500,000 sq.m on Kurokamiyama Hill in the northwest part of Nara City. It is reached in 10 min. by bus from the JR Nara Station.

Mt. Kasuga 74 : This is the generic name for several peaks, the highest reaching 460 m. Since it has been regarded as the abode of the gods from ancient times, the trees are considered sacred and have never been cut down. Hunting is prohibited as well. A pleasant round trip to these mountains is popular with those wishing to admire the beautiful verdure of spring and summer as well as the abundant colors of autumn. The entire route can be covered by car in 1 hr.

Wakakusa Hill: Alt of 342 m, north of Kasuga Taisha Shrine. Unlike Mt. Kasuga, this rise is bare of trees and offers a fine view from the top. The hill is covered with grass, which is burned on the night of January 15 every year. After fires are set around the bottom of the hill, the flames cover the hill, making a fantastic spectacle. This burning of dead grass on the hill is called *yamayaki*.

Shin-Yakushiji Temple 91 : Southwest of Kasuga Wakamiya Shrine, the temple was founded in 747 by Empress Komyo (701-760), the pious consort of Emperor Shomu, in order to pray for the recovery of her husband from an eye infection. The 1.9-m-tall, seated main image is a carved wooden *Yakushi-Nyorai* (a National Treasure)—the Lord of the Eastern "Joruriko" Paradise. This famous statue is installed in the center of an earthen pedestal 7.5 m in circumference and guarded by a circle of the *Junishinsho* (Twelve Divine Generals). These statues are 1.7 m-2.4 m tall, with expressions of great rage; 11 of them are National Treasures. With the exception of the Main Hall (a National Treasure), which is a classic example of late Nara-period (710-784) architecture, all the other buildings in the Shin-Yakushiji Temple compound were reduced to ashes long ago, although the *Shoro* (Belfry) and *Nammon* (Southern Gate) were reconstructed during the Kamakura period (1192-1333). Another priceless treasure is a painting of Nirvana (an Important Cultural Property), which with that of the Kongobuji Temple on Mt. Koya (refer to p.741) constitute a typical pair of portrayals of Nirvana from the late Heian period (794-1185).

Former Site of Heijokyo Palace 74 : 1 km east of Yamato-Saidaiji Station on the Kintetsu Line, 5 min. by bus, or 2.5 km northwest of the JR Nara Station, 15 min. by bus via Kintetsu Nara Station. This area flourished as the political and cultural center of the late Nara period from 710, when Empress-Regnant Gemmyo moved the capital here from the Asuka district, until Emperor Kammu moved the capital in 784 to Nagaoka—southwest of the present Kyoto. The capital city, Heijo, was grandly laid out in imitation of Changan, the capital of the T'ang Dynasty in China. The palace occupied about 1.07 sq.km. Today, 1.02 sq. km of this ancient palace site has been designated as a Special Place of Historical Importance. Halls for exhibiting objects excavated from the site and for preservation of the site as well as for partial architectural reconstructions stand here.

Kairyuoji Temple 74 : About 2 km northwest of the JR Nara Station, or 15 min. by bus via Kintetsu Nara Station. The temple was founded in 731 in accordance with the wishes of Empress Komyo, consort of the Emperor Shomu. The site was formerly the property of Fujiwara-no-Fuhito, father of the Empress. Although almost all of the structures were lost many years ago, the remaining buildings such as the *Seikondo* (Western Main Hall) and *Kyozo* (Sutra Library; both Important Cultural Properties) were renovated to a considerable extent in the 12th century. The construction technique of the wooden, 4-m-tall *Goju-no-Shoto* (Little Five-Story Pagoda; a National Treasure) is quite similar to that of the *Sanju-no-To* (Three-Story Pagoda) at Yakushiji Temple.

Hokkeji Temple: West of Kairyuoji Temple. Empress Komyo established this temple in the mid-eighth century as the headquarters of all the nunneries in the country. The main image is a wooden statue of the *Juichimen-Kannon* (Eleven-Headed *Kannon*; a National Treasure) that is supposed to have been modeled after Empress Komyo by a Hindu artist. The statue, of almost bewitching beauty, is only put on public view on special occasions. Cute little dog-shaped charms are sold at this temple, the Main Hall of which is a 1601 reconstruction. Like Kairyuoji Temple, the grounds were once the property of Fujiwara-no-Fuhito.

Saidaiji Temple (Great Western Temple) 74 : Immediately south of Yamato-Saidaiji Station on the Kintetsu Nara Line. Established in 765 by order of Empress-Regnant Shotoku, the temple is the headquarters of the Shingon-Ritsu sect of Buddhism. The bronze and wooden statues of the Four Heavenly Guardians (Important Cultural Properties) in *Shiodo* Hall were burned so that only part of their legs and the demons under their feet are regarded as relics of the late Nara period (710–784). In former days, the temple, with its many splendid buildings, was one of the "Seven Great Temples of Nara." However, the temple was destroyed by repeated fires, and although it was extensively renovated by the priest Eison, or Kosho-Bosatsu (1201–1290), once again it was consumed by fire. Today, no structure worthy of special note is left standing. The ruins of the gigantic *Toto*, or Eastern Pagoda, will convey some idea of the temple's vast scale of bygone days. The present Main Hall is a reconstruction from 1752 and contains a 1.7-m-tall, standing wooden statue of Sakyamuni (an Important Cultural Property). It was copied at the request of Eison from an image at Seiryoji Temple in Kyoto by Buddhist artist Zenkei. The images of *Monju-Bosatsu* riding on a lion and *Kosho-Bosatsu* are also Important Cultural Properties. The silk scrolls inscribed with the *Juniten* (Twelve Devas) are one of the most highly valued objects of this temple and are included among the National Treasures.

Ochamori, a special tea ceremony in which participants drink from a huge tea bowl of more than 30 cm in diameter, is held here every January 15, the second Saturday and Sunday in April, and the second Sunday in October.

Akishinodera Temple 74 : Located north of Yamato-Saidaiji Station, this temple was founded in 780 in compliance with the wishes of

Emperor Konin. The image of *Gigeiten* (an Important Cultural Property) is quite famous. Its dry-lacquer head dates back to the late Nara period, while the remaining wooden parts are attributed to the Kamakura period (1192–1333). The original buildings were all burned down in battle in 1135, and the only surviving building, the *Kodo* (Lecture Hall), now serves as the Main Hall. An excellent example of Nara-period architecture, it has been designated as a National Treasure.

Museum Yamato Bunkakan ⟦74⟧: The structure stands on a pine-covered hill near Gakuen-mae Station on the Kintetsu-Nara Line. The museum's 2,000-piece collection is principally made up of examples of the different arts of Far Eastern countries, including paintings, sculptures, ceramics and lacquerware, among which are four National Treasures as well as many others that are Important Cultural Properties. Centered around a small bamboo garden, the exhibition galleries are so designed that visitors are free from the formalities often observed at other museums, enabling them to relax and enjoy the artwork. At the nearby Nakano Art Museum, famous works by modern painters are on display.

Mt. Ikoma ⟦74⟧: This peak soars over the border between Nara and Osaka. With an altitude of 642 m, the mountain can be ascended by cable car running from Kintetsu Ikoma Station or by automobile on the parkway called the "Shigi-Ikoma Skyline." Hozanji Temple on the eastern slope is also called Ikoma-Shoten. Since it is believed that worship here will promote commercial prosperity and matrimonial harmony, there is an unending stream of worshippers. There is an amusement park on the mountain peak, which commands an excellent view.

Toshodaiji Temple ⟦92⟧: Located near Nishinokyo Station on the Kintetsu Kashiwara Line, the temple was founded in 759 by the famous priest Chien Chen (688–763) of the T'ang Dynasty of China (known as Ganjin in Japan). It is the headquarters of the Ritsu sect of Buddhism. The *Kondo* (Main Hall; a National Treasure) is 29 m from east to west and 15 m from north to south. The magnificent beauty of its architectural style has led it to be considered one of the most valuable structures of the late Nara period (710–784). The main image is the celebrated 3.3-m-high, dry-lacquer statue of *Birushana-Butsu* (Vairocana; a National Treasure) sitting on a pedestal. The largest image of its kind, it is attributed to T'an Ching and Szu T'o, the two ablest disciples of Chien Chen. The halo was originally decorated with a thousand small Buddhas, but only 864 remain. According to temple records, the walls and pillars of the hall were decorated with 2,000 images of Sakyamuni, but not a trace remains. To the left of *Birushana-Butsu* is a wooden, dry-lacquer-coated *Senju-Kannon* (Thousand-Handed *Kannon*; a National Treasure) that stands 5.4 m tall. It is the largest known example of this kind of sculptural technique. At present, 953 hands remain. On the right side of *Birushana-Butsu* is a wooden, 3.7-m-tall, dry-lacquer-coated statue of *Yakushi-Nyorai* (a National Treasure). *Birushana-Butsu* is preceded on both sides by *Bonten* (Brahma) and *Taishakuten* (Indra). Both of these latter statues are National Treasures and stand 1.9 m high. At the right end of the hall is a sitting, wooden image of *Dainichi-Nyorai* (another form of Vairocana). This Important Cultural Property measures 3.5 m high and is one of the finest works of its kind.

Originally the Assembly Hall of the Nara Court, the *Kodo* (Lecture Hall; a National Treasure) was donated to the temple. It was rebuilt in 759, and although it has undergone many repairs, it is still a valuable example of palace architecture. Of the many treasures in the Lecture Hall, the most important is the principal image, a seated, 2.8-m-tall figure of *Miroku-Butsu* (an Important Cultural Property). The *Koro* (Drum Tower; a National Treasure), also known as *Shariden* (Hall of Buddha's Ashes), is located between the *Kondo* (Main Hall) and the *Raido* (Prayer Chapel). The Prayer Chapel and the *Sobo* (Priest's Quarters) are under the same roof of an elongated building that has been designated as an Important Cultural Property. The *Kyodo* (Sutra Library) and *Hodo* (Treasure House; National Treasures), east of the Prayer Chapel, were built in the *Azekura*-style at the time of their original construction.

In the *Mieido* (Founder's Hall; an Important Cultural Property), northeast of the Lecture Hall, is enshrined a seated, dry-lacquer statue of Chien Chen (a National Treasure) dating from 763. It is only on public view from June 5 to 7. Chien Chen, invited to Japan to ordinate Japanese Buddhists, introduced the Ritsu doctrines to Japan, but he lost his sight through the hardships of traveling from China.

Yakushiji Temple [92]: Situated south of Toshodaiji Temple, this was another of the "Seven Great Temples of Nara." Serving as the headquarters of the Hosso sect of Buddhism, it is noted for its famous *Yakushi-Sanzon* (*Yakushi* Trinity); *Yakushi-Nyorai*, the Lord of the Eastern "Joruriko" Paradise, and his attendants—*Nikko-Bosatsu* and *Gakko-Bosatsu*. These three statues are counted as National Treasures. The temple was founded in Asuka in 680 and moved here in 718. Except for the *Sanju-no-To* (Three-Story Pagoda), all the structures were destroyed by repeated fires, then reconstructed.

The *Kondo* (Main Hall) is a 1976 reconstruction based on the original design of the majestic structure. Besides the aforementioned bronze *Yakushi* Trinity, it contains the main, 2.6-m-tall image, *Yakushi-Nyorai*, seated on a marble pedestal, with the statues of *Nikko-Bosatsu* and *Gakko-Bosatsu* standing on each side. These statues were originally gilded, but centuries of exposure to air and occasional flames have transformed the bronze alloy to such a glossy black that they appear to be lacquered. The design of the pedestal shows Oriental influences brought in over the Silk Road.

The Lecture Hall holds another *Yakushi-Sanzon* (*Yakushi* Trinity; an Important Cultural Property) of nearly the same size and general appearance, but the workmanship is inferior. The *Sanju-no-To* (Three-Story Pagoda), known as the *Toto* (East Pagoda; a National Treasure), was erected no later than 698, measuring 33.6 m high and 9.1 m across the base. Supported by 17 columns, the interior is elaborately painted. It appears to have six stories since each story has an additional wooden roof called *mokoshi*. The unusual architecture and exquisite equilibrium has made the pagoda famous. The colorful *Seito* (West Pagoda) is a 1981 reproduction of the original.

The *Toindo* (East Hall; a National Treasure), at the back of the East Pagoda, was rebuilt in 1285 and contains a famous statue of *Sho* (Holy)-*Kannon*. Standing 1.9 m high, it dates either from the Hakuho period (645–710) like the *Yakushi* Trinity in the Main Hall or immediately thereafter. It is unsure whether it was a gift to the Imperial Court from a king of the Korean Paikche kingdom or was created at the behest of Princess Hashihito, consort of Emperor Kotoku (597–654). The *Bussokudo* (Hall of Buddha's Footprint) is on the south side of the West Pagoda. It contains a stone (a National Treasure) 49 cm long and 14 cm wide that is imprinted with a large footprint worshipped as that of Buddha. It dates back to 753 and affords considerable interest for archaeologists. The *Kisshoten* Portrait (a National Treasure) of this temple, painted in the late Nara period (710–784), portrays the beautiful attire of a contemporaneous woman, but it is only on display during a short period in autumn.

Joruriji Temple 74 : Located in a mountainous area called *Tono-o*, 25 min. by bus to the northeast of Nara. Since nine images of *Amida-Nyorai* are worshipped at this temple, it is also called Kutaiji (Nine Images Temple). All of the gilt, wooden statues with mysterious expressions are National Treasures. They are lined up in the elongated *Hondo* (Main Hall; a National Treasure), built in 1107, and present an overwhelming sight. The beautiful standing figure of *Kisshoten* still retains the bright colors that were applied when it was made during the Kamakura period. It is only on display during certain times of the year. Across the pond is an elegant *Sanju-no-To* (Three-Story Pagoda) dating from the late Heian period (a National Treasure).

Gansenji Temple 74 : Once quite large, this tiny temple to the east of Joruriji Temple was founded by the priest Gyoki (668–749) in 729 at the wish of Emperor Shomu. The massive statue of *Amida-Nyorai* made in 946 and the delicate *Fugen-Bosatsu* riding a white elephant are famous, while the *Sanju-no-To* (Three-Story Pagoda) dates from the Muromachi period (1336–1573)—all Important Cultural Properties. In the area between Joruriji Temple and Gansenji Temple, there are many stone Buddhas scattered about.

Kasagi 74 : About 30 min. by local train from the JR Nara Station on the Kansai Main Line. It is a picturesque spot along the Kizu River. The mineral springs and Mt. Kasagi with its numerous historical sites attract many visitors. Mt. Kasagi (alt. 324 m) is famous as the place where Emperor Godaigo fled from Kyoto, taking refuge from the Hojo Clan. Many cherry trees blossom on the mountain and numbers of gigantic rocks lie exposed, several of which have Buddhist images carved on them. Kasagiji Temple, on the side of the mountain, was an important site for *Miroku* Buddhists, but since it had given sanctuary to Emperor Godaigo, most of the temple was burned in battle. The stone-made *Jusanju-no-To* (13-Story Pagoda) and *Dosho* (bronze bell) that remain are Important Cultural Properties.

Yamato-Koriyama [74] ☎07435: Pop. 92,454. It is famous for the cultivation of goldfish, which are exported in large quantities every year. In addition to flourishing electronics and metal industries, watermelons and strawberries are the specialties of the area. 30 min. from Tennoji Station (Osaka) on the JR Kansai Main Line, or 45 min. from Kyoto on the Kintetsu Kyoto and Kashihara lines.

Jiko-in Temple: Located on top of a hill on the west side of Tomio River, this temple was established in 1663 by Katagiri Sadamasa, founder of the Sekishu-style tea ceremony. The white sand garden in front of the thatched *Shoin* (Study Hall) has large clumps of beautifully clipped azaleas at the south end, with small shrubs spreading out to the east overlooking the Yamato Basin. The Study Hall and the Tea Room are Important Cultural Properties.

Yatadera Temple [74]: Situated on a hill in the western part of the city, the temple is said to have been founded in 673. The main image is a *Jizo-Bosatsu* (*Jizo* Bodhisattva; an Important Cultural Property), which is worshipped by its devotees. The sight of some 6,000 hydrangeas that bloom here from early June to early July is breathtaking.

Horyuji Temple [74/92-93]: Standing to the southwest of Yamato-Koriyama, this is not only one of the oldest existing temples in Japan, it is actually the oldest wooden structure in the world. It is believed to have been founded by Empress-Regnant Suiko (reigned 592–628) and her regent, Prince Shotoku (574–622). Prince Shotoku was the eldest son of Emperor Yomei and a nephew of Empress-Regnant Suiko. One of the "Seven Great Temples of Nara" and the headquarters of the Shotoku sect, this temple is regarded as the source of Japanese art and culture. Consisting of two parts—the *Toin* (East Temple) and the *Saiin* or *Nishi-no-in* (West Temple), it includes nearly 50 important buildings, with the period of their construction ranging from the Asuka period (592–628) to the Edo period (1603–1867). Sixteen of them are National Treasures, while the rest are Important Cultural Properties.

The West Temple is generally mistaken as the entire Horyuji Temple, probably because the East Temple is in a separate enclosure. It can be reached by bus from the JR Horyuji Station on the JR Kansai Main Line.

Nandaimon (Great South Gate) is a National Treasure, rebuilt in 1438. After passing through this front gate to Horyuji Temple, one comes to the *Chumon* (Middle Gate; a National Treasure). With a roofed corridor on either side, the **Middle Gate** serves as the front gate to the *Saiin* (West Temple). It is believed to have been constructed during the early Hakuho period (645–710), following the original architectural style of Horyuji Temple. Unlike other gates, the unusual construction of the Middle Gate is such that the pillars supporting the center divide the entrance into two parts. In the frontal niches, there are a pair of fierce-looking *Kongo-Rikishi* (Deva Kings), who are usually placed to guard the gates of Buddhist structures. These statues were completely renovated in 1964, with the one on the right painted red and the one on the left black to symbolize light and darkness. The famous **Kondo** (Main Hall; a National Treasure) standing inside the Middle Gate is one of the oldest wooden buildings in the world, measuring 9.1 m long, 7.3 m wide and 17.8 m high. Like the Middle Gate, it is constructed with massive pillars with entasis and double-roofed with tiles plus a *mokoshi*, or extra wooden roof. The ceiling is coffered, but the original arabesque decorations are hardly visible now.

The **Main Hall** houses several Buddhist images and other art objects, the most noteworthy being the bronze *Shaka-Sanzon* (Sakya Trinity; a National Treasure), cast in 623. The central figure of Sakyamuni, stands 87 cm high and is flanked by two Bodhisattvas: *Yakuo* and *Yakujo*. Famous as a representative masterpiece of Asuka sculpture, the Trinity has all the characteristic features, including, for example, the naive yet august countenance. The artist was the Buddhist sculptor, Tori-Busshi. Other important images include the bronze *Yakushi-Nyorai* (a National Treasure), which once was claimed to have been cast in 607 by order of Empress-Regnant Suiko and Prince Shotoku but has proved to be a little newer; the bronze statue of *Amida-Nyorai* (an Important Cultural Property); the wooden statues of the *Shitenno-Ritsuzo* (Four Heavenly Guardians; National Treasures), and the wooden statues of *Kisshoten* and *Bishamonten* (National Treasures).

The walls of the Main Hall once displayed several treasured frescoes of international renown. Created anonymously, they were severely damaged by fire in 1949, but they have since been restored to their exact representation. The painting from the only undamaged wall can be seen in the Horyuji Treasure House. **Goju-no-To** (Five-Story Pagoda; a National Treasure) is also among the oldest wooden buildings in the world. It still has the same timber used in its construction some 1,300 years ago. The 34-m-tall structure with a *mokoshi* has a very solid presence. The *Shumisen*, or Mt. Sumeru, a legendary peak towering from the sea in the center of the buddhist world, is on the first floor around the central pillars. Clay images on each of the four sides of the *Shumisen* represent different Buddhist stories: "The Exchange of Questions and Answers between *Yuima* and *Monju*" on the east, "The Cremation of Sakyamuni's Bones" on the west, "*Miroku* Paradise" on the south and "Buddha's Entry into Nirvana" on the north.

The **Daikodo** (Great Lecture Hall; a National Treasure), north of the Five-Story Pagoda, contains a *Yakushi-Sanzon* (*Yakushi* Trinity; National Treasures) made of gilt wood. The original building burned down in 925 when a thunderbolt caused a fire, with the present structure dating from 990. The central image of the trinity, *Yakushi-Nyorai*, is 2.5 m tall, while his two attendants are each 1.7 m tall. Statues of the *Shitenno-Ritsuzo* (Four Heavenly Guardians; Important Cultural Properties) can also be found here along with the *Kyozo* (Sutra Library) to the west of the Great Lecture Hall and the *Shoro* (Belfry) to the east—both National Treasures.

Shoryo-in (Sacred Spirit Hall; a National Treasure) stands just outside the east corridor of the Main Hall. It contains a wooden statue of Prince Shotoku (84 cm tall) sitting in the costume of his office as regent (a National Treasure) as he was at the age of 45. The north part of the *Shoryo-in* Hall, *Higashi-muro* (a National Treasure), was one of the quarters of the priests. *Gofuzo* (a National Treasure), east of *Shoryo-in* Hall, is a high-floored treasure repository of great importance that contains some works of art donated to Horyuji Temple by various emperors as well as by Prince Shotoku.

To the east of *Gofuzo* stands the *Daihozoden* (Great Treasure Hall). Constructed to look like an *Azekura*-style storehouse of piled up logs, the ferroconcrete buildings were completed in April 1941—the 1,320th anniversary of the death of Prince Shotoku. The storehouses, which are moisture/fire-proof, display and preserve treasures formerly contained in the *Gofuzo* and other parts of Horyuji Temple.

The North Storehouse holds the *Yumetagai-Kannon* (a National Treasure), which was believed to have the power of changing bad dreams into good ones; a sandalwood statue of the *Kumen-Kannon* (Nine-Headed *Kannon*; a National Treasure); a graceful *Roku-Kannon* (Six-Bodied *Kannon*), and the famous wooden statue of *Kudara-Kannon* (a National Treasure). This last masterpiece is 2.1 m high. Many other bronze images, swords, small pagodas, masks and objects used on Buddhist altars are also on display.

Included in the display in the South Storehouse are a brocade called *Shokko Nishiki*, a portrait of Prince Shotoku, the small fresco that was originally part of the decoration of the Main Hall, and the angels and phoenixes that were once part of the canopy over the principal image in the Main Hall. The most famous of all the treasures are Lady Tachibana's Miniature Shrine and the *Tamamushi-no-Zushi* (Miniature Shrine of the Golden Beetle). Lady Tachibana's Shrine (a National Treasure) contains a bronze *Amida-Sanzon* (Amitabha Trinity; National Treasure) revered by Lady Tachibana, mother of Empress Komyo (701-760), the consort of Emperor Shomu (701-756). The trinity is set upon three lotus blossoms growing from a holy pond ingeniously represented by a bronze plate engraved with waves and lotus leaves.   The shrine is admired as a masterpiece of early Hakuho-period (645-710) art. It measures 2.8 m high, while the main image of *Amida* is 50 cm. The latter image is attended by 30-cm-tall images of *Kannon* and *Seishi* with gentle faces that are quite memorable.

The *Tamamushi-no-Zushi* (a National Treasure) is a small, palace-style shrine on a high pedestal with a height totaling 2.3 m.   The origin of the name derives from the fact that the edges of the miniature building were profusely pasted with the multicolored wings of "*tamamushi*" beetles (chrysochroa eleganses), pressed down with exquisite metal openwork of honeysuckle arabesques, although the insect wings have crumbled into dust with the passage of time. The shrine and pedestal are coated with black lacquer and covered with scenes from Buddhist legends painted with a kind of lead monoxide, oil, pigment, composed chiefly of a mixture of yellow and vermilion with a little green. The front doors of the shrine are painted with Deva Kings, the doors on both sides are decorated with *Bosatsu* and the rear is covered with paintings of three pagodas, the sun, the moon, angels, phoenixes and arhats.   The frames of the pedestal are delineated with arabesques and clouds, while the frontage is decorated with a scene of burning incense to pay homage to the ashes of Buddha enshrined in the center, where they are surrounded by paintings of priests, legendary animals and ascending angels. The rear is painted with *Shumisen*, or Mt. Sumeru—the legendary peak said to have risen from the sea in the center of the world—and many other objects. The sides show incidents in the life of Sakyamuni. He is shown on one side giving himself up to a demon in order to learn part of the Gatha, or Buddhist verse, and on the other allowing himself to be eaten in order to feed a hungry tiger cub.

A short distance from the *Chumon* (Middle Gate) is the *Todaimon* (Great East Gate; a National treasure) of the West Temple. Proceeding east from the *Todaimon*, one will come upon the East Temple, which includes the *Yumedono*, the *Dempodo* (Sermon Hall) and the *Shoro* (Belfry)—all National Treasures. It also contains the *Raido* (Prayer Hall), *Eden* (Picture Hall) and *Shariden* (Hall of Buddha's Ashes), which are all Important Cultural Properties. The *Toin* (East Temple) grounds were originally the site of Ikaruga Palace, built by Prince Shotoku in 601 as the place where he resided until his death in 622. Subsequently, the palace fell into ruin and was replaced in 739 by a temple built by the priest Gyoshin. It was dedicated to Prince Shotoku and his family.

Yumedono, the main hall of the East Temple, is said to be the most beautiful octagonal building in Japan. *Yumedono* means "Hall of Dreams" and was so named because Prince Shotoku used to come here to meditate when he came across a passage too difficult to understand during his annotation of the Lotus Sutra, the Vimalakirti-nirdesa Sutra and the Shoman Sutra. Legend has it that he was always helped on such occasions by a venerable sage who appeared from the east. The main image of the hall is the historic *Guze-Kannon*, a gilt, wooden standing statue. A National Treasure, the statue is 1.8 m tall, which is said to have been the height of Prince Shotoku. It is prized as one of the most beautiful representations in the country and until 100 years ago it was covered with cloth to keep it out of sight. It can now be viewed from April 11 to May 5 and from October 22 to November 3. There is a mysterious expression on the face and an elaborate openwork crown. *Yumedono* also contains a fine, dry-lacquer statue of the founder of the temple—the abbot Gyoshin (d. 750)—as well as a superb clay image of the priest Dosen (d. 876), who repaired the building. Both statues are National Treasures. There are two buildings to the north of *Yumedono*: the Hall of Buddha's Ashes is on the right and the Picture Hall is on the left. The Picture Hall is so named because it contained a number of sliding screens covered with paintings depicting Prince Shotoku's life from birth till death. At present, they are on display at the Tokyo National Museum. **Dempodo** (Sermon Hall) was the residence of Lady Tachibana and was donated to the temple in 739. In this hall, which actually corresponds to the lecture hall in other temples, are a wooden *Amida-Sanzon* (Amitabha Trinity) on the east side, a dry-lacquer Amitabha Trinity in the center and another wooden Amitabha Trinity on the west side. All three works are from the late Tempyo period (729-749) and are Important Cultural Properties. Several carved wooden statues of the late Heian period (794-1185) are also preserved here.

Chuguji Temple: Northeast of the Sermon Hall, this well-known nunnery contains an imposing, wooden, 1.8-m-tall *Miroku* (Maitreya) or, according to the temple records, a *Nyoirin-Kannon*. The statue, with its right hand gently touching its cheek and its graceful expression, is a National Treasure. Another attraction of Chuguji Temple is the oldest embroidery sample existing in Japan and shows *Tenjukoku*, or the "Land of Heavenly Longevity," where Prince Shotoku is said to have gone. Generally called the "Tenjukoku Shucho Mandala," this priceless artwork is a National Treasure. Of the original 4.8 m-long Mandala, two remaining fragments were combined to form a partial restoration measuring 1.1 m by a little over 90 cm. Although it may be difficult to imagine the complete work from these fragments, they are still a valuable source of information on the industrial arts and pictorial style of the Asuka period (592-628).

Horinji Temple: About 1 km northeast of Horyuji Temple. This ancient temple is said to have been founded in 621 by Prince Yamashiro-no-Oe, the eldest son of Prince Shotoku, as a place to pray for his father's recovery. The original main image of the Main Hall, a figure of *Yakushi-Nyorai* (an Important Cultural Property), can now be seen in the Lecture Hall, which also serves as a repository. The statue is an example of the Tori-Busshi sculpture style. The 3.6-m-high main image in the *Kodo* (Lecture Hall) is a colorful wood *Juichimen-Kannon* (Eleven-Headed *Kannon*; an Important Cultural Property) from the early part of the Heian period (794–1185). Also lined up in the *Kodo* are colorful wood statues of the *Kokuzo-Bosatsu* in a style similar to that of *Kudara Kannon, Kisshoten, Sho-Kannon* and *Jizo*—all Important Cultural Properties. The *Sanju-no-To* (Three-Story Pagoda) is a 1975 construction erected in the style of the original buildings and based on traditional methods.

Hokkiji Temple ☐74☐: Located in Okamoto, northeast of Horinji Temple. Also called Okamotodera Temple, it is 20 min. on foot from Horyuji Temple. It is believed to have been converted from a palace in 638 by Prince Yamashiro-no-Oe. The *Kondo* (Main Hall) and pagoda are set up in reverse positions to those of Horyuji Temple. This *Sanju-no-To* (Three-Story Pagoda; a National Treasure) is the main attraction. It is now the oldest remaining example of a three-story pagoda, with construction said to have commenced in 685 and finished in 706. Standing 24 m high, this valuable relic of Buddhist architecture is a classic example from the Hakuho period (645–710).

Fujinoki Tumulus: 350 m west of Horyuji Temple. It is believed to have been created some time in the mid-sixth century. The stone coffin, which was exceptionally fortunate enough to have remained intact, was opened in 1988 and found to contain the remains of two people, ornaments, weapons and cloth. The coffin itself is covered with superb openwork, representing a find that is priceless in archaeological terms.

Oji ☐74☐: A key transportation point in Nara located on the border of Osaka. It is a junction for the JR Wakayama Line and Kintetsu Ikoma and Tawaramoto lines.

Tatsuta River: About 2 km north of the JR Oji Station. The river is celebrated for its more than 10,000 maple trees along the banks, producing autumn tints that are often praised in Japanese poetry. Buses connect the riverside spots with Horyuji Temple and other nearby places of interest.

Mt. Shigi ☐74☐: Alt. 437 m. 3.5 km northwest of the JR Oji Station. It can be reached by bus from Shigisan-shita Station on the Kintetsu Ikoma Line. From Uehommachi in Osaka, the Kintetsu Line runs to Shigisan-guchi and connects to the cable car. On the summit is Chogosonshiji Temple, also known by the same name as the mountain, i.e. Shigisan (Mt. Shigi). Serving as the headquarters of the Shigisan-Shingon sect, it is set picturesquely on the cliffs facing east. Tradition has it that the temple was founded by Prince Shotoku (574 –622). It is dedicated to *Bishamonten*, one of the Four Heavenly Guardians of Buddhism, who is clad in armor, holds a spear in one hand and has a miniature pagoda in the other. Three picture scrolls entitled "The Illustrated History of Shigisan Temple" in the possession of Chogosonshiji Temple are National Treasures. The present temple buildings were erected by Toyotomi Hideyori (1593-1615), son of Hideyoshi (a military ruler of Japan), in the Keicho era (1596-1615) after the original structures were destroyed by fire. Souvenir shops selling papier-mâché tigers unique to the temple line the approaching path. There is a splendid view of Yamato Plain from the observation platform on the mountain top.

Tenri 74 ☎07436: About 10 km south of Nara, or about 15 min. on the JR Sakurai Line. The city with its population of 65,076 is the home of the Tenrikyo Shinto sect and is known for the head shrine opened here in 1908 by Nakayama Miki. It is the location of Tenri University and the associated library, which has a massive collection, including many National Treasures and Important Cultural Properties. There is also the Tenri Sankokan, with data on folk customs, transportation and many other subjects from all over the world.

Isonokami Shrine 74 : 1.5 km east of the JR Tenri Station, or 7 min. by bus. The shrine is dedicated to Futsunomitama-no-Okami. According to legend, this god is a divine sword which was presented to Emperor Jimmu by Takakuraji-no-Mikoto, a Shinto deity of the Kumano region. The *Haiden* (Oratory), one of the oldest existing oratories, is a National Treasure constructed during the early part of the Kamakura period (1192-1333), while the two-level gate is an Important Cultural Property. In the main building, there is an unusual six-branched sword, a National Treasure, with an inscription stating it was presented from the Paikche Court of Korea in the fourth century. The shrine is the starting point of the popular Yamanobe Trail.

Yamanobe Trail: A 15-km historical trail originated before the Nara period (710-784). There are many shrines and temples of historical importance and Emperors' tumili along the way. This is a wonderful trail for history lovers.

Chogakuji Temple 74 : 15 min. by bus from the JR Tenri Station. The wooden, highly animated *Amida-Sanzon* (Amitabha Trinity) from the late Heian period (794-1185) is famous. Together with the two-level gate at the entrance, also from the Heian period, they are Important Cultural Properties.

Emperor Sujin's Mausoleum 74 : A gigantic, ancient keyhole-shaped tumulus, extending for a total of 240 m and surrounded by a water-filled moat. Emperor Keiko is buried in a 300-m-long tumulus immediately its south.

Omiwa Shrine 74 : Also called Miwa Myojin, the shrine is located at the foot of the picturesque Mt. Miwa (alt. 467 m). Omononushi-no-Kami, the god of Mt. Miwa, is enshrined here. One of the oldest shrines in Japan, its major characteristic is the lack of a main hall found at most shrines. The Oratory was built by the fourth Tokugawa Shogun, Ietsuna, in 1664. The deity worshipped here is also the god of *sake*.

Sakurai 74 ☎07444: Pop. 59,853. 20 km from Nara. Besides being an important transportation center of the district, it is also a base for sightseeing trips to the many shrines, temples and historical sites in the area. The Kintetsu Osaka Line, JR Sakurai Line and many bus lines pass through the city, which is also a market for lumber products and a supplier of wooden fittings.

Tanzan Shrine ⎣74⎦: Situated 6 km south of Sakurai, 30 min. by bus from Sakurai Station. Set halfway up Mt. Tonomine, the shrine is dedicated to Fujiwara-no-Kamatari (614–669), the founder of the Fujiwara family, and was established by Priest Jo-e (d. 714), eldest son of Kamatari. Comprising many fine buildings, the shrine grew in importance as the power of the family increased. The main shrine was rebuilt many times up to 1850. The shrine is sometimes called the Nikko Shrine of the Kansai District because of the magnificence of its painted colors. The sight of the many hanging lanterns in the oratory is quite beautiful. By the gate, there is a wooden *Jusanju-no-To* (13-Story Pagoda) dating from 1532 and believed to be the only one of its kind in existence. All of these buildings are Important Cultural Properties. The mountainside abounds in maple trees, setting the countryside ablaze in autumn.

Hasedera Temple ⎣74⎦: About 6 km east of Sakurai, or 800 m north of Hasedera station on the Kintetsu Osaka Line. The temple is nestled in the mountains. Said to have first originated in 686, with present structures dating from 727, it is the headquarters of the Buzan school of the Buddhist Shingon sect and the eighth Station on the 33-Temple Pilgrimage in the Former Western Provinces. The main image in the Main Hall (dating from 1650) is a wooden statue of the *Juichimen-Kannon* (Eleven-Headed Kannon) about 8 m high. Since it used to be a favorite resort of the Court nobles of Nara, the area is rich in fine scenery and classical relics. The temple is noted for its numerous cherry trees and peonies, with their blossoms attracting large crowds.

Muroji Temple ⎣74⎦: Set back deep into the mountains 8 km southeast of Kintetsu Muroguchi-Ono Station, it is thought to have been constructed late in the eighth century. The delicate, 16.2-m-high *Goju-no-To* (Five-Story Pagoda) and *Kondo* (Main Hall), both National Treasures, are in the classic style of the early Heian period. The Main Hall contains a thick, 3.4-m-tall wooden statue of Sakyamuni (a National Treasure) from the same period as the building, 90-cm-tall statues of the *Junishinsho* (Twelve Divine Generals; Important Cultural Properties) and other Buddhist images. The seated image of Sakyamuni (a National Treasure) in the *Mirokudo* Hall (an Important Cultural Property) is particularly famous. The temple is also known for the beautiful rhododendron blossoms that bloom in early May.

Ko-ochidani Valley ⎣74⎦: Known for its scenic rock formations, the valley is situated 8 km southeast of Nabari Station on the Kintetsu Osaka Line. The valley is especially beautiful in autumn, when the rocky cliffs that overhang the stream are covered with colored leaves. Oku(Inner)-Ko-ochidani Valley is a little further on. There, the river banks are lined with columnar rock formations, with names like *Kabuto* (Warrior's Helmet) Cliff and *Byobu* (Screen) Rock, creating picturesque scene. On the west side of the mountain are the 48-Akame Waterfalls along the 4-km walking trail. 25 min. by bus from Kintetsu Nabari Station.

Ueno 74 ☎0595: Pop. 59,948. An old castle town on the Meihan (Nagoya-Osaka) National Highway, or National Highway 25. The most convenient stations are Iga-Ueno Station on the JR Kansai Main Line and Ueno-shi Station on the Kintetsu Iga Line. *Iga-yaki* earthenware, braided cords and *sake* are among the many items produced here. The three-story donjon standing in Hakuho Park on the former site of Ueno Castle is a 1953 reproduction of the original 1611 structure. The first and second floors are a museum, while the third is an observation platform. Matsuo-Basho Memorial Hall, situated near the entrance to Hakuho Park, contains the bronze statue and related data of Basho (1644–1694), master of *haiku* (17-syllable poems, refer to p.158 and 160) and a native of this region. The house where he was born and *Minomushian*, a small house that he loved, are both still standing in the town.

Ninja Mansion is one of the strongholds of those masters of guerrilla warfare, the *ninja*. At a glance, it appears nothing more than an ordinary home, but inside there are reversible doors, escape routes, hidden rooms and many other secret contrivances. Visitors can also see the tools and weapons used by the *ninja* as well as printed materials related to them. There were two groups of *ninja*: the Iga school, which developed in this area, and the Koga school, which developed in the Koga region to the north.

Asuka

This ancient capital was the seat of government until the new Nara Heijokyo capital was established. Many emperors ruled here, and many political powers rose and fell. The remains of this history can still be found today. Since bicycle rental shops usually stand in front of the major Kintetsu stations, the one here provides a convenient way to see the historical sites scattered around town.

Asukadera Temple (Ango-in Temple) 74 : 10 min. by bus from Kintetsu Kashihara-Jingumae Station. The temple is known for the bronze, seated figure of Sakyamuni, commonly called the *Asuka-Daibutsu* (Asuka Great Buddha). It was established by Soga-no-Umako (d. 626), the political and religious leader of his time(refer to p.117). Cast by Buddhist artist Tori-Busshi in 606, this is the oldest existing Buddhist image in Japan and is an Important Cultural Property. Even though it has been badly damaged and imperfectly repaired, it has retained the characteristics of its day. After the new capital was set up in Heijo (the old name of Nara) in 710, this temple was moved there and was named Gankoji Temple. The original Asukadera Temple remained here and was renamed Moto(Original)-Gankoji Temple. However, it gradually crumbled to ruins, and today only part of the priests' quarters, Ango-in, remains.

Okadera Temple ⬚74⬚: 15 min. by bus from Kintetsu Kashihara-Jingumae Station. Properly called Ryugaiji Temple, it is a place of worship for the Buzan school of the Shingon sect. Its origin is traced to Okamoto Palace, which Prince Kusakabe, the son of ancient ruler Emperor Temmu, donated to Priest Gien (d. 728) for use as a monastery. Later, Kobo-Daishi restored it from dilapidation as a monastery for the Shingon sect. It is the seventh Station on the 33-Temple-Pilgrimage in the Former Western Provinces. The main image, a clay figure of *Nyoirin-Kannon*, is 4.5 m tall. Regarded as an early Heian-period (794–1185) piece, it has been designated as an Important Cultural Property. The lacquer-coated, seated wooden image of Priest Gien, a masterpiece of the Nara period, is a National Treasure that can now be seen at the Nara National Museum.

Ishibutai Tumulus ⬚74⬚: 15 min. by bus from Kintetsu Kashihara-Jingumae Station, to the south of Okadera Temple. Built in the seventh century and an excellent specimen of the enormous tombs of ancient times, it probably had a square base and rounded top. The covering earth has disappeared, leaving the stone ceiling and side walls exposed. Constructed with more than 30 blocks weighing about 75 tons each, the stone tomb is believed to have been part of a huge mausoleum surrounded by moats and dikes. It is probably dedicated to Soga-no-Umako since he lived nearby.

Tachibanadera Temple: 10 min. by bus from Kintetsu Kashihara-Jingumae Station. One of the seven Buddhist monasteries attributed to Prince Shotoku (574–622), it stands on what is believed to have been the birthplace of the prince, having once occupied a vast area. There were corridors with gates, a pagoda and a large number of buildings, but now all that remains is the *Taishido* (Prince's Hall), which was reconstructed in 1864, the *Hondo* (Main Hall) and a few other structures. The Prince's Hall houses a seated, wooden image of the prince (an Important Cultural Property) that was carved in the Muromachi period. The monastery is a sanctuary for the Tendai sect, and its precincts are a Place of Historical Importance. In one corner stands a stone that is carved with what are said to be the faces of good and evil.

Emperor Jimmu's Mausoleum: Said to be the final resting place of Japan's first Emperor, Jimmu. Fenced off and surrounded by a double line of moats, his tumulus is situated at the foot of Unebi Hill (alt. 199 m), which is believed to have been the site of the Emperor's palace.

Kashihara Shrine ⬚74⬚: Near Emperor Jimmu's Mausoleum. The shrine was built in 1889 of timbers that were formerly part of the Imperial Palace in Kyoto and dedicated to Emperor Jimmu and his consort, Empress Himetatara-Isuzu-Hime. The shrine is about 500 m from Kashihara-Jingumae Station.

Takamatsuzuka Tumulus: Located in the southern part of Asuka, the mound was excavated in 1972. Believed to have been constructed in the seventh century, it was the site of one of the most important archaeological discoveries in Japanese history—a collection of richly colored murals dating back over 1,300 years. These paintings of groups of human and animal figures show the distinct influence of Chinese and Korean culture. After the murals were unearthed in a stone chamber in the tumulus, they were sealed off and a reproduction was created in the original states of its discovery and origin. Together with the model of the stone chamber in actual size, they are on display at Mural Hall at the neighboring plot.

Asuka Historical Museum: 500 m northeast of Asukadera Temple. It centers around several Asuka-related themes—the remains of the palaces, temples and tumuli in general, and the Takamatsuzuka Tumulus. The exhibits include excavated objects, models and panels set up so as to afford an understanding of ancient Asuka. It is an annex of the Nara National Cultural Properties Research Institute. Another place exhibiting many of the relics unearthed around Nara Prefecture is the Museum Affiliated to Nara Prefectural Kashihara Archaeological Institute about 500 m from Kashihara Shrine.

Imaimachi: 10 min. on foot from Yamato-Yagi Station on the Kintetsu Osaka Line. Some 80% of the houses among the 800 dwellings in this town retain the same facades as when they were built during the Edo period (1603–1867). Among the houses behind the white walls that line both sides of the narrow road, eight are Important Cultural Properties. Some of these homes are open to the public.

Tsubosakadera Temple 75 : 4 km east of Tsubosakayama Station on the Kintetsu Yoshino Line, 10 min. by bus. This name is the popular label for Minami (South)-Hokkeji Temple and is said to have been founded in the eighth century by the priest Benki of Hokoji Temple in Nara. It is a monastery of the Shingon sect. The main image, a wooden *Senju-Kannon* (Thousand-Handed *Kannon*), is famous for a miracle related in the *joruri* puppet drama "Tsubosaka Reigenki" (lit. miraculous virtue story). This is the sixth Station on the 33-Temple Pilgrimage in the Former Western Provinces. The *Sanju-no-To* (Three-Story Pagoda) was constructed in 1497. Other attractions include a fragrance flower garden for those with impaired vision and a huge, 20-m-tall (including the pedestal), stone *Kannon* sent as a gift from the government of India.

Taimadera Temple 74 : Near Taimadera Station on the Kintetsu Minami (South)-Osaka Line. One explanation for the origins of this temple is that it was founded in 612 and was moved to its present location in 684. The present Main Hall or *Mandarado* (Mandala Hall; a National Treasure) was erected in 1242. The most important object here is a reproduction of the famous mandala of Buddhist paradise painted in 763. Legend has it that the original was the work of Chujo-Hime, the daughter of Fujiwara-no-Toyonari (706–765), who wove it from lotus threads while she was serving as a nun at the temple. She died on May 14, and on this day 25 Bodhisattvas appeared to welcome her to paradise. A parade takes place to revive the event each year. Another important structure of this temple is *Kondo* that was reconstructed in 1184 and contains an enshrined image of the seated figure of *Miroku-Bosatsu* (a National Treasure) from the early Nara period (710–784). Pagodas stand to the east and west—both National Treasures from the late Nara period or immediately thereafter. Within the *Naka-no-Bo* (Central Priests' Quarters) adjoining the temple are a beautiful garden and a teahouse.

Yoshino Mountain Region [75]

The Yoshino Mountain region includes, in order from the east, the Daiko Mountains, the Omine Mountains and the Obako Mountains—all running from north to south. The Yoshino River runs north and the Kitayama River flows south between the Daiko and the Omine Mountains, while the Totsukawa River runs south between the Omine Mountains and the Obako Mountains. National Highways 168 and 169 run along each of the river valleys. At the north end is the Yoshino Valley. This mountainous region covers the greater part of Nara Prefecture, a portion of which has been set aside as the Yoshino-Kumano National Park.

Yoshino [76] : This is a small town with a population of 14,181 on the crest of a ridge extending to the heart of the Yoshino Mountain region. The area is famous for its cherry blossoms, and for two weeks out of the year this otherwise quiet town bustles with visitors attracted by the beauty of the blossoms. The best route to Yoshino is by the Kintetsu Yoshino Line from Abenobashi (Osaka) to Yoshino (terminal station via Kashihara-Jingumae), and then by cable car. Those driving may use National Highway 169. The famous cherry trees, said to number in the tens of thousands, are divided into four large groves known as *Hitome-Sembon* (One Thousand Trees at a Glance). The first grove, near the terminal of the Yoshinoyama cable car, is *Shimo-no-Sembon* (Lower Thousand Trees), the second is *Naka-no-Sembon* (Middle Thousand Trees), the third is *Kami-no-Sembon* (Upper Thousand Trees) and the fourth is *Oku-no-Sembon* (Inner Thousand Trees). Most of them are white mountain cherry trees. The trees of the lower grove usually bloom in early April, those in the middle and upper groves during mid-April, and the inner grove in late April. A cherry-blossom festival called *Hanakueshiki* is held here every April 11 and 12.

The trees have been preserved as sacred ever since the priest En-no-Ozunu carved the image of the god *Zao-Gongen* on one of the trees. En-no-Ozunu, a priest of the seventh century who made Mt. Sanjogatake his headquarters, managed to make the trees objects of special care by warning people not to injure them if they truly valued the trees' existence. New trees were planted from time to time until the entire hillside was covered with them. In the early years of the Meiji period (1868–1912), many of them were cut down, but this actually promoted new growth and gave them their present appearance. Down through the centuries, the cherry trees of Yoshino have been supported through the efforts of many believers. On an elevation 1.5 km to the southwest of Kintetsu Yoshino-Jingu Station stands Yoshino Shrine, dedicated to Emperor Godaigo (1288–1339). A little further on is the tomb of Murakami Yoshiteru, a faithful retainer who sacrificed his life in 1333 to save that of his lord, Prince Morinaga (1308–1335), a son of Emperor Godaigo. A bit further still is a cluster of houses strung along both sides of a steep ridge so that the third floors of many houses are on a level with the road and serve as shops. The floor below is the living quarters, while the first floor is a storeroom. This type of construction is called *Yoshino-date*.

Kimpusenji Temple: The headquarters of the Kimpusen-Shugen-honshu sect. After the original temple buildings were burned down, the present structures were erected in 1455. *Zaodo*, the Main Hall, rises to a height of 27.7 m, making it the second-largest, ancient, wooden edifice in Japan. Surpassed in size only by *Daibutsuden* Hall in Nara, it is a National Treasure. The pair of *Kongo-Rikishi* (Deva Kings) at the gate were made in the late Kamakura period (1192–1333). To the right of *Zaodo* is the site of the palace where three emperors of the Yoshino Court lived in the early 14th century.

A little further south along the road are two shrines: Yoshimizu Shrine and Katte Shrine. In the oratory of the latter shrine, Shizuka, mistress of Minamoto-no-Yoshitsune (1159–1189; a famous general of the Minamoto Clan), performed her famous dance. Further up the road on the left is Nyoirinji Temple. According to tradition, Kusunoki Masatsura (1326–1348), son of the celebrated Masashige (a loyal retainer of Emperor Godaigo), inscribed a poem and the names of 143 of his men on the temple door before he led them on his last fight for the Imperial cause. Behind the temple is the mausoleum of Emperor Godaigo.

Chikurin-in Temple is south of Katte Shrine. The garden here is said to have been designed by Sen-no-Rikyu (1522–1591), originator of the tea ceremony. A little further beyond is *Hana Yagura* (lit. Flower Tower), which commands a splendid view of the Upper Thousand Trees. Further inward is Yoshino-Mikumari Shrine, rebuilt in 1604 by Toyotomi Hideyori. A typical example of Momoyama-period shrine architecture, its structures are Important Cultural Properties. A little way up the hill stands Kimpu Shrine, and to the right of that is the site of the hermitage of the famous priest-poet Saigyo (1118–1190). This is also the location of the fourth grove of cherry trees, *Oku-no-Sembon*.

Mt. Sanjogatake (Mt. Omine) ⬛75 : Alt. 1,719 m. Located about 24 km southeast of Yoshino, this is considered to be the most holy peak of the Omine Mountains and is the only mountain in Japan where women, even today, are not allowed to tread as ascetics. These mountains extend 50 km from north to south between the Totsu and Kitayama rivers, tributaries of the Kumano River, and were developed as a religious training ground. *Nishi-no-nozoki*, where trainees are required to lean over a cliff hundreds of meters high, is one of the magnificent sights. The main hall of Ominesanji Temple on the summit is famous because of a gold Buddhist image excavated from beneath it. On clear days, Mt. Fuji can be seen in the distance from here. The most common method of ascent is to take a bus for 1 hr. 35 min. from Shimoichi-guchi Station on the Kintetsu Yoshino Line to Dogawa. The ascent from there takes about 4 hrs.

Odaigahara Plateau 75 : A tableland with an altitude ranging from 1,654 to 1,695 m. It sits on the border between Nara and Mie prefectures, 64 km southeast of Nara. Frequently cloaked in mist, it is a high-precipitation area with an average rainfall of 4,700 mm a year. Bamboo grass covers the plain, rhododendrons and moorwart grow here and fallen trees are covered with moss. The western edge is cut off by Daijagura, a group of jagged cliffs. There are many beautiful waterfalls in Osugi Valley, where the the Miyakawa River has its source, while the gorge itself is one of the most imposing in Japan. It takes 2 hrs. 15 min. by bus from Yamato-Kamiichi Station on the Kintetsu Yoshino Line. During the appropriate season, there are lodging facilities available for mountain climbers and casual hikers.

Area 6. Southern Kii Peninsula

The southwest portion of the Kii Peninsula provides an ideal holiday resort. It is blessed with a mild climate, beautiful views of the coast and numerous spas as well as ancient temples and shrines. Besides, it is also only a short distance from Osaka. The Kumano district in the south is one of the most popular tourist spots, containing the grand Dorokyo Gorge, the famous Nachi Waterfall and the picturesque coastlines of Kushimoto and Katsuura. The Kumano district was combined with the Yoshino District to form Yoshino-Kumano National Park in 1936.

TRANSPORTATION

Visitors from Osaka may take a JR limited express train from Tennoji (some trains originate at Shin-Osaka) on the Hanwa Line (up to Wakayama) and Kisei Main Line (after Wakayama) destined for Shingu via Gobo, Kii-Tanabe, Shirahama, Kushimoto and Kii-Katsuura. The total elapsed time is 4 hrs. For those coming from Nagoya, take a JR limited express train bound for Kii-Katsuura via Shingu on its Kansai Main Line, Ise Railway's tracks and the Kisei

Main Line—a 4-hr. 10-min. trip. There are also flights to Shirahama from Tokyo and Nagoya. Highways include National Highway 26 to Wakayama and National Highway 42, which follows the peninsular coast. From Gojo in Nara Prefecture, National Highway 168 passes through the mountains, coming out at Shingu.

Wakayama 76/94-① ☎0734

Pop. 400,143. The capital of Wakayama Prefecture. Two railways connect Osaka and Wakayama; 45 min. by limited express from Tennoji Station to Wakayama Station on the JR Hanwa Line, or 1 hr. by express from Namba Station to Wakayamashi Station on the Nankai Electric Railway. A branch of the JR Kisei Main Line runs between Wakayama Station and Wakayamashi Station in 6 min. (3.3 km).

The area was once called Kii Province, or Kishu. Since the lord of Kishu originated from one of the sons of Tokugawa Ieyasu, the special position of those successive lords in relation to the Tokugawa Shogunate gave them political and military influence over western Japan. A seaside industrial district occupies the area around the mouth of the Kinokawa River, where metals, chemicals, traditional textiles and furniture are produced.

Wakayama Castle 94-① : Located in the center of the city, the castle was built in 1585 by order of Toyotomi Hideyoshi (1536–1598). The present three-story donjon is a 1958 reconstruction as the original was destroyed by air raids during World War II. Besides a museum and an observation platform within the donjon itself, Momijidani Garden, designed in the early part of Tokugawa period, on the north side of the donjon is famed for its beautiful landscape, making effective use of its undulation. The prefectural museum on the former castle grounds preserves and displays many National Treasures and Important Cultural Properties supplied from shrines and temples around the prefecture. Kata, about 15 km northwest of Wakayama, and Tomogashima Island, off its coast, are famous for swimming and fishing.

Wakanoura 76 : 25 min. by bus from Wakayamashi Station on the JR and Nankai lines or 40 min. from the JR Wakayama Station. Wakanoura, with its extension Shin-Wakanoura, has long been regarded as one of the most scenic places in the region. Take the ropeway up Mt. Takazushi for an excellent view of the entire area.

Kimiidera Temple 76 : 600 m from the JR Kimiidera Station or 35 min. by bus from the JR Wakayama station or Wakayamashi Station on the JR and Nankai lines. The second Station on the 33 Temple Pilgrimage in the Former Western Provinces, this temple was founded in 770 by Iko, a Chinese priest of the T'ang Dynasty, and is the headquarters of the Guse-Kannon sect of Buddhism. *Romon* (Tower Gate), a Belfry, *Tahoto* (Pagoda), a wooden statue of Thousand-Handed *Kannon*, two wooden images of Eleven-Headed *Kannon* and two other statues are all Important Cultural Properties.

The temple grounds contain about 400 cherry trees, three-fourths of which are *higan-zakura*—an early flowering variety that blooms in late March. The view of Wakanoura and Awaji Island from here is excellent.

Kii Fudoki-no-Oka (Hill of Local History and Topography) is a group of more than 500 tumuli in a park about 2 km east of the city. Some of stone vaults can be entered. The park contains old houses brought from all over the prefecture as well as a museum of archaeological and folk history.

Southern Kii Peninsula

Negoroji Temple 76 : Headquarters of the Shingi-Shingon sect of Buddhism, 8 km east of Kii Station on the JR Hanwa Line. It was founded in 1130 by priest Kakuban or Kokyo-Daishi (1095-1143). The extensive grounds are said to have once contained more than 2,700 temples, but the area was ravaged by fighting with Toyotomi Hideyoshi. It was reconstructed in 1623. Among the many buildings now standing, *Tahoto*, a National Treasure, or the Two-Story Pagoda constructed in 1515, is the largest of its type still standing. The garden with its many stones has been designated as a Place of Scenic Beauty. The cherry blossoms of early April are famed for their beauty.

Kokawadera Temple 76 : The temple is located 20 km east of Wakayama and 800 m north of Kokawa Station on the JR Wakayama Line. Founded in 770, it had more than 500 structures during its heyday, but all of them were burned in 1585 as a result of attacks by Toyotomi Hideyoshi. The Main Hall was reconstructed in 1720, with a famous garden in front that has many rocks and azaleas. This is the third Station on the 33 Temple Pilgrimage in the Former Western Provinces. The scroll depicting the history of Kokawadera Temple is thought to date from the early Kamakura period and is a National Treasure, but it is not on public display.

Mt. Koya 76 : The name for the mountain mass with an altitude of 900 m in the eastern part of the Nagamine mountains, which are part of the Kii Mountain Chain. It is included in the Koya-Ryujin Quasi-National Park. The mountain has a plateau extending 6 km from east to west and 3 km from north to south. A town centered around Kongobuji Temple, a temple founded in 816 by Kukai (774-835), is situated on the plateau. Kukai, also known as Kobo-Daishi, was the great founder of the Shingon sect. The temple grounds extend over an area of almost 1 sq.km and are covered with dense forest. Fires have frequently occurred, but 53 temple lodgings and more than 100 temple buildings still remain in the town today. Many people come here to escape the summer heat. From Namba (Osaka), take the Nankai Koya Line express for 1 hr.30 min. to Gokurakubashi Station, ride up the cable car and then take a bus for 15 min. If one takes the

JR Wakayama Line, transfer to the Nankai Koya Line at Hashimoto.

When taking the cable car toward the halfway point up the mountain, the first thing that will appear is *Nyonindo* (Women's Hall). Until the restrictions were lifted in 1872, women were prohibited from entering the temple proper and had to stop here. Cedars and *Koya-maki* or Koya black pines grow in profusion in this area.

Kongobuji Temple, the headquarters of the Koyasan-Shingon sect of Buddhism, was originally a general name for the whole region of Mt. Koya, but now it only refers to this chief temple. The screens painted by the Kano school artists and the rhododendrons in the garden are special attractions.

Danjo-Garan Temple is 300 m west of Kongobuji Temple. *Kompondaito* (Large Central Tower), the most imposing building on Mt. Koya, is part of this temple. It was built in 1937 with five figures of Buddha enshrined inside and brightly colored paintings of Buddhist religious subjects covering the walls and poles. Right next to it is *Fudodo* Hall (a National Treasure), built in 1198. A light, airy structure, it is the oldest building remaining on Mt. Koya. Other buildings such as the Main Hall, East Tower, West Tower and *Miedo* (Sacred Portrait Hall) stand nearby. A portrait of Kukai is the main image in *Miedo*.

Reihokan (Treasure House) contains a standing statue of *Hachidai Doji*, attributed to Unkei (a National Treasure), a picture of Amitabha welcoming the souls (a National Treasure) and other temple treasures, totaling as many as 25,000. *Daimon*, the Two-Story Gate that stands in the western end of the grounds, was built in 1705 and is 25 m tall. It is the main gate to Mt. Koya. Kitan Straits, Awaji Island and even Shikoku Island can be seen when standing in front of the gate.

East of the temple group is Ichinohashi Bridge, the first bridge to *Okuno-in*, or Kukai's mausoleum. The avenue from Ichinohashi Bridge to the mausoleum is lined on both sides with numerous tombs and memorial stones of believers of all classes, including some of the most celebrated figures of Japanese history. Just behind Ichinohashi Bridge is a replica of the famous Nestorian Monument of Sian, China. It was erected in 1911 by Mrs. G.A. Gorden, an Irish woman who had once served as lady-in-waiting to Queen Victoria. Near the end of the approach is *Gomado* (Holy Fire Hall), an old temple containing a seated wooden image of Fudo that is an Important Cultural Property. Close by is *Gokusho*, the building where offerings to the mausoleum are cooked, and behind that is *Torodo* Hall, a ferro-concrete building containing over 3,000 *toro* (lanterns) that were all dedicated by devotees. The mausoleum is behind *Torodo* and contains the ashes of Kukai, while next to that is the octagonal *Nokotsudo* (Charnel House), where the remains of those who wish to rest near Kukai are consecrated.

Kainan 76 ☎0734: Pop. 50,272. Located 10 km from Wakayama, this industrial city is known for a type of lacquerware called *Kuroe-nuri*. Petroleum, chemical, spinning and print-dyeing industries also flourish here.

Chohoji Temple 76 : About 2 km east of Shimotsu Station on the JR Kisei Main Line. Founded in the year 1000, it is the historical burial ground for the successive lords of the Tokugawa branch family that ruled the Kii Province (now, Wakayama Prefecture). The Main Gate built in 1388, Main Hall of 1311 and the Two-Story Pagoda are all National Treasures.

Arida 76 ☎0737: Pop.35,737. About 25 km from Wakayama, the city, especially the Minoshima area at the mouth of the Arida River, is famous for the cultivation of mandarin oranges and the production of mosquito coils. In fact, these mandarin oranges, popularly known as *Kishu-Mikan*, are regarded as one of the finest in Japan. Many petrochemical-related industries can also be found here. In the surrounding area, seven stone stupas remain to indicate that this was once the area in which priest Myoe (1173-1232), an eminent leader of the Kegon sect of Buddhism, was active. It has been designated as a Historical Site. Jomyoji Temple, about 2 km southwest of Mino-shima Station on the JR Kisei Main Line, was founded in 806 by a Chinese priest of the T'ang Dynasty named Nyoho. It contains a main hall and two-story pagoda from the late Kamakura period (1192 -1333), which are Important Cultural Properties, as well as many ancient Buddhist statues.

Yura is famous for Kokokuji Temple, also known as the Komuso Temple. Komuso is a priest of the Fuke sect of Buddhism. The priests would cover their faces with woven, basket-like hats, play the *shakuhachi* (a bamboo flute) and ask for alms. They held a special position in Edo-period (1603-1867) society.

Gobo 76 ☎0738: Pop. 29,262. Located at the mouth of the Hidaka River, this small industrial town is known for the production of lumber, paper and mahjong tiles. To the west of the city is Enju Kaigan (Coast) Prefectural Park, which features a scenic, 6-km-long beach called Enjugahama, which is covered with white sand and bordered by a pine forest. Benten Island, which lies off the coast on the way to Cape Hinomisaki, is a nesting ground for black-tailed gulls.

Dojoji Temple 76 : Located east of Gobo. Popular for its association with the story of Anchin and Kiyohime, a favorite *kabuki* drama that should be seen by anyone interested in old Japanese legends. Founded in 701 by Ki-no-Michinari at the request of Emperor Mommu, the Main Hall, an Important Cultural Property, was reconstructed during the Muromachi period (1336-1573). The main image is a wooden statue of *Senju-Kannon* (Thousand-Handed Kannon) made during the late Heian period (794-1185). It stands 3.6 m high. The temple also possesses a scroll illustrating the story of Anchin and Kiyohime and several Buddhist statues—all Important Cultural Properties.

The story is about a youthful monk named Anchin, who made a pilgrimage every year to Kumano Shrine. On the trip he would spend the night at the house of a yeoman whose daughter Kiyohime fell in love with him. One day she revealed her feelings and he promised to return her love on his return journey from Kumano. On the way back, however, Anchin went by the house without stopping, whereupon the girl changed herself into a giant snake and chased him. Anchin rushed into Dojoji Temple and hid himself under a bell that had not yet been hung. The snake entwined itself around the bell until the metal turned red-hot and then slithered away and vanished in the Hidaka River, not far from the temple. When the bell was raised, only a few charred bones could be found.

Minabe ⬜76⬜: About 60 km directly south of Wakayama. It is famed for having Japan's largest plum grove, which is said to contain some 300,000 trees. During the blossoming season in late January to early February, numerous visitors are attracted from the Osaka area. The pickled fruit is a famous local specialty. About 60 km northeast of Minabe is Ryujin Spa (1 hr.55 min. by bus from Kii-Tanabe Station on the JR Kisei Main Line). The alkaline spring bubbles forth from the upper reaches of the Hidaka River among the mountains, with a dip in its waters reputedly capable of making the bather beautiful.

Tanabe ⬜76⬜ ☎0739: Pop. 71,683. About 100 km from Wakayama on the JR Kisei Main Line. Protected from the north wind by the mountains and facing Tanabe Bay in the south, Tanabe provides a healthy climate in winter, while the summer heat is tempered by sea breezes that make the nights especially cool. It is known as the birthplace of Benkei, the most loyal retainer of Minamoto-no-Yoshitsune and a popular figure in *kabuki* plays. Among Tanabe's many good swimming beaches, Ogigahama, with its long stretches of pine trees and nearby islets, is the most popular.

National Highway 311, which passed through the mountainous region from Tanabe to Kumano, is also known as Nakaheji (Middle Pilgrimage Road), while the route from Tanabe to Hongu along the coast is called Oheji (Main Pilgrimage Road) or Umiheji (Seaside Pilgrimage Road). Pilgrims coming to worship at the temples and shrines of the Kumano district have traveled both roads since ancient times.

Shirahama ⬜76⬜: A large spa to the south across the bay from Tanabe. It can be reached from Tennoji in Osaka in 2 hrs. by limited express on the JR Kisei Main Line—a distance of 167 km. It is a 10-min. bus ride from Shirahama Station to the center of the spa town. The hot water of the various springs in Shirahama is piped to the many *ryokan* and public bathhouses. The waters are efficacious against rheumatism, neuralgia, female complaints and gastroenteric ailments. There are many places of interest in and around the spa, including Senjojiki, a huge rock formation, and Sandanheki, a breathtaking, 50-m-high cliff that extends along the beach. Other attractions include an aquarium with the experimental facilities of Kyoto University, Shirahama Energy Land with displays of pictures of future city life using only natural energy, a life-sized electric dinosaur and three-dimensional movies, a hothouse of tropical plants at Hama Blanca and the Kishu Museum with a fine collection of such *ukiyo-e* masters as Utamaro and Hokusai. Swimming can be enjoyed on Shirara Beach during summer. Adventure Land contains a safari park with some 2,300 animals of 200 species roaming about freely and Marine World with dolphin and seal shows as well as an aquarium.

Tsubaki Spa 76 : Situated 8 km south of Shirahama. It is perched high on the rocky coast, commanding a fine view of the seascape. The waters are efficacious for the treatment of nervous afflictions and rheumatism.

The coast from Shirahama to Kushimoto is called the Kareki-nada Coast and supports a growth of temperate-climate plants—a Natural Monument—as well as many various-shaped boulders.

Kushimoto 76 : About 160 km from Wakayama on the JR Kisei Main Line. This is a fishing port on the neck of Cape Shionomisaki. Scenic *Hashikui-Iwa* is a row of more than 40 rocks of all sizes in a regular line extending for about 700 m in the ocean directly facing Oshima Island. They resemble the supports of a bridge (*hashikui*); hence, the name.

The ocean west of Kushimoto has been designated as a marine park. The marine observation tower, standing 140 m offshore, permits visitors to descend 6.3 m below the waterline to see the coral and fish. A glass-bottomed boat is also available. The Marine Pavilion has an aquarium with 50 types of coral and 350 kinds of fish.

Cape Shionomisaki 76 : About 6 km south of the JR Kushimoto Station, 20 min. by bus, at the southernmost tip of Honshu, at 33°26' north latitude. The white lighthouse, built in 1878, stands on a grassy flat and has a light that sweeps over the ocean for a distance of 35 km.

Oshima Island is about 2 km off the coast of Kushimoto and can be reached by boat in 10 min. Sub-tropical plants grow in the warm climate of the island, which is lined with towering cliffs on the south side. A monument to the 581 Turkish sailors of the Erutogroru, a warship that was wrecked off the east coast of the island in 1890, has been erected on Cape Kashino.

Taiji 76 : A fishing port 20 km northeast of Kushimoto that was known as the center of the whaling industry in the Kumano District. In Kujirahama Park, 5 min. by bus from Taiji Station on the JR Kisei Main Line, are a whaling boat museum and a whale museum that has exhibits on the many species of whales, their physical make-up, artifacts and models that tell the history of whaling, etc. These museums allow visitors to come in contact with an important segment of local history.

Kii-Katsuura 76 : Like Shirahama, Kii-Katsuura is one of the most prominent hot-spring areas in the southern Kii District. 3 hrs. 30 min. on the JR limited express from Tennoji in Osaka—a distance of 248 km—or, 4 hrs. 10 min. on the JR limited express from Nagoya—a distance of 224 km. Although the shoreline is complex, the city has flourished because of its excellent natural harbor. It is also conveniently located for going on a sightseeing tour of the many landmarks in the area. Hot springs are ubiquitous and many of *ryokan* are equipped to accommodate a large number of guests. People often take a boat to the tip of the peninsula or Nakanoshima Island. The mineral waters are efficacious against rheumatism, neuralgia, female complaints and skin diseases. Bokido, a famous large spa inside a cavern facing the ocean, makes visitors forget about returning home because of its soothing, relaxing bathing. A view of the area can be obtained from Noroshiyama Park.

Outside the bay is a group of islands called Ki-no-Matsushima, named for their rough, wild beauty that resembles Matsushima in the Tohoku District. Yukawa Spa is located near Yukashigata Cove southwest of the city.

Mt. Nachi ⬚76⬚ : 30 min. by bus north from Katsuura Spa via Nachi Station on the JR Kisei Main Line. Kumano-Nachi Shrine, Seigantoji Temple and Nachi Waterfall are cloaked in the greenery of the Nachi Primeval Forest, a Natural Monument.

Nachi Waterfall is approached by descending a flight of stone steps lined with cedars, then passing through a *torii* gate. It is the largest of the many waterfalls in the Nachi River, with a 133-m drop.

Kumano-Nachi Shrine ⬚76⬚ : It consists of five main shrines in a row at the top of a long flight of stone steps. They are constructed in the *Kumano-zukuri*, or Kumano style. Considered one of the three most important shrines in the district along with Kumano-Hayatama Shrine and Kumano Hongu Shrine, it has attracted numerous worshippers since ancient times. The treasure house contains a sacred sword donated in 1636 by Tokugawa Yorinobu, the lord of the Kii Tokugawa branch family, and an ancient bronze seal, both of which are Important Cultural Properties. The famous fire festival that takes place on July 14 includes a long procession of torches.

According to legend, Seigantoji Temple originated when priest Ragyo arrived here from India and constructed a small shrine. It then became the headquarters of the Kumano Yamabushi (mountain priests) and is the first Station on the 33 Temple Pilgrimage in the Former Western Provinces. The Main Hall (an Important Cultural Property), standing next to Kumano-Nachi Shrine, was constructed in 1587, while the vermilion, three-story pagoda is a 1972 reconstruction. The principal image of the Main Hall is *Nyoirin-Kannon*.

Shingu ⬚76⬚ ☎0735: Pop. 36,616. Located about 200 km from Wakayama at the mouth of the Kumano River. This is the southeast extremity of Wakayama Prefecture. Lumber and paper manufacture are the chief industries. Kumano-Hayatama Shrine is quite ancient and one of the three most important shrines in the area. Many of the ancient mirrors, boxes, statues and other treasures preserved here are National Treasures or Important Cultural Properties, some of which are on public display. The giant, 20-m-tall *maki* (a kind of podocarpus), which has been designated as a Natural Monument, can be seen here.

Next to the JR Shingu Station lie the graves of Ch'in Hsu Fu and his seven retainers who, according to legend, were sent to Japan in the third century B.C. by Ch'in, the first emperor of China, in search of medicine that would provide immortality.

Dorokyo Gorge 〔76〕: This gorge is created by the Kitayama River, a tributary of the Kumano River, and is considered to be one of the most beautiful gorges in Japan. To ride the water-jet excursion boat through it, take a bus for 45 min. from Shingu Station on the JR Kisei Main Line. The sides are sheer cliffs and fantastically shaped rocks lie scattered about. The outstanding features in the continuous, breathtaking beauty include *Byobu-Iwa* (lit. "Screen Rock"), which is 20 m tall and 87 m wide, and the Kankyoku Rapids, which have a depth of 21 m. The lower reaches for about 1 km are called *Shimo* (Lower)-*Doro*, while *Kami* (Upper)-*Doro* is a 2-km section in the upper reaches. A round trip can be made in 2 hrs. *Doro* means "deep, quiet waters." Azaleas and rhododendrons blossoming between the cracks in the rocks from May to June and the autumn leaves are especially beautiful.

Kumano 〔77〕 ☎05978: Pop. 24,119. 20 km northeast of Shingu, adjoining Mie Prefecture. The coastline along the way is called Shichirimihama, a gentle curving beach lined with sand. In striking contrast, part of the north coast is jagged, including a grotesque rock formation called Onigajo (Demon Castle). Good timber and mandarin oranges are produced here.

Kumano Hongu Shrine 〔76〕: Situated along National Highway 168, which runs from Shingu to Gojo in Nara Prefecture. It takes 1 hr. 20 min. by bus from the JR Shingu Station. The grounds of this serene, ancient shrine are filled with buildings.

Kawayu Spa 〔76〕: South of Kumano Hongu Shrine. As the name, which means "Hot Water River," indicates, hot water bubbles up from the bed of the Oto River, a tributary of the Totsukawa River. One has only to dig a hole in the riverbed to take a dip in a hot spring.

Yunomine Spa 〔76〕: About 2 km from Kumano Hongu Shrine, along National Highway 311, which connects Hongu and Tanabe. Historically, people have come here to purify their bodies before praying at the shrine. Today, it is said that the waters have a beautifying effect.

Totsukawa: This town is in Nara Prefecture and can be reached by heading north on National Highway 168 from Yunomine Spa. The 297-m-long and 54-m-tall Tanise Suspension Bridge crosses the river here. Totsukawa Spa, Tozenji Spa and many other hot springs are clustered along the river.

Area 7. Kobe and Vicinity

Kobe 79/88-89 ☎078

Pop. 1,426,156. Kobe is the capital of Hyogo Prefecture and, combined with Osaka, Amagasaki, Nishinomiya and Ashiya, forms a contiguous urban area along the north coast of Osaka Bay. The JR Tokaido Main Line runs to all five of these cities, which are linked by the JR, Hankyu and Hanshin lines. Kobe (Shin-Kobe) can be reached from Tokyo on the Shinkansen in 3 hrs. 20 min.—a distance of 590 km—and from Nagoya in 1 hr.20 min.—a distance of 224 km.

In the same way that Yokohama serves the east, Kobe is the west gateway to international trade. A substantial share of total exports and imports are handled in Kobe. In terms of population, it is the sixth-largest city in Japan and second only to Osaka in the Kinki District. Protected by a range of hills in the north, it enjoys a very temperate climate, making it a favorite place to live for expatriates.

Administratively, Kobe is divided into eight wards: Chuo, Higashi-Nada, Hyogo, Kita, Nada, Nagata, Suma and Tarumi. The city spreads from east to west along the north shore of Osaka Bay, hemmed in at the back by mountains. The business district extends along the waterfront, while the residential district is in the hills. Kobe proper is contained within Chuo Ward. It is divided into two regions: Yamate (or Bluff) and Kaigan-dori (or Waterfront). Between these two districts are located some well-known shopping streets such as Motomachi, Sannomiya, "Tor Road" and "Sanchika Town"—a mall extending from the basement of the Sannomiya Station. The three main JR stations in Kobe are Shin-Kobe, Sannomiya and Kobe. Out of the three, the most convenient for visiting tourists is Sannomiya because it is situated near the piers and in the heart of the city, where many banks, shipping companies and major foreign and Japanese business offices are located, although some offices are now also on Port Island. There are many souvenir shops lining the streets to serve the numerous tourists that flock to the city. Kobe is also a mecca for gourmets. Not only Japanese food but Western, Chinese and the cuisines of many other countries are all delicious, not to mention the famous Nada *sake*, superb Kobe beef and many other local specialties.

HISTORY

The history of Kobe is as old as the history of Japan. In ancient times, it was known as Muko. Muko-no-Tomari (Muko Port), part of what is now Hyogo Port, was a good, natural port. It served as a window through which Chinese and Korean culture entered Japan in those days. In the 12th century, military leader Taira-no-Kiyomori (1118–1181) moved the capital from Kyoto to Fukuhara (now, western Kobe) to try and bring prosperity to Japan through foreign trade, carrying out a huge port construction plan. The capital lasted only six months, but its port, Hyogo, prospered and continued to do so. For a time in the 16th century, ships bound for Osaka made it a port of call. By 1788 it had a population of 19,580, which increased significantly after the port of Kobe was opened to foreign trade on January 1, 1868.

It was for the sake of political expediency to evade many voices opposed to the opening of Hyogo to foreign trade that Kobe, a port somewhat northeast of Hyogo, was opened, as in the case of Yokohama, which developed as an open port in lieu of Kanagawa. At that time, Hyogo was the capital of the prefecture and Kobe a suburb, but as the years passed and the port increased in importance, Kobe eventually absorbed Hyogo.

A railway between Osaka and Kobe opened in 1874. Some years later, work began on the San-yo Line to link Kobe with Shimonoseki at the western tip of Honshu. When the predominance of Kobe was recognized in 1889, the city was granted a charter which incorporated Hyogo. The Sino-Japanese War (1894-1895) and the Russo-Japanese War (1904-1905) spurred the development of the port. When Yokohama's silk trade collapsed temporarily after the earthquake of 1923, much of the country's silk business was diverted to Kobe. During World War II, Kobe was the target of air raids that devastated two-thirds of the city. Kobe recovered rapidly after the war, however, expanding and absorbing neighboring towns and villages into the municipality. Port Island, a man-made island, was completed in 1981, and now Rokko Island is nearing completion (scheduled in 1992).

INDUSTRIES AND TRADE

As a major port, Kobe handled 12.6% of the nation's exports in 1989 totaling some ¥4.9 trillion, and 8.3% of the imports, exceeding ¥2.5 trillion. Kobe's principal exports are machinery, metals, iron and steel products, fibers and textile products, and office appliances as well as VTRs. Imported goods include clothing, fruit, vegetables, marine products, organic compounds, nonferrous metals and petroleum.

The industry of Kobe developed along with its port, with Kobe and its neighboring cities forming part of the Hanshin (Osaka-Kobe) Industrial Zone. The main industries are the heavy ones such as iron and steel, rolling stock, shipbuilding and machinery. Also significant are the food processing, chemicals, electronics, sugar manufacturing, flour milling and *sake* brewing industries.

TRANSPORTATION

Railways: Sannomiya is the city's transportation center. The JR Tokaido Main Line heads eastwards for Osaka and Kyoto, while for the westwards it becomes the JR San-yo Main Line from Kobe and then extends to Suma and Akashi. The Hanshin Main Line runs from Motomachi to Umeda in Osaka via Sannomiya and Ashiya. The Hankyu Kobe Line runs from Sannomiya to Umeda. Limited express trains on both of the latter lines reach Umeda in about 30 min.

To the west, the Kobe Rapid Transit Railway runs between San-nomiya and Sumaura-koen, traveling partway on the tracks of the Hankyu, Hanshin and San-yo electric railways. From Nishidai, the San-yo Electric Railway goes west to Himeji (1 hr.5 min. by limited express), passing the famous seaside resorts of Suma and Akashi en route.

The Kobe Electric Railway runs from Shinkaichi, where it is linked with the Kobe Rapid Transit Railway, to Arima Spa and Sanda on the JR Fukuchiyama Line. Sannomiya and Shin-Kobe on the JR San-yo Shinkansen are 2 minutes apart on the municipal subway, which extends further to Tanigami on the Kobe Electric Railway and to Seishin-chuo via Minatogawa-koen in the opposite direction.

The computer-run Portliner leaves Sannomiya for a circular run on Port Island, while the Rokkoliner plies between the JR Sumiyoshi Station and Rokko Island.

Airport Buses: Buses to Osaka International Airport leave JAL and ANA Sannomiya offices and from Portopia Hotel on Port Island, each arriving in 30 min.

Ferries: In addition to the long-distance ferries to Shikoku, Kyushu and Okinawa, a car ferry also operates between Kobe and Shanghai, China. The Kobe-Naka (Middle) Pier can be reached on foot in 10 min. from the JR Motomachi Station, but Higashi-Kobe Port (Uozaki, Aoki and Rokko Island piers) must be reached by bus from the JR Ashiya Station.

Highways: The Hanshin Expressway and National Highways 2 and 43 run parallel through the area. The Meishin Expressway joins the Hanshin Expressway at Nishinomiya, while the No.2 Shimmei Highway runs in the direction of Akashi.

Sightseeing Bus Tours: The Bureau of Transportation offers several kinds of half-day tours of the major tourist attractions in and around the city. All guided tours are provided in Japanese only. Schedules depend on the day of week and time of year. For information and reservations, call or visit the City Tourist Information Office.

ANNUAL EVENTS

Irizomeshiki (Hot-Spring Opening Ceremony): January 2 at Arima Spa. In order to commemorate the occasions when one Buddhist priest opened the spa and another later restored it, their wooden images are placed in a portable shrine, carried through the streets of the town by priests and *geisha*, and are given the year's first bath.

Tsuinashiki (Ceremony to Drive Away Evil Spirits): February 3–4 at Nagata Shrine in Nagata Ward. On the eve of *Setsubun* at the beginning of spring, seven "devils" dance about holding flaming torches.

Nanko Festival: May 25 at Minatogawa Shrine in Chuo Ward. Held in memory of Kusunoki Masashige, a loyal general popularly known as "Nanko-san." During divine services, traditional folk songs are sung. May 25 is the day Masashige died a hero's death in 1336.

Kobe Festival: The third weekend in May. The festival is held to offer congratulations for the city's prosperity. One of the many events is a colorful parade of thousands of citizens complete with baton twirlers and brass bands.

Kobe Port Fireworks Festival: The last Saturday in July or the first Saturday in August near the Kobe Port Terminal. The colorful explosions light up the summer night sky.

Takigi Noh: August 1–2 at Nagata Shrine in Nagata Ward. The outdoor performance of *noh* plays by torchlight creates a mysterious beauty.

Refer to the supplement for details regarding the "i" **System Information Center** in Kobe.

PLACES OF INTEREST

Chuo Ward

Sannomiya ⟨79⟩ : Sannomiya Station is the center of transportation, where the JR, Hankyu and Hanshin lines as well as the subway and Portliner all stop. Hankyu and Sogo department stores, the Kobe Newspaper Company and other major commercial establishments are also concentrated in this area. The underground "Sanchika Town" is a mall, where some 150 specialty shops offer fashion garment and gourmet food. Immediately west of "Sanchika Town" is Sannomiya Center Street—an arcade lined with clothing, shoe and many other kinds of shops. It is the representative shopping district of Kobe. The 50-m-wide road extending from the station to Kaigan-dori Road is called Flower Road because it has flowers growing along both sides and in the median strip. The Kobe City Hall stands on the west side of the road, while north of it is a flower clock 6 m across. The totem pole standing next to the flower clock was a gift from the city of Seattle, Washington, USA, Kobe's sister city. In the park on the south side of the city hall stands a statue of Wencesalos de Moraes (1854–1929), the Portuguese consul general who introduced many things about Japan to his home country. The Kobe City Museum, 8 min. on foot from Sannomiya Station, has a collection that shows the antiquities, history and folk culture of the area as well as a famous collection of 16th- and 17th-century pictures of Portuguese and Spanish influence. The area around Daimaru Department Store was once the site of the foreign residential community that developed after the Treaty of Amity and Commerce were signed by England, America, France and two other countries in 1858. This area became a center for the development of Kobe. A gas lamp and a monument showing the old residential area stands in front of Daimaru Department Store. Motomachi, the shopping district that continues west of Sannomiya Center Street, is characterized by the sedate atmosphere found only in shops that have been around for a long time. The south side of the eastern part of this road is called Nanking-machi (China town) because there are many Chinese restaurants and food stores among the numerous restaurants and bars in the area.

Kobe Port 88-89 : One of the most prominent international ports in Japan. Some 12,000 foreign ships annually make this a port of call through which some 44 million tons of freight pass. The port covers quite a large area including many piers with berths, with ten Shinko piers lining the center. Maya Wharf, consisting of four piers, is located to the east. Further to the east on a man-made island named Rokko Island, which is still under construction, a container wharf and ferry wharf are already in operation. To the south on Port Island, another man-made island, a container wharf is on the western side of the island, while three additional wharfs are on the eastern side. To the west is Naka Pier, where passenger liners ply to Awaji Island, Shikoku, Kyushu and Okinawa. Further to the southwest are three Hyogo piers, where domestic and international trade flourishes. When *Meriken Hatoba* (American Pier), located to the northeast of Naka Pier, was constructed in 1868, it was in front of the American consulate at that time; hence, the name. *Meriken* Park is a 150,000-sq.-m area between Naka Pier and Meriken Hatoba that was made by filling in the ocean between the two. Kobe Port Tower, the Kobe Maritime Museum, a hotel, a multi-purpose hall, restaurants and many other facilities as well as a lawn square and observation platform are all located here. A sightseeing boat that circles the Kobe Port area leaves from a dock next to Port Tower.

Kobe Port Tower 88 : An hourglass-shaped, 108-m-high tower. A panoramic view can be enjoyed from its five-story, glass-enclosed observatory. The Kobe Maritime Museum has models, video films and objects related to ships, the port and the ocean. Its white clipper-and-wave motif pipe facade is beautiful.

Port Island 88-89 : A 4.36-sq.-km, man-made island that is linked to Pier No. 4 by the red, double-arched Kobe Ohashi Bridge. The island was constructed over a period of 15 years by filling in the ocean with earth shaved off the mountain in the northern part of the city. It was completed in 1981. The unmanned Portliner is run by computer between the JR Sannomiya Station and the island. On the island are Portopia Land with its giant, 63-m-high ferris wheel and a loop-coaster, the UCC Coffee Museum exhibiting data on coffee, the Kobe Science Museum, which includes one of the best planetariums in the world, the Port Island Sports Center, the International Conference Center Kobe and the Kobe Trade Promotion Center as well as Fashion Town with its concentration of fashion-related manufacturers. It is 15 min. on the Portliner from Sannomiya Station to Shimin-Hiroba Station.

International Conference Center: Situated on the northern part of Pier No. 4, standing 26 stories high. It contains various organizations concerned with external trade, commerce and manufacturing.

Ikuta Shrine 88 : 500 m northwest of Sannomiya Station. Said to have been founded by Empress Jingu on her return from the Korean campaign in the third century, it is dedicated to the goddess Wakahirume-no-Mikoto. The name, Kobe, was derived from "Kambe," the area donated for this shrine by the Imperial Court. The newly reconstructed shrine buildings are attractive with vermilion paint. In back of the shrine is a grove of camphor trees, while the area from the shrine to Sannomiya Station is full of restaurants and bars, providing a lively night scene.

Kitanocho 88 : The Bluff district centering around Yamamoto-dori Street and Kitano-dori Street is usually called Kitanocho. It is known for some 30 Western-type buildings called *yokan* or *ijinkan* that were built from the later Meiji period (1868-1912) to the early Taisho period (1912-1926). The buildings still remain, creating a special atmosphere. "Tor Road," a fashionable shopping mall, runs from north to south between the western edge of Kitanocho and Sannomiya Center Street. Once used by expatriates going between their homes and their trading firms in the foreign settlement, this flourishing street is now lined with high-class boutiques and nice restaurants. Shin-Kobe Oriental City is a 37-story building in front of Shin-Kobe Station on the JR Shinkansen in the western part of Kitanocho. The three basement floors and first three floors above ground contain the shopping mall, which includes the 627-seat Shin-Kobe Oriental Theater as well as boutiques, restaurants and a disco—a total of some 200 establishments. The upper part of the building is a hotel.

Soraku-en Park 88 : 2 min. on foot from Yamate Subway Station. The azaleas are superb in this 20,000-sq.-m Japanese garden. The former Hassam (a trader from Great Britain) residence, built in 1902, and a red brick building that was once the barn of the Kodera family (the former owner of this property) stand in the park. Both buildings are Important Cultural Properties.

Minatogawa Shrine 88 : Situated 300 m north of Kobe Station, the shrine is popularly known as "Nanko-san" and is dedicated to Kusunoki Masashige, a loyal military strategist (1294-1336). He died in this area after being defeated in his attempt to uphold the cause of Emperor Godaigo against Ashikaga Takauji (1304-1358), who later founded the Ashikaga Shogunate. On the shrine grounds is a monument inscribed with the words "Ah, Here Lies the Faithful Kusunoki!" that was erected in 1692 by Tokugawa Mitsukuni, the lord of the Mito Tokugawa branch family. There are many camphor trees on the grounds, evidently because Kusunoki means camphor tree.

Suwayama Park 88 : Located on the 180-m-high Suwayama Hill on the northern side of the city center. It provides a splendid view of the city and port. There is an observatory named Kinseidai (Venus Observatory) since that is where French astronomer P.T.C. Jansen observed the planet of that name in 1874. It is linked to the park by the Venus Bridge, which is shaped like the figure 8.

Hyogo, Nagata, Nada and Higashi-Nada Wards

Shinkaichi 88 : The name of the area, which means new ground, is derived from the fact that it was created by reclaiming an old bed of the Minato River at the beginning of this century. The quarter has a number of *pachinko* (pinball game) parlors, movie theaters, bars and restaurants. In the northern part of Minatogawa Park are a bronze statue of Kusunoki Masashige, an outdoor concert hall and a fountain. It is right next to Kosoku Shinkaichi Station on the Kobe Kosoku (Rapid Transit) Railway.

Nagata Shrine 88 : 200 m north of Kosoku Nagata Station. Legend has it that the deity worshipped here, Kotoshironushi-no-Mikoto, wanted to be enshrined in a village in Nagata where the clucking of chickens could be heard. This led to the custom of offering chickens to the temple and several of them can be seen on the grounds even today. Many people come to this ancient temple on New Year's or *Setsubun* (February 3 or 4) to pray for business prosperity and good fortune.

Oji Park 89 : Covering some 20,000 sq.m, the park has a track-and-field area, a gymnasium, a pool, a zoo and many other recreational facilities. The former Hunter residence (an Important Cultural Property) northeast of the zoo was British trader E. H. Hunter's (1843–1917) home, moved here from Kitano. It is a large and beautiful two-story brick building of the Meiji period. The park is also known for its multitude of cherry trees. The park is close to Hankyu Oji-Koen Station. The Hyogo Prefectural Museum of Modern Art next to Oji Park houses a collection of some 3,000 works by artists from all over the world, especially those from Hyogo Prefecture.

Sawanotsuru Museum 89 : 7 min. on foot from Hanshin Oishi Station. The equipment for brewing *sake* as well as the process and history of *sake*-brewing are displayed inside a former *sake* warehouse built more than a century ago. Similar exhibits can be seen at the Kikumasamune Sake Production Memorial Museum near Hanshin Uozaki Station and the Hakutsuru Sake Brewery Museum near Hanshin Sumiyoshi Station.

Hakutsuru Fine Art Museum 89 : 15 min. on foot from Hanshin Mikage Station. Situated at the foot of Mt. Rokko, the magnificent two-story, Japanese-style building faces the Sumiyoshi River. The collection of some 1,000 Chinese and Japanese ancient art objects includes two National Treasures and more than twenty Important Cultural Properties. The Chinese bronzes of the Yin and Xizhou periods and the collection of ceramics ranging from the Han to the Ming dynasties are especially fine. The Kosetsu Museum of Art contains tea-ceremony articles as well as calligraphy, paintings, swords and other traditional Japanese arts, including about twenty Important Cultural Properties.

Rokko Island 89 : A man-made island east of Port Island, covering an area of 5.8 sq.km. Construction of a ferry dock, container berths, shopping and residential districts, and recreational facilities is under way, with completion scheduled for 1992.

Suma and Tarumi Wards

Suma Rikyu Koen (Detached Palace Park): Covering some 150,000 sq. m. The park's main attraction is the fountains, with the 474 fountain nozzles creating a wide variety of water designs. During summer, the water is illuminated with colored lights at night, creating a beautiful fantasy world. It is 10 min. on foot from Tsukimiyama Station on the San-yo Electric Railway.

Suma Temple: Properly called Fukushoji Temple. It is said to have been founded in 886 at the request of Emperor Koko. The wooden image of the Eleven-Headed *Kannon* of the Muromachi period (1336 –1573) is an Important Cultural Property. 5 min. on foot from Sumadera Station on the San-yo Electric Railway.

Suma Kaihin (Beach) Park: Located east of the JR Suma Station, it extends for about 2 km through pine groves to the sandy banks of the Myohoji River. In summer the beach is open for swimming. Suma Beach Aquarium, one of the largest aquariums in Japan, is situated in the park.

Sumaura Park [79]: An 87,000-sq.-m natural park, near Sumaura-koen Station on the San-yo Electric Railway. It includes Mt. Hachi-buse, where some 1,000 cherry trees grow, and Sumaura Beach. To mark the battle fought here in 1184 between the Minamoto Clan and the Taira Clan, there is a "Battle Beach" marker and a memorial to Taira-no-Atsumori, who died here. A ropeway runs 464 m from Sumaura-koen Station with a short connecting ride on a "carlator" to the top of Mt. Hachibuse (alt. 246 m). At the peak is a rotating observatory that commands an extensive view of Suma, Maiko and Akashi beaches as well as Awaji Island. A chairlift carries visitors to the summit of neighboring Mt. Hatafuri. Kobe Sports Park is close to Kobe-Sogoundojo Subway Station. Having served as the main grounds for the 1985 Universiad Kobe, it contains a track-and-field area and other facilities suitable for competitive, international events. Green Stadium Kobe at the northwest end of the park is an ultra-modern baseball stadium.

Goshikizuka Tumulus: Between Tarumi and Kasumigaoka stations on the San-yo Electric Railway. The 194-m-long tomb is shaped like a keyhole. It has been restored, surrounded by stones and decorated with *haniwa* (clay figures) as it was when first made.

Maiko Park: Disembark at Maiko Station on the JR San-yo Main Line at the west end of Kobe to arrive at this 23,000-sq.-m prefectural park along the waterfront. It adjoins Sumaura Park in the east and Akashi Park in the west, with a lovely view available of Awaji Island just across the Akashi Straits. The three-story, octagonal building in the center of the park is the Sun Yat-sen Museum Hall. Sun (1886–

1925) was the leader of the Chinese Revolution of 1911 and this hall exhibits personal articles and data concerning him.

Nishi Ward

Taisanji Temple: 5 min. by bus from Ikawadani Subway Station. This Tendai-sect Buddhist temple is said to have been founded by Jo-e, son of the Fujiwara family patriarch, Kamatari (614–669). The Main Hall is an imposing building of the late Kamakura period (1192 –1333) and has been designated as a National Treasure. There are many buildings such as *Niomon* Gate (an Important Cultural Property) that were reconstructed in the Muromachi period, *Sanju-no-To* (Three-Story Pagoda) and *Amidado* Halls, which contains many Important Cultural Properties such as an image of Amitabha. The grounds are surrounded by dense forest through which a fresh mountain stream flows.

Municipal Kobe Winery: 10 min. by bus from Seishin-chuo Subway Station. Commonly called the Wine Castle, a southern European-type, white-walled building stands on a small hill. Inside is a wine factory, a wine museum displaying various European wines and several kinds of wine glasses, a restaurant at which Kobe wine and Kobe beef are served, and lodging accommodations.

Nyoiji Temple: 8 min. by bus from Seishin-Chuo Station. The temple is said to have been founded in 645 by Hodo, the legendary hermit who rode in on a purple cloud from India. *Amidado* Hall, Three-Story Pagoda and *Monjudo* Hall are all Important Cultural Properties. Constructed in 1385, the Three-Story Pagoda, in particular, is thought to be a beautifully balanced building from a design point of view.

Mt. Rokko 79 : Alt. 931 m. The highest peak in the mountain chain that spreads approximately 30 km from the northeast to southwest, north of the cities of Kobe, Ashiya and Nishinomiya. Other high peaks in the chain are Mt. Kabuto (alt. 309 m.) in the east and Mt. Maya (alt. 699 m.) and Mt. Hachibuse in the west. One can reach the top by taking a bus from Hankyu Rokko Station (15 min.), the JR Rokkomichi Station (20 min.) or Hanshin Mikage Station (30 min.) to Rokko Keiburu(Cable car)-shita Station, from where it is another 10-min. ride by cable car. Or one may take a 30-min. bus ride from Hankyu Rokko Station from April to July. If coming by car from Ashiya, take the Royu Driveway to Arima or the Omote-Rokko Driveway, which passes by Rokko Keiburu-shita Station. From the summit, one can look over Osaka Bay and see distant Awaji Island in the easternmost part of the Inland Sea. Small ponds and thickets of trees are scattered about on the flats or on the spacious summit. For recreation, there are restaurants, hotels, golf courses, an alpine botanical garden, observatory, ranch and more. There is also a striking view of the harbor and the city lights at night. In summer, hydrangeas burst into riotous bloom. The 18-hole golf course on the summit is the oldest in Japan, dating back to 1903. The development of the area as a resort, including the golf course, was largely due to the British trader Arthur H. Groom. Today, a number of Osaka and Kobe residents, both Japanese and non-Japanese, have summer homes on the mountain. The numerous ponds attract campers in summer and skaters in winter. In winter, man-made snow is used for the ski grounds, whereas in other seasons "pla-snow" made of polyethylene plastic is provided for skiing. The revolving observatory at the top, which offers an excellent view of the entire surrounding area, is known as "Jukkoku (Ten Provinces) Observatory." Rokko Bokujo (Mt. Rokko Ranch) is located between Mt. Rokko and Mt. Maya. Barns and silos stand about on the ranch, designed after those in the Swiss Alps. Milk cows and sheep greet visitors. The ranch also has the Kobe Cheese Hall, where many different kinds of cheese can be sampled and the cheese-making process can be observed.

Mt. Maya 　79　: Alt. 702 m. The mountain was so-named because Tenjoji Temple, dedicated to Sakyamuni's mother, Maya, is located here. To reach the top, it is a 20-min. bus trip from Sannomiya, a 5-min. cable car ride from Maya Keiburu(Cable car)-shita Station and then 5 min. further on the ropeway. On a hill named Kikuseidai, meaning "platform to scoop up the stars," one can gaze at the beautiful nightscape, with twinkling lights scattered about like starts. Mt. Futatabi, 468 m above sea level, is directly north of Kobe Port. Many Kobe residents take their daily constitutional by hiking up and down the mountain. Beyond the thickly wooded slopes is Shuhoga-hara, a 20,000-sq.-m plain surrounded by verdure. The entire area comprises Futatabisan Park. Just below is Dairyuji Temple, where a wooden *Nyoirin Kannon* (an Important Cultural Property) is enshrined. A cemetery for foreigners lying just beyond the park was moved here from the city in 1952. The name, Mt. Futatabi or Futatabisan (Twice-Visited Mountain) is derived from the fact that Kobo-Daishi (774-835), who introduced Shingon-sect Buddhist doctrines to Japan, visited the mountain twice—on his way to China in 804 and upon his return in 806.

Kita Ward

Kobe Municipal Arboretum: Located along National Highway 428, the park covers more than 1 sq.km. Inside, some 1,200 species of plants from all over the world are grown according to their country of origin, with a path meandering between them. The Arboretum Exhibit Hall contains data on all kinds of trees, butterflies specimens from all over the world and other natural history displays.

Arima Spa 　78　: The resort is situated on the north side of the Rokko mountains, 40 min. from Minatogawa Station in Kobe on the Kobe Electric Railway Arima Line. By bus, it is less than 1 hr. from Umeda in Osaka, 40 min. from Sannomiya or 30 min. from Takarazuka. It was recorded that in the seventh century even the Emperors

came to bathe in the hot springs at Arima and that Toyotomi
Hideyoshi (subjugator of all feudal lords in the Azuchi-Momoyama
period) had the bathing facilities repaired for his enjoyment. Situated
at an altitude of 360 m, the area remains comparatively cool in
summer, while cherry blossoms can be enjoyed in spring and the
changing leaves can be viewed in autumn. There are approximately
25 *ryokan* or Japanese-style inns to choose from, many of which are
quite large. The top of Mt. Rokko is connected with Arima Spa by
ropeway or, if driving, by either the Ura-Rokko Driveway or the
Royu Driveway.

Sanda 78 ☎0795: Pop. 45,205. Located north of Arima Spa, the
city can be reached in 1 hr. by the Kobe Electric Railway Sanda Line
from Shinkaichi in Kobe or in 50 min. from Osaka on the JR Fukuchiyama Line. Situated in the the Sanda Valley, the area is famous
for its high-quality Sanda rice and the breeding of Sanda cattle.
Electric appliance factories can also be found in the area, but at the
same time, it is quickly developing as a bedroom community for the
Hanshin (Osaka-Kobe) area. Yotakuji Temple, 40 min. by bus from
Sanda, is famous for its iris garden.

Akashi, Himeji and Vicinity

The region west of Kobe was once called Harima. The JR San-yo
Main Line and the San-yo Shinkansen serve as trunk lines for the
many branch lines that cover the area. The roads include National
Highway 2, and National Highway 250, which runs along the coast,
as well as No. 2 Shimmei Expressway, Kakogawa Bypass, Himeji
Bypass and the San-yo Expressway (partially open).

Akashi 79 ☎078: Pop. 261,035. Located about 20 km west of Kobe,
the city can be reached in less than 20 min. on the JR San-yo Main
Line or in about 30 min. on the San-yo Electric Railway from Kobe.
The San-yo Shinkansen stops at Nishi(West)-Akashi Station. It
occupies the west end of the Hanshin Industrial Zone and the east
part of the Harima Industrial Zone, with transportation equipment,
construction equipment, electrical equipment and similar industries
thriving here. As one might guess from the fame of Akashi octopus
and Akashi sea bream, marine products are also a specialty. The 135°
eastern meridian by which Japan Standard Time is calculated passes
through Akashi, and the marker and an observation platform can be
found atop the 54-m-high observation tower at the Akashi Municipal
Planetarium. Akashi faces Awaji Island across the Akashi Straits,
and construction of the Akashi Straits Bridge is under way, with
completion planned for 1998. Akashi Park, north of Akashi Station,
contains the remains of the Akashi Castle, constructed in 1619. Two
of the original turrets (Important Cultural Properties) still remain
intact. The cherry blossoms of early April and the chrysanthemum
show in mid-October are popular attractions. Tennis courts and
other sports facilities are provided.

Akashi Municipal Planetalium: Situated north of Hitomaru-mae Station on the San-yo Electric Railway part way up Hitomaru Hill. In addition to the observation tower mentioned above, it exhibits interesting models and data about the universe. Planetarium shows are also held here.

Nearby is **Kakinomoto Shrine**, dedicated to the famous "Man-yo-shu" poet Kakinomoto-no-Hitomaro (? - ?). A monument inscribed with his poetry stands on the grounds. Gesshoji Temple, founded by the great priest Kobo-Daishi, is also located here.

Yakushi-in is an old Buddhist temple 700 m west of Dentetsu-Uozumi Station on the San-yo Electric Railway. It is popularly called Botandera (Peony Temple) because of the many peonies that bloom here from late April.

Kakogawa [79] ☎0794: Pop. 233,720. An industrial city situated along the lower reaches of the Kakogawa River, it supports flourishing chemical, machinery and textile factories. Since the city has a long history, there are many old temples scattered about. It takes 35 min. from Kobe on the JR San-yo Main Line. **Kakurinji Temple** is 10 min. by bus from the JR Kakogawa Station. Founded in 587 at the command of Prince Shotoku (574–622), it houses many ancient treasures. *Hondo* (Main Hall) and *Taishido* (Prince's Hall) are National Treasures, while the Belfry and three other buildings are Important Cultural Properties. The beautiful bronze statue of Prince Shotoku is thought to have been made in the Hakuho period (late seventh–eighth century).

Takasago [70] ☎0794: Pop. 92,207. Located in the delta, where the mouth of the Kakogawa River empties into the Harima-nada Sea. Steel and iron as well as machinery and petroleum factories thrive in this industrial city. The twin pine trees in the Takasago Shrine compound were the inspiration for the *noh* play "Takasago," passages of which are often recited at weddings and other auspicious occasions. The present trees are the fifth generation of the originals.

Miki [78] ☎07948: Pop. 74,311. 50 min. from Kobe-Shinkaichi Station on the Kobe Electric Railway Ao Line. It is located near the Mino River, a tributary of the Kakogawa River. Saws and other carpentry tools and knives as well as machine tools are produced here.

Ono [78] ☎07946: Pop. 45,670. Located midway up the Kakogawa River, the city is known for the production of abacuses and hardware in addition to the cultivation of agricultural products. Jodoji Temple, 15 min. by bus from Ono Station on the Kobe Electric Railway Ao Line, can be reached in 1 hr. from Minatogawa Station in Kobe. The temple was founded at the end of the 12th century by priest Chogen who was in charge of the reconstruction of the Todaiji Temple of Nara. Both *Jodo* Hall, erected in 1194, and the Amitabha Trinity, enshrined in the hall, are National Treasures. The Amitabha Trinity is believed to be the work of the famous Buddhist sculptor Kaikei.

The spacious temple grounds also contain *Yakushido* Hall (an Important Cultural Property) as well as many other buildings that house the temple treasures, a large part of which are also Important Cultural Properties.

Kasai 78 ☎07904: Pop. 52,748. 1 hr. from Kakogawa Station on the Hojo Railway. In addition to agricultural activities, textiles and electric appliances are also produced here. At Rakanji Temple, 20 min. on foot from Hojo Station, are a group of more than 400 stone figures (*Gohyakurakan*) representing the disciples of Buddha who attained Nirvana. Although they all have different expressions and shapes, each one stands about 1 m tall. Their origin remains a mystery despite the fact that some believe they were made sometime in the 16th or 17th century.

Ichijoji Temple: About 4 km from Hokkeguchi Station on the Hojo Railway. It was founded in 650 by the legendary hermit Hodo, who is said to have come from India. The *Sanju-no-To* (Three-Story Pagoda), a National Treasure, was built in 1174. Among the many buildings are *Myokendo* Hall and three other Important Cultural Properties. The temple possesses many treasures, too. It is the 26th Station on the 33 Temple Pilgrimage in the Former Western Provinces.

Lake Tojo 78 : A man-made lake in Tojo Town with an area of 550,000 sq.m. A sightseeing boat cruises the surface, while fish swimming below tempt the angler. The cherry blossoms and autumn leaves around the lake are beautiful in their respective seasons. There is an amusement park on the lake shore called Tojoko Land.

Nishiwaki 78 ☎0795: Pop. 38,722. 1 hr. from Kakogawa by the JR Kakogawa Line. It is the center for Banshu (old Harima Province) weaving, especially gingham tablecloths and figured broadcloth, both of which are noted for their quality. Much of this cloth is exported from Kobe Port. The city is also famous for the manufacture of fish hooks. Located at 135°E. longitude and 35°N. latitude, it is sometimes called the navel of Japan.

Himeji 70 ☎0792: Pop. 450,374. 50 min. on the JR San-yo Main Line, 20 min. on the Shinkansen, or 1 hr. by limited express on the San-yo Electric Railway from Kobe. A former castle town, Himeji is the leading industrial and commercial city as well as the transportation center of the Harima Plain. Factories include iron and steel, machinery, hardware, electric appliances, chemicals, matches, rubber goods and foodstuffs. The production of leather goods is also a traditional industry.

Himeji Castle 70 : A 15-min. walk north of Himeji Station on a low hill called Himeyama. The history of the castle began in the 14th century with a fort built by Akamatsu Sadanori, the local lord, at the foot of the hill. Later, Toyotomi Hideyoshi built a castle with a three-story donjon to serve as his headquarters for the attack on the Chugoku District (western Honshu). The present castle was built in the 17th century. This gorgeous castle consists of a main tower that appears to be only five stories from the outside but actually has six stories on the inside, with smaller, three-story keeps connected by covered passages—all designated as National Treasures. In addition, there are many turrets, corridors, gates and walls in the complex construction, most of which are Important Cultural Properties. Considered the acme of design and architecture for feudal castles, it is called Shirasagijo (Egret Castle) because the entire structure, from the five-story main tower to the walls, is plastered in white. It looks like the silhouette of the large bird often seen in the rice fields on the plain. From the castle, the Ieshima Islands can be seen floating in the Harima-nada Sea. The northeast part of the castle grounds has been converted into a park with many flowering trees and shrubs such as plums, peaches, cherry trees, azaleas and wisteria.

Tegarayama Park is on the top of a hill 5 min. by bus from the JR Himeji Station. It has such facilities as a botanical garden, an aquarium, a pool and a library. The observation platform offers an excellent view of the Inland Sea. Himeji Central Park, a 1.9-sq.-km leisure center, is 30 min. by bus from Himeji Station, while nearby is a popular, safari-style zoo, where some 300 animals roam freely within a large, sprawling enclosure.

Hiromine Shrine: Standing atop a graceful hill (alt. 311 m) 3 km north of Himeji Station. It can be reached with a 15-min. bus ride from Himeji Station and then an additional 40-min. walk. Said to have been founded in the eighth century, it is dedicated to Susano-o-no-Mikoto and his son, Isotakeru-no-Mikoto, both Shinto deities. It is thought to be the main shrine for the Yasaka Shrine (popularly called Gion Shrine) in Kyoto. Also called Hiromine Tenno, the main hall is an Important Cultural Property.

Mt. Shoshazan: Located 8 km northwest of the JR Himeji Station with an altitude of 363 m. It is famed for **Enkyoji Temple** on its summit. Founded in 966 by a priest Shoku (910-1007), the temple was once one of the three largest Tendai-sect Buddhist seminaries, ranking with Enryakuji Temple on Mt. Hiei near Kyoto and Daisenji Temple on Mt. Daisen in Tottori Prefecture. Many fine buildings stand among the cedars and cypresses that form the sanctuary, including *Daikodo* (Main Lecture Hall) and *Jyogyodo* (Training Hall), both of which are Important Cultural Properties. This is the 27th Station on the 33 Temple Pilgrimage in the Former Western Provinces. A ropeway goes to the mountaintop, which offers a spectacular view of the surrounding scenery. A bus from the JR Himeji Station will carry one to Shosha Station in 25 min. for transfer to the ropeway for a 4-min. ride.

Ikaruga Temple, 30 min. by bus from Himeji Station, was founded by Prince Shotoku (574-622), who also founded Horyuji Temple in Nara. The Three-Story Pagoda, rebuilt in 1565, as well as many of the Buddhist images and paintings are Important Cultural Properties.

Tatsuno ⟦70⟧ ☎0791: Pop. 41,702. 30 min. from Himeji by the JR Kishin Line. A castle town of the Wakisaka family in feudal days. Many of the *samurai* mansions and old wooden houses can still be seen in this tranquil town, which is also famous for the production of soy sauce and *somen* (thin noodles) as well as *ramen* (Chinese-style noodles) and macaroni. Tools and data related to the production of soy sauce are on exhibit in the Usukuchi Tatsuno Shoyu Museum along with video tapes introducing the actual process of production. Tatsuno Park spreading out to the west of the city is a famous site for viewing cherry blossoms. Shuentei House, which stands in the park, is the former villa of the Wakisaka family, the feudal lord of this district. Tatsuno Castle has been restored at the foot of the mountain in the northern part of the city.

Aioi ⟦70⟧ ☎07912: Pop. 38,244. Both the JR San-yo Main Line and the Shinkansen stop here. Facing Aioi Bay, the fine natural port can provide safe anchorage for 10,000-ton-class ships. The city is also known for its shipbuilding industry.

Ako ⟦97⟧ ☎07914: Pop. 52,193. Located about 10 km southwest of Aioi. It is widely known for the production of salt, but in recent years it has developed as an industrial town through the production of firebricks, fishing nets, medicine and cement. It is also quite famous for its association with the story of the "47 Loyal Samurai" who, in 1702, avenged the death of their lord, Asano Naganori (*daimyo*, or feudal lord, of Ako), by killing Kira Yoshinaka who disgraced their lord (refer to p.382). There are many historical sites associated with these loyal retainers throughout the city.

Kagakuji Temple: 10 min. on foot from Banshu-Ako Station on the JR Ako Line. It is the family temple of the Asanos and the leader of the 47 *samurai*, Oishi Yoshio (commonly called Oishi Kuranosuke), who was the chief retainer of the Asano Clan. One of the temple gates was moved here from Ako Castle. Although the graves of the 47 *ronin* are in Tokyo, the tombs and wooden images of the 47 loyal *samurai* as well as treasures and documents associated with the vendetta are kept here. At the site of Ako Castle are the original stone walls and a restored main gate and turret as well as *Nagayamon* Gate, which was part of the mansion of Oishi Kuranosuke.

Oishi Shrine: Dedicated to Oishi and his 46 followers. It contains a hall, where wooden images of the devoted vassals are arrayed, and a treasure hall. On December 14, the anniversary of the date that vengeance was taken on Kira Yoshinaka, a senior official of the Tokugawa Shokunate, in 1702, there is a parade of the "47 Loyal Samurai" from the castle site to the station along with many other big events. Ako City Museum of History, near Oishi Shrine, contains exhibits related to Ako such as salt production, the 47 *samurai* and Ako Castle.

Cape Ako: Lying 4 km southeast of the station (15 min. by bus), is a scenic cape jutting out into Harima-nada Sea. Covered with beautiful pine trees and fantastic rocks, it provides a magnificent view of the Inland Sea, Ieshima Islands, Shodo Island and the mountains of Shikoku. The coast is popular for swimming and fishing.

Section VI. Western Honshu
(Chugoku District)

Western Honshu, also known as the Chugoku District, is composed of the five prefectures of Hiroshima, Okayama, Shimane, Tottori and Yamaguchi. The Chugoku District is subdivided into two distinct regions by the Chugoku Mountain Chain: San-yo (Okayama, Hiroshima and southern half of Yamaguchi) in the south facing the Inland Sea and San-in (Tottori, Shimane and northern half of Yamaguchi) in the north on the coast of the Japan Sea.

With a serpentine coastline, salubrious climate and a well-developed transportation network, San-yo is one of the most highly developed areas in Japan. This area is known for its lovely seascapes formed by the many islands that dot the Inland Sea. The San-yo District originally developed with agriculture, stock farming, salt making and fishery industries. However, as the district lies along important sea routes and is favored with an abundant supply of labor, there has been tremendous growth in such modern industries as cement, chemical fertilizer, metal, machinery, oil refining, chemical fiber and shipbuilding.

The main transportation routes are the JR San-yo Shinkansen and San-yo Main Line, the Chugoku Expressway that passes through various mountain ranges, and the San-yo Expressway, partially completed and opened to traffic along the coast, as well as National Highway 2.

The San-in District, located north of the San-yo District, has a severe climate with less sunshine in winter. However, due to the effects of the warm Tsushima Current, even in January the average temperature is at least 3°C, and there is not an excessive amount of snow. The mountains almost stand on the coastline, leaving few plains or open areas. The area is covered with hot-spring spas. The main industries in the San-in District are fishery, agriculture and stock farming, although the metal and pulp industries flourish in some parts. The main transportation routes are the JR San-in Main Line and National Highways 9 and 191.

The San-yo and San-in districts are linked by several JR lines and national routes that pass through the Chugoku Mountain Chain. The most convenient of these is the Hakubi Line running between Okayama in San-yo and Yonago in San-in.

Area 1. Okayama, Kurashiki and Surrounding Areas

This area is located in the eastern part of the San-yo District and is characterized by the calm Inland Sea and beautiful, natural landscapes. The transportation routes include the JR San-yo Main Line and Shinkansen, the Hakubi Line running north from Kurashiki, and the Seto-Ohashi Line to Shikoku as well as National Highway 2 and National Highway 180, which runs parallel to the Hakubi Line. These are supplemented by the parts of the San-yo Expressway that have been opened and the Seto-Chuo Expressway that crosses over the Inland Sea.

Bizen ⟨97⟩ ☎0869: Pop. 31,882. This area is best known for *Bizen-yaki* pottery. The Bizen Pottery Museum displays examples and reference material on Bizen Pottery. Craftsmen can be seen working at the *Bizen-yaki* Pottery Center and the Kei Fujiwara Art Museum (named after the *Bizen-yaki* master, Fujiwara, honored as a Living National Treasure). Many craft stores and kilns offer good opportunities to see fine pieces of work. Bizen is 40 min. from Okayama by the JR Ako Line. Get off at Imbe Station.

The former Shizutani School was built by local lord Ikeda Mitsumasa in the 17th century to provide the common people with an opportunity for education. The large lecture hall is designated as a National Treasure, while the Confucian temple and stone wall are designated as Important Cultural Properties. 10 min. by bus from Yoshinaga Station on the JR San-yo Main Line.

South of Bizen lies Osafune, famous for the Japanese swords produced here. Demonstrations of the actual forging process of swords are given twice a month at the Bizen Osafune Museum.

Ushimado ⟨97⟩: This town is located southwest of Okayama facing the Inland Sea, 1 hr.10 min. by bus from the JR Okayama Station. This area is known for the local cultivation of olives, affording a superb view of the Inland Sea beyond the olive trees. The area offers a full range of recreational facilities, including swimming on the beach and a yacht harbor. Surrounded by hills and looking down on the ocean, the Main Hall of Honrenji Temple was built in 1492 and has been designated together with the *Chumon* (Middle Gate) and other buildings as an Important Cultural Property.

Okayama ⟨97/100-101⟩ ☎0862

Pop. 579,593. Okayama is one of the principal industrial and cultural centers in the Chugoku District. Okayama may be reached by the JR Tokaido and San-yo Shinkansen from Tokyo in 3 hrs. 50 min. (733 km), from Nagoya in 2 hrs. (367 km) and from Osaka in 40 min. (177 km). By plane, it takes 1 hr. and 20 min. from Tokyo.

The Okayama Prefectural Government Office is located here. During the Edo period, this city developed as a castle town under the Ikeda family. Local industries include textiles, foodstuffs, metal and rubber, while the principal agricultural products are peaches, grapes and other fruits. The area is also well known for the "i" (a kind of rush) grass it produces for use in *tatami* mats. The city is served by many train lines, including the JR Seto-Ohashi Line that goes to

Shikoku, and by National Highways 2, 30, 53 and 180. Ferries leave from Okayama Port to Shodo Island.

Refer to the supplement for details regarding the "i" **System Information Center** in Okayama.

PLACES OF INTEREST

Koraku-en Garden 101 : Located along the Asahi River about 2 km east of the JR Okayama Station, it can be reached by bus in 20 minutes. Along with Kairaku-en in Mito and Kenroku-en in Kanazawa, this garden is one of the three best landscape gardens in Japan. With a total area of 133,000 sq.m., the garden was built in 1700 by the local lord Ikeda Tsunamasa in the Enshu landscape style of strolling gardens. The garden houses a tea ceremony house, several ponds, a small waterfall and elegantly designed landscapes. As the seasons change, pine trees, maples, cherry trees and plum trees reach their peak of beauty.

Okayama Castle 101 : In direct contrast to the white-walled Himeji Castle, also known as Egret Castle, the black walls of Okayama Castle have earned it the name of Crow Castle. The castle can be seen from the garden across the Asahi River. Originally built in 1573, the castle's two remaining original turrets have been designated as Important Cultural Properties. The donjon and entrance were rebuilt in 1966, with the former housing a research material hall.

There are several museums in the surrounding area. These include the Hayashibara Art Museum, which displays swords, ceramics and other craftwork as well as *noh* costumes handed down from the Ikeda family, armor, and other items registered as National Treasures and Important Cultural Properties; the Okayama Municipal Museum of Near Eastern Art with a collection of over 2,000 pieces of ancient earthenware and pottery; the Yumeji Provincial Art Museum, which houses famous portraits by Takehisa Yumeji, popular artist and poet, and the Okayama Prefectural Museum with its collection of *Bizen-yaki* ceramics.

The Ikeda Zoo is located at the foot of Mt. Kyoyama on the northwestern side of the city. The Kyoyama Ropeway leads to the peak, where an observatory affords a beautiful view of the area. 15 min. by bus from Okayama Station and 3 min. by ropeway.

Saidaiji Temple 97 : Located south of Saidaiji Station, which is 20 min. east of Okayama on the JR Ako Line. It can also be reached by bus from Okayama Station in 30 min. This temple is dedicated to *Senju* (Thousand-Handed) *Kannon* and was built around the year 770. The *Eyo* Festival and the *Hadaka* (Naked) *Matsuri* are held here late at night on the third Saturday of February. Half-naked young men cleanse themselves in cold water, make their way through the crowds to the temple and try to grab wooden branches called *shingi* that are thrown by monks. It is believed that whoever succeeds in retaining the *shingi* will have a happy life.

Okayama and neighboring Soja make up the ancient province of Kibi, an area that is covered with ancient shrines and grave mounds. **Kibitsu Shrine**: A 10-min. walk from Kibitsu Station on the JR Kibi Line. It is dedicated to Kibitsuhiko-no-Mikoto, who is said to have played an active role in this area. In the Muromachi period (1336–1573), Shogun Ashikaga Yoshimitsu rebuilt the Main Hall in the year 1425 in the large-scale *Kibitsu-zukuri* style. The shrine is an example of Shinto architecture with clear influences of Buddhist temples. The *Haiden* (Oratory) was also built in the same period and is quite unique in structure. Both have been designated as National Treasures. Refer to p.198. The 300-m cloister is beautiful. Nearby is the Kibitsuhiko Shrine honoring the same deity.

Tsukuriyama Burial Mound: About 45 min. by bus from Okayama Station. Measuring 350 m long and 30 m high, this is the fourth largest site of its kind in Japan. About 3 km to the west is another grave mound 286 m long that bears the same name of Tsukuriyama Grave Mound. The overall area is called Kibiji Fudoki (Local History and Topography)-no-Oka Hills and contains a national temple named Bitchu Kokubunji Temple, built in 741 under the direction of Emperor Shomu. *Goju-no-To* (Five-Story Pagoda) was rebuilt during the Edo period and is registered as an Important Cultural Property. Craftwork unearthed in the region is displayed at the Kibiji Local History Museum and the Kibi Archaeological Hall.

Soja ⬜97 ☎08669: Pop. 52,634. This area has many ancient ruins. The local industry is mainly pharmaceutical manufac-turing, textiles and casting. **Hofukuji Temple** is 10 min. by bus from Soja Station on the JR Kibi Line or Hakubi Line.

It has *Sanju-no-To* (Three-Story Pagoda), which was built in 1376 and is designated as an Important Cultural Property. Many other halls also remain. This temple is also known for a legend concerning the famous priest-painter Sesshu (1420–1506), who trained here as a novice. Legend has it that, as a punishment for laziness, he was bound to a pillar in the main hall. He drew a picture of a mouse on the floor with his tears. The mouse then came to life and freed him by chewing through his ropes.

Gokei Gorge is 30 min. from Soja Station by bus. A tributary of the Takahashi River, the Makitani River flows through here surrounded on both sides by granite cliffs over 500 m long. In autumn the changing colors of the leaves are beautiful.

Kurashiki ⬜97 ☎0864

Pop. 416,052. Located in the western part of Okayama Prefecture, Kurashiki is 193 km from Osaka. Known for the lovely, white walls of its buildings, this city developed as a port town along the Kurashiki River. As the central industrial city in the Okayama Plain, this area has textiles, petroleum, steel, machinery, pharmaceutical, cement and other industries. Mizushima, south of the city, is one of the most important coastal industrial zones in Japan. Kurashiki also lies in the center of this area's most active cultural and artistic regions, housing many displays of artistic pieces. The JR Hakubi Line that starts from Okayama and heads for Yonago in San-in separates here in Kurashiki from the San-yo Main Line.

Refer to the supplement for details regarding the "i" **System Information Center** in Kurashiki.

PLACES OF INTEREST

Ohara Museum of Art: Located 1 km southwest of Kurashiki Station. It was built in 1930 by Ohara Magosaburo (1880–1943, president of Kurashiki Spinning Industries). The white, two-story, ferroconcrete main hall is built in the style of ancient Greek temples and houses a collection of European art gathered by Ohara that includes important works by El Greco, Corot, Rodin, Gaughin, Picasso and others. The annex has a collection of works by modern Japanese artists who painted in Western styles, while exhibits of pictures and sculpture can be found in the basement. Other attractions include pottery by Bernard Leach and Tomimoto Kenkichi, wood-block prints by Munakata Shiko, dyed goods by Serizawa Keisuke and other handicrafts. There is also a hall of Oriental art with displays of ancient Chinese art.

Kurashiki Museum of Folk Craft: Standing a short distance to the southeast of the Ohara Museum. It is a two-story complex that makes use of rice granaries from the Edo period, and with its white walls and black tiles on the roof, it is a beautiful building. The collection of over 8,000 folkcraft articles includes ceramics, dyed goods, lovely mats, wooden craftwork, bamboo craftwork, textiles and other crafts from Japan and abroad.

Kurashiki Archaeological Museum: A white building across from the folkcraft museum. It displays over 700 objects unearthed at archaeological digs in this area as well as ancient objects from the Andes Civilization.

In addition to these, there is the Kurashiki Ninagawa Museum with its collection of ancient Greco-Roman art as well as the Japanese Rural Toy Museum displaying primitive toys from Japan and abroad. The Ivy Academic Hall in the former factory of Kurashiki Spinning Industries (a red-brick building) has the Kurabo Memorial Hall, with its collection of material on the development of spinning techniques in the area, the Torajiro Kojima Memorial Hall, with the paintings of Kojima Torajiro, who assembled the Ohara collection, a restaurant, a hotel and other facilities. The Ohashi House, located a few minutes from the Ohara Museum, has been preserved from the middle of the Edo period and is open to the public. It has been designated as an Important Cultural Property.

South of Kurashiki lies Kojima at the southwestern edge of the

Kojima Peninsula, serving as the base for the Honshu side of the Seto-Ohashi Bridge. It can be reached by rapid train on the JR Honshi-Bisan Line in 25 min. from Okayama or in 50 min. by bus from Kurashiki. The Seto Ohashi Memorial Museum of Bridge in the shape of an arch bridge is near Kojima Station. Here, one can find a 1-500th scale reproduction of the Seto-Ohashi Bridge, a model of London Bridge and a reproduction of the Rialto Bridge, whose construction was unsuccessfully attempted 400 years ago in Venice. In the underground Picture Hall, a film about the bridge is shown. Next to the Memorial Museum is a park with examples of many Japanese bridges.

Washuzan Hill 97 : 133 m in altitude. Known as one of the best locations from which to view the Inland Sea. From the top, one can command a fine view of many islands dotting the surface of the emerald sea and the beautiful formation of the Seto-Ohashi Bridge extending across to Shikoku. 1 hr.10 min. by bus from Kurashiki and 1 hr.20 min. from Okayama.

Rendaiji Temple: Located 30 min. by bus from Kojima Station on the JR Honshi-Bisan Line, this temple was the site of the Yuka Daigongen faith, which drew both from Shinto and Buddhism. Attractions include the main hall and several towers with the paintings of Maruyama Okyo (1773-1795, a noted artist) on the sliding doors of the guest hall. In spring the cherry blossoms are lovely, while the changing of the colors of leaves in autumn is impressive.

Seto-Ohashi Bridge 97 : This new bridge connects Kojima in Honshu with Sakaide in Shikoku. It is composed of 11 bridges connecting Hitsuishi Island, Iwaguro Island, Yoshima Island and Mitsugo Island, all belonging to the Shiaku Islands. Completed in 1988, the bridge has a total length of 12.307 km. Railcars cross over on the lower level, while automobiles use the upper level. It is the longest bridge in the world that can accommodate both trains and automobiles. The Minami-Bisan Bridge, which makes up a part of the construction, is 1,723 m long and is the fifth-largest suspension bridge in the world. The Hitsuishijima Bridge and Iwagurojima Bridge are twin, cable-stayed bridge. Their interesting forms and the Yoshima Truss Bridge are quite pleasing to the eye. Excursion boats leave from Okayama to see the bridges. The design and construction of these bridges were achieved through the use of advanced technology on elevated constructions to ensure that they can resist wind force and earthquakes, and to support many automobiles and railcars.

Tamano 97 ☎0863: Pop. 75,322. Known for its shipbuilding industry, this city is located in the southeastern part of the Kojima Peninsula. Uno was once a very important port for those crossing over to Shikoku. Since the completion of the Seto-Ohashi Bridge, however, it has become less important, but there are still many boats and ferries crossing from here. Shibukawa Beach with approximately 1 km of white sand and pine trees is about 30 min. by bus from Uno. It is possible to swim at this natural seaside setting. The Tamano Marin Museum has a display of fish common to the Inland Sea.

Takahashi 97 ☎0866: Pop. 25,759. A former castle town located approximately 35 km north of Kurashiki. In addition to stock farming and agriculture, Christmas decorations and *Hinaningyo* dolls are made here. The Takahashi River is known for its *ayu* or sweetfish. Former *samurai* residences still remain intact in some areas, with one even being opened as the Takahashi Samurai Residence. Some town areas still contain old family residences. A 10-min. walk from Bitchu-Takahashi Station brings one to the **Raikyuji Temple** with its garden, built at the beginning of the Edo period by Kobori Enshu. Among others, it contains many beautiful azaleas. The **Bitchu-Matsuyama Castle** is 10 min. by taxi from the station, with an additional 20-min. walk required to reach the top of Mt. Gagyu at an elevation of 420 m. The castle was built in 1683, and *Niju-no-To* (Two-Story Pagoda), the donjon and parts of the earthen wall have been designated as Important Cultural Properties. The Mount Gagyu Natural Monkey Park has wild monkeys that run free.

Niimi 97 ☎0867: Pop. 27,737. Located upstream along the Takahashi River. To the south is a limestone deposit called the Atetsudai. Limestone-related industries abound in this area, which is also blessed with many stunning caves and valleys. The area is also active in stock farming and forestry. Niimi can be reached in 1 hr.5 min. from Okayama by limited express on the JR Hakubi Line. **Ikurado Cave** is 10 min. by train from Niimi to Ikura, transferring to a bus with another 30 min. ride. Measuring 1,200 m in length and 90 m high, this limestone cave and the adjoining valley are beautiful. Approximately 15 km east of Ikura Cave is the Makido cave (a stalactite cave).

Tsuyama 97 ☎0868: Pop. 86,773. Located approximately 60 km from Okayama, this town developed at the crossroads of road and rail transportation between the San-yo and San-in districts. This area on the upstream basin of the Yoshii River is active in traditional industries and is directly connected to Osaka by the Chugoku Expressway. It is also known for the interest in Western learning that developed here during the final years of the Edo period. The ruins of Tsuyama Castle, which stood until 1873, can be found among the hills in the central part of the city. Here, Kakuzan Park is filled with more than 5,000 cherry trees, azaleas, wisterias and other lovely foliage. The **Shuraku-en Garden** was built in 1657 as a garden attached to the local lord's villa based on the Sento Imperial Palace in Kyoto. The combination of ponds, ancient buildings and natural settings is elegant. It is 10 min. by bus from the JR Tsuyama Station. In the city, one can visit Nakayama Shrine, whose Main Hall was built in the unique Nakayama style. The Sojagu Shrine was built in the prevailing style in the 16th century. Both shrines are registered as Important Cultural Properties. Ruins of ancient dugout dwellings from the Yayoi period (over 2,000 years ago) that were found in a part of the city called Numa have been partially restored.

Yunogo Spa 97 : Located approximately 16 km southeast of Tsuyama, 40 min. by bus from the JR Tsuyama Station along the Yoshino River in the mountains. The Yunogo Spa is one of the three spas of the **Mimasaka Spas Area**, the other two being Okutsu Spa and Yubara Spa. There are many golf courses nearby.

Okutsu Spa 97 : Situated 32 km north from Tsuyama Station, it can be reached in 1 hr.10 min. by bus. The hot-spring waters range 26–43°C in temperature and are said to be efficacious against gastroenteric disorders, neuralgia and other ailments. Nearby is the lovely Okutsu-kyo Gorge, which runs for 3 km along the Okutsu River. Katsuyama is an old small castle town in the mountains. Located about 40 km to the west of Tsuyama, it is the entrance to Mt. Hiruzen. The Kamba-no-Taki Waterfall is 5 km north of Chugoku-Katsuyama Station on the JR Kishin Line and can be reached in 15 min. by bus. The beauty of the 140-m falls has earned a reputation surpassing that of all other waterfalls in the district.

Yubara Spa 97 : Approximately 20 km north of Chugoku-Katsuyama Station (35 min. by bus) in the mountains, with many deluxe *ryokan*. The Koma (Top) Museum with a collection of 3,000 tops from Japan and abroad is located in this spa town. There is also a preservation center for great salamanders, which have been designated as Natural Monuments. Lake Yubara, a 15-min. drive from the hot-spring town, is an artificial lake created by the damming of the Asahi River.

Mt. Hiruzen 97 : The three peaks of Kami (Upper)-Hiruzen (alt. 1,202 m), Naka (Middle)-Hiruzen (alt. 1,122 m) and Shimo (Lower)-Hiruzen (alt. 1,101 m) rise from west to east in Okayama and Tottori prefectures. The three peaks are all approximately 1,200 m in altitude, with Kami-Hiruzen being the highest and Shimo-Hiruzen the lowest. Shimo-Hiruzen is shaped like a lava dome and is certainly the loveliest of the three. The mountains are covered with untouched, beech tree forests and many clusters of high-altitude mountain flora. Mt. Daisen and the distant Japan Sea can be seen from the peak. In the southern foothills of Mt. Hiruzen, the Hiruzen Plateau spreads 14 km from east to west and 5.5 km from north to south at an elevation of 600 m.

Area 2. Central San-yo District

This area lies along the coast of the Inland Sea and is served by the JR San-yo Main Line, San-yo Shinkansen and Kure Line, which runs along the coast from Mihara. The area is served by National

Highway 2 and National Highway 185, which passes Takehara on the way to Kure.

Fukuyama ⬜97 ☎0849: Pop. 364,281. Located approximately 60 km west from Okayama, Fukuyama can be reached from there in 25 min. by the JR San-yo Shinkansen. It is linked to Kurashiki by the San-yo Expressway. Fukuyama developed on the eastern side of Hiroshima Prefecture as a castle town. It is now a large, industrial city. Matsunaga, in the western part of the city, is the largest manufacturing region in Japan of *geta* (traditional Japanese wooden clogs). The Japan Footwear Museum is located here.

Directly north of Fukuyama Station is Fukuyama Castle, which contains the *Fushimi* Tower and *Sujigane* (lit. metal reinforcement) Gate taken from Fushimi Castle in Kyoto. Both are registered as Important Cultural Properties. An exhibition hall is located in the donjon, rebuilt in 1966. The castle grounds are also known for their many cherry trees. On the eastern side of the castle is the Fukuyama Museum of Art with its display of 20th-century European art, especially Italian art.

Myo-o-in Temple, located only 10 min. from the station by bus, was built in 807. *Goju-no-To* (Five-Story Pagoda) and the Main Hall, both built in the 14th century, are registered as National Treasures.

Refer to the supplement for details regarding the "i" **System Information Center** in Fukuyama.

Tomonoura ⬜97 : Located 30 min. by bus from Fukuyama Station, this port town faces lovely Sensui, Benten and Kogo islands. In the Edo period, Taichoro was built as an inn to accommodate official messengers from Korea arriving to greet a new *shogun*. Ankokuji Temple and Nunakuma Shrine are registered as Important Cultural Properties. The 600-year-old pine tree of the Hosenji Temple is one of the attractions here. Tomonoura's special *sake* called Homeishu is made from glutinous rice and is known as a medicinal drink containing 16 types of herbal medicines. A unique tourist attraction of this area is the *tai* (sea bream) net. During the whole month of May, tourists can observe the fishing of sea bream as a net strung between two boats is used to catch the sea bream that have come in from the ocean to spawn.

Abuto Kannon Temple: Located 4 km from Tomonoura at the edge of the Nunakuma Peninsula. Abutoguchi can be reached in 50 min. by bus from Fukuyama Station plus a 15-min. walk to the temple. Many people come to this temple to pray for safety on the seas. It is built at a 28-m height on a rocky jetty and affords a uniquely beautiful view. It is said that long ago an envoy from Korea visited this temple with offerings of rice and paper.

Mirokunosato: 30 min. by bus from the JR Fukuyama Station. This area has a 2,100,000-sq.-m resort with leisure facilities that include a training center equipped with lodging accommodations and meeting rooms, a well-equipped sports center with athletic grounds and a soccer field as well as Shinshoji Temple, which is used for spiritual training.

Onomichi 96 ☎0848: Pop. 100,224. Located directly west of Fukuyama, Onomichi can be reached by the JR San-yo Shinkansen in about 2 hrs. from Osaka (255 km), transferring at Fukuyama to the JR San-yo Main Line in additional 17 min. This town developed as a port town on the Inland Sea. As the town is situated in an area where the mountains and sea meet, it has many steep slopes. Many boats depart for the islands of the Inland Sea as well as for Imabari and Matsuyama in Shikoku. A project is under way to construct a bridge spanning the Inland Sea between Onomichi and Imabari in Shikoku. When completed, it will be one of the three large bridges crossing the Inland Sea. Eventually, it will be composed of several sections, two of which have already been completed. The Onomichi Ohashi Bridge connects Onomichi with Mukai Island, which, in turn, is connected to Innoshima Island by the Innoshima Ohashi Bridge.

Senkoji Park: Situated northeast of Onomichi Station on the JR San-yo Main Line. Containing Senkoji Temple, built in 806 on Mt. Daiho, the park can be reached by the Nagaeguchi Ropeway, which is a 5-min. bus ride from the station, or directly from the station by bus in 20 min. The park is known for its 10,000 cherry trees and a splendid view of the Inland Sea. Also located here are the Onomichi City Art Museum, the Onomichi Castle Museum with its collection of material from castles all around Japan and the Kikuningyo Hall that exhibits *kikuningyo* dolls (dolls made from chrysanthemum flowers). A special attraction is the Literature Path, with the stones inscribed with verses from the works of great Japanese poets and writers.

Jodoji Temple: Located in the eastern part of the city, it can be reached by bus from the station in 5 min. Originally built in 616, the Main Hall was rebuilt in 1327, while the *Tahoto* Pagoda was rebuilt in 1329. Both were built in a refined style and are designated as National Treasures. Many other temple structures and Buddhist images are designated as Important Cultural Properties. The temple garden is splendid, too. Onomichi has many other ancient temples, including Saigokuji Temple, Tenneiji Temple and Saikoji Temple, none of which should be missed.

Mihara 96 ☎0848: Pop. 85,002. Mihara is 12 km from Onomichi and 15 min. by the JR San-yo Main Line. The JR San-yo Shinkansen also stops here, and this city serves as the junction for the JR San-yo Main Line and Kure Line. Located on a small plain surrounded by mountains, the city faces the Inland Sea. After Kobayakawa Takakage (a famous warlord) built Mihara Castle in 1567, the city developed around it as a castle town. Parts of the castle walls and the ruins of the moat still remain. It has developed into one of the principal industrial regions of the Chugoku District with many rayon, machinery, shipbuilding, cement and other factories. Mt. Fudekage (alt. 313 m) faces the sea southwest of Mihara Station, offering a clear view of the Inland Sea. There is a road to the summit.

Buttsuji Temple: 45 min. by bus from Mihara Station. It is the headquarters of the Buttsuji school of the Buddhist Rinzai sect. When it was built in 1397, it was surrounded by many structures, but the only remaining original building is the famous *Jizodo* Hall, which is registered as an Important Cultural Property.

Takehara ☐96☐ ☎08462: Pop. 36,195. Located 26 km from Mihara and about 30 min. by the JR Kure Line, Takehara developed as a salt-making town during the Edo period. Although it is presently an industrial area, the old section of town still remains intact and has been designated as a Preservation Area for Traditional Japanese Architecture. It is sometimes called "Little Kyoto." The "Greenpia" Yasuura is located 20 km to the west. A 10-min. bus ride from Yasuura Station on the JR Kure Line will take one to this resort area with its many sports facilities, amusement parks, camping grounds and other recreational facilities.

Area 3. Hiroshima and Surrounding Areas

Hiroshima ☐96/98-99☐ ☎ 082

Pop. 1,049,168. Of the cities west of Kobe, Hiroshima is the second-largest city after Fukuoka. The Hiroshima Prefectural Government Office is located here, and many governmental, economic, educational and information services for the entire Chugoku District are performed in Hiroshima. The city developed on the delta of the Ota River at the mouth of Hiroshima Bay. The six tributaries of the Ota River flow through the city on their way to Hiroshima Bay.

HISTORY

In 1591 Mori Terumoto (1553-1625), a feudal lord, built a castle at this site and called it "Hiroshima-jo" (lit. Broad-Island Castle). Thus, the area became known as Hiroshima. After the successive reigns of the Mori and Fukushima families, the Asano family took over sovereignty of the district until the end of the Edo period. Under their rule, local industries prospered and a castle town developed.

In 1868 Imperial rule was restored, spelling an end to the reign of the Asano family. In 1889 a municipal government was established and construction work was completed on Hiroshima Port. In 1894 railways connecting Kobe and Shimonoseki were completed, and the San-yo Line began operations.

During the Sino-Japanese War of 1894-1895, the Imperial headquarters was established in Hiroshima Castle, and the city grew as a center of land and marine transportation. As the city continued to expand, it attracted many government offices, schools and large factories to the city and surrounding areas. Before the outbreak of

World War II, the city had a population of 344,000 (1940 National Census), making it the seventh largest city in Japan. At 8:15 a.m. on August 6, 1945, a U.S. atomic bomb was dropped on Hiroshima. The city was instantaneously demolished and approximately 200,000 people were killed.

On August 6, 1947, citizens of Hiroshima held the first three-day peace festival based on the theme of "No More Hiroshimas." It has since become Hiroshima's most important annual event. With the enforcement in 1949 of the Hiroshima Peace Memorial City Construction Law, rehabilitation progressed rapidly under long-range city planning so that today the city has regained its status as an important industrial area in Japan.

INDUSTRY

Local industry is centered on automobile, metal and shipbuilding industries, with many large-scale factories lining the coast. Hiroshima Bay is also well known for the quality of its *nori* (dried seaweed) cultivation and oyster beds.

TRANSPORTATION

Transportation to Hiroshima: Hiroshima can be reached from Tokyo in 1 hr.30 min. by plane or 4 hrs. 35 min. by the JR Shinkansen (895 km). It takes 1 hr.40 min. from Shin-Osaka Station (339 km) and 1 hr.25 min. from Hakata Station in Fukuoka (282 km) by the JR Shinkansen. The JR Geibi Line connects it with the Japan Sea coast. Long-distance buses travel the distance from Tokyo in 12 hrs.

Transportation within Hiroshima: Several streetcar lines of Hiroshima Electric Railway fan out across the city from Hiroshima Station; moreover, the web of bus services also covers the city and its vicinity. The Hiroshima Bus Center at Kamiyacho is one of the important hubs of the network, with bus services to distant cities in the San-in District also available from the Center. It takes 35 min. by bus to Hiroshima Airport. Hiroshima Port in Ujina in the southern part of the city can be reached by streetcar from the JR Hiroshima Station in 25 min. Boats leave for Kure and Miyajima as well as Takamatsu, Imabari and Matsuyama in Shikoku.

Places of interest such as the Shukukeien Garden, Hiroshima Castle, Peace Memorial Park and the Atomic Bomb Dome—all conveniently located within 1-2 km from the station.

Refer to the supplement for details regarding the "i" **System Information Center** in Hiroshima.

PLACES OF INTEREST

Shukukeien Garden: Located 700 m west of Hiroshima Station, this garden was originally designed in 1620 by Asano Nagaakira, a feudal lord who ruled this district. It later developed into its present form to cover an area of 40,000 sq.m. Registered as a Scenic Place, it is situated on the Kyobashi River, from which water is drawn to make streams and ponds within its enclosure. The islets and bridges, the swimming carp and the surrounding woods combine to lend a special beauty to the garden.

Its name, which literally means "miniature landscape gardens," was chosen because it was laid out in imitation of Hsi Hu, or West Lake—a beautiful expanse of water and parkland situated west of Hangchou, the capital of Chekiang Province in central China. The Hiroshima Prefectural Museum of Art is next to the park.

Hiroshima Castle [98]: Situated 1.5 km west of Hiroshima Station, the castle—also called *Rijo* (Carp Castle)—was completed in 1591 by Mori Terumoto, a feudal lord. Ownership of the castle changed from Mori to Fukushima Masanori, another feudal lord, in 1600 and again to Asano Nagaakira in 1619. After that, the castle served as the Asano family residence for about 250 years until the Meiji Restoration.

The donjon of the castle was registered as a National Treasure until 1945, when the entire castle was destroyed by the atomic bomb. However, on the occasion of the Hiroshima Rehabilitation Exposition held in 1958, the five-story donjon was reconstructed in its former shape for exhibiting the history of Hiroshima, with the surrounding area being used as a public park. From the top of the donjon, visitors can see the entire city, Hiroshima Bay and Miyajima Island.

Hiroshima Museum of Art [98]: Located directly south of Hiroshima Castle, this museum has a collection of over 150 important works by artists since the days of impressionism. These include works by Courbet, Monet, Cezanne and Renoir as well as by modern Japanese painters and sculptors of both Japanese and Western styles.

Atomic Bomb Dome (Ruins of the Industry Promotion Hall) [98]: Located 2 km west of Hiroshima Station facing the Motoyasu River, the dome stands on the east side of Aioi Bridge—the approximate epicenter of the atomic explosion on August 6, 1945. The concrete section was burnt and melted, leaving the skeletal steel frame exposed to the sky. The bomb exploded approximately 600 m above the dome and destroyed everything within a radius of 3 km. The dome, which was majestic and beautiful before the blast, is the only atomic-bombed building remaining in the city. It is administered by the city and serves as a grim reminder of the horrors of war.

Peace Memorial Park [98]: Situated 2 km southwest of Hiroshima Station, this park was laid out after the war at the northernmost corner of the delta island separating the effluence of the Ota River into two additional branches—the Motoyasu and Honkawa rivers. The park contains a modern-style Peace Memorial Hall, Peace Memorial Museum, International Conference Center, Hiroshima, Memorial Cenotaph for Victims of the Atomic Bomb and many other memorial monuments.

At the southernmost end of the park, the Honkawa River is spanned by the West Peace Bridge and the Motoyasu River by the Peace Bridge. Both bridges, which have projecting railings, were designed by Noguchi Isamu (a sculptor, the son of the poet Yone Noguchi). From this sector of the park, the 100-m-wide Peace Boulevard leads to Hijiyama Park in the east. Trees that have been donated from around Japan and abroad line both sides and the center section of the boulevard.

The Peace Memorial Museum is a modern, piloti-style building with displays of glass and roofing materials that were deformed by the atomic blast, a shadow printed on the stone steps by the radiation in the shape of a human body and numerous terrifying materials—all testifying to the devastation of the bomb and prompting the visitor to make a vow for universal peace.

The Memorial Cenotaph for Victims of the Atomic Bomb consists of a huge vault shaped like the figurine clay saddle found in ancient tombs under which lies a stone chest containing a list of the names of those killed by the atomic bomb. On the front of the chest is an epitaph inscribed in Japanese which means "Repose ye in peace for the error shall not be repeated." The cenotaph was designed by Tange Kenzo, the world-renowned architect, so that anyone standing in front of it can see through the vault to the Atomic Bomb Dome beyond. Moreover, by turning around, one can see the Peace Memorial Hall, thus enabling one to encompass all the atomic bomb-related objects from a single position. The memorial peace fire some 50 m from the cenotaph will continue to burn until the day when nuclear weapons disappear from the world.

Hijiyama Park ⌊98⌋: Located 1.5 km south of Hiroshima Station, this park forms a small hill in the eastern part of the city. A drive leads to the summit, and from the southern crown a visitor can obtain a fine view of most of the city, including Peace Boulevard. In one corner is the Hiroshima City Museum of Contemporary Art, designed by Kurokawa Kisho. The museum contains over 450 works by Henry Moore, Andy Warhol, Ikeda Masuo and others. The hillside is covered with many cherry trees, making it a popular place in the city for viewing cherry blossoms in spring.

The Asa Zoological Park is located in the northern part of the city and can be reached by bus in 45 min from Hiroshima Station. Approximately 170 species and a total of 1,000 African and other animals are kept within the zoo's extensive, 140,000-sq.-m area. On the other hand, the Hiroshima Municipal Botanical Garden is situated in the western part of the city and may be reached in 40 min. by bus. One of the largest botanical gardens in Asia, it has a collection that includes 8,200 species and a total of 190,000 plants from around the world.

Kumano, located on the eastern side of Hiroshima, is known for its local production of brushes. With an annual production of 125,000,000 brushes for calligraphy, art, and cosmetic purposes, Kumano has over 70% of the Japanese market for brushes. Many brushes are manufactured for export as well. Kawajiri lying east of Kure is also known for brush manufacturing.

Kure ⬚96⬚ ☎0823: Pop. 221,240. This is the central station of the JR Kure Line, which connects Kaitaichi with Mihara on the San-yo Main Line. It is located approximately 25 km from Hiroshima on the east side of Hiroshima Bay. In the west is Etajima Island, while to the south is Kurahashi Island. After a naval station was set up in Kure Port in 1889, this area developed quickly as a naval port. During World War II, large naval vessels and military facilities were built at factories here. Since the war, the region has remained active with shipbuilding, steel, machinery, metal and other heavy industries. Locally produced specialties include *Nikata yasuri* (files) and grind-stone. Ferries connect Kure and Nikata ports in the city with Shikoku.

Irifuneyama Memorial Hall is located 1 km southeast of the station in the former official, Western-style residence of the commander of Kure Naval Station. The museum exhibits naval displays and research materials on Kure and the surrounding area. The Ondo-no-Seto Straits are located 7 km south of Kure Station (30 min. by bus) and separate Mainland and Kurahashi Island. Although they are only 70 m wide, the straits are noted not only for their important position on the sailing route in the southeastern part of Hiroshima Bay, but also for their rapid currents and the great number of ships passing through. Legend has it that Taira-no-Kiyomori (1118–1181) managed to excavate the straits in a single day, recalling the setting sun by beckoning it with a wave of his fan. Kiyomori was head of the Taira Clan, and in a park that looks down on the straits a stone tablet that bears his image was erected in his honor. The Seto-Ohashi Bridge that crosses over the Ondo-no-Seto Straits is 172 m long and allows the passage of 500,000-ton-class vessels. The bridge leads on either side to an elevated highway and makes a striking appearance against the natural scenery.

Nikyukyo Gorge is a lovely gorge on the upper reaches of the Kodai River 10 km northeast of Kure Station and can be reached by bus in 45 min. Many waterfalls cascading down the cliffs on either side of the river lend a unique beauty to the gorge. Numerous potholes, designated as Natural Monuments, can be found here. Nikokyo Gorge lies north of the station, 10 min. by bus. Stretching over a 2-km area upstream of the Nikogawa River, it is the same type of recreational site for visitors as Nikyukyo.

Etajima Island in Hiroshima Bay has a total land surface of 30 sq. km. The Naval Academy was established here in 1888 and continued to train cadets until 1945. At present, the Maritime Self-Defense Force First Service School is located here among many old stone and brick buildings. One of these buildings is open to the public as an educational reference hall, displaying many artifacts and research materials from the former Imperial Navy.

Higashi-Hiroshima 96 ☎0824: Pop. 87,778. Saijo, the center of Higashi-Hiroshima, is approximately 30 km to the east of Hiroshima and can be reached by train on the JR San-yo Main Line in 33 min. This area, known for its local production of *sake*, has many white-walled, *sake* storage houses. *Sake* production began in 1675 and some of the local brands are popular throughout the nation. It is also known for its *Saijogaki* (Saijo persimmons) crops. The Aki Kokubun-ji Temple, designated as a Historical Site, is 500 m from Saijo Station. In the past, the western part of Hiroshima Prefecture was known as Aki Province.

Miyajima 96

Also called Itsukushima, it is an island about 31 km in circumference and 30 sq.km in area. It is noted for the Itsukushima Shrine built on supports extending into the sea. The landscape, including the shrine, has been famed since olden times as one of Japan's three most beautiful sights, the other two being Matsushima near Sendai and Amanohashidate in Miyazu Bay on the Japan Sea coast.

Miyajima has excellent swimming beaches and many pleasant paths for strolling. The temperature is mild even in summer, when it is relatively cool at night. The island is also noted for its cherry blossoms—at their peak in early April—as well as for the changing colors of leaves in autumn. Tame deer roam the island, as in Nara.

An ancient religious regulation, observed up to the time of the Meiji Restoration (1868), forbade any rituals related to death from being performed on the island. Although this restriction is no longer in force, the dead are always buried at Ono on the opposite shore.

The island can be reached by a 25-min. ride from Hiroshima to Miyajimaguchi on the JR San-yo Main Line and a 5-min. walk to the pier, from where ferry boats cross over to the island in 10 min. Ferry service is also available directly from Hiroshima Port in 25 min.

At Miyajimaguchi stands the Miyajima Tower, a 50-m-high structure topped by a revolving observation platform that offers a fine view of the island, the city and the Inland Sea.

Itsukushima Shrine 99 : A 10-min. walk from the pier, this shrine is dedicated to the three daughters of Susano-o-no-Mikoto, a Shinto god—Princesses Ichikishima-Hime, Tagori-Hime and Tagitsu-Hime. The shrine is said to have been constructed in 593, with the present foundation being laid by Taira-no-Kiyomori around the year 1168. The buildings, which have been reconstructed several times, presently consist of the Main Shrine and several secondary shrines and buildings, all connected by wide corridors and galleries. These stretch above the sea so that when the tide comes in, the whole edifice appears to float on the water's surface. Reconstructed during the 13th and 14th centuries, the Main Shrine consists of four parts: the *Honden* (Main Hall), where the goddesses are enshrined; *Heiden* (Inner Sanctum), where only priests may enter; *Haiden* (Oratory), open for all, and *Haraiden* (Purification Hall). The Main Hall, *Heiden, Haiden,* and *Haraiden* and the corridors have been designated as National Treasures. The ordinary dances (*kagura*) of the shrine are performed in the *Heiden,* but the festival dances (*Bugaku*) are performed on the large, open-air platform in front of the shrine. Well known for their ancient origins, these dances are performed to Japanese Court music (*gagaku*) on special, ritual occasions.

Just beyond the entrance to the shrine is the Marodo (Guest) Shrine, rebuilt in 1241 as a small model of the Main Shrine. It is designated as a National Treasure. Okuni Shrine is dedicated to the mythical Shinto god Okuninushi-no-Mikoto (refer to p.799), while Tenjin Shrine along the west-side gallery is dedicated to an eminent scholar and statesman, Sugawara Michizane (845–903, refer to p.843). The arched bridge near the exit symbolizes the Bridge of Heaven in Japanese mythology. A great *torii* gate stands 16 m high in the water 160 m from the Main Shrine. It was rebuilt in 1975 and designated as an Important Cultural Property.

The *noh* stage with a *hashigakari* (passageway) and a dressing room is constructed of plain wood and roofed with Japanese cypress bark. Originally built in 1568, it was reconstructed during the Edo period and is the oldest of all *noh* stages extant in Japan. It has been designated as an Important Cultural Property.

Senjokaku: Lit. Hall of One Thousand Mats. It is the old building to the north of the shrine. Actually, it contains about 450 mats and was dedicated to the shrine in 1587 by Toyotomi Hideyoshi (1536–1598), who is said to have had the hall constructed using only the best wood from camphor trees. Since 1872 the Senjokaku has served as the Hokoku Shrine, dedicated to Toyotomi Hideyoshi. It belongs to Itsukushima Shrine. *Goju-no-To* (Five-Story Pagoda) close-by soars to a height of 27.6 m. Thatched with the bark of Japanese cypress, it was built in 1407. Both have been designated as Important Cultural Properties.

Treasure Hall: Near the west gallery across the small stream of the Mitarashigawa River stands the Treasure Hall, a modern earth-quake- and fire-proof structure containing approximately 3,500 objects. These include more than 130 treasures designated as National Treasures or Important Cultural Properties such as the 33 illustrated scrolls with Buddhist precepts donated by the family of Taira-no-Kiyomori and known as impressive works of art.

Lanterns: In the galleries are several bronze lanterns. For a fee, the shrine authorities will have all these lanterns lighted especially for group visitors. The scene at high tide on a moonless night is especially impressive.

Festivals: The following are some of the most important festivals and events held at this shrine every year: *Kangensai* (Orchestra Festival) is held late in July (June 17 according to the lunar calendar), when stately barges bearing *mikoshi* (portable shrine) as well as priests and musicians cross the bay with other gaily decorated boats in a colorful progression, and *Tamatori Matsuri* (Ball-Catching Festival), or *Ennen-sai* (Longevity Festival) is held in the middle of August in which men and boys dive into the sea to retrieve a sacred wooden ball about 70 cm. in circumference which is released by a priest from a swinging platform set up in the sea. Whoever recovers the ball may keep it as well as other prizes and is assured a long, happy life.

Daiganji Temple: This temple was built west of the shrine in 802. Belonging to the Koyasan-Shingon sect of Buddhism, its principal image—*Benzaiten* (Goddess of Fortune)—is popularly known as "Itsukushima Benten." It also has several wooden statues of Buddha and his disciples, which are designated as Important Cultural Properties.

The Miyajima Municipal History and Folklore Museum is located on the property of an Edo-period merchant family, offering a display of over 2,000 ancient articles. The building itself is recognized as having great historical value.

The Miyajima Public Aquarium displays over 450 species of tropical and fresh-water fish and presents sea lion shows.

Momijidani (Maple Valley) Park, a 15-minute walk from the pier, is a quiet retreat situated on a hillside among a grove of maple trees. There are several tea houses and *ryokan* in this valley.

Mt. Misen: With an altitude of 530 m, this is the highest peak on the island. The summit can be reached in 20 min. by a 1.7-km ropeway ride from Momijidani behind Itsukushima Shrine plus a short hike. Near the summit is the *Misen Hondo* (Main Hall) surrounded by large stones. The primeval forest here is preserved as a Natural Monument. There is a splendid view from the summit of Hiroshima, the nearby mountains and the innumerable islets and boats.

Yuki Spa [96]: This quiet, hot-spring resort situated in the valley of the Utsuodani River west of Hiroshima can be reached directly by bus from the Hiroshima Bus Center at Kamiyacho in 1 hr. 40 min. In summer the croaking of frogs and the brilliant glimmering of fireflies are a special attraction. Known as a bathing spot for the feudal lord of Hiroshima, this spa and nearby Yunoyama Spa are popular with hikers. Both are radon spas. To the southwest of Yuki Spa is Iwakura Spa, also accessible by bus from the Bus Center in 1 hr.30 min.

Nishi (West)-Chugoku Plateau Quasi National Park [96]: This park, 285.53 sq.km in area, sprawls over a vast mountainous region that extends into the three prefectures of Hiroshima, Shimane and Yamaguchi. It is known for the magnificent scenic beauty presented by a range of 1,000-m-high mountains with a number of deep ravines and gorges, including Sandankyo Gorge.

Sandankyo Gorge [96]: Designated as an Outstanding Scenic Place, it is situated on the upper reaches of the Ota River, 73 km northwest of Hiroshima. Accessible by bus from the Hiroshima Bus Center in 2 hrs. 10 min, the gorge is noted for its scenic beauty, especially that of its many fine waterfalls. The gorge extends for approximately 16 km. Points of interest include Sarutobi, an area where two cliffs are separated by a 2-m gap, and beautiful Nidantaki, Sandantaki, Kuro-fuchi and Mitsudaki falls. Some parts are covered by boat, from which the beautiful scenery can be appreciated at its best.

Area 4. Chugoku Mountain Area

Along JR Geibi and Kisuki Lines

Hiroshima and Matsue, the capital city of Shimane Prefecture on the Japan Sea Coast, are connected by the JR Geibi and Kisuki lines traversing the Chugoku Mountain Chain. Direct express trains cover the distance of 214 km in about 5 hrs. National Highway 54 runs along this route and can be accessed from the Chugoku Expressway at the Miyoshi Interchange.

Miyoshi [96] ☎08246: Pop. 39,209. Located 1 hr.20 min. (69 km) by express from Hiroshima on the JR Geibi Line, the Miyoshi Basin is blessed with an extensive area of farmland rich in riverside attractions. Three meandering rivers meet and combine to form the Gonokawa River—the longest in the Chugoku District, which flows to the Japan Sea. Located in the heart of the basin, Miyoshi originally developed as a castle town, but has always played an important role as a center of transportation connecting the San-in and San-yo districts.

Miyoshi is a commercial and industrial city as well as a distribution center for lumber. The main attractions of the city include the cherry blossoms at Ozekiyama Park and the ancient tomb mounds of Jo-rakuji Temple near Kamisugi Station, 8 min. from Miyoshi by the JR Geibi Line. The burial ground forms a park known as Miyoshi Fudoki(Local History and Topography)-no-Oka Hill. Besides the Hiroshima Prefectural Museum of History and Folkcrafts and ancient houses, the 400-year-old tradition of cormorant fishing is carried out in summer at the confluence of the three rivers.

Hiba-Dogo-Taishaku Quasi-National Park [96-97]: Designated in 1969, this park covers a large mountainous region of 78.08 sq.km on the borders of Tottori, Shimane and Hiroshima prefectures. It is divided into two sections: Mts. Hiba, Dogo, and Sentsu in the central part of the Chugoku Mountain Chain and Taishakukyo Gorge. The park attracts skiers, hikers and campers because of its richly varied scenic beauty, including extensive prairies, plateaus and swamps, beech forests, fresh verdure and vivid, natural colors.

Mt. Hiba, soaring to an altitude of 1,240 m, and its foothills contain the Hiroshima Kemmin-no-mori (Prefectural Citizen's Forest), which can be reached in 45 min. by bus from Bingo Saijo Station on the JR

Geibi Line. This area is popular with skiers and campers. The beech forest here is designated as a Natural Monument. The foot of Mt. Dogo (alt. 1,269 m) can be reached in 20 min. by bus from the JR Bingo-Ochiai Station, with a lift going part of the way up the mountain. Many mountain flora and fauna, especially butterflies, can be seen, with the azaleas appearing particularly beautiful when they bloom in early summer. This area is also popular with skiers and campers.

Shobara `96` ☎08247: Pop. 22,630. This area is accessible in 40 min. from Miyoshi to Bingo-Shobara by the JR Geibi Line, but it can also be reached from the Shobara Interchange on the Chugoku Expressway. North of the city is Mt. Shoko, which has deposits of agalmatolite. There are many clay and ceramic factories in the surrounding area. The city is noted for the Hiba cattle raised here as well as the cherry trees in Ueno Park near Bingo-Shobara Station. It is also the starting point for the famous Taishakukyo Gorge to the west.

Taishakukyo Gorge `96` : Located 55 min. by bus from Shobara Bus Center. A 35-min. bus ride from Tojo Station on the JR Geibi Line brings one to a marvelous area in which magnificent limestone tablelands are carved in this valley. The area is blessed with limestone caves, sharp cliffs and natural bridges all along its 15-km stretch. In particular, the Ombashi Bridge is 70 m long and 18 m wide with a height of 40 m. Downstream is the smaller Membashi Bridge. The name of this narrow valley was taken from the Eimyoji Temple, which is dedicated to *Taishakuten*, one of the guardian deities of Buddhism. The downstream area has been dammed to form the artificial Lake Jinryu, which has a circumference of 24 km. Sightseeing boats on the lake leave from Inuse. The whole area is well known for the maple tree leaves that change color in autumn.

Nita is well known for the Nita cattle raised here. This town, along with neighboring Yokota, is famous for its production of Unshu abacuses. The *Oni-no-Shitaburui* Valley is located 15 min. by bus from Izumo-Minari Station on the JR Kisuki Line. This 3-km-long, V-shaped valley is filled with fine examples of granite. Huge, strangely shaped rocks known as *Otenguiwa* (Big, Long-Nosed Goblin Rock) and *Kotenguiwa* (Small, Long-Nosed Goblin Rock) line the valley. In autumn this area is especially beautiful when the leaves begin to change colors.

Area 5. Western San-yo District

Iwakuni to Shimonoseki

Otake `96` ☎08275: Pop. 33,701. Located 40 min. (36 km) southwest of Hiroshima Station on the San-yo Main Line, this area was an important naval base during World War II, but it has since become an industrial city. Its many factories now produce chemical fiber, paper and petrochemical products as part of the Inland Sea Industrial Zone along with the adjacent city of Iwakuni.

Iwakuni ☐96☐ ☎0827: Pop. 111,298. Located at the eastern edge of Yamaguchi Prefecture and only 41 km from Hiroshima, Iwakuni is served by the JR San-yo Shinkansen in the western part of the city. It is the junction for the JR Gantoku Line, which leads to Tokuyama, and the San-yo Main Line, which follows the coastline.

The city developed as a feudal town when the Kikkawa family began construction of Iwakuni Castle at the beginning of the 17th century. With the establishment of factories for rayon, other chemical fibers and pulp as well as petroleum refineries, it has become an important industrial city. Among the tourist attractions are the Kintai Bridge with five spans, Iwakuni Castle in Momoyama-style with smacks of European architecture, carp in the Nishiki River, Kikko Park with its rich, historical assets, and Momijidani Park with its abundance of appealing scenery.

Iwakuni Port is equipped with facilities for docking 10,000-ton-class vessels.

Kintai Bridge: Located approximately 5 km west of Iwakuni Station, 15 min. by bus. The bridge was originally constructed by Kikkawa Hiroyoshi (a feudal lord of the district) in 1673. Because of its resemblance in shape to an abacus, the bridge is called *Sorobambashi*, which means "Abacus Bridge." It was destroyed by a flood in 1950 and reconstructed in 1953 as an exact duplicate of the original. The bridge is 193 m long, 5 m wide, and 12 m above the water at its highest point. No nails are used at all; instead, cramps and wires are employed as fasteners.

During the three months from June to August, demonstrations of cormorant fishing are held under the bridge.

Kikko Park is located next to Kintai Bridge amid the ruins of the former clan residence. The park houses former *samurai* residences and the Nishimura Museum, which displays ancient *samurai* armor and weapons.

Iwakuni Castle: Originally built by Kikkawa Hiroie. Its construction was begun in 1601—the year after the lord was transferred from Izumo Province (now, a part of Shimane Prefecture) to his fief, the present Iwakuni—and was completed in 1608. Unfortunately, however, it was destroyed in 1615 by order of Iemitsu, the third Tokugawa Shogun. The castle was left in a dilapidated condition for nearly 350 years, but in 1962 the donjon was reconstructed in Momoyama-style with a strain of European architectural design—a very unique castle for Japan. The castle stands on Shiroyama Hill, connected by a ropeway to Kikko Park that takes 3 min. to reach the top.

Yanai ☐96☐ ☎0820: Pop. 37,181. Located south of Iwakuni, this area developed as a port of trade between Japan and China, with many old parts of the town still intact today. Straight out from the port is

Yashiro Island, also known as Oshima (lit. Big Island). With a total land area of 139.7 sq.km, it is the third-largest island in the Inland Sea. The opposite coast of Obatake is connected by the Oshima-Ohashi Bridge. Yashiro Island is known for the cultivation of mandarin oranges. In 1943 the Imperial Navy battleship Mutsu sunk mysteriously in the vicinity. A memorial museum of the ship stands here.

Hikari 96 ☎0833: Pop. 48,938. Located 1 hr.40 min. (96 km) from Hiroshima on the San-yo Main Line, Hikari has achieved remarkable development as an industrial city. Located in the city are the factory of Nippon Kokan K.K. (one of the biggest steel producing companies in Japan), which began operations after World War II on the site of the former naval arsenal, and other factories producing pharmaceuticals and other products.

Nearby Murozumi, a well-known beach resort in the Chugoku District, has a long stretch of pine trees along its shore.

Kudamatsu 96 ☎0833: Pop. 54,117. 1 hr.47 min. or 103 km from Hiroshima by the JR San-yo Main Line. This area specializes in the heavy and chemical industries, producing automobiles, steel and iron, and petroleum products. It is also active in farming and fishing. Measuring 36 km in circumference, it faces Kasado Island, and abounds in curious rocks and lovely creeks. The island is connected to the mainland by the 156-m-long Kasado Ohashi Bridge—a picturesque, crimson-painted structure. Yashiro is located 5 km northwest of Takamizu Station on the JR Gantoku Line. Late every October, flocks of *nabezuru* or white-tufted cranes migrate here from Siberia for refuge until early March. The birds are under protection as Natural Monuments. Nearby Mitsuo Spa is surrounded by mountains on three sides and is characterized by a pastoral atmosphere.

Tokuyama 96 ☎0834: Pop. 110,823. This flourishing seaport is located 40 min. (89 km) by the JR San-yo Shinkansen from Hiroshima. It can be reached from Yamaguchi by the San-yo Expressway. An important naval fuel depot was located in the city before the end of World War II. Together with Kudamatsu to the east along the Inland Sea coast, it has been turned into a large industrial zone in the postwar years based on the development of heavy and chemical industries manufacturing such products as caustic soda, steel plates and petroleum. It is especially known for the naphtha-refining plants that form the core of the petro-chemical industry located here.

With Tokuyama Bay, which is protected from southeasterly and westerly winds by the Oshima Peninsula and the islands of Senjima, Kurokami and Otsu, the city is the largest trading port in Yamaguchi Prefecture. The summit of Mt. Taika, 2 km from Tokuyama Station, commands a clear view of the industrial zone as well as the island-studded sea. Kurokami Island off the city's coastline produces granite that is used throughout the country. Most of the stones used in constructing the National Diet Building in Tokyo came from this island.

Hofu ⟨96⟩ ☎0835: Pop. 118,396. Located 2 hrs. 30 min. (115 km) by local train from Hiroshima, this city was the center of Suo Province (now, a part of Yamaguchi Prefecture) in ancient times. Although the city has long been known as a production center for salt, it has recently developed into an industrial city, spurred by the rapid progress of the chemical industry in synthetic fibers, liquors and drugs.

Hofu Temmangu: Standing 1 km north of the station, dedicated to Sugawara Michizane (845–903), a scholar-statesman of the early Heian period. An imposing shrine rebuilt in 1963, it is said to have originally been constructed in 904. A scroll painting illustrating the life of Michizane together with a wooden statue of *Dainichi-Nyorai* (a Buddhist diety) are listed among the treasures of the shrine. This shrine and the Temmangu Shrine of Kitano in Kyoto as well as Dazaifu in Fukuoka Prefecture are called Japan's Three Temmangu.

In the city, the Suo Kokubunji Temple, including seven Buddhist images (an Important Cultural Treasure) and the former residence of the Mori family with a museum that houses a painting of Sesshu (refer to p.767), are interesting, too. In the surrounding area, Mt. Ohira (alt. 631 m) can be reached from Hofu Station by bus in 20 min. plus a 6-min. ropeway ride. The summit affords a superb view of the surrounding area. At the foot of the mountain is Amidaji Temple, an annex to the Todaiji Temple in Nara. It was built in 1197, and the 3-m-high steel tower *Tetsuhoto* (lit. steel treasure pagoda), among many other precious properties, is designated as a National Treasure.

Ogori ⟨96⟩: Situated 133 km from Hiroshima and can be reached by the JR San-yo Shinkansen in 45 minutes. It prospers as the transportation center of this area: the JR Yamaguchi Line leads to Masuda via Tsuwano, an old castle town, while the JR Ube Line goes to Ube; National Highways 2 and 9 merge here and the Chugoku Expressway passes north of the city at the Ogori Interchange, and buses leave for Hagi, Akiyoshido Cave and Yuda Spa. The town, which extends along the lower reaches of the Fushino River, is active in producing farming tools and furniture.

Yamaguchi ⟨96/103-②⟩ ☎0839

Pop. 124,308. 25 min. (13 km) on the JR Yamaguchi Line from Ogori. It is approximately 5 km from the Yamaguchi Interchange of the Chugoku Expressway to the center of the city. The capital of Yamaguchi Prefecture, this city was once called the "Western Kyoto" because of its many shrines, the most famous of which is Yasaka Shrine, originally built in 1370. *Sagimai*, or the Heron Dance, is the main attraction of the shrine's annual week-long festival beginning on July 20. It is protected as an Intangible Cultural Property. *Ouchi-nuri* lacquerware and ball-shaped *Ouchi-ningyo* dolls are very popular local specialties.

HISTORY

The history of Yamaguchi Prefecture dates back to the 14th century when it passed into the hands of the Ouchi family. The family increased its prosperity, building numerous, splendid temples and buildings in imitation of those in Kyoto, which the city somewhat resembles in topography. It was at the height of its glory in the 16th century, when a Spanish Christian Jesuit missionary, Francisco de Xavier (1506-1552), paid a visit to this city.

In 1557 the city passed into the control of Mori Motonari (1497-1571), who governed the area with his base in Hiroshima. However, his grandson, Mori Terumoto, was exiled from Hiroshima to Hagi on the Japan Sea coast because he had fought on the side of the defeated Toyotomi forces in the decisive Battle of Sekigahara in 1600. Although this resulted in a decline in the prosperity of the city, it rose to prominence again in 1863 when it became one of the bases of operations of the Meiji Restoration.

PLACES OF INTEREST

Kameyama Park ⌈103-②⌉: Located 1.5 km north of the JR Yamaguchi Station, it can be reached by bus in 3 min. It is situated on a hill—the site of the villa of the Ouchi family. Covering an area of 58, 300 sq.m, it is not only noted for its cherry blossoms, azaleas and maple leaves, but also for the fine view of the city it commands. The bronze statues in the park represent famous members of the Mori Clan, who took part in the Meiji Restoration.

St. Xavier Memorial Church ⌈103-②⌉: A Roman Catholic church built in the Romanesque style at the top of Kameyama Hill. Its vestibule is modeled after that of Xavier Castle in Navarra, Spain, where the saint was born. Two tall towers rise at the rear. The 25 stained-glass windows were made in Spain. The cathedral was built in 1951 to celebrate the 400th anniversary of the visit to Japan by the saint, who arrived in Kagoshima, Kyushu, in 1549 to introduce Christianity to Japan (refer to p.881). In 1551 he began his evangelical work in Yamaguchi with the permission of the local feudal lord, Ouchi Yoshitaka. He was granted the Daidoji Temple for use as a church and stayed there for five months.

St. Xavier Monument, located 2.5 km northeast of the station, was erected in 1926 in the garden of the ruins of the Daidoji Temple in Kanakoso. Made of granite, it is in the shape of a cross, 6 m high, with a bust of Xavier embedded in the center.

Rurikoji Temple ⌈103-②⌉: Situated approximately 3 km north of the station with its *Goju-no-To* (Five-Story Pagoda). It was built in 1442 with a height of 31.2 m. The tower has large eaves and is quite graceful and stable. It has been designated as a National Treasure. The surrounding gardens boast many *ume* (Japanese plum) and cherry trees.

Joeiji Temple: Located approximately 4 km northeast of the center of the city, it is known for the landscape garden designed by the famous priest-painter Sesshu in the 15th century (refer to p.767).

Yuda Spa ☐103-②☐ : Located west of Yamaguchi Station, it is one of the best hot-spring resort areas in the Chugoku District. Equipped with many modern facilities, the spa can easily be reached through the local transportation network and receives visitors all year round. The Akiyoshido Cave, Akiyoshi Plateau and Chomonkyo Gorge are popular tourist spots in the vicinity.

Chomonkyo Gorge ☐96☐ : Situated about 20 km from Yamaguchi or 35 min. by the JR Yamaguchi Line in the upstream reaches of the Abu River, which flows to the Japan Sea. The beauties of the gorge were first pointed out by Mr. J. Gauntlett around 1911, when he was a professor at Yamaguchi Higher Commercial School. Although the Chomonkyo Gorge extends for approximately 10 km, a 5.5-km stretch from Chomonkyo Station to Ryugubuchi is commonly considered as the gorge by tourists. This area consists of fantastically shaped rocks, cascades, deep pools, holes and a stalactic grotto. The foliage along the gorge displays gorgeous tints in autumn.

Akiyoshidai Plateau Quasi-National Park ☐96☐ : Akiyoshidai Plateau is the largest karst topography in Japan with an area of 130 sq. km. The park occupies 45.3 sq.km, the major part of which has been designated as a Special Natural Monument.

On the extensive, elevated region stretching in mild undulations for about 300 m above sea level, visitors can see a variety of elements of karst topography such as karrenfeld (rows of tomblike rocks of limestone exposed from the earth's surface), doline (a basin in a limestone district), uvale (several dolines unified into one large basin), polje (upland hollow), ponor (a basin with a hole at the bottom through which running water drops underground) and a lime grotto. All these formations have been created by limestone erosion caused by rainwater and underground water containing carbonic acid gas. Among the many lime grottoes, the Akiyoshido Cave is perhaps the most striking example.

Akiyoshido Cave ☐96☐ : Located 30 km from Yamaguchi Station, this cave can be reached by bus in 55 min. or from Ogori in 45 min. This is one of the many stalactic caves of the Akiyoshidai Plateau and one of the largest of its kind in the world. The entrance to the cave is at the south end of the plateau. Opening towards the east, the entrance is 24 m high and 8 m wide. Inside, it is about 60 m wide on an average and 150 m at its widest. The average height is 30 m with a maximum height of 80 m. Its total length is said to be 10 km, of which about 1 km permits passage by people. The cave offers a rich variety of beautiful scenery with its rivers, waterfalls, and deep pools as well as a series of well-developed stalactites, stalagmites and stone pillars. Water oozing through the cave's limestone walls redeposits the limestone in the form of stalactites. The cave may easily be explored in any season as the temperature is always around 17°C. Mercury lamps have been installed. At Kurodani, visitors may exit the cave onto the Akiyoshidai Plateau by elevator (80 m). A science museum on the plateau also serves as a scientific research institute with a large collection of stalactites and stuffed animals from species found in the cave as well as research materials on stalactites, stalagmites, and the local flora and fauna, topography and climate.

Ube 96 ☎0836: Pop. 172,068. Until 1967 when the Coal Mine of Ube Industries was closed, this area was the largest undersea coal mining area in Japan. At present such products as urea for chemical fertilizers, ammonium sulphate, synthetic resins, cement and caustic soda are manufactured here.

Tokiwa Park: A 15-min. ride by bus from Ube Shinkawa Station on the JR Ube Line. It is a recreation center situated in a lovely setting around the artificial Lake Tokiwa, 12 km in circumference. The lake is inhabited by some 500 swans of eight different species and over 1.5 million carp. Over 3,000 exhibits of machinery and research material are exhibited in the local Coal Museum. In the basement is a model coal mine shaft, while on the roof is an observation tower made from a coal shaft.

Onoda 96 ☎0836: Pop. 46,170. Located to the west of Ube. The Onoda Cement Co. Ltd. was established in 1881 as the first and largest private enterprise in Japan to engage in the manufacture and export of cement. Nowadays, its industries turn out such products as cement, sulphuric acid and chemical fertilizers as well as drugs and ceramics—all contributing to the prosperity of the city. The area is also noted for being one of the largest producers of acid-proof ceramics in Japan.

Shimonoseki 96 ☎0832

Pop. 259,391. Shimonoseki can be reached from Hiroshima by the JR San-yo Shinkansen in approximately 1 hr. (223 km). Formerly called Akamagaseki, or Bakan, the city lies at the southwest extremity of the island of Honshu. It is connected by three tunnels and the Kammonkyo Bridge with Moji on the opposite coast in Kyushu and serves as the western gateway to the Inland Sea. The city is a vital land and sea traffic link. Its port is divided into commercial and fishing, sectors. The latter serves as a base for deep-sea fishing, obtaining some of the best catches in the country. Consequently, many factories in the city are engaged in the production of processed sea food as well as frozen and canned sea food. The metal, shipbuilding and chemical industries also prosper here. The Kampu Ferry Co., Ltd. provides daily service between Shimonoseki and Pusan in the Republic of Korea.

HISTORY

Shimonoseki is famous in connection with the tragedy of the Taira (Heike) Clan, which was exterminated by the Minamoto (Genji) Clan in the famous sea battle of Dannoura off the beach of the city in 1185.

Dominated by Choshu Clan or Mori Clan, Shimonoseki was also the scene of one of the most dramatic incidents before the Meiji Restoration. Rallying under the slogan "Expel the barbarians," members of the Choshu Clan began firing on Western ships passing through the Shimonoseki Straits in 1863 and eventually sealed off the straits. In retaliation for these attacks, a combined allied fleet of British, French, Dutch and American warships bombarded the Shimonoseki forts in 1864, severely damaging them after three days of action. The incident is called the Shimonoseki Incident, or the Bakan War, and forced the Mori Clan of Choshu or Nagato Province (now, a part of Yamaguchi Prefecture) to realize the necessity of opening up the country. The Mori Clan later entered into an agreement with the Shimazu Clan of Satsuma Province (now, Kagoshima Prefecture) to form one of the two major forces of the Meiji Restoration bringing about an end to the Tokugawa Shogunate. Furthermore, the Sino-Japanese Treaty of Peace was signed at Shimonoseki in 1895.

PLACES OF INTEREST

Kameyama Hachimangu Shrine: Situated 2.3 km east of Shimonoseki Station (10 min. by bus) and dedicated to Emperors Chuai, Ojin and Nintoku and Empress Jingu. It is noted for its fine view of the straits.

Akama Jingu Shrine: Standing 2.2 km east of the station (10 min. by bus), the shrine is dedicated to the infant Emperor Antoku (1178-1185), who shared the fate of the Taira Clan at the battle of Dannoura when he was drowned. The vermilion-lacquered gate is very picturesque. The grand festival of the shrine, known as *Sentei-sai*, is held annually from April 23 to 25, with a parade of women clad in ancient *kimonos* on the 24th. Dannoura is a beach along the straits, 1 km east of the Akama Jingu Shrine, and is known as the battlefield of the Heike (Taira) and Genji (Minamoto) clans. Along the shore, one can find small crabs, popularly called *heike-gani* (Heike crabs) because the creases on their shells resemble the anguished faces of the defeated Heike warriors.

Mt. Hinoyama: Alt. 268 m. Towering near the entrance to the Kammon Automobile Tunnel. A 10-min. bus ride from Shimonoseki Station and a 425-m ropeway ride will bring visitors to the summit. "Hinoyama Parkway" (a toll road) also leads to the top, where a park overlooks the ancient battlefield of Dannoura and commands a fine view of northern Kyushu across the straits. In summer a fine view can be enjoyed at night.

Chofu: The town of Chofu is located on the eastern side of Shimonoseki and can be reached by bus, either from Shimonoseki Station in 25 min. or from Chofu Station on the JR San-yo Main Line in 5 min. This area is said to have had deep connections with Emperor Chuai (reigned 192-200), who is said to have sojourned here with his consort, Empress Jingu, while on his way to quell a rebellion in Kyushu. The Iminomiya Shrine stands on the ruins of Toyourano-miya, which was once the seat of the government of Nagato Province (now, a part of Yamaguchi Prefecture) during the Nara period (710–784). As it was a castle town of the Mori Clan, a few, large *samurai* residences still remain here. The Kozanji Temple, built in 1327, is an ancient Buddhist sanctum with a fine example of ancient roof architecture. It is designated as a National Treasure.

The Shimonoseki Municipal Aquarium is located 7 min. by bus from Chofu Station or 20 min. by bus from Shimonoseki Station. A three-story concrete building, it displays over 400 species of salt- and fresh-water fish and tropical fish. Connected with the aquarium is an amusement park on the Sotoura seashore that is equipped with a variety of recreational facilities.

Sumiyoshi Shrine: 20 min. by bus from Shimonoseki Station. It is said to have been founded by Empress Jingu. The Main Hall, rebuilt in 1370, has an extremely wide front side, which is characteristic of its specialized architectural style. It has been designated as a National Treasure and contains a bronze bell designated as an Important Cultural Property as well as many other treasures.

Area 6. Eastern San-in District

Toyo-oka to Izumo

Toyo-oka 97 ☎07962: Pop. 47,406. Toyo-oka can be reached from Kyoto in about 2 hrs. 30 min. (149 km) by limited express on the JR San-in Main Line. This city is the junction for the Kitakinki-Tango Railway Miyazu Line that continues to Nishi-Maizuru via Amano-hashidate. The city is situated in the center of the basin of the same name and is surrounded by the Chugoku Mountain Chain, with the Maruyama River valley to the east and the fertile fields of the Izushi Basin to the southeast. Toyo-oka is the political, economic and tourist center of the Tajima District (now, a part of Hyogo Prefecture), with the Gembudo Cave and Kinosaki Spa lying to the north. The city is famous for its cattle breeding and wickerwork made of Japanese basket osiers, which grow in the neighboring marshes. It produces most of such wickerwork manufactured in Japan.

Gembudo 97 : A basaltic cave about 70 m wide and 10 m deep. Facing the Maruyama River, it can be reached in 15 min. by bus from Toyo-oka Station. Said to have been formed 1.6 million years ago by volcanic activity, it consists of many large stones jutting down from the ceiling.

Kinosaki Spa 97 : Located 158 km from Kyoto, about 2 hrs. 40 min. by limited express on the JR San-in Main Line, or 184 km from Osaka about 2 hrs. 50 min. by limited express on the JR Fukuchiyama Line. One of the nearest of those in the San-in District to Kyoto and Osaka, this spa has gained great popularity among Kansai residents. It is surrounded by mountains on three sides and is open to the east where the Maruyama River flows to the north towards the Japan Sea. It is only 7 min. by ropeway from the spa town to the top of Mt. Daishi, whose surrounding area is known for its beautiful view. Located on the mountain are the Onsenji Temple, whose Main Hall has been designated as an Important Cultural Property, and the museum with its display of ancient Buddhist artifacts. The spa has been known since the seventh century. In the past it consisted of seven public baths. All of the local *ryokan* have their own baths, while the tradition of public outdoor bathing continues. The water ranges 40–70°C in temperature and is efficacious against gastroenteric ailments, female disorders and neuralgia.

Hiyoriyama Park: Located 10 min. by bus from the JR Kinosaki Station. Mt. Hiyori faces the sea. A marine park has been constructed on the reefs with dolphin and penguin shows and fishing holes. Glass-bottomed boats for underwater observation are in service in spring, summer and autumn.

Kasumi 97 : About 3 hrs. from Kyoto by limited express on the JR San-in Main Line. The coast near Kasumi is known for its picturesque rock formations and is the most magnificent, jagged coastline in the San-in District. The area from here west to Hamasaka, known as Tajima-Mihonoura, is studded with many sea-eroded caves and reefs of great beauty. Visitors can enjoy 30- to 90-min. excursion-boat tours out to sea in all seasons except winter.

The Daijoji Temple is located 1.5 km south of Kasumi Station and can be reached in 5 min. by bus. Often called the Okyodera Temple, this temple is well known among lovers of Japanese art as it houses many paintings by Maruyama Okyo (1733–1795) and his disciples. Many of them are designated as Important Cultural Properties. Maruyama Okyo was a landscape artist who achieved a realistic style and founded the Maruyama school. The temple is said to have been founded by a famous priest named Gyoki during the eighth century.

The Amarube Steel Bridge connects Yoroi and Amarube along the San-in Main Line. It is 41.5 m high and 309 m long. There is a lovely view of Amarube hamlet below from a train crossing the bridge.

Yumura Spa 97 : Located 25 min. by bus from Hamasaka Station on the JR San-in Main Line and 2 hrs. 45 min. from Osaka by direct bus. As it is a mountain spa, the hot water gushes forth abundantly, causing a mist to rise above the Haruki River as it enters. The water, which reaches temperatures up to 98°C, can be used in cooking *tofu* (bean curd) and vegetables. It is a famous spa with a long history that dates back to its discovery in the year 848. Closer to Hamasaka Station (2–3 km) is Hamasaka Spa.

Uradome Bay is 7 min. by bus from Iwami on the San-in Main Line, with the Uradome Coast spreading out 15 km from east to west in a jagged line and the bay at its center. The western side is covered with caves, steep cliffs and rocks. Iwamoto is 10 min. by bus from Iwami

Station, from which excursion boats depart in all seasons but winter. The eastern side has many beaches that are suitable for swimming. Iwai Spa is located 3 km southeast of Iwami and can be reached in 10 min. by bus. This spa is said to have been visited by aristocrats and nobles from Kyoto as early as the year 859.

Tottori 97/102-① ☎0857

Pop. 139,087. Tottori can be reached by limited express on the JR San-in Main Line from Kyoto in 3 hrs. 50 min. (231 km). From Osaka, it takes about 4 hrs. 10 min. by the JR limited express (256 km). The JR San-in Main Line and Imbi Line from Tsuyama join here. In addition to National Highway 9, National Highway 29 leads to the Chugoku Expressway's Yamazaki Interchange and National Highway 53 to the Tsuyama Interchange. By plane it takes 1 hr.20 min. from Tokyo and 50 min. from Osaka.

Tottori is the second-largest city in the San-in District and the capital of Tottori Prefecture. Lying on the lower reaches of the Sendai River, it originally developed as a castle town and is characterized by *ryokan* with hot-spring spas, which is unusual in an urban area. Many shrines, temples and historical monuments have been preserved. Local traditions include the puppet shows of Entsuji Temple and *Nagashibina*, in which people float their paper dolls on the river, praying that evil spirits may be carried away.

Local industry and agriculture includes raising fruit, crabs, bamboo work and Japanese paper. In the vicinity of Tottori are many orchards of Japanese pear trees, yielding an abundance of *Nijusseiki* pears.

Among the points of interest in the city are the Tottori Folk Art Museum, the Kannon-in Garden surrounding a pond (1.2 km north of the station), the O-ochidani Shrine with beautiful halls designated as an Important Cultural Properties (1.5 km northeast of the station), Tottori Prefectural Musuem (2 km north of the station) and other interesting places. Tottori Castle once stood on a hill east of the museum with part of the stone walls still remaining. The area is now Kyusho Park. There is a splendid view of the city, the dunes and the Japan Sea.

Tottori Sand Dunes 97 : Lying 5 km from the station, 20 min. by bus. The coast along the Japan Sea runs for 16 km from east to west and is 2 km wide from north to south, with the Sendai River flowing down its center. The sand dunes are rich in soft, rippling patterns formed by the wind, with the best view said to be at sunrise. In summer the shore is well suited for swimming. In the vicinity are many shallot and pear gardens.

About 11 km west of Tottori Station (25 min. by bus) is a secluded spa called Yoshioka with simple, thermal springs of 30–50°C. Nearby is the Koyama Pond with a 16-km circumference.

Hamamura Spa [97] : This hot-spring resort is located near Hamamura Station on the San-in Main Line and is well known because of the folk song "Kaigara-bushi." The nearby coast is suitable for bathing.

Kurayoshi [97] ☎0858: Pop. 51,892. During the Nara period, this area was the center of Hoki Province (now, the western part of Tottori Prefecture). It can be reached by JR limited express from Kyoto in 4 hrs. 30 min. and from Osaka in 4 hrs. 40 min. (296 km). The Chokokuji Temple is famous for its votive pictures, approximately 50 in number, as well as for some 10,000 azaleas. There are many other old temples.

Lake Togo: Situated 4 km northeast of Kurayoshi, with **Togo Spa** on its southeastern shore. On the western shore is **Hawai Spa**. Togo Spa is a 5-min. walk from the JR Matsuzaki Station, while Hawai Spa is 20 min. from the JR Kurayoshi Station by bus or 10 min. by boat from Matsuzaki Port. Since the lake abounds with *wakasagi* (a kind of smelt) and *funa* (crucian carp), it is popular with local fishermen. It is even possible to fish out of the windows of some of the *ryokan* along the shore.

Misasa Spa [97] : 25 min. by bus from Kurayoshi Station on the JR San-in Main Line. The water in this spa bubbles up along the Misasa River. Although there are many deluxe *ryokan* or Japanese-style inns, this spa is one of the best in the San-in District. At night, bars are quite lively. The area is known for the high levels of radium found in the hot-spring water. The Institute for Study of the Earth's Interior, Okayama University is also located here. The water is 40–85°C in temperature and is said to be especially efficacious against rheumatism, neuralgia and diseases of the digestive organs.

Sambutsuji Temple: About 8 km from the spa on Mt. Mitoku (alt. 900 m). Founded by an ascetic around 700, its Main Hall, *Monjudo*, is designated as an Important Cultural Property. In the back of the shrine behind its many other buildings is the *Okunoin* (Inner Hall). Located in a large grotto, this structure is also called *Nageiredo* (Thrown-in Hall) because it is said to have been thrown into the mountain by the ascetic through the miraculous power of Buddhism. Many treasures, including the statue of *Zaogongen*, a Buddhist deity —an Important Cultural Property—are stored in the treasury.

Sekigane Spa: Located approximately 7 km south from Kurayoshi, it is a tranquil hot-spring resort in the northern part of Sekigane. Ranking second in radium content next to Misasa Spa, it lies midway on the bus route from Kurayoshi to Mt. Hiruzen.

Daisen-Oki National Park [97] : This park is centered around Mt. Daisen (alt. 1,729 m) and is known for the coastal beauty of the Shimane Peninsula, which is best exemplified by Mihonoseki, the area around Izumo Taisha Shrine, the extinct volcano of Mt. Sambe and the Oki Islands. The park has its own unique attractions, including thickly wooded slopes, a large variety of plants, and many rare birds and insects.

Mt. Daisen (lit. Great Mountain) 97 : Popularly known as the Mt. Fuji of Hoki Province (now, a part of Tottori Prefecture), Mt. Daisen is the highest peak in the Chugoku District. It has two faces: when viewed from the west, Mt. Daisen resembles the graceful cone of Mt. Fuji, but when seen from the north or south side, it presents a picture of rugged, rocky crags. Buses are available from Yonago Station on the JR San-in Main Line to the Daisenji Temple (50 min.) situated halfway up the mountain. It can also be reached by bus from Daisenguchi Station on the JR San-in Main Line in 35 min. Founded in 718, the temple was the center of the Tendai sect. It once had three towers and 42 buildings, but most were dismantled early in the Meiji period due to governmental order and now only ten structures remain. Only the *Amidado* Hall from the Kamakura period retains the old architecture. It is designated as an Important Cultural Property. The temple contains a bronze statue of the Eleven-Headed *Kannon*, six other Buddhist images and a miniature iron shrine—all listed as Important Cultural Properties. After climbing steep stone steps for 10 min. from the temple, one will reach the Ogamiyama Shrine's *Okumiya* (Inner Hall), which is a magnificent structure that has been designated as an Important Cultural Property. Although it takes approximately 2 hrs. 30 min. to reach the summit from the temple, the climber is rewarded with a beautiful view of the Shimane Peninsula, Mt. Hiruzen and the Oki Islands once he reaches the top. North of Daisenji Temple is Mt. Goen, also known for its fine view. The summit can be reached after a 30-min. hike from the temple. There is also a lift. Because its slopes are so gentle, Mt. Daisen provides some of the best ski slopes and camp grounds in western Honshu as well as a superb excursion area with a high level of accommodation facilities.

Masumizu Plateau: 3.5 km south of Daisenji Temple, well known by hikers, campers and skiers. Accessible by bus from Daisenji Temple in 10 min., it affords a superb view of Mt. Daisen and the Shimane Peninsula.

Kagamiganaru: Lying at the southeastern foothills of Mt. Daisen. Surrounded by mountains, this plateau is ideal for hiking, camping and skiing. It can be reached by car in 25 min. from Masumizu Plateau.

Yonago 97 ☎0859: Pop. 131,367. 5 hrs. 20 min. from Kyoto and 5 hrs. 40 min. from Osaka by JR direct limited express. But the fastest way to the San-in District further west of Yonago by rail is to take the JR San-yo Shinkansen to Okayama and transfer there to the Hakubi Line. By taking this route, one can reach Yonago from Osaka in about 3 hrs. 20 min. Yonago can also be reached by air from Tokyo in 1 hr.20 min. or from Osaka in 1 hr. The Chugoku Express-way's Niimi Interchange leads to National Highway 180, which goes to Yonago (75 km). This old castle town is now flourishing as the

foremost city in the San-in District in terms of commerce and industry. It is known for a famous spa called Kaike and scenic Yumigahama Beach. The ruins of Yonago Castle 1 km west of the station
have been transformed into a park. The views of Nakanoumi Lagoon
and Mt. Daisen are magnificent.

Kaike Spa 97 : Located about 5 km northeast of Yonago Station, it
can be reached by bus in 20 min. It faces Miho Bay, with a stretch
of pine trees along the shore and Mt. Daisen visible in the distance.
Many modern, well equipped *ryokan* serve visitors to the area.

Yumigahama 97 : Also called Yomigahama or Kyuhin. Washed by
the Japan Sea, it is a wide strip of land that extends for some 20 km
on Miho Bay, with thousands of old pine trees along the sandy beach
adding their beauty to the scenery. The Hama-Kasuri Folkcraft
Museum with displays of splashed-pattern fabrics originally made
here is a 5-min. walk from Misakiguchi Station on the JR Sakai Line.

Sakaiminato 96 ☎0859: Pop. 38,287. Located 18 km to the northwest of Yonago, Sakaiminato is the terminal of the JR Sakai Line,
which runs along Yumigahama from Yonago. With one of the best
ports in the San-in District, Sakaiminato is known for the lumber
imports that pass through it. It is also a fishery base for the area
around the Oki Islands, including the processing of marine products.
Regular boat service is available from here to the Oki Islands.

Mihonoseki 97 : Mihonoseki can be reached from Sakaiminato by
bus in 30 min. by passing over a 1,714-m-long bridge. Buses also reach
here from Matsue in 1 hr.15 min. Lying at the eastern extremity of
the Shimane Peninsula, this fishing port on the Japan Sea was once
used to collect taxes from boats entering the port, as is evident from
its name, which literally means "Barrier at Miho."

Miho Shrine: Dedicated to Kotoshironushi-no-Mikoto, the eldest son
of Okuninushi-no-Mikoto, the deity of Izumo Taisha Shrine. The
architectural style used in the Main Hall, built in 1813, is known as
the Miho style. The hall has been designated as an Important
Cultural Property. The local deity is also known as Ebisu, the god of
wealth and protector of fishermen and boats. The Treasure Hall
contains ancient musical instruments designated as Important Tan-
gible Folk Cultural Properties. There are also displays of ancient
boats. Just to the east is Bukkokuji Temple with five Buddhist
images designated as Important Cultural Properties.

Gohon-Matsu (Five Pines) Park: A 5-min. walk from Mihonoseki
and another 3 min. by lift. This resort area is named for the five large
pine trees that once stood here. Although all have died, one is still
standing. The pine trees are known from the song "Seki-no-Gohon-
Matsu (The Five Pines of the Barrier)" and a second generation of
five pine trees now stands nearby. The park affords a splendid
panoramic view of Mt. Daisen and the Oki Islands.

Yasugi 96 ☎08542: Pop. 32,721. Located west of Yonago, it is the
seat of Hitachi Metals, Ltd., which continues the production of steel

according to ancient Japanese refining techniques using *tatara* or foot bellows. This town is well known for the "Yasugibushi" folk song and its humorous dance, both of which comically describe the gestures of a fisherman trying to catch a slippery *dojo* or loach. The area is also known for the local production of stone garden lanterns. The Wako Memorial Museum, located 1 km west of Yasugi Station, displays materials related to *tatara* steel manufacturing.

Kiyomizu Temple, located 15 min. by bus from the station, includes a Main Hall (an Important Cultural Property), *Sanju-no-To* (Three-Story Pagoda) and many other halls. A splendid landscape garden and teahouse are also here.

In the southeastern section of Yasugi is **Saginoyu Spa**, a small hot-spring resort that can be reached by bus in 20 min. **The Adachi Museum of Art** here houses great works by masters of modern Japanese painting, including Yokoyama Taikan, and a collection of ceramic craftwork. The spacious landscape gardens with white sand, plants and stones are truly beautiful.

Matsue $\boxed{96/102\text{-②}}$ ☎0852

Pop. 139,478. Located 352 km from Kyoto, Matsue faces Nakanoumi Lagoon and Lake Shinji on either side. It is the capital of the prefecture and connecting one of the principal cities of the San-in District. The JR Shinkansen and connecting limited express service is available from Osaka via Okayama in 3 hrs. 45 min. Long-distance buses from Tokyo and Hiroshima are also available.

Matsue is well known among foreigners and Japanese people because of its association with Lafcadio Hearn (1850-1904), who adopted the name of Koizumi Yakumo when he was naturalized as a Japanese.

Refer to the supplement for details regarding the "i" **System Information Center** in Matsue.

PLACES OF INTEREST
Lafcadio Hern's Old Residence $\boxed{102\text{-②}}$: Hern came to Matsue in 1890 and lived for one year and three months as an English teacher at Matsue Middle School. The house in which he lived is near the moat of the old castle and has remained unchanged since he left Matsue. Hearn's impressions of Japan are found in the essay entitled "In a Japanese Garden," included in the volume "Glimpses of Unfamiliar Japan." He is also well known as a writer of ghost stories. The Koizumi Yakumo Kinenkan, a memorial hall dedicated to Hearn, stands next door to his former house. It has a good collection of his manuscripts and other valuable articles—all suggestive of his life in Japan and his efforts to interpret Japan to the world.

Matsue Castle $\boxed{102\text{-②}}$: Standing on Kamedayama Hill 2 km west of Matsue Station. It was first built in 1611 by Horio Yoshiharu, one of Toyotomi Hideyoshi's lords. The five-level, six-story donjon, built in

1642, has been designated as an Important Cultural Property and is celebrated for its extensive view of the surrounding countryside that includes Lake Shinji and Mt. Daisen. Shiroyama Park, surrounding the castle grounds, has many cherry trees. North of the Matsue Castle moat are many ancient *samurai* residences, some of which are open to the public. The Tanabe Art Museum has a collection of tea-ceremony articles. Lafcadio Hern's old residence is nearby. The Meimeian teahouse with its thickly thatched roof, which is quite striking, is also close by.

Kanden-an 102-② : A hermitage located in the mountains north of the city. It has a famous teahouse of the same name and has been designated as an Important Cultural Property. It takes 20 min. to get here by bus from the station.

Other attractions in Matsue include the Shimane Prefectural Museum near the castle and **Yaegaki Shrine** devoted to Princess Kushinada and Susano-o-no-Mikoto in the suburbs to the south. These deities are famed for their part in a legend about the slaying of a gigantic serpent. **Kamosu Shrine** has a Main Hall, built in the 14th century and designated as a National Treasure. The whole area has been set aside as the Yakumotatsu Fudoki(Local History and Topography)-no-Oka Hill, with historical ruins and archaeological materials displayed in the Fudoki-no-Oka Museum.

Lake Shinji 102-② : This lake is 80 sq.km in area and has a circumference of 44 km. It is the sixth-largest lake in Japan, abounding with fish. It has picturesque scenery, especially on the islet called Yomegashima (Bride's Island), with an excursion around the lake by sightseeing boat regarded as one of the best ways to view the lake and islet scenery. On the northern side of the lake is Matsue Spa, where there are many modern *ryokan* or Japanese-style inns. 15 min. by bus from Matsue Station.

Nakaumi Lagoon 96-97 : This lagoon, also called Nakanoumi, has a total area of 99 sq.km and a circumference of 84 km. Situated between Lake Shinji to the west and Miho Bay on the east, it is connected with both bodies of water.

Daikonjima Island 96 : Located approximately in the center of Nakanoumi Lagoon, with an total area of 6 sq.km. This volcanic island is famous for the local cultivation of Korean ginseng and tree peonies. Many tourists visit the island from the end of April to early May, when the tree peonies are in bloom. It can be reached by bus in 50 min. from Matsue.

Kukedo Caves: Formed from a fault in the seabed and wave erosion by the Japan Sea. Shin(New)-Kukedo Cave is 30 m high, 20 m wide, and 200 m long and can be traversed by a small boat. Kyu(Old)-Kukedo Cave is 30 m high and 10 m deep. The Kukedo Caves can be reached by bus in 50 min. from Matsue Station.

Tamatsukuri Spa 96 : This spa is west of Matsue, 6 min. from Tamatsukuri-Onsen Station on the JR San-in Main Line or 20 min.

from Matsue Station by direct bus. There are many well-equipped *ryokan* with gardens and baths in this spa town along the Tamayu River. *Magatama* (an ancient accessory) have been made here since ancient times, with a museum displaying many specimens. The town still produces blue agate.

Izumo 96 ☎0853: Pop. 82,001. Approximately 30 km west of Matsue, about 40 min. by the JR San-in Main Line or 54 min. by Ichibata Electric Railway. This city and its surrounding area are engaged in agriculture, livestock farming and commerce as well as the textile and lumber industries. It is connected with Tokyo and Osaka by JR direct sleeper trains as well as by air routes. The Izumo Folkcraft Museum, which can be reached by bus in 15 min., displays folkcraft items not only from the San-in District, but from the rest of the country as well.

Tachikuekyo Gorge 96 : Situated about 10 km south of Izumoshi (Izumo City) Station, it is famous for its curious rock formations created by the weathering and erosion of andesite. The gorge stretches for about 1 km near the upper reaches of the Kando River, where 100–150-m-high cliffs line the sides, which are decorated with plants shaped like curved *bonsai* trees (dwarfed trees).

Hirata 96 ☎0853: Pop. 31,373. Located northeast of Izumo, it can be reached in 20 min. from Izumoshi Station by the Ichibata Electric Railway.

Gakuenji Temple: The Tendai-sect Temple founded towards the end of the sixth century. It houses many fine examples of Buddhist art, several of which are designated as Important Cultural Properties. The spacious precincts of the temple are noted for their fine maple trees. 8 km west of the Ichibata Electric Railway Hirata Station, about 25 min. by bus.

Ichihata Temple 96 : Also known as Ichihata Yakushi (Buddhist deity). The temple is a 9-min. bus ride from Ichihata-guchi Station, which is a 9-min. ride from Hirata or 25 min. from Matsue-Onsen Station on the Ichibata Electric Railway. Said to have been founded in 894, it is believed that eye diseases can be cured through divine grace at this temple. As it is situated high up on a mountain, the view of the surrounding area and mountains is superb. The tree peonies and azaleas are lovely.

Izumo Taisha Shrine (Grand Shrine of Izumo Province) 96 : Located 8 km northwest of Izumo City, it can be reached from Matsue-Onsen Station by the Ichibata Electric Railway in 1 hr. It is one of the oldest shrines in Japan and is dedicated to Okuninushi-no-Mikoto, a Shinto deity who is traditionally credited with the introduction of medicine, sericulture and the art of farming. According to tradition, he is said to have founded and ruled a state in this district. However, he bequeathed this area to the descendants of Amaterasu-Omikami, a heavenly deity, who, in return, built a large castle for him to live in afterwards. This castle later developed into Izumo Taisha Shrine. Situated in the midst of old pine trees, the Main Hall stands at the foot of Mt. Yakumo. Designated as a National Treasure, it was originally built in 1744 in a unique architectural style called *Taisha-zukuri*. The large-scale design of the 24-m-high hall is said to have once called for a height of 50 m. Around this Main Hall are many smaller shrines and halls that give the entire area a solemn atmosphere. Many important objects are on display in the Treasure Hall, including the *Makietebako* jewel box (a National Treasure). The priests who serve at this shrine are said to be the descendants of Amaterasu-Omikami's second child, Ame-no-ho-Hinomikoto. In ancient times, the Imperial Court appointed the chief priest as the governor of this district. The post of chief priest is hereditary. People make pilgrimages here all year round, but especially from May 14 to 16, on November 23 and from October 11 to 17 (lunar calendar), when *Kamiari-sai* or, the God Assembly Festival is held. A unique feature of this shrine is the long, rectangular buildings on both sides of the Main Hall, which are said to have been the houses of the gods. Legend has it that every year in the tenth month of the lunar calendar, all of the gods in Japan gathered here to discuss the current state of affairs. October was thus called *Kannazuki* (Month without Gods) in all other parts of Japan except here in Izumo Province (now, Shimane Prefecture), where it was called *Kamiarizuki* (Month with Gods).

Cape Hinomisaki and Hinomisaki Shrine ⬚96⬚: Located at the end of a beautiful, 6-km-long coastline contiguous to Inasahama Beach, which is known as a good swimming beach. The shrine was built in 1644. Its hall is designated as an Important Cultural Property. Offshore near the shrine are Iwanojima and Fumishima islands, known for the black-tailed gulls that inhabit them. On the cape stands a 44-m-high lighthouse, the highest in Japan. The surrounding area has been designated as a marine park and can be explored from a glass-bottomed boat.

Oki Islands ⬚96-97⬚: This cluster of volcanic islands lying from 40–80 km north of Shimane Peninsula are partially included in the Daisen-Oki National Park. The islands, with a total area of 350 sq. km, are divided into the two major groups of Tozen and Togo. The islands were famous as a place of exile. The ex-Emperor Gotoba attempted to upset the Hojo Regency and restore the Emperor's actual supremacy, but he was defeated and banished to Tozen Island by the Hojos, where he died in 1239. Emperor Godaigo also had to spend about a year in exile on Togo Island. As a result, the islands abound in historical relics. The most interesting place to see is the Kuniga Coast on Nishinoshima Island. Eroded by the waves of the Japan Sea, the rough, 13-km-long, basaltic rock coast contains many caves, crags and rough cliffs. The 258-m-high Matengai (skyscraping) Cliff is impressive. The area can be explored by excursion boats and hiking paths. The Chibuakakabe Coast on Chiburi Island, and the Shirashima and Jodogaura coasts on Togo, all offer magnificent scenery. Since ancient times, there have been many annual events held on the Oki Islands, including a type of cattle wrestling called *Ushitsuki* on Togo. Authentic *Ushitsuki* is held twice a year—on September 1 and October 13, but for the sake of tourists it is also held on April 29 and August 15. In July and August, passengers on scheduled sightseeing buses may have a chance to observe it. It takes 3 hrs. from Shichirui Port on Shimane Peninsula to Urago Port on Tozen and 3 hrs. 20 min. to Saigo Port on Togo by ferry. Boats sail from Sakaiminato as well. Air service is available from Osaka (1 hr. 10 min.), from Izumo (30 min.) and from Yonago (25 min.) to Togo.

Area 7. Western San-in District

Oda to Shimonoseki

The western part of the San-in District is served mainly by the JR San-in Main Line and National Highways 9 and 191.

Oda 96 ☎08548: Pop. 37,761. The city lies in the central part of Shimane Prefecture and faces the Japan Sea to the north. Since olden times, it has been engaged in commerce, including the distribution of lumber as well as agricultural and marine products. Blessed with magnificent, coastal scenery and the hot springs around the foothills of Mt. Sambe, it has now developed into a modern tourist resort area. It is 29 min. by limited express on the JR San-in Main Line from Izumoshi to Odashi (Oda City) Station.

The ruins of the Iwami Silver Mine: 30 min. by bus from Odashi Station. Opened in the 14th century, the mine came under the direct control of the ruling Tokugawa Shogunate during the Edo period. The mine was closed in 1923. At present the remains of the Omori Magistrate's Office (now transformed into a museum), old temples, and the ruins of the mine tunnels serve to chronicle the history of the mine through the centuries. The town of Omori itself is of great interest as a reflection of Japanese towns of the past.

Sambe Spa: Situated 20 km southeast of Odashi Station (40 min. by bus) in the southern foothills of Mt. Sambe. Located on high ground, the spa is a base for exploring Mt. Sambe and is known for its beauty as well as for being one of the best summer resorts in the San-in District.

Mt. Sambe 96 : With an altitude of 1,126 m, this extinct volcano is also known as Iwami-Fuji. From Sadamenomatsu, 35 min. from Odashi Station by bus, it takes 1 hr.30 min. to climb to the top of O (Male)-Sambe (alt. 1,126 m.)—the highest of the seven peaks of Mt. Sambe. From Sambe Spa, it takes 1 hr. to climb Me(Female)-Sambe, the second-highest peak (alt. 957 m). A convenient road called the "Iris Line" cuts across the plateau at the foot of the mountain.

Yunotsu Spa 96 : Located near a harbor that opens on the Japan Sea, 35 min. by local train from Odashi on the San-in Main Line. In the center of this spa town is the Yunotsu Tenryokan Museum, which features exhibits of tools from the old Iwami Silver Mine and local craftwork.

Gotsu 96 ☎08555: Pop. 27,963. Located approximately 70 km from Izumoshi by limited express (1 hr.16 min.) on the JR San-in Main Line and 4 hrs. 5 min. from Hiroshima by bus, this is the junction for the JR Sango Line on its way to Miyoshi. Situated at the mouth of the Gonogawa River—the longest in the Chugoku District, it has developed as one of the busier commercial ports along the Japan Sea coast. As a source of good-quality potter's clay, it has been extensively engaged in the ceramic industry since olden times. A large quantity of Iwami tile and pottery known as *Iwami-yaki* are produced here. Many factories have also been established for the production of paper pulp.

Arifuku Spa 96 : Lying south of Gotsu Station (35 min. by bus). Nestled in a narrow valley and surrounded by mountains on three sides, it boasts abundant thermal waters ranging in temperature from 40–47°C, which are efficacious against rheumatism, neuralgia and injuries.

Senjokei Gorge: A 15-min. drive from Kawado Station on the JR Sango Line. The gorge extends for about 5 km along the upper stream of the Hiwa River. The sides are covered with quartz stones in rough and ragged formations that are quite impressive.

Dangyokei Gorge 96 : 15 min. by bus from Imbara Station on the JR Sango Line. A tributary of the Gonokawa River, the Nigori River runs through it for 4 km. The foundation of quartz crystals is exposed to form marvelous waterfalls and deep water pools here, too.

Hamada 96 ☎0855: Pop. 48,992. Hamada is located 89 km from Izumoshi and can be reached in 1 hr.23 min. by limited express on the JR San-in Main Line or from Hiroshima in 3 hrs. 40 min. by bus. The city has flourished as a port town since olden times and it had particularly assumed a position as a castle town since 1619. Now, it has developed into an important fishing and commercial port, especially for offshore fishing.

With well-equipped port facilities, the Hamada Fish Market is said to be the largest in the San-in District. In addition to processed marine products, the area is known for Iwami tile and pottery.

Masuda 96 ☎0856: Pop. 53,092. Located 140 km from Izumoshi or about 2 hrs. 5 min. by limited express on the San-in Main Line. It is the junction of the JR San-in Main Line and Yamaguchi Line, which connects with the JR San-yo Main Line at Ogori. It takes 3 hrs. 10 min. by express bus from Hiroshima. National Highway 9 runs along the Japan Sea coast and leads to Yamaguchi from here. National Highway 191 follows the coast to Shimonoseki.

The city is the commercial center for the western extremity of

Shimane Prefecture. Its primary commercial activity consist of agriculture and forestry, including the production of lumber and coastal fishery. It is also a center for plywood and chemical fiber. Other local specialties include *ayu* (sweetfish) from the Takatsu River, Ams melons, summer mandarin oranges, grapes and *Sesshu-yaki* pottery.

Mampukuji Temple: Approximately 3.5 km east of Masuda Station, 10 min. by bus. The grand Main Hall, built in the 14th century, has been designated as an Important Cultural Property. The garden is said to have been designed with many stones by Sesshu (1420–1506), a famous priest-painter (refer to p.767).

Ikoji Temple: Standing 500 m to the east of Mampukuji, the temple was originally built in 1363. The garden and its pond are also said to have been designed by Sesshu. The magnificent temple entrance is quite impressive.

Kakinomoto Shrine: Situated 2 km west of Masuda Station on the side of Takatsu Hill. Although this shrine is said to have been founded early in the eighth century, few details are known about the life of the famous poet, Kakinomoto-no-Hitomaro, who is the deity of the shrine. It is said that he returned to the Province of Iwami (now, Shimane Prefecture), his native town, in his later years and settled down till his last days. Nearby Man-yo Park has a collection of over 150 species of trees and flowers that are mentioned in the "Man-yo-shu," the oldest collection of Japanese poems (refer to p.153). Next to the shrine is Lake Banryu, famous as a boating lake.

Tsuwano [96]: This small castle town at the western end of Shimane Prefecture is known as the Little Kyoto of the San-in District. Located along the JR Yamaguchi Line that connects the San-yo and San-in districts (31 km from Masuda and 63 km from Ogori), the town stretches along the banks of the Tsuwano River. To the east is Mt. Aono and in the west is Mt. Shiroyama. Around Tonomachi, the center of town, are former *samurai* residences and ancient, white-walled houses that offer a glimpse of the past as well as colorful carp that fill the creeks along the streets. Located on what was once a field of *tsuwabuki* or Japanese silverleaves, the town dates back to the late Kamakura period. During the Edo period, the local clan was quite small. Because of its farsighted respect for education, however, the level of local culture had been raised so much that it had become as influential as a large clan. The town still has many reminders of these olden times. Since the town is quite small, it can easily be explored on foot or by rented bicycle. The *Sagimai* (Heron Dance) held on July 20, 24 and 27 at the Yasaka Shrine is known for its elegance and simplicity.

The Industrial Museum stands just east of the station and displays materials on traditional local industry—Japanese paper manufacturing and *sake* brewing.

The Folk Customs Museum, known as Yorokan, is located in a

gorgeous, old building surrounded by white walls and latticework. This was the site of the local school built by the lord of the Kamei Clan in 1786. The curriculum covered various academic fields; e.g., literature, mathematics and medicine as well as martial arts to produce many important Japanese historical figures. It is the birth-place of Mori Ogai (1862–1922), an eminent writer, doctor and army surgeon of the Meiji period (1868–1912), and Nishi Amane (1829–1897), a noted philosopher, lived here for 18 years in his youth. At present it is used as a library and research center. The regional history museum, built in the Meiji period, is found at the south end of the Ohashi Bridge and displays historical, art and craft materials from the town.

Otometoge (Pass of the Virgin) Memorial Church of St. Mary is on the slope of Mt. Otome behind the JR Tsuwano Station. Under the repressive policies of the government during the Meiji period, 153 Christian martyrs were killed here. The Christian followers detained at Korinji Temple were, until freedom of religion was allowed in 1873, persecuted night and day, with 59 followers forced to renounce their belief and 36 killed. The stained-glass windows completed in 1983 depict the horrors of those persecuted during this period of repression.

The path to Yomeiji Temple, located to the southwest of Tsuwano Station, is paved with moss-covered, stone steps and lined with magnificent trees on either side. In 1420 the fifth lord of the Yoshimi Clan, Yorihiro, built the ancient temple, which developed as the family temple. Although it was ravaged by fire twice, the elegant, thatched-roof Main Hall and many other imposing halls still remain.

Taikodani-Inari Shrine stands on the northern side of Mt. Shiro-yama. In 1773 the seventh lord of the Kamei Clan, Norisada, built it to pray for the fortunes of the castle and the peaceful life of the local people. It invited the deity of the Fushimi Inari Shrine in Kyoto. A series of *torii* gates lead to the vermilion shrine in a tunnel-like formation that presents a beautiful, somber image. The view of the town below is impressive.

The **ruins of Tsuwano Castle**, or *Sambommatsu* (Three Pines) Castle, are located near the west side of town at an altitude of 367 m on Mt. Shiroyama. It used to be a typical mountain castle. In 1295, the first lord of the Yoshimi Clan, Yoriyuki, built the castle in a project that required 30 years to complete. It was regarded as a very beautiful castle until 1874, when it was destroyed. With many maple trees on the site, it is popular as a historical park that commands a fine view of Mt. Aono directly in front and Tsuwano Town below.

Tsuwano Folks Arts Museum "Jingasa" is located on the western side of the Tsuwano River and displays over 150 examples of *jingasa* or headpieces used by soldiers in feudal days, a procession of *Sagimai* (Heron Dance) dolls, handmade goods and crafted articles.

Hagi 96 ☎08382

Pop. 51,529. It takes approximately 3 hrs. 20 min. to Higashi(East)-Hagi from Izumoshi by express on the JR San-in Main Line. This port city is the fishing center of this district. Higashi-Hagi Station is located at the center of the city, which originally developed as a feudal castle town on the delta of the Abu River. Surrounded by hills on the east, south and west sides, it presents a picturesque view. Besides the fisheries and food industry for *kamaboko* (boiled white fish paste) and other processed marine products, the city is noted for its production of summer mandarin oranges and its 360-year-old tradition of *Hagi-yaki* pottery.

From 1604 it prospered as the castle town of the Mori family for 260 years until the headquarters of the feudal lord's government was transferred to Yamaguchi in 1863. It was particularly noted as the hometown of such famous people as Yoshida Shoin, Takasugi Shinsaku, Ito Hirobumi, Yamagata Aritomo, Kido Takayoshi and many others, all of whom played an important role in the period of the Meiji Restoration. Buses leave from Ogori and pass through Yamaguchi on their 1-hr. 35-min. trip here. It takes about 1 hr.50 min. by bus from Tsuwano.

PLACES OF INTEREST

Kumaya's Art Museum: A 20-min. walk from Higashi-Hagi Station to the west. The three-building complex was built in 1768 and displays excellent examples of old Japanese art and *Hagi-yaki* pottery. The oldest piano in Japan, a gift from a famous German physician named Philipp Franz von Siebold (1796–1866), is also on display here.

Ruins of Hagi Castle: Lying 4.5 km west of Higashi-Hagi Station on the foothills of Mt. Shizuki. Some stone walls and the moat are all that now remain. Hanae Tea Room, which once was the teahouse of the clan lord's villa, is still used by tourists and groups for tea ceremonies. The castle ruins are still quite popular because of the many cherry trees that blossom here in spring. At the entrance to the castle ruins is the Hagi Old Document Museum, with reference materials on the local area's history, and the Hagi Pottery Hall, which has elegant displays of this special type of ceramics craftwork produced only in this area. Also in the area are the remains of the large residence of the chief retainer of the Mori Clan.

Kikuya Residence: Standing 500 m southwest of Kumaya's Art Museum. This old mansion was built in the Edo period as the residence of a rich, local merchant. It has been designated as an Important Cultural Property and is open to visits by the public.

Shoin Shrine: Situated 1 km southeast of Higashi-Hagi Station and dedicated to Yoshida Shoin (1830–1859), a famous thinker-educator who is well known to Western readers through Robert Louis Stevenson's short sketch in his "Familiar Studies of Men and Books," in which he lavishes high praise on Shoin. In the precincts is the building of Shoka-Sonjuku, a small village school where he had taught for two years and six months before he was executed by the Tokugawa Shogunate government. Shoin was greatly interested in educating young minds, and among his pupils were Ito Hirobumi, Yamagata Aritomo and Inoue Kaoru, all of whom played important roles in the government after the Meiji Restoration of 1868.

Tokoji Temple: Located east of Shoin Shrine as the family temple of the Moris. There are many excellent examples of halls built in the style of the Obaku Zen sect. Among them is the large Main Hall, which was built in 1698 and is designated as an Important Cultural Property. Behind this hall are hundreds of stone lanterns to honor the graves of five lords of this clan. A similar cemetery is located west of Hagi Station at the Daisho-in Temple, where many stone lanterns also stand to mark the graves of seven other former clan lords.

The Myojin Lagoons: Covering an area of 11,780 sq.m in the eastern foothills of Mt. Kasayama, 5 km north of Higashi-Hagi Station. The lagoons are connected underground with the sea and are noted for the saltwater fish that inhabit them. The lagoons, which form a sort of natural aquarium, were once used for pleasure boating by the feudal lords. Mt. Kasayama is formed by a volcanic lava dome that lies on top of a shield volcano. With a summit of 112 m in altitude, it is indeed a small volcano. It has a crater of 30 m in diameter and 30 m in depth. Besides offering an impressive view, the area is also known for its many camellia trees.

Kita-Nagato Kaigan (Coast) Quasi-National Park [96]

With a total area of 80.21 sq.km, this park includes most of the Japan Sea coast in Yamaguchi Prefecture, extending 90 km between Esaki and Susa Bay in the east and Yuya Bay in the west and including sections of Hagi and Nagato cities. The park boasts of the scenic locations and magnificent views of Omishima Island, Susa Bay and other islets. The Japan Sea coast is especially popular with visitors for the rugged beauty of its precipices, caves, stone columns and fantastic rock formations.

Susa Bay: The bay contains about 70 islands, while a stretch of its coastline extending for approximately 100 m is marked by precipices, rugged rock formations of granite and many crags and coastal caves. With its varied topography of rocks and islands, the area offers many points of interest for geologists. Excursion boats rounding the bay are available from May to August. A 5-min. walk from Susa Station on the JR San-in Main Line.

Nagato [96] ☎08372: Pop. 26,673. Located 215 km from Izumoshi Station, this is the junction for the JR Mine Line that leads to Asa on the JR San-yo Main Line. Local industries include agriculture, forestry, and fishery, especially *Senzaki kamaboko* (boiled white fish paste) and other processed marine products.

Omishima Island 96 : A total area of 18 sq.km and a circumference of 30 km. An 8-min. bus ride from Nagatoshi Station on the JR San-in Main Line takes visitors to Senzaki, which is connected by a bridge with the island 200 m across the strait. The northern coast of the island is known for its beauty and the 100-m-high cliffs formed by the rough waves, the stone tunnels, caves, stone columns and reefs—all spread out in a grand panorama. Excursion boats are available from Senzaki.

Ohibi, at the center of the island, is noted for the Saienji Temple with its magnificent gate and for the original summer mandarin orange tree growing on the property of a local resident, Mr. Nishimoto. The tree measures about 1 m in circumference and about 6 m in height. Although it has grown weak with age, it still bears fruit every year.

It is said that the tree grew from the seed of a summer mandarin orange that drifted ashore and was picked up by a woman of the old Nishimoto family around 1774. It is also said that summer mandarin oranges, which are now a specialty of the Hagi District, first began to grow around 1805 from the seeds of this fruit from Omishima Island. The site and the tree have been designated as a Historic Site and Natural Monument. On the eastern side of the island stands Seigetsu-an, a Buddhist temple, whose grounds include the Whale's Grave—a tombstone over 2 m tall erected in 1692. Whaling off the coast of Omishima Island was an important part of the local area's economy and way of life from the early part of the 17th century. When whale embryos were sometimes found inside the bodies of captured whales, the local people, out of piety, buried them behind this gravestone—a custom that was maintained until the 1870s. This site has also been designated as a Historic Site.

Yumoto Spa 96 : This spa is located 500 m southeast of Nagato-Yumoto Station on the JR Mine Line. The spa is popular as a recreation resort with beautiful scenery and the clean waters of the Otozure River. There are many large, well-equipped *ryokan*. Nearby is Daineiji, an ancient temple, as well as the Fukagawa Kiln, one of the main kilns of *Hagi-yaki* pottery.

Tawarayama Spa: 40 min. by bus from Nagatoshi Station. This mountain spa is known to be efficacious against rheumatism, neuralgia and other illnesses.

Kawatana Spa 96 : Located 2 km east of Kawatana-Onsen Station on the JR San-in Main Line, this spa is quite popular due to its relatively close proximity to Shimonoseki (25 km). Types of accommodations range from deluxe *ryokan* to simple facilities that cater mainly to those coming for the medicinal benefits of the spa for the treatment of rheumatism and neuralgia. At the entrance to the spa town is the Karasuyama Folk-Crafts Museum, with displays of over 12,000 items representing numerous folkcraft styles from all over Japan.

Section VII. Seto-Naikai (Inland Sea) and Shikoku

SETO-NAIKAI (Inland Sea)

Outline of Seto-Naikai (Inland Sea)

The long expanse of water lying among Honshu, Shikoku and Kyushu is called "Seto-Naikai" (lit. Sea within Channels) in Japanese and the "Inland Sea" in English. Really a chain of five seas linked together by channels, it is one of the most picturesque bodies of water in the world. The Seto-Ohashi Bridge was completed in 1988, connecting Honshu and Shikoku for both automotive and rail traffic. It is expected to greatly enhance the progress of the industrial sector in Shikoku. The Inland Sea is generally accepted as extending from Osaka Bay in the east to the Kammon Straits in the west. The sea is about 500 km long and measures 64 km at its widest point (from north to south) and 6.4 km at its narrowest. It is connected to the Kii Channel in the east by means of the Kitan and Naruto straits, which, in turn, are connected to the Pacific Ocean. The Hoyo Straits and Bungo Channel lie between Shikoku and Kyushu to the southwest, connecting the Inland Sea to the Pacific Ocean. The Kammon Straits open into the Japan Sea on the extreme northwest. Geologists believe that Shikoku and Kyushu were once joined to Honshu but were separated by volcanic disturbances. The line of the fracture is fringed by a chain of volcanoes—all extinct except Mt. Aso in Kyushu, which is supposed to have been the center. The peaks of the extinct volcanoes and the 600 islands scattered through the sea create a scene of great natural beauty. The red *torii* gate and green pines rising from the islands' granite rocks present many exquisite scenes of diverse character. The Inland Sea is comparatively shallow, seldom surpassing a depth of 40 m, with the deepest sections located at the west end of the Kammon Straits and the Akashi Straits. There are very strong tidal currents in the Hoyo and Kammon straits. In the Naruto Straits, opposing currents over an uneven bottom create a myriad of whirlpools, forming a scene of mysterious beauty.

The Inland Sea was once abundant with marine life, including *tai* (sea bream), *sawara* (Spanish mackerel), *karei* (flounder), *saba* (mackerel), *aji* (saurel), *bora* (mullet), *iwashi* (sardines), *ebi* (shrimp), *tako* (octopus), *ika* (squid), *kaki* (oysters) and *wakame* (seaweed). But excessive fishing and pollution have taken their toll, and there is fear that all fishing may someday dry up. Today, fishermen not only catch fish, but cultivate them as well. *Tai* (sea bream), a favorite fish in Japan, enter the Inland Sea from April to June for spawning, and in their migration have to negotiate some strong currents. This, coupled with the abundance of organic matter in the water on which they feed, accounts for their delicious flavor.

The principal products of the Inland Sea coastal districts include salt and citrus fruit. Olives and soy beans on Shodo Island are also famous. Granite is quarried on many of the smaller islands. Heavy industry is also flourishing, especially in Sakaide and Niihama on Shikoku. The San-yo District's Inland Sea coast (on the Honshu Side) is one of the most prominent heavy-industry districts in Japan. Some of the islands in the western sector have terraced fields that extend nearly to the top of the hills. There, mandarin oranges and other fruit are grown. Because the coastline along the Inland Sea is heavily populated, it has played a prominent part in the history of Japan. The sea served as a road that bound the culture of Kyushu to that of the Kinki District—the two great cradles of culture in ancient Japan.

Area 1. Seto-Naikai (Inland Sea)

Seto-Naikai National Park 104

Seto-Naikai National Park was established in 1934 and was later enlarged to 628.4 sq.km. The park is coterminous with the Inland Sea. Numerous islands, beautiful beaches and coastal platforms with superb maritime views all lie within the boundaries of this national park. Originally, only the most beautiful part of the waterway extending from Shodo Island on the east to Tomo and Tadotsu on the west was included in the park. Scenic points such as the Kankakei Gorge in Shodo Island, Mt. Goken, and Yashima Peninsula in Shikoku and Tomonoura, Sensui Island, Cape Abuto and Washuzan Hill in Honshu all lie within this area. Indented with many coves, the coastline refreshes the eye with clean, white sand and radiant green pines. Numerous islets dot the sea—some large enough to be inhabited by thousands of people, others hardly bigger than rocks, all creating a wonderful effect of light and shade on the sea.

The park was later expanded to include the following areas: Sumoto, Yura, Fukura and Mt. Yuzuruha on Awaji Island; Murotsu Beach (near Aioi) and Nishijima Island (off the coast of Murotsu) in Hyogo Prefecture; part of Naruto in Tokushima Prefecture; Zozusan Hill on which stands Kotohiragu Shrine (Kagawa Prefecture); part of Omishima Island and Ikuchi Island off the coast of Mihara; part of Osaki-Kami (Upper) and Osaki-Shimo (Lower) islands off the coast of Takehara; Miyajima, famous for Itsukushima Shrine, in Hiroshima Prefecture; Kurokami Island and Kasato Island off the coast of Tokuyama in Yamaguchi Prefecture, and Mt. Takasaki (near Beppu) and part of Himeshima Island (off the coast of the Kunisaki Peninsula) in Oita Prefecture, Kyushu.

Seto-Naikai National Park is one of two national parks in Japan that extend for the most part over the sea, the other being Saikai National Park in Kyushu. The romantic beauty of this sea can best be enjoyed by steamer, though occasional glimpses of it may be caught from train windows on the JR San-yo Main Line on Honshu or the JR lines on Shikoku. The national highways also provide excellent opportunities to experience the magnificent landscape. But perhaps the ultimate view is from the Seto-Ohashi Bridge. The best time to see the park is from early summer to autumn.

Boat Trips on the Inland Sea

The main ship lines running through the Inland Sea from east to west will be introduced here. Those leaving from Honshu for Shikoku will be dealt with in another section.

1) Six 3,000-ton ships operated by the Kansai Steamship Co. ferry passengers on the Osaka–Kobe–Sakate (Shodo Island)–Taka-matsu–Imabari–Matsuyama–Beppu route. Althogh many pass through the Inland Sea at night, the Osaka–Takamatsu-bound ships pass through during the day.

2) The Kobe–Matsuyama–Oita Diamond Ferry Line runs 1–2 ships at night.

3) Kobe–Kokura Hankyu Ferry Line has one departure a day.

4) Osaka–Higashi Kobe–Kawanoe–Niihama route of the Shikoku Central Ferry Boat Line has one departure a day.

A pleasure cruise among the myriads of islands during the daylight hours is a most enjoyable experience. The Akinada Line, operated by the Seto-Naikai Steamship Co., runs from March to November and cruises the Hiroshima–Miyajima–Omishima–Ikuchi Island route.

Awaji Island ⌑105⌑

Covering an area of 592.9 sq.km., this is the largest island in Seto-Naikai (Inland Sea) as well as one of the nation's most thickly populated islands. According to myth, this was the first island the gods gave birth to when creating Japan. It has many shrines and temples, puppet plays and other cultural properties. The island is shaped like a triangle pointing north with no high mountains. Since most of the land is composed of fertile plains, agricultural production, especially vegetables, thrives, with most of the produce being supplied to the Hanshin (Osaka–Kobe) area. Marine products are also harvested in abundance. The island is separated from Honshu by the Akashi Straits in the north and the Kitan Straits in the east. It is also separated from Shikoku by the Naruto Straits in the southwest, except for the enormous, 1,629-m-long Onaruto Bridge connecting the two areas. Located on the east coast, Sumoto is the main city on the island, serving as the center for administration and transportation as well as the starting point for sightseeing.

The high-speed boat from Kobe is a convenient way to get to Awaji Island, reaching Sumoto in 1 hr. 20 min. The ferry from Akashi to Iwaya only takes 25 min. and runs frequently. There is also a ferry from Fuke, southwest of Osaka, to Sumoto that takes 1 hr. 20 min. A bus leaves from Tokushima in Shikoku and goes to Fukura–Sumoto

–Tsuna via the Onaruto Bridge (1 hr. 20 min.).

Sumoto 105 ☎0799: Pop. 44,879. This is the largest city on Awaji Island and the seat of its administration. The chief products are buttons, roofing tiles, onions and other agricultural products. Mt. Mikuma (alt. 133 m) lies to the south of the city, about 15 min. by bus. The summit was the site of Sumoto Castle, with a magnificent view from the donjon, reconstructed in 1928. The foothills of Ohama Park offer excellent beaches for swimming as well as hot springs for relaxing.

Fukura 105 : Located on the southwest coast of the island in a deep cove, it can be reached by bus from Sumoto in 40 min. This is the site of the famous *Naruto uzushio* (whirlpools). Besides the view from a sightseeing boat, they can also be observed from the 23-km-long South Awaji Island Toll Road (commonly called the "Uzushio Road"). The highlights of the area are Cape Naruto and the Onaruto Bridge Museum, which contains scientific exhibits on whirlpools and presents traditional puppet performances, *ningyo-joruri*, as well.

Senkoji Temple 105 : Established in the tenth century, it stands on the peak of Mt. Senzan, a mountain with an altitude of 448 m in the center of the island. It is a temple of the Koyasan-Shingon sect of Buddhism. The main image is *Senju-Kannon* (Thousand-Handed *Kannon*), the goddess of mercy. The temple also possesses a *Dosho* (Bronze Bell), cast in 1283, that has been designated as an Important Cultural Property. The building dates from the 17th century. A 15-min. bus ride from Sumoto will take one to the foot of the mountain. The summit can be reached by an additional 20-min. climb. The west coast of the island offers beautiful seascapes at Goshikihama (Five-Colored Beach) and Keino-Matsubara. This area is 50 min. by bus from Sumoto. Extending for 4 km, Goshikihama (Five-Colored Beach) is named for the variety of colored beach pebbles. Keino-Matsubara is a large grove of pine trees about 3 km long and 600 m wide, highlighted by the contrasting white sand. Swimming and camping are possible at both beaches.

Shodo Island 105

Lying 27.2 km to the northeast of Takamatsu on Shikoku, Shodo Island is the second-largest island in the Inland Sea, with an area of 170 sq.km. Since most of the island is mountainous, it is blessed with ravines, plateaus and other scenic aspects of nature. Recently, moreover, it has become known as an ideal beach resort for swimming and fishing. Tonosho Port, the main entrance to the island, is 40 min. by high-speed boat from Okayama on Honshu or 35 min. from Takamatsu on Shikoku. The island has other ports, including Sakate (a port of call for the Osaka/Kobe–Beppu ferry), Kusakabe, Fukuda, Obe and Ikeda. There is a ferry service from Honshu and Shikoku to these ports as well. The main products of the island are soy sauce, *somen* (thin wheat noodles) and olives, which have been grown here for nearly a century. The island is also famous for its quarries, and most of the stones used for the walls of Osaka Castle, erected in the 16th century, were quarried from this island. Tourism is concentrated in the middle, from Choshikei Gorge to Kankakei Gorge. In Choshikei Gorge, wild monkeys roam the valleys and the Choshi Waterfall cascades down a rocky cliff. The skyline road runs between here and Kankakei Gorge via Utsukushi-no-Hara Plateau (alt. 770 m). Shihozashi lookout provides an excellent view of Honshu, Shikoku and the Inland Sea. Kankakei Gorge (lit. Cold and Misty Valley) is a group of mountain peaks with fantastically shaped rocks formed by weathering and erosion, and unusual clusters of plants. The changing leaves in November are especially beautiful. The summit of the precipice, called Shibocho, can be reached either by a ropeway from the base or a highway called the "Blue Line." A bus is also available from Tonosho via Choshikei Gorge in 1 hr.25 min. Nearby, visitors can enjoy beach resorts such as Futagoura and Gimpaura in Tonosho, and Silver Beach on the north coast. Tonosho is the busiest port town on the island and the starting point for most of the sightseeing tours on Shodo Island by motorcoach. Tour coaches have Japanese guides and take about 5-7 hrs. to complete a tour. One of the typical tour routes covers Tonosho-Heiwa-no-Gunzo (Group Statue of Peace)-Peacock Park-Nampudai Point-Silver Beach-Choshikei Gorge-Kankakei Gorge-Taiyo-no-Oka (lit. Sun's Hill)-Tonosho.

SHIKOKU
Outline of Shikoku

Shikoku, one of Japan's four main islands, is divided administratively into four prefectures—Tokushima, Kagawa, Ehime and Kochi. They correspond to the four historical provinces of Awa, Sanuki, Iyo and Tosa, for which Shikoku (lit. Four Provinces) was named.

Shikoku covers an area of 18,780 sq.km. Several mountain ranges extend from east to west through the central portion of the island, the most prominent peaks of which are Mt. Ishizuchi (alt. 1,982 m) and Mt. Tsurugi (alt. 1,955 m). There are many long rivers: the longest, Yoshino River (194 km), empties into the Kii Channel on the east coast and the second longest, Shimanto River (192 km), empties into Tosa Bay in the south. Being an island, Shikoku has many distinct differences from Honshu. Especially during spring, travelers to Shikoku will often come across Buddhist pilgrims, usually dressed in simple, white clothing and white mittens and leggings. They are followers of the Buddhist priest Kukai, posthumously named Kobo-Daishi, who was born in Sanuki Province (now, Kagawa Prefecture) in 774. Devotees come from all over Japan to make a pilgrimage to the 88 Sacred Places (Buddhist temples founded by or closely related to Kobo-Daishi). They are scattered all through the island, including

23 in Awa (now, Tokushima Prefecture), 16 in Tosa (now, Kochi Prefecture), 26 in Iyo (now, Ehime Prefecture) and 23 in Sanuki (now, Kagawa Prefecture). Popular since the beginning of the Edo period (1603–1867), this pilgrimage used to take 45–60 days to complete on foot. Many present-day pilgrims, however, utilize modern transportation and are able to complete their journey in about 2 weeks. Even today, about 100,000 people annually take special coach tours to make this pilgrimage.

Although smaller in area than Hokkaido or Kyushu, Shikoku is in no way inferior as a holiday destination, abounding in places that will interest the tourist. To cite just a few, Shikoku includes the scenic Inland Sea coast that forms a part of Seto-Naikai (Inland Sea) National Park, the Seto-Ohashi Bridge, which demonstrates the beauty of modern engineering, and Yashima Tableland, a 12th-century battlefield of major historical importance. In Ashizuri-Uwakai National Park on the southwest coast, one can enjoy mysterious seascapes and oddly shaped rocks. Some highlights include Kotohira with Kotohiragu Shrine and an ancient Kabuki theater, Tokushima of *Awa-Odori* (folk dance) fame, Takamatsu with the beautiful Ritsurin Park, Kochi for its dog fighting, Matsuyama well known for Dogo Spa and the fighting bulls of Uwajima.

There are also three quasi-national parks in Shikoku: Ishizuchi, Tsurugi and Muroto-Anan Coast.

TRANSPORTATION

Transport Connections with Honshu

Shikoku is well provided with a varied means of transportation to and from Honshu.

By Land: With the opening of the Seto-Ohashi Bridge, JR trains now travel directly to Shikoku. The rapid train, "Marine Liner," runs from the JR San-yo Main Line and Shinkansen Station in Okayama to Takamatsu (1 hr.), while limited expresses go to Matsuyama (3 hrs. 10 min.) and Kochi (3 hrs.). The "Marine Liner" has an observation car (surcharge required). There is also a long-distance bus from Tokyo and Osaka to Takamatsu, Imabari, Matsuyama, Yawatahama, Uwajima and Tokushima.

By Air: There are four airports in Shikoku—at Takamatsu, Tokushima, Kochi and Matsuyama. Flights leave from Tokyo to all of these airports, taking 1 hr.10 min. to 1 hr.20 min. Osaka is connected with all four airports by frequent flight service in 30–50 min. In addition, there are flights from Fukuoka, Miyazaki and Kagoshima to some of these four airports.

By Sea: There are ferries from most of the main cities on Honshu. Most of them travel at night and arrive in Shikoku the next day. From Tokyo, ferries of the Nihon Enkai Ferry Co. go to Kochi via Katsuura (on Kii Peninsula) in 21 hrs. 20 min, while ferries of the Ocean Tokyu Ferry Co. bound for Kokura (Kyushu) also stop at Tokushima. From Kobe and Osaka, refer to the Inland Sea Routes on p.810.

There are too many services to list all those crossing the Inland Sea from north to south, but the main lines include Uno-Takamatsu, Shimotsui-Marugame, Onomichi-Imabari or Matsuyama, Mihara-Imabari, and Hiroshima-Matsuyama or Imabari.

Transportation within Shikoku

JR lines, other railways and buses pass through Shikoku. Although expressways cover only a fraction of the island, a national highway network is being developed.

JR: The main lines are the Yosan Line (Takamatsu-Uwajima), which follows along the north coast, the Kotoku Line (Takamatsu-Toku-shima) along the northeast coast, the Tokushima Line (Tokushima-Awa-Ikeda) from the east coast to the center of the island and the Dosan Line (Takamatsu-Kubokawa) from the north coast across to the south coast.

There are three local lines: Takamatsu-Kotohira Electric Railway in Takamatsu and its vicinity, Iyo Railway for Matsuyama and vicinity and Tosa-Kuroshio Railway, which runs between Kubokawa and Nakamura.

Highways: National Highway 11 running Tokushima-Takamatsu-Matsuyama, 32 running Kawanoe-Kochi and 33 running Kochi-Matsuyama are the main highways. For sightseeing, National Highway 55, which circles Cape Muroto, and Highway 56, which approaches Cape Ashizuri, are both popular scenic routes. The Matsuyama Expressway runs 49 km along National Highway 11 from Zentsuji to Doi as well.

Buses: There are several intra-island, long-distance buses—Taka-matsu - Tokushima, Takamatsu - Kochi, Takamatsu - Matsuyama, Kawanoe-Matsuyama, Imabari-Matsuyama and Dogo Spa (Matsu-yama)-Yawatahama.

Area 2. Kagawa Prefecture

Kagawa occupies most of the northeastern part of the island and includes Shodo Island and more than a hundred other islands in the Inland Sea. Most of the prefecture is coastal plain with no mountains over 1,000 m in altitude. The landscape is characterized by many irrigation reservoirs that dot the plain. Since ancient times, great quantities of wheat have been cultivated here and made into *udon*, a type of noodle that has now become famous as *Sanuki Udon*.

Takamatsu ☐ 105/106-① ☎ 0878

Takamatsu is the capital of Kagawa Prefecture with a population of 327,655. It is the gateway to both overland and water transporta-tion, with all types of transportation from Honshu arriving here. With the completion of the Seto-Ohashi Bridge, direct train services from Tokyo and Okayama have started, allowing easier access to the city.

Takamatsu was established in 1587 and served as the seat of the Matsudaira Clan through the Edo period. Today, it is the home of many administrative offices and large companies as well as the administrative and economic center of Shikoku.

Regular sightseeing bus tours are conducted in Japanese. One tour covers Yashima, Ritsurin Park, Marugame Castle, Tokiwa Park, Zentsuji Temple and Kotohira in 8 hrs. 45 min. There is a half-day tour that covers Yashima and Ritsurin Park in 3 hrs. 50 min. The tours leave from Takamatsu Pier.

Refer to the supplement for details regarding the "i" System Information Center in Takamatsu.

PLACES OF INTEREST

Tamamo Park 106-①: Near Takamatsu Pier, facing the Inland Sea. It was the site of Takamatsu Castle, built in 1588 by Ikoma Chikamasa (a feudal lord), later becoming the residence of the Matsudaira Clan. The tides of time have not left much of the castle, but the three turrets and one gate remaining have been designated as Important Cultural Properties.

Ritsurin Park 106-①: Situated 2 km south of the JR Takamatsu Station, it was the site of the villa of the lord of the Matsudaira Clan. Covering an area of about 750,000 sq.m, it is skillfully laid out to harmonize with the surrounding natural forest of magnificent pine trees. It also includes fountains and fantastically shaped rocks, providing an excellent example of Japanese landscape gardening that rivals Koraku-en in Okayama. A zoo and folk musuem are located in the park precincts.

Megijima Island 105: Located about 2 km north of Takamatsu in the Inland Sea, the island is only 8 km in circumference. Associated with the legend of "Momotaro," it is widely known as Onigashima (Demon Island). Momotaro and his three followers—a dog, a monkey and a pheasant—are said to have subdued a den of demons here. A good view of the Inland Sea can be obtained from atop a hill. A ferry service between Takamatsu and the island takes 20 min.

Yashima 105: Situated 6 km east of Takamatsu, this was formerly an island but is now connected to the Shikoku mainland. Yashima could almost be called a mesa—it is a long, thin strip of lava table-land extending northward, with an altitude of 293 m. The summit of the slope is nearly flat and can be ascended from Takamatsu by bus or cable car. The bus terminates at Nanrei (South Hill), the site of Yashima Temple and an aquarium. The temple contains many relics from the naval battles between the rival Taira and Minamoto clans that occurred in the nearby sea during the 12th century. A pleasant promenade lined with red pines leads from Nanrei to Hokurei (North Hill), taking about 30 min. on foot. The view of Takamatsu, Mt.

Goken and the Inland Sea is magnificent. There is a collection of traditional houses and folk art gathered from all over the island of Shikoku in "Shikoku Village" at Nanrei.

The ruins of the temporary refuge of Emperor Antoku (1178–1185) and the Taira Clan still remain on Yashima.

In 1182 Taira-no-Munemori, third son of Kiyomori (chief of the Taira Clan), was pursued by the Minamoto Clan and fled here from Kyoto with his clansmen and the infant Emperor Antoku (son of Munemori's sister). At Yashima they enlisted the aid of lords from Shikoku and the San-yo District and thus regained their strength. They later transferred their headquarters back to Fukuhara in Kobe, but were defeated again by Minamoto-no-Yoshitsune (commander of the Minamoto forces) and fled back to Yashima. Yoshitsune continued to win, forcing the Taira Clan to flee even further west. From Yashima they fled to Shimonoseki and were finally destroyed at Dannoura in 1185.

Mt. Goken [105]: Alt. 366 m. It is 5 min. by the Takamatsu-Kotohira Electric Railway (popularly abbreviated as Kotoden) from Yashima and consists of a few serrated peaks. There is a cable car to the mountain peak, where a visitor can look out over Takamatsu and Yashima. Yakuriji Temple stands on the mountain as well.

Eastern Kagawa Prefecture

Shidoji Temple [105]: 30 min. from Takamatsu on the JR Kotoku Line or 35 min. on the Kotoden Line. The 86th Station on the 88-Temple Pilgrimage in Shikoku lies 700 m northeast of the JR Shido Station. It is said to have been established in the seventh century and became famous through the legend of a diver, portrayed in the *noh* play "Ama," who found treasure in the ocean depths. The statues of the *Kongo-Rikishi* (Deva Kings), the image of Buddha and the paintings portraying the history of the temple in the main hall are among the many Important Cultural Properties here.

Tsuda Pine Grove: 4 km of beach along the coast of Tsuda. The trees in the *kuromatsu* (black pine) grove stand with incredible grace. This is also the Prefectural Kinrin Park, popular with local bathers in summer. 50 min. from Takamatsu on the JR Kotoku Line. There also are such interesting places to visit as Chofukuji Temple, which has an image of Buddha (an Important Cultural Property), Shirotori Shrine and its priest's villa, as well as Shionoe Hot Springs for lodgings.

Western Kagawa Prefecture

Goshiki Plateau [105]: This lava tableland, located in the western part of Kagawa, juts out into the Inland Sea. It affords a great view, with the Inland Sea Folk History Museum, a prefectural natural history museum and a National Vacation Village all looking out over the ocean. A temple in the western part called Shiramineji, the 81st

Station on the 88-Temple Pilgrimage in Shikoku, was erected to pacify ex-Emperor Sutoku's vexation over having lost the battle for succession in the 12th century.

Sakaide 105 ☎0877: 22 km west of Takamatsu, with a population of 65,764. Lying above the delta of the Aya River, the city was once a center for salt production. However, with progress in the reclamation of the ocean, it has become an industrial zone for chemicals as well as ships, machinery and processed foods. Tokiwa Park, located atop a hill northwest of the city, offers a superb view of the Shiwaku Islands.

Seto-Ohashi Bridge 97 : Opened to traffic in April 1988, the Bridge connects Honshu and Shikoku. Actually, it is a generic name for a series of six bridges, including (in order from north to south) Shimotsui-Seto, Hitsuishijima, Iwagurojima, Yoshima, Kita(North)-Bisan-Seto and Minami(South)-Bisan-Seto. Connecting Kojima in Okayama Prefecture on Honshu with Sakaide in Kagawa Prefecture on Shikoku, the Bridge took 100 years to realize since its original conception and ten years to complete since the start of construction at a total cost of ¥1.1 trillion. The bridge holds both rail and highway traffic, with a toll road on top and the JR tracks below. The six bridges are all painted pure white, each constructed with a beautiful design that reflects against the blue waters of the Inland Sea.

By JR, it takes 15 min. from Kojima to Utazu, or by car, there is an 18.5-km-long toll road. The best way to fully experience the beauty of the bridge is either from the water or from the air. An excursion boat leaves from Kojima Port (1 hr.), Takamatsu Port (2 hrs. 30 min.), Marugame Port (1 hr.) and Sakaide Port (1 hr.10 min.). A helicopter tour is also available from Gold Tower in Utazu. There is a large drive-in facility on Yoshima Island, the only rest area on the bridge. The excursion boat from Yoshima Island takes 30 min.

Gold Tower: Immediately north of the JR Utazu Station. The tower is 158 m high with a facade of gold half-mirrors. There is an excellent view of Seto-Ohashi Bridge from the observation platform.

Marugame 105 ☎0877: About 30 km west of Takamatsu, with a population of 75,262. This old castle town was once the landing port for pilgrims to Kotohiragu Shrine. Even today there is passenger boat service from Shimotsui and Fukuyama. The specialty of the town is *uchiwa*, a kind of rounded, non-folding fan. About 1 km to the south of the JR Marugame Station lie the ruins of Marugame Castle, built in 1597. A three-story donjon and *Otemon* (Main Gate) are still intact and have been designated as Important Cultural Properties. The stone wall has a beautiful curve in it that is sometimes called "the fan pitch."

Tadotsu 105 : A port town about 35 km from Takamatsu, serving as the junction for the JR Dosan Line. The Japan *Shorinji Kempo* Headquarters is to the west of the JR Tadotsu Station in Momoyama. This is a unique martial art that was introduced from China. The site of the villa of the feudal lords who ruled this area is to the north in Toryo Park, which is now famous for its cherry trees.

Zentsuji 105 ☎0877: Pop. 37,415. 6 km from Tadotsu and about 40 km from Takamatsu. Zentsuji is famous for its association with Kobo-Daishi (774–835), who introduced the Buddhist Shingon doctrines to Japan.

Zentsuji Temple 105 : Located 1.2 km to the west of Zentsuji Station on the JR Dosan Line, it is the headquarters of the Zentsuji school of the Shingon sect. This is the birthplace of Kobo-Daishi, who founded the temple in 813. It is said that the temple grounds originally belonged to Saeki Zentsu, father of the great priest. The temple building was reconstructed in the 17th century. The East Temple grounds contain *Goju-no-To* (Five-Story Pagoda) and *Shoro* (Belfry). The Main Hall, called *Kondo* or *Yakushido*, contains a 4.8-m-tall wooden image of *Yakushi-Nyorai*, the god of medicine. The Five-Story Pagoda, which stands 45.6 m high, was reconstructed in 1882. The West Temple grounds are also called the *Tanjo-in* (Birth Temple), with many halls clustered around *Miedo* (Main Hall). The treasure house to the left of *Miedo* exhibits many National Treasures and Important Cultural Properties, including Buddhist religious articles brought back from China by Kobo-Daishi as well as donations from various Emperors. The two large camphor trees on the grounds are said to have been growing here since the temple was founded. Zentsuji Temple is the 75th Station on the 88-Temple Pilgrimage in Shikoku.

Kotohira 105 : 45 km from Takamatsu on the JR Dosan Line, 40 min. by limited express. It can also be reached by the Kotoden Line (1 hr.10 min.) or by bus (1 hr.40 min.). It is well known for Kotohiragu Shrine, popularly known as "Kompira-san."

Kotohiragu Shrine 105 : Located 1 km west of the JR Kotohira Station, halfway up Zozusan Hill. Long flights of granite steps lead up to the shrine, which is dedicated to the Shinto deity Omononushi-no-Mikoto. It is believed this god protects seafarers and voyagers. Worshippers approach the shrine at the *Sando* Entrance through a great gate in the midst of a grove of cherry trees. An additional 20-min. climb brings the visitor to the *Shoin* (Study Hall), built in 1659. The paintings that decorate the doors and alcoves of the building are the work of a famous landscape artist, Maruyama Okyo (1733–1795). These paintings and the building itself are Important Cultural Properties. There are many other paintings and ancient images of Buddha in the treasure house to the east. The path to the left of the Study Hall leads to *Chadokoro* (Tea House). From here it is another long and arduous climb to Asahi-no-Yashiro (Rising-sun Hall). It contains several famous carvings of people, animals, birds and flowers, representing the finest workmanship of the early 19th century. The central part of the grounds includes *Hongu* (Main Hall), *Emaden* (Votive-Picture Hall) and *Gagakuden* (Sacred Music Hall). It is another half-hour walk to the inner shrine. The entire grounds are densely wooded with cedar, pine, camphor and other ancient trees. The 1-km ascent to *Hongu* (Main Shrine) takes about 1 hr. The annual festival of Kotohiragu Shrine is held October 9–11.

Kanemaruza Theater: Standing on the left side of the main approach to Kotohiragu Shrine. Erected during the 19th century, this is the oldest extant theater in Japan. The two-story wooden structure has a stage 10.9 m long as well as a hand-turned revolving stage, a mezzanine and all the other elements of a proper playhouse. It is an Important Cultural Property, with performances held here on an irregular basis.

Manno Pond: About 1.5 km northeast of Shioiri Station on the JR Dosan Line, one stop from Kotohira. The pond is the oldest of the reservoirs in Japan being utilized for irrigation. It has an area of 1.5 sq.km, a circumference of 19.7 km and a maximum depth of more than 30 m. It was excavated between 701 and 704 to supplement the inadequate water supply of the district.

Kan-onji 105 ☎0875: Pop. 46,279. 57 km from Takamatsu on the JR Yosan Line. There is also a non-stop bus from Kotohira. Kotohiki Park is located on the coast 1.5 km to the north of Kan-onji Station. The 59-m-high Kotohiki Hill is in the center, while on the beach the contrast of the white sand with the pine grove is an appealing sight. There is a road and a trail to the top of the mountain, where a visitor will find Kotohiki-Hachiman Shrine. If one looks down toward the shore from here, the shape of a giant coin will be seen carved out of the sands on the beach. Called *Kan-ei-Tsuho*, this coin circulated during the 17th century. The trench design is 122 m across from east to west and 90 m across from north to south, with a circumference of 345 m that encloses an area of 30,000 sq.m. When the lord of the fief was touring his lands in 1633, the local residents dug out this coin design overnight to welcome him. The trenches are repaired every spring and autumn. Kan-onji Temple, located at the foot of the mountain, was established during the Nara period (710–784). It belongs to the Koyasan-Singon sect. The Important Cultural Properties here include *Kondo* (Main Hall), images of Buddhas and Buddhist paintings. Jinne-in Temple, on the same grounds, is also an Important Cultural Property. It is the 68th Station on the 88-Temple Pilgrimage in Shikoku, while Kan-onji Temple is the 69th—an unusual coincidence to have two stations located within the same confines.

Area 3. Ehime Prefecture

Ehime Prefecture occupies the northwestern end of Shikoku. The northern part faces the Inland Sea, where Omishima Island and the rest of the Geiyo Island Chain lie. In the west, the 40-km-long

Sada-Misaki Peninsula stretches out toward Kyushu, cut off by the Hoyo Straits. The south is mountainous. Mt. Ishizuchi in the east, historically of religious significance, has now been made a quasi-national park. Matsuyama, Ozu, Uwajima and other castle towns together with Dogo Spa make this a popular area with tourists.

Matsuyama ⸢104/107-①⸥ ☎ 0899

Pop. 437,062. Serving as the capital of Ehime Prefecture, the city lies just about in the middle of the prefectural coastline and can be reached by limited express on the JR Yosan Line in 2 hrs. 40 min. from Takamatsu (195 km) or 3 hrs. 10 min. from Okayama (215 km) over the Seto-Ohashi Bridge. It takes 1 hr.25 min. by air from Tokyo and 50 min. from Osaka. For those who are driving, it is 160 km along National Highway 11 from Takamatsu. Iyo Railway trains as well as buses run through the town. The city is also connected to the San-yo side of Honshu and Kyushu by ship. There are three ports: Takahama, Mitohama and Horie. Matsuyama was founded when an Inland Sea navy commander built a castle here in the 14th century. Moreover, it served as a castle town from the 17th century through the Edo period. As a result, the cultural and historical roots run deep. Matsuyama was the birthplace of many modern *haiku* poets, including Masaoka Shiki (1867–1902) and Takahama Kyoshi (1874–1959). One of the three oldest spas in Japan, Dogo is located in the eastern part of the city and serves as a base for tourists. The spa town is famous for *Iyo-kasuri* (a type of woven cotton cloth with splashed patterns) and other traditional crafts as well as a variety of delicious local dishes.

Horinouchi Park ⸢107-①⸥ : 500 m to the east of the station. The park, in fact, comprises the entire grounds of Matsuyama Castle, including all of Mt. Katsuyama (or Mt. Shiroyama)—a picturesque, densely wooded (except for the peak) hill rising in the center of the city. A ropeway takes visitors to the top from the eastern base in 3 min. The summit offers an extensive view of the surrounding countryside. The park also contains the Prefectural Art Museum and its Bansuiso Annex, a French-style building constructed in 1922. The museum displays pictures, calligraphy and craftwork created by Ehime natives.

Matsuyama Castle ⸢107-①⸥ : Dating from 1602, this is one of the best preserved castles in Japan. It is enclosed by four gates and stone walls. The Donjon (an Important Cultural Property) is now a spacious, three-story building, the greater part of which is used as an art museum. Exhibits include old palanquins, armor, swords and other items that once belonged to the Matsudaira Clan (one of the branches of the Tokugawa family) of the Matsuyama area.

Shikido ⸢107-①⸥ : Located on the precincts of Shoshuji Temple, 2 km southeast of the JR Matsuyama Station. This is a replica of the home of Masaoka Shiki, a *haiku* poet master of the Meiji period who was born in Matsuyama. The house contains many articles associated with his literary works.

Dogo Spa 104 : About 5 km to the northeast of the JR Matsuyama Station. 20 min. by Iyo Railway train or bus. Literary references to the area date from the eighth century, making this one of the oldest spas in Japan. It is a spot of activity on the quiet mountain slope, with more than 100 *ryokan*, or Japanese-style inns as well as gift shops and restaurants concentrated here. The hot spring has water that is colorless and odorless—a relaxing place to bathe. Dogo Park, to the south of the spa, is situated on the site of an ancient castle and is famous for its cherry trees. Shiki Memorial Museum is located here. Isaniha Hachiman Shrine, with a splendid Main Hall (an Important Cultural Property), and Hogonji Temple are located nearby, making this an ideal place for a walk. Dogo Spa Honkan (Main Building) is a tall, dignified, wooden, public bathhouse constructed in 1891. It is crowned by a drum tower called Shinrokaku. Inside are two separate baths called Kaminoyu and Tamanoyu, with rest areas for each bath. An annex, called Yushinden, was added to accommodate the Imperial Family during its visits.

Ishiteji Temple: The 51st Station on the 88-Temple Pilgrimage in Shikoku is located 1 km east of Dogo Spa. Founded in 728 and rebuilt during the Kamakura period, the temple is an excellent example of the exquisite combination of Chinese and Japanese architectural techniques. *Niomon* (a gate guarded by the two Deva Kings) is a National Treasure, while *Hondo* (Main Hall) and several other facilities on the grounds are Important Cultural Properties.

Oku(Inner)-Dogo Spa: About 4 km to the north of Ishiteji Temple. It can be reached from Matsuyama in 30 min. by bus. The hot-spring waters are similar to those of Dogo Spa. At the rear, there is an amusement park and a ropeway to the top of the mountain, where one can obtain a panoramic view of Matsuyama.

Takahama Port 104 : Also called Matsuyama Kanko Port, it is situated on the northwest coast of Matsuyama and can be reached in 25 min. by the Iyo Railway. It is an important port for ships on the Inland Sea, with the Osaka/Kobe–Beppu vessels of the Kansai Steamship Co. and Kobe–Oita ferries of the Diamond Ferry Co. calling here. Taisanji Temple, the 52nd Station on the 88-Temple Pilgrimage of Shikoku, is east of the port, while Gogojima Island is about 2 km offshore and can be reached by ship in 10 min. The island is known for its fruit cultivation, with the citrus, peach, and loquat blossoms and fruit providing their seasonal beauty. A "Ship Dance" staged aboard ship each October 6 is really a play performed in pantomime. It has been designated as a prefectural Intangible Cultural Property.

Eastern Ehime Prefecture

Omogokei Gorge 104 : Situated along the upper reaches of the Omogo River, the gorge is about 70 km southeast of the JR Matsuyama Station. A bus goes to Kammon, the entrance of the gorge (2 hrs. 20 min. from Matsuyama). The beauty of the gorge is in the blue, meandering streams, strangely shaped rocks, waterfalls and narrow ravines. The excursion course runs from Kammon to Goraiko Falls via Kamehara Cliff and Momijigahara Plain. The verdure of spring and red tints of autumn are especially beautiful. The "Ishizuchi Skyline" toll road runs 18 km from Kammon to Tsuchigoya on the eastern face of Mt. Ishizuchi. A karst called Shikoku Karst to the west of Omogokei Gorge is a big plateau spreading for about 25 km from east to west on the borders of Ehime and Kochi prefectures.

Hojo ☐ 104 ☐ ☎0899: Adjoining the north end of Matsuyama, Hojo has a population of 30,022. It is a rural town where mandarin orange cultivation and chicken breeding thrive. Kashima is a beautiful island 400 m off the west coast with more than 200 kinds of plants and wild deer. There is an excellent swimming beach and hiking course. It can be reached in 3 min. by ferry.

Imabari ☐ 104 ☐ ☎0898: Pop. 123,393. 2 hrs. by limited express on the JR Yosan Line from Takamatsu, or 160 km on National Highway 11. The busy trading port is in the northern part of Ehime Prefecture on the northeast coast of the Takanawa Peninsula, which juts out into the Inland Sea. Originally the castle town of the Imabari Clan, it is now so commercially successful that it is sometimes called the "Osaka of Shikoku." The manufacture of cotton textiles is the main industry, especially towels, accounting for 64% of the total towel production in Japan, or ¥86 billion worth (1988). It also lies at the southern end of a new bridge that will connect Shikoku and Onomichi on Honshu in 1998. Principal places of interest include Fukiage Park, 1.6 km southeast of the station, where the remains of the Imabari Castle can be seen. The donjon has been restored. Karako Beach and the Sakurai Coast, 5 km to the southeast, have gentle waves ideal for swimming. There is a National Vacation Village at Sakurai. If one wishes to experience the beauty of the many islands in the Inland Sea, a visit to the following two places is recommended: Hashihama Park and Mt. Itoyama. Hashihama Park is situated on a hill 4 km to the north of Hashihama Station on the JR Yosan Line, next to Imabari. The cherry blossoms in spring make this a beautiful scenic spot on the Inland Sea. The summit also offers an excellent view of the Kurushima Straits. Mt. Itoyama, a 97-m peak on the east side of Hashihama Port, offers a fine view of the Kurushima Straits. In the vicinity is a park, where a bridge between Imabari and Onomichi will be erected.

Kurushima Straits ☐ 104 ☐: A narrow passage between Imabari and Oshima Island. It is known for the tumultuous whirlpools formed by the ebb and flow of the tides, with the maximum speed of currents—18 km per hour at Kurushima—ranking second only to that of Naruto —22 km per hour. Nevertheless, many ships, both large and small, pass safely through Kurushima Straits, guided by a current-signal station situated on a small island in the straits.

Oyamazumi Shrine 104 : 1 km east of Miyaura on Omishima Island, about 15 km off the coast of the Takanawa Peninsula, where Imabari is situated. Miyaura Port is connected by regular boat service to Imabari (1 hr.) and Onomichi (35 min. by hydrofoil). Dedicated to the guardian gods of seafarers, the shrine is said to have been founded during the prehistoric period. Plagued by repeated fires, the present building dates from 1427. This was a popular place to worship for Emperors and *shogun*, who donated armor, swords and many other precious items. Today, they are preserved in the treasure house, which contains a total of eight National Treasures and more than 100 Important Cultural Properties. This means that 80% of the armor designated as National Treasures or Important Cultural Properties in Japan belongs to this shrine.

Toyo 104 ☎0898: Pop. 34,253. 19 km from Imabari or about 30 min. to Nyugawa Station on the JR Yosan Line. Agriculture and fishery are the main industries, but since it was designated as a "New Industrial City," the number of factories has increased. Traditionally, Toyo is known for the production of large quantities of tradi-tional, high-quality, Japanese-style paper.

Saijo 104 ☎0897: 1 hr.40 min. from Takamatsu or 1 hr.10 min. from Matsuyama by JR limited express. Saijo is 50 km along National Highway 11 from Matsuyama. With a population of 57,275, it has developed as an industrial city by utilizing the abundant water resources available. It is also the entrance to Ishizuchi Quasi-National Park.

Ishizuchi Quasi-National Park 104 : Located about 30 km to the southwest of Saijo, Mt. Ishizuchi towers 1,982 m high—the highest peak not only in Shikoku but in all of western Japan. The quasi-national park spans the mountain and Omogokei Gorge for a total area of 106.83 sq.km. The bus from Iyo-Saijo Station on the JR Yosan Line arrives at the ropeway station halfway up the mountain in 1 hr, with another 8 min. required to reach the ropeway terminal. It takes 2 hrs. 45 min. to climb the 4.5 km to the summit from the ropeway terminal. This can also be accomplished from the Omogokei Gorge side at Tsuchigoya, which is 2 hrs. or 4 km away. In the old days, the mountain was the site of pilgrimages, with the popular Ishizuchi Shrine Main Hall at the base, Joju Shrine in the middle and Chojo Shrine at the peak. The white-clad pilgrims usually climb between July 1-10. Alpine plants blanket part of the summit, from which there is a fine view of the Inland Sea to the north, Tosa Bay to the south and most of Shikoku.

Niihama 104 ☎0897: Pop. 132,764. The city can be reached in 1 hr. 25 min. by limited express on the JR Yosan Line from either Taka-matsu or Matsuyama. This was formerly one of the most prosperous trading ports in Shikoku, due in part to the Besshi Copper Mine, opened by the founders of the Sumitomo family (modern industrialists) in 1691. The area has continued to serve as an important base for Sumitomo Metal Mining Co., but Besshi Mine was closed in 1973. There are many factories producing metals, machinery and chemical products along the coast of the Hiuchi-nada Sea, an area that constitutes the nucleus of the industrial development of the eastern district of Ehime Prefecture.

Iyo-Mishima 104 : It has a population of 39,272, while Kawanoe to the east has a population of 39,488. The two cities are located along the JR Yosan Line, with paper production flourishing in both. There are many pulp, paper and paper-processing factories scattered about. *Mizuhiki*, decorative strings made of Japanese paper for tying presents, are a specialty. Local sights include Lake Kinsha, 10 km south of Iyo-Mishima Station. Iyo-Mishima Shrine, the source of the city's name, is also located here. Sankakuji Temple, the 65th Station on the 88-Temple Pilgrimage in Shikoku, can be reached by bus in 35 min. from the JR Kawanoe Station plus an additional 45-min. walk. It is believed that worshipping at the temple will ensure safe childbirth.

Southwestern Ehime Prefecture

Iyo 104 ☎0899: Pop. 30,070. The port town, located to the south of Matsuyama, was once called Gunchu. The specialty is dried bonito. It can be reached from Matsuyama on the Iyo Railway in 25 min. Tobe, to the west of Iyo, is known for a type of porcelain called *Tobe-yaki*. Approximately 60 kilns here turn out exquisitely painted white porcelain that is sold both domestically and overseas. A ceramics museum is located along National Highway 379 running through the town.

Ozu 104 ☎0893: 56 km to the southwest of Matsuyama, 50 min. by limited express on the JR Yosan Line, or 55 km on National Highway 53. The population is 39,620. With the Ozu Basin enclosed on all four sides by mountains and the Hiji River running through the city, a landscape of such beauty is created that it is sometimes called the "Little Kyoto of Iyo Province (now, Ehime Prefecture)." Until the Meiji period (1868-1912), Ozu was a castle town, with the remains of the castle lying in Shiroyama Park. Takayama Menhir, Mt. Tomisu Dolmen and other gigantic, ancient, stone relics are a sight to see. Cormorant fishing is done on the Hiji River from June 1 to September 20. A popular autumn tradition is *Imotaki* (stewing of taro root and chicken) in the dry riverbed.

Yawatahama 104 ☎0894: Pop. 39,625. Fishery has long flourished in the area. Today, it is known as the base for deep-sea trawling. 1 hr.10 min. from Matsuyama by limited express on the JR Yosan Line, or 79 km on National Highway 56 or 378. This port town is located on the southwest coast at the base of the Sada-Misaki Peninsula and connected by ferry to Kyushu. The trip to Beppu takes 3 hrs. 30 min. The climate is warm, with terraces of mandarin oranges cultivated on the mountainsides, creating a unique landscape in the area. On the

820-m-high summit of Mt. Kinzan, 16 km to the north of the JR Yawatahama Station or 1 hr. by bus, stands Shussekiji Temple, founded in the eighth century. The temple grounds are cloaked in natural forest. The Inland Sea, Mt. Ishizuchi and even the mountains of Kyushu can be seen from the summit.

Cape Sada ☐104☐: The tip of the Sada-Misaki Peninsula, which stretches thinly from Yawatahama westwards toward the Hoyo Straits. This narrow, 40-km-long peninsula is only 6 km wide at the most and a mere 500 m at the narrowest point. National Highway 197 runs to the tip, where Misaki Town and the port, the central features of the peninsula, are located. There is a lighthouse and a forest of wild *ako*, a kind of banyan tree (a Natural Monument), at the edge of the cape, where a gorgeous view of the ocean can be obtained. From Yawatahama to Misaki Town, it takes 1 hr.5 min. by bus or 1 hr.20 min. by boat.

Uwajima ☐104☐ ☎0895: Pop. 69,621. Located 1 hr.45 min. from Matsuyama by limited express on the JR Yosan Line or 115 km along National Highway 56, this is the main city in southwestern Ehime Prefecture. From the 16th century through the early Meiji period, this was a castle town as well as a cultural and industrial center. Today, it is a port town, with fishery, the processing of marine products, mandarin orange cultivation and dairy farming providing the main industries. It is also the nucleus of the Nan-yo (South Ehime Prefecture) Recreation City Plan. Uwajima Castle has a three-story, 17th-century donjon. Tensha-en Garden, 2 km southwest of the JR Uwajima Station, served as a retreat for the seventh lord of the clan in feudal days. There are many kinds of bamboo, wisteria and irises growing here. The Dekoboko (lit. "Bumpy") Temple Museum of sexual culture is also quite unique. Uwajima is famous for Togyu, or bullfights, which take place at the Municipal Bull Ring seven times a year. Two bulls test their strength, *sumo*-style, by locking horns. The bulls are ranked according to their previous performances, as in traditional *sumo* wrestling, and are even taught certain techniques. The *Yasshika* (Eight Deers) Dance and *Ushionin* (Ox-Monster) Parade are performed at the autumn festival of Uwatsuhiko Shrine (October 29).

Nan-yo Recreation City: Uwajima together with the nearby towns and villages of Yoshida, Tsushima, Uchiumi, Misho, Nishiumi and Johen are jointly developing an area to give the public an opportunity to enjoy the beauty of the Uwa Sea. The projected completion date is 1995. The beautifully jagged coastline is the habitat of many rare animals such as *nihon kawauso*, or Japanese otter (a Protected Animal), and rare landscapes such as the stone-walled village of Sotodomari.

Area 4. Kochi Prefecture

Kochi Prefecture occupies the southern half of Shikoku and faces the Pacific Ocean, sandwiched between Cape Muroto and Cape Ashizuri. All the rivers run south, with the basins opening up into flat, cultivated plains. The mountains of north Shikoku form a wall, making the climate of Kochi Plain warm and rainy. The area is known as a region in which two annual crops of rice can be harvested, but recently vegetable and fruit cultivation has been thriving. Fishery is the principal industry along the coast, especially deep-sea fishing of bonito and tuna. *Katsuobushi* or dried bonito, commonly used in Japanese cooking, is noted as the local specialty. Unique local cuisine such as *sawachi* cuisine and events such as dog fighting are offered. *Sawachi* cuisine is a lavish assortment of fish and vegetables served in four separate dishes and arranged naturally on a large platter.

Kochi ⌷105/107-②⌷ ☎ 0888

Pop. 313,357. Located near the middle of the Pacific side, Kochi is the capital of Kochi Prefecture. The town spreads out along the back of the deep inlet known as Urado Bay. It can be reached in 2 hrs. 45 min. from Takamatsu by limited express on the JR Dosan Line. It is 135 km down National Highway 32. There is also a direct limited express from Okayama on the JR San-yo Main Line or the Shinkansen over the Seto-Ohashi Bridge, taking about 3 hrs. There are flights from Tokyo, Osaka, Nagoya and Fukuoka, and ferry service from Tokyo and Osaka.

Kochi was a castle town from the 16th century, developing as the base from which the feudal lords ruled Tosa Province (now, Kochi Prefecture). Today, it remains as the largest commercial city in the district, based on thriving tertiary industries such as wholesaling, retailing, servicing and tourism. The shopping district is concentrated around Harimaya Bridge. Here, there are many places to savor *sawachi* cuisine and bonito, the specialties of Kochi. Lodging facilities are plentiful, making Kochi an excellent starting place from which to go sightseeing on Cape Muroto and Cape Ashizuri.

Refer to the supplement for details regarding the "i" **System Information Center** in Kochi.

Kochi Park ⌷107-②⌷ : 1.5 km southwest of the JR Kochi Station. Situated in the center of the city, this is the site of Kochi Castle. Now the main attraction in the park, the castle was erected in 1603 by the lord of Tosa Province, Yamanouchi Kazutoyo. The donjon, reconstructed in 1747 with three levels and six floors, and the 14 other buildings are Important Cultural Properties. There is an extensive view of the city from the top of the donjon. The Kyodo Bunka

Kaikan Public Museum is also located in the park.

Godaisan Park [105]: Situated about 5 km southeast of the station, the park is situated on a 145-m-high hill that offers a fine view of the city and Urado Bay to the west. There is an old Shingon-sect temple called Chikurinji Temple, surrounded by a beautiful Edo-period garden. The Main Hall, or *Monjudo*, and the 19 wooden images of *Monju-Bosatsu*, the bodhisattva of wisdom and intellect, are Important Cultural Properties. Said to have been founded in 724 by the priest Gyoki, it is the oldest temple in Kochi Prefecture and the 31st Station on the 88-Temple Pilgrimage in Shikoku.

The Prefectural Makino Botanical Garden lies at the foot of the stone steps leading to the temple. The gardens are a memorial to Makino Tomitaro (1862-1957), a native of Kochi Prefecture and a botanist who made great contributions to his field. Some 1,000 tropical plants grow in the greenhouses here. In addition, there is a fossil museum and the Makino Library, which houses a collection of 42,000 rare books.

Katsurahama Park [105]: 13 km south of Kochi Station. Stretching along the mouth of Urado Bay on the Pacific coast, the park is 30 min. by bus from the Harimayabashi Bus Terminal. The coastline is white sand bordered by green pines, while nicely formed rocks in key positions dress up the landscape. It was famous as a place for viewing the moon, but it is now better known as a good place for swimming. The Tosa Token (Dog fighting) Center is located in the park, with matches staged twice a day. The unique Tosa long-tailed cock (a Protected Animal), with plumes extending as far as 6-8 m, can be seen here. An aquarium and a shell museum are also located on the grounds. Urado Ohashi Bridge, 1,480 m long, extends from Katsurahama Beach to the east coast of Tanesaki.

Eastern Kochi Prefecture

Nangoku [105] ☎0888: Pop. 47,432. Adjoining the eastern edge of Kochi. A 25-min. ride from Kochi on the JR Dosan Line will bring one to Gomen Station in Nangoku. Rice is harvested twice a year, and hothouse cultivation of vegetables and fruit flourishes in this rural town. The Nishijima Horticulture Complex, 2 km north of the station, is especially large. The hothouses are open for tourists and the produce can be sampled. Long-tailed cocks, raised in the Shinohara area to the south of the station, can be observed at the Chobikei Center, which specializes in breeding these beautiful birds.

Kokubunji Temple: This temple of the Shingon sect is 4 km northwest of the JR Gomen Station. It was founded in 739 by the celebrated priest Gyoki (668-749). The *Hondo* (Main Hall, reconstructed in 1558) houses *Bonsho* (Bell; an Important Cultural Property). Its two wooden images of *Yakushi-Nyorai*, the god of medicine, are also Important Cultural Properties. It is the 29th Station on the 88-Temple Pilgrimage in Shikoku.

Ryugado Cave [105]: This massive stalactite cave can be reached from Kochi by traveling for 30 min. on the JR Dosan Line to Tosa-Yamada. To reach the cave, which is 8 km to the east of the station, one can board a bus from Tosa-Yamada Station, which takes 20 min., or a bus from Kochi that takes 1 hr. It is also accessible from Noichi on the "Ryugado Skyline" (a toll road), 9 km to the northeast.

The cave meanders inward for about 4 km, with its widest chamber measuring about 180 sq.m. In one domed, cupola-like section, the cave ceiling is 30 m high. The limestone pillars and stalactites, shaped by tiny rivulets of water dripping from the ceiling, are well formed, providing excellent geological specimens. The cavern was discovered in 1931. Archaeologists have unearthed a number of clay dishes presumed to be used by prehistoric cave dwellers. The cave has been designated as a Historic Site and a Natural Monument. The Ryugado Museum stands by the cave entrance.

Aki [105] ☎08873: Pop. 24,746. 40 min. by bus from Gomen Station, 40 km on National Highway 55 from Kochi. Agriculture thrives in Aki, which is also the center for the intensive cultivation of vegetables. This is the birthplace of the founder of the Mitsubishi *zaibatsu* (financial clique), Iwasaki Yataro (1834–1885). Besides the Municipal Historical Folk Museum and the Municipal Calligraphy Museum located here, *Uchiharano* pottery is also made in Aki.

Large Cedar in Osugi: A large cedar in the Yasaka Shrine precincts 500 m to the west of Osugi Station on the JR Dosan Line. It has split trunks, which are called Southern Large Cedar and Northern Large Cedar. The former is 68 m high and 30 m around at the base, while the latter is 57 m high and 15 m around at the base. Known as the largest cedar in Japan and believed to be more than 3,000 years old, the massive tree has been designated as a Special Natural Monument.

Burakuji Temple: 1 km north of Otaguchi Station on the JR Dosan Line. The Main Hall, called *Yakushido*, was built in 1151. Designated as a National Treasure, it is a classic example of late-Heian-period (794–1185) architecture. Inside are wooden images of *Yakushi-Nyorai* (the god of medicine and the main object of worship here), *Amida-Nyorai* and *Shaka-Nyorai*, all of which are Important Cultural Properties.

Cape Muroto [105]: The cape is located at the southeastern edge of Kochi Prefecture on the eastern tip of Tosa Bay. It can be reached from Kochi by bus in 2 hrs. 20 min. or in 1 hr.40 min. by bus from Mugi Station on the JR Mugi Line. Kannoura, 39 km to the northeast of the cape, is the port where ferries arrive from Kobe and Tosa-Shimizu. It takes 1 hr. by bus from Kannoura to Cape Muroto, which is noted for the wild, romantic scenery along the rocky coast. It has been designated as a Scenic Place. Lately, the Muroto-Anan Kaigan (Coast) Quasi-National Park has become a popular sightseeing attraction. *Ubame-gashi* (holm oaks), *aogiri* (parasol trees) and other subtropical trees as well as seaside plants growing in clusters on the cape are preserved as a Natural Monument. A good view of the cape scenery can be obtained along the "Muroto Skyline" road (about 4 km).

Hotsumisakiji Temple: Also called Higashidera or Eastern Temple, it stands near the tip of the headland behind the lighthouse. The temple was founded in 807 by Kobo-Daishi, and relics related to him have been found in the vicinity. This is the 24th Station on the 88-Temple Pilgrimage in Shikoku. It contains three Buddhist images designated as Important Cultural Properties. The temple also serves as a youth hostel.

Kongochoji Temple: The 26th Station of the Pilgrimage is often called Western Temple. The treasure house here contains many Important Cultural Properties. There is also a building called the Geishokan that chronicles the history of whaling.

Western Kochi Prefecture

Ino 104 : 11.4 km northwest of Kochi. Spreading along the basin of the Niyodo River, the town can be reached from Kochi by streetcar in 30 min. Since the early 17th century, Ino has been known for the production of handmade paper called *Tosa-gami*. The paper is made from *mitsumata* (paper mulberry) and other tree barks with beautiful yet durable results. At the Handmade Paper Museum on the banks of the Niyodo River visitors can try the process of papermaking with their own hands.

Yokonami-Sanri 104 : Uranouchi Bay is a lake-like inlet of scenic beauty extending for 12 km embraced by the Yokonami Peninsula. The tranquil, fjord-like waters are excellent for fishing and swimming. Usacho, the center of Tosa City (pop. 33,030), is located on the north at the mouth of the bay and can be reached from Kochi in 1 hr. by bus or 25 km via National Highway 56. The 645-m-long Usa-Ohashi toll bridge spans the mouth of the bay, while the "Yokonami Kuroshio (lit. Black Current) Line," an 18.9-km-long highway, slices across the Yokonami Peninsula. The view of the quiet inland sea to the north and the magnificent outer ocean to the south is a pleasing contrast. Green Pia Tosa-Yokonami (a recreation facility) and a hotel are located on the north shore.

Sakawa 104 : This town, northwest of Tosa, can be reached from Kochi in 1 hr. on the JR Dosan Line or 25 km down National Highway 33. There is a bus from Matsuyama (2 hrs. 25 min.). This is the town where Makino Tomitaro (refer to p.827) was born, and Makino Park is dedicated to his memory. Seizan Library specializes in resources related to the Meiji Restoration.

Nakamura 104 ☎08803: Pop. 36,182. Located in the southwestern part of Kochi Prefecture. Spreading along the Shimanto River, this city serves as a base for sightseeing on Cape Ashizuri. There is a direct limited express from Kochi on the JR Dosan Line/Tosa

Kuroshio Railway (1 hr.55 min.) or 108 km on National Highway 56. The town is centered around the basin of the Shimanto River, the second-longest river (192 km) in Shikoku and regarded as the most beautiful of all the rivers in Japan. The city was established in 1468, when Ichijo Norifusa, an Imperial Court noble and former chief advisor to the Emperor, came to live here and modeled the city after Kyoto. This is why it is called the "Little Kyoto of Tosa Province (now, Kochi Prefecture)." Many venerable temples can be found in Nakamura.

Tosa-Shimizu 104 ☎08808: Pop. 22,592. Situated at the base of Cape Ashizuri on the southwestern edge of Shikoku. 1 hr. by bus from Nakamura Station on the Tosa Kuroshio Railway or 35 km down National Highway 321. There is a direct bus from Kochi and a boat from Kochi Port. Fishery is the main industry, with much of the catch consisting of bonito, tuna and yellowtail. In fact, dried bonito is a local specialty. This is the birthplace of John Manjiro (Nakahama Manjiro), who was rescued from a shipwreck by an American whaler in the mid-19th century, went to America and brought new knowledge back to Japan—a country still bottled up by a policy of isolationism.

Ashizuri-Uwakai National Park 104 : Established in 1972, the park covers 109.7 sq.km from Cape Ashizuri in Kochi Prefecture to Uwajima in Ehime Prefecture, including the southern coast of Shikoku and the ocean that borders it. It has the beauty only seen on a wild frontier.

Cape Ashizuri 104 : Located 18 km southeast of Tosa-Shimizu, it can be reached by bus in 40-45 min. There are 70-m-high cliffs covered with clusters of camellias, holm oaks, and other subtropical plants at the tip of the cape. A trail circles the cape (about 2 hrs.), with a magnificent view of the ocean from the lighthouse area.

Kongofukuji Temple: Established in 822 by Kobo-Daishi, the temple stands behind the lighthouse. It also serves as a youth hostel. The *Hondo* (Main Hall) and *Tahoto* Pagoda are still standing in the compound of this ancient temple, which is the 38th Station on the 88-Temple Pilgrimage in Shikoku. The main image is a *Senju-Kannon* (Thousand-Handed Goddess of Mercy). There is a natural grove of *ako* (banyan) trees surrounding Matsuo Shrine on the west coast that has been designated as a Natural Monument.

Tatsukushi and Minokoshi 104 : Tatsukushi is 24 km west of Cape Asizuri, or 20 min. by bus from Tosa-Shimizu. It is a 30-min. round trip to Minokoshi by boat from Tatsukushi. Both Tatsukushi and Minokoshi are protruding, sea-eroded plateaus of strangely shaped, reddish-brown sandstone formed through erosion caused by the wind and waves. Fossilized sand, marked by waves, and coral reefs can be seen. The Ocean Gallery in Tatsukushi displays some 3,000 kinds of (or a total of 80,000) shells, including many rare specimens. The Coral Museum, the Ashizuri Ocean Museum with its collection of ocean plants and animals from Tosa Bay, the Ashizuri Seabed Museum with a 17-m-high observation deck and a 7-m-deep, ocean-floor observation hall are all attractions not to be missed.

The name Minokoshi (lit. Fail to Notice) is derived from the fact that the area was located in such an inaccessible place that one could not help but overlook it; but now, it is possible to go here by glass-bottom boat.

Sukumo 104 ☎08806: Located in southwest Kochi Prefecture on the border with Ehime Prefecture, the town has a population of 26,014. It can be reached from Nakamura Station on the Tosa Kuroshio Railway in 45 min. by bus, or 90 km down National Highway 321. From Uwajima there is a rapid bus that arrives in 1 hr. 50 min. or, if driving, it is 60 km on National Highway 56. Facing Sukumo Bay, the excellent natural harbor was a major international trading port during the 16th century and is still a leading distribution center for coral, fish and shellfish. Sukumo Mound, where Jomon-period (the New Stone Age) artifacts have been found, is northwest of the town.

Area 5. Tokushima Prefecture

Located in eastern Shikoku and facing the Kinki District across the Kii Straits, Tokushima has been greatly influenced by the ancient culture of the Kinki region. The Yoshino River, which runs from east to west across the prefecture, is the longest river (194 km) in Shikoku and serves as the border to the wild Mt. Tsurugi region to the south. Traditional specialties of the area are indigo and high-quality refined sugar. The northern coast is industrial, while fishery thrives in the south.

Tokushima 105/106-② ☎ 0886

Serving as the capital of Tokushima Prefecture, the city has a population of 258,245. It can be reached from Takamatsu in 1 hr. 15 min. by limited express on the JR Kotoku Line or by driving 77 km along National Highway 11. There is also an express from Awa-Ikeda on the JR Tokushima Line that will arrive in 1 hr.20 min. Planes fly from Tokyo and Osaka, while ferry service is available from Osaka, Kobe and Wakayama.

The city is located at the mouth of the Yoshino River and until the Meiji Restoration of 1868, it was the castle town of the Hachisuka Clan that included all of Awa Province (now, Tokushima Prefecture) and Awaji Island. The main industries are cotton textiles and woodwork, especially furniture. The *Awa-chijimi* (cotton crepe) and indigo dye are local specialties.

Tokushima is also noted for the *Awa-Odori* dance and *ningyo-joruri* (puppet shows). The dance, said to date from about 400 years ago, is performed annually from August 12-15 by more than 50,000 people, who dance enthusiastically through the streets to the accompaniment of *samisen* (or *shamisen*; a three-stringed instrument), drums and flutes.

The performances of the puppet show are presented between farming seasons by farmers skilled in this art. There is a puppet theater in the city.

Tokushima is also closely associated with Wenceslao de Moraes (1854-1925), who came to Japan in 1893 as a member of the Portuguese Navy and remained as a consular officer. After retiring, he took up residence in Tokushima as it was the home of his wife, Fukumoto Yone. Moraes devoted the rest of his life to the study of things Japanese and authored 16 literary works in Portuguese. His tomb is in Cho-onji Temple, about 1 km southwest of the JR Tokushima Station. There is also a monument dedicated to Moraes in Bizan Park (See below).

Site of Awa Jurobei House 106-② : 7 km north of Tokushima Station, situated at the mouth of the Yoshino River. This is the location of the house of Awa Jurobei, the well-known character featured in the *joruri* play "Keisei Awa-no-Naruto" written by Chikamatsu Monzaemon, a famous playwright of the Edo period. Awa Puppet Theater is situated in the compound.

Tokushima Park 106-② : Located 400 m east of the station, the park occupies the greater part of Shiroyama Hill in the center of the city where the castle once stood. The castle was originally constructed around 1586 by Hachisuka Iemasa, a feudal lord, but all that remains of the castle is the stone wall and foundation stones. A garden of the former lords on the south side of the park has been designated as a "Scenic Place." It is divided into two kinds of gardens: a rock garden that uses the blue rocks of Awa and a pond landscape garden.

Bizan Park 106-② : 1 km southwest of Tokushima Station. Situated on the slope of Otaki Hill, this park is famous for its beautiful cherry blossoms. A ropeway takes visitors in 7 min. to the summit (alt. 277 m), where one can obtain a distant view of Awaji Island, the Yoshino River and the surrounding mountains. A well-paved road also leads to the leisure center at the top. The Prefectural Museum as well as the 25-m-tall Peace Memorial Pagoda, erected in 1958, are at the foot of the hill. Dedicated to the victims of World War II, the pagoda contains a collection of local artifacts from Southeast Asian countries and is said to possess a small quantity of Buddha's ashes. The house in which Moraes lived is at the eastern base of the hill.

Yoshino River 104-105 : The water source of the longest river in Shikoku is near Mt. Ishizuchi (alt. 1,982 m)—the highest peak in Shikoku. Traversing 194 km through three prefectures (Ehime, Kochi and Tokushima), it ultimately flows into the Kii Channel through several mouths. Tokushima is located at one of these effluents.

Along the upper and middle reaches are scenic spots such as Oboke and Koboke, while the Iyadani Gorge runs along its tributary, the Iya River.

Jorokuji Temple: About 9 km south of Tokushima Station, 20 min. by bus. This is a Buddhist temple established in 650. An elaborate wooden image of *Sho*(Holy)-*Kannon*, said to be the work of the priest Gyoki (670–749), is 4 m 80 cm tall or *joroku* by the old Japanese measurement; hence, the name of the temple. *Kannondo* Hall, where the image stands, the two-story gate and *Hondo* (Main Hall) have all been designated as Important Cultural Properties.

Naruto ⌷105⌷ ☎0886

Pop. 65,223. This port town is located in the northeastern part of the prefecture. From Tokushima, it can be reached in 40 min. on the JR Naruto Line, in 30 min. by bus along National Highway 11 with the distance of 11 km. From Takamatsu, it takes 1 hr.40 min. on the JR Kotoku Line, transferring to the Naruto Line at Ikenotani. There are also boat services from Kobe and Awaji Island. If driving, one can get to Awaji Island by crossing the Onaruto Bridge. This is the take-off point for seeing the whirlpools of Naruto. Industries include salt, seaweed and their processing.

Naruto Straits ⌷105⌷: Popularly called "Awa-no-Naruto" (lit. Roaring Gateway of Awa Province), the straits separate Awaji Island from Shikoku and connect Seto-Naikai (Inland Sea) with the Pacific Ocean. The inward and outward currents rushing through this narrow passage between the Inland Sea and the Kii Channel sometimes reach a speed of more than 20 km per hour. Because of the 1 –2 m difference in water levels, the onrushing water forms hundreds of foaming whirlpools of all sizes, some as large as 20 m in diameter, creating a tremendous roar. Rocks dividing the narrow channel stimulate the wildness of the water. The whirlpools peak during the new and full moons, but sightseeing boats run throughout the year, allowing observation at close range.

Naruto Park ⌷105⌷: Situated about 8 km to the northeast of the JR Naruto Station, the park lies on the northern edge of Ogejima Island. It can be reached by bus from Naruto Station in 20 min. Besides the picturesque view of the sandy beach facing the ocean and the pines groves, there is an excellent view of the whirlpools from the top of the hill, which can be reached by the lift. The Onaruto Bridge connecting this park to Cape Naruto and Awaji Island was completed in 1985. The 1,629-m-long suspension bridge can hold both automotive and rail traffic, but currently only motor traffic passes over it. The Onaruto Bridge Construction Memorial Museum, where the ocean floor can be seen and natural phenomena like the whirlpools are explained, is at the foot of the bridge.

German Village Park: Located in the southwestern part of the city. During World War I, German prisoners of war were kept in this part of the city called Oasacho. The park was created to commemorate those soldiers. In addition to German Bridge, there are two memorials—German Tombs and the German House displaying relics of the day.

Western Tokushima Prefecture

Dochu (Earth Pillars) ⎡105⎤ : 1 hr.10 min. from Tokushima on the JR Tokushima Line to Anabuki and then an additional 15-min. bus ride to the northeast. *Dochu* (Earth Pillars) were formed when the slope of an alluvial fan eroded, exposing the layers of the earth. The pillars are 12-18 m tall, with stones and weeds on top. They have been given different names based on their shapes. As a valuable geological phenomenon, they have been designated as a Natural Monument. Similar pillars are said to exist in the Tyrol in central Europe and the Rocky Mountains of North America.

Mt. Tsurugi ⎡105⎤ : Alt. 1,955 m. The second-highest peak in Shikoku, Mt. Tsurugi together with Tsurugikyo Gorge and Iyakei Gorge constitutes Tsurugi-san (Mountain) Quasi-National Park (212 km²). Mt. Tsurugi is the main peak in the Tsurugi mountains. Called the roof of Shikoku, it has held religious significance since ancient times. The meaning of *Tsurugi* is sword, but the shape of the mountain is rounded and feminine. For mountain climbing, take a bus from Sadamitsu Station on the JR Tokushima Line to Tsuzurodo (1 hr.10 min.). It is a 3-hr. 40-min. hike to Minokoshi. Use the lift from Minokoshi to Nishijimasawa, and then it is only a 40-min. climb to the summit. Alpine flora carpets the surrounding area of the summit, from which there is an incredible view extending as far as the Kii Peninsula in the east, Cape Muroto in the south, the Inland Sea in the north and the Shikoku mountains in the west. A descent to Koritori can be made in 3 hrs 30 min. There is a bus to Anabuki Station on the JR Tokushima Line from the Kawakami-Shako Bus Stop, a 40-min. walk from Koritori.

Tsurugikyo Gorge ⎡105⎤ : A ravine of the Anabuki River, a main tributary of the Yoshino River that runs along the route from Anabuki to Mt. Tsurugi. It is about 33 km long and is composed of Sho (Minor)-Tsurugikyo Gorge and Dai (Major)-Tsurugikyo Gorge.

Iyakei Gorge ⎡105⎤ : This ravine follows along another major tributary of the Yoshino River, the Iya River. Awa-Ikeda, a junction for the JR Dosan Line and the JR Tokushima Line, is the entrance. Awa-Ikeda can be reached from Takamatsu by limited express on the JR Dosan Line in 1 hr.15 min. or by driving 55 km along National Highway 32. From Tokushima, it can be reached by express on the Tokushima Line in 1 hr.20 min. or 72 km by car on National Highway 192.

Iya Valley extends 45 km from Iyaguchi, 16 km south of Awa-Ikeda, to Sugeoi via Kyojo. There are sheer, 100-m-high cliffs along both sides of the riverbank. The verdure of spring and the reddish tints of autumn are exquisite. Iya Spa in the gorge is reached by a 200-m descent in a cable car. There is an outdoor hot-spring bath at the bottom of the ravine.

The local residents are said to be descendants of the Taira Clan; defeated at Yashima by the Minamoto Clan in 1185 and isolated from the rest of the world, they have many unique customs. To facilitate contact within their village, they built the famous Iya-no-Kazura Bashi (lit. Vine-made Suspension Bridge) in the deep valley. Made of silvervine, the bridge near Zentoku is 42 m long, 2 m wide, and rises 15 m above the water surface. There is another one in Nagoro. Buses leave from Awa-Ikeda Station for Zentoku (1 hr.) and Nagoro (2 hrs. 40 min.). In addition, there is a 5.7-km toll road from Oboke Station on the JR Dosan Line or a bus that takes in 1 hr.

Oboke and Koboke 105 : These are two ravines located near the stations of the same names on the JR Dosan Line. It is more worthwhile to visit Oboke in the south than Koboke in the north. Oboke can be reached from Awa-Ikeda in 25 min. by express on the JR Dosan Line. Located on the upper reaches of the Yoshino River, it is the most representative of the gorges in Shikoku. This 3-km-long gorge offers the diverse beauty of its strangely shaped rocks. From 1.5 km north of Oboke Station, a riverboat shoots down to Dotoko in 20 min. It is a 2-km stroll from here to Koboke.

Southern Tokushima Prefecture

Komatsushima 105 ☎08853: This port town of 44,716 adjoins Tokushima on the southeastern edge of Shikoku. From Tokushima take the JR Mugi Line to Minami-Komatsushima (20 min.) or drive 10 km down National Highway 55. Ferries run from Osaka and Wakayama. There are many textile and pulp factories in this industrial port.

Tatsueji Temple 105 : Situated 300 m southwest of Tatsue Station on the JR Mugi Line, this temple is the 19th Station on the 88-Temple Pilgrimage in Shikoku. It contains a color-painted Gautama Buddha and two attendants, all designated as Important Cultural Properties.

Kakurinji Temple: Situated 12 km southwest of Tatsue Station, it is the 20th Station on the 88-Temple Pilgrimage in Shikoku. Nestled in a thickly wooded grove of ancient cedars, the temple contains a standing wooden image of *Jizo-Bosatsu*, the divine guardian of children, travelers and pregnant women. It is an Important Cultural Property.

Anan 105 ☎0884: Pop. 60,769. From Tokushima, the city is 35 min. by express on the JR Mugi Line or a 25-km drive down National Highway 55. Located at the mouth of the Nakagawa River, it faces Tachibana Bay. Since it has been designated as a "New Industrial City," efforts are being made to develop paper and chemical production. Yahoko Shrine, 10 min. by bus from the city, is believed to have been founded during the latter part of the Heian period (794-1185). It

houses two wooden images of Shinto deities that have been designated as Important Cultural Properties.

Muroto-Anan Kaigan (Coast) Quasi National Park 105 : Occupying an area of 72.2 sq.km, the park is highlighted by a 200-km-long
seashore stretching along the southeast coast of Shikoku from Anan
in the north to Cape Muroto in the south. Although somewhat
inaccessible, the area is rich in natural beauty with many cliffs and
inlets as well as clusters of subtropical plants. It is inhabited by huge
turtles.

The JR Mugi Line starts at Tokushima and extends southward to
Kaifu. An express will arrive in Mugi in 1 hr.35 min., or it is a 70-km
drive along National Highway 55. Places of interest around Anan
include the lookout on 247-m-high Mt. Tsunomine and Cape Gamoda
at the eastern tip of Shikoku. Cape Gamoda, known as the nesting
ground of the turtles, is an excellent camping ground and is accessible
by car or boat.

Turtles also come to nest on the beach at Hiwasa. A turtle
Museum stands nearby. The coast of Semba-Kaigai (lit. Sea Cliff), an
ideal spot for fishing with beautiful pine groves, is 4 km south of here.
There is an excursion boat. Disembark at Hiwasa Station on the JR
Mugi Line. A toll road called the " Minami-Awa (South Tokushima)
Sun Line" follows along the coast from Hiwasa to Mugi. Mugi has
a diversely beautiful coastline, while Oki-no-Oshima, in the offing, is
reached by sightseeing boat. The huge area from the north to east
side of the island is a big Marine Park. Lying 20 km to the south,
Mitoko Bay is famed for its seascape similar to that of Matsushima
in the Tohoku District—one of the three most beautiful sights in
Japan. Takegashima Marine Park is also nearby. A bus goes from
Mugi Station to Cape Muroto (only one service a day).

Section VIII. Kyushu and Okinawa

Kyushu, lying southwest of Honshu, is the third largest of Japan's four main islands. Including smaller adjacent islands, it covers an area of 44,296 sq.km or 11.3% of Japan's total land mass, and has a population of 12.2 million. The narrow Kammon Straits between Honshu and Kyushu can be crossed by four routes: two railway tunnels, an expressway tunnel and a suspension bridge. On the east, the Bungo Channel separates the island from Shikoku, with the East China Sea stretching out to the west. In the south, the Satsunan Islands extend toward Okinawa.

The inland part of Kyushu is mountainous, with many peaks soaring to 1,700 m, including Mt. Kuju, Mt. Sobo and Mt. Kirishima. The highest is Mt. Miyanoura (alt. 1,935 m) on Yakushima Island. There is a countless number of scenic attractions in Kyushu, each with its own unique appeal. Kyushu is characteristically rich in beautiful seacoasts and various types of hot-spring resorts, including more than 150 well-known spas with an abundance of hot mineral waters. Kyushu has played an important part in cultural development from the very beginning of Japanese history. Besides its historical remains that have served as the basis for mythological legends, the island has traditionally been the site of interchange with foreign countries (especially China and the Korean Peninsula).

PARKS

There are five national parks: Saikai, Unzen-Amakusa, Aso-Kuju, Kirishima-Yaku and Iriomote. Saikai National Park extends from Sasebo and Hirado to the Goto Islands in the west. Unzen-Amakusa National Park covers the entire Shimabara Peninsula, Upper-and Lower-Amakusa islands, and other small islands. Aso-Kuju National Park contains Mt. Aso, which has the world's largest caldera, and the Kuju Mountain Mass. Kirishima-Yaku National Park, which is bordered by Mt. Kirishima of mythological legend as well as the Satsuma and Osumi peninsulas, includes Kinko Bay with an active volcano, Sakurajima and Yakushima Island lying to the South. A marine national park is formed by Iriomote Island and the southern part of the Yaeyama group of islands.

There are eleven quasi-national parks: Kita-Kyushu, Genkai, Iki-Tsushima, Yaba-Hita-Hikosan, Nippo-Kaigan(Coast), Sobo-Kata-muki, Kyushu Chuo-Sanchi (Central Mountains), Nichinan-Kaigan(Coast), the Amami-Gunto(Islands), Okinawa-Senseki(Old Battlefields) and Okinawa-Kaigan(Coast).

HISTORY

Kyushu is considered as the cradle of Japanese civilization. Tradition says that the first Japanese Emperor, Jimmu, launched his eastward expedition by sea from the Province of Hyuga (now,

Miyazaki Prefecture) and laid the foundation for the Yamato Court somewhere south of Nara in 660 B.C. From around the fourth century onward, Kyushu figured prominently as the center of traffic with Korea and China, with a distinctive culture flourishing around Dazaifu—the political focal point of the island at the time. Kyushu is also invariably associated with the abortive Mongol invasions. Kublai Khan's two futile attempts to invade Japan were made at Hakata (now, Fukuoka) in 1274 and 1281(refer to p.91).

After Japan adopted an isolationist policy in 1635, Nagasaki became the only porthole through which foreign cultures trickled into Japan. In 1637 some 40,000 rebellious Japanese Christians were wiped out in a final stand at Shimabara, leaving behind many tragic stories of martyrdom. During World War II, Nagasaki had the misfortune of being atom-bombed three days after Hiroshima, but it has since been restored to its former position as Japan's leading shipbuilding port and the center of Catholicism. For administrative purposes, Kyushu is divided into seven prefectures—Fukuoka, Kagoshima, Kumamoto, Miyazaki, Nagasaki, Oita and Saga.

TRANSPORTATION

Transportation to Kyushu

The main gateway to Kyushu is Fukuoka (the JR station is called Hakata). The JR Tokaido-Sanyo Shinkansen goes to Hakata, taking 5 hrs. 47 min. from Tokyo by the fastest bullet train (Shinkansen) and about 3 hrs. from Osaka. Kyushu has six airports—Fukuoka, Oita, Kumamoto, Nagasaki, Miyazaki and Kagoshima. All of them are closely connected with Tokyo, Osaka and other major cities by direct flights. Fukuoka, Nagasaki, Kagoshima and Kumamoto have international airports, with flights to/from Southeast Asia, China, Guam, Saipan and Australia. The leisurely traveler will be delighted by the boat trip he can take through the Inland Sea from Osaka or Kobe to Beppu. Car ferry is also available from Tokyo to Kokura, from Osaka to Oita, Miyazaki and Kagoshima, from Kobe to Miyazaki, etc.

Transportation within Kyushu

There are three JR trunk lines starting from Hakata (Fukuoka): the Kagoshima Main Line that runs via the west coast to Nishi-Kagoshima, the Nippo Main Line that travels along the east coast to Beppu, Miyazaki and over to Nishi-Kagoshima, and the Nagasaki Main Line that goes all the way to the western tip of Nagasaki. The eastern and the western Parts of Kyushu are tied together by the Kyudai Main Line running between Kurume and Oita, and the Hohi Main Line between Kumamoto and Oita. Airlines fly from Fukuoka to Miyazaki and Kagoshima, and from Nagasaki to Miyazaki and Kagoshima. Smaller aircraft fly from Fukuoka, Nagasaki and Kagoshima to the surrounding islands. An expressway network covering Kyushu is currently under construction. The Kyushu Expressway extends from Kitakyushu to Hitoyoshi via Fukuoka,

Kumamoto, and from Ebino to Kagoshima. The Nagasaki Expressway runs through to the Oita Expressway, traversing Kyushu from
Nagasaki to Hita and from Yufuin to Beppu, while the Miyazaki
Expressway has opened between Ebino and Miyazaki (As of April
1990). Several bus companies offer long-distance service via expressways connecting major cities. Coastal ship routes are mostly concentrated on the west coast, especially in the area around the Amakusa
Islands. There are also ships leaving from Kagoshima Port to the
Satsunan Islands and Okinawa.

Area 1. Fukuoka Prefecture

Fukuoka Prefecture is in the northern part of Kyushu, separated
from Honshu only by the narrow Kammon Straits. The Onga River
flowing northward and the Chikugo River flowing westward form a
basin in this plain, which has been inhabited since the fourth century.
Kitakyushu on the northern end is a port town and a major heavy-
industry center. The Chikuho coal fields in the east-central region
were once a mining center, but they are now on the decline. Except
along the Ariake Coast, the south is an agricultural region where tea
and fruit are grown.

Fukuoka ⌷108/112-113⌷ ☎ 092

Pop. 1,169,145. Serving as the capital of Fukuoka Prefecture, this
is the largest city in Kyushu. It covers the area along the Hakata Bay
Coast and the main part of Fukuoka Plain. The city is divided by the
Nakagawa River, with Hakata area to the east and Fukuoka area to
the west and the entire city is named Fukuoka. Hakata was formerly
called Nanotsu (Port of Na). This port town had a close relationship
with the Chinese mainland, supporting a large merchant population
during the feudal days. On the other hand, Fukuoka was the location
of the residences of the *samurai* or castle town under the Kuroda
Clan.

Many ancient shrines and temples are found in the city along with
several parks, creating a spacious atmosphere. Fukuoka offers many
excellent opportunities for marine recreation such as Shikanoshima
Island and Umi-no-Nakamichi Seaside Park (which separates the bay
from the open sea). The commercial district is located in Nakasu,
between the Nakagawa River and the Hakata River. Hotels and
restaurants serving such local specialties as *fugu* (blowfish) and
tori-no-mizutaki (chicken stew) line the streets. The river banks here
bustle with popular street stalls, which serve delicious snacks like
fried dumplings, Chinese noodles and barbecued chicken. Tenjincho
and Shintencho near Nishi Nippon Railroad (generally abbreviated as
Nishitetsu) Fukuoka Station make up the shopping district.

TRANSPORTATION
Transportation to Fukuoka

About 6 hrs. from Tokyo or 3 hrs. from Osaka on the JR Shinkan-sen. 1 hr.40 min. from Tokyo or 1 hr.5 min. from Osaka by air. The airport is conveniently located 15 min. by bus from downtown. If traveling by automobile, it is 648 km from Osaka down the Chugoku Expressway, then switching to the Kyushu Expressway. It is 64 km from Kokura.

Transportation within Fukuoka Area

In addition to the JR San-yo Shinkansen, trains on the Kagoshima, Nippo and Nagasaki main lines also arrive at the JR Hakata Station. There are frequent departures for Kumamoto, which can be reached in about 1 hr.30 min. by limited express. The terminal of Nishitetsu is the Nishitetsu Fukuoka Station, from where there are frequent departures for Omuta. There are two bus terminals: one at the Fukuoka Kotsu Center in front of the JR Hakata Station and the other at the Fukuoka Bus Center in Tenjin near the Nishitetsu Fukuoka Station. Intercity and intracity buses leave from both terminals, some going as far as Nagasaki, Kumamoto and Miyazaki. The No. 1 Subway Line runs from Hakata Station to Meinohama, directly connecting with the JR Chikuhi Line as far as Nishi-Karatsu. The No. 2 Subway Line extends from Kaizuka to Nakasu, connecting with the No. 1 Subway Line at Kawabata. Boats for Iki, Tsushima and nearby islands depart from Hakata Port.

Regular Sightseeing Buses

The city tour of Fukuoka covers the main sights in 3 hrs. 10 min, including Port Tower, Hakozaki Shrine, Fukuoka Art Museum and Kushida Shrine. There are also two-four tours to Shikanoshima Island and Dazaifu Temmangu Shrine.

LOCAL SPECIALTIES AND EVENTS

Fukuoka is rich in history and many of the traditional crafts and events have been preserved.

The most famous crafts are the *Hakata-Ningyo* Doll and *Hakata-Ori* weaving. *Hakata-Ningyo*, clay dolls with a 400-year tradition, possess an elegant yet colorful beauty. *Hakata-Ori* is a type of brocade weaving originally brought from China in the 13th century and mainly used for *obi*(sashes).

Fukuoka has some interesting fetes and festivals, of which *Don-taku*, *Hakata Yamagasa* and *Tamaseseri* are the most distinctive and colorful.

Dontaku: May 3-4. The main event is a costume parade, but the *niwaka* (a type of improvised comedy done with masks) and dance performed on the specially erected stage are also highly enjoyable.

Hakata Yamagasa: July 1-15. A festival to honor the guardian god of Fukuoka at Kushida Shrine. Magnificent, gorgeously decorated floats called *Yamagasa* are set up along the streets. They are carried through the city by young men on the 15th—the last day of the festival.

Tamaseseri: January 3. A very masculine fete held at Hakozaki Shrine. Two contesting teams fight half-naked for a purified wooden ball, with the winning team offering the ball to the deities of the shrine.

Refer to the supplement for details regarding the "i" **System Information Center** in Fukuoka.

PLACES OF INTEREST

Sumiyoshi Shrine 113 : Located on a hillside 800 m southwest of the JR Hakata Station. One of the oldest Shinto shrines in Kyushu, it was a favorite place of worship for seafarers. The *Honden* (Main Hall), reconstructed in 1623, is an Important Cultural Property. The annual festival from October 12-14 includes *sumo* matches.

Shofukuji Temple 113 : North of Hakata Station on the banks of the Ishido River. It was founded in 1195 by Eisai (1141-1215), who first introduced Zen doctrines and tea-plant seeds into this country after four years of study in China. It is the oldest Zen Buddhist temple in Japan, belonging to the Myoshinji School of Zen Buddhism. The *dosho* (Korean-style bronze bell) is an Important Cultural Property, while the entire temple grounds have been designated as a Historical Site.

Fukuoka Castle 112 : This imposing castle was completed in 1607 after seven years of work by the head of the Kuroda Clan. The donjon has been lost, but the front gate, turret and tenement gate remain. The municipal stadium and the Heiwadai Baseball Stadium are located here in an area that is open to the public as Maizuru Park.

Ohori Park 112 : 4 km west of the JR Hakata Station. Formerly the site of the moats of Fukuoka Castle, the park has a large pond where boating and fishing can be enjoyed. Beautiful willows and azaleas fringe the pond. A huge sundial was erected in 1959. Fukuoka Art Museum in the southeast part of the park contains the famous Imperial gold seal from the Chinese Emperor of the first century, treasures from the Kuroda Clan, the Matsunaga collection of tea utensils and many other valuable items.

Nishi (West) Park 112 : Located 5 km west of Hakata Station. This scenic spot, with some 4,000 cherry trees as well as azaleas, attracts crowds of people in season. The hill provides a fine view of Hakata Bay and the Genkai-nada Sea.

Minami (South) Park 112 : 4 km southwest of the JR Hakata Station in the Hirao Hill region. Pine, chinquapin and camphor trees provide a thick blanket of green. The municipal zoo and botanical garden are located in the park.

Higashi (East) Park 113 : Situated 2 km north of the JR Hakata Station. A monument commemorating the Mongol Invasions of 1274 and 1281(refer to p.91) as well as bronze statues of Emperor Kameyama (the emperor at the time of invasions) and Nichiren, the founder of the Nichiren sect, (who prayed for victory) stand amidst a grove of pines.

Hakozaki Shrine ⌈113⌋: Located 3 km north of the JR Hakata Station. Also called Hakozaki Hachiman, the Shinto shrine was founded in 923. It is one of the most famous Hachiman shrines in Japan. *Haiden* (Oratory) and *Honden* (Main Hall), both built in 1546, *Romon* (Two-Story Gate), constructed in 1594 without using a single nail, and the stone *torii* gate, constructed in 1609, are all Important Cultural Properties. The shrine is noted for the festival of *Tamaseseri* (refer to p.841). The *Hojo-e* Festival from September 12–18 is also famous. *Hojo* means the release of captive birds or animals, and many pigeons are released into the sky during this festival.

Kashiigu Shrine ⌈108⌋: Dedicated to the ancient Emperor Chuai (reigned 192–200), who dispatched troops to the Korean Peninsula, and his empress, Jingu. *Honden* (Main Hall), rebuilt in 1801, is an Important Cultural Property. Venerable pines and chinquapins are scattered through the grounds.

Umi-no-Nakamichi: A 12-km-long sandbar that embraces Hakata Bay to the west of Fukuoka City, with Shikanoshima Island lying at its tip. It can be reached by bus from Fukuoka in 1 hr.15 min. or by a municipally operated ferry from Hakata Port in 45 min. A nationally managed coastal park is constructed with six pools, a plaza and an animal park. Shikanoshima Island is where the gold seal of ancient Japanese history was unearthed in 1784. The gold seal is believed to have been conferred by the Chinese Emperor in A.D. 57 to the Japanese Emperor in return for his tribute. The 165-m-high Shiomidai Plateau provides a good view of the Genkai-nada Sea to the north and Hakata Bay to the south. The island coast offers excellent swimming spots, and there is a National Vacation Village at the northern tip with lodgings and sports facilities.

Genkai Quasi-National Park ⌈108⌋: The marine park covers 111 sq. km along the Genkai-nada Sea. It extends 90 km from east to west, from the coast of Wakita in Fukuoka Prefecture to the Higashi-Matsuura Peninsula in Saga Prefecture, and includes some twenty islands off the coast. Covered with luxuriant black pines, the coastline is characterized by cliffs of basalt. It is one of the ideal recreation areas in northern Kyushu. Ruins of the stone walls used for defense against the Mongol invasion of 1281 can be seen.

Keya-no-Oto (Great Cave of Keya) ⌈108⌋: Located on the western tip of Itoshima Peninsula, 30 min. by bus from Chikuzen-Maebaru Station on the JR Chikuhi Line. A gigantic, 64-m-tall rock, composed entirely of basalt, juts out into the ocean, the northeast side of which forms a cave mouth 10 m high and 18 m across. When the sea is calm, it can be penetrated for a distance of about 50 m by boat.

Munakata Grand Shrine ⌈108⌋: Standing 22 km to the northeast of Fukuoka, 15 min. by bus from Togo Station on the JR Kagoshima

Main Line. The shrine actually consists of three shrines: Hetsu Shrine on the Kyushu mainland, Nakatsu Shrine on Oshima Island and Okitsu Shrine on Okinoshima Island. Three goddesses have been enshrined here since ancient times. *Honden* (Main Shrine) and *Haiden* (Oratory) at Hetsu Shrine are Important Cultural Properties. Okinoshima Island is covered with the remains of ancient religious ceremonies. Of the many artifacts from the fourth and fifth centuries that have been excavated, then collected at Hetsu Shrine, most are National Treasures.

The coast that continues northeast of Shikanoshima Island is excellent for swimming and fishing.

Southern Fukuoka Prefecture

Futsukaichi Spa ⬛108⬛ : 25 min. by JR from Hakata or 15 min. by Nishitetsu limited express. Nishitetsu forms a junction here with the train heading for Dazaifu. There are twenty *ryokan* or Japanese-style inns here at the spa, which has flourished from the days of Dazaifu (see below). Mt. Tempai, a 258-m-high hill to the southwest of the spa, is said to be where Sugawara Michizane (see below) offered prayers to the Emperor in Kyoto.

Dazaifu Temmangu Shrine ⬛108⬛ : Standing 500 m, or 5 min. on foot to the northeast of Dazaifu Station. This terminal station for the Nishitetsu Dazaifu Line is a 40-min. journey from Fukuoka via Nishitetsu-Futsukaichi. Established in 905 and dedicated to Suga-wara Michizane (or Tenjin, Sugawara's deified name), this is the main shrine of the Temmangu shrines found throughout Japan. The present Main Shrine, a beautiful, lacquered edifice constructed in 1590, has been designated as an Important Cultural Property. Since Tenjin is the god of scholarship, the Temmangu shrines all over Japan are busy throughout the year with students praying for success on their exams.

The grounds shelter many plum trees, a favorite of Michizane, including the *Tobi-Ume* (lit. Flying Plum Tree), which is said to have flown to the shrine from the garden in Michizane's former residence in Kyoto to follow him into exile. The plum trees blossom in mid-February. The shrine's *Tsuina* festival, held on the night of January 7, has two main parts: the *Usokae* ceremony in which carved birds (bullfinch) are exchanged and the *Onisube* ceremony to smoke out a demon. The *Shinko* ceremony is held from September 23–25.

Sugawara Michizane (845–903) was the greatest scholar of Chinese literature of his day. After reaching a top post at the Imperial Court in Kyoto, he was demoted through the intrigues of a rival to the post of vice governor general of Kyushu. After reaching his place of exile, he never left his residence and devoted himself entirely to study. He was posthumously deified and worshipped all over Japan as a guardian god of scholarship.

Remains of Dazaifu Governmental Offices (Office of the Governor General of Kyushu): Established in the seventh century as an outpost of the Nara (later Kyoto) Court, the office existed through the 14th century. Located 2.5 km north of the Futsukaichi Station on the JR Kagoshima Main Line, it is now an historical park. The stone foundations of the main chambers of state, the east and west chambers, and several gates are among the total of 71 remains. It has been designated as a Place of Historical Importance.

Kanzeonji Temple: When it was completed in 746, the temple consisted of many buildings. It was the largest temple in western Japan and a center for Buddhist worship. The present *Kodo* (Lecture Hall) and *Kondo* (Main Hall) were reconstructed in the 17th century and have been designated as Important Cultural Properties. Besides the many images of Buddha and art objects in the storehouses, the *dosho* (bronze bell) in the *Shoro* (Belfry) dates from the seventh century and is a National Treasure.

Kurume ☐108☐ ☎0942: Pop. 224,262. The city is located 28 min. by limited express from Fukuoka on the JR Kagoshima Main Line, 30 min. by Nishitetsu limited express, or 45 km along the Kyushu Expressway. Situated in the southwestern part of Fukuoka Prefecture in the middle section of the Chikugo River, it serves as a commercial and communication center of the Tsukushi Plain. The JR Kyudai Main Line trains leave for Oita and Beppu on the east coast of Kyushu, with the express taking about 2 hrs. 50 min.

Kurume was formerly the castle town of the Arima Clan and is known for a kind of woven cotton cloth called *Kurume-gasuri*, but now there are many large rubber factories. *Kurume-gasuri* is indigo-dyed fabric with white splashed patterns. It has been produced for 180 years with a popularity that continues today.

Suitengu Shrine: About 300 m to the west of the JR Kurume Station along the Chikugo River. Founded in 1185, the shrine is dedicated to Emperor Antoku. It is believed to afford protection from calamities at sea and promote easy childbirth. The River Festival is held here from May 5-7.

Chikugo River ☐108-109☐: Originating in the Kuju Mountain Chain, flowing through the Tsukushi Plain and emptying into the Ariake Sea, this is the longest river in Kyushu (143 km). Fertile farmland spreads out along both banks, and many hot springs can be found around it, including Harazuru with a sulphurous content, Funagoya with a carbonated content, Chikugogawa, Yoshii and several others. Funagoya Spa is also famous for fireflys. There is a total of about 30 *ryokan* around the four spas. Cormorant fishing is famous around the Chikugo River.

Koishiwara: Located at the eastern edge of Fukuoka Prefecture, the village can be reached in 2 hrs. 10 min. by bus from Fukuoka. It is about 45 km along the Kyushu Expressway from Dazaifu Interchange. More than 50 kilns are producing *Koishiwara-yaki* pottery in Koishiwara. *Koishiwara-yaki* is handmade pottery mainly colored brown or gray. Many ancient examples can be seen at the Koishiwara Kogeikan Hall.

Yame 108 ☎0943: Pop. 40,375. Yame is the commodity distribution center for the southern part of Fukuoka Prefecture. The cultivation of Japanese green tea, called *Yame-cha*, and chrysanthemums (grown with electric lighting) are flourishing industries in addition to special Japanese paper and stone lanterns. As the largest tumulus in Kyushu, Iwatoyama lies to the northwest of the town. It is believed to be the grave of Tsukushi-no-kimi, a local headman in the sixth century. Stone figures of people and horses and *haniwa* (clay figures) have been excavated here. There are some 200 other tumuli in the area, of which eight have been designated as Historical Sites.

Omuta 108 ☎0944: Pop. 154,987. Located at the southwestern edge of Fukuoka Prefecture. About 50 min. on a JR limited express from Fukuoka or about 1 hr. on a Nishitetsu limited express. Having developed as a coal town since the 15th century, it became the largest in Japan when Mitsui Mining Co. set up operations in 1889. Today, most of the coal veins have run dry, but chemical and metal industrial complexes have been set up in the area. Miike Port, which formerly flourished as the loading point for shipping coal, was constructed in an unusual lock style to maintain the depth of the water inside the lock constant at 8.5 m or more at low tide. The difference in the ebb and flow of the tide from the Ariake Sea, which the port faces, ranges up to 5.5 m. It is located 3 km from the JR and Nishitetsu Omuta Station, with ferrys today setting off from here over the Ariake Sea to Shimabara Peninsula. Shimabara can be reached by speedboat in 50 min. A tour boat also cruises the Ariake Sea.

Yanagawa 108 ☎0944: Pop. 45,198. Located at the mouth of the Chikugo River, this was a castle town during the feudal period. It can be reached from Fukuoka in 20 min. by Nishitetsu limited express. Taking a boat through the waterways that criss-cross the town is an enjoyable way to sightsee. This is also the birthplace of poet Kitahara Hakushu (1885–1942), who portrayed the nostalgic riverside landscape of Yanagawa in his works. A waterway tour takes 1 hr.10 min. Yanagawa is famous for *kabayaki* (broiled eel in a sweet soy-based sauce) and seafood cuisine made from *mutsugoro* or mudskippers and *kuchizoko* or sole from the Ariake Sea.

Tachibana Villa (Ohana): Located in the southwestern part of Yanagawa. This villa erected by the head of the Tachibana Clan in 1697 consists of several buildings, including a *shoin*-style study, a Western-style building from the early Meiji period and a modern hotel. The garden that enfolds it is called Shoto-en and is modeled after Matsushima near Sendai, which is one of the three most beautiful sights in Japan. Many wild ducks roost here during winter. The library has displays of helmets, armor, dolls and other objects used by the *daimyo* (feudal lord).

Kitakyushu 109 ☎093

Pop. 1,029,724. Located on the northern edge of Kyushu with an area of 480.6 sq.km, Kitakyushu is the seventh-largest city in Japan. In 1963 the new city of Kitakyushu was created by merging five existing cities—Kokura, Moji, Tobata, Yahata and Wakamatsu, reducing each of them to the status of a ward although they each retain something of their former urban character. Today, the center of administration and commerce is in Kokura, Moji is a strategic marine transportation center, Yahata is an iron and steel manufacturing district, in Tobata steel manufacturing and deep-sea fishing flourish and Wakamatsu is a bedroom community.

Kokura can be reached on the JR Shinkansen from Tokyo in 5 hrs. 40 min. (1,109 km), from Osaka in 2 hrs. 45 min. (556 km) and from Fukuoka in 55 min. (69 km) by limited express on the JR Kagoshima Main Line. Harbors include Hiake in Kokura and Moji. A car ferry runs from Tokyo and Kobe to Kokura, while the ferry from Osaka goes to Moji Port. If traveling by automobile, it is a 584-km trip from Osaka along the Chugoku and Kyushu expressways. From Kokura, Moji can be reached in 10 min., Tobata in 10 min. and Yahata in 20 min. on the JR Kagoshima Main Line. To Wakamatsu, take the JR Kagoshima Main Line at Orio, transfer to the JR Chikuho Main Line and ride for 16 min. There is also a bus from Kokura taking 15 min.

Kitakyushu ranks with Keihin, Chukyo and Hanshin as one of the largest industrial districts in Japan, with its iron and steelmaking industries and other heavy industries. It also thrives as a manufacturing center for such products as petrochemicals, electrical machinery and food chemicals. There are not a few sights worth visiting such as the Kammon Straits and Hiraodai in the suburban city area. Local products include cutlery, *uni* or sea urchin and *wakame* or seaweed. One of the most famous annual events is *Gion-Daiko* (Big Drum-Beating) Contest in the *Kokura-Gion* Festival for three days from the third Saturday in July. Moji Port Festival is from May 4-6.

Kammon Straits 109 : Flowing between Shimonoseki on Honshu and Moji Port on Kyushu, the channel connects the Inland Sea with the Genkai-nada Sea. Hayatomo, the narrowest part of the channel, is a mere 670 m wide, with a depth of 20 m. The first tunnel dug under the straits was the Kammon Tunnel on the JR San-yo Main Line completed in 1942, followed by a tunnel for automobile traffic in 1958 and the Shin-Kammon Tunnel for the JR Shinkansen in 1974. The Shin-Kammon Tunnel is 18,675 m long, 880 m of which is under the ocean floor.

Kammon Bridge: A 1,068-m-long suspension bridge connecting Dannoura, Shimonoseki in Yamaguchi Prefecture, and Mekari (Moji Ward) in Kitakyushu. The bridge hovers 61 m above the water so that 100,000-ton ships can easily pass under it. It ties together the Chugoku Expressway on Honshu and the Kyushu Expressway on

Kyushu. The six-lane bridge is solely for automobile traffic.

Mekari Park 109 : The park atop on the 175-m-high Mt. Kojo commands a picturesque view of the straits and Kammon Bridge. Many tourists throng the park in spring to admire the cherry trees and azaleas in bloom. The Peace Pagoda at the east end of the park was erected in 1958 through an endowment from Myanmar (Burma) for the repose of the souls lost during World War II in Southeast Asia. A bus is available from the JR Mojiko Station (15 min.) and then a 15 –20-min. walk.

Mekari Shrine: Located on the coast below Mekari Park, the shrine is dedicated to the guardian god of the ocean, and is famous for the *Mekari Shinji* Festival that is held early in the morning of January 1 by the lunar calender. Priests go to the ocean, reap a type of seaweed called *wakame* and offer it to the gods.

Kokura Castle 109 : Standing 700 m southwest of the JR Kokura Station, it was constructed in 1602 by feudal lord Hosokawa Tadaoki. It once had an imposing donjon, 148 turrets and 48 gates, but the castle was destroyed by fire during the Meiji Restoration of 1868. A four-story, five-layer donjon and some turrets were reconstructed in 1959. Part of the grounds is now occupied by Katsuyama Park as well as modern municipal government offices, Municipal Hall, the library and other cultural and recreational facilities.

Kitakyushu Quasi-National Park 109 : Established in 1972, it includes karst-shaped Hiraodai and Sembutsu Stalactite Grotto as well as Mt. Hobashira in Kokura, the northern coast of Wakamatsu, Mt. Fukuchi (alt. 901 m) where the Agano pottery kilns are located, and Agano Gorge.

Hobashira Natural Park: Located to the south of Yahata Ward. Mt. Sarakura (alt. 622 m) is centrally situated in the chain running through this natural park that includes Mt. Gongen, Mt. Hanao and Mt. Hobashira. A cable car runs from the bus terminal to the top of Mt. Hobashira, and from here, it is a 1-hr. 30-min. hike to the summit of Mt. Sarakura. Besides the natural scenic environment of the park, the view of the Kitakyushu area is magnificent. Kawachi Reservoir is located at the southern base and a concentration of workshops producing ceramics, furniture, weaving, lacquerware and other traditional crafts called Kyushu Mingei (Folk Art) Village is nearby. It is possible to observe the artisans at work.

Hiraodai: Located on the southeastern edge of Kitakyushu, this is a karst (limestone plateau) measuring 6 km from north to south and 2 km from east to west. From the top, exposed limestone and many small caves make this a fascinating sight. The main attraction is the Sembutsu Stalactite Grotto, which can be penetrated 1,200 m, but only 480 m of this is open to visitors. However, the cave runs inward even deeper, and it is still unclear how far it really extends. There is lighting for the first 900 m. Inside, stalactites, stalagmites and stone pillars offer a singular spectacle. It can be reached from Kokura by bus in 1 hr. and takes about 2 hrs. 30 min. to cover.

Dokai Bay: Both banks of the inlet, 6 km from west to east and 1 km from north to south, are lined with steel, cement and other factories. Wakamatsu lies to the north and Tobata to the south, but they are connected by a 2,068-m-long bridge, Wakato Ohashi, of which 680 m is suspended. The bridge was completed in 1962.

Takatoyama Park: Located in eastern Wakamatsu, the peak has an altitude of 120 m and offers an excellent view of Kitakyushu. An observation platform and a pagoda containing Buddha's ashes stand in the park. The azaleas are especially beautiful.

Mt. Hikosan ☐109☐ : Towering along the prefectural border be-tweeen Fukuoka and Oita, this mountain has an altitude of 1,200 m. The volcanic range is divided into three peaks: Kita(North), Naka(Central) and Minami(South). Much of the nature in the area is well preserved and the mountain abounds in flora and fauna, making it a delightful retreat in summer and skater's paradise in winter.

Hikosan Shrine monasteries and priests' quarters dot the mountain-side from midway up to the peak and are popular with pilgrims. A 25-min. bus ride from Hikosan Station on the JR Hita-Hikosan Line (1 hr.25 min. from Kokura) takes one to Jingushita. It is a 1-hr. 30-min. climb to the summit. The entrance to the shrine is marked by the bronze *Kane-no-Torii* Gate dating from 1637. A stroll along the stone-paved path lined with cherry trees leads to *Hoheiden* Hall. The large wooden structure was erected in 1616 and, along with the *torii* gate, is an Important Cultural Property. The treasure house is situated at the back of the hall. One of the oldest Shinto centers in Kyushu, Hikosan Shrine is reputed to have been founded by En-no-Ozunu, a priest who lived in the late seventh century. It rose to fame as the headquarters of the Shugendo sect of Buddhist exorcists. By that time, the shrine had lost its purely Shinto aspects and merged with Buddhism. There were said to be 3,000 dwelling quarters on the grounds during the 16th century, with the position of chief abbot often being filled by an Imperial prince. When the Buddhist elements were eliminated after the Meiji Restoration of 1868, the buildings fell into decay.

Area 2. Saga Prefecture

A small prefecture in the western part of Kyushu, facing the Genkai-nada Sea in the north and the Ariake Sea in the south. The largest city in the north is Karatsu, an ancient port town. The Saga Plain in the southern portion is criss-crossed by creeks with a land-scape that is said to be similar to Chiangnan in China. It is known as one of the major potteries in Japan along with *Arita*, *Imari* and *Karatsu* ware.

Saga ⌐108/114-①⌐ ☎ 0952

Pop. 166,599. The capital of Saga Prefecture, this was a castle town for the Nabeshima Clan during the feudal period. Since the JR Kagoshima Main Line forms a junction with the Nagasaki Main Line at Tosu, Saga can be reached from Fukuoka (Hakata) by limited express in 40 min. (54 km) or 1 hr.25 min. from Nagasaki (101 km). It is a 54–55-km drive from Fukuoka to the Saga-Yamato Interchange on the Nagasaki Expressway. Saga being an agricultural distribution center, its commercial sector is flourishing. Many ancient camphor trees line the streets, reminding the visitor of its feudal past. A folk dance festival with 500-year-old history, *Menfuryu* is held in mid-October at the Saga and Matsubara shrines—both 1.5 km south of Saga Station. Youths wearing devil masks and dangling a drum from their shoulders dance to the accompaniment of music played on drums and gongs.

Hokuzan Dam Prefectural Park: Located about 20 km north of Saga, the park has a reservoir formed by Hokuzan Dam, which was built for irrigating farmland. Surrounded by mountains, the park has a rich scenic beauty as well as such man-made features as a suspension bridge, an observatory and an amusement zone. Boats are available for pleasure trips around the reservoir.

The Yoshinogari Archaeological Site: These extensive ruins of an ancient village were uncovered in 1989. The village was believed to have been settled in the latter half of the Yayoi period (B.C. 3C to A. D. 3C). This discovery was important because it indicated that there were considerably large communities in this part of northern Kyushu during the Yayoi period. History records that during this period, a country known as Yamatai-koku existed somewhere in present-day Japan. There have been two main theories as to whether this country existed in Yamato (present-day Nara) or in the northern part of the island of Kyushu, and this discovery gave considerable credence to the Kyushu theory. Yoshinogari is currently being set up as an historical park. The archaelogical findings themselves are on display. Refer to p.84.

Taku Shrine ⌐108⌐: Dedicated to Confucius. The wooden structure with Chinese elements was built in 1708 and is an Important Cultural Property. In addition to Confucius, the four philosophers—Mencius, Tseng-tsu, Tsu-su and Ku-tsu—are honored here. It is 4 km north of Taku Station on the JR Karatsu Line, 10 min. by bus.

Yutoku Inari Shrine ⌐108⌐: One of the three largest *inari* (tutelary shrines) in Japan and the largest in Kyushu. Set against Mt. Ishikabe, the *Honden* (Main Hall) is a vermilion-painted, Chinese-style building. Founded in 1687, it is famous for the beauty of the cherry trees and azaleas in blossom. 4 km south of Hizen-Kashima Station on the JR Nagasaki Main Line, 10 min. by bus.

Takeo ⌐108⌐ ☎0954: Pop. 35,201. 25 min. from Saga by limited express on the JR Sasebo Line to Takeo-Onsen Station. This is a popular spa-resort town, whose hot springs are located to the north-west of the JR Takeo-Onsen Station and can be reached in 10 min. on foot. The town is situated at the foot of Mt. Horai, with a vermilion gate tower like the undersea "Ryugu Palace" of legend standing at the entrance. There are approximately 35 *ryokan* or Japanese-style inns in the area. Originally a villa for the lord of the Nabeshima Clan, Mifuneyama Gardens are especially popular when the cherry trees and azaleas are in bloom. There is also a grove of 10,000 plum trees at the eastern foot of the mountain.

Ureshino Spa: Another flourishing spa community, hemmed in by hills 14 km south of Takeo (35 min. by bus). The hot-spring water is soothing to the skin and said to be efficacious against neuralgia, women's afflictions and dermatological ailments. There are some 65 *ryokan*. In the Fudoyama section of town stands an enormous tea tree, measuring 2.6 m around the base. Said to be 300 years old, it has been designated as a Natural Monument as Japan's largest tea tree. The spa is also noted for its production of fine, light-flavored tea, widely known as "Ureshino Tea."

Arita 108 ☎0955: Pop. 14,388. 1 hr.20 min by limited express from Fukuoka on the JR Sasebo Line or 15 min. from Takeo-Onsen Station. Arita is a pottery town with about 150 kilns, lying in a narrow valley along the Arita River. In addition to the famous Kakiemon, Imaemon and Gen-emon kilns, Koransha and Fukagawa porcelain are also produced here. A pottery fair is held from April 29 –May 5, with countless stores displaying their wares and attracting more than 400,000 people from all over Japan. Kyushu Ceramic Museum stands on a hill 600 m southwest of Arita Station, offering exhibits with a historical perspective of the ceramics of Arita and all of Kyushu. The museum is rich in superb examples of the past, including the Kambara Collection of 101 antique Imari pieces bought back from overseas collectors.

Other museums for ceramics-lovers are the Arita Ceramic Museum and the Aritamachi History Folk-Art Museum.

Arita is where white porcelain was first produced in Japan. In 1616 a Korean potter by the name of Lee San P'ing introduced the art of manufacturing porcelain to Arita. Broken pieces of porcelain found at old kiln sites have been identified as the remains of elegant, Korean-style bowls in daily usage. Overglaze color decoration, introduced later by Chinese potters, was improved upon by Kaki-emon, who succeeded in creating overglaze decoration in persimmon red—his trademark. Kakiemon's early masterpieces are considered priceless. Increasing sophistication of the art soon attracted the attention of Dutch traders on Dejima Island in Nagasaki, who export-ed them abroad in large quantities. It was not until the Philadelphia Exhibition of 1876, however, that *Arita-yaki* (Arita ceramics) began to attract widespread public attention. Today, large quantities of this porcelain are being exported. It is the exceptionally fine clay and translucent glazes that produce such a superior product.

Imari [108] ☎0955: Pop. 62,171. Located 13 km north of Arita or 25 min. by the Matsuura Railway. This port town lies facing horseshoe-shaped Imari Bay. As the ceramics produced at Arita have been shipped from here since the 16th century, Arita ceramics are called *Imari-yaki*. *Nabeshima-yaki* (Nabeshima ceramics) started production at Okawachiyama, southeast of Imari, in the 17th century. A ceramics fair is also held here from April 1-5.

Nabeshima-yaki Kilns: 15 min. by bus from Imari Station. The Imari-Arita Traditional Crafts Center and Imari Ware Exhibition Center are located near the entrance, while the mountain at the back has been designated as the Nabeshima Fief Kiln Park. During feudal days, the porcelain production method was so treasured that a check-point was set up to prevent the technology (especially, colored decoration) from being stolen. There are about 30 kilns on the hilly road leading to the west that produce celadon porcelain and *Iro* (Colored) *Nabeshima*.

Karatsu [108] ☎0955: Pop. 79,489. About 1 hr.20 min. by the JR Chikuhi Line from Fukuoka or 60 km on National Highway 202, 1 hr. 45 min. by bus. Located in the northwestern portion of Saga Prefecture and facing Karatsu Bay, this port town has been a center for trade and commerce with China and Korea since ancient times. It is still a busy port for fishing in the neighboring seas as well as one of the most popular summer resorts in Kyushu. It also serves as a base for exploring the beauty of the Genkai Quasi-National Park and is known as the home of *Karatsu-yaki* (Karatsu pottery).

Karatsu-yaki is especially treasured by devotees of the tea ceremony. It was developed in the last decade of the 16th century when Toyotomi Hideyoshi (1536-1598), returning from his campaign in Korea, brought back potters among his captives. Today, there are about 20 working kilns.

Karatsu-kunchi of Karatsu Shrine is an annual event, which is held from November 2-4. It is said to have begun over a hundred years ago when a local inhabitant modeled a float after those of the *Gion* Festival in Kyoto. At present, 14 huge, gorgeously decorated floats and giant papier-mâché figures of lions, helmets, fish and ships are drawn through the city by groups of young men in colorful costumes to the accompaniment of lively music. These spectacular floats can be seen on permanent display in the Karatsu Civic Hall next to Karatsu Shrine.

Kinshoji Temple: This Buddhist Temple of the Rinzai sect lies 600m northwest of the JR Karatsu Station. Chikamatsu Monzaemon (1653 -1724), one of Japan's foremost playwrights, is said to have served his novitiate here.

Maizuru Park: Situated 1.5 km to the northeast of the JR Karatsu Station, the park stands on the grounds of what was once Karatsu

Castle. A five-story donjon was reconstructed in 1966, inside of which is a local museum. From the top floor, there is an excellent view of Niji-no-Matsubara and Karatsu Bay.

Niji-no-Matsubara 108 : Located at the foot of Kagamiyama Hill, the area is noted for a stretch of white, sandy beach called Matsu-uragata, along which is a grove of *Kuromatsu* (black pines). It is one of the most picturesque landscapes in Japan because of the interesting shapes of the trees and some historical legends. The beach is also popular as a bathing resort.

Kagamiyama Hill 108 : Alt. 284 m. A road runs from Niji-no-Matsubara right to the summit, which has been turned into a park. According to legend, Otomo-no-Sadehiko was ordered to lead an expedition to Korea in the middle of the sixth century, but he tarried at Matsuura in Hizen Province (now, Saga Prefecture). He fell in love with the daughter of a powerful local family named Princess Sayohime. She was so reluctant to part from him that she climbed Kagamiyama Hill, where she took off her kerchief and waved it until the ships vanished over the horizon. Her intense grief at his absence transformed her into a stone, after which the hill was called *Hire-furiyama* (Kerchief-Waving Hill). The small temple dedicated to *Benten*, one of the Seven Gods of Prosperity, commemorates this ancient romance.

Nanatsugama 108 : Situated at Yakataishi, 14 km northwest along the scenic coast from Karatsu Station. The famed seven caves in the joined columnar cliffs have been designated as a Natural Monument. These caves are of basaltic formation and may be entered by boat on calm days. From Karatsu, it is 40 min. by bus to the entrance and then a 30-min. walk. A glass-bottomed boat offers a 1-hr. 10-min. cruise from Yobuko.

Yobuko ☎0955: Situated 13 km northwest of Karatsu, this fishing port lies at the north end of Higashi Matsuura Peninsula. It faces Kabe Island where an ancient shrine is dedicated to Matsura-Sayohime, the heroine of the legend mentioned above. Besides its many restaurants and *ryokan* serving delicious seafood cuisine, it has a morning market, where fresh fish are sold.

Remains of Nagoya Castle 108 : 50 min. by bus from Karatsu. Toyotomi Hideyoshi had this castle built in 1592 to serve as an advance base from which he sallied forth on his expeditions to Korea. In addition to the donjon, there were entrenchments and encamp-ments in those days, with more than 300,000 soldiers said to have resided here. It has been designated as a Special Place of Historical Importance. The stone walls and paving stones are about all that remain today.

Cape Hado 108 : This cape jutting off the northern edge of Higashi(East)-Matsuura Peninsula can be reached by bus from Kara-tsu in 1 hr. A people's Lodge and camping grounds are located on a grassy plateau together with an ocean observation tower. The sea here has been designated as part of the Genkai Marine Park, with the waters providing a home for tropical fish, lush tropical seaweed and red coral. One way to see this area is to take the glass-bottomed boat from Yobuko, which passes by on the way to Nanatsugama.

Area 3. Nagasaki Prefecture

Nagasaki Prefecture is on the western edge of Kyushu facing the East China Sea. Forty-five percent of the prefecture consists of detached islands such as Iki, Tsushima and Goto(Goto Islands). The shoreline is complex and irregular. On the mainland portion of the prefecture are volcanic mountains such as Unzen and Taradake. Dominated by mountains, the limited agricultural land is intensively cultivated with rice, mandarin oranges, etc., although marine products are the main industry. There is little heavy industry except for the shipbuilding in Nagasaki and Sasebo.

Nagasaki 108/116-117 ☎ 0958

Pop. 444,061. The capital of Nagasaki Prefecture. It is on the west coast of Kyushu at the mouth of the Uragami River, where it empties into Nagasaki Bay. The bay is a deep inlet extending about 5 km from the open sea to the shore and protected by a group of islands at the entrance. Sheltered on three sides by thickly wooded hills, the city is open toward the west. The eastern waterfront teems with commercial activity, while the residential areas rise terrace upon terrace on the hillsides.

Historically, it was the only port in Japan left open to foreign trade by the Tokugawa Shogunate during the period of isolation from 1639 to 1859.

When Nagasaki, together with Hiroshima, was atom-bombed during World War II, the greater part of the city was almost completely demolished. Restoration of the city, however, has been remarkable since the war so that it has now become quite as prosperous as before the war.

Nagasaki serves as the western gateway for Japan's most popular international tourist itinerary, following a route across Kyushu and through the Inland Sea from Nagasaki to Osaka or Kyoto via Unzen-Amakusa National Park, Kumamoto, Aso National Park and Beppu. In addition to its many historic places, annual events and local cuisine, the city and its environs are also very rich in scenic beauty. The climate is mild and invigorating, with an equable temperature in winter and temperate sea breezes in summer.

TRANSPORTATION

About 2 hrs. by limited express from Fukuoka on the JR Nagasaki Main Line or 150 km along the Kyushu Expressway, Nagasaki Expressway and National Highway 34. There are also buses from

Fukuoka and Kumamoto. JR has long-distance sleeper services from Tokyo (1,331 km) and Osaka (774 km) taking about 18 hrs. and 11 hrs. 40 min., respectively. Nagasaki International Airport is situated on the man-made island in Omura Bay. It takes 1 hr.40 min. from Tokyo to Nagasaki by air and 1 hr.10 min. from Osaka. Flights are also available to and from Nagoya, Okinawa, Kagoshima, Miyazaki, Tsushima and Fukue. Air China also operates flights from Shanghai to Nagasaki. It takes 55 min. by bus from Nagasaki to the airport. The city has good streetcar, bus and taxi services. There are two bus terminals; one in front of the JR Nagasaki Station and the other at the Nagasaki Bus Co. head office in Shinchi. Ferries depart from Nagasaki Port to the Goto Islands.

HISTORY

Until the 12th century, Nagasaki was called Fukaenoura or Tamanoura. It was renamed when the district was given as a fief to Nagasaki Kotaro, but in those days it was just a lonely fishing village. It did not develop much until it became an important trading port in 1571 and began attracting trading ships from Portugal, Spain and Holland. Japanese traders soon made it their home port for trade with China and Southeast Asia. In 1587 it was placed under the direct control of Toyotomi Hideyoshi (1536–1598), who ruled a unified Japan, and from this time on, Nagasaki was governed by prefects appointed by the central government established by Tokugawa Ieyasu, Hideyoshi's successor, in Edo (now, Tokyo).

With the expulsion of the Portuguese and Spaniards in 1639, only the Dutch and the Chinese were allowed to continue trading at Nagasaki, the former being confined to the small island of Dejima in the Bay of Nagasaki. All through the period of seclusion, however, foreign learning filtered into Japan through Nagasaki, particularly in medicine, botany and the military arts. When the country was opened in 1859, Nagasaki attained major, if only temporary, importance as a center of Western learning as many ambitious youths flocked here. With the rise of other seats of learning, however, Nagasaki gradually lost its intellectual primacy and popularity.

ANNUAL EVENTS

Hata-age: April 1. A kite-flying festival is held in the surrounding hills, with kite-flyers trying to sever the strings of each other's kites by cleverly manipulating their own. The strings are sometimes reinforced with small pieces of broken glass to make cutting easier.

Peiron: June–August. Annual boat races held in and around Nagasaki. The *Nagasaki Peiron* held on the fourth Sunday in July is especially festive. The racing boats are of peculiar construction—long, narrow and shallow, suggestive of the whalers of the past. Ten or more boats compete in the race, each manned by more than 30 oarsmen.

Bon Matsuri: August 13-15. The Festival of the Departed Souls or sometimes known as the Feast of Lanterns. It is observed with more solemnity at Nagasaki than at most other places. Lanterns are lit at all the cemeteries because it is believed that the souls of the departed revisit their earthly homes during this period. On the third night, miniature boats are provided with lanterns and food for the departed souls and then set adrift in the sea so that loved ones can use them to return to the other world.

Okunchi: October 7-9. Held at Suwa Shrine and regarded as one of the most distinctive Shinto festivals in Japan. During these three days, the streets are filled with processions and the exotic Dragon Dance of Chinese origin is performed to music. Stages are erected in various locations where jugglers and other performers entertain the crowds thronging the streets from the surrounding countryside. It has been designated as an Intangible Folk Culture Asset.

NAGASAKI CUISINE

Known as *shippoku* cuisine, it includes elements of both Chinese and European cooking. There is a Chinatown in Shinchi with a high concentration of Chinese restaurants. *Nagasaki champon* and *sara-udon* are popular noodle dishes using lots of seafood. Sponge cake, called *kasutera* (a Portuguese inheritance), is another Nagasaki specialty.

Refer to the supplement for details regarding the "i" **System Information Center** in Nagasaki.

PLACES OF INTEREST

Site of Martyrdom of the Twenty Six Saints of Japan 117 : Located on a hill in Nishizaka Park in front of the JR Nagasaki Station. Six foreign missionaries and 20 Japanese Christians were crucified here on February 5, 1597, for defying the decree prohibiting Christianity promulgated by Toyotomi Hideyoshi, the military ruler at the time.

Legend has it that for 80 days after the crucifixion, the martyrs looked like sleeping angels, showing no signs of death. As the days passed, many miracles occurred, attracting the attention of local residents, who fenced off the execution site, planted many trees and built a large cross in the center. In May 1949 on the occasion of the quadricentennial of St. Francisco de Xavier's arrival in Japan(refer to p.881), the area was designated as Nishizaka Park. Since then it has become the custom for Christians, not only in Nagasaki but from all over Japan, to gather in the park to commemorate the day of martyrdom (February 5) through prayer. A monument to the 26 martyrs, with their figures carved in relief, and a memorial hall were built in 1962—the 100th year since their canonization.

Nagasaki Park 117 : Formerly called Suwa Park, it is located on a hillside northwest of the city, about 1.5 km from the JR Nagasaki Station. The park contains the Nagasaki Prefectural Library, which is known for its many valuable books and documents on the history and development of Nagasaki Port. There are many objects in the park that commemorate interchange with foreign countries such as a banyan tree planted by General Ulysses S. Grant (former president of the U.S.) and Mrs. Grant, and memorials to three scholars who introduced medicine and botany to Japan during the period of isolation—German physician and naturalist Engelbert Kaempfer (1651–1716), Swedish botanist Carl Peter Thunberg (1743–1822) and German surgeon Philipp Franz von Siebold (1796–1866).

Suwa Shrine ⟨117⟩: Adjoining Nagasaki Park, the shrine is noted for its *Okunchi* Festival. A climb up its 73 stone steps brings one to the shrine precincts, where a panoramic view of the entire city and port can be obtained.

Meganebashi (Spectacles Bridge) ⟨117⟩: 1.5 km south of the JR Nagasaki Station. The bridge, which spans the Nakajima River flowing through the center of the city, is so named because of its double arches. Erected in 1634 by Chinese priest Nyojo, the second abbot of Kofukuji Temple, it is the oldest foreign-style stone bridge in Japan. It has been preserved in its original state and is an Important Cultural Property.

Kofukuji Temple: A Zen temple of the Obaku sect. Known as the Chinese Temples, it was established by and made the family temple of Chinese (especially Nanjing) residents. Itsunen (1601–1668), the third abbot of the temple, introduced Chinese painting to Nagasaki. The temple is a 10-min. walk from Kokaido-mae Streetcar Stop.

Kodaiji Temple: A Zen temple of the Soto sect, south of Kofukuji Temple. The temple precincts contain a 7-m-high image of Buddha and the tombs of Takashima Shuhan (1798–1866), who introduced Western military science and gunnery into Japan, and Ueno Hikoma (1837–1904), a native of Nagasaki and the first Japanese photographer. (He opened a photo studio in 1862)

Sofukuji Temple ⟨117⟩: Established in Imakagomachi in 1629 as the first Zen temple of the Obaku sect in Japan, with a Chinese priest as abbot. The gate tower, built to represent *Ryugu* (a sea-bottom paradise in an ancient Japanese legend), and other structures are fine examples of the magnificent architecture of the late Ming Dynasty (1368–1644). The original Second Gate and the *Honden* (Main Hall) have been designated as National Treasures. Many of the worshippers originally come from Fuzhou in China.

Dejima ⟨117⟩: This artificial island was constructed at the order of the Tokugawa Shogunate to isolate the Portuguese traders. After the expulsion of Portuguese in 1641, Dutch traders were moved from Hirado to this island for seclusion. Today, the foreshore has been filled in so that Dejima has lost most of its distinguishing features. However, a clubhouse utilized by expatriates was moved here to serve as a museum with a 19th-century garden.

Confucian Temple ⟨117⟩: Founded in 1893. The reconstructed temple, which is architecturally Chinese, containing a Chinese historical museum with exhibits of Chinese art and crafts. A 5-min. walk from the Ishibashi Streetcar Stop.

Oura Catholic Church ⌈117⌉ : Located 2.6 km south of the JR Nagasaki Station. The church is of Gothic architecture, with an octagonal spire. It was completed in 1865 under the supervision of Petit Jean, a French missionary, in memory of the 26 Martyrs crucified in 1597. The church has been designated as a National Treasure as the oldest structure of Christian faith in Japan. 5min. on foot from Bentembashi Streetcar Stop.

Glover Garden ⌈117⌉ : 500 m west of Oura Catholic Cathedral, looking down over Nagasaki Port. At the end of the 19th century, this was a foreign residential district, and the Glover Mansion and many other Western-style buildings from the Meiji period stand within the premises of the park. It covers 30,000 sq.m, with a moving sidewalk through part of the park. The old Glover House, a wooden colonial building constructed in 1863, is said to have been the setting for Puccini's opera "Madame Butterfly." Stone-built Alt Mansion, Ringer House and the former Mitsubishi No. 2 Dock House (removed from Mitsubishi Shipbuilding Yard) are other features of the park. 10 min. on foot from the Oura Catholic Church.

Peace Park ⌈116⌉ : Situated in Matsuyamacho, north of the JR Nagasaki Station. The park was laid out to commemorate the exact spot of the atomic explosion at 11:02 a.m. on August 9, 1945. It contains the Nagasaki International Culture Hall, which was built in 1955 under the Nagasaki International Culture City Law promulgated in 1949. It is a steel-framed, ferroconcrete structure with six stories above ground, a basement and a beautiful garden in front. The building contains a hall, conference room, municipal museum, data room on the atomic explosion and restaurant. The annex is an auditorium that can accommodate 1,000 persons.

Another feature of the park is the bronze Peace Statue. This unique male figure representing peace measures 9.7 m high and rests on a 4-m-tall pedestal.

Urakami ⌈116⌉ : Noted as the area where large numbers of Christians retained their faith despite persecution by the Tokugawa Shogunate. Christianity was never entirely eradicated from Kyushu during the 18th century, and at the time of the Meiji Restoration in 1868, many people re-acknowledged their Christian faith. The Urakami Catholic Church was dedicated in 1914 after 32 long years of construction work, although the two towers at the entrance were not completed until 1925. Until it was destroyed by the atomic bomb, this was the largest church in the Far East, with a seating capacity of 600. A new ferroconcrete structure with seating for 1,300 people was completed in 1959.

Mt. Inasa Park ⌈116⌉ : To the west of the city, the mountain (alt. 333 m) commands a fine view of the city and harbor. The night view is also superb. An aerial cable car goes to the top in 5 min.

Nagasaki Aquarium: Located 6 km south of the city in Aba. The aquarium opened in 1959, displaying 5,500 fish of 380 species from along the Kyushu coast. 30 min. by bus from the JR Nagasaki Station.

Nagasaki Peninsula [108]: A long narrow peninsula projecting to the southwest of the city of Nagasaki. A ferry runs to Tomioka on the Amakusa Islands from Mogi Port on the east coast (1 hr.10 min.).

Cape Waki in Nomozaki at the tip of the peninsula is the home of Nomozaki Marine Land, which contains a shell museum displaying 8,000 kinds of shells and a prefectural, subtropical botanical garden. 1 hr.10 min. by bus from the JR Nagasaki Station.

Unzen-Amakusa National Park [108]

Covering Mt. Unzen in the middle of the Shimabara Peninsula and the Amakusa Islands to the south, the park has an area of 255 sq. km. It was designated as a national park in 1934. Unzen is a volcanic region with an abundance of hot springs, while from late April to late May the wild azaleas attract many visitors with their colorful blossoms. Kami Island and Shimo Island, the two main islands among the Amakusa Islands, are connected to the Kyushu mainland through a series of five bridges. The seascape of the west coast, where many Christian relics can be found, is spectacular. Amakusa will be refferred to in the later section.

Isahaya [108] ☎0957: Pop. 88,393. Situated at the neck of the Shimabara Peninsula, this old castle town serves as its entrance. From Nagasaki, it can be reached in 20 min. by limited express on the JR Nagasaki Main Line or by bus in 50 min. From Fukuoka a limited express will arrive in 1 hr.45 min.

Mt. Unzen [108]: An extinct volcano chain in the central portion of the Shimabara Peninsula. The main peaks include Mts. Myoken, Nodake, and the highest, Fugen, with an altitude of 1,359 m. Panoramic views from these peaks are particularly impressive because of the unusual scenery of the peninsula. The seasonal aspects of Mt. Unzen deserve particular mention for among its glories are the splendid display of azaleas in May, the brilliant foliage of the maples in autumn and the "silver thaw" in winter when the trees are coated with ice.

Delightful excursions to Nitta Pass (alt. 1,100 m) between Mts. Myoken and Nodake can be made in 30 min. by bus from Unzen Spa. A ropeway leads to the top of Mt. Myoken, which commands an extensive view. Mt. Fugen is about a 1 hr.-climb from the top of Mt. Myoken.

Unzen Spa ☎ 0957: Located at an altitude of 700 m near the southwest base of Mt. Unzen. There are three groups of hot springs at the spa: Furuyu, Shinyu and Kojigoku. The abundant waters are said to be efficacious against neuralgia and rheumatism. There are 24 *ryokan* or Japanese-style inns, and because of the refreshing summer climate (rarely surpassing 27°C), the area was originally developed as a resort for foreigners and includes many stylish hotels. The spa can be reached by bus from the JR Nagasaki Station in 2 hrs. 10 min. or from the JR Isahaya Station in 1 hr.20 min.

Unzen Jigoku (Hell): The area in the east behind the hot-spring town contains thirty solfataras and fumaroles, the water from which overflows into a pond that is constantly agitated. Everywhere are beds and mounds of whitish earth, from which rise dense clouds of steam, while the paths are bordered with streams stained many colors by the chemicals in the water. The area, which can be reached by a 30-min. walk from Onsen Shrine, was a site of martyrdom for Christians in the 17th century.

Lake Shirakumo: Located 500 m to the southwest of the spas. Lying at the foot of Mt. Kinugasa, the lake offers boating and good camping grounds in summer.

Obama Spa 108 ☎0957: Situated on the eastern shore of Chijiwa Bay at the southwestern foot of Mt. Unzen, the spa serves as the gateway to Mt. Unzen. It can be reached by bus in 1 hr. 50 min. from the JR Nagasaki Station or 55 min. from the JR Isahaya Station. The water is abundant and can be safely drunk. Besides some 35 *ryokan* along the seashore, swimming and windsurfing are popular activities on Chijiwa Bay. The Unzen National Vacation Village with a hotel and sports facilities lies 5 km to the south of the spa.

Shimabara 108 ☎0957: Pop. 45,074. The city is reached in 1 hr. from Isahaya by the Shimabara Railway or 1 hr.20 min. by bus. From Nagasaki, it is 1 hr.55 min. by bus, or a drive of 70 km along National Highways 34, 57 and 251. There is also a speedboat from Omuta in Kumamoto Prefecture (taking 50 min.) and a ferry from Misumi arriving in 1 hr.

The city is located on the east coast of the Shimabara Peninsula, with Mt. Mayuyama (alt. 819 m) at the rear. It faces Kumamoto Prefecture across the Ariake Sea. During the feudal period, this was a castle town, with remains of the castle and the former mansions of the *samurai* still visible. The sea along the coast is dotted with a group of tiny islands called the Tsukumo Isles (lit. ninety-nine islets). Created by an eruption of Mt. Mayuyama in 1792, they form a landscape of special beauty. There are hot springs, and the seafood is delicious in this tourist town.

Shimabara Castle 108 : Located 400 m west of Shimabara Station on the Shimabara Railway. These are the ruins of the castle built by *daimyo* (feudal lord) Matsukura that is associated with the Christian uprising (Shimabara Rebellion, refer to p.860) from 1637 to 1638. The five-story donjon was reconstructed in 1964 and serves as a museum on Christianity in Japan. One of the turrets has been turned into the Kitamura-Seibo Memorial Museum. Kitamura is the sculptor who created the Peace Statue in Nagasaki Park.

Along the Shimabara Railway: Starting at Isahaya on the JR Nagasaki Main Line, this line circles the peninsula along the coast via Shimabara and arrives at Kuchinotsu Port on the southern tip. The district is full of historic interest because of its connection with the persecution of the Christians in the early 17th century. The ruins of Hara Castle 500 m east of Harajo Station are particularly famous. The "Shimabara Rebellion" began in December 1637, when the peasants of the district rose up against heavy taxes and the prohibition of Christianity by the Tokugawa Shogunate. The uprising was led by Amakusa Shiro, who thought he was the son of God. Some 37,000 believers seized Hara Castle. The Shogunate in Edo had to bring in 125,000 troops to take back the castle. In February of the following year, the rebels were finally quelled, slaughtered to the last man, woman and child. Today, the ruins of the inner citadel and the stone walls remain, with a cross and the statue of Amakusa Shiro standing in the castle precincts.

It takes 1 hr. from Shimabara by Shimabara Railway to get to Kuchinotsu Port on the southern tip, or one can take a 30-min. ferry ride from Oniike Port on Amakusa. This was a port for foreign trade during the early years of the Edo period.

Northern Nagasaki Prefecture

Omura ⎡108⎤ ☎0957: Pop. 71,898. Situated along the east coast of Omura Bay, this was the headquarters of Christian *daimyo* Omura, thriving as a foreign trade port during the early years of the Edo period. The main industries today are dairy products as well as pottery (bricks) and pearl culture. About 45 min. from Nagasaki by rapid train on the JR Omura Line.

Nagasaki Holland Village ⎡108⎤ : A tourist attraction located on the east coast of the Nishi-Sonogi Peninsula, which embraces Omura Bay. It can be reached by bus from Nagasaki in 55 min. or from Sasebo in 40 min. It consists of three zones called Broemendam, Hoorn (along National Highway 206) and Willemstadt, located on the opposite bank of a cove. Besides a windmill and a marine museum, the sailing ship Prince Willem is also moored in Broemendam Zone. Hoorn Zone has a museum of Dutch culture amidst the facade of a port town. Willemstadt Zone, a re-created 17th-century Dutch town, includes the city, the outlying rural villages and a port. A wooden paddle-wheel steamer cruises around Omura Bay.

An admission ticket for Holland Village allows one to enter the nearby Nagasaki Bio-Park, with a 300,000-sq.-m zoo and botanical garden containing 450 animals of 85 species.

Sasebo ⎡108⎤ ☎0956: Pop. 248,958. About 1 hr.50 min. by limited express on the JR Sasebo Line from Fukuoka, or 100 km along Kyushu Expressway and National Highway 35. From Nagasaki, it is about 1 hr.40 min. away by rapid train. From Nagasaki Airport on the man-made island, 1 hr.20 min. by boat. If leaving Nagasaki by car, take National Highways 206, 202 and 35 for 75 km. A sleeper limited express travels directly from Tokyo, arriving in 17 hrs. 50

min. and from Osaka in 11 hrs. 30 min.

This port city is located on the northern part of Omura Bay and serves as the gateway to Saikai National Park. Japan Maritime Self-Defense Force and U.S. Navy bases are located here. With an area of 33 sq.km, Sasebo is the port of call for many large ships and is now developing as a port for international trade. Shipbuilding is the major industry here.

Saikai National Park 108

Covering an area of 246.53 sq.km. The park includes part of Hirado Island, the Kujukushima Islands (lit. Ninety-nine isles) and a portion of the Goto Islands. It is characterized by a jagged coastline, with these numerous tiny islands dotting the blue sea. This is also the area where there are many descendants of so-called Secret Christians who went into hiding and maintained the faith during the Tokugawa regime.

Mt. Yumihari: Located west of Sasebo. The top of this 361-m-high peak offers a panoramic view of the Kujukushima Islands. 25 min. by bus from Sasebo Station.

Kujukushima Islands 108 : More than 170 small islets lying close together on a stretch of sea between Hirado Island and the Kyushu mainland. The area is noted for subtropical plants. A 50-min. cruise leaves from Kashimae Port, 6 km west of Sasebo, but the scheduled boat to Hirado also offers a good view of the islets.

Saikai Bridge 108 : A 316-m-long, 42-m-high arched bridge between Hario Island at the mouth of Omura Bay and the Nishi-Sonogi Peninsula. The tide in the Hario Straits under the bridge reaches ten knots (about 19 kph.), with a 3-10-m diameter whirlpool forming in the swift currents. There is an amusement park near the eastern span of the bridge. 40 min. by bus from Sasebo Station.

Hirado 108 ☎0950: A 171-sq.-km island located off the northwestern edge of the prefecture and separated only by a narrow strait. The population is 27,993. From Sasebo, 1 hr.20 min. by Matsuura Railway to Hirado-guchi Station and then by bus across Hirado Bridge in 15 min. Or, one can take a bus from Sasebo Station in 1 hr.35 min. The ferry from Sasebo (Kashimae Port) arrives in 1 hr.5 min.

Hirado was developed as a port of international trade by the feudal Matsuura Clan when the Portuguese landed here in 1550, making it the first such harbor in Japan. The Dutch, English and Spanish later built trading houses here. With the closing of the country to foreign intercourse, these houses were shut down, the Dutch alone being allowed to remain at Dejima (Nagasaki). Markers at Hirado identify the sites of the former English and Dutch houses.

Hirado Kanko Museum: Displaying documents related to Christianity, international trade and isolationism in Japan. There is a heart-rending letter from a girl of mixed parentage exiled to Jagatara (Jakarta of today) by the policy of isolation (the Jakarta Letter) soliciting permission to return to Japan.

Sakikata Park: Located on a hill that commands a panoramic view of the harbor. Memorials to Francisco de Xavier (Jesuit missionary, who arrived in Japan in 1549, refer to p.881) and William Adams (also known as Miura Anjin, an English navigator employed by the Tokugawas, refer to p.441) stand in the park. It is popular with admirers of Hirado azaleas.

Matsuura Historical Museum: A castle-like building standing on a stone base northwest of the harbor. It was once a villa for the lord of the Matsuura Clan, but now serves as a museum, housing a collection of traditional armor and objects related to the suppression of Christianity.

Ruins of Hirado Castle: Located to the south of the harbor on a hill called Kameoka Park. This was the fortified residence of the Matsuura Clan. The donjon and other parts of the castle were reconstructed in 1962.

Senrigahama Beach: An area 8 km southwest of Hirado, 15 min. by bus. The beautiful white expanse of sand makes this an excellent beach for swimming. Cheng Ch'eng-kung (Koxinga), who fought to restore the Ming Dynasty, was born here in 1624. A marker commemorates the site of the house and a grave stone contains a dedication. Cheng died in Taiwan in 1663.

The villages of hidden Christians are scattered on the west and south coasts of Hirado and Ikitsuki Island to the northwest. There are many relics related to their martyrdom.

Goto Islands, Iki and Tsushima

Goto Islands (lit. Five Islands) 108 ☎0959: A chain of some 140 islands of all sizes are scattered off the northwest coast of Kyushu comprising a total area of about 690 sq.km. As the name denotes, it consists of the five larger islands of Fukue, Hisaka, Naru, Wakamatsu and Nakadori. The largest city is Fukue on Fukue Island with a population of 30,591. By plane, Fukue can be reached from Nagasaki in 35 min. or from Fukuoka in 55 min. The ferry from Nagasaki takes 3 hrs. 50 min., and from Fukuoka 13 hrs.

Fishery is the main industry of the islands based on large catches of *buri* (yellowtail) and *tai* (sea bream). Since stockbreeding also flourishes, it is no wonder that Goto beef is famous for its excellent flavor. Places of interest include ruins containing various Christian artifacts, the scenic beauty of the jagged coastline and the marine park of Wakamatsu Island.

Iki-Tsushima Quasi-National Park 108 : The park is composed of the Iki Island with its sea-eroded cliffs and the Tsushima Islands, with their jagged, ria-type coastline. These islands have a unique history and customs as the frontier region that served as a bridge between Japan and the Korean Peninsula.

Iki Island 108 ☎09204: A round island 16 km off the northern coast of the Kyushu mainland with an area of 139 sq.km and a population of 38,856. The main city, Gonoura, can be reached from Fukuoka by speedboat in 1 hr.30 min. There is also an airport (20 min. by bus from Gonoura), which can be reached by a flight from Fukuoka in 30 min. The island offers Shinjo Shrine, where the remains of the Mongol Invasion of 1274 and 1281 (refer to p.91) can be seen, and Mt. Dakenotsuji, which has an observation platform. Fishery is the main industry, with *uni* or sea urchin and dried squid as the specialties.

Tsushima Islands 108 ☎09205: Islands lying some 60 km north-west of Iki Island across the Tsushima Straits. They were originally a single island, but during the Edo period, a narrow passage called the Manzeki Gut was cut through the island, dividing it into two: Kami (Upper) Island and Shimo (Lower) Island. The two islands cover a total area of 709.6 sq.km and have a population of 47,026. The principal town is Izuhara on the east coast of Kami Island, which can be reached by ferry from Fukuoka in 5 hrs. or from Gonoura on Iki Island in 2 hrs. 15 min. By air, flights from Fukuoka arrive in 35 min. and those from Nagasaki in 45 min. The airport is in the northern part of Kami Island along National Highway 382.

The Tsushima Islands, both Kami Island and Shimo Island, are mountainous, with fishery and forestry as the main industries. Places of interest include remains of the So Clan, who ruled Izuhara; the Manzeki Observation Platform, which overlooks the jagged coastline along the Manzeki Gut, and Watatsumi Shrine, the principal shrine of old Tsushima Province. The Korean Peninsula can be seen from Waniura—the northernmost tip of the islands.

Area 4. Kumamoto Prefecture

Kumamoto Prefecture lies along the west coast of central Kyushu. A world-famous volcano, Mt. Aso, sits in the eastern part of the prefecture, while the Amakusa Islands lie in the west, separated by the Ariake and Shiranui seas. There are many hot springs, both in the mountains and along the coast. The main industries include agriculture, forestry and dairy farming, while chemicals, machinery and other manufacturing industries are being developed along the coast.

Kumamoto 109/115-① ☎ 096

Pop. 559,418. The capital of Kumamoto Prefecture, located at the center of the west coast of Kyushu. The city spreads out in the Kumamoto Plain along the Shirakawa River, which flows down from Mt. Aso, and is often called the "City of Woods and Water." It developed as a castle town around the fortress of the Hosokawa Clan. Today, not only is Kumamoto the prefectural center for administration, commerce and transportation, it is also, like Fukuoka, one of Kyushu's bustling, pivotal cities. The shopping center is around the Kami-and Shimo-Toricho district.

TRANSPORTATION

From Fukuoka, Kumamoto can be reached in 1 hr.30 min. by limited express on the JR Kagoshima Main Line, 2 hrs. by bus, or 105 km along the Kyushu Expressway. From Beppu in the east, an express on the JR Hohi Main Line will take 3 hrs. 10 min., a bus 4 hrs., or 150 km along "Yamanami Highway" and National Highway 57. From Nishi(West)-Kagoshima in the south, there is a JR limited express arriving in 2 hrs. 50 min., or one can drive 211 km along National Highway 3. A direct sleeper limited-express from Tokyo arrives in about 17 hrs. (1,295 km), and that from Osaka in 10 hrs. 33 min. (739 km). The airport lies to the east of the city (55 min. by bus). A flight from Tokyo will take 1 hr.35 min. and from Osaka 1 hr.5 min.

Refer to the supplement for details regarding the "i" **System Information Center** in Kumamoto.

PLACES OF INTEREST

Kumamoto Castle 　109 ： One of the most famous castles in Japan. It was completed in 1607 after six years of work supervised by Kato Kiyomasa (1562–1611), then lord of Higo Province (now, Kumamoto Prefecture). Standing on a low hill called Chausuyama, 2 km northeast of the JR Kumamoto Station, the castle has been dubbed "Ginnan (Gingko Nut) Castle" because an enormous gingko tree, said to have been planted by Kiyomasa, grows here.

In 1877 the castle was besieged by a rebel army from Kagoshima led by Saigo Takamori. Although a large part of the castle was burned, the loyal forces triumphed after holding out for 50 days until relief arrived to aid in defeating the rebels (refer to p.881). The stone walls, watchtowers and fences that remain are Important Cultural Properties. The donjon reproduced in 1960 has a museum. Miyukizaka, the sloping path leading up to the castle, is noted for its avenue of cherry trees. 10 min. by bus from Kumamoto Station.

Kato Shrine 　115-① ： Directly north of Kumamoto Castle. The shrine is dedicated to the founder of Kumamoto City and builder of Kumamoto Castle, the brave soldier Kato Kiyomasa. Among the shrine treasures are an *eboshi* (a hat worn in Court)-shaped helmet, sword and war drum used by Kiyomasa himself. Kiyomasa's grave is at Hommyoji Temple, about 3 km north of Kumamoto Station. This temple is affectionately called "Seishoko-san (Mr. Lord Kiyomasa)" by local residents.

Fujisaki Hachimangu Shrine 　115-① ： 4 km northeast of Kumamoto Station, 10 min. by bus. Founded in 935, the shrine is dedicated to Emperor Ojin and his mother, Empress Jingu. The annual festival held September 11–15 features a parade of warriors in ancient costumes and a roundup of horses.

Suizenji Park 〔115-①〕: The landscape garden laid out in 1632 in the villa for the lord of the Hosokawa Clan, who took control of the district from the Kato Clan. Located in the southeastern part of the city, it can be reached by bus in 15 min. from the Kumamoto Kotsu (Transportation) Center. Covering 690,000 sq.m, the park features a crystal-clear pond and a landscape garden modeled after Mt. Fuji and Lake Biwa. *Kokindenju-no-Ma*, a teahouse moved from the Katsura Imperial Villa in Kyoto, stands by the bank of the pond.

Lake Ezu: About 600 m south of Suizenji Park is a large, gourd-shaped lake about 6 km in circumference. Fed by an exceptionally cold spring from the park, it is well stocked with carp, crucian carp and eels. The lake is famous as the origin of a rare species of fresh-water laver called *Suizenji-nori*. A prefectural zoo is located along the shores of the lake.

Tatsuda Natural Park: 10 min. on foot after a 20-min. bus ride from the JR Kumamoto Station. This is the site of Taishoji Temple, the family temple of the Hosokawas. The moss garden and spring-fed pond surrounded by clusters of cypress take the visitor back 300 years in time. Koshoken, the teahouse in the garden, was designed and constructed by Hosokawa Tadaoki (1563-1645). Its latticed paper doors contain no skirting, and the alcove parts have wave patterns, providing a good sample of Tadaoki's refined artistic taste.

Amakusa Islands 〔108〕

More than 70 islands of all sizes in the ocean off the south coast of the Shimabara Peninsula. The largest is Amakusa-Shimo (Lower) Island with an area of 610 sq.km, followed by Amakusa-Kami (Upper) Island with an area of 235 sq.km. Northern Amakusa-Shimo Island faces the Shimabara Peninsula over the Hayasaki Straits; the south-eastern part looks at the mainland of Kyushu over the Shiranui Sea, while the Amakusa Sea, which continues into the East China Sea, touches the west coast. Amakusa-Kami Island lies east of Amakusa-Shimo Island, with bridges connecting the two islands. In addition, eastern Amakusa-Kami Island is connected by bridge to Oyano Island and then to the Kyushu mainland on the Uto Peninsula over the Misumi Straits. These are part of the Amakusa Five Bridges. The islands are mountainous, with most of the peaks having an altitude of around 500 m. The main industries are agriculture, forestry and fishery. It is an excellent place to visit because of the natural beauty of the coastline and the abundance of Christian relics. The islands are part of the Unzen-Amakusa National Park.

TRANSPORTATION

The most common way to get to the islands is to take the bus that leaves from Kumamoto (Kotsu Center and JR Station) and then cross the Amakusa Five Bridges to arrive at Hondo. It takes 2 hrs. 30 min., traversing National Highways 3, 57, 266 and 324 over 90 km. There are many ferries operating among all the major islands: Minamata-

Hondo, 2 hrs; Shimabara–Matsushima, 1 hr. 30 min.; Kuchinotsu–Oniike, 30 min.; Minamata–Ushibuka, 1 hr. 25 min.... and many more. The main mode of transportation on the islands is by bus.

Amakusa Five Bridges ⌷108⌷: A group of bridges connecting the Amakusa Islands and the Kyushu mainland at Misumi. Each one is designed and color-schemed to match the landscape. Completed in 1966, they extend a total of 12 km. The route is sometimes called the "Pearl Line."

Amakusa-Matsushima ⌷108⌷: This designation after scenic Matsushima near Sendai covers 20 islets of a variety of sizes scattered between Oyano Island and Amakusa-Kami Island. Pearls are cultivated here by utilizing many quiet coves. There is a 40-min. boat tour that leaves from Matsushima Port. Mt. Sengan (alt. 162 m) southeast of the port commands a panoramic view of the area.

Hondo ⌷108⌷ ☎0969: Pop. 41,687. Located on the east edge of Amakusa-Shimo Island, the city is the center of administration and culture as well as tourism for the islands. There are also many Christian relics, including Martyrs Park on the site of Hondo Castle, where a monument stands in dedication to the dead of the Shimabara Rebellion. The Christian museum here provides an excellent way to experience the days of the revolt. The coastline has an excellent beach, with an underwater aquarium situated on the north coast.

North and West Coast of Amakusa-Shimo Island: Tomioka on the north coast of Amakusa-Shimo Island is a good port with an old castle at the edge of the island. By heading south along the west coast, one will find the stones used in producing Amakusa stoneware. 30 min. from Tomioka by bus (1 hr.5 min. from Hondo) is Shimoda Spa, where 100-m-high cliffs extend along Myoken-ura Bay. A marine park and two Catholic churches, Oe and Sakitsu, are located here. There were many hidden Christians in this area.

Ushibuka ⌷108⌷: 1 hr.20 min. by bus from Hondo. Located at the southern end of Amakusa-Shimo Island, it sits directly in front of Nagashima Island in Kagoshima Prefecture. This is a fishing town with some orange cultivation. On the small cape south of town is a marine park with a 1-hr. 20-min. tour offered by glass-bottomed boat.

Southern and Western Kumamoto Prefecture

Yatsushiro ⌷109⌷ ☎0965: Pop. 109,221. 20 min. from Kumamoto by limited express on the JR Kagoshima Main Line, 1 hr.10 min. by bus, or 42 km along the Kyushu Expressway. It is located in the western part of the prefecture at the mouth of the Kumagawa River on the Shiranui Sea (Yatsushiro Bay). Besides large factories for paper, cement and many other products a lot of pomelos, watermelons and other agricultural products are also produced here. Nearby are the famous *Koda-yaki*, or *Yatsushiro-yaki*, pottery kilns.

Shiranui Sea: The ocean that lies south of Yatsushiro, extending beyond Nagashima Island of Kagoshima Prefecture. It is known for the *shiranui* (lit. strange lights on the sea), which appears in the middle of the night from late summer through early autumn.

Hinagu Spas 108 : Discovered in 1409, this resort consists of some 30 *ryokan*. The waters are efficacious against neuralgia. The Amakusa Islands can be seen from the shore. The spas can be reached from the JR Yatsushiro Station in 20 min. by bus.

Minamata 108 ☎0966: Pop. 35,463. This city is an industrial center in the southern part of the prefecture and the birthplace of the nitrogen-fixation industry in Japan. 1 hr.10 min. from Yatsushiro by limited express on the JR Kagoshima Main Line. Ferries to Hondo and Ushibuka in the Amakusa Islands leave from here. There are two spas in the area: Yunoko along the north coast and Yunozuru at the foot of the mountains in the southeast.

Hitoyoshi 109 ☎0966: Pop. 41,194. 1 hr.25 min. by express on the JR Hisatsu Line or 57 km on National Highway 219 from Yatsushiro. Located in the southern part of the prefecture, it is situated along the Kumagawa River that flows through the Hitoyoshi Basin. This was a castle town from the Edo period. There are hot springs along the banks of the Kumagawa River, attracting many visitors. The specialties of the region are the fish caught from the Kumagawa River and *Kuma-Shochu* (liquor). To the north of the city lies the tiny village of Itsuki, known through a popular Japanese lullaby of the same name.

Kumagawa Rapids: Some of the fastest rapids in Japan, equaling the speed of those of the Mogami River and Fuji River, and creating a power that is harnessed into hydroelectric power. Its source is the massive 1,722-m-high Mt. Ichibusa that towers over the border between Kumamoto and Miyazaki prefectures. The river is 144 km long.

A rapids-shooting boat goes down the river, leaving from the opposite shore of where the remains of Hitoyoshi Castle stand, and runs down 18 km to Osakama. On the way are Shuri-no-Se, Futamata-no-Se, and many other rapids and pools, making this quite a thrilling ride. The song that the helmsman sings while pulling the oar is the Itsuki lullaby.

Kyushu-Chuo Sanchi (Mountains) Quasi-National Park: Forming the spine of the Kyushu Mountain Chain, the park region spans both Miyazaki and Kumamoto prefectures. The mountain altitudes range from 1,200–1,700 m. Covered with a primeval, glossy-leaved forest, the terrain provides a rough mountain beauty. The main peaks are Mt. Kunimi and Mt. Ichibusa. The gorge in Aya in the southwestern part of Miyazaki is also included. The park covers an area of 270.96 sq.km.

Eastern and Northern Kumamoto Prefecture and Aso

Tamana 108 ☎0968: Pop. 46,061. This garden city lies in the northern part of the prefecture and can be reached from Kumamoto

by the JR Kagoshima Main Line in 30 min. There are many prehistoric tumuli scattered around the area. Tamana Spa is located on the
edge of town.

Etafunayama Tumulus: In Kikusuimachi to the north of Tamana. A
high cultural value is accorded to this tumulus, where a straight
sword inscribed with the silversmith's name (believed to be from the
early fifth centry) was unearthed.

Yamaga ⌈108⌉: A spa town that is famous for a mid-summer festival
held on August 15 and 16 in which the Lantern Dance is performed.
Nabeta Cave Tumili Group is another attraction of the city, where
paintings and sculptures of high cultural value were found.

Tsujun Bridge ⌈109⌉: 1 hr.20 min. away from Kumamoto by bus.
Constructred in 1854, this single-arched stone bridge is in Yabe. A
water pipe runs through the 75.6-m-long bridge, with water spouting
from the drainage mouth in the center. The water is drained only on
Saturdays, Sundays and holidays from September to November. The
bridge is an Important Cultural Property.

Aso-Kuju National Park ⌈109⌉: This alpine park includes two
characteristic sets of volcanoes: Mt. Aso and Mt. Kuju. It also
includes Mt. Tsurumi, which surrounds Beppu Spa and Mt. Yufu.
Covering a total area of 726.8 sq.km, it straddles both Kumamoto and
Oita prefectures. Amidst the magnificent mountain scenery are
gentle plateaus that are treasure-houses of wild azaleas and other
alpine plants. There are abundant hot springs in the area as well.

Mt. Aso ⌈109⌉: A common designation for five peaks of which Mt.
Nakadake (alt. 1,323 m) is active and Mt. Kishima (alt. 1,321 m), Mt.
Eboshi (1,337 m), Mt. Takadake (highest peak, 1,592 m) and Mt.
Nekodake (1,408 m) are extinct. These five peaks create a central
volcanic cone with broad plateaus (crater basins or calderas)—Aso
Valley on the north and Nango Valley on the south. They contain
three towns with 53,000 residents where agriculture and tourism are
the main sources of income.

The outer crater that surrounds the volcanic cone and crater basin
is about 700 m high—extending 24 km from north to south and 18 km
from east to west—and has a circumference of 128 km. Thus, it is the
largest caldera in the world. This gigantic caldera was formed some
80,000-100,000 years ago, but the central volcanic cone only took on
its present form a few thousand years ago.

Mt. Nakadake: The center of the volcanic cone, remaining an active
volcano today. There is a gap from the peak to the west, with a cone
circumference of 4 km and a depth of 100 m. Underground rumblings
resonate through the area and smoke wafts upward. Two ropeways
lead to the crest, but they are closed down when volcanic activity is
particularly violent.

There are two routes of ascent—from the east and from the west.
The western route begins by taking a bus from Aso Station on the JR
Hohi Main Line (1 hr. by express from Kumamoto) for 35 min. One

passes through a spacious grassy plain called *Kusasenri*—the remains of the crater of Mt. Eboshi, used as pasture in summer and ski grounds (with artificial snow) in winter. A bus from Kumamoto goes directly to Mt. Aso in 2 hrs. It is 4 min. to the crater by ropeway.

The eastern route also begins by bus, from Miyaji Station on the JR Hohi Main Line (1 hr.15 min. by express from Kumamoto), with a 15-min. bus ride and 6 min. by ropeway to the crater. Sensuikyo Gorge, famous for the wild azaleas called "Miyama-Kirishima," lies near Asosan-Higashi Station.

Mt. Takadake is 4 km to the east of Mt. Aso, while Mt. Eboshi is 1.2 km from Kusasenri. Both can only be reached on foot.

Mt. Aso Volcanic Museum: Standing at Kusasenri, it has a large TV monitor showing the activity of the Mt. Nakadake crater.

Aso Shrine: 1 km north of the JR Miyaji Station. The oldest shrine in Kumamoto Prefecture, it is dedicated to the guardian god of the Aso area. The main shrine was constructed in 1835. The Fire Ceremony is annually held on March 19.

Hot Springs in Aso: Located about halfway up Mt. Eboshi at an altitude of 820 m, Yunotani is the highest of the spas in the Aso district and commands an extensive view of the Kumamoto Plain and Mt. Unzen beyond the Ariake Sea. The waters are 71-84°C. There is a golf course nearby and many modern hotels in the area. 20 min. by bus from the JR Akamizu Station. The Aso Pension Village is also nearby. Aso-Uchinomaki Spa is located in the crater basin near Uchinomaki Station. It commands a good view of the outer crater and the central volcanic cone. There are some 35 *ryokan* or Japanese-style inns here. Aso-Akamizu Spa is a 5-min. walk from Akamizu Station. There are two rather plush *ryokan* or Japanese-style inns with pools, golf courses and other recreational facilities.

There are also isolated hot springs in Nango Valley at the southern foot of Mt. Aso. Tochinoki, Tarutama and Jigoku each have only one or two *ryokan* around, but large-scale public facilities are available in the south at Green Pia Minami-Aso and in the east at Minami(South)-Aso National Vacation Village.

Daikampo Peak: A 936-m-high summit on the Aso outer crater. 30 min. by bus from the JR Aso Station. This is the best observation point for a magnificent view of the Aso Valley, the central volcanic cone and the Kuju Mountain Chain to the northeast. National Highway 212 runs by the peak.

Tsuetate Spa: Located on the border between Kumamoto and Oita prefectures. It takes 2 hrs. 40 min. by bus from Kumamoto and 50 min. by bus from Hita in Oita Prefecture. Surrounded by cedar mountains and located in a valley through which a river runs, this spa is efficacious against nervous disorders and external abrasions. The waters are very hot. There are some 30 *ryokan* in this area, which serves as a base for sightseeing around Mt. Aso.

Area 5. Oita Prefecture

Oita Prefecture occupies the northeastern part of Kyushu and faces the Inland Sea. Its southern part faces Shikoku across the Hoyo Straits. The coastal regions are favored with a mild climate brought by warm ocean currents, while the winter is quite severe in the western highland region, which is located amidst the volcanic Yaba-kei Gorge and Kuju Mountain Chain. Forestry is the main industry, with little flat land available. Oita is celebrated throughout Japan for its *shiitake* mushroom production. There are many hot springs such as those at Beppu, and excellent accommodations are available for the traveller.

Oita ☐ 109/115-② ☎ 0975

Pop. 396,942. Serving as the capital of Oita Prefecture, the city is located on the east coast of the Kyushu mainland. It evolved as a castle town for Otomo Sorin (1530–1587), the Christian *daimyo* (feudal lord) who controlled all of northern Kyushu. Today, it is the center of the prefecture's administration and communication as well as an important industrial complex of the heavy and petroleum industries. **Transportation**: Oita can be reached from Fukuoka in 3 hrs. 15 min. by limited express on the JR Kagoshima and Nippo main lines. From Kumamoto, an express on the JR Hohi Main Line will arrive in 2 hrs. 50 min. By air it is 1 hr.30 min. from Tokyo and 55 min. from Osaka. The Oita Airport is located on the southern shores of the Kunisaki Peninsula and is connected with the city center by hovercraft in 25 min. or by bus in 1 hr.10 min.

Beppu ☐ 109 ☎0977

Pop. 130,299. The city is known throughout Japan for its abundant hot springs. It is located on the east coast of the prefecture along Beppu Bay, with Mt. Tsurumi and Mt. Yufu rising in the west. The city contains eight different spas: Beppu, Hamawaki, Kankaiji, Kannawa, Myoban, Kamegawa, Horita and Shibaseki. There are a total of around 520 lodging facilities in the area, although none are available at either Hamawaki or Horita. There are nine types of spring waters. Medical treatment is also available. Experimental agricultural facilities that utilize hot-spring water have been set up by the prefecture. Bamboo work and geyserite are some of the local specialties. A crowd of participants gather annually for the Beppu-Oita Marathon in February.

TRANSPORTATION

From Fukuoka, Beppu can be reached by limited express on the JR Kagoshima and Nippo main lines in 2 hrs. 30 min., by express bus in

3 hrs. 50 min. From Kumamoto, one can take an express on the JR Hohi Main Line, which arrives in 3 hrs., a bus arriving in 3 hrs. 55 min., or drive 148 km using National Highway 57 and "Yamanami Highway." From Oita Airport, Beppu is 40 min. away by hovercraft or 50 min. by bus.

Beppu Port serves as the eastern gateway by sea into Kyushu. Car ferries sail from Osaka and Kobe in 13 hrs. and from Hiroshima in 8 hrs. 30 min. It takses 10 min. by bus from the JR Beppu Station to Beppu International Tourist Port.

There are five city sightseeing bus tours that circle *Jigoku* (Hell) hot springs, Mt. Takasaki, Marine Park and other major sights. Regular sightseeing buses for the Kunisaki Peninsula and Usuki also depart from Beppu. The bus terminal is in Kitahama.

HOTSPRINGS

Every day 130,000 kl of hot water boils up from 2,800 different openings. Among the eight spas, Kannawa and Kankaiji have unique characteristics. Kannawa is 6.4 km north of the JR Beppu Station near the Jigoku region, and so much steam is emitted that it is utilized for cooking. Kankaiji, 3.6 km west of Beppu Station, is halfway up Mt. Tsurumi and commands a magnificent view of Beppu Bay. Geyserite is found in the Myoban Spa area.

There are numerous public baths, both privately and municipally owned. Of the latter, Takegawara-Onsen at Hamawaki Spa is especially popular, offering the sand baths that Beppu is famous for. A more deluxe atmosphere can be found at privately owned Suginoi Palace at Kankaiji Spa, where a theater, art museum, pool, bowling center and other attractions center around the enormous bath.

Refer to the supplement for details regarding the "i" **System Information Center** in Beppu.

PLACES OF INTEREST

Beppu Jigoku (Hell) Group: A kind of volcanic formation in which hot water and mud are spewed into the air. They are so named since they seem to graphically portray hell as one might imagine it. The most active of the *Jigoku* geysers explodes with thunderous noises and ejects mud more than a foot into the air. There are several such places throughout the city, but the largest is *Umi*(Sea)-*Jigoku* at a depth of 120 m and a temperature of 94°C. The mud of *Chinoike* (Blood Pond)-*Jigoku* is quite red. It has a depth of 165 m and a temperature of 93°C. *Tatsumaki* (Tornado)-*Jigoku* is a geyser that spurts more than 50 m high every 20 min. and has a temperature of 100°C. In addition, a visitor can see cobalt blue and milky white geyserite. There is a convenient sightseeing bus service that includes several of the *Jigoku*.

Mt. Takasaki ⟨109⟩: The 628-m-high mountain area located southeast of Beppu, forming the border between Oita and Beppu. The area is named "National Park, Mt. Takasaki" where wild monkeys roam, begging for food from tourists. Schools of fish swim in a 61-m-long circular tank at Oita Marine Palace, which faces the ocean. The aquatic shows performed here are highly popular. It takes 20 min. by bus from Beppu.

Kijima Plateau: About 12 km southwest of Beppu, 35 min. by bus. Located at the southern foot of Mt. Tsurumi (alt. 1,375 m), the area has been developed as an Inner-Beppu resort. Lake Shidaka is good for boating. There is a ropeway that reaches the top of Mt. Tsurumi in 10 min. In addition to a spacious observation platform for viewing the surrounding area, the wild azaleas of spring and winter frosts are exquisite.

Yufuin 109 ☎0977: A spa town on a basin along the Yufu River located 11 km west of Beppu. It has an altitude of 480 m and a refreshing climate, rarely rising above 27°C even in summer. It takes 1 hr.10 min. by bus from Beppu. There are about 60 *ryokan* and a folk art village.

Yunohira Spa, especially efficacious against stomach ailments, and Tsukahara Spa, where many come to take healing baths, are both located nearby.

Mt. Yufu 109 : Alt. 1,583 m. An extinct volcano that is popularly known as "Bungo-Fuji" for its resemblance to Mt. Fuji. Bungo is the old name of the present Oita Prefecture. The summit is divided into two peaks, offering a magnificent view of Beppu Bay and Yufuin. The frost flowers are also beautiful. It is 15 min. by bus from Yufuin Station to the point of ascension, with the climb taking about 2 hrs.

African Safari: About 10 km north of Beppu or 1 hr. by bus. This natural animal park covers 11.5 sq.km of smooth grassy plain on the Ajimu Plateau. Approximately 1,300 animals of 69 species graze freely in the compound, while visitors observe them from the windows of a tour bus. It is divided into zones for bears, tigers, giraffes and two other zones, and features shows of trained animals.

Kunisaki Peninsula, Yabakei Gorge and Vicinity

Kunisaki Peninsula 109 : Forming the northern boundary of Beppu Bay, the rounded peninsula extends 35 km from north to south and 30 km from east to west. Mt.Futago (alt. 720 m) rises in the center, with gorges radiating on all sides. There are many Buddhist relics from ancient times through the Middle Ages such as the many stone stupas called "*Kunisaki-To*" scattered throughout the area. Some of the famous temples and Buddhism treasures include Maki-Odo Temple with its figure of Buddha from the Fujiwara period during the 10–12th centuries (an Important Cultural Property), Fukiji Temple (a National Treasure), the *Magaibutsu* (an Image of Buddha carved on a cliff; an Important Cultural Property) at Kumano and the largest temple on the peninsula—Futagoji Temple. The area is best covered by driving by oneself, but the sightseeing bus from Beppu is a convenient alternative. Kitsuki on the southern coast of the peninsula was a castle town, with the old castle now restored. Many residences of *samurai* still remain.

Usa Shrine ☐109☐ : Located uptown in Usa (pop. 51,761), facing the Suo-nada Sea. From Fukuoka, it can be reached in 1 hr.55 min. or from Beppu in 55 min. by limited express to Usa Station, then a 10-min. bus ride. This is the main shrine of all the Hachimangu shrines found throughout Japan. The ancient shrine has been revered by the Imperial Family since the eighth century. The precincts are about 50,000 sq.m, and the Main Hall peers through dense growths of massive trees. The Main Hall (a National Treasure), consisting of three connected buildings, is an edifice with vermilion columns, white walls and a cypress-bark roof. It was reconstructed in 1861.

Nakatsu ☐109☐ ☎0979: Pop. 65,684. Situated in the northernmost part of the prefecture, the city spreads out along the mouth of the Yamakuni River at the Suo-nada Sea. From Fukuoka, it can be reached in 1 hr.35 min., or from Beppu in 55 min. by limited express on the JR Nippo Main Line. The Nakatsu Plain is a commercial and transportation center, with the city originally evolving as a castle town. The ruins of the castle with a reconstructed donjon can be found 1 km northwest of the station. Fukuzawa Yukichi, who was active during the Meiji Restoration, was originally a *samurai* of the Nakatsu Clan. A memorial dedicated to him stands in the park among the ruins of the castle, with the remains of his former residence situated 500 m further east. The town also serves as a gateway to Yabakei Gorge.

Fukuzawa Yukichi (1835–1901), who studied Dutch and English in his youth, opened a school in Edo (now, Tokyo) in 1858 that later developed into the present Keio Gijuku University. Fukuzawa published many books that contributed to the advancement of Western learning.

Yaba-Hita-Hikosan Quasi-National Park ☐109☐

The park includes the scenic Yabakei Gorge, Mt. Hikosan (famous as a training ground for the followers of Buddhist asceticism) and the riverside town, Hita. It was established as a quasi-national park in 1950 and covers an area of 850.23 sq.km. Each part of the park area has deep literary and historical connotations in addition to beautiful landscapes.

Yabakei Gorge ☐109☐ : Located on the upper reaches of the Yamakuni River. The region extends 36 km from east to west and 32 km from north to south. The gorge was formed by the erosion of lava, with clear waters running through the narrow ravines topped by towering peaks. Maples grow in abundance, presenting the beauty of fresh green leaves in spring and that of red leaves in autumn. The rhododendrons in May are also magnificent. Yabakei Gorge is divided into Hon-Yabakei, Shin-Yabakei and eight other valleys. Regular sightseeing buses that tour Yabakei Gorge depart from the

JR Nakatsu, Beppu and Bungo-Mori Stations.

Hon(Proper)-Yabakei Gorge: The area from Ao-no-Domon to Morizane Spa, 35 min. by bus from the JR Nakatsu Station. Ao-no-Domon is a tunnel cut through a big rock. It is said that the tunnel was completed in 1764 by a Buddhist priest named Zenkai, who took 30 years to finish the job. Rakanji Temple, a Buddhist temple of the Soto sect founded in 1337, is located 2 km southeast of Ao-no-Domon. There are 3,770 stone images, including figures of the 500 disciples of Buddha or *Gohyaku* (lit. Five hundred) *Rakan*, who achieved Nirvana. The area is called Rakanji-Yabakei Gorge.

Shin(Inner)-Yabakei Gorge: Extending along the Yamautsuri River, a tributary of the Yamakuni River. 1 hr.20 min. from the JR Nakatsu Station by bus. Sheer cliffs line both sides of the narrow canyon, with a splendid view of the gorge obtainable from an observation point called *Hitome-Hakkei* (lit. Eight Views at a Glance). There is a 7-km-long hiking trail to Ifuku in Ura (Back)-Yabakei Gorge.

Oku(Deep)-Yabakei Gorge: Extending 16 km along the route that connects Morizane Spa in Yabakei Gorge and Mt. Hikosan. It forms deep valleys with dense trees.

Hita 109 ☎0973: Pop. 65,402. About 1 hr.30 min. by express on the JR Kyudai Main Line from Fukuoka. It is located on the northwestern edge of the prefecture where the Mikuma River flows into the Hita Basin. During the Edo period, the magistrate office here supervised the territories in Kyushu under the direct control of the Edo Shogunate government. Hita's claim to fame rests chiefly on its serene atmosphere coupled with its scenic surroundings. Hita is also called "Kyoto in Kyushu" because of the resemblance of its scenery to that of Kyoto. Besides thriving lumbering and woodworking industries, the area is also known for the production of folk pottery called *Onda-yaki*.

The city abounds in hot springs, with some ten *ryokan* or Japanese-style inns making use of them. Tourists enjoy cormorant fishing on the Mikuma River from late May to mid-October, while savoring a meal of freshly caught of *ayu* (sweet fish) on traditional-style roofed boats.

Taio Gold Mine: Located 38 km southwest of Hita near the borders of Oita, Kumamoto and Fukuoka prefectures, this was famed as the largest gold mine in Asia until it closed down in 1972. It takes 2 hrs. 10 min. from the JR Hita Station by bus. This once-thriving mine has now been revitalized as a mining museum, with a 1-km-long shaft lined with machinery used in mining and dioramas recreating the mining process.

Amagase Spa 109 : North of Amagase Station on the JR Kyudai Main Line. *Ryokan* or Japanese-style inns lie clustered around the Kusu River. There are six outdoor baths by the river that are open to public, with waters that are efficacious against rheumatism.

Southern Oita Prefecture

Usuki ⬜109 ☎0972: Pop. 39,474. 45 min. from Oita on the JR Nippo Main Line. It is located at the point furthest inland on the deep Usuki Bay. Soy sauce brewing and shipbuilding are the prime industries.

Usuki Stone Buddhas: Southwest of the town, 15 min. by bus from Usuki Station on the JR Nippo Main Line. The area is designated as a Special Place of Historical Importance. The group of Buddhas were carved in the 9-12th centuries and are divided roughly into four groups: Hoki, Dogasako, Sannosan and Furuzono. There are a total of 60 images, with those of the Furuzono Group portraying the Vairocana Buddha considered as the best.

Onagara Stalactite Grotto: 50 min. by bus from Saeki Station on the JR Nippo Main Line. The cave is 700 m long and has clusters of stalactites and stalagmites.

Furen Stalactite Grotto: Located in the southeastern part of the prefecture along the north bank of the Notsu River. 1 hr. by bus from Oita. The grotto is 500 m long and contains stalactites, stalagmites and stone pillars of all shapes, including the 1,500-sq.-m Ryugujo or the Palace of the Sea God with the 10-m-high Kyoshuho peak towering above it.

Taketa ⬜109 ☎09746: Pop. 21,235. About 1 hr.5 min. from Oita by express on the JR Hohi Main Line or 40 km along National Highways 210 and 442. Located in the southwestern part of the prefecture, this former castle town is famous as the birthplace of writer-painter Tanomura Chikuden (1777-1835) and the composer of "Kojo-no-Tsuki" (The Moon on a Ruined Castle)—Taki Rentaro (1879-1903). Agriculture and forestry are the main industries, with saffron regarded as a local specialty. The ruins of the Oka Castle lie in the eastern part of town, 7 min. by bus from the station. It is said that the castle inspired Taki in his composition of "Kojo-no-Tsuki." Today, only stone walls remain on the cliffs surrounded by a river, but on clear days it is possible to see the Kuju Mountain Chain and Mt. Sobo.

Sobo-Katamuki Quasi-National Park ⬜109⬜: The mountain chain that covers the southern part of Oita Prefecture and extends over the border into Miyazaki Prefecture. Mt. Sobo has an altitude of 1,756 m. The mountains are covered with primeval forests of beeches and spruces among which goats, antelope, boar and other wild animals roam. The climb begins from Kobaru, a 40-min. bus ride from Taketa, and takes 3 hrs. 40 min. to complete. Mt. Katamuki is in the east and has three peaks, while Takachiho Gorge to its south is well known for its weird rock formations and its association with various myths. It is said that the gorge and its vicinity form the Cradle of Japan.

Yamanami Highway ⬜109⬜: A part of the Trans-Kyushu Highway. The toll road extends for 52 km from Mizuwake Pass in Oita

Prefecture to Mt. Aso, cutting through the heart of Aso-Kuju National Park. It averages an altitude of 1,000 m, the highest point being 1,333 m at Makinoto Pass. The magnificent throughway passes through Senomoto Plateau, where it intersects with National Highway 442, and Handa Plateau, and lets one look over Mt. Kuju and Mt. Aso at close range. Among the many unique spas along the road, Sujiyu is located 50 min. by bus from Bungo-Nakamura Station on the JR Kyudai Main Line. It is famous for the hot waterfalls that drop down to massage the bodies of the bathers. Kan-no-Jigoku (lit. Cold Hell) is only 14°C, but the low temperatures are said to be good for the skin.

There are several bus services that use the "Yamanami Highway," connecting Beppu to Kumamoto in 4 hrs., with some routed near the crater of Mt. Aso. Bus services continue further west to Kumamoto, the Amakusa Five Bridges and on to Nagasaki via Unzen. It takes 6 hrs. 40 min. from Mt. Aso to Nagasaki.

Kuju Mountain Chain: A large mountain chain in the southwest part of Oita Prefecture. The main peak is Mt. Kuju, which, with an altitude of 1,791 m, is the highest mountain on the Kyushu mainland. Mt. Hossho, Mt. Mimata, Mt. Daisen and several other peaks are in the 1,700 m-range and 35 peaks are over 1,000 m high. The Kuju mountains are tholoid volcanoes with irregular shapes. Handa Plateau in the north and Kuju Plateau in the south abound in hot springs, while clusters of wild azaleas called *Miyama-Kirishima* bloom throughout the area.

It is a 1-hr. 45-min. climb to the top of Mt. Kuju from Makinoto Pass on "Yamanami Highway." An ascent of Mt. Daisen takes 1 hr. 30 min. from Hokkein Spa, the saddle between this peak and Mt. Mimata. Hokkein Spa has a lodge at an altitude of 1,303 m and is popular with mountain climbers. Many alpine plants grow in the area. It can be reached by a 40-min. bus ride from the JR Bungo-Nakamura Station to Kuju Tozanguchi (mountaineering gateway) and a 1-hr.30-min. climb on foot.

Nippo Kaigan(Coast) Quasi-National Park 109 : Covering the coastal line from Saganoseki Peninsula east of Oita to Mimitsu in Hyuga City, Miyazaki Prefecture. The area around the Hoyo Straits consists of a wild, jagged coastline preserved in its natural state.

Area 6. Miyazaki Prefecture

The east coast of Kyushu, facing the Hyuga-nada Sea where the Japan Current flows. The climate is mild with an annual average temperature of 17°C, while precipitation reaches about 2,700 mm. Most of its 7,735 sq.km of area are mountainous with Obi cedar, and *shiitake* mushrooms and other forms of forestry comprising the common occupational pursuit. There is small coastal plain to the north and south, where the forced cultivation of vegetables occurs. Since it is believed that Miyazaki is the legendary stage of the birth of Japan as a nation, there are many tourist sights related to the legend.

Miyazaki 110/118-119 ☎ 0985

Pop. 283,896. The capital of Miyazaki Prefecture. Situated in the southern part of the Miyazaki Plain at the mouth of the Oyodo River, the city boasts pure air and clean streets. Washingtonia palms, phoenix, camphors and other kinds of plants grow along the main boulevard, Tachibana-dori. The city has a highly commercial atmosphere. Miyako-City (Bus Terminal) on the south bank of the Oyodo River is the center of transportation. Miyazaki is the center of tourist activities in the region, with some 150 hotels and *ryokan* or Japanese-style inns. Popular souvenirs include ancient clay figurines called *haniwa*, Aoshima-bina dolls and *shiitake* mushrooms.

TRANSPORTATION

From Fukuoka, the city is about 6 hrs. away by limited express on the JR Nippo Main Line, 5 hrs. 35 min. by bus, or 325 km down the Kyushu and Miyazaki expressways. From Beppu, it is about 3 hrs. 40 min. by limited express on the JR Nippo Main Line, or 219 km along National Highway 10. A bus runs from Kumamoto in 4 hrs. 40 min. The airport is 4 km south of the city and is connected by a 25-min. bus ride. By air, it is 1 hr.45 min. from Tokyo, 1 hr. from Osaka and 40 min. from Fukuoka.

Refer to the supplement for details regarding the "i" System Information Center in Miyazaki. .

PLACES OF INTEREST

Miyazaki Shrine 118 : Situated 2 km north of Miyazaki Station, 10 min. by bus. The shrine is dedicated to Emperor Jimmu, first Emperor of the Yamato Court. The shrine buildings standing on the spacious grounds were constructed in 1907. Miyazaki Prefectural Museum contains a valuable collection of *haniwa* and stone implements of archeological interest.

Heiwadai Park 118 : Situated on a 60-m-high hill northwest of the city. A "Peace Pagoda" stands on the lawn, surrounded by a flower garden. The pagoda is 37 m tall, and the foundations are made of stones sent from all over the world by Japanese expatriates. The Haniwa Garden is located north of the pagoda, with 400 clay reproductions of *haniwa* lining the path.

Saitobaru Tumuli Group 110 : 1 hr. by bus from Miyazaki, 25 km to the northwest. A total of 311 tumuli of all sizes dot the plateau of this Special Place of Historical Importance. The burial mounds were made in the fifth–sixth centuries and many *haniwa* have been excavated here. Enclosed by a double moat, the tumulus called *Osaho-zuka* is the largest, with a total length of 219 m and a height of 18 m. A museum to the west of the plateau displays the artifacts excavated here.

Northern Miyazaki Prefecture

Hyuga ⌷110⌷ ☎0982: Pop. 59,734. This industrial port city is in the northeastern part of the prefecture. Since the area is blessed with abundant water resource and electrical power, many kinds of factories operate here, including fiber, food products and sugar. The port is called Hosojima (Hyuga Port). From Miyazaki, a limited express on the JR Nippo Main Line takes 1 hr. and a bus takes 2 hrs. to cover the 67 km along National Highway 10. Car ferries arrive here from Kawasaki in Kanagawa Prefecture (21 hrs.) and from Osaka and Kobe (15 hrs.).

Prized stones for the Japanese board game "go" are made here (especially the white ones) from the clamshells collected at nearby Okuragahama Beach.

Nobeoka ⌷110⌷ ☎0982: Pop. 133,930. Situated in the northern part of the prefecture, this is the largest industrial city on the east coast of Kyushu, with the chemical industrial complex of Asahi Chemical Industry and its related enterprises operating here. It spreads out at the mouth of the Gokase River, which abounds in *ayu* (sweet fish). From Miyazaki, 1 hr.20 min. by limited express on the JR Nippo Main Line. From Fukuoka, a JR limited express takes 4 hrs. 45 min. (325 km). A bus leaves from Kumamoto arriving in 4 hrs. 10 min.

Takachiho ⌷110⌷ ☎0982: Located on the upper reaches of the Gokase River, near the border between Oita and Kumamoto prefectures. The legend says that this is the birthplace of Japan as a nation. From Nobeoka, it can be reached in 1 hr.50 min. by express bus, or 56 km of driving along National Highway 218. From Kumamoto, 2 hrs. 50 min. by bus.

The main landmark is Takachihokyo Gorge, a V-shaped ravine formed through the erosion of the Aso lava plateau by the Gokase River. There is a 600-m-long trail along the gorge, which contains the 17-m Manai Falls and other natural wonders.

Southern Miyazaki Prefecture

Nichinan Kaigan (Coast) Quasi-National Park ⌷111⌷: Extending 90 km down the east coast from Miyazaki to Cape Toi and including Shibushi Bay in Kagoshima Prefecture. Affected by the Japan Current and mild climate, many subtropical plants grow here.

Aoshima Island ⌷110⌷: A tiny island of 1.5 km in circumference lying about 14 km south of Miyazaki, connected with the mainland by a 300-m-long bridge. It is celebrated for its luxurious growth of tropical and subtropical plants. The island is surrounded by eroded sandstone and shale boulders that protrude from the sea between the waves. It is 40 min. by express bus from Miyazaki. On the mainland side of the bridge stands the Kodomo-no-Kuni ("Children's Land")—an amusement park. There are some 15 *ryokan* along the beach.

Saboten (Cactus) Garden: 18 km south of Aoshima Island. 500 species of cacti grow in the 500,000-sq.-m garden.

Udo Shrine ⌷110⌷: 30 km south of Aoshima Island. It takes 1 hr. 20 min. by express bus from Miyazaki via Aoshima Island. The shrine is dedicated to the father of Jimmu, the first Emperor of Japan. The vermilion Main Hall is situated in a large cave—an unusual setting for a shrine. Since the cave opens on a cliff facing the sea, the view from the shrine is magnificent.

Nichinan ⌷110⌷ ☎0987: Pop. 51,139. 1 hr.20 min. by the JR Nichinan Line from Miyazaki to Aburatsu, the gateway of the city. Located south of Miyazaki, the town is composed of a fishing port, Aburatsu, and an old castle town, Obi. It is famous for a species of cedar known as Obi cedar. Pulp production is a thriving industry. The ruins of Obi Castle and the old quarters of the town are worth visiting.

Cape Toi ⌷111⌷: A tableland some 300 m above sea level, projecting into the Pacific Ocean at the southeastern extremity of Miyazaki Prefecture and embracing Shibushi Bay. More than 100 wild horses graze freely on Misaki (Cape) Pasture here. Favored with a mild climate throughout the year, fern palms grow wild around Misaki Shrine. The horses and fern palms are protected as Natural Monuments. Toi Lighthouse, capable of throwing a 1.3 million candlepower light, stands at the edge of the cape. Inspection tours are available. 2 hrs. 45 min. by express bus from Miyazaki, or 45 min. by bus from Kushima Station on the JR Nichinan Line.

Miyakonojo ⌷110⌷ ☎0986: Pop. 131,930. Situated in the southern part of Miyazaki Prefecture, in the heart of the Miyakonojo Basin. Agriculture, forestry and livestock breeding are the main industries. From Miyazaki, a limited express on the JR Nippo Main Line takes 50 min. or 34 km along the Miyazaki Expressway. From Kagoshima, a JR limited express takes 1 hr.15 min. or 155 km along the Kyushu and Miyazaki expressways.

Area 7. Kagoshima Prefecture

The lower part of the Kyushu mainland. Islands like Tanegashima, Yakushima and Amami-Oshima in the southern sea are part of Kagoshima Prefecture. During the feudal period, the area was under the control of the Shimazu Clan, who maintained the isolationist policy by closing the province border to the people of other provinces. The Kirishima Volcano Group sits in the center of the northern part. Kagoshima Bay (also called Kinko Bay) is enclosed by the Osumi Peninsula on the east and the Satsuma Peninsula on the west, while the active volcano on Sakurajima rises in the middle of the Bay. Kagoshima Prefecture has the third-longest coastline in Japan, and fishery is thriving. Visitors admire the scenic beauty of volcanic landscapes and extensive seascapes.

Kagoshima 111/120 ☎ 0992

Pop. 528,598. The capital of Kagoshima Prefecture as well as the center of transportation for southern Kyushu. The city evolved as a castle town under the Shimazu Clan from 1341 until the Meiji Restoration in 1868 for a total of 527 years.

The city is also known for its association with several leaders of the Meiji Restoration, including Saigo Takamori (1827-1877) and Okubo Toshimichi (1830-1878). Saigo became a national hero when he rebelled in 1877 against the Imperial government he had helped to restore and tragically had to commit *harakiri*.

The city sits on the east bank of Kinko Bay facing the active volcano, Sakurajima. The Taniyama district to the south of the city center has been developed as an industrial zone. The shopping district centers around Temmonkan Street. There are many unique local dishes such as *tonkotsu* (pork rib) cuisine and *Kagoshima ramen* (Chinese noodles). Local specialties include silk pongee, *Satsuma-yaki*(ceramics), *shochu* (liquor) and bamboo ware. *Satsuma-yaki* is a type of pottery made on the east coast of the Satsuma Peninsula. Production began in 1598 when Shimazu Yoshihiro brought potters over from Korea. The crackled white ground tinged with yellow is often glazed with gorgeous patterns, making this pottery popular both at home and abroad.

TRANSPORTATION

Two main lines of the JR Kagoshima (west coast) and Nippo (east coast) meet here, making the city a starting point for exploring the Satsuma and Osumi peninsulas, Amami-Oshima Island and the Satsunan Islands. National Highways 3 (west coast) and 10 (east coast) also meet in Kagoshima. A JR limited express takes 4 hrs. 25 min. from Fukuoka (318 km) or 2 hrs. 10 min. from Miyazaki (126 km). The direct sleeper limited express from Tokyo takes 20 hrs. 35 min. (1,494 km), while that from Osaka takes 13 hrs. 53 min. (938 km). All these trains terminate at Nishi(West)-Kagoshima Station.

The Kagoshima Airport is on the north bank of Kinko Bay and can be reached from the city center in 1 hr. by bus; 36 km along the Kyushu Expressway. By air, 1 hr.55 min. from Tokyo, 1 hr.10 min. from Osaka or 40 min. from Fukuoka. There are also flights departing for Hong Kong and Seoul.

Kagoshima Port is situated on the east coast of Kinko Bay facing Sakurajima, with boats departing here for islands in the south and Okinawa. Car ferries from Osaka also docks here (20 hrs. 45 min.).

Refer to the supplement for details regarding the "i" **System Information Center** in Kagoshima.

PLACES OF INTEREST

St. Xavier Church 120 : Erected in 1949 on the 400th anniversary of the landing of St. Xavier in Kagoshima. The church stands in

Xavier Park near the Takamibaba Streetcar Stop. His bust and a hall commemorating his arrival are also located in the park.

St. Francisco de Xavier (1506-1552), a Spanish Jesuit missionary, landed in Kagoshima in 1549 after a stormy voyage from Malacca. With the permission of the Lord of Satsuma, he preached Christianity during his 10-month stay here. This was Japan's first contact with Christianity. Later, he visited Hirado, Yamaguchi, Kyoto and Oita to evangelize, finally leaving Japan in 1551.

Shiroyama Park 120 : Situated on a 107-m-high hill, 1.5 km north-east of Nishi-Kagoshima Station (25 min. by bus). It was formerly the site of the castle of the lord who ruled this district in the 14th century. The summit affords an extensive view of Kagoshima Bay, including the graceful volcano Sakurajima and the dormant volcano Mt. Kaimon (also known as Satsuma-Fuji). Behind the hill is the cave where Saigo Takamori committed *harakiri* with his followers when *Seinan-no-Eki* or the Kagoshima Rebellion collapsed in 1877.

Iso Garden 110 : Situated in Iso, 5.5 km northeast of the JR Nishi-Kagoshima Station. It takes 25 min. by bus. This garden was the grounds of a villa erected by the lord of the Shimazu Clan in the mid-17th century. Sea water from Kagoshima Bay flows into the pond, while the artificial hill was made to resemble Sakurajima in this magnificent garden. The villa, containing a drawing room with a main alcove and side alcove, is located near Iso Hill. There is an amusement park on the hill with a ropeway to the top.

The Shoko-Shuseikan Museum is adjacent to the garden. It was once a factory established by Lord Shimazu Nariakira (1809-1858) in 1852 to produce armaments and promote the weapons industry. It was the largest in the country at the time and had a work force of 1,200. Today, it is a museum that tells of the 700-year Shimazu family history.

Sakurajima 110 : Once an island in Kagoshima Bay, but now a peninsula. The flow of lava from a massive volcanic eruption in 1914 dammed up the narrow channel in the east that once separated the island from the Kyushu mainland. The former island bears a consid-erable resemblance to the Shimabara Peninsula, formed by eruptions from the Unzen volcanoes. Sakurajima has erupted scores of times since the first one was recorded in 708.

Although from a distance the volcano appears to have only a single cone, it actually has three peaks—Kitadake (North Peak, alt. 1,118 m), Nakadake (Middle Peak, alt. 1,110 m) and Minamidake (South Peak, alt.1,060 m). Each peak has a crater from which lava has poured out over the years to form the main body of the island (now, peninsula). However, only Minamidake is active now.

Since Sakurajima is blessed with a mild climate, oranges, loquats and many other fruit are cultivated here. A specialty of the "island" is the *Sakurajima daikon*—a giant white radish growing to about 50 cm in diameter and weighing 45 kg. It is usually pickled and sold as a souvenir. There is frequent ferry service from Kagoshima Port reaching Sakurajima in 15 min. A bus to Furusato Spa on the south coast of the "island" arrives in 20 min. The hot-spring waters are slightly salty at Furusato Spa, where four *ryokan* are operated. A regular sightseeing bus covers Sakurajima in 3 hrs.

Satsuma Peninsula

Ibusuki ⎡111⎤ ☎0993: Pop. 32,066. A hot-spring resort on the southeast coast of the Satsuma Peninsula. 1 hr. by the JR Ibusuki-Makurazaki Line, 1 hr.40 min. by bus, or 45 km along National Highway 226 from Kagoshima. A ferry leaves from nearby Yamagawa Port for the Osumi Peninsula on the opposite shore.

Ibusuki Spa ⎡111⎤: There are many hot springs along the 10-km-long Ibusuki coast, but Ibusuki Spa ranks with Beppu in fame and size. The main area is called Surigahama, famous for the sand baths on the coast. There are municipally run sand baths where bathers, clad only in a cotton *kimono*, lie down and are covered with sand warmed in the hot-spring water. The water temperature ranges 60-85°C. Efficacious against gastroenteric disorders and rheumatism. There are a total of 800 springs which spout 120,000 tons of water a day. There are 50 *ryokan* and a National Vacation Village on the northern coast.

Cape Nagasakibana ⎡111⎤: Jutting out from the southernmost tip of the Satsuma Peninsula the cape offers an excellent view of Mt. Kaimon. On a clear day, Tanegashima and other southern islands can be seen across the Pacific Ocean. Part of the cape is a subtropical botanical garden called "Parking Garden." 35 min. by bus from Ibusuki.

Mt. Kaimon ⎡111⎤: A dormant conoid volcano in the southeastern part of the Satsuma Peninsula with an altitude of 922 m. Its beautiful conical shape has led it to being called "Satsuma-Fuji." An ascent takes about 2 hrs. There is a natural park at the eastern foot of the mountain where Tokharian horses frolic in the grass among the subtropical plants. Tokharian horses are wild horses from the Tokhara Islands to the south of Yakushima Island.

Lake Ikeda ⎡111⎤: The largest lake in Kyushu lies 8 km west of Ibusuki. It has a circumference of 19 km and an area of 11 sq.km. It is a caldera lake, unusual in that the volcanic cone can be seen at the bottom of the lake. Mt. Kaimon is reflected in the bright, clear lake waters. A public health resort called "Green Pia Ibusuki" is located on the east coast, offering a wide range of sports facilities and accommodations.

Samurai House, Chiran ⎡111⎤: Located in the south-central portion of the Satsuma Peninsula. 1 hr.15 min. by bus from Kagoshima or 30 min. by bus from Makurazaki. During the feudal period, this was a castle town for the local lord under the Shimazu Clan, and many of the warrior class had homes here. These houses with small but beautiful gardens still remain. The former site of Chiran Air Base, where *kamikaze* fighters left on their one-way sorties during World War II, is also nearby. Specialties are tea and oranges.

Makurazaki ☐111☐ ☎0993: This fishing town on the south coast of the Satsuma Peninsula serves as a base for bonito and other deep-sea fishing. The annual bonito catch averages around 90,000 tons. The bonito are dried and made into flakes—one of the many activities of the thriving marine-products processing industry. From the JR Nishi-Kagoshima Station, a train takes 2 hrs. 40 min., while a bus takes 1 hr.40 min. A bus from the JR Ijuin Station takes 1 hr.40 min.

Bonotsu ☐111☐ ☎0993: Located on the southwestern tip of Satsuma Peninsula, 25 min. by bus from Makurazaki. In the eighth–tenth centuries, officials and envoys to China left from this ancient harbor, and during the years of isolation it was the base for secret trading by the Shimazu Clan. It is now a quiet fishing port, with a magnificent view of the picturesque bay.

Fukiagehama ☐110☐: On the west coast of the Satsuma Peninsula. The sand dunes stretch a total of 40 km from Kushikino to Kaseda, with widths ranging 1-3 m and a high point of 47 m. Pines grow in the sand, adding a wild touch to the landscape. There is a 2.5-km-in-circumference lake, called Lake Satsuma, in the middle of this stretch of sand. 30 min. by bus from Ijuin Station on the JR Kagoshima Main Line.

Sendai ☐110☐ ☎0996: Pop. 71,710. It takes 40 min. from Nishi-Kagoshima Station by limited express on the JR Kagoshima Main Line. Located in the center of the basin along the lower reaches of the Sendai River, it is a distribution center for agricultural products. Populated since ancient times, Nitta Shrine northwest of the town is dedicated to Ninigi-no-Mikoto, a mythological figure who, according to legend, descended from Heaven. His purported grave is behind the shrine.

The Koshiki Islands lie 50 km out into the ocean off the west coast. Ferries bound for the islands leave from Kushikino Port, 10 min. from Sendai by JR.

Izumi ☐110☐ ☎0996: Pop. 39,913. This country town is located at the northern edge of Kagoshima Prefecture. Large crops of citrus fruit are cultivated here. 1 hr.25 min. by limited express on the JR Kagoshima Main Line from Nishi-Kagoshima or 1 hr. 30 min. from Kumamoto. Izumi Plain, to the northwest of the city bordering the Shiranui Sea, is known for the many kinds of cranes that migrate here from Siberia. From October to March, white-naped cranes, black cranes and especially hooded cranes—a total of some 6,000 birds—nest here. Many other varieties of wild birds accompany them. 35 min. by bus from Izumi Station. An observation station is provided.

Kirishima and Osumi Peninsula

Kirishima-Yaku National Park ☐110-111☐: Covering a vast area of

537 sq.km, it contains incredible natural beauty. The park extends from the Kirishima Mountain Chain in the northern part of Kagoshima to Yakushima Island in the south sea. It also includes the tips of the Satsuma and Osumi peninsulas that enclose Sakurajima and Kagoshima Bay.

Kirishima Mountain Chain 110 : A volcanic range of 23 large peaks in southern Kyushu. It is roughly divided into eastern and western sections, with Mt. Takachiho (alt. 1,574 m) marking East Kirishima and Mt. Karakuni (alt. 1,700 m) marking West Kirishima, separated by 16 km. The range cuts through the border between Kagoshima and Miyazaki prefectures, with Ebino and Ikoma, two large plateaus, lying on the Miyazaki side.

The park is cloaked with silver firs, hemlocks and other coniferous trees and groves of red pines. Miyama-kirishima (wild azaleas), Kirishima-mizuki (dogwood) and other flowering plants also bloom in abundance. The volcanoes form an unusual landscape with craters, crater lakes and hot springs dotting the area. The largest of the crater lakes is Onami, which lies on the southwestern face of Mt. Karakuni and has a circumference of 2 km. The blue-green lake water forms an exquisite contrast with the surrounding scenery.

The base for sightseeing would be either Kirishima Spa at the southwest foot or the Ebino Plateau on the northwest face. The "Kirishima Skyline" highway runs between them. Kirishima Shrine on the southeastern foot is another base, with the driveway running either to Kirishima Spa or to the Ebino Plateau via "Kirishima Skyline."

Ascent of Mt. Takachiho: A 40-min. bus ride from the JR Kirishima-Jingu Station to Takachihogawara. The hike from here takes 1 hr. 30 min. At the summit stands a halbert that is said to have been thrust upright when the mythological Ninigi-no-Mikoto descended to Earth from Heaven. The view from here is excellent no matter which way one looks. There is a visitors' center in Takachihogawara.

Ascent of Mt. Karakuni: From the Karakunidake-tozanguchi (gateway for mountaineering) on Ebino Plateau, taking 1 hr.30 min. From the Onami-tozanguchi to Lake Onami, it takes 40 min. and another 1 hr. to the peak. The crater at the top has a high lip and the bottom is overgrown with weeds and moss. The view from here is even more extensive than that from Mt. Takachiho.

Kirishima Shrine 110 : Standing to the south of the Kirishima mountains nestled in a grove of venerable cedars, the shrine is dedicated to Ninigi-no-Mikoto, grandson of the highest goddess, Amaterasu, and great-grandfather of the first Emperor, Jimmu. It takes 15 min. by bus from Kirishima-Jingu Station on the JR Nippo Main Line. An express bus from Nishi-Kagoshima Station will arrive in 1 hr.30 min. Kirishima-Jingu Spa is near the shrine.

Kirishima Spas Area 110 : A general name for a group of hot springs scattered around the southwest face of the Kirishima Mountain Chain. There are many divergences of the water source, with the temperature ranging 40-97°C. Maruo Spa forms an accommodation center with some 15 *ryokan*. Iodani and Hayashida spas have only one *ryokan* each, but they are both large facilities with spacious baths. 2 hr.10 min. from the JR Nishi-Kagoshima Station by bus to Hayashida Spa. The other spas are an additional 5-10-min. bus ride.

Ebino Plateau [110]: Situated northwest of Mt. Karakuni at an altitude of 1,200 m, surrounded by Mt. Koshiki and Mt. Kurino. The northern part is dotted with crater lakes such as Lake Fudo, Lake Rokkannon and Lake Byakushi, while the southern side contains the bus terminal and visitors' center among groves of red pines. There are hot springs here as well as accommodations. There are also many rare plants and animals on the plateau, making it an excellent location for camping and hiking. It will take 1 hr.30 min. to go around all the lakes.

From Hayashida Spa, it takes 30 min. by bus; from Miyazaki, 2 hrs. 30 min. by express bus, and from Kobayashi Station on the JR Kitto Line, 1 hr. by bus. The bus from Kobayashi Station passes through the Ikoma Plateau on the way. *Nanohana* or rape blossoms are beautiful in spring, while the cosmos brightly color the plains in autumn.

Shibushi Bay [111]: Situated on the northeastern coast of the Osumi Peninsula. The port in Shibushi (pop. 20,063), a major coastal town, has long prospered. The coast of Cape Daguri on the east side of the town is noted as a beautiful swimming resort with long, white-sand beaches. Lodgings and camping facilities are available. It takes 3 hrs. from Miyazaki to Shibushi, the terminal station on the JR Nichinan Line, or 1 hr.30 min. by bus from Miyakonojo. A ferry from Osaka will arrive in Shibushi Port in 15 hrs. 40 min.

Kanoya [111] ☎0994: Pop. 76,389. The central city on the Osumi Peninsula. 45 min. by bus from Tarumizu Port on the Kagoshima (Kinko) Bay (35 min. by ferry from Kagoshima Port). The city is set on a plateau formed from volcanic ash. Many of the fields are irrigated with sprinkler systems. Just like Chiran, the Kanoya Air Base—now used by the Maritime Self-Defense Force—was also the site from where *Kamikaze* fighters left on their one-way sorties during World War II.

Uchinoura [111]: Located on the east coast of the Osumi Peninsula or the south coast of the land mass enclosing Shibushi Bay. In 1962 the Kagoshima Space Center (Rocket Center), was built here and serves as the headquarters for space research in Japan. The area bustles when rockets lift off. The observatory south of town covers 70,000 sq.m on the Nagatsubo Plateau and includes satellite telemeter reception equipment and parabola antennas. The Uchu Kagaku Shiryokan (Space Science Museum) at the entrance shows the progress of development. 1 hr.30 min. by bus from Kanoya.

Cape Sata [111]: The tip of the Osumi Peninsula. Access is from

Odomari, a town 1 hr.50 min. by bus from Kanoya. A 20-min. bus ride via "Sata Misaki(Cape) Road Park" brings one to the cape. There is a 1-hr. hiking trail at the tip of the cape. When one hikes clear of the lush jungle complete with *ako* (banyan trees) and *sotetsu* (fern palms) there is an excellent view of Mt. Kaimon to the west and Tanegashima Island and Yakushima Island over the ocean to the south. On the east coast is a marine park, where table coral and tropical fish such as cobalt sea bass and butterfly fish can be seen.

Satsunan Islands

The arc of islands stretches from Tanegashima Island about 40 km off the mainland of Kyushu to Yoron Island near Okinawa Main Island. It extends as far as 450 km over the Pacific Ocean including Tanegashima, Yakushima, Amami and Tokunoshima islands. All these islands belong to Kagoshima Prefecture. Separated from the Kyushu mainland, these islands are rich in local color and natural beauty. They are connected to Kagoshima by boat and airplane.

Tanegashima Island ⬚110⬚ ☎09972: 447 sq.km in area. This long narrow island from north to south is the northernmost of the Satsunan Islands. The main city is Nishino-omote (pop. 21,673), a port on the northwest coast. 3 hrs. 30 min. by ferry from Kagoshima. The airport is in the center of the island and can be reached from Kagoshima in 40 min. It is 50 min. by bus from the airport to Nishino-omote.

In 1543 three Portuguese drifted ashore here. They were the first to teach the Japanese the use of firearms, which accordingly were called *Tanegashima* after the name of the place where they were introduced. A memorial to this effect stands in Wakasa Park, south of Nishino-omote. A memorial to the introduction of the firearms also stands in Cape Kadokura on the southern edge of the island at the spot where the three Portuguese drifted ashore. Tanegashima Space Center is at the southeast end of the island. There are two rocket launch pads on capes Takezaki and Osaki and a space development exhibition hall at the entrance gate. The exhibition hall displays panels and models showing the development of space exploration and includes audio-visual facilities.

Yakushima Island ⬚110⬚ ☎09974: An almost perfectly round island about 30 km southwest of Tanegashima Island with an area of 500 sq. km. Kyushu's highest peak, the 1,935-m-high Mt. Miyanoura towers magnificently over the center of the island. Although the climate is subtropical with high precipitation, snow sometimes accumulates on the summit of Mt. Miyanoura. The largest town is Kamiyakucho, where Miyanoura Port is located, on the north coast. It is about 4 hrs. by boat from Kagoshima Port. The airport is near the east coast and can be reached from Kagoshima in 40 min. by air. The bus from the airport to Miyanoura takes 20 min. The starting point for intra-island buses is Ambo on the east coast (35 min. by bus from Miyanoura). Yaku-sugi (cedar) Land Nature Reserve lies about 16 km inland from Ambo at an altitude of 1,000 m. Here, hiking trails ranging from 30 min. to 2 hrs. pass through groves of ancient cedars (more than 1,000 years old) called *Yaku-sugi*. The oldest, the Buddha Cedar, in Yaku-sugi Land is about 2,500 years old. The *Yaku-sugi* have been designated as Natural Monuments. The annual rings formed within the trees are detailed and the wood is fine-grained, making it resistant to rot. Thus, the cedar is manufactured into furniture, household utensils and flower arrangement bowls. It is 16 km from Ambo by a woodland path, about 1 hr. by car.

Along the Mt. Miyanoura ascent, one can see the oldest *Yaku-sugi* in Japan: the Jomon Cedar, which is said to be 7,200 years old.

Amami Gunto (Island Chain) Quasi-National Park 111 : The main islands in the Amami Island Chain are Amami-Oshima, Kikai-jima, Tokunoshima, Okinoerabu and Yoron. They are all subtropical with warm temperatures and plenty of rain. The abundance of nature is apparent in the beautiful blossoms of the fern palms, bougainvillea and hibiscus trees as well as in the coral reefs in the clear blue sea. The local customs, similar to those of Southeast Asia, are quite diffferent from those of the mainland and quite interesting.

Amami-Oshima Island 110 : The north end of the island chain, with an area of 819 sq.km. It is long and narrow from north to south, the southern part having a jagged, ria-type coastline. Oshima Straits, which separates this island and the neighboring Kakeroma Island (77 sq.km), has been designated as a marine park, and glass-bottomed boats make excursions upon its waters. Specialties include Oshima pongee (handwoven silk fabric), brown sugar and papayas. The lobsters here are delicious.

Naze (pop. 46,587, ☎ 0997) on the west coast is the administrative, commercial and cultural center of the islands. The ferry from Kagoshima arrives at Naze in 11 hrs. 10 min. There are also boats from Tokyo, Osaka and Naha. The airport is in Kasari Town on the northeast coast, with a flight from Kagoshima taking 55 min. and from Okinawa, 1 hr.10 min. The bus from the airport to Naze takes 55 min. Intra-island buses start from in front of Amami Kotsu Co. Head Office in Naze. The sightseeing bus tour of the island takes 8 hrs.

Tokunoshima Island 111 : Located southwest of Amami-Oshima with an area of 248 sq.km. Agriculture is thriving, and the production of sugarcane surpasses that anywhere else on the islands. The coast is beautiful, and, in addition to the swimming at San on the northwest coast, there are spots of striking natural beauty such as Cape Kanami at the northern end and Cape Inutabu at the southwestern end. Port Kametoku on the east coast can be reached from Naze by boat in 4 hrs. 20 min. The airport is on the west coast, with flights from Kagoshima (1 hr.) and Amami-Oshima (30 min.). The sightseeing bus covers the island in 7 hrs. 30 min.

Kikaijima, Okinoerabu and Yoron islands are all developing marine resorts. Except among true lovers, they are relatively unknown as excellent spots for diving, beach fishing and trawling. There is an airport on each of these islands connecting them to Kagoshima, Amami-Oshima and Okinawa.

Area 8. Okinawa Prefecture and Ryukyu Islands

Lying 685 km off the southern end of the mainland of Kyushu. This arc of islands divides the Pacific Ocean and the East China Sea, extending all the way to Taiwan. There are more than sixty islands between the main island, Okinawa, in the north and Yonaguni Island at the southwestern end. The prefecture covers a total area of 2,255.85 sq.km and has a population of 1,229,726. The capital is Naha on the main island.

Okinawa is a typical Japanese subtropical region with a generally warm climate and many typhoons in autumn. The cherry blossoms bloom in late January, while the swimming season is from April to October. The islands are popular because of the beautifully clear ocean water. Marine resort facilities have been set up on each island, providing a perfect base for sports and nature appreciation on both land and sea. There is one national park, Iriomote, and two quasi-national parks, Okinawa-Kaigan(Coast) and Okinawa Senseki(Old Battlefields).

HISTORY AND CULTURE

Mention of the islands appears in Chinese documents from the seventh century. Once called the Ryukyus, these islands were unified into a kingdom in the 12th century, while a dynasty was established in the 15th century by the Sho Clan, who made Shuri the capital. By the 17th century, the islands had come into the joint possession of China and the Shimazu Clan of Japan, later becoming a prefecture of Japan during the Meiji period. It was the place of a brutal battle during World War II, resulting in many casualties. The islands were placed under American military control from 1945-1972, then restored to Japan on May 15, 1972.

In terms of culture, Okinawa used to have unique Japanese manners and customs mingled with Chinese elements, but today the islands are completely assimilated with Japanese culture. However, the past mores are retained in its ancient religion and traditional arts. Ryukyu Dancing, one of the traditional arts, is seen throughout the year. There are dinner shows offering dance performances. Ryukyu women with wide sleeves and narrow *obi* dance gracefully to the accompaniment of drums, *samisen* (three-stringed instrument) and flutes. The most famous dances are "Tanchame" and "Asatoya Yunta."

ANNUAL EVENTS

Juriuma: Celebrated in Tsuji, Naha, on January 20 of the lunar calendar. Over 100 dancing girls wearing colorful folk costumes parade through the streets to the accompaniment of gongs, *samisen*, flutes and drums.

Haryusen or Hary: A festival centered around prayers to the sea god for a big catch and the safety of fishermen. Held on May 3-5 in Tomari Port in Naha and Itoman, it features a boat race, with 12 rowers and a steersman manning each boat.

Eisa: Held on July 13-16 of the lunar calendar in Okinawa City. It is a very masculine event in which young men dance and shout to the accompaniment of *jabisen* (a *samisen* with a snakeskin-covered sound box) and drums.

A tug of war: Held on August 15 of the lunar calendar in Itoman and on October 9-10 in Naha. Two teams of men pull against each other with a giant, rice-straw rope 60 cm in diameter and some 500 m in length.

INDUSTRIES

Although agricultural products (rice and sugar cane) and livestock (cows and pigs) still make up the major portion of the area's economic production, tourism is starting to play an increasingly important role in the Okinawan economy. There are few factories yet, but recently petroleum, cement and other large-scale plants have developed along the coast. The traditional crafts, *awamori* (millet brandy) and other food products provide good souvenirs.

Specialties: *Bingata* is the dyeing of cotton, linen and silk by a traditional technique using a mixture of pigments and vegetable dyes. Considered one of the most colorful among all of Okinawa's traditional arts, it takes even an experienced craftsman at least two weeks to dye a small piece of cloth since the dyeing process requires concentration, patience and careful finger work. The color dyes are of bright hue, and their patterns feature animals, plants, landscapes and geometrical designs. It is possible to watch this dyeing process at workshops in Shuri, Naha (20 min. by taxi from Kokusai-odori Street, or International Street).

Ryukyu Ceramic is a traditional ceramic art with a 400-year-long history. Originally introduced from China, the ceramic technique is now based on the use of a red clay found in the northern part of the main island of Okinawa. Since the ceramics are baked in Tsuboya in Naha (10 min. by taxi from Kokusai-odori Street), they are also known as *Tsuboya-yaki* ware. Simply designed articles of daily use are produced here in large numbers.

Bashofu is a good-quality cloth peculiar to Okinawa made from banana-tree fibers. Based on a history of 600 years, *Bashofu* is dyed by a process that takes 15 days, with another week required to weave the cloth. The woven cloth is mainly used for *kimono*, *obi* and cushions.

Ryukyu lacquerware is another typical art of Okinawa. *deigo* wood is generally used for the crafted item on which lacquer made from Kucha earth is applied. This lacquerware is characterized by its light weight and the absence of discoloration and cracks.

Ryukyu-kasuri cloth, *mon-ori* (a type of weaving using a raised pattern in colors on warp), glassware, leather work, coral and shell crafts are also regarded as typical Okinawan products.

Okinawa Main Island

As the largest island in the prefecture and the main island in the Ryukyu Island Chain, it is called Okinawa-Honto (Main Island). It is long and thin, measuring 135 km from north to south, 10 km from east to west, and rimmed by coral reefs. The south-central area is a plain, where Naha and other cities are situated. There are many mountains in the north (of which Mt. Yonaha (alt. 503 m) is the highest) with stunted development. Bus is the main form of transportation on the island.

Naha ⌊111/114-②⌋ ☎ 0988

Pop. 309,536. As the largest city in Okinawa Prefecture, it is the area's political, economic and cultural center. It lies on the west coast of the southern part of the island and includes the former capital of the Ryukyu Kingdom, Shuri. The prefectural offices, Okinawa Development Bureau, other governmental branches and the mass media are concentrated in this large, bustling city. The shopping district is focused around the Kokusai-odori Street and Heiwa-dori Street area. There are some 140 hotels and other accommodations.

TRANSPORTATION
Transportation to Naha

The major mode of transportation in and out of Okinawa is flying. The Naha International Airport is located 15 min. by bus from the city center. Flights leave for Guam, Honolulu, Los Angeles, Hong Kong and Taiwan among others. JAL, ANA and JAS all service Naha from major city centers on the mainland. A flight takes 2 hrs. 30 min. from Tokyo, 2 hrs. from Osaka or 1 hr.35 min. from Fukuoka. There are also flights from Nagasaki, Kagoshima, Oita, Miyazaki and Kumamoto in Kyushu.

Ferry service is available from Tokyo (52 hrs.) and Osaka (34 hrs.), some of which include stops at the Amami Islands. A ship from Hakata Port in Fukuoka takes 30 hrs. 30 min. and one from Kagoshima Port takes 25 hrs. Ryukyu Kaiun and Arimura Sangyo are the major operators in the area.

Inter-Island Transportation

Since there is no train service in Okinawa, buses and taxis are the only alternatives. The Naha Kotsu bus terminal is next to Naha Port. The bus network is well provided and service is frequent.

Regular Sightseeing Buses: City tour of Naha; southern old battle-fields; central and northern area, EXPO'75 Memorial Park, etc. (guided tours in Japanese only). Most of them are full-day tours and operated all year round.

Refer to the supplement for details regarding the "i" **System Information Center** in Naha.

PLACES OF INTEREST

Shureimon Gate: 6 km east of Kokusai-odori Street. This "Gate of Courtesy" is regarded by native residents as a familiar symbol of Okinawa. The gate was built in the early 16th century to serve as a secondary gate for Shuri Castle. The present structure is a reconstruction completed in 1958. At first glance, it looks Chinese, but it is truly representative of Ryukyuan architecture.

Tamaudon: 200 m west of Shureimon Gate. These are the tombs of the Sho family—the royal family of the former Ryukyu Kingdom. There are three large tombstones. The center one contains coffins, the left one the remains of kings and queens and the right one the remains of princes, princesses and consorts. They are designated as Important Cultural Properties.

Sonohiyan Utaki: A stone gate located next to Shureimon Gate. It was built in 1511 by the Ryukyuan royal family as an offering to the god of prophecy. According to legend, this god was able to foresee any mishap that might befall the king when he left home.

This stone gate is also a typical example of Okinawan stone architecture. The Chinese gabled-roof, stone rafters and fish-tail ridgepole crests show a beautiful harmonization between the diverse elements of Chinese and Japanese aesthetics.

Okinawa Prefectural Museum: A 10-min. walk north of Shureimon Gate. The museum exhibits some 1,000 examples of the arts of Okinawa—sculptures, folkloric items and archaeological relics. Here, one can obtain a good, general idea of the unique culture of Okinawa.

Okinawa Senseki (Old Battlefields) Quasi-National Park 111 : It covers an area of 31.3 sq.km between Itoman and Gushikamison in the southern part of the main island of Okinawa. There are 67 monuments within the park, including *Himeyuri-no-To* (lit. Star Lily-of-the-Valley Tower) on Mabuni Hill and a memorial tower dedicated to the 244,136 Okinawan war dead of World War II. The Peace Memorial Hall and a Museum also stand on the grounds.

Itoman ☎ 09899: Pop. 49,301. Located 12 km south of Naha. It is the center of the fishing industry for the waters of the Pacific south of Japan. The city is also noted for the production of sugarcane. Hakugindo Hall, built to encourage bountiful harvests and safe sea voyages, is in the northern part of town. Originally an offering to this same god, the Haryusen Boat Race, held on May 4 of the lunar calendar, is a popular, well-known event that attracts many tourists.

The southern part of the city is largely included within the Okinawa Old Battlefields Quasi-National Park.

Gyokusendo Cave: A stalactite cave located 12 km southeast of Naha with a total length of 4 km. An 800-m section is open to the public. It is the third-largest cave in Japan after Akiyoshido Cave in Yamaguchi Prefecture and Ryusendo Cave in Iwate Prefecture. The cave is worth visiting for its scientific elements as well as its scenic beauty. There are some 900,000 stalagmites and stalactites around transparent streams where bats nest. The echoing footsteps in the tranquil caves conjure up visions of distant, primitive ages. A sub-tropical botanical garden nearby is thick with lush growths of sago, coconut palms and subtropical flowers.

Urasoe ☎ 0988: Located 9 km northeast of Naha with a population of 88,340. This was the political center of the Okinawa Islands from the 12th to 15th centuries. Although the city was destroyed during World War II, reconstruction is complete and the city is growing rapidly. Many trading companies and factories have sprung up in the business and industrial sections. Sights include historical relics such as the ruins of Urasoe Castle and a royal mausoleum built in the 13th century. Urasoe Castle is located 12 km northeast of Naha on a hill east of Urasoe. This was once the castle site of the feudal lords who ruled the entire area during the 13th and 14th centuries. Nothing remains now to remind one of the fierce battles fought here during World War II. Today, this is a park commanding a breathtaking view of the Pacific and the East China Sea.

Nakagusuku Castle: Lying 22 km northeast of Naha is Nakagusuku in the south-central part of the main island of Okinawa. The castle was built in 1438 by Gosamaru, reputed to be the most skillful castle architect in Okinawa. The stone wall, stretching almost 1 km around the castle site, retains its original shape. The site has now been made into Nakagusuku Park.

Nakamura-ke Major Cultural Assets: 10 min. on foot from Naka-gusuku Park. This house miraculously escaped damage during the war. As a typical Okinawan home of the mid-18th century, it attracts many visitors today. Perhaps the most distinguishing characteristic is that it was built without a single nail. A high stone-and-wood fence encloses the 1,500-sq.-m grounds. It is an Important Cultural Property.

Okinawa ☎ 09893: Pop. 106,950. Located in the central part of the main island of Okinawa, 24 km northeast of Naha. Formerly called Koza, this is the second-largest city in Okinawa. It takes 1 hr. by bus from Naha. Since the town sprang up around the U.S. Kadena Air Force Base, English signboards flood the town, and U.S. military servicemen and their families out shopping or enjoying themselves are frequently seen. Kadena Air Base is one of the most important U.S. military bases in Asia. The Southeast Botanical Garden in the northern part of the city has a total area of 400,000 sq.m. It includes an insect zoo, a water park that covers six ponds and botanical gardens containing some 2,000 species of tropical and subtropical plants.   In addition, a giant amusement park called Okinawa "Kodomo-no-Kuni" (Children's World) is located on a hill overlooking the Pacific in the southern part of town.   It features a zoo that includes the Iriomote wildcat, (a Special Natural Monument) and the crested eagle (a Natural Monument).

Okinawa Kaigan(Coast) Quasi-National Park 111 : Covering a total area of 102 sq.km, the park stretches 80 km along the coast from Nagahama Beach to Nago Bay, and from Unten in Nakijin on the eastern tip of the Motobu Peninsula to Cape Hedo at the northern-most tip of the island.   Onna Village is in the center of the park.

There are many beaches in the park.   From the south—Moon, Tiger, Manza, Kariyushi, Emerald, Okuma and others, where swimming, diving, yachting, water-skiing, surfing, deep-sea fishing and seashell gathering can be enjoyed from April to November.   The beaches are cut off by cliffs in places and are covered with tiny grains of coral.   The clear ocean waters change from emerald to blue to deep indigo, depending on the depth and amount of sunlight.   There are deluxe resort hotels with first-class facilities on each of the beaches. Visitors come to relax here from all over Japan.

Okinawa Kaichu (Marine) Park: Located 59 km northeast of Naha, the park has a total area of 190,000 sq.m that covers the southern end of Nago Bay and Cape Busena.   It features an underwater observatory, where coral and tropical fish can be viewed in their natural habitat 6 m under the ocean.   There is also the Shell Exhibition Hall, which contains many species of shells found along the seacoast.

Nago ☎0980: Located almost in the middle of the main island at the neck of the Motobu Peninsula.   The city covers an area of 210.9 sq. km and has a population of 51,580.   It is 69 km northeast of Naha (2 hrs. 20 min. by bus) and is the largest city in the region.   There are banks, business offices, hospitals, breweries and pineapple processing factories.   Many typical, old Okinawan houses remain in the area since damage from the war was slight.   On the southeastern outskirts of the city, tall 300-year-old *gajumaru* (banyan) trees can be seen. Nago Castle is located 15 min. on foot from the center of the city. This was the site of the castle residence of the Nago Clan, who ruled the district during the 14th century.   Along both sides of a long flight of stone steps leading to the castle site are rows of densely planted cherry trees that burst into bloom from late January to early February.   At this time of the year, an annual cherry blossom festival is held.   The site commands a panoramic view of Nago, the Motobu Peninsula and the Kunigami Mountain Range.

Okinawa Memorial Nation Government Park: Located on the tip of the Motobu Peninsula.   Commemorating the Exposition of 1975, the park lies on the original fairgrounds, called Emerald Park.   The 770,000-sq.-m site contains an aquarium, an ocean culture center, an amusement park called Expo Land, the "Aquapolis" (artificial float-ing island) and many other attractions. Swimming is possible on the Emerald Beach, an artificial sandy shore in front of Expo Land. An excursion in a glass-bottomed boat is available. 1 hr.20 min. by bus from Nago.

Ie Island 111 : 8 km northwest of the Motobu Peninsula, 40 min. by ferry from Motobu Port, a peanut-shaped island 22 km in circumfer-ence. The island was a bloody battlefield for the Japanese and American forces during World War II. The north side is formed by 60-m-high precipices and jutting coral reefs, but the south and east coasts around the Youth Travel Village are sandy beaches popular with swimmers, fishermen and campers. Mt. Tatchu (alt. 172 m), the island's only rocky mountain, is located on the east side of the island. It can be climbed in about 1 hr. The summit commands an exquisite panorama of the main island and the Motobu Peninsula.

Cape Hedo: 61 km north of Nago, the northernmost tip of the main Island of Okinawa. On a clear day, one can enjoy a view of the Amami Island Chain. On the way to the cape are the Kayauchi-Banta Cliffs, a magnificent marine landscape.

Islands South of Okinawa Main Island: These include the Kerama Island Group (Kerama, Zamami, Tokashiki, etc.) and Kume Island. Each one has beautiful white beaches enclosed in coral, but Ifu Beach on Kume Island is a particularly fine campground. It can be reached in 35 min. by plane from Naha. There are four resort hotels.

Miyako and the Yaeyama Island Chains

Miyako Island 111 : 320 km southwest of the Main Island of Okinawa, or 45 min. by plane from Naha. This is the largest of the eight islands of the Miyako Island Chain, with an area of 158.6 sq.km and roughly triangular in shape. The main city is Hirara in the north with a population of 33,631 (☎ 09807). The bus services fork out from Hirara city center to three corners of the island. Since much of the island is covered with sugarcane fields, there are many sugar-processing plants. In recent years, tourism has become a fast-growing industry on the island, which is blessed with many historical relics and white sandy beaches (famed for its star-shaped sand).

The beaches, so beautiful that they are sometimes called "Sports-man's Heaven," include Maehama Beach, where a good resort hotel stands, as well as Painagama Beach, Sunakawa Beach and Shigira Beach. These beaches are a mecca for surfing and scuba diving. In late April, the whole island becomes the site of the triathlon games.

Ishigaki Island 111 : About 430 km southwest of Okinawa Island, the principal island of the Yaeyama Island Chain with an area of 227 sq.km. Mt. Omoto (alt. 525 m), the highest peak in the prefecture, soars up in the middle of the island, while Hirakubo Hill rises in the northeast. The whole island belongs to Ishigaki City (pop. 42,535. ☎ 09808), with the port located in the southwest. Since the island was undamaged by war, it retains many aspects of old Okinawa, with its streets laid out in a chequerboard pattern and old walled houses lined up along them. The main industries are the cultivation and processing of pineapple and sugarcane as well as bonito fishing. It takes 55 min. by air from Naha, or 25 min. from Miyako Island.

Miyara-Donchi Residence, Ishigaki House Garden and Gongendo Shrine have been made Important Cultural Properties because they show the life-style of the Ryukyuan nobility. Kabira Bay on the north coast has an incredibly exquisite beach facing the emerald green waters dotted with tiny islets. Palms grow wild in Kabira Park, and black pearls are cultivated here. Sukuji Beach in the northwest is another popular beach with sports facilities. It takes 40 min. by bus from Ishigaki City.

Taketomi Island: A 6.7-sq.-km island 6 km west of Ishigaki Island, taking 10 min. by ferry from Ishigaki Island. Numerous red-walled, thatched houses are scattered throughout the landscape, creating an atmosphere of days gone by. Many historical relics and traditional customs have been retained.

Kohama Island ⌈111⌉: About 14 km southwest of Ishigaki Island. With a circumference of only 12 km, this tiny island can be reached by ferry from Ishigaki Island in 35 min. Cape Biruma on the south coast is the location of a marine sports center called Yamaha Resort "Haimurubushi."

Iriomote National Park ⌈111⌉: The park consists of several small islands in the southern part of the Yaeyama Islands—Iriomote, Kohama, Taketomi, Kurojima, Aragusuku and Nakanokan—all covering a total area of 125 sq.km. The attraction of the park lies in the mangroves, nipa palms, other subtropical plant groves and the tropical fish that swim among the coral reefs. There are also many unusual animals, including the Iriomote wildcat (a Special Natural Monument), the crested eagle and many different kinds of butterflies.

Iriomote Island ⌈111⌉: About 15 km west of Ishigaki Island. With an area of 290.3 sq.km, this island is second in size only to Okinawa Island in the prefecture. The entire island is covered with primeval jungle, the only inhabited areas being along the north and east coasts. The main villages are Ohara on the southeast coast and Funaura and Shirohama on the west coast, all of which are connected by bus. It takes 45 min. by ferry from Ishigaki Island. To see the island, one must either walk or have a car, but a boat tour along the Nakama River or Urauchi River is another alternative.

Even further south is Hateruma Island (in fact, it is the southernmost point in Japan) and Yonakuni Island to the west (the westernmost point in Japan). Both can be reached by plane from Ishigaki Island.

Supplement

TOURIST INFORMATION SERVICES
("i" System Information Centers)

JNTO TOURIST INFORMATION CENTERS (TIC)

Tokyo Office: Kotani Bldg., 1-6-6, Yurakucho, Chiyoda-ku, Tokyo
Tel. (03) 3502-1461

New Tokyo Int'l Airport Office: Airport Terminal Bldg., Narita, Chiba Pref.
Tel. (0476) 32-8711

Kyoto Office: 1st fl., Kyoto Tower Bldg., Higashi-Shiokojicho, Shimogyo-ku, Kyoto
Tel. (075) 371-5649

"i" System Information Centers

City	Office	Address	Tel.
SAPPORO	Sapporo City Tourism Department	Sapporo City Office	(011) 211-2376
	Sapporo City Tourist Office	JR Sapporo Station	(011) 221-0013
HAKODATE	Hakodate Tourist Information Center	12-14, Wakamatsu-cho	(0138) 23-5440
MORIOKA	Kita-Tohoku Sightseeing Center	1-48, Morioka-Ekimae dori	(0196) 25-2090
SENDAI	Sendai Tourist Information Office	JR Sendai Station	(022) 222-4069
YAMAGATA	Yamagata City Information Center	JR Yamagata Station	(0236) 31-7865
	Yamagata Tourist Information Center	Yamagata Airport	(0237) 47-3111
AIZU-WAKAMATSU	Aizu-Bandai District Tourist Information Center	2-8-8 Omachi	(0242) 32-0688
	Tsurugajo Castle Tourist Imformation	Tsurugajo Castle	(0242) 27-4005
UTSUNOMIYA	Utsunomiya City Tourist Information	JR Utsunomiya Station	(0286) 36-2177
NIKKO	Nikko City Tourist Information Center	Tobu Nikko Station	(0288) 53-4511
	Nikko Historical Museum	591, Miyuki-cho	(0288) 53-3795
TSUCHIURA	Tsuchiura City Tourist Information Center	JR Tsuchiura Station	(0298) 21-4166
TSUKUBA	Tsukuba Information Center	Tsukuba Bus Terminal	(0298) 55-7155
NARITA	Narita City Information Office	JR Narita Station	(0476) 24-3198
	Narita Tourist Pavilion	383-1, Nakamachi	(0476) 24-3232
CHIBA	Chiba Convention Bureau Information Center	Japan Convention Center	(0472) 96-0535
YOKOHAMA	Kanagawa Prefectural Tourist Assn.	Silk Center, Yamashita-cho	(045) 681-0007
	Yokohama Int'l Tourist Assn.	Silk Center, Yamashita-cho	(045) 641-4759
	Yokohama Municipal Tourist Assn.	JR Shin-Yokohama Station	(045) 473-2895
	Yokohama Tourist Information	JR Yokohama Station	(045) 441-7300
ATAMI	Atami Tourist Information Center	JR Atami Station	(0557) 82-3053
ITO	Ito Station Tourist Information Center	JR Ito Station	(0557) 37-3291
	Ito City Tourist Information Center	1-8-3 Yukawa	(0557) 37-6105
FUJIYOSHIDA	Fujiyoshida Information Center	Fuji-Yoshida Bus Terminal	(0555) 22-7000

KAWAGUCHIKO	Kawaguchi-ko Ekimae Information Center	89 Funatsu, Kawaguchi-ko-machi	(0555) 72-0346
	Yamanashi Prefectural Fuji Visitors' Center	6663-1 Funatsu- Kemmar-ubi Kawaguchiko-machi	(0555) 72-0259
MATSUMOTO	Matsumoto City Tourist Information Center	1-1-1 Fukashi	(0263) 32-2814
NIIGATA	Tourist Information Center	JR Niigata Station	(025) 241-7914
TOYAMA	Toyama City Imformation Center	JR Toyama Station	(0764) 32-9751
TAKAYAMA	Hida Tourist Information Office	JR Takayama Station	(0577) 32-5328
NAGOYA	Nagoya Station Tourist Information Center; Nagoya Station	JR Nagoya Station	(052) 541-4301
	Nagoya City Tourist Information Center; Chunichi Bldg.	Chunichi Bldg., Sakae 4-1-1, Naka-ku	(052) 262-2918
	Nagoya City Tourist Information Center; Kanayama	1-17-18, Kanayama, Naka-ku	(052) 323-0161
	Nagoya Int'l Center	Nagoya Int'l Bldg., Nakamura-ku	(052) 581-5678
HIKONE	Hikone City Information Center	JR Hikone Station	(0749) 22-2954
OTSU	Otsu City Tourist Information Office	JR Otsu Station	(0775) 22-3830
NARA	Kintetsu Nara Station Tourist Information Office	Kintetsu Nara Station	(0742) 24-4858
	Nara City Tourist Center	23-4 Kami-sanjomachi	(0742) 22-3900
	Sarusawa-Ike Information Center	4-49 Noborioji-cho	(0742) 26-1991
KANAZAWA	Kanazawa City Tourist Information Office	JR Kanazawa Station	(0762) 31-6311
OSAKA	Osaka Municipal Tourist Information Center	JR Osaka Station	(06) 345-2189
	Osaka Tourist Information Center	JR Shin-Osaka Station	(06) 305-3311
	Tourist Information Service	Osaka Kokusai Hotel, Chuo-ku	(06) 941-9200
	World Travel Plaza	Kintetsu Dep. Store, Abeno-ku	(06) 624-1111
KOBE	Kobe Int'l Tourist Assn.	Kotsu Center Bldg., Sannomiya	(078) 392-0020
SHIRAHAMA	Shirahama Tourist Information Center	JR Shirahama Station	(0739) 42-2900
HIMEJI	Himeji City Information Center	JR Himeji Station	(0792) 85-3792
OKAYAMA	Okayama City Tourist Information Office	JR Okayama Station	(0862) 22-2912
	Okayama Int'l Plaza	Koseicho 3-1-15	(0862) 22-0457
KURASHIKI	Kurashiki-kan Hall Tourist Information Center	Chuo 1-4-8	(0864) 22-0542
	Kurashiki Station "i" Information Center	JR Kurashiki Station	(0864) 26-8681
FUKUYAMA	Fukuyama Tourist Information Center	JR Fukuyama Station	(0849) 22-2869
ONOMICHI	Onomichi Tourist Information Center	JR Shin-Onomichi Station	(0848) 22-6900
HIROSHIMA	Hiroshima City Tourist Assn.	Peace Memorial Park, Naka-ku	(082) 247-6738
MATSUE	Matsue Tourist Information Center	JR Matsue Station	(0852) 27-2598
TAKAMATSU	Takamatsu City Tourist Information Center	1, Hamano-cho	(0878) 51-2009
MATSUYAMA	Matsuyama City Tourist Imformation	JR Matsuyama Station	(0899) 31-3914
	EPIC Imformation Center	8 Horinouchi	(0899) 43-6688
KOCHI	Kochi Station Imformation Center	JR Kochi Station	(0888) 82-1634

FUKUOKA	Fukuoka City Tourist Information	JR Hakata Station	(092) 431-3003
	Fukuoka Int'l Assn.	1-7-11, Tenjin, Chuo-ku	(092) 733-2220
IMARI	Imari City Tourist Association	619 Shinten-cho	(0955) 22-6820
ARITA	Arita-cho Information Center	JR Arita Station	(0955) 43-3942
TAKEO	Takeo City Information Center	JR Takeo-Onsen Station	(0954) 22-2542
URESHINO	Ureshino City Information Center	JR Ureshino-Onsen Bus Center	(0954) 42-0336
BEPPU	Beppu City Tourist Information	JR Beppu Station	(0977) 24-2838
NAGASAKI	Nagasaki City Tourist Information	1-88, Onoue-cho	(0958) 23-3631
	Nagasaki Prefecture Tourist Federation	Nagasaki Kotsu Sangyo Bldg.	(0958) 26-9407
KUMAMOTO	Kumamoto Airport Information Office	Kumamoto Airport	(096) 232-2810
	Kumamoto City Tourist Office	JR Kumamoto Station	(096) 352-3743
MIYAZAKI	Miyazaki City Tourist Information Center	JR Miyazaki Station	(0985) 22-6469
KAGOSHIMA	Kagoshima City Tourist Service	JR Nishi-Kagoshima Station	(0992) 53-2500
	Kagoshima Prefectural Tourist Federation	Kagoshima Sangyo Kaikan	(0992) 23-5771
NAHA	Naha City Tourist Center	Naha Airport	(0988) 57-6884

AIRLINES

Code	Airlines	Tokyo Tel. (03)	Narita (0476)	Osaka (06)	Fukuoka (092)	Nagoya (052)
AA	American Airlines	3214-2111	—	264-6308	—	—
AC	Air Canada	3586-3891	—	227-1180	—	—
AF	Air France	3475-1511	32-7710	201-5161	713-1565	551-4141
AI	Air India	3214-1981	32-7690	264-1781	471-7172	583-0747
AN	Ansett Airlines of Australia	3214-6876	—	—	—	—
AQ	Aloha Airlines	3216-5877	—	341-7241	—	—
AR	Aerolineas Argentinas	3433-1195	—	—	—	—
AS	Alaska Airlines	3407-8386	—	—	—	—
AV	Avianca	3567-0230	—	282-1151	—	563-5881
AY	Finnair	3222-6801	32-7600	363-0270	—	—
AZ	Alitaria Airway	3580-2181	32-7811	341-3951	—	551-5411
BA	British Airlines	3593-8811	32-7222	345-2761	411-2432	971-2221
CA	Air China	3505-2021	32-3941	946-1702	472-8383	—
CI	China Airlines	3436-1661	—	—	471-7788	—
CO	Continental Airlines	3281-7426	32-8832	—	—	—
CP	Canadian Airlines Int'l	3281-7426	32-7763	346-5591	481-1855	—
CX	Cathay Pacific Airways	3504-1531	32-7650	245-6731	441-1811	962-6931
DL	Delta Air lines	5275-7000	—	243-2525	—	561-6161
EA	Eastern Air lines	3592-1634	—	—	—	—
EG	Japan Asia Airways	3455-7511	32-3921	223-2222	733-3111	563-4141
EI	Irish Airlines	3582-8886	—	—	—	—
ET	Ethiopian Airlines	3281-1990	—	—	—	—
EW	East-West Airlines	3214-6876	—	—	—	—
FJ	Air Pacific	3593-7030	32-8815	262-1691	761-1821	561-6061
GA	Garuda Indonesia	3593-1181	32-7860	445-6985	—	222-4771
GF	Gulf Air	3563-3288	—	282-1151	—	563-5881
IA	Iraqi Airway	3264-5501	—	—	—	—
IB	IBERIA Airlines of Spain	3582-3631	32-7861	347-7201	—	—
IR	Iran Air	3586-2101	32-8842	—	—	—
IT	Air Inter	3475-2211	—	—	—	—
JD	Japan Air System	3438-1155	—	345-2828	272-5511	212-1155
JL	Japan Airlines	5489-1111	—	203-1212	271-4411	563-4141
KA	Hong Kong Dragon Airlines	3589-5315	—	—	—	—

KE	Korean Air	3211-3311	32-7561	264-3311	441-3311	586-3311
KL	KLM Royal Dutch Airlines	3216-0771	32-7905	345-6691	751-3209	582-0811
KQ	Kenya Airways	3214-4595	—	—	—	—
LH	Lufthansa German Airlines	3580-2111	32-7511	345-0231	—	561-2428
LR	Lacsa	3276-0794	—	—	—	—
LW	Air Nevada	3404-9909	—	—	—	—
MH	Malaysia Airlines	3503-5961	32-8850	245-7123	733-6006	—
MS	Egyptair	3211-4521	32-7840	341-1575	—	—
NH	All Nippon Airways	3272-1212	—	372-1212	474-1212	971-5588
NW	Northwest Airlines	3432-6000	32-7411	228-0747	751-7770	562-0867
OA	Olympic Airways	3583-1911	—	—	—	—
ON	Air Nauru	3581-9271	—	—	—	—
OS	Austrian Airlines	3582-2231	—	—	—	—
PK	Pakistan Int'l Airlines	3216-6511	32-7882	341-3106	—	—
PR	Philippine Airlines	3593-2421	32-8846	444-2541	—	—
QF	Qantas Airways	3593-7000	32-8815	262-1691	761-1821	561-6061
RG	Varig-Brazilian Airlines	3211-6751	32-7890	341-3571	714-7558	565-1641
SK	Scandinavian Airlines	3503-8101	32-7311	348-0211	713-7581	561-6913
SN	Sabena Belgian World Airlines	3585-6151	32-7850	341-8081	—	251-1733
SQ	Singapore Airlines	3213-3431	32-7591	364-0881	481-7007	565-5539
SR	Swissair	3212-1016	32-7311	345-7851	431-7291	582-0551
SU	Aeroflot Soviet Airlines	3434-9671	32-3944	—	—	—
SV	Saudia	3591-9081	—	—	—	—
TE	Air New Zealand	3287-1641	32-7613	212-8990	—	—
TG	Thai Airways Int'l	3503-3311	32-7311	202-5161	481-4881	963-8585
TK	THY Turkish Airlines	3595-2901	—	—	—	—
TN	Australian Airlines	3216-5828	—	—	—	—
UA	United Airlines	3817-4411	32-8275	271-5951	—	571-5488
UL	Air Lanka	3573-4261	32-8586	—	—	—
UT	UTA French Airlines	3593-0773	—	345-0616	—	—
VP	VASP	3211-2071	—	—	—	—
VS	Virgin Atlantic Airways	3435-8330	32-4675	—	—	—
YR	Scenic Airlines	3354-7281	—	—	—	—

HOTEL

388 government registered hotels, all members of the Japan
Hotel Association are listed in alphabetical order of their location.

LOCATION HOTEL NAME	ADDRESS	TELEPHONE
HOKKAIDO		
ASAHIKAWA		
Asahikawa Terminal	Miyashita-dori	(0166) 24-0111
New Hokkai	Gojo-dori	24-3111
Toyo	Shichijo-dori	22-7575
Asahikawa Palace	Nanajo-dori	25-8811
CHITOSE		
Nikko Chitose	Honcho	(0123) 22-1121
FURANO		
Furano Prince	Kitanominecho	(0167) 23-4111
HAKODATE		
Hakodate Kokusai	Ote-machi	(0138) 23-8751
Hakodate Royal	Omoricho	26-8181
Hakodate Harbor view	Wakamatsu-cho	22-0111
KUSHIRO		
Kushiro Pacific	Sakaecho	(0154) 24-8811
OBIHIRO		
Obihiro Grand	Nihsi-Nijo, Minami	(0155) 22-4181
OTARU		
Otaru Kokusai	Inaho	(0134) 33-2161
SAPPORO		
Alpha Sapporo	Minami-Ichijo, Chuo-ku	(011) 221-2333
ANA Hotel Sapporo	Kita-Sanjo, Chuo-ku	221-4411
Century Royal	Kita-Gojo, Chuo-ku	221-2121
Fujiya Santus	Kita-Sanjo, Chuo-ku	271-3344
Keio Plaza Hotel Sappro	Kita-Gojo, Chuo-ku	271-0111
New Otani Sapporo	Kita-Nijo, Chuo-ku	222-1111
Sapporo Grand	Kita-Ichijo, Chuo-ku	261-3311
Sapporo Park	Minami-Jujo, Chuo-ku	511-3131
Sapporo Prince	Minami-Nijo, Chuo-ku	241-1111
Sapporo Royal	Minami-Shichijo, Chuo-ku	511-2121
Sapporo Tokyu	Kita-Shijo, Chuo-ku	231-5611
Sunroute New Sapporo	Minami-Nijo, Chuo-ku	251-2511
Sapporo Koraku-en	Nishi 8 cho	261-0111
TOMAKOMAI		
East Japan	Irifunecho	(0144) 34-7211
Tomakomai Hotel New Oji	Omote-machi	33-6121
AOMORI Pref.		
AOMORI		
Aomori Grand	Shin-machi	(0177) 23-1011
HACHINOHE		
Hachinohe Grand	Bancho	(0178) 46-1234
Hachinohe Park	Fukiage	43-1111
Hachinohe Plaza	Kashiwazaki	44-3121
HIROSAKI		
New Castle	Kami-Sayashi-machi	(0172) 36-1211
TOWADA		
Towada Fujiya	Higashi-Sambancho	(0176) 22-7111
Towada Prince	Towadako, Kosaka-machi Kazuno-gun	75-3111

AKITA Pref.

AKITA
Akita Castle	Naka-dori	(0188) 34-1141
Akita New Grand	Naka-dori	34-5211
Akita terminal	Nakadori	31-222

IWATE Pref.

MORIOKA
Higashi-Nihon	Odori	(0196) 25-2131
Morioka Grand	Atagoshita	25-2111
Royal Morioka	Saien	53-1331

MIYAGI Pref.

ISHINOMAKI
Ishinomaki Riverside	Fudocho	(0225) 96-5411

SENDAI
Koyo Grand	Honcho	(022) 267-5111
Miyagi Dai-ichi	Tsutsujigaoka	297-4411
Sendai	Chuo	225-5171
Metropolitan Sendai	Aoba-ku	268-2525
Sendai Plaza	Honcho	262-7111
Sendai Tokyu	Ichibancho	262-2411

YAMAGATA Pref.

YAMAGATA
Onuma	Kojirakawa-machi	(0236) 32-1111
Yamagata Grand	Honcho	41-2611

FUKUSHIMA Pref.

FUKUSHIMA
Tatsumiya	Sakae-machi	(0245) 22-5111

KORIYAMA
Koriyama View	Naka-machi	(0249) 24-1111

NIIGATA Pref.

MYOKO
Akakura Kanko	Myoko-Kogen, Nakakubiki-gun	(0255) 87-2501

NAGAOKA
Nagaoka Grand	Higashi-Sakanouecho	(0258) 33-2111
New Otani Nagaoka	Dai-machi	37-1111

NIIGATA
Bandai Silver	Bandai	(025) 243-3711
The Italia-ken	Nishibori-dori	224-5111
Niigata Grand	Shimo Okawamae	228-6111
Niigata	Bandai	245-3331
Niigata Toei	Benten	244-7101
Okura Hotel Niigata	Kawabatacho	224-6111

YUZAWA
Naeba Prince	Mikuni, Yuzawa-machi, Minami-Uonuma-gun	(0257) 89-2211

TOCHIGI Pref.

NASU
Nasu Royal	Takaku-Otsu, Nasu-machi	(0287) 78-2001

NIKKO
Nikko Kanaya	Kami-Hatsuishi-machi	(0288) 54-0001
Nikko Lakeside	Chugushi	55-0321
Nikko Prince	Shobugahama, Chugushi	55-0661

UTSUNOMIYA
Utsunomiya Grand	Nishiharacho	(0286) 35-2111
Utsunomiya Royal	Eno-machi	33-0331

GUMMA Pref.

IKAHO
Hashimoto	Ikaho-machi, Kitagunma-gun	(0279) 72-2035

KUSATSU
Village	Kusatsu, Kusatsu-machi, Azuma-gun	(0279) 88-3232

HOTEL

MAEBASHI
Gumma Royal	Ote-machi	(0272) 23-6111
Mercury	Otomo-machi	52-0111

IBARAKI Pref.

KASHIMA
Kashima Central	Onohara, Kamisu-machi, Kashima-gun	(0299) 92-5511

MITO
Mito Keisei	Sannomaru	(0292) 26-3111
Mito Plaza	Suifucho	31-8111
Sannomaru	Sannomaru	21-3011

OARAI
Oarai Park	Isohama Oarai-machi, Higashi-Ibaraki-gun	(0292) 67-2171

TSUKUBA
Tsukuba Dai-ichi	Azuma	(0298) 52-1112

SAITAMA Pref.

HONJO
Saitama Grand	Minami-moto-machi, Honjo	(0495) 21-2111

OMIYA
Palace Omiya	Omiya	(048) 647-3300

CHIBA Pref.

CHIBA
Chiba Grand	Chiba-Minato	(0472) 41-2111
Chiba Keisei	Honchibacho	22-2111
Chiba New Park	Chiba-Minato	42-1111
New Tsukamoto	Chiba-Minato	43-1111

FUNABASHI
Sungarden Lalaport	Hamacho	(0474) 31-7531

NARITA
Holiday Inn Tobu Narita	Tokko	(0476) 32-1234
Narita View	Kosuge	32-1111
Nikko Narita	Tokko	32-0032

URAYASU
Sunroute Plaza Tokyo	Maihama	(0473) 55-1111
Daiichi Tokyo Bay	Maihama	55-3333
Sheraton Grande	Maihama	55-5555
Tokyo Bay Hilton	Maihama	55-5000

TOKYO

HACHIJOJIMA
Hachijojima Taiyo	Mitsune, Hachijo-machi, Hachijo Island	(04996) 2-3111

TACHIKAWA
New Plaza	Akebonocho	(0425) 22-6191

TOKYO
Akasaka Prince	1-2, Kioicho, Chiyoda-ku	(03) 3234-1111
Akasaka Tokyu	2-14-3, Nagatacho, Chiyoda-ku	3580-2311
ANA Hotel Tokyo	1-12-33, Akasaka, Minato-ku	3505-1111
Asakusa View	3-17-1, Nishiasakusa, Taito-ku	3842-2111
The Capital Tokyu	2-10-3, Nagatacho, Chiyoda-ku	3581-4511
The Century Hyatt Tokyo	2-7-2, Nishi-Shinjuku, Shinjuku-ku	3349-0111
Daiei	1-15-8, Koishikawa, Bunkyo-ku	3813-6271
Diamond	25, Ichibancho, Chiyoda-ku	3263-2211
Fairmont	2-1-17, Kudan-Minami, Chiyoda-ku	3262-1151
Gajoen Kanko	1-8-1, Shimo-Meguro, Meguro-ku	3491-0111
Ginza Dai-ichi	8-13-1, Ginza, Chuo-ku	3542-5311
Ginza Nikko	8-4-21, Ginza, Chuo-ku	3571-4911
Ginza Tokyu	5-15-9, Ginza, Chuo-ku	3541-2411
Grand Palace	1-1-1, Iidabashi, Chiyoda-ku	3264-1111
Haneda Tokyu	2-8-6, Haneda-kuko, Ota-ku	3747-0311
Hill-Top	1-1, Kanda Surugadai, Chiyoda-ku	3293-2311
Holiday Inn Tokyo	1-13-7, Hatchobori, Chuo-ku	3553-6161
Imperial	1-1-1, Uchisaiwaicho, Chiyoda-ku	3504-1111
Keio Plaza Inter Continental	2-2-1, Nishi-Shinjuku, Shinjuku-ku	3344-0111
Kokusai Kanko	1-8-3, Marunouchi, Chiyoda-ku	3215-3281
Metropolitan	1-6-1, Nishi-Ikebukuro, Toshima-ku	3980-1111

Miyako Hotel Tokyo	1-1-50, Shiroganedai, Minato-ku	3447-3111
New Meguro	1-3-18, Chuocho, Meguro-ku	3719-8121
The New Otani	4-1, Kioicho, Chiyoda-ku	3265-1111
Okura	2-10-4, Toranomon, Minato-ku	3582-0111
Pacific Meridien Tokyo	3-13-3, Takanawa, Minato-ku	3445-6711
Palace	1-1-1, Marunouchi, Chiyoda-ku	3211-5211
Royal Park	Kakigara-cho, chuo-ku	3667-1111
Shiba Park	1-5-10, Shibakoen, Minato-ku	3433-4141
Sunroute Tokyo	2-3-1, Yoyogi, Shibuya-ku	3375-3211
Takanawa	2-1-17, Takanawa, Minato-ku	3443-9251
Takanawa Prince	3-13-1, Takanawa, Minato-ku	3447-1111
Takanawa Tobu	4-7-6, Takanawa, Minato-ku	3447-0111
Tokyo	2-17-18, Takanawa, Minato-ku	3447-5771
Tokyo Hilton International	6-6-2, Nishi-Shinjuku, Shinjuku-ku	3344-5111
Tokyo Hotel Urashima	2-5-23, Harumi, Chuo-ku	3533-3111
Tokyo Marunouchi	1-6-3, Marunouchi, Chiyoda-ku	3215-2151
Tokyo Prince	3-3-1, Shiba Park, Minato-ku	3432-1111
Tokyo Station	1-9-1, Marunouchi, Chiyoda-ku	3231-2511
Tokyukanko	2-21-6, Akasaka, Minato-ku	3582-0451
Yaesu Fujiya	2-9-1, Yaesu, Chuo-ku	3273-2111

KANAGAWA Pref.

ATSUGI
Atsugi Royal Park	Naka-machi	(0462)21-0001

CHIGASAKI
Pacific Hotel Chigasaki	Higashi-Kaigan Minami	(0467)82-1141
	(temporarily closed)	

HAKONE
Fujiya	Miyanoshita, Hakone-machi	(0460)2-2211
Hakone Hotel Kowaki-en	Ninotaira, Hakone-machi	2-4111
Hakone Kanko	Sengokuhara, Hakone-machi	4-8501
Hakone Prince	Moto-Hakone, Hakone-machi	3-7111
Kagetsu-en	Sengokuhara, Hakone-machi	4-8621
Odakyu Hakone Highland	Shinanoki, Sengokuhara, Hakone-machi	4-8541
Yama	Moto-Hakone, Hakone-machi	3-6321
Yumoto Fujiya	Yumoto, Hakone-machi	5-6111

KAMAKURA
Kamakura Park	Sakanoshita	(0467)25-5121

KAWASAKI
Kawasaki Nikko	Nisshincho, Kawasaki-ku	(044)244-5941

OISO
Oiso Prince	Kokufu-Hongo, Oiso-machi, Naka-gun	(0463)61-7111

YOKOHAMA
Aster	Yamashitacho, Naka-ku	(045)651-0141
Bund	Shin-Yamashita, Naka-ku	621-1101
Empire	Matanocho, Totsuka-ku	851-1431
The Hotel Yokohama	Yamashitacho, Naka-ku	662-1321
New Grand	Yamashitacho, Naka-ku	681-1841
Satellite Hotel Yokohama	Yamashitacho, Naka-ku	641-8571
Shin Yokohama	Shin-Yokohama, Kohoku-ku	471-6011
Yokohama Tokyu	Minami-Saiwaicho, Nishi-ku	311-1682

YOKOSUKA
Yokosuka	Yonegahama-dori	(0468)25-1111
Kannonzaki Keikyu	Hashirimizu	41-2200

SHIZUOKA Pref.

ATAMI
New Fujiya	Ginzacho	(0557)81-0111

FUJI
Grand Fuji	Heigaki-Honcho	(0545)61-0360

HAMAMATSU
Concorde Hamamatsu	Moto-Shiro-machi	(0534)57-1111
Grand Hotel Hamamatsu	Higashi-Iba	52-2111
Hamamatsu Meitetsu	Itaya-cho	52-5111

HAMANA-KO
Sunza Villa	Kiga, Hosoe-machi, Inasa-gun	(05352)2-1171

HOTEL

ITO
Izukogen Izumigo Plaza	Sakihara, Futo	(0557) 51-1666
Kawana	Kawana	45-1111

IWATA
Iwata Grand	Iwai	(05383) 4-1211

NIHONDAIRA
Nippondaira	Mabase, Shimizu	(0543) 35-1131

SHIMODA
Shimoda Tokyu	Shimoda	(05582) 2-2411

SHIZUOKA
Shizuoka Grand Hotel Naka-jimaya	Konya-machi	(0542) 53-1151

YAIZU
Yaizu Grand	Hamatome	(0546) 27-1121

YAMANASHI Pref.

FUJI LAKES
Fuji View	Katsuyamamura, Minamitsuru-gun	(0555) 83-2211
Highland Resort	Shin-Nishihara, Fuji-Yoshida	22-1000
Mt. Fuji	Yamanaka, Yamanakakomura, Minamitsuru-gun	62-2111
New Yamanakako	Yamanaka, Yamanakakomura, Minamitsuru-gun	62-2311
Yamanakako	Yamanakakomura, Minamitsuru-gun	62-2511

KOFU
Konaya	Chuo	(0552) 35-1122

NAGANO Pref.

HAKUBA
Hakuba Tokyu	Happo, Hakubamura Kita-Azumi-gun	(0261) 72-3001

KARUIZAWA
Karuizawa Prince	Karuizawa, Karuizawa-machi, Kitasaku-gun	(0267) 42-8111
Mampei	Sakuranosawa, Karuizawa-machi, Kitasaku-gun	42-2771

NAGANO
Nagano Hotel Saihokukan	Agata-machi	(0262) 35-3333
Nagano Kokusai Kaikan	Agata-machi	34-1111
Nagano Royal	Chitose 1 chome	28-2222

SHIGA HEIGHTS
Okushiga-Kogen	Okushiga-kogen, Yamanouchi-machi, Shimotakai-gun	(0269) 34-2034
Shiga-Heights	Hirao, Yamanouchi-machi, Shimotakai-gun	34-2111

SHINANO-OMACHI
Kuroyon Royal	Taira, Omachi	(0261) 22-1530

TATESHINA
Heidi	Tateshina-kogen, Chino	(0266) 67-2001
Artland Tateshina	Kitayama, Tateshina-kogen, Chino	67-2626

GIFU Pref.

GIFU
Gifu Grand	Nagara	(0582) 33-1111
Nagaragawa	Nagaraukaiya	32-4111

TAKAYAMA
Hida Hotel plaza	Hanaoka-machi	(0577) 33-4600
Takayama Green	Nishino-isshikicho	33-5500

AICHI Pref.

INUYAMA
Meitetsu Inuyama	Kita-Koken, Inuyama	(0568) 61-2211

NAGOYA
Castle Plaza	Meieki, Nakamura-ku	(052) 582-2121
International Hotel Nagoya	Nishiki, Naka-ku	961-3111
Meitetsu Grand	Meieki, Nakamura-ku	582-2211
Meitetsu New Grand	Tsubakicho, Nakamura-ku	452-5511
Nagoya Castle	Hinokuchicho, Nishi-ku	521-2121
Nagoya Dai-ichi	Meieki, Nakamura-ku	581-4411
Nagoya Fuji Park	Nishiki, Naka-ku	962-2289
Nagoya Kanko	Nishiki, Naka-ku	231-7711

Nagoya Miyako	Meieki, Nakamura-ku	571-3211
Nagoya Terminal	Meieki, Nakamura-ku	561-3751
Nagoya Tokyu	Sakae, Naka-ku	251-2411

OKAZAKI

Meitetsu Okazaki	Kosei-dori Nishi	(0564)23-3111
Okazaki Grand	Koseicho	23-5481
Okazaki New Grand	Koseicho	21-5111

TOYOHASHI

Toyohashi Grand	Ekimae-Odori	(0532)55-6221
Holiday Inn Toyohashi	Fujisawacho	48-3131

TOYOTA

Toyota Castle	Shimobayashicho	(0565)31-2211

MIE Pref.

KASHIKOJIMA

Shima Kanko	Kashikojima Agocho, Shima-gun	(05994)3-1211

NAGASHIMA

Nagashima	Urayasu, Nagashimacho, Kuwana-gun	(0594)45-1111

TOBA

Toba Hotel Kokusai	Toba	(0599)25-3121

YOKKAICHI

Yokkaichi Miyako	Nishishinchi	(0593)52-4131

TOYAMA Pref.

TATEYAMA

Tateyama	Murodo, Ashikuraji-Tateyama-machi, Nakaniikawa-gun	(0766)65-3333
Tateyama Kokusai	Hara, Oyama-machi, Kaminiikawa-gun	81-1111

TOYAMA

Meitetsu Toyama	Sakurabashi-dori	(0764)31-2211
Toyama Dai-ichi	Sakuragicho	42-4411

ISHIKAWA Pref.

KANAZAWA

Holiday Inn Kanazawa	Horikawa-machi	(0762)23-1111
International Hotel Kanazawa	Onuka-machi	96-0111
Kanazawa Miyako	Konohanacho	61-2111
Kanazawa New Grand	Takaoka-machi	33-1311
Kanazawa Sky	Musashi-machi	33-2233
Kanazawa Tokyu	Korinbo	31-2411

FUKUI Pref.

FUKUI

New Yours	Ote	(0776)24-3200
Yours Hotel Fukui	Chuo	25-3200

HAKUI

Fukui Palace	junka	23-3800

SHIGA Pref.

HIKONE

Ohmi Plaza	Matsubaracho	(0749)22-2111

MORIYAMA

Lake Biwa	Imahamacho	(0775)85-2511

OTSU

Biwako	Yanagasaki	(0775)24-1255

KYOTO Pref.

KYOTO

Fujita Kyoto	Nishizume, Nijo-Ohashi, Kamogawa, Nakagyo-ku	(075)222-1511
Gimmnod	Takakura Oike-dori, Nakagyo-ku	221-4111
Holiday Inn Kyoto	Nishihirakicho, Takano, Sakyo-ku	721-3131
International Hotel Kyoto	Nijo-Aburanokoji, Nakagyo-ku	222-1111
Keihan Kyoto	Nishi-Sannocho, Higashi-Kujo, Minami-ku	661-0321
Kyoto	Kawaramachi-Oike, Nakagyo-ku	211-5111
Kyoto Century	Shiokoji-sagaru, Higashi-no-Toin-dori, Shimogyo-ku	351-0111

HOTEL

Kyoto Dai-ni Tower	Shiokoji-sagaru, Higashi-no-Toin-dori, Shimogyo-ku	361-3261
Kyoto Grand	Shiokoji Higashi Horikawa-dori, Shimogyo-ku	341-2311
Kyoto Palaceside	Shimodachiuri-agaru, Karasuma-dori, Kamigyo-ku	431-8171
Kyoto Park	Sanjusangendo Mawari-machi, Higashiyama-ku	525-3111
Kyoto Royal	Ebisumachi, Kawara-machi, Sanjo, Nakagyo-ku	223-1234
Kyoto Tokyu	Kakimotocho, Gojo-sagaru, Horikawa-dori, Shimogyo-ku	341-2411
Kyoto Tower	Higashi-shiokoji, Karasuma-Shichijo-sagaru, Shimogyo-ku	361-3211
Miyako	Sanjo Keage, Higashiyama-ku	771-7111
Mt. Hiei	Ipponsugi, Hieizan, Sakyo-ku	701-2111
New Hankyu Kyoto	Higashi-shiokoji, Shiokojishin-machi, Shimogyo-ku	343-5300
New Kyoto	Horikawa-Maruta-machi, Kamigyo-ku	801-2111
New Miyako	Nishi-Kujoincho, Minami-ku	661-7111
Sunflower Kyoto	Higashi-Tennocho, Okazaki, Sakyo-ku	761-9111
Kyoto Brighten	Kamikyo-ku	441-4411

NARA Pref.

NARA

Fujita Nara	Shimo-Sanjocho	(0742) 23-8111
Nara	Takabatakecho	26-3300
Nara Royal	Hokkejicho	34-1131
Yamatosanso	Kawakamicho	26-1011

WAKAYAMA Pref.

SHIRAHAMA

Green Hill Shirahama	Shirahamacho, Nishimuro-gun	(0739) 42-2733

OSAKA Pref.

IKEDA

Crevette Airport	Kuko	(06) 843-7201

OSAKA

ANA Sheraton Hotel Osaka	Dojimahama, Kita-ku	(06) 347-1112
Do Sports Plaza	Minami Semba, Chuo-ku	245-3311
Echo Osaka	Abeno-suji, Abeno-ku	633-1141
Hanshin	Umeda, Kita-ku	344-1661
Holiday Inn Nankai Osaka	Shinsaibashi-suji, Chuo-ku	213-8281
International Hotel Osaka	Hon-machi, Chuo-ku	941-2661
Miyako Hotel Osaka	Uehon-machi, Tennoji-ku	773-1111
New Hankyu	Shibata, Kita-ku	372-5101
New Hankyu Annex	Shibata, Kita-ku	372-5101
New Otani Osaka	Shiromi, Chuo-ku	941-1111
Nikko Osaka	Nishi-Shinsaibashi, Chuo-ku	244-1111
Osaka Castle	Kyomachi, Tenmabashi, Chuo-ku	942-2401
Osaka Dai-ichi	Umeda, Kita-ku	341-4411
Osaka Grand	Nakanoshima, Kita-ku	202-1212
Osaka Hilton	Umeda, Kita-ku	347-7111
Osaka Kokusai	Hommachi, chuo-ku	941-2661
Osaka Korakuen	Minami Semba, Chuo-ku	251-2111
Osaka Riverside	Nakanocho, Miyakojima-ku	928-3251
Osaka Terminal	Umeda, Kita-ku	344-1235
Osaka Tokyu	Chaya-machi, Kita-ku	373-2411
The Plaza	Oyodo-Minami, Kita-ku	453-1111
Royal	Nakanoshima, Kita-ku	448-1122
Tennoji Miyako	Hidenincho, Tennoji-ku	779-1501
Toyo	Toyosaki, Kita-ku	372-8181

TOYONAKA

Osaka Airport	Nishi-machi, Hotarugaike	(06) 855-4621
Senri Hankyu	Higashi-machi, Shin-Senri	872-2211

HYOGO Pref.

HIMEJI

Himeji Castle	Hojo	(0792) 84-3311

KOBE

Kobe Portopia	Minatojima-Nakamachi, Chuo-ku	(078) 302-1111
Shin Kobe Oriental	Kitano-cho, chuo-ku	291-1121
Oriental	Kyomachi, Chuo-ku	331-8111

Rokko Oriental	Nishi Taniyama, Rokkosancho, Nada-ku	891-0333
Rokkosan	Minami-Rokko, Rokkosancho, Nada-ku	891-0301
Sannomiya Terminal	Kumoi-dori, Chuo-ku	291-0001

TAKARAZUKA
Takarazuka	Umenocho	(0797) 87-1151

ITAMI
Itami Dai ichi	Chuo	(0727) 77-1111

TOTTORI Pref.

TOTTORI
New Otani Tottori	Ima-machi	(0857) 23-1111

YONAGO
Yonago Kokusai	Kamocho	(0859) 33-6611

SHIMANE Pref.

MATSUE
Ichibata	Chidoricho	(0852) 22-0188

OKI
Oki Plaza	Minatomachi, Saigocho, Oki-gun	(08512) 2-0111
Setouchi Kojima	Fukiage, shimotsui	73-7711

OKAYAMA Pref.

KURASHIKI
Kurashiki Kokusai	Chuo	(0864) 22-5141
Mizushima Kokusai	Mizushima-Aobacho	44-4321
Setouchi Kojima	Fukiage, Shimotsui	73-7711

OKAYAMA
New Okayama	Ekimaecho	(0862) 23-8211
Okayama Grand	Funabashi	33-7777
Okayama Kokusai	Kadota, Hon-machi	73-7311
Okayama Plaza	Hama	72-1201
Okayama Royal	Ezucho	54-1155
Okayama Tokyu	Daiku	33-2411

TSUYAMA
Tsutama Kokusai	Sange	(0868) 23-1111
Tsuyama Plaza	Yokoyama	23-4311
Tsuyama Kakuzan	Higashi shin-machi	25-2121

HIROSHIMA Pref.

FUKUYAMA
Fukuyama Grand	Nishi-machi	(0849) 21-5511
Fukuyama Castle	Sannomarucho	22-2121

HIROSHIMA
ANA Hotel Hiroshima	Naka-machi, Naka-ku	(082) 241-1111
Hiroshima City	Kyobashicho, Minami-ku	263-5111
Hiroshima Grand	Kami-Hatchobori, Naka-ku	227-1313
Hiroshima Kokusai	Tate-machi, Naka-ku	248-2323
Hiroshima River Side	Kaminoboricho, Naka-ku	228-1251
Hiroshima Station	Matsubaracho, Minami-ku	262-3201
Hiroshima Terminal	Matsubaracho, Minami-ku	262-1111
New Hioroden	Osugacho, Minami-ku	263-3456

KURE
Kure Hankyu	Hon-dori	(0823) 21-1281

YAMAGUCHI Pref.

HAGI
Hagi Grand	Furuhagicho	(08382) 5-1211

SHIMONOSEKI
Sanyo	Mimosusogawa	(0832) 32-8666
Shimonoseki Grand	Nabecho	31-5000

YAMAGUCHI
New Tanaka	Yuda-onsen	(0839) 23-1313

KAGAWA Pref.

SAKAIDE
Sakaide Kokusai	Irifunecho	(0877) 46-8111

HOTEL

SHODOSHIMA
Shodoshima International	Tonoshocho, Shozu-gun	(0879) 62-1441

TAKAMATSU
Keio Plaza Hotel Takamatsu	Chuocho	(0878) 34-5511
Rich Takamatsu	Furujin-machi	22-3555
Takamatsu Grand	Kotobukicho	51-5757
Takamatsu Kokusai	Kitacho	31-1511

TOKUSHIMA Pref.

TOKUSHIMA
Astoria	Ichibancho	(0886) 53-6151
Tokushima Park	Tokushimacho	25-3311

EHIME Pref.

IMABARI
Imabari Kokusai	Asahi-machi	(0898) 22-3355

MATSUYAMA
ANA Hotel Matsuyama	Ichibancho	(0899) 33-5511
Kokusai Hotel Matsuyama	Ichibancho	32-5111
Oku-Dogo	Sue-machi	77-1111

NIIHAMA
Lady bird	Kubotacho	(0897) 33-1000

KOCHI Pref.

KOCHI
Kochi Dai-ichi	Kitahon-machi	(0888) 83-1441
New Hankyu Kochi	Hon-machi	73-1111

FUKUOKA Pref.

FUKUOKA
ANA Hotel Hakata	Hakata-ekimae, Hakata-ku	(092) 471-7111
Hakata Miyako	Hakataeki Higashi, Hakata-ku	441-3111
Hakata Shiroyama	Nakasu, Hakata-ku	281-2211
Hakata Tokyu	Tenjin, Chuo-ku	781-7111
New Otani Hakata	Watanabe-dori, Chuo-ku	714-1111
Nishitetsu Grand	Daimyo, Chuo-ku	771-7171
Station Plaza	Hakata-ekimae, Hakata-ku	431-1211
Takakura Hotel Fukuoka	Watanabe-dori, Chuo-ku	731-1661
Tokyo Dai-ichi Hotel Fukuoka	Nakasu, Hakata-ku	281-3311

KITA-KYUSHU
Kokura	Sembacho, Kokurakita-ku	(093) 531-1151
Kokura Station	Asano, Kokurakita-ku	521-5031
New Tagawa	Furusenbacho, Kokurakita-ku	521-3831

OMUTA
Omuta Garden	Asahi-machi	(0944) 51-1111

SAGA Pref.

KARATSU
Karatsu Seaside	Higashi-Karatsu	(0955) 73-5185

SAGA
New Otani Saga	Yoko-machi	(0952) 23-1111

NAGASAKI Pref.

NAGASAKI
Nagasaki Grand	Manzai-machi	(0958) 23-1234
Nagasaki Tokyu	Minamiyamate-machi	25-1501
New Tanda	Tokiwa-machi	27-6121
Parkside	Heiwa-machi	45-3191
New Nagasaki	Daikokucho	26-8000

UNZEN
Unzen Kanko	Unzen, Obamacho, Minami-Takagi-gun	(0957) 73-3263

OITA Pref.

BEPPU
Kamenoi	Chuo-machi	(0977) 22-3301
Nippaku	Kitahama	23-2291
Suginoi	Minami-Tateishi	24-1141

OITA

Odakyu Century Oita	Funaicho	(0975) 36-2777
Oita Dai-ichi	Funaicho	36-1388
Oita Nishitetsu Grand	Maizuru-machi	36-1181

YUFUIN

Kuju Lakeside	Kawanishi, Yufuincho, Oita-gun	(0977) 84-3151

KUMAMOTO Pref.

ASO

Aso Kanko	Yunotani, Choyomura, Aso-gun	(0957) 73-3263

KUMAMOTO

Kumamoto Hotel Castle	Joto-machi	(096) 326-3311
Kumamoto Kotsu Center	Sakura-machi	354-1111
New Sky	Higashi-Amidaji-machi	354-2111

YATSUSHIRO

Yatsushiro Royal	Hon-machi	(0965) 34-1111

MIYAZAKI Pref.

KIRISHIMA

Ebino Kogen	Suenaga, Ebino	(0984) 33-1155

MIYAZAKI

Miyazaki Kanko	Matsuyama	(0985) 27-1212
Phoenix	Matsuyama	23-6111
Plaza Miyazaki	Kawaharacho	27-1111
Seaside Hotel Phoenix	Hamayama, Shioji	39-1111
Sun Hotel Phoenix	Hamayama, Shioji	39-3131

KAGOSHIMA Pref.

IBUSUKI

Ibusuki Kanko	Junicho	(0993) 22-2131
Ibusuki Royal	Junicho	23-2211

KAGOSHIMA

Kagoshima Hayashida	Higashi-Sengokucho	(0992) 24-4111
Kagoshima Sun Royal	Yojiro	53-2020
Kagoshima Tokyu	Kamoike-shincho	57-2411
Shiroyama Kanko	Shinshoincho	24-2211

KIRISHIMA

Hayashida Onsen	Takachiho, Makizonocho, Aira-gun	(0995) 78-2911

OKINAWA Pref.

ISHIGAKI

Miyahira	Misakicho	(09808) 2-6111
Nikko Yaeyama	Okawa	3-3311

KUMEJIMA

EEF Beach	Aza Janado, Nakazatoson, Shimajiri-gun	(098985) 7111

MOTOBU

Royal View	Ishikawa, Motobucho, Kunigami-gun	(0980) 48-3631

NAHA

Ekka	Ameku	(0988) 68-3135
Naha Tokyu	Ameku	68-2151
Okinawa Fuji	Nishi	68-1118
Okinawa Grand Castle	Yamakawacho, Shuri	86-5454
Okinawa Harbor View	Izumizaki	53-2111
Okinawa Miyako	Matsukawa	87-1111
Pacific Hotel Okinawa	Nishi	68-5162
Seibu Orion	Asato	66-5533

ONNASON

Manza Beach	Serakaki, Onnason, Kunigami-gun	(09896) 5-1211
Moon Beach	Maeganeku, Onnason, Kunigami-gun	5-1020

YOUTH HOSTELS

★: open not throughout the year

Name	Locationg & Address	Telephone
HOKKAIDO		
★Wakkanai	Komadori, Wakkanai	(0162)23-7162
Wakkanai Moshiripa	Chuo, Wakkanai	(0162)24-0180
★Rebun Funadomari	Funadomari, Rebun Isl	(01638)7-2717
Rebun	Kafuka, Rebun Isl.	(01638)6-1608
★Momoiwa-so	Kafuka, Rebun Isl.	(01638)6-1421
★Rishiri Green Hill	Oshidomari, Rishiri Isl	(01638)2-2507
Obira Boyodai	Obira-machi, Rumoi	(01645)6-2631
Haboro Choritsu	Sakae-cho, Haboro	(01646)2-1460
Shiokari-onsen	Shiokari, Wassamu	(016532)2168
Asahikawa	kamui, Asahikawa	(0166)61-2751
Shirogane Center	Shirogane-onsen, Biei-cho	(0166)94-3131
Furano White	Kitanomine, Furano	(0167)23-4807
Daisetsu-zan Shirakabaso	Higashikawa-machi Kamikawa-gun	(0166)97-2246
Sounkyo	Sounkyo, Kamikawa	(01658)5-3418
Hamatonbetsu	Hinode Hamatonbetsu	(01634)2-3108
Mashike Syokanbetsu	Shokanzawa Mashike	(01645)3-2396
★Rubeshibe	Asahichuo, Rubeshibe	(0157)42-2268
Bihoro	Motomachi, Bihoro	(01527)3-2560
Saroma-kohan	Hamasaroma, Saroma	(01587)6-2515
Gensei-kaen	Kitahama, Abashiri	(0152)46-2630
Koshimizu	Hamakoshimizu, Koshimizu	(0152)64-2011
Shari	Bunko-cho, Shari-machi	(01522)3-2220
Shiretoko	Utoro-onsen, Shari-machi	(01522)4-2034
Shiretoko Youth Guest House	Utoro-onsen, Shari-machi	(01522)4-2764
★Iwaobetsu	Iwaobetsu, Shari-machi	(01522)4-2311
Rausu	Honcho, Rausu-machi	(01538)7-2145
★Kussharo-ko	Kawayu-nibushi, Teshikaga	(01548)3-2415
Nomura Kawayu	Kawayu, Teshikaga	(01548)3-2037
Mashu-ko	Genya, Teshikaga	(01548)2-3098
Akan-kohan	Akan-kohan, Akan-machi	(0154)67-2309
Akan-angel	Akan-kohan, Akan-machi	(0154)67-2309
Nonaka-onsen	Moashoro, Ashoro	(01562)9-7454
Shibetsu-machi	Shibetsu, Shibetsu-machi	(01538)2-2407
Nemuro	Koyo-cho, Nemuro	(01532)2-2825
Akkeshi-aikappu	Wangetsu-cho, Akkeshi	(0153)52-2054
Hamanaka	Sakaki-machi, Hamanaka	(0153)64-2055
Kuhsiro	Tsurugadai, Kushiro	(0154)41-1676
Kushiro Makiba	Kawakita, Kushiro	(0154)23-0852
Obihiro	Higashi 2-jo, Obihiro	(0155)22-7000
Erimo-misaki	Erimo-misaki, Erimo	(01466)3-1144
★Niikappu	Takae, Niikappu	(01464)7-2317
Sapporo House	Kita-ku, Sapporo	(011)726-4235
★Sapporo Miyagaoka	Chuo-ku, Sapporo	(011)611-9016
Sapporo Lions	Chuo-ku, Sappro	(011)611-4709
Otaru Tengu-yama	Mogami, Otaru	(0134)34-1474
Bikuni	Bikuni, Shakotan	(0135)44-2610
Shakotan	Yobetsu, Shakotan	(0135)46-5051
Shakotan Kamoi	Kamoenai Furuu-gun	(0135)77-6136
Shimamaki	Shimamakimura, Shimamakigun	(01367)4-5264
Niseko	Asahi, Kucchan-cho	(0136)22-0553
Nakayama Toge	Nakayamatoge, Kimobetsu	(0136)33-2668
Showa-shinzan	Sobetsu-onsen, Sobetsu	(01427)5-2283
Kitayuzawa	Otaki-mura, Usu-gun	(014268)6552
Noboribetsu Kannon-ji	Noboribetsu-onsen	(01438)84-2359
Akashiya-so	Noboribetsu-onsen	(01438)4-2616
Kanefuku	Noboribetsu-onsen	(01438)4-2565
★Noboribetsu-Ekimae	Noboribetsu	(01438)3-1039
Muroran	Miyuki-cho, Muroran	(0143)44-3357
Shiraoi	Hinode-cho, Shiraoi	(0144)82-2302
Shikotsu-ko	Shikotsu-kohan, Chitose	(0123)25-2311
Utonai-ko	Uenae, Tomakomai	(0144)58-2153
Ikusanda Onuma	Onuma-cho, Kameda-gun	(0138)67-3419
Yano Ryokan	Fukuyama, Matsumae-cho	(01394)2-2525

AOMORI

Wakinosawa	Wakinosawa, Shimokita	(0175) 44-2341
★Shiriyazaki	Higashi-dori, Shimokita	(0175) 47-2941
Kawayo Green	Mukaiyama, Shimoda-machi	(0178) 56-2756
Oirase	Yakeyama, Towadako-machi	(0176) 74-2031
Hakubutsu-kan	Towada-kohan, Towadako-machi	(0176) 75-2002
Towada	Hakka, Towada-kohan	(0176) 75-2603
Fukaura	Oka-machi, Fukaura	(01737) 4-2459
Hirosaki	Mori-machi, Hirosaki	(0172) 33-7066

IWATE

Hachimantai	Matsuo, Iwate	(0195) 78-2031
Tono	Tsuchibuchi, Tono	(01986) 2-8736
★Noda	Noda-mura, Kunohe-gun	(0194) 78-2314
Suehiro-kan	Suehiro-cho, Miyako	(0193) 62-1555
Miyako Kimura	Kuroda-cho, Miyako	(0193) 62-2888
Hanamaki	Kudashizawa, Hanamaki	(0198) 25-2458
Motsu-ji	Osawa, Hiraizumi	(0191) 46-2331
Rikuzen Takada	Takada Matsubaya, Rikuzentakada	(0192) 55-4246
Morioka	Takamatsu, Morioka	(0196) 62-2220
Shizukuishi	Nagayama, Shizukuishi	(0196) 93-2854

MIYAGI

Kinkazan-jinja	Ayukawahama, Oshika	(02254) 5-2264
Matsushima	Nobiru, Naruse	(0225) 88-2220
Sendai Chitose	Odawara, Sendai	(022) 222-6329
Sendai Akamon	Kawauchi, Sendai	(022) 264-1405
Kimura-ya-ryokan	Fukuoka, Shiroishi	(02242) 6-2161
Minami-zao	Shichigashuku-machi	(0224) 37-2124
Sendai Onnai	Kashiwagi, Sendai	(022) 234-3922
Karakuwa	Nakai, Karakuwa-machi	(02263) 2-2490
Sendai Dochu-an	Onoda, Sendai	(022) 247-0511

AKITA

★Towada	Towada-kohan, Kosaka-machi	(0176) 75-2603
Kuromori-so	Towada-oyu, Kazuno	(0186) 37-2144
Oga	Kitaurayumoto, Oga	(0185) 33-3125
Akita	Asahiminami, Akita	(0188) 23-5100
Monzen	Hunakawako, Oga	(0185) 27-2823
Tazawako	Obonai, Tazawako-machi	(0187) 43-1281
Matsuba	Nishiki, Senboku-gun	(0187) 48-2201
Kamataya Ryokan	Kotobuki, Yokote	(0182) 32-2584
Kisakata-seinen-no-ie	Irikonoma, Kisakata	(0184) 43-3154

YAMAGATA

Sawaguchi Ryokan	Tobishima, Sakata	(0234) 95-2246
Tsuruoka	Sanze, Tsuruoka	(0235) 73-3205
Yamagata	Kurosawa, Yamagata	(0236) 88-3201

FUKUSHIMA

Taira	Taira, Iwaki	(0246) 34-7581
★Tokiwa	Taira, Iwaki	(0246) 21-2226
Azuma-kogen Fukushima	Machiniwasaka, Fukushima	(0245) 91-1412
Ura-Bandai	Goshikinuma, Urabandai	(0241) 32-2811
Bandai-Yuai-Sanso	Hayama, Inawashiro	(0242) 62-3424
Misato	Ryozen-machi, Date-gun	(0245) 86-1828
Aizu-no-sato	Aizu-shiokawa-cho	(0241) 27-2054
Tadami	Tadami, Minami-Aizu-gun	(0241) 82-2526

IBARAKI

Kaba-sanso	Nagaoka, Makabe-cho	(0296) 55-1928
Tsukuba-san	Hatori, Makabe-cho	(0296) 54-1200
Tsukuba-sanso	Tsukuba, Tsukuba	(0298) 66-0022
Itako-so	Uwado Ushibori	(0299) 64-2510
Mito Tokuda	Nikoda, Tomobe	(02967) 7-3113
Tsuchiura-Masuo	Komatsu, Tsuchiura	(0298) 21-4430

TOCHIGI

Shirakaba-so	Yumoto, Shiobara	(02873) 2-2565
Nasu-kogen	Yumoto, Nasu-machi	(0287) 76-1615
Nikko	Tokorono, Nikko	(0288) 54-1013
Nikko Daiyagawa	Nakahatsuishi-Machi, Nikko	(0288) 54-1974
Shinko-en	Kiwadajima, Imaichi	(0288) 26-0951

GUMMA

Oze Tokura	Tokura, Katashina-mura	(0278) 58-7421
Haruna-kogen	Harunasan, Haruna	(0273) 74-9300
Gonzan-so Noen	Okuwa, Naganohara	(0279) 85-2028
Kusatsu-Kogen	Kusatsu-machi, Agatsuma-gun	(0279) 88-3895

Akagi-paos	Akagi-mura, Seta-gun	(0279) 56-5731
SAITAMA		
Kamakita-ko	Gongendo, Moroyama-machi	(0492) 94-0219
Hanno	Futayanagi, Hanno-shi	(0429) 72-4018
Chichibu	Otaki-mura, Chichibu	(0494) 55-0056
CHIBA		
Inuboso	Inubosaki, Choshi	(0479) 22-1252
Tateyama	Mera, Tateyama	(0470) 28-0073
Hiranoya	Shinobe, Futtsu	(0439) 87-2030
Kujukurihama Shirako	Sorigane, Shirako-machi	(0475) 33-2254
Chiba-shi	Yasashido, Chiba	(0472) 94-1850
Kofuso	Kofudai, Ichihara	(0436) 36-2770
TOKYO		
TokyoYoyogi	Yoyogi, Shibuya-ku	(03) 3467-9163
Takao	Takao, Hachioji	(0426) 61-0437
Mitake	Mitake, Ome	(0428) 78-8501
Mihara-sanso	Motomachi, Oshima	(04992) 2-1111
Miyakejima Ako	Miyake-mura, Miyakejima	(04994) 5-0100
Ogasawara	Chichijima, Ogasawara	(04998) 2-2692
Tokyo Kokusai	Kaguragashi, Shinjuku-ku	(03) 3235-1107
College Town Hachioji	Owada-machi, Hachioji-shi	(0426) 48-2111
KANAGAWA		
Kanagawa	Nishi-ku, Yokohama	(045) 241-6503
Jogashima	Misaki, Miura	(0468) 81-3893
Kamakura Kagetsuen	Sakanoshita, Kamakura	(0467) 25-1238
Shonan	Naka-kaigan, Chigasaki	(0467) 82-2401
Sagami-ko	Yose, Sagamiko	(04268) 4-2338
Hakone Soun-zan	Gora, Hakone-machi	(0460) 2-3827
★Manazuru	Manazuru-machi	(0465) 68-3580
NIIGATA		
Kado-yonezawa-ya	Sugatani, Shibata	(0254) 29-2008
★Konsen-ji	Takeno-machi, Nishi Kanbara-gun	(0256) 72-3339
Myoko-ji	Maki-machi Nishi Kanbara-gun	(0256) 77-2025
★Shomyoji	Teradomari-machi Mishima-gun	(0258) 75-2301
Kashiwazaki	Higashi-minato, Kashiwazaki	(0257) 22-5740
Myochi-ji	Kujiranami, Kashiwazaki	(0257) 23-6484
Muikamachi	Oguriyama, Muika-machi	(0257) 72-2842
Tsuchitaru-Sanso	Tsuchitaru, Yuzawa	(0257) 87-3188
Kiyotsu-kyo	Nakazato, Nakauonuma-gun	(0257) 63-2431
Ikeno-ya	Ikenotaira, Myokokogen	(0255) 86-2116
Kazashima-kan	Katanoo, Ryotsu, Sado	(02592) 9-2003
★Ogi-Sakuma-so	Ogi-machi, Ogi, Sado	(0259) 86-2565
Sotokaifu	Aikawa-machi, Sado	(0259) 78-2911
Senkaku-so	Aikawa-machi, Sado	(0259) 75-2011
★Sado Hakusan	Sawada-machi, Sado	(0259) 52-4422
TOYAMA		
Tenkyo-ji	Oienosho, Asahi-machi	(0765) 82-0580
Sugita	Senjugahara, Tateyama	(0764) 82-1754
Toyama	Hamakurosaki, Toyama	(0764) 37-9010
Karashima-so	Kitao-machi, Himi	(0766) 72-0097
Zuiryu-ji	Seki-hon-machi, Takaoka	(0766) 22-0179
EcchuGokayama	Kamitaira, Higashitonami	(0763) 67-3331
ISHIKAWA		
Tsukumo-wan	Ogi, Uchiura-machi	(0768) 74-0150
Sosogi Kajiyama	Machino, Wajima	(0768) 32-1145
Wajima Choraku-ji	Shinbashidori, Wajima	(0768) 22-0663
Oku-noto	Ushitsu, Noto-machi	(0768) 62-0436
Ryugo-ji	Sakami, Togi-machi	(0767) 42-0401
Notominazuki	Monzen-machi, hoshi-gun	(0768) 46-2022
Kanazawa	Suehiro-machi, Kanazawa	(0762) 52-3414
Matsui	Kata-machi, Kanazawa	(0762) 21-0275
FUKUI		
Tojinbo	Nishiki, Mikuni-cho	(0776) 82-5400
Fukuiken Fujin-seinen Kaikan	Ote, Fukui	(0776) 22-5920
Eihei-ji-monzen Yamaguchi	Shihi, Eiheiji	(0776) 63-3123
Echizen-Kaigan	Kuriya, Echizen-machi	(0778) 37-1033
Mihama-so	Hayase, Mihama	(0770) 32-0301
★Obama	Aoi, Obama	(0770) 52-2158
YAMANASHI		
★Doshi-kan	Doshi-mura, Minamitsuru-gun	(0554) 52-2015
Fuji Yoshida	Fujiyoshida	(0555) 22-0533

★Kawaguchi-ko	Kawaguchiko	(0555) 72-1431
★Fuji-sai-ko	Ashiwada, minamitsuru	(0555) 82-2616
Yamanaka-ko Marimo	Yamanakako, Minamitsuru	(0555) 62-4210
Isawa-onsen	Yamazaki, Isawa	(0552) 62-2110
Kofu	Kamiobina-machi, Kofu	(0552) 51-8020
★Koun-kaku	Sutama-machi, Kitakoma	(05514) 5-0442
Kiyosato	Kiyosato, Takane-machi	(0551) 48-2125
Minobu-sanso	Umedaira Minobu-machi	(05566) 2-0213

NAGANO

Togari-kanzan-so	Ota, Iiyama	(0269) 65-2094
Kumanoyu	Kumanoyu, Shigakogen	(0269) 34-2311
Nojiri-ko	Nojiri, Shinano-machi	(0262) 58-2501
Togakushi-kogen Yokokura	Chusha, Togakushi	(0262) 54-2030
Kyoju-in	Motoyoshi-machi, Nagano	(0262) 32-2768
★Karuizawa	Kyu-karuizawa, Karuizawa	(0267) 42-2325
Fuji-ya	Aoki-mura, Chiisagata-gun	(0268) 49-3115
Tateshina Shirakaba Kogen	Megamiko, Tateshina	(0267) 55-6601
Shirakaba-ko	Kitayama, Chino	(0266) 68-2031
Suwa-ko	Takagi, Shimosuwa	(0266) 27-7075
Kizaki-ko	Taira, Omachi	(0261) 22-1820
★Utsukushigahara Sanjiro	Iriyamabe, Matsumoto	(0263) 31-2021
Asama-onsen	Asama-onsen, Matsumoto	(0263) 46-1335
Oishi-kan	Shirahone-onsen, Azumi-mura	(0263) 93-2011
Norikura-kogen	Suzuran, Azumi-mura	(0263) 93-2748
Komagane	Akao, Komagane	(0265) 83-3856
Shimojo Land	Shimoyo-mura, Shimoina-gun	(0539) 67-3111
Kiso Ryojoan	Kisofukushima	(0264) 23-7716
Azumino	Kashiwabara, Hotaka-cho	(0263) 82-4265
Komoro	Minamigahara, Komoro	(0267) 23-5732
Ueda Mahoroba	Bessho-onsen, Ueda	(0268) 38-5229

GIFU

Hida Takayama-tenshoji	Tenshoji, Takayama	(0577) 32-6354
Nenoue Kogen Kohan-no-yado	Nenouekogen, Nakatsugawa	(0573) 65-4643
Hokono-ko	Higashino, Ena	(0573) 65-3534
Gujo-tosen-ji	Nakatsubo, Hachiman-cho	(05756) 7-0290
★Hirugano-kogen	Takasu-mura, Gujo-gun	(05757) 3-2011
Gifu	Kamikanosan, Gifu	(0582) 63-6631
Hida Furukawa	Takano, Furukawa-machi	05777-3-6177

SHIZUOKA

Gotenba	Higashiyama, Gotenba	(0550) 82-3045
Ito	Kawana, Ito	(0557) 45-0224
Izu-okawa	Okawa, Higashiizu	(0557) 23-1063
Irori-so	Amagi-Yugashima	(0558) 85-0108
Kiya-Ryokan	Nakaizu-cho	(0558) 83-0146
Takasagoya-ryokan	Toi, Toi-machi	(0558) 98-0200
Amagi-haris Court	Nashimoto, Kawazu-machi	(05583) 5-7253
Gensu	Shimokamo, Minamiizu-machi	(05586) 2-0035
Sanyo-so	Naka, Matsuzaki	(0558) 42-0408
Fumotono-ie	Sugita, Fujinomiya	(0544) 27-4314
Miho	Miho, Shimizu	(0543) 34-0826
Hamana-ko	Arai-machi, Hamana-gun	(05359) 4-0670
Shuzenji	Shuzenji-machi	(0558) 72-1222
Sayo-no-nakayama	Kanaya-machi	(05474) 6-3284
Kanzan-ji-murakushi	Murakushi, Hamamatsu	(0534) 89-2801
Omaezaki	Omaezaki	(0548) 63-4518
Sakuma Yoshizawa	Yoshizawa Sakuma	(0539) 67-3111
Totaru	Totari, Ito	(0557) 45-2591

AICHI

Soezawa-onsen Yamano-ie	Taguchi, Shitara-cho	(05366) 2-0520
Chita Hanto	Onoura, Mihama-cho	(0569) 87-0435
Inuyama	Tsugao, Inuyama	(0568) 61-1111
Nagoya	Chikusa-ku, Nagoya	(052) 781-9845
Aichi-ken Seinen-kaikan	Naka-ku, Nagoya	(052) 221-6001
Hazukannon	Higashihazu, Hazu	(0563) 62-2297

MIE

Gozaisho	Gozaisho, Komono-machi	(0593) 92-2264
Atago-san	Atago, Matsuzaka	(0598) 21-2931
Taiko-ji	E, Futami-cho	(05964) 3-2283
Ise-shima	Anagawa, Isobe	(05995) 5-0226
Kumano-shi seinen-no-ie	Arima, Kumano	(05978) 9-0800

SHIGA

Shizugatake	Kinomoto	(0749) 82-2493
Kaizu-tenjinja	Kaizu, Makino	(0740) 28-0051
Kajuji	Maruyama, Omihachiman	(0748) 32-2938
Omi-kiboga-oka	Kitasakura, Yasu-cho	(0775) 87-2201
Tatehaya-jinja	Kizu, Shin-asahi-cho	(0740) 25-3018
Wanihama-seinen-kaikan	Minamihama, Shiga-cho	(0775) 94-4203
Saikyo-ji	Sakamoto, Otsu	(0775) 78-0013
Otsu center	Yamagami-cho, Otsu	(0775) 22-8009

KYOTO

Utano	Ukyo-ku, Kyoto	(075) 462-2288
Higashiyama	Higashiyama-ku, Kyoto	(075) 761-8135
Kaijusen-ji	Reihei, Kamo-cho	(077476) 2256
Amanohashidate	Nakano, Miyazu	(07722) 7-0121
Amanohashidate Kanko-kaikan	Ogaki, Miyazu	(07722) 7-0046
Tango-Hanto	Taiza, Tango-cho	(07727) 5-1529
Kyoto Ohara	Sakyo-ku, Kyoto	(075) 744-2721
Kitayama	Kita-ku, Kyoto	(075) 492-5345

OSAKA

Hattori Ryokuchi	Toyonaka	(06) 862-0600
Gyokusen-ji	Nose, Toyono-gun	(0727) 34-0844
Osakashiritsu Nagai	Higashi Sumiyoshi-ku, Osaka	(06) 699-5631
Sayama Yuen	Tondabayashi	(0723) 65-3091
Kawachi-Nagano	Kawachinagano	(0721) 53-1010

HYOGO

Inagawa Sanso	Yatouenoyama, Kawanishi	(0727) 51-3565
Ashiya	Okuike, Ashiya	(0797) 38-0109
Kobe-tarumi	Tarumi-ku, Kobe	(078) 707-2133
Chorin-ji	Zaimoku-cho, Akashi	(078) 911-4727
Yotaku-ji	Yotakuji, Sanda	(07956) 6-0401
★Kazan-in	Ninji, Sanda	(0795) 66-0125
Chusho-in	Takamatsu, Nishiwaki	(0795) 22-9398
Kiyomizu-dera Shukuin	Yashiro, Kato-gun	(0795) 45-0025
Amarube	Amarube, Kasumi-cho	(0963) 4-0031
Hamasaka	Shiroyamaenchi, Hamasaka	(07968) 2-1282
Moroyose-so	Moroyose, Hamasaka	(07968) 2-1279
Tegarayamaseinen-no-ie	Himeji	(0792) 93-2716
Joun-ji	Murotsu, Mitsu-machi	(07932) 4-0030
Seppiko-zan	Yamanouchi, Yumesaki-cho	(07933) 8-0003
Ruri-ji	Funakoshi, Nanko-cho	(0790) 77-0450
Asahi-ryokan	Gunge, Ichinomiya	(0799) 85-0018
★Sumoto sempuku-ji	Sakae-machi, Sumoto	(0799) 22-3309
★Awaji	Minami-awaji	(0799) 52-0460
Kobe Mudo-ji	Kita-ku, Kobe	(078) 581-0250

NARA

Nara	Horen-cho, Nara	(0742) 22-1334
Naraken Seishonen Kaikan	Handahiraki-cho, Nara	(0742) 22-5540
Senko-ji	Narukawa Heguri-cho	(07454) 5-0652
Kizo-in	Yoshino-machi	(07463) 2-3014
Yamanobe	Yanagimoto, Tenri	(07436) 6-2770

WAKAYAMA

Katsuragi	Katsuragi-cho	(0736) 22-0825
Henjoson-in	Koyasan, Koya-cho	(0736) 56-2434
Shiono-misaki	Shionomisaki, Kushimoto-cho	(07356) 2-0570
Taiji	Taiji-machi	(07355) 9-2636
Nachi	Nachikatsuura-cho, Higashimuro-gun	(07355) 2-0584
Shingu Hayatama	Kami-honmachi, Shingu	(0735) 22-2309
Kajika-so	Kawayu, Hongu-machi	(07354) 2-0518
Arida	Suhara, Yuasa-machi	(0737) 62-4536
Ohgigahama	Shinyashiki, Tanabe	(0739) 22-3433
Misaki Lodge	Shionomisaki, Kushimoto-cho	(07356) 2-1474

TOTTORI

Wakasa Hyonosen	Tsukuyone, Wakasa-cho	(0858) 82-1700
Koho-ji	Shimoasozu, Hawai-cho	(0858) 35-2054
Daisen	Daisen-cho	(0859) 52-2501
Yamanomura	Miyaichi, Kofu-cho	(0859) 75-2359
Yonago-minami	Saihaku-cho	(0859) 66-3410

SHIMANE

Okino-shima	Fuse-mura, Oki	(08512) 7-4321
Takuhi	Nishinoshima, Oki	(08514) 6-0860
Chibu	Chibu, Oki	(08514) 8-2355

Matsue	Kososhi-cho, Matsue	(0852) 36-8620
Tachikue-kyo	Ottachi, Izumo	(0853) 45-0102
Ebisuya	Shinmondori, Taisha	(0853) 53-2157
Jofuku-ji	Nima-cho, Nima	(08548) 8-3019
Tsuwano	Tsuwano, Kanoashi-gun	(08567) 2-0373

OKAYAMA

Nihonbara-kogen	Ichiba, Shoboku-cho	(0868) 36-2165
Daisho-ji	Daishoji, Sakuto-cho	(08687) 6-0001
Hiruzen-masudaya	Yatsuka, Maniwa-gun	(0867) 66-3102
Niimi-higashiya	Niimi	(0867) 72-0021
Okayama Ken Seinen-kaikan	Tsukura, Okayama	(0862) 52-0651
Kurashiki	Mukaiyama, Kurashiki	(0864) 22-7355
Washu Zan	Obatake, Kurashiki	(0864) 79-9280
Kasaoka-ya	Nishihon-machi, Kasaoka	(08656) 3-4188
Manabe-santora	Manabeshima, Kasaoka	(08656) 8-3515
Takahashi	Tera-machi, Takahashi	(0866) 22-3149

HIROSHIMA

Dogo-sanso	Misaka, Saijo-cho	(08248) 4-2132
M. G.	Yanoonsen, Joge-cho	(084762) 3244
Setoda	Setoda-machi	(08452) 7-0224
Hiroshima	Higashi-ku, Hiroshima	(082) 221-5343
Miyajimaguchi	Ono-machi, Saeki,gun	(0829) 56-1444
Hiroshima Sakamachi	Saka-machi, Aki-gun	(082) 885-0700
Miyoshi	Miyoshi-cho	(08246) 3-1759
Tomo Monte	Notohara, Numaguma	(0849) 87-1230
Ikuchi-jima-tarumi	Setoda-machi	(08452) 7-3137
Higashi Hiroshima	Higashi Hiroshima	(0824) 29-0305

YAMAGUCHI

Yuno-onsen	Yono, Tokuyama	(0834) 83-2104
Hagi	Horinouchi, Hagi	(08382) 2-0733
Akiyoshidai	Akiyoshi, Shuho-cho	(08376) 2-0341
Ube Tokiwa-kohan	Kamiube, Ube	(0836) 21-3613
Shimonoseki Hinoyama	Mimosusokawa, Shimonoseki	(0832) 22-3753
Iwakuni	Yokoyama-cho, Iwakuni	(0827) 43-1092
Yamaguchi	Miyanokami, Yamaguchi	(0839) 28-0057
Jinjo-ji	Era, Toyota-cho	(08376) 6-0286

TOKUSHIMA

Tokushima	Ohara, Tokushima	(0886) 63-1505
Komatsujima Chitose	Komatsujima	(08853) 2-0155
Anraku-ji	Kamiita-cho	(0886) 94-2046
Hiwasa	Hiwasa-cho	(08847) 7-0755

KAGAWA

Tsuda	Tsuda, Tsuda-cho	(087942) 4033
Takamatsu-yashima-sanso	Yashimanaka-machi, Takamatsu	(0878) 41-2318
Takamatsu-shi	Okamoto-cho, Takamatsu	(0878) 85-2024
Kotohira Seinen-no-ie	Kawanishiotsu, Kotohira-cho	(0877) 73-3836
Kaigan-ji	Nishi-shirakata, Tadotsu-cho	(0877) 33-3333
Shodoshima Olive	Olive-mura, Uchiumi-cho	(0879) 82-4584

EHIME

Shin-hase-dera	Sangawa-cho, Iyomishima	(0896) 25-0202
Kanmon	Omogo-mura	(089258) 2311
Ozu Kyodokan	Ozu-Sannomaru, Ozu	(0893) 24-2258
Uwajima	Atagokoen, Uwajima	(0895) 22-7177
Mannen-so	Matsuno-cho, Kitauwa-gun	(0895) 43-0205
Matsuyama	Dogo-himezuka, Matsuyama	(0899) 33-6366

KOCHI

Higashi-dera	Murotomisaki, Muroto	(08872) 2-0366
Jofuku-ji	Otoyo-machi, Nagaoka-gun	(0887) 74-0301
Wakamiya Taiheiyo Kogen	Tosayamada-cho	(08875) 3-2993
Kochi-ekimae	Kitahon-cho, Kochi	(0888) 83-5086
Iwamoto-ji	Mogushi, Kubokawa-cho	(08802) 2-0376
Ishimi-ji	Yasunami, Nakamura	(0880) 35-3033
Kongofuku-ji	Ashizurimisaki, Tosashimizu	(08808) 8-0038
Fujii-dera	Misaki, Tosashimizu	(08808) 5-0120
Odo	Kashiwajima, Otsuki-cho	(08807) 6-0222
Shirao-jinja	Ashizurimisaki, Tosashimizu	(08808) 8-0324
Sukumo	Hashigami-cho, Sukumo	(0880) 64-0233

FUKUOKA

Kita-kyushu	Yahata-ku, Kitakyushu	(093) 681-8142
Yakiyama-kogen	Yakiyama, Iizuka	(0948) 22-6385
Runowaru	Sataka-machi	(09446) 2-2423

YOUTH HOSTELS

Dazaifu	Dazaifu	(092)922-8740
SAGA		
Niji-no-matsubara	Kagami, Karatsu	(0955)72-4526
Takeo	Takeo-cho, Takeo	(0954)22-2490
Sagaken Seinen-kaikan	Hinode, Saga	(0952)31-2328
NAGASAKI		
Hiradoguchi	Okubomen, Tabira-cho	(0950)57-1443
Oranda-zaka	Higashiyamate, Nagasaki	(0958)22-2730
Nagasaki	Tateyama-cho, Nagasaki	(0958)23-5032
Shimabara	Shimokawagiri-cho, Shimabara	(0957)62-4451
Tsushima Seizan-ji	Izuhara-machi, Tsushima	(09205)2-0444
Nagasaki Nanpoen	Hamahira-cho, Nagasaki	(0958)23-5526
Goto	Miiraku-cho, Matsura	(0959)84-3151
Uragami-ga-oka	Joei-cho, Nagasaki	(0958)47-8473
KUMAMOTO		
Senomoto-kogen	Senomoto, Minamioguni	(0967)44-0157
Aso	Bochu, Aso-machi	(0967)34-0804
★Kumamoto YMCA Aso Camp	Kurumagaeri, Aso-machi	(0967)35-0124
Murataya-ryokan	Takamori-machi	(09676)2-0066
Suizenji	Hakusan, Kumamoto	(096)371-9193
Kumamoto-shiritsu	Shimazaki, Kumamoto	(096)352-2441
Amakusa	Hondo-cho, Hondo	(0969)22-3085
Ichifusa	Mizukami, Kuma-gun	(0966)46-0520
OITA		
Beppu	Kankaiji-onsen, Beppu	(0977)23-4116
Kunisaki-hanto Kunimi	Imi, Kunimi-machi	(0978)82-0104
Yamaguniya	Honyabakei-machi	(09795)2-2008
Hita-ohyama	Nishi-oyama, Oyama-machi	(0973)52-2134
MIYAZAKI		
Iwato Furusato	Iwato, Takachiho-cho	(0982)74-8254
Takachiho	Mitai, Takachiho-cho	(0982)72-3021
Yamatoya	Mitai, Takachiho-cho	(0982)72-2243
Gokase Shiraiwa	Kuraoka, Gokase-cho	(0982)83-2820
Miyazakiken-fujin-kaikan	Asahi, Miyazaki	(0985)24-5785
Aoshima	Oryuzako, Miyazaki	(0985)65-1657
Nichinan-kaigan	Kumaya, Nichinan	((0987)27-0113
Miyakonojo	Tohoku-cho, Miyakonojo	(0986)38-0022
Toi-misaki	Toinomisaki, Kushima	(0987)76-1397
KAGOSHIMA		
Kagoshima Ken Fujin-kaikan	Shimoarata, Kagoshima	(0992)51-1087
Sakura-jima	Sakurajima	(0992)93-2150
Ibusuki	Omura, Ibusuki	(0993)22-2758
Tamaya	Yunohama, Ibusuki	(0993)22-3553
Yoronto Takakura-so	Yoron-Isl.	(09979)7-2273
Okinoerabu	Wadomari-cho	(09979)2-2024
Fukiage-hama	Hiyoshi-cho Hioki	(0992)92-3455
OKINAWA		
Naha	Ounoyama, Naha	(0988)57-0073
Naha-harumi	Tomari, Naha	(0988)67-3218
Tamazono-so	Asato, Naha	(0988)67-5377
Maeda misaki	Onna-mura, Kunigami-gun	(09896)4-2497
Yashima-ryokan	Tonojo, Ishigaki	(09808)2-3157
Takana-ryokan	Taketomi	(09808)5-2151
Irumote-so	Uehara, Taketomi	(09808)5-6255
Iriomote-jima Midori-so	Uehara, Taketomi	(09808)5-6526
Trek Ishigaki-jima	Hoshino, Ishigaki	(09808)6-8257

PACKAGE TOURS
(As of October 1990)

Sunrise Tour Series by Japan Travel Bureau

Japan Travel Bureau:1-13-1 Nihombashi, Chuo-ku, Tokyo TEL (03)3276-7777
Notes: 1) If the tour does not return to the point of origin, the tour terminal place is underlined.
2) The tour fares of superior and deluxe tours are indicated by single and double asterisks respectively.
3) Tokyo Kabuki Night (A130/B130) is operated only when Kabuki drama is staged.

Tours in Tokyo

Tour Name	Tour Code	Tour Fare	Single Extra	Meals Incl.	Places to Visit ( ) indicates number of overnight stays	Departure
Tokyo Morning	A010	¥3,910			Tokyo Tower, Tea Ceremony, Imperial Palace Grounds, Flower Arrangement, Pearl Gallery	Daily
Tokyo Afternoon	A020	¥3,910			Imperial East Garden, Meiji Shrine, Tea-time at "Furusato Restaurant", Tokyo Tower	Daily
Dynamic Tokyo	A060	¥11,030		lunch	Tokyo Tower, Imperial Palace Plaza, Asakusa Kannon Temple, Meiji Shrine, Barbecue lunch, Pearl Gallery	Daily (Mar.-Sep.)
Panoramic Tokyo	A100	¥9,980		lunch	Tokyo Tower, Imperial Palace Plaza, Asakusa Kannon Temple, Barbecue lunch, Pearl Gallery	Daily
Tour to Tokyo Disneyland	A050	¥8,630			Approx. 7-hour free time at Tokyo Disneyland	Sun. Mon. Wed. Fri. Sat. (Feb.-Mar. & Nov.-Dec.) except Nov.28, Dec 5 & 12. Sun. Mon. Fri. Sat. (Jan. & Apr.-Oct.) except Nov.28, Dec 5 & 12 8:50 AM- Around 6:00 p.m.
Fascinating Night	A140 B140	¥11,050 ¥ 7,960		dinner —	Shows at Restaurant and Cabaret "Matsubaya" and "Shogun"	Daily

PACKAGE TOURS

Kabuki Night	A130 B130	¥12,970 ¥10,180		dinner —	Sukiyaki Dinner (A130 only) . Kabuki, Geisha Entertainment	Daily
Bright Night	A190	¥8,970		dinner	Tokyo Tower, Tempura Dinner, Geisha Entertainment	When "Kabuki Night" not operated
Industrial Tokyo	A080	¥9,980		lunch	〈Tue. Course〉 Tokyo Stock Exchange, Lunch at "Kawahara Restaurant". Isuzu Motors Ltd. Fujisawa Factory 〈Thu. Course〉 Ride on monorail to Haneda Airport, Japan Air Lines Maintenance Base, Lunch at "kawahara Restaurant", Isuzu Motors Ltd. Fujisawa Factory	Tue. & Thu. except the beginning of January, certain national holidays, the end of December, and a few other days in July and August.
Village Life & Crafts	A090	¥10,300		lunch	Agricultural cooperative association, Bonsai Garden, Lunch at "Mansei Restaurant", Making of traditional dolls and fishing rods & Daruma	Wed. (Apr. - Oct.)

Tours from Tokyo

Nikko 1 Day	F500	¥18,000		lunch	Nikko	Daily except May. 18& Oct. 17
Nikko 2 Days	F510	¥27,000	¥6,500	1 lunch	Nikko	Same as above (F 500)
Kamakura & Hakone 1 Day "By Bullet"	F700	¥18,000		lunch	Kamakura, Hakone	Daily except Jan.2, Apr.28-May.6, Aug.11-16, Sep. 22-24, Nov.3 & 23-25
Kamakura & Hakone	F770	¥14,500		lunch	Kamakura, Hakone	Mon.-Fri. (Mar.19-Nov.22) except May.21, Apr.30-May.4, Aug.13-16, Sep.24 & Oct.10.
Kamakura & Hakone 2 Days	F710	¥26,800	¥5,600	1 lunch	Kamakura, Hakone	Daily except Jan.1, 2, Apr.27-May 6, Aug.10-16, Sept. 21-24, Nov.2, 3, & 22-25

Mt.Fuji & Hakone 1 Day By "Bullet"	F800	¥18,500		lunch	Mt. Fuji, Hakone	Daily (Mar.-Nov.) except Nov. 3 (Sat. Sun. Jan. 15 & Feb. 11 only in Jan. Feb. & Dec.)
Mt. Fuji & Hakone 1 Day By Motorcoach	F880	¥15,000		lunch	Mt. Fuji, Hakone	Mon.-Fri (Mar.-Nov.) except Mar. 21, May. 1-5, Aug. 11. 14-16, Sep. 15, Oct. 10 ,Nov. 3 & 23
Mt. Fuji & Hakone 2 Days	F800-HX1	¥26,800	¥5,300	1 lunch	Mt. Fuji, Hakone	Daily (Mar. -Nov.) except Jan. 1, 2, Apr. 27-May. 6, Aug. 10-16, Sept. 21-24, Nov. 2, 3, & 22-25
Sunrise Express 1 Day Kyoto	QT1	¥46,500 ¥58,500**		lunch	Kyoto	Daily
Sunrise Express 2 Days Kyoto & Nara	QT2	¥65,000 ¥68,000* ¥82,500**	¥5,200 ¥7,200 ¥9,600	1 lunch	Kyoto (1) , Nara	Daily
Sunrise Express 3 Days Kyoto & Nara	QT3	¥74,500 ¥81,500* ¥98,500**	¥10,400 ¥14,400* ¥19,200**	2 lunches	Kyoto (2) , Nara	Daily
Sunrise Holiday 2 Days	HT2	¥48,800 ¥51,300* ¥64,500**	¥5,200 ¥7,500* ¥9,600**	1 lunch	Kamakura (HT2A) or Mt. Fuji (HT2B) , Hakone, Kyoto (1)	HT2A; Daily except Jan. 2, Apr. 28-May 6, Aug.11-16, Sept. 22-24. 23. 24, Nov. 3 & Dec. 23-25 HT2B; Daily Mar. - Nov.22 & Mar. 3, 4, 10, 11
Sunrise Holiday 3 Days	HT3	¥66,000 ¥70,600* ¥77,900**	¥10,400 ¥15,000* ¥19,200**	1 lunch	Kamakura (HT3A) or Mt. Fuji (HT3B) , Hakone, Kyoto (2) , Nara	HT3A; Same as above (HT2) HT3B; Daily, Mar. 17-Nov. 22, & Mar. 3, 4, 10, 11 except Jan. 2, Apr. 28-May. 6, Aug. 11 -16, Sep. 22-24. Nov. 3 & 23-25
Sunrise Holiday 4 Days	HT4	¥86,500 ¥95,700* ¥111,000**		2 lunches	Kamakura (HT4A) or Mt. Fuji (HT4B) , Hakone (1) , Kyoto (2) , Nara	HT4A; Daily but omit Kamakura Jan. 2, Apr.28-May.6 ,Aug. 11-16, Sept. 22-24. & Nov. 3 & 23-25 HT4B; Daily Mar. 17 -Nov.25 & Mar. 3, 4, 10, 11, except Apr. 28-May. 6, Aug. 11-16, Sep. 22 -24. & Nov. 3, 23-25

PACKAGE TOURS

Sunrise Holiday 5 Days	HT5	¥125,400 ¥134,900* ¥145,500**		3 lunches	Kamakura (HT5A) or Mt. Fuji (HT5B), Hakone (1), Toba (1) Ise, Kyoto (2), Nara	HT5A; Daily Mar. 17–Nov.20 but omit Kamakura Apr. 28–May. 6, Aug. 11–16, Sep 22–24. & Nov. 3 HT5B; Daily Mar. 17–Nov. 20 except Apr. 28–May. 3, Aug 11–12, Sep. 22 & Nov. 3
Sunrise Holiday 8 Days	HT8	¥231,100	¥37,700	4 lunches	Kamakura (HT8A) or Mt. Fuji (HT8B), Hakone (1), Toba (1), Ise, Nara, Kyoto (3), Hiroshima (1), Fukuyama, Osaka (1)	Tue. & Sat. (Mar. 18–Nov. 11) HT8A & HT9A: Operated but omit Kamakura, Apr. 29, May. 2. 6, Aug. 12. 15, Sep. 16 & 23 HT8B & HT9B:
Takayama & Kanazawa 5 Days	TK5	¥199,000	¥24,000	4 b'fasts 2 dinners	Lake Shirakaba, Matsumoto (1), Tsumago, Takayama (1), Kanazawa (1), Awara Spa (1), Kyoto	Tue. (Apr. 3, 10, 17, 24 Oct. 2, 9, 16, 23, 30)
Tohoku 3 Days	F490	¥225,000	¥19,000	1 b'fast 1 dinner	Matsushima, Sendai (1) Togatta, Mt. Zao, Kaminoyama Spa (1), Yonezawa, Fukushima	Daily (May. 7–Oct. 19)
Hokkaido 4 Days	F900	¥199,000	¥29,400	3 b'fasts 1 lunch 2 dinners	Sapporo (1), Nakayama Pass, Lake Toya (1), Noboribetsu Spa (1), Shiraoi, Chitose Airport	Daily (Apr. 16–Oct. 31)

Tours in/from Kyoto

Kyoto Morning	N270	¥5,000			Nijo Castle, Golden Pavilion, Imperial Palace, Kyoto Handicraft Center	Daily
Kyoto Afternoon	N280	¥5,000			Heian Shrine, Sanjusangendo Hall, Kiyomizu Temple	Daily
Kyoto 1 Day	P280	¥10,400		1 lunch	Nijo Castle, Golden Pavilion, Imperial Palace, Heian Shrine, Sanjusangendo Hall	Daily
Kyoto Special Night	N260	¥9,300		dinner	Tempura dinner, Tea Ceremony, Gion Corner	Wed. & Sat. (Apr. -Nov.)

"Maiko" & "Geisha" Night	N230	¥58,000		dinner	Traditional Performing Art	Daily except the 1st & 3rd Sundays of everymonth
Nara Afternoon	N310	¥5,700			Todaiji temple, Deer Park, Kasuga Shrine	Daily (Feb.–Dec.)

Tours from Osaka

Afternoon Tour to Kyoto	P850	¥8,900			Heian Shrine, Sanjusangendo Hall, Kiyomizu Temple	Sat. Sun. and national holidays (Apr.-Oct.)

Tours from Kyoto/Osaka

Pearl Island & Ise 1 Day	M300	¥23,600		lunch	Ise, Toba, Ise Jingu Shrine	Daily (Mar. 19–Nov.22)
Hiroshima & Miyajima 1 Day	S1	¥49,000			Hiroshima, Miyajima, Itsukushima Shrine	Sun. & Thu. (Mar. 22–Nov. 22)
Sunrise Eastbound 1 Day	ET1	¥37,900		lunch	Ise, Toba, Tokyo	Daily (Mar. 19-Nov. 22)
Sunrise Eastbound 2 Days	ET2	¥47,700	¥5,000	1 lunch	Ise, Toba (1), Tokyo	Daily (Mar. 19-Nov. 21)
Inland Sea 2 Days	S2	¥98,000	¥5,000	1 lunch	Hiroshima (1), Miyajima, Inland Sea Islands	Sun. & Thu. (Mar. 22,Nov-22)
Inland Sea 3 Days	S3	¥142,000	¥12,000	1 b'fast 2 lunches 1 dinner	Hiroshima (1), Miyajima, Inland Sea Islands, Tomonoura (1), Kurashiki, Okayama	Sun. & Thu. (Mar. 22–Nov.22)
Northern Kyushu 5 Days	NT5	¥248,000	¥22,000	2 lunches	Fukuoka (1), Beppu (1), Mt. Aso, Kumamoto (1), Amakusa, Unzen, Nagasaki (1)	Sat. (Mar. 24,Nov. 17)
Northern Kyushu & Inland Sea 7 Days	NT7	¥325,000	¥32,000	3 lunches	Fukuoka (1), Beppu (1), Mt. Aso, Kumamoto (1), Unzen, Amakusa, Nagasaki (1), Hiroshima (2), Fukuyama	Sat. (Mar.24-Nov. 17)

Tour from Fukuoka

Northern Kyushu 5 Days	T5	¥204,000	¥22,000	2 lunches	Fukuoka (1), Beppu (1), Mt. Aso, Kumamoto (1), Amakusa, Unzen, Nagasaki (1)	Sat. (Mar. 24-Nov. 17)

PACKAGE TOURS

Imperial Coachman Tour Series By Japan Amenity Travel
Japan Amenity Travel : 6-2-10 Ginza, Chuo-ku, Tokyo TEL (03) 3573-1011

Tours from Tokyo

Tour	Code	Price		Meals	Places	Schedule
1-Day Nikko Country Tour	NCT01	¥14,100 ¥16,200		— Lunch	Nikko	Daily (Apr. 1–Nov. 30)
1-Day Mt. Fuji Hakone Tour	ICT01	¥16,500 ¥18,500		— Lunch	Mt. Fuji, Hakone	Daily (Mar. 1–Nov. 30)
1-Day Mt. Fuji Hakone Tour	ICT01	¥16,500 ¥18,500		— Lunch	Mt. Fuji, Hakone	Daily
2-Day Mt. Fuji Hakone Tour	ICT02	¥27,300 ¥40,100	¥5,000	— 1B'fast 1 lunch 1 dinner	Mt. Fuji (Mar. 1–Nov. 30) or Kamakura (Jan 5–Feb.28. Dec 2–26.), Hakone (1)	Daily (Mar. 1–Nov. 30) Tue. Thu. Sat. & Sun. (Jan. 5–Feb. 28 & Dec. 2–26)
2-Day Hakone Kyoto Tour	HXT 02	¥47,900 ¥49,900	¥5,000	— 1 lunch	Mt. Fuji (Mar. 1–Nov. 30) or Kamakura (Jan. 6–Feb.27, Dec. 1–25), Kyoto (1)	Same as above (ICT02)
3-Day Hakone Kyoto Nara Tour	ICT03	¥63,700 ¥86,000	¥10,000	— All inclusive	Mt. Fuji (Mar. 1–Nov. 30) or Kamakura (Jan. 6–Feb. 27, Dec. 1–25) , Hakone (1) , Kyoto (1)	Same as ICT02
4-Day Hakone Toba Kyoto Tour	ICT04	¥92,300 ¥125,600	¥15,000	— All inclusive	Mt. Fuji (Mar. 1–Nov. 30) or Kamakura (Jan. 6–Feb. 27, Dec. 1–25) , Hakone (1) , Ise shima (1), Kyoto (2)	Same as ICT02
5-Day Hakone Ise-Shima Kyoto Tour	ICT05	¥107,100 ¥149,800	¥20,000	— All inclusive	Mt. Fuji (Mar. 1–Nov. 30) or Kamakura (Jan. 5–Feb. 28, Dec. 2–26) Hakone (1), Ise shima (1) , Kyoto (2)	Same as ICT02
1-Day Kyoto Superexpress Tour	KXT 01	¥44,800 ¥46,900		— Lunch	Kyoto	Daily
2-Day Kyoto Nara Superexpress Tour	KXT 02	¥54,600 ¥56,700	¥5,000	— 1 lunch	Kyoto (1) , Nara	Daily
3-Day Kyoto Nara Superexpress Tour	KXT 03	¥70,000 ¥74,200	¥10,000	— 2 lunches	Kyoto (2) , Nara	Daily

Tours from Kyoto

Tour	Code	Price			Places	Schedule
Kyoto Morning Tour	KAM	¥5,000			Nijo Castle, Old Imperial Palace, Golden Pavilion	Daily

922

Tour	Code	Price	Price 2	Meals	Visits	Schedule
Nara Afternoon Tour	NRA	¥5,000			Kasuga Shrine, Deer Park, Todaiji Temple	Daily

Tours from Kyoto/Osaka

Tour	Code	Price	Price 2	Meals	Visits	Schedule
5-Day Japan East Bound Tour	JET05	¥86,000	¥26,400		Kyoto (2), Tokyo (2)	Daily except Dec. 28-Jan. 4
2-Day Inland Sea Tour	KIT02	¥98,000	¥5,000	1 lunch	Hiroshima (1), Miyajima Inland sea	Thu. & Sun. (Mar. 22-Nov. 24)
3-Day Inland Sea Tour	KIT03	¥142,000	¥12,000	1 b'fast 2 lunches 1 dinner	Hiroshima (1), Inland Sea, Tomonoura (1), Kurashiki, Okayama	Thu. & Sun. (Mar. 22-Nov. 24)
5-Day Kyoto/ Osaka Departure	KRT X05	¥248,000	¥22,000	3 lunches	Fukuoka (1), Beppu (1), Mt. Aso, Kumamoto (1), Unzen Nagasaki (1)	Sat. (Mar. 24-Nov. 17)

Tour from Fukuoka

Tour	Code	Price	Price 2	Meals	Visits	Schedule
5-Day Fukuoka (Hakata) Departure	KRT05	¥204,000	¥22,000	3 lunches	Fukuoka (1), Beppu (1), Mt. Aso, Kumamoto (1), Unzen Nagasaki (1)	Sat. (Mar. 24-Nov. 17)

Japan Holiday Tour Series by Hankyu Express International

Hankyu Express International : NKK Bldg. 2-18-2 Shimbashi, Minato-ku, Tokyo TEL (03) 3459-9080
Note: If the tour does not return to the point of orgin, the tour terminal place is underlined

Tours from Tokyo

Tour	Code	Price	Price 2	Meals	Visits	Schedule
1-Day Kamakura & Hakone Tour	H1	¥14,900		lunch	Mt. Fuji, Hakone	Daily (Mar. 20-Nov. 20)
2-Day Mt. Fuji & Hakone Tour	H2	¥25,200	¥5,800	lunch	Mt. Fuji, Hakone (1)	Daily (Mar.20-Nov.19)
2-Day Kyoto Tour	H3	¥47,900	¥5,900	lunch	Mt. Fuji, Hakone, Kyoto (1), Nara (Optional ¥7,800)	Daily (Mar. 20-Nov. 29) except Apr. 28-May. 6, Aug. 11-16, Sep. 15,16, 22-24, Oct. 10 & Nov. 3-4)
3-Day Kyoto Tour	H4	¥69,000	¥11,700	2 lunches	Mt. Fuji, Hakone (1), Kyoto (1), Nara	Same as above (H3)
4-Day Kyoto Tour	H5	¥77,000	¥17,600	2 lunches	Mt. Fuji, Hakone (1), Kyoto (2), Nara	Same as H3
2-Day Quick Tour	Q2	¥70,000	¥5,900	2 lunches	Mt. Fuji, Hakone, Kyoto (1), Nara	Same as H3
3-Day Quick Tour	Q3	¥78,000	¥11,800	2 lunches	Mt. Fuji, Hakone, Kyoto (2), Nara	Same as H3

| 6-Day Highlight Tour | HL6 | ¥137,000 | ¥36,400 | 2 lunches | Tokyo (3), Nikko, Hakone, Mt. Fuji, Kyoto (2), Osaka | Daily (Mar. 20- Nov. 17) |
| 7-Day Highlight Tour | HL7 | ¥159,000 | ¥42,200 | 3 lunches | Tokyo (3), Nikko, Hakone (1), Mt. Fuji, Kyoto (2), Nara, Osaka | Same as above (HL6) |

Japan Holiday Tour Series by Japan Gray Line

Japan Gray Line : 3-3-3 Nishi-Shimbashi, Minato-ku, Tokyo TEL (03) 3433-5745
Note: Samurai Night Tour (T-N1) is operated Only when Kabuki drama is staged

Tours from Tokyo

Tokyo Morning Tour	T-M	¥3,900			Tokyo Tower, Imperial East Garden, Asakusa, Ginza	Daily
Tokyo Afternoon Tour	T-A	¥4,300			Meiji Shrine, NHK Broad Casting Center, Diet Bldg., Pearl Gallery	Daily
Tokyo One Day Tour	T-O	¥9,200 ¥7,200		lunch —	A combined tour of "Morning" & "Afternoon" at a reduced Fare	Daily
Geisha Party Tour	T-N3	¥10,200			Geisha Party	Nightly
Happening Night Tour	T-H2	¥14,300		dinner	Sukiyaki or steak dinner, Revue, Geisha Party	Nightly except Sun
Royal Night Tour	T-R	¥7,900			Sukiyaki or Steak dinner, Kabuki theater.	Nightly
Samurai Night Tour	T-N1	¥10,200			Kabuki drama, Geisha Party	Nightly
1Day Mt. Fuji & Hakone Tour	T-S	¥14,900		lunch	Boat cruise on Lake Ashi, Hakone Ropeway	Daily

Japan Holiday Tour Series by Kinki Nippon Tourist

Kinki Nippon Tourist : 19-2 Kanda-Matsunagacho, Chiyoda-ku, Tokyo TEL (03) 3255-6535

Tours from Kyoto

| Kyoto Morning Tour | 101 | ¥4,800 | | | Nijo Castle, Golden Pavilion, The Old Imperial Palace | Daily (Mar. 1- Nov. 30) |
| Kyoto Afternoon Tour | 202 | ¥4,800 | | | Kodai Yuzen-en, Kiyomizu Temple, Heian Shrine | Same as above (101) |

Nara Afternoon Tour	303	¥5,700			Todaiji Temple, Deer Park, Kasuga Grand Shrine, Treasure Museum of Kasuga Grand Shrine-Round trip by train	Same as 101
Kyoto One Day Tour	502	¥10,000			Combination of 101 & 202	Same as 101
Kyoto & Nara One Day	503	¥11,000			Combination of 101 & 303	Same as 101

Note: Japan Holiday Tour Series are operated by a consortium of 18 leading travel agents.

Japan Holiday Tour Series by Tobu Travel

Tobu Travel: 3-4-12 Nihombashi, Chuo-ku, Tokyo TEL (03)3272-1806

Tours from Tokyo

1 Day Trip to Nikko	N-1	¥18,000		b'fast lunch	Nikko	Daily except Dec. 30-Jan. 4
2 Day Trip to Nikko	N-2	¥24,700	¥5,200	1 b'fast 1 lunch	Nikko (1)	Same as N-1

FOREIGN DIPLOMATIC DELEGATIONS

SAPPORO

American Consulate General, 28 Nishi, Kita-Ichijo, Cho-ku	011-641-1115
Austrian Honorary Consulate, c/o Senshuan Seika K.K. 3-17 Nishi, Minami-Sanjo, Chuo-ku	261-7964
Belgian Honorary Consulate, c/o Nichiryo-Seipan K.K. 18-5-1 Tukisamu-Higashi-Ichijo, Toyohira-ku	852-0110
Brazilian Honorary Consulate, Ito Bldg., 4 Nishi, Kita-Shijo, Chuo-ku	251-0717
China Consulate-General, 23-15 Nishi, Minami-Jusanjo Chuo-ku	563-5563
Finnish Honorary Consulate, 10-1 Nijo, Hiragishi, Toyohira-ku	822-7693
French Honorary Consulate, c/o Shingu-Shoko, 2-7-1 Kotoni, Nishi-ku	0134-24-1311
German Honorary Consulate(Federal Republic of Germany), Hokaido-Denryoku K.K., 1-2 O-Dori Higashi Chuo-ku	011-251-1111
Korean Consulate General, 21-9-1 Nishi, Kita-Sanjo, Chuo-ku	621-0288
Philippine Consulate-General, Ishii-Bldg., 13 Nishi, Kita-Yonjo, Chou-ku	211-1133
Soviet Consulate General, 12-826 Nishi, Minami-Juyojo, Chuo-ku	561-3171
Swedish Honorary Consulate, c/o SapporoToshikaihatsu Kosha K.K.Hinode Bldg. 4 Nishi, 1 Minami, Chuo-ku	231-6060

HAKODATE

Italian Honorary Consulate, 22-15 Wakamatsucho,	0138-23-8211

SENDAI

Korean Consulate, 5-5-22 Kamisugi	022-221-2751
Swedish Honorary Consulate, c/o 77 Bank, 3-3-20 Chuo, Aoba-ku	022-267-1111

MITO

Costa Rican Honorary Consulate, 2-62-1 Migawa,	0259-51-5221

UTSUNOMIYA

Costa Rican Honorary Consulate-General, 3-2-3 Ekimae-Tori	0286-34-4311

TOKYO

Algerian Embassy, 2-10-67 Mita, Meguro-ku	03-3711-2661
American Embassy, 1-10-5 Akasaka, Minato-ku	3224-5000
Apostolic Nunciature, 9-2 Sanbancho, Chiyoda-ku	3263-6851
Arabian Embassy 1-5-4 Aobadai, Meguro-ku	3770-8021
Argentine Embassy, Chiyoda House, 2-17-8 Nagatacho, Chiyoda-ku	3592-0321
Australian Embassy, 2-1-19 Mita, Minato-ku	5232-4111
Austrian Embassy, 1-1-20 Moto-Azabu, Minato-ku	3451-8281
Bangladesh Embassy, 2-7-45 Shirogane, Minato-ku	3442-1501
Belgian Embassy, 5 Nibancho, Chiyoda-ku	3262-0191
Belize Honorary Consulate, #1208 1-11-4 Nishi-Azabu, Minato-ku	3403-6963
Bolivian Embassy, Kowa38 Bldg., 4-12-24 Nishi-Azabu, Minato-ku	3499-5441
Bolivian Honorary Consulate, 1-7-22 Hirakawa-cho Chiyoda-ku	3221-6221
Brazilian Embassy, 2-11-12 Kita-Aoyama, Minato-ku	3404-5211
British Embassy, 1 Ichibancho, Chiyoda-ku	3265-5511
Brunei Darussalam Embassy, 6-5-2 Kita-Shinagawa, Shinagawa-ku	3447-7997
Bulgarian Embassy, 5-36-3 Yoyogi, Shibuya-ku	3465-1021
Cameroon Embassy, 9-12 Nanpeidaimachi, Shibuya-ku	3496-1125
Canadian Embassy, 7-3-38 Akasaka, Minato-ku	3408-2101
Central African Embassy, 32-2 Ooyamacho, Shibuya-ku	3460-8341
Central African Honorary Consulate-General, Senpaku-Shinkou Bldg., 1-15-16 Torano-mon, Minato-ku	3502-2371
Chilian Embassy(Consulate-General), Nippon-Seimei-Akabanebashi, 3-1-14 Shiba, Minato-ku	3452-7561
Chinese Embassy, 3-4-33 Moto-Azabu, Minato-ku	3403-3380
Colombian Embassy, 3-10-53 Kamioosaki, Shinagawa-ku	3440-6451
Costa Rican Embassy, Kowa38 Bldg, .4-12-24 Nishi-Azabu, Minato-ku	3486-1812
Costa Rican Honorary Consulate-General, 1 Izumicho Kanda Chiyoda-ku	3864-2075
Cote d'Ivoire Embassy, Kowa38 Bldg., 4-12-24 Nishi-Azabu, Minato-ku	3499-7021
Cuban Embassy, 3-16-23 Higashi-Gotanda, Shinagawa-ku	3449-7511
Cyprian Honorary Consulate-General, Kowa-Hitotsubashi Bldg., 3-7-1 Kanda-Nishikicho, Chiyoda-ku,	3294-9100
Czechoslovakian Embassy, 2-16-14 Hiroo, Shibuya-ku	3400-8122
Danish Embassy, 29-6 Sarugakucho, Shibuya-ku	3496-3001
Danish Honorary Consulate, Dai10-Toyo-Kaiji Bldg., 2-31-7 Nishi-Shinbashi, Minato-ku	3459-8230

Djibouti Embassy, 9-10 Nampeidaicho, Shibuya-ku	3496-6135
Dominican Embassy, Kowa38 Bldg., 4-12-24 Nishi-Azabu, Minato-ku	3499-6020
Dominican Consulate-General, Kowa 38 Bldg., 4-12-24 Nishi-Azabu, Minato-ku	3499-6010
Ecuadorian Embassy, Kowa38 Bldg., 4-12-24 Nishi-Azabu, Minato-ku	3499-2800
Ecuadorian Honorary Consulate, TOC Bldg., 7-22-7 Nishi-Gotanda, Shinagawa-ku	3494-2130
El Salvadorian Embassy, Kowa38 Bldg., 4-12-24 Nishi-Azabu Minato-ku	3499-4461
Ethiopian Embassy, 1-14-15 Midorigaoka, Meguroku-ku	3718-1003
Fijian Embassy, Noa Bldg., 2-3-5 Azabudai, Minato-ku	3587-2038
Finnish Embassy, 3-5-39 Minami-Azabu, Minato-ku	3442-2231
French Embassy (Consulate-General), 4-11-4 Minami-Azabu, Minato-ku	3473-0171
Gabonese Embassy, 1-12-11 Kami-Osaki, Shinagawa-ku	3448-9540
Gambian Honorary Consulate-General, Hayama Bldg., 1-3-14 Hirocho, Shibuya-ku	3444-7806
German Embassy(Federal Republic of Germany), 4-5-10 Minami-Azabu, Minato-ku	3473-0151
Ghananian Embassy, 28Mori Bldg., 4-16-13 Nishi-Azabu, Minato-ku	3409-3861
Greek Embassy, 3-16-30 Nishi-Azabu, Minato-ku	3403-0871
Guatemalan Embassy, Kowa38 Bldg., 4-12-24 Nishi-Azabu, Minato-ku	3400-1830
Haitian Embassy(Consulate-General), Kowa38 Bldg., 4-12-24 Nishi-Azabu, Minato-ku	3486-7070
Honduran Embassy, Kowa38 Bldg., 4-12-24 Nishi-Azabu, Minato-ku	3409-1150
Honduran Honoary Consulate, Hazamagumi Bldg., 2-5-8 Kita-Aoyama, Minato-ku	3405-1111
Hungarian Embassy, 2-17-14 Mita, Minato-ku	3798-8801
Icelandic Honorary Consulate, c/o Shintozai K.K., 1-5-17 Harumi, Chuo-ku	3531-8776
Indian Embassy, 2-2-11 Kudan-Minami, Chiyoda-ku	3262-2391
Indonesian Embassy, 5-2-9 Higashi-Gotanda, Shinagawa-ku	3441-4201
Iranian Embassy, 3-10-32 Minami-Azabu, Minato-ku	3446-8011
Iraqurian Embassy, 8-4-7 Akasaka, Minato-ku	3423-1727
Ireland Embassy, Kowa25 Bldg., 8-7 Sanbancho, Chiyoda-ku	3263-0695
Ireland Honorary Consulate, Mitsui-Busan Bldg., 1-2-1 Ote-Machi, Chiyoda-ku	3285-7723
Israeli Embassy, 3 Nibancho, Chiyoda-ku	3264-0911
Italian Embassy, 2-5-4 Mita, Minato-ku	3453-5291
Jordanian Embassy, Chiyoda-House, 2-17-8 Nagata-cho, Chiyoda-ku	3580-5856
Kenyan Embassy, 3-24-3 Yagumo, Meguro-ku	3723-4006
Kiribati Honorary Consulate, Marunouchi Bldg., 2-4-1 Marunouchi, Chiyoda-ku	3201-3487
Korean Embassy, 1-2-5 Minami-Azabu, Minato-ku	3452-7611
Kuwait Embassy, 4-13-12 Mita, Minato-ku	3455-0361
Laotian Embassy, 3-6-2 Minami-Magome, Ota-ku	3778-1660
Lebanese Embassy, Chiyoda-House, 2-17-8 Nagatacho, Chiyoda-ku	3580-1227
Liberian Embassy, 6-5-3 Kita-Shinagawa, Shinagawa-ku	3441-7138
Libyan Arab Embassy, 10-14 Daikanyamarcho, Shibuya-ku	3477-0701
Luxemburger Embassy, T. S. Bldg 2-1 Nibancho, Chiyoda-ku	3265-9621
Luxemburger Honorary Consulate-General, c/o Nippon-Kogyo Bank K.K., 1-3-3 Marunouchi, Chiyoda-ku	3214-1111
Malagasy Embassy, 2-3-23 Moto-Azabu, Minato-ku	3446-7252
Malaysian Embassy, 2-1-11 Minami-Azabu, Minato-ku	3280-7601
Maldives Honorary Consulate, Technical Associate Bldg., 11-3 Mitoshiro, Chiyoda-ku	3292-3320
Maltese Honorary Consulate, c/o Hakubi-Kyoiku-Kaikan, 1-15-6 Kita-Otsuka, Toshima-ku	3917-1161
Malian Honorary Consulate, c/o Kanematsu-Kosho K.K., 2-14-1 Kyobashi, Chuo-ku	3562-8256
Mauritian Honorary Consulate, c/o Mitsubishi-Shoji K.K., 2-6-3 Marunouchi, Chiyoda-ku	3211-8569
Mexican Embassy, 2-15-1 Nagatacho, Chiyoda-ku	3581-1131
Monaco Honorary Consulate-Genaral, Mitsubishi-Shoji Bldg., 2-6-3 Marunouchi, Chiyoda-ku	3211-4994
Mongolian Embassy, 21-4 Kamiyamacho, Shibuya-ku	3469-2088
Moroccan Embassy, Silver Kingdom Mansion 3-16-3 Sendagaya, Shibuya-ku	3478-3271
Myamar Embassy, 4-8-26 Kita-Shinagawa, Shinagawa-ku	3441-9291
Nepalese Embassy, 7-14-9 Todoroki, Setagaya-ku	3705-5558
Netherlands Embassy, 3-6-3 Shiba-Koen, Minato-Ku	3431-5126
New Zealand Embassy, 20-40 Kamiyamacho, Shibuya-ku	3467-2271
Nicaraguan Embassy, Kowa38 Bldg., 4-12-24 Nishi-Azabu, Minato-ku (Consulate General)	3499-0400 / 3499-0404
Nigerian Embassy, 2-19-7 Uehara, Shibuya-Ku	3468-5531
Niger Honorary Consulate, c/o Shigen-Kaihatsu Bldg., 2-3-4 Akasaka, Minato-ku	3505-6371
Norwegian Embassy, 5-12-2 Minami-Azabu, Minato-ku	3440-2611

FOREIGN DIPLOMATIC DELEGATIONS

Norwegian Honorary Consulate-General, Niko-Sanno Bldg., 2-5-3 Akasaka, Minato-ku	3584-7711
Omani Embassy, 3-16-3 Sendagaya, Shibuya-ku	3402-0877
Pakistani Embassy, 2-14-9 Moto-Azabu, Minato-ku	3454-4861
Panamanian Embassy(Consulate-General), Kowa38 Bldg., 4-12-24 Nishi-Azabu, Minato-ku	3499-3741
Papua New Guniea Embassy, Mita Kokusai Bldg., 1-4-28 Mita, Minato-ku	3454-7801
Paraguayan Embassy(Consulate-General), Asahi-Kami-osaki Bldg., 3-5-8 Kami-Osaki, Shinagawa-ku	3447-7496
Peruvian Embassy, 4-4-27 Higashi, Shibuya-ku	3406-4240
Peruvian Honorary Consulate, 2-31-11 Kabukicho, Shiju-ku	3200-9911
Philippine Embassy, 11-24 Nampeidaicho, Shibuya-ku	3496-2731
Polish Embassy, 2-13-5 Mita, Meguro-ku	3711-5224
Portuguese Embassy, Olympia Annex, 6-31-21 Jingu-Mae, Shibuya-ku	3400-7907
Qatar Embassy, 6-16-22 Shirogane, Minato-ku	3446-7561
Romanian Embassy, 3-16-19 Nishi-Azabu, Minato-ku	3479-0311
Rwandan Embassy, Kowa38 Bldg., 4-12-24 Nishi-Azabu, Minato-ku	3486-7800
Rwandan Honorary Consulate-General, Shinjuku-Center Bldg., 1-25-1 Nishi-Shinjuku,Shinjuku-ku	3342-2886
San Marino Honorary Consulate-General 4-11-7 Nishi-Azabu, Minato-ku	3498-8427
Saudi Arabian Embassy, 1-53 Azabu-Nagasakacho, Minato-ku	3589-5241
Senegalese Embassy, 1-3-4 Aobadai, Meguro-ku	3464-8451
Seychelles Honorary Consulate-General, c/o The-Card K.K., 2-4-1 Ginza, Chuo-ku	3561-8002
Singaporean Embassy, 5-12-3 Roppongi, Minato-ku	3586-9111
South African Consulate-General Zenkyoren Bldg., 2-7-9 Hirakawacho, Chiyoda-ku	3265-3366
Soviet Embassy, 2-1-1 Azabudai, Minato-ku	3583-4224
Spanish Embassy, 1-3-29 Roppongi, Minato-ku	3583-8531
Sri Lankain Embassy, 1-14-1 Akasaka, Minato-ku	3585-7431
Sri Lankain Honorary Consulate-General, 74 Ichigaya-Yakuojicho, Shinjuku-ku	3526-1787
Sudanse Embassy, 6-6-20 Minami-Aoyama, Minato-ku	3406-0811
Swazilands Honorary Consulate-General, c/o Yoshida-Industry K.K., 1 Kanda-Izumicho, Chiyoda-ku	3864-2075
Swedish Embassy, 25Mori Bldg., 1-4-30 Roppongi, Minato-ku	3582-6981
Swiss Embassy, 5-9-12 Minami-Azabu, Minato-ku	3473-0121
Syrian Arab Embassy, 6-19-45 Akasaka, Minato-ku	3586-8977
Tanzanian Embassy, 4-21-9 Kami-Yooga, Setagaya-ku	3425-4531
Thai Embassy, 3-14-6 Kami-Oosaki, Shinagawa-ku	3441-7352
Tongan Honorary Consulate-General Sempaku Shinko Bldg., 1-15-16 Toranomon, Minato-ku	3502-2371
Tunisian Embassy, 1-18-8 Wakaba, Shinjuku-ku	3353-4111
Turkish Embassy, 2-33-6 Jingu-Mae, Shibuya-ku	3470-5131
United Arabian Embassy, Kotsu Anzen Kyoiku Bldg., 3-24-20 Nishi-Azabu, Minato-ku	3478-0650
Uruguayan Embassy, Kowa38 Bldg., 4-12-24 Nishi-Azabu, Minato-ku	3486-1888
Venezuelan Embassy, Kowa38 Bldg., 4-12-24 Nishi-Azabu, Minato-ku	3409-1501
Vietnamese Embassy, 50-11 Motoyoyogi, Shibuya-ku	3466-3311
Western Samoan Honorary Consulate-General, Marunouchi Bldg., 2-4-1 Marunouchi, Chiyoda-ku	3211-7604
Yemeni Arab Embassy, Kowa38 Bldg., 4-12-2 Nishi-Azabu, Minato-ku	3499-7151
Yugoslavia Embassy, 4-7-24 Kita-Shinagawa, Shinagawa-ku	3447-3571
Zairean Embassy, 3-53-17 Sendagaya, Shibuya-ku	3423-3981
Zambian Embassy, 3-9-19 Ebisu, Shibuya-ku	3445-1041
Zimbabwean Embassy, 5-9-10 Shirogane-dai, Minato-ku	3280-0331

YOKOHAMA

Argentine Consulate General, Silk Center Bldg., 1 Yamashitacho Naka-ku	045-641-4194
Colobian Honorary Consulate, Daiichi-Kensetsu Bldg., 2-12-6 Tsuruyacho, Kanagawa-ku	312-8461
Danish Honorary Consulate General, Marsk Bldg., 18 Nippon-O-Dori Naka-ku	651-1591
El Salvadorian Honorary Consulate-General, Asahi-Bldg., 1-3 Honcho, Naka-ku	211-1371
Korean Consulate General, 118 Yamatecho, Naka-ku	621-4531
Mexican Honorary Consulate, Sangyo-Boueki Center-Bldg., 2 Yamashitacho, Naka-ku	671-7277
Netherlands Honerary Consulate, 25 Yamashitacho Naka-ku	651-1661
Norwegian Honorary Consulate, 23 Yamashitacho, Naka-ku	641-0141
Swedish Honorary Consulate, 75-2 Yamashitacho, Naka-ku	671-9478
Thai Honorary Consulate, Silk Center Bldg., 1 Yamashitacho, Naka-ku	212-7750

KOFU

Costa Rican Honorary Consulate-General, c/o Kofu-Shiten Tokyo-Sowa-Bank, 2 -4-20 Aioi	0552-32-7811
French Honorary Consulate, 2-4-20 Aioi	32-7811

NIIGATA

Korean Consulate-General, Maruyama Bldg., 3-1-63 Yoneyama	0252-43-4771

NAGOYA

Belgian Honorary Consulate, c/o Toyota-Tsusho K.K., 4-7-23 Meieki, Nakamura-ku	052-584-5056
British Honorary Consulate 3-21-24 Nishiki, Naka-ku	211-1111
Brazilian Honorary Consulate, c/o Nippon-Tokushu Tougyo K.K., 14-18 Takatsujicho, Mizuho-ku	872-5911
Costa Rican Honorary Consulate-General, 1-23-22 Izumi, Higashi-ku	952-2111
Ecuadorian Honorary Consulate, 1-23 Tomeicho, Chikusa-ku	781-8295
French Consular Agency, 3-92-2 Asaoka-cho Chikusa-ku	782-6768
German Honorary Consulate (Federal Republic of Germany), 1 Toshincho, Higashi-ku	951-8211
Korean Consulate General, 9-25 Higashi-Ozone, Higashi-ku	935-9221
Mexican Honorary Consulate, 1-6-1, Sannomaru, Naka-Ku	232-1605
Netherlands Honorary Consulate, c/o Amano-Sefyaku K.K., 1-2-7 Nishiki, Naka-ku	211-3033
Portuguese Honorary Consulate 1-23-22 Izumi, Higashi-ku	952-2111
Thai Honorary Consulate, 3-6-29 Nishiki, Naka-ku	963-3001
Swedish Honorary Consulate, c/o Tokai-Bank Honten 3-21-24 Nishiki, Naka-ku	211-1111

KYOTO

Brazilian Honorary Consulate, c/o Shimazu-Sesakusho, 1 Nishinokyo-Kuwabaracho, Chukyo-ku	075-823-1111
Italian Honorary Consulate-General, c/o Urasenke Konnian, Ogawa-Dori, Teranouchi-Agaru, Kamigyo-ku	431-3111
Mexican Honorary Consulate, c/o Kyoto-Gaikokugo-Daigaku, 6 Saiinkasame-cho, Ukyo-ku	312-3388
Peruvian Honorary Consulate, 613 Hampoji-maecho Ogawa-Dori Teranouchi-Agaru, Kamigyo-ku	431-3111
Portuguese Honorary Consulate, Horikawa-Dori, Kuramaguchi-Agaru	432-5158

OSAKA

American Consulate-General, 2-11-5 Tenman, Kita-ku	06-315-5900
Australian Consulate-General, Osaka-Kokusai Bldg., 2-3-13 Azuchimachi, Chuo-ku	271-7071
Austrian Honorary Consulate-General, c/o Ito-Chu-Shoji K.K., 4-1-3 Kyutaro, Chuo-ku	241-3011
Belgian Consulate-General, Osaka-Kokusai Kouryu-Bldg., 8-2-6 Uehonmachi, Tennouji-ku	773-5289
Bhutanese Honorary Consulate, Nippon-Golf Bldg., 1-5 Kamiyamacho, Kita-ku	313-0417
British Consulate-General, 3-6-1 Awajimachi, Chuo-ku	231-3355
Burundian Honorary Consulate, Nishizawa K.K., 2-5-8 Bingocho, Chuo-ku	208-5400
Canadian Consulate-General, Daisan-Matsutoyo Bldg., 2-2-3 Nishi-Shinsaibashi, Chuo-ku	212-4910
Chad Honorary Consulate, 3-5-19-411 Kitahama, Chuo-ku	231-5841
Chile Honorary Consulate, Osaka-Ekimae Daiichi-Bldg., 3-1-1000, Umeda, Kita-ku	341-5050
Chinese Consulate-General, 3-9-2 Utsupohoncho, Nishi-ku	445-9482
Comoros Honorary Consulate, c/o Nishizawa K.K., 2-5-8 Bingocho, Chuo-ku	208-5400
Danish Honorary Consulate, Suntory-Bldg., 2-1-40 Doujima-Hama, Kita-ku	346-1285
El Salvadorian Honorary Consulate, c/o Toyobo K.K., 2-2-8 Dojimahama, Kita-ku	348-3183
Finnish Honorary Consulate, Dojima Bldg., 2-6-8 Nishi-Tenman, Kita-ku	361-0938
France Consulate-General, Obayashi-Bldg., 4-33 Kitahama-Higashi, Chuo-ku	946-6181
Gabonese Honorary Consulate, c/o Nishizawa K.K., 2-5-8 Bingomachi, Chuo-ku	208-5400
Guatemalan Honorary Consulate, 2-7-914 Konagawacho, Chuo-ku	761-7206
Italian Consulate-General, MID-Tower, 2-1-61 Shiromi, Chuo-ku	949-1161
Korean Consulate General, 2-3-4 Shinsaibashi, Chuo-ku	213-1401
Luxemburgian Honorary Consulate, c/o Sumitomo-Shintaku Bank, 4-5-33 Kita-hama, Chou-ku	220-2121
Madagascar Honorary Consulate, Suntory Bldg., 3-14-5 Kitabatake, Abeno-ku	653-3577
Mexican Honorary Consulate Suntory Bldg., 2-1-40 Dojimahama, Kita-ku	343-0050
Pakistan Honorary Consulate, c/o Marubeni K.K., 2-5-7 Hommachi, Chuo-ku	266-2483
Panamanian Honorary Consulate-General, Moriyama Bldg., 6-13-7 Fukushima-ku	455-8082

FOREIGN DIPLOMATIC DELEGATIONS

Portuguese Honorary Consulate, Sakaisuji-Inahata Bldg. 1-15-14 Minami-Funaba, Chuo-ku ... 267-6090

Singaporean Consulate-General, Osaka-Kokusai Bldg., 2-3-13 Azuchimachi, Chuo-ku ... 261-5131

Soviet Consulate General, 1-2-2 Nishi-Midorigaoka, Toyonaka-ku ... 848-3452

Spanish Honorary Vice-Consulate, 1-13 Hashimotocho, Abeno-ku ... 661-9068

Sri Lanka Honorary Consulate-General, Kamiya- Shimido Bldg., 1-12-40 Esaka-cho, Suita-shi ... 338-0230

Swiss Consulate-General, Dohoku-Dai Bldg., 1-2-5 Dojima, Kita-ku ... 344-7671

Thai Honorary Consulate, c/o Konoike-Higashi Bldg., 3-6-9 Kita-Kuhoji-cho Chuo-ku ... 243-5563

Turkish Honorary Consulate-General, 3-14-5 Kitabatake Abeno-ku ... 653-3577

Ugandan Honorary Consulate, c/o Osaka-International K.K., 2-3-9 Bakuroucho, Chuo-ku ... 262-1661

KOBE

Bolivian Honorary Consulate, 4-7-7 Kitanocho, Chuo-ku ... 078-221-1663

Brazilian Consulate-General, Nittsei-Kawasaki Bldg., 2-1-18 Nakamachi-Dori, Chuo-ku ... 341-7731

Chilean Honorary Consulate, Tajima Bldg., 4-2-8 Isobe-Dori, Chuo-ku ... 251-1878

Colombian Honorary Consulate, 5-1-6 Taamon-Dori, Chuo-ku ... 341-0103

Costa Rican Honorary Consulate-General, 7-1-19 Morikitacho, Higashinada-ku ... 453-0217

Danish Honorary Consulate, 6-1 Nishi, Kouyocho, Higashinada-ku, ... 857-0251

El Salvadorian Honorary Consulate, c/o Ueshima-Coffee, 5-1-6 Tamon-Dori, Chuo-ku ... 341-3606

German Consulate General Kobe International House 8-1-6 Goko-dori, Chuo-ku ... 232-1212

Honduran Consulate-General, c/o Ueshima-Coffee K.K., 5-1-6 Tamon-Dori, Chuo-ku ... 361-8805

Indian Consulate-General, Kokusai-Boueki Center-Bldg., 4-1-8 Isobe-Dori, Chuo-ku ... 241-8116

Indonesian Consulate-General, KatoBldg., 76-1 Kyomachi, Chuo-ku ... 321-1654

Korean Consulate General 2-21-5 Nakayamate-Dori, Chuo-ku ... 221-4853

Netherlands Consulate-General, Kobe-C.I.T. Bldg., 5-1-14 Hamabe-Dori, Chuo-ku ... 232-3400

Norwegian Honorary Consulate-General, Hatobacho, Chuo-ku ... 331-3563

Panamanian Consulate-General, Yamamoto-Bldg., 71 Kyomachi, Chuo-ku ... 392-3361

Paraguayan Honorary Consulate-General, 5-1-6 Tamon-Dori, Chuo-ku ... 361-8816

Philippine Consulate General, Taiwa-Bldg., 18-1 Akashimachi, Chuo-ku ... 331-9471

Portuguese Honorary Consulate, 1-3-18 Sowacho, Nada-ku ... 851-9538

Swedish Honorary Consulate, Hayashi-Daiichi Bldg., 2-13-3 Shimo-Yamate-Dori, Chuo-ku ... 331-4518

Uruguayan Honorary Consulate, c/o Ishimitsu-ShojiK.K. Iwaya-Minamimachi, Nada-ku ... 861-7787

HIROSHIMA

Brazilian Honorary Consulate, 3-1 Shinchi, Fchumachi, Aki-gun ... 0822-82-1111

British Consulate, 1-3-8 Kamiyacho, Naka-ku ... 247-5151

Danish Honorary Consulate, Hiroshima-Andelsen, 7-1 Hon-Dori, Naka-ku ... 247-2403

UBE

Thai Honorary Consulate, 2-194-1 Kogushi ... 0836-32-2277

SHIMONOSEKI

Korean Consulate-General, 2-13-10 Higashi-Yamato ... 0832-66-5341

TOKUSHIMA

Portuguese Honorary Consulate, 4-3-5 Minamisako, ... 0886-25-2400

FUKUOKA

American Consulate, 2-5-26 Ohori, Chuo-ku ... 092-751-9331

Belgin Honorary Consulate, c/o Fukuoka-Bank, 2-13-1 Tenjin, Chuo-ku ... 711-1315

British Honorary Consulate, c/o Nishi-Nippon Bank, 1-3-6 Hakata-Ekimae, Hakata-ku ... 411-2525

Chinese Consulate-General, 1-29-2 Chigyo-Hama, Chuo-ku ... 713-1121

French Honorary Consulate, Kotobukiken Bldg., 2-10-16 Hakataeki-Higashi, Hakata-ku ... 431-0331

German Honorary Consulate(Federal Republic-Germany), c/o Seibu-Gasu K.K., 2-13-20 Kego, Chuo-ku ... 731-2211

Indonesian Honorary Consulate, c/o Kyushu-Denryoku K.K. 2-1-82 Watanabe-Dori, Chuo-ku ... 761-3031

Italian Honorary Consulate, c/o Fukuoka-City Bank, 3-1-1 Hakata-Ekimae, Hakata-ku ... 441-2222

Korean Consulate-General 1-29-7 Chigyohama, Chuo-ku ... 772-0461

Thai Honorary Consulate, c/o Iwataya K.K., 2-11-1 Tenjin, Chuo-ku ... 721-1111

KITA-KYUSHU

Mexican Honorary Consulate, 1-14 Nakamachi, Moji-ku	093-321-9211

NAGASAKI

Brazilian Honorary Consulate, Taiyo-Gyogyo K.K., 8-23 Asahimachi	0958-61-7111
Chinese Consulate-General, 5-3 Aburagimachi,	49-3311
French Consular Agency, 3-10 Dejimacho	23-1224
Netherlands Honorary Consulate, Nagasaki-Jidosha K.K., Shinchimachi	26-1111
Portuguese Honorary Consulate, c/o The 18th Bank., 1-11 Doza-machi	24-1818

KAGOSHIMA

Peruvian Honorary Consulate, c/o Yamamoto-Kogyo K.K., 11-5 Chuo-ku	0992-58-3144

NAHA

Bolivian Honorary Consulate, 46 Onoyamacho	0988-59-0434
Brazilian Honorary Consulate, c/o Okinawa-Rattkawear Bldg., 1-7-10 Asato	67-1333
Korean Consulate, 2-15-3, Kumochi	67-6940
Peruvian Honorary Consulate, Kokuba-Bldg., 3-21-1 Kumochi	63-2324

URAZOE

American Consulate-General, 2564 Nishihara,	0988-76-4211
Paraguayan Honorary Consulate, Bakurei-Bldg., 2556 Nishihara	76-0195

GINOWAN

Philippine Honorary Consulate, 877 Oyama	0988-97-3624

JAPANESE EMBASSIES, CONSULATES-GENERAL AND CONSULATES ABROAD

("E" stands for Embassy, "CG" for
Consulate-General, "C" for Consulate.)

Country	Address	Telephone
NORTH AMERICA		
U. S. A		
Washington D. C. (E)	2520 Massachusetts Avenue, N. W. Washington D. C. 20008-2869	(202) 939-6700
Agana(CG)	Suite 604, Guam Int'l Trade Center Bldg. 590 South Marina Drive Tamuning, Guam 96911	646-1290
Anchorage(CG)	550 West 7th Avenue, Suite 701 Anchorage, Alaska 99501	(907) 279-8428
Atlanta(CG)	Suite 1501, 400 Colony Square Bldg. 1201 Peachtree Street, N. E. Atlanta, Georgia 30361	(404) 892-2700
Boston(CG)	Federal Reserve Plaza, 14th Floor 600 Atlantic Avenue Boston, Massachusetts 02210	(617) 973-9772
Chicago(CG)	737, North Michigan Avenue, Chicago, Ilinois 60611	(312) 280-0400
Honolulu(CG)	1742 Nuuanu Avenue, Honolulu, Hawaii 96817-3294	(808) 536-2226
Houston(CG)	First Interstate Bank Plaza, Suite 5300, 1000 Louisiana Street, Houston, Texas 77002	(713) 652-2977
Kansas City(CG)	2519 Commerce Tower 911 Main Street Kansas City, Missouri 64105-2076	(816) 471-0111
Los Angeles(CG)	250 East First Street, Suite 1507, Los Angeles, California 90012	(213) 624-8305
New Orleans(CG)	Suite 2050, One Poydras Plaza, 639 Loyola Avenue, New Orleans, Louisiana 70113	(504) 529-2101
New York(CG)	299 Park Avenue, New York, N. Y. 10171	(212) 371-8222
Portland(CG)	2400 First Interstate Tower, 1300 S. W. 5th Avenue, Portland, Oregon 97201	(503) 221-1811
Saipan(C)	4th Floor, Nauru Bldg., Susupe Saipan, Marianas Islands 96950	234-7201
San Francisco(CG)	50 Fremont Street, Suite 2300, San Francisco, California 94115	(415) 777-3533
Seattle(CG)	601 Union Street, Suite 500, Seattle, Washington 98101	(206) 682-9107
CANADA		
Ottawa(E)	255 Sussex Drive, Ottawa, Ontario K1N 9E6	(613) 236-8541

EMBASSY

Edomonton (CG)	2480 Manulife Place, 10180-101 Street, Edomonton, Alberta T5J 3S4	(403)422-3752
Montreal(CG)	600, rue de la Gauchetièreéouest, Suite, 1785 Montréal, Québec H3B 4L8	(514)866-3429
Toronto (CG)	Toronto-Dominion Centre, Suite 2702, Toronto, Ontario, M5K 1A1	(416)363-7038
Vancouver(CG)	900 Board of Trade Tower, 1177 West Hastings Street, Vancouver, B. C., V6E 2K9	(604)684-5868
Winnipeg(CG)	730-215 Garry Street, Credit Union Central Plaza, Winnipeg Manitoba, R3C 3P3	(204)943-5554

CENTRAL & SOUTH AMERICA

ARGENTINA
Buenos Aires(E)	Avenida Paseo Colón 275, 9-piso Buenos Aires	30-2561

BRAZIL
Brasilia(E)	Avenida das Nações, Lote 39 70425 Brasília, D. Federal	242-6475
Belem(CG)	Travessa Padre Eutíquio 2112, 66010 Belém, Pará	222-1900
Curitiba(CG)	Rua Marechal Deodoro, 630 Edifício CCI, 18 andar, 80000 Curitiba, Paraná	224-3861
Manaus(CG)	Rua Ferreira Pena, 92 69000 Manaus, Amazonas	232-2000
Porto Alegre(CG)	Avenida João Obino, n-467-Bairro Petrópolis, 90000 Porto Alegre, Rio Grande do Sul	34-1299
Recife(CG)	Avenida Dantas Barreto, 191 Edifício Santo Antônio 3-andar, 50010 Recife, Pernambuco	224-1930
Rio de Janeiro(CG)	Praia do Flamengo, 200, 10-, andar 22210 Rio de Janeiro, RJ	265-5252
Sao Paulo(CG)	Avenida Paulista, 475 5-~8-andar, 01311 Saõ Paulo-SP	287-0100

CHILE
Santiago(E)	Avenida Providencia 2653, 19- piso, Casilla 2877, Santiago	2321807

COLOMBIA
Bogotá(E)	Carrera 7 No 74-21, Edifício Seguros Aurora, Bogota	255-0300

MEXICO
Mexico City(E)	Paseo de la Reforma No.395, Col. Cuauhtemoc 06500 México, D. F.	211-0028

PANAMA
Panama(E)	Calle 50 y Calle 61, Edifício Don Camilo, Apartado No. 1411, Panamá 1	63-6155

PERU
Lima(E)	Avenida San Felipe 356, Jesús María, Lima	63-0000

EUROPE

AUSTRIA
Vienna(E)	1040 Wien, Argentinierstrasse 21	5017102~8

BELGIUM
Brussels(E)	Avenue des Arts 58, 1040 Bruxelles	513-9200

DENMARK
Copenhagen(E)	Oslo Plads 14, 2100, Copenhagen ø.	26-33-11

FINLAND
Helsinki(E)	Yrjönkatu 13 00120 Helsinki 12	644206

FRANCE
Paris(E)	7, Avenue Hoche, 75008-Paris	4766-02-22
Marseilles(CG)	70, Avenue de Hambourg, 13008 Marseille	91-73-45-55

GERMANY
Bonn(E)	Bundeskanzlerplatz, Bonn-Center HI-701, 5300 Bonn 1	5001
Berlin(E)	Wachtelstrasse 8, 1000 Berlin 33	832-70-26
Frankfurt(CG)	Hamburger Allee 2-10 6000 Frankfurt am Main 90	770351
Hamburg(CG)	Rathausmarkt 5, 2000 Hamburg 1	333017-0
Düsseldorf(CG)	Immermannstr. 45, 4000 Düsseldorf, 1. c/o. Deutsch-Japanisches Center	35-33-11
Munich(CG)	Prinzregentenplatz 10, 8000 München 80	47-10-43

GREECE
Athens(E)	2-4, Messoghion Avenue, Athens Tower Bldg. 21st Fl., Athens	775-8101

IRELAND
Dublin(E)	22, Ailesbury Road, Dublin 4	69-40-33

ITALY
Roma(E)	Via Quintino Sella 60,00187 Roma	481715
Milan(CG)	Via F. Turati 16/18, 20120, Milano	29002316

NETHERLANDS
Hague(E)　　　　Tobias Asserlaan 2, 2517 KC The Hague　　　　3469544
NORWAY
Oslo(E)　　　　Parkveien 33-B, 0244, Oslo 2　　　　55-10-11
PORTUGAL
Lisbon(E)　　　　Rua Mouzinho da Silveira, No.11 1200, Lisboa　　　　3523485
U.S.S.R.
Moscow(E)　　　　Kalashny Pereulok 12, Moscow　　　　291-85-00
Nakhodka(CG)　　No.9, Ulitsa Lunacharskogo, Nakhodka, Primorsky　　5-63-60
　　　　　　　　Krai, 692900
Leningrad(CG)　　Nab. Reki Moiki 29, Leningrad　　　　314-14-34
SPAIN
Madrid(E)　　　　Calle de Joaqún Costa, 29 28002-Madrid　　　　262-55-46
Barcelona(CG)　　Ediffcio Banca Catalana, Planta 3 Avda. Diagonal 662-　(93)204-7224
　　　　　　　　664-08034 Barcelona
SWEDEN
Stockholm(E)　　Gärdesgatan 10, 115 27 Stockholm　　　　663-0440
SWITZERLAND
Berne(E)　　　　43, Engestrasse, 3012 Berne　　　　24-08-11
Geneva(CG)　　　10, Avenue de Budé, 1202 Genève　　　　34-84-00
UNITED KINGDOM
London(E & CG)　101-104, Piccadilly London, WIV 9FN　　　　465-6500

ASIA

CHINA
Beijing(E)　　　　7 Ri Ten Rd., Jian Guo Men Wai, Beijing　　　　532-2361
Shanghai(CG)　　1517 Huai hai Rd. Central, shanghai　　　　4336639
HONG KONG
Hong Kong(CG)　25th Fl., Bank of America Tower 12, Harcout Road,　5221184
　　　　　　　　Central
INDIA
New Delhi(E)　　50-G, Chanakyapurn, New Delhi　　　　6876564
Bombay(CG)　　　No. 1, M.L. Dahanukar Marg, Cumballa Hill, Bombay　4933857
　　　　　　　　400 026
Calcutta(CG)　　12, Pretoria Street, Calcutta, 700071　　　　22-2241
Madras(CG)　　　60, Mayor Ramanathan Salai, Chetput Madras 600 031　865594
INDONESIA
Jakarta(E & CG)　Jalan M. H. Thamrin 24, Jakarta　　　　324308
Surabaya(CG)　　Jalan Sumatera No.93, Surabaya　　　　44677
REPUBLIC OF KOREA
Seoul(E)　　　　18-11, Chunghak-Dong, Chongro-ku, Seoul　　　(733)5626
Pusan(CG)　　　No. 1147-11, Choryang-Dong Dong-ku, Busan　　465-5101
MALAYSIA
Kuala Lumpur(E)　No. 11, Pesiaran Stonor, off Jalan Tun Razak, Kuala　2438044
　　　　　　　　Lumpur
Penang(CG)　　　No. 2, Biggs Road, 10350 Penang　　　　368222
PAKISTAN
Islamabad(E)　　Plot No. 53-70, Ramna 5/4, Diplomatic Enclave 1, Is-　820181
　　　　　　　　lamabad
Karachi(CG)　　　233, Raja Ghazanfar Ali Khan Road, E. I. Lines, Karachi　511331
PHILIPPINES
Manilla(E & CG)　375 Senator Gil J. Puyat Avenue, Makati, Metro Manila　818-9011
SINGAPORE
Singapore(E)　　16, Nassim Road, Singapore, 1025　　　　2358855
SRI LANKA
Colombo(E)　　　No. 20, Gregory's Road, Colombo 7　　　　693831
THAILAND
Bangkok(E)　　　1674, New Petchburi Road, Bangkok 10310　　　252-6151
Chiang Mai(C)　　14 Boonruangrit Road, Chiangmai　　　　221-451

MIDDLE & NEAR EAST

IRAN
Tehran(E)　　　　Bucharest Avenue, Corner of the 5th Street, Tehran　623396
IRAQ
Baghdad(E)　　　Hay Babil 929/17/70, Baghdad　　　　7195156
ISRAEL
Tel Aviv(E)　　　Asia House, 4, Weizman Street 64 239 Tel-Aviv　　257292

EMBASSY

LEBANON
Beirut(E)	Immeuble Olfat Salha, Bldg. Corniche Chouran, Beyrouth	810408

SAUDI ARABIA
Riyadh(E)	A-11 Diplomatic Quarter, Riyadh	488-1100
Jeddah(CG)	Palestine Road, Jeddah	6652402

TURKEY
Ankara(E)	Resit Galip Caddesi 81, Gaziosmanpasa, Ankara	1460500

AFRICA

ALGERIA
Alger(E)	1, Chemin Macklay, El-Biar, Alger	78-63-41

ARAB REPUBLIC OF EGYPT
Cairo(E)	3rd Floor, Cairo Center Bldg. 2, Abdel Kader Hamza St. Garden City, Cairo	3553962

REPUBLIC OF SOUTH AFRICA
Pretoria(CG)	200 Standard Plaza, 440 Hilda Street, Hatfield, Pretoria	342-2100

OCEANIA

AUSTRALIA
Canberra(E)	112 Empire Circuit, Yarralumla, Canberra A. C. T. 2600	2733244
Melbourne(CG)	3rd Floor, "Holland House", 492 St. Kilda Road, Melbourne 3004. Victoria	867-3244
Perth(CG)	21st. Fl., The Forrest Centre, 221 St., Geoge's Terrace, Perth W. A. 6000	321-7816
Sydney(CG)	Level 34, State Bank Centre, 52 Martin Place, Sydney, N. S. W. 2000	231-3455
Brisbane(C)	17th Floor, Comalco Place, 12 creek Street, Brisbane, Queensland 4000	221-5188

NEW ZEALAND
Wellington(E)	7th Fl., Norwich Insurance House, 3-11 Hunter St., Wellington 1	731-540
Auckland(CG)	6th Fl., National Mutual Center Bldg. 37-45, Shortland Street, Auckland, 1	303-4106
Christchurch(CV)	1st Fl., General Bldg., 77 Hereford Street, Christchurch 1	665-680

SISTER CITIES IN JAPAN

Japanese City	Affiliated City	Country	Date of Affiliation
Abashiri	Port Alberni	Canada	Feb, 9, 86
Akashi	Vallejo	Calif., U. S. A.	Dec, 9, 68
Akita	Lanchou	China	Aug, 5, 82
Akita	Passau	Germany	Apr, 8, 84
Amagasaki	Augsburg	Germany	Apr, 7, 59
Arida	Delano	Calif., U. S. A.	Aug, 26, 65
Asahikawa	Bloomington	Ill., U. S. A.	Oct, 11, 62
Asahikawa	Suweon	Korea	Oct, 17, 89
Ashiya	Montebello	Calif., U. S. A.	May, 24, 61
Atami	San Remo	Italy	Nov, 10, 76
Atsugi	New Britain	Conn., U. S. A.	May, 31, 83
Beppu	Beaumont	Tex., U. S. A.	May, 20, 85
Beppu	Mogpo	Korea	Oct, 1, 84
Beppu	Rotorua	New Zealand	Jul, 10, 87
Chiba	Asuncion	Paraguay	Jan, 1, 70
Chiba	Houston	Tex, U. S. A.	Oct, 24, 72
Chiba	Kezon	Philippines	Nov, 9, 72
Chiba	North Vancouver	Canada	Jan, 1, 70
Chichibu	Antioch	Calif., U. S. A.	Oct, 9, 67
Chichibu	Gangreung	Korea	Feb, 16, 83
Chichibu	Linfen	China	Oct, 7, 88
Chitose	Anchorage	Alaska., U. S. A.	Jun, 20, 68
Chosi	Coos Bay	Ore., U. S. A.	Feb, 10, 83
Chosi	Legaspi	Philippines	Jun, 27, 85
Dazaifu	Puyo	Korea	Apr, 20, 78
Ebetsu	Gresham	Ore., U. S. A.	May, 20, 77
Esashi	Shepparton	Australia	Mar, 3, 79
Fujieda	Penrith	Australia	Nov, 3, 84
Fujimi	Sabac	Yugoslavia	Oct, 23, 82
Fujinomiya	Santa Monica	Calif., U. S. A.	Jul, 21, 75
Fujisawa	Kunming	China	Nov, 5, 81
Fujisawa	Miami Beach	Fla., U. S. A.	Mar, 5, 59
Fujisawa	Windosr	Canada	Dec, 2, 87
Fujiyoshida	Chamonir Mt Blanc	France	Oct, 9, 78
Fujiyoshida	Colorado Springs	Colo., U. S. A.	Mar, 16, 62
Fukaya	Fremont	Calif., U. S. A.	Jan, 26, 80
Fukui	Fullerton	U. S. A.	Nov, 5, 89
Fukui	Hangchow	China	Nov, 23, 89
Fukui	New Brunswich	N. J., U. S. A.	May, 25, 82
Fukuoka	Auckland	New Zealand	Jul, 24, 86
Fukuoka	Bordeaux	France	Nov, 8, 82
Fukuoka	Ipoh	Malaysia	Mar, 21, 89
Fukuoka	Oakland	Calif., U. S. A.	Oct, 13, 62
Fukuroi	Hillsboro	Ore., U. S. A.	Aug, 3, 88
Funabashi	Hayward	Calif., U. S. A.	Nov, 7, 86
Funabashi	Odense	Denmark	Apr, 6, 89
Furano	Schladming	Austria	Feb, 23, 77
Futtsu	Carlsbad	Calif., U. S. A.	Oct, 25, 88
Gifu	Campinas	Brazil	Feb, 22, 82
Gifu	Cincinnati	Oha., U. S. A.	May, 11, 88
Gifu	Firenze	Italy	Feb, 8, 78
Gifu	Hanagchou	China	Feb, 21, 79
Gotenba	Beaverton	Ore., U. S. A.	Oct, 22, 87
Gotenba	Chambersburg	Pa., U. S. A.	Aug, 22, 60
Hadano	Pasadena	Tex., U. S. A.	Sep, 29, 64
Hagi	Ulsan	Korea	Oct, 29, 68
Hakodate	Halifax	Canada	Nov, 25, 82
Handa	Midland	Mich., U. S. A.	Jun, 5, 81
Handa	Port Macquarie	Australia	Apr, 14, 90
Hanno	Brea	Calif., U. S. A.	Jan, 5, 81
Hanyu	Baguio	Philippines	Jun, 19, 68
Hashimoto	Rohnert Park	Calif., U. S. A.	Nov, 7, 83
Hashimoto	Taian	China	May, 13, 87
Higashihiroshima	Marilia	Brazil	Nov, 29, 80

935

Higashimurayama	Independence	Missuri, U. S. A.	Jan,	26,	78
Higashiosaka	Berlin, Wedding	Germany	Aug,	12,	59
Higashiosaka	Glendale	Calif., U. S. A.	Sep,	23,	60
Hikone	Ann Arbor	Mich., U. S. A.	Mar,	28,	69
Himeji	Adelaide	Australia	Apr,	19,	82
Himeji	Charleroi	Belgium	Jul,	13,	65
Himeji	Curitiba	Brazil	May,	14,	84
Himeji	Phoenix	Ariz., U. S. A.	Nov,	3,	76
Hino	Redlands	Calif., U. S. A.	Jul,	15,	63
Hirara	Maui	Hawaii, U. S. A.	Jun,	24,	65
Hiroshima	Chungching	China	Oct,	23,	86
Hiroshima	Hannover	Germany	May,	27,	83
Hiroshima	Honolulu	Hawaii, U. S. A.	Jun,	15,	59
Hiroshima	Volgograd	U. S. S. R.	Sep,	28,	72
Hitachi	Birmingham	Ala., U. S. A.	Apr,	23,	82
Hitachi	Tauranga	New Zealand	Apr,	18,	88
Hondo	Encinitas	Calif., U. S. A.	Sep,	22,	88
Hyuga	Weifang	China	Feb,	25,	86
Ibaraki	Minneapolis	Minn., U. S. A.	Oct,	22,	80
Ibusuki	Rockhampton	Australia	Nov,	21,	80
Ichikawa	Gardena	Calif., U. S. A.	Nov,	6,	62
Ichikawa	Medan	Indonesia	Nov,	4,	89
Iida	Charle Mézières	France	Aug,	5,	88
Ikeda	Launceston	Australia	Nov,	1,	65
Imabari	Panama	Panama	Mar,	2,	77
Inazawa	Olympia	Greece	Aug,	22,	87
Iruma	Walfratshausen	Germany	Oct,	14,	87
Isahaya	Athens	Ten., U. S. A.	Apr,	25,	86
Isehara	La Mirada	Calif., U. S. A.	Sep,	21,	81
Isesaki	Springfield	Miss., U. S. A.	Jul,	18,	86
Isesaki	Maanshan	China	Nov,	9,	89
Ishinomaki	Civitavecchia	Italy	Oct,	12,	71
Itami	Hasselt	Belguim	Apr,	5,	85
Ito	Rieti	Italy	Jul,	21,	85
Ito	Gillingham	U. K.	Aug,	10,	82
Iwai	Pine Bluff	Ark., U. S. A.	Nov,	9,	86
Iwakuni	Everett	Wash., U. S. A.	Aug,	1,	62
Iwamizawa	Pocatello	Ida., U. S. A.	May,	20,	85
Iwanuma	Napa	Calif., U. S. A.	Feb,	15,	73
Iwata	Dagupan	Philippines	Feb,	19,	75
Iwata	Mountain View	Calif., U. S. A.	Jun,	4,	76
Izumo	Santa Clara	Calif., U. S. A.	Oct,	11,	86
Joetsu	Lilienfeld	Austria	Oct,	7,	81
Kadoma	Eindhoven	Netherlands	May,	27,	66
Kadoma	São Jose dos Compos	Brazil	Apr,	13,	73
Kaga	Dundas	Canada	Mar,	21,	68
Kagoshima	Changsha	China	Oct,	30,	82
Kagoshima	Napoli	Italy	May,	3,	60
Kagoshima	Perth	Australia	Apr,	23,	74
Kaizuka	Culver City	Calif., U. S. A.	Apr,	29,	65
Kakegawa	Eugene	Ore., U. S. A.	Aug,	3,	79
Kakogawa	Maringa	Brazil	Jul,	2,	73
Kamakura	Nice	France	Nov,	9,	66
Kameoka	Jandira	Brazil	Nov,	3,	85
Kameoka	Knittelfeld	Austria	Apr,	14,	64
Kameoka	Stillwater	Okla., U. S. A.	Nov,	3,	85
Kanazawa	Buffalo	N. Y., U. S. A.	Dec,	18,	62
Kanazawa	Ghent	Belguim	Oct,	5,	71
Kanazawa	Irkutsk	U. S. S. R.	Mar,	20,	67
Kanazawa	Nancy	France	Nov,	6,	72
Kanazawa	Porto Alegre	Brazil	Mar,	20,	67
Kanazawa	Suchou	China	Jun,	13,	81
Kan-onji	Appleton	Wisc., U. S. A.	Jan,	27,	88
Kashiwa	Torrance	Calif., U. S. A.	Feb,	20,	73
Kasugai	Kelowna	Canada	Feb,	5,	81
Katano	Collingwood	Canada	Nov,	3,	81
Kawagoe	Offenbach	Germany	Aug,	24,	83
Kawagoe	Salem	Ore., U. S. A.	Aug,	1,	86
Kawasaki	Baltimore	Md., U. S. A.	Jun,	14,	79
Kawasaki	Rijeka	Yugoslavia	Jun,	23,	77
Kawasaki	Shenyang	China	Aug,	18,	81

Kawasaki	Wollongong	Australia	May, 18, 88
Kesennuma	Puntarenas	Costa Rica	May, 22, 78
Kiryu	Biella	Italy	Oct, 12, 63
Kiryu	Columbus	Ga., U. S. A.	Apr, 25, 78
Kitakami	Concord	Calif., U. S. A.	Oct, 25, 74
Kitakata	Wilsonvill	Ore., U. S. A.	Oct, 16, 88
Kitakyushu	Incheon	Korea	Dec, 20, 88
Kitakyushu	Norfolk	Va., U. S. A.	Jul, 14, 59
Kitakyushu	Tacoma	Wash., U. S. A.	Jun, 8, 59
Kitakyushu	Tailien	China	May, 1, 79
Kitami	Elizabeth	N. J., U. S. A.	Jun, 12, 69
Kitami	Jinju	Korea	May, 10, 85
Kobe	Brisbane	Australia	Jul, 16, 85
Kobe	Marseille	France	Jul, 2, 61
Kobe	Riga	U. S. S. R.	Jun, 18, 74
Kobe	Rio de Janeiro	Brazil	May, 19, 69
Kobe	Seattle	Wash., U. S. A.	Oct, 21, 57
Kochi	Fresno	Calif., U. S. A.	Feb, 11, 65
Kochi	Wuhu	China	Apr, 19, 85
Kofu	Chengtu	China	Sep, 27, 84
Kofu	Des Moines	Iowa., U. S. A.	Aug, 16, 58
Kofu	Lodi	Calif., U. S. A.	Apr, 11, 61
Kofu	Pau	France	Aug, 18, 75
Kohama	Kyongju	Korea	Feb, 13, 77
Komaki	Wyandotte	Mich., U. S. A.	Mar, 22, 63
Komatsu	Suzano	Brazil	Jul, 11, 72
Komatsu	Vilvoord	Belgium	May, 15, 74
Koriyama	Brummen	Neatherland	Jun, 25, 88
Koshigaya	Campbelltown	Austlaria	Apr, 11, 84
Kuji	Franklin	Ind., U. S. A.	Oct, 5, 60
Kuji	Klaipeda	U. S. S. R.	July, 9, 89
Kumamoto	Kueilin	China	Oct, 1, 79
Kumamoto	San Antonio	Tex., U. S. A.	Dec, 28, 87
Kumano	Bastos	Brazil	Dec, 8, 72
Kurashiki	Christchurch	New Zealand	Mar, 7, 73
Kurashiki	Kansas City	Mo., U. S. A.	May, 20, 72
Kurashiki	St. Pö lten	Austria	Sep, 29, 57
Kure	Bremerton	Wash., U. S. A.	Sep, 22, 69
Kurobe	Macon	Ga., U. S. A.	May, 10, 77
Kurobe	Sneek	Netherlands	Sep, 10, 70
Kuroishi	Wenatchee	Wash., U. S. A.	Oct, 5, 71
Kuroishi	Yongchou	Korea	Aug, 17, 84
Kurume	Hofei	China	May, 12, 80
Kusatsu	Pontiac	Mich., U. S. A.	Aug, 2, 78
Kushikino	Salinas	Calif., U. S. A.	May, 27, 79
Kushima	Ibiuna	Brazil	May, 21, 87
Kushiro	Burnaby	Canada	Sep, 9, 65
Kushiro	Kholmsk	U. S. S. R.	Aug, 27, 75
Kyoto	Boston	Mass., U. S. A.	Jun, 24, 59
Kyoto	Firenze	Italy	Sep, 22, 65
Kyoto	Guadalajara	Mexico	Oct, 20, 80
Kyoto	Hsian	China	May, 10, 74
Kyoto	Kiev	U. S. S. R.	Sep, 7, 71
Kyoto	Köln	Germany	May, 29, 63
Kyoto	Paris	France	Jun, 15, 58
Kyoto	Zagreb	Yugoslavia	Oct, 22, 81
Maizuru	Nahotoka	U. S. S. R.	Jun, 21, 61
Maizuru	Tailien	China	May, 8, 82
Marugame	Pasing	Philippines	Nov, 4, 71
Matsudo	Box Hill	Australia	May, 12, 71
Matsumoto	Katmandu	Nepal	Nov, 17, 89
Matsumoto	Salt Lake City	Utah., U. S. A.	Nov, 29, 58
Matsuto	Columbia	Miss., U. S. A.	Mar, 7, 88
Matsuura	Mackay	Australia	Jul, 22, 89
Matsuyama	Freiburg	Germany	Apr, 4, 89
Matsuyama	Sacramento	Calif., U. S. A.	Aug, 18, 81
Miki	Visalia	Calif., U. S. A.	May, 18, 66
Minami-Ashigara	Tilburg	Neatherland	Jun, 4, 89
Misawa	Wenatchee	Wash., U. S. A.	Oct, 4, 81
Mishima	Pasadena	Calif., U. S. A.	Jul, 24, 57
Mito	Anaheim	Calif., U. S. A.	Jan, 21, 77

Mitsuke	Mairinque	Brazil	Sep,	7, 73
Miyazu	Delray Beach	Fla., U. S. A.	Sep,	29, 77
Miyazu	Nelson	New Zealand	May,	7, 76
Mizunami	Liling	China	Jan,	14, 87
Mizunami	Selb	Germany	Sep,	28, 66
Monbetsu	Newport	Ore., U. S. A.	Apr,	8, 66
Mo-oka	Glendale	Calif., U. S. A.	Oct,	1, 88
Moriguchi	New Westminster	Canada	Apr,	10, 63
Morioka	Victoria	Canada	May,	23, 85
Moriyama	Adrian	Mich., U. S. A.	Aug,	3, 89
Moriyama	Kauai Is.	Hawaii., U. S. A.	Jan,	31, 75
Muko	Hangchou	China	Sep,	27, 85
Muko	Saratoga	Calif., U. S. A.	Nov,	16, 84
Nagahama	Augsburg	Germany	Apr,	11, 59
Nagai	Bad Säckingen	Germany	Sep,	8, 83
Nagano	Clearwater	Fla., U. S. A.	Mar,	14, 59
Nagano	Shihchiachuang	China	Apr,	19, 81
Nagaokakyo	Arlington	Mass., U. S. A.	Sep,	21, 84
Nagaokakyo	Ningpo	China	Apr,	21, 83
Nagaoka	Fort Worth	Tex., U. S. A.	Nov,	9, 87
Nagasaki	Fuchou	China	Oct,	20, 80
Nagasaki	Middelburg	Netherlands	Oct,	17, 78
Nagasaki	Porto	Portugal	May,	26, 78
Nagasaki	Saint Paul	Minn., U. S. A.	Dec,	7, 55
Nagasaki	Santos	Brazil	Jul,	6, 72
Nagoya	Los Angeles	Calif., U. S. A.	Apr,	1, 59
Nagoya	Mexico City	Mexico	Feb,	16, 78
Nagoya	Nanching	China	Dec,	21, 78
Nagoya	Sydney	Australia	Sep,	16, 80
Nago	Hillo	Hawaii, U. S. A.	Jun,	13, 86
Naha	Fuchou	China	May,	20, 81
Naha	Honolulu	Hawaii., U. S. A.	Jan,	10, 61
Naha	Sao Vicente	Brazil	Oct,	23, 78
Nakatsugawa	Registro	Brazil	Aug,	4, 80
Nanao	Bratsk	U. S. S. R.	Dec,	11, 70
Nanao	Chin Hsien	China	Apr,	13, 86
Nanao	Kimchon	Korea	Oct,	16, 75
Nanyo	Nanyang	China	Oct,	6, 88
Narashino	Tuscaloosa	Ala., U. S. A.	Apr,	26, 86
Nara	Hsian	China	Feb,	1, 74
Nara	Kyongju	Korea	Apr,	15, 70
Nara	Toledo	Spain	Sep,	11, 72
Nara	Versailles	France	Nov,	14, 86
Narita	Hsienyang	China	Sep,	14, 88
Naruto	Ruhneburg	Germany	Apr,	18, 74
Natori	Guararapes	Brazil	May,	31, 79
Nayoro	Lindsay	Canada	Aug,	1, 69
Nemuro	Sitka	Alaska., U. S. A.	Dec,	19, 75
Neyagawa	Newport News	Va., U. S. A.	Jul,	1, 82
Neyagawa	Oakville	Canada	Apr,	6, 84
Nichinan	Portsmouth	N. Hamp., U. S. A.	Sept,	5, 85
Niigata	Galveston	Tex., U. S. A.	Jan,	28, 65
Niigata	Haerhpin	China	Dec,	17, 79
Niigata	Khabarovsk	U. S. S. R.	Apr,	23, 65
Nikko	Palm Springs	Calif., U. S. A.	Jul,	30, 69
Nirasaki	Fairfield	Calif., U. S. A.	Oct,	28, 71
Nirasaki	Kiamusze	China	Oct,	10, 84
Nishinomiya	Spokane	Wash., U. S. A.	Sep,	13, 61
Nishiwaki	Renton	Wash., U. S. A.	Jul,	11, 69
Nobeoka	Medford	Mass., U. S. A.	Aug,	29, 80
Noshiro	Wrangell	Alaska., U. S. A.	Dec,	16, 65
Numazu	Kalamazoo	Mich., U. S. A.	Jul,	1, 63
Numazu	Yüehyang	China	Apr,	5, 85
Obihiro	Seward	Alaska., U. S. A.	Mar,	27, 68
Oda	Daejeon	Korea	Nov,	14, 87
Odawara	Chulavista	Calif., U. S. A.	Nov,	8, 81
Oita	Aveiro	Portugal	Oct,	10, 78
Okawa	Pordenone	Italy	Sep,	19, 87
Okaya	Mt. Plesant	Mich., U. S. A.	Jun,	14, 65
Okayama	Loyang	China	Apr,	6, 81
Okayama	Plovdiv	Bulgaria	Apr,	28, 72

Okayama	San Jose	Calif., U. S. A.	May,	26, 57
Okayama	San Jose	Costa Rica	Jan,	27, 69
Okazaki	Newport Beach	Calif., U. S. A.	Nov,	27, 84
Okazaki	Uddevalla	Sweden	Sep,	17, 68
Omachi	Innsbruck	Austria	Feb,	18, 85
Ome	Boppard	Germany	Sep,	24, 65
Omihachiman	Grand Rapids	Mich., U. S. A.	Aug,	4, 86
Omura	Shanghai	China	Aug,	31, 84
Ono	Lindsay	Calif., U. S. A.	Feb,	17, 73
Osaka	San Francisco	Calif., U. S. A.	Oct,	7, 57
Osaka	Sao Paulo	Brazil	Oct,	27, 69
Osakasayama	Ontario	Ore., U. S. A.	Oct,	27, 74
Ota	Burbank	Calif., U. S. A.	Feb,	14, 84
Ota	Yingkow	China	Sep,	26, 87
Otaru	Dunedin	New Zealand	Jul,	25, 80
Otaru	Nahotoka	U. S. S. R.	Sep,	12, 66
Otsu	Interlaken	Switzerland	Oct,	1, 78
Otsu	Lansing	Mich., U. S. A.	Oct,	1, 69
Otsu	Würzburg	Germany	Feb,	13, 79
Owase	Prince Rupert	Canada	Sep,	26, 68
Rumoi	Ulan Ude	U. S. S. R.	Jul,	5, 72
Saga	Warren County	N. Y., U. S. A.	Sep,	23, 88
Sagae	Andong	Korea	Feb,	4, 74
Sagae	Giresun	Turkey	Jun,	25, 88
Sakado	Dothan	Alab., U. S. A.	Mar,	26, 88
Sakai	Berkeley	Calif., U. S. A.	Nov,	3, 67
Sakaide	Sausalito	Calif., U. S. A.	Feb,	2, 88
Sakata	Zheleznogorsk-Ilimskii	U. S. S. R.	Oct,	8, 79
Saku	Avalon	France	Jul,	14, 76
Sapporo	München	Germany	Aug,	28, 72
Sapporo	Portland	Ore., U. S. A.	Nov,	17, 59
Sapporo	Shenyang	China	Nov,	18, 80
Sasebo	Albuquerque	New Mexico, U. S. A.	Nov,	1, 72
Sasebo	Coffs Habor	Australia	Jun,	6, 88
Sasebo	Hsiamen	China	Oct,	27, 83
Sayama	Chungju	Korea	Jul,	4, 73
Seki	Moji Das Cruzes	Brazil	May,	20, 69
Sendai	Acapulco	Mexico	Oct,	23, 73
Sendai	Changchun	China	Oct,	27, 80
Sendai	Minsk	U. S. S. R.	Apr,	6, 73
Sendai	Rennes	France	Sep,	6, 67
Sendai	Riverside	Calif., U. S. A.	Mar,	9, 57
Shimada	Húzhóu	China	May,	30, 87
Shimada	Richmond	Calif., U. S. A.	Dec,	12, 61
Shimane	Wanaka	New Zealand	Jul,	28, 83
Shimizu	Stockton	Calif., U. S. A.	Mar,	9, 59
Shimoda	New Port	Rhod., U. S. A.	May,	17, 58
Shimonoseki	Chingtao	China	Oct,	3, 79
Shimonoseki	Istanbul	Turkey	May,	16, 72
Shimonoseki	Pusan	Korea	Oct,	11, 76
Shimonoseki	Santos	Brazil	Oct,	6, 71
Shin-gu	Santa Cruz	Calif., U. S. A.	Dec,	25, 74
Shiojiri	Mishawaka	Ind., U. S. A.	Jun,	5, 72
Shirakawa	Compiégne	France	Oct,	20, 88
Shizuoka	Omaha	Neb., U. S. A.	Apr,	1, 65
Soka	Carson	Calif., U. S. A.	Nov,	19, 79
Suita	Bankstown	Australia	Mar,	9, 89
Suita	Moratuwa	Sri Lanka	Jul,	20, 82
Susaki	Castanhal	Brazil	Oct,	1, 79
Susono	Frankston	Australia	Feb,	22, 82
Suwa	Amboise	France	Mar,	4, 87
Suwa	St. Louis	Miss., U. S. A.	Sep,	23, 74
Suwa	Wörgl Kundl	Tyrol, Austria	Sep,	27, 60
Suzu	Pelotas	Brazil	Sep,	17, 63
Tachikawa	San Bernardino	Calif., U. S. A.	Dec,	23, 59
Tajimi	Terre Haute	Ind., U. S. A.	May,	12, 62
Takaishi	Romita	Calif., U. S. A.	Oct,	29, 81
Takamatsu	St. Petersburg	Fla., U. S. A.	Oct,	5, 61
Takamatsu	Tour	France	Jun,	3, 88
Takaoka	Chinchou	China	Aug,	10, 85
Takaoka	Fort Wayne	Ind., U. S. A.	Apr,	8, 77

Takaoka	Mirandopolis	Brazil	Oct,	19,	74
Takasaki	Battle Creek	Mich., U. S. A.	Jul,	1,	81
Takasaki	Chenste	China	Oct,	6,	87
Takasaki	Santo Andre	Brazil	Oct,	2,	81
Takatsuki	Manila	Philippines	Jan,	25,	79
Takayama	Denver	Colo., U. S. A.	Jul,	29,	60
Takeda	San Lorenzo	Paraguay	Oct,	28,	73
Tamano	Chungju	Korea	Aug,	3,	81
Tateyama	Bellingham	Wash., U. S. A.	Jul,	11,	58
Tendo	Marlborough	New Zealand	Jul,	7,	89
Tendo	Marostica	Italy	Apr,	22,	89
Tenri	Bauru	Brazil	Apr,	18,	70
Tenri	La Serena	Chile	Oct,	1,	66
Toba	Santa Barbara	Calif., U. S. A.	Mar,	24,	66
Toda	Kaifeng	China	Aug,	21,	84
Tokamachi	Como	Italy	Feb,	27,	75
Toki	Faenza	Italy	Oct,	22,	79
Tokorozawa	Decatur	Ill., U. S. A.	May,	6,	66
Tokushima	Leiria	Portugal	Oct,	15,	69
Tokushima	Saginaw	Mich., U. S. A.	Dec,	23,	61
Tokuyama	Sao Bernardo do Campo	Brazil	Apr,	23,	74
Tokyo	Beijing	China	Mar,	14,	79
Tokyo	Djakarta	Indonesia	Oct,	23,	89
Tokyo	New South Wales	Australia	May,	9,	84
Tokyo	New York	N. Y., U. S. A.	Feb,	29,	60
Tokyo	Paris	France	Jul,	14,	82
Tokyo	Seoul	Korea	Sep,	3,	88
Tomakomai	Napier	New Zealand	Apr,	22,	80
Tondabayashi	Bethlehem	Pa., U. S. A.	Apr,	10,	64
Tono	Salerno	Italy	Aug,	8,	84
Tosa	Itaituba	Brazil	Aug,	5,	89
Tosashimizu	New Bedford	Mass., U. S. A.	Dec,	2,	87
Tosashimizu	Fairhaven	Mass., U. S. A.	Dec,	2,	87
Tosayamada	Lago	Flo., U. S. A.	Jul,	11,	69
Toyama	Durham	N. Cal., U. S. A.	Jun,	13,	89
Toyama	Moji Das Cruzes	Brazil	Nov,	8,	79
Toyonaka	San Mateo	Calif., U. S. A.	Oct,	8,	63
Toyota	Detroit	Mich., U. S. A.	Sep,	21,	60
Tsu	Chenchians	China	Jun,	11,	84
Tsu	Osasco	Brazil	Oct,	18,	76
Tsukuba	Cambridge	Mass., U. S. A.	May,	8,	84
Tsukuba	Irvin	Calif., U. S. A.	Aug,	3,	89
Tsukuba	Summer Land	Canada	Sep,	7,	85
Tsuru	Henderson Ville	Tenn., U. S. A.	May,	18,	83
Tsuruga	Nahotoka	U. S. S. R.	Oct,	11,	82
Tsuruga	Tonshae	Korea	Apr,	13,	81
Tsuruoka	New Brunswick	N. J., U. S. A.	Jun,	10,	60
Ube	Newcastle	Australia	Nov,	21,	80
Uji	Hsienyang	China	Jul,	24,	86
Uji	Nuwara Eliya	Sri Lanka	Apr,	12,	86
Urawa	Chengchou	China	Oct,	12,	81
Urawa	Hamilton	New Zealand	May,	14,	84
Urawa	Toluca	Mexico	Oct,	2,	79
Urayasu	Orlando	Fla., U. S. A.	Nov,	4,	89
Ushiku	Whitehorse	Canada	Apr,	19,	85
Usuki	Kandy	Sri Lanka	Feb,	27,	67
Utsunomiya	Chichihaerh	China	Sep,	30,	84
Utsunomiya	Manukau	New Zealand	Feb,	24,	82
Utsunomiya	Orléans	France	May,	7,	89
Wakayama	Bakersfield	Calif., U. S. A.	Jul,	14,	61
Wakayama	Jeju	Korea	Nov,	12,	87
Wakayama	Richmond	Canada	Mar,	31,	73
Warabi	El Dorado	Calif., U. S. A.	Mar,	26,	75
Yaizu	Hobart	Australia	Feb,	17,	77
Yamagata	Kitzbühel	Austria	Feb,	17,	63
Yamagata	Swan Hill	Australia	Aug,	6,	80
Yamaguchi	Pamplona	Spain	Feb,	19,	80
Yamatotakada	Lismore	Australia	Aug,	7,	63
Yanagawa	Berderwiede	Netherlands	Oct,	24,	73
Yao	Bellevue	Wash., U. S. A.	Nov,	17,	69
Yao	Shanghai	China	Sep,	13,	86

Yokkaichi	Long Beach	Calif., U. S. A.	Oct,	7,	63
Yokkaichi	Marquette	Mich., U. S. A.	Aug,	13,	79
Yokkaichi	Tienchin	China	Oct,	28,	80
Yokohama	Bombay	India	Jun,	26,	65
Yokohama	Constantsa	Roumania	Oct,	12,	77
Yokohama	Lyon	France	Apr,	7,	59
Yokohama	Manila	Philippines	Jul,	1,	65
Yokohama	Odessa	U. S. S. R.	Jul,	1,	65
Yokohama	San Diego	Calif., U. S. A.	Oct,	29,	57
Yokohama	Vancouver	Canada	Jul,	1,	65
Yokosuka	Brest	France	Nov,	26,	70
Yokosuka	Corpus Christi	Tex., U. S. A.	Oct,	18,	62
Yokosuka	Fremantle	Australia	Apr,	25,	79
Yonezawa	Moses Lake	Wash,. U. S. A.	May,	1,	81
Yonezawa	Taubate	Brazil	Jan,	28,	74
Yotsukado	Livermore	Calif., U. S. A.	Apr,	19,	77
Yubari	Fushun	China	Apr,	19,	82
Zentsuji	El Dorado	Ark., U. S. A.	Sep,	30,	64

Index

Index

Index

Index

Hiruzen, Mt. 771
Hisaya Odori Park, Nagoya 576
Hishikawa Moronobu 96,186
Historical Village of Hokkaido 279
Hita 874
Hitachi 557
Hitachi-Daigo 558
Hitachi-Ota 557
Hitotsugi-dori Street, Tokyo 385
Hitoyoshi 867
Hitsuji-ga-Oka 280
Hiunkaku 199
Hiyoriyama Hill, Toba 591
Hiyoriyama Park, Kinosaki 792
Hiyoriyama Park, Sakata 337
Hiyoshi Shrine 707
Hobashira Natural Park 847
Hofu 786
Hofu Temmangu 786
Hofukuji Temple 767
Hogen Monogatari 90,157
Hojo 822
Hojo-in Temple 702
Hojo Masako 429
Hojo Sadatoki 438
Hojo Takatoki 432
Hojo Tokimune 91,438
Hojo Tokiyori 439
Hojo Yoshitoki 513
Hojoki 157
Hokaiji Temple 699
Hokekyo 123
Hokekyoji Temple 413
Hokkai Soran Matsuri 275
Hokkaido Jingu Matsuri 275,279
Hokkaido Shrine 279
Hokkaido University 277
Hokkaido University Botanical Gardens 277
Hokkeji Temple 722
Hokkiji Temple 731
Hokoji Temple 600,683
Hokoku Shrine 683
Hokokuji Temple 436
Hokuriku District 19
Hollyhock Festival, Kyoto 38
Home Stay 66
Home Visit System 64
Homma Museum of Art 337
Hommoku Jazz Festival, Yokohama 418
Hommonji Temple 396
homongi 219
Hon-ami Koetsu 205,658
Hon-Yabakei Gorge 874
Hondo 866
Honen-in Temple 676
Honen, priest 122
Hongakuji Temple 419
Hongu Shrine, Nikko 538
Honji-suijaku 122
honjin 611
Honnoji Temple 672
Horai 216
Horaiji Temple 598
Horikiri Iris Garden 402
Horinji Temple 694,730
Horinouchi Park, Matsuyama 820
Horyuji Temple 726
   Daihozoden 728
   Daikodo 728
   Gofuzo 728
   Goju-no-To 727

Kondo 727
Kyozo 728
nandaimon 726
Shoro 728
Shoryo-in 728
Shumisen 727
Yumedono 729
Hoshakuji Temple 650
Hosho-in Temple (Osu Kannon) 576
Hosokawa Katsumoto 92,692
Hosso sect 123
hot springs 82
Hotaka, Mt. 500
Hotsumisakiji Temple 829
Hozu-River boat trip 694
Hozuki Ichi 371
Hyakumangoku 617
hyakunin-isshu 32
Hyuga 878
[I]
"i" System Information Center 63
iaijutsu 222,227
Ibaraki 649
Ibuki, Mt. 604
Ibusuki 882
Ibusuki Spa 882
Ichihata Temple 799
Ichijo, Emperor 88
Ichijo Norifusa 830
Ichijodani Ruins of Asakura Family 628
Ichijoji Temple 760
Ichikawa 412
Ichikawa Danjuro 161
Ichikawa Danjuro I 172
Ichikawa Danjuro IX 174
Ichikawa Sadanji II 255
Ichinomiya 579
Ichinoseki 326
IDC (International Digital Communications, Inc.) 41
Idemitsu Museum of Arts 373
Ie Island 894
Iemitsu's Mausoleum 545
Iga-yaki 734
Ihara Saikaku 160
Ii Naosuke 98,418,709
Iimori Hill 351
Iiyama 523
Iizaka Spa 348
Iizuna Plateau 519
ijinkan 753
Ikaho 504
Ikaruga Temple 761
Ike-no-Taiga 97,185
ikebana 212
Ikebukuro 399
Ikeda, Hokkaido 304
Ikeda, Lake 882
Ikeda, Osaka 648
Ikenobo Senkei 671
Iki Island 862
Iki-Tsushima Quasi-National Park 862
Ikoji Temple 803
Ikoma, Mt. 723
Ikukunitama Shrine 646
Ikurado Cave 770
Ikuta Shrine 752
Imabari 822
Imaichi 533
Imaihama Spa 481
Imaimachi 736

948

Index

Index

Index

Index

Index

Index

Index

963

Index

Index

ABBREVIATIONS USED ON THE MAPS

LEGEND

J R=Japan Railway
P R=Private Railway
N H=National Highway
L R=Local Road
T R=Toll Road
Exwy=Expressway
S R=Sea Route

C.=Cape
Is.=Island
Isls=Islands
L.=Lake
Mt.=Mount
Pen.=Peninsula
Pref.=Prefecture
      Prefectural
R.=River
Wf.=Waterfall

Bldg.=Building
Dept.=Department
EL=Electric
RY=Railway
Gym.=Gymnasium
IC=Inter Change
Int'l=International
JCT=Junction
Met.=Metropolis
St.=Street
Sta.=Station
Univ.=University

The abbreviations above are used on the following map pages.

MAPS AND PLANS

HOKKAIDO ❶

❷

NORTHEASTERN
HONSHU

❸

❺

WEST CENTRAL HONSHU ⑭ ⑮ ⑬

❹

❻

EAST CENTRAL HONSHU

❼

WESTERN HONSHU ⑪

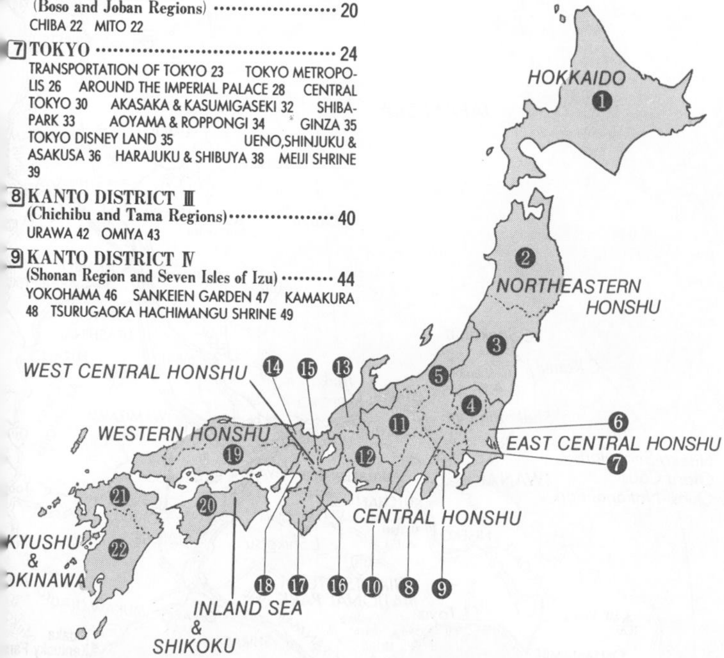

WESTERN HONSHU ⑲

⑫

KYUSHU
& ㉑

OKINAWA ㉒

⑳

CENTRAL HONSHU

⑱ ⑰ ⑯ ⑩ ❽ ❾

INLAND SEA
&
SHIKOKU

LEGEND

J	R
P	R
N	R
L	R
T	R
Exwy	
S	R

∴ Scenic Sites

0   20   40   60km

C.Noshappu   C.Soya
WAKKANAI
238
Rebun Is.   Sarobetsu Natural   BAKKAI
Flower Garden
Mt. Rishiri   Beniya Natura
1721   Flower Garde
Rishiri Is.   TOYOTOMI
RISHIRI-REBUN-SAROBETSU   HORONOBE
NATIONAL PARK
Teshio R.   UTANAI
OTOINEPPU
Yagishiri Is.
Teuri Is.   Haboro   NAYORO
L.Shumarinai   40
SHIBETSU
232   289   WASSAM
HOROKANAI
MASHIKE   RUMOI
RUMOI   ASAHIKAWA
C.Ofuyu   MAIN   FUKAGAWA   12
LINE
1491
Mt. Shakambetsu   BIEI
231   TAKIKAWA   AKABIRA
ASHIBETS
JAPAN SEA   SASSHO LINE   SUNAGAWA
UTASHINAI
BIBAI   FURANO
C.Shakotan   MIKASA
C.Kamui   Mt. Shakotan   Ishikari R.   IWAMIZAWA
1255   OTARU   SAPPORO   YUBARI
Shakotan Pen.   EBETSU   237
YOICHI   CHITOSE
Niseko-Shakotan-   Jozankei Spa   KITA HIROSHIMA
Otaru Coast   IWANAI   KUTCHAN
Quasi-National Park   230   Mt. Eniwa   ENIWA OIWAKE
NISEKO   L.Shikotsu   CHITOSE   274
Mt. Yotei   276
1893   SHIKOTSU-TOYA   MUKAWA   Saru R.
Mt. Kariba   NATIONAL PARK   Hidaka
1520   L.Toya   TOMAKO   Kentucky Far
Orofure   MAI
OSHAMAMBE   Mt. Showa   Pass   SHIRAOI
Mt. Usu   HIDAKA-MOMBETSU
Uchiura Bay   NOBORIBETSU   NIIKAPPU
Noboribetsu Spa   SHIZUNAI
YAKUMO   MURORAN   C. Chikyu   HIDAKA-MITSU
277
MORI
Mt. Komagatake
Okushiri Is.   1131
Oshima Pen.   Onuma Quasi-National Park
277   ONUMA
ESASHI   Kameda Pen.
Mt.Esan
HAKODATE
Yunokawa Spa
228   KIKONAI
Matsumae   Tsugaru Straits
Pen.
Seikan Tunnel   AOMORI
To Niigata·Tsuruga·Maizuru   PREF.   To Sendai·Tok

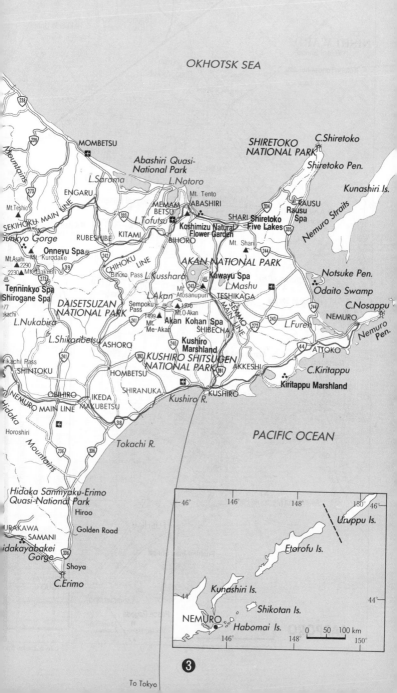

HOKKAIDO

OKHOTSK SEA

MOMBETSU

Abashiri Quasi-National Park

L.Saroma

L.Notoro

SHIRETOKO NATIONAL PARK

C.Shiretoko

Shiretoko Pen.

Kunashiri Is.

ENGARU

Mt.Teshio

Mt. Tento

MEMAM BETSU

ABASHIRI

RAUSU

Rausu Spa

Nemuro Straits

SEKIHOKU MAIN LINE

L.Tofutsu

SHARI

Shiretoko Five Lakes

Junkyo Gorge

RUBESHIBE

KITAMI

Koshimizu Natural Flower Garden

Mt.Asahi

Kurodake

BIHORO

Mt. Shari

Onneyu Spa

CHIHOKU LINE

2290

2230

Hakuun

Bihoro Pass

AKAN NATIONAL PARK

Mt. 244

Notsuke Pen.

Tenninkyo Spa

Shirogane Spa

L.Kussharo

Kawayu Spa

L.Mashu

Odaito Swamp

C.Nosappu

L.Akan

Atosanupuri

TESHIKAGA

NEMURO

L.Nukabira

DAISETSUZAN NATIONAL PARK

Sempoku Pass

1499

SEMMO MAIN LINE

L.Furen

Nemuro Pen.

Mt. O-Akan

Mt. Me-Akan

Akan Kohan Spa

SHIBECHA

ASHORO

Kushiro Marshland

ATTOKO

L.Shikaribetsu

KUSHIRO SHITSUGEN NATIONAL PARK

AKKESHI

C.Kiritappu

SHINTOKU

HOMBETSU

Kiritappu Marshland

OBIHIRO

IKEDA

SHIRANUKA

KUSHIRO

Horoshiri

MAKUBETSU

Kushiro R.

PACIFIC OCEAN

Tokachi R.

Hidaka Sanmyaku-Erimo Quasi-National Park

Hiroo

URAKAWA

SAMANI

Golden Road

idakayabakei Gorge

Shoya

C.Erimo

To Tokyo

46°   146°   148°   150°   46°

Uruppu Is.

Etorofu Is.

44°

Kunashiri Is.

Shikotan Is.

NEMURO

Habomai Is.

0   50   100 km

146°   148°   150°

44°

❸

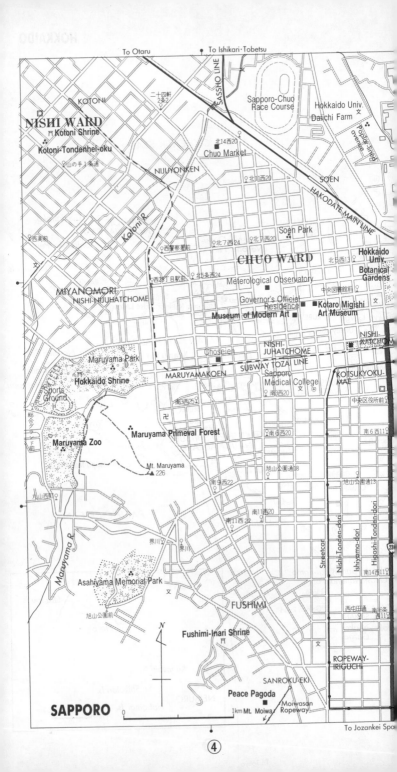

To Otaru · To Ishikari・Tobetsu

SASSHO LINE

Sapporo-Chuo Race Course

Hokkaido Univ. Daiichi Farm

Poplar-lined avenue

KOTONI

二十四軒 2条2

NISHI WARD

Kotoni Shrine

Kotoni-Tondenhei-oku

山の手1条通

北14西20

Chuo Market

NIJUYONKEN

北川西20

SOEN

HAKODATE MAIN LINE

Kotoni R.

西高前

Soen Park

北7西24

北7西20

西警察署前

CHUO WARD

北日西13

Hokkaido Univ. Botanical Gardens

MIYANOMORI
NISHI-NIJUHATCHOME

西2丁目駅前

北3条西24

Meterological Observatory

中央図書館前

Governor's Official Residence

Museum of Modern Art ■

Kotaro Migishi Art Museum

Maruyama Park

Choseien

NISHI-JUHATCHOME

NISHI-JUTCHOM

Hokkaido Shrine

MARUYAMAKOEN

SUBWAY TOZAI LINE

Sapporo Medical College

KOTSUKYOKU-MAE

Sports Ground

南3西25

南2西20

中央区役所前

Maruyama Primeval Forest

南6西11

Maruyama Zoo

Mt. Maruyama
△ 226

南9西22

旭山公園通18

旭山公園通13

丸山西

南11西20

南11西26

Maruyama R.

界川

泉川

Streetcar

Nishi-Tonden-dori

Ishiyama-dori

Higashi-Tondan-dori

南14西11

Asahiyama Memorial Park

旭山公園前

FUSHIMI

西中田通

南11条

N

Fushimi-Inari Shrine

ROPEWAY-IRIGUCHI

SANROKU-EKI

Peace Pagoda

Moiwasan Ropeway

SAPPORO

0   1km Mt. Moiwa

④

To Jozankei Spa

HOKKAIDO

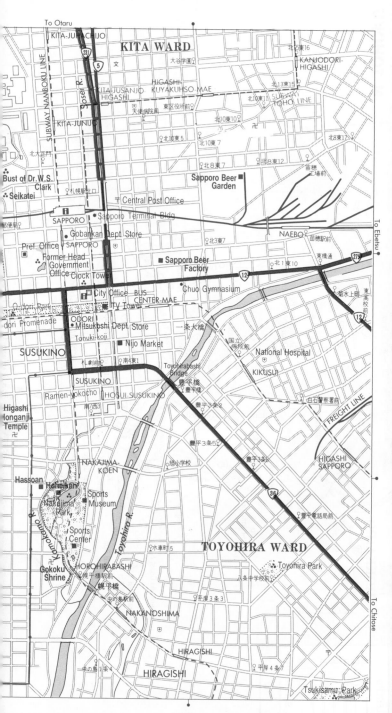

To Otaru

KITA-JUICHIJO

KITA WARD

大谷学園 文

SUBWAY NAMBOKU LINE

Jōsei R.

JUICHIJUSANJO HIGASHI

HIGASHI-KUYAKUHSO-MAE

KANJODORI-HIGASHI

北9東16

北13東15

SUBWAY TOHO LINE

天使病院前

東区役所前

北10東9

北8東17

KITA-JUNIJO

北10東5

北10東7

北10東7

北8東12

北大正門

苗穂

工場前

Bust of Dr.W.S. Clark

Seikatei

札幌駅前

北8東7

Sapporo Beer Garden

Central Post Office

郵便局

SAPPORO

Sapporo Terminal Bldg

NAEBO

苗穂駅前

Gobankan Dept Store

北3条7

Pref. Office SAPPORO

Former Head Government Office Clock Tower

■ **Sapporo Beer Factory**

北1東10

東橋通

To Ebetsu

City Office BUS CENTER-MAE

Chuo Gymnasium

菊水上町

東橋校前

TV Tower

Odori Park

ODORI

Mitsukoshi Dept. Store

一条大橋

国立

病院前

National Hospital

dori Promenade

Tanuki-koji

■ Nijo Market

SUSUKINO

札幌前

南4東1

Toyohirabashi Bridge

KIKUSUI

SUSUKINO

豊平橋

豊平橋

白石警察署前

FREIGHT LINE

Ramen-yokocho

HOSUI-SUSUKINO

南西3

豊平3条2

Higashi Honganji Temple

豊平3条5

豊平3条7

HIGASHI SAPPORO

Hassoan

■ Hoheikan

NAKAJIMA-KŌEN

旭小学校

Nakajima Park

Sports Museum

Sports Center

Toyohira R.

Toyohira-gawa R.

TOYOHIRA WARD

水車町5

Toyohira Park

豊平電話局前

八条中学校前

Gokoku Shrine

HOROHIRABASHI

幌平橋駅前

鰍平橋

中の島駅前

平岸3条3

To Chitose

NAKANOSHIMA

HIRAGISHI

HIRAGISHI

平岸4条7

中の島1条4

Tsukisamu Park

⑤

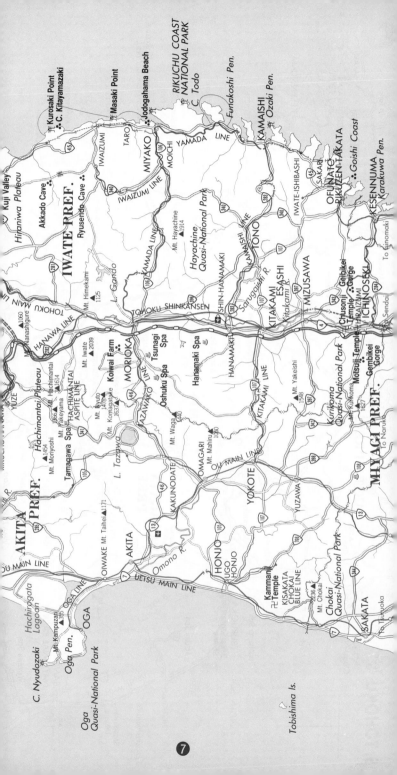

7

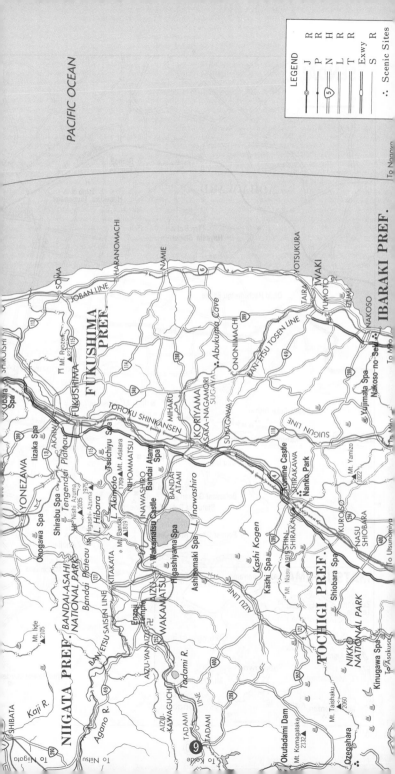

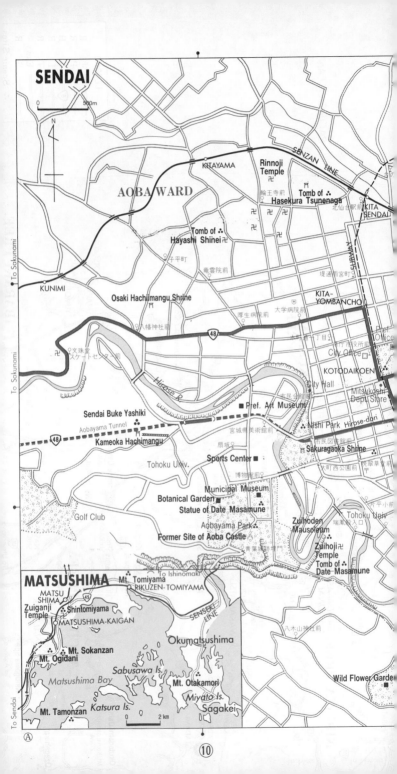

SENDAI

0 500m

N

AOBA WARD

KITAYAMA

SENZAN LINE

Rinnoji Temple
輪王寺前
Tomb of Hasekura Tsunenaga
北仙台駅前 KITA-SENDAI

卍 卍 卍 卍

Tomb of Hayashi Shinei 卍

子平町

竜雲院前

Osaki Hachimangu Shrine
八幡神社前

KITA-YOMBANCHO

KUNIMI

48

大学病院前
厚生病院前

本町一丁目 Pref. Office
市役所前 City Office
KOTODAIKOEN

文珠堂
スケートセンター前

卍

Hirose R.

City Hall
市民会館前
Mitsukoshi Dept. Store

Pref. Art Museum

Sendai Buke Yashiki

Nishi Park Hirose-dori

Aobayama Tunnel
宮城県美術館前
市民図書館前
Sakuragaoka Shrine
扇坂

Kameoka Hachimangu

Tohoku Univ.

Sports Center
博物館前

大町西公園前

Municipal Museum

Botanical Garden

Statue of Date Masamune

青葉城資料展示館前

Zuihoden Mausoleum
瑞鳳殿入口
Tohoku Univ.

Golf Club

Aobayama Park

Former Site of Aoba Castle

Zuihoji Temple 卍
Tomb of Date Masamune

MATSUSHIMA

MATSUSHIMA CITY

Mt. Tomiyama
To Ishinomaki
RIKUZEN-TOMIYAMA

45

Zuiganji Temple
卍 Shintomiyama
MATSUSHIMA-KAIGAN

SENSEKI LINE

Okumatsushima

Mt. Sokanzan

Mt. Ogidani

Sabusawa Is.

Matsushima Bay

Mt. Otakamori

Miyato Is.
Sagakei

Mt. Tamonzan
Katsura Is.

0 2 km

八木山橋社前

Wild Flower Garden

Ⓐ

⑩

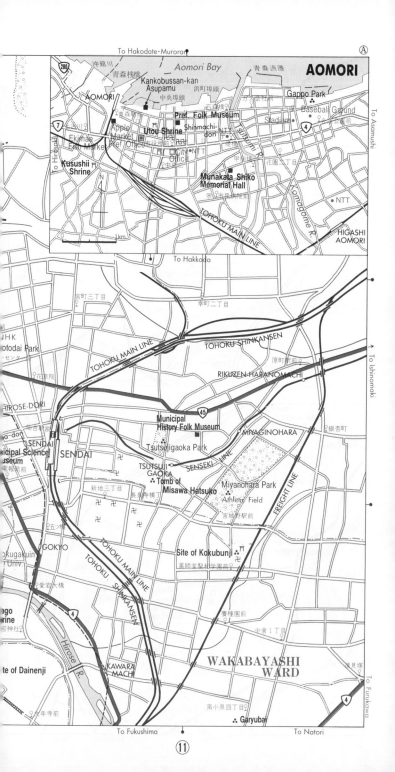

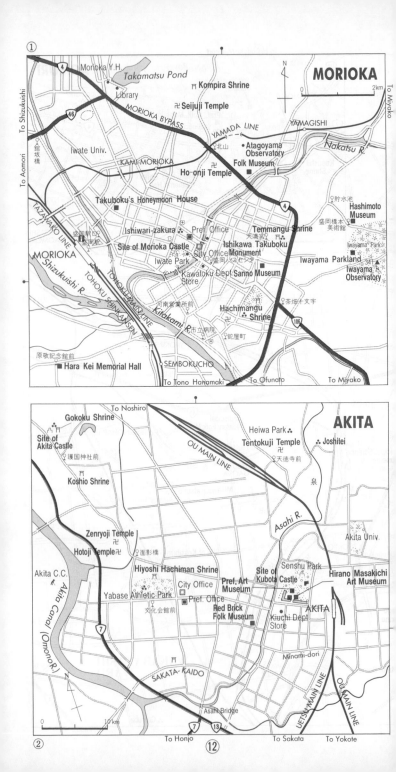

①

To Shizukuishi
To Aomori
To Miyako

Morioka Y.H.
Takamatsu Pond
Library
Kompira Shrine
MORIOKA BYPASS
Seijuji Temple
YAMADA LINE
YAMAGISHI
北山
Atagoyama Observatory
Nakatsu R.
Iwate Univ.
KAMI-MORIOKA
Folk Museum
Ho-onji Temple
Takuboku's Honeymoon House
Hashimoto Museum
盛岡橋本美術館
TAZAWAKO LINE
盛岡駅
Ishiwari-zakura
Pref. Office
天満宮
Temmangu Shrine
Ishikawa Takuboku Monument
Iwayama Park
MORIOKA
Site of Morioka Castle
City Office
盛岡バスセンター
Iwayama Parkland
Iwayama Observatory
Shizukuishi R.
TOHOKU SHINKANSEN
TOHOKU MAIN LINE
Iwate Park
Kawatoku Dept. Store
Sanno Museum
茶畑十文字
Kitakami R.
河南省業所前
Hachimangu Shrine
市立病院
鉈屋町
原敬記念館前
Hara Kei Memorial Hall
SEMBOKUCHO
To Tono Hanamaki
To Ofunato
To Miyako

②

To Noshiro
Gokoku Shrine
Heiwa Park
Tentokuji Temple
Joshitei
Site of Akita Castle
護国神社前
OU MAIN LINE
天徳寺前
泉
Koshio Shrine
Asahi R.
Akita Univ.
Zenryoji Temple
Hotoji Temple
面影橋
Akita C.C.
Hiyoshi Hachiman Shrine
City Office
Senshu Park
Site of Kubota Castle
Hirano Masakichi Art Museum
Akita Canal (Omono R.)
Yabase Athletic Park
Pref. Art Museum
文化会館前
Pref. Office
Red Brick Folk Museum
AKITA
Kiuchi Dept. Store
Minami-dori
SAKATA-KAIDO
Asahi Bridge
UETSU MAIN LINE
OU MAIN LINE
To Honjo
To Sakata
To Yokote

⑫

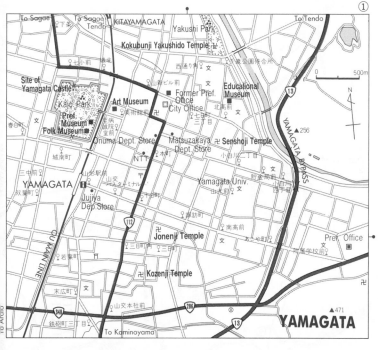

To Sagae　To Sagae　KITAYAMAGATA　To Tendo
一丁末　Tendo
Yakushi Park
Kokubunji Yakushido Temple 卍
西通り町 文
城北公園総合所
山新ビル前
Site of
Yamagata Castle
Kajo Park
Art Museum
美術館前
Former Pref.
Office
City Office
三丁目
Educational
Museum
北前町
13
▲256
YAMAGATA BYPASS
Pref.
Museum
Folk Museum
春日町 文
城南町
Onuma Dept. Store
NTT
本町
Matsuzakaya
Dept. Store
Senshoji Temple 卍
小白川二丁目
文
貯金局前
YAMAGATA
山形駅前
山交
バスターミナル
十日町
Yamagata Univ.
山大前
文
双葉町前
Jujiya
Dep Store
諏訪前
112
南高前
Jonenji Temple 卍
三日町前 三日町
あ や町二丁目
開明学校前
Pref. Office
卍
若葉町
Kozenji Temple 卍
末広町
848
山交本社前
286
鉄砲町三丁目
13
To Araoi
To Kaminoyama
▲471

YAMAGATA

0   500m
N

To Iizaka Spa 岳代清水　To Shiroishi　To Sendai
Matsu R.
Sports Center
▲268
Shinobuyama Park
TOHOKU SHINKANSEN
Mt.Shinobu
Haguro Shrine
Pref.
Art Museum
MORIAI
Moriai Sports
Park
Gassan
Shrine
Iwayakannon 卍
Shinobugaoka
Green Park
TOHOKU MAIN LINE
Pref. Cultural Center
君谷前
115
OU MAIN LINE
Kuronuma Shrine
文化センター入口
To Yonezawa
製作所前
18
SONEDA
保健所前
競馬場前
岡部
To Soma
City Office
Race Course
Abukuma R.
FUKUSHIMA
Ito Yokado
4
役所大手
Fukushima
Kotsu
NTT
Municipal Folk
Museum
To Nihommatsu
Nakago Dept. Store
大町
Su R.
Shinjoin
Temple
Pref. Office
卍
Momijiyama Park
渡利船場
Jokoji Temple 卍
115
天神渡
渡利小
渡利
143▲

FUKUSHIMA

0   500m
N

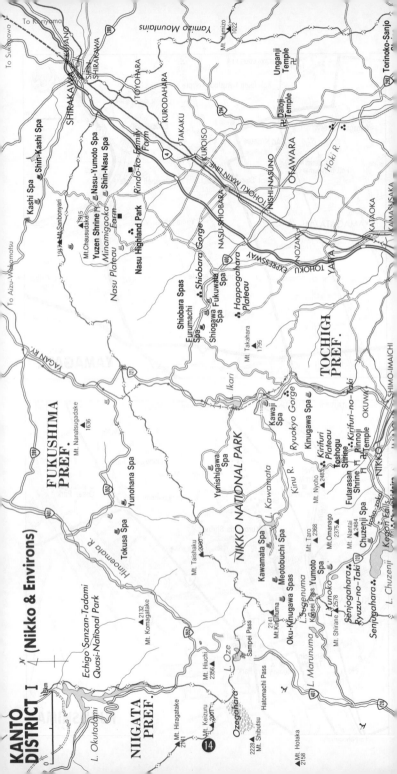

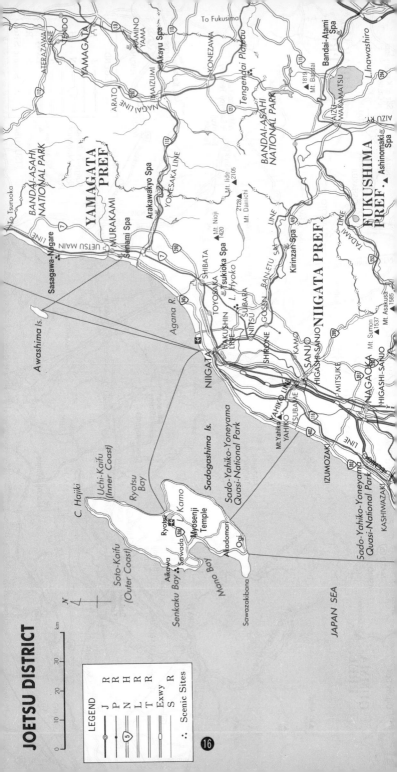

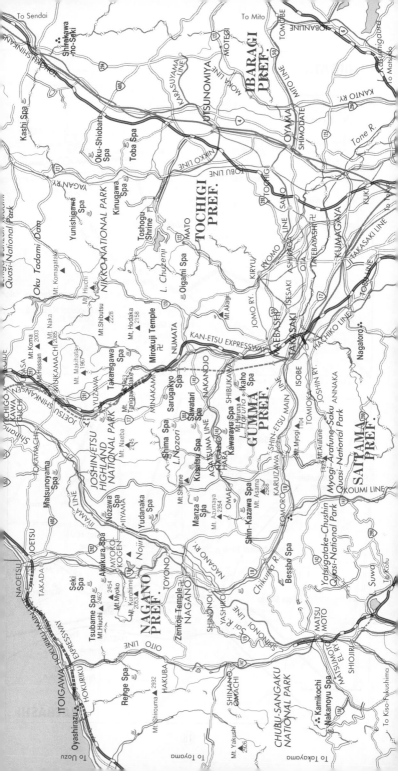

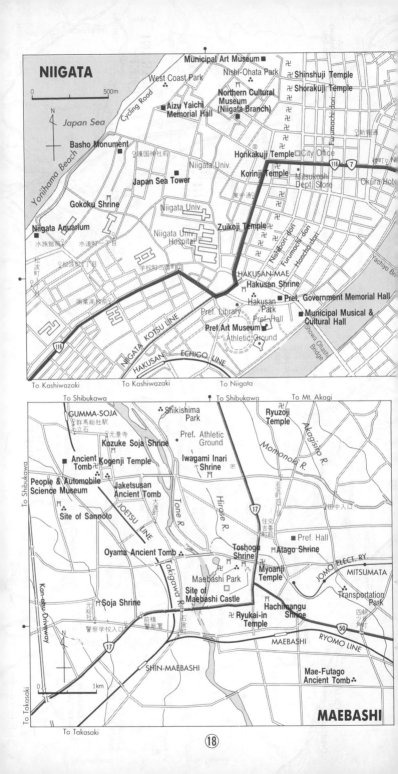

NIGATA

0 ⟶ 500m

N

Japan Sea

Municipal Art Museum ■
Nishi-Ohata Park
卍 Shinshuji Temple
卍 Shorakuji Temple
West Coast Park
Northern Cultural Museum (Niigata Branch)
Aizu Yaichi Memorial Hall ■
Cycling Road
卍
卍
卍
新潟駅前 ❑
卍
Basho Monument ■
卍
Honkakuji Temple 卍 ❑City Office
116 7
Niigata Univ.
Korinji Temple 卍
Mitsukoshi Dept. Store
Okura Hote
Japan Sea Tower ■
Gokoku Shrine ■
Niigata Univ
Zuikoji Temple 卍
Yachiyo Bri
Niigata Aquarium ■
Niigata Univ Hospital
水族館前❑
水道町一丁目
松波町
HAKUSAN MAE
Hakusan Shrine
卍
Pref. Government Memorial Hall ■
Pref. Library ■
Hakusan Park
Municipal Musical & Cultural Hall ■
Pref Hall
Pref. Art Museum ■
Athletic Ground
Showa Ohashi Bridge
116
NIIGATA KOTSU LINE
HAKUSAN
ECHIGO LINE
To Kashiwazaki
To Kashiwazaki
To Niigata

To Shibukawa
To Shibukawa
To Mt. Akagi

Shikishima Park
GUMMA-SOJA
群馬総社駅
北立石
元景寺
Pref. Athletic Ground
Ryuzoji Temple 卍
Kozuke Soja Shrine ■
Kogenji Temple
Iwagami Inari Shrine
Momonoki R.
Arogisho R.
Ancient Tomb ■
People & Automobile Science Museum ■
Jaketsusan Ancient Tomb
大渡町
JOETSU LINE
Tone R.
Hirase R.
17
Site of Sannoto ■
住友吉岡町前
田中入口
Pref. Hall ■
Oyama Ancient Tomb ■
Toshogu Shrine
Atago Shrine ■
Myoanji Temple
JOMO ELECT. RY
MITSUMATA
Kan-etsu Driveway
Takigawa R.
Maebashi Park
Soja Shrine ■
元総社前
前橋警察署
Site of Maebashi Castle
Transportation Park
四
警察学校入口前
石倉町
Hachimangu Shrine
Ryukai-in Temple 卍
50
17
MAEBASHI
RYOMO LINE
SHIN-MAEBASHI
Mae-Futago Ancient Tomb
1km
N
To Takasaki
To Takasaki
MAEBASHI

⑱

To Niigata Airport

Shinano R.

350

345

魚市場前

佐渡汽船前

Numatari

宮浦中学前

345

Bandai

Bandai
Bridge

Daiei •
Bus Terminal

• Rainbow Tower

•Isetan Dept Store

Tsurui Art Museum

越信病院前

本町通り

水島町

Central Post
Office

7

新潟駅前

NIIGATA

駅南口

Industrial Exhibition
Center

SHIN-ETSU MAIN LINE

ECHIGO LINE

JOETSU SHINKANSEN

笹口二丁目

To Suibara

To Futarasan Shrine

To Niitsu

Nagaoka

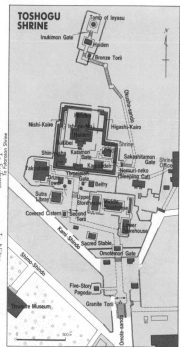

TOSHOGU SHRINE

Tomb of Ieyasu

Inukimon Gate

Haiden

Bronze Torii

N

Okariba-sando

Nishi-Kairo

Ishino-Ma

Haiden

Higashi-Kairo

Jubei

Karamon
Gate

Shrine

Shinyosha

Kaguraden

Takukido

Yomeimon
Gate

Sakashitamon
Gate

Nemuri-neko
(Sleeping Cat)

Shrine
Office

Drum
Tower

Belfry

Sutra
Library

Upper
Storehouse

Middle
Storehouse

Covered Cistern

Second
Torii

Kami-Shindo

Sacred Stable

Lower
Storehouse

Omotemon Gate

Shimo-Shindo

Five-Story
Pagoda

Granite Torii

Treasure Museum

Onote-sando

W.C.

500

To Rinnoji Temple

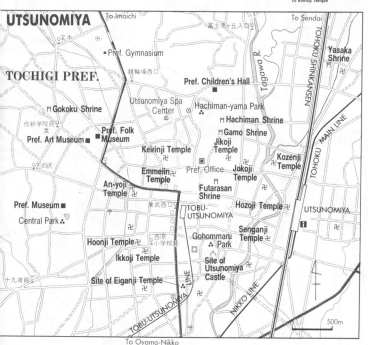

UTSUNOMIYA

To Imaichi

To Sendai

富士見ヶ丘入口

TOCHIGI PREF.

本

• Pref. Gymnasium

競輪場西口

Pref. Children's Hall

Utsunomiya Spa
Center

Hachiman-yama Park

Hachiman Shrine

Yasaka
Shrine

Gokoku Shrine

作新学院前
文

Pref. Art Museum ■

左右の沢

Pref. Folk
Museum

Gamo Shrine

Keirinji Temple

Jikoji
Temple

Kozenji
Temple

Emmelin
Temple

Pref. Office

Jokoji
Temple

An-yoji
Temple

東武西口

Futarasan
Shrine

Pref. Museum ■

Central Park

TOBU-
UTSUNOMIYA

Hozoji Temple

UTSUNOMIYA

Senganji
Temple

Hoonji Temple

西原

小学校前

Gohommaru
Park

Ikkoji Temple

Site of
Utsunomiya
Castle

Site of Eiganji Temple

十九夜前

TOBU-UTSUNOMIYA LINE

NIKKO LINE

TOHOKU SHINKANSEN

TOHOKU MAIN LINE

Tagawa R.

500m

To Oyama-Nikko

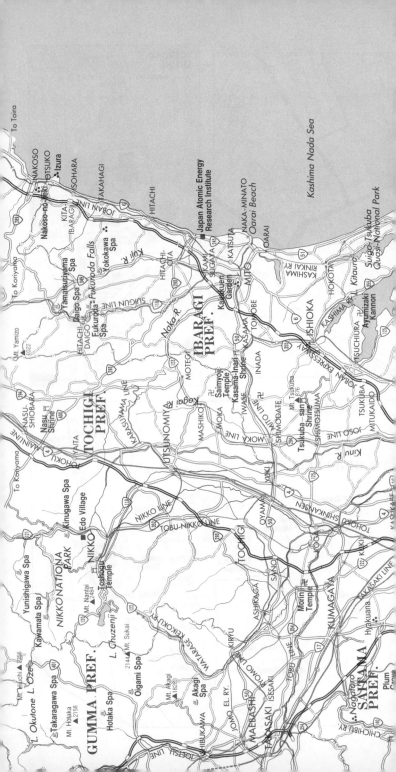

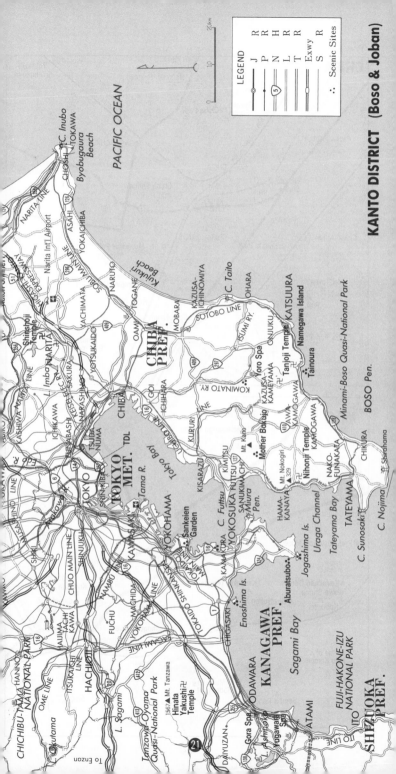

KANTO DISTRICT (Boso & Joban)

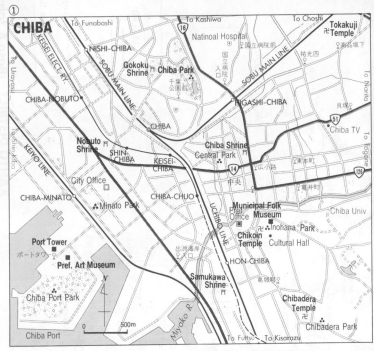

① CHIBA

To Funabashi
To Kashiwa
To Choshi

Natinoal Hospital

国立病院前
国立病院
入口

SOBU MAIN LINE

Tokakuji Temple
商品坂下

KEISEI ELECT. RY.

NISHI-CHIBA

Gokoku Shrine

Chiba Park

千葉公園前

To Urayasu

CHIBA-NOBUTO

SOBU MAIN LINE

CHIBA

HIGASHI-CHIBA

祐光四

To Narita

貝塚

51

Chiba TV

Nobuto Shrine

SHIN-CHIBA

KEISEI-CHIBA

Chiba Shrine
Central Park

広小路

14

東本町

126

To Shin-Akita

KEIYO LINE

City Office

CHIBA-MINATO

Minato Park

CHIBA-CHUO

UCHIBO LINE

電井町

Municipal Folk Museum

Pref. Office

Inohana Park

Chiba Univ

Port Tower
ポートタワー

Pref. Art Museum

出洲海岸

Chikoin Temple

Cultural Hall

HON-CHIBA

葛城町

N

Chiba Port Park

Samukawa Shrine

Chibadera Temple

0   500m

Chiba Port

Miyako R.

To Futtsu   To Kisarazu

Chibadera Park

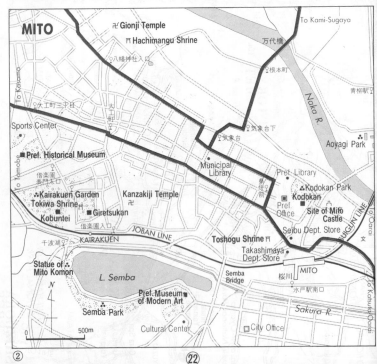

MITO

To Kami-Sugaya

Gionji Temple

Hachimangu Shrine

万代橋

八幡神社入口

根本町

Naka R.

青柳駅

To Kasawa

大工町三丁目

大町

気象台下

気象台

Aoyagi Park

Sports Center

Pref. Historical Museum

To Tomobe

偕楽園表門入口

Municipal Library

県庁前

Pref. Library

Kodokan Park

Kairakuen Garden
Tokiwa Shrine

Kanzakiji Temple

Kodokan

Kobuntei

Giretsukan

偕楽園入口

Pref. Office

Site of Mito Castle

KAIRAKUEN

JOBAN LINE

Toshogu Shrine

Seibu Dept. Store

SUIGUN LINE

千波湖

Takashimaya Dept. Store

To O-Arai

Statue of Mito Komon

L. Semba

MITO

桜川

水戸駅南口

To Katsuta/O-Arai

Semba Park

Pref. Museum of Modern Art

Semba Bridge

N

Sakura R.

0   500m

Cultural Center

City Office

② ㉒

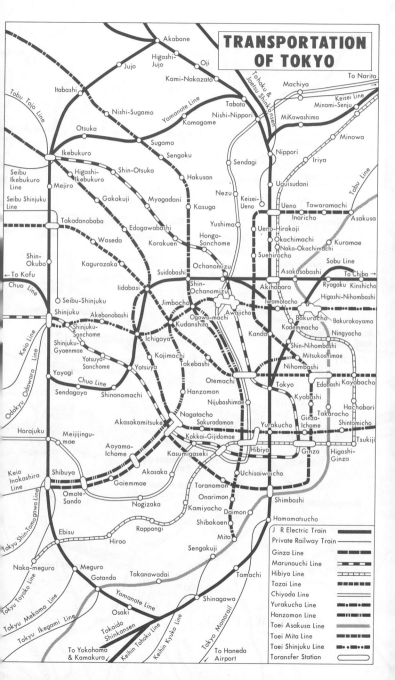

TRANSPORTATION OF TOKYO

To Narita

J R Electric Train
Private Railway Train
Ginza Line
Marunouchi Line
Hibiya Line
Tozai Line
Chiyoda Line
Yurakucho Line
Hanzomon Line
Toei Asakusa Line
Toei Mita Line
Toei Shinjuku Line
Transfer Station

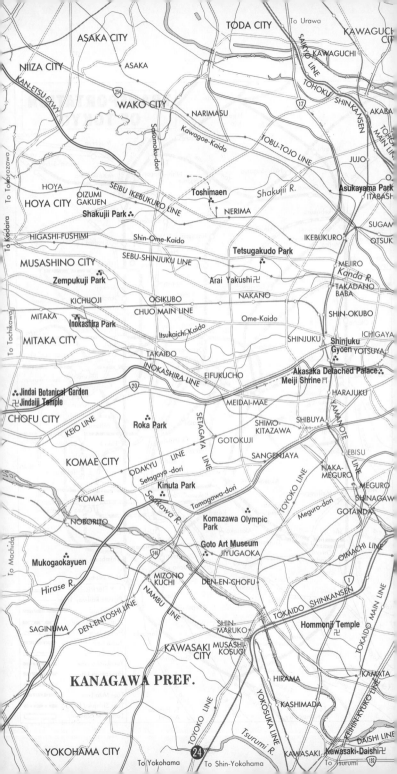

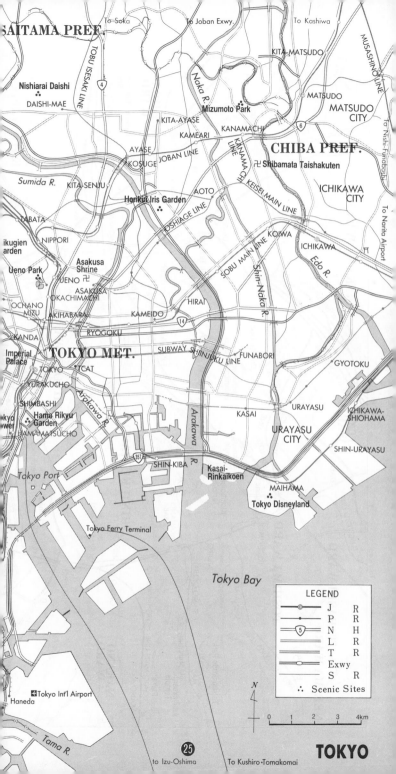

SAITAMA PREF.

To Soka
To Joban Exwy.
To Kashiwa

KITA-MATSUDO

TOBU ISESAKI LINE

Nishiarai Daishi
DAISHI-MAE

Naka R.

MUSASHINO LINE

MATSUDO

MATSUDO CITY

To Nishi-Funabashi

Mizumoto Park

KITA-AYASE

KANAMACHI

KAMEARI

CHIBA PREF.

KAMEARI

KANAMACHI LINE

卍 Shibamata Taishakuten

AYASE

JOBAN LINE

KOSUGE

Sumida R.

KITA-SENJU

AOTO

KEISEI MAIN LINE

ICHIKAWA CITY

Horikiri Iris Garden

TABATA

OSHIAGE LINE

KOIWA

To Narita Airport

ikugien arden

NIPPORI

SOBU MAIN LINE

ICHIKAWA

Edo R.

Ueno Park

Asakusa Shrine

UENO 卍

Shin-Naka R.

OCHANO MIZU

ASAKUSA
OKACHIMACHI

AKIHABARA

HIRAI

KANDA

KAMEIDO

14

RYOGOKU

Imperial Palace

TOKYO MET.

SUBWAY SHINJUKU LINE

FUNABORI

GYOTOKU

TOKYO

TCAT

YURAKUCHO

Arakawa R.

URAYASU

ICHIKAWA-
SHIOHAMA

SHIMBASHI

Hama Rikyu Garden

KASAI

 kyo wer

HAMA-MATSUCHO

URAYASU CITY

SHIN-URAYASU

357

Tokyo Port

SHIN-KIBA

Arakawa R.

Kasai-
Rinkaikoen

MAIHAMA

Tokyo Disneyland

Tokyo Ferry Terminal

Tokyo Bay

LEGEND

⊚	J	R
•	P	R
⑤	N	H R
	L	H R
	T	R
	Exwy	
	S	R
∴	Scenic Sites	

N

0 1 2 3 4km

Tokyo Int'l Airport

Haneda

Tama R.

㉕

to Izu-Oshima

To Kushiro·Tomakomai

TOKYO

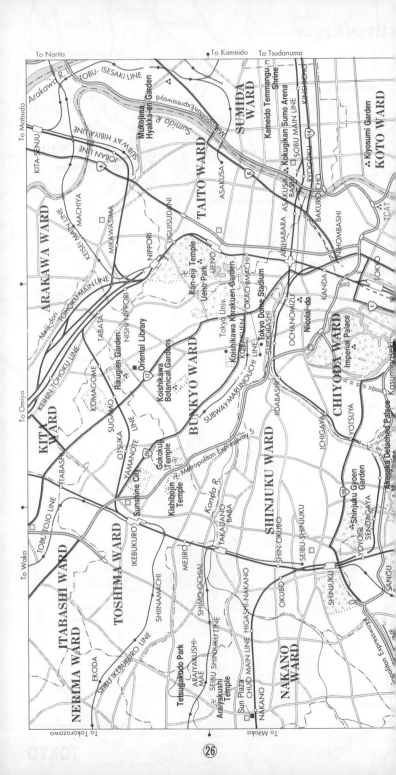

To Narita   To Kameido   To Tsudanuma

To Matsudo

To Omiya

To Woko

To Tokorozawa

To Mitaka

To Misaka

TOBU- ISESAKI LINE
Arakawa R.
KITA-SENJU
JOBAN LINE
SUBWAY HIBIYA LINE
Mukojima Hyakka-en Garden
Metropolitan Expressway6
Sumida R.

SUMIDA WARD
Kameido Temmangu Shrine
Kokugikan Sumo Arena
SOBU MAIN LINE
RYOGOKU
KINSHICHO

Kiyosumi Garden
KOTO WARD
TCAT

KEISEI MAIN LINE
MACHIYA
MIKAWASHIMA
ARAKAWA WARD
TOHOKU MAIN LINE
Meijidori
NIPPORI
NISHI-NIPPORI
KEIHIN-TOHOKU LINE
TABATA
KOMAGOME
SUGAMO
OTSUKA
YAMANOTE LINE

TAITO WARD
ASAKUSA
UGUISUDANI
Kan-ei-ji Temple
UENO
Ueno Park
Tokyo Univ.
Oriental Library
Rikugien Garden
Koishikawa Korakuen Garden
KORAKUEN
Koishikawa Botanical Gardens
SUIDOBASHI
SUBWAY MARUNOUCHI LINE
Tokyo Dome Stadium
OKACHIMACHI
AKIHABARA
NIHOMBASHI
BAKUROCHO
KANDA
OCHANOMIZU
Nicolai-do
TOKYO

AKABANE

KITA WARD
ITABASHI
TOBU TOJO LINE
NERIMA WARD
EKODA
SEIBU IKEBUKURO LINE
IKEBUKURO
Sunshine City
Gokokuji Temple
Kishibojin Temple
TAKADANO BABA
Kanda R.
Metropolitan Expressway 5

BUNKYO WARD

CHIYODA WARD
Imperial Palace
Akasaka Detached Palace
Kasumigaseki

ITABASHI WARD
SHIINAMACHI
MEJIRO
SHIMO-OCHIAI
ARAI-YAKUSHI-MAE
SEIBU SHINJUKU LINE
TOSHIMA WARD
Tetsugakudo Park
Araiyakushi Temple
Sun Plaza
NAKANO
CHUO MAIN LINE
HIGASHI-NAKANO
OKUBO
SHIN-OKUBO
SEIBU-SHINJUKU
TAKADANO BABA

SHINJUKU WARD
ICHIGAYA
YOTSUYA
Shinjuku Gyoen
YOYOGI
SENDAGAYA
SHINJUKU

NAKANO WARD

Akasaka Detached Palace
SANGU
Shinjuku Gyoen Garden
Metropolitan Expressway

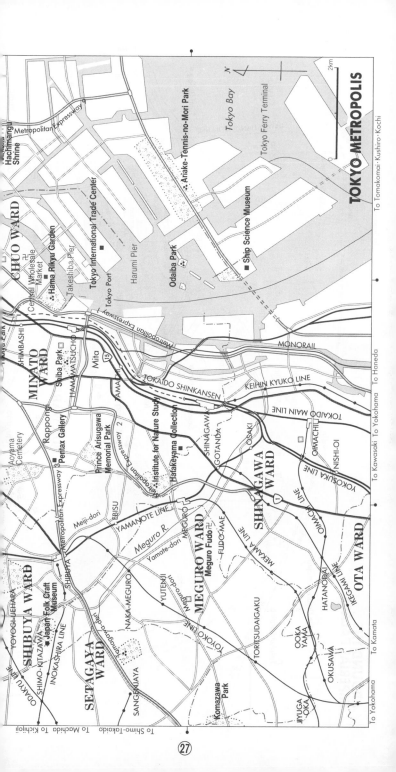

TOKYO METROPOLIS

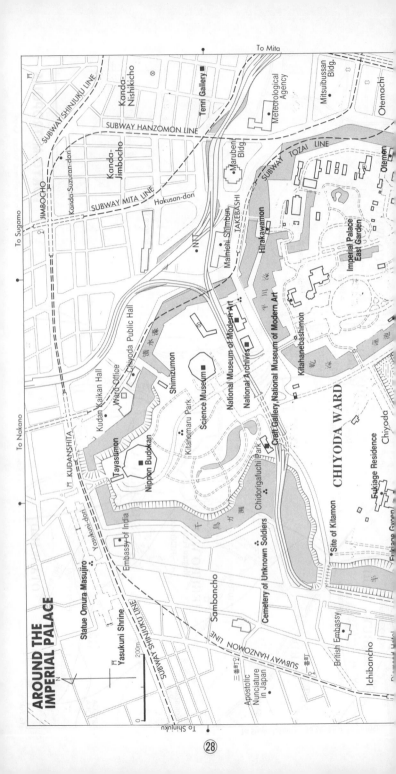

AROUND THE IMPERIAL PALACE

N

200m

To Shinjuku
To Nakano
To Sugamo
To Mita
To Mita

JIMBOCHO

Kanda-Nishikicho
Temi Gallery ■

SUBWAY SHINJUKU LINE

SUBWAY HANZOMON LINE

Kanda-Jimbocho

Kanda-Suzuran-dori

SUBWAY MITA LINE

Hakusan-dori

Meteorological Agency

Mitsuibussan Bldg.

Otemachi

Marubeni Bldg.

SUBWAY TOZAI LINE

Mainichi-Shimbun

TAKEBASHI

Hirakawamon

NT

Chiyoda Public Hall

SUBWAY SHINJUKU LINE

KUDANSHITA

清水濠

Ward Office

Kudan Kaikan Hall

ShimiZumon

Science Museum ■

National Museum of Modern Art ■

National Archives ■

Craft Gallery, National Museum of Modern Art ■

Kitahanebashimon

Imperial Palace East Garden

Otemon

平川濠

乾濠

蓮池

CHIYODA WARD

Kitanomaru Park

Tayasumon

Nippon Budokan ■

Chidorigafuchi Park

千鳥ヶ淵

Site of Kitamon

Fukiage Residence

Chiyoda

Yasukuni-dori

Embassy of India

Statue Omura Masujiro

Yasukuni Shrine

Cemetery of Unknown Soldiers

Sambancho

SUBWAY HANZOMON LINE

三番町

Fukiage Gyoen

半蔵濠

British Embassy

Ichibancho

Apostolic Nunciature in Japan

⑳

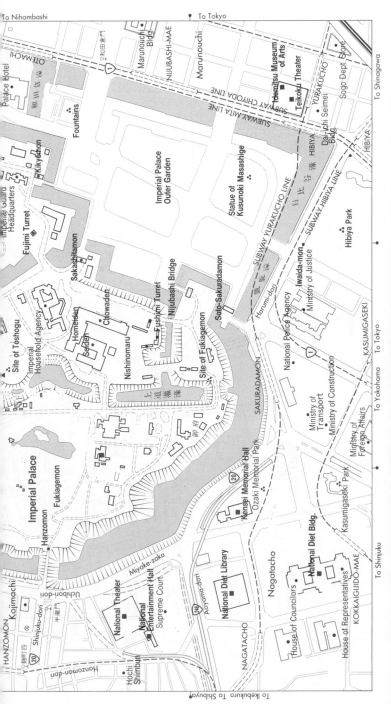

To Naka-Meguro   To Akasaka

SUBWAY HIBIYA LINE

Jisshi Park

6

Shuto Expressway 1

Bank of Fuji
Museum

Kabuto Shrine

Tokyo Stock
Exchange

Nihombashi

SHIN-NIHOMBASHI

Edo-dori

MITSUKOSHI-MAE

Nihombashi Bridge

Edobashi
Bridge

Kanda

17

SOBU MAIN LINE

Mitsui Main Bldg.

Mitsukoshi
Dept. Store

Money Museum

MITSUKOSHI-MAE

To Ueno

KANDA

Bank of Japan

SUBWAY HANZOMON LINE

YAMANOTE-KEIHIN-TOHOKU LINE

1

Japan Bldg.

Shin-Nittetsu
Bldg.

SUBWAY TOZAI LINE

Kanko Bunka Library

Eitai-dori

Tekko Bldg.

To Ikebukuro

Soboni-dori

CHIYODA WARD

Tokyo Int'l Post Office

Communications
Museum

Electronic

Communication
Science Museum

Tokyo-Shigai
Telephone &
Telegraph Office

Shin-Otemachi Bldg.

Marunouchi Hotel

JR East Japan

JTB Bldg.

Tekko Bldg.

To Kita-Senju

Nihon Keizai Shimbun

Keidanren Hall

Yomiuri Shimbun

OTEMACHI

OTEMACHI

Otemachi Bldg.

JR MARUNOUCHI LINE

Hongo-dori

Hibiya-dori

OTEMACHI

To Sugamo To Shibuya

Meteorological
Agency

Mitsui Seimei Bldg.

IBM Information
Science Museum

OTEMACHI

SUBWAY CHIYODA LINE

Takebashi-Kaikan
Hall

Otemon

Palace Hotel

NKK

AIU

OTEMACHI

Wadakuramon

Fountains

To Nakano

30

CENTRAL TOKYO

CHUO WARD

To Nishi-Funabashi
To Ueno

Kabutocho

Yamatane Museum of Art

KAYABACHO

SUBWAY HIBIYA LINE

HATCHOBORI

Hatchobori

Yaesu-dori

NIHOMBASHI

SUBWAY ASAKUSA LINE

Showa-dori

Takashimaya Dept. Store

SUBWAY GINZA LINE

Bridgestone Museum of Art

Yaesu-dori

Kokusai Kanko Kaikan Bldg.

Yaesu Underground Shopping Center

Chuo-dori

TAKARA-CHO

Daimaru Dept. Store

ANA

JAS

Yaesu Book Center

Meijiya

KYOBASHI

Fuji Center

INAX Gallery

Ginza

TOKYO

Tokyo Station Hotel

Sorobon-dori

Fujiya Hotel

Site of Kyobashi

Hotel Seiyo

SUBWAY YURAKUCHO LINE

To Shi-kiba

GINZA-ITCHOME

To Shibuya

Central Post Office

Marunouchi Yaesu Bldg.

Tokyo Metropolitan Office

Nisseki Bldg.

Tokyo Kotsu Kaikan

Printemps Ginza

To Shinjuku

Mitsubishi Shoji

Marunouchi Bldg.

Mitsui Bldg.

NIIJUBASHI-MAE

Mitsui Bldg.

Tokyo Chamber of Commerce and Industry

Tokyo Kaikan

Marunouchi

Idemitsu Museum of Arts

Teikoku Theater

YURAKUCHO

Sogo Dept. Store

Yurakucho Center Bldg.

To Ginza

SUBWAY MITA LINE

HIBIYA

Yurakucho Bldg.

HIBIYA

Hibiya Chanter

To Shinagawa

Hibiya-dori

To Omotesando

To Ikebukuro

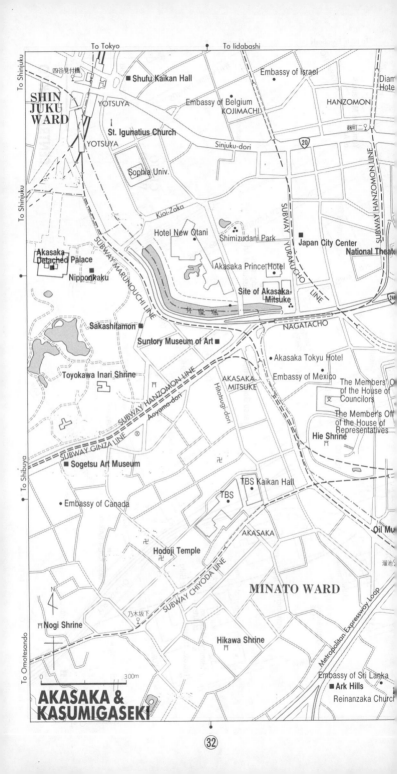

To Tokyo
To Iidabashi
To Shinjuku
四谷見付橋
■ Shufu Kaikan Hall
Embassy of Israel
Diam
Hote
SHIN
JUKU
WARD
YOTSUYA
Embassy of Belgium
KOJIMACHI
HANZOMON
■ St. Ignatius Church
YOTSUYA
Sinjuku-dori
麹町二☆
20
To Shinjuku
Sophia Univ.
Kioi-Zaka
Hotel New Otani
Shimizudani Park
Japan City Center
National Theate
SUBWAY MARUNOUCHI LINE
SUBWAY HANZOMON LINE
SUBWAY YURAKUCHO LINE
Akasaka
Detached Palace
Nipponkaku
Akasaka Prince Hotel
Site of Akasaka
Mitsuke
弁慶堀
■ Sakashitamon
NAGATACHO
246
■ Suntory Museum of Art ■
• Akasaka Tokyu Hotel
AKASAKA
MITSUKE
• Embassy of Mexico
The Members
of the House of
Councilors
SUBWAY HANZOMON LINE
Toyokawa Inari Shrine
Aoyama-dori
Hitotsugi-dori
文
The Member's Off
of the House of
Representatives
SUBWAY GINZA LINE
Hie Shrine
卍
■ Sogetsu Art Museum
卍
• Embassy of Canada
TBS Kaikan Hall
TBS
To Shibuya
Oil Mu
AKASAKA
卍
Hodoji Temple
卍
SUBWAY CHIYODA LINE
MINATO WARD
Metropolitan Expressway Loop
N
乃木坂下
卍 Nogi Shrine
溜池
To Omotesando
0   300m
Hikawa Shrine
卍
Embassy of Sri Lanka
■ Ark Hills
AKASAKA &
KASUMIGASEKI
Reinanzaka Churc

SHIBA PARK

Embassy of Holland

御成門中

ONARIMON

新橋六

Children's Park

Japan Red Cross

Shiba Daimon

芝大門

二天門

Tokyo Prince Hotel

Shiba Park Hotel

Ward Office

Tokyo Tower

Shiba Daijingu Shrine

TV Tokyo

Zojoji Temple

Sutra Library

DAIMONI

Shiba Park

World Trade Center Bldg.

Toshogu Shrine

HAMAMA TSUCHO

ABC Kaiken Hall

N

赤羽橋

Yubin Chokin Hall

MINATO WARD

SHIBA-KOEN

Inari Shrine

300m

芝二

0

金杉橋

NTT

To Mita

Tokyo Grand Hotel

To Shinagawa

To Haneda

Shiba Detached Palace Garden

National Diet

Ministry of Transport

Ministry of Justice

OKKAIGIJIDO-MAE

SUBWAY MARUNOUCHI LINE

Kasumigaseki Park

KASUMIGASEKI

Ministry of Foreign Affairs

Hibiya Park

KASUMIGASEKI

IKAIGIJIDO-MAE

HIBIYA

CHIYODA WARD

Ministry of Agriculture, Forestry and Fisheries

Ministry of Health and Welfare

KASUMIGASEKI

Hibiya Outdoor Music Hall

Ministry of Finance

To Ginza

Ministry of International Trade and Industry

Hibiya Library

Ministry of Education

Mitsui Kasumigaseki Bldg.

Hibiya Public Hall

Ministry of Posts and Telecommunications

NTT Bldg

TORANOMON

UCHISAIWAICHO

佐久間町

SUBWAY GINZA LINE

西新橋

assy of U.S.A.

SHIMBASHI

Hotei Okura

Okura Shukokan Museum

SHIMBASHI

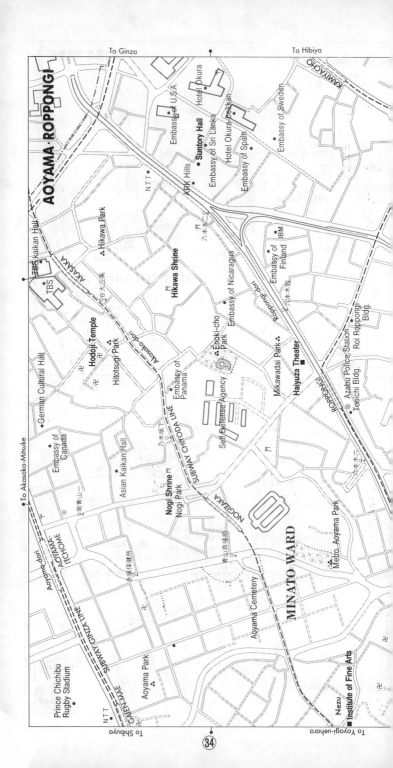

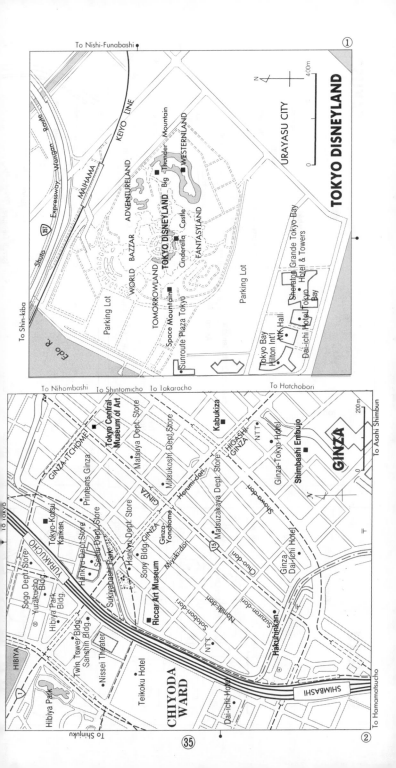

①

TOKYO DISNEYLAND

To Nishi-Funabashi •

To Shin-kiba

Edo R.

Shuto Wangan Route Expressway

(357)

KEIYO LINE

MAIHAMA

Parking Lot

WORLD BAZZAR

ADVENTURELAND

Big Thunder Mountain

WESTERNLAND

TOKYO DISNEYLAND

Cinderella Castle

FANTASYLAND

TOMORROWLAND

Space Mountain

Sunroute Plaza Tokyo

Parking Lot

URAYASU CITY

Tokyo Bay Hilton Int'l

NK Hall

Dai-ichi Hotel Tokyo Bay

Sheraton Grande Tokyo Bay

Hilton Hotel & Towers

N

400m

②

GINZA

To Nihombashi   To Shintomicho   To Takaracho

To Hatchobori

To Tokyo

To Asahi Shimbun

CHIYODA WARD

To Shinjuku

To Hamamatsucho

Tokyo Central Museum of Art

GINZA-ITCHOME

Matsuya Dept. Store

Kabukiza

Printemps Ginza

Mitsukoshi Dept. Store

GINZA

HIGASHI-GINZA

NTT

Ginza-Tokyo Hotel

Harumi-dori

Shimbashi Embujo

Tokyo-Kotsu Kaikan

Hankyu Dept. Store

Seibu Dept. Store

Sony Bldg.

Ginza Yonchome

GINZA

Miyuki-dori

Showa-dori

YURAKUCHO

Sogo Dept. Store

Yurakucho Bldg.

Hibiya Park Bldg.

Sukiyabashi Park

Riccar Art Museum

(15)

Matsuzakaya Dept. Store

Chuo-dori

Ginza Dai-ichi Hotel

HIBIYA

Twin Tower Bldg.

Sanshin Bldg.

Nissei Theater

Sotobori-dori

Namiki-dori

Suzuran-dori

NTT

Hakuhinkan

Hibiya Park

Teikoku Hotel

Dai-ichi Hotel

SHIMBASHI

200m

N

35

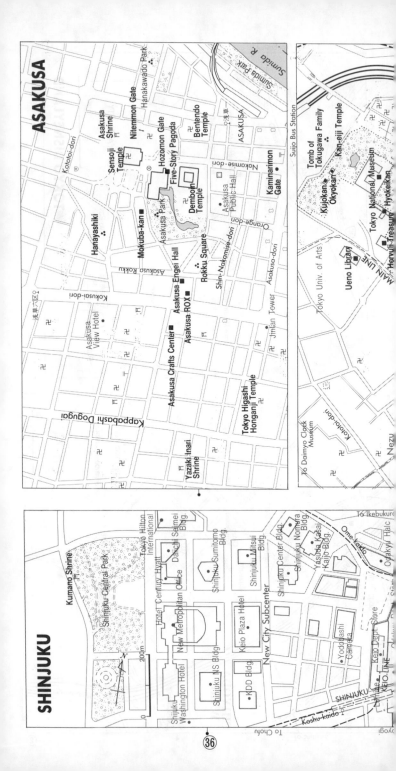

ASACUSA

Sumida R.

Kototoi-dori

Asakusa Shrine

Nitenmon Gate

Hanakawado Park

Sensoji Temple

Hozomon Gate

Five-Story Pagoda

Bentendo Temple

ASAKUSA

Hanayashiki

Mokuba-kan

Asakusa Park

Dembōin Temple

Nakamise-dori

Asakusa Engei Hall

Asakusa Rokku

Rokku Square

Asakusa Public Hall

Kaminarimon Gate

Shin-Nakamise-dori

Orange-dori

Asakusa-dori

Kokusai-dori

Asakusa View Hotel

Asakusa Crafts Center

Asakusa ROX

Asakusa Engei Hall

Jintan Tower

Kappabashi Dougai

Tokyo Higashi Honganji Temple

Yazaki Inari Shrine

Suijo Bus Station

Tomb of Tokugawa Family

Kujokan Okyokan

Tokyo National Museum

Hyokeikan

Horyuji Treasure Kan-eiji Temple

Tokyo Univ. of Arts

MAIN LINE

Ueno Library

To Daimyo Clock Museum

Kototoi-dori

Nezu

SHINJUKU

Kumano Shrine

Tokyo Hilton International

Shinjuku Central Park

Daiichi Seimei Bldg.

Hotel Century Hyatt

New Metropolitan Office

Shinjuku Sumitomo Bldg.

Shinjuku Mitsui Bldg.

Keio Plaza Hotel

Shinjuku Center Bldg.

Shinjuku Nomura Bldg.

Yasuda Kasai Kaijo Bldg.

New City Subcenter

Shinjuku Washington Hotel

Shinjuku NS Bldg.

KDD Bldg.

Ome Kaido

To Ikebukuro

Odakyu Halc

Yodobashi Camera

SHINJUKU

KEIO LINE

Keio Dept. Store

To Chofu

Koshu-kaido

N

0 200m

UENO

To Asakusa

Ward Office

TOHOKU SHINKANSEN
YAMANOTE-KEIHIN TOHOKU LINE
TOHOKU LINE

SUBWAY GINZA LINE

TAITO WARD

SUBWAY HIBIYA LINE

To Nihombashi

National Science Museum

National Museum of Western Art

-Kan

Ueno Park

UENO

Tokyo Metropolitan Festival Hall

Takeno-dai

Art Museum

Ueno Royal Museum

Kan-eiji

Kiyomizudo Temple

Statue of Saigo Takamori

Ueno Dept. Store

Marui Store

Ameya Yokocho

Ameyoko Center Bldg.

OKACHI MACHI

Belfry

KEISEI UENO

Five Story Pagoda

Toshogu Shrine

Shitamachi Museum

Suijo Ongakudo Hall

UENO HIROKOJI

Ueno Zoo

Mono Rail

Bentendo Temple

Shinobazu Pond

YUSHIMA

To Otemachi

Hotel Ogaiso

Aquarium

Yushima Tenjin

Yayoi Kaikan Hall

BUNKYO WARD

Yokoyama Taikan Memorial Hall

Shinobazu-dori

N

200m

UENO

YAMANOTE-CHUO-SAKYO LINE

Limine 2 My City

Studio Alta

Kabukicho

Ward Office

Hanazono Shrine

Golden-gai

Konica Plaza

Kinokuniya Book Store

SHINJUKU-SANCHOME

Yasukuni-dori

Shinjuku-Rokuchome

Mitsukoshi Dept. Store

Isetan Dept. Store

Isetan Park City

Koseinenkin Hall

Marui

SUBWAY SHINJUKU LINE

SUBWAY MARUNOUCHI LINE

20

To Shinjukugyoen-mae

③⑦

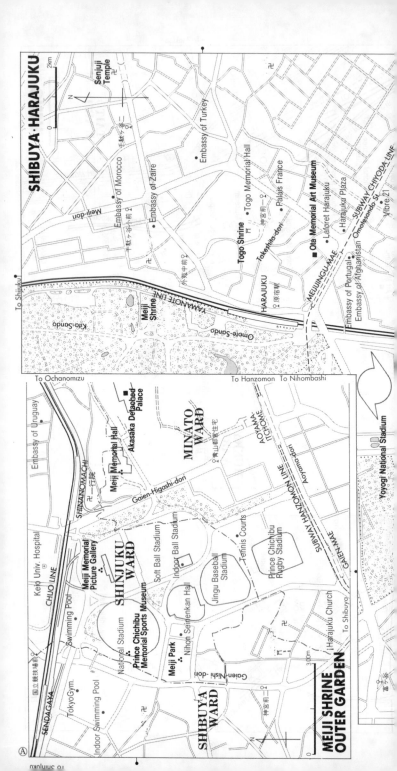

SHIBUYA · HARAJUKU

Senjuji Temple 卍

To Shibuya

Embassy of Morocco ·
Meiji-dori
千駄ヶ谷一
Embassy of Zaire ·

Embassy of Turkey ·

Togo Memorial Hall ·
Palais France ·
千駄ヶ谷二 ◌

神宮前 ◌
Togo Shrine 卍
Takeshita-dori

■ Ota Memorial Art Museum

外苑中前 ◌

Laforet Harajuku ·
Harajuku Plaza ·
MEIJINGU-MAE
Omotesando St.
SUBWAY CHIYODA LINE
HARAJUKU
Fibre 21
◌ 原宿駅

Embassy of Portugal ·
Embassy of Afghanistan ·

YAMANOTE LINE

Meiji Shrine

Kita-Sando
Omote-Sando

To Hanzomon   To Nihombashi

To Ochanomizu

Embassy of Uruguay ·
千駄町
SHINANOMACHI

Meiji Memorial Hall ■
Akasaka Detached Palace

Keio Univ. Hospital ⊕
CHUO LINE

Meiji Memorial Picture Gallery 🎷

MINATO WARD

Gaien-Higashi-dori

Swimming Pool

SHINJUKU WARD

Soft Ball Stadium

青山都営住宅

AOYAMA ITCHOME
青山一丁目駅
Aoyama-dori

SUBWAY HANZOMON LINE

Indoor Ball Stadium

Prince Chichibu Memorial Sports Museum 🎷

国立競技場前 ◌
SENDAGAYA

National Stadium

Nihon Seinenkan Hall

Jingu Baseball Stadium

Tennis Courts

Prince Chichibu Rugby Stadium

GAIEN-MAE

To Shibuya

Harajuku Church

TokyoGym.

Indoor Swimming Pool

Meiji Park 🎷
卍

神宮前 ◌

Gaien-Nishi-dori

SHIBUYA WARD

MEIJI SHRINE OUTER GARDEN

300m

Ⓐ

To Shinjuku

N   2km

Yoyogi National Stadium

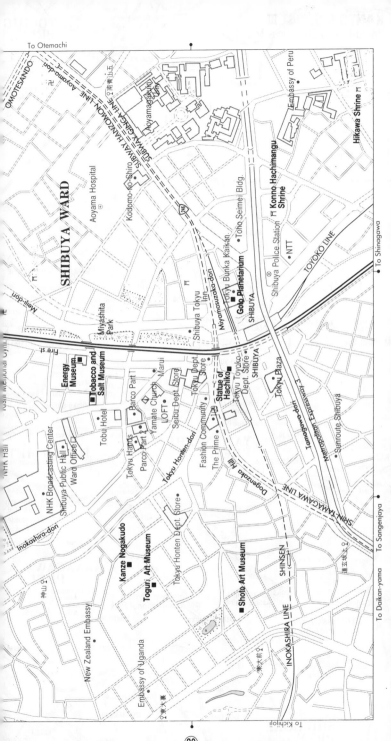

To Otemachi

OMOTESANDO

SHIBUYA WARD

SUBWAY HANZOMON LINE
SUBWAY GINZA LINE
Aoyama-dori

Aoyama Hospital

Kodomo-no-Shiro

Embassy of Peru

Hikawa Shrine

Konno Hachimangu Shrine

Toho Seimei Bldg.

TOYOKO LINE

To Shinagawa

Shibuya Police Station

NTT

Meiji-dori

Miyashita Park

Tokyu Bunka Kaikan

Miyamasuzaka-dori

Goto Planetarium

SHIBUYA

Shibuya Tokyu Inn

Fire st.

Energy Museum

Tobacco and Salt Museum

NHK Hall

NHK Broadcasting Center

Shibuya Public Hall

Ward Office

Tobu Hotel

Parco Part 1

Yamate Church

LOFT

Marui

Seibu Dept. Store

Tokyu Dept. Store

Statue of Hachiko

Tokyu Toyoko Dept. Store

SHIBUYA

Tokyu Plaza

Tokyu Hands

Parco Part 2

Tamagawa-dori

Metropolitan Expressway 3

Sunroute Shibuya

Tokyu Honten-dori

Fashion Community

The Prime

Dogenzaka Hill

Inokashira-dori

Kanze Nogakudo

Toguri Art Museum

Tokyu Honten Dept. Store

Shoto Art Museum

SHINSEN

SHIN-TAMAGAWA LINE

To Sangenjaya

New Zealand Embassy

Embassy of Uganda

INOKASHIRA LINE

To Daikan-yama

To Kichijoji

㊴

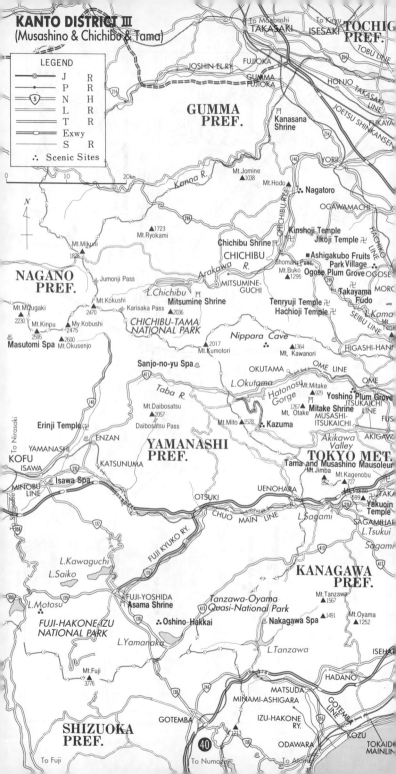

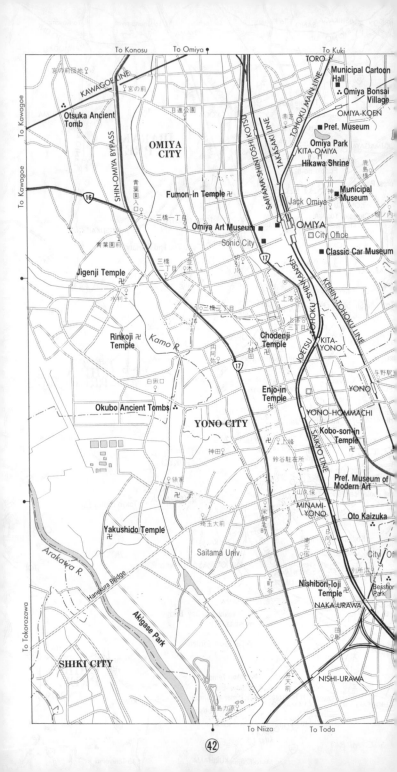

To Konosu　To Omiya　To Kuki
TORO

Municipal Cartoon Hall
Omiya Bonsai Village

OMIYA-KOEN

Pref. Museum

KAWAGOE LINE

Otsuka Ancient Tomb

Omiya Park
KITA-OMIYA
Hikawa Shrine

OMIYA CITY

SHIN-OMIYA BYPASS

Fumon-in Temple

Jack Omiya

Municipal Museum

16

Omiya Art Museum

OMIYA

City Office

Sonic City

Classic Car Museum

17

Jigenji Temple

Rinkoji Temple

Kamo R.

Chodenji Temple

KITA-YONO

17

Enjo-in Temple

YONO

YONO-HOMMACHI

Okubo Ancient Tombs

YONO CITY

Kobo-son-in Temple

SAIKYO LINE

Pref. Museum of Modern Art

MINAMI-YONO

Oto Kaizuka

Yakushido Temple

City Of

Arakawa R.

Saitama Univ.

Besshor Park

Nishibori-Ioji Temple

NAKA-URAWA

Hanakura Bridge

Akigase Park

SHIKI CITY

NISHI-URAWA

To Tokorozawa

To Niiza　To Toda

TOHOKU MAIN LINE
TAKASAKI LINE
SAITAMA-SHINTOSHI KOTSU
JOETSU TOHOKU SHINKANSEN
KEIHIN-TOHOKU LINE

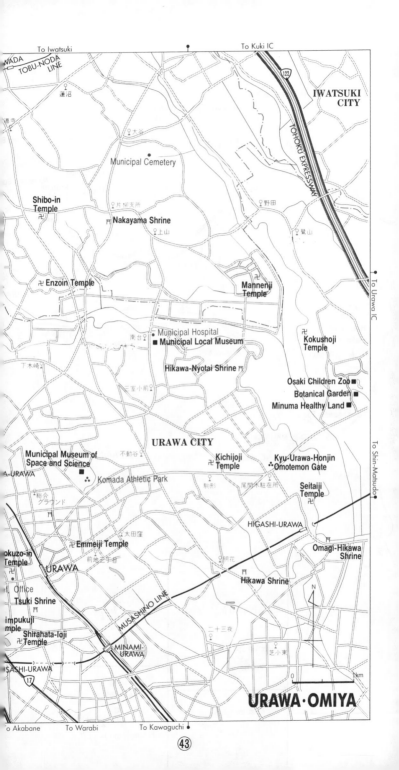

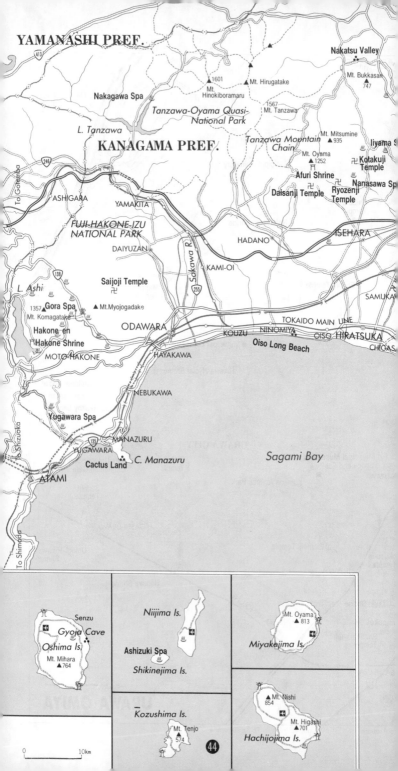

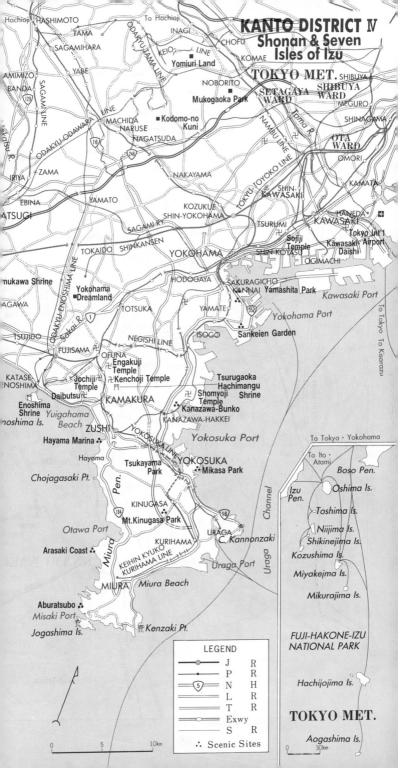

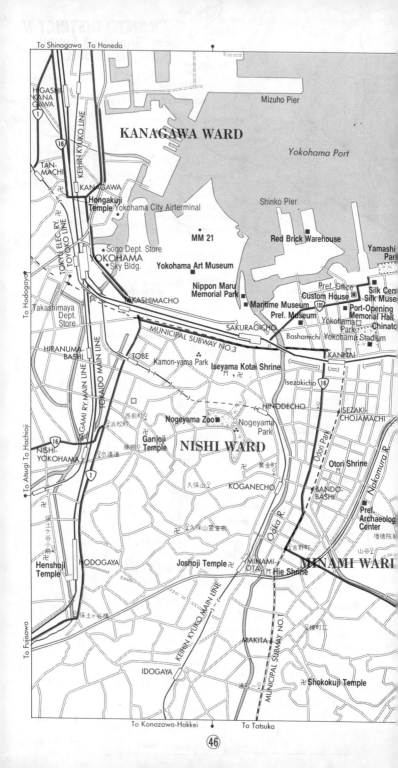

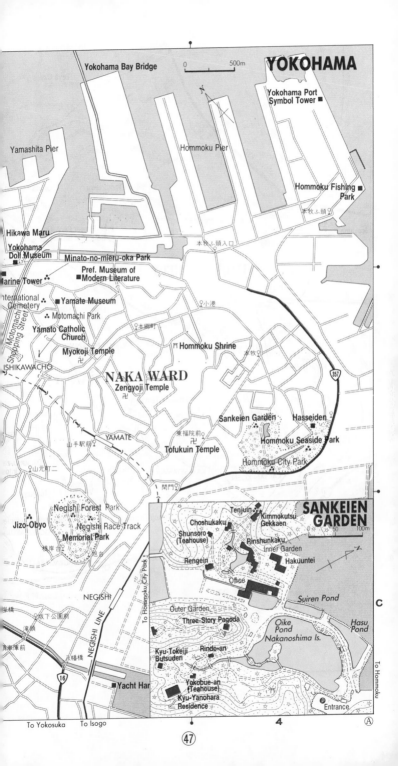

YOKOHAMA

Yokohama Bay Bridge

0 500m

Yokohama Port Symbol Tower ■

Yamashita Pier

Hommoku Pier

Hommoku Fishing Park ■

本牧ふ頭

Hikawa Maru

Yokohama Doll Museum

Minato-no-mieru-oka Park

本牧ふ頭入口

Marine Tower

International Cemetery

Pref. Museum of Modern Literature

Yamate Museum

小港

Motomachi Park

本牧町

Yamato Catholic Church

Myokoji Temple 卍

Hommoku Shrine 卍

本牧

NAKA WARD

Zengyoji Temple 卍

357

東福院前

Sankeien Garden

Hasseiden

ISHIKAWACHO

YAMATE

山手駅前

Tofukuin Temple

Hommoku Seaside Park

Hommoku City Park

山元町二

間門

Negishi Forest Park

Jizo-Obyo

Negishi Race Track

Memorial Park

根岸台

池

SANKEIEN GARDEN

0 50 100m

Tenjuin

Choshukaku

Kimmokutsu Gekkaen

Shunsoro (Teahouse)

Rinshunkaku

Inner Garden

Rengein

Hakuuntei

Office

NEGISHI

To Hommoku City Park

Suiren Pond

C

Outer Garden

Three-Story Pagoda

Oike Pond

Nakanoshima Is.

Hasu Pond

NEGISHI LINE

坂下公園前

滝頭

Kyu-Tokeiji Butsuden

Rinde-an

食庫前

入幡橋

16

Yokobue-an (Teahouse)

Kyu-Yanohara Residence

Entrance P

To Hommoku

Yacht Har

To Yokosuka   To Isogo

4

Ⓐ

(47)

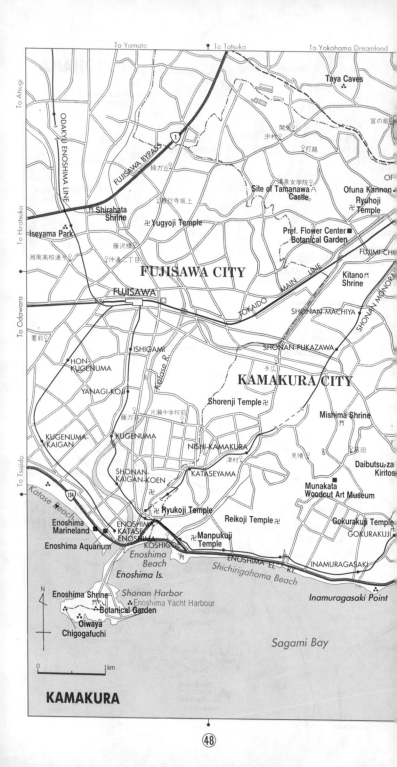

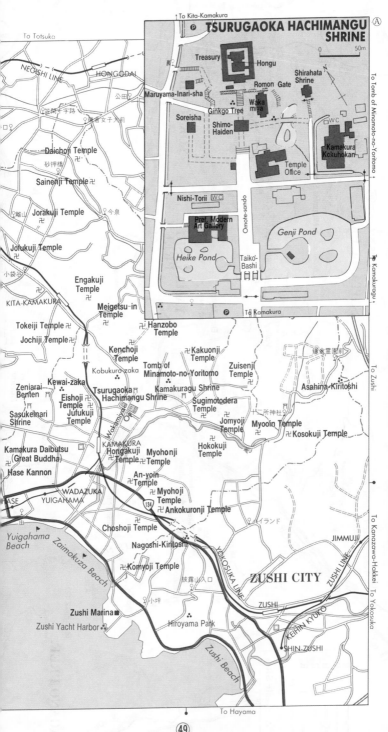

To Kita-Kamakura

TSURUGAOKA HACHIMANGU SHRINE

Ⓐ

0 ——— 50m

To Totsuka

NEGISHI LINE

HONGŌDAI

公田北

笠間十字路

鎌倉女子大前

Daichoji Temple

砂押橋

Sainenji Temple 卍

今泉

Jorakuji Temple 卍

鎌山

小袋谷

Jofukuji Temple 卍

Engakuji Temple

KITA-KAMAKURA

Meigetsu-in Temple

Tokeiji Temple 卍

Jochiji Temple 卍

Hanzobo Temple

Kenchoji Temple

Kobukuro-zaka

Kewai-zaka

Zeniarai-Benten

Eishoji Temple

Tsurugaoka Hachimangu Shrine

Jufukuji Temple

Sasukeinari Shrine

Kamakura Daibutsu (Great Buddha)

Hase Kannon

HASE

WADAZUKA

YUIGAHAMA

Yuigahama Beach

Zaimokuza Beach

Zushi Marina ■

Zushi Yacht Harbor

Treasury

Hongu

Shirahata Shrine

Maruyama-Inari-sha

Romon Gate

Wakamiya

Ginkgo Tree

Soreisha

Shimo-Haiden

Kamakura Kokuhokan

Temple Office

WC

Nishi-Torii WC

Omote-sando

Pref. Modern Art Gallery

Genji Pond

Heike Pond

Taiko-Bashi

To Kamakura

To Kamakura

Kakuonji Temple

Zuisenji Temple

Tomb of Minamoto-no-Yoritomo

Kamakuragu Shrine

Sugimotodera Temple

Asahina-Kiritoshi

Jomyoji Temple

Myooin Temple

Kosokuji Temple

十二所神社

鎌倉霊園入口

To Zushi

Hongakuji Temple

Myohonji Temple

Hokokuji Temple

KAMAKURA

An-yoin Temple

Myohoji Temple

Ankokuronji Temple

134

Choshoji Temple

Nagoshi-Kiritoshi

ハイランド

YOKOSUKA LINE

ZUSHI CITY

JIMMUJI

To Kanazawa-Hakkei

To Yokosuka

Komyoji Temple

披露山入口

小坪

Hiroyama Park

ZUSHI LINE

ZUSHI

SHIN-ZUSHI

KEIHIN KYUKO

Zushi Beach

To Hayama

To Tomb of Minamoto-no-Yoritomo

To Kamakuragu

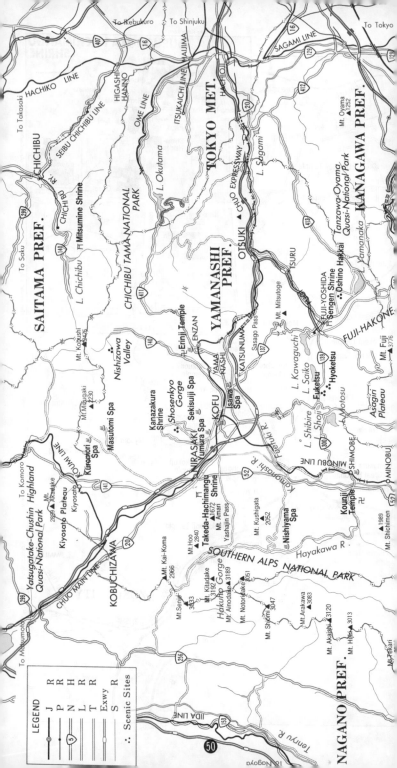

CHUBU DISTRICT II
(Fuji Hakone & Izu)

Oshima Is.
Mt. Mihara ▲764

Sagami Bay

Hatsushima Is.

To Niijima Is.

To Nagoya

Ensho Nada Sea

KOZU
ODAWARA
C. Manazuru
Izusan Spa
ATAMI
Nishikigaura
DAIJIRO
USAMI
KAWANA
Jogasaki Beach
Atagawa Spa
Inatori Spa
Imaihama Spa
Shirahama Beach
C. Tsumeki

Hakone-
Yumoto Spa
GORA
Myojogatake
Mt. Komagatake ▲
Mt. Kamiyama ▲
Mifo-Hakone
Hakone
KINOMIYA
ITO LINE
Hatake Spa
ITO
Mt. Omuro
Ippeki
Mt. Nunomi
IZU
KYUKO
RY.
Rendaiji
REMDAIJI
SHIMODA
C. Iro

NAT'L
SUSONO
MISHIMA
IZU-HAKONE RY.
Izu Skyline
SHUZENJI
Amagi Mountains
Yugashima Spa
Amagi Pass
Mt. Amagi ▲1406
Yugano Spa
Osawa Spa
Shimogamo Spa
C. Hagachi

PARK
Mt. Ashitaka ▲1505
TOMEI EXPRESSWAY
SHIN-FUJI
NIRAYAMA
OHITO
Shuzenji Spa
IZU-NAGAOKA
MIO
Heda
Mt. Daruma
Kano R.
Joren Falls
Matsuzaki Spa
Matsuzaki
Kawazu Nanadaru
Sengammon
Tensodo Cave
Dogashima

Fujisan-Hongu
Sengen Shrine
FUJINOMIYA
Taisekiji
Temple
Fuji R.
FUJI
TOKAIDO SHINKANSEN
Tagonoura Port
Sembon-Matsubara
NUMAZU
C. Ose
C. Osc
Toi Spa
Suruga Bay

SHIZUOKA
PREF.

Sumatakyo Gorge
L. Ikawa
IKAWA
Sessokyo Gorge
Sessokyo Spa
SENZU
Abe R.
OIGAWA RY.
382
362

SHIMIZU
Miho-no-Matsubara
Nihondaira
Kunozan Toshogu Shrine
Loess Ruins
Okuzure Coast
Kinozan-Ho
SHIZUOKA
Saiokuji Temple
(Togeppo)
YAIZU
FUJIEDA BYPASS
FUJIEDA
Oi R.
SHIMA
DA
Omaezaki Point
Nan-en Sand Dunes

Nomarinoike Pond
To Toyohashi
Oguni Shrine
KANAYA
Sayo-no-Nakayma
Makinohara Tableland
asuisai
Temple
RYU-
MANAKO RY.
FUKUROI
Son-eiji Temple
KAKEGAWA
150
1

0   10   20Km

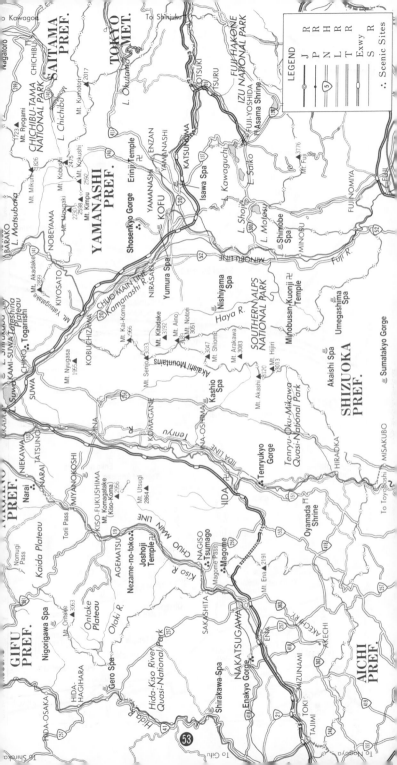

① SHIZUOKA

To Umegashima Spa

To Hamamatsu

Route 1

Sannomiya Shrine

Rinzaiji Temple

Shizuhatayama Hill

Johoku Park

Shimmei Shrine

Zuiryuji Temple

Sengen Shrine

Municipal Cultural Treasure Museum

Tenshoji Temple

Tokoji Temple

Kumano Shrine

Atago Shrine

Ren-eiji Temple

NHK

Gofukumachi-dori

Sumpu Park

Site of Sumpu Castle

Gokoku Shrine

Pref. Office

Iseman Dept. Store

Shotoku-dori

SHIN-SHIZUOKACHO

HIYOSHI CHO

Kiyomizu Park

Yunoki Park

Hodaiin Temple

Seibu Dept. Store

Shin-Shizuoka Center Matsuzakaya

OTOWACHO

KASUGACHO

YUNOKI

Sumpu Museum

SHIZUOKA Dept. Store

SHIZUOKA

TOKAIDO SHINKANSEN

TOKAIDO MAIN LINE

To Senzu

To Yaizu - Shimada

Hon-dori

To Shimizu

To Hamamatsu

To Shimizu

0 500m

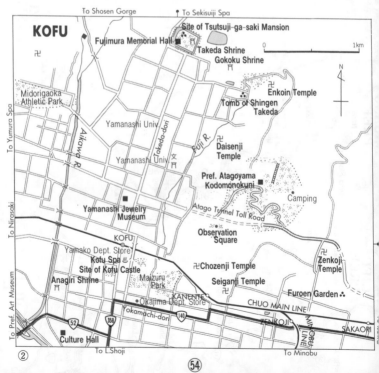

KOFU ②

To Shosen Gorge

To Sekisuiji Spa

Site of Tsutsuji-ga-saki Mansion

Fujimura Memorial Hall

Takeda Shrine

Gokoku Shrine

Midorigaoka Athletic Park

Enkoin Temple

Tomb of Shingen Takeda

Yamanashi Univ.

Aikawa R.

Takeda-dori

Fuji R.

Daisenji Temple

Yamanashi Univ.

Pref. Atagoyama Kodomonokuni

Camping

Yamanashi Jewelry Museum

Atago Tunnel Toll Road

Observation Square

Zenkoji Temple

KOFU

Yamako Dept. Store

Kofu Spa

Site of Kofu Castle

Chozenji Temple

Seiganji Temple

Furoen Garden

Anagiri Shrine

Maizuru Park

Okajima Dept. Store

KANENTE

CHUO MAIN LINE

Culture Hall

Yokamachi-dori

Route 140

ZENKOJI

SAKAORI

To Yumura Spa

To Nirasaki

To Pref. Art Museum

Route 52

Route 358

To L.Shoji

To Minobu

MINOBU LINE

0 1km

N

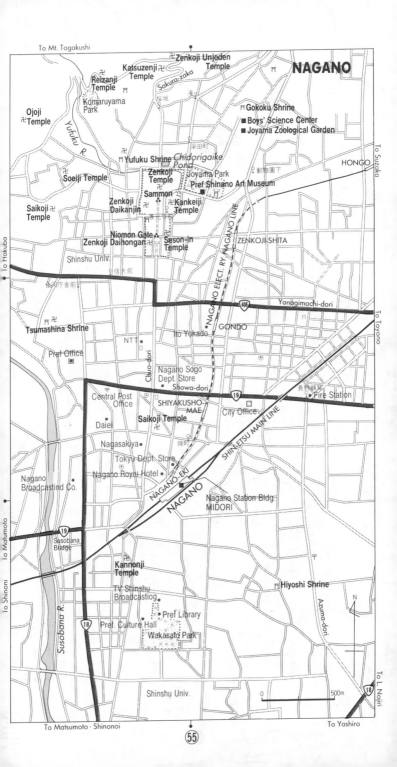

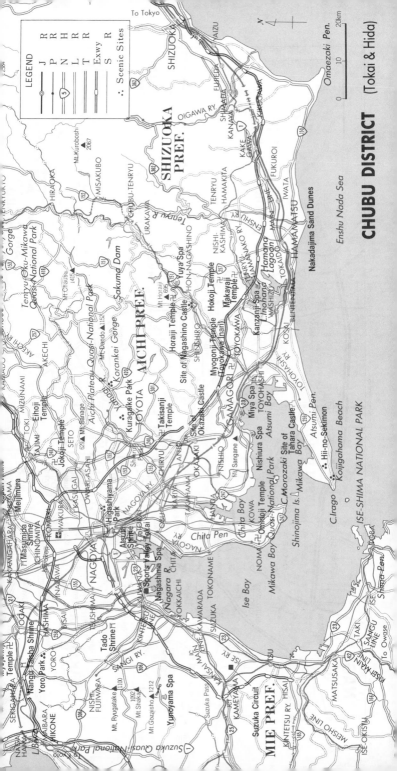

CHUBU DISTRICT (Tokai & Hida)

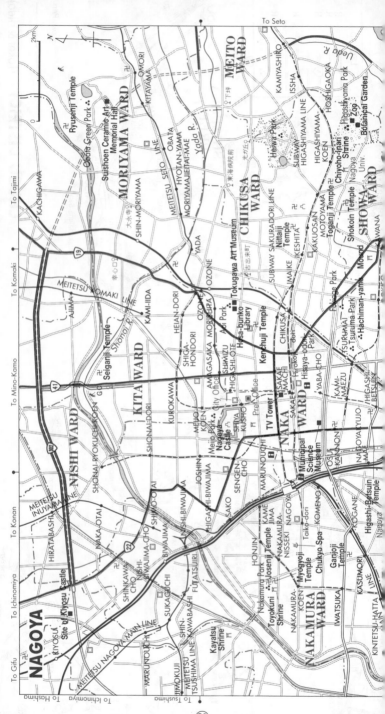

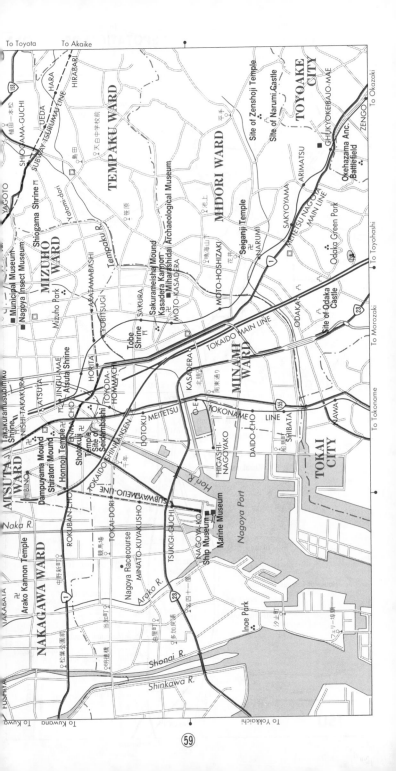

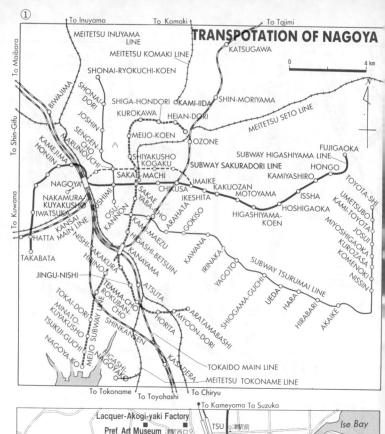

① TRANSPOTATION OF NAGOYA

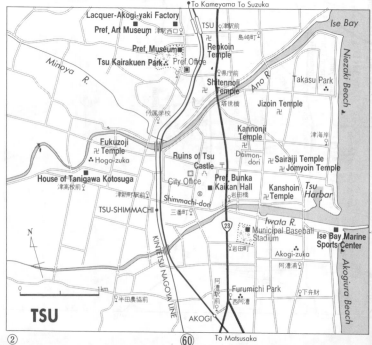

② TSU

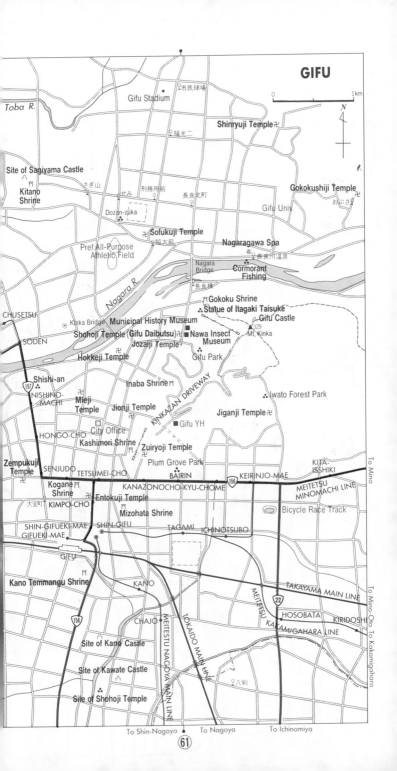

GIFU

Toba R.

Gifu Stadium

市民球場

Shinryuji Temple 卍

福光二

Site of Sagiyama Castle

Kitano Shrine

さぎ山

せみ

刑務所前

長良北町

Gokokushiji Temple

おぶさ

Gifu Univ

Dozan-zuka

Sofukuji Temple 卍

長大前

Nagaragawa Spa

長良川温泉

Pref All-Purpose Athletic Field

Nagara Bridge

Cormorant Fishing

Nagara R.

長良橋

Gokoku Shrine

Statue of Itagaki Taisuke

CHUSETSU

Kinka Bridge

Municipal History Museum

Gifu Castle

329

Mt. Kinka

SODEN

Shohoji Temple (Gifu Daibutsu) 卍

Nawa Insect Museum

Jozaiji Temple 卍

Hokkeji Temple

Gifu Park

Shishi-an

157

Inaba Shrine 卍

NISHINO-MACHI

Mieji Temple

Jionji Temple 卍

Iwato Forest Park

KINKAZAN DRIVEWAY

Jiganji Temple 卍

City Office

Gifu YH

HONGO-CHO

Kashimori Shrine

Zuiryoji Temple

Zempukuji Temple 卍

SENJUDO

Plum Grove Park

BAIRIN

KITA-ISSHIKI

Kogane Shrine

TETSUMEI-CHO

KANAZONOCHO KYU-CHOME

156

KEIRINJO-MAE

MEITETSU MINOMACHI LINE

Entokuji Temple

大宝町

KIMPO-CHO

Mizohata Shrine

Bicycle Race Track

SHIN-GIFUEKI-MAE

SHIN-GIFU

TAGAMI

ICHINOTSUBO

GIFUEKI-MAE

GIFU

To Mino

Kano Temmangu Shrine

KANO

TAKAYAMA MAIN LINE

MEITETSU

22

HOSOBATA

KIRIDOSHI

CHAJO

TOKAIDO MAIN LINE

KAKAMIGAHARA LINE

To Mino-Ota To Kakamigahara

MEITETSU NAGOYA MAIN LINE

Site of Kano Castle

Site of Kawate Castle

八剣

Site of Shohoji Temple

To Shin-Nagoya

To Nagoya

To Ichinomiya

61

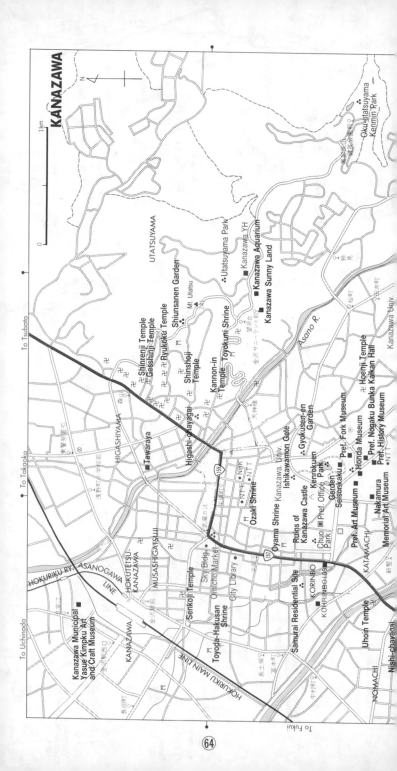

KANAZAWA

N

1km
0

To Tsubata
To Takaoka
To Uchinada
To Fukui

UTATSUYAMA

Oku-utatsuyama
Kenmin Park

Kanazawa YH
Utatsuyama Park
Kanazawa Aquarium
Kanazawa Sunny Land

Shinrenji Temple
Gesshinji Temple
Ryukoku Temple
Shiunsanen Garden
Mt. Utatsu
Shinshoji Temple
Kannon-in Temple
Toyokuni Shrine

Higashi-chayagai
Tawaraya

HIGASHIYAMA

Asano R.

Hoenji Temple
Kanazawa Univ.

Gyokusen-en Garden
Pref. Folk Museum
Honda Museum
Pref. Nogaku Bunka Kaikan Hall
Pref. History Museum

Kenrokuen Park
Ishikawamon Gate
Seisonkaku
Pref. Art Museum
Nakamura Memorial Art Museum

Oyama Shrine
Kanazawa Univ.
Ozaki Shrine
Ruins of Kanazawa Castle
Pref. Office
Chuo Park
KATAMACHI

HOKUTETSU KANAZAWA
MUSASHIGATSUJI
Sky Bldg.
Omicho Market
City Library
Senkoji Temple

HOKURIKU RY. ASANOGAWA LINE

KANAZAWA
Toyoda-Hakusan Shrine
HOKURIKU MAIN LINE

Kanazawa Municipal Yasue Kimpku Art and Craft Museum

Samurai Residential Site
KORINBO
Uhoin Temple
NOMACHI
Nishi-chayagai

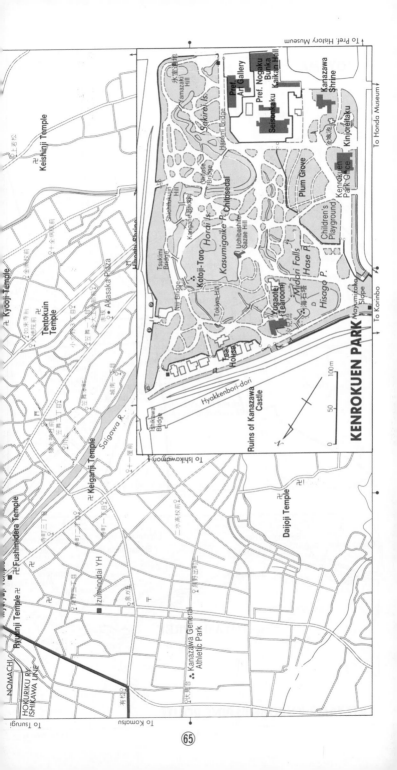

KENROKUEN PARK

To Pref. History Museum
To Honda Museum
To Korinbo
To Ishikawamon
To Shikawamon
To Komatsu
To Tsurugi

Keishiji Temple
Kyooji Temple
Tentokuin Temple
Akasaka Plaza
Hirooji Shrine
Saigawa R.
Izuminodai YH
Keiganji Temple
Fushimidera Temple
Ryuolji Temple
NOMACHI
HOKURIKU RY ISHIKAWA LINE
Kanazawa General Athletic Park
Daijoji Temple

Pref. Art Gallery
Pref. Nogaku Bunka Kaikan Hall
Seisonkaku
Kanazawa Shrine
Kinjoreitaku
Kenrokuen Park Office
Hase P.
Children's Playground
Plum Grove
Midori Falls
Hisago P.
Mayumizaka Slope
Kasumigaike P.
Chitosedai
Horai Is.
Kotoji-Toro
Uchibashitei
Sazae Hill
Yugaotei (Tearoom)
Tokiwa-taki
Niji Bridge
Tokiwa Hill
Tsukimi Bridge
Kangate Bridge
Shichifukujin Hill
Yamazaki Hill
Sekirei Is.
Hanami Bridge
Shiose Bridge

Hyakkenbori-dori
Ishikawa Bridge
Ruins of Kanazawa Castle

0 50 100m

N

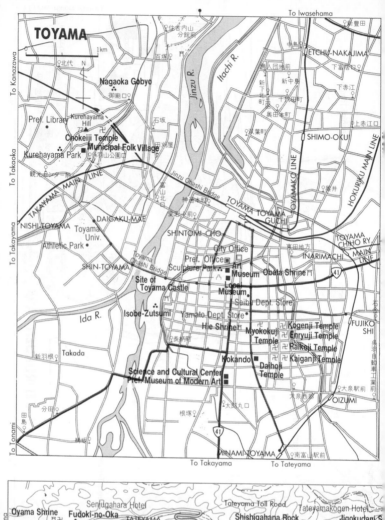

TOYAMA

1km

N

To Iwasehama
To Toyoda

ETCHU-NAKAJIMA

Jinzu R.
Itachi R.

Nagaoka Gobyo

Pref. Library

Kurehayama Hill

Chokeiji Temple

Municipal Folk Village

Kurehayama Park

To Kanazawa

To Takaoka

To Takayama

TAKAYAMA MAIN LINE

SHIMO-OKUI

HOKURIKU MAIN LINE

OYAMAKO LINE

Jinzu Ohashi Bridge

TOYAMA

TOYAMA GUCHI

DAIGAKU-MAE

NISHI-TOYAMA

Toyama Univ.

Athletic Park

SHIN-TOYAMA

Toyama Ohashi Bridge

SHINTOMI-CHO

City Office

Pref. Office

Sculpture Park

Art Museum

Obata Shrine

TOYAMA CHIHO RY. MAIN LINE

INARIMACHI

41

Site of Toyama Castle

Local Museum

Isobe-Zutsumi

Seibu Dept. Store

Yamato Dept. Store

Hie Shrine

Myokokuji Temple

Kogenji Temple

Enryuji Temple

Raikoji Temple

Kaiganji Temple

FUJIKOSHI

Ida R.

Takada

Kokando

Daihoji Temple

Science and Cultural Center
Pref. Museum of Modern Art

OIZUMI

41

MINAMI-TOYAMA

To Tonami

To Takayama
To Tateyama

TATEYAMA KUROBE ALPINE ROUTE

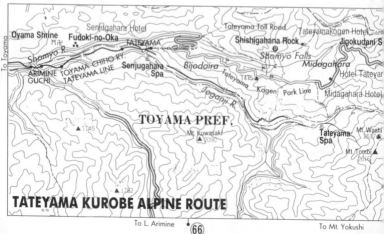

Oyama Shrine
Fudoki-no-Oka

Senjugahara Hotel

TATEYAMA

Tateyama Toll Road

Tateyamakogen Hotel

Shishigahara Rock

Jigokudani S

To Toyama

Shomyo R.

ARIMINE GUCHI

TOYAMA CHIHO RY. TATEYAMA LINE

Senjugahara Spa

Bijodaira

Shomyo Falls

Midagahara

Hotel Tateyar

Joganji R.

Tateyama Kogen Park Line

1415

Midagahara Hotel

TOYAMA PREF.

Mt. Kuwasaki

Tateyama Spa

Mt. Washi

Mt. Tombi

To L. Arimine

66

To Mt. Yokushi

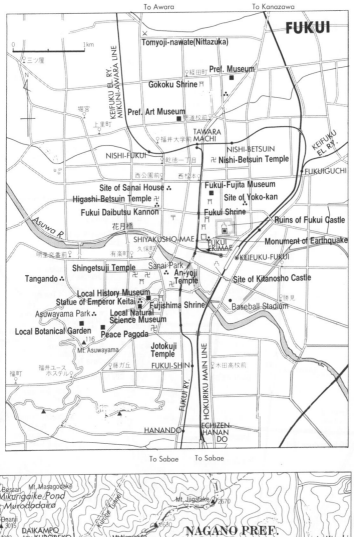
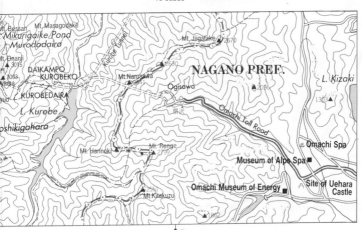

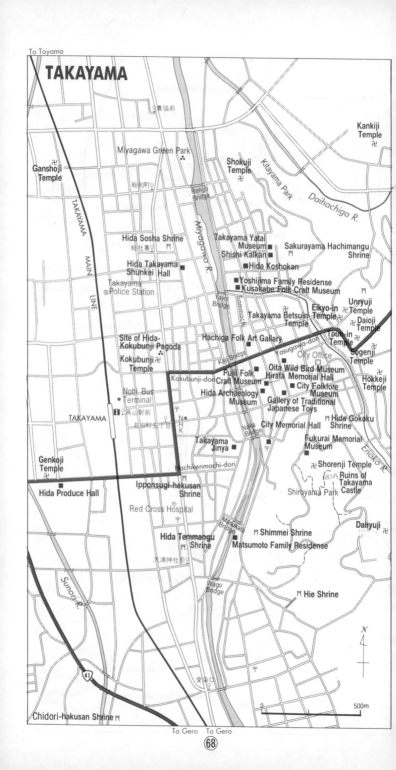

TAKAYAMA

To Toyama

Kankiji Temple 卍

Miyagawa Green Park

Shokuji Temple 卍

Kitayama Park

Daihachiga R.

Ganshoji Temple 卍

二鳥協前

総和町1丁

Rengi Bridge

Hida Sosha Shrine 卍

Takayama Yatai Museum
Shishi Kaikan ■

Sakurayama Hachimangu Shrine 卍

Hida Takayama Shunkei Hall

総社裏1丁

■ Hida Koshokan

Takayama ⊗Police Station

Takayama Police Station

Yoshijima Family Residense
Kusakabe Folk Craft Museum

Miyagawa R.

Unryuji Temple 卍

Eikyo-in Temple 卍 Daioji Temple 卍

Yayoi Bridge

Sammachi

Takayama Betsuin Temple

Toun-in Temple

Site of Hida-Kokubunji Pagoda

Hachiga Folk Art Gallary

Yasugawa-dori

Sogenji Temple 卍

Kokubunji Temple 卍

Kiji Bridge

City Office

Kokubunji-dori

Fujii Folk Craft Museum

Oita Wild Bird Museum
Hirata Memorial Hall

Hokkeji Temple 卍

Nohi Bus Terminal

高山駅前

Hida Archaeology Museum

City Folklore Museum

Gallery of Traditional Japanese Toys

Enoko R.

TAKAYAMA

谷田町五丁目

N•HK

City Memorial Hall

Hida Gokoku Shrine 卍

Takayama Jinya

Fukurai Memorial Museum

Genkoji Temple 卍

Nakae Bridge

Shorenji Temple 卍

Ruins of Takayama Castle

Hachikenmachi-dori

■ Hida Produce Hall

Ipponsugi-hakusan Shrine 卍

Shiroyama Park

Red Cross Hospital

Hida Temmangu Shrine

Masukata Bridge

Shimmei Shrine 卍

Daiyuji 卍

天満神社前

Matsumoto Family Residense

Sunori R.

Wago Bridge

Hie Shrine 卍

愛宕町口

N

41

〒

0   500m

Chidori-hakusan Shrine 卍

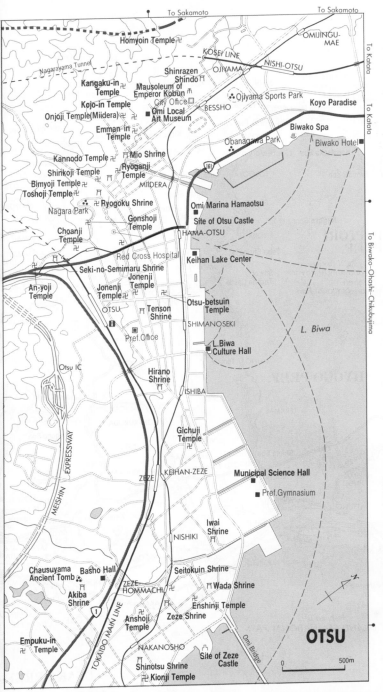

To Sakamoto
To Sakamoto

OMIJINGU-MAE

Homyoin Temple 卍
KOSEI LINE
OJIYAMA
NISHI-OTSU
To Katata

Nagarayama Tunnel
Shinrazen Shindo 卍

Kangaku-in Temple
Mausoleum of Emperor Kobun 卍
City Office 🏛
Ojiyama Sports Park
Koyo Paradise
To Katata

Kojo-in Temple
Omi Local Art Museum
BESSHO
Biwako Spa

Onjoji Temple(Miidera) 卍
Biwako Hotel ■

Emman-in Temple
Obanagawa Park

Kannodo Temple 卍
Mio Shrine
161

Shirikoji Temple 卍
Ryoganji Temple
Omi Marina Hamaotsu

Bimyoji Temple 卍
MIIDERA
Site of Otsu Castle

Toshoji Temple 卍
Ryogoku Shrine
HAMA-OTSU

Nagara Park
Gonshoji Temple

Choanji Temple 卍
Red Cross Hospital
Keihan Lake Center

Seki-no-Semimaru Shrine
Jonenji Temple

An-yoji Temple
Jonenji Temple
Otsu-betsuin Temple

OTSU 🏛
Tenson Shrine
SHIMANOSEKI
L. Biwa

Pref.Office
L.Biwa Culture Hall

Otsu IC
Hirano Shrine
ISHIBA

To Biwako-Ohashi-Chikubujima

Gichuji Temple

KEIHAN-ZEZE
Municipal Science Hall

ZEZE
Pref.Gymnasium

NISHIKI
Iwai Shrine

Chausuyama Ancient Tomb
Basho Hall
Seitokuin Shrine

Akiba Shrine
ZEZE-HOMMACHI
Wada Shrine

1
Enshinji Temple
Zeze Shrine

Anshoji Temple

Empuku-in Temple 卍
NAKANOSHO
Site of Zeze Castle

Shinotsu Shrine
Omi Bridge

Kionji Temple
OTSU

0   500m

MEISHIN EXPRESSWAY
TOKAIDO MAIN LINE

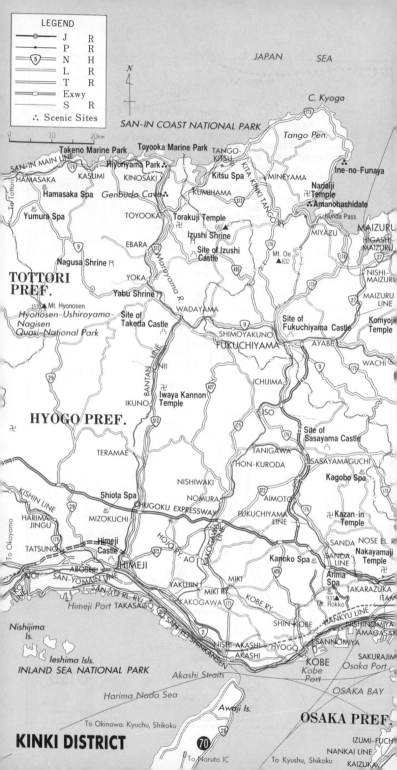

KINKI DISTRICT

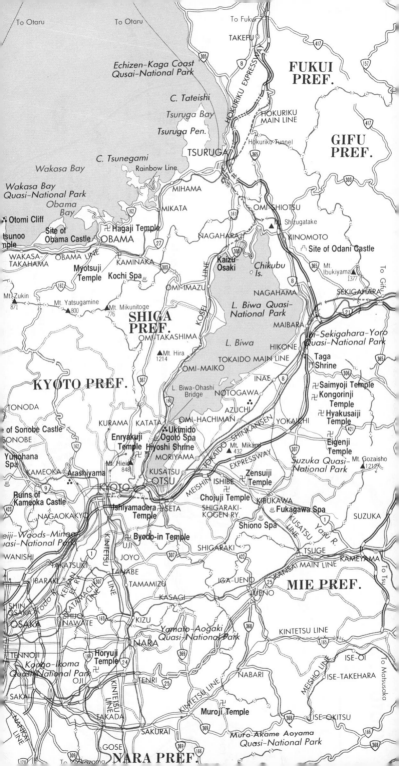

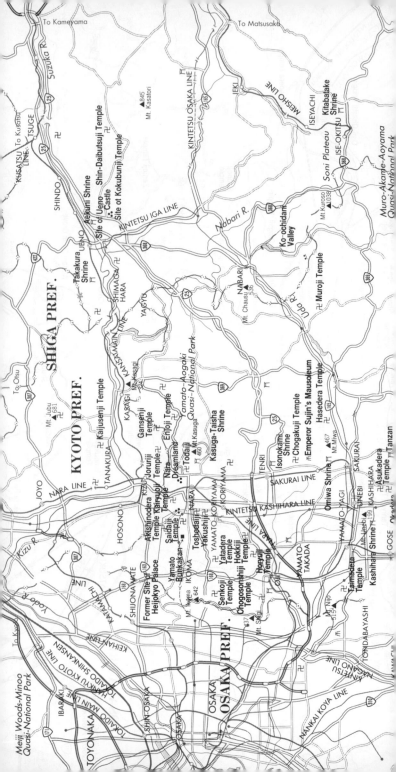

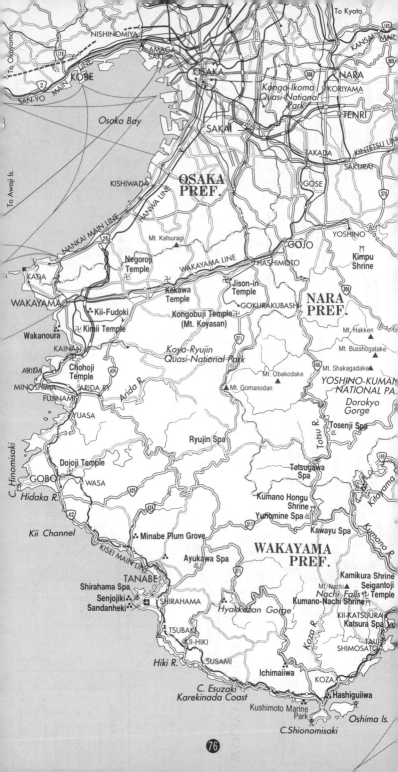

KII PENINSULA

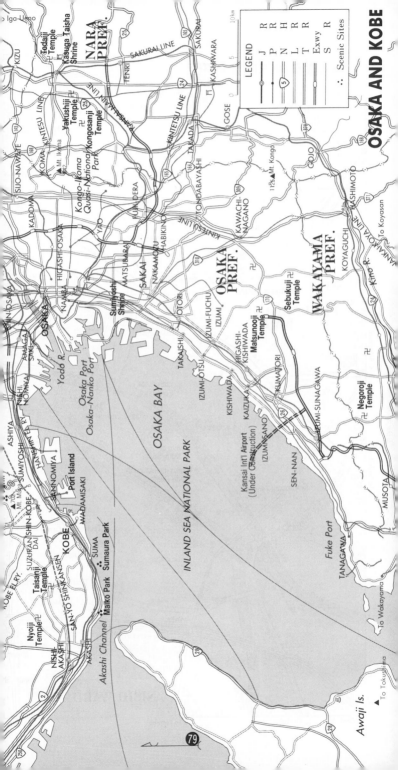

OSAKA AND KOBE

LEGEND

◉	J R
●	P R
	N H
	R
	L R
	T R
Exwy	
⑤	S R
∴	Scenic Sites

0   10km

NARA PREF.

OSAKA PREF.

OSAKA PREF.

WAKAYAMA PREF.

OSAKA BAY

INLAND SEA NATIONAL PARK

Osaka Port
Osaka-Nanko Port

Kansai Int'l Airport
(Under Construction)

KOBE

Port Island

Awaji Is.

To Tokushima

To Wakayama

To Koyasan

Todaiji Temple
Kasuga Taisha Shrine
Yakushiji Temple
Kongosanji Temple
Kongo-Ikoma Quasi-National Park
Mt. Ikoma
Mt. Kongo
Sumiyoshi Shrine
Sebukuji Temple
Matsunooji Temple
Negoroji Temple
Taisanji Temple
Nyoji Temple
Sumaura Park
Maiko Park
Mt. Maya
Mt. Rokko
Mt. Kabuto-san
Mt. Kongo

Yodo R.
Kino R.

Osaka Bay
Akashi Channel

KIZU
SUJO-NAWATE
KOMA
KADOMA
HIGASHI-OSAKA
NABA
SHIN-OSAKA
OSAKA
AMAGA-SAKI
NISHI-NOMIYA
ASHIYA
SUMIYOSHI
SHIN-KOBE
SANNOMIYA
WADAMISAKI
SUMA
SUZURAN-DAI
SAN-YO SHINKANSEN
NISHI-AKASHI
AKASHI
KOBE ELRY

IGA-UENO
TENRI
SAKURAI
KASHIHARA
TAKADA
GOSE
GOJO
KASHIMOTO
KOYAGUCHI
TONDABAYASHI
KAWACHI-NAGANO
FUJIIDERA
YAO
NAKAMOZU
MATSUBARA
HABIKINO
SAKAI
OTORI
IZUMI-FUCHU
IZUMI
HIGASHI-KISHIWADA
KISHIWADA
KAIZUKA
KUMATORI
IZUMISANO
SEN-NAN
IZUMI-SUNAGAWA
TANAGAWA
MUSOTA
TAKASHI
IZUMI-OTSU
Fuke Port
Nanko Port

SAKURAI LINE
KINTETSU LINE
KINTETSU LINE
NANKAI LINE
HANSHIN ELRY
NANKAIKOYA LINE

79

OSAKA (NORTH QUARTER)

Shin-Yodo R.

Nanban Bunkakan Hall

D.D House

Hankyu Terminal Bldg

Urae Park

Osaka Tower

The Symphony Hall

Acty Osaka

Hilton Plaza

Shogi Museum

NISHI-UMEDA

Osaka Maru Bldg

Ryotokuin Temple

FUKUSHIMA
WARD

FUKUSHIMA

Sonezaki-Shi

HANSHIN-NODA

FUKUSHIMA

Birth Place of
Fukuzawa Yukichi

Pref.
Modern Art
Center

Osaka Univ.

HIGOBASHI

Site of
Kurayashiki

NO DA

Osaka International
Trade Center

Gokurakuji Temple

Osaka Science
Technology Center

Utsubo Park

Kita-

HOMMACHI

Aji R.

AWAZA

Chuo-dori

Ikasuri Shrine
Minami

HANSHIN EXPRESSWAY HIGASHI-OSAKA LINE

Namba Sh

NISHI WARD

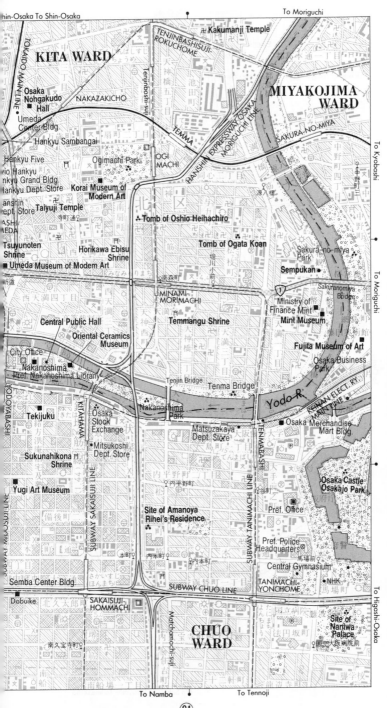

To Moriguchi

Shin-Osaka To Shin-Osaka

KITA WARD

Kakumanji Temple

TENJINBASHISUJI-
ROKUCHOME

**MIYAKOJIMA
WARD**

NAKAZAKICHO

Osaka
Nohgakudo
Hall

Umeda
Center Bldg.

SAKURA-NO-MIYA

TEMMA

Hankyu Sambangai

To Kyobashi

Ogimachi Park

OGI
MACHI

Hankyu Five

io Hankyu
nkyu Grand Bldg.
Hankyu Dept. Store

Korai Museum of
Modern Art

anshin
ept Store Taiyuji Temple

Tomb of Oshio Heihachiro

ASHI
EDA

Tomb of Ogata Koan

Sakura-no-miya
Park

Tsuyunoten
Shrine

Horikawa Ebisu
Shrine

Sempukan

To Moriguchi

Umeda Museum of Modern Art

UMINAMI-
MORIMACHI

Ministry of
Finance Mint

Sakuranomiya
Bridge

Central Public Hall

Temmangu Shrine

Mint Museum

Oriental Ceramics
Museum

City Office

Fujita Museum of Art

Nakanoshima
Pref. Nakanoshima Library

Osaka Business
Park

KITAHAMA

Tenjin Bridge   Tenma Bridge

Yodo R.

YODOYABASHI

Tekijuku

Osaka
Stock
Exchange

Nakanoshima
Park

Osaka Merchandise
Mart Bldg.

KEIHAN ELECT. RY.
MAIN LINE

Sukunahikona
Shrine

Mitsukoshi
Dept. Store

Matsuzakaya
Dept. Store

SUBWAY SAKAISUJI LINE

Osaka Castle
Osakajo Park

Yugi Art Museum

SUBWAY TANIMACHI LINE

Site of Amanoya
Rihei's Residence

Pref. Office

Pref. Police
Headquarters

To Higashi-Osaka

Semba Center Bldg.

Central Gymnasium

TANIMACHI-
YONCHOME

NHK

SUBWAY CHUO LINE

Dobuike

SAKAISUJI-
HOMMACHI

Site of
Naniwa
Palace

Matsomachi-suji

**CHUO
WARD**

南久宝寺町

To Namba   To Tennoji

(81)

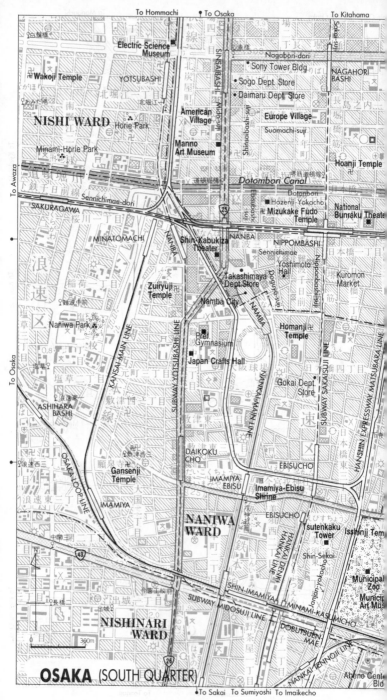

Electric Science Museum

卍 Wakoji Temple

YOTSUBASHI

Nagabori-dori

Sony Tower Bldg.
Sogo Dept. Store
Daimaru Dept. Store

NAGAHORI BASHI

NISHI WARD

Horie Park

American Village

Europe Village

Suomachi-suji

Minami-Horie Park

Manno Art Museum

Hoanji Temple 卍

Dotombori Canal

Dotonbori

SAKURAGAWA

Sennichimae-dori

Hozenji-Yokocho

National Bunraku Theatre

Mizukake Fudo Temple

To Awaza

To Osaka

MINATOMACHI

NANBA

Shin-Kabukiza Theater

NANBA

NIPPOMBASHI

Sennichimae

Kuromon Market

Yoshimoto Hall

Zuiryuji Temple

Takashimaya Dept. Store

Namba City

NANBA

Homanji Temple 卍

Naniwa Park

Pref. Gymnasium

Japan Crafts Hall

Gokai Dept. Store

ASHIHARA BASHI

DAIKOKU CHO

IMAMIYA-EBISU

EBISUCHO

Gansenji Temple

Imamiya-Ebisu Shrine

IMAMIYA

NANIWA WARD

EBISUCHO

Tsutenkaku Tower

Isshinji Tem

Shin-Sekai

Municipal Zoo

Municipal Art Mus

NISHINARI WARD

SHIN-IMAMIYA

MINAMI-KASUMICHO

DOBUTSUEN MAE

Abeno Cent Bld

OSAKA (SOUTH QUARTER)

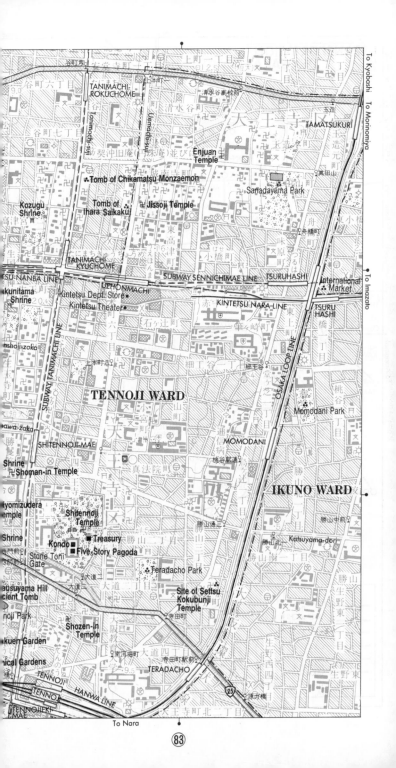

To Kyobashi

To Momomiya

TANIMACHI-
ROKUCHOME

TAMATSUKURI

清水谷高校前

清水谷町

谷町六丁目

上町一丁目

上本町2.5

玉造

真田山

Énjuan
Temple

■·Tomb of Chikamatsu Monzaemon

Sanadayama Park

谷町七丁目

Tanimachi-suji

Uemachisuji

契沖由庵(契冲庵)並び

Kozugu
Shrine

Tomb of
Ihara Saikaku

·Jissoji Temple

2舟橋町

東高津町

小橋町

To Imazato

TANIMACHI
KYUCHOME

SUBWAY SENNICHIMAE LINE

TSURUHASHI

International
Market

SU-NANBA LINE

UEHONMACHI

石ヶ辻町

KINTETSU NARA LINE

TSURU
HASHI

kunitama
Shrine

Kintetsu Dept.
Store

Kintetsu Theater·

赤

東上

OSAKA LOOP LINE

桃谷

nshojizoka

SUBWAY TANIMACHI LINE

本町3

細工谷

堀越町

Momodani Park

TENNOJI WARD

真法院町

MOMODANI

桃谷駅通2

awa-zaka

SHITENNOJI-MAE

勝山通2

IKUNO WARD

Shrine
■·Shoman-in Temple

勝山中町2

yomizudera
emple

Shitennoji
Temple

Katsuyama-dori

Shrine

Kondo ■ ■·Treasury
■·Five-Story Pagoda

勝山一丁目

勝山

Stone Torii
Gate

大道二

·Teradacho Park

生野西

atsuyama Hill
cient Tomb

·Site of Settsu
Kokubunji
Temple

noji Park

Shozen-in
Temple

 kuen Garden

nical Gardens

TENNOJI

勝山生野東

HANWA LINE

2南河場町

大道 四丁目

寺田町駅前2

TERADACHO

源ヶ橋

25

天王寺町北一丁目

TENNOJI
EKI
MAE

To Nara

㊂

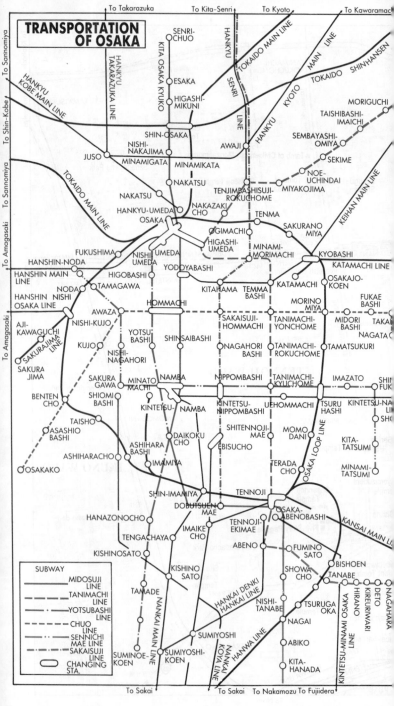

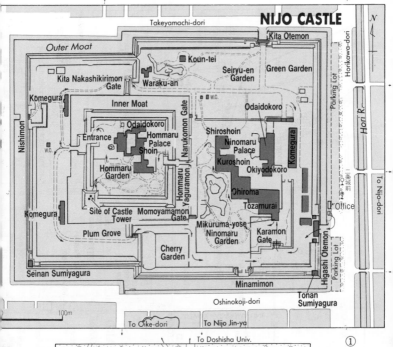

NIJO CASTLE

Takeyamachi-dori

Outer Moat

Kita Otemon

Horikawa-dori

Hori R.

N

Koun-tei

Seiryu-en Garden

Green Garden

Parking Lot

Kita Nakashikirimon Gate

Waraku-an

Komegura

Inner Moat

W.C.

Odaidokoro

W.C.

Nishimon

Entrance

Odaidokoro

Hommaru Palace Shoin

Narukomon Gate

Shiroshoin

Ninomaru Palace

Kuroshoin

Odaidokoro

Komegura

Hommaru Garden

Okiyodokoro

To Nijo-dori

Hommaru Yaguramon

Komegura

Site of Castle Tower

Momoyamamon Gate

Ohiroma

Tozamurai

Office

Plum Grove

Mikuruma-yose Ninomaru Garden

Karamon Gate

Higashi Otemon

Parking Lot

Seinan Sumiyagura

Cherry Garden

Minamimon

Tonan Sumiyagura

Oshinokoji-dori

100m

To Oike-dori

To Nijo Jin-ya

①

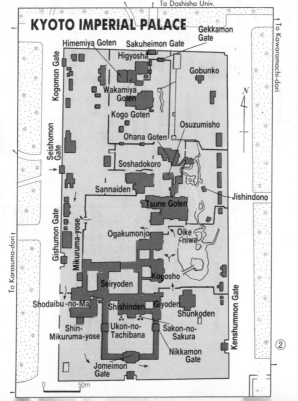

To Doshisha Univ.

KYOTO IMPERIAL PALACE

Gekkamon Gate

To Kawaramachi-dori

Himemiya Goten

Sakuheimon Gate

Higyosha

Kogomon Gate

Gobunko

Wakamiya Goten

N

Kogo Goten

Seishomon Gate

Ohana Goten

Osuzumisho

Soshadokoro

To Karasuma-dori

Sannaiden

Tsune Goten

Jishindono

Gishumon Gate

Mikuruma-yose

Ogakumonjo

Oike-niwa

Seiryoden

Kogosho

Shodaibu-no-Ma

Shishinden

Giyoden

Shunkoden

Kenshummon Gate

Shin-Mikuruma-yose

Ukon-no-Tachibana

Sakon-no-Sakura

Jomeimon Gate

Nikkamon Gate

0   50m

②

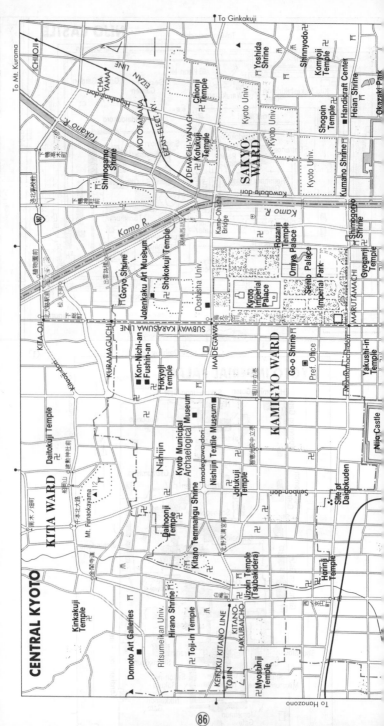

CENTRAL KYOTO

To Mt. Kurama

To Ginkakuji

KITA WARD

SAKYO WARD

KAMIGYO WARD

Kinkakuji Temple

Domoto Art Galleries

Daitokuji Temple

Ritsumeikan Univ.

Hirano Shrine

Toji-in Temple

KERFUKU KITANO LINE

TOJIIN

KITANO-HAKUBAICHO

Myoshinji Temple

Uizoin Temple (Tsubakidera)

Kitano Temmangu Shrine

Daihoonji Temple

Nishijin

Mt. Funaokayama

▲112

Kyoto Municipal Archaeological Museum

Nishijin Textile Museum

Imadegawa-dori

Jofukuji Temple

Horinji Temple

Site of Daigokuden

Senbon-dori

Nijo Castle

Hokyoji Temple

Kon-Nichi-an
Fushin-an

KURAMAGUCHI

KITA-OJI

SUBWAY KARASUMA LINE

Goryo Shrine

Jotenkaku Art Museum

Shokokuji Temple

Doshisha Univ.

Shimogamo Shrine

Takano R.

Kamo R.

EIZAN LINE

ICHIJOJI

CHA-YAMA

Higashioji-dori

MOTOTANAKA

EIZAN ELECT. RY.

DEMACHI-YANAGI

Kofukuji Temple

Chionji Temple

Yoshida Shrine

Shinnyodo

Komyoji Temple

Kyoto Univ.

Kyoto Univ.

Kyoto Univ.

Handicraft Center

Shogoin Temple

Kumano Shrine

Helan Shrine

Okazaki Park

Kawabata-dori

Kamo-Ohashi Bridge

Rozanji Temple

Omya Palace

Sento Palace

Imperial Park

Shimogoyo Shrine

Gyoganji Temple

MARUTAMACHI

Kyoto Imperial Palace

Go-o Shrine

Pref. Office

Yakushi-in Temple

Kitaotachiuri-dori

Omiyadori

Kamidachiuri-dori

Nakadachiuri-dori

To Hanazono

86

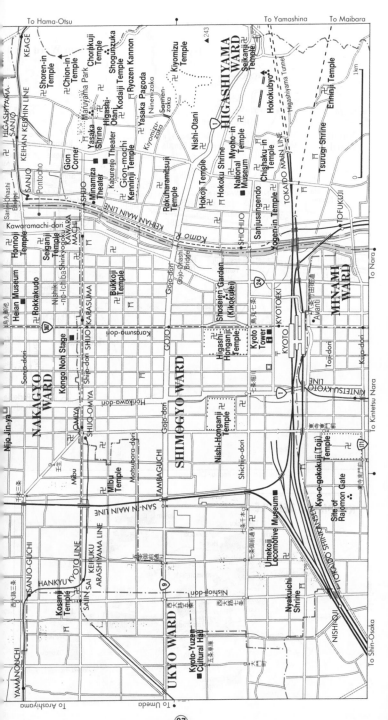

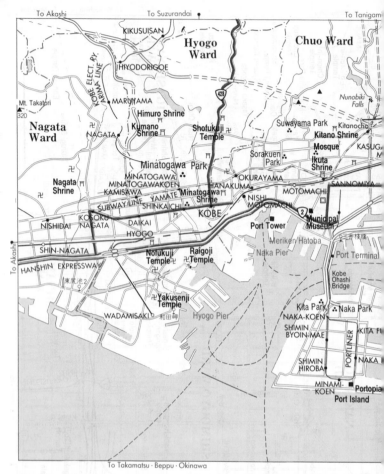

To Akashi
To Suzurandai
To Tanigam

KIKUSUISAN

Hyogo Ward

Chuo Ward

HYODORIGOE

KOBE ELECT. RY. ARIMA LINE

MARUYAMA

Himuro Shrine

Nunobiki Falls

Mt. Takatori
320

Nagata Ward

NAGATA

Kumano Shrine

Shofukuji Temple

Suwayama Park

Kitanocho

Kitano Shrine

Mosque

KASUGA

Sorakuen Park

Ikuta Shrine

Minatogawa Park

MINATOGAWA
MINATOGAWAKOEN
KAMISAWA

OKURAYAMA

HANAKUMA

MOTOMACHI

SANNOMIYA

Nagata Shrine

Minatogawa Shrine

NISHI MOTOMACHI

SUBWAY LINE
YAMATE
SHINKAICHI

KOBE

Municipal Museum

KOSOKU
NISHIDAI
NAGATA

DAIKAI

HYOGO

Port Tower

NoFukuji Temple

Raigoji Temple

Meriken/Hatoba
Naka Pier

SHIN-NAGATA

HANSHIN EXPRESSWAY

To Akashi

Port Terminal

Kobe Ohashi Bridge

Yakusenji Temple

WADAMISAKI

Hyogo Pier

Kita Park
Naka Park

NAKA-KOEN

SHIMIN BYOIN-MAE

KITA FU

SHIMIN HIROBA

PORTLINER

NAKA

MINAMI-KOEN

Portopia
Port Island

To Takamatsu · Beppu · Okinawa

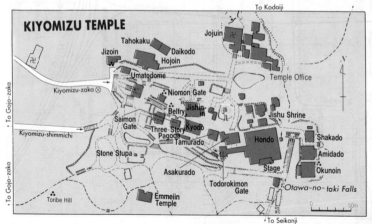

KIYOMIZU TEMPLE

To Kodaiji

Tahokaku

Jojuin

Jizoin

Daikodo

Hojoin

Temple Office

N

Umatodome

Kiyomizu-zaka ⊗

To Gojo-zaka

Niomon Gate

Belfry

Jishin in

Jishu Shrine

Saimon Gate

Three-Story Pagoda

Kyodo

Kiyomizu-shimmichi

Tamurado

Hondo

Shakado

Stone Stupa

Asakurado

Amidado

To Gojo-zaka

Stage

Okunoin

Todorokimon Gate

Otawa-no-taki Falls

Emmeiin Temple

Toribe Hill

0   50m

To Seikanji

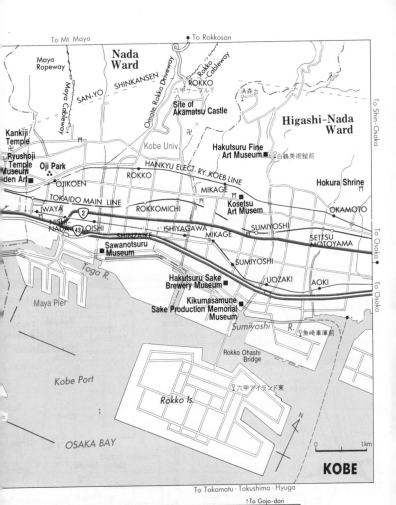

KOBE map

To Mt. Maya
To Rokkosan

Nada Ward

Maya Ropeway

SHINKANSEN
SAN-YO

Omote Rokko Driveway

ROKKO
Rokko Cableway
六甲ケーブル下
湯森台

Site of Akamatsu Castle

Higashi-Nada Ward

Kobe Univ.
卍

Kankiji Temple
Ryushoji Temple Museum den Art

Oji Park

OJIKOEN

Hakutsuru Fine Art Museum
白鶴美術館前

Hokura Shrine

HANKYU ELECT. RY. KOEB LINE
ROKKO

MIKAGE

TOKAIDO MAIN LINE

ROKKOMICHI

Kosetsu Art Musem

OKAMOTO

IWAYA
NISHI NADA
2
43
OISHI
SHINZAIKE
ISHIYAGAWA
MIKAGE
SUMIYOSHI

SETTSU MOTOYAMA

Sawanotsuru Museum

SUMIYOSHI

Toga R.

Maya Pier

Hakutsuru Sake Brewery Museum

UOZAKI
AOKI

Kikumasamune Sake Production Memorial Museum

Sumiyoshi R.
魚崎車庫前

Rokko Ohashi Bridge

Kobe Port

Rokko Is.

六甲アイランド東

OSAKA BAY

To Shin-Osaka
To Osaka
To Osaka

N

0 — 1km

KOBE

To Takamatu · Tokushima · Hyuga

NISHI-HONGANJI TEMPLE

To Gojo-dori

Koro

To Shimabara

Tearoom

Hyakka Pond

Sutra Library

Amidado (Main Hall)

Amidado Gate

Horikawa Canal

To Higashi-Honganji

N

North Noh Stage
Kuroshoin

Shiro Shoin

Goeido (Daishido)

Goeido Gate

Kokei Garden

Tekisuien

Horikawa-dori

Temple Office

South Noh Stage

Kokaku dai
Hiunkaku

Koshoji Temple

Karamon Gate

0 — 100m

To Omiya-dori
To Shichijo-dori

89

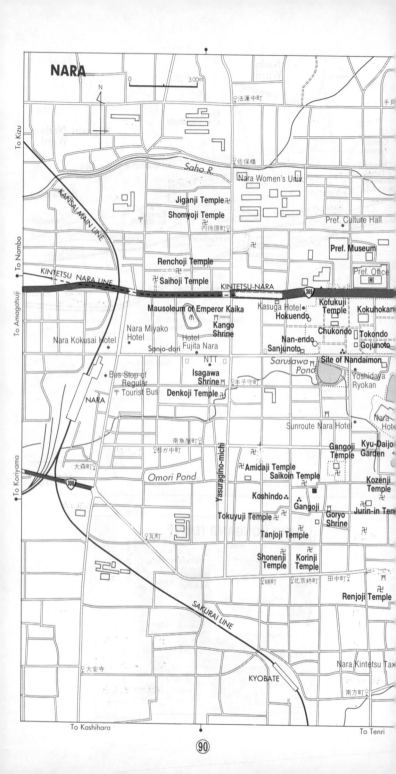

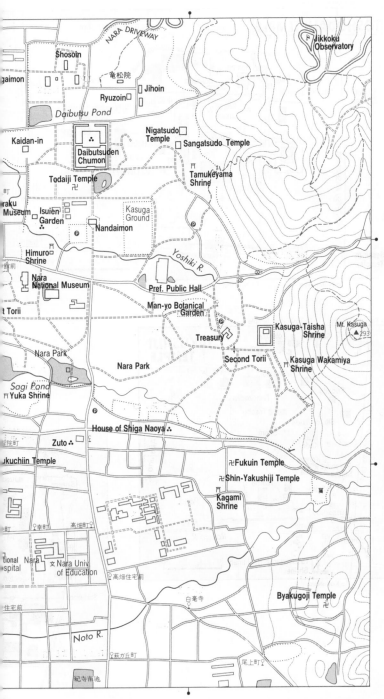

Jikkoku Observatory

NARA DRIVEWAY

Shosoin

竜松院

Ryuzoin

Jihoin

~gaimon

Daibutsu Pond

Kaidan-in

Nigatsudo Temple

Sangatsudo Temple

Daibutsuden Chumon

Tamukeyama Shrine

Todaiji Temple 卍

~raku Museum

Isuien Garden

Kasuga Ground

Nandaimon

Himuro Shrine

間門

Nara National Museum

Yoshiki R.

Pref. Public Hall

~t Torii

Man-yo Botanical Garden

Kasuga-Taisha Shrine

Mt. Kasuga ▲293

Treasury

Second Torii

Kasuga Wakamiya Shrine

Nara Park

Nara Park

Sagi Pond

Yuka Shrine

House of Shiga Naoya ∴

Zuto ∴

~kuchiin Temple

卍 Fukuin Temple

卍 Shin-Yakushiji Temple

Kagami Shrine

院町

幸町

高畑町

~tional Nara ~spital

文 Nara Univ of Education

高畑住宅前

白毫寺

住宅前

Byakugoji Temple 卍

Noto R.

萩ガ丘町

尾上町

紀寺画池

TOSHODAIJI TEMPLE

To Yamato-Saidaiji

Ganjinwajo Gobyo

N

Mieido

Hombo

Daigoi

Jizodo

Site of Kaizando

Kyu-Kaizando

Kaigakuln

Site of Saimon

Site of Jikido

Higashi-muro
Treasure House

Kaidan

Kodo

↑Koro

Raido

Sakai Pond

Shoro

Kondo

Sutra Library

KINTETSU KASHIHARA LINE

W.C.

Akishino R.

Munizoin

Temple Office

♨

Seson-in Temple

←

極楽橋

Nandaimon

0   50   100 m

↓

To Nishinokyo   To Yakushiji Temple

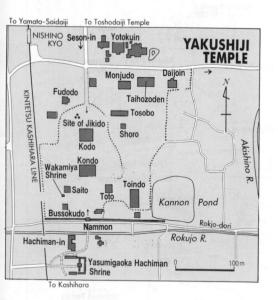

To Yamato-Saidaiji   To Toshodaiji Temple

NISHINO KYO   Seson-in   Yotokuin

↓

YAKUSHIJI TEMPLE

Monjudo   Daijoin   →

Fudodo

Taihozoden

N

Site of Jikido

Tosobo

Kodo

Shoro

Akishino R.

Kondo

Wakamiya Shrine

Saito

Toindo

KINTETSU KASHIHARA LINE

Toto

Kannon Pond

Bussokudo ↑

Nammon

Rokjo-dori

Hachiman-in

Rokujo R.

Yasumigaoka Hachiman Shrine

0   100 m

To Kashihara

Yakushibo

Saiendo

Jizo

Sut Lib

Nishimuro

Goji Sangyoin

Hojuin

Chuin

Benter Pond

Saidaimon

Oyuya

♨

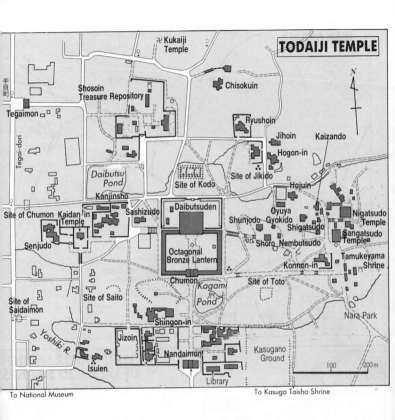

TODAIJI TEMPLE

Kukaiji Temple

Chisokuin

Shosoin Treasure Repository

Tegaimon

Tegai-dori

Ryushoin

Jihoin

Kaizando

Hogon-in

Site of Jikido

Hojuin

Daibutsu Pond

Site of Kodo

Kanjinsho

Oyuya

Nigatsudo Temple

Sashizudo

Daibutsuden

Shunjodo

Gyokido

Shigatsudo

Sangatsudo Temple

Site of Chumon

Kaidan-in Temple

Shunjodo

Shoro

Nembutsudo

Senjudo

Octagonal Bronze Lantern

Tamukeyama Shrine

Konnon-in

Chumon

Kagami Pond

Site of Toto

Site of Saidaimon

Site of Saito

Yoshiki R.

Shingon-in

Nara Park

Jizoin

Nandaimon

Kasugano Ground

Isuien

Library

100   200 m

To National Museum

To Kasuga Taisha Shrine

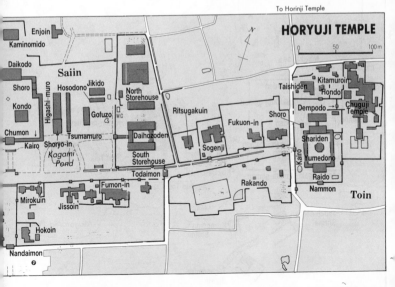

To Horinji Temple

HORYUJI TEMPLE

Enjoin

Kaminomido

Daikodo

Saiin

50   100 m

Shoro

Kondo

Higashi-muro

Hosodono

Jikido

North Storehouse

Taishiden

Kitamuroin

Hondo

Chumon

Gofuzo

WC

Ritsugakuin

Dempodo

Chuguji Temple

Kairo

Tsumamuro

Fukuon-in

Shoro

Shoryo-in

Daihozoden

Shariden

Kagami Pond

South Storehouse

Sogenji

Kairo

Yumedono

Todaimon

Raido

Mirokuin

Fumon-in

Rakando

Nammon

Jissoin

Toin

Hokoin

Nandaimon

⑬

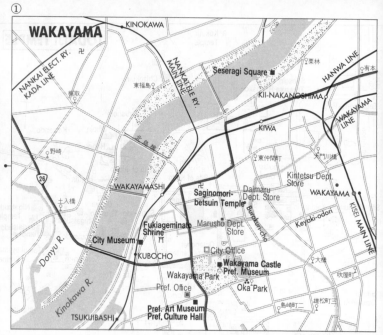

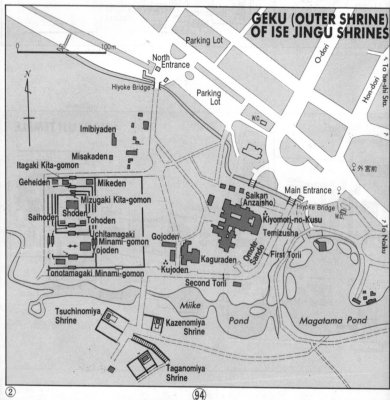

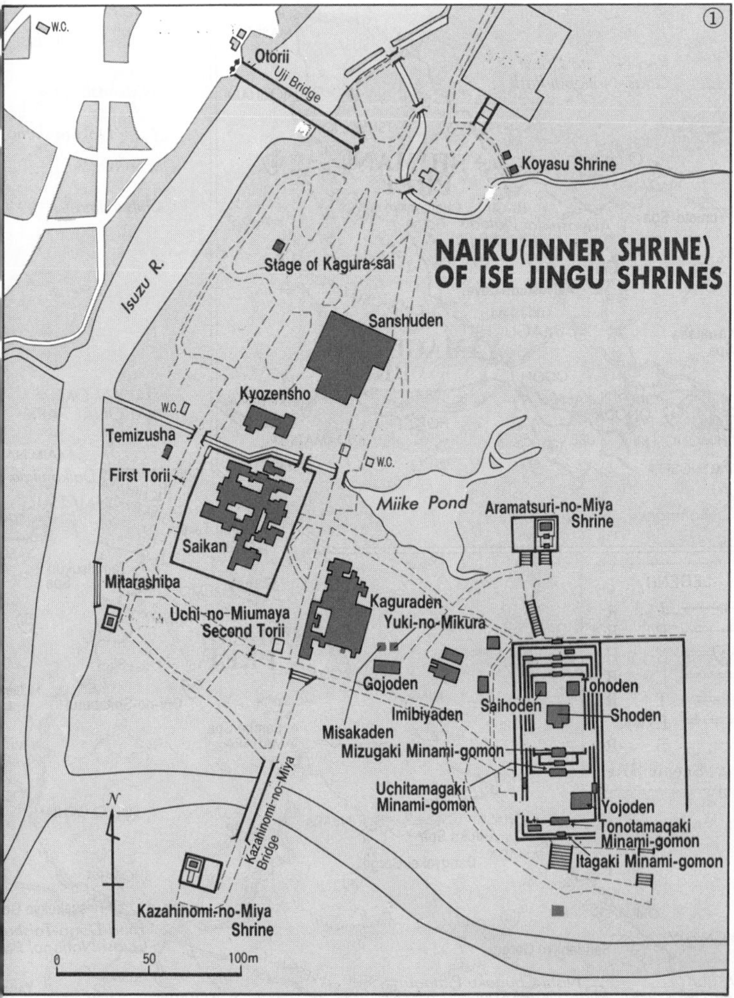
①
NAIKU(INNER SHRINE) OF ISE JINGU SHRINES
W.C.
Otorii
Uji Bridge
Koyasu Shrine
Isuzu R.
Stage of Kagura-sai
Sanshuden
Kyozensho
W.C.
Temizusha
W.C.
First Torii
Miike Pond
Aramatsuri-no-Miya Shrine
Saikan
Mitarashiba
Kaguraden
Uchi-no-Miumaya
Second Torii
Yuki-no-Mikura
Gojoden
Tohoden
Saihoden
Shoden
Imibiyaden
Misakaden
Mizugaki Minami-gomon
Uchitamagaki Minami-gomon
Yojoden
Tonotamaqaki Minami-gomon
Itagaki Minami-gomon
Kazahinomi-no-Miya Bridge
Kazahinomi-no-Miya Shrine
N
0
50
100m

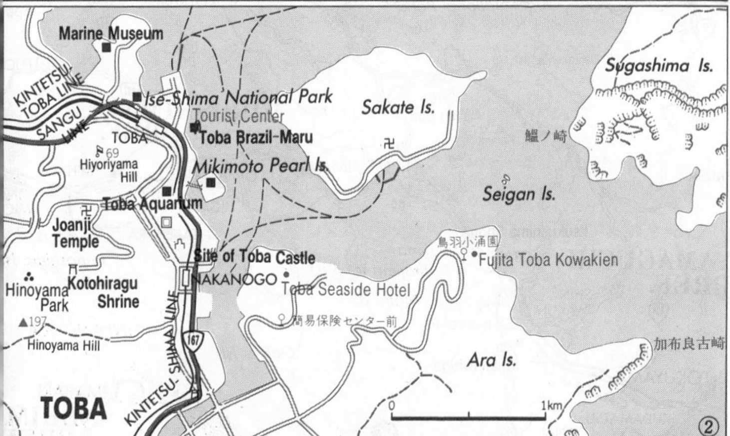
Marine Museum
KINTETSU-TOBA LINE
SANGU LINE
Ise-Shima National Park
Tourist Center
Toba Brazil-Maru
TOBA
69
Hiyoriyama Hill
Mikimoto Pearl Is.
Toba Aquarium
Joanji Temple
Site of Toba Castle
NAKANOGO
Hinoyama Park
Kotohiragu Shrine
197
Hinoyama Hill
167
KINTETSU-SHIMA LINE
TOBA
Sakate Is.
Sugashima Is.
鳳ノ崎
Seigan Is.
鳥羽小涌園
Fujita Toba Kowakien
Toba Seaside Hotel
商易保険センター前
加布良古崎
Ara Is.
0
1km
②

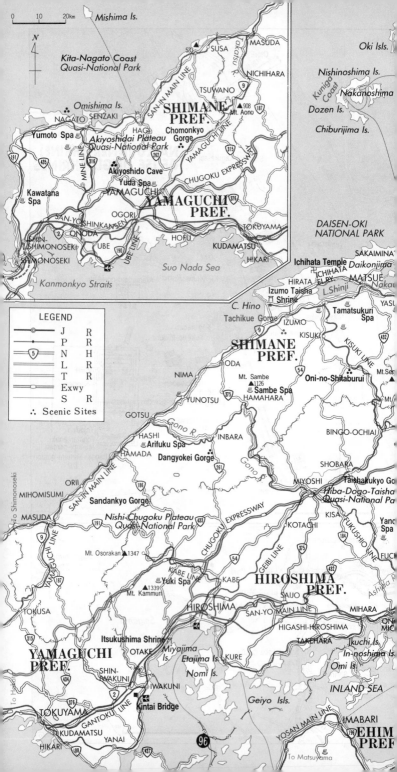

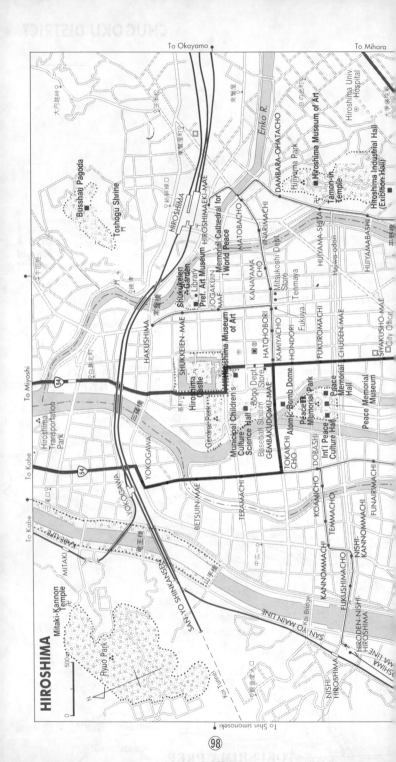

HIROSHIMA

Mitaki-Kannon Temple

Mitaki

Ryuo Park

500m

To Kabe

To Kabe

To Miyoshi

To Kabe

54

54

Hiroshima Transportation Park

YOKOGAWA

YOKOGAWA

BETSUIN-MAE

TERAMACHI

KANNONMACHI

NISHI-KANNONMACHI

FUKUSHIMACHO

NISHI-KANNONMACHI

FUKUSHIMA-NISHI-HIROSHIMA

HIRODEN-NISHI-HIROSHIMA

KANNONMACHI

FUNAIRIMACHI

SAN-YO SHINKANSEN

KABE LINE

MITAKI

SAN-YO MAIN LINE

Kai Bridge

To Shin simonoseki

Busshari Pagoda

Toshogu Shrine

HIROSHIMA

HAKUSHIMA

SHUKKEIEN-MAE

Shukkeien Garden

Library
Pref. Art Museum

JOGAKUIN-MAE

Memorial Cathedral for World Peace

HIROSHIMA-EKI-MAE

MATOBACHO

KANAYAMA-CHO

UNARIMACHI

Mitsukoshi Dept. Store

Tenmaya

Fukuya

KAMIYACHO

HATCHOBORI

HONDORI

FUKUROMACHI

CHUDEN-MAE

SHAKUSHO-MAE

City Office

Enko R.

To Okayama

To Mihara

Hiroshima Univ Hospital

DAMBARA-OHATACHO

Hijiyama Park

Hiroshima Museum of Art

Tamon-in Temple

Hiroshima Industrial Hall (Exhibition Hall)

HIJIYAMA-SHITA

HIJIYAMA-MAE

Hijiyama-dori

HIJIYAMABASHI

Hiroshima Museum of Art

SHUKKEIEN-MAE

Hiroshima Castle

Central Park

Municipal Children's Culture Science Hall

Baseball Stadium

GEMBAKUDOMU-MAE

Bogo Dept. Store

TOKAICHI-MACHI

Atomic-Bomb Dome

DOBASHI

Peace Memorial Park

Peace Memorial Hall

Peace Memorial Museum

Int'l Peace Culture Hall

KOAMICHO

TEMMACHO

N

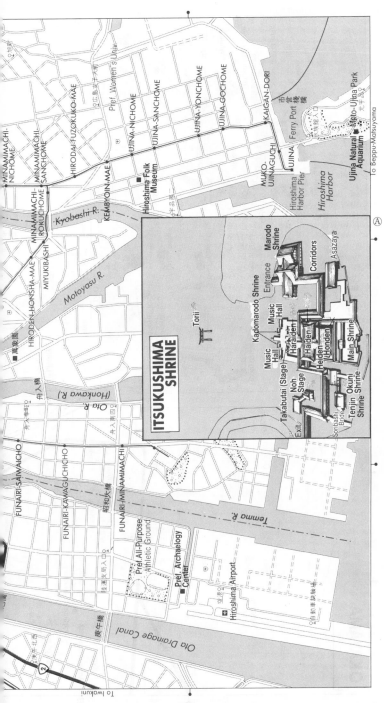

ITSUKUSHIMA SHRINE

Torii ⛩

Kadomarodo Shrine
Marodo Shrine
Music Hall
Entrance
Corridors
Asazaya
Music Hall
Takabutai (Stage)
Noh Stage
Haraiden
Haiden
Heiden
Honden
Main Shrine
Exit
Tenjin Shrine
Okuni Shrine
Sorihashi Bridge

(A)

MINAMIMACHI-NICHOME
MINAMIMACHI-SANCHOME
MINAMIMACHI-ROKUCHOME
HIRODEN-HONSHA-MAE
MIYUKIBASHI
Kyobashi R.
KEMBYOIN-MAE
HIRODA-FUZOKUKO-MAE
UJINA-NICHOME
Pref. Women's Univ.
UJINA-SANCHOME
UJINA-YONCHOME
UJINA-GOCHOME
KAIGAN-DORI
MUKO-UJINAGUCHI
UJINA
Hiroshima Folk Museum
Motoyasu R.
Ota R. (Honkawa R.)
FUNAIRI-SAIWAICHO
FUNAIRI-KAMAGUCHICHO
FUNAIRI-MINAMIMACHI
Temma R.
Ota Drainage Canal
Pref. All-Purpose Athletic Ground
Pref. Archaeology Center
Hiroshima Airport
Hiroshima Harbor Pier
Hiroshima Harbor
Ferry Port Pier
Ujina Natural Aquarium
Moto-Ujina Park

To Iwakuni
To Beppu-Matsuyama

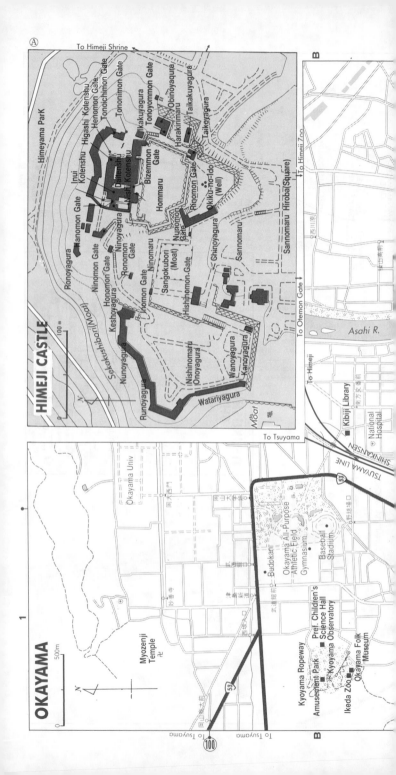

OKAYAMA

N

500m

Okayama Univ

Myozenji
Temple 卍

Kyoyama Ropeway
Amusement Park ■
Kyoyama Observatory
Ikeda Zoo

Pref. Children's
Science Hall

Okayama Folk
Museum

Okayama All-Purpose
Athletic Field
Budokan ●
Gymnasium

Baseball
Stadium ●

To Tsuyama
To Tsuyama
(100)

B

To Himeji

TSUYAMA LINE

SHINKANSEN

Kibiji Library

National
Hospital ⊕

To Himeji Zoo

To Otemon Gate

Asahi R.

B

Ⓐ

To Himeji Shrine

HIMEJI CASTLE

100 m

N

Himeyama ParK

Ronoyagura

Hanomon Gate

Inui
Kolenshu Higashi Kolenshu
Henomon Gate
Tonoichimon Gate
Tononimon Gate
Tonoyommon Gate
Obinoyagura
Taikakuyagura
Ikakuyagura

Nishi Kolenshu
Daitenshu
Bizemmon Gate
Hommaru
Rinomon Gate
Harakirimaru
Taikoyagura

Ninomon Gate
Honomon Gate
Ronomon Gate
Ninoyagura
Keshoyagura

Ninomon Gate
Ihomon Gate

Ninomaru
Nunomon Gate
Okiku-no-ido
(Well)

Sangokubori
(Moat)

Chinoyagura

Hishinomon Gate

Sannomaru

Sannomaru Hiroba(Square)

Nunoyagura
Nishinomaru
Wanoyagura
Onoyagura
Kanoyagura

Runoyagura

Watariyagura

Sekakushibori(Moat)

Hanomon Gate

To Tsuyama

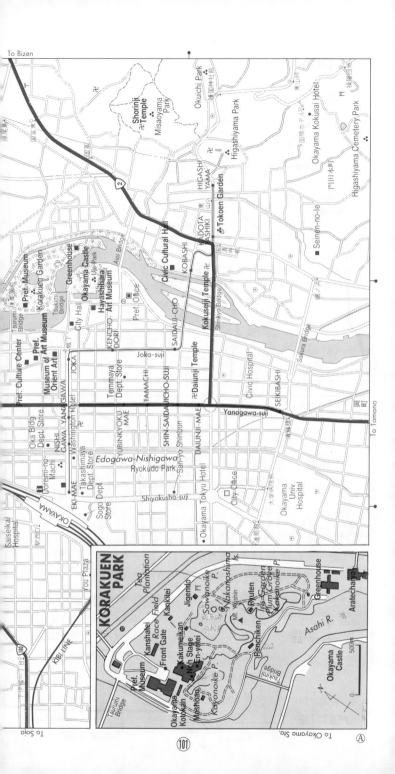

To Bizen

Shorinji Temple

Misaoyama Park

Okuichi Park

Higashiyama Park

Okayama Kokusai Hotel

Higashiyama Cemetery Park

Pref. Museum

Korakuen Garden

Greenhouse

Okayama Castle

Hayashibara Art Museum

Civic Cultural Hall

Tokoen Garden

HIGASHI YAMA

DOTA KASHIKI

KOBASHI

Kokuseiji Temple

Seinen-no-ie

Pref. Culture Center

Pref. Museum of Art Museum

Orient Art

City Hall

Pref. Office

KENCHO-DORI

SAIDAIJI-CHO

Shinkyo Bridge

Sakura Bridge

Aoi Bridge

Tsukimi Bridge

Joka-suji

Oka Bldg. Dept. Store

Temmaya Dept. Store

TAMACHI

Daiunji Temple

Civic Hospital

SEKIBASHI

NISHI GAWA

YANAGAWA

Washington River

YUBINKYOKU-MAE

SHIN-SAIDAIJICHO-SUJI

DAIUNJI-MAE

Yanagawa-suji

To Tamano

Doremi-no-Machi

Takashimaya Dept. Store

Edogawa-Nishigawa

Ryokudo Park

San-yo Shinbun

City Office

EKI-MAE

Sogo Dept. Store

Okayama Tokyu Hotel

Shiyakusho-suji

Okayama Univ. Hospital

OKAYAMA

Saiseikai Hospital

Tour Plaza

KIBI LINE

Tsukumi Bridge

To Sola

KORAKUEN PARK

Tea Plantation

Pref. Museum

Race Field

Kanshatei

Front Gate

Kankitei

Jigendo

Sawanoike P.

Nakanoshima Is.

Ryuten

Mt. Yushin

Plum Grove

Garden

Kakomeikan

Noh Stage

En-yotei

Benchiken

Katsuonoike P.

Greenhouse

Asahi R.

Okayama Kotokan

Mushiozan

Kayonoike P.

Tsukimi Bridge

Okayama Castle

Aratechayo

500 m

To Okayama Sta.

Ⓐ

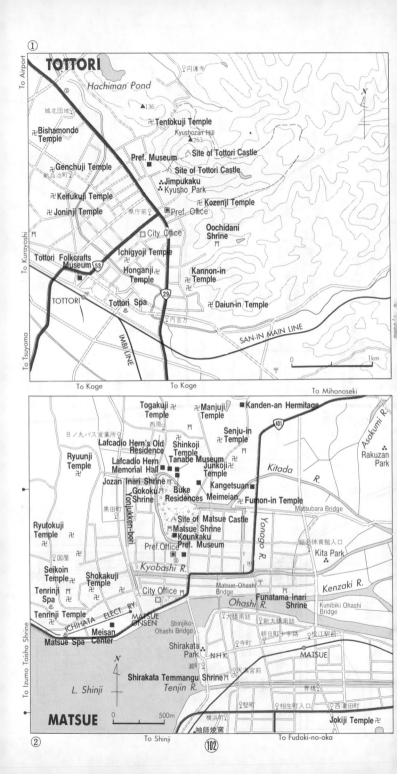

① **TOTTORI**

To Airport

Hachiman Pond

城北団地

▲136

卍 Tentokuji Temple

Kyushozan Hill
▲263

卍 Bishamondo Temple

🏛 Pref. Museum

🏯 Site of Tottori Castle

卍 Genchuji Temple

新品治町

Site of Tottori Castle

:. Jimpukaku
• Kyusho Park

卍 Keifukuji Temple

卍 Joninji Temple

県庁前

🏛 Pref. Office

卍 Kozenji Temple

Oochidani Shrine

To Kurayoshi

☐ City Office

Tottori Folkcrafts Museum

53

Ichigyoji Temple

卍 Honganji Temple

卍 Kannon-in Temple

To Tsuyama

TOTTORI

Tottori Spa

29

卍 Daiun-in Temple

市内吉方

SAN-IN MAIN LINE

IMBY LINE

0 _____ 1km

To Koge   To Koge

To Mihonoseki

② 卍 Togakuji Temple   卍 Manjuji Temple   ■ Kanden-an Hermitage

日ノ丸バス営業所

西原

卍 Senju-in Temple

431

Asokumi R.

Lafcadio Hern's Old Residence

Shinkoji Temple

Kitada

Rakuzan Park

Ryuunji Temple 卍

Lafcadio Hern Memorial Hall

Tanabe Museum

卍 Junkoji Temple

R.

Jozan Inari Shrine
Gokoku Shrine

Buke Residences

■ Kangetsuan

Meimeian • ■ Fumon-in Temple

黒田町

Site of Matsue Castle

Yonago R.

Matsubara Bridge

Ryutokuji Temple 卍

Matsue Shrine
■ Kounkaku

Kita Park

国屋

Pref.Office

Pref. Museum

総合体育館入口

Seikoin Temple 卍

Kyobashi R.

Kenzaki R.

Shokakuji Temple

☐ City Office

Matsue-Ohashi Bridge

Funatama Inari Shrine

Tenrinji Spa

MATSUE ONSEN

Ohashi R.

Kunibiki Ohashi Bridge

Tenrinji Temple 卍

CHIHATA ELECT. RY.

Shinjiko-Ohashi Bridge

新太橋南詰

松江駅前

Meisan Center

大橋南詰

朝日町十字路

MATSUE

Matsue Spa

Shirakata Park

寺町

NHK

天満宮前

堺橋

N

避難口

Shirakata Temmangu Shrine

Tenjin R.

相生町入口 西灘田町

L. Shinji

0 _____ 500m

堅町

横浜町

Jokiji Temple 卍

MATSUE

神師焼窯

To Izumo Taisha Shrine

To Shinji   To Fudoki-no-oka

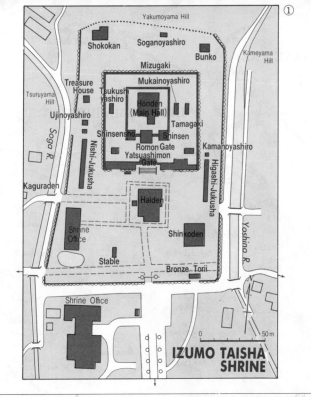

IZUMO TAISHA SHRINE

Yakumoyama Hill

Shokokan
Soganoyashiro
Bunko

Kameyama Hill

Mizugaki

Mukainoyashiro

Tsuruyama Hill

Treasure House
Tsukushi-yashiro

Honden (Main Hall)

Tamagaki

Ujinoyashiro

Shinsensho
Shinsen

Nishi-Jukusha

Romon Gate
Yatsuashimon Gate

Kamanoyashiro

Soga R.

Kaguraden

Haiden

Higashi-Jukusha

Yoshino R.

Shrine Office

Shinkoden

Stable

Bronze Torii

Shrine Office

0   50 m

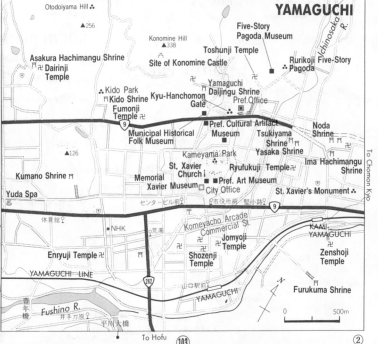

YAMAGUCHI

Otodoiyama Hill
▲256

Ichinosaka R.

Konomine Hill
▲338

Five-Story Pagoda Museum

Toshunji Temple

Rurikoji Five-Story Pagoda

Asakura Hachimangu Shrine
Dairinji Temple

Site of Konomine Castle

Kido Park
Kido Shrine
Kyu-Hanchomon Gate

Yamaguchi Daijingu Shrine
Pref. Office

Fumonji Temple

Pref. Cultural Artifact Museum

Noda Shrine

⑨ Municipal Historical Folk Museum

Tsukiyama Shrine

Yasaka Shrine

▲126

Kameyama Park

Kumano Shrine

St. Xavier Church

Ryufukuji Temple

Ima Hachimangu Shrine

Memorial Xavier Museum

Pref. Art Museum
City Office

St. Xavier's Monument

Yuda Spa

センタービル前

市役所前 堅小路 ⑨

NHK

荒高

Komeyacho Arcade
Commercial St.

KAMI-YAMAGUCHI

Enryuji Temple

Jomyoji Temple

Zenshoji Temple

YAMAGUCHI LINE

262

Shozenji Temple

山口駅前

YAMAGUCHI

To Chomon Kyo

Fushino R.
豊年橋
井手ガ原

平川大橋

Furukuma Shrine

0   500m

To Hofu   103

②

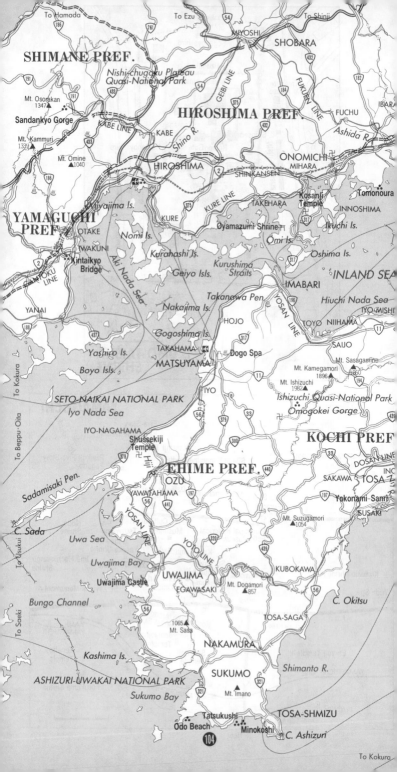

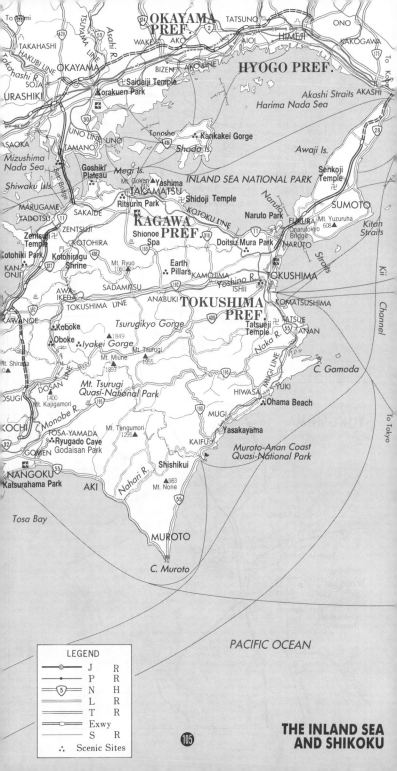

THE INLAND SEA
AND SHIKOKU

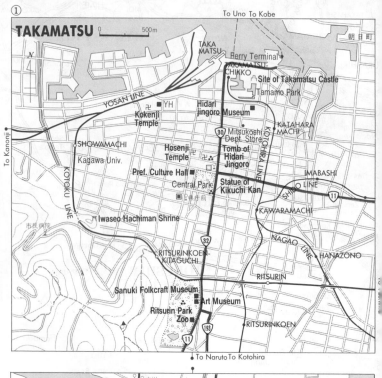

①

TAKAMATSU

0 ⎯⎯⎯ 500m

To Uno To Kobe

朝日町

TAKA MATSU

Ferry Terminal

TAKAMATSU-CHIKKO

Site of Takamatsu Castle

Tamamo Park

YOSAN LINE

KATAHARA MACHI

YH

Kokenji Temple

Hidari jingoro Museum

30 Mitsukoshi Dept. Store

KOTOHIRA LINE

To Kanonji

SHOWAMACHI

Kagawa Univ.

Hosenji Temple

Tomb of Hidari Jingoro

IMABASHI

Pref. Culture Hall

Central Park

市庁前

Statue of Kikuchi Kan

SHIJO LINE

11

KOTOKU LINE

市民病院

Iwaseo Hachiman Shrine

KAWARAMACHI

32

NAGAO LINE HANAZONO

RITSURINKOEN-KITAGUCHI

RITSURIN

Sanuki Folkcraft Museum

Art Museum

Ritsurin Park Zoo

193

RITSURINKOEN

11

To Naruto To Kotohira

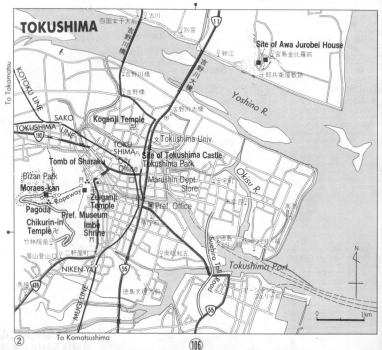

TOKUSHIMA

四国女子大前

古川

別宮

11

Site of Awa Jurobei House

宮島金比羅前

鈴江

十郎兵衛屋敷跡

吉野川橋

吉野川大橋

Yoshino R.

吉野橋

To Takamatsu

KOTOKU LINE

吉野川大橋

SAKO

Kogenji Temple

TOKUSHIMA LINE

192

TOKU SHIMA

文 Tokushima Univ.

Tomb of Sharaku

TOKU SHIMA City Office

Site of Tokushima Castle

Tokushima Park

Okisu R.

Bizan Park

Moraes-kan

Ropeway

Marushin Dept. Store

安宅

Pagoda

Zuiganji Temple

Pref. Office

高松

Chikurin-in Temple

Pref. Museum

Imbe Shrine

竹林院前

徳島前

Suehiro Toll Road

南昭和五

Tokushima Port

NIKEN-YA

55

眉山登山口

二軒屋町

N

馬場

438

徳島文理大前

0 ⎯⎯⎯ 1km

BIZAN LINE

55

To Komatsushima

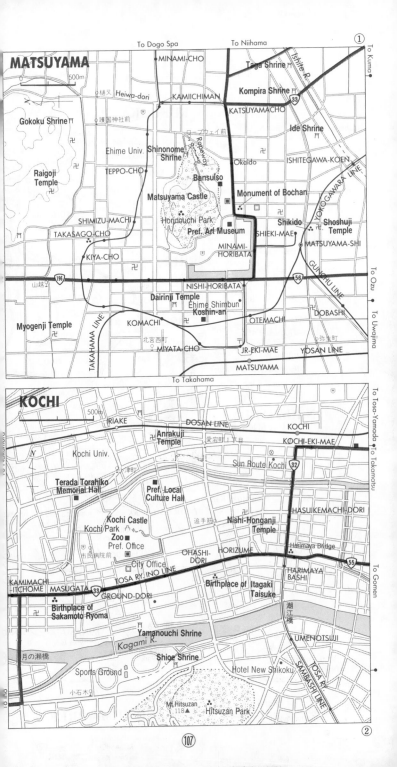

MATSUYAMA

500m

To Dogo Spa   To Niihama   ①   To Kuma

MINAMI-CHO
Taga Shrine
Ishite R.
Kompira Shrine
33
Heiwa-dori
KAMIICHIMAN
KATSUYAMACHO
Gokoku Shrine
護国神社前
Ide Shrine
樋又
Ehime Univ.   Shinonome Shrine
Okaido
ISHITEGAWA-KOEN
TEPPO-CHO
Raigoji Temple
Bansuiso
YOKOGAWARA LINE
Matsuyama Castle
Monument of Bochan
SHIMIZU-MACHI
Horinouchi Park
Shikido
Shoshuji Temple
TAKASAGO-CHO
Pref. Art Museum
SHIEKI-MAE
MATSUYAMA-SHI
KIYA-CHO
MINAMI-HORIBATA
GUNCHU LINE
山越え   196
56
To Ozu
To Uwajima
NISHI-HORIBATA
Dairinji Temple
Ehime Shimbun
DOBASHI
Koshin-an
Myogenji Temple
TAKAHAMA LINE
KOMACHI
OTEMACHI
北宮西町
弥生町
MIYATA-CHO
JR-EKI-MAE
YOSAN LINE
MATSUYAMA
To Takahama

KOCHI

500m
IRIAKE
DOSAN LINE
KOCHI
To Tosa-Yamada
To Takamatsu
Anrakuji Temple
愛宕町1丁目
KOCHI-EKI-MAE
N
Kochi Univ.
Sun Route Kochi
32
Terada Torahiko Memorial Hall
Pref. Local Culture Hall
HASUIKEMACHI-DORI
Kochi Castle
追手筋2丁目
Nishi-Honganji Temple
Kochi Park
Zoo
Harimaya Bridge
Pref. Office
市民病院前
OHASHI-DORI
HORIZUME
55
To Gomen
City Office
TOSA RY. INO LINE
HARIMAYA BASHI
KAMIMACHI ICHOME
MASUGATA
33
Birthplace of Itagaki Taisuke
潮江橋
To Ino
Birthplace of Sakamoto Ryoma
GROUND-DORI
UMENOTSUJI
TOSA RY.
Yamanouchi Shrine
Kagami R.
SAMBASHI LINE
月の瀬橋
Shioe Shrine
Sports Ground
Hotel New Shikoku
小石木町
Mt.Hitsuzan
118▲
Hitsuzan Park

②

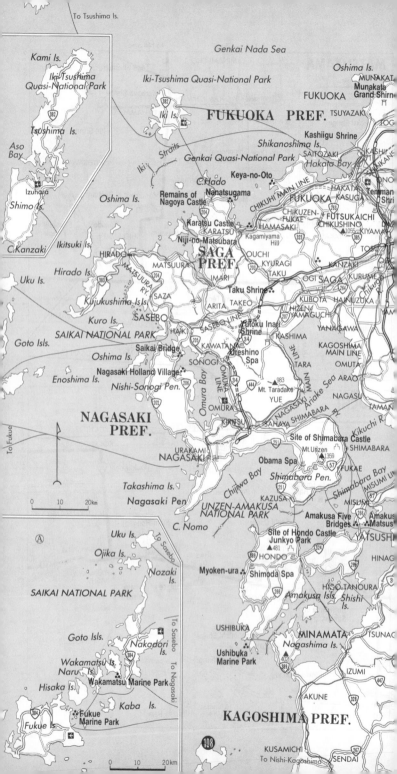

NORTHWESTERN KYUSYU

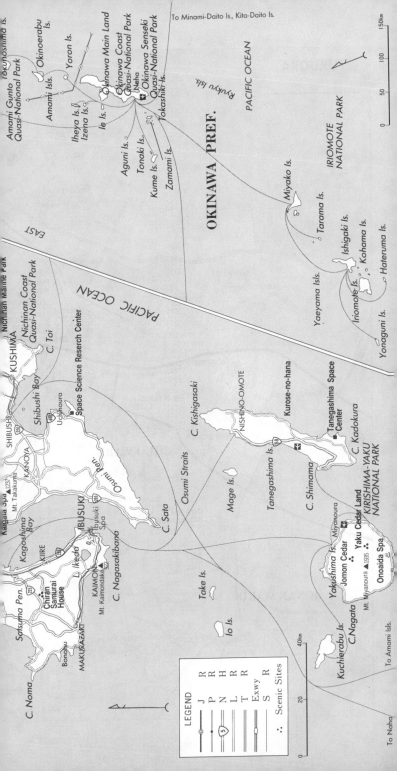

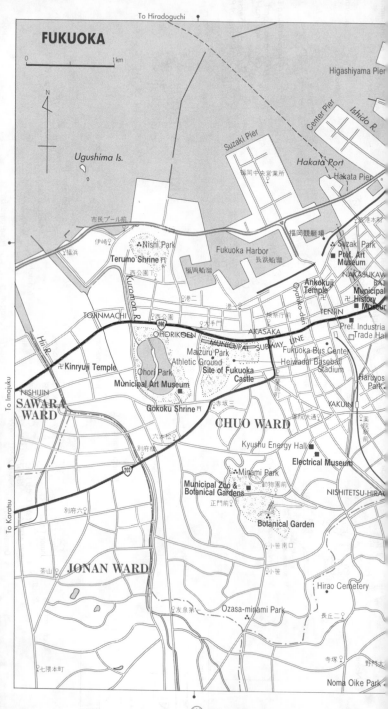

FUKUOKA

0   1km

N

To Hiradoguchi

Higashiyama Pier

Ugushima Is.

Center Pier

Ishido R.

Suzaki Pier

Hakata Port

市民プール前

福岡中央営業所

Hakata Pier

東公園本原

伊崎

Nishi Park

福岡競艇場

Terumo Shrine

Fukuoka Harbor

長浜船溜

Suzaki Park

■ **Pref. Art Museum**

福浜

西公園

福岡船溜

NAKASUKAW BA

Ankokuji Temple

■ **Municipal History Museu**

oyariko-dōn

TENJIN

TOINMACHI

西公園

港二

水手門

検察庁前

赤坂

□ Pref. Industria Trade Ha

OHORIKOEN

AKASAKA

MUNICIPAL   SUBWAY   LINE

Kinryuji Temple

Maizuru Park

Fukuoka Bus Cente

Athletic Ground

Heiwadai Baseball Stadium

Haruyos Park

Ohori Park

Site of Fukuoka Castle

NISHIJIN

Municipal Art Museum

YAKUIN

SAWARA WARD

Gokoku Shrine

赤坂三

To Imajuku

六本松

CHUO WARD

別府核

美術前

Kyushu Energy Hall

202

別府

Electrical Museum

Minami Park

動物園前

To Karatsu

Municipal Zoo & Botanical Gardens

NISHITETSU-HIRA

別府六

正門前

JONAN WARD

Botanical Garden

茶山

小笹南口

Hirao Cemetery

小笹

友泉第

Ozasa-minami Park

長丘二

七隈本町

寺塚

野門大

Noma Oike Park

112

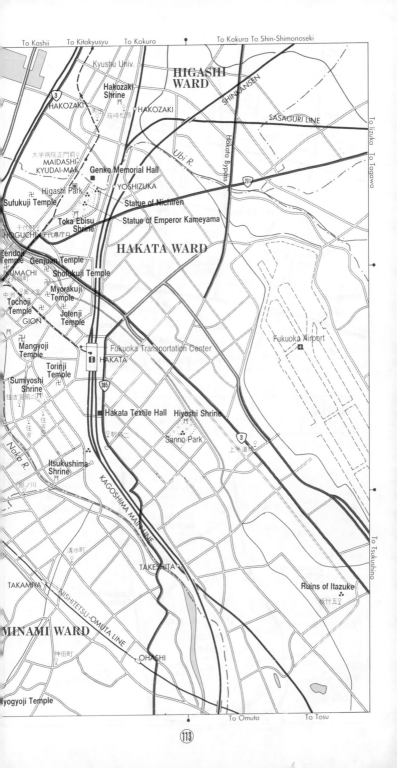

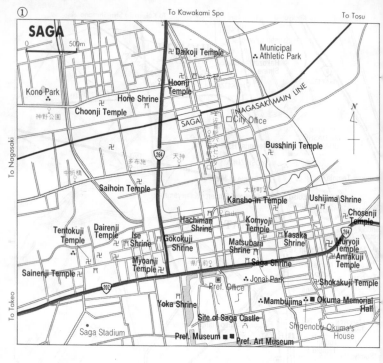

① **SAGA**

To Kawakami Spa
To Tosu

0 500m

Daikoji Temple

Municipal Athletic Park

Kono Park

Hoonji Temple

Horie Shrine

Choonji Temple

NAGASAKI MAIN LINE

SAGA

City Office

Busshinji Temple

To Nagasaki

Saihoin Temple

Kansho-in Temple

Ushijima Shrine

Tentokuji Temple

Dairenji Temple

Hachiman Shrine

Komyoji Temple

Chosenji Temple

Ise Shrine

Gokokuji Shrine

Matsubara Shrine

Yasaka Shrine

Muryoji Temple

Myoanji Temple

Anrakuji Temple

Sainenji Temple

Saga Shrine

Shokakuji Temple

To Takeo

Yoka Shrine

Pref. Office

Jonai Park

Mambujima

Okuma Memorial Hall

Site of Saga Castle

Shigenobu Okuma's House

Saga Stadium

Pref. Museum

Pref. Art Museum

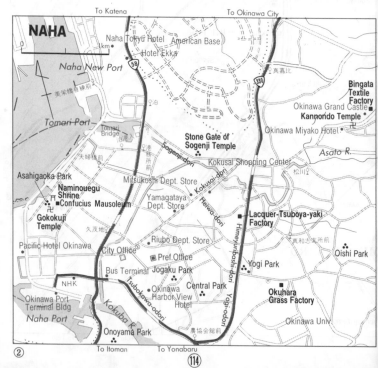

NAHA

To Katena
To Okinawa City

0 1km

Naha Tokyu Hotel

American Base

Hotel Ekka

Naha New Port

Bingata Textile Factory

Okinawa Grand Castle

Kannondo Temple

Okinawa Miyako Hotel

Tomari Port

Tomari Bridge

Stone Gate of Sogenji Temple

Asato R.

Kokusai Shopping Center

Asahigaoka Park

Mitsukoshi Dept. Store

Naminouegu Shrine

Confucius Mausoleum

Yamagataya Dept. Store

Lacquer-Tsuboya-yaki Factory

Gokokuji Temple

Pacific Hotel Okinawa

Riubo Dept. Store

City Office

Pref. Office

Yogi Park

Oishi Park

Bus Terminal

Jogaku Park

Central Park

Okuhara Grass Factory

NHK

Okinawa Harbor View Hotel

Okinawa Port Terminal Bldg

Naha Port

Onoyama Park

Okinawa Univ.

To Itoman
To Yonabaru

② (114)

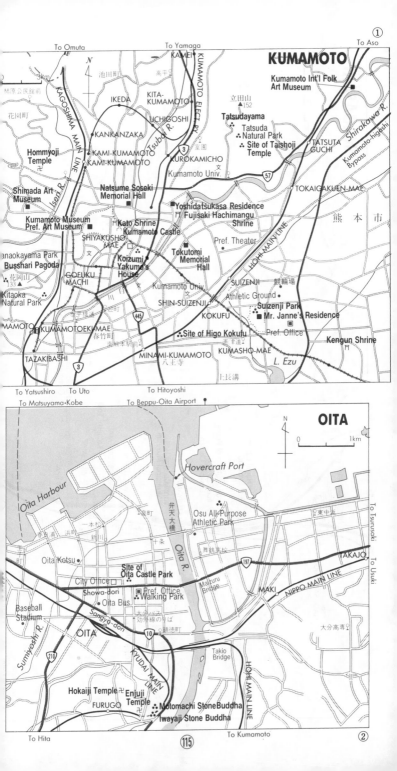

KUMAMOTO ①

To Omuta　To Yamaga　To Aso

KAMEI
立田山 152

Kumamoto Int'l Folk
Art Museum

Tatsudayama

Tatsuda
:・Natural Park
:・Site of Taishoji
Temple

TATSUTA
GUCHI

Shirakawa R.

Kumamoto-higashi
Bypass

IKEDA
KITA-
KUMAMOTO
UCHIGOSHI

KANKANZAKA

KUROKAMICHO
文
Kumamoto Univ.

57

TOKAIGAKUEN-MAE

**Hommyoji
Temple**

KAMI-KUMAMOTO
KAMI-KUMAMOTO

**Shimada Art
Museum**

**Natsume Soseki
Memorial Hall**

Yoshidatsukasa Residence
門 **Fujisaki Hachimangu
Shrine**

熊　本　市

**Kumamoto Museum
Pref. Art Museum**

Kato Shrine
Kumamoto Castle
SHIYAKUSHO-
MAE

Pref. Theater

anaokayama Park
Busshari Pagoda

**Koizumi
Yakumo's
House**

**Tokutomi
Memorial
Hall**

GOFUKU
MACHI

Kumamoto Univ.
文

SUIZENJI 競輪場
Athletic Ground

Kitaoka
Natural Park

SHIN-SUIZENJI

Suizenji Park
■ **Mr. Janne's Residence**

MAMOTO
KUMAMOTOEKI-MAE

KOKUFU

Pref. Office

Kengun Shrine
門

TAZAKIBASHI

3

MINAMI-KUMAMOTO
八王寺

Site of Higo Kokufu

KUMASHO-
MAE

L. Ezu

To Yatsushiro　To Uto　To Hitoyoshi

To Matsuyama・Kobe　To Beppu-Oita Airport

OITA

N
0　　　1km

Hovercraft Port

Oita Harbour

**Osu All-Purpose
Athletic Park**

To Tsurusaki

Oita R.

TAKAJO
To Usuki

Oita Kotsu

**Site of
Oita Castle Park**

197

Matsuru
Bridge

MAKI

NIPPO MAIN LINE

City Office

Pref. Office
Showa-dori　**Walking Park**
Oita Bus

**Baseball
Stadium**

Sangyo-dori

OITA

10

Sumiyoshi R.

210

KYUDAI MAIN LINE

Takio
Bridge

HOH MAIN LINE

Hokaiji Temple 卍
**Enjuji
Temple**

FURUGO

Motomachi Stone Buddha
Iwayaji Stone Buddha

To Hita

To Kumamoto

②

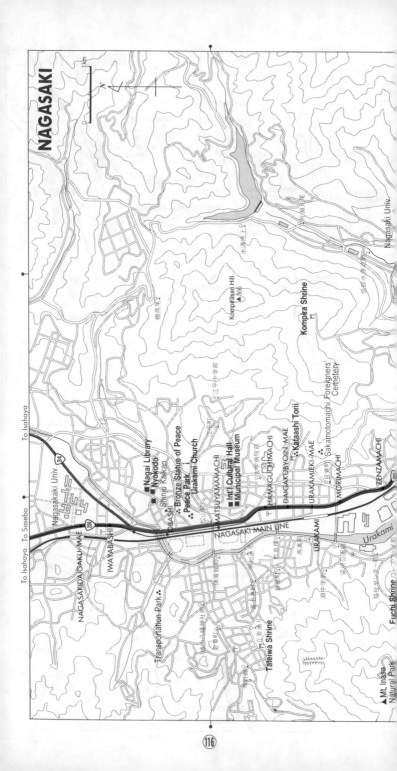

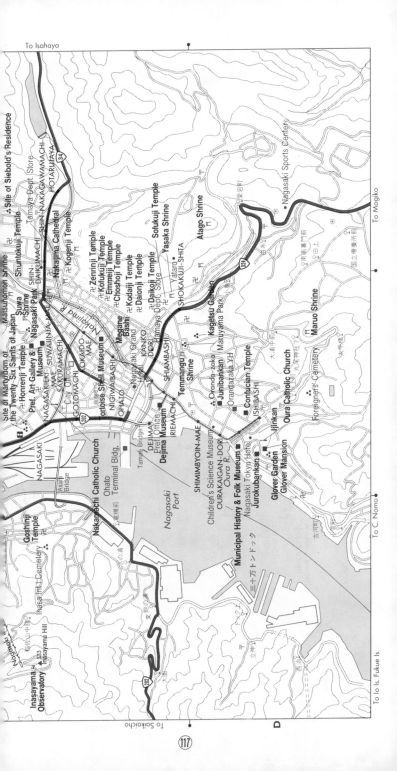

To Isahaya

Site of Siebold's Residence

Tamaya Dept. Store

SHIN-NAKAGAWAMACHI

HOTARUJAYA

34

Shuntokuji Temple

Matsunomori Shrine

SHIN-DAIKUMACHI

Suwa Shrine

Nagasaki Park

Nakajima Cathedral

Kogenji Temple

Site of Martyrdom of the Twenty-Six Saints of Japan

Honrenji Temple

Suwajinja-mae

Pref. Art Gallery & Museum

Zenrinji Temple

Kofukuji Temple

Nagasaki Sports Center

To Mogiko

Sotukuji Temple

Emmeiji Temple

Choshoji Temple

Kodaiji Temple

Daionji Temple

Atago Shrine

Yasaka Shrine

Daikoji Temple

Yataro Dept. Store

SHOKAKUJI-SHITA

Nagasaki-eki

City Office

NAGASAKIEKI

SAKURAMACHI

OKADO-MAE

Megane Bashi

Nakajima R.

SUWAJINJA-MAE

GOTOMACHI

NIGIWAIBASHI

OHATO

KANKO DORI

Hamano-machi

Nagasaki Grand Hotel

Tortoise Shell Museum

Nagasaki Tokyu Hotel

Kagetsu Garden

202

Maruyama Park

Maruo Shrine

SHIAMBASHI

Temmangu Shrine

RIEMACHI

Oranda-zaka

Junibankan

124

Pref. Office

DEJIMA

Orandazaka YH

Confucian Temple

Tamaya Bridge

Dejima Museum

SHIMIMBYOIN-MAE

Nakamachi Catholic Church

Ohato Terminal Bldg.

Asahi Bridge

Children's Science Museum

OURAKAIGAN-DORI

Oura R.

Oura Catholic Church

NAGASAKI

Foreigners' Cemetery

Nagasaki Port

Municipal History & Folk Museum

Jurokubankan

ISHIBASHI

Jinkan

Glover Garden

Glover Mansion

Goshinji Temple

To C. Nomo

Inasayama Observatory

Inasayama Hill

Inasa Int'l Cemetery

Nagasaki R.

三十六万トンドック

202

To Io Is. Fukue Is.

To Saikaicho

(117)

D

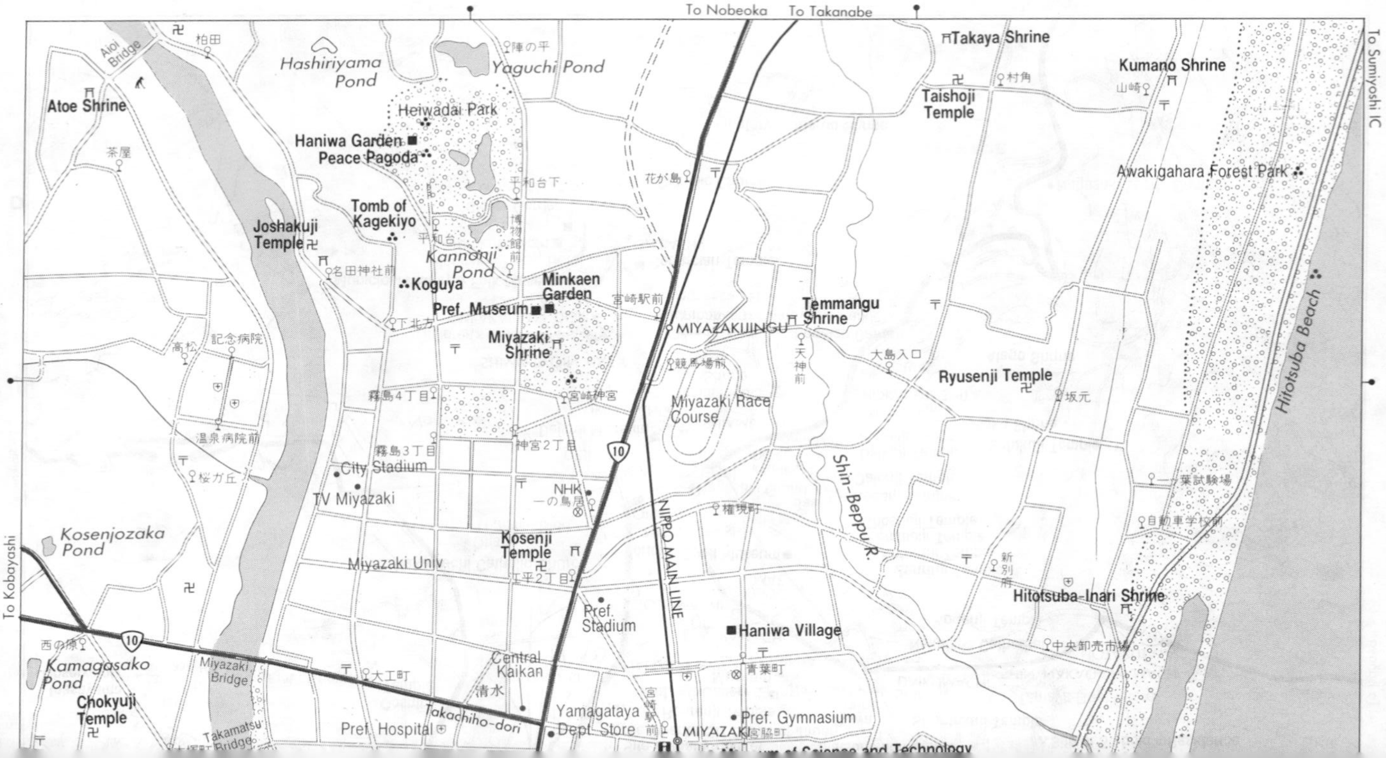

To Nobeoka
To Takanabe
To Sumiyoshi IC
To Kobayashi
Atoe Shrine
Aioi Bridge
柏田
Hashiriyama Pond
Yaguchi Pond
陣の平
Heiwadai Park
Haniwa Garden
Peace Pagoda
茶屋
平和台下
Tomb of Kagekiyo
Joshakuji Temple
平和台
博物館前
Kannonji Pond
名田神社前
Koguya
Minkaen Garden
宮崎駅前
Pref. Museum
下北方
Miyazaki Shrine
MIYAZAKIJINGU
Temmangu Shrine
天神前
競馬場前
花が島
高松
記念病院
温泉病院前
霧島4丁目
宮崎神宮
Miyazaki Race Course
霧島3丁目
神宮2丁目
City Stadium
TV Miyazaki
桜ガ丘
NHK
一の鳥居
権現町
Kosenjozaka Pond
Kosenji Temple
Miyazaki Univ.
上平2丁目
NIPPO MAIN LINE
Shin-Beppu R.
Pref. Stadium
Haniwa Village
青葉町
Central Kaikan
清水
Yamagataya Dept. Store
宮崎駅前
MIYAZAKI
Pref. Gymnasium
Pref. Hospital
Takachiho-dori
Miyazaki Bridge
Takamatsu Bridge
大工町
西の原
Kamagasako Pond
Chokyuji Temple
Takaya Shrine
Taishoji Temple
村角
Kumano Shrine
山崎
Awakigahara Forest Park
Hitotsuba Beach
大島入口
Ryusenji Temple
坂元
一葉試験場
自動車学校前
新別府
Hitotsuba-Inari Shrine
中央卸売市場
10

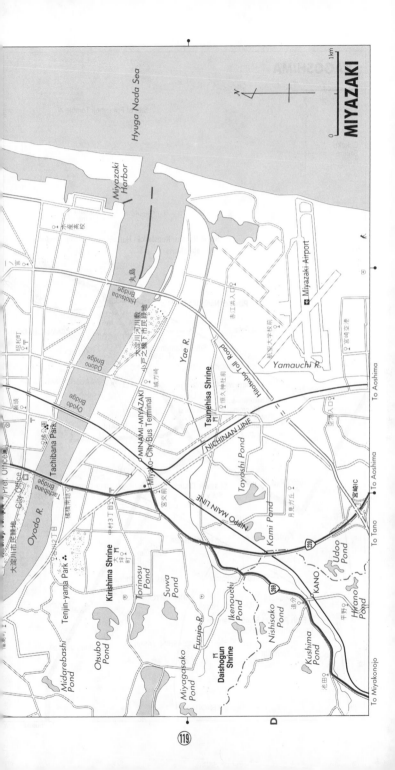

MIYAZAKI

Hyuga Nada Sea

Miyazaki Harbor

Miyazaki Airport

0   1km

N

Hirotsuba Bridge

丸島

Yae R.

Odono Bridge

Oyodo Bridge

大淀川河川敷緑地

小戸之橋下市民緑地

昭和町〒

Oyodo R.

波頭

Tachibana Bridge

Tachibana Park

大淀川市民緑地

MINAMI-MIYAZAKI

Miyako-City Bus Terminal

中村3丁目〒

City Office

Post Office

Kirishima Shrine

Tenjin-yama Park

Otsubo Pond

Midarebashi Pond

Miyagasako Pond

Torinosu Pond

Suwa Pond

Fururyu R.

Ikenouchi Pond

Daishogun Shrine

Kushima Pond

Nishisako Pond

Hisisako Pond

Hirano Pond

Udoo Pond

Kami Pond

Tayoshi Pond

Tsunehisa Shrine

宮文前

月見ヶ丘〇

NICHINAN LINE

NIPPO MAIN LINE

Hiroba Toll Road

城ヶ崎

直久神社前

空港入口〇

赤江大学校前

宮崎大学校前

宮崎空港

Yamauchi R.

KANO

平野〇

池田〇

遠介

〒

220

269

To Miyakonojo

To Tano

To Aoshima

To Aoshima

宮崎IC

To Aoshima

D

⑪⑨

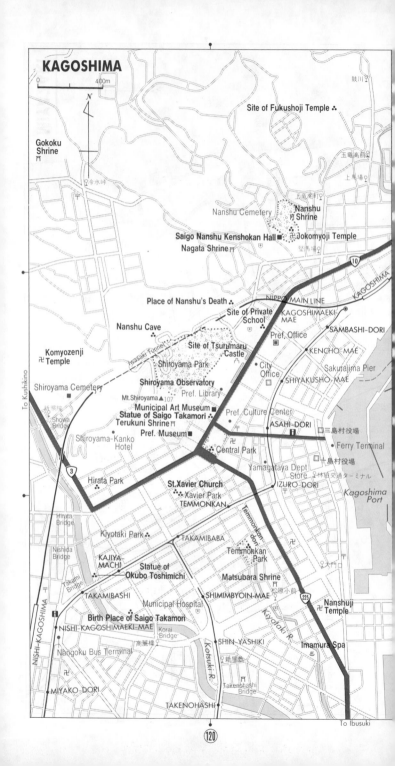

KAGOSHIMA

0   400m

N

Gokoku
Shrine

Site of Fukushoji Temple

玉竜高前

上竜場

Nanshu Cemetery

Nanshu
Shrine

Saigo Nanshu Kenshokan Hall

Jokomyoji Temple

Nagata Shrine

Place of Nanshu's Death

NIPPO MAIN LINE

KAGOSHIMAEKI-
MAE

KAGOSHIMA

Nanshu Cave

Site of Private
School

Pref. Office

SAMBASHI-DORI

Komyozenji
Temple

Site of Tsurumaru
Castle

KENCHO MAE

Iwasaki Tunnel

Shiroyama Park

City
Office

Sakurajima Pier

SHIYAKUSHO-MAE

Shiroyama Cemetery

Shiroyama Observatory

Pref. Library

Mt.Shiroyama▲107

Municipal Art Museum

Pref. Culture Center

三島村役場

Showa
Bridge

Statue of Saigo Takamori

Terukuni Shrine

ASAHI-DORI

Ferry Terminal

To Kushikino

Pref. Museum

三島村役場

Shiroyama-Kanko
Hotel

Central Park

Yamagataya Dept
Store

県交通ターミナル

Hirata Park

St.Xavier Church

IZURO-DORI

Kagoshima
Port

Xavier Park

TEMMONKAN

Hirata
Bridge

Kiyotaki Park

TAKAMIBABA

Temmonkan
Park

Nishida
Bridge

KAJIYA-
MACHI

Statue of
Okubo Toshimichi

Matsubara Shrine

Takami
Bridge

TAKAMIBASHI

Municipal Hospital

SHIMIMBYOIN-MAE

松原小前

225

Nanshuji
Temple

Birth Place of Saigo Takamori

NISHI-KAGOSHIMAEKI-MAE

Korai
Bridge

SHIN-YASHIKI

Imamura Spa

高麗橋

Nangoku Bus Terminal

新屋敷

MIYAKO-DORI

Takenohashi
Bridge

TAKENOHASHI

To Ibusuki

120

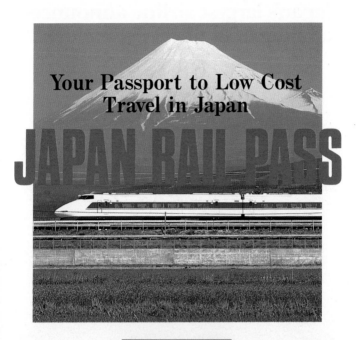

Your Passport to Low Cost Travel in Japan

JAPAN RAIL PASS

Super savings…up to 50 percent — even more!

Stylish travel on Japan's famous JR railway system: high-speed trains, locals, even buses

Covers the entire country: 13,000 miles of railways all over the four major islands

Special tourist-only bargain—not sold in Japan (advance purchase required)

Prices:

JAPAN RAIL PASS	GREEN		ORDINARY	
	Adult	Child	Adult	Child
7-DAY	¥37,000	¥18,500	¥27,800	¥13,900

14-DAY and 21-DAY passes are also available.
Actual price depends on exchange rate at the time of purchase.

Valid as of March 1991

Where to purchase: Japan Travel Bureau, Nippon Travel Agency, Kinki Nippon Tourist, Tokyu Tourist Corporation, Japan Airlines, and their associated agencies.

JR JAPAN RAILWAYS GROUP

Japan's largest airline announces a bouquet of new destinations.

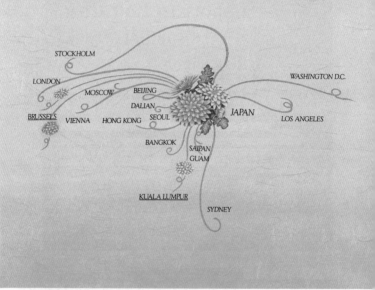

Can flying ever be a beautiful experience?

Over 30 million loyal passengers who fly ANA every year will attest that it can be.

Now you can enjoy our refreshingly intuitive service and attention to detail en route from Tokyo to Paris or Brussels, and from Nagoya to Kuala Lumpur.

It means ANA now flies to 17 cities worldwide, as well as 30 domestic destinations.

Put in perspective, we not only fly more passengers than any other Japanese airline, we're number eight in the world.

What's more, the style to which an ANA flight accustoms you can be continued once you've landed, courtesy of the luxurious ANA hotel chain; 24 hotels in Japan and 7 worldwide.

Rather than wilting when you travel, stay fresh with ANA.

ANA
All Nippon Airways
Japan's best to the world.

INTERNATIONAL RESERVATIONS:
- TOKYO (03) 3272-1212 ● OSAKA (06) 372-1212 ● NAGOYA (052) 971-5588
- SAPPORO (011) 281-1212 ● FUKUOKA (092) 474-1212 ● OKINAWA (0988) 61-1212

DOMESTIC RESERVATIONS:
- TOKYO (03) 5489-8800 ● OSAKA (06) 534-8800 ● NAGOYA (052) 962-6211
- SAPPORO (011) 231-5131 ● FUKUOKA (092) 411-2211 ● OKINAWA (0988) 66-5111

TAKE A CLOSE LOOK AT TOKYO.
You'll See Many of the Good Things Japan Has to Offer. Meet Its People, and Meet the Real Japanese.

Sunrise Tours jointly operated by JTB and Hato Bus let you travel in luxury and enjoy the sights, culture and history of Tokyo, Kamakura, Hakone and Mt. Fuji.

Most popular among our big excursion lineup are:
- Tokyo Morning
- Tokyo Afternoon
- Dynamic Tokyo
- Kabuki Night
- Industrial Tokyo
- Village Life & Crafts
- Kamakura-Hakone 1 Day
- Mr. Fuji-Hakone 1 Day

For reservations, contact your travel agent or

JAPAN TRAVEL BUREAU, Inc.
Licensed Travel Agent No. 64

HATO BUS
An Associated Member of American Sightseeing International/US Gray Line

A century of unmatched service. An unbeatable location.

Since our founding in 1890 the Imperial Hotel has been defining and redefining the standard for hospitality in the Japanese tradition. We set the standard. We made it our tradition. And we covetously uphold both, for guests who won't settle for less. This, and a location near the central business district and the fabulous, fashionable Ginza. An unmatched tradition. An unbeatable location. No wonder the Imperial remains the imperative choice among the world's most discriminating travelers.

IMPERIAL HOTEL
TOKYO

A member of
The Leading Hotels of the World®

Information: Call our New York office, (212) 692-9001, Los Angeles office, (213) 627-6214,
or London office, (71) 930-2710. Reservations: Contact Japan Travel Bureau Int'l, The Leading Hotels
of the World, Nikko Hotels Int'l, Utell Int'l, Preferred Hotels Worldwide, SRS-Steigenberger
Reservation Service, Groupe des Hôtels Concorde, or any Japan Air Lines office.
Direct telex Imperial: 26816 IMPHO J or facsimile: (03) 3581-9146. Tel: (03) 3504-1111.

Japanese elegance, defined. Tokyo's Hotel Okura.

Elegance. In Japan, it's characteristic of the best hotels. But nowhere is it more prevalent than at Tokyo's Hotel Okura.

Each of the Okura's guest rooms bears signs of this elegance. Rooms feature soothing colors. Soft, indirect lighting. And plush furnishings. Entirely in keeping with our desire to create a refined blend of traditional Japanese and Western design.

Dining at the Okura includes an enviable choice of eight restaurants, with French, Chinese and Japanese as the featured cuisines.

Of course, our definition of elegance must include mention of service. And truly it is this, above all else, that confirms the Okura's position as Tokyo's preeminent hotel.

Hotel Okura
TOKYO

2-10-4 Toranomon, Minato-ku, Tokyo 105, Japan
TEL: (03) 3582-0111 FAX: (03) 3582-3707

A member of *The Leading Hotels of the World*®

Only one hotel in Tokyo has a 400-year-old decompression chamber.

Tokyo is one incredibly fast-paced city. But you can still get away from it all. Just stay at The Hotel New Otani. And escape the pressures of the fast lane in our 10-acre, 400-year-old Japanese garden. Over the years, leaders of industry and government from many nations have walked its peaceful pathways. The New Otani. There really is no place like it.

FOR RESERVATIONS AND INFORMATION
THE NEW OTANI INTERNATIONAL SALES OFFICES

Toll-free
(800) 421-8795 (U.S. & Canada), (800) 273-2294 (in California only)

Los Angeles
120 S. Los Angeles St., Los Angeles, CA 90012, U.S.A.
Tel.: (213) 629-1114, Telex: 4720429 NEWOTANI LSA, Fax: (213) 620-9808

New York
520 Madison Ave., New York, NY 10022, U.S.A.
Tel.: (212) 308-7491, Telex: 12059 NEWOTANI NYK, Fax: (212) 980-1932

London
The Kiln House, 210 New Kings Road, London SW6 4NZ, England
Tel.: (071) 731-4231~3, Telex: 8950113 LUXURY G, Fax: (071) 384-1507

Hong Kong
Luk Kwok Centre, 16th Flr., 72 Gloucester Road, Wanchai, Hong Kong
Tel.: 5292723, Telex: 86025 NPE HX, Fax: 8613549

Tokyo
4-1, Kioi-cho, Chiyoda-ku, Tokyo 102, Japan
Tel.: (03) 3265-1111, Telex: J24719 HTLOTANI, Fax: (03) 3239-2632

> **Airline Access Codes**
> **(New Otani Tokyo only)/U.S. & Canada**
> Apollo NO9730, Sabre NO9051, Pars SI390,
> System One SITYO390, Datas II SI390,
> Sahara UITYO0323

HOTEL NEW OTANI TOKYO

TOKYO · OSAKA · LOS ANGELES · HONOLULU · SINGAPORE · BEIJING · SOFIA

The Largest International Credit Card Company in Japan

	●TOKYO	✆(03)3294-8111	
●PARIS	✆(1)42 86 06 01	●HONOLULU	✆(808)971-8111
●LONDON	✆(071)491-8004	●GUAM	✆(671)646-1294
●ROME	✆(06)481-5556	●HONG KONG	✆3667211~2
●LOS ANGELES	✆(213)629-8111	●BEIJING	✆(1)513-9837
●NEW YORK	✆(212)332-8111	●SINGAPORE	✆734-0096
●CHICAGO	✆(312)222-0045	●BANGKOK	✆(662)231-0970
●SAN FRANCISCO	✆(415)956-8111	●SYDNEY	✆(02)247-6399

Fine tune
your finances with Fuji expertise.

To harmonize your finances in the midst of today's
rapidly changing business environment,
Fuji Bank offers its proven expertise
in all aspects of financial management.
As the pre-eminent bank in world markets,
Fuji will help keep your finances in perfect pitch.

Your international banking professionals

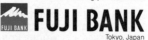 **FUJI BANK**

Tokyo, Japan

Overseas Network
London, Manchester, Düsseldorf, Frankfurt, Munich, Zürich, Brussels, Luxembourg, Paris, Milan, Madrid, Amsterdam, New York, Los Angeles,
Chicago, Houston, Seattle, San Francisco, Atlanta, Miami, Toronto, Montreal, Mexico City, Grand Cayman, São Paulo, Colombia, Bahrain, Tehran,
Seoul, Singapore, Hong Kong, Jakarta, Manila, Bangkok, Kuala Lumpur, Beijing, Shanghai, Dalian, Guangzhou, Shenzhen, Sydney, Melbourne

Heller Financial, Inc., Heller Overseas Corporation

AT YOUR SERVICE, WORLDWIDE.

Whether you're traveling for business or pleasure in Japan, the level of service you've come to expect can be found at the following first class hotels which welcome the Diners Club® card.

The New Otani (Tokyo)

Imperial Hotel (Tokyo)

Hotel Okura (Tokyo)

Hotel New Grand (Yokohama)

The Plaza (Osaka)

Royal Hotel (Osaka)

Kyoto ANA Hotel (Kyoto)

Kobe Portopia Hotel (Kobe)

Hotel Alpha Sapporo (Sapporo)

Hotel Nagoya Castle (Nagoya)

Nishitetsu Grand Hotel (Fukuoka)

®Diners Club is a registered service mark of Diners Club International Ltd.

DINERS CLUB OF JAPAN For card information, please call ☎(03)3499-1311
Shibuya Head Office Service Center: 13-7, Shibuya 1-chome, Shibuya-ku, Tokyo

BRINGING YOU
THE JOYOUS HARMONY
OF JAPAN—
A DISTINGUISHED
NEW WHISKY DELIGHT

SUNTORY
BLENDED WHISKY
"HIBIKI"
響

SUNTORY
WHISKY

ALC 43% by VOL. 750ml

YAMAZAKI
—THE FRONTIER OF LIGHT
AND MILD PURE MALT WHISKY,
NURTURED OVER
12 YEARS
TO THE LULLABY
OF KYOTO

SUNTORY
PURE MALT WHISKY
"YAMAZAKI"
山崎

SUNTORY
PURE MALT
WHISKY
AGED 12 YEARS
山崎

ALC 43% by VOL. 750ml
Drinking by minors is prohibited.

MIKIMOTO
The Originator of Cultured Pearls.
Since 1893.

● TOKYO: MAIN STORE: GINZA, Tel.3535-4611・Imperial Hotel Arcade Tel.3591-5001・
  Hotel Okura Arcade Tel.3584-4664・Akasaka Tokyu Hotel Plaza Tel.3581-9585
● YOKOHAMA: Motomachi Tel.681-3801 ● NAGOYA: Sakae Tel.261-1808
● KYOTO: Shijo st., Kawaramachi Tel.251-1281 ● OSAKA: Shin Hankyu Bldg. Tel.341-0247
● KOBE: Kobe Int'l House Tel.221-0062 ● TOBA: Mikimoto Pearl Island
● NEW YORK ● PARIS ● LONDON ● SWITZERLAND ● HONG KONG
● Tax free for tourists © 1991

SONY

1958
TR-610
AM Radio

32 years ago, the world's most excitin portable radio had six transistors. Now it has 31,758!*

1991
ICF-SW1
Multi-band Radio

In 1958 Sony took the transistor out of the laboratory and put it in pepole pockets with the landmark TR-610. And, in doing so, brought radio out of the livir room and into the hands and hearts of millions around the world.

During the last three decades, both Sony and portable radio have come a lor way. The ICF-SW1 is about the same size as the TR-610, but mounts 31,758 transistors. A more than 5000-fold increase! This Sony multi-band does a l more, too. Like receiving MW, LW and FM stereo broadcasts anywhere in th world—and SW from all over the world. At the same time, its advanced digit tuning and other sophisticated features make early efforts seem primitive b comparison. Yet the design philosophy is the same: to pack more performanc into ever smaller packages.

* Built-in ICs converted into equivalent number of transistors

Another tiny triumph of technology from Sony

We have two treasures: curiosity and ROBO.

Secret hiding places in a vacant lot, a shooting star, a new puppy down the block, pretty flowers, first love. Kids like us are full of curiosity, and ROBO is the electronic play tool we like best. The ROBO lineup includes an easy-to-operate cassette player, a radio that floats on water, a sing-along system with electronic fanfare, and a whole lot more. They're all made of brightly colored ABS resin that's safe for kids. Even better, ROBO helps us to learn about the world of grown-ups while we play. Wherever we go, whatever we do, ROBO is sure to be nearby.

OKI... leading the way since 1881.

In 1881, Kibataro Oki, founder of Oki, manufactured the first telephone in Japan.

In 1881, only five years after
Alexander Graham Bell invented the telephone,
Kibataro Oki manufactured the first telephone in Japan
Since then, Oki has been a leader
in the telecommunications field for 110 years.

OKI

Oki Electric Industry Co., Ltd.
Tokyo. Japan

Head Office: 10-3, Shibaura 4-chome, Minato-ku, Tokyo 108, Japan Tel: +81-3454-2111

Our balanced viewpoint has become second nature.

One of the world's largest construction companies is also just a good neighbor.
Because Taisei Corporation's first priority is building lively communities. And that means considering the natural environment as well as human needs.
It's a balance that has helped us come up with new technologies and original ideas. Ones that are going places.

TAISEI CORPORATION

25-1, Nishi-Shinjuku 1-chome, Shinjuku-ku, Tokyo 163

Everything you need to see Japan......JTB

Live your travel dream.
We are Japan's travel experts,
you just relax and enjoy.

For Your Travelife

JAPAN TRAVEL BUREAU

The New Official Guide : JAPAN

ザ・ニューオフィシャルガイド・ジャパン

印　刷　　1991年 3 月 1 日
発　行　　1991年 3 月15日

編集兼　　内　藤　錦　樹
発行人

発行所　　JTB日本交通公社出版事業局
〒101 東京都千代田区神田鍛冶町3-3 大木ビル8階
編集部 ☎ 東京03-3257-8303

図書のご注文はJTB出版販売センターへ
〒101 東京都千代田区神田須田町1-28
タイムビル 3 階
☎ 03-3257-8337

編集協力　　株式会社 る る ぶ 社

写真植字　　株式会社 デ ン プ ロ
・製版

印刷所　　凸 版 印 刷 株 式 会 社

本書の掲載地図は、国土地理院発行の地形図を使用し調
整したものです。

ISBN4-533 01681-2

WORLD TIME CHART

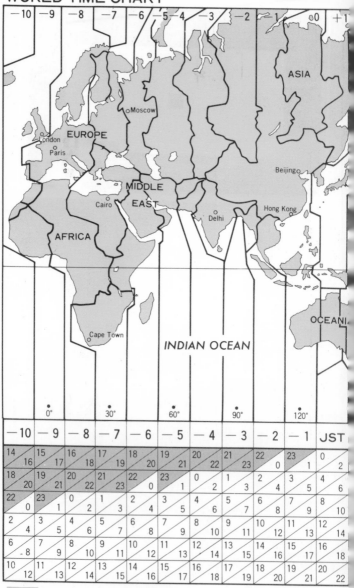

−10	−9	−8	−7	−6	−5	−4	−3	−2	−1	JST
14/16	15/17	16/18	17/19	18/20	19/21	20/22	21/23	22/0	23/1	0/2
18/20	19/21	20/22	21/23	22/0	23/1	0/2	1/3	2/4	3/5	4/6
22/0	23/1	0/2	1/3	2/4	3/5	4/6	5/7	6/8	7/9	8/10
2/4	3/5	4/6	5/7	6/8	7/9	8/10	9/11	10/12	11/13	12/14
6/-8	7/9	8/10	9/11	10/12	11/13	12/14	13/15	14/16	15/17	16/18
10/12	11/13	12/14	13/15	14/16	15/17	16/18	17/19	18/20	19/21	20/22

Shows previous day to Japan Standard Time (JST)

KING ALFRED'S COLLEGE

LIBRARY